KW-169-055

90 0819439 X

WITHDRAWN
FROM
UNIVERSITY OF PLYMOUTH
LIBRARY SERVICES

7 Day

University of Plymouth Library
Subject to status this item may be renewed
via your Voyager account
http://voyager.plymouth.ac.uk
Tel: (01752) 232323

The Politics of Belgium

For too long Belgium remained an unexplored terrain by comparative political scientists. Belgium's politics were best known through the writings of Arend Lijphart, who considered it a model case of consociationalism. Over the past ten to fifteen years, the analysis of consociationalism has been complemented by a more detailed coverage of Belgium's spectacular transformation process from a unitary into a federal state, moving rapidly now to disintegration. Likewise, several peculiar aspects of Belgian politics, such as the record fragmentation of its party system, have been covered in edited volumes or international journals. However, given the complexity of the Belgian configuration of political institutions and actors, any inclusion of particular aspects of the Belgian case in comparative work calls for an in depth and integrated understanding of the broader political system.

This is the first book which provides such an analysis. It brings together a team of 19 political scientists and sociologists who aim to explain the dynamics and incentives of institutional change and seek to analyze the intricate interplay between the main institutional components of the Belgian body politic. The sociological, political and institutional determinants and the consequences of the "federalisation" process of Belgium is the central theme that links each of the individual chapters. This book will be essential reading for students who want to understand the politics of Belgium and for anyone with a strong interest in West European Politics, comparative politics and comparative federalism.

This book was published as a special issue of *West European Politics*.

Marleen Brans is Associate Professor in Public Administration at the Public Management Institute of the Katholieke Universiteit Leuven, Belgium. She teaches public administration, policy analysis, and comparative public policy.

Lieven De Winter is Professor at the Political and Social Science Department of the Université Catholique de Louvain where he chairs the Centre de Politique Comparée.

Wilfried Swenden is Lecturer in Politics at the University of Edinburgh, UK. His current research interests are in comparative federalism and regionalism, in particular intergovernmental relations and territorial party politics.

The Politics of Belgium

Institutions and policy under bipolar and centrifugal federalism

Edited by Marleen Brans, Lieven De Winter and Wilfried Swenden

Routledge
Taylor & Francis Group

LONDON AND NEW YORK

First published 2009 by Routledge
2 Park Square, Milton Park, Abingdon, Oxon, OX14 4RN

Simultaneously published in the USA and Canada
by Routledge
270 Madison Avenue, New York, NY 10016

Routledge is an imprint of the Taylor & Francis Group, an informa business

© 2009 Edited by Marleen Brans, Lieven De Winter and Wilfried Swenden

Typeset in Times by Value Chain, India
Printed and bound in Great Britain by CPI Rowe, Chippenham, Wiltshire

All rights reserved. No part of this book may be reprinted or reproduced or utilised in
any form or by any electronic, mechanical, or other means, now known or hereafter
invented, including photocopying and recording, or in any information storage or
retrieval system, without permission in writing from the publishers.

British Library Cataloguing in Publication Data
A catalogue record for this book is available from the British Library

ISBN10: 0-415-48453-7
ISBN13: 978-0-415-48453-4

UNIVERSITY OF PLYMOUTH

900819439X

West European Politics Series

Edited by **Klaus H. Goetz**, *University of Potsdam, Germany,* **Peter Mair** - *European University Institute, Italy and* **Gordon Smith** - *London School of Economics and Political Science, UK*

West European Politics has established itself as the foremost journal for the comparative analysis of European political institutions, politics and public policy. Its comprehensive scope, which includes the European Union, makes it essential reading for both academics and political practitioners. The books in this series have originated from special issues published by West European Politics.

Immigration Policy in Europe
The politics of control
Edited by Virgine Guiradon and *Gallya Lahav*

Norway in Transition
Transforming a stable democracy
Edited by Oyvind Osterud

Policy Change and Discourse in Europe
Edited by Claudio M. Radaelli and *Vivien Schmidt*

Politics and Policy in Greece
The challenge of 'modernisation'
Edited by Kevin Featherstone

France's Political Institutions at 50
Edited by Emiliano Grossman and *Nicolas Sauger*

Interest Group Politics in Europe
Lessons from EU studies and comparative politics
Edited by Jan Beyers, Rainer Eising and *William A. Maloney*

Italy – A Contested Polity
Edited by Martin Bull and *Martin Rhodes*

European Politics
Pasts, presents, futures
Edited by Klaus H. Goetz, Peter Mair and *Gordon Smith*

Contents

Notes on Contributors

Jan Beyers is Professor at the Department of Political Science, University of Antwerp. His research and publications focus on Belgian European policy, European institutions and decision-making. His publications have appeared in journals such as *International Organization*, the *Journal of Common Market Studies, the European Journal of Political Research, Comparative Political Studies and European Union Politics*.

Jaak Billiet is Professor Emeritus at the Centre for Survey Methodology of the Katholieke Universiteit Leuven. His research focuses principally on the domain of quality control of survey research with special attention to the modelling of measurement errors. The subject of his research is connected to the relation between voting behaviour and changes in values and political attitudes, including ethnocentrism.

Marleen Brans is Associate Professor at the Public Management Institute of the Katholieke Universiteit Leuven, where she teaches public administration, policy analysis, and comparative public policy. She has published refereed journal articles and chapters in edited volumes on local government reform, civil service systems, comparative public administration, and the policy work of civil servants. Her current research interests include policy-making reform, the relation between science and policy-making, and financial rewards for public office.

Peter Bursens is Associate Professor and Jean Monnet Chair at the Department of Political Science University of Antwerp. His research focuses on issues of Europeanisation, preference formation and foreign policy. His publications include books, book chapters and articles in journals such as *Scandinavian Political Studies, Comparative European Politics and the Journal of European Integration*.

Bea Cantillon has been Professor at the University of Antwerp since 1998. She teaches social policy and the welfare state and has published widely on a range of issues relating to poverty, social security and the welfare state. She has acted as a consultant to, among other organisations, the OECD and the European Commission. She serves on the Research Committee of the International Social Security Association.

Veerle De Maesschalck is a research assistant at the Department of Sociology of the University of Antwerp and a member of the Centre for Social Policy Herman Deleeck (University of Antwerp). Her PhD research focuses on the territorial aspects of social redistribution.

Stefaan De Rynck is European Commission Official and part-time Lecturer at the College of Europe in Bruges. De Rynck has authored articles and books on regions, cohesion policy, local employment initiatives, and policy change in education and environmental policies.

Kris Deschouwer is currently Professor of Political Science at the Free University of Brussels. His most recent book – co-authored with Michael Keating and John Loughlin – is *Culture, Institutions and Economic Development. A Study of Eight European Regions* (Edward Elgar, 2003). He is currently involved in a research programme assessing the effects of the increasing complexity of political institutions on democratic political representation.

Lieven De Winter is Professor at the Université Catholique de Louvain, in the Department of Political and Social Sciences, where he teaches comparative politics, methodology, and the Belgian political system. He has taught at the Universities of Bergen, Trento, Leiden, and Barcelona. His research interests include parliamentary politics, coalition governments, and regionalist parties. He has published numerous peer reviewed journal articles and chapters in edited volumes. Recent publications include *Coalition Formation and Governance in Belgium* (Oxford University Press, 2000) and *Les partis autonomistes et régionalistes. Le rétrécissement* (Edition Sciences Po, 2005).

Karolien Dezeure holds master degrees in Political Science and Social Policy Analysis. She is Research Assistant at the Policy Research Centre - Governmental organization in Flanders, at the University College Ghent, where she prepares a PHD on "Citizen participation in Flemish cities: deliberative democracy between practices and attitudes."

Patrick Dumont is researcher in political science at the newly created Université du Luxembourg, member of the Centre de Politique Comparée of the Université Catholique de Louvain and of the Board of the Association Belge de Science politique – Communauté française. Recent research projects focus on the (de)-selection of government ministers (coordination of an international network of scholars led by K. Dowding, London School of Economics) and the impact of the European Union on member states' political structures, processes and public policy.

André-Paul Frognier is Professor at the Department of Politics and International Relations of the Université Catholique de Louvain. He is President of the Belgian Francophone Association of Political Science. He teaches comparative politics, science policy, political sociology and methodology. His main research interests are the study of elections and the operation of governments, on which subjects he has published several books and many journal articles and book chapters.

Maarten Theo Jans studied Political Sciences at the Free University of Brussels, where he teaches several courses including 'Multi-level Governance in the European Union', 'Institutions and Policy', 'Data Analysis' and 'Institutional Conflict Regulation'. His main research interests are European governance, federalism and institutional conflict regulation. He has published book chapters and articles on conflict regulation, federalism and intergovernmental relations.

Bart Maddens is Associate Professor at the Centre for Political Research in the Faculty of Social Sciences at the Katholieke Universiteit Leuven. His main research interests include issue-voting, national identity, ethnocentrism and institutional reforms. Recent publications include articles in peer-reviewed journals such as *West European Politics*, *Electoral Studies* and the *Journal of Representative Democracy*. He is also the editor of *Res Publica*, a Belgian political science journal.

Jeroen Maesschalck is Lecturer in Criminal Justice Administration at the Institute for Criminology at the Katholieke Universiteit Leuven. He is also Research Fellow in Integrity of Governance at the Free University Amsterdam and co-chair of the Study Group on Ethics and Integrity of Governance of the European Group of Public Administration (EGPA). His international publications include articles on public sector ethics and scandals in *Public Administration*, the *International Public Management Journal* and *Public Integrity*.

B. Guy Peters is Maurice Falk Professor of American Government at the University of Pittsburg. He is honorary professor at the University of Strathclyde and at the City University of Hong Kong, and Senior Fellow at the Canadian Centre for Management Development. He teaches comparative politics and policy. He has published over 30 books and more than 70 refereed journal articles on comparative public administration and policy.

Stijn Rottiers is a researcher at the Centre for Social Policy Herman Deleeck, University of Antwerp. His current PhD research focuses on minimum protection and social justice in Europe.

Wilfried Swenden is Lecturer in Politics at the School of Social and Political Studies, Department of Politics, University of Edinburgh. His current research and teaching interests are in the field of comparative federalism and regionalism, in particular territorial party politics and intergovernmental relations. He is the author of *Federalism and Regionalism in Western Europe: A Comparative and Thematic Analysis* (Palgrave, 2006) and of recent articles in *Publius: The Journal of Federalism*, *Regional and Federal Studies*, *Journal of Common Market Studies* and *West European Politics*.

Marc Swyngedouw is full Professor in political sociology and methodology at the University of Leuven (Belgium). He is chair of the Centre for Sociological Research (CESO) at the faculty of Social Sciences and is director of the Institute of Social and Political Opinion research (www.kuleuven.be/ispo). His research interests include quantitative and qualitative methodology, ethnic minorities, political sociology, extreme right and populist parties, comparative research methodology and public opinion. He has published in the following journals: *Quantity and Quality, West European Politics, Electoral Studies, Revue Internationale de Politique Comparée, Revue Française de Science Politique, Journal of Ethnic and Migration Studies, European Sociological Review, Ethnicities*.

Diederik Vancoppenolle is Doctor-Assistant in public policy and public management - University College Ghent. His doctorate focused on the policy-making role of civil servants. He is also coordinating several training sessions on policy and policy-making for students and civil servants.

Steven Van de Walle is Associate Professor at the Department of Public Administration, Erasmus University Rotterdam. His research interests include citizens' perceptions of the public sector, citizen–government relations, governance indicators and comparative public administration. His recent articles on these topics have been published in *International Review of Administrative Sciences, Public Management Review, International Journal of Public Administration, Public Performance and Management Review and the Journal of Comparative Policy Analysis*.

Gerlinde Verbist is senior researcher at the Centre for Social Policy Herman Deleeck, University of Antwerp. She has a PhD in Applied Economics. Her main research interests include microsimulation modelling and applications, measurement of income inequality and redistribution, higher education funding policies, and the interaction between taxes and the welfare state.

Christian de Visscher has held several positions in the Belgian civil service (at both federal and regional levels) before being recruited as a professor in public administration by the Université Catholique de Louvain in 1998. He teaches public administration and public management both at Master's and PhD levels and is also involved in Executive Masters for professional civil servants. From 2000 to 2003, he chaired the Department of Political and Social Sciences of his University. His research interests lie in the field of public sector management in Belgium and in Western Europe.

The Politics of Belgium: Institutions and Policy under Bipolar and Centrifugal Federalism

WILFRIED SWENDEN, MARLEEN BRANS and
LIEVEN DE WINTER

For too long Belgium remained an unexplored terrain by comparative political scientists. This lack of visibility was partly due to the community of Belgian political scientists itself. Frequently, they described the Belgian political system by using idiosyncratic concepts that were not readily translatable to Anglo-Saxon, academic and comparative discourse (De Winter *et al.* 2006). Neologisms that featured in the description of the *sui generis* character of the Belgian polity included *verzuiling* or *pillarisation*, whiplash parties, dissociative federalism, partitocracy or New Political Culture. Belgium's politics were best known through the writings of Arend Lijphart, who considered it a model case of consociationalism. Over the past 10–15 years, the analysis of consociationalism has been complemented by a more detailed coverage of Belgium's spectacular transformation process from a unitary into a federal state. Likewise, several peculiar aspects of Belgian politics, such as the exceptional fragmentation of its party system, have been increasingly covered in edited volumes or international journals. However, given the complexity of the Belgian configuration of political institutions and actors, any inclusion of particular aspects of the Belgian case in comparative work calls for an in-depth and integrated understanding of the broader political system. Therefore, this volume deals not only with the dynamics and incentives explaining institutional change, but also with the intricate interplay between the main institutional components of the Belgian political system.

Federalism as a Connecting Theme

The sociological and institutional determinants and the consequences of the federalisation process in Belgium are the central themes that link the individual contributions. To what extent has the Belgian federal model been capable of attenuating ethno-nationalist conflict? Has the institutional shape of federalism contributed to the overall stability and sustainability of the Belgian political system? Or has the centrifugal and bipolar logic of Belgian federalism triggered a dynamic that inevitably undermines the very survival of the Belgian state and nation, both in its institutional configuration and in its performance?

Table 1 provides a schematic overview of the federalisation of Belgium since 1970. It offers general background information against which the individual studies may be situated.

Belgium is a clear example of *federalisation by disaggregation*. As such, the Belgian experience of federalism is very different from federal systems which emerged from the coming together (Stepan and Linz 1996) or *aggregation* of formerly independent states. Therefore, when speaking of federalisation or federalising a policy or competence we mean the transfer of that policy or competence from the centre to the regions; we use centralisation to denote a movement in the opposite direction. Furthermore, we use the term regions to refer to the newly created meso-level of government, situated between local or decentralised units of government (municipalities and provinces) and the federal centre. Although some readers (in particular international relations scholars) may object to the use of 'region', it is in line with standard usage in political science literature. Yet, for three reasons, the Belgian regions are a particular example of regional government.

First, the Belgian regions are entrusted with considerable political, legal and spending autonomy and by now are very close to being constitutionalised units of a federal state (in fact the 1993 constitutional reform already recognised Belgium as a federal state made up of Regions and Communities). Among the group of European regions, they assume a prominent place in REGLEG, the association grouping the Regions with Legislative Powers. Second, competencies were federalised to two different sets of regions: three Regions and three Communities. (In this issue, we will only capitalise Region/ Regional whenever we refer to the competencies, institutions or policies of the

TABLE 1

BELGIAN FEDERALISM (1970–PRESENT)

'State Reforms'	1970	1980	1988–89	1992–93	2001–present
Central machinery preparing for federalism	➤ Most constitutional laws pertaining to federalism require special majorities in federal parliament ➤ Parity in federal cabinet and consensus rule between both language groups, Alarm bell procedure	➤ Court of Arbitration created (operational since 1984): can test compliance of federal and regional legislation with certain constitutional provisions as well as with federal special majority laws determining autonomy of the Regions and Communities	➤ Strengthening of intergovernmental machinery: Deliberation Committee and possibility of cooperation agreements between centre, Regions and Communities ➤ Powers of Court of Arbitration extended ➤ Federal government retains control over institutional autonomy Brussels Capital Region (consociational rules)	➤ Constitution recognises Belgium as a federal state, made up of Regions and Communities ➤ Senate reform: provincial senators are replaced with Community senators (elected to Community Councils)	➤ Further Senate reform envisaged ➤ Transformation of Court of Arbitration into a full-scale Constitutional Court envisaged
Political autonomy of the Communities and Regions	➤ Flemish, Francophone and German-speaking Communities created ➤ Community Councils made up of Dutch-speaking and Francophone members of national	➤ Small Community executives no longer answerable to national executive Advisory role ➤ German-speaking Community expanded to legislative role (decrees)	➤ Agreement on exercise Community competencies in Brussels (Community Councils and executives composed from Dutch- and French-speaking	➤ Agreement on indirect election of Community Councils on the basis of directly elected regional parliaments (members of Community Council cease to be	➤ Since 2003, election of federal parliament and regional parliaments are uncoupled ➤ Flemish receive guaranteed minimum representation in Brussels Regional Parliament

(continued)

TABLE 1
(*Continued*)

'State Reforms'	1970	1980	1988–89	1992–93	2001–present
	∧ parliament, small executives emanate from Councils, but answerable to national executive Community Council German-speaking Community directly elected since 1973, but initially only advisory role ∧ No agreement on creation Regions with legislative power	∧ Agreement on operationalisation Flemish and Walloon Regions with legislative powers ∧ Regional Councils not directly elected but composed from Flemish and Walloon MPs in national parliament; regional executives answerable to Regional Councils ∧ Flemish Community and Flemish Region merge	∧ members of the directly elected Brussels Regional Council ∧ Agreement on operationalisation Brussels Capital Region, with directly elected council	∧ members of national parliament) French Community can transfer legislative powers (education) to Walloon Region and French Community Commission (Brussels) ∧ Walloon and Flemish Councils (Parliament) directly elected	
Community competencies	∧ Use of language and cultural policy (legislative capacity in the case of Francophone and Flemish Communities only)	∧ 'Personalised' matters added (health policy and assistance to individuals)	∧ Education added	∧ Social assistance policies expanded ∧ Foreign policy (including treaties) in all spheres of domestic competence	

(continued)

TABLE 1
(*Continued*)

'State Reforms'	1970	1980	1988–89	1992–93	2001–present
Regional competencies		⋏ Employment policy, public investment, economic development, housing policy and structural planning	⋏ Scientific research, transport policy	⋏ Inter-municipal cooperation for provision of utilities; ⋏ Transport; ⋏ Road construction and waterways ⋏ Aspects of foreign trade, energy and most of agricultural policy ⋏ Foreign policy (including treaties) in all spheres of domestic competence	⋏ Agricultural policy + foreign trade ⋏ Transfer development aid to Regions planned
Spending autonomy Regions and Communities	⋏ Unconditional grants	⋏ Unconditional grants ⋏ Regions and Communities spend 8% of total public budget	⋏ Unconditional grants ⋏ Regions and Communities spend close to 30% of total public budget	⋏ Unconditional grants ⋏ Regions and Communities spend approx. 34% of total public budget	⋏ Unconditional grants ⋏ Regions and Communities spend more than federal government (excluding federal interest payments on public debt)

(continued)

TABLE 1
(*Continued*)

'State Reforms'	1970	1980	1988–89	1992–93	2001–present
Tax-raising autonomy Regions and Communities	➤ Nil entirely funded on the basis of central grants	➤ Nil: but shared tax revenues complement central grants	➤ Shared tax revenue component dominates ➤ Limited fiscal autonomy for Regions only (inheritance tax)	➤ Shared tax revenue component dominates ➤ TV and radio tax revenues, as well as eco-taxes transferred to Regions	➤ Shared tax revenue component dominates ➤ Communities remain without fiscal autonomy ➤ Fiscal autonomy Regions expanded (possibility to reduce or surcharge income tax rate) ➤ Regions raise approximately 20% of what they spend

Sources: Committee of the Regions (2003) and Alen and Muylle (2003: 341–99); table compiled by Wilfried Swenden.

Flemish, Walloon and/or Brussels Capital Regions. Whenever the term region is not capitalised it is meant to reflect the competencies, institutions or policies of the Regions and Communities.) Unlike Regions, Communities do not have a clear territorial basis, but use language as their main criterion.

Finally, the Belgian regions are relatively homogeneous units in what is a heterogeneous, multinational state. Therefore, some regions, Flanders in particular, have embarked upon a project of nation-building which puts it in the same category as stateless nations such as Catalonia, Scotland or the Basque Country. Various contributions will touch upon this social basis underpinning the Belgian federalisation process: are Flemish and Walloon political cultures really as different as public opinion leaders often make us believe and do differences in political culture also underpin policy divergences in administrative reform and public policy overall?

Sociological and Institutional Determinants of Policy-Making in Belgium

The contributions in this volume are grouped in two parts. A first set of papers discusses the principal sociological and institutional determinants of policy-making in Belgium. Since federalism is the central theme, it is also the subject of the first contribution. Wilfried Swenden and Maarten Theo Jans analyse why and how Belgium became federal. Yet, as they explain in detail, the boundaries of the Regions and Communities strongly overlap. Since Flanders and Wallonia are the most important players in the federation and the party system is structured along linguistic lines, it is said that the Belgian federation is a dyadic or bipolar federation. What are the strengths and weaknesses of such a federal system and does the Belgian federal system contain inbuilt mechanisms to sustain Belgium as a federal political entity? Put differently, what is the *finalité politique* – or durable equilibrium – of the Belgian federalisation process? Is federalism – along other factors such as the role of Brussels, the monarchy, national identity, public debt and social security – a strong enough glue to hold Belgium together?

While federalism may assume a central place in the work of most comparativists who study contemporary Belgium, for long the country has drawn the attention of scholars – in particular Arend Lijphart – who considered it as a prime example of consociationalism (Lijphart 1977, 1984, 1999). In his contribution, Kris Deschouwer first discusses to what extent consociationalism really was a permanent feature of the pre-federal Belgian political system. He then analyses whether consociationalism still lives on in contemporary Belgian federalism. Has the transformation of Belgium into a federal state not in fact decreased the consensus character of the Belgian polity, making the latter more majoritarian in character? Can we transfer the notion of societal segments and pillars with a primary ideological connotation to segments with a predominantly territorial meaning? Furthermore, can we explain institutional stability by referring to elite attitudes? Should we attribute the ability to govern the complex Belgian centre to specific institutional features which make the absence of a negotiated compromise unattractive for all partners?

Belgian federalism emerged as an institutional device to accommodate growing ethnic tensions between Flemish- and French-speakers. One could assume that the presence of two different political cultures is both a cause and a further consequence of federalisation. In their contribution, Jaak Billiet, Bart Maddens and André-Paul Frognier analyse to what extent the political culture in both language communities is effectively different, with regard to national identity and a number of variables such as church attendance, trust in political institutions, pillarisation as a predictor of voting behaviour and attitudes towards foreigners. Are both language communities really so far apart that one could speak of the presence of two different political cultures in one country, or are inter-community differences relatively small?

Belgium has one of the most fragmented party systems of any modern democracy. This is not due to changes in the electoral system, but to the emergence of ethno-regionalist parties. In fact, the rise of the latter put the traditional parties under such pressure that they also split along linguistic lines. While ideological pillars still retain a crucial role in the provision of health care, employment protection and education, the 'pillar parties' with which they are associated no longer succeed in engendering almost complete voter loyalty. The rise of the Greens and the extreme right further balkanised the party system and boosted electoral volatility. On the linguistic cleavage, Belgium has become a clear-cut example of what Sartori (1976: 131–216) labelled polarised pluralism, although on the socio-economic and denominational divide, competition is more centripetal. In their contribution, Lieven De Winter, Marc Swyngedouw and Patrick Dumont analyse voting behaviour in what are effectively two autonomous and incongruent party systems – a Flemish and a francophone one. Furthermore they discuss and explain coalition behaviour at the federal and regional levels of government.

Next to a consociational democracy, Belgium has also been frequently identified as a 'partitocracy'. Lieven De Winter and Patrick Dumont analyse how parties have responded to the extreme fragmentation of the Belgian party system and the increasing needs for multilevel coordination. Both authors discuss a number of gradual adaptations of the Belgian *particratie* (or as they call it *party-archy*) which reduced the negative consequences of the grip of political parties on government and thus prevented a collapse of the *party-archic* system. Has federalisation changed the role of the Belgian parties as principals rather than as agents of the Belgian polity? Has the role of parties changed in determining who can be elected to parliament and what coalitions will be made at the federal and regional levels of government?

Policy Performance and Policy Reform

The federalisation of Belgium was not only meant to attenuate tensions between Flemish- and French-speakers in the Belgian federation. Ultimately, a federal structure was also meant to enhance policy-making, facilitate policy reform and improve the overall effectiveness of public policy in Belgium. The second set of papers discusses to what extent Belgian federalism may have lived up to these expectations, and also touches upon the impact of Europeanisation on the policies of the federal and regional levels of government.

In their contribution, Marleen Brans, Christian de Visscher and Diederik Vancoppenolle first discuss recent administrative reforms at the regional and federal levels of government. They analyse whether the possibility to carve out different administrative regimes at the federal and regional levels reflect as well as instil different administrative cultures. They assess to what extent efforts of administrative reform on which the Flemish government embarked relatively soon after its creation also influenced more recent efforts at the federal level and in Wallonia. In turn, are recent changes in the public service driven by international trends such as New Public Management? Furthermore, have proposals for administrative reform led to a depoliticisation of the top administrative echelons?

In the 1990s, Belgium moved into the limelight of the international media because of a few high profile corruption cases and policy failures in vital policy areas such as policing or food quality control. Sometimes, these corruption cases and policy failures developed into full blown scandals. In their contribution, Jeroen Maesschalck and Steven Van De Walle examine the effect of political culture and federalism on corruption and policy failures and their impact on the likelihood of such occurrences becoming scandals. They first ask whether there are significant differences between Dutch- and French-speakers in the perception and tolerance of corruption. They then discuss what could be the independent effect of federalism on explaining corruption and policy failure in Belgium. Do political elites at the federal and regional levels of government learn from each other in terms of developing suitable strategies to combat corruption and prevent policy failure? Or do they rather put forward further federalisation as the key to the avoidance of future policy failure and scandal? In the case of the latter, an important opportunity that can arise from operating federal systems of government is largely lost.

Policy learning and transfer frequently emerge from a situation of policy divergence and experimentation. The dual Belgian federal system certainly creates ample opportunities for such diversity. Stefaan De Rynck and Karolien Dezeure analyse and explain policy divergence in education and health care. For each policy they discuss similarities and differences between both communities in the choice of policy goals, policy instruments and the setting of these instruments. In expenditure terms, education is the largest regional (Community) budgetary item. Is policy divergence in education policy between Flanders and the French Community caused by differences in the structure and education preferences of the regional education providers, by divergent views of the key party actors or by discrepancies between what the providers and the party actors want? Have the Flemish and French Communities learned from each other, or does education policy increasingly run on divergent tracks? The article also looks at health policy, which in contrast to education policy is scattered between the federal and regional levels of government. Room for policy divergence in health policy is largely limited to the choice of policy instruments, since the policy goals are mostly determined by a federal regulatory framework. Does this lead to frictions and policy duplication between both levels and do such frictions give rise to demands for more regional autonomy or for a centralisation of health policy?

Although the Belgian centre may have been hollowed out as a result of federalisation, it still controls the entire social security system, including its funding. Social security, much more so than the mechanisms which underpin the funding of the Regions and Communities, is the most significant mechanism of inter-regional redistribution in the Belgian federation. Bea Cantillon, Veerle De Maesschalk, Stijn Rottiers and Gerlinde Verbist analyse where these transfers originate from (demographic factors, differences in socio-economic performance or differences in the level of benefits) and what size they represent. Do transfer payments spark a debate on federalising (aspects) of the social security system and what are the prospects of such reforms being implemented? Situating the Belgian example within the comparative literature on the political economy of federalism they assess the pros and cons of federalising social security from the viewpoint of accountability, effectiveness and equity.

Although the regions may have gained significant autonomy in a wide array of competencies, the policies of the European Union constrain the federal and regional levels alike. In their contribution Jan Beyers and Peter Bursens analyse how the European Union affects the nature of Belgian federalism. Does Europeanisation mitigate the dual character of the Belgian federation? To what extent are the Belgian regions involved in the formulation, decision-making and implementation of EU policies which affect their domestic set of competencies? Finally, does Europeanisation in fact strengthen the role of the centre vis-à-vis the regions or merely alter the extent to which both levels need to cooperate with one another?

By way of concluding, B. Guy Peters reviews all contributions in this volume from the viewpoint of the comparativist. Is the Belgian federalisation process really as unique as Belgian political scientists claim or it merely a prominent example in a growing universe of federalising countries? His conclusion brings together the points from the different contributions that matter most for comparative politics, policy and public administration. By positioning the Belgian case in a broader comparative perspective, he evaluates what comparativists and institutional designers might learn from Belgium, from both an empirical and normative point of view.

Acknowledgements

The contributions to this volume were first presented at a Workshop in Brussels on 9–10 December 2005. We wish to acknowledge the Royal

Flemish Academy of Belgium for Science and the Arts and the Scientific Research Committee of the Fund for Scientific Research – Flanders (programme on Methodology of Comparative and Longitudinal Research into Social Change) for supporting our workshop, financially and logistically. We also wish to thank Hans Daalder, Charlie Jeffery, B. Guy Peters, Daniel-Louis Seiler, Philippe Van Parijs and Hans Vollaard who, as external discussants, provided invaluable comments on the set of papers presented at this workshop.

References

Alen, André, and Koen Muylle (2003). *Compendium van het Belgisch Staatsrecht*. Mechelen: Kluwer.

Committee of the Regions (2003). *Devolution in the European Union and the Candidate Countries: Belgium*, available at http://www.cor.eu.int/en/documents/progress_democracy.htm

De Winter, Lieven, André-Paul Frognier, Karolien Dezeure and Marleen Brans (2006). 'Belgium: From One to Two Political Sciences?', in Hans-Dieter Klingemann (ed.), *The Current State of Political Science in Western Europe*. Berlin: Wissenschaftszentrum.

Lijphart, Arend (1977). *Democray in Plural Societies. A Comparative Exploration*. New Haven, CT: Yale University Press.

Lijphart, Arend (1984). *Democracies: Patterns of Majoritarian and Consensus Democracy in Twenty-One Countries*. New Haven, CT: Yale University Press.

Lijphart, Arend (1999). *Patterns of Democracy. Government Forms and Performance in Thirty-Six Countries*. New Haven, CT: Yale University Press.

Sartori, Giovanni (1976). *Parties and Party Systems. A Framework for Analysis*. Cambridge: Cambridge University Press.

Stepan, Alfred C., and Juan J. Linz (1996). *Problems of Democratic Transition and Consolidation. Southern Europe, South America and Post-Communist Europe*. Baltimore, MD: Johns Hopkins University Press.

PART I:
SOCIOLOGICAL
AND INSTITUTIONAL
DETERMINANTS
OF POLICY-MAKING

'Will It Stay or Will It Go?' Federalism and the Sustainability of Belgium

WILFRIED SWENDEN and MAARTEN THEO JANS

In this article, we situate Belgian federalism in a comparative perspective and analyse its contribution to the sustainability of Belgium. The study is divided into three sections. In the first section, we set out the structure of Belgian federalism and analyse why the federalisation of Belgium did not start until 1970. In the second section, we highlight the specificities of Belgian federalism when put into a comparative perspective and discuss the political dynamics that underpin its further development. In the third section, we list the assets and liabilities of federalism for holding Belgium together, and bring in additional factors that may add to the sustainability of Belgium. On the basis of these assessments we will – cautiously – attempt to predict the political future of Belgium and the contribution of federalism therein.

Why Federalism?

Unlike most of the traditional federations, Belgium did not form as the result of a 'coming together' of various states, cantons or colonies into one political unit. As in Spain, in Belgium federalism was perceived as a device to 'hold together' (Linz and Stepan 1996) what had become a multinational democratic state. Yet, unlike Spain, Belgium did not devolve powers to newly established regional entities until 1970, that is, more than 50 years after all male Belgian citizens obtained suffrage. Furthermore, by then the centre had long recognised the multi-linguistic nature of the Belgian state. Thus, a first question which concerns us is why federalism is of such recent vintage and why federalism emerged when many of the linguistic grievances which featured so prominently on the agenda of the Flemish Nationalists in the late nineteenth and early twentieth century were already resolved.

This question can only be answered if we put the federalisation of Belgium into a broader historical perspective and take into account the events which socialised the political agents and influenced their political motives when federalism took off (Witte *et al.* 2000). First, it took considerable time and effort before Dutch was recognised as one of three official Belgian languages and as the only public language of Flanders. This achievement would not have been possible without the mobilising force of the Flemish Movement, a movement that was closely linked (but not exclusively confined to) Flemish Catholicism. The intransigence of the Belgian centre in recognising Dutch as the only public language of Flanders; in enforcing language laws to this effect; and in offering Dutch-speakers a place in the centre commensurate with their demographic strength (executive and legislative representation, representation in the civil service, military, higher courts and foreign office) contributed to transforming the Flemish Movement from a cultural into a *national* movement, seeking a form of Flemish self-rule. Several Flemish activists who had been socialised into the more linguistically averse climate of the inter-war period were not willing to reconsider their loyalty vis-à-vis the Belgian state despite the latter's accommodation of their initially non-territorial grievances. Flemish and Belgian nationalism were increasingly perceived as mutually incompatible goals.

Second, until the late 1950s, Belgian politics was rife with ideological and socio-economic conflict. In the case of the former, such conflicts pitted Catholics against Socialists and Liberals; in the case of the latter they confronted Socialists with Liberals (with the Catholics somehow split between two camps). These ideological and socio-economic cleavages were more salient than the language cleavage, and also cross-cut it (Lijphart 1977; Deschouwer this volume). The widespread secularisation of Belgian society since the 1960s *and* the accommodation of ideological grievances by granting self-rule to the ideological pillars created a climate in which ideological conflict lost much of its salience (Huyse 1970). Although the consociational mechanisms which contributed to this ideological peace are still in place, the ebbing of the ideological cleavage itself opened up space for political mobilisation along linguistic lines.

Third, in the 1960s, Flemish per capita GDP overtook that of Wallonia for the first time. This strengthened the bargaining position of the Flemish in the centre, for instance, in securing the Flemish character of the Brussels suburbs or in preventing the adoption of socio-economic recovery packages that stood to benefit the suffering Walloon economy. Like many other early industrialised regions of Western Europe, the Walloon coal and steel industries were facing a painful reconversion process. In light thereof, the Walloon Social Democrats and union leaders were hoping to secure funding from the centre. The latter refused it, partly because Flemish union leaders (and Social Democrats) did not support their actions.

Finally, in 1962–63, language laws were adopted which entrenched the character of language zones as Dutch, French, German or bilingual (Dutch and French). Although these laws confirmed legislation that was put in place in the 1930s, they changed the method for determining what language zones a municipality should belong to (Witte and Van Velthoven 2000). This proved to be a particularly contentious issue in and around Brussels. Shortly after it became the capital of the then still officially francophone state, Brussels turned into a predominantly French-speaking urban agglomeration surrounded by Dutch-speaking territory. Improved transport after World War II and immigration from outside Belgium also changed the linguistic composition of the suburbs. Until 1948, language censuses determined whether a city or municipality should remain within its language zone. If the share of adult citizens reporting to speak the language of another zone (i.e. French) was higher than 30 per cent, a municipality could acquire a bilingual character or (for higher percentages even) switch to the other language group. Flemish speakers contested these censuses because they worked against their interests in the Brussels suburbs. The language laws of 1962–63 'froze' the language zones and dispensed with the language census as a method for demarcating the borders. Although some suburbs were forced to offer language facilities in French, they remained a part of the Dutch-speaking language zone (Janssens 2001).

The demarcation and entrenchment of the language zones sparked heated debates in and around Brussels. Ethno-regionalist parties emerged which defended the French-speaking character of Brussels and its suburbs (*Front Democratique des Francophones* – FDF) or insisted on keeping the suburbs Flemish (*Volksunie* or *People's Union* – VU). Concurrently, the *Rassemblement Wallon* (RW), a Walloon ethno-regionalist party, campaigned in favour of more socio-economic autonomy for Wallonia, enabling Wallonia to devise the socio-economic policies which it was refused by the centre. These ethno-regionalist forces clearly illustrate two different types of nationalism: cultural-linguistic (Flanders) and socio-economic (Wallonia). At the height of their electoral successes, the FDF received close to 40 per cent of the vote in and around Brussels, the VU close to 20 per cent in Flanders and the RW close to 15 per cent in Wallonia. The rise of these parties put the state-wide Belgian party organisations – Socialists, Liberals and Christian Democrats – under such pressure that all of them broke up along linguistic lines between 1968 and 1978. Without an organisational linkage with the ideologically related parties across the language border, parties were free to adopt a radical approach vis-à-vis the other language group and take away much of the electoral support for FDF, VU or RW. However, the regionalisation of the party system increased the salience of the ethno-regionalist cleavage and thus created the conditions for federalism. In Belgium, the split of the parties *precedes* the transformation of the Belgian state from a unitary into a federal one. In this sense, the Belgian experience does not support the thesis that changes in the territorial structure of the state cause shifts in the territorial structure of the party system (Chhibber and Kollman 2004). Rather, political elites have used federalism as a mechanism to recapture lost electoral support and control policies for which consensus was lacking at the national level (Tsebelis 1990; Van Houten 2004).

Belgian Federalism: Institutional Architecture and Dynamics

The transformation of Belgium into a federal state took several decades. Table 1 in the introduction to this volume provides a schematic overview of that process. We have summarised the main features of Belgian federalism in the following points.

A Federation Based on Communities and Regions

The intensity of the language cleavage explains why the first steps towards devolution resulted in granting some autonomy to three language Communities (the Dutch-, French- and German-speaking[1]) and not to ten administrative provinces. Provinces existed from 1831 and by 1970 each had had directly elected assemblies and executives for a considerable period of time. Autonomy for the language communities complied much better with the demands of the Flemish nationalists. However, devolving powers to language communities was always going to be difficult in Brussels, where both language groups live side by side. Furthermore, French-speakers were less united in their drive towards regional autonomy. For French-speakers who lived in and around Brussels, linguistic concerns played the upper hand. French-speakers elsewhere were more likely to support regionalism as a means to increase autonomy in socio-economic matters. In addition to being more weakly developed than its Flemish counterpart, Walloon nationalism was driven more strongly by a desire to expand socio-economic rather than cultural autonomy.

The more fragmented aspirations of the French-speaking Belgians and the presence of two distinct drivers of regionalism gave rise to a very complex and asymmetric form of federalism. The creation of three language Communities – Flemish-, French- and German-speaking – complied with the Flemish demands for more cultural autonomy. This was so despite its economic dominance when federalism set in. The territorial boundaries of these Communities are *not* clear-cut: the Flemish and French Communities stretch into Brussels. This in part *non-territorial* form of federalism sets Belgium apart from other federations where the territorial nature of the subunits is unambiguous.

In contrast, the creation of three Regions follows a strictly territorial logic. Regions comply better with the aspirations of the leading Walloon politicians, who prioritised regional autonomy in socio-economic matters. The Flemish and Walloon Regions acquired legislative powers in 1980, the Brussels Capital Region not until 1988–89 – at least ten years after a form of Community autonomy was agreed upon. This delay reflected the fears of the Flemish party leaders who believed that a federal structure built on three Regions would turn the state-wide Flemish demographic majority on its head. In Brussels Flemish-speakers represent barely 15 per cent of the population. Therefore, the Flemish only consented to turning Brussels into a third Region after it was agreed that the Dutch-speaking minority in Brussels would be offered consociational protective devices similar to those from which the French-speaking minority benefited at the federal level (Deschouwer this volume; Swenden and Brans 2006). Furthermore, although Brussels was granted regional status in 1989, in legal terms the legislative acts which emanate from the Brussels Capital Region ('ordinances') do not stand on equal terms with those deriving from the other regional assemblies ('decrees'). Ordinances are subject to limited judicial review by the ordinary courts (Alen and Ergec 1993).

Federalism as a Top-Down Process

The federalisation of Belgium has occurred in steps, did not start from a clear blueprint (it took 18 years before all the federal units were fully operational) and has been managed from the centre. Any formal decision to increase the powers of the regions rests with the central parliament alone, albeit often with special majorities (see Deschouwer this volume). The political elites who controlled the central executive (i.e. the ministers in the central executive and the leaders of the parties which they represent) played the lead role in turning Belgium into a federal state. Paradoxically, whereas since 1993 the regional parliaments must endorse international treaties which affect their domestic competencies, their approval is not yet required for proposed changes to the constitution or special majority laws affecting their competencies (see Deschouwer this volume for the meaning of special majorities). The major language communities hold a mutual veto power in the centre. This way, the French-speakers ensured that their demographic (and increasingly also socio-economic) minority position would not lead to their political marginalisation. That said, the input of the Brussels Capital Region, let alone the German-speaking Community at that level is minimal. Since federal MPs represent linguistically split parties which do not campaign across the language border, they are not likely to scale back the current levels of regional autonomy. The requirement that both language groups must approve changes to the federal structure of Belgium largely compensates for the Senate's failure to represent specific Community or Regional interests.

Federalism without Fragmenting Political Control

Next to ensuring that reforming the state is a prime responsibility of the actors in central government, central party elites have been reluctant to weaken or fragment their political control, *horizontally* (at the central policy level) and *vertically* (between the centre and the regions). Federalism requires horizontal checks on the powers of the central government, for instance through a second chamber which seeks to represent regional interests or a Constitutional Court which tests the compliance of federal legislation with (constitutional) rules that specify the competencies of the centre and the regions. Most senators are directly elected simultaneously with the lower house and their election also determines the *party political* distribution of the Community senators (i.e. a much smaller group of senators who reside in the Community parliaments). Consequently, the likelihood of incongruent bicameralism (Lijphart 1999) is very low. Furthermore, a Constitutional Court was not created until 1984. The Court still does not have the power to test the compliance of federal and regional legislation with *all* constitutional articles and half of its membership is made up of retired politicians (who must have served at least five years as federal MPs or members of a regional parliament).

The desire to minimise political fragmentation *vertically* is reflected by the long lasting indirect election of the most important regional legislatures. Until 1995 these were made up of directly elected MPs who served in the central lower house or Senate and were split up into separate Dutch and French language groups. Hence, in Belgium, regional political institutions developed more slowly than in the UK and Spain, where the devolution of competencies immediately coincided with the creation of directly elected parliaments. Although the Flemish and Walloon parliaments have been directly elected since 1995, their election coincided with that of the federal parliament until 2003. Until then, parties could simultaneously steer federal and regional election campaigns, pre-select candidates for both sets of elections and form federal and regional coalition governments thereafter.

Political Asymmetry and Incongruence in a Bipolar Federal Context

By 1992–93, the regions had acquired a respectable set of competencies which made them among the most important regional players in Europe, but politically they were only just approaching adolescence. Until 2003, most parties chose to participate in government (or opposition) at *both* levels (see Swenden 2002 for some exceptions). At the federal level the linguistically split parties preferred to cooperate with the ideologically most similar party across the language border, creating *symmetrical* coalitions. For instance, the Flemish Social Democrats could be pulled into a federal coalition government because their much larger sister across the language border would take part in it. Subsequently, the Flemish Social Democrats could use their participation in the federal government as leverage for entering the Flemish regional government, making its composition *congruent* with that of the federal government. The logic could work the other way around as well: an early consensus on the formation of a regional government could determine the party make-up of a federal government. The latter would then comprise the French- and Flemish-speaking parties in the two main regional governments (De Winter 2006). Despite differences in the regional party systems (and occasionally also in the magnitude and direction of electoral swings within each party system after each set of federal/regional elections), symmetrical federal and congruent federal–regional coalition governments were formed. Although such a practice facilitated the management of the Belgian federal system, it also clipped the wings of the more regionalist inclined members of a regional government.

Since 2003, federal and regional elections have been uncoupled, but the elections of the regional legislatures still take place on the same day. The outcome for the 2004 regional elections was markedly different from the federal election outcome one year earlier. For the French-speaking Social Democrats, the clear winner in French-speaking Belgium, the result of the 2004 elections offered a strategic opportunity. They could 'divide and rule' by throwing out the Liberals from all regional coalition governments and forging a coalition with the Christian Democrats in Wallonia and the Christian Democrats and Greens in Brussels instead. The Liberals remained in coalition with the Social Democrats at the federal level. In Flanders, the rising support of the extreme right wing *Vlaams Belang* and the pledge of the Flemish Greens not to take part in a coalition government after their dramatic losses in 2003, resulted in a Grand Coalition of Christian Democrats, Liberals and Social Democrats, with the Christian Democrats assuming the premiership.

The formation of such party politically incongruent governments is common practice in other federations, such as Austria, Australia, Canada, Germany and the US. Where regional coalition governments are formed that best reflect the electoral swings in the regional party systems, progress is made from the viewpoint of electoral accountability. Yet in Belgium such a practice was always going to be difficult. The de facto bipolarity of the federation implies that Flanders and Wallonia carry more weight at the federal policy level than, say, even North-Rhine Westphalia in Germany or New South Wales in Australia. Furthermore, while providing them with strategic opportunities, party leaders must coordinate the role of being a government party at one level and an opposition party at another. Had there been state-wide parties with separate regional party branches, different party leaders and executives could have steered policies at both levels, and a larger degree of intra-party dissent would have been easier to swallow.

Asymmetric Federalism

The concurrent presence of Regions and Communities gave rise to an *asymmetric* form of federalism. Brussels is a Region, but it is not a Community of its own. In Community affairs, the authority of the Flemish and French Communities extends into Brussels. The Flemish and the French Community parliaments enact *primary* legislation in Community policies that cater for the needs of the Flemish- and French-speakers in the capital. However, the Brussels Regional parliament is split into Dutch- and French-speaking language groups and each language group can propose *supplementary* legislation (secondary legislation) with a view to implementing Flemish or French Community policies in the Region (when acting accordingly these language groups constitute 'language commissions' known respectively as the Flemish Community and the French Community Commission). Where Community policies are not clearly distinguishable on a linguistic basis (for instance, some subsidised retirement homes may seek to accommodate Dutch- *and* French-speaking people), the consent of the Dutch and French language groups in the Brussels Regional parliament and executive is required (hence, the Flemish and the French Community Commissions constitute a Joint Community Commission). In this sense, the members of the Brussels Regional parliament put on two hats: *legislators* in Regional policies of the Brussels Capital Region and *administrators* in Community policies within the same region (Swenden and Brans 2006).

The Dutch-speakers who are based in Brussels represent less than 3 per cent of the total group of Dutch-speakers and tend to identify more readily with Flanders than with Brussels. Therefore, as early as 1980, a decision was made to merge the Flemish Community and Region into one 'Community' governed by a single parliament and executive. Conversely a French-speaking Community parliament and executive still exist alongside a Walloon Regional parliament and executive. This reflects the much larger demographic weight of the Brussels based French-speakers in the total pool of French-speaking Belgians (approximately 18 per cent) and the distinct socio-economic and political preferences of the French-speakers who live in Brussels and Wallonia. The former generally do not identify with Wallonia and tend to side less with the Social-Democrats. The 'distinct' status of the (French-speaking) *Bruxellois* within the Belgian *Francophonie* is illustrated further by the internal organisation of the French-speaking parties which have retained distinct branches for Brussels and Wallonia (unlike the Flemish parties which lack separate Brussels branches).

In Flanders, then, the *Community* principle dominated the *Regional* principle, in line with the more linguistic concerns that drove Flemish nationalism. In French-speaking Belgium, *Regions* have not only consolidated but have also gained further strength. The French Community has ceded some of its legislative authority in educational policy to the French Community Commission in Brussels and the Walloon Region. The French Community now also lives by the name *Communauté Bruxelles-Wallonie*, symbolising the presence of dual identities in French-speaking Belgium. Although Communities and Regions are recognised by the constitution, disagreements remain on what principle should ultimately prevail in the organisation of the Belgian federal state. This goes some way to explaining why Regions or Communities do not yet have regional constitutions proper. An early attempt by the Flemish parliament to draft a Flemish constitution made this clear: the Flemish constitutional draft would have stripped the Regions (particularly Brussels) of most of their powers and elevated the status of the Communities. By doing so, the proposed Flemish constitution would have violated the federal constitution (Clement *et al.* 1996).

Extensive Regional Policy Autonomy, But Limited Fiscal Autonomy

By comparative standards, the Regions and Communities have built up an extensive policy portfolio (see Table 1 in the introduction to this volume). In expenditure terms, the federal government still outspends the regions (Quebec Commission 2001). That picture alters, however, if we take into account that a large share of federal money is used to pay interest on the overall public debt. Furthermore, public finance statistics frequently catalogue federal grants to regional or sub-regional governments as a federal expenditure item. If we consider the latter as matters of regional expenditure instead, regions outspend the federal government by a fifth (NBB accounts 2005). Although the Belgian regions can spend unconditionally, their high levels of spending autonomy are not matched with commensurate levels of fiscal or taxation autonomy. In this regard, the autonomy of the Belgian regions is very small (Watts 1999; Swenden 2006). Communities are entirely dependent on federal grants because their partly 'non-territorial' character rules out tax autonomy. In contrast, since Regions have a more clearly identifiable territorial basis, their levels of fiscal autonomy could be more easily extended (in the Flemish case, that revenue could be used for Community purposes as a result of the institutional merger between Region and Community). Today Regions remain dependent from federal grants or shared tax revenues (VAT and personal income) for about three-quarters of their expenditures. Despite the non-conditional character of these grants, the Flemish Region, in particular, is keen on increasing its degree of Regional fiscal autonomy. Regional fiscal autonomy would benefit Flanders, at present the most affluent Belgian region. Echoing the view of some scholars of fiscal federalism, the Flemish government argues that regional fiscal autonomy would strengthen the link between tax-spender and tax-raiser, and thus increase overall levels of accountability (Ter-Minissean 1997).

Dual Federalism, But No Coherent Policy Packages

The cumbersome process of decision-making among Flemish and franco-phone members of the national government combined with the historical drive towards regional autonomy led to a distinctly dual type of federal system. The centre was carefully carved up between the two linguistic groups and their corresponding regional governments. Federal and regional competencies were divided as sharply and precisely as possible in order to decrease the volume of decisions which Flemish and francophone politicians must take together. The volume of concurrent or shared competencies has been kept to an absolute minimum. Federal and regional laws stand on equal footing and are subject to the constitution (or Special Majority Laws) only. Competencies attributed to either level of government are as a general rule of an exclusive nature, in which one level of government is solely responsible for legislating and administrating policy. Belgian federalism was construed to require as little intergovernmental cooperation as possible.

However, in part reflecting today's complex social realities, dual federalism remained a fiction. Furthermore, different policy aspects are often attributed to different levels of government. In this sense, federal and regional governments cannot operate in completely watertight zones if their policies intend to generate real impact. As Poirier (2002) documents, social insurance (e.g. unemployment insurance, health insurance) is federal, but preventive health care is a Community competence; labour market policy is scattered between the Communities and Regions (Communities coordinate professional training, but the Regions are responsible for the placement of unemployed people); the Communities are responsible for education, but the Regions coordinate school transport, the federal government pays out teacher's pensions and recognises professional qualifications; the federal government controls the railway system and regulates air traffic and the use of Brussels international airport, but the regions are responsible for other transport channels and the Communities organise personal access programs for people with reduced mobility. Furthermore, as Beyers and Bursens attest in this volume, Europeanisation regularly forces the regions into coopera-tion on policies which the Belgian constitution clearly assigns exclusively to the regions. Consequently, the federal and regional levels of government had to devise some mechanisms which allow them to prepare or take binding or advisory decisions on matters requiring cooperative action. The appropriate intergovernmental machinery was created in 1988.

Intergovernmental Relations as Inter-Executive and Intra-Party Relations

As is common practice in most parliamentary federations, the leading intergovernmental forums bring together members from the federal and regional *executives* (Smiley and Watts 1985). Intergovernmental relations can take the form of horizontal (inter-regional) cooperation between two or more regional governments, or may involve federal–regional cooperation. In the latter case, the federal government may seek the agreement of one, several or all of the regional partners (Community and Regional governments). The best known instrument of intergovernmental coordination is the Deliberation Committee. It brings together the federal Prime Minister, six federal ministers and six ministers who represent the Regional and Community governments. The Committee only convenes when a meeting is called for by the chair (federal Prime Minister) or a regional (Community or Regional) minister (about ten meetings every year). It has 60 days in which to work out a compromise and operates as a compromise-building measure of last resort. The latter explains its relatively low success rate (only about a third of all conflicts which the Committee was asked to consider between 1995 and 1997 generated a unanimously adopted compromise solution; Jans and Tombeur 2000: 153). The number of successfully concluded cooperation agreements outweighs the number of compromises emerging from the Deliberation Committee, possibly because agreements require the consent of fewer actors and sometimes touch upon issues of lower political salience. Between 1988 and 1998, when Belgian federalism was still moving out of its infancy, no less than 126 cooperation agreements were concluded (Jans and Tombeur 2000: 149).

In addition to the Deliberation Committee, a wider set of mechanisms of information-sharing or consultation between the various (levels of) government exists. For instance, the federal (special majority) law which regulates the financing of the regions contains no less than 18 clauses which prescribe their involvement in federal decision-making (Poirier 2002). In addition, numerous provisions require that information must be exchanged or that the regions must be heard or associated with federal decisions which affect their interests. Although the federal government must not always take the advice of the regions into consideration, a failure to hear their opinion could render its decisions illegal. In addition to the Deliberation Committee, these consultation and coordination requirements are fulfilled in 16 Interministerial Conferences, which bring together ministers with related portfolios from the different governments.

The increasingly incongruent nature of the Belgian federal and regional coalition governments complicates the resolution of intergovernmental tensions. Until 2004, the federal government was the most appropriate forum to solve them since its members represented parties which also participated in regional government. Failure to reach consensus on an issue that pitted French- against Dutch-speakers would result in its 'freezing' until further attempts to comprise were made. In the worst-case scenario, parties would dissolve federal parliament and call early federal elections (Jans 2001a, 2001b). Since 2004, an agreement among the leaders of the parties in federal government may prove insufficient to produce a solution to intergovernmental conflict. By the same token, a failure to agree within the federal government no longer triggers the virtual standstill of the entire political system. The federal government may collapse but the regional governments are not necessarily directly affected by federal immobilism. Not all parties in a conflict will suffer the consequences of continued disagreement with the federal government (parties which exclusively participate in a regional government may even benefit from it – Scharpf 1988). Formal mechanisms of intergovernmental dispute resolution will become more visible, albeit that they may not necessarily be more successful. Both in the Deliberation Committee and the Interministerial Conferences decisions can only be reached by consensus, and without the direct threat of governmental instability the intergovernmental arena has until today proven ineffective in settling conflicts. Without intergovernmental agreement, sidelined parties are more likely to contemplate judicial review and/or litigation to strengthen their case in the intergovernmental arena – as has been a recurrent feature in Spain (Agranoff and Gallarin 1997; Braun 2000). The so-called 'DHL crisis', which paralysed the federal government in the autumn of 2004, provides a powerful illustration of this. The federal government failed to secure agreement with the Brussels, Flemish and Walloon governments on adjusting environmental norms and flight paths so that the courier firm DHL could expand its hub at Brussels international airport (Gelders and Facon 2004 for an in-depth analysis).

Federalism and its Contribution to 'Holding Together' Belgium

The Assets of Belgian Federalism

Belgian federalism has not been without its virtues. First, federalism contained acute tensions between Flemish- and French-speakers resulting in fewer mass demonstrations that can be directly linked to the regional cleavage (Hooghe 2004: 63–4) and in growing federal coalition stability. Second, federalism has enabled regions to tailor policies to their specific needs, allowing clear policy divergences to emerge in policies such as education and the environment (De Rynck 2005). Third, federalism has been more cost constraining when compared with some conflict-solving mechanisms that were used when all decisions were still centralised. There is less scope to practise the infamous 'waffle-iron strategy' whereby alleged benefits for one language group had to be matched by commensurate benefits for the other group (just as a waffle iron consists of two symmetrical parts, central benefits had to be divided equally between both language groups irrespective of their objective need). Now, regional governments are in charge of most important distributive and public procurement policies (except for social security and defence). Fourth, the emptying of distributive prerogatives at the federal level, either through regionalisation or by EU prohibition (e.g. state subsidies) left the linguistic communities with little to disagree about at the federal level. The end of 'waffle-iron politics' contributed to a reduction in overall public debt. In 2005, total public debt fell below 100 per cent of GDP levels, down from 135 per cent in the early 1990s. Federal governments have run balanced budgets for several successive years. If this trend continues federal governments will have less to spend on interest payments and can spend more on social security, health policy, the modernisation of the judiciary and civil service or other areas in which they remain competent. The centre could compete with the regions in a more straightforward manner because it would be less restrained by its current role as the main public debt manager. Ironically, to reduce overall public debt levels would also reduce the cost of separatism, as the discussion on how to split the debt between the major communities would become less painful. Finally, although it is not easy to pinpoint the independent effect which federalism has had on public opinion, the transformation of Belgium into a federal state has not increased popular support for independence (see Billiet *et al.* this volume). Identity surveys demonstrate that Flemish and Walloon citizens often display complementary or dual identities. In recent years, the share of citizens who exclusively identify with the region in which they live, let alone propagate regional independence, has not substantially increased. Furthermore, in Flanders at least, the younger cohorts are more willing to identify with Belgium, possibly because they lack first-hand experience with linguistic discrimination.

The Liabilities of Belgian Federalism

Are the above virtues sufficiently strong to sustain Belgium as a federation? We identify four major features of the Belgian federal system that reduce its sustainability and are likely to lead to a further unravelling of the centre.

First, federalism was built to pacify tensions between two language communities, but the structure of federalism perpetuates this bipolarity insofar as Flanders and Wallonia are the dominant players and only occasionally Brussels constitutes a significant third. Bipolar or dyadic federations do not usually stand a high chance of survival (Fillipov *et al.* 2004). The structure of Belgian federalism accentuates the bipolarity that was already present in the Belgian party system. Parties which do not have to canvass for support among members of the other language community will be tempted to outbid the other parties on ethno-regionalist issues. Even regional elections may be dominated more by a debate on which steps to take in the next round of constitutional reform talks than on the policy portfolio which the regions already control. As Pieter Van Houten (2004: 17) puts it, 'a party system with mostly regional organised parties implies that a territorial cleavage will be very salient for the population, as it now has effectively been institutionalised in the political system. Consequently, more and more issues will be framed and discussed in territorial terms, and the region will become the primary point of reference in political debates'. Although Belgium had only recently become a federal state, the party programmes of the

Flemish Christian-Democrats and Liberals already endorse the notion of a 'confederal Belgium'. Subsequent electoral gains for the extreme right wing and Flemish nationalist *Vlaams Belang* may beef up the 'ethno-regionalist' rhetoric of the other non-state-wide parties even further.

Second, the bipolar logic is taken straight into the federal government which is composed solely of members representing monolingual political parties. The consociational and anti-majoritarian devices that operate at that level may function as significant institutional shock-absorbers. However, at best they mitigate, but do not reverse, the centrifugal logic of Belgian federalism. Therefore, not only the regional, but also federal politicians assess the relevance of the centre from the viewpoint of its cost and benefits to their respective language communities. In its most extreme manifestation, disenchanted federal politicians can threaten 'to go it alone' if the interests of the language group which they represent are not served. Belgium experienced its first potential case of regional unilateralism in a 1991 arms exports licensing dispute (Jans 2001a). The francophone Moureaux, then vice prime minister, threatened to have the Walloon regional government unilaterally sign export licences if the Flemish politicians failed to compromise.

Third, and related to the previous point, the bipolar federal system and the bifurcated party system raise the legitimate question: who still speaks for the centre? Media is a competence of the Communities and all public media are split along linguistic lines. There are few institutions of symbolic significance left along which a Belgian identity can be sustained or constructed. One such institution is the monarchy, a central institution which has grudgingly come to terms with the new Belgian federal realities. Contemporary monarchs construct Belgium as a multicultural nation-state, with a centre that seeks to bridge the divide between both communities while acknowledging the right of each to some level of autonomy. In his public addresses Albert II has repeatedly emphasised how learning the language of the other community can serve to bridge the divide between both communities. Conversely, separatism ('overt or hidden') constitutes 'an impoverishment' and runs against the vocation of Belgium as a multicultural nation (Maddens and Vanden Berghe 2003: 612–13). Thus, the monarchy serves as a federal tool for mobilising the Belgian public against more regional autonomy, let alone secession.

Fourth, although we find less inter-community conflict within the Belgian federation, the capacity of the system to deal with its linguistic conflicts has also been reduced. In the past, most instances of conflict regulation took place during the federal government coalition formation. Non-agreement or failed joint decision-making once the federal government was in place led to its collapse. In other words, negotiations on ethno-linguistic issues almost always developed in a context where disagreement caused dire consequences for all involved. The Belgian unitary state combined the absence of unilateral venues to achieve policy outcomes with strong pressures to conclude mutually acceptable compromises. In the federal system these two characteristics have been watered down, thereby reducing Belgium's capacity to cope with outstanding conflictual issues. The presence of strong regional authorities stimulates unilateral approaches and asymmetric coalitions reduce the regional concerns for federal government stability.

Forces that Bind

Placed against these weaknesses, we see four forces, none of which are directly related to federalism, that serve to slow down the process of unravelling.

First, the consociational mechanisms in the centre can be used to slow down regional autonomy where proposed changes work against the interest of the members of *one* community. For instance, granting more fiscal autonomy or regionalising health or social security legislation would harm the interest of the French-speakers who can use their federal veto powers to protect their interests. Second, despite the emergence of a class of politicians who have spent a considerable portion of their career at the regional level, a federal political career remains attractive. Belgian politicians also 'hop' back and forth between the federal and regional levels (Fiers 2001; De Winter *et al.* this volume). Although recurrent level-hopping may be questionable from the viewpoint of democratic accountability, it socialises politicians into the codes and practices of federal and regional governance. Third, any suggestion to dissolve Belgium would have to touch upon the thorny issue of Brussels, a Region in which the Dutch- and French-speaking communities retain a common interest. Symbolically and socio-economically, Brussels is of vital importance to Flanders. Its economy generates employment for 650,000 people, 350,000 of whom commute from Flanders to the capital on a daily basis. Needless to say, the international and European vocation of Brussels adds strategic weight to a Flemish presence there. The Flemish Region has made Brussels its capital, and thus chose as its capital a city which strictly speaking is not situated even within its territorial boundaries. Fourth, as alluded to above, so far there is little evidence to support the view that public opinion has warmed up to separatism (see Billiet *et al.* this volume). Not only in the Basque Country, but also in Quebec, Catalonia or Scotland, support for regional autonomy (and the exclusive identification patterns with the region) is much higher than in Flanders, let alone in Wallonia (Keating 2001; Gunther *et al.* 2004). Yet identities are malleable: will this support for Belgium persist without state-wide parties or media to speak up for Belgium? Recent surveys already document that a majority of the Flemish citizens wish to extend the autonomy of the Flemish Region. Almost half of Flemish citizens support the partial federalisation of social security or health care (Meersseman *et al.* 2002). Although demographic trends may jeopardise the quasi-free provision of social services, by regionalising these policies (including the mechanisms which underpin their financing) their delivery could be easily safeguarded in Flanders – at the expense of the Walloons (see Cantillon *et al.* this volume).

Whither Belgium?

Where does this leave us? We see the following scenario unfolding. In the run-up to the 2007 general elections, representatives of the Flemish parties will seek to obtain further constitutional changes. They are likely to put forward as their core demands the federalisation of health policy and child benefits, extending the levels of regional fiscal autonomy and the split of the Brussels–Halle–Vilvoorde constituency into a homogenous Flemish and a bilingual Brussels constituency.[2] In addition, Flemish politicians who consider taking part in the next federal coalition government will also demand the 'transfer' of policies which at present Flanders only controls in part. The French-speakers will veto some of these changes (particularly the federalisation of health care or more fiscal autonomy without more inter-regional fiscal equalisation). They will strike back by raising some demands that are unacceptable to the Flemish (for instance extending the borders of bilingual Brussels to include some of the suburbs), but they will also concede to some demands. Unlike previous rounds of constitutional reform, the negotiations will more explicitly involve representatives from the regional governments, particularly if the current situation of incongruence between the federal and regional governments were to persist. The unravelling of the Belgian centre will continue, but at a pace that holds the middle between what the Flemish demand and the French-speakers are willing to concede.

Yet with Brussels as an important 'institutional' hyphen linking both language communities and with the 'rules of the game' at the federal level this process could still go on. Furthermore, it is worth remembering that the federal government (and increasingly also the European Union) still controls important policies such as social security, defence, the judiciary, most of health and taxation policy, air and railway transport and certain aspects of foreign policy, external trade, agriculture, development aid, energy and environmental policy.

In the long run, federalism may turn out to be the institutional device which fostered the 'velvet transition' of Belgium from a unitary into a confederal state. The two major language communities may still play a role in the co-governance of Brussels and the centre may retain its role as a 'mailbox' on European issues (see Beyers and Bursens this volume). With its HQ in Brussels, the EU will be keen to keep the Belgian process of unravelling relatively clean and smooth. Although the transition to a confederal order may be questionable from the viewpoint of institutional stability, for the student of ethnic conflict management that outcome is not an entirely unrespectable one.

Notes

1. Next to the Flemish and French communities, a German-speaking community comprising 70,000 inhabitants in formerly German territory which was ceded to Belgium after World War I received recognition.

2. At present, Brussels and its suburbs (which are located in territory belonging to the Flemish Region) constitute a single electoral constituency for federal and European elections. Most Dutch-speaking parties advocate splitting this constituency into one Flemish constituency (containing the suburbs) and one bilingual constituency (containing the territory of the Brussels Capital Region).

References

Agranoff, R., and Ramos Gallarín (1997). 'Toward Federal Democracy in Spain: an Examination of Intergovernmental Relations', *Publius: the Journal of Federalism*, 27:4, 1–38.

Alen, André, and Rusen Ergec (1993). *Federal Belgium after the Fourth State Reform*. Brussels: Belgian Ministry of Foreign Affairs.

Braun, D. (2000). *Federalism and Public Policy*. Aldershot: Ashgate.

Chhibber, Pradeep, and Ken Kollman (2004). *The Formation of National Party Systems. Party Aggregation in Canada, Great Britain, India and the United States*. Princeton, NJ: Princeton University Press.

Clement, Jan, Wouter Pas, Bruno Seutin, Geert Van Haegedooren and Jeroen Van Nieuwenhove (1996). *Proeve van Vlaamse Grondwet*. Bruges: Die Keure.

De Rynck, Stefaan (2005). 'Regional Autonomy and Education Policy in Belgium', *Regional and Federal Studies*, 15:4, 485–500.

De Winter, Lieven (2006). 'Multi-level Party Competition and Coordination in Belgium', in Dan Hough and Charlie Jeffery (eds.), *Devolution and Electoral Politics*. Manchester: University of Manchester Press, 76–95.

Fiers, S. (2001). 'Carrièrepatronen van Belgische parlementsleden in een multi-level omgeving (1979–99)', *Res Publica: Belgian Journal of Political Science*, 53 (Winter 2001), 171–92.

Filippov, Mikhail, Peter C. Ordeshook and Olga Shvetsova (2004). *Designing Federalism. A Theory of Self-Sustainable Federal Institutions*. Cambridge: Cambridge University Press, 2004.

Gelders, David, and Pedro Facon (2004). 'Het nachtvluchtendossier: een complexe materie voor beleid en communicatie', *Burger, Bestuur and Beleid*, 1:4, 317–64.

Gunther, Richard Montero, José Ramón and Joan Botella (2004). *Democracy in Modern Spain*. New Haven, CT: Yale University Press.

Hooghe, Liesbet (2004). 'Belgium: Hollowing the Center', in Ugo M. Amoretti and Nancy Bermeo (eds.), *Federalism and Territorial Cleavages*. Baltimore, MD: Johns Hopkins University Press, 55–92.

Huyse, Luc (1970). *Passiviteit, pacificatie en verzuiling in de Belgische politiek*. Antwerp: Standaard Wetenschappelijke Uitgeverij.

Jans, Maarten Theo (2001a). 'Federalism and the Regulation of Ethnonational Conflict. Joint Decision-making in the Canadian Federation and the Belgian Unitary State', unpublished PhD dissertation, Vrije Universiteit Brussel.

Jans, Maarten Theo (2001b). 'Leveled Domestic Politics. Comparing Institutional Reform and Ethnonational Conflicts in Canada and Belgium (1960–89)', *Res Publica: Tijdschrift voor Politologie*, 43:1, 15–36.

Jans, Maarten Theo, and Herbert Tombeur (2000). 'Living Apart Together: The Belgian Intergovernmental Cooperation in the Domains of Environment and Economy', in Dietmar Braun (ed.), *Public Policy and Federalism*. Aldershot: Ashgate, 142–76.

Janssens, Rudi (2001). *Taalgebruik in Brussel. Taalverhoudingen, taalverschuivingen en taalidentiteit in een meertalige stad*. Brussels: VUB Press.

Keating, Michael (2001). *Nations against the State. The New Politics of Nationalism in Quebec, Catalonia and Scotland*, 2nd ed. Basingstoke: Palgrave Macmillan.

Linz, Juan J., and Alfred C. Stepan (1996). *Problems of Democratic Transition and Consolidation. Southern Europe, South America and Post-Communist Europe*. Baltimore, MD: Johns Hopkins University Press.

Lijphart, Arend (1977). *Democracy in Plural Societies: A Comparative Exploration*. New Haven, CT: Yale University Press.

Lijphart, Arend (1999). *Patterns of Democracy. Government Forms and Performance in Thirty-Six Countries*. New Haven, CT: Yale University Press.

Maddens, Bart, and Kristine Vanden Berghe (2003). 'The Identity Politics of Multicultural Nationalism: A Comparison between the Regular Public Addresses of the Belgian and Spanish Monarchs (1990–2000)', *European Journal of Political Research*, 42, 601–27.

Meersseman, E., J. Billiet and A. Depickere (2002) 'De Communautaire Items. De Opinie van de Vlamingen over de Staatsstructuur en hun (etno)territoriale identiteit', *ISPO Bulletin*, 49, Department of Sociology, KULeuven.

NBB (National Bank of Belgium) accounts (2005). Public Finance Statistics, available at: <http://www.nbb.be/belgostat>.

Poirier, Joanne (2002). 'Formal Mechanisms of Intergovernmental Relations in Belgium', *Regional and Federal Studies*, 12:3, 24–5.

Quebec Commission (2001). 'Intergovernmental Fiscal Relations: Germany, Australia, Belgium, Spain, United States and Switzerland', Background Paper for the International Symposium on Fiscal Imbalance, Commission sur le déséquilibre fiscal, Government of Québec, 13–14 September 2001.

Scharpf, Fritz W. (1988). The Joint-decision Trap: Lessons from German Federalism and European Integration, *Public Administration*, 66:3, 239–78.

Smiley, Donald V., and Ronald L. Watts (1985). *Intra-State Federalism in Canada*. Toronto: University of Toronto Press.

Swenden, Wilfried (2002). 'Asymmetric Federalism and Coalition-Making in Belgium', *Publius: The Journal of Federalism*, 32:3, 67–88.

Swenden, Wilfried (2006). *Federalism and Regionalism in Western Europe: A Comparative and Thematic Analysis*. Basingstoke: Palgrave Macmillan.

Swenden, Wilfried, and Marleen Brans (2006). 'The Hyphenated State. Multi-Level Governance and the Communities in Belgium: the Case of Brussels', in M. Burgess and H. Vollaard (eds.), *Territoriality in the European Union*. London: Routledge, 120–44.

Ter-Minissian, Teresa (1997). 'Intergovernmental Relations in a Macro-economic Perspective: An Overview', in Teresa Ter-Minissian (ed.), *Fiscal Federalism in Theory and Practice*. Washington, DC: International Monetary Fund, 3–24.

Tsebelis, George (1990). *Nested Games*. Berkeley and Los Angeles: University of California Press.

Van Houten, Pieter (2004). 'Public Opinion and Regional Autonomy Demands in Catalonia and Flanders: Some Comparative Observations', paper presented at PSA Territorial Politics Conference, 'UK Devolution in Comparative Perspective', Glasgow, 7–9 January 2004.

Watts, Ronald L. (1999). *Comparing Federal Systems in the 1990s*, 2nd ed. Kingston: Queen's University Press.

Witte, Els, and Harry Van Velthoven, H. (2000). *Language and Politics. The Situation in Belgium in a Historical Perspective*. Brussels: VUB Press.

Witte, Els, Jan Craeybeckx and Alain Meynen (2000). *Political History of Belgium*. Brussels: VUB Press.

And the Peace Goes On?
Consociational Democracy
and Belgian Politics
in the Twenty-First Century

KRIS DESCHOUWER

Consociational democracy is a concept coined in the 1960s to define a special type of political regime. It was introduced to solve the puzzle of democratic stability in deeply divided countries. It means 'government by elite cartel to turn a democracy with a fragmented political culture into a stable democracy' (Lijphart 1969: 216). In the early days of consociational democracy theory, Belgium was seen as one of its foremost examples. In this contribution we would like to see whether and to what extent the Belgian political system of the early twenty-first century can still be considered a consociational democracy. In other words, can consociational democracy theory still teach us something about Belgium, and, conversely, can the Belgian case teach us something about the status and the usefulness of the theory?

The questions are inevitably related. Consociational theory has travelled a lot, both in time and in space, constantly taking on board a wide variety of new meanings. For a concept that had from the very beginning a rather fuzzy status, that was probably not the best thing to do. This story about Belgian consociationalism will therefore have to say something about the theory itself. That is the reason for the double question and the double aim: learning from the theory and learning from the case.

A Classical Case of Consociationalism

The first systematic account of Belgium as a consociational democracy was offered by Huyse (1971). In order to demonstrate that Belgium does indeed belong to this category, he defines it by using four indicators: political stability, segmentation (pillarisation), elite behaviour and political passivity. This immediately illustrates the problematic status of the theory. These four indicators for checking whether Belgium belongs to the category of consociational democracies uses the dependent variable of the theory (stability), the independent variable (elite behaviour), the societal character- istic making alternative techniques of decision-making necessary (fragmen- tation) and one favourable condition (passivity). Actually, Huyse follows the logic of the later work of Lijphart (1984, 1999), in which he introduces consensus democracy as a type of democracy identified on the basis of a number of institutional variables.

Huyse looks at a very specific and limited period of Belgian political history: 1944–61. His reason for not going further back in history is the – at that time – lack of reliable data on the functioning of the system. His end point – 1961 – is a deliberate choice. That date marks the end of a period and the beginning of a new one. It is the end of a long period of conflict between the denominational segments or pillars, with the School Pact as its end point. After 1961, social conflicts and ethno-linguistic conflicts became more important. Whether the post-1961 period can also still be labelled as consociational will be discussed later.

The evidence found by Huyse is fairly mixed. The stability of the regime goes without saying: it did not collapse and was not confronted with a high degree of political violence (although there was some street violence during the concluding days of the royal question – see also below). Looking at the longevity of the governmental coalitions offers a slightly different picture: an average life time of one year and three months. With eight different govern- ments, the period 1944–50 is quite unstable. The average lifetime of cabinets in the 1950s was two years and seven months (Huyse 1971: 188). Looking at the political personnel in the executive, Huyse finds much more stability. Although there were 13 cabinets between 1944 and 1961, there were only eight Prime Ministers, four Ministers of Foreign Affairs and seven Ministers of Finance. This is an indicator of the fact that individual members of the poli- tical elite did play a crucial role in keeping the Belgian system on the tracks.

Huyse's analysis of the Belgian segmentation, which he labelled *pillarisation*, stresses the fact that the pillars are not very strong structures. They are a strong and solid network of *organisations* (see also Huyse 1987) but are unable to be the leading actors of long-lasting conflicts between the segments. Relying also on Lorwin (1966) and Van den Brande (1963), he stresses the fact that the Belgian cleavages – religious, economic and ethno-linguistic – are cross-cutting, and therefore neutralise each other. Each pillar – the Catholic, the Socialist and the (much smaller) Liberal – is internally divided by at least one of the other conflict dimensions. This can be considered as one of the explanations, together with the consociational prudent leadership, of the stability of the regime. Towards the end of the so-called School War (1957–58), the Christian labour movement asked that more attention be paid to social and economic problems, and in doing so reduced the strength of the Catholic pillar and pushed the leaders of the Catholic pillar towards a solution of the school conflict. It is interesting to note that the pillars in Belgium have been built on a combination of religious and economic cleavages, and that the ethno-linguistic cleavage cuts across both of these.

Looking at elite behaviour, Huyse describes the way in which the principle of *proportionality* is used in many different spheres of society. This principle is the most important device of accommodation between the conflicting groups. He also sees evidence of a prudent attitude among the elites. In particular the political parties play a major role in negotiating the way out of political crises. Every party has a number of individuals – sometimes not centre stage – with this crucial capacity of finding compromises when needed.

Huyse adds to this that the ability of the elites to rely on techniques of prudent leadership is made possible by the great amount of freedom enjoyed by elites and thus the high degree of non-involvement of citizens. Selection of political personnel (drafting of electoral lists) is under the firm control of the party leaders. The press is linked to the pillars and does not critically scrutinise the activities of the parties. And the citizens are mainly linked to their pillar organisations and parties by means of patronage rather than by ideological mobilisation. That means that on all four indicators there is enough evidence to classify Belgium as a consociational democracy.

There are, however, two qualifications here. The first is the fact that the cross-cutting cleavages are an important brake on the escalation of conflicts. The explanation is thus not elite behaviour only. The other qualification is the fact that between 1944 and 1961 there were two deep and long crises. The first was the royal question between 1944 and 1950 (especially 1950) and the second was the school question between 1954 and 1958. During the build-up of these conflicts, several attempts to avoid the escalation by using classical three-party negotiations failed. Only when the crisis reached its highest point did the braking mechanisms – cross-cutting cleavages and prudent leadership – seem to function properly.

The royal question started in 1940, when King Leopold III and the cabinet disagreed on the way to deal with the German invasion. The King decided to stay in the country and tried to form an alternative cabinet under

German occupation. When Brussels was liberated in 1944, the King had been taken away by the German forces. His brother Charles became regent and the discussion began on whether Leopold could return to the throne. Catholics defended the return of the King, while Socialists and Liberals refused. In 1950 the Christian Democrats won an absolute majority in the parliament and decided to organise a referendum asking whether the King should return. The referendum result was 57% in favour, but there was only a majority in Flanders. Brussels and Wallonia – the industrial and thus Socialist areas – voted no. When the King came back, several demonstrations turned violent, with three persons killed. That was the point at which the elites of the three major parties and of the trade unions decided to stop the conflict and to seek a compromise. Finally Leopold was forced to leave the throne in favour of his son Beaudoin. The majoritarian Christian Democrats – majority in the parliament and majority in the referendum – in the end decided not to use the full power they had won.

The school question followed a similar pattern of a majoritarian attempt to win, and then a negotiated agreement using proportional distribution. When the Christian Democratic Party lost its parliamentary majority in 1954, a coalition of Socialists and Liberals – the two secular parties – was formed against the Christian Democrats, with their joint position on the school question – defending the public schools against the Catholic schools – as the most important glue. These attempts to boost the public schools against the Catholic schools led to a huge mobilisation of the Catholic pillar organisations and finally to the ending of the conflict by a three-party agreement called the School Pact. The major ingredient of this agreement was a (quasi) proportional distribution of the financial means between the two school networks and the setting up of a three-party commission to monitor all future educational policy.

Consociationalism is thus *not a constant feature* of Belgian post-war politics. The picture one gets is very mixed, with fairly long periods of crisis and attempts to solve them in a majoritarian, non-consociational way (Lorwin 1966; Seiler 1997). When the crisis deepens, the elites finally decide to opt for the consociational devices: power-sharing and thus mutual veto, proportional distribution and – in the case of the school question – segmental autonomy. This raises an interesting problem, again related to the theory of consociationalism and to its explanatory power. Can one say that there is something like a consociational *tradition* in Belgian politics? Does the political culture (at elite level) favour the use of non-majoritarian techniques of decision-making? Apparently this culture or tradition surfaces at certain moments, but disappears afterwards.

That is also the picture one gets when looking further back in history. The very first time a Socialist minister entered the cabinet was in 1917. This grand coalition of the three traditional parties was of course in the first place a consequence of the war. After the war, however, the first typically consociational agreement was reached. The war had brought the ethno-linguistic tensions to the forefront, and demands by the labour movement for universal (male) suffrage were likely to be voiced more strongly after the war. Anticipating the potential social unrest, the leaders of the three parties met – on the initiative of the King – and concluded in 1918 the so-called Pact of Loppem (referring to the name of the castle where the agreement was reached). The major decision was to introduce universal suffrage immediately for the first post-war elections, and to change the constitution afterwards. This seems to be the first evidence of the self-denying prophecy, of the elites learning that accommodation is a better strategy to keep the system going. But one cannot say that this marks the beginning of a tradition. The wartime grand coalition was ended in 1921, and in the following 15 years the Socialists remained firmly in opposition (except for 18 months in 1925–26). Only in 1935, again at a moment of high crisis – the devaluation of the currency – was a new grand coalition formed, which lasted until the end of the war.

Whether there is a tradition of consociationalism in Belgium is thus difficult to answer. There are certainly a number of striking examples of high-tension conflicts that are solved in a consociational way. But the periods in between deserve as much attention as the moments of consociational crisis management. The problem of 'history' or 'tradition' as explanatory variables is that one can always go and look for the historic period that fits the story, ignoring the episodes that contradict it. Explaining why some elites in some countries at some moments opt for consociational techniques, and why other elites opt for other methods, remains one of the crucial questions (and weaknesses) of the consociational theory. Before coming back to the matter of explaining elite behaviour, we need to look at more recent periods to see whether Belgium after 1961 still displays consociational features.

A Consociational Federation

On the occasion of the 150th anniversary of the Belgian state in 1980 a symposium on 'Belgium: The Bicultural State and Society' was organised in Berkeley. It resulted in a volume edited by Arend Lijphart (1981a). In his introductory chapter he immediately clarifies the matter: 'Belgium can legitimately claim to be the most thorough example of consociational democracy, the type of democracy that is most suitable for deeply divided societies' (Lijphart 1981b: 1). And again: 'In fact, contemporary Belgian democracy is a more perfect example of the consociational ideal than British democracy is of the majoritarian ideal' (Lijphart 1981b: 4). This bold statement is based on an analysis of Belgian politics using the *institutional characteristics* that would appear in Lijphart's 'Democracies' in 1984. This focuses primarily on the institutions, and not on the societal aspects (segmentation) or on the relations between society and institutions. The label consociational democracy is then replaced by consensus democracy.

This approach simultaneously limits and expands the scope of the theory. It is limiting because it looks in the very first place at the interplay of the institutions, at indicators of a non-majoritarian or power-sharing logic. Explaining the genesis of these institutions or why they are more likely to come about under certain circumstances (favourable conditions) is largely removed from the theory. Actually, Lijphart develops much more interest in measuring and assessing the *effects* of consensus democracy, defending it as a better type of democracy, a more peaceful, kinder and gentler democracy (Lijphart 1999).

On the other hand, this move from consociational to consensus democracy also broadens the scope. It allows a search for mechanisms of power-sharing in a wider range of societies, not limited to the deeply divided smaller European democracies like the Netherlands, Austria and Belgium. When the theory was first coined, it actually looked back at a way of functioning that was coming to an end. Lijphart (1968) expected the Netherlands to move towards a more 'normal' centripetal democracy, and Huyse (1971) asserted that after 1961 a new period had begun in which the ethno-linguistic tensions could be politicised precisely because the old cleavages (especially the religious cleavage) had been healed (see also Huyse 1981). The original theory has from the very beginning been expanded to other parts of the world, to a broader set of institutions and to other cleavage types (Andeweg 2000).

Costa and Magnette (2003) warn that using the notion of consensus democracy for countries or political systems (like the European Union) that do not belong to the classical cases of consociationalism leads to a problematic stretching of the notion of 'segment' (see also Chryssochoou 1994). In particular, the expansion of consensus democracy to federal systems means moving away from ideological or denominational segments to *territorial* segments: member states in the case of the EU or sub-states in the case of federal systems. Evaluating the degree of consociationalism in Belgium after 1961 means looking at the way in which the ethno-linguistic tensions have been dealt with. The nature of the societal division that needs to be bridged at the elite level differs from the classical religious and social divisions. When Lijphart stated in 1981 that Belgium is the best model of consociationalism, he referred especially to the new institutions organising relations between the two language groups: the granting of autonomy to the language groups and the devices for protecting minorities. Although it is important to keep in mind the nature of the segments and the ways in which they are represented in central decision-making, the most important question we would like to answer for post-1961 Belgium is: do we still see – perhaps only at crucial moments – evidence of non-majoritarian decision-making?

The modern Belgium is a federal system. Lijphart (1999) has included a number of typically federal characteristics in his notion of consensus democracy, partly because he built the ideal type on the basis of Switzerland, Belgium and the EU. We will, however, only search for the presence of consociational techniques in the processes of decision-making in the centre of the state: power-sharing, veto power and segmental autonomy as a solution (and not in the first place as a problem).

Moving from the 'old' to the new ethno-linguistic cleavage is not a total change. The territorial division of the country is not new, and has exerted its influence on the way in which the 'old' consociationalism functioned. That can, for instance, be seen when looking at the shape and organisation of the pillars. The Catholic pillar with the Christian Democratic Party as its political actor has always been much stronger and better organised in the Dutch-speaking north of the country. Indeed, Christian democracy has always been very strong in Flanders. In 1961 the CVP-PSC (now renamed as CDh for the Francophone and CD&V for the Flemish party) polled 50.3% in Flanders and only 31% in Wallonia, while the Socialist Party polled 46% in Wallonia and only 29.6% in Flanders. That means that a grand coalition of the two most important pillarised parties was always to some extent also a grand coalition of the two major language groups. The linguistic and territorial divide cuts across the other cleavages, but not in an orthogonal way. The old cleavages also partially coincide with the ethno-linguistic divide. The royal question especially was thus not only a conflict in which the two major parties and pillars where confronting each other, but also one in which the two regions were displaying very divergent preferences. The old consociationalism thus already had a strong territorial flavour (Deschouwer 1994; 2002a).

Moving towards more regional autonomy therefore created two entities in which the two major political forces of the country – the Christian Democrats and the Socialists – became even stronger. It is a feature that has certainly facilitated state reform and that therefore also explains why these two political families were the driving forces behind decentralisation. Actually, they did not in the first place defend far-reaching devolution or the implementation of a fully-fledged federalism. They rather tried to contain the ethno-linguistic conflict, and removing some contentious competencies from the centre seemed a good way to do this. It also allowed at the same time the demands of the regionalist parties to be taken into account (see Swenden and Jans this volume). The split of the Belgian parties into two unilingual parties reinforced this process. The now autonomous Flemish Christian Democrats and francophone Socialists were the leading forces of their regions. Taking away powers from the centre therefore meant a transfer of those powers to a level where both major political forces would still be able to control them. The segments of the ethno-linguistic conflicts are territorial, but the territories have a meaning that remains firmly linked – because of their partial coinciding – with the old pillarised segmentation.

The Institutional Obligation to Opt for Consensus

A very important turning point in the political history of Belgium is the constitutional reform of 1970. It marks the beginning of what would later become a federal state, but also – much more important – introduced a number of devices that would determine the way in which subsequent reforms will have to be implemented. In the first place the 1970 reform introduced a neat division between the language communities *at the elite level*. Every member of the national parliament belongs now to either the Dutch-speaking or to the French-speaking group. This division builds on the linguistic border-line that was fixed in 1963 (until then the borderline – dividing the country into a Dutch-speaking, a francophone, and a bilingual area (Brussels) – moved according to the results of a language census organised every decade). An MP elected in a unilingual constituency would now automatically belong to that language group. Only the MPs elected in a bilingual constituency (Brussels – Halle – Vilvoorde) can choose freely to which group they belong. But the end result is a parliament in which the representatives are supposed to represent *their own language group*. That is an important (and not the last) institutional change assuming that the country is divided into language groups and that each language group has its own elites, its own representatives.

The division of the parliament into language groups was then used to define a few new rules of decision-making. For constitutional changes related to the institutional architecture of the state (written down in so-called Special Majority Laws – see Deschouwer 2005) a double majority was to be required. That means a two-thirds majority of all the MPs present (the normal rule for any constitutional change) and a majority in each language group. That was a fairly high threshold to be passed by all the constitutional reforms towards a further federalisation of the Belgian state.

Still at the level of the parliament, a special device was introduced to protect the francophone minority: the alarm bell procedure. Whenever 25% of the MPs of a language group considered a proposal potentially harmful to their interests, they could activate the alarm bell. In that case, the debates in the parliament were to be suspended and the national government would be asked to propose a solution within 60 days. The alarm bell procedure has never been used, but there have been a few threats to do so. Actually the alarm bell procedure obliges both language groups to find a negotiated solution rather than one in which one group wins. Hence, the Dutch speakers cannot use their demographic majority to impose their will on the francophones. They need at least one-quarter of the francophone votes. The francophones – being the demographic minority – also need to convince at least one-quarter of the Dutch speakers in order to reach the 50% majority needed to accept a proposal in the parliament. Both groups have since 1970 been condemned to find a negotiated way out of all conflicts.

At the level of the government, the 1970 reform also introduced a clear division between the language groups and an obligation to cooperate. The Belgian government needs to contain an equal number of francophone and Dutch-speaking (senior) ministers, with the Prime Minister as the only person not counted as belonging to one of the groups (although since 1978 he has always been a Dutch speaker).

These are the outlines of the institutional framework in which Belgium had to function after 1970. And what followed has been – not too surprisingly – an alternation of deep crises and highly imaginative compromises. Gradually these compromises have given birth to what would be in 1993 officially labelled a federal state. The federal result was however not deliberate. On the contrary, the first reforms – especially those of 1970 – were attempts to contain the ethno-linguistic tensions and to avoid a movement towards federalism. Only radical regionalist parties saw federalism as a desirable solution for the Belgian linguistic division.

The gradual evolution towards a federal state was thus reached in the classical Belgian way, by letting the tension build up and then finally opting for compromise. That also explains why the federal construction is hybrid (Swenden and Jans this volume), including both Regions and Communities, with a basically territorial logic, but also important exceptions in Brussels and its periphery. There has never been a clear agreement on what the end point of the reforms should be. Every reform came about in an attempt to keep the system going.

The consecutive constitutional changes (changes to the Constitution and changes relating to Special Majority Laws) do follow a clear logic though. It is the logic of *separation*. There is the granting of autonomy to Regions and Communities, receiving an increasing number of central competencies. More important for us is the systematic reliance on the principle of 'politics of presence' (Philips 1995). Both linguistic segments are given their own elites, with a decreasing number of political actors finding themselves in a position or in an institution where the bridges between both segments can be built. We already found this logic in the 1970 constitutional reform. At that time two of the three major political parties were still national and thus bilingual or bi-community parties. Yet in the early 1970s the Liberal Party fell apart and in 1978 the Socialist Party split. New (relevant) parties created afterwards (Greens; right-wing extremists) will always limit their activity to only one of the two now totally split party systems. Political elites – even those elected in the bilingual constituency – are elites of their own segment only.

When in 1979 the European Parliament was for the first time elected directly by the citizens, an electoral system was set up that again assumed that MEPs should be MEPs of one language group only. The country was divided into two constituencies: a Dutch-speaking one for inhabitants of Flanders and Brussels (and periphery) and a francophone one for the inhabitants of Wallonia and Brussels (and periphery). The number of seats available for each language group was fixed. Exactly the same system was introduced for the election of the new Senate after 1995: 25 senators elected by the Dutch speakers and 15 elected by the francophones.

When in 1988 an agreement was reached about the institutions of the Brussels Capital Region, it reflected this same logic. Parties participating in the elections for the regional parliament have to make clear to which language group they belong. A candidate on a list of a party belonging to one language group can afterwards never be a candidate for a party of the other group. For the distribution of the seats, the votes are first counted by language group, in order to see how many seats each of them should receive. And then the seats are distributed within the language groups. A later reform in 2002 fixed the number of seats for each language group, leaving the rest of the institutional logic unchanged (Deschouwer 2002b; Pilet 2005). Governing the Brussels Region can only be done if and when both language groups agree. Indeed, the institutions of Brussels are very much like those of the Belgian state: separation of elites into two language groups, an equal number of ministers for each language group (except for the Prime Minister) and an alarm-bell procedure to protect the (here Dutch-speaking) minority. The major difference between Brussels and the federal state in general is the absence in Brussels of a territorial separation of the language groups. The Dutch-speaking minority is scattered all over the Region.

Why Does It Still Work?

Given this neat and increasing separation between the segments, both at the level of society and at the level of the political elites, we need to explain how these elites have always been able to find their way out of conflicts and tensions that seemed to be too tense to solve. The end of the Belgian system has been frequently predicted (especially in the 1970s), and generally those were the times when a new compromise was reached. This fluctuation between conflict and compromise is a fundamental characteristic of the Belgian consociational democracy, whether the segments are the old pillars and parties or the language communities. And that brings us back to the key question: why does the system work despite these deep conflicts? What explains the emergence of prudent leadership and the willingness to bargain, given the fact that very often this willingness seems to be lacking? And can or will this go on in the future?

To answer those questions we might in the first place rely on consociational theory itself. Yet its explanatory power has never been its strongest asset. Lijphart (1977) has suggested a (varying) list of favourable conditions that might facilitate the emergence and success of a consociational democracy. Many debates and discussions have revealed that in fact none of these can really be considered to be either a necessary or a sufficient condition (Bogaards 1998; Pappalardo 1981). For our purposes we could look at the conditions that change when the segmentation and accommodation is based on ethno-linguistic and territorial rather than on denominational and socio-economic segments. That means that two conditions clearly become less favourable. In the first place, there is a majority segment, which was not the case in the 'old' consociationalism. The majority segment is, however, a minority group in Brussels, which might compensate for this. The second problem is the socio-economic difference between the north and the south of the country. And, indeed, the Flemish demographic majority and economic power does put pressure on the smooth functioning of the Belgian system. Yet with some of the conditions becoming less favourable, we do not have a strong explanation for the fact that the consociational federation has so far been functioning in a rather stable way. Government instability has been very high during the 1960s and 1970s, with an average cabinet duration of 16 months between 1965 and 1981. Since 1981, the average has been 38 months (even 43 without one short-lived caretaker government in 1991–92), with all cabinets since 1991 continuing to the end of their mandate.

What can explain this renewed stability of the system? Rather than looking at favourable conditions, we suggest looking at the political institutions. Jans (2001) has shown convincingly, by comparing the managing of the Canadian ethno-linguistic conflict with the Belgian one, that the institutional setting in which the actors have to play their game is a very powerful independent variable for explaining the outcomes of negotiating processes (see also Scharpf 1988). Two aspects of the institutional context are important: the decision rules and the default options. The rules of the game refer to the way in which a decision can be reached: either by a majority vote or by unanimity. The default option is what happens if no agreement can be found. Jans makes a distinction between a single policy paralysis and a generalised policy paralysis. The first means that the topic on which the actors try to find an agreement will remain pending, will be frozen until new negotiations can be started, while other processes of decision-making in other policy domains can go on. A generalised policy paralysis means total gridlock, a situation in which no decision-making is possible in any policy domain.

The crucial difference, then, between the Canadian and Belgian institutions is not the obligation to reach unanimity, but the default options. The federal logic in Canada means that the absence of an agreement on the constitutional changes requested by Quebec does not lead to a generalised policy paralysis. The political actors – leaders of the regional and federal governments – can 'go home' and continue their business as usual. If the Belgian elites have managed to reach consecutive agreements over incompatible demands from both language communities that is to be explained by the fact that the price – to be paid by all – for non-agreement is very high. And that is the result of the fact that Belgium is – or was – a *unitary state*. In the unitary state the arena for decision-making is the national government and parliament. The rules of the game are consociational, that is, no unilateral action or majoritarian decision is possible. That is the direct consequence of the mutual vetoes and high thresholds introduced in 1970. Either there is a compromise that is acceptable for both communities, or there is no longer any government.

This quite dramatic default option gives every actor in the game a powerful weapon, which cannot, however, be used constantly. Yet when one of the language communities – i.e. the governing parties of that community – really wants to put an issue on the agenda and really wants a solution to be found, it can put a lot of pressure on the other community. Refusing to negotiate means either the end of the government coalition or the post-ponement of the formation of a new coalition. Important steps in the reform of the state have therefore always been taken by a government trying to survive or during the formation of a new government. Of course the governing parties could also agree not to negotiate because they felt that the solution was – for the time being – too far away. If they agreed not to exert pressure and preferred the formation or continuation of the coalition over a constitutional reform, the conflict would remain unsolved (as, for instance, with the statute of Brussels during the 1980s). But when the tension was really high and one of the actors wanted a constitutional reform, there was a quasi-obligation for the other to accept the negotiation and to try to find a solution. The Belgian elites – i.e. the party leaders of the governing parties – have used a wide variety of techniques to avoid total gridlock: agreeing to disagree, log-rolling, splitting the difference, waffle-iron policy, asymme-trical constructions (Jans 2001; Covell 1993). The result of these agreements is the thoroughly reformed state that was labelled 'federal' in 1993.

We can thus explain the success rate of conflict management in Belgium by looking at the institutional context obliging the elites – a fairly small number of top politicians – to rely on complex compromises for getting rid of mutual vetoes in a system where majoritarian decision-making is impossible and where ongoing confrontational tactics are counterproductive. The crucial institution in which these successes were achieved was the national government, and thus among the party leaders and top ministers of the governing parties. When these governing parties did not have enough parlia-mentary votes to reach the thresholds (double majorities) for implementing a reform, the coalition had to be (temporarily) broadened and the extra partners had to be involved in the negotiations and the compromises.

Time and time again the institutional devices introduced in 1970 to protect the francophone minority proved to be crucial. One might wonder why the majority accepted these devices, since they have in a dramatic way put a 'bolt' on Flemish power in Belgium. The demographic majority could not be used anymore as a political majority. Indeed, Flemish nationalists refer to the 1970 constitution as the 'bolt constitution'. Introducing devices to protect the francophone minority had been high on their agenda throughout the 1960s. That was the decade during which Flemish power became really visible and was used several times. During the 1960s, the economic decline of the old Walloon industry became very clear and led to the fear that the Belgian state would favour the newer, booming Flemish economy. The population in Flanders was younger and growing more rapidly than the Walloon, which led to extra seats for Flemish representatives in parliament. the language laws of 1962–63, which required knowledge of the second language for an increasing number of civil servants, clearly offered more job opportunities for the (more bilingual) Dutch speakers. In the national government there was already the informal rule that there should be an equal number of Dutch speakers and French speakers, which led to the fear that the Dutch speakers might claim even more government seats. In 1968 the Catholic University of Leuven (geographically located in Flanders) split along linguistic lines and forced the francophone part to create a new francophone university (Louvain-la-Neuve) in the south of the country. This 'Leuven Vlaams' decision (which also meant the end of the unitary Belgian Christian Democratic Party) was a traumatic event for the Belgian francophones. And finally, during the discussions on the creation of Regions and Communities, the Flemings obtained the limitation of the Brussels Region to the boundaries already fixed in 1963, while francophones would have liked a larger Brussels. When in 1970 the new articles of the constitution were once again discussed and finally accepted, it almost went without saying that these devices for protecting the minority had to be part of it. And they have proven to be extremely important for the functioning of Belgium since 1970 and for the way in which the decentralisation of powers could be expanded.

The result of these reforms has been the creation of a truly federal state. That is therefore the institutional setting in which the system needs to function today. Does the Belgian federation then still contain institutional devices fulfilling the same pacifying function? The rules of 1970 are limited to decision-making at the federal level and in the federal government.

The Regional and Community governments have come to life very slowly, and it is only since 1995 that they have been elected directly (1989 for the Brussels Region). Yet the 1995 and again the 1999 regional elections were organised in a very peculiar setting: these elections coincided with the election of the federal parliament and were therefore only quasi-regional (Versmessen 1995; Deschouwer 2000). But more important still, the horizontal and vertical simultaneity of the regional and federal elections allowed the deliberate formation of symmetrical and congruent coalitions, creating an institutional environment very close to the one of the old unitary state (see Swenden and Jans this volume).

The vertical disconnection of the elections from 2003 onwards has radically changed the institutional context. Incongruent coalition governments which have formed since have created a newly relevant forum of conflict and decision-making: intergovernmental relations. In a context of congruence, intergovernmental relations (i.e. relations between governing parties at different levels) are basically overlapping with relations within the federal government. The parties involved are exactly the same. The federal government thus remains the real centre. Yet in a context of incongruence the federally governing parties are not in full control any more. They need to talk to other parties with which they govern (or not) at the other level.

Yet, despite a new forum and logic of conflict and decision-making, the basic rules have not really changed. The rule of the game is still unanimity, is still a common agreement between the representatives of the two language groups. It is required in the federal government and it is required to reach intergovernmental agreements. For the latter there is no formal obligation to reach consensus, but with only two players in the game the choice is always between agreement between the two (thus mutual veto) or non-agreement. The crucial difference is, however, the default option when inter-governmental negotiations fail: a single policy paralysis. Only the topic on which no agreement can be reached remains unsolved. Regional and federal governments can go on with other matters belonging to their area of com-petence. And there have indeed been a number of negotiations ending with a non-decision, and some surprise that the non-decision did not lead to the usual dramatic gridlock and obligation to find a way out, but to nothing more than the simple end of the negotiations and the freezing of the problem. The DHL case (see Swenden and Jans this volume) is the prime example of such an intergovernmental conflict to date.

Can the Peace Go On?

Looking ahead to assess the future (consociational) functioning of the Belgian system is hazardous. The disconnection of the elections at the different levels and the functioning of incongruent coalitions are recent features. The new games to be played in this context are not yet clear, whether for the political actors or for the political scientists. The games to be played are certainly more complex, involving different parties having different relations with each other at different levels. That is to a certain extent a normal situation for parties in a federal country, but the Belgian parties find themselves in a very peculiar situation because there are no longer any federal parties. There are no federal political elites accountable to the Belgian population. Society, parties and institutions are neatly split along the linguistic borderline. And still some actors have to bridge the division at the elite level and need to do so in a consociational, in a non-majoritarian way.

A first possible scenario for the future is a learning process. The federal dynamics, with regions going their own way not only for policy-making but also for the composition of the governing coalitions, are there to stay. The formation of congruent coalitions might still be an option, but with elections at the two levels following a different cycle, incongruence seems to be the most likely situation. That requires the ability to see its possibilities and constraints. The most important element is the disappearance of the single forum of decision-making in which the others can eventually be forced to negotiate if they want to avoid a total paralysis and gridlock of the system. That means that confrontational strategies to prepare the negotiations and to build up the pressure are likely to be counterproductive, since the other side can simply refuse to negotiate. And since the other side cannot be forced to negotiate, it has to be tempted into negotiations. The various techniques used in the past are still available, such as log-rolling, side payments and waffle iron. One can thus envisage a learning process in which the elites realise that – even more than before – an accommodating attitude is the only way to solve problems. That would be a scenario in which the consociational attitudes become a more permanent feature of the system, rather than surfacing when the tensions are extremely high.

On the other hand, all parties in Belgium only speak to the voters belonging to their own segment. In a situation of incongruence there will always be federal opposition parties able and willing to defend a more radical position. If there are relevant parties with no or very low coalition potential they will happily blame the others for being traitors, for promises they communicated to their voters and for reneging on their promises when they search for compromises with the enemy. The presence of a strong right-wing extremist, populist and separatist party on the Flemish side is weakening the elites who would be ready to adopt a more prudent, cooperative and compromising attitude.

The formation of a new federal government furthermore could remain a moment at which the segmental elites can force each other to accept negotiations. The default option is then no federal government, while the regional governments can be formed or can go on. This situation has so far never occurred, but one can imagine that it could be easier than before to live – at least for a while – with a caretaker government at the federal level.

A second scenario is one that has been suggested by political leaders on several occasions. It is the return to simultaneous elections at the federal and the regional levels. All coalitions can then be formed simultaneously and can be made – if the election results permits it – as congruent as possible. The political personnel can be pooled and used at the level where they are needed. Intergovernmental and federal intra-governmental relations will again be a matter of the same small group of party elites, striking an agreement with each other to take on board the issues on which they can find solutions and to keep away the matters on which no agreement can be found.

Belgium would then still be a consociational democracy as it has been since 1970, and it would – according to its constitution – also be a federal system. But the consociational flavour would be far more pronounced than the federal one. It would be a system in which the linguistically divided segments have some policy autonomy, but where the crucial autonomy is to be found among the leaders who keep the system going. Belgium would then still, and again, be a country governed by an 'elite cartel to turn a democracy with a fragmented political culture into a stable democracy' (Lijphart 1969: 216).

References

Andeweg, Rudy B. (2000). 'Consociational Democracy', *Annual Review of Political Science*, 3, 509–36.

Bogaards, Matthijs (1998). 'The Favourable Factors for Consociational Democracy: A Review', *European Journal of Political Research*, 33, 475–596.

Chryssochoou, Dimitris N. (1994). 'Democracy and Symbiosis in the European Union: Towards a Confederal Consociation', *West European Politics*, 17:4, 1–14.

Costa, Olivier, and Paul Magnette (2003). 'The European Union as a Consociation? A Methodological Assessment', *West European Politics*, 26:3, 1–18.

Covell, Maureen (1993). 'Political Conflict and Constitutional Engineering in Belgium', *The International Journal of the Sociology of Language*, 104, 65–86.

Deschouwer, Kris (1994). 'The Decline of Consociationalism and the Reluctant Modernization of the Belgian Mass Parties', in Richard S. Katz and Peter Mair (eds.), *How Parties Organize: Adaptation and Change in Party Organizations in Western Democracies*. London: Sage, 80–108.

Deschouwer, Kris (2000). 'Belgium's Quasi-regional Elections of June 1999', *Regional and Federal Studies*, 10:1, 125–32.

Deschouwer, Kris (2002a). 'Falling Apart Together. The Changing Nature of Belgian Consociationalism, 1961–2000', in Jurg Steiner and Thomas Ertman (eds.), *Consociationalism and Corporatism in Western Europe. Still the Politics of Accommodation?* Special issue of *Acta Politica*, 37, 68–85.

Deschouwer, Kris (2002b). 'Getrennt zusammenleben in Belgien und Brüssel', in *Jahrbuch des Föderalismus 2002*. Baden-Baden: Nomos Verlaggesellschaft, 275–87.

Deschouwer, Kris (2005). 'Kingdom of Belgium', in John Kincaid and Alan Tarr (eds.), *Constitutional Origins, Structure, and Change in Federal Countries*. Montreal and Kingston: McGill-Queen's University Press, 48–75.

Huyse, Luc (1971). *Passiviteit, pacificatie en verzuildheid in de Belgische politiek*. Antwerpen: Standaard Wetenschappelijke Uitgeverij.

Huyse, Luc (1981). 'Political Conflict in Bicultural Belgium', in Arend Lijphart (ed.), *Conflict and Coexistence in Belgium. The Dynamics of a Culturally Divided Society*. Berkeley: Institute of International Studies, University of California, 107–26.

Huyse, Luc (1987). *De verzuiling voorbij*. Leuven: Kritak.

Jans, Maarten Theo (2001). 'Leveled Domestic Politics. Comparing Institutional Reform and Ethnonational Conflicts in Canada and Belgium (1960–89)', *Res Publica*, 43:1, 37–58.

Lijphart, Arend (1968). *The Politics of Accomodation: Pluralism and Democracy in the Netherlands*. Berkeley: University of California Press.

Lijphart, Arend (1969). 'Consociational Democracy', *World Politics*, 21:2, 207–25.

Lijphart, Arend (1977). *Democracy in Plural Societies: A Comparative Exploration*. New Haven, CN: Yale University Press.

Lijphart, Arend, ed. (1981a). *Conflict and Coexistence in Belgium. The Dynamics of a Culturally Divided Society*. Berkeley: Institute of International Studies, University of California.

Lijphart, Arend (1981b). 'Introduction: The Belgian Example of Cultural Coexistence in Comparative Perspective', in Arend Lijphart (ed.), *Conflict and Coexistence in Belgium. The Dynamics of a Culturally Divided Society*. Berkeley: Institute of International Studies, University of California, 1–12.

Lijphart, Arend (1984). *Democracies: Patterns of Majoritarian and Consensus Government in Twenty-one Countries*. New Haven, CN: Yale University Press.

Lijphart, Arend (1999). *Patterns of Democracy. Government Forms and Performance in Thirty-Six Countries*. New Haven, CT: Yale University Press.

Lorwin, Val (1966). 'Belgium. Religion, Class and Language in National Politics', in Robert A. Dahl (ed.), *Political Oppositions in Western Democracies*. New Haven, CT: Yale University Press, 147–87.

Pappalardo, Adriano (1981). 'The Conditions for Consociational Democracy: A Logical and Empirical Critique', *European Journal of Political Research*, 9, 365–90.

Philips, Anne (1995). *The Politics of Presence: The Political Representation of Gender, Ethnicity and Race*. Oxford: Clarendon Press.

Pilet, Jean-Benoît (2005). 'The Adaptation of the Electoral System to the Ethno-linguistic Evolution of the Belgian Consociationalism', *Ethnopolitics*, 4:4, 397–411.

Scharpf, Fritz W. (1988). 'The Joint-decision Trap: Lessons from German Federalism and European Integration', *Public Administration*, 66:3, 239–78.

Seiler, Daniel-Louis (1997). 'Un système consociatif exemplaire: la Belgique', *Revue Internationale de Politique Comparée*, 4:3, 601–24.

Van den Brande, A. (1963). 'Elements for a Sociological Analysis of the Impact of the Main Conflicts on Belgian Political Life', *Res Publica*, 9:3, 535–52.

Versmessen, Elke (1995). 'In the Kingdom of Paradoxes: The Belgian Regional and National Elections of May 1995', *Regional and Federal Studies*, 5:2, 239–46.

Does Belgium (Still) Exist? Differences in Political Culture between Flemings and Walloons

JAAK BILLIET, BART MADDENS and
ANDRÉ-PAUL FROGNIER

Belgium's neighbours sometimes look at Belgium with some curiosity. Does that small country where Europe's capital is based really still exist? Many observers are under the impression that Belgium is in the process of falling apart in the wake of repeated constitutional reforms. Some have the impression that Belgians find it difficult to participate in any kind of activity as one nation. For instance, in its representation in the standing committees of the European Science Foundation, Belgium is the only country to send a delegation from both language communities. In the European Social Survey, Belgium is also the only country incapable of compiling its data under the leadership of one national coordinator. Is this image of a slow disintegration played out in reality? Or is Belgium a country capable of maintaining its unity despite its cultural differences, thanks to the high level of autonomy of its composite parts and the original solutions it has found?

The topics discussed in this article touch upon this question. In a number of areas and developments, we go in search of what divides Belgians and what unites them. In so doing, we look not only at behaviour and beliefs as areas in which the inhabitants of the different regions are different or alike; we also look at some structural developments which may or may not favour the preservation of a political entity. The development of two separate party systems, together with the almost complete separation of cultural life – the media in particular – are certainly trends which are gradually dividing the country. A difference can also be seen in the extent to which the citizens of the different regions identify with the Belgian nation or the sub-nation. However, we can also see similarities. It has long been taken for granted that Flanders is Catholic and Christian democrat, Wallonia unbelieving and socialist, and Brussels liberal and free-thinking. At both ideological and philosophical levels, this stereotypical picture is increasingly being eroded. At the religious level, the differences between the regions are shrinking and de-pillarisation is increasing, although pronounced links still exist between social organisations and the political parties. Another stereotypical picture that points towards separation is the idea that Flemings are more right-wing and xenophobic, a notion that is nurtured by the existence of a large extreme right-wing party in Flanders. Francophones, then, are supposed to be left-wing and much more open, but they allegedly have less faith in political institutions and the government. We will see, however, that the reality is much more subtle. This is the common thread running through this discussion.

The Development of Two Separate Party Systems

As described more in detail by De Winter, Swyngedouw and Dumont (this volume), the most striking feature of the Belgian party system is that since the end of the 1970s, there is no longer a single party system, but two distinct party systems, one Flemish and one francophone. On the Flemish side, we currently find Christian-democratic CD&V (*Christian Democratisch & Vlaams*, previously called CVP), the social-democratic SP.a (*Socialistische Partij anders*, previously SP), the liberal VLD (*Vlaams Liberalen en Democraten*, previously PVV), the Greens (*Groen*, previously AGALEV), the separatist and xenophobic *Vlaams Belang* (previously *Vlaams Blok*, and finally the *Volksunie* (VU, which split in 2000 into the independent N-VA, *Nieuw Vlaams Alliantie*, and the 'postnationalist' Spirit).

The first five party families can also be found, although at different strengths, on the francophone side: the Christian-democratic CdH (*Centre démocrate humaniste*, previously PSC), the social-democratic PS (*Parti Socialiste*), the liberal MR (*Mouvement Réformateur*, previously PRL), the Greens (Ecolo), and the xenophobic *Front National* (FN).

Apart from Brussels and the surrounding area, Flemish and francophone politics form two different worlds. The media report only to a limited extent on the politics of the other region. It is unusual for a politician from another region to be interviewed or to participate in a political debate. Most citizens are therefore scarcely involved, if at all, in the politics of the other region and their knowledge of it is extremely limited (Dewachter 1996: 136).

The Development of Two Separate Societies

The emergence of two separate party systems is not, of course, an isolated phenomenon, but reflects a broader social development in which the Flemish and francophone regions are drifting further apart. This increasing divergence has led to a situation where the sense of common political community required for the continued existence of unitary political parties has gradually disappeared.

Many factors have contributed to this social duality in Belgium. Firstly, the language difference, which for a long time was the main reason behind Flemish–Walloon conflicts. Belgium has been able to function perfectly well as a bilingual nation. However, this was mainly because the Flemish political, economic and cultural elite was largely francophone until the nineteenth century and, subsequently, increasingly bilingual. The Flemish elites remained closely involved in francophone social and cultural life, read the French-language newspapers and communicated fluently with their largely monolingual French-speaking compatriots. For the middle classes, too, knowledge and use of French were taken for granted. This gradually became less true as Flanders – following the language legislation – became officially monolingual Dutch-speaking. The youngest generations of Flemings, unlike their parents and grandparents, have grown up and become socialised in a monolingual Dutch environment. Moreover, they are much more focused on the Anglo-Saxon world, which means that French has literally become more of a foreign language. The most tangible consequence of this development is that virtually no French-language newspapers are read in Flanders and virtually nobody there watches francophone Belgian television channels. Likewise, very few Walloons or francophone Brussels residents follow the Flemish media (Dewachter 1996: 134–5). The three communities each have their own stations (VRT for the Flemish Community, RTBF for the French Community and BRF for the German Community), while the commercial radio and television stations are also monolingual.

Primarily as a result of this media gap, two different cultures have gradually emerged, with diverging social sensitivities, fashions and customs. This trend towards cultural divergence was institutionalised and, at the same time, enhanced by the subsequent reforms of the state . Cultural policy was one of the first competences, as far back as 1970, to be devolved to the communities. In 1989, the communities were also given authority over education. This brought about a separation between Flemish, French and German education systems. Even in bilingual Brussels, the French-speaking and Dutch-speaking education networks are entirely separate. This means that the central Belgian authority has barely any policy instruments to promote or socialise a shared Belgian culture, assuming the existence of a political will to do so.

The fact that citizens know nothing about the other region and are becoming increasingly alienated from it, leads logically to a decline in inter-regional mobility. Relatively few Flemings or Walloons look for jobs in the other region, which prevents optimum harmonisation between demand and supply on the Belgian labour market and increases unemployment (Nationale Bank van België 2004: 57–9). Related to this, the number of mixed Flemish–Walloon marriages is also very low. In 1991, only 7.4 per cent of men and 7.6 per cent of women in Flanders had a marriage partner from another region. In Wallonia, these percentages are a little higher – 19 per cent and 15.3 per cent respectively – but this also includes those Walloons whose marriage partner comes from the largely francophone Brussels Region (Bartiaux and Wattelar 2002: 91–5).

The Identity of Flemings and Walloons

Due to the unconsolidated process of nation-building in Belgium, identification with the nation has always been relatively weak, even before the start of the federalisation process. As a result of the successive constitutional reforms, moreover, the Belgian nation has met with competition from the Walloon and Flemish entities, which also appeal to the citizens' sense of identity. The Flemish government, in particular, occasionally pursues a genuine policy of nation-building, aimed at creating a Flemish national consciousness. In this way, the new Flemish institutions to some extent take over the role which was long played by the *Vlaamse Beweging* (Flemish Movement). This policy is also a way for the Flemish government to legitimise itself. On the French-speaking front, this desire for a (sub-) national sense of identity is much less obvious. This is because, on the one hand, Belgian identity is seen as less problematic than in Flanders, but also because no uniform object of identification is present. On the Flemish side, the Flemish Region and the Flemish Community have merged, as a result of which a single sub-nation has emerged, with one government and one parliament. By contrast, the Walloon Region and the French Community form two separate institutions. Advocates of a subnational consciousness are fighting different corners: some prefer to advocate a Walloon regional consciousness while others primarily want to promote identification with what is known as the *Communauté Wallonie-Bruxelles*. This division – at the levels of both the institutions and the policy visions – is one of the reasons why subnational or regional consciousness is relatively limited in Wallonia.

The more recent survey results using the 'Moreno' question indicate that a large proportion of Walloons (39.1 per cent) attaches equal importance to Walloon and Belgian identity (Table 1). For a relative minority, however, Belgian identity is to a greater or lesser extent more significant. Compared to this, the group for which Walloon identity is more important is very small

(11.9 per cent). In Wallonia, Belgian feelings are somewhat stronger among young people and the more highly educated but, in general, the correlation between national consciousness and background characteristics is weak (De Winter 2003).

If we look at the development over time of territorial identities (Table 2), using the question 'With which level do you identify most?', we find that in Wallonia the absolute majority that identifies with Belgium increases steadily, while identification with the region or community continues to decrease.

In Flanders, Belgian national consciousness has been put under pressure most by a form of subnational consciousness, although we do notice an important shift over time. While before 1986 most Flemings identified in the first place with Flanders, Belgium has become the first choice since 1986, and for more than an absolute majority in the last decade. Here too, it does not seem to be true that the Belgian sense of identity is gradually being eroded as

TABLE 1

IDENTIFICATION WITH BELGIUM AND THE REGION, IN FLANDERS AND WALLONIA, 2003 (VERTICAL PERCENTAGES)

	Flanders	Wallonia
Only Fleming/Walloon	7.4	3.6
More Fleming/Walloon than Belgian	23.9	8.3
As much Fleming/Walloon as Belgian	42.8	39.1
More Belgian than Fleming/Walloon	14.0	18.2
Only Belgian	11.9	30.8
N	1204	731

Source: ISPO/PIOP, 1999 (samples weighted by age, gender, education and vote).

TABLE 2

FEELINGS OF BELONGING IN FLANDERS ON BASIS OF HIERARCHICAL QUESTION IN THE 1979–2003 PERIOD (PERCENTAGE OPTING FOR A SPECIFIC LEVEL AS FIRST CHOICE)

	1979	1980	1981	1982	1986	1992	1996	1999	2003
Wallonia									
Belgium	54.3	59.4	61.3	57.4	57.6	69.0	71.4	73.3	67.9
Francophone Community	15.7	16.2	17.0	15.6	10.7	11.4	9.2	4.9	6.1
Walloon Region	18.4	17.4	15.0	17.7	15.7	12.2	10.0	10.7	10.3
Province	2.0	0.7	1.0	1.4	2.2	0.0	0.7	1.7	2.2
City/commune	9.4	6.3	5.8	7.8	11.9	7.4	8.7	9.2	10.1
Flanders									
Belgium	34.35	40.12	37.26	34.81	43.89	43.09	53.42	56.9	53.8
Flemish Community/ Region	44.99	44.44	47.36	48.52	32.57	40.53	25.59	27.3	29.3
Province	1.94	1.85	2.16	2.22	3.17	3.07	3.25	2.1	3.6
City/commune	18.71	13.58	13.22	14.44	20.36	13.31	17.71	13.5	12.3

Source: ISPO/PIOP, 1999 (samples weighted by age, gender, education and vote); Regioscopes I to VI (Delruelle and Frognier 1983).

the federalisation process continues. Also, if we look at the Moreno question (Table 1), most Flemings do not regard Belgian and Flemish identities as conflicting, but as complementary. In 2003, a relative majority of 43 per cent felt just as much Fleming as Belgian. In addition, however, another 31.3 per cent felt more or exclusively Flemish, compared to a somewhat smaller group of 25.9 per cent who felt more or exclusively Belgian (De Winter 2002). In other words, the group with a dominant regional or subnational identity is significantly larger than in Wallonia. In Flanders, a clear link exists between level of education and national consciousness, but it is the reverse of the situation in Wallonia: the higher the educational level, the more a person identifies with Flanders. By contrast, national consciousness is not linked to age (De Winter 2002; Maddens *et al.* 1994).

In the Brussels Region, we find more or less the same pattern as in Wallonia: identification with Belgium prevails, albeit to a slightly lesser extent. The fact that Brussels is home to many European institutions and is often regarded as the capital of Europe is reflected in a stronger sense of European identity among the inhabitants of Brussels. Thirty per cent of these strongly identify with Europe as opposed to only 21.9 per cent in Wallonia and 12.8 per cent in Flanders (Billiet *et al.* 2000: 24).

At the same time, these clear differences between Flemings and francophones should be put into perspective, taking into account that in Flanders, Wallonia and Brussels identification with the country or region occupies only a subordinate place in the broader sense of identity. By far the most Belgians (36.1 per cent) identify first and foremost with a primary group (such as family, friends or neighbours). This is followed by ideological groups and associations, with which 15.3 per cent and 9.8 per cent respectively feel most closely linked. Political entities, such as country, region or community, only rank fourth, with 5 per cent (Billiet *et al.* 2000: 18–19).

The degree of national or subnational consciousness is, of course, closely entwined with the political attitude to constitutional reform and the level of autonomy for the provinces. This is why the stronger subnational feelings in Flanders are also translated into more outspoken support for the further federalisation of Belgium. By the end of the 1990s, 60.7 per cent of Flemings were in favour of increasing the autonomy of the regions to a certain degree, within the Belgian state (Table 3). In fact, 33.8 per cent were in favour of dividing up social security – one of the last supporting pillars of the unitary Belgium – compared to 34.8 per cent against (Meersseman *et al.* 2002). Nonetheless, only a small minority of Flemings, about 12 per cent, is in favour of separatism and complete Flemish independence. Another minority of 14.5 per cent advocates a complete return to a unitary Belgium to the detriment of the regions, while 12.7 per cent wants to return some powers to the centre.

It should also be pointed out that only a few Flemings regard the Flemish/ Walloon issue as a political priority and take it into consideration in their voting behaviour. In the 1999 elections, only 2.2 per cent mentioned it in the

TABLE 3
ATTITUDE WITH REGARD TO THE DESIRED STATE STRUCTURE
IN 1999, BY REGION (VERTICAL PERCENTAGES)

	Flanders	Wallonia
Return to unitary Belgium	14.5	46.7
Federal state with more powers for the central authority than now	12.7	13.9
Federal state with more powers for the communities and regions than now	28.1	14.6
Federal state with as many powers as possible for communities and regions	32.6	19.3
Separatism	12.0	5.5
N	1760	1112

Source: ISPO/PIOP, 1999 (samples weighted by age, gender, education and vote).

broad sense as one of the reasons for their choice of a party (Swyngedouw *et al.* 2001: 7). With this in mind, it may be surprising that a radical separatist party is currently the largest in Flanders. However, *Vlaams Belang* draws voters mainly on the basis of the issues of immigrants and security and less on the basis of the Flemish/Walloon issue. At the same time, since the disappearance of the VU, this issue has become somewhat more important among the *Vlaams Belang* electorate.

In Wallonia, those favourably disposed towards Belgium are significantly more numerous than in Flanders. No fewer than 46.7 per cent are out-and-out advocates of a return to a unitary Belgium, while an additional 13.9 per cent want to maintain federalism, but with a strengthening of the central authority (Table 3). By contrast, 33.9 per cent are in favour of a strengthening of the regions within the Belgian state and a mere 5.5 per cent are separatists (De Winter 2003). In Wallonia, only 12.4 per cent are in favour of dividing up social security. This should come as little surprise because it is particularly the less prosperous Walloon Region which has an interest in a federally organised social security system and also because the Walloon political elite is strongly against splitting it up.

On the whole, it appears that, despite the growing social duality referred to above, a Belgian feeling still exists and has actually been on the rise in recent years. This should be seen as a latent undercurrent in public opinion, which can be sporadically activated by emotionally charged events. For example, whenever Belgium does well in the football World Cup or if a 'Belgian' final is played at the Roland Garros tennis tournament, then the Belgian tricolour is flown proudly and everyone is Belgian again, rather than Flemish or Walloon. Following the Dutroux case in 1996 and the ensuing 'white march' in Brussels, a strong feeling of national solidarity was evident. However, the most pronounced demonstration of Belgian feelings took place in 1993 following the death of King Baudouin. The fact that the Belgians mourned their deceased monarch *en masse* was regarded by observers as a sign that Belgian national consciousness is still widespread and deep-rooted, whatever form it may take.

The latter also provides a good illustration of the importance of the monarchy as a symbolic bond between Flemings and Walloons. Around 52 per cent of Belgians in 2003 agreed with the statement, 'we should be happy that we have a King because the country would fall apart otherwise'. Here too, however, major differences are evident between Flanders, where only 43 per cent are of this opinion, and Wallonia, where 63 per cent subscribe to this view. As Belgium is institutionally dismantled and social duality increases, the role of the monarchy as a unifying factor actually seems to be growing. This is facilitated by the fact that the royal house can rely on considerable popularity throughout the country. Nonetheless, the monarchy is not entirely immune to the growing dualism in Belgian society. For a long time, it was particularly in the predominantly socialist Wallonia that the monarchy was contested, while the more conservative Flanders took up the defence of the monarchy. This contrast was most clearly expressed during the post-war royal question. In a referendum on the return of Leopold III to the throne in 1950, a majority of Flemings voted in favour and a majority of Walloons against. However, in recent decades, the roles seem to have been reversed and support for the monarchy is more widespread in Wallonia than in Flanders. In Flanders, we observe that support for the monarchy decreased during the 1990s: in 1990, 62.1 per cent of Flemings still believed that Belgium needed a King but by 2003 that had shrunk to 52.7 per cent. In Wallonia, the proportion responding positively to this question is currently significantly higher than in Flanders, at 71 per cent, while it was comparable in 1990 (59.6 per cent). This is perhaps related to the fact that the monarch, in strongly defending the unity of the country and explicitly rejecting the more radical demands for increased regional autonomy, fits in more closely with Walloon than with Flemish public opinion. This is also why Flemings sometimes have the impression that the monarch serves primarily francophone interests. For instance, in 2001, 46.3 per cent of Flemish 18 year olds agreed with the statement that the King was much closer to francophones than to Dutch-speakers, compared to only 17 per cent who rejected this statement (Maddens *et al.* 2002: 559).

Secularisation in Belgium: Increasing Similarity?

Belgium is known as a Catholic country. In 1846, the first census in Belgium registered 99.8 per cent of the population as Catholic. By 2003, according to the European Social Survey (ESS), this figure was only 43 per cent of the population aged over 15. In Flanders, half of the population still refers to itself as Catholic but in Wallonia and Brussels only one in three inhabitants still professes membership of the Catholic Church. Of course, this comparison between 1846 and the present does have its shortcomings. In 1846, the survey dealt with those actually baptised Catholic, while the ESS relates to subjectively considering oneself Catholic. For this reason, we would do better to compare the present figures with similar surveys. In 1981, the European Value Study (EVS) still registered 72 per cent Catholic. Less than ten years later, in the EVS for 1990, this was only 55 per cent, after which it declines to a minority of around 43 per cent in 2003. At the same time, half of the Belgians included in the ESS claim that they do not (or no longer) belong to any church. This places Belgium, of the 22 countries that participated in the ESS, in a central position between Greece and Poland as the most religious countries and the Czech Republic and Sweden at the other extreme.

These data are in line with a recent study by the sociologist of religion, Dobbelaere; using the church statistics, he reached approximately the same conclusion regarding weekly church attendance (around 10 per cent in 1998). He also observes that little difference is evident among the regions (Dobbelaere 2003: 10). Until the 1980s, major differences still existed among the populations of Flanders, Wallonia and Brussels. Dobbelaere also demonstrates that the proportion of marriages still celebrated in church has fallen to 50 per cent. Christian burials have also declined, but the percentage is still around 80 per cent. This can partly be explained by differences in age as far as church involvement is concerned. In the generation aged over 60, according to the recent ESS data for Belgium, 31 per cent still go to church every week, but this figure drops to 9 per cent among those aged 45–60. In the age groups under 45, weekly religious practice is below 4 per cent. In this age group, the number of inhabitants of Belgium who never participate in religious services and who do not regard themselves as religious is well over 50 per cent. Among 45–60 year olds, 42 per cent do not belong to any religion but in the category aged over 80 this figure is only 27 per cent. This indicates that secularisation is taking place chiefly among the generations that have not yet reached the age of 60 (in other words, baby-boomers). If we assume that abandoning the church is mainly a phenomenon affecting young adults, this would fit in with the findings of Dobbelaere (2003), which place the most rapid decline in church involvement during the 1960s and 1970s. The decline took place more quickly in Flanders than in the rest of the country so that, as stated above, the differences between the regions in terms of church involvement have diminished. In the 2003 electoral survey, the figures for weekly religious practice are so similar that no significant difference can be seen: 9.5 per cent in Flanders, 8.7 per cent in Wallonia and 10.9 per cent in Brussels. The fact that Brussels is now at the same level is related to the presence of Muslims.

Of course, weekly participation in religious services is not the whole story. We know from research that many people still take part in public religious services regularly, or at least during the major religious festivals. As far as Belgium is concerned, in addition to the more than 10 per cent of weekly practising believers, another 8 per cent participate regularly and 15 per cent only take part in services on major religious Holy Days (e.g. Christmas, Easter, All Saints). In addition, many more people come into contact with religious services mainly within the context of funerals. It could be said that, at such times of loss, most people still come into contact with the church.

Secularisation, De-pillarisation and Voting Behaviour

Despite growing secularisation among Flemings and francophone Belgians, church involvement continues to exert a strong influence on voting behaviour for certain parties. Thanks to successive electoral surveys, we have a reasonably good picture of the composition of the electorates of political parties by church involvement and membership of social organisations in the various regions, spanning a period of 13 years. Table 4 shows the net effects of voting for each party, in the 2003 parliamentary elections, depending on the level of church involvement. The column percentages on the right (total) give the distribution of all votes cast by the voting populations of Flanders and Wallonia. The row at the top of each table section gives the distribution of these populations by church involvement. We present the effects as differences between the average percentage of votes for a party and the net percentage of votes for that party within each category of voters. The net percentages (or odds) of votes for a party are usually a good deal lower than the observed percentages because the other characteristics, such as age and health insurance fund, have been removed. In the table, all effects of more than five percentage points are given in bold. This makes it easy to see where a party has scored considerably below or above its average.

TABLE 4

NET EFFECTS OF VOTING FOR EACH PARTY BY CHURCH INVOLVEMENT
IN FLANDERS AND WALLONIA IN 2003, EXPRESSED AS DEVIATIONS
FROM THE GRAND MEAN OF EACH PARTY

Flanders 2003	None (11.1%)	Free thinker (6.7%)	Non-practising (46.6%)	Irregular churchgoer (20.7%)	Regular churchgoer (11.9%)	Total*
Agalev	+0.47	+4.92	−0.13	+0.45	−2.38	3.9%
CD&V	−12.18	−16.85	−4.09	+10.12	+25.82	20.9%
N-VA	+0.44	−2.95	−0.60	+1.09	−0.54	4.6%
SP.A-Spirit	+10.90	+11.03	−1.07	−4.54	−3.59	23.6%
VLD	+1.73	−3.72	+4.07	−4.86	−11.22	24.3%
Vlaams Blok	−1.59	−0.29	+1.53	+3.78	−10.29	17.9%

Wallonia 2003	None (13.4%)	Free thinker (11.7%)	Non-practising (42.0%)	Irregular churchgoer (16.9%)	Regular churchgoer (11.8%)	Total*
CDH	−9.94	−10.30	−1.78	+7.40	+17.20	15.2%
Ecolo	+5.85	−1.88	−3.59	+1.99	−1.05	7.3%
FN	−4.95	+10.01	+3.54	−5.07	−4.92	5.5%
MR	−2.53	−13.47	−0.30	+6.62	+8.62	28.0%
PS	+5.27	+9.27	+4.40	−5.82	−18.22	36.1%

ISPO data: N = 1.213 in Flanders and 777 in Wallonia.

*Calculated based on all voters, blank and spoiled votes included, but these are not shown in the table. Those of 'other' religions are not included because of their low numbers.

Involvement in church life in Flanders remains an important predictor of voting for the CD&V, although the overall influence of religious involvement is declining. Table 4 shows that, in Flanders, the net odds of voting for the CD&V in 2003 is indeed more than twice as high as the average (0.474 compared to 0.205). Furthermore, it is striking that being of no religion or liberal (free-thinker) has a strong effect on the chance of voting for SP. a-*Spirit* or for Agalev. The VLD has the highest net odds among non-practising voters. The net odds of a vote for the *Vlaams Blok* is the smallest among devout voters. We know from the ISPO surveys[1] that, until 1999, the *Vlaams Blok* had more success among non-believers and, in 1991, among liberals (Billiet *et al.* 2000) but, in 2003, this seemed to have changed. For the first time, the *Vlaams Blok* probably obtained more votes than the average from the (irregularly) practising Catholics, while that chance is no higher than the average among voters who claim no religious conviction and among liberals.

In Wallonia, the odds of voting *Front National* is apparently much larger among voters who refer to themselves as 'liberal'. It is still true that, in Wallonia, being of no faith or liberal still strongly favours the socialist vote and prevents voting for the Christian democrats. Voters in Wallonia who regularly go to church are only half as likely to vote for the PS than the average odds in the electorate as a whole. The exact opposite is true for devout Catholics. In Wallonia, the MR has considerably higher odds among practising and devout Catholics. The effects on a vote for the CDH are even higher but the net odds of voting for the MR are higher among these Catholics than the net percentage of a vote for the CDH. These data indicate that de-pillarisation, in the sense of the separation of voters from their traditional, pillarised party, had advanced further in Wallonia in 2003 than in Flanders, if the criterion of the relationship between church involvement and (reported) voting behaviour is used.

A similar trend towards de-pillarisation, with some differences in pace between Flanders and Wallonia, depending on whether we look at sociological Catholics or socialists, can also be seen in membership of a trade union and health insurance fund. The declining predictability of voting behaviour based on membership of socialist organisations is advancing more rapidly in Flanders than in Wallonia. This can be deduced from the differences in odds of members of a Christian or socialist trade union, or of Christian or socialist health insurance funds of voting for the Christian democrats or socialists respectively, depending on the generation to which they belong (under or over 45).[2] In both the younger and older generations, the link between membership of a trade union and the political party associated with it is stronger among socialists than Christian democrats. The ideological colour of a trade union perhaps remains a predictor of voting behaviour, but de-pillarisation is felt more strongly among both Flemings and francophones in the generations aged under 45 because, on average, fewer votes are cast for Christian democrats or socialists. Among the youngest generation of members of the Christian trade union in Wallonia, in 1999 the PSC no longer gained an advantage because the odds of voting for the socialists was equally high. This indicates that in Wallonia the PSC and, subsequently, the CDH are losing trade union votes to the socialists, a clear sign of de-pillarisation (Billiet 2006). Membership of health insurance funds shows a similar picture but, in Wallonia, this remains a very strong predictor of voting for the socialists, among both older and younger generations. In Wallonia, the socialist pillar remains firm (Billiet 2006).

The increasing detachment of voting behaviour from membership of social organisations was associated in Flanders, between 1999 and 2004, with the growth of the *Vlaams Blok*, a party at odds with the traditional divisions on the electoral landscape.

The Attitude of Belgians towards Newcomers

In the special Eurobarometer of 1997, Belgium was presented as the country with the most racists among all European countries investigated at the time. Why is this? Thanks to the ESS, we currently have more reliable data about a large number of aspects of attitudes towards immigrants and asylum-seekers. The picture is more subtle. We have been following the development of attitudes towards foreigners almost constantly since 1989. What are the main findings?

One aspect that was repeatedly examined between 1989 and 2003 is the feeling of being threatened by the presence of immigrants in terms of employment, social provisions and culture. As far as this aspect is concerned, few differences exist between Flemings and francophones and not much has changed over the years. Around 1998, the economic threat had diminished somewhat but, subsequently, these feelings became as strong as they were 15 years ago. Almost six out of ten Belgians have the feeling that 'their' social security is being threatened by the presence of foreigners and this feeling is stronger in Wallonia than in Flanders and Brussels. For instance, in 2003, four out of ten Flemings were of the opinion that immigrants who were long-term unemployed should be forced to leave, but this was less the case than in francophone Belgium, where half of the adult population is of this opinion. Things are slightly different in terms of cultural threat. Almost four out of ten Belgians feel threatened in their cultural individuality but that is just as much the case in Flanders as in Wallonia, but much less pronounced in Brussels. Where political rights are involved, such as the municipal voting right granted last year to foreigners who have been in Belgium legally for more than five years, various studies show that the vast majority of Flemings opposes this (between 60 and 65 per cent) while in Wallonia and Brussels around 45 per cent are against. More francophones (67 per cent) than Flemings (50 per cent) are of the opinion that people who come to live in Belgium should have the same rights as everyone else. Over 57 per cent of francophones claim to have some friends from another country; among Flemings this is considerably lower (37 per cent).

In other words, quite a few differences are still evident between the regions depending on the specific aspect that is related to immigration. Flemings usually feel somewhat more threatened in their cultural individuality and are less likely to seek out social contact with foreigners. In francophone Belgium, particularly in Wallonia, where the economic situation is the most problematic, people feel most threatened at economic level and in terms of social provisions.

The attitude towards asylum-seekers is another aspect that has been examined recently. Do Flemings have a different attitude towards asylum-seekers than their southern compatriots? In order to answer this question, we use the data from the ESS. This face-to-face survey, conducted in 2002 among 1,899 Belgians, contains a large number of items about admission policy and about the subjects of immigration and asylum. Members of the French-speaking community seem to hold a more tolerant attitude than their northern neighbours. As far as admission policy is concerned, Belgians are, in general, not very favourably disposed towards admitting many people from outside Belgium, no matter what their characteristics – the same or a different ethnic group, rich or poor. When forced to choose, people were more inclined to accept immigrants from poorer countries rather than people from richer countries. A minority of around 15 per cent simply does not want to admit anyone else. These findings provide a subtle picture of the admission or reception of foreigners. Most Belgians appear to be receptive to arguments in favour of accepting asylum-seekers, as long as their number is not too high.

Most Belgians agree on a number of aspects of the asylum issue. For instance, 68 per cent of Belgians believe that Belgium has proportionately far too many asylum-seekers. The majority of Belgians (61 per cent) is also of the opinion that asylum-seekers should be granted permission to work in Belgium while their asylum applications are being processed. On this point, virtually no differences exist between Flemings and francophones. A narrow majority of 56 per cent does not agree that the government should be flexible when assessing asylum applications and does not advocate the right to family reunification for recognised refugees; this percentage is considerably higher in Flanders (over 67 per cent). Francophones are also somewhat more inclined to provide financial support (30 per cent compared to 19 per cent of Flemings) and to allow family reunification (36 per cent compared to 23 per cent) and only half as many francophones (20 per cent) as Flemings (40 per cent) agree with housing asylum-seekers in closed centres (Meireman *et al.* 2004). With respect to various aspects of asylum policy and immigration, the Belgians are not so different from the Dutch. They rank approximately in the middle of the 22 European countries that participated in the first round of the European Social Survey. The Nordic countries are generally more open and the southern and central European countries more closed towards immigration.

Social and Political Trust

A final set of political views attracting our interest relates to confidence in the future and in others, including politicians and institutions. We prefer to report the figures of the 1999 election survey since the list of institutions was then much larger than in 2003. Significant changes in 2003 are reported in the text.

Following the Dutroux case in the mid-1990s, confidence in institutions and in the police took a serious blow. Among all institutions, education and the King could rely most on the confidence of the Flemish population. In research following the 1995 elections, in other words before the infamous summer of 1996, over 70 per cent of Flemings still had a high or very high degree of confidence in education and 50 per cent in the King. In 1999 in Flanders, education still retained the same level of support, but confidence in the King fell considerably to 41 per cent (Table 5). In Wallonia, confidence in the King remained at more or less the same level and in Brussels it actually rose by five percentage points compared to 1995. Trust in the King rose more than ten percentage points by 2003 in Brussels and Wallonia. In Wallonia and Brussels, by the end of the 1990s, citizens had less confidence in education (around 55 per cent) than in Flanders and this remained reasonably stable between 1995 and 1999. This cannot be separated from the limited resources on which the French Community can rely as a result of the economic situation and the successive strikes suffered by the education system over this period.

TABLE 5

CONFIDENCE IN SOCIAL INSTITUTIONS IN THE BELGIAN REGIONS IN 1999
(PERCENTAGES OF HIGH AND REASONABLY HIGH CONFIDENCE)

Institution	Flanders	Wallonia	Brussels	Total
Education system	72.6	55.0	52.2	65.5
Preferred political party[ns]	47.5	43.8	51.3	46.5
King	41.3	52.2	49.6	45.5
Federal police (*Rijkswacht*)	38.1	29.7	24.6	34.4
Banks	37.7	24.0	28.1	23.4
Federal Parliament	19.1	25.8	27.8	21.9
European Parliament	18.2	25.0	30.0	21.2
The press	16.3	28.1	23.6	20.6
Trade unions	18.3	20.3	22.5	19.2
The government	17.1	24.2	22.3	19.8
Church[ns]	18.3	20.3	16.7	18.8
Central administration	12.3	23.8	16.0	16.3
The judicial authorities	13.9	19.9	17.5	16.1
Employers' organisations	11.7	14.3	12.9	12.7
Political parties[ns]	8.2	11.1	11.2	9.4
N	2,179	1,483	577	4,239

Note: **ISPO/PIOP** data from 1999 electoral research. All differences are statistically significant.
[ns]Not statistically significant at level 0.01.

Confidence in the justice system (judicial authorities) was already low in 1995 in Belgium (19 per cent) and fell even further in 1999 (16 per cent) and it remains low in 2003. The decline in confidence in the judicial authorities took place mainly in Flanders and Brussels. Confidence in the federal police (then still the *Rijkswacht*) also fell from 41 per cent in 1995 to only 34.4 per cent in 1999. The most striking aspect is that this decline in confidence in the federal police of over ten percentage points was evident primarily in Wallonia and Brussels. This is not surprising, since it was chiefly the *Rijkswacht* in Brussels and Wallonia that was involved in the investigative work relating to the missing children. In francophone public opinion, the police fell short in many respects. The general figure for 2003 is about the same, and there are no longer differences between the regions in trust in the federal police.

It is noticeable that confidence in a number of institutions such as the federal parliament, the European Parliament, the press, the government and the central administration is higher in francophone Belgium than in Flanders. The fact that the European Parliament scores the highest in Brussels is, of course, related to the fact that much European activity takes place in the capital, which produces tangible advantages for many citizens. Confidence in the banks is higher in Flanders. Public opinion there is obviously less left-leaning. In the ISPO/PIOP survey[3] from 1999, confidence in the political parties scores poorly in general throughout the country but we see a sharp contrast with confidence in the preferred political party. Evidently, people still have confidence in the parties for which they vote. The trust in the preferred political party is somewhat higher in 2003, but confidence in the government or the federal parliament has remained almost unchanged.

In addition to information about confidence in institutions, we have data about the images citizens have of politicians and the political system. In particular, Wallonia stands out for its very negative picture of political life. In answer to the question about spontaneous reaction to the word 'politics', in 1999 57 per cent of Walloon voters responded with 'distrust', 'aversion' and 'boredom'. In Flanders and Brussels, the figure is a good ten percentage points lower. Proportionately fewer Walloon than Flemish voters are satisfied with democracy. This remained fairly stable in 1996 and 1999. The electoral survey of 1996 showed that Walloon voters had more markedly negative feelings towards politicians and elections. More than Flemings, they felt that promises would not be fulfilled and that little consideration was given to the wishes of the voters. This dismal view of politicians improved a little in 1999 and 2003. Differences still exist between Flemings and francophones, but they are somewhat less pronounced than in 1996.

The feeling of political impotence and distrust has always been more strongly held in Wallonia and Brussels than in Flanders, but this is not only the case for lack of confidence in politics. The allegation that most people disappoint once you get to know them was endorsed by a quarter of Flemish voters in 1996, but in Wallonia the figure was considerably higher, at 38 per cent. The general feeling of distrust also seems to have grown in Flanders. In 1989, 42 per cent of adult Flemings agreed with the statement, 'Nowadays you really do not know whom you can trust'. In 1996, this had risen to 59 per cent, but in Wallonia, in the same period, this figure was over 68 per cent. Deeper research shows that this view is closely correlated with an attitude that expressed confusion, the feeling of complexity and uncertainty about the future. This general feeling of social confusion was a little stronger in Wallonia around 1996 but, subsequently, it diminished again and francophone Belgium presented a less unfavourable picture. In 1999 and 2003, half of Flemings still expressed this general distrust of others but, in Wallonia, this had fallen to approximately 44 per cent. Apparently not everything evolves in the same direction. This observation is a good starting point for thinking about how we should understand these tendencies in differing public opinions.

The Values of Flemings and Francophones

The European Social Survey examines the ten 'universal values' from Schwartz (1992, 2003), using 21 verbal 'portraits'; these are short descriptions in which the respondent has to indicate how strongly he or she identifies with each portrait. An attempt was made to measure more concisely the extensive instrument used to measure every value based on four items. These basic values are independence, universalism, charity, tradition, conformity, security, power, success, hedonism and meeting challenges. In Schwartz's research, these ten values can be traced back to two main dimensions: openness to change versus conservatism, on the one hand, and self-enhancement versus self-transcendence, on the other. Since the value set was severely limited, it is not possible to reconstruct the ten original values using measuring models in a way that is equivalent for all 22 countries in the ESS. During a presentation at the first conference of the European Association for Survey Research, researchers presented a model with seven values that is equivalent for all countries (Davidov and Schmidt 2005). This model is obtained by merging universalism with charity, tradition with conformity and power with success. We will use this model. Below is a brief description of each of the seven values. We then examine to what extent Flemings and francophones differ in average scores and whether the effect of the language group is still evident after controlling for other relevant characteristics.

- *Universalism and charity*: believing it important that everyone in the world be treated equally and have equal opportunities, that people try to understand one another, that they care for the environment and that people devote themselves to the welfare of people around them;

- *Tradition and conformity*: always following the rules, upholding the customs acquired during one's upbringing and always acting modestly and properly;
- *Power and success*: attaching much importance to money and material success, being admired by others and acquiring influence and recognition so that others do what he or she wants;
- *Security*: believing that it is important to live in a secure environment and knowing that one is protected by a strong state;
- *Hedonism*: taking every opportunity to pursue pleasure and to enjoy and indulge oneself;
- *Independence*: being creative and wanting to do everything in an original way, feeling free and making decisions independently;
- *Taking on challenges*: always going in search of new things, looking for adventure as well as being prepared to take risks.

These are descriptions to which people attach great importance and the exercise involves indicating, on a six-point scale, how strongly the respondent resembles them. All value scales consist of two to five indicators and are constructed so that they vary between 0 (least similar) and 10 (most similar). The internal consistency or reliability of these scales is not strong, but moderate to weak. This is because each description contains more than one idea and is fairly complex.[4] Table 6 presents a summary of the average scores for Flemings and francophones. The differences are statistically significant in six of the seven cases (0.01 at α level). In order to assess the size of the differences, we look once again at neighbouring countries.

With the exception of traditionalism/conformity and the security value, francophones achieve consistently higher scores than Flemings. This is particularly true of the values of independence and being willing to take on challenges and adventures. Flemings score significantly lower on these aspects. Francophones are also on average somewhat more focused on enjoying life and they also attach greater importance to having material success and influence. As far as the values of universalism and charity are

TABLE 6
AVERAGE SCORES (OUT OF 10) FOR SEVEN VALUES AMONG FLEMINGS (N = 1245) AND FRANCOPHONES (N = 651) IN THE EUROPEAN VALUES SURVEY OF 2002

Group	Univ. & charity	Trad., conform	Power, success	Security	Hedonism	Independence	Challenges
Francophones	9.97	6.46	5.22	7.22	7.22	7.65	5.74
Flemings	9.76	6.45	4.87	6.99	6.75	7.07	5.03
Difference	0.20	0.01	0.35	0.24	0.47	0.58	0.71
T value	3.02	0.08	3.83	2.46	4.78	6.77	6.39
prob. >|t|	0.003	0.933	<0.001	0.014	<0.001	<0.001	<0.001

concerned, francophones also score somewhat higher, but the difference is very small.

To what extent can these differences be attributed to membership of a linguistic community? In order to examine this question, we must control for other relevant characteristics that are present to varying degrees in the two population groups. We examine whether the linguistic group still has an effect on the values after controlling for characteristics such as gender, age, level of education, church involvement, professional situation and urbanisation. We do this using multivariate regression analyses with the values as dependent variables. The first noticeable aspect is that the values can only be explained to a very limited extent by the characteristics mentioned. The explained variance usually fluctuates between 5 and 10 per cent. Only the values of tradition and conformity (18 per cent explained variance) and taking on challenges (16 per cent) are better explained. As was the case for the averages, the linguistic group has no effect on the value of tradition and conformity. In other cases, being French-speaking still seems to lead to somewhat stronger identification with the stated values.

The question is, of course, whether the differences found in values are sufficiently pronounced to attach any importance to them. If we compare the scores for Flemings and Walloons with those of their neighbours – the Dutch, Germans, French and British – it appears that, all things considered, the differences between Flemings and Walloons are not so large after all.

Conclusion

We have seen above that quite a few differences in public opinion still exist between Flemings and francophone Belgians. Are these related to differences in national character? If this were the case, these differences would be stable. We have seen, however, that some opinions vary from survey to survey. Answers to opinion questions are shaped by the convictions that are most salient to the respondents at the time of questioning and this salience is related to presence in the media (Zaller 1992). For this reason, it is better to attribute differences in public opinion to political and economic circumstances and events that are specific to the region, such as the economic situation in Wallonia or approval of the actions of the *Gendarmerieijkswacht* in francophone public opinion. These contextual characteristics are more important than national character. Some differences indicate a stable trend and these can be ascribed to the predominant political climate in public opinion in the various regions. The fluctuations in confidence in democracy and the government can be related to policy experiences in the period preceding the electoral survey. The differences in political views do not have a significant impact on the assessment of the pace at which Belgium is apparently disintegrating. We even saw that some differences of opinion between Flemings and Walloons were actually reversed over a period of ten years.

The different ways in which Flemings and francophones regard new-comers is slightly more stable but here, too, we saw that, in some respects, the Walloons feel more economically threatened than Flemings, while in other areas francophone Belgium demonstrates a higher degree of openness. This difference can be explained on historical grounds, as Wallonia has a much longer experience with immigration than Flanders. The presence of an extreme right-wing party, which, in public opinion, keeps the subject of immigration alive, can also be proposed as an explanation.

We found a number of differences in values with which people identify. Taken together, these values are embraced somewhat more actively by francophone Belgians, but the differences are not so pronounced when compared to neighbouring countries.

According to the political scientist Karl Deutsch (1953), social commu-nication is the essence of nation-building. A nation stands or falls by the extent of internal communication between its members. From this perspective, it is difficult to call Belgium a nation by French standards, which is typical of multicultural polities. This is particularly strong in Belgium as the minority (French and German speakers) as well as the majority group (Flemish) react as a menaced minority. The two regions increasingly form separate circuits of communication and are therefore growing socially further apart, as indicated above. The emergence of two separate political systems is the logical consequence of this far-reaching social development rather than its cause. It is true, however, that political developments – the institutional dismantling of the Belgian unitary state and the creation of two separate party systems – have confirmed the trend towards social divergence in recent decades. As a result of far-reaching constitutional reforms, the central government no longer has the policy tools to stop these developments, let alone reverse them. Moreover, it is generally accepted that even more powers will be transferred from the federal government to the regions and communities in the near future. Consequently, it is to be expected that Flanders and francophone Belgium will grow further apart in the future.

However, this does not have to mean that Belgium will cease to exist as a country. Belgium's 175-year history and the historical solidarity between Flemings and Walloons have left their mark. This is expressed, in particular, in a continued and widespread Belgian feeling, although this is considerably stronger in Wallonia than in Flanders, and in a number of shared values. The emotional ties to Belgium remain, in both regions, an important counterbalance to the centrifugal forces, both institutional and social. In addition, these forces are also contained by the fact that an over-arching Belgian political and economic elite still exists, which uses its not inconsiderable, albeit significantly reduced power to maintain the unity of the country. The still-popular monarchy plays a key role in this respect. The likelihood of Belgium dividing into two separate states therefore is not very high in the medium term. The country may, however, evolve into a looser confederate or bi-national union, where the regions have very broad autonomy and continue to decide mutually on a number of community matters.

At the same time, the concept of the state will lose much of its significance one way or another in the future. The classical nation-state concept is largely outdated as a result of economic and cultural globalisation and increasing interdependence. Institutionally, this development is most strongly expressed in the European integration process. With this in mind, the question of whether the state of Belgium will continue to exist needs to be put into perspective. In the long term, the question will probably not be so much whether Belgium will continue to exist as a sovereign state, but whether either Flanders and Wallonia or Belgium will become the member states of the European federation in the making. Who knows, maybe Belgium will come up with a creative compromise for this dilemma too.

Notes

1. ISPO is the Institute for Social and Political Opinion Research in the Dutch-speaking part of Belgium.
2. This is covered in detail in a recent study about de-pillarisation by J. Billiet (2006).
3. PIOP is the Institute for Political Opinion Research in the French-speaking part of Belgium.
4. The scales with four or five statements have an alpha reliability of 0.60 to 0.68. The correlations between the pairs of statements are higher than 0.43, with the exception of the 'independence' value, where the two items only correlate at 0.30.

References

Bartiaux, F., and C. Wattelar (2002). *Algemene Volks- en Woningtelling op 1 maart 1991. Nuptialiteit*, Monograph no. 5A. Brussels: National Statistical Institute.

Billiet, J. (2006). 'Verzuiling en ontzuiling', in E. Witte and A. Meynen (eds.), *De geschiedenis van België na 1945*. Antwerp: Standaard Uitgeverij, 221–364.

Billiet, J., R. Doutrelepont and M. Vanderkeere (2000). 'Types van sociale identiteiten in België: convergenties en divergenties', in K. Dobbelaere, M. Elchardus, J. Kerkhofs, L. Voyé and B. Bawin-Legros (eds.), *Verloren zekerheid. De Belgen en hun waarden, overtuigingen en houdingen*. Tielt: Lannoo, 17–53.

Davidov, E., P. Schmidt and S. Schwartz (2005). 'Valves in Europe: A Multiple Group Comparison with 20 Countries Using the European Social Survey 2003', paper presented at the 1st EASR Conference, Barcelona, July 2005.

Delruelle, N., and A.-P. Frognier (1983). 'Opinion publique et les problèmes communautaires', *Regioscope* IV, C.H. du CRISP, nos. 991–2.

Dewachter, W. (1996). 'La Belgique d'aujourd'hui comme societé politique', in A. Dieckhoff (ed.), *Belgique: la force de la désunion*. Brussels: Editions Complexe, 105–42.

De Winter, L. (2002). 'De ondraaglijke lichtheid van het Belg- of Vlaming-zijn: het enigma van etno-territoriale identiteiten in Vlaanderen', in M. Swyngedouw and J. Billiet (eds.). *De kiezer heeft zijn redenen. 13 juni 1999 en de politieke opvattingen van Vlamingen*. Leuven: Acco, 215–32.

De Winter, L. (2003). 'Sire, il y a encore des Belges ...', in A.P. Frognier and A.M. Aish (eds.), *Elections, la rupture? Le comportement des Belges face aux élections de 1999*. Brussels: De Boeck Université, 110–33.

Deutsch, K.W. (1953). *Nationalism and Social Communication. An Inquiry into the Foundations of Nationality*. Cambridge, MA: MIT Press.

Dobbelaere, K. (2003). 'Trends in de katholieke godsdienstigheid eind 20ste eeuw: België vergeleken met West- en Central- Europese landen', *Tijdschrift voor Sociologie*, 24:1, 9–36.

ISPO/PIOP (1995). *1995 General Election Study Belgium. Codebook and Questionnaire*. Leuven/ Louvain La Neuve: ISPO/PIOP.

ISPO/PIOP (1999). *1999 General Election Study Belgium. Codebook and Questionnaire*. Leuven/ Louvan La Neuve: ISPO/PIOP.

Maddens, B., R. Beerten and J. Billiet (1994). *O dierbaar België? Het natiebewustzijn van Vlamingen en Walen*. Leuven: ISPO/SOI.

Maddens, B., J. Tommissen, D. Vanhee, W. Van Mierloo and K. Weekers (2002). 'In de ban van de koning? Een verkennend survey-onderzoek naar de structuur van de attitudes van Vlaamse scholieren tegenover de monarchie', *Res Publica*, 54:4, 549–73.

Meersseman, E., J. Billiet and A. Depickere (2002). 'De communautaire items. De opinie van de Vlamingen in 1999 over de staatsstructuur en hun (etno)territoriale opvattingen', *ISPO Bulletin* 2002/48. Leuven: Department of Sociology.

Meireman, K., B. Meuleman, J. Billiet, H. De Witte and J. Wets (2004). *Tussen aanvaarding en weerstand. Een sociologisch onderzoek naar houdingen tegenover asiel, opvang en migratie*. Brussels: Federal Science Policy/Academia Press.

Nationale Bank van België (2004). *Annual Report 2003. Part I: Financial and Economic Development*. Brussels: NBB.

Schwartz, S.H. (1992). 'Universals in the content and structure of values: theory and empirical tests in 20 countries', in M. Zanna (ed.), *Advances in Experimental Social Psychology*, volume 25. New York: Academic Press, 1–65.

Schwartz, S.H. (2003). 'A Proposal for Measuring Value Orientations across Nations. Suggestions for the ESS core Module', available at http://www.europeansocialsurvey.org/

Swyngedouw, M., E. Meersseman and J. Billiet (2001). 'Motieven in partijkeuze. De nationale verkiezingen van 13 juni 1999. Results of the VRT-Tijd-ISPO exit poll', *ISPO Bulletin* 2001/42. Leuven: Department of Sociology.

Zaller, J.R. (1992). *The Nature and Origins of Mass Opinion*. Cambridge: Cambridge University Press.

Party System(s) and Electoral Behaviour in Belgium: From Stability to Balkanisation

LIEVEN DE WINTER, MARC SWYNGEDOUW and
PATRICK DUMONT

This article addresses the evolution of the Belgian polity from its unitary and stable period up until the mid-1960s to the present situation of high fragmentation of the party system and centrifugal tendencies of parties and electoral behaviour. The absence of integration between Flemish- and French-speaking parties, the importance of the community cleavage at the level of party elites, and observed divergences in the weight of other cleavages at the level of the electorate all point to the fact that, despite state and electoral reforms, the polities of the two main regions have increasingly diverged and now display deeply entrenched differences.

Evolution of Fragmentation of Party System

The Belgian party system started out as a two-party system in the nineteenth century, opposing the Catholics and liberals basically on the issue of the religious neutrality of the bourgeois state. After the breakthrough of the socialists at the end of that century and the politicisation of the socio-economic left–right cleavage, the Belgian party system constituted a clear-cut example of a two and a half party type (Blondel 1968) until 1965, in which the three traditional parties, Christian Democrats (*Parti Social Chrétien–Christelijke Volkspartij*, Christian Peoples Party–Social Christian Party, PSC-CVP), Socialists (*Parti Socialiste Belge–Belgische Socialistische Partij*, Belgian Socialist Party, PSB-BSP) and Liberals (*Parti Libéral–Liberale Partij*, Liberal Party, PL-LP) alternately shared governmental office in different coalition combinations (De Winter and Dumont 1999).

In the 1960s and 1970s, the number of parties represented in Parliament rose dramatically from four in 1949 to 14 in 1981 (see Tables 1 and 2). Since then, in spite of a slight decrease in the number of parties (currently ten), the degree of fragmentation continuously rose until 1999 (reaching a European record value of 9.1 effective parties, down by 2.1 to 7.0 in 2003). With successive reforms – turning Belgium into a federal state – the party system broke up into two linguistic segments between which there is no electoral competition, in spite of increasing ideological polarisation between them.[1] Since this break-up, no national parties have existed. It is the Flemish party system that mainly caused the high degree of fragmentation recorded at the federal level. For instance, whereas in 1999 the effective number of parties amongst the Flemish linguistic group of the Chamber was 5.2, it was only 3.8 in the French-speaking one.

The de facto regionalisation of the party system occurred in several waves. First the ethno-regionalist parties broke through in the 1960s – the *Volksunie* (People's Union, VU) in Flanders, the *Rassemblement Wallon* (Walloon Rally, RW) in Wallonia, and the *Front Démocratique des Franco-phones* (Francophone Democratic Front, FDF) in the Brussels Region. By the early 1970s, they obtained 20 per cent of the Flemish and Walloon vote, and 40 per cent of the francophone vote in Brussels. Second, the growing saliency of the linguistic and regional cleavage on which their success was based internally divided the Christian Democrat, Liberal and Socialist unitary parties, and each traditional party split into two organisationally and programmatically independent Flemish- and French-speaking branches (respectively in 1968, 1972 and 1978). These parties were bound to split up because of increasing internal clashes between Flemings and francophones, and because internal compromises with regard to regional and linguistic issues did not satisfy their respective electorates in Flanders, Wallonia and Brussels, as the ethno-regionalist parties offered more attractive regionally tailored programmes. Third, at the end of the 1970s, another wave of expansion of the party system occurred through the emergence of the Flemish

TABLE 1

RESULTS OF ELECTIONS FOR THE CHAMBER OF REPRESENTATIVES, 1945–2003

Year	PSC/CVP		PSB/BSP		PL/LP		FDF	RW	PCB	VU	AGALEV	Ecolo	VB	UDRT	FN	ROSSEM	Volatility
	CVP	PSC	SP	PS	VLD	PRL											
1946	42.5		31.6			8.9			12.3								
1949	43.6		29.8			15.3			7.5	2.1							8.10
1950	47.7		34.5			11.2			4.8								8.85
1954	41.1		37.3			12.1			3.6	2.2							6.85
1958	46.5		35.8			11			1.9	2							4.95
1961	41.5		36.7			12.3			3.1	3.5							4.95
1965	34.5		28.3			21.6			4.6	6.7							15.80
1968	22.3	9.4	28			20.9	2.2		3.3	9.8							5.95
1971	21.9	8.2	27.2		9.5	7.2	5.9		3	11.1							6.85
1974	23.3	9.1	26.7		10.4	6	11.4		3.2	10.2							3.25
1977	26.2	9.8	27		8.5	7.8	10.9		2.1	10				0.9			6.35
1978	26.1	10.1	12.4	13	10.4	6	7.1		3.3	7			1.4	2.7			6.20
1981	19.3	7.1	12.4	12.7	12.9	8.6	7.3		2.3	9.8	2.3	2.2	1.1	1.2			14.35
1985	21.3	8	14.6	13.8	10.7	10.2	4.2		1.2	7.9	3.7	2.5	1.4	0.1			9.75
1987	19.5	8	14.9	15.7	11.5	9.4	1.2		0.8	8	4.5	2.6	1.9				4.30
1991	16.8	7.7	12	13.5	12	8.1	1.2		0.1	5.9	4.9	5.1	6.6		1	3.2	12.35
1995	17.2	7.7	12.6	11.9	13.1	10.3	1.1			4.7	4.4	4.	7.8		2.3		6.70
1999	14.1	5.9	9.5	10.2	14.3	10.1				5.6	7	7.4	9.9		1.5		10.90
2003	13.25	5.5	14.9	13	15.36	11.4				3.1	2.5	3.07	11.6		2		12.67

TABLE 2
NUMBER OF SEATS BY PARTIES, CHAMBER OF REPRESENTATIVES, 1945–2003

Year	PCB/KPB	PSB/BSP PS	PSB/BSP SP (a)	E	A (b)	RW	FDF	PSC/CVP PSC (c)	PSC/CVP CVP (c)	VU (d)	PL/LP PRL (e)	PL/LP VLD	UDRT	FN	VB (f)	Others (g)	Effective Number of parties	Total seats
1946	23		**69**						**92***		17					1	2.9	202
1949	12		66						**105***		**29**						2.8	212
1950	7		77						**108***		20						2.5	212
1954	4		**86**						**95***	1	**25**					1	2.6	212
1958	2		84						**104***	1	21						2.5	212
1961	5		**84**						**96***	5	20						2.7	212
1965	6		**64**			2	3		**77***	12	48					2	3.6	212
1968	5		**59**			5	7	**19**	**50***	20	47						5.0	212
1971	5		**61**			14	10	**20**	**47***	21	20	14					5.9	212
1974	4		59			13	9	**22**	**50***	22	9	**21**				3	5.8	212
1977	2		**62**			5	**10**	**24**	**56***	**20**	14	17				2	5.2	212
1978	4	**32**	**26**			4	**11**	**25**	**57***	14	14	22	1			1	6.8	212
1981	2	35	26	2	2	2	6	**18**	**43***	20	**24**	**28**	3		1		7.7	212
1985	0	35	32	5	4	0	3	**20**	**49***	16	**24**	22	1		1		7.0	212

(continued)

TABLE 2
(*Continued*)

Year	PCB/KPB	PSB/BSP		E	A (b)	RW	FDF	PSC/CVP		VU (d)	PL/LP		UDRT	FN	VB (f)	Others (g)	Effective Number of parties	Total seats
		PS	SP (a)					PSC (c)	CVP (c)		PRL (e)	VLD						
1987	0	**40**	**32**	3	6	0	3	**19**	**43***	**16**	23	25	0		2		7.2	212
1991	0	**35**	**28**	10	7	0	3	**18**	**39***	10	20	26	0	1	12	3	8.4	212
1995	0	**21**	**20**	6	5	0	(e)	**12**	**29***	5	18	21	0	2	11		8.1	150
1999	0	**19**	**14**	11	**9**	0	(e)	10	**22***	8	**18**	**23**	0	1	15		9.1	150
2003	0	**25**	**23**	4	0	0	(e)	8	21	1	**24**	**25**	0	1	18		7.0	150

In bold: the parties that composed the governments that were formed after an election.

(a) Became the SP.A (*Socialistische Partij-anders*) in 2001 and formed an electoral cartel since 2003 with SPIRIT, formerly part of the Flemish nationalist VU.

(b) Agalev (the Flemish Greens) became *Groen!* in 2004.

(c) Both the Christian Democrat parties changed names in 2001. The CVP became CD&V (*Christen-Democratisch en Vlaams*) and the PSC became CDH (*Centre Démocrate Humaniste*, Humanist Democrat Centre).

(d) The VU split in 2001. Its successor was the NV-A, first as a standalone party, then in an electoral cartel for the 2004 regional and European elections with the CD&V.

(e) In 1993 the FDF joined the PRL to create the PRL-FDF federation, that would become the PRL-FDF-MCC federation with the arrival of a splinter group from the PSC. In 2003 the federation became the MR (*Mouvement Réformateur*).

(f) In November 2004 the VB became the *Vlaams Belang* (Flemish Interest).

(g) From 1973 to 1979, the Brussels federation of the Liberal Party seceded. They eventually joined back the Walloon Liberals when the PRL was formed in May 1979. In 1991, Flemish businessman Jean-Pierre Van Rossem managed to get elected with two other candidates from his list.

separatist and xenophobe *Vlaams Blok* (Flemish Bloc, VB), the poujadist *Union Démocratique pour le Respect du Travail–Respect voor Arbeid en Democratie* (UDRT-RAD), and the Green parties (Agalev in Flanders and Ecolo in the francophone areas). These evolutions were recognised in the new federal state structures created by the different stages of the state reforms (Martiniello and Swyngedouw 1998).

Hence, since 1978 (the split-up of the last traditional party), there have been two distinct party systems: a Flemish and a francophone one. In the Flemish constituencies, only Flemish parties compete for votes, and as a rule they do not present any lists in the Walloon constituencies (and vice versa). Only in the Brussels–Halle–Vilvoorde (Brussels and periphery) constituency do these two party systems overlap, and Flemish as well as francophone parties compete, at least potentially, for the same set of voters.[2] These two party systems differ in terms of the type of parties that are active, as well as their electoral strength and evolution.

The splitting of the Belgian party system into two quasi-autonomous regional party systems further strengthens the centrifugal tendencies in the Belgian polity. Thus, in Sartori's terms, the current Belgian situation clearly represents a case of extreme multipartyism. As far as the direction of competition between the two regions is concerned, it does not take the polarised *type* for religious and socio-economic founding cleavages, but it certainly does for the most prominent linguistic cleavage. On this cleavage, almost all the Flemish parties are situated at the pole of defence of Flemish interests, while the francophone parties are situated at the pole of the defence of francophone/Walloon interests. Only the Flemish and francophone Green parties remain situated near the centre, as they kept until 2003 a unitary parliamentary group in the federal Parliament and generally aimed at developing a common programme on linguistic/regional problems. Even in this party family, however, in recent times there have been signs of growing tensions on these issues. Note that within the two party systems the different cleavages carry different weights (Swyngedouw 1995 and below). So the left–right dimension in the francophone party system is much more relevant than in the Flemish one, where all the main parties take a centre position on this cleavage.

The Impact of the Electoral System

Under the current system, introduced in 2003, the number of constituencies is 11, equalling the number of provinces plus the large capital constituency Brussels–Halle–Vilvoorde.[3] District magnitude varies from four to 22. Parties in each constituency normally nominate a number of candidates equal to the number of representatives to be elected.

Since 1995, the Senate has consisted of 71 members, of whom 25 and 15 are directly elected in two huge constituencies, the Flemish and Francophone Community, respectively, which only overlap in the Brussels Region. Added to this are 21 delegates of the Communities to the federal Senate: the 'Flemish Parliament' and the 'Francophone Community Council' each nominate ten members and the Council of the German-speaking Community nominates one. Finally, ten senators are co-opted by the first two types of senators. Thus voters have direct influence on the selection of 40 out of 71 senators.

The electoral reform of 2003 has simplified the allocation of seats considerably, by applying the d'Hondt system in each of the 11 constituencies. Also, a 5 per cent threshold at the provincial constituency level was introduced, abolishing the former system of 30 constituencies with second-tier allocation held at the provincial level.

The recent reduction of the party system, bringing the effective number of parties down from 9.1 to 7.0, is only partially due to the introduction of the 5 per cent threshold at the provincial district level.[4] While thresholds had been debated only sporadically as a means to reduce party system fragmentation, it became a salient issue within the wider political reform project of the Liberal–Socialist–Green coalition launched in 1999. One of the facilitating factors was that for the first time in decades, several parties had become so small that they became potential targets for elimination by threshold, at least in some constituencies. Apart from the small *Front National*, the potential victims were the successor parties to the Flemish-nationalist *Volksunie*, which after a decade of struggle for survival decided to split in 2000. From its ashes rose the postnationalist left-liberal SPIRIT, which, in order to survive the electoral threshold, has formed since the 2003 elections an electorally beneficial cartel with the Flemish Socialists, while the traditional faction calling for the independence of Flanders formed the *Nieuw-Vlaamse Alliantie* (N-VA). Apart from its leader, this party did not gain any parliamentary representation at the federal level. More importantly, the Flemish Greens – which as a government party had voted to adopt the threshold – were annihilated, while the French-speaking Greens were only left with a handful of representatives and senators. However, this bloodshed was due to simple electoral losses rather than to the threshold.[5] Still, the 2003 massacre certainly enhanced feelings of insecurity amongst minor parties and pushed them to look for alternatives, including the conclusion of electoral cartels. For the 2004 Flemish regional elections, the Greens were invited by the Socialists to form an electoral cartel but eventually declined, the N-VA concluded such a cartel with the Flemish Christian Democrats, while the small ultra-liberal VIVANT formed a cartel with the VLD.

With the disintegration of the *Volksunie*, all Flemish parties but the Greens now contain a considerable proportion of former VU-MPs, either as cartel or fully integrated. This 'volksunie-sation' of the parties is also reflected in some party name changes: in 1992 the liberals changed from *Partij voor Vrijheid en Vooruitgang* (Party for Liberty and Progress) into the *Vlaamse Liberalen en Democraten* (Flemish Liberals and Democrats, VLD), in 2001 the CVP became *Christen Democratisch en Vlaams* (Christian Democratic and Flemish, CD&V), in 2000 the Socialist Party became

Socialistische Partij Anders (SP.A). On the francophone side, most of the members of the defunct regionalist RW joined the *Parti Réformateur Libéral* (Liberal Reformist Party, PRL) and the *Parti Socialiste* (PS), and in 1993 the francophone communitarian FDF formed a cartel with the PRL, which was subsequently renamed *Mouvement Réformateur* (Reformist Movement, MR) in 2002.

The recent changes in the electoral system (number of constituencies, their size, the introduction of the threshold and suppression of second tier allocation) also resulted in a considerable net gain of disproportionality.[6] Gallagher's least square index nearly doubled from 2.85 in the 1999 general elections for the Chamber to 5.05 at the 2003 elections, whereas the average value of this index according to Lijphart (1994: 160) was 3.23.

The provincialisation of the district magnitude for the Chamber since 2003, together with the regionalisation of the Senate constituencies since 1995, have in one decade drastically shifted the power of candidate selection to a higher, if not the highest level of decision-making within parties. Before 1995, in each party, the 30 constituency parties were quite autonomous in selecting their representatives to Parliament, empowering usually local bosses, but in some parties also the rank-and-file membership. The central party leadership already decided on candidate selection for the region-wide constituencies used for the Senate and the European Parliament. Due to the recent drastic reduction of the number of constituencies, it now also acquired a stronger say in the composition of the lists for the Chamber. Formally the latter are decided by the provincial party organisations, but this level never was powerful in Belgian parties, and thus traditionally is more subject to national party interference, regularly parachuting strong vote catchers to head the province-wide list. Often hardworking backbenchers are bypassed by 'surprise' candidates attracting a lot of media attention.

However, the national party electorate continues to offer a territorially balanced ticket between the subregions in each province. Hence, provincial constituencies do not necessarily widen the communication gap between elected officials and citizens, but mainly allow better exploitation of the region-wide popularity of the parties' main figureheads and non-political TV celebrities (such as leaders of humanitarian or environmental NGOs, but also sports personalities, singers or fashion models).

Lack of Integration between Flemish and Francophone Parties

At the federal level, most parties are organised in a similar way: a congress as the supreme, sovereign party body, in charge of main programmatic orientations and endorsing government participation (Deschouwer 1992). The party executive, usually nominated by the congress delegates, takes care of the day-to-day management, under the leadership of the party president (who is elected either by the congress or by a general poll of the members). In each party, the parliamentary group is considered a delegate/agent of the party principal. Finally, there are the powerful and well-equipped party research centres. When the traditional parties split, some provisions were installed to secure coordination between the regional successor parties, like common research centres or common parliamentary group (meetings). However, after a few years, most of these initiatives became obsolete.

Only the Green parties – Agalev and Ecolo – do not fit this process. As they were founded after the traditional parties had already split, they decided from the beginning to set up a non-state-wide party organisation. But the Greens established an elaborate system of cross-party cooperation, including a joint federal executive, joint parliamentary group meetings, joint member congresses, joint meetings of the Councils of the Constituency Parties, and instruments of coordination when they were both participating in the federal government (1999–2003). However, in practice only the former two functioned regularly and government participation eventually led to conflicts between parties. The loss of national representation for the Flemish Greens after the 2003 elections has further undermined these forms of cooperation (De Winter 2006).

Intraparty Multilevel Coordination and Leadership Concentration

Within each party, the most important territorial subdivisions are the constituency parties. In most francophone parties, the Brussels constituency party enjoys a particular status in the party's organisational framework in terms of holding separate conferences, guaranteed representation in the federal executive committee, etc. This is not the case for the Flemish parties, which, apart from the VB, do not give special status to their Brussels constituency parties.

Before the direct elections of the regional parliaments (1995), all members of the community and regional parliaments (apart from Brussels and the German-speaking one) were also members of the Chamber or the Senate. One week they would sit as a member of the federal Parliament, the other week as a regional/community MP. Through this personal combination of mandates, coordination between the parliamentary party groups' (PPG) positions at the federal and sub-federal levels did not pose a major problem. Since 1995, this system of 'double hat' has no longer been operational, as positions at the two legislative levels are not longer compatible. Hence, the working environments of senators, representatives and regional/community MPs have become strictly separated. Evidently, this proliferation of separate PPGs poses a serious problem of party policy coordination (De Winter and Dumont 2000).

This is especially problematic in the Belgian federal system in which there are no federal parties, which, as in Germany, could play a coordinating role between subfederal party sections. Therefore the federal and subfederal PPGs have to be brought into tune more than in other federal systems. Since the end of the double mandate, divergent views between national and regional MPs are more and more frequent, not only with regard to regional/

linguistic conflicts, but also to socio-economic issues as well as democratic reform. Hence, parties have installed coordination mechanisms in order to harmonise the positions of their four to six parliamentary groups and secure support for the executives at different levels.[7]

Multilevel coordination can occur at the top of party hierarchy, at the level of the party executive or the PPGs, or at a policy decentralised level. Oligarchic coordination usually occurs through regular meetings between the party president and the group chairs. Regarding coordination at the level of the party executives, all parties include their PPG chairpersons in the party executive (except the VB), as well as most regional or federal ministers. In practice, a much larger number of members of the party executive are MPs or ministers, chosen by their constituency party to sit as their delegates in the party executive. In about half of the parties, the president of the national party organisation attends the plenary meetings of his PPG in the Chamber more or less regularly, but not those of the PPGs in other assemblies. Some groups hold occasional joint meetings of all PPGs. At the beginning or/and the end of every parliamentary session, parties usually organise study weekends where their parliamentarians can meet. Last, but not least, there is decentralised coordination for different policy sectors. In most parties, there are a large number of standing and *ad hoc* working groups (usually headed by an MP from the level that is most suitable for the policy issue), in which MPs from different PPGs work together with the experts from the party research centre, the PPG staff members and external experts (academics, civil servants or interest group representatives) to prepare the party's positions and initiatives on specific policy areas. Most of these groups are not permanent; they largely depend on the current or potential saliency of the issue at stake.

The party leadership also influences federal and regional cabinet decision-making through direct formal and informal contacts between the presidents of the government and supporting parties during which decisions are reached that are binding for ministers and PPGs. Many crucial conflicts have been solved by way of such party leader summits. Agreements reached at these summits are presented as political pacts, not amendable by the cabinet or by the PPGs.

Regional ministers and parliamentary groups are generally less represented, consulted and involved with federal party organs. As a result, regional ministers and minister-presidents are more often subjected to the authority of the federal party executive and party leader than federal ministers (Massart 2001). Regarding the effectiveness of all these formal and informal arenas for position articulation and aggregation, the end result seems positive, as party discipline in Parliament has remained very high.[8]

In some parties, there has been a recent fusion of power between party leadership and governmental leadership. The MR federal vice-prime minister also became party leader in 2004, keeping his position in the federal government, while the PS president became minister-president of the Walloon Region in 2005, keeping his post as party leader. The VLD and

CD&V nominated low-key figures on the position of the party leadership when the real leaders decided to head the federal and Flemish governments respectively. These personnel changes tend to shift power from the organisational leadership to the party in government, and thus may weaken the coordinating capacities of party organisation leaders.

Party Competition in Belgium and Different Regions

Major societal changes, such as growth of neutral mass media, depillarisation, higher educational attainment, secularisation, globalisation and economic crisis, have undermined the grip of political parties on their natural constituencies. Whereas before the 1960s party supporters were mostly loyal to the party of their pillar, overall volatility has since increased slowly but erratically. Of the seven general elections held since 1981, five surpassed the 10 per cent level of volatility (Table 3). However, traditional aggregate measures of volatility only indicate the minimal estimate of the real volatility as it occurred at the level of the voter, because many shifts are not registered at the aggregate level (Swyngedouw 1989). Post-electoral studies and exit polls give a more accurate idea of the real change of voters between two successive elections. While between the 1981 and 1985 federal elections in Flanders approximately 13.5 per cent of the voters changed party, 32 per cent did so between the elections of 1991 and 1995 and 34 per cent between 1995 and 1999 (Swyngedouw and Beerten 1999). Similar high figures of micro-level volatility are found between 1999 and 2003 (Swyngedouw *et al.* 2007). In the French-speaking part of Belgium we find

TABLE 3
EXTERNAL VOLATILITY, HOUSE OF REPRESENTATIVES ELECTIONS, 1946–2003

	Volatility	Flemish parties	French-speaking parties	Difference
1949	8.10			
1950	8.85			
1954	6.85			
1958	4.95			
1961	4.95			
1965	15.80			
1968	5.95			
1971	6.85			
1974	3.25			
1977	6.35			
1978	6.20			
1981	14.35	7.35	5.60	1.75
1985	9.75	5.00	3.45	1.55
1987	4.30	2.15	1.40	0.75
1991	12.35	8.25	3.70	4.55
1995	6.70	4.10	2.55	1.55
1999	10.90	6.50	4.40	2.10
2003	12.67	8.01	4.67	3.34

comparable figures, with 36 per cent volatility between 1991 and 1995 (Swyngedouw and Frognier 1999) in Wallonia.

Besides or across the three traditional cleavages (left–right, denominational, linguistic), new cleavages or sub-cleavages have emerged. While a distinction is generally accepted between the economic left–right (taxes, organisation economy, etc.) and the socio-cultural left–right (abortion, euthanasia, homosexuality, adoption rights for homosexuals, etc.), there is some debate as to whether or not the socio-cultural left–right includes the materialist–post-materialist dimension, which separates the Green parties from the other parties (Swyngedouw 1992; Elchardus and Pelleriaux 1998; Kitschelt 1989). Next, as in other European countries (Kitschelt 1995; Grunberg and Schweisguth 1997; Kriesi *et al.* 2006), we observe a new political divide featuring opposition on the question of granting new citizens of immigrant origin the same social, political and cultural rights as native Belgians. Authors and politicians use divergent labels for this divide, researchers also differ on the question whether this divide should be considered a new cleavage as understood by Lipset and Rokkan (1967). We labelled it as the universalist–particularist dimension (Swyngedouw 1995). Although no recent reliable large-scale data measuring party positions on these cleavages are available, one can hypothesize that on the economic left–right cleavage (taxes, private versus public initiatives, etc.) the Flemish parties are positioned more to the right than their francophone party family members. Furthermore, all mainstream parties tend to converge around the centre to centre-left position on economic matters. This facilitated the formation of the previous rainbow coalition (between Social Democrats, Liberals and Greens) and the current federal purple coalition (between Social Democrats and Liberals). This convergence is less obvious regarding the socio-cultural left–right divide. The recent controversy concerning the right of homosexuals to adopt children indicated that francophone parties' positions were generally more conservative than those of the Flemish parties. On these socio-cultural issues, extreme right and Christian democratic parties are clearly more conservative than the other parties in Flanders as well as in francophone Belgium.

On both sides of the linguistic border, the universalist–particularist divide opposes the extreme right parties (VB and FN) to all other parties, although in Flanders some mainstream parties are also sensitive to calls from sectors of the electorate for protective measures for Belgians and for pushing back immigration. For instance, in 2004 the VLD strongly opposed the parliamentary decision to grant suffrage at the municipal elections to non-EU residents (Ivaldi and Swyngedouw 2006).

The successors of the three traditional parties have drifted apart on the regional and linguistic divide. On this cleavage we find at the extreme Flemish-nationalist pole the *Vlaams Belang* and to a lesser extent the VU (and its successor parties N-VA and SPIRIT, which are now part of electoral cartels with mainstream parties), followed by the CD&V, VLD, SP-A, with

Groen! as the most moderate. At the extreme francophone pole we find the FDF, followed by the PS, PRL, CdH, with Ecolo as the most moderate.

When running for the federal and regional elections (both were held on the same day until 2003), we find little programmatic differentiation within the parties. At the first direct elections for the regional assemblies in 1995, most parties formulated a specific regional/community electoral manifesto. In 1999, only the PS produced separate documents for the federal and regional/community elections (De Winter 2006). However, in the manifestos for the 2003 federal elections, which for the first time did not coincide with regional elections, most parties formulated proposals regarding policy areas for which the federal level was no longer competent, and as such would not be affected by the outcome of the federal vote. As the voters are little aware of the division of competencies between levels, parties tend to formulate programmes 'fitting all levels', just as European campaigns usually run on domestic matters (Ackaert *et al.* 1996).

In recent decades, two of the three traditionally cross-cutting cleavages have lost salience for a significant part of the electorate. The denominational cleavage between Catholics and free-thinkers and between opinions about the desirability of the separation of church and state once most structured voting behaviour. The cleavage positioned the Socialist and Liberal parties against the Christian Democrats. From the 1960s onward, this cleavage lost weight and by the turn of the century its relevance for structuring voting behaviour was seriously restricted.[9] At the level of religious identification, in Flanders about 78 per cent and in Wallonia about 71 per cent of the voters say they do not have any denomination, or identify themselves as irregular or marginal Catholic. Only the regular churchgoers (mostly belonging to the older generation), who represent about 12 per cent of the population in both language communities and still vote predominantly for the Christian democratic parties, and the free-thinkers, who represent 7 per cent of the voters in Flanders and 11 per cent in Wallonia and mostly vote for the social democratic parties, are the categories for which this cleavage remains important in voting behaviour.

A similar, but less marked, development affects the left–right cleavage. Observers point out that the main parties are converging around the centre-left of the left–right divide. On an 11-point scale (0: right–10: left) the whole Flemish electorate has a mean score of 6.4, and only one electorate significantly deviates from this mean. These are the voters of the liberal VLD with a score of 5.4. So, most voters are situated at the centre-left, which is not surprising as there is little discussion over the general economic and social policy within the Flemish Community at party elite level (Swyngedouw *et al.* 2007). On the francophone side, given the fact that the economic situation is far worse than in Flanders, we find a slightly higher electoral relevance of the left–right cleavage opposing the social democratic PS to the liberal MR. In both communities, however, we see that the position of the voter on issues related to the left–right cleavage (e.g. free entrepreneurship versus control on entrepreneurship, social equality, economic progressiveness) adds significantly to the explanatory power of voting behaviour models (Frognier and Mouchart, 2003; Billiet *et al.* 2007).

Structural and Attitudinal Dispositions of Voting Behaviour

Using the data from the (post-electoral) national election study of Belgium (Swyngedouw *et al.* 2004), it is possible to draw a reliable picture of the socio-demographic and attitudinal variables that characterise the different electorates (Swyngedouw *et al.* 2007). We discuss, in turn, results for Flanders and for Wallonia (the complex Brussels case is not analysed).

We start by fitting a multinomial logistic regression including the generally accepted socio-demographic variables such as age, education, profession, income, gender, religious involvement, membership of socio-cultural organisations (as a proxy for social capital – Putnam 1993), ideological affiliation of health insurance fund, and of trade union/or professional organisations (the two latter as proxies for the measurement of pillarisation). Table 4 produces the best fitting model, using Kaufman and Schervish (1986) to transform additive logit parameters to absolute proportions (see Swyngedouw 1989).

Using the L^2/df estimate to investigate the relative importance of the different significant variables, it becomes clear that the proxy for pillarisation – type of heath insurance companies – is by far the most important variable to predict voting behaviour in Flanders 2003. It is followed by religious involvement, education and gender. Finally, age and type of trade union/professional organisation are also significant. Note that none of the traditional socio-economic variables such as profession or income have a significant influence on voting behaviour in Flanders. Table 5 gives us a view of how these significant variables exactly influence the vote (see notes to the table) and help us to draw the profile for each party electorate. The liberal VLD is characterised by a rather young electorate, with a medium level of education, mostly affiliated to the liberal health insurance fund, liberal trade union or other professional organisations.

TABLE 4

BEST FITTING MULTINOMIAL LOGISTIC REGRESSION MODEL OF SOCIO-DEMOGRAPHIC VARIABLES OF FLEMISH VOTERS FOR THE CHAMBER OF REPRESENTATIVES, 18 MAY 2003

Characteristics	df	L^2	p	L^2/df
Intercept	6	81.82	<.0001	
Age (categorical)	30	56.16	0.0026	1.87
Gender	6	13.99	0.0297	2.33
Education	18	46.25	0.0003	2.57
Religious involvement	30	77.34	<.0001	2.58
Membership health insurance fund	18	149.15	<.0001	8.29
Membership trade union and professional organisations	24	45.58	0.0050	1.90

Likelihood ratio Chi-square (L^2) = 2140.29; df = 3480; p = 1.000.

TABLE 5
NET EFFECTS OF SOCIO-DEMOGRAPHIC VARIABLES ON FLEMISH VOTERS
FOR THE CHAMBER OF REPRESENTATIVES, 18 MAY 2003 (%)

Characteristics	VLD	SPA	CD&V	Vlaams Blok	N-VA*	Agalev
General average (election results including blank/ invalid vote)	23.04	22.53	20.16	17.19	4.59	3.85
Age						
18–24	23.85	**32.22**	12.33	18.83	5.91	3.64
25–34	**31.12**	23.96	14.30	19.48	3.32	2.99
35–44	23.38	14.74	20.30	18.10	4.73	5.07
45–54	19.62	26.95	16.72	14.82	5.03	6.06
55–64	24.13	22.98	18.38	16.97	7.65	5.54
65–85	18.17	19.92	**32.35**	15.86	2.42	0.60
Religious involvement						
None	24.48	**32.40**	8.44	15.42	5.70	4.46
Free Thinker	19.56	**33.87**	3.51	17.44	1.63	8.21
Other religions (non-Catholic)	**38.62**	16.64	1.36	17.41	12.04	3.63
Marginal Catholic	26.75	21.12	16.54	18 59	4.03	4.35
Irregular church going Catholic	18.79	18.32	29.51	**21.15**	5.55	1.52
Regular church going Catholic	12.32	20.35	**44.81**	6.73	3.92	2.62
Education						
Lower	18.95	18.91	**26.70**	**25.74**	1.60	0.86
Lower secondary	25.58	20.37	19.92	19.31	3.39	2.66
Higher secondary	24.24	23.57	16.20	16.71	6.02	3.38
Higher	23.52	**26.61**	19.07	7.22	6.67	8.61
Gender						
Men	23.27	20.96	19.37	**20.91**	4.94	2.36
Women	22.81	24.04	20.92	13.60	4.26	5.29
Membership health insurance fund						
Christian	20.41	16.68	**30.21**	15.26	4.69	4.80
Socialist	14.55	**44.06**	5.81	19.84	0.79	2.10
Liberal	**66.62**	5.14	0.92	16.77	5.75	2.39
Other	25.08	17.96	12.51	21.76	11.53	3.77
Membership trade union or profession organisation						
Christian trade union	14.26	**24.93**	25.75	20.12	4.02	4.18
Socialist trade union	16.97	21.54	12.23	**22.76**	2.28	7.03
Liberal trade union	**28.69**	11.60	25.26	8.81	1.96	3.28
Other (professional oragnisation)	**28.36**	18.66	**36.49**	4.66	5.66	1.56
No member	26.53	22.73	18.56	16.37	5.30	3.27

(Estimate on basis of logit model from Table 4; reference category = other small parties) (N = 1063).
*N-VA (New Flemish Alliance) Flemish nationalist.
Example: the liberal VLD has a general election result of 23.04% but in the category of the voters aged between 25 and 34 its share is 31.12%.
Values in bold for categories in which the party electorate is overrepresented.

The social democratic SP.A has a young and middle aged voting public, with a rather high educational level, originating from the socialist trade union and seeing themselves as free-thinkers. The Christian democratic CD&V has a rather old electorate, with rather low educational level, mostly members of the Catholic health fund and Catholic trade union or other professional organisations. They identify themselves as regular churchgoers. The extreme right *Vlaams Blok* voter is rather young, with a low educational level, masculine, affiliated to the socialist trade union and the other (i.e. the independent Flemish nationalist) health insurance fund and identifying as irregular churchgoers (notice the quasi-absence of regular churchgoers in their electorate).

Following Lazersfeld (1955), we add attitudinal variables to the best fitting socio-demographic model. Table 6 shows that the three most important attitudinal variables explaining voting behaviour in Flanders in 2003 are: ethnocentrism, Flemish nationalism and political alienation, followed by economic progressiveness and post-materialism. Table 7 gives the additive logistic parameters from the model of Table 6 and contrasts the voters of the different parties with the voters of the extreme right party *Vlaams Blok* (serving as reference category). A negative sign indicates that the probability of a vote for the VB exceeds that of the other party, a positive

TABLE 6

BEST FITTING MULTINOMIAL LOGISTIC REGRESSION MODEL OF SOCIO-DEMOGRAPHIC AND ATTITUDINAL VARIABLES OF FLEMISH VOTERS FOR THE CHAMBER OF REPRESENTATIVES, 18 MAY 2003

Characteristics	df	L^2	p	L^2/df
Intercept	6	99.97	<.0001	
Age (categories)	30	76.94	<.0001	
Religious Involvement	30	73.34	<.0001	
Membership health insurance fund	18	124.16	<.0001	
Membership trade-unions and professional org	24	36.84	0.0454	
Ethnocentrism	6	88.04	<.0001	14.67
Political alienation	6	64.64	<.0001	10.77
Economic progressiveness	6	42.55	<.0001	7.09
Flemish autonomy	6	76.43	<.0001	12.74
Post-materialism	6	41.20	<.0001	6.87

Likelihood ratio Chi-square $(L^2) = 2660.89$; df $= 6138$; p $= 1.000$.

TABLE 7

DIRECT SIGNIFICANT NET EFFECT OF ATTITUDINAL VARIABLES ON FLEMISH VOTERS FOR THE CHAMBER OF REPRESENTATIVES, 18 MAY 2003

Characteristics	VLD/ *Vlaams Blok*	SP.A-SPIRIT/ *Vlaams Blok*	CD&V/ *Vlaams Blok*	N-VA/ *Vlaams Blok*	Agalev/ *Vlaams Blok*
Ethnocentrism	−0.38***	−0.57***	−0.53***	−0.44***	−0.99***
Political alienation		−0.34***			−0.27*
Economic progressiveness	−0.16*	0.26***			
Flemish autonomy	−0.28***	−0.25***	−0.23***	0.27**	−0.23*
Post-materialism		0.15*		−0.22*	0.56***

*Significance at .05 level (p < .05); **significance at 0.01 level (p < .01); ***significance at .001 level (p < .001).
(Additive logistic regression parameters), under controle socio-demographic variables (model of Table 6).

sign points to the opposite. For example, the more one is ethnocentric, the higher the probability of one voting for the VB. This actually holds for all contrasts of the *Vlaams Blok* with any other party (as all estimates are negative), so from the attitudinal point of view, VB voters are more ethnocentric than any other electorate (before those of respectively the VLD, the N-VA, the CD&V, the SP.A and the Greens). The VB voter is also more politically alienated and less post-materialist than the voters of the SP.A and the Greens. He/she defends Flemish autonomy more than liberal, social democratic, Christian democratic and Green voters, but less than the voters of the N-VA. Last but not least, the VB voter is less economically conservative than the liberal voters.

As far as the Walloon voter is concerned, Table 8 presents the best fitting model for the socio-demographic variables and also points to the fact that the proxy variable for pillarisation (membership health insurance fund) is the most important determinant (using the L^2/df measure), followed by education, religious involvement and membership of trade union. Comparing L^2/df across the Flemish and Walloon voter model, differences are rather limited, even though we observe that in Wallonia age and gender are insignificant. Note that in both regions the socio-economic variables – EGP (see Erikson *et al.* 1979), income – are not significantly related to voting behaviour. Table 9 give us the profile of the different parties.

The liberal MR is overrepresented amongst irregular and regular churchgoers, the more highly educated and members of the liberal health insurance fund. The PS electorate is overrepresented amongst free-thinking and marginal Catholic voters, the less well educated and members of both the socialist trade union and the socialist health insurance fund. Put differently, the PS electorate is still firmly entrenched in the socialist pillar. The Christian democratic (CDH) voters are found more amongst irregular and regular churchgoers, and tend to be more highly educated. They are more often members of the Catholic health insurance fund. The Green voter (Ecolo) is predominantly secular, to a lesser degree a non-Catholic believer, is highly educated and tends to be a member of the Catholic trade union.

Turning to the attitudinal dispositions to vote for a party, we observe (Table 10) the emergence of a totally different model than for the Flemish

TABLE 8

BEST FITTING MULTINOMIAL LOGISTIC REGRESSION MODEL OF SOCIO-DEMOGRAPHIC VARIABLES OF WALLOON VOTES FOR THE CHAMBER OF REPRESENTATIVES, 18 MAY 2003

Characteristic	df	L^2	p	L^2/df
Intercept	4	31.41	<.0001	
Education	12	48.42	<.0001	4.04
Religious Involvement	20	74.13	<.0001	3.71
Membership health insurance fund	12	84.62	<.0001	7.05
Membership trade union or professional organisation	12	37.04	0.0002	3.09

Likelihood ratio Chi-square $(L^2) = 549.77$; df $= 700$; p $= .913$.

TABLE 9

NET EFFECT ESTIMATES OF SOCIO-DEMOGRAPHIC VARIABLES ON WALLOON
VOTERS FOR CHAMBER OF REPRESENTATIVES, 18 MAY 2003 (%)

Characteristic	MR	PS	CDH	Ecolo
Overall average	26.68	34.18	14.46	6.97
Religious involvement				
None	23.09	29.69	4.46	**12.34**
Free thinkers	14.44	**45.63**	4.93	5.61
Other religions (non-Roman Catholic)	21.90	21.36	8.39	**19.32**
Marginal Catholic	27.86	**40.14**	12.87	3.88
Irregular church going Catholic	**33.61**	31.96	**21.70**	8.88
Regular church going Catholic	**31.41**	17.23	**33.46**	4.57
Education				
Lower	10.42	**54.70**	12.16	6.14
Lower-secondary	27.24	38.89	10.62	3.37
Higher secondary	27.69	27.77	15.06	8.51
Higher	**39.96**	19.26	**19.35**	**9.01**
Membership health insurance fund				
Christian	26.62	19.35	**28.67**	6.74
Socialist	18.87	**54.14**	8.47	6.05
Liberal	**49.90**	11.14	2.14	8.24
Other	30.29	33.89	7.05	8.27
Type of trade union or profession organisation				
Christian trade Union	22.06	33.12	14.62	**9.28**
Socialist trade Union	13.11	**64.07**	9.34	4.65
Other (professional organisation)*	26.60	40.63	8.52	5.51
No member	30.44	27.14	16.07	7.24
N	165	227	121	67

(Logit model from Table 8. reference category = other small parties) (N = 626).
*The small liberal trade union is included in the 'Other' category.

TABLE 10

BEST FITTING MULTINOMIAL LOGISTIC REGRESSION MODEL OF
SOCIO-DEMOGRAPHIC AND ATTITUDINAL VARIABLES OF WALLOON
VOTERS FOR THE CHAMBER OF REPRESENTATIVES, 18 MAY 2003

Characteristics	df	L^2	p	L^2/df
Intercept	4	26.67	<.0001	
Education	12	28.83	0.0042	
Religious involvement	20	65.41	<.0001	
Membership health insurance fund	12	86.66	<.0001	
Membership trade union or professional organisation	12	25.19	0.014	
Political alienation	4	29.9	<.0001	7.48
Utilitarian individualism	4	10.8	0.0289	2.70
Defence of environment	4	17.76	0.0014	4.44
Economic progressiveness	4	49.47	<.0001	12.37

Likelihood ratio Chi-square (L^2) = 1399.65; df = 2E3; p = 1.000. (N = 616).

case. Only the variables of political alienation and economic progressiveness appear in both regions (but contrary to Flanders, the latter is more important than the former in Wallonia). The long-standing and rather strong presence of the Green party Ecolo might be the result of the environmental awareness of a part of the electorate. A final attitudinal variable that seems to explain the behaviour of the Walloon electorate is utilitarian individualism – a measure which taps the importance one gives to personal advantages and concerns.

Table 11 contrasts the different francophone parties to the Green party, the main challenger of the traditional parties. We notice that the Ecolo voter is less politically alienated than those of the MR and the CDH (the PS electorate does not differ from the Ecolo voters in this respect). On the other hand, Ecolo voters are more utilitarian individualists than the voters of the traditional parties, but care more for the environment. Finally, the social democratic PS has the most economic progressive electorate, followed by Ecolo. The most economically conservative are the MR voters followed by those of the CDH.

Multilevel Coalition Formation

The most striking feature of multilevel coalition formation is the strong symmetry one finds between the coalition composition patterns between the regional and federal levels, and as a consequence, also between the executives of the different regions and communities (De Winter *et al.* 2000). This double symmetry may appear surprising given the different strengths of the main party families in the three regions and communities (see Table 1), which strongly affects the bargaining power of each family in the different arenas.

First, in spite of the fact that since the 1970s former unitary parties are organisationally autonomous, parties belonging to the same traditional party family have up to now always been together in government or in opposition at the federal level. This search for federal symmetry meant that often a coalition included a surplus party of relatively small size, that is, the sister party of a main party of the other side of the linguistic border (especially the PSC and SP vis-à-vis the *incontournable* CVP and PS respectively).

Second, as far as numerically possible, coalitions at the regional level also include the same parties as those forming the coalition at the federal level. Until 1999, elections at both levels were held simultaneously, so party

TABLE 11
DIRECT SIGNIFICANT NET EFFECT OF ATTITUDINAL VARIABLES ON
WALLOON VOTERS FOR THE CHAMBER OF REPRESENTATIVES, 18 MAY 2003

Characteristic	MR/Ecolo	PS/Ecolo	CD&H/Ecolo
Political alienation (POLAL)	0.16*	0.02	0.11*
Utilitarian individualism (INDIV)	0.18*	0.25**	0.15*
Defence of environment (ENVIR)	−0.20*	−0.28**	−0.12*
Economic progressiveness (ECONS)	−0.41***	0.18*	−0.15*

(Additive logistic regression parameters), under control of socio-demographic variables (model of Table 10).
*Significance at .05 ($p < .05$); **Significance at .01 ($p < .01$); ***Significance at .001 ($p < .001$).

negotiators (party presidents, some *ministrables* party leaders, and party experts), who were largely the same at both levels, managed to link the formation bargaining processes and were able to force the inclusion of their party in executive coalitions at both levels.[10] Only when for numerical reasons symmetry was excluded were asymmetric formulae tolerated.[11]

These symmetries were induced by formal rules as well as by norms of reciprocity and common interest. During the period after the first constitutional reforms (1971–80), the ministers responsible for regional and community matters were formally part of the national executive, and therefore were selected during the formation of the federal government. In the first legislative term after the second reforms (1981–85), the regional/community ministers constituted cabinets outside the federal government. However, during a transition period of one legislative term, these regional/community executives had to be constituted in a proportional way between the main parties. Evidently, these formal rules induced symmetry. For each party it remained profitable in policy terms to bring in its sister party, as this inclusion reinforced the weight of a party family's programmatic preferences in the government agreement. Second, the office costs of bringing in the surplus sister parties are basically paid by the (non-sister) parties of the other linguistic camp. In fact, the 1970 constitutional parity rule stipulated that the Council of Ministers is equally composed of Flemish- and French-speaking members (not taking the PM and the junior ministers into account).

Still, for a variety of reasons specific to each party family, the norm of double symmetry weakened in the 1990s, and all parties except the Greens and Socialists declare that asymmetric government should be feasible in principle. Thus they are willing to let down their sister party on the other side of the linguistic border for the sake of guaranteeing their own governmental participation. In practice, up until 2004, double symmetry remained the rule. At the first regional elections decoupled from national elections (which had been held in 2003), major changes intervened: in the Walloon Region, the French-speaking Community and Brussels the PS decided to switch partners and exclude the liberals at all levels, opening the door instead to the CDH (former PSC). This change was a major one, as the PS had chosen in 2003 to keep on working at the federal level with the liberals. On the Flemish side, the three main parties (cartels) had to join forces to avoid a participation of the VB to the regional government. As the CD&V (former CVP) won the 2004 elections, it even took the minister-presidency of the Flemish Region, whilst it remained absent (like the CDH) in the federal government.

Participation in the federal executive has long been considered the main office reward. Although usually the negotiations on a policy programme at the regional formation process runs faster than at the federal level (the latter including more parties and contentious issues), efforts were often made to synchronise the conclusion of government formations (the nomination of ministers), following the informal principle that the deals regarding one level would only become valid when there was agreement at all levels (multilevel package deals).

The predominance of the federal executive also affects multilevel ministerial career patterns. First, level hopping is more frequent for executive careers than legislative ones. In 1999, of all 55 federal and regional ministers, a third had been elected at the wrong level! However, the direction of the hopping also evokes a more hierarchical top-down or *parachutage* model (Massart 2001).[12] For instance, after the 1999 elections, most regional or community prime ministers had been elected as federal MPs. Moreover, after the 2004 regional elections, only ten out of the 21 federal ministers and secretaries of state kept exactly the same ministerial portfolios as they had received a year before, when the national government was formed. Overall, there were eight new ministers (or secretaries of state) appointed to the federal government and three of the original team were reshuffled. Some leading federal ministers opted for the regional executives. Four of the departing federal ministers went to the Flemish government and one took over the minister-presidency of the French-speaking Community government. On the other hand, one can also discern a bottom-up career path, from regional/community to the federal executive. When it was formed, the Verhofstadt II government comprised four out of 14 ministers drawn from the regional/community government at which level they had performed well in the 1999–2003 period, and therefore were rewarded with a promotion to the federal level. Thus federal formations may also trigger major reshuffles of the regional and community executives.

Conclusion

Successive institutional reforms in Belgium towards the creation of a federal state have not reduced the fragmentation and centrifugal tendencies of the Belgian polity. The two quasi-autonomous regional party systems that resulted from the splitting of the Belgian party system display clear differences in terms of the type of parties that are active, as well as their electoral strength and development. These differences result from the relative weight or societal cleavages in the two main regions. The left–right dimension is still the most relevant for electoral behaviour in Wallonia, whereas in Flanders ethnocentrism and political alienation have become the main factors, with Flemish autonomy being the most prominent of the traditional Belgian cleavages at work. The lack of integration and coordination between Flemish- and French-speaking parties further reinforces the tendency towards the growing apart of the two polities.

As remains of unitary characteristics, such as coordination between the party organisations of the Greens or efforts towards the building of symmetric coalitions between the federal and regional executives, have been recently undermined or even abandoned, sporadic initiatives towards forms of reunification (the recreation of national parties, electing a proportion of federal MPs in a national constituency, etc.) have emerged. These are, however, not considered seriously by Belgian political elites. The latter prefer to envisage reforms to enhance the legitimacy of the political personnel (direct election of mayors, codes of conduct) and of political decisions (by introducing forms of direct democracy). Last but not least, measures aimed at halting the ever growing success of the extreme right, such as the abolishment of compulsory voting (assuming that citizens would rather not vote than express a protest vote) or the decision to stop public financing for racist parties, are also on the political agenda. If these reforms are undeniably inspired by a will to protect the democratic system from its challengers, they may simply have the effect of breaking the thermometer that measures citizen dissatisfaction. Moreover, they may well have no influence, even indirect, on the balkanisation of Belgian polities and the deeply entrenched potential for division of the country.

Notes

1. This does not mean that the Flemish and Walloon party systems are drifting apart. A recent analysis by Deschouwer (2005) shows that in terms of party families, the party landscape in north and south is very different, but electoral swings in north and south have only been diverging between the late 1960s and the early 1980s. Before and after this period the general logic is one of parties of the same families gaining or losing together.
2. The splitting of this electoral district has become one of the symbolic reforms called for by Flemish nationalists and by now endorsed by all Flemish parties represented in Parliament. Negotiations took place at the federal level in 2005 but collapsed as the SP.A's electoral cartel partner, the nationalist SPIRIT, refused to accept the compensations demanded by the French-speaking parties in return for this splitting.
3. The number of constituencies for the elections to the Chamber was 30 in the 1945–93 period, district magnitude varying from 2 to 33 in the Brussels constituency, electing overall 212 deputies. At the 1995 and 1999 elections, the 150 deputies were elected through PR in 20 constituencies, varying between 2 and 22 seats.
4. The second-tier threshold system combined with small constituencies which was in use before 2003 actually put the average effective threshold for many parties over 10% and for the smallest constituencies sometimes over 20% (Blaise *et al.* 2003; Vander Weyden 2005). Only in the large constituencies of Brussels, Antwerp and Liège was the practical threshold lower than the current 5% formal provincial threshold.
5. Of the nine Chamber seats lost by Agalev, only two can be attributed to the new electoral threshold, while it made the NVA lose one seat (out of two). None of the other parties suffered from the threshold.
6. The number of seats allocated to constituencies is proportional to the number of legal inhabitants in the constituencies, not the number of Belgians or voters. This leads to a certain overrepresentation of Wallonia, and especially Brussels, given the higher number of non-Belgians residing in these regions. This malapportionment due to the bonus given to francophone parties artificially boosts disproportionality.
7. Flemish parties have at most four PPGs (Chamber, Senate, Flemish and Brussels Parliaments). Francophone parties have at most six groups (Chamber, Senate, Walloon, Brussels Legislature, French- and German-speaking Community Parliaments). The number of MEPs is usually too small to be considered a group. In addition, they have great freedom of manoeuvre vis-à-vis the domestic party organisation (Raunio 2002).
8. Detailed analysis of Chamber rebellions in the 1991–99 period (Depauw 2000) indicates that in the 1991–95 term, community problems were the policy sectors that triggered most intraparty dissent in absolute terms. However, given the large number of institutional reforms proposals voted in that period, in relative terms it is one of the least conflictual.

9. This is illustrated by the change in the share of vote for the Christian democratic parties. Where at the end of the 1950s they had almost an absolute majority in the country, in 2003 the CDH has about 14.3% of the vote in Wallonia and the CD&V 20.1% in Flanders.

10. The formations of the Martens VIII (in 1987–88) and Verhofstadt I (in 1999) governments were clear examples of the linkages between the federal and regional processes of coalition formation.

11. This was for instance the case in the Brussels regional executive from 1989.

12. The Flemish government was until the 2003 federal elections chaired by a member of the Chamber, and counted another two federal MPs and one MEP. Also the head of the Brussels Region government was a member of the Chamber, while his colleague from the French Community government was a senator. The former aspired to a position in the federal government in 1999, and had to be pressured to take up a 'lower-level' prime ministerial office at the regional level!

References

Ackaert, J., L. De Winter and M. Swyngedouw (1996). 'Belgium: An Electorate on the Eve of Desintegration', in C. Van der Eijk and M. Franklin (eds.), *Choosing Europe? The European Electorate and National Politics in the Face of Union*. Ann Arbor: University of Michigan Press, 59–77.

Blaise, P., J. Brassinne de la Buissière and V. de Coorebyter (2003). 'Les réformes électorales sous la législature 1999–2003', *Courrier hebdomadaire du CRISP*, 1790–91.

Blondel, Jean (1968). 'Party Systems and Patterns of Government in Western Democracies', *Canadian Journal of Political Science*, 1, 180–203.

Depauw, Sam (2000). 'Fractiecohesie en effectiviteit van parlementen', *Res Publica*, 4, 503–19.

Deschouwer, Christian (1992). 'Belgium', in R.S. Katz and P. Mair (eds.), *Party Organizations. A Data Handbook*. London: Sage, 121–98.

Deschouwer, K. (2005). 'The Regionalization of National Electoral Politics? An Explorative Analysis of Belgium and Spain', paper prepared for presentation at the workshop *Territorial Party Politics*, University of Edinburgh, 28–29 October.

De Winter, Lieven (2006). 'Multi-Level Party Competition and Co-ordination in Belgium', in D. Hough and C. Jeffrey (eds.), *Devolution and Electoral Politics*. Manchester: Manchester University Press.

De Winter, Lieven, and Patrick Dumont (1999). 'The Belgian Party System(s) on the Eve of Disintegration', in David Broughton and Mark Donovan (eds.), *Changing Party Systems in Western Europe*. London and New York: Pinter, 183–206.

De Winter, L., and P. Dumont (2000). 'Belgium: Subjects of Partitocratic Dominion', in Knut Heidar and Ruud Koole (eds.), *Parliamentary Party Groups in European Democracies*. London: Routledge, 106–30.

De Winter, L., A. Timmermans and P. Dumont (2000). 'Belgium: On Government Agreements, Evangelists, Followers, and Heretics', in Wolfgang C. Müller and Kaare Strøm (eds.), *Coalition Government in Western Europe*. Oxford: Oxford University Press, 300–55.

Elchardus, M., and K. Pelleriaux (1998). 'De polis verdeeld – Hoe de kiezer links en rechts herdefiniëren', in M. Swyngedouw, J. Billiet, A. Carton and R. Beerten (eds.), *De (on) redelijke kiezer*. Leuven: Acco.

Erikson, R., J.H. Goldthorpe and L. Portocarero (1979). 'Intergenerational Class Mobility in Three Western European Societies: England, France and Sweden', *British Journal of Sociology*, 34, 303–43.

Frognier, A.-P., and M. Mouchart (2003). 'Wallonie: l'impact des positions sociales, des clivages et des enjeux sur le vote en 1999', in A.-P. Frognier and A.M. Van Vaerenbergh (eds.), *Élections la rupture?, Le comportement des Belges face aux élections de 1999*. Bruxelles: de Boeck, 13–27.

Grunberg, G., and E. Schweisguth (1997). 'Libéralisme culturel et libéralisme économique (Cultural and Economic Liberalism)', in D. Boy and N. Mayer (eds.), *L'électeur Français en question*. Paris: CEVIPOF.

Ivaldi, G., and M. Swyngedouw (2006). 'Rechtsextremismus in populistischer Gestalt: Front National und Vlaams Blok (Comparing the extreme right in Belgium and France: Party ideology, electoral success and party system change)', in Frank Decker (ed.), *Populismus. Nützliches Korrektiv oder Gefahr für die Demokratie?* Wiesbaden: VS-Verlag für Sozialwissenschaften, 121–43.

Kaufman, L.R., and P.G. Schervish (1986). 'Using Adjusted Crosstabulations to Interpret Log-Linear Relationships', *American Sociological Review*, 51, 717–33.

Kitschelt, H. (1989). *The Logic of Party Formation, Ecological Politics in Belgium and West Germany*. Ithaca, NY: Cornell University Press.

Kitschelt, H. (1995). *The Radical Right in Western Europe. A Comparative Analysis*. Ann Arbor: The University of Michigan Press.

Kriesi, H., E. Grande, R. Lachat, M. Dolezal, S. Bornschier and T. Frye (2006). 'Globalization and the Transformation of the National Political Space: Six European Countries Compared', *European Journal of Political Research*, 45.

Lazarsfeld, P.F. (1955). 'Interpretation of Statistical Relations as a Research Operation', in P.F. Lazarsfeld and M. Rosenberg (eds.), *The Language of Social Research. A Reader in the Methodology of Social Research*. Glencoe, IL: The Free Press.

Lijphart, A. (1994). *Electoral Systems and Party Systems. A Study of Twenty-Seven Democracies, 1945–1990*. Oxford: Oxford University Press.

Lipset, S.M., and Stein Rokkan (1967). 'Cleavage Structure, Party Systems and Voter Alignments: An Introduction', in S.M. Lipset and S. Rokkan (eds.), *Party Systems and Voter Alignments*. New York: Free Press, 1–64.

Martiniello, Marco, and Marc Swyngedouw, eds. (1998). *Où va la Belgique? Les soubresauts d'une petite democratie européenne*. Paris: L'Harmattan, 269.

Massart, F. (2001). 'Le leadership régional et communautaire en Belgique fédérale', in A. Smith and C. Sorbets (eds.), *Leadership et arrangements territoriaux*. Science de la Société, Université de Toulouse II.

Putnam, Robert (1993). *Making Democracy Work: Civic Traditions in Modern Italy*. Princeton, NJ: Princeton University Press.

Raunio, T. (2002). 'Why European Integration Increases Leadership Autonomy within Political Parties', *Party Politics*, 8, 405–22.

Swyngedouw, Marc (1989). 'De keuze van de kiezer. Naar een verbetering van de schattingen van verschuivingen en partijvoorkeur bij opeenvolgende verkiezingen en peilingen', dissertation, Leuven/Rotterdam, SOI/BMG.

Swyngedouw, Marc (1992). 'L'essor d'Agalev et du Vlaams Blok', *Courier Hebdomadaire du CRISP*, 1362.

Swyngedouw, Marc (1995). 'Les nouveaux clivages dans la politique Belgo-Flamande', *Revue Française de Science Politique*, 45, 775–90.

Swyngedouw, Marc, and Roeland Beerten (1999). 'De fragmentatie van het kiezerskorps in Vlaanderen. Verschuivingen 1991–95 en 1995–99', *I.S.P.O. Bulletin* 1999/34.

Swyngedouw, Marc, and André-Paul Frognier (1999). 'Les transferts de voix: 1991–95', in A.-M. Aisch and A.-P. Frognier (eds.), *Des élections en trompe-l'oeil: Enquête sur le comportement électoral des Wallons et des Francophones*. Bruxelles: De Boeck, 35–46.

Swyngedouw, Marc, Lieven De Winter, André-Paul Frognier, Jaak Billiet, B. Goeminne, P. Baudewijns and A.-S. Berck (2004). *General Election Study Belgium. Codebook: Questions and Frequency Tables*. Leuven/Louvain-la-Neuve: ISPO-PIOP.

Swyngedouw, Marc, Jaak Billiet and B. Goeminne (2007). 'De federale verkiezingen van 2003' (working title). Leuven: Universitaire Pers Leuven (accepted for publication).

Vander Weyden, Patrick (2005). 'Conceptueel kader voor de analyse van kiessystemen. Toepassing op België, Spanje, Portugal, Hongarije en Roemenië', *IPSoM-Bulletin* 2005/10.

Do Belgian Parties Undermine the Democratic Chain of Delegation?

LIEVEN DE WINTER and PATRICK DUMONT

Party-archy and the Complexity of Multilayered Multipartisan Governance

The main particularity of party government in Belgium, which like Italy is often labelled a partitocracy (De Winter, Della Porta and Deschouwer 1996), is the overwhelming role played by organised political parties. While political parties were already predominant in the 1970s, their role was enhanced by two processes. First, the dramatically increasing fragmentation of the party system (see De Winter *et al.* this volume) raised the question of cabinet instability. Second, the federalisation process created an entirely new chain of democratic delegation and accountability in the regions and communities, each of which has its own directly elected legislature, an executive headed by a prime minister, and a civil service.

Our main thesis is that in order to guarantee a minimal degree of multi-level policy cohesion and stability, governmental parties had to minimise the interference of other political actors: voters, party rank-and-file, MPs, individual ministers, civil servants, and even the judiciary, by controlling elite recruitment and institutionalising particular coalition maintenance mechanisms. Policy-making within parties became highly centralised in the hands of the party executive – mainly the party president and his entourage.

The Predominance of Party Government

The Fight against Government Instability

Since the early 1970s, Belgium has undoubtedly had the most complex coalition bargaining system in Western Europe, and government formation has become its most crucial decision-making stage. Its party system is the most fragmented in Western-Europe in terms of effective number of parliamentary parties (6.9 on average since 1968), with the highest average number of parties in government (4.4 on average since 1968), the largest number of relevant policy dimensions (at least three) and an extremely long government formation process (Müller and Strom 2000: 561). In fact, in the period before government formation became so complex, the process consumed less than half the time: rising from an average of about 20 days in the 1946–66 period to an average of about 43 days between 1968 and 2003. The increase is even clearer for post-electoral formations: an average of 27.6 days between 1946 and 1966 compared to 66.4 days in the subsequent period. Before 1968, the mean number of parties in government was 1.8; in the 1968–2003 period it was 4.4.

One reason why coalition formation takes so long is that often several attempts need to made. The average for the period 1946–2003 is 1.4 unsuccessful attempts. If we consider only the cabinets preceded by elections, the average increases to 2.2 failed attempts. When no elections are held, it takes only 0.7 unsuccessful attempts on average. The number of unsuccessful attempts at forming a coalition has risen over time (from on average 1.1 in the 1946–66 period to 1.6 in 1968–2003). But calculated only on the basis of post-election coalitions, the increase in unsuccessful attempts is more dramatic, from on average 1.1 attempts in 1946–66 to 2.8 afterwards. Hence, 1968 (which coincides with the splitting up of the first traditional party, CVP/PSC, and the first profound government crisis over a linguistic issue, i.e. the splitting of the Catholic University of Louvain) constitutes a turning point in the process, a qualitative jump away from the rather simple logic of government formation in a 'two and a half' party system.

The large and increasing number of relevant (in Sartori's sense) parties increases uncertainty and the potential for shirking, thus undermining cabinet stability. Hence, in order to reduce agency loss, parties have developed an elaborate set of *ex ante* and *ex post* delegation control mechanisms, which tend to reduce cabinet ministers to pure party agents. Governmental decision-making – since the introduction of coalition government after the First World War – is extremely collective. Even though, with 37 governments since 1946, cabinet instability approaches the Italian 'pathological' case (Müller and Strom 2000: 561), some aspects of coalition formation were rather simple, as the pivotal and largest party family, the Christian Democrats, was typically the driving force in the formation process, usually choosing its coalition partners between Socialists and Liberals. Thus, this party family was in power from 1958 to 1999, and in that period had to yield the premiership to another party for one year only. Since 1999, it has lost this privileged position and has not been part of the federal government. In general terms, with all post-electoral governments since 1987 lasting for more than three years of the four-year mandate period, government stability has grown in the two last decades.

Government Formation: Composition, Programme, Selection of Ministers

The electoral responsiveness of coalition bargaining is very low, with parties taking office more often after electoral losses than after gains. Electoral accountability is low as well, as voters are hardly ever called upon to indicate which parties should govern after a government breaks down (De Winter *et al.* 2000).

Formally, the making of a new cabinet starts with the King's consultations with the main parliamentary parties. The King can then appoint a *formateur*, though he usually appoints an *informateur* first, or sometimes a mediator if the political situation is exceptionally difficult. In practice, the largest party usually takes the initiative, if it is willing to do so.

The result of interparty negotiations is embodied in the coalition policy programme, which since the late 1960s is usually published as an annex to the official 'government declaration' verbally delivered by the PM to Parliament. Its length has grown over time – often more than 100 pages (De Winter *et al.* 2000). While they are essentially packages of policy agreements, coalition agreements sometimes also contain statements about competencies and behavioural rules the coalition members are expected to follow. The 1992 and 1995 agreements concluded with a statement that 'also for all matters not included in the coalition agreement the majority parties have agreed to observe the classic rule of consensus within the cabinet and in parliament'. This meant that majority MPs and ministers could only launch new policies when their initiative was explicitly approved by all coalition parliamentary parties or by the full cabinet, respectively.

But many other matters are negotiated during government formation. First, because the Constitution did not restrict the number of ministers until 1995, the number of government members varied considerably, depending on the number of parties and factions in the coalition (Frognier 1993). Second, some government coordination mechanisms (e.g. cabinet committees and relations between senior and junior ministers) are also usually decided during coalition formation negotiations. Finally, since the early 1970s, the distribution of patronage resources are also included in government formation talks (De Winter 2006).

The coalition composition and policy agreement become definitive after they have been submitted to each coalition party's National Congress – the parties' supreme decision-making body. Congress decisions morally bind the entire party (rank-and-file members, MPs, ministers, party executives and party leader) to the coalition contract. They therefore constitute a core element in coalition maintenance and in the delegation from parties and their parliamentary groups to their agents in cabinet. Hence, any party organ's criticism of the policy of ministers of other parties can be condemned as a breach of party discipline, as long as the policy is mentioned in the coalition agreement. Thus, the coalition agreement not only ties coalition parties to each other, but also enhances discipline within each coalition party. These congresses are made up of representatives selected at the level of the communal or constituency party organisations. In practice, all top- and mid-level party elites are amongst those selected. No party congress has ever rejected a coalition agreement.

The votes taken indicate a usually large consensus on government composition and agreement, with some notorious exceptions. This large consensus is rarely due to the attractiveness of the policies the new government promises to implement, or the brilliance with which the party negotiators present the deal to the rank-and-file. It is mainly due to the fact that a large number of congress participants have – directly or indirectly – an interest in their party gaining or maintaining power. First, most top party leaders, but also some backbenchers, are appointed to the cabinet – appealing to every office-seeking politician. Second, MPs support the government because participation facilitates their individual and collective constituency service. Third, the party *intelligentsia* is awarded positions in the ministerial cabinets and promotions into the highly politicised public sector. Fourth, intraparty factions not only welcome any government favourable to their demands, but can often also nominate the ministers representing their interest, and appoint trustees in the relevant cabinets and administrations. Finally, most constituency party organisations can put some of their administrative personnel on the state payroll by 'parking' them in the ministerial cabinets (De Winter, Frognier and Rihoux 1996). Hence, it is not at all surprising that party congresses usually approve government participation by overwhelming majorities, even in the case of ideologically incoherent coalitions.

Portfolio distribution is formally the final stage in the formation process. The distribution of portfolios amongst partners is decided first, followed by the nomination of specific ministers. In both cases the party presidents are the main or sole decision-makers. Though the largest party usually claims the office of prime minister and most parties have specific portfolio preferences, portfolio allocation nonetheless involves interparty bargaining to satisfy a complex set of demands.[1] Still, ministers are generally seen as delegates of their party leaders, as each party president decides who will occupy the party's positions in government. Even for the ministers of his own party, the PM is only the coordinator of this complex allocation process. Nearly all ministers are recruited from the Parliament, which hinders the selection of non-partisan specialists or technicians (De Winter 1991).

Once the PM, ministers and state secretaries have been sworn in by the King, there is a customary parliamentary investiture (until 1995, in both Chambers), which since 1945 has been won by all cabinets except one. Voting discipline is very high. Since the coalition programme and configuration are approved by the national party congresses before the government is invested, a negative vote by the parliamentary majority would openly defy their parties' supreme decision-making bodies.

The Collective Nature of Cabinet Decision-making

There are no legal texts concerning internal cabinet rules, except for a few articles in the Constitution, such as the 'parity' rule requiring the cabinet to have equal numbers of Dutch- and French-speaking members, not taking the PM and the junior ministers into account. There exists a text called 'Practical Instructions of the Council of Ministers'. The 1985 version (Alen and Dujardin 1986: 532–4), which is still operational, stipulates that the cabinet not only debates and decides on 'overall governmental policy', but also on all bills ministers want to introduce in Parliament, all ministerial decisions with 'important budgetary repercussions', and all matters that could 'jeopardise government solidarity'. The latter rule brings most matters decided by individual ministers under collective cabinet responsibility and gives coalition parties effective veto power over policies proposed by ministers of other parties. In fact, the objection of one party or minister to a certain policy proposal is sufficient to force a discussion by the full cabinet, followed by a decision taken by consensus. In addition, for each matter that may 'involve the government as a whole', ministers must consult the relevant cabinet committee or the cabinet. Also, ministers are not supposed to make declarations about matters that fall under their colleagues' competencies and which might embarrass them. Even in their own jurisdiction, they must be 'extremely discreet' about making public statements as long as the government has not yet decided the matter. Finally, ministers should not make any declaration or take any action expressing a personal point of view that challenges the government's stance. Thus, by constitutional convention, cabinet decisions are taken by consensus formulated by the Prime Minister. The 1985 principles state that a minister, when he does not agree with a cabinet decision supported by a 'fundamental' majority, has two alternatives: accept it without public dissent, or resign. These operational rules suggest that Belgian ministers are not at all policy dictators in their jurisdictions (as suggested by Laver and Shepsle 1996). Every policy initiative of any significance must be scrutinised and approved by the entire cabinet.

However, the vague formulations of these rules leave the PM and his vice-PMs with some discretion (Timmermans 1994). In addition, while these stringent rules were in various degrees effective in the Martens and Dehaene governments (1978–99), the Verhofstadt I cabinet cherished the 'open debate culture', which led to a cacophony of different opinions voiced by ministers and their supporting parties before any collective government position was defined.

The PM chairs the cabinet and its secretariat, controls the cabinet agenda and acts as its main coordinator (Frognier 1997). Vis-à-vis his vice-PMs, the PM is only a *primus inter pares*. Each coalition party (including, in the most recent governments, the PM's party) usually has one vice-PM, who is in charge of a large department. They act as cabinet frontbenchers of their parties – and constitute the so-called *Kerncabinet*. This inner cabinet, chaired by the PM, meets quite regularly (sometimes more than once a week), and constitutes a forum in which coalition parties reach major decisions on conflictual matters, which the full cabinet then formally ratifies. To assist them in their cabinet leadership role, vice-PMs are equipped with a 'ministerial cabinet for general policy' of about 50 to 70 staff members, who follow the decision-making of other ministers and safeguard the party's interest.

Until 1992, when they were abolished, cabinet committees prepared the cabinet's collective decisions. Cabinet committees included not only the relevant ministers, but usually also a representative of each coalition party, regardless of their actual departmental competencies. Therefore, each party was fully informed about the decisions that were under preparation.

The number and the competencies of junior ministers (a position that has existed since 1960) are decided collectively by the formation negotiators. Until 1991, junior ministers often did not belong to the same party as their senior, or – in the days of the unitary traditional parties – often came from a different linguistic wing of the party. In these cases, junior ministers tended to operate as 'watchdogs' over their ministers. The junior ministers' decision-making autonomy was often relatively high and rested on the overall balance of power between coalition parties. This watchdog system led to so many conflicts between ministers and their juniors that between 1991 and 1999 they always belonged to the same party.

Supporting parties can also monitor cabinet decision-making through direct formal and informal contacts between leaders of the party organisations, such as interparty summits which are called to reach compromises that aggregate a large number of conflictual issues. This reduces the problems of shirking once a party has seen its preferred policies implemented – a problem that is particularly likely to plague large coalitions. In many cases compromises can only be reached by solving 'in one stroke' all or most unresolved problems in a wide variety of policy areas. Sometimes these decisions acquire the status of political pacts (School pact, Culture pact, and a wide number of constitutional reform pacts), which cannot be amended by the cabinet or by the parliamentary majority.

In addition, in all parties, most ministers and junior ministers regularly attend the weekly meetings of their party executive. Even more important are their weekly meetings with the party chairman (who, according to party statutes, cannot be a cabinet member) and top party leaders (De Winter 1993). At these meetings, the cabinet agenda is carefully scrutinised, and the positions to be defended by the ministers are defined. Also, when important issues or new facts are unexpectedly raised during a cabinet meeting, the meeting is sometimes suspended in order to allow ministers to phone their party leader for advice, or the matter is deferred to the next meeting.

In addition, ministers have large personal staffs ('ministerial cabinets') paid for by the state. The size of ministerial cabinets ranges from several dozen to over 200 members. In the traditional parties, most top cabinet members are appointed by party headquarters, including the *chef de cabinet*, the minister's main advisor. This enables party leaders to install their 'men of confidence' as monitoring and information channels in the immediate entourage of their ministers. The *chefs de cabinet* often remain in charge of a department longer than do ministers. As a reward for their party service, they often advance to the top of the civil service, or become MPs or minister. The core of a ministerial cabinet constitutes about ten policy collaborators who are the main personal political advisors of the minister.[2] The members of the ministerial cabinet prepare their minister's own projects and positions on issues to be raised in forthcoming cabinet meetings or in cabinet committees on which the minister serves, formulate potential compromises that the minister can propose, and also prepare the minister's positions for parliamentary appearances. Some advisors specialise in the policy area of another department, usually when a coalition party has a particular interest in a policy area in which it does not have any ministers. Finally, the ministerial cabinet, especially its lower-level staff, is responsible for running the clientelist machinery, especially in the minister's electoral constituency. Dozens of ministers' staff members also work directly and exclusively for the party.

In 1999, an ambitious reform of the administration (the so-called Copernicus reform) was initiated by the unprecedented 'rainbow coalition' of liberals, socialists and the Greens. Especially the Greens – which had never taken office before – aimed at a reduction in the size and power of ministerial cabinets in favour of the regular civil service (Walgrave *et al.* 2004). Only a few months after this government took office it decided to abolish the ministerial cabinets *tout court* and to rely on the civil service for policy advice. Yet the abolishment of the ministerial cabinets did not really succeed, and the next government of socialist and liberal parties that took office in June 2003 reinstated the ministerial cabinets.

The Weakness of Other Veto Players

Parliament: The Price of Party Discipline

Since the 1960s, Belgium has followed a difficult path toward federalism. A 1993 constitutional amendment transformed Belgium into a federal country based on three linguistic communities (Flemish, French and German, a tiny minority) and three regions (Flanders, Brussels and Wallonia). Since 1995, the Senate has lost several competencies[3] and has evolved into a 'reflection chamber' and a meeting place between the federal and regional/community levels of government. Hence, the shift from symmetrical to asymmetrical bicameralism (Lijphart 1999: 212) has weakened the veto power of the Senate.

Parliamentary government in Belgium can only function properly if the MPs of the numerous majority parties are able to guarantee permanent support for the government. Until the introduction of the constructive motion of censure in 1995, the cabinet had to mobilise a majority of votes from the majority parties on every single governmental initiative introduced in Parliament (because any defeat would have 'morally' obliged the government to resign). Consequently, parliamentary groups are very disciplined in voting (Depauw 2000). Apart from investiture voting, there are no systematic longitudinal data available, but disparate data spanning the 1954–98 period suggest that also on ordinary legislative activities, discipline comes close to *Kadaverdisziplin*.[4] 'Alternative majorities' (which include the votes of some opposition parties and exclude some of the majority parties) might have existed on specific issues, but have never been used in the postwar period (at least on government-initiated proposals), because doing so would trigger the downfall of the government. Hence, members of the majority are permanently faced with the dilemma of having to approve government actions unconditionally, or forcing the cabinet to resign.

Formal and informal party constraints further enhance voting discipline. First, party investiture votes force all party bodies into loyalty to the agreement. Second, according to the statutes of all parties, supreme authority is given to the party's national congress, and between congresses to the party executive. In most party executives a majority of members are MPs, but they do not generally consider themselves delegates of the parliamentary party (De Winter and Dumont 2000). In addition, most party statutes define the role of their public office-holders as mere agents of the party. In almost all parties, MPs must ask permission from their group (leader) to introduce a private member's bill or amendment, hold interpellations, or support a bill sponsored by another party. The parliamentary group can explicitly sanction voting rebellions in a variety of ways – from a simple warning to expulsion from committees, the parliamentary party group, and/or the party and deselection.

The small staffs of individual MPs and the relatively well subsidised party research centres add to the MP's dependency on his party organisation. MPs often rely on information provided by their research centre in drafting bills, amendments and interpellations. For most policy sectors, a group of paid experts and volunteer specialists associated with the party research centres prepare the party's proposals in collaboration with the MPs who specialise in these areas. Thus, MPs to a large extent depend on their party's brain trust.

In comparison with the powerful inter- and intraparty tools that parties use to monitor the government, the traditional tools for parliamentary monitoring of the executive (legislation and various oversight devices) seem quite ineffective (De Winter 1998). In parliamentary systems, Parliament can monitor government behaviour through the role it plays in government legislation (including budget bills). An even more powerful steering tool is for Parliament to pass its own legislation. In spite of the fact that committees in both Chambers are specialised and permanent, this potentially strong committee structure (Mattson and Strøm 1995) has not prevented the function of legislation being largely usurped by the executive. A large majority of successful bills are introduced by the government rather than by individual MPs. However, in spite of their declining role in legislation, the average individual MP has engaged increasingly in law-initiating activities. The relative decline of the legislative function of Parliament is due to the fact that a decreasing proportion of the bills and amendments introduced by MPs is enacted. In contrast, government bills and amendments are generally successful.[5] The low success rate of private member's bills is primarily due to the detailed and extensive government agreements. The only private member's bills that have a chance to become law are issues not mentioned in the government programme but on which members of the coalition parties can nevertheless agree. Hence, successful private member's bills are usually of little policy importance and are often motivated entirely by a desire to claim credit for specific legislation. Since majority parties occupy most legislative leadership positions and can therefore set its plenary and committee agenda, government bills usually get priority treatment. Finally, given the increasing complexity of the decision-making process and the need for rapid decisions, the executive increasingly resorts to delegated legislation.

Apart from budget control, votes of censure and committees of investigation, the main parliamentary tools of government control are written and oral questions and interpellations. Over past decades the House has become increasingly active with regard to these activities. Nonetheless, the majority's duty to promote government stability has considerably undermined Parliament's control function. In fact, about half of the questions are simple demands for information, often inspired by mere vote- or publicity-seeking motives. Moreover, because ministers' responses to questions are not followed by debate, the usefulness of questions for controlling the government and ministers is limited.

Interpellations are questions put to the government or a minister on a matter of general importance, and can be followed by a motion for debate between the interpellant and the government, which can include a proposal not to grant the government the confidence of the House. However, interpellations increasingly focus on minor aspects of particular government policies and are inspired by a member's personal electoral concerns. The House tends to relegate them to public committee meetings. Only interpellations of a general nature or of exceptional political importance are still held in plenary session.

Before the 1989 reforms, departmental budget bills (indicating planned expenditures for the coming year) were usually submitted quite late – after the budget year had already begun. Thus, most of the money was spent before the final budget was approved. In addition, budget bills were usually rushed through the Chambers by the government majority. Parliament's budgetary oversight of the executive therefore became something of a farce. Since 1989, the rules governing the government's budget bill have been changed to strengthen parliamentary oversight. The budget process ends with parliamentary approval of the Law on Accounts, which includes a financial report from the Audit Office. This requires the introduction of a bill to that effect during October following the end of the fiscal (i.e. calendar) year. The vote on this law was originally intended to provide an opportunity to assess government policy. Yet because passage of the Law on Accounts often occurs several years later, it has become a mere formality, not least because the responsible government is usually no longer in power. In addition, the Audit Office's report evaluates the regularity and legality of government expenditures, rather than their efficacy and necessity.

Until the 1980s, parliamentary committees of investigation (which have the same powers as an examining magistrate) were quite rare, as majority MPs – in solidarity with the government – were reluctant to allow investigations that could embarrass a specific minister or the entire government. In addition, even when a committee of inquiry concluded that a minister was politically responsible for certain failures, the minister did not resign as long as he was supported by his party. However, while the House created only nine such committees in the entire 1880–1988 period, since then it has established roughly one each year. They have developed into an alternative instrument of parliamentary oversight and draw considerable publicity.

The Belgian Parliament is characterised by a lack of institutionally provided resources to individual MPs. First, until 1987 most MPs did not have a private working space inside Parliament. Second, the House counts (in 2004) 636 permanent employees, of which only about a quarter have a university degree. Of the latter, only those working for the Legislative Service and the Library (about a third of the university-trained employees) can provide intellectual assistance to individual MPs. Each permanent committee has just one or two secretaries who – time permitting – can also act as research assistants. Apart from these services, no collectively provided staff is available to individual members. Third, only in 1981 was each MP allocated funds for employing a full-time helper paid at the level of *clerk*. In most cases, these assistants only perform secretarial work (correspondence, filing, individual constituency service), and very few are involved in the preparation of parliamentary work. Since May 1995, MPs are also allocated funds for recruiting a full-time collaborator paid at the level of university-trained civil servants. However, in most parliamentary parties, these staff have been pooled and attached to the party research centre, where they work for the party as a whole. In fact, specialised policy preparation committees operate in each party research centre (financed mainly by the parliamentary group contributions). MPs often rely on information provided by their research centre as far as the drafting of bills, amendments and interpellations is concerned. For most policy sectors, a group of permanent experts and volunteering specialists associated with the party research centre prepares the party's policy proposals in collaboration with the MPs specialised in these fields. Thus, MPs are to a large extent dependent on their party's braintrust, because they do not have alternative resources at their disposal.

These structural constraints undermine MPs' ability to represent the policy preferences of their voters. First, the highly fragmented and multidimensional party system obliges MPs to position themselves programmatically on more dimensions and issues than ever before. Given their strict obligation to underwrite the national party manifesto, it is not easy to adopt a profile that best suits their specific constituencies. In addition, majority MPs are obliged to honour the coalition agreement. Many MPs try to circumvent these structural constraints by generating electoral support through non-policy-related activities – for example, case work, local office-holding, pork-barrel politics and local symbolic representation. This also explains the rather high levels of parliamentary absenteeism in the Belgian Parliament (De Winter 1992). Case work used to constitute an activity in which Belgian MPs invested considerable amounts of time. This was, on the one hand, related to the clientelist political culture in Belgium and electoral payoffs, and, on the other, to the wide variety of services MPs could offer given parties' control over most sectors of public life. However, since the end of the 1980s, case work has declined. This may be due to the devolution of many competencies to the regional and community level and the direct election of regional MPs since 1995, and thus the potential emergence of an autonomous class of active constituency servants. Survey research indicates a general decrease in the capacities of elected officials to deliver the goods to their clients, especially in Flanders.[6]

Another non-policy form of representation is the *cumul local*, that is, holding a local elected office together with a seat in Parliament. This belongs to one of the traditions of Belgian parliamentary behaviour and represents a wider tendency towards localism within the political culture. In 1999, about six out of ten representatives combined their parliamentary mandate with a local office. Of those, half were members of the local council, while the other half held office at the executive level, as mayor or alderman (the latter are elected by the city council, the mayor is appointed by the Minister of the Interior on the proposal of the city council). Apart from the Greens, all parties tried to exploit the 'dual mandate', as far as the recruitment reservoir and statutory arrangements permitted. As a consequence, representatives tend to spend a considerable proportion of their time on local duties.

Finally, Belgian MPs invest a great deal in symbolic responsive behaviour and spend about half of their working time in the constituency, as the distance between the capital and the constituency is for most MPs less than an hour's drive and most MPs tend to return to their constituency home every evening. They attend meetings and social gatherings organised by a wide variety of local and constituency organisations, groups and institutions (such as chambers of commerce and trade unions, pensioners, cultural, sports, youth or women organisations and local government boards). In addition, they traditionally spend their evenings and weekends inaugurating buildings, distributing prizes at schools, attending festivities, dedications, *vernissages* (private inaugurations), balls, receptions, openings of commercial and cultural initiatives, sports manifestations, fairs, even funerals and weddings. This 'flower pot' function is considered one of the electorally most effective activities.

However, the recent increase in the territorial size of the constituencies has undermined the capacities of MPs to engage in these small-scale activities. With province- or even region-wide constituencies, constituency service and active participation in the social life of the constituency becomes unmanageable (too many clients to serve, too many local events to attend), the impact of local office negligible, and the pork barrel too diffused. We do notice a serious decline in time devoted to constituency case work, local office and constituency party work (De Winter 2002). This suggests that MPs are trying to reach wider audiences in the enlarged constituencies in order to attract preference votes, rather than using the traditional local channels, and are employing the regional and national media, especially television, as their first instrument of communication with potential voters.

In addition, with the decline of the major cleavages (at least regarding the left–right and denominational divide, see De Winter *et al.* this volume), parties encounter more and more problems adopting an original policy programme. Hence, election victories are believed to depend more on presenting attractive candidates than on promising policies. Therefore, most parties invest in new media-attractive candidates, such as pretty women, well-assimilated candidates of foreign origin and, increasingly, children of famous politicians, most categories lacking political experience. In 1999, turnover skyrocketed as less than half (74/150) of the deputies were deputies in the previous term (Fiers 2000).

This turnover weakens social cohesion, familiarity and political trust amongst MPs, which may undermine the efficacy of committee work. However, it is too soon to grasp the effect on governance. But given the complexity of political decision-making in Belgian consociationalism, vital bargaining and compromising skills are usually only acquired through long parliamentary experience. Hence, the traditional capacity of accommodation and pacification of the Belgian elites may be jeopardized (Lijphart 1981).

Civil Service: Party Control over the Public Sector

The ministerial cabinets are the main link between the minister and his civil servants. The excessive use of ministerial cabinets is partially due to the politicisation of the civil service, which often creates tensions when top civil servants belong to a different party than their minister. In fact, about three out of four higher civil servants are party members – 60 per cent being Christian democrats (Dierickx and Majersdorf 1993: 151). The high degree of politicisation of the civil service is a traditional feature of Belgian consociationalism, which became more institutionalised and pervasive during the 1970s due to the fragmentation of the party system (De Winter 1981, 2006). Two types of interparty negotiations govern the distribution of civil service promotions between governmental parties. First, the distribution of top positions (director-general and secretary-general) is decided by the government collectively. Second, promotions of lower ranks of university-trained civil servants are decided by an unofficial interparty committee, in which each coalition party is represented. For each vacancy, the committee considers the candidates for promotion and the support each one has from a coalition party. In principle, each coalition party has a quota of nominations (approximately proportional to its parliamentary strength) that is usually fixed in a secret protocol annexed to the coalition agreement. Only when there is no partisan candidate does the committee nominate the candidate proposed by the board of directors of the ministerial department.

Given this encompassing politicisation, ministers feared that they could not unconditionally rely on the loyalty of their civil servants. Hence, until the early 1990s, ministerial cabinets carried out most policy development, verification of policy implementation, and mediation with interest groups (Hondeghem 1996: 51–8). The civil service, including high-level civil servants, basically only provided the cabinet with the information necessary for policy planning and policy and department management (except for personnel policy, which was also controlled by the ministerial cabinets). Many *cabinetards* go back and forth between the ministerial cabinets and the civil service, with cabinet service quickening promotion in the civil service, and the civil service acting as a waiting room for the politically active whose party is in opposition (Dewachter 1992: 237; Decat *et al.* 2004).

A similar exchange operates between ministerial cabinets, on the one hand, and the judiciary and the public enterprises, on the other.

However, since the late 1980s, and especially after the breakthrough of the extreme right in the 1991, 'Black Sunday' elections and the subsequent calls for a 'new political culture', there has been a general move towards accountability and depoliticisation of the civil service. As a consequence, at the present time, about five in six higher civil servants are appointed on the proposal of the departmental board of directors (Hondeghem 1996: 60). In addition, the ministerial staffs are now required to meet regularly with their top civil servants. In the past, ministerial staffs tended to work with civil servants loyal to their party, often bypassing the departments' hierarchy. Higher civil servants have been made more responsible for the management of their departments, are regularly evaluated, and can now be sanctioned (or even fired) for poor performance. The role of the departmental secretary-general has been enhanced in budgeting, personnel policy and policy implementation. As a consequence, ministers now tend to have much more direct contact with their top civil servants. The emancipation of the higher civil service has been enhanced by the reduction of the overall size of the ministerial cabinets by half, basically due to the introduction of a constitutional amendment limiting the number of ministers to 15, and by the transfer of competencies to regions and communities. However, empirical analysis suggests that the so-called Copernicus reforms do not seem to have fundamentally altered the old ways. The power relations between politics and administration have not fundamentally changed (De Visscher 2004: 179–80).

Given the encompassing party patronage in the civil service, it comes as no surprise that in public, semi-public and quasi-autonomous enterprises and services, parties (together with trade unions) interfered with the recruitment and promotion of personnel, at different levels (ranging from the janitor in a public kindergarten to the chairman of the board of directors of the Belgian national airline). Not only were all members of the board of directors of all (semi-)public enterprises nominated by political parties, political patronage was widespread at the lower levels too. In the 1990s, several of the main public enterprises were given more autonomy (including airlines, telephone, railways, ferries, post, some public banks and credit institutions). Management contracts between the minister and public managers heading these enterprises were concluded. They stipulate the objectives of the service and the financial means allocated by the minister in charge. Managers themselves can decide how to allocate these resources and achieve their goals. Also, private sector participation puts a check on direct ministerial or party interference in policy-making and, in particular, personnel recruitment. With the Copernicus reforms, the top managers of these enterprises are subject to the new recruitment system. Yet, many of the new managers have a political pedigree, and their board of directors are still largely nominated by parties. Hence, while top managers have acquired much more autonomy in running their public enterprise (including personnel policy), political parties keep control over the nominations of the top managers and the board of directors. Finally, in comparative perspective, the Belgian National Bank scores low on political autonomy (Lijphart 1999). Although the National Bank is formally autonomous, there has been a symbiotic relationship between the governor and the top echelons of the government.

Judiciary: Weak Constitutionality Checks and Politicisation of Recruitment

Belgian legal culture has traditionally opposed judicial review of the constitutionality of laws (Lijphart 1999: 41). Ordinary courts cannot review the constitutionality of laws, though they exercise judicial control over administrative actions. Only two specialised courts exercise some authority with regard to the constitutionality of legal rules. First, the Council of State is an advisory court that can express an opinion on the constitutionality of government or private member's bills. It does not express an opinion on the policy goals or means of a bill and its decisions are non-binding. General bills initiated by the government must be submitted to the Council of State by the respective ministers. The initiative to submit a draft bill may also come from Parliament. In other cases asking for this court's advice is optional. Hence, out of all rules for which an opinion might be requested, only 20 per cent are submitted to the Council of State. Although it has no formal judicial power, its advice has gained moral weight since 1970, when constitutional reform began to dominate the political agenda. Nonetheless, when there was a solid consensus between coalition parties, the governmental majority has on occasion not hesitated to pass a bill or amendment that the Council had judged unconstitutional.

Second, the Court of Arbitration was established in 1984 in order to determine whether legislative rules issued by federal, regional and community assemblies were enacted in compliance with the Constitution and its enabling legislation. In 1988, its competencies were enlarged to include reviewing the compliance of legislative rules with fundamental rights enumerated in three constitutional articles: the principles of equality, non-discrimination, and the right to and freedom of education. The Court exercises its jurisdiction through annulment proceedings that may be initiated by the executive or legislative bodies of the federal, regional or community levels of government or by any legal or natural person. In such cases, the Court's rules are binding. In practice, the Court has interpreted its new competence broadly, including all cases of discrimination and violation by federal, regional and community legislative assemblies of constitutional rights and other rights granted in international treaties. It has, therefore, evolved into a genuine constitutional court, though it has limited policy competence.

Recruitment to the courts, and especially the constitutional ones, is heavily subject to party patronage (De Winter 2006). Although there is no strong evidence that judges recruited through party patronage are easily influenced by party pressure, their partisan recruitment and career dependence raise questions about the independence and political neutrality of the 'third branch'. Yet, there have also been changes in the judiciary. In 1991, recruitment to the judiciary was made conditional upon success in entrance examinations, although the Minister of Justice could still freely choose between the candidates that passed the tests. Only in 1998 was it decided to depoliticise the promotion of judges by transferring the minister's powers of nomination to a more neutral and pluralist Council of the Judiciary (De Winter 2002).

Conclusion: The Unavoidable Concentration of Power in the Hands of Party Leaderships

The extreme fragmentation of the Belgian party system in combination with increasing need for multilevel coordination have enhanced the position of political parties in the Belgian polity. In that sense, Belgium has become even more partitocratic than in the heyday of the 1970 and 1980s. On the other hand, some of the clientelistic and patronage excesses were reduced in the 1990s, and restored to some degree the legitimacy of Belgian partitocracy.[7] While the Italian *partitocrazia* suddenly imploded in the early 1990s, the Belgian *particratie* underwent a number of gradual adaptations, which reduced the negative consequences of the grip of political parties on central government and thus prevented a collapse of the partitocratic system. To some degree they restored the governability of the country.[8] Still, even while major corrections have been made, it is debatable whether these are sufficient to overcome public dissatisfaction with the way parties have run the country in recent decades.

The heavy burden of the repayment of the huge public debt (137 per cent of GDP in 1993)[9] will remind the population for decades of the dysfunctions[10] of the Belgian partitocracy and will long undermine the legitimacy of the main political parties, as the payment of the interest on this debt, let alone its repayment, reduces enormously government's policy-making capacity and the possibility to react to and meet new societal needs.[11]

The Belgian partitocracy violates the ideal-type chain of parliamentary delegation in many ways, insofar as political parties play a predominant role at each stage. They channel the delegation of power from voters to MPs, from Parliament to the cabinet, from the collective cabinet to individual ministers, and from ministers to their civil servants. Many actors in the parliamentary chain of delegation have been reduced to mere party agents of party principals. To some extent, partitocracy is unavoidable and even functional for political system stability. Given the extremely high fragmentation, a minimum level of government stability and coherence requires power to be concentrated in the hands of a small number of actors. Autonomous MPs, ministers, top civil servants, and to some extent judges and courts, could 'spoil' the complex and delicate process of delegation, and even contribute to its collapse.

On the other hand, the costs of partitocracy are high, and partitocratic practices carried to their extreme have undermined political legitimacy and governability. Since the 1991 'Black Sunday' elections, institutional reform and democratic refinement have been high on the political agenda. This has produced a large number of institutional reform proposals (De Winter and Brans 2003). Amongst those that have been effectively implemented, one finds restrictions on the accumulation of local executive offices by MPs, closing loopholes with regard to private party financing, lowering the ceiling on campaign spending for individual candidates, allowing groups of citizens to introduce a 'popular legislative initiative' to Parliament, re-evaluating and simplifying existing legislation, increasing citizens' access to public administrators, increasing the transparency, responsiveness, responsibility and efficacy of public administration, (partially) depoliticising civil service recruitment and promotions, and drafting a code of conduct for MPs that would curtail their clientelistic intervention in public administration.[12]

To conclude, mainly since the early 1990s, Belgium has witnessed a gradual decline in the informal system of partitocratic delegation. Thus, some formal agents (the cabinet, top civil servants, some MPs) are gradually regaining autonomy. Renewal seems to have started. Yet survey research indicates that political reform has dropped off the citizens' agenda. Moreover, as the elections of 2003 and 2004 produced another Black Sunday, institutional reform aimed at fighting partitocracy has largely vanished from the overall political agenda, probably for the next half decade.

Notes

1. With the growing number of governing parties and the complexity of institutional constraints, the allocation of cabinet and junior ministerships is ruled by detailed arrangements. Each position has a specific weight and parties have drawing rights proportional to their parliamentary strength. To fine-tune the bargain, new positions are sometimes created (like government commissioners in 1999 and 2003), payoffs at the level of the regional and community executives are sometimes included in the negotiations as well as the Belgian seat in the European Commission.
2. A very large majority (86% in the 1970–99 period) were party members and about half declared themselves to be active militants of their party (Suetens and Walgrave 2001). The number of these policy advisors (of which 81% have a university degree) in the federal plus the regional ministerial cabinets rose from around 300 to 900 in the 1970–99 period. Apart from these substantial aids, a ministerial cabinet typically consists of almost 40 technical and administrative collaborators: secretaries, chauffeurs and cleaning personnel.
3. As of 1995 only the House of Representatives can invest or dissolve a government, approve the budget, and conduct interpellations of ministers. All government bills are introduced in the House. Despite this, the Senate and the House remain equally competent as regards constitutional and other institutional reforms, regional and linguistic matters, ratification of treaties, and the organisation of the judiciary. The Senate is exclusively competent for conflicts between the national and regional/community legislatures. The Senate has the right to discuss and amend bills approved by the House, but the latter has the final word, even on bills initiated by the Senate.

4. At investiture votes (1945–99), 0.6% of the majority deputies voted against the new government and its government agreement (De Winter *et al.* 2000).
5. Roughly speaking, about nine out of ten of all legislative proposals originate from parliamentary initiative, but of those, only one out of ten becomes a bill. The proportion of private member's bills in the total amount of approved bills has increased from about less than one in five in the 1960s to about one in four since the 1980s.
6. In 1991, about 21% of respondents declared themselves to have applied in the previous four years for 'a politician's help for the solution of one or more personal problems', against only 12% in 2003. In 1991, 69% of these clients found that the politician's involvement had helped to resolve their problem, against 61% in 2003 (own calculations). In 1991, 53% declared themselves to have voted for this politician in the previous parliamentary elections, against 52% in 2003. In the 1978–81 period, the average Flemish member of the House of Representatives treated 1,979 cases, against only 461 in 1996. The francophone representatives treated 1,040 cases in 1996, against 2,492 in 1978–81.
7. Survey research indicates that a large majority of Belgian citizens believe that parties and politicians are not responsive to the policy preferences of ordinary citizens (ISPO-PIOP 1999 post-electoral survey). This public disaffection with Belgian parties reached an alarming degree at the end of the 1980s, as reflected in the breakthrough of the extreme right and other protest parties.
8. However, while satisfaction with democracy took a dramatic dip in 1997 (minus 34% to 19%, the lowest in the EU), it has recovered surprisingly quickly, to even above the European average (De Winter and Türsan 2001). Trust in political institutions has followed this trend (with trust in government, parliament, the parties and public administration approaching again the European average), but trust remains dramatically low for the judiciary, police, army and the church.
9. In the 1990s Belgium had the highest level of public debt of the 15 EU members (in 1993, 137.1% of GDP and still at 94.7% in 2004). In 1993 the repayment of this debt absorbed 11.1% of GDP or 28.4% of the federal budget (as most of this debt was incurred by the federal government), but has decreased to 4.8% of GDP by 2004, or 9.6% of the federal budget. The Maastricht norms forced the governments of the 1990s to cut public expenditures severely, leaving little space for innovative policies (Belgium has one of the lowest rates of public investment in research and development) or for expanding social security benefits, hiring new civil servants or increasing their pay. Finally, during the Dutroux affair, it also scored the lowest with regard to citizen satisfaction with the functioning of democracy (Eurobarometer, 47.1).
10. Direct interferences with the operation of the civil service has rendered obsolete the use of objective cost/benefits analyses for public investments, government subsidies to industries in decline, new social security measures aimed at satisfying old and new needs, etc. (Varone *et al.* 2005).
11. For the last 6 years, Belgium has produced a balanced budget.
12. The Flemish Parliament promulgated such a code in 1997, drafted by Dr. De Winter, which has gradually become the standard for similar codes being drafted by other national, provincial and local assemblies. Also many parties have drafted codes of proper conduct, which are usually stricter than the current consensus, and in which each party to some extent tries to put into practice for its own elected officials the principles they would like to impose on the entire political class (De Winter and Dumont 2000).

References

Alen, André, and Jean Dujardin (1986). *Casebook Belgisch Grondwettelijk Recht*. Brussels: Story-Scientia.
Decat, A., C. Pelgrims and A. Hondeghem (2004). *Het glazen plafond bij de overheid. Een case study naar de selectie van de federale topmanagers*. Rapport Instituut voor de Overheid, D/2004/10107/015, Katholieke Universiteit Leuven.

Depauw, Sam (2000). 'Fractiecohesie en effectiviteit van parlementen', *Res Publica*, 4, 503–19.

De Visscher, C. (2004). *La relation entre l'autorité politique et la haute administration*. Gent: Academia Press.

Dewachter, Wilfried (1992). *Besluitvorming in Politiek België*. Leuven: Acco.

De Winter, Lieven (1981). 'De Partijpolitisering als Instrument van de Particratie. Een Overzicht van de Ontwikkeling Sinds de Tweede Wereldoorlog', *Res Publica*, 23, 53–107.

De Winter, Lieven (1991). 'Parliamentary and Party Pathways to the Cabinet', in Jean Blondel and Jean-Louis Thiébault (eds.), *The Profession of Government Minister in Western Europe*. London: Macmillan.

De Winter, Lieven (1992). 'The Belgian Legislator', unpublished PhD thesis. Florence: European University Institute.

De Winter, Lieven (1993). 'The Links between Cabinets and Parties and Cabinet Decision-Making', in Jean Blondel and Ferdinand Müller-Rommel (eds.), *Governing Together*. London: Macmillan.

De Winter, Lieven (1998). 'Parliament and Government in Belgium: Prisoners of Partitocracy', in Philip Norton (ed.), *Parliaments and Governments in Western Europe*. London: Frank Cass.

De Winter, Lieven (2002). 'Political Corruption in Belgium', in M. Bull and J. Newell (eds.), *Corruption in Contemporary Politics*. London: Macmillan, 93–105.

De Winter, L. (2006). 'Sixty Years of Party Patronage in the Belgian Partitocracy: Quantitative and Qualitative Transformations, Paper presented at the workshop Political Parties and Patronage of the Joint Sessions of Workshops of the ECPR, Nicosia, 25–30 April.

De Winter, Lieven, and Marleen Brans (2003). 'Belgium: Political Professionals and the Crisis of the Party State', in Jens Borchert and Jürgen Zeiss (eds.), *The Political Class in Advanced Democracies*. Oxford: Oxford University Press, 45–66.

De Winter, Lieven and Patrick Dumont (2000). 'Belgium: Subjects of Partitocratic Dominion', in Knut Heidar and Ruud Koole (eds.), *Parliamentary Party Groups in European Democracies*. London: Routledge.

De Winter, Lieven, and Huri Türsan (2001). 'The Belgian Presidency 2001', Research and Policy Paper 13, Notre Europe, Paris.

De Winter, Lieven, Donatella Della Porta and Kris Deschouwer (1996). 'Comparing Similar Countries', *Res Publica*, 38, 215–36.

De Winter, Lieven, André-Paul Frognier and Benoît Rihoux (1996). 'Belgium: Still the Age of Party Government?', in Jean Blondel and Maurizio Cotta (eds.), *Party and Government*. London: Macmillan.

De Winter, Lieven, Arco Timmermans and Patrick Dumont (2000). 'Belgium: On Government Agreements, Evangelists, Followers, and Heretics', in Wolfgang C. Müller and Kaare Strøm (eds.), *Coalition Government in Western Europe*. Oxford: Oxford University Press.

Dierickx, Guido, and Philippe Majersdorf (1993). *La Culture Politique des Fonctionnaires et des Hommes Politiques en Belgique*. Brugge: Vanden Broele.

Fiers, Stefaan (2000). *Vijftig jaar volksvertegenwoordiging. De circulatie onder de Belgische parlementsleden 1946–95*. Brussels: Koninklijke Vlaamse Academie van België voor Wetenschappen en Kunsten.

Frognier, André-Paul (1993). 'The Single Party/Coalition Distinction and Cabinet Decision-Making', in Jean Blondel and Ferdinand Müller-Rommel (eds.), *Governing Together*. London: Macmillan.

Frognier, André-Paul (1997). 'Belgium: A Complex Cabinet in a Fragmented Polity', in Jean Blondel and Ferdinand Müller-Rommel (eds.), *Cabinets in Western Europe*, 2nd ed. London: Macmillan.

Hondeghem, Annie (1996). 'De Politieke en de Ambtelijke Component in het Openbaar Bestuur', in Rudolf Maes and Kathleen Jochmans (eds.), *Inleiding tot de Bestuurkunde*. Brussel: Studiecentrum Open Hoger Onderwijs.

Laver, Michael, and Kenneth Shepsle (1996). *Making and Breaking Governments*. Cambridge: Cambridge University Press.

Lijphart, Arendt (1981). *Conflict and Coexistence in Belgium: The Dynamics of a Culturally Divided Society*. Berkeley: University of California.

Lijphart, Arendt (1999). *Patterns of Democracy*. New Haven, CT: Yale University Press.

Mattson, Ingvar, and Kaare Strøm (1995). 'Parliamentary Committees', in Herbert Döring (ed.), *Parliaments and Majority Rule in Western Europe*. Frankfurt am Main: Campus and New York: St. Martin's Press.

Müller, Wolfgang C., and Kaare Strøm (eds.) (2000). *Coalition Government in Western Europe*. Oxford: Oxford University Press.

Suetens, Mik, and Stefan Walgrave (2001). 'Belgian Politics without Ministerial Cabinets?', *Acta Politica*, 36, 180–205.

Timmermans, Arco (1994) 'Cabinet Ministers and Parliamentary Government in Belgium. The Impact of Coalitional Constraints', in Michael Laver and Kenneth A. Shepsle (eds.), *Cabinet Ministers and Parliamentary Government*. Cambridge: Cambridge University Press.

Varone, F., S. Jacob and L. De Winter (2005). 'Polity, Politics and Policy Evaluation in Belgium', *Evaluation*, 11, 253–73.

Walgrave, S., T. Caals, M. Suetens and K. De Swert (2004). 'Ministerial Cabinets and Partitocracy. A Career Pattern Study of Ministerial Cabinet Members in Belgium', PSW Paper 2004/7, Politieke Wetenschappen, Universiteit Antwerpen.

PART II:
POLICY PERFORMANCE
AND POLICY REFORM

Administrative Reform in Belgium: Maintenance or Modernisation?

MARLEEN BRANS, CHRISTIAN DE VISSCHER and
DIEDERIK VANCOPPENOLLE

As a major employer, the federal civil service served for a long time as a model for other sectors. Many of the practices observed at the national level, therefore, also characterised other levels in the public sector. However, the redistribution of competencies between levels of government severely decreased the importance of the federal civil service. Large numbers of civil servants were transferred from the federal to the subnational state level as a result of the federalisation process. In 2000, 29.7 per cent of civil servants worked at the federal level (federal government and particular bodies, such as courts, army, federal police), but only 6.8 per cent were employed in the ministries (Federaal Ministerie van Ambtenarenzaken 2001). Not only had the federal civil service been severely reduced, but the most dynamic sectors of government had been transferred to the regions and communities. The federal level was left with some classic departments, such as Finance and Justice, with the Ministry of Justice having an especially strong reputation for its conservatism. This certainly had an impact on the capacity for innovation, and the federal level seemed more resistant to change than the new administrations. At the subnational level, the federalisation process created opportunities for innovation. Without the constraints of past legacies, and unhampered by the serious budgetary problems which the federal level faced, the new institutions at the subnational state level had the opportunity to prove themselves. Within a common framework (General Principles of the Public Servants Statute), the communities and regions were also given far-reaching autonomy in their personnel management (Brans and Steen 2006).

During the 1990s, Flanders built up an image as a pioneer in administrative reform, whereas both the federal and the French-speaking governments came to be seen as laggards in an OECD context. For the federal administration, it took a crisis and a drastic change in the coalition to produce a radical and far-reaching reform agenda. Also in Wallonia, administrative reform efforts took off at the start of the new millennium. In this article, we first describe the content of administrative reform for four cases, the Flemish Community, the Walloon Region, the French-speaking Community, and the federal administration. We group the different reform efforts under four subjects of reform: organisation, personnel, strategy and budgeting. The second part outlines the main similarities and differences, and the final part explores possible explanations for divergence and convergence in administrative reform.

Before starting the analysis, we would like to point out the limits of this article. First, public sector reform is very broad. In this article, we only deal with reforms aimed at improving the internal operation of administrations. We do not analyse the structural transformation of the state itself (see Swenden and Jans this volume), or changes to the relationship with citizens and civil society. Local government reform (Brans 1992) and changes in intergovernmental relations also fall outside the scope of the analysis. Second, reform is both discourse and action. We try as much as possible to distinguish between the rhetoric of reform and reform action. Since several reform efforts are in the process of being implemented or changed in the process of implementation, it is too early to assess the achievements for each reform component. Third, the analysis is not exhaustive as to the inclusion of all subnational administrations. We have omitted administrative reform in the Brussels Region and the German-speaking Community from the analysis. Throughout the article, we use 'French-speaking governments' to denote the governments of the French-speaking Community and the Walloon Region, which unlike the Flemish Region and Community have kept separate legislative, executive and administrative institutions (see Swenden and Jans this volume). Finally, the search for explaining convergence and divergence remains speculative to a great extent, since not many reliable indicators exist for independent variables.

Administrative Reform in Flanders, Wallonia and the Federal Government

Four Components of Reform

Table 1 describes four components of administrative reform in Flanders, the French-speaking governments, and the federal government: organisation, personnel, strategy, and finance (for data on Flanders and the French-speaking governments see Vancoppenolle and Legrain 2003; for the federal government see Hondeghem and Depré 2005). Many of the reform components have been introduced in a fragmented and incremental way. There are two exceptions. Both the federal government and Flanders launched comprehensive reform packages at the start of the new millennium. The comprehensiveness of a reform launch, however, does not guarantee comprehensive implementation, as the next section shows.

Comprehensive Reform in the Federal Government: Launch and Backlash

In February 2000, after a new purple–green (composed of Social Democrats, Liberals and Greens) government had been formed, the Minister of the Civil Service in conjunction with the Prime Minister launched a plan to modernise the federal administration. The press quickly called it the 'Copernicus plan', a label which the minister keenly adopted since it corresponded with the government's ambitious discourse on modernisation. The astronomer Copernicus had caused a revolution in showing that not the earth but the sun was the centre of the universe. Similarly, the Copernicus plan was to convert the federal administration from a closed, rigid bureaucracy into a modern, customer-oriented organisation with the citizen at its centre instead of the administration. The central catalysts for this Copernican change were to be the radical revision of the organisational structure, the strengthening of the administration's managerial and policy roles, and the introduction of a modern human resources (HR) policy. Copernicus would also radically change the status of senior civil servants, in terms of both the conditions of appointment and rewards.

   As to organisation changes, under Copernicus the traditional ministries became 'Federal Government Services' (FGS), and secretaries-general were replaced by 'Chairs of the Management Committee'. Directors-general no longer preside over the old-fashioned 'Administrations' but over 'Operational Directorates'. Copernicus also introduced a number of new structural interfaces, such as the policy board, and policy units. The policy board is presided over by the minister and is responsible for a number of managerial tasks as well as for assisting the minister in drafting and monitoring the execution of his or her policy programmes. At the same time, each FGS is endowed with a new policy formulation unit, put in charge of the coordination and integration of policy advice and evaluation. The introduction of these units was to coincide with the radical substitution of ministerial cabinets by greatly reduced personal secretariats, and the transfer of the

TABLE 1

OVERVIEW OF ADMINISTRATIVE REFORMS IN FLANDERS, THE FRENCH-SPEAKING COMMUNITY, WALLOON REGION AND THE FEDERAL GOVERNMENT

Subject of Reform	Flanders	French-speaking Community (CFWB) and Walloon Region (RW)	Federal Administration
ORGANISATION	1991: Installation of one single ministry with matrix structure – distinction between horizontal (internal focus on administrative procedure and civil service) and vertical departments (external focus) – coordination assigned to College of Secretaries-General: – in charge of general management and interdepartmental coordination – one secretary-general takes the cabinet's secretariat 1993–96: HOOP (Homogenous organisational development plans) – aim to analyse organisational objectives and processes – consequences: new organisational chart and flattening of the organisational structure from 400 services to 130 – followed by PIP (process implementation plans) and PEP (personnel plans) – 'without PIP no PEP': personnel assigned only after improved implementation processes. 2000–...: *Beter Bestuurlijk Beleid* (better administrative policy)	1989: RW Creates a second ministry (MET), in contrast with other regions who keep single ministries 1990–98: RW (Quality Project) – analysis processes to align them with organisational missions – establishment of direction for management aid to assure permanent internal audit (not prolonged) 2001: Board table project – one shot external audit – defines objectives for all services – aims to create permanent management evaluation tool 1996: CFWB: merges ministries under one single SG – aims for better coordination – horizontal staff functions (personnel, civil service, budget and finances) under one SG – college of general administrations in charge of conflict regulation – transversal cells for better coordination 2000: CFWB: consideration of more autonomy for services and two horizontal services – not implemented	1985–89: Modernisation project – State secretary for modernising the public service added to the PM – installation of modernisation cells in different ministries – creation of modernisation secretariat 1989: Appointment of Minister of Civil Service 1989: Creation of College of Secretaries-General (strengthened in 1993) – meant as joint management unit across federal ministries – meant to smoothen politico-administrative relations – halfhearted implementation 2000: Launch of Copernicus Project – radical revision of organisational structure with new structural interfaces with policy boards and policy units – aims at abolishing ministerial cabinets at the benefit of strengthening policy role of administration (later omitted from revision) – introduction of business process re-engineering (improvement projects, BPRs);

(continued)

TABLE 1
(Continued)

Subject of Reform	Flanders	French-speaking Community (CFWB) and Walloon Region (RW)	Federal Administration
			– analysis of working process, organisational design, and personnel allocation in line with organisational missions
PERSONNEL	– restructuring along principles of agencification – aim at reducing ministerial cabinets – introduce a one-to-one relationship between ministers and 13 policy domains – create policy boards for coordination and policy planning		
	1995: PLOEG (plan, lead, organise, evaluate, be evaluated) – introduces individual targets and evaluations – introduces new pay systems that honours individual performance	1996: CFWB – introduction of functional evaluation 2001: CFWB: audit of human resources functions	1989: Introduction of new mobility plan – Creation of Ministry of Public Affairs and Office for Organisation and Management – introduction of evaluation system
	1997: PEP (personnel plans) – qualitative and quantitative analysis of personnel engaged in processes – PEPs overrule the more formal 'cadre'	– alignment of personnel resources with organisational mission – intended, but not implemented, permanent personnel audit structure	2000 Copernicus – modernisation of central recruitment agency (Selor) – development circles replace evaluation system
	2001: *Beter Bestuurlijk Beleid* – decentralises the HRM functions – introduces new pay system with function weighting – put top civil service on contracts (mandate system)	2001: CFWB: Policy brief of Minister of Public Affairs – new mobility plan – creation of school of public administration – top civil servants are put on contract (mandate system) 2002: RW: Code de la Fonction Publique – created interdepartmental units for drafting function profiles, and elaboration of individual objectives	– old grading system replaced by function weighting – new pay system – competency management (later substituted for certified education) – radical improvement of top civil service pay (later reduced) – top civil servants put on contracts (mandate system)

(continued)

TABLE 1
(*Continued*)

Subject of Reform	Flanders	French-speaking Community (CFWB) and Walloon Region (RW)	Federal Administration
STRATEGY	1992: Introduction of ministerial policy plans and policy letters to parliament 1995: launch of strategic planning – introduction of long term policy planning – setting of strategic and operational targets involves both civil servants and members of ministerial cabinets 1999: Adoption of the strategic planning method – better adaptation to the political cycle 1999: Administration contribution to the government agreement – administration drafts a note on existing policies, implementation difficulties, and future challenges	– puts top civil servants on contract (mandate system) 2000: RW: Launch of the 'Contrat d'Avenir' – macro-strategic document covering all the regional competences – translation of general objectives in sub-objectives – drafted with the help of consultants, after consultation with citizens and socio-economic actors – no input from the administration – no integration between strategic objectives and internal operational objectives from board tables	2000 Copernicus introduces layered strategic planning – strategic plan of government and individual ministers – translation in 6-year management plans drafted by chairs of management committees – 3-year operational policy plans include financial, personnel, and investment plans – professionalisation of policy work and integration in the budgetary process is pending
FINANCE	1992–96: piloting of DMA (*Doelmatigheidsanalyse*) – method aims at enhancing the visibility of costs of actions – introduces performance management in the structure of the budget – cartography of means, performances, activities and impacts of administrative units and	1999: CFWB: Quality monitoring by Secretariat-General for budgetary and financial audit – not a fully fledged internal financial auditor 2000: RW and CFWB: launch of WALCOMFIN project – joint project for modernising financial management	1985: Programme budgeting 1990–95: Zero-based budgeting 2000 C – launches new budget and control system – more strategic and operational autonomy and budgetary spending for ministries – creation of internal audit cells for each ministry

(*continued*)

TABLE 1
(*Continued*)

Subject of Reform	Flanders	French-speaking Community (CFWB) and Walloon Region (RW)	Federal Administration
	comparison with preset objectives – encounters bureaucratic-political opposition but leaves traces in the methods used by the Inspection of Finance 2003: Decree on *Financial and Budgetary Reform* – adoption of performance budgeting – new budgetary structure with reflection of objectives of departments and agencies – policy effects reports are linked to annual budgets – accounting system with cost-analytical components – highly dependent on coherence between policy notes, policy letters and contracts and commitments of agencies – implementation planned by 2007	– new ICT for accounting – introduction of double entry-bookkeeping	– full implementation is pending – no explicit performance orientation – introduction of double entry bookkeeping (reconsidered under current minister) – insecure implementation – double entry bookkeeping not promoted by the current minister – monitoring not performance focused

Sources: Ministère de la Communauté française 1996; Ministère de la Region wallonne 1996; Bouckaert and Auwers 1999; Communauté française 1999; Dujacquier 1999; Ministerie van de Vlaamse Gemeenschap 1999; Stemmans 1999; Deloitte & Touche 2000; Gouvernement wallon 2000a, b, c; Taminaux 2000; Victor and Stroobants 2000; Federaal Ministerie van Ambtenarenzaken 2001; Vancoppenolle 2001; Demotte 2002; Le Soir 2002; de Visscher 2004; Hondeghem and Depré 2005; Feyt and Maréchal 2005.

tasks of those cabinets to the administration (Brans *et al.* 2006), a component of the plan which was later omitted.

The modernisation of the human resources management (HRM) function was one of the main pillars of the Copernicus reform of the early 2000s. Many changes were implemented. The central recruitment secretariat was transformed into a modern selection agency, Selor. Personnel planning was introduced. The old evaluation system was replaced by development circles. The old grading system was replaced by functions, with function weighing as a new perspective on remuneration. Copernicus also adopted the international trend towards competency management, although in the course of its implementation, this got watered down, with competency measurement being substituted by certified education.

As to top functions, the changes introduced by Copernicus were far-reaching. Copernicus radically altered the status and rewards of top civil servants. Both the chairs of the federal government services and the grades directly below are appointed by mandate, on the basis of modern-style assessments. The chairs of the management committees are put on six-year contracts, which exceeds legislative terms by two years. An exception was made for the PM's Chancellery, whose chair will serve four years, which is justified with reference to the strong political character of this office. The rewards of office also changed. The salaries for the very top – the chairs of the management committee – almost trebled, although this was later corrected by 30 per cent (Brans and Steen 2006).

The Copernicus modernisation of the HR function put strong emphasis on flexibility and differentiation (Hondeghem and Depré 2005). The confrontation of these values with a more traditional articulation of values such as equality, legality and objectivity by the first new coalition to follow the Copernicus legislature led to a reconsideration of several Copernican changes. Competency measurements were substituted by qualifications, the rewards for top offices were reduced, and several aspects of the HR function were recentralised.

Strategic planning was introduced to federal ministries in the framework of Copernicus. Ministries were given substantial autonomy in developing policy strategies. Copernicus conceived policy planning in a layered fashion. First comes a strategic plan which comprises the strategic policy options of the government and the individual ministers. The translation of these options is laid down in a management plan drafted by the Chair and the management team of the ministries, with a time perspective of six years. Operational policy plans, in turn, have a three-year perspective and should lead to financial, personnel and investment plans. Research by the Court of Auditors (Rekenhof 2004: 125; Conings and Sterck 2005: 223) shows that the federal ministries have indeed made a start with management and operational plans, but a number of aspects still await further professionalisation, such as the formulation of objectives and the choice and availability of indicators. The extent to which these plans will not merely result in a new bureaucracy depends on a further professionalisation of policy work by the administration as well as the will to integrate them firmly in the budgetary process.

Copernicus also launched a new budget and control system, coupled to the enlargement of the ministries' strategic and operational autonomy and budgetary spending. Each ministry is endowed with an internal audit cell, charged with the monitoring of economy and efficiency. Several of the Copernicus components have been decreed by law, but implementation is incomplete and on some points insecure. The structure of the budget is not explicitly performance oriented, in that performance information remains an internal management instrument, rather than a basis for external accountability. As to accounting, a law of 2003 imposes double entry bookkeeping as an instrument to make the economy, efficiency and effectiveness of government actions more visible, but the implementation is not promoted by the current Minister of Finance. Monitoring, too, is hitherto not too performance focused and often limited to financial information. The decentralised audit cells are operational in only a few ministries, and the full implementation is expected to take a couple of years (Conings and Sterck 2005).

Comprehensive Reform in the Flemish Government

In 2000, the Flemish government came up with a new ambitious plan labelled BBB (*Beter Bestuurlijk Beleid*), or better administrative policy in which it envisaged completely restructuring its organisation along principles of agencification. The Flemish civil service would be structured around 13 policy domains. Each policy domain would have the same structural components: a core department for policy-making with several internal and external agencies for the execution of policies. This separation was consistent with a decoupling of the policy cycle. Each unit would be responsible for clear and measurable objectives. Core departments would be responsible for policy design, and ministerial cabinets would be reduced in number. Coordination and policy planning were to be assured by a new unit, the Policy Board. The Policy Board would consist of senior civil servants and be presided over by the minister. BBB was decreed by the Flemish Parliament, and is, at the time of writing, in the process of being implemented.

The BBB package also comprises HRM changes. One is the decentralisation of the HRM function, the second a new remuneration system with function weighting, the principles of which were approved by the Flemish government in 2001. The third was the mandate system, which put top civil servants on contract.

In 2004, the Flemish Parliament enacted a financial reform decree (*Comptabiliteitsdecreet*), which imposes a new budgeting and accounting system and a new system of internal control and internal audit. Flanders has thus adopted performance budgeting, the most important components of which, pending implementation, are: a new budgetary structure in which the objectives and actions of departments and agencies are reflected, policy effects reports linked to annual budgets, and an accounting system with a cost-analytical component. The new system is quite ambitious in that its quality is highly dependent on coherence between policy notes, policy letters, and the contracts and commitments of agencies. Implementation is planned by 2007.

Maintainers, Modernisers and Hybrids

This section first summarises similarities and differences in the content of reforms as presented in Table 1, starting from internationally observed trends in administrative reform. Next it attempts to classify the different cases.

Reform Content: Similarities and Differences

As to organisational reforms, at least three trends can be observed internationally: a greater decentralisation and operational specialisation; a reform of the relationship between politics and administration; and a reconsideration of interorganisational relations within the administration. In Flanders, these tendencies are clearly observed. The single Ministry of the Flemish Community makes place for smaller and more autonomous entities. The matrix structure of 1991 and the BBB reform of 2000 confirm this trend. The reorganisation uses principles of internal and external privatisation, with a contractualised relationship between core departments and agencies. The federal government did not explicitly engage in agencification, but did significantly restructure its ministries, including operational services. It appears that the French-speaking community too, briefly entertained the idea of restructuring its administration into smaller autonomous services, whereas the Walloon Region has not considered such a reform at all. As to linking process to structure, Flanders seems to have a relatively long tradition of seeking to improve internal processes, and the definition of organisational objectives. These procedural reforms are either absent in francophone Belgium or subject to consultants' work, not involving civil servants' inputs. The federal level in turn, has made a good start with business process re-engineering plans, now called improvement plans, with a substantial participation of civil servants at all levels.

Organisational reforms in Flanders also envisage a reconsideration of politico-administrative relations, in that it is planned to reduce ministerial cabinets, and create a more direct relation between civil servants and the minister. The abolition of ministerial cabinets was one of the cornerstones of the Copernicus reform, but it failed. In Wallonia, the abolition of ministerial cabinets is not a reform issue.

International trends in personnel reform include decentralisation to vertical departments and line managers, greater mobility and flexibility, rewarding performance, and a HRM specific to the top of the administration. As to the timing of reform trajectories, Flanders took an early start with modernising its HRM, followed by the federal government, and next by the governments in Wallonia. The content of trajectories differs in several components. In Flanders, PLOEG and PEP introduced greater flexibility and attention to individual performance, whereas the more recent BBB reform seeks to decentralise HRM. The federal Copernicus plan included initiatives to modernise HRM, with greater attention to competency and individual performance, although several elements were changed during the process of implementation. In francophone Belgium, the Community made a start with functional evaluation, and there is a more modest move towards rewarding civil servants' individual performance. As in the implementation changes to the Copernicus plan, there is a preference for formal qualifications instead of competency assessments, also evident in plans to create a Regional School of Public Administration in the Walloons. In 2002, the Walloon Region introduced a number of HRM novelties, such as evaluation and the setting of individual objectives. They also picked up the idea of mandates or contracts for the top level of the administration, as did the other administrations. But here too, a closer look at the reform content shows that seemingly similar trajectories hide important differences. It is striking that in both Flanders and at the federal level, the contractualisation of top officials goes hand in hand with an organisational delegation of responsibility, whereas it seems that in the Walloon governments no such tandem of trajectories exists. A further difference is that, unlike in Flanders and the federal administration, contracts in the Walloon government are congruent with the time of a legislature, which puts top officials closer to the spoils.

As to the strategic dimension of reform, international trends include the coupling of micro-, meso-, and macro-planning, more attention to results and impacts, and a greater involvement of civil servants in the formulation of strategies. The Flemish trajectory of strategic reform is very different from the one of the French-speaking governments. Since the early 1990s, Flanders has experimented with professionalised policy planning, later integrated in a strategic planning format. Moreover, the administration itself is involved in strategy formulation, and its contribution at the time of coalition formation makes it an active partner in strategic planning. Also the introduction of a strategy board is evidence of an involvement of the top administration in strategic policy issues. In Wallonia, too, there is a trend towards strategic planning, but with a greater disconnection between the work of consultants, cabinets and the administration. Also striking is the use in Flanders of a wide range of policy documents, which do not have linguistic equivalents in French. The strategic components of the Copernicus reform come closer to the Flemish experience, but at the moment the drafting of strategic and operational policy plans risks engendering a new kind of policy bureaucracy, if not integrated with the policy work of ministerial cabinets. There is one component of policy professionalisation that seems to have a stronger foothold in Wallonia, that is policy evaluation, which is generally weakly institutionalised in Belgium (Varone *et al.* 2005).

In its financial management reform trajectory, Flanders has the most comprehensive plans in following international trends to a greater focus on performance, new bookkeeping systems, and audits, followed by Copernicus at the federal level, although in the latter case there seems to be a reconsideration of the value of double-entry bookkeeping. The francophone governments, too, are in the process of revising their financial management, but the reform seems less geared to an integration of the budgetary and policy cycle.

Different Trajectories of Reform

In their comparative study of public management reform across OECD countries, Pollitt and Bouckaert (2003) grouped the reform trajectories of countries into four categories. A first group follows a strategy of maintaining the status quo as much as possible, by taking steps to make current structures and practices work better. They tighten up structures and processes rather than restructuring them. A more adventurous group are the modernisers, who make moves towards performance budgeting, greater strategic planning, extensive decentralisation, and a loosening of personnel rigidities, without giving up the career civil service. A third group they identified as marketisers. This group also wants to make fundamental reforms but hold a particular view on the nature of change, that is, the introduction of competition and market mechanisms in the public sector. Apart from importing markets, these countries also introduce contractual appointments and performance pay for civil servants. The fourth group, in which no country could be safely classified but whose ideas have been flirted with by neo-liberal parties (Pollitt and Bouckaert 2003: 98), are minimisers, who seek to downsize and privatise as much as possible.

Pollitt and Bouckaert (2003) classified Belgium in the group of continental modernisers, but their analysis comprised the federal level only. Given the timing and content of reform trajectories, we would like to classify the Flemish government as early modernisers in the Belgian context. We agree with Pollitt and Bouckaert that the federal government is a moderniser, but only from 1999 onward, before which it could be safely classified in the maintenance group. It is interesting to observe that the Copernicus reform was to some extent a hybrid in that it was strongly influenced by the New Public Management (NPM) discourse, and expected a lot from the introduction of market-type mechanisms, particularly by opening up top positions to applicants from the private sector. The federal government, we could say, launched a radical modernisation trajectory, some components of which were later thrown off course, by the reinvention of ministerial cabinets and the rearticulation of classical civil service career characteristics (Brans *et al.* 2006). The francophone governments, in turn, have only recently ventured into modernisation plans, but a striking difference with both Flanders and the federal government is that reform efforts are more fragmented and not part of a comprehensive reform package that seeks to integrate several components. This is clear in the disjointed use of strategic planning and board tables, or the introduction of mandates without a structural reorganisation. It is also clear that the francophone governments, unlike Flanders and the federal government, were never, like France (Pollitt and Bouckaert 2003: 99), much impressed with the Anglophone NPM discourse and ideas of marketisation.

Explaining Similarities and Differences: Structure, Culture, and Entrepreneurs

There is no single model of administrative reform, and little middle range theory. Most analysts will point at the explanatory variables such as external pressures, political choice, institutional constraints, and administrative traditions (see Toonen 2001: 474–5). In this article, we choose to apply five possible sets of variables (see also the model in Pollitt and Bouckaert 2003) as a checklist for exploration: political-institutional structure, politico-administrative culture; role of policy entrepreneurs; external events and socio-economic conditions.

Political-Institutional Structure

Comparative studies of administrative reform show that the speed and severity of reform are influenced by the nature of the executive, on the one hand, and the location of portfolios or responsibilities for reform within the executive, on the other. The first variable does not offer much to explain convergence in the Belgian context. All executives of the cases studied are coalition governments, not single-party governments as in the so-called pioneering cases of modernisation and marketisation. The second variable has more promising explanatory value. The launch of administrative reform has more force when carried forward by central actors in government, such as the Minister of Finance or the Prime Minister. Both in Flanders and in the federal Copernicus reform there was a strong link between the Minister responsible for Public Affairs and a central cabinet figure. In Flanders in the 1990s, this was the Minister responsible for the Budget; in the federal case the Prime Minister put his weight behind the Copernicus reform. In the executives in francophone Belgium, such links between champions of reform have been absent.

Another feature of the political-institutional structure that may favour or hamper administrative reform is the degree of coordination and fragmentation, combined with the structuring influence of initial path dependency.

These features explain to some extent the differences in the timing and scope of reform between Flanders and the Walloons. The degree of fragmentation is much bigger in Wallonia. The fact that the francophone Regional and Community institutions never merged may explain the narrower scope of reform and the lack of uniformity across the administrations. We can also safely speculate that the political insecurity over the future of the Region and the Community did not encourage the launching of administrative reform. It seems that the early merger of the Community and Regional administration in one single Flemish ministry fostered a more positive climate for administrative reform. Admittedly, recent reform efforts in Wallonia include some experiments with joint projects, such as the Walcomfin financial management project involving both the regional and community administrations, but the implementation clearly risks suffering from coordination deficits.

Politico-administrative Culture

There are many references to differences in politico-administrative culture in public and political discourse. Flanders is culturally closer to the Netherlands, and the Walloon culture more closely resembles the French. In the press, such considerations were repeatedly used to explain the failure of some of the Copernicus components at the federal level. A clash between francophone and Flemish administrative culture would have thrown the Copernicus trajectory off course. Is there evidence to support these speculations? In their book, Pollitt and Bouckaert (2003) used one of the few available sets of national culture indicators to explain different administrative traditions supporting different (non-)trajectories of reform. Hofstede's (2001) cultural indicators are very useful, if a bit outdated, for speculating on the impact of national cultures on administrative reform (see Table 2). Particularly the power distance index and the uncertainty avoidance index can be used to support different administrative traditions. High scores on power distance and insecurity avoidance seem to go hand in hand with *Rechtstaat* traditions, which articulate legality and administrative law. Lower power distance and risk avoidance scores are characteristic of a more pragmatist managerial tradition, which is less resistant to administrative change.

TABLE 2
CULTURAL INDICATORS FOR BELGIUM, FLANDERS, THE WALLONIA,
THE NETHERLANDS AND FRANCE

Dimensions	Flanders	Belgium	Wallonia	Netherlands	France
Power distance	61	65	67	38	68
Uncertainty avoidance	97	94	93	53	86
Individualism-Collectivism	78	75	72	80	71
Masculine–feminine	43	54	60	14	43

Source: Hofstede (2001: 501).

According to Hofstede (2001: 63), the Belgian national culture closely resembles French culture. Fortunately, Hofstede (2001: 501) also engaged in collecting cross-linguistic differences in multi-lingual countries, including Belgium. His evidence shows that the cultural gap between the Netherlands and Flanders is somewhat smaller than that between the Netherlands and French-speaking Belgium, but the gap is still very wide. Inglehart (1990) came to a similar conclusion in his values study. If we take a closer look at the differences between Flanders and Wallonia, Hofstede's (2001) evidence on power distance and risk avoidance becomes even less conclusive in supporting allegations of different administrative cultures. Power distance is indeed a bit smaller in Flanders, but its extremely high score on risk avoidance should make its culture very resistant to change, which our cases have shown it is not. Overall, Flanders closely resembles Wallonia.

On the basis of Hofstede's data we can conclude that subnational culture is not a strong indicator for divergence in administrative reform. At the same time, we must admit that Hofstede's data are outdated (late 1970s, early 1980s) and may not reflect cultural change over time, which could have occurred in the context of 20 years of devolution.

For the federal level, no similar data exist on cultural differences between francophone and Flemish civil servants. There is, however, some research (Willems *et al.* 2003) that gives evidence of the dominance of a culture of avoidance and opposition, which may be used to explain the resistance of civil servants to welcoming the Copernicus reforms with open arms. There are also some other indicators that point at a different reception of the reforms by francophones within the federal administration. The francophone socialist civil service union was very militant in organising opposition against the HRM components of the reform, and articulated classic principles of personnel regulation such as seniority and equality against mechanisms to do away with such rigidities. Quite early in the implementation process they were joined in their manifesto by several Walloon socialists, who effectively blocked the final implementation of one of the cornerstones of the Copernicus personnel plans (Hondeghem and Depré 2005). Piraux (2004) analysed differences between francophone and Dutch-speaking federal civil servants on the basis of the Artemis surveys the government organised on workplace participation in the Copernicus reform. According to Piraux, Dutch-speaking civil servants were more enthusiastic about the reform than their francophone counterparts. Piraux interprets the results as evidence that Dutch speakers are more receptive to the Anglo-Saxon managerial culture.

The available evidence on politico-administrative culture is hence not conclusive. We have no clear indicators of distinct culture in Flanders and Wallonia, but for the federal level we do have some indirect evidence of different attitudes to reform.

There are other dimensions of political culture that may be explanations of differences in administrative reform. One such dimension would be the extent of partitocracy (de Visscher 2003) or party-archy (De Winter and Dumont this volume). We hypothesise that the extent of party-archy is greater in Wallonia, due to the monopolist position of the Walloon socialists. There are at least three indicators that confirm stronger party control over the French-speaking administrations: contractual employment, size of ministerial cabinets, and constituency service. First, with 38 per cent in the Walloon Region and 46 per cent in the French-speaking Community administration, flexible contractual employment is more prominent than at the federal and Flemish levels (21 per cent and 18 per cent respectively) (Destexhe *et al.* 2003; GERFA 2006). This allows for more partisan recruitment than does tenured employment, for which recruitment requires competitive examinations. Second, the size of ministerial cabinets is bigger in the French-speaking administrations, and they spend 2.26 times more on these interfaces than does Flanders (*La Libre Belgique* 2004; Bastaits *et al.* 2004). A third, albeit indirect indicator is higher constituency service on the part of francophone MPs (in 1996 francophone MPs had 1,040 constituency interventions, whereas Flemish MPs counted on average 461 constituency interventions, De Winter 1996).

The greater the hold of political parties over the administration, the greater the resistance against reform. Politicians will resist administrative reforms that reduce their control, as the Walloon Socialists did with the intended abolition of ministerial cabinets (although many other ministers were halfhearted supporters of this change, too). But, indirectly, party-archy also fosters another source of opposition against administrative reform. As a guarantee against favouritism and arbitrariness on the side of politicians, trade unions will defend classic civil service features against flexible HRM. At first sight, one may be puzzled by the fact that both francophone governments have operationalised the mandate system, which signifies a clear break with senior civil service careers. At the same time, however, the nature of the term of the contracts differs from the other governments' mandates. Since it is legislature congruent, it promises to increase the hold of politicians over the top administration, which they can treat as benefits. In Hood's (2001) terms, the bargain between politicians and bureaucrats then becomes hybrid again, not one that clearly separates political and administrative responsibilities (see de Visscher 2003).

Policy Entrepreneurs

Structure and culture may serve as facilitators of or obstacles to reform. In addition, the role of particular actors may explain divergence. Of course, reforms, if they are to be successful, will need to survive individual actors. But in championing change, and launching reform, the latter can make a big difference. For Flanders and the federal level we find the same policy entrepreneur, one who had earlier promoted significant change in educational policy (De Rink and Dezeure this volume). The minister who championed administrative change in Flanders in the 1990s became Minister of Public Affairs in 1999 and launched the Copernicus reform at the federal level. In terms of policy diffusion, he functioned as a transfer agent between two levels of government, creating opportunities for lesson-drawing. There is little evidence of policy learning and transfer between the two subnational levels or between the federal and the francophone administrations. It also seems that there were no real policy entrepreneurs in the field of administrative reform on the Walloon side, and nor was there much continuity in who held the offices for Public Affairs.

There are two more sets of actors that need to be taken into account. Civil servants themselves, and external actors that diffuse reform ideas. In Flanders, particularly in the more recent BBB reform, top civil servants seem to have acted as agents for change. In the absence of an empirical test, we speculate that this is less the case at the federal level and in the francophone administrations. Pollitt and Bouckaert (2003) also call attention to the role of policy diffusers. The broader the range of policy advice on administrative reform, the more diffusion of reform ideas will occur. It is true that Flemish reforms have had both high levels of consultant involvement and substantial academic input, with the latter having been institutionalised in a five-year research pillar on administrative organisation. The Copernicus reforms were preceded by academic studies of administrative reform commissioned by government, and at the same time extensively employed consultants. Copernicus also relied heavily on concepts of administrative reform diffused by OECD. In Wallonia, it seems that the range of policy advice on administrative reform is less, and mainly limited to consultants, drawn from a narrower reservoir than at the federal and Flemish levels. There is very little commissioned academic research on the issue of reform, which may also contribute to a more limited diffusion of reform ideas in francophone Belgium.

External Pressures

External pressures, too, can influence the nature and timing of reforms. It is safe to say that pressures to reach the Maastricht norms kept the federal government concerned during much of the 1990s with what we call *maintenance*, with a focus on budgetary savings. Positive socio-economic conditions at the start of the millennium, in turn, may have contributed to a more positive climate for reform, while there are signs that a deterioration of economic growth from 2003 onward explains the hesitance over implementing the budgetary reform plans. We agree with Pollitt and Bouckaert (2003) that to some extent socio-economic changes can put reforms on the agenda but at the same time blow reform trajectories off course.

What also seems to create windows of opportunities are crises and major changes in coalition. Both occurred in 1999 at the federal level. In the aftermath of a severe food safety crisis (Maesschalck and Van de Walle this volume), the perception of a failing government gave a positive impetus to major reform efforts by the new coalition. We do not find much evidence of the differential impact of crises in Flanders and the Walloons, except perhaps for a perception of a crisis of democracy in Flanders after consecutive electoral victories by the extreme right in the 1990s, fostering a climate in which the New Political Culture movement (Maesschalck and Van de Walle this volume) came to include components of administrative reform. Finally, socio-economic differences between Flanders and Wallonia do not offer much explanatory material for differences in administrative reform.

Conclusion: Institutional Insecurity, Entrepreneurs, and Parties Yet Again?

The introduction of separate administrations in federal Belgium created different arenas and opportunities for administrative reform. In comparative perspective, Flanders took an early start to modernise its administration and consolidated several reform components in a comprehensive package in 2000. The federal government, after having been locked in a period of maintenance and incremental reform efforts, embarked upon a radical reform trajectory in 1999, but not until after a serious food safety crisis and consecutive dramatic change in coalition had created the necessary window of opportunity. The Flemish and federal modernisation trajectories share a number of tendencies, such as a greater receptiveness to the international and national diffusion of public sector reform discourse, policy entrepreneurship in the portfolio of the same Minister of Public Affairs, and centrally located links between change agents. The federal case clearly shows how comprehensive reform plans do not guarantee comprehensive implementation, as several of Copernicus' pivotal reforms were watered down or even rejected in the course of implementation. Cases in point are the reinvention of ministerial cabinets as indispensable interfaces between politicians and the civil service, the rearticulation of classic civil service career systems, and the pending implementation of new financial management.

Several of the factors that facilitated the modernisation of the Flemish and federal administrations have been absent in the French-speaking administrations, which we classified at late modernisers. The institutional insecurity over Community and Regional administrations together with discontinuity in executive leadership have not been conducive to entrepreneurship for administrative reform, either on the part of politicians, or on the part of the senior civil service. Academic diffusion of reform ideas has been more limited, too, and NPM discourse less popular. Whereas there was some policy transfer from Flanders to the federal government, the Copernicus experience at the federal level only supported negative lesson-drawing in the French-speaking governments. In general terms, differences in political culture between Flanders and the Wallonia are not conclusive indicators for receptiveness or resistance against international ideas of administrative reform. Yet, at the meso level, we do believe that the degree of partisan control in politico-administrative relations offers a promising venue for explaining variation of reform, particularly for those organisational, HRM and strategic components that go to the heart of the relationship between politicians and civil servants.

Acknowledgements

The title refers to maintenance and modernisation as two of four types of trajectories of public sector reform identified by Politt and Bouckaert (2003) in their comparative study of public sector reform.

References

Bastaits, Sebastien, Vinciane Dermien and Robert Deschamps (2004). *Dépenses de la Flandre, de la Wallonie et de Bruxelles: comparaison interrégionale des budgets 2004*. Namur: Centre de recherches sur l'économie Wallonne.

Bouckaert, Geert, and Tom Auwers (1999). *De modernisering van de Vlaamse Overheid*. Brugge: Die Keure.

Brans, Marleen (1992). 'Theories of Local Government Reorganization', *Journal of Public Administration*, 70:3, 429–51.

Brans, Marleen, and Trui Steen (2006). 'From Incremental to Copernican Reform? Changes to the Position and Role of Senior Civil Servants in the Belgian Federal Administration', in Edward C. Page and Vincent Wright (eds.), *From the Active to the Enabling State*. Basingstoke: Palgrave, forthcoming.

Brans, Marleen, Christophe Pelgrims and Dieter Hoet (2006). 'Comparative Observations on Tensions between Professional Policy Advice and Political Control in the Low Countries', *International Review of Administrative Sciences*, 72:1, 57–71.

Communauté française (1999). 'Les nouvelles structures du Ministère. SGABF: Pistes de réflexion sur son fonctionnement', *SGABF. Second rapport d'activités*, 1er novembre 1998 au 31 août 1999.

Conings, Veerle, and Miekatrien Sterck (2005). 'De financiële Hervorming als Hefboom voor Resultaatsgericht Management', in Annie Hondeghem and Roger Depré (eds.), *De Copernicushervorming in Perspectief. Veranderingsmanagement in de Federale Overheid*. Brugge: Vandenbroele, 223–56.

Deloitte & Touche (2000). *Audit de la Gestion globale des ressources humaines du Ministère de la Communauté française* – Descriptif de l'offre.

Demotte, Rudy (2002). 'Une modernisation participative par objectifs', Document de travail, Bruxelles.

Destexhe, Alain, Alain Eraly and Eric Gillet (2003). *Démocratie ou particratie? 120 Propositions pour refonder le système belge*. Liège: Editions Labor.

De Visscher, Christian (2003). 'Le Coup dans L'Eau de Copernic: Réforme de la Haute Fonction Publique, Nouvelle Gestion Publique et Particratie en Belgique', 14th Colloque International de la Revue 'Politique et Management Public'.

de Visscher, Christian (2004). *La relation entre l'autorité politique et la haute administration*. Gent: Academia Press.

De Winter, Lieven (1996). 'Party Encroachment on the Executive and Legislative Branch in the Belgian Polity', *Res Publica*, 2, 325–52.

Dujacquier, Isabelle (1999). 'Les commissions d'accompagenement du ministère. Entretien avec Léon Zaks', *La Plume du Coq*, 37, 15–16.

Federaal Ministerie van Ambtenarenzaken (2001). *Overzicht van de personeelssterkte in de overheidssector*. Brussel.

Feyt, Annemie, and Maya Maréchal (2005). 'Les Fonctions de Management', *Administration Publique*, 3–4, 270–6.

GERFA (Group d'étude et de réforme de la fonction administrative) (2006). *Diagnostic*, 236.

Gouvernement wallon (2000a). *Contrat d'Avenir pour la Wallonie*. Namur.

Gouvernement wallon (2000b). 'Cahier des charges relatif à la mise en œuvre d'une évaluation globale mixte de la fonction publique conduisant à la mise en place d'un processus d'évaluation mixte permanente', *Communiqué du Gouvernmenent*, 14 September 2000.

Gouvernement wallon (2000c). 'Informatique administrative', *Communiqué du Gouvernement*, 26 May 2000.

Hofstede, Geert (2001). *Culture's Consequences. Comparing Values, Behaviour, Institutions, and Organizations Across Nations*, 2nd ed. Thousand Oaks, CA: Sage.

Hondeghem, Annie, and Roger Depré, eds. (2005). *De Copernicushervorming in Perspectief. Veranderingsmanagement in de Federale Overheid*. Brugge: Vandenbroele.

Hood, Christopher C. (2001). 'Control, Bargains and Cheating: The Politics of Public Service Reform', *Journal of Public Administration Research and Theory*, 12:3, 309–32.

Inglehart, Ronald (1990). *Culture Shift in Advanced Industrial Society*. Princeton, NJ: Princeton University Press.

Le Soir (2002). 'Demotte veut une administration en ligne', *Le Soir*, 13 June 2002.

La Libre Belgique (2004). 'Les Cabinets Mammouth s'Expliquent', *La Libre Belgique*, 23 December 2004.

Ministère de la Communauté française (1996). *Le nouveau système d'évaluation des agents du Ministère de la Communauté française. Guide à l'usage des évaluateurs*. Bruxelles.

Ministerie van de Vlaamse Gemeenschap (1999). *Bijdrage Vlaamse Administratie aan het regeerprogramma van de aantredende Vlaamse Regering*.

Ministère de la Region wallonne (1996). *S'engager dans une démarche qualité*. Namur.

Piraux, Alexandre (2004). 'Copernic, Son Imaginaire et ses Pratiques', *Pyramides*, 8, 29–51.

Politt, Christopher, and Geert Bouckaert (2003). *Public Management Reform. A Comparative Analysis*, 2nd ed. Oxford: Oxford University Press.

Rekenhof (2004). *161ste Boek van het Rekenhof: Deel 1*. Brussels: Rekenhof.

Stenmans, Alain (1999). *La transformation de la fonction publique en Belgique*. Bruxelles: CRISP.

Taminaux, Willy (2000). 'Note d'orientation relative au régime des mandats', Note de Gouvernement, 16 November 2000.

Toonen, Theo A.J. (2001). 'Public Sector Reform in Comparative Perspective: Creating Open Villages and Reinventing the Politics of Administration', in B. Guy Peters and Jon Pierre (eds.), *Politicians, Bureaucrats and Administrative Reform*. London: Routledge: 183–201.

Vancoppenolle, Diederik (2001). *De modernisering van de Vlaamse en de Waalse administratie. Kritische analyse van het Ministerie van de Vlaamse Gemeenschap en de administraties van het Waalse gewest en de Franse Gemeenschap*. Leuven: KULeuven.

Vancoppenolle, Diederik, and Amaury Legrain (2003). 'Le New Public Management en Belgique: Comparaison des Réformes en Flandres et en Wallonie', *Administration Publique*, 2, 112–28.

Varone, Frederic, Steve Jacob and Lieven De Winter (2005). 'Polity, Politics and Policy Evaluation in Belgium', *Evaluation*, 11, 253–73.

Victor, Leo, and Eric Stroobants (2000). *Beter besturen: Reorganisatie van de Vlaamse Overheid*. Brussel: Ministerie van de Vlaamse Gemeenschap.

Willems, Ingrid, Ria Janvier and Eric Henderickx (2003). *Copernicus tussen de regels door: de cultuur en de verwachtingen van het federale overheidspersoneel*. Gent: Academia Press.

Policy Failure and Corruption in Belgium: Is Federalism to Blame?

JEROEN MAESSCHALCK and STEVEN VAN DE WALLE

Belgian politics seemed to have become synonymous with corruption, scandal and policy failure in the 1990s (Maesschalck 2002). The murder of socialist politician André Cools in 1991 marked the start of a scandal-ridden decade. The investigation into his killing led to the discovery of the Agusta–Dassault corruption scandal over bribes that had been paid in the procurement of helicopters for the military. The scandal caused the indictment of several politicians and forced the resignation of NATO Secretary-General and former Belgian Vice-Prime Minister Willy Claes. The Dutroux scandal in the mid-1990s had an even greater impact on the country's national mood and international image. The perceived incompetence of the police and the judiciary in dealing with a major paedophilia and child murder case led to massive popular outrage, reaching a peak in the 'White March' in Brussels: the largest protest march in Belgian post-war history. In 1999, it appeared that the administration had been unable to detect or prevent contamination of poultry, leading to the so-called dioxin scandal. Since the scandal emerged just before the elections, it contributed to a historic shift in the ruling coalition, with the Christian Democrats moving to the opposition benches for the first time in decades. These are just a few illustrations of the size and the impact of scandals in 1990s Belgium.

In this article we distinguish between corruption, policy failure (or fiasco) and scandal. Friedrich defines the first as 'deviant behaviour associated with a particular motivation, namely that of private gain at public expense' (Friedrich 1989: 15). As we emphasise *political* corruption, we will particularly focus on such deviant behaviour that implicates public officials. Compared with corruption, policy failure is a much broader concept, since it can mean 'a negative event that is perceived by a socially and politically significant group of people in the community to be at least partially caused by avoidable and blameworthy failures of public policymakers' (Bovens and 't Hart 1996). As such, policy failures can occur without malicious intent. In the examples listed above, the Agusta–Dassault bribes exemplify corruption; the failures in the Dutroux investigation illustrate a policy failure or fiasco. Finally, we consider scandal as a social and political construction that might be triggered by policy failure or fiasco. Many problems are not followed by scandal (Thompson 2000) and sometimes scandals are triggered by occurrences that, in other circumstances, would hardly be seen as problematic.

Seeking to provide a thorough explanation of the occurrence of corruption, policy failure and scandal in 1990s Belgium would be inappropriately ambitious within the scope of the present article. Of all three occurrences, this article will focus particularly on corruption. Furthermore, we will mainly emphasise the explanatory value of two variables. The first variable considers to what extent the (perception) of corruption is related to the coexistence of two different political cultures (Flemish and Walloon) in one state. Using survey data, we will analyse whether the Flemish are more prone to corrupt behaviour than the Walloons or vice versa. The second variable is the key variable linking the various contributions in this volume: federalism. Has the federalisation of Belgium, and, in particular, the peculiar structure which Belgian federalism acquired, affected the (perception) of corruption, policy failure and scandal? Or has Belgian federalism changed the institutions in such a way that they become more vulnerable to corruption, failure and scandal? (See Boin and 't Hart 2000 for the notion of 'institutional vulnerability'.)

How Corrupt is Belgium?

While qualitative analysis of the types of corruption occurring in Belgium has been made elsewhere (e.g. De Winter 2003; De Ruyver *et al.* 1999), we will focus on quantitative data. Between 1973 and 2003, De Winter (2003) counted about 100 important political corruption cases in Belgium. In 2003, 56.2 per cent of the Flemish agreed that you need 'connections' to get something done by government or the public administration, and just 13.4 per cent disagreed (Van de Walle 2007). Detailed empirical research on corruption in Belgium is scarce, however. In a European comparative perspective, perceptions of corruption in Belgium are quite high. In the 2005 Transparency International Corruption Perceptions Index Belgium was ranked 19th (http://www.transparency.org), above only Spain, Portugal and Italy out of the other Western European countries. 'Scandalitis' is a word that refers to an atmosphere of constant scandals, and was regularly used with reference to Belgian politics in the 1990s. But is Belgium's image of being a corrupt state correct, and why is corruption perceived to be higher in Belgium than in, say, Sweden?

Figure 1 shows the development in perceived corruption in Belgium. The right-hand vertical scale indicates the country's score on the Transparency International Corruption Perceptions Index, where 10 stands for low levels of perceived corruption. The left-hand scale shows answers from the Flemish administration's yearly surveys on social and cultural change (http://aps.vlaanderen.be). A representative sample of respondents in the Flemish Region (n = about 1,500) had to pick from a list of 22 potential problems the five most important ones. In 1997, almost 40 per cent included (political) corruption in this list, while 6.5 per cent of respondents identified corruption as the most important problem. The figure suggests a change to lower levels of perceived corruption or at least a return to normalcy after a period of high perceived corruption.

Judicial statistics show a similar trend. Yante (2003) analysed judicial statistics before 1993, and found a clear decrease in the number of convictions for administrative corruption in the period between 1985 and 1992 as compared

FIGURE 1
PERCEIVED CORRUPTION IN BELGIUM-FLANDERS, 1996–2005

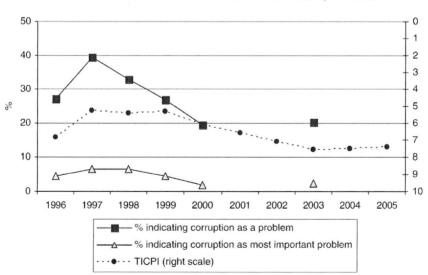

Source: Administratie Planning en Statistiek (http://aps.vlaanderen.be) and Transparency International (http://www.transparency.org).

to the preceding periods. At the same time, he observed a tendency towards more severe punishment, albeit many cases of active corruption only lead to a probationary sentence. More recent judicial statistics confirm this downward trend (Figure 2). Obviously, these statistics only refer to cases where corruption was actually discovered, reported, investigated and punished.

In the second round of the European Social Survey (ESS), 1,778 Belgians were interviewed on a broad range of issues (Jowell *et al.* 2005). The survey also included a number of items on corruption and bribery. Unsurprisingly, for reasons of social desirability, the number of respondents admitting to having offered a bribe to public officials is very low (just 14 people out of 1,770 over the past five years). However, the number of experiences with public officials asking for a bribe is equally low. A similar phenomenon has been reported with regard to experienced corruption in interactions with police officers (Van Kesteren *et al.* 2000). At the same time, however, the 2004 survey on social and cultural change in Flanders revealed that 17.5 per cent of Flemish citizens thought that many or almost everyone in the public administration was involved in corruption (Carton *et al.* 2005). Hence, there seems to be a difference between actual experience of corruption and the general image or perception.

The ESS surveys not only asked about actual occurrence of corruption, but also about attitudes. When asked how they evaluate a public official asking someone for a favour or bribe in return for their services, 94 per cent of Belgians answer that they consider this wrong. This percentage is similar

FIGURE 2

CONVICTIONS FOR ACTIVE AND PASSIVE BRIBERY IN BELGIUM, 1993–2003

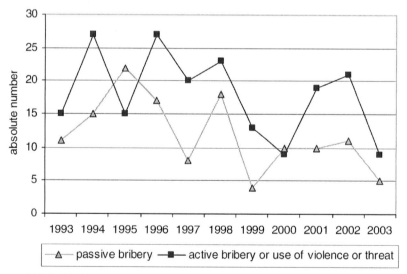

Source: FOD Justitie, Dienst Strafrechterlijk Beleid, Statistisch Steunpunt (http://www.dsb-spc.be).

to that for the other countries which participated in the ESS. A similar question in the 1999–2000 European Values Survey did not reveal much between-country variation either. The ESS statement on whether you should always strictly obey the law even if this means missing good opportunities, however, showed the Belgians to be the most flexible of nations, with just 47 per cent agreeing. This is over 17 percentage points below the average for 17 European countries. This is quite interesting, especially when compared to the findings on attitudes to bribe-taking reported above. Yet there are variations in the attitudes towards corruption. The 1995 Belgian General Election Study revealed that Belgians have more problems with politicians asking for money for granting government contracts than with politicians who merely accept money. Also, corruption was considered worse when these politicians used the money for their personal election campaign as compared to when they gave it to their party (Beerten *et al.* 1997).

In sum, although survey evidence of attitudes towards, and occurrence of, corruption shows some differences with other European countries, there is no strong evidence that Belgium would be as dramatically corrupt as is sometimes suggested. The limited evidence available also suggests a downward trend since the late 1990s. When it comes to corruption perception, Belgium tends to score fairly low in a European perspective, but perception-based data should always be interpreted with great caution.

Are there Regional Differences in Attitudes towards Corruption?

Pujas and Rhodes (1999a: 689) wonder whether there is a clean north and a corrupt south in Europe, or whether there is a 'southern syndrome' (1999b: 41). They show how the Transparency International Corruption Perceptions Index suggests the existence of two groups of countries in Europe: a northern Protestant one and a southern Catholic one. Yet, they conclude, this does not explain why some countries have managed to eradicate corruption while others, geographically close, have not. They define Belgium as a northern country and have difficulties in explaining high levels of perceived corruption.

A more common argument, however, is that Belgium is on the border between the two groups, consisting of two separated administrative cultures (see also Brans *et al.* this volume): a southern one in French-speaking Wallonia, and a northern one in Dutch-speaking Flanders, although traces of a 'southern' culture are also said to be found in, until recently largely Catholic, Flanders. If this is the case, different approaches to corruption should be found in the two regions: high corruption and high acceptance in the south, and lower corruption and lower acceptance in the north.

Differences in Perceived Corruption

We first test whether corruption is perceived differently by Dutch- and French-speakers. We rely on data from the 1995 and 2003 Belgian General

Election Studies,[1] because of the large samples. The 1995 study contains several corruption-related issues, inspired by a series of corruption scandals in the first half of the 1990s. The 2003 survey contained a question on the perceived extent of bribe-taking among politicians. Rather than merely looking at the region in which respondents reside (Flanders, Wallonia, Brussels), we use the language in which the interview was conducted, precisely because we want to look at differences in political culture, which correspond more to linguistic than territorial lines. We first test differences in perceived corruption and then look at differences in public attitudes towards corruption.

When looking at the 1995 survey, French- and Dutch-speakers clearly differ in their perception of political corruption: French-speakers are more likely to state that politicians are more corrupt than other people (see Table 1). This difference remains significant when controlling for sex, age, education and income. Also in the 2003 survey, French-speakers perceive political corruption in Belgium to be considerably higher than Dutch-speakers (see Table 2). Language remains an important determinant of perceived corruption after controlling for sex, education, and age.

Differences in Attitudes towards Corruption

In the 1999 European Values Study (Inglehart *et al.* 2005), a question was included on the justifiability of accepting bribes in the course of one's duties. Two-thirds of the Belgians thought this could never be justified (one on a

TABLE 1

PERCEIVED CORRUPTION AMONG POLITICIANS IN BELGIUM, ACCORDING TO LANGUAGE OF RESPONDENT, 1995

	French	Dutch
Politicians more corrupt than other people	41.5	30.2
Politicians less corrupt than other people	1.6	2.7
Politicians not more or less corrupt than other people	56.9	67.1

Source: Belgian General Election Study 1995 (N = 3,557), weighted for region, age and sex.

TABLE 2

PERCEIVED CORRUPTION AMONG POLITICIANS IN BELGIUM, ACCORDING TO LANGUAGE OF RESPONDENT, 2003

How widespread do you think corruption such as bribe taking is among politicians in Belgium?	French	Dutch
Very widespread	50.4	24.5
Quite widespread	42.6	55.2
Not very widespread	3.1	15.4
It hardly happens at all	3.9	4.8

Source: Belgian General Election Study 2003 (N = 2,225).

one to ten scale), and only a small minority was tolerant towards accepting bribes. There is, however, a small but significant difference between French- and Dutch-speakers, with the French-speakers more often opting for the extreme option (75.6 per cent never justified), and the Dutch speakers more often found in categories 2–6 (62.1 per cent in category 1). In a multivariate analysis including socio-economic status, age, sex, education and the size of one's town, language remains the main determinant of attitudes towards bribes. We find a similar trend in the 1995 General Election Study: French- speakers consider different types of political corruption (politicians accept- ing or asking money for government contracts, for personal use, or for party use) less acceptable than Dutch-speakers, again controlling for socio- demographics in a multivariate analysis (sex, age, education and income).

Finally, the 2005 European Social Survey also contained a number of items related to corrupt behaviour. Two of these were briefly discussed above: how respondents evaluate a public official asking someone for a bribe in return for their services, and what respondents think about the statement 'you should always strictly obey the law even if this means missing good opportunities'. Figures 3 and 4 disaggregate the responses for the three Regions. In the Flemish Region, 1,028 people were interviewed, in the Walloon Region 597 and in the Brussels Region 153.

Bivariate analysis shows differences between the three Regions in Belgium, with inhabitants of the Flemish Region being slightly more tolerant towards public officials asking for bribes. The Flemish were also less likely to agree that one should always strictly obey the law even if it

FIGURE 3
ATTITUDES TOWARDS OBEYING THE LAW: YOU SHOULD ALWAYS OBEY THE
LAW

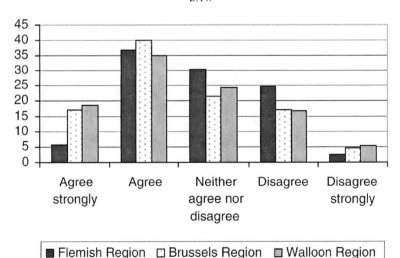

■ Flemish Region   □ Brussels Region   ▨ Walloon Region

FIGURE 4
ACCEPTANCE OF BRIBERY

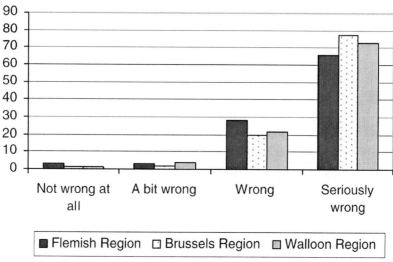

Source: European Social Survey, round 2, 2005.

means missing good opportunities. The differences remain (albeit small), when controlling for a number of socio-demographics such as gender, education, age and self-reported level of urbanisation of domicile.

In conclusion, French-speaking Belgians seem to perceive more corruption than their Dutch-speaking counterparts, but tolerance towards corruption is lower among French-speakers. As for the latter, it is unclear whether the difference in tolerance is due to political culture or to a reaction against higher levels of perceived corruption. However, the small differences that do exist repeatedly falsify the proposition of a Flemish culture, which, because of its adherence to a northern political culture would be less tolerant towards corruption. This interesting observation is an obvious avenue for further research into the actual prevalence of corruption in the two parts of the country. In any case, bearing in mind the small differences between the two language communities, we can conclude that there is at first sight little indication of a clash of political cultures when it comes to corruption and that it may be hard to explain corruption by referring to regional culture.

Explaining Corruption

In line with the focus of this volume, we want to investigate whether Belgian-style federalism could go some way in explaining why the 1990s saw several cases of corruption. Yet, before we delve into federalism, we would list a few factors that are frequently mentioned as contributing or contextual factors to explaining corruption in Belgium.

First and foremost, many authors refer to the complex of interrelated cultural factors that include fairly low trust in democratic institutions (e.g. Van de Walle 2007), relatively high tolerance towards breaking the law (e.g. Gibson and Caldeira 1996), and a culture of clientelistic relations between politicians and their voters for both individual favours and advantages for their constituency. Factors like these create a context that facilitates corrupt practices.

Second, in each of the Belgian regions, political parties and their presidents play a pivotal role. Until the end of the 1980s, the governing parties strongly controlled promotion in the civil service (De Winter 2003: 99), thus creating a possible avenue for dubious dependencies between politics and individual administrators. Political parties also had a strong impact on actual policy-making, particularly through the *ministerial cabinets*: the ministers' personal political advisors, often former party officials, seconded public servants or representatives of interest groups (see e.g. Pelgrims 2001). '[A]s they are central to departmental decision-making and are staffed by party loyalists, ministerial cabinets are evidently useful sites for organizing illicit activities' (De Winter 2003: 99).

Third, in an analysis of corruption in Belgium, Frognier (1986) considered consociationalist systems as more prone to corruption. Likewise, Lijphart, in his analysis of consociational systems, pointed out that 'it may be hypothesised that the greater clarity of responsibilities in majoritarian democracies inhibits corruption and that the consensus system's tendency to compromise and "deal-making" fosters corrupt practices' (Lijphart 1999: 289). Yet his empirical analysis of 36 countries did not reveal significant effects. Pujas and Rhodes (1999a) also argue that political competition does not function properly in a consociational system, because inter-party agreement is bought, and because there is no real control when you always cooperate with the same people. The ruling group will thus insulate itself from outside scrutiny, even if many parties are involved (Frognier 1986). The strong distinction between the ideological pillars in the Belgian consociational system, which have lived on after the federalisation of Belgium, and the close ties between a political party and a diversity of organisations within the same pillar (trade unions, public health bodies, professional organisations, and even market actors such as banks, architects or firms) lead to long-term alliances that are sensitive to political corruption, particularly when parties required extensive funding. For example, investigations into the role of Leo Delcroix in a number of high-profile scandals revealed that, as party secretary for the Flemish Christian Democrat party, he was at the centre of a network of friendly companies that also involved dubious forms of party financing.

Fourth, party fragmentation could in theory decrease opportunities for corruption, as complex coalition governments require more actors to be bribed and there is a higher risk of one of the parties blowing the whistle on illicit behaviour. Yet, although Belgium has one of the most fragmented party systems in Europe (see De Winter *et al.* this volume), for two reasons, it is very doubtful that this had a negative impact on corruption. For starters, party fragmentation coincided with spiralling costs in election campaigning, contributing to the Agusta–Dassault and a number of other party finance scandals (De Winter 2000). Furthermore, all the main parties seemed to share the fear of a 'chain of denunciation' (Frognier 1986) and thus 'signed' an 'implicit non-aggression pact' (De Winter 2003: 98) prohibiting the reporting of corrupt behaviour.

Some recent changes justify cautious optimism. A very important factor was a law in 1989 reducing the need for (illicit) party financing by strongly increasing government donations and capping the cost of election campaigns. Moreover, the 1990s saw a significant decrease in the politicisation of the judiciary and the administration through independent assessments of candidates. Meanwhile, administrations at different levels are experimenting with preventive measures of ethics management (Maesschalck 2005). A whistle-blowing act has been approved at the Flemish level (Maesschalck and Ornelis 2003) and is under consideration at the federal level. In the spring of 2006, a number of scandals were uncovered involving political and administrative behaviour in both Flanders and Wallonia in the past. Devastating as these revelations are, this behaviour is now public and appears to have stopped, which is a positive sign.

The reasons that are listed above fall beyond the scope of federalism. Yet would federalism, Belgian-style, have had an independent effect on the incidence of corruption? In the literature the empirical evidence of a link between federalism and corruption is shaky at best, and there are theoretical arguments to both support and reject such a relationship. For instance, using perception indicators, Treisman (2000: 401) found federal states to be more corrupt than unitary states. He also found that 'countries with more tiers of government tend to have higher perceived corruption' (Treisman 2002: 1), but the results were not straightforward. Federalism effects often disappear when other variables are included in the models (Bohara *et al.* 2004). This paragraph briefly discusses two mechanisms through which federalism might have an impact on corruption.

The first mechanism refers to proximity. Federalism is said to bring government closer to the people. This has at least two, contradictory, effects. Proximity increases accountability and control and might thus reduce corruption. Yet at the same time it stimulates more frequent and closer interaction and thus more opportunity for corruption (see e.g. Rose-Ackerman 2004). The relevance of this mechanism for Belgium will depend on how one interprets proximity. First, if one focuses on the quantitative dimension of the argument and on literal proximity in the sense of close interaction between political and bureaucratic officials and citizens, then the relevance seems very limited. Population size of the regions suggests it probably does not matter all that much whether we are dealing with a federalised or a unitary Belgian state. While Belgium has almost 10.5 million inhabitants (as of July 2005), the Flemish Region still has 6 million, and the Walloon 3.4 million. It is therefore unlikely that this federalism or regionalism would lead to greater proximity between citizens and politicians.

Furthermore, one could also interpret proximity in terms of values and political culture. In this sense, proximity might indeed have the two contradictory effects mentioned above. On the one hand, if principal (electorate) and agent (political and bureaucratic officials) share more values, it will be easier for the former to control the latter. On the other hand, shared values could make it easier for both parties in the interaction to actually engage in corrupt practices, because the availability of information on the other's motives and values lowers transaction costs and the risks of a corrupt encounter. Yet this argument only holds for Belgium if there are significant differences between the two main communities in political culture and particularly in attitudes towards corruption. Evidence for the latter is, as we discussed above, very weak.

The second mechanism refers to the increased competition that federalism allegedly creates. Public choice approaches attribute high levels of corruption to a lack of competition in the political arena, because competition is said to reduce politicians' discretionary power and 'diminish the value of bribing officials' (Bohara *et al.* 2004: 485). Thus, because of its scattered power structure, a federal structure requires that a large number of actors are bribed instead of just one, making it more difficult to influence decisions, but possibly leading to an increase in the total number of corrupt deeds (Treisman 2000: 407). Also, because there is a larger number of actors to extract bribes from the population or other actors (Treisman 2000: 433), political competition (both within and between parties) is likely to have the effect of keeping the level of bribes low (Shleifer and Vishny 1993: 610). Yet competition in a federal structure can also increase corruption: it makes constituents or clients less dependent on politicians or bureaucrats, because they can replace politicians or bring their case to another bureaucrat (Montinola and Jackman 2002: 147, 151). In a (federal) system with much political competition one only needs to bribe a segment of government to influence decisions.

In order to assess the relevance of these arguments about increased competition for the case of Belgian federalism, it is important to distinguish between those policies that are still entirely assigned to the national level (e.g. defence), policy areas which are shared by the regional and federal levels (e.g. employment) and policies which are entirely regional (e.g. education).

First, the arguments above are clearly relevant for those policy areas that are still entirely at the federal level, since federal decisions require the agreement of the two major language communities and the non-state-wide parties represented in the federal coalition government. However, these mechanisms were present at the outset of Belgium's federalisation process (see Deschouwer this volume) and therefore cannot be attributed to the latter as such.

Second, Belgian federalism minimises the occurrence of shared, or con-current, competencies (although different slices of a policy area, such as employment policy, are often attributed to different levels of government). 'Joint-decision' federations may increase the likelihood of corruption, since they make more officials, with less decisive power and with allegiances to different (levels of) government(s) responsible for policy implementation.

Third, the arguments presented above are not relevant for those policy areas in which the regions have gained full competence. In fact, one could argue that, compared with the situation prior to federalisation, the number of actors to be bribed has been reduced and their decision-making power increased. In the Belgian unitary state, the decision to initiate a large public infrastructure project required a complex balancing of regional interests (as is still the case for the federal policies described above). Yet 'waffle-iron' strategies became redundant in competencies that are entirely regional, as decision-makers gained the power and the budget to tailor policies to their own needs. The balancing act for these devolved competencies is thus much less complex and mainly depends on agreement within the governing coalition at the regional level, leading to fewer potentially corruptible decision-makers, but with more power. On the other hand, the federalisa-tion of Belgium initially reduced competition at the regional level. Without directly elected regional parliaments until 1995, federalisation contributed to strengthening the power of some pillar parties in the region in which they received most electoral support. For instance, in Wallonia, federalisation consolidated the hegemony of the Parti Socialiste and in Flanders it initially strengthened the role of the Christian Democrats. Traditionally, these are the strongest pillar parties which maintain strong links to a number of important auxiliary associations in health and education policy.

The Impact of Federalism on Policy Failure in Belgium

Federalism was introduced in Belgium to prevent the reoccurrence of a number of policy failures that emerged in the 1970s and 1980s. We will discuss these failures by means of a typology of three typical 'general failure types' that was developed by Boin and 't Hart (2000). They explain how these failure types (respectively crisis by ignorance, crisis by rigidity and crisis by failed intervention) act as endemic factors that contribute to a legitimacy gap between societal norms and performance and thus to policy failure. When applying this framework to Belgium, we can see how federalism was introduced as a means to avoid crises of all three general failure types.

First, a crisis by ignorance occurs when 'the dominant coalition in the sector fails to identify an externally perceived need for adaptation or reform' (Boin and 't Hart 2000). It is not difficult to find policy fields that have been neglected as a consequence of the political elite's occupation with the federalisation process in the 1970s and 1980s. During the Dutroux crisis in the mid-1990s, for example, many senior politicians admitted that problems in the police and justice sector had been largely ignored because the political elites were preoccupied with federalisation. For the same reason, administrative reform was long kept off the political agenda (Van de Walle *et al.* 2005; Brans *et al.* this volume).

A crisis by rigidity occurs 'when environmental changes are noted and understood, but the dominant coalition in the sector is unable to go beyond gradualist adaptation in its response' (Alink *et al.* 2001: 297). Despite its unitary status, pre-1970 Belgium was already marred with ideological, sociological and linguistic cleavages which regularly paralysed decision-making in the centre. Change was only possible through small incremental steps, leading to an equilibrium that was only infrequently punctuated by a pact. Although such pacts could pave the way for more drastic changes, these often arrived at the expense of enormous political efforts. An example of an area where this immobilism as a consequence of the complex structure occurred is the field of public finance and particularly the growing national debt. Although most actors realised the need for drastic cutbacks, the complex Belgian system did not allow for the kind of serious measures that were necessary, particularly in a context where problems were often solved by throwing money at them, for example in the 'waffle iron' tradition. Federalisation has reduced this complexity, creating more room for decisive action when needed (admittedly, the budgetary criteria imposed by the Maastricht Treaty also played an important role in enforcing budgetary discipline).

Finally, a crisis by failed intervention occurs when problems are addressed in the wrong way: 'applying the wrong solutions to the right problem or applying the right solutions to the wrong problem' (Boin and 't Hart 2000). Despite variations in political culture and socio-economic development, the unitary state did not create much room for policy differentiation. A good policy for one part of the country could take the form of a failed intervention for the other, for example, because the economic circumstances were entirely different. Federalisation enabled more focused and appropriate policies, at least for those policies in which the regions gained exclusive competence, reducing the chance of such types of failed intervention.

Yet, although federalisation may have reduced the chance of policy failures, federalism is not without risks either. First, a new version of a crisis of ignorance becomes possible. In those policy areas where competencies are clearly assigned to the regional level, there is a risk that the regions will develop their own idiosyncratic policies without knowing anything about policies in the other region, thus forgoing the opportunity for synergies or running the risk of contradictory policies. Other than at the federal level, there is little room for regular interaction between politicians representing the two language groups and the (linguistically) split media do not report extensively on the policies of the region that is associated with the other language group.

Second, a new form of the crisis of rigidity also becomes possible. Having fought so long to acquire some competencies, regions may be very protective of them, rigidly following their own convictions even if it is obvious that an open-minded and flexible cooperation with the other region or the federal level would drastically increase policy effectiveness. Policy areas which are scattered between various levels or governments (such as environmental policy) are particularly prone to such risk, as the Belgian federal model cannot force the regions into binding cooperation agreements (see Swenden and Jans this volume). Furthermore, the Flemish government, in particular, may be prone to such behaviour, as it emphasises a rhetoric of '*wat we zelf doen doen we beter*' ('what we do ourselves, we do better'). Systematic policy coordination only takes place in areas that are deeply affected by Europeanisation (see Beyers and Bursens this volume) and a widely shared attitude of '*Bundestreue*' (federal comity) is still missing from the Belgian federal context.

The Impact of Federalism on Scandal in Belgium

Despite the media's focus on the facts behind a scandal, most authors do not see scandals as exceptional events, emanating from an objective fact or change. The 1990s featured a high incidence of scandals, not only in Belgium, but also elsewhere in the West. Most authors treat scandals as constructions, and point at the political opportunity structure as an explanation for their emergence: 'The appearance of a crisis is a political act, not a recognition of a fact or a rare situation' (Edelman 1988: 31).

The Belgian case seems to be no exception to this apparent broader trend of scandal-proneness. The early 1990s saw the emergence of a discourse on 'the confidence gap' between citizen and government. The phrase was coined by then opposition politician (and since 1999 federal Prime Minister) Guy Verhofstadt and assumed its full strength as a widely shared problem definition after the dramatic 1991 elections, in which the extreme right-wing party *Vlaams Blok* gained a spectacular increase in votes. Situations previously not generally defined as problematic suddenly became so. The air was filled with cries for a 'New Political Culture' that would eradicate power politics, and do away with much of the backroom decision-making.

Not all Belgian scandals in the 1990s can simply be reduced to changes in sensitivity or expectations, or to the political games that constructed them. The Agusta–Dassault corruption revelations followed the murder of socialist politician André Cools, the first national politician to be murdered in Belgium since communist leader Julien Lahaut in 1950. Rumour spread that the murder was related to a broad culture of fraud and corruption, and even mafia involvement. Despite the actual killers being imprisoned, no satisfactory motive has been found for the murder, but many corrupt practices have been uncovered during the investigation. This makes the Agusta case different from more 'mainstream' corruption cases.

The abuse and killing of several young girls by a well-known and previously convicted sex offender, Marc Dutroux, hardly can be qualified as an average policy failure either. Against the background of the huge public outrage surrounding his arrest in 1996 and a widely held (but never proved) assumption that there were networks of powerful people who protected him, his short-lived accidental escape in April 1998 counts as one of the most absurd and shocking events in the history of Belgian criminal policy.

We now turn to federalism and its potential impact on three different stages in the development of a scandal: problem definition, scandal expansion and scandal coping or solution. With regard to problem definition, one should note that not all problems become scandals. Brändström and Kuipers (2003) identified the violation of crucial 'core values' as a prerequisite for incidents to develop into crises and to initiate a process of blaming. In Belgium, many problems are framed as resulting from deep-rooted differences in political culture, especially when it comes to issues of corruption or the management of public sector institutions. As such, the attempt to accentuate differences in political culture rather than federalism as an institutional variable underpins the making of several scandals. Above, we suggested that survey evidence for the existence of different regional attitudes towards corruption is weak. Yet the two language communities have deep-rooted stereotypes of each other, and frequently refer to these in the political discourse. Any event that confirms these stereotypes (e.g. 'a corrupt south') has a higher propensity to draw attention, and to develop into a scandal. In fact, recent years show that virtually all public policy issues can be framed in terms of a Flemish–Walloon juxtaposition, from administrative reform to tobacco advertising on sports events or the right of non-EU citizens to vote.

The rise of the extreme right in Flanders further contributed to this development. Since the arrival of the extreme right-wing *Vlaams Blok/ Belang*, cases of corruption are now widely used to generate political conflict. As a permanent opposition party (at least until now), the *Vlaams Belang* has no interest in maintaining the cosy backroom politics associated with consociationalism and thus has its hands free to frame any problematic occurrence as a scandal. Moreover, the party's extreme Flemish nationalist stance typically leads it to frame problems in terms of a clean Flanders that is deprived of its means by a corrupt and lazy south. Yet this rhetoric is not confined to extreme right parties. Regional identity has become a major element in the political game, and in the party-political game, often in a misguided attempt to win back votes from the extreme right.

With regard to an increase in scandal, it is noted that growing political competition has a great effect on this. However, as discussed above, federalism has not necessarily increased competition in the Belgian political system, certainly not until 2003, when federal elections were decoupled for the first time from regional elections. Even the strength of the extreme right in Flanders seems to have a double, contradictory effect on the level of scandal. On the one hand, they take a strong interest in expanding scandals, thus increasing pressure on the other parties to arrive at a 'collective definition of the deviance as scandalous' (Sherman 1978: 64). On the other hand, by their quantitative strength (and as a consequence of the so-called *cordon sanitaire*, that is, the agreement of all the other parties not to enter in coalition with the *Vlaams Belang*), they force virtually all traditional parties together in coalition governments, thus effectively reducing the scope for competition between those parties.

Finally, as a young multi-ethnic federal state, debates about the future development of the federal system feature prominently in the political discourse, no matter what is the policy issue at hand. In the bipolar Belgian federation, Belgian political actors (particularly in Flanders) routinely and systematically present more federalism as the means to put emerging scandals to rest. This creates the risk that other, potentially more relevant, solutions are routinely overlooked.

Conclusion: So what has Federalism to do with it?

Our analysis suggests that Belgian federalism has a limited impact on the occurrence of corruption, policy failure and scandal. With regard to the former, we demonstrated differences in the acceptance of corruption between the two different language communities. Yet we could not present objective data to demonstrate that corruption is more frequent in Flanders than in Wallonia or vice versa. Other factors, such as the escalating needs for party finance in the 1980s and the consociational elitist political system which has been governed by a 'junta of party presidents', are likely to play a much larger role in explaining why Belgium often suffers from a corrupt image. However, federalism may have created some favourable conditions insofar as it reduced the complexity of political decision-making in the regions and increased electoral accountability. The decoupling of federal and regional elections increased opportunities to 'throw out the rascals'. On the other hand, in Flanders, the *cordon sanitaire* effectively reduced the levels of political competition by forcing all the other political parties (except for the Greens) into a grand coalition government.

The process of federalising Belgium absorbed much energy of the political leaders and put a brake on necessary reforms, for instance in the police and justice sectors, thereby increasing incidences of policy failure. Although still an ongoing process, the scope of competencies that are fit for decentralisation (other than social security and health) is much reduced, and the regions can expend more energy to tailor policy solutions to the political preferences of the regional electorates they represent. The low incidence of shared policy competencies in the Belgian federation further increases the scope for policy divergence and experimentation. On the other hand, infrequent interaction between regional governments which cross-cut the language divide and a desire of the Flemish to 'do things their way' constrain opportunities for policy transfer and learning. Frequently, more regional autonomy is seen as the best solution to policy failure and scandal, whereas alternative and potentially more cost-efficient solutions are often overlooked.

Our analysis suggests that many of the undesirable consequences that are commonly attributed to federalism might in fact be due to the coexistence of different cultures in Belgium, independent of federalism. Yet this claim remains only a hypothesis and is an obvious avenue for further research. Hard evidence of how the presence of different political cultures affects policy failures and scandal remains very limited, mainly because empirical research on inter-regional differences in civil and political culture is lacking. Most research comparing the regions focuses on differences in national/ regional or ethno-territorial identities (e.g. Billiet *et al.* 2003; De Winter *et al.* 1998), not on attitudes towards corruption or similar issues. Therefore, this would be an important avenue for further research.

Focusing on one explanatory variable, as we did with federalism, always carries a certain risk of bias, an exaggeration of the power of the variable to explain the dependent variables (corruption, policy failures and scandal) to the detriment of other potential explanatory variables. We have made efforts to avoid such biases, for example by referring to the impact of depillarisation and the rise of the extreme right, but an obvious avenue for further research consists of more thorough analyses that are system- atically open for other explanations. The latter could include theoretically codified narrative accounts (see e.g. Maesschalck 2002 for such an analysis of the Dutroux scandal and its impact on police reform) or could rather focus on a limited number of explanatory factors, based on the study of a fairly large number of cases (see e.g. Bovens *et al.* 2001).

Acknowledgements

Steven Van de Walle would like to thank the Campbell Public Affairs Institute at the Maxwell School of Citizenship and Public Affairs (Syracuse University) for its hospitality when writing this article, and the National Fund for Scientific Research-Flanders (FWO Vlaanderen) for its financial support. Both authors would like to thank Wilfried Swenden and Sanneke Kuipers for their helpful comments.

Note

1. The data/tabulations utilised in this publication were made available by the ISPO and PIOP- Interuniversity Centres for Political Opinion Research, sponsored by the Federal Services for Technical, Cultural and Scientific Affairs. The data were originally collected by Jaak Billiet, Marc Swyngedouw, Ann Carton and Roeland Beerten (ISPO) for the Flemish voters and André-Paul Frognier, Anne Marie Aish-Van Vaerenbergh, Serge Van Diest and Pierre Baudewyns (PIOP) for the French-speaking. Neither the original collectors of the data nor the Centre bears any responsibility for the analysis or interpretations presented here.

References

Alink, Fleur, Arjen Boin and Paul 't Hart (2001). 'Institutional Crises and Reforms in Policy Sectors: The Case of Asylum Policy in Europe', *Journal of European Public Policy*, 8:2, 286–306.

Beerten, Roeland, Jaak Billiet, Ann Carton and Marc Swyngedouw (1997). *1995 General Election Study Flanders-Belgium: Codebook and Questionnaire*. Leuven: ISPO Interuniversitair Steunpunt voor Politieke-Opinieonderzoek KULeuven.

Billiet, Jaak, Bart Maddens and Roeland Beerten (2003). 'National Identity and Attitude Toward Foreigners in a Multinational State: A Replication', *Political Psychology*, 24:2, 241–57.

Bohara, Alok K., Neil J. Mitchell and Carl F. Mittendorff (2004). 'Compound Democracy and the Control of Corruption: A Cross-country Investigation', *The Policy Studies Journal*, 32:4, 481–99.

Boin, Arjen, and Paul 't Hart (2000). 'Institutional Crises and Reforms in Policy Sectors', in H. Wagenaar (ed.), *Government Institutions: Effects, Changes and Normative Foundations*. Boston: Kluwer Academic Publishers, 9–31.

Bovens, Marc, and Paul 't Hart (1996). *Understanding Policy Fiascoes*. New Brunswick, NJ and London: Transaction.

Bovens, Marc, Paul 't Hart and B. Guy Peters (2001). *Success and Failure in Public Governance. A Comparative Analysis*. Cheltenham: Edward Elgar.

Brändström, Annika, and Sanneke Kuipers (2003). 'From "Normal Incidents" to Political Crises: Understanding the Selective Politicization of Policy Failures', *Government and Opposition*, 38:3, 279–305.

Carton, Ann, Hendrik Van Geel and Sara De Pelsemaeker (2005). 'Basisdocumentatie Sociaal-Culturele Verschuivingen in Vlaanderen 2004'. Brussel: Ministerie van de Vlaamse Gemeenschap, Administratie Planning en Statistiek.

De Ruyver, Brice, Frederik Bullens, Tim Vander Beken and Nathalie Siron (1999). Anti-corruptiestrategieën. De aanpak van corruptie en beïnvloeding bij de bestrijding van de hormonendelinquentie en de vleesfraude: een case study. Antwerpen: Maklu.

De Winter, Lieven (2000). 'Political Corruption in the Belgian Partitocracy: (Still) an Endemic Disease?' EUI Working Paper RSC No. 2000/31.

De Winter, Lieven (2003). 'Political Corruption in Belgium', in Martin J. Bull and James L. Newell (eds.), *Corruption in Contemporary Politics*. Houndmills: Palgrave Macmillan, 93–105.

De Winter, Lieven, André-Paul Frognier and Jaak Billiet (1998). 'Y a-t-il encore des Belges? L'évolution des identités politiques des Wallons, des Bruxellois et des Flamands', in Marc Swyngedouw and Marco Martiniello (eds.), *Où va la Belgique? Les Soubresauts d'une petite Démocratie européenne*. Paris: L'Harmattan, 123–36.

Edelman, Murray (1988). *Constructing the Political Spectacle*. Chicago: University of Chicago Press.

Friedrich, Carl J. (1989). 'Corruption Concepts in Historical Perspective', in A.J. Heidenheimer, M. Johnston and V.T. LeVine (eds.), *Political Corruption. A Handbook*. New Brunswick, NJ: Transaction Publishers, 15–24.

Frognier, André-Paul (1986). 'Corruption and Consociational Democracy: First Thoughts on the Belgian Case', *Corruption and Reform*, 1, 143–8.

Gibson, James L., and Gregory A. Caldeira (1996). 'The Legal Cultures of Europe', *Law and Society Review*, 30:1, 55–87.

Inglehart, Ronald, Miguel Basanez, Jaime Díez-Medrano, Loek Halman and Ruud Luijkx (2005). *Human Beliefs and Values: A Cross-Cultural Sourcebook on the 1999–2005 Values Surveys*. México: Siglo XXI editores.

Jowell, R., and the Central Co-ordinating Team, European Social Survey 2004/2005 (2005). *Technical Report*. London: Centre for Comparative Social Surveys, City University. Data retrieved from the Norwegian Social Science Data Services (NSD).

Lijphart, Arend (1999). Patterns of Democracy: Government Forms and Performance in Thirty-Six Countries. New Haven, CT: Yale University Press.

Maesschalck, Jeroen (2002). 'When do Scandals Have an Impact on Policy Making? A Case Study of the Police Reform Following the Dutroux Scandal in Belgium', *International Public Management Journal*, 5:2, 169–93.

Maesschalck, Jeroen (2005). *Een ambtelijk integriteitsbeleid in de Vlaamse overheid*. Leuven: Steunpunt Bestuurlijk Organisatie Vlaanderen.

Maesschalck, Jeroen, and Frank Ornelis (2003). 'Een interdisciplinaire analyse van de klokkenluidersproblematiek in de openbare sector', *Tijdschrift Voor Bestuurswetenschappen En Publiek Recht*, 58:8, 535–57.

Montinola, Gabriella R., and Robert W. Jackman (2002). 'Sources of Corruption: A Cross-National Study', *British Journal of Political Science*, 32, 147–70.

Pelgrims, Christophe (2001). *Ministeriële kabinetsleden en hun loopbaan. Tussen mythe en realiteit*. Brugge: Die Keure.

Pujas, Véronique, and Martin Rhodes (1999a). 'A Clash of Cultures? Corruption and the Ethics of Administration in Western Europe', *Parliamentary Affairs*, 52:4, 688–702.

Pujas, Véronique, and Martin Rhodes (1999b). 'Party Finance and Political Scandal in Italy, Spain and France', *West European Politics*, 22:3, 41–63.

Rose-Ackerman, Susan (2004). 'The Challenge of Poor Governance and Corruption', Copenhagen Consensus Challenge Paper.

Sherman, Lawrence W. (1978). *Scandal and Reform: Controlling Police Corruption*. Berkeley: University of California Press.

Shleifer, Andrei, and Robert W. Vishny (1993). 'Corruption', *The Quarterly Journal of Economics*, 108:3, 599–617.

Thompson, John B. (2000). Political Scandal: Power and Visibility in the Media Age. Cambridge: Polity Press.

Treisman, David (2000). 'The Causes of Corruption: A Cross-National Study', *Journal of Public Economics*, 76, 399–457.

Treisman, David (2002). 'Decentralization and the Quality of Government', unpublished paper, UCLA.

Van de Walle, Steven (2007). 'Perceptions of Corruption as Distrust? Cause and Effect in Attitudes Towards Government', in Leo Huberts, Carole Jurkiewicz and Jeroen Maesschalck (eds.), *Ethics and Integrity of Governance: Perspectives across Frontiers*. Cheltenham: Edward Elgar, forthcoming.

Van de Walle, Steven, Nick Thijs and Geert Bouckaert (2005). 'A Tale of Two Charters: Political Crisis, Political Realignment and Administrative Reform in Belgium', *Public Management Review*, 7:3, 367–90.

Van Kesteren, J.N., P. Mayhew and P. Nieuwbeerta (2000). Criminal Victimisation in Seventeen Industrialised Countries: Key-Findings from the 2000 International Crime Victims Survey. The Hague: Ministry of Justice, WODC.

Yante, Jean-Marie (2003). 'La Corruption dans l'Administration belge aux XIXe et XXe siècles', in Seppo Tiihonen (ed.), *The History of Corruption in Central Government*. Amsterdam: IOS Press, 65–82.

Policy Convergence and Divergence in Belgium: Education and Health Care

STEFAAN DE RYNCK and KAROLIEN DEZEURE

Due to the far-reaching federalisation of policy competences, Belgium allows for a structured binary comparison of policy convergence or divergence between Flanders and Wallonia. The purpose of this article is to compare the policies of Flanders and Wallonia and to detect to what extent policies converge or diverge. The questions that inform this paper are: has policy divergence occurred since federalisation or not? If so, in what direction have policies changed and with what intensity? How can one explain intensity and direction of policy divergence and the observed patterns of similarity and variation between two regional political systems in the same national context? These questions will be studied in two very different policy domains in order to control for the sector-specificity of observed impacts. The structure of this article is as follows. First, we will briefly sketch two different views on what drives policy convergence and divergence. Next, we apply our framework to two cases, namely education and health care. In the last section we summarise the scope and drivers for policy divergence in both of these policy sectors.

Policy Convergence or Policy Divergence: A Theoretical Framework

Convergence and Divergence: A Definition

Convergence and non-convergence both have their own logics. Knill (2005) describes policy convergence as any increase in the similarity between one or more characteristics of a certain policy (e.g. policy objectives, policy instruments, policy settings) across a given set of political jurisdictions (supranational institutions, states, regions, local authorities) over a given period of time. Policy convergence thus describes the end result of a process of *policy change* over time towards some common point, regardless of the causal process. Other approaches expect opposite consequences from the same process. As such, divergence can be defined as the dissimilarity between one or more characteristics of a certain policy across a given set of political jurisdictions and over a given period of time. Policy divergence can also be considered as an end result of a process of *policy change* over time towards an uncommon point. Just as policy convergence, policy divergence can have several dimensions: there can be divergence due to the different policy goals in the two regions (third order), due to the fact that different policy instruments are used (second order) or because of the different settings of instruments (first order).

Causes of Convergence or Divergence

With respect to causal mechanisms driving convergence, five central aspects can be found. First, cross-regional policy convergence might simply be the result of similar, but independent, responses of different countries or regions to comparable problem pressures (e.g. ageing societies, environmental pollution or economic decline) (Collier and Messick 1975). Second, several studies emphasise convergence effects stemming from the imposition of policies. Imposition refers to constellations where countries or international organisations force other countries to adopt certain policies by exploiting asymmetries in political or economic power. Third, emphasis is placed on the harmonisation of national policies through international or supranational law. Countries and the regions within them are obliged to comply with international rules on which they have agreed in multilateral negotiations. Fourth, regulatory competition emerging from the increasing economic integration of European and global markets has been identified as important for the mutual adjustment of policies across countries and regions. Fifth, cross-regional policy convergence can simply be caused by communication (for example: transregional and/or transnational) (Knill 2005). A sixth and last hypothesis suggests that states which follow comparable pathways of social and economic development will naturally move towards common policies and policy instruments ('societal convergence') (Lowi 1964).

The divergence thesis, when focusing on its causes, concentrates on the stability of specific national characteristics such as differences in national policy styles (Richardson 1982), the stability of institutional arrangements and the importance of path dependence (Busch 2002; Busch and Jörgens 2005). Greer (2005), who emphasises in particular the policy styles, starts with the basic formula of a policy outcome which is a combination of a problem (that seems to demand a response), a politician (who can and might actually do something) and a policy (something to do). If one of the three is absent, it is unlikely that anything will happen. When the three come together, a 'window of opportunity' opens in which something happens, and a policy is likely to be the result. Looking at the systematic differences in the sources of problems, policies and politics gives us a rough estimate of the likelihood of policy divergence. Greer concludes that the key to under-standing policies, and the key to understanding the likelihood of policy varia-tion over time, is to look at the systemic regularities in problems, politics and policy in each country. To the extent that these differ between two polities, we should expect that the policy outcomes will differ. Pierson (2000) underlines the concept of path dependency. In this view, positive returns to scale, network externalities and feedback effects can lead to equilibrium outcomes that are very stable (lock-in). Therefore, the costs of change are prohibitively high and consequently change is very rare (Jordan *et al.* 2005).

Triggers for Policy Divergence

Many different approaches to policy change coexist in the literature. In this article we compare the policies between the Flemish- and French-speaking Communities in education and health policy and examine the question if there is policy divergence between both Communities. As such we deal with a 'what question': what in the national policy legacy changed? If policy divergence between policy sectors and regions can be found today, it will be explained by tracing the dynamics of the policy process since federalisation. In order to understand the dynamics of the impact of regional government on public policy, the analysis concentrates on opportunities for reform and actors as key analytical concepts. The structuration of the policy process that leads to and affects the nature of reform will also be considered, parti-cularly by taking account of the level of polarisation in a policy system and the strategies employed to deal with this polarisation. Obviously, the way in which a policy process is structured is, in part, a legacy from the past, but it is also partly affected by agency and becomes, in analytical terms, a moving target.

The analysis of divergence is built on different factors. First, the question emerges whether there are particular opportunities that are necessary conditions to trigger and support a drive for divergence. Policy entrepre-neurs need opportunities for reform in order to promote change. Oppor-tunities for reform can emerge through external shocks and strain (Sabatier and Jenkins-Smith 1999), which can point to the inadequacy of established policy, or change social demands and the utility of social and political resources. Party adaptation is a second type of opportunity for reform. It alters the opportunity structure for actors within the policy system. Finally, routine politics, such as the budgetary process, offers changes for advancing reform.

Second, political and administrative actors, or 'policy entrepreneurs',[1] are needed to seize opportunities for change. They will invest political capital in the risk of changing policy, hoping to receive a return in the form of 'good policy' and, possibly, more selective benefits. They will try to seize opportunities to push through their policy alternative. Entrepreneurs will try to build a reputation as credible policy-makers that will help them in organising coalitions for change. Such a reputation will depend on their credibility in honouring agreements, their initial action when taking office and their image with those who tend to be sceptical about a proposed direction. Policy entrepreneurs are embedded in a specific organisational context. They operate from within political parties, executives, legislatures, the civil service or social groups (Aberbach *et al.* 1981).

This article focuses on government-based entrepreneurship, whereby more radical divergence is likely to involve entrepreneurship within the executive. The organisational embeddedness of entrepreneurs will affect their capacity for action. Also, some organisations will nurture entrepreneurship more than others. With regard to political parties, their position and role in the established order and their level of internal cohesion will be crucial in determining whether or not entrepreneurship will be encouraged. A weak link with the past and high internal cohesion foster the emergence of entrepreneurs within the party. In contrast, a party that is implicated in the established order and/or internally heterogeneous will offer a less encouraging organisational environment for risk-takers. In addition, the level of polarisation which is seen as largely exogenous to entrepreneurial action can restrict the possibility for successful change. The level of polarisation amongst policy participants is crucial for coalition-building and new policy choice. A high level of polarisation in the policy system increases the risk and reduces the chances of successful change (Sabatier and Jenkins-Smith 1993).

Policy Convergence and Divergence in Belgium

As an empirical test case, this study chooses education and health care policy. Within these two cases, a substantial number of actual and potential policy changes are analysed. These policy areas seem particularly suitable to the task at hand for a number of reasons. First, education is one of the most important federalised competencies. It accounts for almost half of public expenditure at the regional level (De Rynck 2002). In contrast to this, unlike most other federal countries, most matters concerning health care are the responsibility of the federal government (Onderzoeksgroep Sociale Zekerheid 2002 1994). However, as we will illustrate below, Communities have some discretionary powers in implementing health care policy.

Second, the education sector had experienced a long period of policy stability or even stalemate before federalisation, notwithstanding an evolving policy environment. Hence, the potential for policy divergence was high when federalisation occurred. In addition, health care experienced long-term stability until the 1990s. Thereafter, the Flemish parties started to discuss its potential 'federalisation' (Palsterman 2005).

Third, attributing policy divergence to political action could easily be countered by arguing that a radically different policy context impinged upon the political institution. Therefore, the policy challenge in both Communities needed to be similar. Education, particularly since the research limits itself to compulsory education, and health care are a good choice from this perspective as both policy areas are faced with comparable policy challenges in both Communities.

Fourth, the two cases satisfy a fourth criterion, namely that sectors have to be very different from each other. The rationale for a cross-sectoral comparison is to ensure that the investigation of the impact of regional government on public policy extends beyond the logic of a single sector.

Policy Convergence and Divergence in Education

Federalisation

The 1988 reforms expanded the power of the Communities over education except for a few issues. The beginning and end of the study year, minimum requirements for diplomas and teacher's pensions were issues in which the federal level retained legislative and administrative competence (Erk 2003). In 1988, the rewriting of the constitution took place during the federal coalition-building process involving five future government parties. In contrast to their ideological counterparts, Flemish Social Democrats and French-speaking Christian Democrats did not hold a pivotal power position in their Communities. They demanded strong protection of their constituencies as a precondition for federalisation. Thus, the mode of federalisation was strongly affected by long-standing distrust amongst various groups within both the Flemish and French Communities. In order to diminish distrust, the five-party coalition introduced new provisions in the constitution which reduced the autonomy of the Communities in education policy.

The new 1988 Constitution safeguards minority rights in both Communities and defines the framework of budgetary allocation to different types of schools (Catholic schools versus state schools). The new text entrenched the principles of an earlier compromise (the so-called School Pact). This pact allowed both public (state) and private (Catholic) schools to expand with public money and stipulated that material considerations should not hinder parental choice between both types of schools. Furthermore, cost-free access to both types of schooling, within 'a reasonable distance' was to be offered throughout Belgium. Hence, the national policy legacy entrenched in the 1958 compromise School Pact heavily affected the constitutional choice in 1988. In addition, new provisions made the general constitutional principle of equality more explicit for education by stating that 'pupils, parents, school personnel and school bodies' are equal before the law. Another type of national protection for minority groups was the introduction of the Constitutional Court, which became the guardian of the new provision. The new constitution also stipulated that the legislature should regulate the organisation of, and the subsidies for, education, thereby formally ending the possibility that issues would be settled only by the executive branch in deals among political parties.

Perhaps the most important constraint imposed by the national level on regional education policy was the definition of the financial framework, which was strongly affected by the fiscal austerity of the 1980s and by a political struggle in the south between regionalist and French Community-oriented Socialists. The central government established a double austerity norm until the end of 1998, whereby total expenditure could never grow faster than inflation and the nominal deficit could never be higher than the previous year. In this context, the government formation process fixed the bulk of Community revenues at the level of 1988 education expenditure, with expenditure growth until 1998 based only on the annual rate of inflation. The total federal grant to the Communities dropped as a percentage of GDP every year. OECD estimates that while Belgian education expenditure amounted to more than 6 per cent of GDP until the mid-1980s, it had fallen to around 5 per cent by 1995. Education as a share of total government expenditure dropped from around 15 per cent in the mid-1980s to around 10 per cent by 1995. This occurred largely beyond the control of the respective Community governments who took charge of the sector. Indeed, Communities have no fiscal powers and can only borrow within a tightly defined federal framework. As a result of the national finance agreement and the regional political situation, the Flemish education budget showed a higher annual increase compared to that of the French Community. The budgetary situation worsened towards the end of the 1990s for both Communities, when budgets grew only marginally compared to inflation. But, the Flemish had more leeway in all of this because they could transfer money that came into the regional treasury to schooling, given that the Region and the Community had been merged.

The constitutional changes of 1988 were the outcome of a long historical process. The active definition of the freedom of education principle has important consequences for regional discretion, most notably by imposing financial appropriations beyond the control of regional decision-makers. At the same time, Communities were being forced into a tight budgetary straitjacket by the national level. The freedom of education principle also limits the freedom of the Communities to condition the use of public money designated for private schools.

Policy Divergence in the Communities since 1988

During the 1990s important differences emerged in how the two Communities conduct education policy, with regard to both the organisation of delivery and the quality of schooling.

Delivery of Education

The Flemish and French Communities have opted for a different course in organising the delivery of compulsory schooling. In Flanders, changes in the planning system testify to a new view of the role of the state. In the French Community, changes consolidated the national policy legacy, and attempts at moving away from that legacy have failed. In the Flemish Community, a public agency (the Autonomous Council for Community Education, ARGO) was established to supervise schooling on behalf of the Flemish executive. A detailed political agreement between the party presidents of the four major Flemish parties defined the agency's structure and tasks. However, the internal structure of ARGO reflected the high levels of mutual distrust over education insofar as a highly politicised and centralised organisation was created. The initial reform envisaged a radical reform ten years later. The 1998 reform strengthened local autonomy and allowed for more differentiation between ARGO schools. This started to undermine the integrated character of the state school system, and depoliticised central decision-making. In short, the reform strengthened the influence of parents and/or other civil society representatives as a control mechanism for the more extensive powers granted to school professionals at the new supra-local level. Flemish policy also established a framework for schools to cooperate better in school associations that are jointly responsible for education supply. Within this context, policy decisions hesitantly pushed for stronger cooperation amongst schools belonging to different types of providers. Thus, in Flanders, advocates of a centralised delivery by the regional state were marginalised.

By contrast, in the French Community, no structural changes were made and the traditional role of the state remained intact. The belief that equity depends on a strong public service remained central for the Socialist Party and underpinned its belief in the pivotal role of the state bureaucracy in education delivery. Despite the budgetary strain and the decline in the attendance of public secondary schools, policy to reform secondary education delivery failed in the French Community. A proposal, presented by the president of the Parti Socialiste (PS) and the Socialist Minister of Education in 1992, included the idea of giving the monopoly for delivering public education at primary level to the municipalities. The purpose was to put the French Community government in a more independent position with respect to the whole education field, with less direct involvement in organising delivery. However, within the French-speaking Social

Democrats, provincial and municipal executives mobilised against the proposal, partly for fear of losing control of teacher recruitment, and partly to avoid a decline in local power. There was a mobilisation against the anticipated involvement of parents in school management, an issue which Flemish policy-makers regarded as self-evident but which some French Community Socialists called an unacceptable 'semi-privatisation' (Samson and Serafini 1997). Thus, reforms failed largely due to discontent within the French-speaking Social Democratic community, in spite of backing from party leaders. Under pressure from the statist faction, the current manifesto of the PS foresees that only directly elected representatives can be responsible for school management, excluding the creation of any agency type of reform.

The developments in education policy reflect the growing policy divergence between the Communities during the 1990s. Divergence also appears in policy changes related to human and financial resource allocation. The Flemish Community moved towards more local flexibility and decentralisation, at least in the second half of the 1990s, whereas the French Community confirmed or even strengthened the national policy legacy of centralisation.

Regulating Quality

We now turn to policy divergence in the regulation and quality of schooling. In Flanders, a pattern of reform towards regulating results achieved and relaxing procedural regulations since 1989 can be observed. Perhaps the most important effect of the creation of a new agency to deliver public education was the redefinition of the role of the Community government as a more impartial regulator between providers. Indeed, the Minister of Education ceased being the general manager of one of the competitors. This in turn, enabled a stronger and more credible role for the state in regulating quality, also for non-state schools. A group of entrepreneurs within the civil service seized upon this structural change as a reform opportunity. An independent expert commission was set up in 1989 with members from Catholic and non-Catholic backgrounds in addition to government advisors and school inspectors. The commission's main conclusions were enshrined in a 1991 decree, which increased the government's role and diminished the power of organising authorities in defining curricula and monitoring school output. The reform provided for performance targets defined by Flemish government which all education providers should incorporate as minimum standards. It left school autonomy for study programmes and teaching methods intact, but imposed the deliverables. Crucially, in addition to the results that pupils should attain, the reform also gave the state control over how schools operate to obtain these results. Under the national regime, expanding the inspectorate's role would have been unimaginable due to its strong association with the state school Community. At the same time, the commission set out a subtle procedure in four steps with the aim of altering power relations in favour of state actors.

Proposing draft performance targets was the sole prerogative of an independent government service which reported directly to the Minister of Education. The process of negotiating on the performance targets mainly displayed a clash between the Flemish government and the Catholic schools. The latter rejected any interference in the contents of teaching and in pedagogic freedom. Despite the fact that the role of the government was rather weak, it was partly compensated by the independence of this new service for education development, whose sole right of initiative to propose targets proved to be a powerful weapon in the deliberations (De Rynck 2005).

The French Community inherited the same national policy legacy for school targets and quality controls as in Flanders. Compared to Flanders, the pressure to tackle this situation was higher. Both the variation in performance between schools and the incidence of school failure are higher, showing more acute problems of unequal treatment between children and insufficient school quality in specific cases.[2] Hence, the challenge for installing stronger external control, or at least for designing a system that induces schools to improve their performance, was more acute in 1988. Policy change however, was less forthcoming compared to Flanders. Although the French Community government decided in 1997 to develop performance targets along ideas similar to those which had guided policy in Flanders, the policy process and actual result differed. There were much lower levels of controversy in developing targets, which was certainly related to the most remarkable difference with the Flemish Community, namely the lack of a strong link between the new targets and government inspection. Reform in the French Community has not yet been linked to external control of schools. An organisational restructuring of the inspectorate did not take place. Also the indicators used to assess the performance of students and schools in relation to the new standards have not been developed yet (De Rynck 2005).

Explaining Divergence in Educational Policy

The federalisation of this policy sector has been accompanied by increasing differences between the two education policies. As such we can speak of a third-order change in the Flemish Community where policy goals and instruments were altered. The internal renewal of political parties within the regional party systems is crucial to understanding the variation in policy change between both Communities, in particular the differences in Social Democratic party adaptation. In Flanders, party renewal offered entrepreneurs an opportunity to push for policy changes and gave them more space to take risks compared to their French-speaking colleagues. In the French Community, potential policy entrepreneurs tried to seize upon financial strain as an opportunity to obtain radical reform, but failed. This was related to the higher capacity for dissent within the French-speaking Social Democrats, or, in other words, to the higher risk inherent in change. In Flanders, the Social Democrats moved towards accepting religious-based diversity in education. The party reacted to a steady decline in voters at the end of the 1970s by opening its ranks to progressive Catholics. This movement was promoted by some actors who would later become key players in Flemish education policy. As a result of internal party renewal, support within the party for the idea of a state monopoly on education waned. In contrast, the French-speaking Social Democrats reached their electoral peak in 1987 with 44 per cent of the regional vote, reviving the age-old dream of an absolute majority, now confined to the regions. No compelling need for party adaptation emerged, at least not in the sense of opening up to progressive Catholics and abandoning the classic state school constituency. In 1988, after seven years in opposition, the French-speaking Social Democrats had no interest in reducing state powers for education delivery, but rather wanted to use them to expand their power base. In sum, the key driving force for education policy divergence rested in the regional party systems, hence in region- rather than sector-specific factors (De Rynck 2002, 2005).

Policy Convergence and Divergence in Health Care

The (Non)-federalisation of Health Care

Despite 20 years of federalisation, health insurance has remained a federal competence. The financing and the basic regulation concerning the insurance of sickness and invalidity and medication have largely remained federal. However, since 1980, some aspects of health care policy have been entrusted to the Communities: the bulk of preventive medicine, the implementation of hospital standards set at the federal level, part of the financing of hospital investment, and the coordination of home care. As such, the Communities could be considered as an 'applying' and 'executive' government. In addition, a constitutional reform in 1993 further complicated the situation by allowing the transfer of responsibilities in this policy field from the French-speaking Community to the Walloon Region and the French-speaking Community in Brussels (i.e. the French-speaking Community Commission – see Swenden and Jans this volume). As a consequence, there is a complicated structure which requires intergovernmental coordination in health policy (European Observatory on Health Care Systems 2000).

Solidarity in financing and equity in access to and utilisation of health care has been an important consideration in shaping the Belgian system of financing and delivering health care (Van Doorslaer *et al.* 2001). Callens and Peers (2003) describe six important features of the Belgian health care system. First, Belgium has a well organised system that is, in comparison with the surrounding countries, of good quality. Second, the system is financed on the basis of compulsory solidarity: citizens must have public insurance coverage through membership of private, non-profit sickness funds. Third, health care coverage through health care institutions is elaborate and constantly expanding. This applies to people, as well as to infrastructure and services. Fourth, Belgian health care operates on the basis of free choice: patients can freely choose their health insurance fund and health care provider. Fifth, the insurance package is defined explicitly through a complex process of negotiations within the National Institute for Sickness and Disability Insurance (RIZIV/INAMI). Each year representatives of the sickness funds and the health care providers negotiate a detailed free schedule for each type of service, the so-called *nomenclature*. Last, the government ensures that the services are accessible to all. In fact, Belgium has long achieved virtually universal coverage for a fairly comprehensive package of services. As a result of the compulsory solidarity schemes, access to high-quality medical services is provided at heavily subsidised or even zero-sum prices for most citizens, including the low-income and vulnerable groups (Van Doorslaer *et al.* 2001).

The Contemporary Debate

It is clear that the federal government plays a dominant role in this policy domain. This role has grown historically. In contrast to educational policy, where most of the competencies rest with the Communities, the federal government is the major legislator in health issues. Yet the role of sickness funds and health care providers implies that the decision-making structure in health policy is rather fragmented. The differences in medical practice between different hospitals and different regions remain considerable (Schokkaert and Van de Voorde 2005). Unsurprisingly, therefore, powerful groups within the Flemish-speaking Community in particular have exerted considerable pressure to transfer health care and insurance to the regional, that is, community, level (Palsterman 2005).[3] In Flanders, average income levels are higher and medical per capita expenditures are lower. By contrast, a large majority in the French-speaking south wants to keep health insurance federal.

The entire discussion tends to focus on the difficult question whether these inter-regional differences in medical expenditures are 'justified', that is, linked to differences in mortality, or 'unjustified', that is, linked to differences in medical supply and practice (Schokkaert and Van de Voorde 2005). Of course, the latter discourse is used by some in Flanders to defend splitting it along regional lines. The presence of such political tensions complicates policy-making and policy innovation in health care at the federal level. Schokkaert and Van de Voorde (2005) even speak of 'a sword of Damocles' hanging over the legitimacy of the federal government in health policy. The incoherent division of powers between the federal government and the Communities further compounds this. However, to what extent is there policy divergence between the two Communities? Is there divergence of the third order in health policy as we have seen with education? And to what extent does the federal level prevent further divergence?

Policy Divergence in Health Policy at the Community Level

The Flemish and French Communities have different priorities in medical schooling, in their attitude towards a quota restriction of doctors (*numerus clausus*) and regarding the relevance which is attached to preventive medicine. They also have different attitudes vis-à-vis the principle of 'cascading' or *echelonnering* (the requirement or preference to see a general practitioner who acts as a 'gatekeeper' before patients are referred to a specialist). Divergent views also exist with regard to the organisation of the curative sector and the relevance of post-graduate training for doctors and dentists (the latter is more developed in Flanders than in French-speaking Belgium; Ponette 2004). We briefly touch upon each of these aspects.

A first difference stems from the training of medical doctors in medical schools which come under the authority of only one Community, each with considerable freedom (and hence different approaches) in devising medical syllabi (Algemeen Syndicaat voor Geneeskundigen in België 1996). For instance, Van Houdenhove (2001) has argued in *The Lancet* that Walloon and Flemish patients and doctors use different labels to communicate information about distress and ill health. This labelling process is strongly covered by the media. This discrepancy can have an influence on the different ways policies are implemented in the Communities.

Second, Belgium has one of the highest physician/population ratios of the industrialised countries. However, doctors are distributed unevenly across the country. In relative terms, physician density is higher in the French-speaking part of the country (Van Doorslaer *et al.* 2001). Until the mid-1990s, the number of medical practitioners was steadily increasing, putting severe pressure on the average income levels of doctors. However, it took until the end of the 1990s before an attempt was made to restrict the supply of providers under the form of a *numerus clausus* mechanism. This idea had to be implemented in the educational system, however, and schooling is one of the Community competences. The Flemish Community introduced an entrance examination; the French-speaking Community opted for a selection procedure after three years of study. The idea of a *numerus clausus* mechanism has never been generally accepted. This is especially the case in Wallonia because the federal government has formulated the quota in such a way that the existing discrepancy between the north and the south should disappear, but only gradually. Certainly in the short run one should not expect a significant effect of the supply restrictions on health care expenditures (Schokkaert and Van de Voorde 2005).

Third, the Communities are responsible for health promotion and preventive services. The Flemish Community puts much stronger emphasis on preventive care than the French-speaking Community (Vermeulen *et al.* 2001). For instance, the Flemish Community has been active in establishing recent organisations such as the Flemish Health Council (*Vlaamse Gezondheidsraad*), the Flemish Institute for Health Promotion (1991), the local health networks

(LOGOs). Similar types of organisation do not exist in Wallonia. Further-more, only the Flemish government has issued a specific regional law ('decree') in preventive health policy (2003).[4] Further indicators which demonstrate that the prevention idea is more deeply embedded in Flanders are the disproportionally high share of vaccinations and mammograms (Flanders accounts for 75 per cent of the latter; Ponette 2004). First-order change at the Community level, in terms of a greater move to preventive medicine, may thus impact on divergence in curative medicine across the Communities.

Fourth, in Flanders the principle of 'cascading' is applied more widely than in French-speaking Belgium. This emerges when we look at the recent figures documenting medical visits. In 2002, the Flemish Community spent 8 per cent more on doctors' visits than the French Community. In contrast to this, the French-speaking Community spent – in the same year – 14 per cent more on specialist consultations than the Flemish-speaking Community.[5] Moreover, the Global Medical File (a personal file containing each person's medical history kept at a general practitioner's office) is more successful in Flanders than in Wallonia.

Fifth, the Flemish and the French Communities each have their own preferential curative sectors. The French-speaking Community spends 15 per cent more than Flanders on medical radiography, clinical biology, urgency honoraria and internal medicine. Flanders, in turn, spends 15 per cent more than the French-speaking Community on home nursing care, psychiatric hospitals and supported accommodation structures. The use of antibiotics is 30 per cent higher in Wallonia than in Flanders.

We have seen that – despite the fact that health care is mostly a federal matter – there are examples of policy divergence. It is also difficult to align preventive and curative activities because the competences are located at different levels. It is difficult to increase the gatekeeper role of the general practitioner because the idea is less popular in the French than in the Flemish Community. Even a relatively simple measure like the *numerus clausus* for doctors has been implemented differently across both Commu-nities (Schokkaert and Van de Voorde 2005). As a consequence of these differences, the demand for splitting the health care insurance system remains a central theme in Belgian politics.

Explaining Policy Divergence

It is obvious that policy divergence in this policy domain is of a totally different order than policy divergence in education. The decision structure in the Belgian health care system is rather fragmented. It is therefore not easy to deduce the broader policy goal of the decision-makers (Schokkaert and Van de Voorde 2005), which makes it difficult to distinguish whether the policy divergence is a result of the different goals in the two Communities. However, despite the fact that the Communities only have limited competences, it is clear that the (minor) policy changes constitute second- or first-order changes.

There were particular opportunities that triggered and supported a drive for divergence. The fact that a limited number of competences were federalised in 1980 enabled the development of proper Community policies in certain aspects of health policy. Still, even some non-federalised matters were subject to minor change. Now, the major Flemish political parties argue in favour of federalising health care (Palsterman 2005). Despite the fact that Flemish policy entrepreneurs ask for federalisation, two political factors explain the absence of major changes. First, labour unions and the federal employers' organisation have strong incentives to oppose the federalisation of health care, which would deprive them of much of their legitimacy as federal organisations involved in the regulation of social policy and labour relations. Second, the institutional veto point of francophone parties in the federal government as a result of consociational practices there represents a major impediment to federalisation 'because French speakers as a whole view federal social security as vital to the maintenance of their socio-economic status and to the survival of Belgium as a country' (Béland and Lecours 2005; see also Cantillon *et al.* this volume).

Conclusion

The purpose of this article was to compare two policies between the Flemish and French-speaking Communities and to detect to what extent policies converge or diverge. The theoretical considerations about convergence and divergence offer two different perspectives and dynamics for an interpretation of that process, and consequently suggest different outcomes. Our questions were: has policy divergence occurred since federalisation t? If so, in what direction have policies changed and with what intensity? How can one explain intensity and direction of policy divergence and the observed patterns of similarity and variation between two regional political systems in the same national context? These questions were studied in two different policy domains, education and health care, in order to control for the sector-specificity of observed impacts.

Federalisation of education policy in Belgium in 1988 started a process of growing policy divergence. Reforms in the Flemish Community testify to a new view on the role of the state ('the enabling state'), whereas the French Community reproduced the national policy legacy. Political factors are most important to understand this divergence. Political party adaptation appears to be the crucial intervening factor explaining institutional and policy divergence in the case of education policy. Party adaptation creates opportunities for policy entrepreneurs at ministerial level or at a high level in the civil service. Moreover, initial policy changes facilitate further reform as they affect actors' preferences and feasibility assessments of policy alternatives. The combination of these factors emerged in a region-specific manner. Policy divergence was driven by structural features of the new polities combined with more contingent facts, namely policy actors taking advantage of opportunities. Additionally, we should stress that policy divergence should be looked at over a longer period of time and not simply at one specific juncture. The initial changes in Flanders sparked the emergence of new policy alternatives which were previously unthinkable.

Despite the converging pressure from the federal level, there is also some degree of policy divergence between Flanders and French-speaking Belgium in health care policy. Although this case needs further exploration, we can draw some preliminary conclusions. First of all, external events and pressures created the opportunity for health care policy divergence in both Communities. The fact that there are changes, however minor, is not only a consequence of the state structure. Another explanatory variable is that there is party willingness in Flanders, but that there is opposition in Wallonia. As a result of this veto point, more drastic changes are difficult to achieve, a situation perhaps comparable to education policy before 1988. As such, health care represents a major partisan issue. Furthermore, it is a highly polarised theme which is an impediment for divergence.

Notes

1. De Rynck (2002) defines an entrepreneur as a political and social actor who invests his time, resources and reputation in advancing policy change. The essential function of a policy entrepreneur is to link policy solutions to problems. They are the opposite of 'policy brokers' who are more concerned with the system stability than with achieving policy goals (Sabatier 1991).
2. The International Educational Association data on students' performance showed that French Community students performed persistently worse over time in various subjects compared to their Flemish colleagues. More recent surveys (OECD 2004) confirm the large gap between the average student performances in the two regions for several subjects.
3. The regionalisation of social security was an issue for almost all Flemish political parties, except for the Greens (*Groen!*). However, to cite Palsterman (2005: 5): 'La position doctrinale du parti ne préjuge par ailleurs pas de l'importance que la gestion recevra dans l'ordre des priorités, et reste généralement assez vague sur les modalités concrètes de l'opération.'
4. 'Kaderdecreet betreffende het preventieve gezondheidsbeleid, bekrachtigd door de Vlaamse Regering op 21 november 2003', *Belgisch Staatsblad*, 3 February 2004.
5. Answer of Minister R. Demotte on the parliamentary question of Bart Laeremans, Chamber of Representatives, 7 October 2003.

References

Aberbach, Joel A., Bert A. Rockman and Robert D. Putnam (1981). *Bureaucrats and Politicians in Western Democracies*. Cambridge, MA: Harvard University Press.
Algemeen Syndicaat voor Geneeskundigen in België (1996). 'Defederaliseren van de Gezondheidszorg', ASGB-standpunt naar voor gebracht in de hoorzitting van de commissie voor staatshervorming, algemene zaken en verzoekschriften van het Vlaams Parlement op 24 October 1996.
Béland, Daniel, and André Lecours (2005). 'Nationalism, PUBLIC POLICY, and institutional Development: Social Security in Belgium', *Journal of Public Policy*, 23:2, 265–85.
Busch, Andreas (2002). 'Divergence or Convergence? Stage Regulation of the Banking System in Western Europe and the United States', contribution on theories of regulation, Nuffield College, Oxford, 25–26 May 2002.

Busch, Per-Olof, and Helge Jörgens (2005). 'International Sources of Cross-national Policy Convergence – and their Interaction', unpublished Paper, European Consortium for Political Research (ECPR), Granada, Spain.

Callens, Stefaan, and Jan Peers (2003). *Organisatie van de gezondheidszorg*. Antwerpen: Intersentia.

Collier, David, and Richard Messick (1975). 'Prerequisites versus Diffusion: Testing Alternative Explanations of Social Security Adoption', *American Political Science Review*, 69:4, 1299–315.

De Rynck, Stefaan (2002). *Changing Public Policy: The Role of the Regions. Education and Environmental Policy in Belgium*. Brussels: PIE Lang.

De Rynck, Stefaan (2005). 'Regional Autonomy and Education Policy in Belgium', *Regional and Federal Studies*, 15:4, 485–500.

Erk, Jan (2003). '"Wat we zelf doen, doen we beter"; Belgian Substate Nationalisms, Congruence and Public Policy', *Journal of Public Policy*, 23:2, 201–24.

European Observatory on Health Care Systems (2000). *Health Care Systems in Transition: Belgium*. Brussels: WHO European Centre for Health Policy.

Greer, Scott (2005). *Territorial Politics and Health Policy: UK Health Policy in Comparative Perspective*. Manchester: Manchester University Press.

Jordan, Andrew, Rudiger Wurzel and Anthony Zito (2005). 'Convergence and Divergence in New Modes of Environmental Governance in Europe. The Use of Voluntary Agreements in Different Jurisdictions', unpublished paper, European Consortium for Political Research (ECPR), Granada, Spain.

Knill, Christoph (2005). 'Introduction: Cross-national Policy Convergence: Concepts, Approaches and Explanatory Factors', *Journal of European Public Policy*, 12:5, 764–74.

Lowi, Theodore (1964). 'American Business, Public Policy, Case-studies, and Political Theory', *World Politics*, 16, 687–713.

OECD (2004). *Learning for Tomorrow's World, First Results from Pisa 2003*. Paris: OECD.

Onderzoeksgroep Sociale Zekerheid 2002 (1994). *Sociale zekerheid in een federaal België*. Leuven: Acco.

Palsterman, Paul (2005). 'Défédaliser la securité sociale', *CRISP*, 1899, 43.

Pierson, Paul (2000). 'Increasing Returns, Path Dependence, and the Study of Politics', *American Political Science Review*, 94:2, 251–67.

Ponette, Eric (2004). 'Pleidooi voor een integrale Vlaamse Gezondheidszorg', *Secessie*, 15, 22–30.

Richardson, Jeremy (1982). *Policy Styles in Western Europe*. London: Allen & Unwin.

Sabatier, Paul A. (1991). 'Towards Better Theories of the Policy Process', *PS: Political Science & Politics*, 24, 147–56.

Sabatier, Paul A., and Hanke C. Jenkins-Smith (1999). 'The Advocacy Coalition Framework: An Assessment', in Paul A. Sabatier (ed.), *Theories of the Policy Process*. Boulder, CO: Westview Press.

Sabatier, Paul A., and Hanke C. Jenkins-Smith, eds. (1993). *Policy Change and Learning. An Advocacy Coalition Approach*. Boulder, CO: Westview Press.

Samson, Chantal, and Livio Serafini (1997). *Elio di Rupo. De la chrystanthide au papillon*. Brussels: Edition Luc Piré.

Schokkaert, Erik, and Carine Van de Voorde (2005). 'Health Care Reform in Belgium', *Health Economics*, 14, 25–39.

Van Doorslaer, Eddy, J. Buytendijk and José Geurts (2001). 'Income-related Inequalities and Inequities in Health Care Utilisation: Belgium and the Netherlands Compared', *Arch Public Health*, 59, 309–28.

Van Houdenhove, Boudewijn (2001). 'Does Myalgic Encephalomyelitis Exist?', *The Lancet*, 357: 9271, 1899.

Vermeulen, Veerle, Katja Coppens and Katrien Kesteloot (2001). 'Impact of Health Technology Assessment on Preventive Screening in Belgium', *International Journal of Technology Assessment in Health Care*, 17:3, 316–28.

Social Redistribution in Federalised Belgium

BEA CANTILLON, VEERLE DE MAESSCHALCK,
STIJN ROTTIERS and GERLINDE VERBIST

In recent decades, Belgium has been transformed from a unitary into a federal state in which the various Communities and Regions have their own designated areas of competence. In the field of social policy, only social security has remained the responsibility of the central government. However, there have been calls for further federalisation in this area of policy-making. Various arguments have been put forward in favour of such a reform, the most prominent of which is the occurrence of interregional financial transfers and the assumption that these transfers may explain Wallonia's inability to close the socio-economic gap with Flanders. Opponents of further federalisation point out that, among other things, federalisation would result in greater poverty and inequality in Wallonia, a Region that is already disadvantaged in economic terms.

In this contribution we start with an outline of the territorial organisation of social policy in a federalised Belgium. Next, we analyse social transfers between Flanders and Wallonia, focusing on the size and determinants of these transfers. We demonstrate that these transfers have a considerable equalising and anti-poverty effect. In the third section we explore the theoretical arguments for and against federalising social policy in further depth and provide several examples. The last section provides an overview of the discussion and indicates some future policy directions.

The Territorial Organisation of Social Policy in Belgium

As far as the distribution of competences in federal or devolved states in general is concerned, previous research (Poirier and Vansteenkiste 2000; Obinger *et al.* 2005; country-specific studies: on Spain, Moreno and Trelles 2005, Subirats 2005; on the UK, Bulmer *et al.* 2006, Keating 2005, McEwen 2005) has shown that most branches of social security fall within the area of competence of the central authorities. Nonetheless, social policy is increasingly a domain of shared responsibility between various levels of government. While income replacement schemes (unemployment and sickness and invalidity benefits, old age pensions) are mostly a matter for the central government, the regions or states play an important role in cost-compensation schemes (child benefits and health insurance). Moreover, international research has shown that the role of the regions can be greater even in social welfare schemes (see Hölsch and Kraus 2004; Carbonell and Pulido 2004). The Belgian distribution of competences in the field of social policy is broadly consistent with practices in other countries.

In the Belgian federal system, the regions are granted so-called 'assigned' powers, meaning that the Communities and Regions only have power of decision in areas of competence which the constitution or Special Majority Laws have explicitly assigned to them. These assigned powers are laid down in articles 127–140 of the Special Majority Law of 8 August 1980 on institutional reform. The question arises, what impact the Belgian model has had on the division of competences in the field of social policy.[1]

The fundamental changes to the Belgian constitutional structure over recent decades have certainly induced a fragmentation of competences in social policy-making. More specifically, social policy has become a shared responsibility between the various (federal, Regional and Community) governments of the country. Federalising reforms have also generated heterogeneous social policy packages. The Regions are, for example, responsible for important aspects of housing policy (e.g. social housing, rent subsidies) and employment policy (e.g. employment agencies, back-to-work programmes for the unemployed) (see also Leblanc 1990). The Communities, for their part, are competent in so-called person-related matters. These are social services, which involve direct contact between state provider and citizen, such as matters that relate to the health and well-being of those individuals who belong to the respective Communities. Social services include social assistance and large parts of family, health and welfare policy. However, even in these largely federalised competences, the federal government has retained important framework responsibilities, such as the setting of standards for minimum income and assistance to disabled people. Likewise, even though health policy is now a Community matter, social healthcare insurance remains a federal competence. Summarising, the federalisation of Belgium has led to a fragmentation of competences in the field of social policy.

The only social policy area that is still entirely a competence of the federal level of government is the social security system. During consecutive constitutional reforms, social security policy was kept deliberately at the federal level (Cattoir *et al.* 2002; Velaers 1991). The rationale for this decision was the assumption that social security is one of the fundamental instruments for maintaining Belgium's economic and monetary union, that is, for retaining the country's unity. The governing principle is that both income-replacing and cost-covering benefits are a federal competence. This also applies for minimum standards in social assistance (Poirier and Vansteenkiste 2000),[2] although local governments bear a significant share of the costs of this scheme.

With the introduction of the Flemish care insurance system the governing principle of organising interpersonal cash transfers at the federal level has for the first time been abandoned. Under the Flemish care insurance scheme, benefits are awarded to compensate for the costs of non-medical care. It is, in other words, a cost-covering benefit. The French Community deemed this to be a social security scheme and therefore launched an infringement procedure. However, the Court of Arbitration of Belgium overruled this objection. An important part of its argumentation[3] states that, while the Communities are not competent to change the existing social security system (as this is a federal jurisdiction), they can nevertheless develop supplementary schemes if, in terms of content, these tie in with their policy domains. Nevertheless, the fact that the French Community has not stopped challenging the Flemish care insurance scheme indicates that the legal consensus on the division of social competences in Belgium has not been fully accepted.[4]

Next to social security, personal income tax – another important instrument of redistribution – has remained an (almost) exclusive competence of the federal government. The Regions can levy additional assessments or assign tax credits, but this is only possible within certain limits and without touching upon the general progressiveness of personal income taxes (Cattoir *et al.* 2002).

Furthermore, the federal character of both systems also becomes evident in their financing and administrative organisation. Social security contributions and taxes are, after all, collected by a federal body (respectively the National Office for Social Security (of the Self-Employed) and the Federal Public Service Finance). Moreover, these institutions are also responsible for the distribution of the collected means.

With this (almost) exclusive competence in the fields of social security and personal income taxes, the federal government is responsible for by far the most important aspects of income and social redistribution policy in

Belgium. The fact that redistribution is still mainly organised at the highest level generates considerable (indirect) interregional social transfers. These interregional social transfers are the subject of analysis in the next section.

Interregional Transfers within the Belgian System of Social Security

In principle, income redistribution through social security and personal income taxes follows an interpersonal logic. As far as the social security system is concerned, mechanisms of horizontal and vertical solidarity redistribute income between individuals from different risk categories and income groups. As for personal income tax, this redistributes between individuals of different income categories through a system of progressive tax rates, combined with various forms of tax advantages (deductions, allowances, exemptions and credits) (Verbist 2003).

However, in specific situations, the social security and personal income tax systems can also give rise to income redistribution between different regions of the country. To the extent that 1) social risks are unequally distributed between the regions, and/or 2) the capacity to contribute to the collective schemes of social security and income taxes differs strongly between the regions, and/or 3) the different regions have different dominant cultures with regard to the collection and payment of contributions and benefits, the systems of interpersonal redistribution may induce cash transfers between the regions.

For many years, the issue of financial flows between the Belgian Regions has received much attention. Since the 1970s, numerous quantitative studies have been published on such interregional transfers (see among others Van Rompuy and Bilsen 1988, 1993; Dethee 1991; Deleeck *et al.* 1989; Demeester *et al.* 1994; De Boeck and Van Gompel 1998; Van Gompel 2004). Quantitatively, the findings of these studies tend to diverge quite strongly. Nevertheless, they are unanimous in concluding that, for a considerable number of years now, there has been a constant financial flow from the Flemish to the Walloon Region (Deleeck *et al.* 1989) and, since the 1990s, also to the Brussels Capital Region (Van Gompel 2004).

Socio-economic Differences between the Regions

This interregional solidarity follows from important socio-economic differences between Flanders and Wallonia (see Table 1). We focus here mainly on Flanders and Wallonia, since reliable data for Brussels are not

TABLE 1
AVERAGE ECONOMIC GROWTH RATE 1995–2003 (%), BELGIAN REGIONS

Flanders	2.2
Wallonia	1.6

Source: IRES, INR, Regional Accounts, 2005 – Voka.

available; moreover, the debate is mostly about social transfers between these two Regions.

It shows from a comparison of both Regions that Flanders is performing better than Wallonia on a number of socio-economic indicators. For instance, in 2004 the Gross Domestic Product (per capita) of Wallonia amounted to 74 per cent of the GDP of Flanders (Voka 2005). Also the average economic growth rate appears to be much lower in Wallonia than in Flanders: between 1995 and 2003 the average economic growth rate in Wallonia was about 1.6 per cent, compared to 2.2 per cent in Flanders. Moreover, since 1990, the Gross Regional Product has grown in Flanders by 30 per cent against 20 per cent in Wallonia. The average wages are higher in Flanders, but because of higher labour productivity (=GDP per person employed) the labour costs in this region remain 5 per cent below the Walloon level (Table 2).

Flanders is also doing better with respect to labour market performance. Employment rates are considerably higher than in Wallonia (64 per cent compared to 55 per cent – figures for 2004), while the unemployment rates are considerably lower (7.9 per cent versus 19.9 per cent – figures for 2003) (Table 3). As a result of weaker economic and labour market performance Wallonia's primary income per capita is much lower than that of Flanders (Table 4).

TABLE 2
WAGES AND PRODUCTIVITY, BELGIAN REGIONS

Wallonia = 100	GDP/person employed (*labour productivity*)	Wage/person employed (*average wage*)	Labour costs/unit product (*labour costs*)
Flanders	113	107	95
Wallonia	100	100	100

Source: INR, Regionale rekeningen, 2005 (data 2002) – Voka.

TABLE 3
LABOUR MARKET INDICATORS (%), BELGIAN REGIONS

	Employment rate (2004)	Unemployment rate (2003)
Flanders	64.0	7.9
Wallonia	55.5	19.9

Source: Hoge Raad voor de Werkgelegenheid, Annual Report 2004.

TABLE 4
PRIMARY INCOME PER CAPITA, BELGIAN REGIONS

	2003
Flanders	€20,722
Wallonia	€16,535
Brussels	€18,702

Source: Authors' calculations; data INR: regional accounts.

The interregional differences are less obvious with regard to demographic features: both Regions face an ageing population. This trend, however, appears to be more pronounced in Flanders as the share of people aged 65 and over grew faster than in Wallonia over the past decade (by 3 per cent versus 1.7 per cent respectively) (Table 5).

There are, however, significant differences between the northern and the southern parts of the country with respect to life expectancy (Table 6). On average, the life expectancy at birth is two years higher for Flemings than for Walloons. The differences are even more pronounced when life expectancy in good and bad health is considered (Table 7).

These divergences between Flanders and Wallonia are also reflected at the micro-level, namely in the composition of disposable household income. Table 8 presents the level and composition of per capita income in Flanders and Wallonia. Income differences are calculated with respect to the average for Flanders and Wallonia. Differences in disposable income per capita are rather small: 6 per cent in 1997[5] compared to almost 0 per cent in 1985. What is striking, though, is the difference in composition: 64 per cent of

TABLE 5
BASIC INDICATORS OF THE DEMOGRAPHIC SITUATION IN THE REGIONS,
1990–2003

	Population structure (as % of total population)		
	15–64 years	**– 15 years**	**+64 years**
Flanders			
1990	67.9	17.9	14.2
1995	67.0	17.7	15.3
2000	66.3	17.0	16.7
2002	66.0	16.8	17.2
2003	65.9	16.7	17.4
Wallonia			
1990	66.3	18.6	15.1
1995	65.1	18.8	16.1
2000	64.6	18.6	16.8
2002	64.7	18.5	16.8
2003	64.8	18.4	16.8

Source: Van Gompel (2004).

TABLE 6
LIFE EXPECTANCY AT BIRTH IN YEARS, BELGIUM AND ITS REGIONS, 2004

	Men	**Women**	**Men & Women**
Flanders	77.57	82.89	80.27
Wallonia	74.52	81.48	78.04
Brussels	76.29	82.10	79.37
Belgium	76.47	82.36	79.47

Source: Federal Ministry of Economic Affairs – General Directorate Statistics and Economic Information, Section Demography.

TABLE 7

LIFE EXPECTANCY IN YEARS IN GOOD AND BAD HEALTH AT 25, 1991–96/97

	Flemish Region		Walloon Region		Belgium	
	No certificate/ primary education	Higher education	No certificate/ primary education	Higher education	No certificate/ primary education	Higher education
Men						
In bad health	15.6	6.2	21.1	9.5	18.3	8.1
In good health	33.6	47.7	25.1	42.9	29.8	45.2
Women						
In bad health	24.6	10.6	30.8	17.9	26.2	14.5
In good health	30.8	47.8	23.4	39	28.8	43.3

Source: National Action-Plan Social Inclusion 2003–05.

TABLE 8

AVERAGE INCOME PER CAPITA ACCORDING TO INCOME SOURCE, FLANDERS-WALLONIA, 1985–97 (IN EURO PER MONTH)

	1985[1]			1997		
	Flanders	Wallonia	% difference[2]	Flanders	Wallonia	% difference[2]
Total disposable income:	620	620	+7.1	785	740	+5.8
Income from work	420	360	+21.0	505	425	+16.8
Income from social security	170	225	−22.5	225	250	−12.1
Replacement income:	135	190	−24.0	190	220	−12.7
pensions	105	140	−11.7	155	160	−3.2
– pensions non-elderly	25	40	8.7	40	35	10.0
– pensions elderly	75	100	19.0	115	125	−7.4
unemployment	20	25	−80.5	20	35	−56.2
Sickness and invalidity	10	20	−24.9	20	25	−30.3
Child benefits	30	35	−14.4	30	35	−8.6

[1]Figures for 1985 in prices of 1997.
[2]Calculated over the average for Flanders and Wallonia.
Source: SEP-surveys.

disposable per capita income in Flanders is generated through work, with 28 per cent coming from social security, compared to, respectively, 57 and 34 per cent in Wallonia. Thus, the welfare basis is unequal: in 1997, earned income per capita in Flanders was 17 per cent above the average (i.e. €80 per month), whereas in Wallonia social benefits were 12 per cent above the average. These differences in disposable household income are indicative of interregional social transfers, which will be discussed in more detail in the next section.

Size and Determinants of Interregional Transfers

At the macro level, Van Gompel (2004) estimates that, in 2003, transfers from the Flemish Region amounted to €6.6 billion, or 4.2 per cent of Flemish primary income. Around €5.4 billion poured into the Walloon Region, where it constituted 8 per cent of primary income, and €1.2 billion flowed into the Brussels Capital Region, representing 4.3 per cent of primary income there. This total transfer amount of €6.6 billion may be divided into three separate financial interregional flows: 1) the federal budget operations (i.e. the regional distribution of federal receipts and expenditures with respect to those policy fields that remain the exclusive competence of the federal government); 2) social security; and 3) the funding of the Regions (through transfers of a part of federal receipts of personal income taxes and value added taxes). In his study, Van Gompel (2004) defines financial transfers on the basis of the 'fair return' principle: a Region which contributes more in taxes should also benefit relatively more from government expenditures.

An important portion of these flows results from income redistribution through the Belgian social security system (see among others Van Rompuy and Van Bilsen 1988). Although social security flows as a proportion of primary income decreased gradually in Flanders over the 1990s, social security is still the most important source of financial transfers between the Belgian regions: some 57 per cent of total transfers in 2003 are estimated to have originated from social security transfers, whereas federal budget operations and the funding of the regions is thought to have accounted for 23.6 per cent and 19.9 per cent respectively (Van Gompel 2004).

Financial transfers are mainly an expression of the differences in contributory capacities of the Regions and of Regional imbalances in the field of social security. They represent the diversity of the Regions in terms of economic and socio-demographic development (economic growth, population structure, employment, etc.). Although the national regulations apply uniformly to the Regions, differences in demographic, economic or social circumstances as well as divergent behavioural patterns (e.g. with respect to health care) generate *de facto* financial transfers from one Region to another (Deleeck *et al.* 1989). If ability to pay and social risks are unevenly distributed between the Regions, then – from a 'fair return' perspective – social transfers will ensue. This may then be attributed mainly to interpersonal transfers, which are at the heart of social security and personal income taxes (Van Gompel 2004).

At the micro level, we have tried to quantify the possible determinants of interregional transfers (see Deleeck *et al.* 1989 for the methodology). We distinguish three possible factors that may help explain social transfers (Table 9):

a. demographic factors, i.e. differences in age structure and sex; for pensions we also look at family type;
b. number of beneficiaries or income recipients;
c. level of benefits or of income from work.

TABLE 9

CONTRIBUTION OF VARIOUS FACTORS TO THE FLEMISH–WALLOON DIFFERENCE IN SOCIAL SECURITY BENEFITS, 1985–97

	1985				1997			
	Demographic factors	Number of beneficiaries or income recipients	Level of benefits or labour income	Total*	Demographic factors	Number of beneficiaries or income recipients	Level of benefits or labour income	Total*
Labour income	38.3	70.5	-8.8	100	22.4	48.2	29.4	100
Replacement benefits	29.0	39.0	32.0	100 (100)	34.3	39.6	26.1	100 (100)
– unemployment benefits	-11.5	95.2	16.3	100 (15.5)	-5.0	86.4	18.7	100 (54.9)
– sickness and disability	-4.8	69.2	35.5	100 (19.5)	-8.5	116.2	-7.7	100 (23.4)
– pensions for elderly	3.0	54.9	42.1	100 (21.7)	-89.3	226.6	-37.3	100 (-10.6)
– pensions for non-elderly	66.9	-2.8	35.9	100 (43.3)	53.6	-12.9	59.3	100 (32.3)

Source: SEP (1985; 1997).

The various factors sum up horizontally to 100%.

*The figures between brackets and in italic express the contribution of each benefit type to the total difference in replacement incomes between Flanders and Wallonia.

We try to estimate the contribution of each of these factors to the income differences for each income type by using a decomposition analysis. Regional per capita income from a specific source can be calculated as the sum of the weighted incomes per capita within certain categories (for more methodological details on the calculation, see Appendix).

In 1997, more than half of the replacement income gap between the two Regions could be attributed to unemployment benefits (which was much more than the 15 per cent in 1985, see Table 9, last column for each year). The second most influential benefit on the replacement income gap is pensions for the elderly. Also sickness and invalidity benefits contribute positively to the difference, whereas in 1997 pensions for the non-elderly (i.e. early retirement and survival pensions) were more important in Flanders than in Wallonia (in contrast to 1985).

Demographic factors between the two Regions account for 34 per cent of the total variation in replacement incomes, following mainly from the larger number of elderly in Wallonia. The greater number of benefit recipients explains around 39 per cent of the variation, and as this effect is particularly strong among the unemployed and early retired, the cause probably lies in differences in economic development. The discrepancy in benefit level has decreased over the years, but, at 26 per cent, still remains important. The divergence in income from work (and hence the contribution base) is chiefly determined by the number of people at work and by the level of labour income, which also points towards economic factors. The contribution of the level of income from work has increased over the years, whereas the weight of demographic factors has diminished.

To summarise, the major determinant of differences between the two Regions is found in benefits to people of working age: the number of people who do not participate in the labour process for economic or health reasons is larger in Wallonia. Hence, interregional transfers occur under the form of intra-generational solidarity (see also Deleeck *et al.* 1989). For those who promote the federalisation of social security, the existence of these interregional social transfers is an important argument (see Poirier and Van Steenkiste 2000), among other things because it is assumed that today's social transfers may explain Wallonia's inability to close the socio-economic gap with Flanders. On the other hand, opponents argue that a split of social security would lead to more poverty in Wallonia and Brussels and, eventually, in the whole country. This point is analysed in the next section.

Income Inequality

Within the Belgian regions.   Social security benefits have a strong impact on income inequality. Table 10 presents intraregional inequalities for 1985–97, using the traditional Gini measure before and after inclusion of benefits. At the federal level, inequality was reduced by 52 per cent in 1997. The effect was stronger in Wallonia (-55 per cent) than in Flanders (-52 per cent).

Pre-benefit inequality is higher in Wallonia than in Flanders, but thanks to social benefits, inequality levels of disposable income are similar in the two Regions.

Table 11 also includes for 1997 the other steps of the redistributive process, namely social contributions and personal income taxes.[6] Inequality in Wallonia before the entire redistribution process is much higher than in Flanders, however, after redistribution the inequality is almost levelled out. The gap is closed mostly through social security benefits, but personal income taxes also play a significant role. The effect of social contributions on inequality is negligible, due to their mainly proportional structure.

Between the Belgian Regions.   How is inequality between Flanders and Wallonia affected by the redistributive process? To answer this question, we apply here the methodological framework of Ravishankar (2003). Inter-regional redistribution is defined as the percentage reduction in interregional inequality before taxation and transfers thereafter, and calculated by comparing the 'between-group'[7] Theil Index before and after redistribution. Income inequality between Flanders and Wallonia in 1997 was reduced approximately 75 per cent (Table 12; Theil coefficients calculated on the basis of standardised incomes).

TABLE 10
INTRAREGIONAL INEQUALITIES: GINI COEFFICIENTS (STANDARDISED HOUSEHOLD INCOME)

	1985			1997		
	Before	**After**	**% Reduction**	**Before**	**After**	**% Reduction**
Flanders	0.472	0.223	*52.64*	0.491	0.236	*51.91*
Wallonia	0.548	0.226	*58.78*	0.526	0.236	*55.14*
Flanders + Wallonia	0.490	0.211	*56.93*	0.504	0.236	*53.17*

Note: The equivalent household income is calculated by means of the modified OECD scale.
Source: SEP (1985, 1997).

TABLE 11
INEQUALITY REDUCTION THROUGH SOCIAL SECURITY TRANSFERS, EMPLOYEE CONTRIBUTIONS AND PERSONAL INCOME TAXES, FLANDERS AND WALLONIA, 1997

Gini	**Flanders**	**Wallonia**	**Flanders + Wallonia**
Income before taxes and social security contributions and benefits	0.458	0.515	0.478
Income before taxes and social security contributions	0.305	0.324	0.313
Income before taxes	0.293	0.312	0.301
Net income	0.225	0.236	0.230

Source: SEP (1985, 1997).

First-Order Effects of Eliminating Interregional Social Transfers
on Inequality and Poverty

The above calculations indicate that redistribution policies have a considerable impact on both intra- and interregional inequality. We now focus on interregional social transfers in particular and try to demonstrate their effect on inequality and poverty. We use the MISIM microsimulation model to study the impact of the levelling of personal income taxes, social insurance contributions (only employees) and replacement incomes between the two Regions. We include personal income taxes, because they are also an important redistributive instrument in Belgium. The Flemish surplus of social contributions, respectively personal income taxes, is estimated at €20 and €35 per month per capita. The Walloon surplus of income from social security is around €30. In our simulation, taxes, contributions and benefits are levelled across the two Regions in a linear way. In other words, we lower taxes and contributions in Flanders proportionally to the average Walloon level; income from social security in Wallonia, for its part, is lowered proportionally to the Flemish level. This way, we can estimate the redistributive effect of interregional social transfers. As a result of this approach, average household income increases in Flanders by around 7 per cent, whereas it decreases in Wallonia by on average approximately 4 per cent (see Table 13). This translates into a sharp increase in the poverty risk

TABLE 12
INTERREGIONAL INEQUALITIES BETWEEN FLANDERS AND WALLONIA
BEFORE AND AFTER REDISTRIBUTION IN TERMS OF INTER-INEQUALITY
THEIL COEFFICIENTS, 1985–97

	1997
Market income	0.00388
Gross income	0.00141
Taxable income	0.00124
Disposable income	0.00097
Reduction because of redistribution	75%

Source: SEP (1997).

TABLE 13
SIMULATION OF LEVELLING PER CAPITA TAXES AND BENEFITS ACROSS THE
REGIONS

	Flanders		Wallonia		Flanders + Wallonia	
	Present	After levelling	Present	After levelling	Present	After levelling
Average hh. income	100%	107%	100%	96%	100%	103%
Poverty rate	9.7%	9.5%	13.1%	18.3%	10.9%	12.6%
Inequality (Gini)	0.236	0.251	0.236	0.250	0.237	0.254

Source: MISIM-SEP.

in Wallonia from 13 per cent to around 18 per cent. The Gini indicates that such a levelling would lead to greater inequality.

The Optimal Decision-Making Level on Social Redistribution: Key Elements in the Debate

Given the first-order effects of eliminating interregional social transfers from Flanders to Wallonia (see the previous paragraph), we may conclude that social security – from the perspective of social efficiency – should clearly remain a federal matter. This viewpoint is in line with, among other things, the theory of fiscal federalism, according to which social redistribution is best organised at the central level of government.

However, today's massive social transfers may also explain Wallonia's inability to close the socio-economic gap with Flanders. It can be argued that Belgium's uniform social safety net is preventing mobility from Wallonia to Flanders and is stifling economic dynamism in the south. According to this viewpoint, jobseekers from Wallonia have too few incentives to look for work in Flanders, while wage costs in Wallonia are still too high for the region to be able to develop comparative advantages.

Therefore, the federalisation of social security could strengthen efficiency and political legitimacy. The question that arises is what – from the perspective of social equity (poverty reduction) – is the most appropriate level for organising redistribution through social security. In what follows, we consider a number of theoretical perspectives on this matter, though it is not our intention to draw up an inventory of all the arguments that have been put forward. Instead, we shall restrict ourselves to some of the relevant insights drawn from the literature on federalism.

Fiscal Federalism and Comparative Advantages

Conventional economic wisdom suggests that redistribution within a federal system is best organised at the federal level. The basic argument for redistribution at the highest level originates in the observation that there are fundamental constraints on redistribution by lower-level governments, namely labour and capital mobility, resulting in a possible 'race to the bottom' (see among others Tiebout 1956; Oates 1972, 1999; Wildasin 1991, 1994; Peterson 1995).

According to the theory of fiscal federalism, competition between regions makes it impossible to organise a large-scale social redistribution within local territorial units. As, in an open market, labour and capital are mobile, local-level redistribution provides incentives for low-income families to move to states/countries with generous social programmes. Wealthier households will, on the other hand, be inclined to emigrate from these regions because they feel they are bearing the entire burden of redistribution under a system of high taxes and social security contributions (Bertels *et al.* 1994).

Companies, too, may be expected to leave regions where taxes are high. Therefore, regions with generous social protection systems will be confronted with increasing expenditures as well as a narrowing financial base.

In *The Price of Federalism*, Peterson (1995) argues that delegating redistribution, besides welfare mobility, forces each state, or country, into a position in which they compete with each other to be the least attractive to people who need welfare. While local competition might be fine for most other purposes, it is disastrous for welfare policy. Each state, or country, will be racing to downgrade its welfare benefits to repel citizens who rely on public supports for survival. Another reason to consider lowering protection levels is that this could attract high-skilled workers. A 'race to the bottom' could thus be set in motion. Peterson (1995: 128) therefore summarises that 'in a society where both people and business are highly mobile, it makes little sense to leave the marginal cost of welfare provision to lower tiers of government'.

So, according to the theory of fiscal federalism, social redistribution should ideally belong to a higher, (supra)national level. Lower tiers of government, on the other hand, ought to concentrate on economic development policies, including in the fields of education, infrastructure and security. Belgian federalism approximates this ideal: Brussels (like Washington, Berlin and Vienna, for that matter) redistributes through a system of a single, strongly centralised personal income tax, a single social security system and co-financing of social assistance. The Regions or Communities, for their part, concentrate on expenditures for education and economic development.

However, the logic of fiscal federalism does imply that, because of the uniformity of cost of labour and social regulations throughout the federation, possible differences between the regions are artificially sustained. Precisely because of the assumed mobility of labour and capital, and in the absence of social transfers, the socio-economic differences between regions should disappear in the long term, either through labour migration from poor to rich regions, or through the relocation of companies and investments in the opposite direction (Manacorda and Petrongolo 2006). As taxation and social security are primarily a federal matter, and because the formation of wages takes place at the national level, wage differences and variations in wage costs between Flanders and Wallonia are rather marginal. Moreover, one may assume that existing unemployment traps have the effect of limiting the mobility of jobseekers from Wallonia to Flanders (Caruso 2003). The development of comparative advantages and the mobility of labour and capital may thus be hindered by the existence of a universal social protection. The asymmetry that exists in Belgium between the Flemish and the Walloon labour markets may be seen as a confirmation of this assumption. Figures do indeed suggest that interregional housing and labour mobility (two aspects of worker mobility) are rather limited in Belgium. In 2002, interregional housing mobility accounted for only 7 per cent of overall housing mobility, and just one in five of those movements were from Flanders to Wallonia. In 2003, about 14 per cent of all workers in Belgium were employed in a different region than the one in which they lived. The commuting rate was slightly higher in Wallonia (17 per cent) than in Flanders (14 per cent). Thus, the differences have not levelled out over time; quite the opposite, in fact.

The question remains to what extent this is attributable to the existence of a single social security system and the resulting social transfers. After all, there is a lot to be said against the assumption of full mobility of labour and capital. First and foremost, this full mobility assumption presupposes that the economic actors (labour and capital) are well *informed*. However, potential migrants do not have a perfect knowledge of, and insight into, the net benefits they receive in their home country, let alone those they might be entitled to in a given host country. It is, therefore, not self-evident that the economic actors concerned are able to make well-considered choices in relation to the advantages and disadvantages of migration. Possibly, the mobility of labour and capital is hindered by the fact that economic actors are in reality less well informed than assumed in the theory of fiscal federalism. In Belgium, for example, the federalisation of employment services implies that information about job opportunities in other Regions than one's own is rather scarce, since the websites of the Regional employment services advertise very few jobs in other language areas (Caruso 2003).

Second, there may be significant financial/economic, institutional, political and cultural barriers to the mobility of people and companies (Ohlin report 1956; Barnard 2000). Certainly in Belgium, the *cultural divide* between the Regions constitutes a considerable obstacle. Belgium's cultural and linguistic fault-line implies that the cultural attachment of citizens to their own Region – and particularly the fact that a different language is spoken in the other Regions – works as a disincentive to interregional mobility (Caruso 2003). The OECD (2005) also regards the high homeownership rate in Belgium to be an important barrier to labour mobility.

Third, the mobility of labour and capital is in part determined by other factors than cost of labour. Productivity (e.g. thanks to a high-skilled working population), the presence or absence of adequate infrastructure, social peace, trust in government institutions and the like are all elements that may contribute to the attractiveness of a Region. Consequently, a Region where the tax and/or social security burden is on average higher may still be an attractive place to invest.

Because of all these mobility restrictions, it is by no means certain that – as the theory of fiscal federalism predicts – it is impossible to sustain social systems within competing regions, federal states or nations. The development of the social security systems in the member states of the European Union would certainly appear to confirm this. Contrary to the classic economic models, European subsidiarity (with systems of solidarity within relatively small nation states) has proven a much more fertile ground for the development of social security than, for example, the US system of fiscal and social federalism, where social security belongs to the highest federal competence (Cantillon 2004).

Conversely, it is by no means clear to what extent federalising social security would lead to greater capital and labour mobility and thus generate a levelling of regional economic imbalances. After all, the question remains whether a devolved social security system would result in i) diverging social safety nets in the various Regions and, consequently, ii) a substantial reduction in the wage cost in Wallonia. If social security were to be federalised, Wallonia would, theoretically, be able to implement a substantial reduction in its fiscal and parafiscal burden (and thus in the cost of labour). However, politically speaking, such a decision is unlikely, since it would inevitably lead to a dramatic increase in the prevalence of poverty. By European standards, poverty risks in Wallonia are already high and benefit levels relatively low. If, after federalisation, one wanted to retain the present level of social security generosity – which seems a reasonable assumption – contributions in Wallonia would have to increase significantly. For this reason, most Flemish political parties feel that, if such a federalisation of (parts of) the social security system were to be carried through, the solidarity flows from Flanders to Wallonia would have to be retained, though not through a system of interpersonal income redistribution.

The Theory of 'Localness'

However, in addition to the questions raised in relation to the mobility assumption, the perspective of fiscal federalism is also challenged by other theoretical arguments, for which the Belgian case provides some convincing evidence. First, there is the theory of *localness*, which promotes redistribution within smaller, homogenous entities, and thus redistributive activity at lower levels of government. It is argued that, in matters of redistribution, the spatial dimension is important: willingness to redistribute is influenced by the distances within the redistributing population, for reasons of familiarity and efficiency (Pauly 1973). If people feel more strongly that they belong to the same community, they will be more inclined to promote social solidarity. A manifestation of this principle is found in the establishment of the Flemish care insurance system (see also section one). Despite a climate in which the emphasis is on cost containment within the social security system and on reducing the burden of taxation, the Flemish government has nevertheless succeeded, on the basis of a very broad political consensus, in levying a new linear (proportional) contribution.

Second, the theory of fiscal federalism is called into question for *reasons of efficiency*.[8] A first argument in this context is that granting competences (including in relation to social policy and social security) to lower-level public authorities leaves more room for a policy that is adapted to the desires and needs of the various local entities (Jung 2005: 3, Bertels *et al.* 1994: 156). It is, for example, not exceptional for there to be strong differential preferences within a country between such local entities. A decentralised approach would, from this perspective, make it possible to pursue policies that are more closely aligned with the preferences of the regions involved. Moreover, sometimes the socio-economic circumstances of regions can be so divergent that a regionally differentiated socio-economic policy is more desirable. In Belgium, for example, we see that, with regard to unemployment, Flanders wants to focus on low activity rates for the elderly, whereas Wallonia sees the main challenge in youth unemployment (Voka 2005: 7).

A second aspect of the efficiency argument is of a financial nature. Not only may federalisation result in more appropriate policies and better coordinated services at the local level, but the ensuing competition between governments may also result in administrative savings (Jung 2005: 3). From the point of view of a federal state with shared competences, increasing regional fiscal autonomy will result in greater accountability on the part of the regions. In this context, we refer to the current situation in Belgian higher education. While Wallonia has decided to establish a two-year master's programme in the Humanities, the Flemish equivalent will, as a rule, encompass just one year. However, these divergent policy options will have significant financial repercussions for the child benefit system. After all, an additional year of study implies that the students in question will be entitled to a further year of child benefits. As the child benefit system remains a federal matter, the costs associated with this policy option will be borne by the federal authorities, implying that Flanders will have to contribute. In other words, the Walloon government has taken a decision with direct implications for one of the branches of the social security system without having to bear the financial consequences, be it directly or indirectly. A similar situation arises in monitoring the willingness of unemployed persons to work. In Belgium, this is a Regional competence, whereas the financial repercussions of non-work are felt only at the federal level (i.e. the total amount payable in unemployment benefits). The consequences of a less stringent monitoring policy in one Region would thus inevitably have financial repercussions for the other Regions.

A third reason why devolution may be preferable to a centralised social policy relates to the assumption that devolved social policy-making offers a potential for innovation (Jung 2005: 3). This argument stems from the concept of 'laboratories of federalism' (Oates 1999: 1131–4) – or in this case perhaps 'laboratories of social policy' – and was described as follows by James Bryce back in 1888: 'Federalism enables a people to try experiments which could not safely be tried in a large centralised country.'[9] Recent developments in Spain in the field of social policy illustrate this quite well. Seven Spanish regions display high levels of discursive and operative innovation (Catalonia, Galicia, Murcia, Madrid, Navarre, the Basque Country and La Rioja) and six regions exhibiting 'median innovation' (Subirats 2005). On the basis of the Spanish case, Moreno and Trelles (2005: 519) argue that '[t]here is certainly a case for sub-state units to become "laboratories of democracy". It has been claimed that the payoff from innovation exceeds the advantages of uniformity and policy diffusion'. Furthermore, both authors put forward the general criterion that 'the greater the need for innovation (for example a "new" problem or solution), the greater is the rationale for that function to be provided by the sub-state government' (Moreno and Trelles 2005: 519). An example of such policy innovation in Belgium was implemented by the Flemish Minister of Labour. He introduced a new plan to (re)activate mainly low-skilled young unemployed persons (Vandenbroucke 2006). This plan, which leans heavily on a collaboration with local authorities, is currently being tested in 14 cities, and interim results suggest it is a great success.

A final aspect of the 'efficiency' argument concerns the danger of cost accumulation. If the distribution of powers between the various public authorities is not adequately defined or if it leaves room for interpretation, there is a danger that authorities, in their pursuit of greater power and electoral success, might try to compete with one another in providing more and better social programmes. In Belgium, we see that divergences between the Flemish and the Walloon perspectives on the optimal distribution of competence in social security have indeed resulted in unfortunate cost increases (Cantillon 2005). One example in this respect is found in elderly care: in Flanders, a new care insurance system has been established, while at the federal level existing social assistance benefits for care for the elderly have been substantially increased.

Conclusion: Federalisation of Social Policy – But How and How Much?

The federalisation of Belgium has in many respects produced a fragmentation of competences. This has also been the case in the field of social policy, where different policy areas (such as employment, education, health, well-being) have become shared between different levels of government. This results from the fact that just one aspect of Belgian social policy has remained a responsibility of the federal government, namely interpersonal income redistribution through social security contributions and personal income tax. Social security and taxation both work horizontally and they touch, directly or indirectly, upon the competences of the Regions (employment/unemployment benefits) and/or the Communities (child benefit/family and educational policy; health insurance/health prevention; care benefits/social well-being policy).

Because of the large socio-economic differences between the Regions of Belgium, as well as their distinct cultural and behavioural characteristics, these systems of interpersonal redistribution induce interregional cash transfers. In Flanders, per capita contributions are greater than per capita receipts, while in Wallonia the reverse is true. The systems of social security and personal income taxes reduce income inequality between Flanders and Wallonia by about 75 per cent.

Some proponents of further devolution cite these social transfers as a reason for splitting the social security system. Others believe that federalising social security would increase poverty in Wallonia and Brussels. Indeed, our simulation demonstrated that halting social transfers from Flanders to Wallonia would dramatically increase the poverty rate in Wallonia in the short term (from 13 per cent to 18 per cent).

The first-order effects of eliminating interregional social transfers between Flanders and Wallonia suggest that social security – from the perspective of social efficiency – ought to remain a federal competence. This also ties in with the theory of fiscal federalism, according to which social redistribution is best organised at the central level of government. The underlying notion is that social redistribution will be pressurised if it is organised at a lower tier of government, because of labour and capital mobility.

However, the logic of fiscal federalism conversely implies that, given that wage costs and social regulations are uniform throughout the federation, possible differences in the economic dynamism between regions will be artificially maintained. In Belgium, the development of comparative advantages and the mobility of labour and capital may be impeded by the prevailing system of universal social protection. The latter argument is heard increasingly often in the debate on the position of social security within Belgian federalism. The question is, however, to what extent federalising the social security system will lead to diverging social safety nets in the regions and a substantial reduction in the cost of labour in Wallonia. Theoretically, a devolved social security system would allow Wallonia to cut taxes and social security contributions (and thus to reduce the cost of labour). As such a measure would inevitably lead to a dramatic increase in poverty, it would appear to be an unlikely political option.

On the other hand, there are good arguments in favour of extended regional competences within a single federal social security system. Principles such as *localness* (close-knit solidarity), *suitability* (the fact that regions have different needs and preferences) and *efficiency* (the fact that accountability will result in cost saving and that a smaller territorial scope creates more room for policy innovation) suggest that federalising social policy further may generate better outcomes. The Belgian case provides some important examples in this respect.

With regard to the future, it is therefore essential that the Belgian social security system should be integrated into a mature social federalism. Social security, as an instrument of interpersonal redistribution, should remain a federal competence. However, the regions should be made fully aware of their financial accountability for federalised policy strategies. Secondly, all Community competences touching directly or indirectly upon the federal social security system should be the subject of consultation between the competent authorities. Thirdly, where appropriate, the regions should be granted competence over certain social security resources (e.g. child benefits for students) – to be allocated to the Communities using a well-considered distribution code – so that they could be spent in accordance with local needs. In view of the major socioeconomic differences between the Communities and the growing policy divergences in the fields of labour, care and education, it is necessary to align the various policy levels more closely. Europe's approved 'Open Method of Coordination', whereby common objectives are formulated, indicators defined and policy strategies exchanged, could serve as a useful example in this respect.

Appendix: Calculation of the Determinants of Interregional Transfers

Income per capita in region G Y_{pc}^{G} can be written as:

$$Y_{pc}^{G} = \frac{Y^{G}}{N^{G}} = \sum_{i=1}^{n} \left(\frac{N_{i}^{G}}{N^{G}} \sum_{j=1}^{m} \left(\frac{N_{ij}^{G}}{N_{i}^{G}} \frac{Y_{i}^{G}}{N_{ij}^{G}} \right) \right)$$

with Y^{G} = total income mass in region G
   N^{G} = number of individuals in region G
   N_{i}^{G} = number of individuals in category i in region G
   N_{ij}^{G} = number of income recipients in category i in region G
   Y_{i}^{G} = total income mass in category i in region G

We apply this formula to the various income types (income from work; replacement incomes, consisting of unemployment benefits, sickness and disability benefits, pensions, both for elderly and non-elderly). We also calculate the same formula, but under the hypothesis that the national distribution of the various categories applies in the two Regions (with 'national' being Flanders and Wallonia together. We replace the demographic distribution, the proportion of recipients per category and the income level in the regions with their national averages. The contribution of a specific factor to the total difference between Flanders and Wallonia ($Y^{F} - Y^{W}$) can then be written as:

$$\frac{(Y^{F} - Y^{W}) - (Y^{F^*} - Y^{W^*})}{(Y^{F} - Y^{W})}$$

where Y^{F^*}, resp. Y^{W^*}, represents nationally weighted per capita income for Flanders, resp. for Wallonia. This provides a measure for the contribution of a certain factor to the overall difference between Flanders and Wallonia, by estimating how much the difference would decrease if the respective demographic composition, number of benefit recipients and benefit level were the same in the two Regions.

   This measure is unfortunately not independent from the order in which the various factors are taken into account. We have chosen to change the most deterministic factor first, demographic characteristics, and we end with arguably the least deterministic, benefit level (we have performed the calculation in a different order, and the broad patterns remain the same).

Notes

1. Social policy is used here in the broadest sense and is defined as government interventions aiming to maintain, create or change citizens' social conditions of existence and development in relation to general well-being (Deleeck 2003: 290). The most important policy areas in this context are education, housing, income security, working conditions and health provisions.
2. With respect to this last area, it is however worth noting that the communities can grant complementary assistance (Poirier and Vansteenkiste 2000).
3. §B.3.9.3., Case 33/2001 of 13 March 2001, Court of Arbitration of Belgium.
4. See Case 8/2003 of 22 January 2003, and Case 51/2006 of 19 April 2006, Court of Arbitration of Belgium and Judgment 157.168 of 30 March 2006, Supreme Administrative Court of Belgium. Case 51/2006 of 19 April 2006 is still open: 3 prejudicial questions have been put to the European Court of Justice.
5. Unfortunately, at the time of our analysis, more recent data were not available. We plan to update these calculations in the future.
6. As social contributions and personal income taxes are not available in the dataset, they have been calculated by means of the micro simulation model MISIM. MISIM was developed at the Centre for Social Policy (Verbist 2003) and calculates the effect of specific policy measures (i.e. tax-benefit policies) on individual households, using a representative sample of the population.
7. The subgroups correspond with the Belgian regions.
8. It is worth recalling that efficiency, particularly in relation to the organisation of solidarity, is also the leading principle in the fiscal federalism theory, which promotes more central social policy-making.
9. James Bryce in *The American Commonwealth* (1880), cited in Oates (1999: 1132).

References

Barnard, Catherine (2000). 'Regulating Competitive Federalism in the EU? The Case of EU Social Policy', in Jo Shaw (ed.), *Social Law and Policy in an Evolving European Union*. Oxford and Portland, OR: Hart Publishing, 49–69.
Bertels, Jan, Wim Cocquyt, Bart Dierick, Guy Joosten and Anja Vanrobaeys (1994). *Juridisch onderzoek naar de financiële transfers in de sociale zekerheid*. Deel II. Leuven: Acco.
Bulmer, Simon, Martin Burch, Patricia Hogwood and Andrew Scott (2006). 'UK Devolution and the European Union: A Tale of Cooperative Asymmetry?', *Publius: The Journal of Federalism*, 36:1, 75–93.
Cantillon, Bea (2004). *Tussen federalisme en subsidiariteit: de weg naar sociaal Europa*. Brussel: Koninklijke Vlaamse Academie van België voor Wetenschappen en Kunsten.
Cantillon, Bea (2005). 'Est-elle encore sociale et securisante? Reflexions sur l'avenir de la securité sociale en Belgique', *Revue belge de sécurité sociale*, 4, 719–38.
Caruso, Frédéric (2003). 'Spanningen en Inadequaties in België', *Sociaal-Economische Nieuwsbrief*, 78:1, 3–26.
Carbonell, Jesus Ruiz-Huerta, and Jose M. Diaz Pulido (2004). 'Decentralization of Old-Age Benefits in Spain: Lessons from Other Federal Countries', unpublished paper presented at the EISS Conference, Rome.
Cattoir, Philippe, Philippe De Bruycker, Hugues Dumont, Henry Tulkens and Els Witte, eds. (2002). *Autonomie, solidariteit en samenwerking: enkele belangen van het Belgisch federalisme in de 21ste eeuw*. Brussels: Larcier.

De Boeck, Johan Van Gompel (1998). 'Financiële stromen tussen de Belgische gewesten opnieuw bekeken', in Chistine Vanderveeren and Jef Vuchelen (eds.), *Een Vlaamse fiscaliteit binnen een economische en monetaire unie.* Antwerp: Insertia Rechtswetenschappen, 213–33.

Deleeck, Herman (2003). *De architectuur van de welvaartsstaat opnieuw bekeken. Herziene en geactualiseerde uitgave onder leiding van Bea Cantillon en Natascha Van Mechelen.* Leuven: Acco.

Deleeck, Herman, Lieve De Lathouwer and Karel Van den Bosch (1989). 'Regional Differences in the Distribution of Social Security Benefits in Belgium: Facts and Causes', *Cahiers Economiques de Bruxelles*, 123:3, 265–310.

Demeester, Nico, Régine Yvergneaux and Paul Van Rompuy (1994). *Normatieve en macro-economische analyse van de interregionale stromen in de sociale zekerheid, Vlaamse Onderzoeksgroep Sociale Zekerheid 2002.* Leuven: Acco.

Dethee, M. (1991). 'Regionale analyse van de Sociale Zekerheid 1985–89', in Herman Deleeck (ed.), *Sociale Zekerheid en federalisme.* Bruges: Die Keure, 47–95.

Hoge Raad voor de Werkgelegenheid (2004). *Verslag 2004.* Brussel: FOD Werkgelegenheid, Arbeid en Sociaal Overleg.

Hölsch, Katja, and Margit Kraus (2004). 'Poverty Alleviation and the Degree of Centralization in European Schemes of Social Assistance', *Journal of European Social Policy*, 14:2, 143–64.

Jung, Saskia (2005). 'When do Political Actors Agree to Shifts of Social Program Responsibilities in Federal Systems? Selected Social Policy Reforms in Canada and Germany since 1995', unpublished paper presented at the Third Annual ESPAnet Conference, 'Making Social Policy in the Postindustrial Age'.

Keating, Michael (2005). 'Policy Convergence and Divergence in Scotland under Devolution', *Regional and Federal Studies*, 39:4, 453–63.

Leblanc, Simon (1990). *La federalisation de la sécurité sociale.* Brussel: CRISP.

Manacorda, Marco, and Barbara Petrongolo (2006). 'Regional Mismatch and Unemployment: Theory and Evidence from Italy, 1977–98', *Journal of Population Economics*, 19:1, 137–62.

McEwen, Nicola (2005). 'The Territorial Politics of Social Policy Development in Multi-level States', *Regional and Federal Studies*, 15:4, 537–54.

Moreno, Luis, and Carlos Trelles (2005). 'Decentralization and Welfare Reform in Andalusia', *Regional and Federal Studies*, 15:4, 519–35.

Oates, Wallace E. (1972). *Fiscal Federalism.* New York: Harcourt Brace Jovanovich.

Oates, Wallace E. (1999). 'An Essay on Fiscal Federalism', *Journal of Economic Literature*, 37:3, 1120–49.

Obinger, Herbert, Stephan Leibfried and Francis Castles (2005). *Federalism and the Welfare State. New World and European Experiences.* Cambridge: Cambridge University Press.

OECD (2005). *Employment Outlook.* Paris: Organisation for Economic Cooperation and Development.

Ohlin report (1956). *Les aspects sociaux de la coopération économique européenne, Rapport d'un groupe d'experts.* Genève: Bureau international du Travail.

Pauly, Mark V. (1973). 'Income Redistribution as a Local Public Good', *Journal of Public Economics*, 2:February, 35–58.

Peterson Paul E. (1995). *The Price of Federalism.* Washington, DC: The Brookings Institution.

Poirier, Johanne, and Steven Vansteenkiste (2000). 'Het debat over federalisering van de sociale zekerheid in België: spiegel van de wil tot samenleven?', *Belgisch tijdschrift voor Sociale Zekerheid*, 42:2, 337–87.

Ravishankar, Nirmala (2003). 'Regional Redistribution: Applying Data from Household Income Data', LIS working paper 347.

Subirats, Joan (2005). 'Social Exclusion and Devolution among Spanish Autonomous Communities', *Regional and Federal Studies*, 15:4, 471–83.

Tiebout, Charles (1956). 'A Pure Theory of Local Expenditure', *Journal of Political Economy* 64:5, 416–24.

Vandenbroucke, Frank (2006). '"Samen voor Meer Banen": een Vlaams meerbanenplan'. Policy document, Office of the Flemish Minister of Work, Education and Training, 16 January 2006.

Van Gompel, Johan (2004). 'Financiële transfers tussen de Belgische gewesten', mimeo.
Van Rompuy, Paul, and Valentijn Bilsen (1988). 'Tien jaar financiële stromen tussen de Gewesten', *Leuvense Economische standpunten*, no. 45.
Van Rompuy, Paul, and Valentijn Bilsen (1993). 'Regionalisering van de sociale zekerheid', *Leuvense Economische standpunten*, no. 68.
Velaers, Jan (1991). 'Sociale zekerheid tussen unionisme en federalisme', in Herman Deleeck (ed.), *Sociale Zekerheid en federalisme*. Brugge: Die Keure, 47–95.
Verbist, Gerlinde (2003). 'MISIM, een microsimulatiemodel voor personenbelasting en sociale zekerheid', *Economisch en Sociaal Tijdschrift*, 57:3, 221–48.
Voka (Voka – Chambers of Commerce and Industry in Flanders) (2005). 'Op zoek naar een nieuwe Waalse én Vlaamse dynamiek'. Policy document.
Wildasin, David E. (1991). 'Income Redistribution in a Common Labour Market', *American Economic Review*, 81:4, 757–74.
Wildasin, David E. (1994). 'Public Pensions in the EU: Migration Incentives and Impacts', in Arvind Panagariya, Paul R. Portney and Robert Schwab (eds.), *Environmental Economics and Public Policy: Essays in honour of Wallace E. Oates*. Cheltenham: Edward Edgar Publishers.

The European Rescue of the Federal State: How Europeanisation Shapes the Belgian State

JAN BEYERS and PETER BURSENS

One of the major puzzles for contemporary political science is how and to what extent states centralise competences or, on the contrary, shift powers to local, regional, European or international arenas. In this respect, Belgium has been subject to two developments over recent decades. On the one hand, a large number of competences have been transferred to the European level, while, on the other hand, the reform of the Belgian state has led to sub-units with a substantial portfolio of policy competences, including foreign relations. Few other states went through such extensive reforms. This process can be seen as an attempt to adjust the scale of government to reflect better Belgium's political and cultural heterogeneity. At the same time, Belgium became intensively involved in and supportive of the process of European integration. Today it participates fully in all policy areas, including the monetary union, the Schengen Agreements and the emerging common defence policy. Belgium's integration into the European Union can be considered as an attempt to create policy-making venues that increase the territorial scope of market exchange. In sum, the combination of federalisation and European integration results in a system of multilevel governance (MLG) which satisfies two seemingly contradictory considerations, i.e. coping with heterogeneity while at the same time reaping the benefits of an expanded economic market.

This article deals with the impact of EU membership on the Belgian federal polity. How did Belgium adapt to the requirements of its membership of the EU and did this process of adaptation transform Belgian federalism? In particular we substantiate two propositions:

1. European integration forces the governments of regions and communities, and the central government to cooperate. To this end, specific institutional structures are created which enable cooperative practices in day-to-day politics. This trend towards cooperative modes of governance contrasts with the constitutional duality of the Belgian federation.
2. European integration prevents the central government from disappearing. On the contrary, instead of contributing to the hollowing out of the federal level, European integration keeps the federal government and the federal policy-making arena at the centre in some key policy areas.

These two propositions fit into a broader concern with the erosion of central state governments as a result of European integration. Is central state control eroding? Is it true that the regions are strengthened by the process of European integration, that the powers of central governments are incrementally hollowed out, and that over time central governments become an empty shell? We submit that Belgium is a critical case in this respect. If there is one state in which multi-levelness and policy fragmentation are pushed to their extremes, it is Belgium. Yet, in contrast to some writings on this topic, we argue that, despite the increased involvement of regions in European policy-making, despite a large set of devolved competences and despite some cross-border associations of regions within Europe, the political authority of regions remains fairly encased in national or federal arenas.

We frame our research questions and hypotheses within two research agendas: Europeanisation and comparative federalism. Firstly, they fit in the Europeanisation literature as this research agenda deals with how member state structures can be operationalised given the impact of European integration on domestic institutional relations (Ladrech 1994; Goetz 2000; Olsen 2002; Vink 2003; Mair 2004; Graziano and Vink 2006). Europeanisation research can be roughly divided into studies on the impact of European integration on domestic polities, politics and policies. Here, we focus on the politics and polity dimensions: how does the EU level (in interaction with domestic developments) lead to changes in the formal procedures and institutional conditions in different policy areas such as agriculture, environment, social policies and European integration? All these areas are expected to respond to what Goetz (2000) calls 'linkage-adaptation': as governments become more and more implicated in European policy-making, they are expected to adapt their domestic policy-making modes (see also Beyers and Trondal 2004). In addition to the Europeanisation research agenda, our research problem will be situated in the literature on federalism. Such a broader institutional angle is needed in order to avoid the *sui generis* discourse which tends to infect contemporary Europeanisation literature.

The following section presents how we conceptualise our puzzle. In the third part, we turn to the empirical evidence. We present a general overview of how the Belgian federation copes with European policies, and we describe the involvement of the Belgian Regions and Communities in European policies and the domestic coordination mechanisms. Finally, through a comparison of different policy areas we show that the Belgian Regions and Communities are pivotal in some key policy areas (such as environment policies and agriculture policies), but that their role in other policy areas is much more limited (for instance social welfare state policies and European treaty reform). Nonetheless, even in those areas where Regions or Communities are crucial, they are – partly due to EU-level restrictions which reinforce existing interdependencies among the different Belgian levels – unable to act as fully-fledged EU-level players in their own right. We will show that regions often need the federal policy-making arena to put their European policies in practice.

The Europeanisation of Federal Institutional Arrangements

Looking at the Europeanisation literature, one is immediately struck by the abundance of contradictory conclusions and the imprecise assessment of the impact Europe has on domestic polities and the concrete mechanisms at play. Authors often arrive at contradictory conclusions, sometimes even for the same member states. Schmidt (1999: 6), for instance, argues that the EU has greater impact on unitary (and statist) states than on federal (and corporatist) states, because the latter 'have largely maintained the balance between executive, legislature and judiciary as well as between center and periphery'. Other authors, however, have noted a substantial impact on federal states as well. Reflecting in a comparative way on the impact on federal states, Kassim (2005) argues that especially strong, so-called constitutional regions were successful in using the EU to strengthen their position vis-à-vis the federal level. With respect to Spain, Börzel (1999) claims that this country has evolved from a system of competitive regionalism to a system of cooperative or joint federalism because the EU encourages cooperation between the central and regional government levels (for a different view on Spain see Bourne 2003). In contrast, Börzel (1999) argues that in Germany domestic coordination mechanisms merely reflect the existing cooperative institutional setting. Jeffery (2003: 102), also discussing Germany, claims that core features of its cooperative federalism are under increasing European pressure.

Following Börzel (1999: 578) we envisage two basic processes which help to conceptualise the changing balance between central state and regional authorities in a European context. On the one hand, regions can adopt a cooperative strategy which entails that different levels within member states start sharing European policy competences and responsibilities. This intra-state adaptation implies that regions remain hierarchically nested within a domestic institutional framework. This practice resembles what Hooghe and Marks (2003) call type-I MLG or what Jeffery (2000: 4–6) characterises as mobilisation through the existing member state structures. On the other hand, there is a strategy whereby regional authorities separate themselves from the central government by increasingly bypassing or acting beyond the existing member state structures (Jeffery 2000: 4–6). While Börzel labels this as a confrontational strategy, we prefer to call it a separating strategy as 'confrontation' suggests severe and visible conflict among the different levels. Although political confrontations may coincide with a separating strategy, we can also imagine that gradually and incrementally regional authorities maximise their autonomous leverage and that levels of government become increasingly disconnected from each other without major or visible institutional conflicts. If this form of adaptation starts to dominate the EU and its member states, we would experience practices resembling type-II MLG of dispersed, non-hierarchical and autonomous venues of policy-making (Hooghe and Marks 2003). Then the question for this article becomes which adaptation strategy – a separating or a cooperative strategy – can we expect in a member state such as Belgium?

At first sight, there are good reasons to expect a general trend towards a confrontational strategy among the Belgian Regions and Communities. Such an adaptation process would fit nicely in the dual nature of the Belgian federation; the constituent entities of the Belgian federation have exclusive legislative and administrative powers within their jurisdiction. In contrast to the model of cooperative federalism, which prevails in countries such as Austria and Germany, the Belgian regions hardly have to bother about uniform standards imposed by a central government. The non-hierarchical nature of the Belgian federation allows and stimulates autonomous and independent policy-making. In addition to its dual structure, the Belgian federation is characterised by competitiveness. The Belgian federal order is designed in order to protect the rights of ethnic-national and linguistic minorities. Constitutionally, it aims to preserve regional identities and to promote cultural, economic and social diversity. This implies that in its origins the Belgian system is non-cooperative, competitive and centrifugal, in contrast to the German cooperative federal order in which the uniformity of living conditions is constitutionally enshrined.

Another seemingly obvious reason for the likelihood of separating strategies concerns the interaction between EU politics and the division of domestic competences. The more extensive the regional competence cata-logue, the more likely that a region will be affected by EU policy-making. The idea is that, because European institutions create policies which affect the regional tier of government, EU-level rent-seeking behaviour by regional governments will be stimulated (Marks *et al.* 1996). Moreover, especially regions with extensive competences have a strong base from which they can mobilise. They are therefore more likely to shift their political strategies to the European level (Jeffery 2000: 12–15). Consequently, Europeanisation pressures will be uneven and member states will not converge in their adaptation to the EU. Especially heterogeneous member states – which are often regionalised or federal states – are expected to face most adaptation pressures. In these states, local and regional levels become more vocal and try to strengthen their position at the expense of the central government. This idea fits into a more general argument made by Europeanisation scholars who claim that European integration leads to a strengthening and a mobilisation of regions to the disadvantage of central governments (Kassim 2005).

The arguments in favour of the separating hypothesis rely strongly on the notion of a strict division of exclusive powers which creates autonomous levels within the Belgian polity. However, autonomy is never absolute. Several contextual factors stimulate the sharing of competences in dual federations and the emergence of cooperative political practices (Thorlakson 2003). This happens when constitutions allocate similar functions to different political levels and create mixed competence catalogues, when constitutions do not unambiguously assign policy areas or when political levels lack sufficient or proper means to fulfil their functions. As Swenden and Jans (this volume) illustrate for the Belgian case, sorting out policy areas into watertight compartments was a precarious undertaking in Belgium and led to the installation of various cooperation mechanisms (and see Swenden 2004: 197–8). Instead of multiplying separate territorial jurisdictions, policy-makers attempt to constrain the number of territorial jurisdictions by keeping the European access of regions under control and by introducing domestic cooperative devices. Policy-makers systematically circumvent and complement the dual formal nature of the Belgian polity with the creation of new formal and informal links, resulting in what Benz and Eberlien (1999: 333) call a 'hierarchical-sequential ordering of arenas of policymaking'. Without such cooperative devices, regions and the central government would not be able to cope with over-complexity, conflicting operating logics and excessive transaction costs which result from ambiguous and incomplete constitutions. In addition, the dual and competitive nature of the Belgian polity contrasts with the cooperative nature of the European system of governance where competences are shared rather than divided (Hix 1998; Börzel and Risse 2000; Börzel and Hosli 2003; Börzel 2005).

We conclude that our policy areas will illustrate that the EU institutional framework is a contextual factor with substantial implications for the formation of and development in Belgian federal institutional arrangements. In general, domestic adaptation to EU membership implies an advantage for central authorities because especially the central government occupies a gate-keeping position between Europe and the domestic level. In some areas, the central government and the regional governments institutionalise and centralise their intergovernmental cooperation devices at the federal level. These domestic intergovernmental arrangements considerably increase the grip of the regional governments on the central government without necessarily provoking separating or bypassing strategies. In short, the inter-action between domestic federalisation and European integration results in a somewhat paradoxical situation in which regions become dominant power-centres and veto-players, while at the same time the federal level gradually develops into a key policy-making arena (Thorlakson 2003: 17).

Finally, and parallel with our two main propositions, we expect that European adaptation strategies are not uniform within single member states and that especially federal states embody a complex mixture of adaptation strategies. Whereas in unitary states or single-level polities one level may specialise in all areas, in a multi-level system each level functions as a separate niche for specific policy areas and issues. In multilevel systems different levels specialise in different policy areas. One important repercus-sion is that adaptation strategies may vary according to the policy areas in which different governments are specialised. Following the argument described above, we expect therefore that cooperative strategies will prevail more in areas where regions have many capabilities (formal powers, budgetary resources, expertise) and that cooperation will be less relevant in areas where the capabilities of regions are limited. The notion that those who are responsible for specific policy areas are more active in EU rent-seeking behaviour echoes much of the Europeanisation literature, which often claims that different sectors face different adaptation pressures and therefore Europeanise in different ways. Many Europeanisation studies are primarily concerned with policies (for instance how member states adapt their domestic legislation) and consider polity and politics as contextual or background variables (Bursens 2006). However, the Europeanisation literature often arrives at contradictory conclusions because sectoral variation within a polity is not always systematically taken into account. Therefore, we aim to clarify the development of the Belgian federal arrangements by cross-fertilising it with insights from different policy areas.

Central Government versus Sub-states in the Belgian Polity: General Patterns

Formally, the Belgian federation can be characterised as a dual federal system, which implies the exclusive allocation of legislative and adminis-trative powers. Following from this is the gradual constitutionalisation of the *in foro interno, in foro externo* principle. The 1988 state reform introduced this for personally bound community competences (such as language, culture, education), the 1993 reform expanded the principle to regional competences. The *in foro interno, in foro externo* principle gives the Regions and the Communities the right to conduct foreign policies – that is, to conclude and ratify treaties, to represent itself, etc. – within the areas where they are domestically competent. At first sight, one could argue that this principle is a clear feature of a dual competitive federal system; sub-units gain full powers, including foreign policies, in their areas of competence. However, this principle is also one of the clearest examples of how cooperative mechanisms slipped into the dual federal system and balanced its competitive nature. In practice, this principle strengthens the need for cooperation among the regions as well as between the regions and the central government. Why is this so?

First of all, international treaties and international organisations often cover policy areas with a mixed character inside Belgium. The Treaty on European Union (TEU) is, of course, an obvious example, but also the treaties establishing the World Trade Organization, the World Bank, the Organization of Economic Cooperation and Development and the Council of Europe are mixed treaties as they cover composites of areas in which both the regions and the central government have competences (for instance industrial policy, transport, environment and trade). While domestically policy-makers separated jurisdictions and competences, the international environment tends to reconnect these. In addition, because few international organisations or third countries recognise single regions as treaty-making entities, it is practically impossible for regions to conduct their foreign policies completely independent from the federal level. On top of these international constraints, domestic constitutional and administrative provisions oblige regions to use the federal diplomatic network when they conduct their foreign policies. Regions have own foreign representatives, but these officials are integrated and operate within the federal diplomatic network which is still controlled by the federal Foreign Ministry (for an overview see Criekemans 2001). All this triggers cooperative behaviour between regions and the central government and transforms the federal arena into an inter-federal network of regional and federal officials.

More specifically, the fact that several European competences belong to the competence sphere of the Belgian regions is an important factor for Belgium. During the 1980s EU-level supranational institutions gained regulatory competences in policy areas (e.g. the Single European Act) that were domestically transferred to the newly created Belgian Regions and Communities. Environmental policy is one of the most obvious examples. Because of the almost exclusive allocation of powers and because of the absence of a legal norm hierarchy within Belgium, European regulations have to be implemented in many of these areas by the regions or communities and not by the central government. Thus, while Regions and Communities gained sometimes exclusive policy competences, they lost major parts these powers almost immediately because of the continuing process of European integration. Here, we are confronted with a clear institutional misfit between the European and the Belgian polity.

Before dealing with the internal situation, we first need to discuss one specific EU-level institutional development that stimulated the trend towards more cooperation within Belgium. Before 1992, article 146 EEC stipulated that the EU Council of Ministers could only consist of members from national governments and that only national ministers could vote. Anxious to secure their constitutional prerogatives, the German *Länder* and the Belgian Regions and Communities mobilised during the 1991 Intergovernmental Conference (IGC) in order to change this system. At this IGC, the Belgian and the German delegations asked a revision of article 146 EEC into the new article 203 TEU, while the French delegation demanded a guarantee that each member state representative would bind the national state as a whole and not only parts of it. The new article 203 TEU became a compromise between these two concerns. Firstly, it allowed regional ministers to be actively present in the Council meetings. In this sense, it is innovative as it acknowledges that central governments are not necessarily the competent interlocutors at the European level. However, at the same time, each representative in the Council must act as a unitary actor representing the policy position of the member state as a whole and independent from the constitutional status the member state representative enjoys domestically (Franck *et al.* 2003: 73; Kovziridze 2002: 136).[1] In this sense the European institutional order confirms a traditional principle of international law implying that states act in a unitary way at the international level.

Nevertheless, article 203 TEU has substantial consequences for domestic politics in the sense that domestic regional and central authorities are stimulated to develop one single national position to be negotiated in the Council. In this regard, the European level defines European competences as competences that are shared by central and regional authorities within domestic constellations. The fact that regional ministers must represent whole member states (and not single entities), forces regions to remain nested within their member state. A domestic compromise is needed if one wants to achieve anything at the EU level. Regions, therefore, depend strongly on internal arrangements.

In short, the Belgian challenge was to reconcile the foreign policy competences of the Regions and Communities with the European rationale of dealing only with the entire state. In 1994, the Regions, Communities and the central government concluded a Cooperation Agreement on EU policy-making which outlines the internal arrangement for the coordination of common positions and the Belgian representation at the EU level. We summarise the main issues of this agreement.[2]

The most important body in the coordination process is the Directorate European Affairs (DEA) within the federal Ministry for Foreign Affairs. This body organises coordination meetings with representatives from a wide range of federal, Regional and Community ministries.[3] Crucial is that this federal body needs to reach unanimity to back negotiation positions. In case unanimity cannot be reached, the issue is referred to the Inter-ministerial Conference for Foreign Policy (ICFP) and eventually to the Deliberation Committee.[4] This rule is yet another cooperative feature that softens the dual features of the Belgian competitive federal system. Consensus is nearly always reached; only a handful cases are discussed in inter-ministerial meetings and almost no cases are considered at the highest political level of the Deliberation Committee. In practice, a gentlemen's agreement exists, calling upon all participants not to make use of the veto power when their competences are not at stake. This clearly shows that most governments understand that, despite their far-reaching foreign policy competences, a domestic cooperative attitude is needed if they want to be influential actors at the European level.

In sum, the 1994 Cooperation Agreement makes the federal Ministry for Foreign Affairs a crucial player, because it is the central arena for coordination meetings and because all meetings are prepared and chaired by federal administrative and political officials. This makes clear that, despite the extensive competences of the Regions and Communities, the role of the central government remains substantial. At the same time, however, its nature has substantially changed. By incorporating representatives from other government levels and by granting these veto powers, the Foreign Ministry is no longer an exclusive federal agent. It has become a cooperative inter-federal or joint agency within a constitutionally defined dual federal logic.

Central Government versus Sub-states in the Belgian Polity: Sectoral Patterns

Because the overall coordination meetings within the federal Foreign Ministry became overloaded, several sectoral coordination mechanisms were introduced in a series of policy areas (Kerremans and Beyers 1996; Kerremans 2000). These sectoral mechanisms coordinate the Belgian input in lower levels of the Council, the working parties, and appoint the Belgian representatives for these technical negotiations. They also prepare the discussions for the subsequent coordination meetings within the federal Foreign Ministry in which the Belgian input at higher political levels in the Council is determined.

By exploring the domestic organisation of environmental policy, agricultural policy, social policy and treaty revision policy, we substantiate our propositions that adaptation to EU membership implies a development towards cooperative policy practices, consolidates the role of the central government and triggers differentiated cooperative arrangements (see Table 1 for an overview).

The Common Agricultural Policy (CAP) is a policy area where the EU has almost full legislative and executive competences. Moreover, agriculture is one of the few EU policy domains with a redistributive character. This makes domestic implementation pressures different when compared to environmental or social policies. While agriculture is mainly made through

TABLE 1
COMPARISON OF ENVIRONMENT, AGRICULTURE, SOCIAL POLICY AND
EUROPEAN TREATY REVISION

	EU competences	Decision-making mode at EU level	Allocation of competences	Implementation pressure
Environment	Strong regulatory	Largely supranational	Mixed, but predominantly regional	High
Agriculture	Strong regulatory + redistributive	Largely supranational	Mixed, but predominantly regional	Weak
Social policy	Weak regulatory	Weakly supranational and most intergovernmental	Mixed, but predominantly central government	Weak
EU Treaty revision	–	Intergovernmental	Central government	Weak

regulations and decisions, EU environmental policies are largely a matter of directives which need to be transposed by the member states (in Belgium on many occasions by the Regions). At the same time, there is a large difference regarding the implementation cost of social and environmental policies. For several reasons, implementation pressures are considerably lower in social policy: social policies are mostly a prerogative of the central government, the number of social directives is very low and many European social regulations already fit quite well into existing Belgian social law. On the contrary, the implementation pressure for some environmental regulations is fairly high because competences are often mixed and spread over different Belgian levels (although the Regions are generally quite dominant). In addition, the Belgian laggard position in environmental policies enhances the adaptation pressure (Bursens 2002). The overall high implementation cost for regional environmental authorities leads to the necessity to grant Regions substantial involvement in the establishment of the overall Belgian positions.

The impact of Europe on the Belgian polity is not confined to functional policy domains. Federal and regional levels are not only affected by European policies, but also by how different competences are delegated to the EU and how member states can influence European policy-making. The fact that since the Maastricht Treaty regions have direct access to the Council and the transfer of regional competences to the EU level are two clear examples of this impact. The 'revision of EU treaties' cannot be considered as a policy domain like agriculture or environment, but treaty revisions do have substantial consequences for domestic institutional constellations. Given the recurring attempts to revise the European treaties, it is plausible to expect that member states – central and regional governments – adjust their political strategies as well as domestic coordination mechanisms in the function of treaty revisions. Although EU institutional reforms affect all Belgian government levels, treaty revisions are not mentioned in the 1994 Cooperation Agreement. Therefore, coordination takes place on a case by case basis. With respect to the most recent attempt to revise the EU treaties, resulting in the so-called Constitutional Treaty, the IGC was preceded by a Convention. This offers us some interesting variation. The Convention was much more open than traditional IGCs in which central government diplomats play a more vital role than regional officials. In addition to our comparison of EU treaty reforms with traditional policy areas, we also investigate if and how the more open Convention method allowed and stimulated the regional governments to develop a European political strategy.

Environmental Policy

Although the Belgian Regions enjoy full policy competences in most environmental matters, the central government remains competent for important aspects such as product standards, protection against nuclear radiation, waste transit and the marine environment. The involvement of several levels calls for coordination among the three Regions as well as between the central and the regional levels. Typical for the areas where regions have extensive competences is the creation of inter-federal agencies and formal procedures to enable the creation of single Belgian policy positions.

Environmental policy formation takes place within the Coordination Committee on International Environmental Policy (CCIEP), set up by a coordination agreement that dates from 1992. The CCIEP is composed of officials from both federal and Regional environmental ministries and agencies (Bursens 2005; Bursens and Geeraerts 2006). It established a division of labour between a plenary meeting, thematic working groups and technically specialised pilot groups. Most work is carried out in the last two groups and has to be ratified in the plenary meeting. Formally, the central government is a vital player since it is responsible for organising and chairing all meetings. In practice, however, policy positions are usually drafted by officials who meet in small pilot or thematic groups. These officials are appointed by the CCIEP plenary and they can be officials from any government level. Expertise is the most important selection criterion. Because Regions are in charge of the bulk of environmental issues, they often enjoy most expertise, and, therefore, deliver most of the officials. This mode of operation puts Regional agencies *de facto* in charge of a considerable part of environmental policy coordination; the role of the central government is quasi non-existent when European regulation touches upon exclusive Regional competences.

The above concerns policymaking with regard the Council working group level. Once an issue rises to the political level – that is, when a position for the Environment Council must be drafted – the central government regains its central position, since ministerial positions have to be discussed within the Foreign Ministry's DEA. This means that, even when a position must be established with respect to purely federalised competences, the central government sits at the table. Since the DEA decides by unanimity, that is, granting all participants the right of veto, the establishment of each Belgian position is shared by all governmental levels. The representation of Belgium's environmental positions in the Environmental Council is currently carried out by Regional ministers (on a basis of rotation and accompanied by a representative of the federal level) who, according to article 203 TEU, act as representatives of the whole Belgian federation.

The organisation of this quasi hierarchical-sequential ordering of arenas (from CCIEP via DEA via eventually ICFP or Deliberation Committee), is important. Although each step may entail increasing political salience, the decision rule remains exactly the same, namely unanimity. Regions remain nested in a domestic arrangement, but as there is no hierarchically superior level that can unilaterally settle paralysing conflicts, officials are already confronted in the early bureaucratic stage with the consequences of no agreement. The chance that higher levels will be able to solve outstanding conflicts by a unanimous decision is quite small. This stimulates lower level bureaucratic actors to reach agreement and to prevent a political vacuum, while at the same time it increases their autonomy as they are less concerned that they will be effectively overruled by the political level (Hammond 1996; Jans and Tombeur 2000; Jans 2001; Tsebelis 2002). For environmental policy-making this means that decisions taken at the level of the CCIEP, where Regional officials dominate, are usually the prevailing Belgian position during the whole policy-making process.

Agricultural Policy

Agriculture was federalised in various steps, of which the most recent state reform in 2003 led to the transfer of almost all agricultural competences to the Regions. An informal system of sector-based coordination was created as early as 1988, establishing a unanimous decision-making venue for agricultural issues that fell within the competences of the Regions (Kerremans 2000: 48). Soon thereafter, in 1990, regional and federal ministers of agriculture formalised this informal coordination system, including the custom of deciding by unanimity. Similar to the environmental policy field, a special entity was created composed of officials from federal and Regional levels: a Permanent Working Group (PWG) was put in charge of preparing the Belgian position for the EU Agriculture Council and its working groups. In practice, the position of the Regions remained weak, since most substantive expertise and experience remained concentrated in the federal Agriculture Ministry.

Until 1992, the establishment of Belgium's European agriculture policy positions was still strongly dominated by the central government. The 1992 state reform gradually expanded the agricultural competences of the Regions, but the central government remained in charge of the residual competences and most European aspects of agricultural policies (such as price setting and market regulation). Yet the 1994 Cooperation Agreement involved the Regions in all coordination meetings, even granting them veto-power. Belgium's positions in the Agriculture Council and its working groups were de facto prepared and coordinated by the PWG, thus involving representatives from all levels. An agreement reached in the PWG had to be 'ratified' by the Foreign Ministry's DEA, but this mostly took place *post factum*, that is, after Belgian officials had already represented the Belgian position in the Council. In short, after the 1992–94 reforms, a co-decision system emerged in which the regional and the central government established a joint position by unanimity. The federal Agriculture Ministry set the agenda while the Regions discussed the proposal. Although Regions had veto powers in the agricultural domain, they seldom used it.

In 2002, most agricultural competences shifted to the Regions. The federal Ministry of Agriculture was abolished (Beyers *et al.* 2004). As a result, the Regions' position as policy-makers was obviously considerably strengthened. One of the consequences is that from 2002 Belgium's EU positions come down to policy positions agreed upon by two Regions, Flanders and Wallonia.[5] Both now act as veto-players: if one of them disagrees, Belgium cannot take any position in the Council while the central government is unable to hierarchically impose a position in case of such a deadlock. The central government now participates merely as a provider of information and opinions in the domestic coordination process. By the end of 2002, Flanders and Wallonia had created a new agency in order to formalise policy-making between the Regions: the Coordination Office for Agriculture. This agency took over the role of the PWG. The Regions and the central government now second officials from their ministries of agriculture (and for the central government from the Federal Economy Ministry) to this new inter-federal agency which prepares all Belgian interventions in the EU Agriculture Council and its working groups.

Although this picture is correct, it is incomplete. It underestimates the enduring importance of the central government and the relevance of the federal arena as a policy-making venue. Firstly, the central government remains competent for public health aspects of food security as well as for the farmer's financial situation (although central government's policies in this area need assent by the Regions). More important, and in contrast to environmental policy-making, is the central government's representation monopoly, entailing that the central government negotiates on behalf of Belgium in the EU Agriculture Council. As such, the central government functions as an agent or a policy-taker of political positions agreed upon by Flanders and Wallonia. It allows the central government to keep a close eye on the EU level and grants it a substantial information advantage. Equally important is that the Common Agriculture Policy still accounts for nearly 50 per cent of the EU budget. Decisions with regard to the EU budget are not taken in the Agriculture Council, but in the European Council and the

Ecofin Council, in which Belgium is, more than anywhere else, predominantly represented by the central government. The impact of the regions on decisions taken in these venues is very low.

Social Welfare State Policies

Compared to environment and agriculture, the EU is only weakly involved in social welfare state policies. Within Belgium, social policy is covered by both levels. Regions and communities are basically competent for social housing, worker placement and some aspects of unemployment policies, personal aid (child protection, disabled persons) and health care (hospitals, prevention). All social security aspects (family allowances, pensions, child benefits, health care and unemployment insurance), as well as labour market policies and the management of industrial relations, remain centralised at the federal level. In Belgium, social policies emerged during the first half of the twentieth century in the context of strong state centralisation, while the Belgian federal political system was established after social welfare programmes and labour market regulations generated powerful constituencies (mainly nationally organised labour and employers' associations). Therefore, regionalist and nationalist movements had for a long time little institutional leverage on the development of the welfare state (Béland and Lecours 2004: 271).

Typical for the social policy area is, in contrast to agriculture and environment, the absence of one single, overarching cooperation system with regard to EU policies (efforts to create this failed in 1994; Kerremans 2000). Instead, reflecting the fact that over time Regions and Communities gained more responsibilities in social and labour issues, a growing number of specialised agreements covering very specific topics were concluded (De Troyer and Cortese 2004). Because regional social policy competences generally have limited EU relevance, less formal and extensive domestic coordination is needed. Within the existing informal networks, officials from the federal Labour and Employment Ministry play a central role; they consult Regional or Community agencies if relevant issues arise. Representation at the different levels within the EU Council is dominated by the central government; Regions and Communities are only indirectly involved (Kerremans 2000).

Despite growing demands for federalising Belgium's social welfare state policies, social policies remain firmly embedded in the central level (Béland and Lecours 2004). The central government remains competent for wage policies, collective bargaining and social security, which are, in addition, areas that are hardly covered by the European level. This situation is strongly supported by federally organised labour unions and employer unions who manage important branches of the social security system. Decentralisation within Belgium or centralisation at the European level would deprive them of legitimacy in running federal social benefit schemes (Beyers 1998; Beyers and Bursens 2006).

The crucial position of the central government with regard to social policies is not only related to its relationship with the Regions and Communities. Belgium is known for its bipartite neo-corporatism in which labour and employers' unions are key players with regard to wage policies, labour market regulation and social security. Collective bargaining can only take place at the central level and the central government has to be involved as it is its competence to ensure that outcomes of collective bargaining become legally binding. However, the traditional dominance of the social partners started to erode during the 1980s when the central government became a much more active player with regard to social policy-making. Examples are the legislation by decree between 1982 and 1986 in order to improve Belgium's international economic competitiveness, different laws on industrial competitiveness (1989, 1993, 1996), which constrained the ability of social partners to increase wages without taking into account wage increase in Belgium's main trading partners, and the legislation by decree in order to implement the Maastricht criteria during the early 1990s (Witte *et al.* 1997). The laws on industrial competitiveness are especially important as they gradually increased the central government's powers to set the boundaries of social bargaining and enable the central government to unilaterally impose policies if labour and employers' unions are unable to compromise. In addition to these domestic developments, membership of the European Monetary Union led to a fiscal environment wherein strict budgetary rules prevail; the exchange-rate instrument and other national monetary policies disappeared. All this implies that the central government carries a crucial and pivotal responsibility in implementing European monetary policies, a responsibility for which it can only use economic and fiscal instruments. The centralisation of social and economic policies by the central government means that especially the central government, and not the Regions or the Communities, is the key interlocutor for the EU-level institutions with some competences in the social policy domain.

European Treaty Revisions

As mentioned above, the central and regional governments are not only affected by European policies, but also by the way competences are transferred to the EU. European treaties are formally amended in an Intergovernmental Conference (IGC), but the most recent IGC, resulting in the so-called Constitutional Treaty, was preceded by a Convention which functioned as an important agenda-setter for member states' negotiations. The Convention method is much more open and public than a traditional IGC, where central government diplomats are vital. Therefore, it can be expected that regional officials are more able to gain access and influence. Although EU institutional changes impinge on all Belgian government levels, EU treaty reform is not mentioned in the 1994 Cooperation Agreement and, therefore, political coordination can take place on an ad hoc basis. The importance of EU treaty revisions for the Regions and Communities, the increased openness of European treaty reform, as well as the absence of formal domestic coordination mechanisms could encourage a separating strategy among the regions, for instance by allying with other like-minded regions in Europe or by directly addressing other member states or the European institutions.

At the same time, however, just as for the functional policy areas, some form of cooperation among the multiple Belgian governmental levels is equally necessary since paralysing non-agreement on a united Belgian position, and hence the obligation to abstain in IGC negotiations, would deprive Belgium of any influence whatsoever in the important institutional reform debates. Involvement of the Regions and Communities in treaty-making is relevant because of the *in foro interno, in foro externo* principle which entails that treaties that touch upon all government levels have to be ratified by six parliaments.[6]

Despite the absence of formal rules, the preparation of Belgian positions in IGCs is generally coordinated within the setting of the 1994 Cooperation Agreement. Both with respect to the Amsterdam IGC and the Nice IGC (Bursens 2004), the Foreign Ministry (Directorate European Affairs) coordinated the establishment of the Belgian position and operated within the confines of the composition, the formal rules and the informal habits of cooperation that exist in functional policy domains (see above). On top of this, the Belgian Permanent Representation became an informal setting for additional coordination. Especially the Regions and the Communities were fond of this latter development as they consider the Permanent Representation as a representative of the overall Belgian federation and not just an extension of the central government (Kerremans and Beyers 2001).

However, some important qualifications should be made. While for all past IGCs cooperative behaviour was somewhat present during the establishment of the Belgian position, the representation of this position was almost completely in the hands of the central government. Negotiations on the level of the 'Representatives of the Government' were conducted by high-ranked diplomats of the federal Foreign Ministry and one representative of the Belgian Prime Minister. In case Regional or Community issues were on the IGC agenda, the latter could be replaced by one representative of the Regions or the Communities on a rotating basis. Although the rotation forced Regions and Communities to coordinate among themselves, the composition of the Belgian delegation clearly pointed in the direction of central government dominance. During meetings at the ministerial level, regional involvement was not always guaranteed. Finally, Regions and Communities were totally absent in the General Affairs Council and the European Council meetings that discussed the Amsterdam and Nice treaties.

Surprisingly, the central government dominance was even more pronounced during the European Convention in 2002–03 (Bursens 2004, 2005;

Crombez and Lebbe 2006). The Convention formula did not necessarily cause an involvement of the standing coordination bodies (such as those established by the 1994 Coordination Agreement), but could have stimulated the installation of new procedures granting Regions and Communities a more influential role. The Convention procedure was new and the broad, inclusive membership could have triggered a more extensive participation of regional actors. The federal Foreign Ministry, however, managed to organise the establishment of the Belgian position along the lines of previous occasions. In fact, even more than before, the central government was able to nearly monopolise the whole process. For instance, while Germany had a representative from the *Länder* governments in the Convention, the Belgian representation in the Convention was completely determined by the federal government and did not include a direct and visible representative from the Communities or the Regions. Partly referring to their traditionally central position in this area and taking advantage of the absence of formal rules with respect to a Convention in the Cooperation Agreement, the federal government succeeded in a centralised coordination of the Belgian position. Moreover, most of the experts that were interviewed with respect to this issue confirmed that trans-European alliances among regions had only a minor impact on the Convention (Bursens 2004). Generally, the regions preferred to work through their national governments.

Conclusion: The European Union as a Driving Force for Cooperation?

Table 2 summarises our findings. The practice of sectoral European coordination in the environmental policy domain clearly shows cooperative elements. The environmental sector is a policy area in which there are few homogeneous competences within the Belgian federation. Confronted with the external pressures of European integration, this heterogeneity needs to be adjusted by cooperative measures. These are operationalised through a system that allows all competent government levels to take part in position drafting bodies, which grants officials from each level far-reaching coordinating and representative competences and that installs a consensus-seeking policy-making culture. The cooperative practice, however, does not imply that the central government disappears from the scene. On the contrary: our second proposition is also confirmed. Both on the administrative level and on the political level, the central government remains an influential actor, even with respect to issues that do not belong to its competences. With respect to agricultural policies, domestic policy-making has been organised according to three different models since 1988. In a broader sense, the successive development of these models sketches a development in which regions became dominant veto-players. In order to be able to reach a single Belgian position, regions complemented the constitutional provisions with new coordinating institutions, hence again confirming our first proposition. Regarding our second proposition, it is clear that the central government

TABLE 2
DEGREE OF COOPERATION AND FEDERAL DOMINANCE IN BELGIAN
EU POLICY-MAKING

	Degree of cooperation	Degree of federal dominance	Regional capabilities	Dominant pattern	Involvement of regions
Environment	High (especially between regions and the federal level)	Low	High	Non-hierarchical, regions and central government are veto-players	Strong, but not an independent second level player, nested within domestic constellation
Agriculture	High (especially among the regions)	Moderate	High	Non-hierarchical, regions are veto-players	Strong, but still highly dependent on the central government, nested within domestic constellation
Social policy	Low	High	Low	Central government is veto-player	Rather weak
EU Treaty revision	Very low	Very high	Very low	Boundary of sub-state involvement is shaped by the central government	Very weak

kept important powers because of its representation monopoly and because of its indirect access to negotiations over the EU budget. Policy-making with regard to social welfare state policies is very informal and the limited involvement of regions and communities in EU social policy issues does not lead to extensive formal cooperation devices. In addition, and related to the previous point, the central government enjoys a strong position in the social policy area. Finally, Belgium's involvement in European Treaty reform did not alter the core features of its dual federal set-up. The stickiness of Belgian federalism, however, was somewhat softened by the cooperative behaviour of all governmental levels. At the same time, the central position of the federal government in the coordination process, and in particular of the Foreign Ministry, grew stronger during the most recent treaty reforms.

It is striking that we found no strong evidence in support of a separation strategy and even more important is the observation that especially extensive (not minor) regional capabilities coincide with high (not low) levels of cooperative behaviour within Belgium. With regard to social policy and EU Treaty reform, the central government has been able to centralise policy-making. In the area of environmental policies and agriculture, we observe that regional involvement remains nested in the federal state and that the regions themselves centralise joint policy-making through the creation of specialised inter-federal agencies. In short, European integration encourages the federal level, the Regions and the Communities to install cooperation mechanisms within the margins of the constitutional provisions of Belgian dual federalism. Regions and Communities are increasingly important, but do not dispel the central government from the theatre. In both regards, Europeanisation mitigates or softens the dual nature of Belgian federalism and it has stimulated a gradual development towards more cooperative forms of formal and informal governance.

Acknowledgements

The research reported in this article was supported by various research grants in Belgium (Fund for Scientific Research-Flanders, the Federal Government and the Flemish government). The title, inspired by a comment from Hans Vollaard, paraphrases Milward's famous book on the origins of European integration (1995). In addition, but separately to us, Charlie Jeffery used a similar title (Jeffery 2006). We acknowledge the feedback and insights provided by Hans Vollaard, Charlie Jeffery, Arco Timmermans, Paul Nieuwenburg, Jan Erk, Richard Sherman, Asnake Kefale and Wilfried Swenden.

Notes

1. Article 203 TEU does not allow for a decentralised representation in the sense that several sub-units of one member state can defend different policy positions and split their vote accordingly. For example, Belgium cannot split its 12 votes.
2. More details can be found elsewhere (see for instance Beyers *et al.* 2001, 2004; Beyers and Bursens 2006; Bursens and Geeraerts 2006).
3. More precisely: representatives from the federal Prime Minister and federal vice prime ministers, from the regional prime ministers, from the federal and regional ministers of foreign affairs, from the – depending on the agenda – sectoral federal and regional ministers, and from the Belgian Permanent Representation to the EU.
4. These bodies are, respectively, composed of the federal, regional and community ministers for Foreign Affairs (or their representatives) and the federal, regional and community Prime Ministers themselves (for more details see Jans and Tombeur 2000).
5. Legally, three regions – the Flemish, the Walloon and the Brussels Capital Region – have agricultural competences. However, in practice, only Flanders and Wallonia play a role in the preparation of Belgium's position in the European Agricultural Council. Due to its urbanised character, there are nearly no agricultural activities in the Brussels Capital Region.
6. It concerns the Belgian federal parliament (Chamber and Senate), the Flemish parliament, the parliament of the Walloon Region, the parliament of the Francophone Community, the parliament of the German Community and the parliament of the Brussels Capital Region. All these legislatures have to ratify. This is also the reason why under the signature of the Belgian Foreign Ministers of the TEU, one reads, in the three official languages Dutch, French and German, that 'This signature equally commits the French Community, the Flemish Community, the German-Speaking Community, the Walloon Region, the Flemish Region, and the Brussels Capital Region'.

References

Béland, Daniel, and André Lecours (2005). 'Nationalism, Public Policy, and Institutional Development: Social Security in Belgium', *Journal of Public Policy*, 25:2, 265–85.

Benz, Arthur, and Burkard Eberlien (1999). 'Europeanization of Regional Policies: Patterns of Multi-level Governance', *Journal of European Public Policy*, 6:2, 329–48

Beyers, Jan (1998). 'Permissieve consensus, maatschappelijk debat en het draagvlak van de Europese Unie bij de Belgische maatschappelijke organisaties', *Res Publica*, 40, 247–72.

Beyers, Jan, and Peter Bursens (2006). *Europa is geen buitenland. Over de relatie tussen het federale België en de Europese Unie.* Leuven: Acco.

Beyers, Jan, and Jarle Trondal (2004). 'How Nation-States "Hit" Europe. Ambiguity and Representation in the European Union', *West European Politics*, 27:5, 919–42.

Beyers, Jan, Bart Kerremans and Peter Bursens (2001). 'Belgium, the Netherlands, and Luxemburg: Diversity among the Benelux Countries', in Eleanor E. Zeff and Ellen B. Pirro (eds.), *The European Union and the Member States*. London: Lynne Rienner Publishers, 59–88.

Beyers, Jan, Tom Delreux and Caroline Steensels (2004). 'The Europeanisation of Intergovernmental Cooperation and Conflict Resolution in Belgium: The Case of Agriculture', *Perspectives on European Politics and Society*, 5:1, 103–34.

Börzel, Tanja A. (1999). 'Towards Convergence in Europe? Institutional Adaptation to Europeanisation in Germany and Spain', *Journal of Common Market Studies*, 37:4, 573–96.

Börzel, Tanja A. (2005). 'What Can Federalism Teach Us About the European Union? The German Experience', *Regional and Federal Studies*, 15:2, 245–57.

Börzel, Tanja A., and Madeleine Hosli (2003). 'Brussels between Bern and Berlin. Comparative Federalism meets the European Union', *Governance*, 16:2, 179–202.

Börzel, Tanja, and Thomas Risse (2000). 'Who Is Afraid of a European Federation? How to Constitutionalize a Multi-Level Governance System', *Jean Monnet Working Paper*, 6:7, http://www.law.harvard.edu/programs/JeanMonnet/papers/00/00f0101.html

Bourne, Angela K. (2003). 'European Integration and Conflict Resolution in the Basque Country, Northern Ireland and Cyprus', *Perspectives on European Politics and Society*, 4:3, 391–415.

Bursens, Peter (2002). 'Why Denmark and Belgium Have Different Implementation Records: On Transposition Laggards and Leaders in the EU', *Scandinavian Political Studies*, 25:2, 173–95.

Bursens, Peter (2004). 'Enduring Federal Consensus. An Institutionalist Account of Belgian Preferences regarding the Future of Europe', *Comparative European Politics*, 2:3, 320–38.

Bursens, Peter (2005). 'Het Europese beleid in de Belgische federatie: Standpuntbepaling en vertegenwoordiging van de Belgische belangen', *Res Publica*, 55:1, 58–79.

Bursens, Peter (2006). 'State Structures', in Paolo Graziano and Maarten Vink (eds.), *Europeanization: New Research Agendas*. London: Palgrave.

Bursens, Peter, and Kristof Geeraerts (2006). 'EU Environmental Policy-Making in Belgium: Who Keeps the Gate?', *Journal of European Integration*, 28:2, 159–79.

Crombez, Christophe, and Jan Lebbe (2006). 'Policy Processes and Positions for Convention and IGC: Belgium', in Simon Hug and Thomas König (eds.), *Preference Formation and European Constitution-Building*. London: Routledge.

Criekemans, David (2001). 'Het Vlaams buitenlands beleid anno 2002: voortrekkersrol of onbenut?', *Studia Diplomatica*, LIV:5–6, 115–48.

De Troyer, Marianne, and Valter Cortese (2004). 'Federalization and Labor Market Policy in Belgium', in Alain Noël (ed.), *Federalism and Labor Market Policy. Comparing Different Governance and Employment Strategies*. Montréal: McGill-Queen's University Press, 181–233.

Franck, Christian, Hervé Leclercq and Claire Vandevievere (2003). 'Belgium: Europeanisation and Belgian Federalism', in Wolfgang Wessels, Andreas Maurer and Jurgen Mittag (eds.), *Fifteen into One? The European Union and its Member States*. Manchester: Manchester University Press, 69–91.

Goetz, Klaus (2000). 'European Integration and National Executives: A Cause in Search of an Effect?', *West European Politics*, 23:4, 210–31.

Graziano, Paolo, and Maarten Vink (2006). *Europeanization: New Research Agendas*. London: Palgrave.

Hammond, Thomas H. (1996). 'Formal Theory and the Institutions of Governance', *Governance: An International Journal of Policy and Administration*, 9:2, 107–85.

Hooghe, Liesbet, and Gary Marks (2003). 'Unraveling the Central State, but How? Types of Multi-level Governance', *American Political Science Review*, 97:2, 233–43.

Hix, Simon (1998). 'Elections, Parties and Institutional Design: A Comparative Perspective on European Union Democracy', *West European Politics*, 21:3, 19–52.

Jans, Maarten T. (2001). 'Leveled Domestic Politics. Comparing Institutional Reform and Ethnonational Conflicts in Canada and Belgium (1960–89)', *Res Publica*, 43:1, 37–58.

Jans, Maarten T., and Herbert Tombeur (2000). 'Living Apart Together: The Belgian Intergovernmental Co-operation in the Domains of Environment and Economy', in Dietmar Braun (ed.), *Public Policy and Federalism*. Aldershot: Ashgate, 142–76.

Jeffery, Charlie (2000). 'Sub-national Mobilization and European Integration: Does it Make Any Difference?', *Journal of Common Market Studies*, 38:1, 1–23.

Jeffery, Charlie (2003). 'Cycles of Conflict: Fiscal Equalization in Germany', *Regional and Federal Studies*, 13, 22–40.

Jeffery, Charlie (2006). 'A Regional Rescue of the Nation-State? Reflections on Territory and Politics'. Inaugural Lecture at the University of Edinburgh, 28 March.

Kassim, Hussein (2005). 'The Europeanization of Member State Institutions', in Simon Bulmer and Christian Lesquesne (eds.), *The Member States and the European Union*. Oxford: Oxford University Press, 285–316.

Kerremans, Bart (2000). 'Determining a European Policy in a Multi-Level Setting: The Case of Specialized Co-ordination in Belgium', *Regional and Federal Studies*, 10:1, 36–61.

Kerremans, Bart, and Jan Beyers (1996). 'The Belgian Sub-National Entities in the European Union: "Second" or "Third Level Players"?', *Journal of Regional and Federal Studies*, 6:2, 41–55.

Kerremans, Bart, and Jan Beyers (2001). 'The Belgian Permanent Representation to the European Union. Mail Box, Messenger, or Representative?', in Kassim Hussein, Anand Menon, Guy B. Peters and Vincent Wright (eds.), *National Coordination in the EU: The EU Level*. Oxford: Oxford University Press, 191–210.

Kovziridze, Tamara (2002). 'Europeanization of Federal Institutional Relationships in Belgium, Germany and Austria', *Regional and Federal Studies*, 12:3, 128–55.

Ladrech, Robert (1994). 'Europeanization of Domestic Politics and Institutions: The Case of France', *Journal of Common Market Studies*, 32:1, 69–88.

Mair, Peter (2004). 'The Europeanization Dimension', *Journal of European Public Policy*, 11:2, 337–48.

Marks, Gary, François Nielsen, Leonard Ray and Jan Salk (1996). 'Competences, Cracks and Conflicts: Regional Mobilization in the European Union', in Gary Marks, Fritz Scharpf, Philippe Schmitter and Wolfgang Streeck (eds.), *Governance in the European Union*. London: Sage, 40–63.

Milward, Alan (1995). *The European Rescue of the Nation-State*. London: Routledge.

Olsen, Johan P. (2002). 'The Many Faces of Europeanization', *Journal of Common Market Studies*, 40:5, 921–53.

Schmidt, Vivienne A. (1999). 'The EU and Its Member States: Institutional Contrasts and their Consequences'. MPIfG paper 99/7.

Swenden, Wilfried (2004). 'What – *if Anything* – Can the European Union Learn From Belgian Federalism and Vice Versa?', *Regional and Federal Studies*, 15:2, 187–204.

Thorlakson, Lori (2003). 'Comparing Federal Institutions. Power and Representation in Six Federations', *West European Politics*, 26:2, 1–22.

Tsebelis, George (2002). *Veto Players: How Political Institutions Work*. Princeton, NJ: Princeton University Press.

Vink, Maarten (2003). 'What is Europeanisation? And Other Questions on a New Research Agenda', *European Political Science*, 3:1, 63–74.

Witte, Els, Jan Craeybeckx and Alain Meynen (1997). *Politieke geschiedenis van België van 1830 tot heden*. Brussel: Standaard Uitgeverij.

Consociationalism, Corruption and Chocolate: Belgian Exceptionalism

B. GUY PETERS

By definition, every political system is unique but, to paraphrase George Orwell, some are more unique than others. Belgium would certainly fall into the category of the more unique, especially within the context of Western European countries. At first glance that uniqueness is not apparent. As a political system and a social system, it shares many features with its neighbours, both proximate and across the rest of the continent. The political system is a 'normal' multi-party democracy, albeit with a larger number of political parties competing in elections and winning seats in parliament than in most countries. The political system is also parliamentary, with the prime minister and cabinet drawn from the parliament, always in a coalition but coalitions are the common mode of forming governments all across Europe. Again, the coalitions in Belgium are large, but this is perhaps a difference of degree rather than type. The public bureaucracy is also generally professional, with the usual merit criteria for recruiting, retention and promotion.

A more detailed examination, such as that provided by the contributions to this volume, reveals a political system that is indeed unique, and highlights a number of crucial factors that set it apart from most other countries in Europe. The authors in this collection all spend a great deal of time emphasising the distinctive features of Belgian politics, and those peculiarities must be understood if governing in this system is to be understood. In particular, the aggregation of these several factors that differentiate Belgium from other European countries lead one to question whether effective governance is possible. Many factors that one might expect to be important for a stable political system and good governance appear lacking, or at least to be strained, in this country, yet it continues to function and to produce reasonable levels of citizen satisfaction.[1]

In this article I will examine the several important aspects of Belgian politics that distinguish it from other European political systems. These dimensions have been mentioned in several of the contributions to this volume, but they should be placed in a more comparative context in order to understand some of the unique character of politics in Belgium. In some ways, although I will be treating these issues as distinctive, in several cases it may be just that Belgium has reached a point along a dimension towards which other countries may be moving, so that the distinctiveness is to some degree exaggerated. Still, at present, these features do set Belgium apart from most of its neighbours.

Some of the distinctive features of Belgian government appear to comprise barriers to effective governance in Belgium, in comparison with other European states. Therefore, we need to understand not just the distinctive features of this political system, but also their consequences for governance. Further, we need to understand the relative success of the system in governing when confronting those barriers. In comparative terms, this is a case that is characterised by relatively similar outcomes with other countries, yet has significantly different initial conditions and structures. The question, then, is what particular features in political and social life enable it to translate the potential for failure into a successful system of democratic governance, albeit still one that is not as successful as many citizens, and many of the authors in this collection, would like it to be.[2]

To some extent the relative success of the system is easier for a North American to understand than it may be for many Europeans, given that it depends to some extent upon institutionalising difference rather than creating uniformity, but certain aspects of governing that are more familiar in the European context will also be important for the narrative. In particular, the role that political parties play in this story about governance conforms most closely with the tradition, if not necessarily the contemporary reality, of strong and integrated political parties.

Multiple Differences

When Belgium is compared with other industrialised democratic political systems, several apparent differences from other seemingly similar political systems emerge, and help to define the nature of this country's politics. Perhaps the most striking difference is found in the discourse over politics among academics, as well as perhaps among those not in the 'chattering classes'. This difference was manifested in many of the articles in this volume, with a number of the authors discussing questions bordering on survival of the system and the maintenance of the system, rather than merely fine tuning and coping with more immediate policy problems.

One of the most apparent features of politics in Belgium is the important role that political parties continue to play, while in most countries in Europe parties appear to be declining in importance. The evidence (Mair and Van Biezen 2001) is that membership in parties, especially traditional main-stream parties, is declining rapidly. Also, in many parliamentary systems the emphasis has been shifting away from party dominance over government in favour of more personal control by prime ministers and members of the cabinet (Poguntke and Webb 2005).

The characterisation of Belgium as a partitocracy or party-archy helps to capture the role that political parties continue to play in this system, in contrast to others. The meaning of these terms is that the political parties tend to control the allocation of positions and policy choices in government, the appointment of many officials, including judges, and most aspects of governing. While to some degree the same characterisation is true of any modern democracy, the extent of control of parties in Belgium appears to exceed that in most other systems (see De Winter and Dumont this volume). Katz and Mair's (1995) concept of cartel parties that are primarily concerned about maintaining their own collective control over the instrumentalities of government to some extent captures the nature of these parties. Belgian parties, and especially their leaderships, have been able to maintain this central position and to use the state for their own ends, just as the state has to some extent used them to provide some cohesion to the governing process.

The domination of Belgian politics by political party elites is one aspect of the system that may simply point in the direction of where politics in other countries are going, albeit in different manners and at different speeds. Democracy seemingly is becoming ever more an elite phenomenon, with the leaders of political parties and government carrying on their elaborate dances with little connection to the political masses. Much of the discussion of Belgian parties emphasises control by the party 'bosses' and the extremely strong position the party leadership has in assigning office and in negotiating with other parties. To the extent that mass memberships of political parties have become disillusioned and deactivated, then, the domination of party leaders becomes a functional means of maintaining a democracy, albeit one that is very much dominated by this cartel.

The federal nature of Belgian politics means that the party leaders must be thinking about their role in the context of a multi-level governance arrangement, and must conceptualise their role as the cement that binds the various elements of the system together. Again, the complexity of Belgian federalism and presence of both territorial and non-territorial elements in the federal structure are distinctive. They solve a particular set of political problems about representation and about the rights of various communities, but in turn appear to make decision-making in government all the more difficult. Further, the structural solution may be only part of the answer, and maintaining the political peace among the various factions within society appears to be in itself a significant challenge to politicians in a country that remains divided. Again, the Belgian solution is distinctive, but as European countries become more diverse socially and culturally, this may simply be the precursor of other complex solutions.

Barriers to Effective Governance

One of the most important differences from most other countries is the deep social division based on language and culture. The differences between Dutch- and French-speaking Belgians are significant and certainly politicised, and create a political load on the system of government that needs to manage those fundamental differences. Although to some extent the pillarisation of Belgian society has been weakened on the original Catholic/secular dimension, and might be said to be weakening on the linguistic division, that division into the two linguistic communities remains significant. The contributions by Dewinter, Swyngedouw and Dumont and by Billiet, Maddens and Frognier to this volume demonstrate the extent to which the two[3] language communities are divided by more than their different tongues, with rather different orientations toward politics and toward the definition of Belgium as an entity being wrapped up in the cultural differences between the groups. All societies have some social divisions, but those in Belgium appear less capable of being managed through the usual political mechanisms. Indeed, what is striking is that the usual methods for coping with difference may have become part of the problem, as well as part of the solution.

Consociationalism

Like their Dutch neighbours to the north, and the Swiss, Belgians have attempted to manage this division through a consociationalist system, albeit one with features that differentiate it from the other political arrangements of this sort. To some extent consociationalist politics in Belgium has gone through two stages, the first dealing with the conflicts between the Catholic and secular/socialist blocs. With the decline of religiosity and institutionalisation of some structures to accommodate demands for separate service delivery mechanisms, the religious dimension lost some of its salience, to be replaced by a dominant linguistic cleavage.

One of the most important of the differences encountered in the Belgian version of pillarisation and consociationalism is its bilateral nature, and with that the unidimensionality of the arrangement in this case. Especially for the Swiss, there are multiple dimensions (language and religion, as well as to some extent urban–rural) of cleavage and hence some capacity to work together with some segments of society on some issues while being divided on others. While the class dimension of politics may continue to unite Walloon and Flemish citizens across the linguistic border, the underlying cultural differences do keep them apart, and separate a great deal of political life into the two blocs.

The fundamental difference between the Belgian version of consociationalism and that practised in the Netherlands is the rather greater direct connection between the social groupings and the political parties and with government itself. In the other consociational systems, and in most corporatist systems, the relationships among the groups appears to be very much a complement to the mainstream government arrangements of party and parliamentary democracy.[4] Unlike corporatist solutions that generally address economic issues using formal groups, consociationalist solutions tend to be more informal and depend upon elite interactions. The close linkage between the formal and the informal in Belgian politics might be thought to reduce some of the effectiveness of informality in softening the potential for conflict among segments of society.

Belgian consociationalism does have most, but not all, the characteristics that Lijphart (1996) has argued are important for consociationalism to be successful in managing social cleavages. On the one hand, there are a limited number of partners involved in the process that are argued to facilitate bargaining, and it is a relatively small country. On the other hand, however, there is not necessarily a greater identification of the public with Belgium as an entity than with the constituent parts.

Federalism

Federalism represents another dimension of the solution to the governance problems created by the divisions within Belgian society. The federal solution for divisions in society is not unique to Belgium in Europe, as confederation in Switzerland, Germany and Austria, and the proto-federalism of Spain indicate. Federalism in Belgium is not, however, like most other versions of federalism (see Hueglin and Fenna 2006). The rather extreme and complex version of federalism that has been created in response to the divisions within society poses some significant problems for managing society in a coherent and effective manner.

One of the most important features of Belgian federalism is the existence of such a limited number of participants, and the delegation of so many policy areas to the two components. This variety of federal solution might be thought to present two significant governance problems. One difficulty is that the rather complete division into the two components tends to highlight differences. The limited range of federal programmes may provide little sense of unity in the face of the diversity. Further, the Belgian version of federalism tends to make the division of competences rather starkly, not using the shared functions that have provided the means of reconciling the differences among the constituent units in many federal political systems.

Thus, both the structural and behavioural mechanisms for coping with differences and enhancing governance capacity in Belgium may in reality tend to reinforce the differences among the communities, rather than helping to overcome them. Each of the communities may be able to govern within its own geographical realm, but the capacity to cope with more comprehensive governing problems appears to be compromised. As already noted, the absence of much sense of concurrent powers and sharing of sovereignty tends to remove one of the more functional aspects of federal solutions to the governance problems.

Putting the Two Together?

Given that Belgium is both federal and consociational, the question arises as to how these two aspects of governance can be put together and be made to function in a compatible manner. In the case of Switzerland, the two features do seem to function together, with the strongly federal and more weakly consociational elements appearing to work in tandem. There is, however, some evidence that the deeply politicised nature of governing in Belgium may prevent this cooperative action, so that two structural elements designed to mitigate conflict may simply become arenas in which the conflict is played out.

As is pointed out in several of the articles in this volume, Belgian consociationalism tends to build veto-players into the system that may block movements in the federal arrangements that would be more functional for public policy. For example, the current debate over federalising the health services appears to be an instance in which the veto position of one linguistic community has prevented adopting a solution that might be able to match better the preferences of groups with the type of care provided (De Rynck and Dezeure this volume).

And Yet it Moves

Perhaps the most fundamental paradox in Belgian politics, and to some extent a means of summarising the other aspects of the system already discussed, is that the system continues to function, and to make public policy, despite the numerous blockages and barriers that exist. The tone of a number of the articles in this volume on Belgium is one of mild wonder that governance does actually happen in the face of all the possible blockages.

If we begin with the description of the Belgian political system as bilateral federalism and as also being consociational with strong veto players, the outcomes that one would expect from the policy process would be very much what Fritz Scharpf (1988) argued should be expected in the European Union and even in Germany's more cooperative version of federalism – government by the lowest common denominator. The blockages within the system might be expected to produce outcomes that all actors may be able to agree on, but those decisions are rarely decisions that can carry the system forward to better and more effective policies. What I want to understand is the extent to which there are mechanisms that can be used to move the bargaining forward and can produce more positive outcomes.[5]

To some extent the very factors that might be expected to prevent government from being effective are the same ones that enable Belgian government to be reasonably effective. It is not *in spite of* the multiple divisions and the apparent internal difficulties in coalescing that seem to beset this political system, but *because of them*, that governance can occur. The expected outcomes from a federal system in which the choices being made are politicised very strongly, and in which preferences for different types of services are also markedly different,[6] are the lowest common denominator, or no decision at all, but the Belgian political system appears capable of making those decisions. There are failures, and the authors in this collection are more than willing to point them out, but there are failures of this sort in all governments (Bovens *et al.* 2001).

The distinctive nature of political parties and their role in governing is perhaps the most central element for explaining how the system continues to move even in the face of adversity. While conventional approaches to democratic governance might wish to emphasise the central, and especially the autonomous, role of government institutions in governing, in the Belgian case these institutions are dependent upon the parties, and especially upon the leadership of the parties. Thus, in many ways, the central steering roles for governance are located outside, or only partially inside, the formal structures of government.

While a governance arrangement that depends largely on extra-governmental actors is in some ways becoming more important in some policy areas, with the dominance of network models of governing (Sorenson and Torfing 2005), the Belgian case does appear to impose such a model for the full range of decisions, rather than on an issue area by issue area approach. Thus, one of the functions that parties fulfil, that might otherwise be fulfilled by cabinets or prime ministers, is to provide some coherence in governance, both horizontally and vertically. There may be several sources for horizontal collaboration and coherence in a political system, but the vertical sources are more limited in the absence of party systems such as that found here.

In some ways, therefore, Belgium may be better prepared than many European systems for coping with the issues raised by multi-level governance. While the general tendency of multi-level governance arrangements is to make governance even more centrifugal than it might ordinarily be (see Peters and Pierre 2004a), parties may be a strong mechanism for uniting the segments. In the European Union, for example, the absence of a meaningful party system in a multi-level system is a major impediment to effective linking both horizontally and vertically.

Having well-integrated parties, and party leaderships, to supply this cement for the system may therefore make governance of these complex intergovernmental arrangements viable when they might not be so even in a less decentralised system. For example, if Belgium is compared to Spain in terms of its capacity to manage across levels the integration of party elites, it appears to provide the means of managing some of the 'competitive' features of multi-level governance and also to cope with some of the centralising features of the shift (Börzel 1999).

Bilateralism

The stark division of most institutions and issues of governance in Belgium was argued above to present some difficulties in governing, as indeed it may, but to some degree that division may also make governance more likely. As Deschouwer (this volume) mentions in his discussion of consociationalism in Belgium, decisions may be reached because the chance for failure is so high without cooperation. Bargaining situations with more possible coalitions and more opportunities for alliances may be able to produce a much wider range of solutions to policy problems. In this case, the only real option appears to be failure, so the political parties and other relevant actors have to reach some decision, functioning within the 'shadow of entropy'.

Corruption and Clientelism

The dominance of political parties in Belgian political life also lead to another means of providing governance in the face of rather strong obstacles, and this is corruption. The World Bank and numerous other organisations have been waging war against corruption in much of the Third World, and it is difficult to be in favour of corrupt practices in government for any number of normative and practical reasons. That having been said, however, there may be an optimal level of corruption that provides the means for greasing the wheels of the public sector and providing ways of reaching agreements that are better than the lowest common denominator agreements that might be expected, especially in as complex and divided a system as Belgium.

Before singing hymns of praise to corrupt practices in government, I should point out that I am talking about rather mild forms of corruption that in many political systems (including perhaps my own) would not necessarily be considered corrupt. There has been some very significant corruption in Belgian government and politics over time and that can only be condemned. However, the continuing use of patronage and clientelism by political parties and individual politicians is more common and I am arguing, perhaps, also more functional. The party dominance of political life in Belgium has led to the use of political criteria for the appointment of government positions that in many other European political systems would be appointed on a more meritocratic basis.[7] Further, some institutions – notably the cabinets of ministers – appear to exist in part as a place to provide jobs for political friends.[8] As Brans *et al.* (2006; Pelgrims and Brans 2006; see also Brans *et al.*

this volume) have pointed out, although the managerialist ideas contained in the Copernicus reforms might have streamlined Belgian administration, in practice, the maintenance of the cabinets may have been too important for the overall functioning of the system – both for governance and for patronage reasons – to dispense with lightly.

The functional aspect of corruption, in the sense of log-rolling, patronage and clientelistic behaviour, is that it can be used to build coalitions around policy and system maintenance issues that might be less probable were there not this capacity to use side payments. The deeply divided political system, consociational veto players, and the large number of political parties involved, present difficulties for reaching effective decisions that being able to trade off jobs or other benefits can mitigate. As the respondents in surveys discussed by Maesschalck and Van de Walle in this volume point out, knowing people and being connected to political parties may be the best way to get things done. While it may be unfortunate that this is true, and while we may all hope for a future with greater probity and less ascriptive criteria for government performance, still the use of these linkages does provide an alternative, and perhaps more efficient, means for conducting business.

Opaqueness

The conventional wisdom about good government is that the public sector should be as transparent as possible. As was true for the elimination of corruption, many international organisations have been investing a great deal of effort in enhancing the transparency of governing. Everything else being equal, transparency does improve government, making it more accountable to the public, and eliminating opportunities for abuse of power and for corruption.

On the other hand, however, some opaqueness may at time also be a virtue. Consociationalism as a principle or method for governing is to a great extent built on a notion of keeping the nature of the bargains, and especially the process of bargaining, less than fully transparent, the argument being that elites need to have some latitude to bargain in order to be able to make deals that would be impossible were they made more visible. Likewise, the strength of party leaders at all levels of Belgian government enables them to carry out the same sort of bargaining with little direct intervention by either party memberships or the public at large. While this may not be the model of perfect openness and deliberation in a democratic system, and indeed it is very far removed from such a model, it may permit this particular form of democracy to continue to function.

Instability

Finally, the relative instability of governments in Belgium can also be seen as functional for governing. Again, instability is generally seen as a threat to good government, creating a sense of an incapacity to govern. De Winter and Dumont (this volume) speak about the fight against instability among the Belgian parties and political elite, yet to some degree this may be another means of reducing the possibilities for deadlock and blockage in politics.[9] Both citizens and scholars tend to value longevity in governments *a priori*, but merely holding on to office may simply be to produce the type of sub-optimal policy choices that Scharpf (1988) was decrying in his analysis of federalism and the European Union.

Future Challenges to Governance

I have been arguing that Belgium is more than a little different from other European political systems. This difference remains, although there are some tendencies in other political systems, for example the movement towards even greater elite domination of parties, that may make them look more like the Belgian system. The numerous factors that differentiate Belgium from other political systems are often considered dysfunctional, and the extreme fragmentation of the federal arrangements, the vetoes within the consociational system, and the fragmentation of the party system do indeed pose challenges to the capacity to govern.

I have been arguing, however, that the Belgian political system has been able to overcome many of these potential blockages in the system, and factors that might be considered dysfunctional, for example a relatively high level of political corruption (that of a more polite form), may actually contribute to system maintenance of policy performance. That having been said, however, there are also several questions that are looming about the capacity to maintain the system as it has been functioning.

One potential challenge to the continuing success of the governance arrangements in Belgium is the nature of the party systems, its increasing balkanisation, and the increasing strength of the Flemish nationalist parties. The fragmented party system has not mattered too much in the past (but see De Winter *et al.* this volume) so long as all the parties were willing to play the usual parliamentary games. The more extreme *Vlaams Belang* and its much lesser willingness to play those conventional games reduces the capacity to make coalitions, within the Flemish parliament at least. If politics among the parties becomes less cooperative and less consociational, then the capacity to manage in the face of other challenges will be minimised.

Further, the strength of this party and the divergence of party systems in the two segments of the country are reducing the degree of symmetry and compatibility among coalitions ruling at the different levels, in part because elections have been decoupled in time across the levels. As noted above, the links among parties across levels of government, and the tendency of the same political parties to be in government at several levels, has been central in vertical coordination within the political system. De Winter and Dumont (this volume), as well as Swenden and Jans (this volume), point out that these linkages and similarities have been declining, so that bargaining and coordination have become more difficult, and less likely to produce comity across the levels.

Incoherent Federalism

The complexity of federalism, and the allocation of policy portfolios among the central government, the regions and the communities, has to some extent been a virtue for Belgian governance, as argued above, by creating some opaqueness in the actual conduct of governance. At the same time, however, that complexity and the failure to provide for adequate coordination across policy areas, or across a range of components of individual policy areas, may be creating more severe governance problems. Belgium is in the rather awkward position of having incoherent policy packages without having the concepts of concurrent jurisdiction and cooperative federalism that have enabled other federal systems to cope with similar problems.

In almost all contemporary governments there is a drive to improve the coordination and coherence of governing, in part for fiscal reasons and in part to enhance the sense of responsible government for citizens. The creation of 'joined-up government' (Bogdanor 2005) or the 'whole of government approach' has been central to recent reforms of government. Such a coherent style of governing may be impossible in Belgium, despite its own attempts at reform, simply because the bargains that have been reached among the various players in the system will not permit that degree of coordination to arise through usual hierarchical or collaborative mechanisms. To the extent that such coordination is possible, again the only real possibility may be through the activation of political party elites, and issues of coordination are rarely the types of issues that play well for voters at the next election.

A second aspect of the incoherence in the federal structure is the poorly developed nature of the fiscal relationships within the Belgian federation. There is a great deal of division of responsibilities for various policy areas, but much less fiscal autonomy to cope with the problems of financing the responsibilities. Arguably, for a federal system to be effective, the availability of money must match the policy responsibilities, and Swenden and Jans (this volume) question whether this is indeed the case for Belgium.

Economic Change

The shifting economic balance between the linguistic regions of Belgium may also be a potential threat to the existing balance of consociationalism and federalism. The politicisation of many contemporary policy issues along community lines and the differential benefits that those proposed changes might produce for one segment or another of the larger political community may become more contentious if the costs and benefits of economic change and policy changes become more apparent. The Flemish region has been more economically successful over the past several decades than has the Walloon region, and this differential prosperity may generate political tensions.

Again, Lijphart's (1996) ideas about successful consociationalism included some sense of equality, or at least tolerable inequality, among the segments of the consociational arrangement, and if this economic pattern persists the differences may become of a magnitude sufficient to undermine the arrangement. However, as noted above concerning bilateralism, perhaps the major fact that can maintain the largely successful consociational and federal arrangement is that almost any alternative is very bleak indeed.

Summary and Conclusions

The logic of comparative politics involves looking at the similarities and differences among political systems. Describing those factors across political systems is important, but more important is understanding what impact the factors may have on the performance of the political system, and its capacity to govern effectively and democratically (see Peters and Pierre 2004b). Belgium has a number of important similarities with other European political systems, but to some extent those similarities are only skin-deep, and once analysts begin to get under the superficial similarities there are crucial differences. The authors of the individual articles in this volume have performed a valuable service in making those differences evident to non-Belgians (and perhaps to some Belgians) who may not understand the distinctiveness of the country's politics and government.

But comparative politics can, and should, go well beyond describing the differences, and begin to think about their consequences. One of the analytic issues is to determine how the various individual factors identified fit together (or perhaps not) to determine the overall pattern of politics.[10] Further, we can attempt to determine what the effects of these various factors may be on the capacity of the system to generate effective governance. I have attempted to put together a number of factors about Belgian politics and to understand how they contribute to the observed patterns of governing.

Belgium is a particularly interesting case from the perspective of the capacity to govern, given the many things that might intervene to limit that capacity. The system has remained together and functions reasonably well, despite some notable exceptions raised in the contributions to this volume. I have offered some seemingly perverse arguments about why that success has been possible, with the intention of trying to use those arguments to emphasise both the singularity of Belgium as a locus for comparative research and the need to think about the full range of effects of political variables.

Notes

1. The evidence presented in the Billiet, Maddens and Frognier article on political culture in this volume does not point to a population that is exactly enamoured of its government and its government's performance, but when compared to other countries the level of satisfaction is not that low.
2. In the Spring 2005 Eurobarometer survey 65% of Belgians expressed satisfaction with the way in which democracy functioned in their country, in comparison with an average of 53% for all 25 EU countries, and 59% for the other EU-15.
3. The much smaller German-speaking community is not examined separately.
4. Stein Rokkan's (1967) memorable phrase about Norwegian corporate pluralism was that 'Votes count but resources decide', meaning that the interaction of interest groups supplemented party government in the *Storting*.
5. For an earlier discussion of this same issue see Peters (1997).
6. De Rynck and Dezeure in this volume point to the markedly different preferences in medical service delivery between French and Flemish patients, with clear implications for how this policy area, presumed at times to be dominated by science and professionalism, is to be governed.
7. Any number of studies across Europe, however, point to the increasing politicisation of appointment and promotion decisions in public administration.
8. The structures do, of course, have some more instrumental purposes for governing, but their utility as a place for providing 'jobs for the boys (and girls)' cannot be ignored easily.
9. For example, MacRae (1967) pointed out that although governments in Fourth Republic France were extremely unstable, the system was able to govern itself. This was due in no small part to the ability to form coalitions around specific pieces of legislation, and then dissolve and reform to confront the next demand.
10. This 'holism' in comparative politics has become somewhat unfashionable, but it remains important to understand whole systems and their internal dynamics.

References

Bogdanor, Vernon (2005). *Joined-Up Government*. Oxford: Oxford University Press.

Börzel, Tanja (1999). 'Towards Convergence in Europe; Institutional Adaptation to Europeanization in Germany and Spain', *Journal of Common Market Studies*, 37, 573–96.

Bovens, Mark A.P., Paul 't Hart and B. Guy Peters (2001). *Success and Failure in Public Governance*. Cheltenham: Edward Elgar.

Brans, Marleen, Christophe Pelgrims and Hoet Dieter (2006). 'Comparative Observations on Tensions between Professional Policy Advice and Political Control in the Low Countries', *International Review of Administrative Sciences*, 72:1, 57–71.

Hueglin, Thomas O., and Alan Fenna (2006). *Comparative Federalism*. Toronto: Broadview.

Katz, Richard S., and Peter Mair (1995). 'Changing Models of Party Organization and Party Democracy: The Emergence of the Cartel Party', *Party Politics*, 1, 5–28.

Lijphart, Arend (1996). 'The Puzzle of Indian Democracy: A Consociational Interpretation', *American Political Science Review*, 90, 258–68.

MacRae, Duncan (1967). *Parliament, Parties and Society in France, 1946–1958*. New York: St. Martin's.

Mair, Peter, and I. Van Biezen (2001). 'Party Membership in Twenty European Democracies', *Party Politics*, 7, 5–21.

Pelgrims, Christophe, and Marleen Brans (2006). 'An Institutional Perspective on Personal Advisors in Belgium. Political Actors and the Failure to Change an Institution during a Critical Juncture', paper presented at Annual Meeting of NISPACee, Ljubljuana, Slovenia.

Peters, B. Guy (1997). 'Escaping the Joint Decision Trap: Repetition and Sectoral Politics in the European Union', *West European Politics*, 20:2, 22–37.

Peters, B. Guy, and Jon Pierre (2004a). 'Multi-Level Governance and Democracy; A Faustian Bargain?', in Ian Bache and Matthew Flinders (eds.), *Multi-Level Governance*. Oxford: Oxford University Press.

Peters, B. Guy, and Jon Pierre (2004b). 'Is There a Theory of Governance?', paper presented at Triennial Conference of the International Political Science Association.

Poguntke, Tomas, and P. Webb (2005). *The Presidentialization of Politics: A Comparative Study of Modern Democracies*. London: Routledge.

Rokkan, Stein (1967). 'Norway: Corporate Pluralism', in Robert A. Dahl (ed.), *Political Oppositions in Western Democracies*. New Haven, CT: Yale University Press.

Scharpf, Fritz W. (1988). 'The Joint-Decision Trap: Lessons from German Federalism and European Integration', *Public Administration*, 66, 239–78.

Sorenson, Eva, and Jabob Torfing (2005). 'The Democratic Anchorage of Governance Networks', *Scandinavian Political Studies*, 28, 195–218.

Index

ÉTUDES ROMANTIQUES ET DIX-NEUVIÉMISTES
sous la direction de Pierre Glaudes et Éléonore Reverzy
123

La Conquête du Parnasse
par Tristan Corbière

Dominique Billy

La Conquête
du Parnasse
par Tristan Corbière

PARIS
CLASSIQUES GARNIER
2023

Dominique Billy, professeur émérite à l'université Toulouse – Jean-Jaurès, est spécialiste de métrique romane. Ses travaux portent aussi bien sur la poésie des troubadours et des trouvères que sur la poésie française classique et moderne. Auteur de nombreux articles sur la rime et la théorie des vers césurés, il a notamment publié *Les Formes poétiques selon Baudelaire* (Ferney-Voltaire, 2015).

© 2023. Classiques Garnier, Paris.
Reproduction et traduction, même partielles, interdites.
Tous droits réservés pour tous les pays.

ISBN 978-2-406-14149-5 (livre broché)
ISBN 978-2-406-14150-1 (livre relié)
ISSN 2103-4672

À Maguelonne, Aurélie et Arnaut.

En souvenir de notre
passionnante collaboration
sur la verification
de John Cowan,
amical hommage

LISTE DES ABRÉVIATIONS

AJ	*Les Amours jaunes*
acq.	acquisition
BU	*Le Bon Usage de la langue française*, 11ᵉ éd. (GREVISSE, Maurice)
CTC	*Cahiers Tristan Corbière*
DAF	*Dictionnaire de l'Académie Française*, 7ᵉ éd.
DALF	*Dictionnaire de l'ancienne langue française* (GODEFROY, Frédéric)
c.p.o.	césure(s) pour l'œil
dét[.]	déterminant
DHOF	*Dictionnaire historique de l'orthographe française* (CATACH, Nina)
DLF	*Dictionnaire de la langue française* (LITTRÉ, Émile)
DN	*Dictionnaire national*, 14ᵉ éd. (BESCHERELLE, Louis-Nicolas)
FEW	*Französisches Etymologisches Wörterbuch* (WARTBURG, Walther von)
fr.	frères *ou* français
GDU	*Grand dictionnaire universel du XIXᵉ siècle* (LAROUSSE, Pierre)
germ.	germanique
Imp.	Imprimerie
ind.	indicatif
num.	numéral
p.	page(s)
p.s.	première série
PC	*Parnasse contemporain (Le)*
pr.	présent
prép[.]	préposition
rev.	revue
s.	série
s.d.	sans date
s.n.	sans nom (d'éditeur)
s.v.	*sub verbo*
t.	tome
tabl.	tableau
tot.	total

v.	vers
vol.	volume(s)
z.m.c.	zone métriquement contrainte

INTRODUCTION

Une œuvre testamentaire

> Du temps que j'en étais épris,
> Les lauriers valaient bien leur prix.
> A coup sûr, on n'est pas un rustre
> Le jour où l'on voit imprimés
> Les poèmes qu'on a rimés :
> Heureux qui peut se dire illustre !
> BANVILLE, *La Corde roide*[1].

Si l'on ne peut douter de la personnalité tourmentée de Tristan Corbière, ses autoportraits, aussi impitoyables que complaisants, n'en construisent pas moins une image littéraire caricaturale du poète qui doit être interprétée pour elle-même, en rapport avec l'œuvre qu'il nous offre. Ce n'est pas pour rien du reste s'il choisit de donner en frontispice une caricature de lui-même et si l'autoportrait littéraire le plus synthétique qu'il nous livre se trouve dans une épitaphe par laquelle il entend léguer à la postérité l'image que nous lui connaissons, conformément à sa devise exprimée dans le dernier sonnet de *Paris* : « Fais de toi ton œuvre posthume ». Corbière ne pouvait pas se contenter de la forme de l'album que son caractère artisanal condamne à un rayonnement qui ne franchit guère le cercle amical : comme le disait Pétrus Borel en son langage tourmenté, « une nouvelle ère ne date pas pour le poète qui sérieusement ne prend un long essor, que du jour où il tombe au jour ; il faut au Peintre l'exposition, il faut au Barde l'impression[2] ».

---

1   Premier poème d'*Odes funambulesques*.
2   *Rhapsodies*, p. II. L'expression quelque peu tourmentée de la phrase se trouve vaguement "éclaircie" au prix d'un contre-sens dans l'édition posthume de 1868 (Bruxelles) : « une nouvelle ère ne date, pour le poëte qui sérieusement prend un long essor, que du jour *etc.* » Nous n'avons pu consulter la rarissime 2ᵉ éd. (Bousquet, 1833).

Sa fable liminaire affiche justement d'emblée sa satisfaction à se voir
« IMPRIMÉ » – et B. Houzé a suffisamment insisté sur l'importance
du recours aux capitales[3] – avant que sa Muse ne le délaisse, se tournant
vers « une blonde voisine » qui l'invite alors à chanter, ouvrant ainsi le
recueil constitué. Que cette fable ait été ajoutée après la composition de
l'ouvrage comme l'atteste la numérotation des pages[4] n'est pas anodin,
et l'on peut considérer que c'est l'achevé d'imprimer du 8 août 1873,
curieusement revisité en « fini d'imprimer », qui signifia aux yeux de
Corbière son accession au Parnasse avec son avènement dans le paysage
littéraire de son temps.

Une fois imprimé, toutefois, Corbière, « [b]ien entendu, ne se préoccupa
en aucune façon du lançage du livre », car, paradoxalement, comme le
dit Martineau[5] : « Il n'écrivait pas pour le public dont il se moquait ».
Mais en voulant hisser son œuvre sur les étagères de la littérature ins-
tituée, Corbière était conscient que son recueil y détonnerait et qu'il
accomplissait ainsi un geste lourd de conséquences dont l'audace même
le complexait[6], lui qui se présente toujours sous les traits d'un homme
et d'un poète qui ne répond pas aux attentes de la société[7]. Lorsqu'il
veut refermer son livre, il revient à sa Muse, dans la fable finale, « ayant
chanté » – et « déchanté » –, « Pour lui peindre ses regrets / D'avoir fait
– Oh : pas exprès ! / Son honteux monstre de livre », ce à quoi elle lui
répond qu'il aurait mieux fait de « le dire » plutôt que de l'écrire. Cette
boutade n'est certainement pas innocente si l'on songe aux difficultés de
Corbière tant à l'égard de l'orthographe que de la ponctuation, et il est
bien certain que s'il avait suivi les conseils avisés de sa muse, sa poésie
eût été mieux accueillie par des auditeurs qui n'auraient pu seulement
les soupçonner, comme par les éditeurs que son désaveu confronte au
défi de l'établissement de son texte.

Le caractère testamentaire des *Amours jaunes* apparaît dans la structure
même du recueil : la première section – *Ça* – se conclut sur une épitaphe,
tandis que la dernière – *RONDELS POUR APRÈS* – se trouve introduite

---

3   « Corbière créateur d'objets », p. 27.
4   Sur cet aspect du recueil, voir *infra*, p. 111.
5   *Tristan Corbière*, p. 76 et 77.
6   Lescane, « Comment peut-on », p. 109, voit dans la nonchalance du poète à corriger ses
     épreuves « une forme de répugnance à imprimer son manuscrit, sans doute devenu, du
     fait de l'impression, un "honteux monstre de livre" » (voir aussi p. 102-103).
7   Voir notamment les remarques de Mortelette, « Le prédécadentisme », p. 151-152.

par un sonnet qualifié de posthume, soulignant la parenté de ces sections qui « se répondent[8] ». L'ironie du destin ne tarda pas à combler les vœux du poète qui disparut le 1ᵉʳ mars 1875, suivi quelque six mois plus tard de « l'auteur de l'auteur de ce livre », comme Tristan désigne son père dans la dédicace de l'exemplaire qu'il offre à celui qui a financé son recueil[9]. Jules Laforgue l'avait finalement bien compris lorsque, s'interrogeant sur la gloire, il donnait en réponse ce vers d'« Évohé ! fouaille… » ainsi cité : « Voir les planches et puis mourir ! », vers que, dans le recueil, soulignent le détachement (par un tiret) et le recours à l'italique[10].

Le caractère le plus saillant qu'on peut attacher à Tristan Corbière, sur le plan plus proprement poétique, est son antiromantisme, manifesté au travers des pointes et saillies qu'il multiplie envers Lamartine et Hugo dont il fait ses cibles préférées au point d'en faire le fond littéraire sur lequel il entend détacher son je-ne-sais-quoi[11], à une époque où le prestige de ces poètes est loin d'avoir disparu, y compris celui de Lamartine qui s'attire encore de nombreux admirateurs dont certains, jusque dans la mouvance du Parnasse, tels Mme Blanchecotte ou Gabriel Marc, lui rendent encore de vibrants hommages[12]. Et c'est bien Lamartine qui retient le plus son attention, comme si Corbière avait besoin de se démarquer d'un poète avec lequel il avait beaucoup plus d'affinités qu'il ne pouvait en convenir. On songe à Melchior, le héros d'*Un poète de gouttière* de Murger qui « s'était décidé à prendre la lyre[13] » :

> Ses amis encouragèrent sa déplorable manie et le comparaient à Lamartine, et, dans le tête-à-tête, avec sa modestie, qui, comme celle de tant d'autres, n'était que l'hypocrisie de l'orgueil, Melchior s'avouait à part lui, qu'il pourrait bien un jour justifier la comparaison.

---

8   Laroche, *Les voix de la corbière*, p. 95 : « Elles encadrent le recueil et partagent une même fonction métapoétique : elles ont pour tâche de définir la place du poète vis-à-vis de son œuvre et de son public. »

9   Voir Steinmetz, *Une vie à-peu-près*, p. 420, et le chapitre « L'or du père » que consacre Laroche, *op. cit.*, p. 38-42, à la relation tutélaire qui lie le poète à son père, sa dépendance financière et le poids de son héritage onomastique.

10   « Une étude sur Corbière », p. 5.

11   Voir notamment Meitinger, « L'ironie antiromantique » ; Mortelette, « Corbière, Hugo ». Musset est par contre épargné comme le montrent Houzé et Hérisson, *op. cit.*, p. 59.

12   Voir en particulier l'« ode dramatique » intitulée *La Gloire de Lamartine* de G. Marc (1869). Sur l'antilamartinisme de Leconte de Lisle et le thème de l'impassibilité, voir Valazza, *La Poésie délivrée*, p. 33-41.

13   *Scènes de la vie de jeunesse*, p. 170.

Ce n'est pas pour rien que c'est dans un journal – *La Vie parisienne* – qui offre ses pages à une poésie faisant la part belle à l'humour, au pastiche, à la parodie et à la satire dont les poètes romantiques font le plus souvent les frais[14] qu'il choisit de publier sous le pseudonyme de Tristan[15], la même année que *Les Amours jaunes*, huit poèmes, dont des extraits de *Veder Napoli poi mori*[16], les vingt premiers vers du *Fils de Lamartine* et *Vésuves et Cie*, dans des versions au demeurant bien différentes de celles qu'il retient pour son recueil[17]. Il est vrai qu'on y trouve aussi *La Pastorale de Conlie* – adressée à « Maître Gambetta » – dont le ton n'a rien de la satire moqueuse mais bien celui d'une indignation sincère. La présence de ce poème singulier est liée à l'actualité qui n'a pas encore enterré les souvenirs de la guerre de 1870 dont témoignent également, dans la livraison du 22 novembre 1873, les sizains signés « Claude », appelant au financement de monuments commémoratifs[18].

En 1867, Victor Fournel se demandait de quoi il advenait de Lamartine dans la jeune mouvance parnassienne qui lui semblait dominée par le modèle de Baudelaire[19] :

> Et Lamartine ? direz-vous. Démodé, usé, arriéré, renvoyé aux pensionnats de jeunes personnes ! Tout au plus a-t-il à revendiquer dans cette foule deux ou trois fidèles, comme MM. Léon Dierx et André Lemoyne ; il est vrai qu'on pourrait être plus mal partagé. Sa poésie n'est plus assez haute en couleur ; il a le tort d'avoir une âme, de faire du sentiment, de s'attendrir, ce qui est le dernier degré de l'absurde, le comble de la platitude, quelque chose de tout

---

14 Mais aussi Leconte de Lisle ou Coppée.
15 Signature omise pour « *Veder Napoli poi morir* ».
16 Dansel, *Langage et modernité*, p. 43, voit dans le titre imprimé du recueil (*... poi mori*), une tournure dialectale, sans précision, ce qui n'est pas faux si l'on pense à la chute du *e* post-tonique de *veder* (au regard de l'italien standard) mais laisse le problème de *vedi* en suspens. On attendrait en fait *Vedi Napoli poi mori*, selon la forme originale du dicton (souvent avec la conjonction *e* entre les deux syntagmes), ou la forme alternative *Veder Napoli poi morir* comme le fait le rédacteur de *La Vie parisienne* dans sa livraison du 24 mai 1873. On pourrait admettre ici une simple coquille comme celle qui affecte *pourquoi* tronqué de son *i* en fin de vers dans *Le Crapaud* (11), résultant sans doute d'un mauvais calage des caractères d'imprimerie sur la réglette. Toutefois, la version écrite à l'hôtel Pagano, *Vedere Napoli è mori* (Bernardelli, « Il testo contumace », p. 58, n. 42), donne raison à Fongaro pour qui Corbière avait une méconnaissance outrancière de l'italien (« Sur le texte », p. 79).
17 *Cf.* Debauve, « Autour de la publication », p. 60 et n. 25, p. 69.
18 Les autres poèmes sont *Le Garde-côtes* (*Le Douanier*, extrait), *Un cabaret de matelots* (*Le Bossu Bitor*, extrait), *Cris d'aveugle* et *À une demoiselle*.
19 Voir l'extrait publié par Mortelette, *Le Parnasse*, p. 75.

à fait bourgeois et mal porté aux yeux des partisans du Rythme (avec un grand R), du Relief et de la Couleur.

Mais là où les Parnassiens avaient généralement tourné la page, Corbière ne cesse d'y revenir, incapable de s'en détacher, son voyage italien ravivant plus que jamais sa fascination pour le poète passé de mode pour bien des poètes de sa génération. Les références littéraires qu'il nous livre dans *Un jeune qui s'en va* sont du reste toutes centrées sur le mouvement romantique, soit de façon directe, dans des exergues où les citations «ostensiblement tronquées, ridicules, déplacées» lui servent essentiellement à «se démarquer[20]», des mentions souvent explicites, sans parler des pastiches, à travers les figures diverses de Musset, Murger, Lamartine, Moreau et Hugo qui, selon H. Laroche, donne encore à se souvenir au lecteur au travers des citations empruntées à Virgile ou Dante[21] ; soit de façon indirecte, à travers les figures de référence du mouvement, avec Escousse, Gilbert, Byron et Chénier, le marginal Paulin Gagne illustrant une excentricité à laquelle Corbière ne devait pas être tout à fait insensible, tandis que l'assassin Lacenaire ne doit sa citation que pour avoir produit quelques vers qui lui valurent d'illustrer le caractère irréductible et antisocial du poète maudit, parodiant ceux qui, selon l'expression de Murger, «fai[saien]t de la tombe de ces infortunés une chaire du haut de laquelle on prêchait le martyre de l'art et de la poésie[22]». Et dans ces allusions d'*Un jeune qui s'en va*, Corbière emprunte plus précisément la voie du Melchior de Murger qui s'essaie à devenir phtisique pour conquérir la notoriété en écrivant une ode *A l'hôpital* qu'il adresserait à la *Revue des Deux Mondes*, rêvant de susciter l'intérêt du public apitoyé du sort de «ce poëte martyr, de cet autre Gilbert, de ce frère de Moreau qui agonisait sur un infâme grabat, etc., etc.[23]». Si la mention de Baudelaire s'inscrit au milieu de cet arrière-fonds romantique, c'est en référence à sa triste fin. Comme l'a si bien noté A. Foglia[24] : «Antiromantique, le recueil des *Amours jaunes* est dans le même temps hyperromantique, au sens où il reste

---

20   Laroche, *Les voix de la corbière*, p. 130.
21   *Ibid.*
22   *Scènes de la vie de Bohême*, 4ᵉ éd., p. IX.
23   *Scènes de la vie de jeunesse*, p. 175.
24   «Tristan Corbière, enterrement», p. 19 ; voir en particulier p. 19-23 sur la figure de Lamartine.

dans la dépendance maladive des modèles et des voix hanteuses des grands précédents. » La publication du recueil ne met pas pour autant un terme à ses préoccupations, confirmant à sa façon l'adage de Borel selon lequel « tant qu'on garde ces choses là, on y revient toujours, on ne peut s'en détacher[25] ». Cette obsession survivra en effet à la publication du recueil comme en témoignent diverses pages vierges et marges de son exemplaire personnel où, plus que jamais hanté par le souvenir de Murger, ressassé de façon obsessionnelle[26], Corbière établit une « liste de bohêmes » et compose des « proses bohêmes », comme B. Houzé qualifie la première[27], revient sans cesse au *Fils de Lamartine* qu'il tente de réécrire, voire peut-être, au vu de la dispersion de ces essais inaboutis, de désécrire en multipliant les repentirs, avec sans doute un infléchissement de ton relevé par B. Houzé[28]. Tant et si bien qu'on peut se demander si Corbière n'a pas une dette beaucoup plus grande qu'on ne le pense généralement envers Murger[29] qui affectionnait le nom de Tristan dont il usait dans ses nouvelles aussi bien comme patronyme (*Le dessous du panier*) que comme prénom (*Le souper des funérailles*; *Dona Sirène*). C'est ainsi que, dans *Scènes de la vie de Bohême*, on trouve au programme de la fête organisée par Rodolphe et Marcel l'annonce suivante[30] :

A 10 heures, M. Tristan, homme de lettres, racontera ses premières amours.

Doté du prénom de son père, le fils Édouard n'aurait-il pas trouvé dans ce passage le nom qu'il adopte en 1869 pour son épitaphe[31] et dont il use d'abord comme pseudonyme pour signer les poèmes qu'il donne

---

25 *Loc. cit.*
26 Voir Steinmetz, *Une vie à-peu-près*, p. 248 et 451-454, qui parle de « murgérisation ».
27 La seconde étant *L'Atelier*; voir Houzé, « Le dernier Corbière », p. 305 et 312 ; transcriptions p. 313-316 et 318-322.
28 Art. cité, p. 309 ; transcriptions p. 330-335 et commentaire p. 309-310. Cette « ébauche de refonte », comme la qualifie Houzé, se trouve sur les p. 80-85 du recueil, courant de *Pauvre garçon* à *Bonsoir*, bien loin du poème imprimé (p. 197-200). Des matériaux exogènes s'y mêlent p. 81 : *cf. infra*, p. 98-99.
29 C'est ainsi que Steinmetz, « Perspectives », p. 12, « s'étonne fort […] que l'on n'ait pas relu ligne à ligne les *Scènes de la vie de bohême* ».
30 *Scènes de la vie de Bohême*, 4e éd., p. 78.
31 « Épitaphe pour Tristan / Joachim-Edouard Corbière, / philosophe-Epave, mort-né » (il n'est pas certain qu'il ne faille lire avec un tiret « philosophe – Epave, […] ») ; éd. Houzé, *ffocsoR*, p. 28 (f° 24r°). Le passage à la ligne donne déjà à voir un surnom dans « Tristan », dont l'identité à l'état-civil est donnée à la suite.

dans *La Vie parisienne* avant de l'adopter comme prénom pour son recueil, s'affranchissant ainsi symboliquement de la tutelle onomastique que son père avait inscrite dans son état civil[32] ? Et n'y aurait-il pas trouvé également le noyau thématique du titre de son recueil que la tradition critique rattache directement à la tradition ronsardienne ? On peut même se demander dans quelle mesure le tirage sur papier jonquille qui vient refléter le titre du recueil comme B. Houzé a pu le souligner[33], ne vient pas faire écho à la jaquette « en nankin jaune d'or » dont Schaunard se revêtit pour annoncer à ses amis qu'il avait « touché », éblouissant Phémie devant « son amant si élégamment relié[34] », et l'on se souviendra qu'A. Piedagnel saluera précisément l'élégance de l'ouvrage qui fait grand honneur aux éditeurs[35]. Il serait sans doute plus téméraire de voir dans les pages jaunes de ces exemplaires une allusion aux « feuilles jaunes » qui verront partir Francine, terrassée par la tuberculose, mettant un terme à ses amours, Murger poussant même la métaphore jusqu'à « jet[er] sur le lit de la malade une feuille jaune arrachée à l'arbre de la petite cour », feuille qu'elle glisse sous son oreiller en déclarant que c'est la dernière[36], et l'on songera également à l'évocation sans fards du cadavre « jaune et long » de la mère Durand étendu sur un grabat dans *Le Souper des funérailles*[37]. Pour Murger, le jaune évoque en effet la perte de la vie, que ce soit la fanaison des feuilles de l'automne ou la décrépitude des corps que l'on retrouve dans « mes vieux jaunes jumeaux » de l'album Noir[38]. On songe également, dans *Madame Olympe*, aux considérations ironiques du romancier sur les améliorations qu'une « civilisation qui se dit bien organisée » devrait apporter pour éviter les méprises auxquelles s'exposent les jeunes gens qui s'attachent aux pas d'inconnues en les parant de toutes les qualités féminines souhaitables[39] :

---

32   Sur cette tutelle, voir Buisine, « Sans rime ni marine ».
33   « L'ironie coloriste », p. 155-156.
34   *Op. cit.*, p. 266.
35   *Revue de France*, III, 8 (oct. 1873), p. 234 : « Au point de vue matériel, le livre est fort élégant ». Il n'est pas le seul à le relever : voir aussi le c.r. de G. Saint-Amé récemment exhumé par B. Houzé, « La mort de ce pauvre garçon », p. 282.
36   *Op. cit.*, p. 280-284.
37   *Scènes de la vie de jeunesse*, p. 37.
38   Sur les ambiguïtés de l'épithète, voir Degott, « *Les Amours Jaunes* à la lumière de l'album Noir », § 49.
39   *Op. cit.*, p. 203.

Quant aux femmes vieilles, elles devraient être strictement vêtues de jaune des pieds à la tête ; aucune fleur, pas un diamant, nul de ces ornements qui appartiennent à un autre âge.

Mais le titre *Les Amours jaunes*, qui, au demeurant, ne reflète pas la totalité du champ thématique du recueil, ne privilégie-t-il pas le thème des amours impossibles et celui de la mort, mort du poète certes, mais mort de l'amour mêmement[40] ? Quoi qu'il en soit, il ne fait guère de doute que le poète s'est délibérément placé sous le patronage de Murger.

L'antiromantisme de Corbière semble d'autant plus exacerbé qu'il est moins capable de s'abstraire des conventions poétiques que suivaient – avec, certes, davantage de scrupules – ses anti-modèles, conventions qu'il tourne cependant en dérision de toutes les manières possibles, ce qui, d'une manière différente, va dans le sens de la « dichotomie fondamentale » qu'a pu pointer Philip Stephan[41] : « D'un côté, il affiche une pose romantique, avec son nom de plume, "Tristan", son rôle assumé de soupirant rejeté, son exaltation de l'amour et de la souffrance personnelle ; d'autre part, il est délibérément antiromantique dans son humour empreint d'ironie, le détachement du regard qu'il porte sur lui-même et sa vitupération générale de l'école romantique ». S'engouffrant dans l'ouverture pratiquée par Baudelaire, Corbière n'en élargit pas moins considérablement le spectre lexical, registral, morphologique et syntaxique de la langue poétique ainsi que son imagerie, ajoutant ainsi aux griefs que le lectorat averti pouvait déjà lui faire en trompant de tant de façons diverses ses attentes en matière de poésie, mais séduisant d'emblée une nouvelle génération de poètes en quête de rupture.

Je remercie particulièrement Benoît Houzé dont les passionnantes recherches m'ont encouragé à me lancer dans l'aventure du présent ouvrage pour lequel il m'a aidé de son savoir et de ses encouragements.

---

40 Pour les interprétations qui ont jusqu'à présent été données à la qualification des *Amours* de Corbière, voir l'importante synthèse de Houzé dans « L'ironie coloriste » qui ouvre également d'autres pistes, et Roger, *La Muse au couteau*, p. 35-40 (et 40-46).

41 « Structure », p. 334 (trad. nôtre) : « *On the one hand, he strikes a romantic pose, with his pen name, "Tristan," his self-conscious role as a rejected suitor, his exaltation of love and personal suffering; on the other hand, he is deliberately antiromantic in his ironic humor, his detached view of himself, and his general vituperation of the romantic school.* ».

PREMIÈRE PARTIE

UNE ÉDITION BÂCLÉE

Il faut qu'un enfant jette sa bave avant
de parler franc ; il faut que le poète jette
la sienne, j'ai jeté la mienne : la voici !…
il faut que le métal bouillonnant dans
le creuzet rejette sa scorie ; la poésie
bouillonnant dans ma poitrine a rejeté
la sienne : la voici !…
BOREL, *Rhapsodies*, p. I.

Alain Buisine a fort justement pointé une caractéristique de la poétique corbiérienne dans laquelle le ratage, devenu « le seul régime possible de l'écriture » d'un poète qui doit sortir de l'ombre de son père, constitue « une posture originale et inédite[1] », et il est même un critique pour l'apprécier pour ce qu'elle est, dès la parution de l'ouvrage[2]. On doit toutefois s'interroger sur le champ du raté littéraire voulu. Buisine liste ainsi : « douteuses licences orthographiques, à peu-près sémantiques et associations sonores d'un mauvais goût concerté, cascades de calembours approximatifs, déplorables jeux de mots, alliances incongrues, abrupts ressourcements étymologiques, dénaturation d'expressions familières, brisures de rythme, prosodies en porte-à-faux, métriques boîteuses ». Nous pensons en effet pouvoir montrer, dans cette première partie, que les aspects qui ne ressortissent pas de la dimension rhétorique et stylistique n'entrent pas dans ce champ, les particularismes orthographiques des *Amours jaunes* ne se distinguant pas de sa correspondance et étant pour partie redevables de l'influence paternelle quand ils ne trouvent pas des échos dans les pratiques contemporaines, comme, du reste, certains aspects relevant de ce que Buisine désigne par « métriques boîteuses », comme nous le verrons dans les parties suivantes.

L'une des difficultés de comprendre correctement la poésie de Corbière réside dans son caractère brouillon qui se traduit dans *Les Amours jaunes* par une désinvolture marquée tant à l'égard de l'orthographe

---

1   « Sans rime ni marine », p. 136-139.
2   Dans *La Bibliographie contemporaine* ; *cf. infra*, p. 492.

que de la ponctuation et de la typographie, le poète ne s'estimant pas vraiment concerné par ces dimensions qui défient régulièrement les éditeurs confrontés à la question de savoir jusqu'où amender le texte des éditions Glady[3]. Même la confection de la table des matières a été négligée, avec des références entachées d'erreurs diverses, et le sous-titre même intervertit l'ordre des sections *SÉRÉNADE DES SÉRÉNADES et RACCROCS*[4]. L'attention portée aux aspects formels de son recueil peut, dans une certaine mesure, avoir contribué à détourner l'attention des aspects textuels. On se demande dans ces conditions quel peut bien être le sens de l'italique dans l'emploi qu'en fait le poète lors de l'évocation des épreuves de son livre où il semble attirer l'attention sur le sens propre du mot, signant ainsi un cas particulier d'antanaclase : « Nous serons riches à bâiller / Quand j'aurai revu *mes épreuves !* » (*Un jeune qui s'en va*, 47) : qu'il les ait ou non revues, il ne *les* aura pas surmontées. Pour autant, les critiques contemporains sont généralement très discrets sur ces aspects qui ont pourtant dû les indisposer mais qui ne tempèrent pas l'enthousiasme des poètes qui verront dans ce recueil extraordinaire un renouvellement profond de l'expression poétique. Même Verlaine ignore ces imperfections pour se tourner vers la technique poétique dans ses pages aussi élogieuses que superficielles : « Comme rimeur et comme prosodiste il n'a rien d'impeccable, c'est-à-dire d'assommant », oubliant que lui-même, qui recherche alors précisément la perfection en ces matières, se garderait bien de se trouver assommant.

On ne peut écarter d'un revers de la main l'hypothèse de B. Houzé relative à la confection du recueil[5] : « il est possible que le poète l'ait suivie de très près et que les étrangetés de présentation, de ponctuation, de typographie ou même de métrique aient été, sinon "pensées" une à une dans une sorte de "formisme" inversé qui cadrerait mal avec ce que l'on sait de Corbière et ce que l'on dit de lui, du moins acceptées en bloc, sciemment ou orgueilleusement non corrigées, voire invitées dans le texte. » On ne peut toutefois ignorer non plus que cette hypothèse est directement inspirée du parti-pris de J.-P. Bertrand d'offrir aux lecteurs une édition acceptant jusqu'à la moindre singularité typographique du

---

3   Voir en particulier les observations de Bernardelli, « Il testo contumace », p. 47-51, et de Lescane, « Comment peut-on ».
4   Bernardelli, « Il testo contumace », p. 31-32 ; Bernal, « Corbière, les coquilles », p. 39-40.
5   C.r. de l'édition de Bertrand, dans *CTC* 2, p. 344.

recueil original[6]. À la fin du XIXe siècle, un M. Souriau pouvait écrire, songeant à un travail de composition suivi qui se fait ordinairement en deux phases distinctes, composition puis révision[7] : « Quiconque a corrigé des épreuves sait que les protes ont leurs idées à eux sur la ponctuation, et que, dans la lutte sourde qui s'engage entre l'auteur et l'imprimeur sur la marge des placards, ce n'est pas toujours le premier qui l'emporte. » Mais d'un autre côté, quiconque sait les difficultés rencontrées par un Baudelaire avec ses imprimeurs a de la peine à imaginer un auteur aussi brouillon que Corbière passer son temps à l'imprimerie pour guider et corriger les gestes d'un prote tentant de se concentrer sur son métier afin de le contraindre à saper sciemment et illogiquement son travail. Une particularité accessoire peut ici servir d'indice : parmi les indications paratextuelles, il est fréquent de trouver entre parenthèses la mention du lieu, la date ou/et les circonstances d'écriture du poème, mais la parenthèse de clôture en est souvent omise par le prote[8], ce que Yann Bernal évoque comme « [u]ne manie courante dans les manuscrits de Corbière[9] », ce qu'on peut vérifier dans l'album Noir, l'unique fois où Corbière y use de ce genre de mention, soit à la fin du *Bain de mer de madame X*** : « *(Roscoff canicule 67[)]*[10] ». Tout indique que le prote, travaillant de façon linéaire et plus ou moins mécanique, s'est contenté de reproduire ce qui lui était confié, et comme il n'était pas de sa responsabilité de relire les épreuves d'un ouvrage édité à compte d'auteur, les choses seront restées en l'état. Mais cette question particulière des parenthèses non fermées se retrouve dans les divers errements de l'orthographe et de la ponctuation qui s'observent tout aussi bien dans les autographes de Corbière, à tel point qu'il apparaît que l'investissement de Corbière dans le travail d'édition dont Bernal fait état concerne essentiellement le travail de mise en page et l'ornementation du recueil, le poète s'étant pratiquement

---

6 Ce parti-pris n'est pas explicité dans la « Note sur la présente édition », p. 51. Nous y reviendrons p. 97.

7 *L'Évolution du vers français*, p. 152. Sur le plan de travail de l'imprimeur, voir *infra* p. 99-102.

8 Voir ainsi p. 31, 70, 71, 79, 160, 321. Voir aussi la parenthèse ouvrante de trop, p. 296, devant la datation. À noter que ces mentions ne figurent pas toujours entre parenthèses (voir p. ex. p. 135, 148, 192, 193).

9 « Corbière, les coquilles », p. 35, n. 54.

10 Au f° 9r° ; voir le fac-similé publié par Houzé, transcription p. 24-25. On peut également relever une parenthèse non fermée dans « Jeune philosophe en dérive », f° 24r°, transcription p. 28.

désintéressé des aspects orthographiques et ponctuationnels quoiqu'en dît le critique qui ne peut résister au courant des tendances contemporaines d'une philologie alternative qui, faute de pouvoir se résoudre à accepter l'idée que Corbière pût être à ce point négligent, s'ingénie à donner des motivations à nombre de déviances dans des exercices d'interprétation plus ou moins improbables[11], emboîtant le pas d'un Louis Barbey qui, en 1920, considérait que « Corbière est Corbière jusque dans ses fautes, qui sont typiques et voulues, pour la plupart[12] ».

Dans les pages suivantes, nous entendons approfondir l'étude magistrale que Bernardelli a consacrée il y a déjà trente-sept ans au texte « contumace » des *Amours jaunes* et qu'A. Fongaro affina trois ans plus tard en apportant d'importantes précisions. Notre attention portera plus particulièrement sur certains aspects de la ponctuation où nous essaierons de dégager des règles, et sur l'orthographe où nous mettrons en évidence, aux côtés de "fautes" proprement dites, *lapsus calami* ou coquilles, et de graphies incertaines, l'existence, aux côtés de la norme, de graphies alternatives légitimées par l'usage de grands écrivains. Nous tenterons également de montrer ce qu'il convient de penser des prétendues "rimes pour l'œil" de Corbière avant de revenir sur la question des rapports du poète et du prote.

---

11   Voir ainsi, en particulier, art. cité, p. 26-30 sur les bourdons – réels ou supposés – qui « propose[raient] une échappée, une prolongation de l'aire poétique corbiérienne, ménage[ant] dans l'expression un *jeu*, dans tous les sens du terme, notamment celui de l'espace » ; p. 33-34 la justification de la métathèse dans *maletot* ; la conclusion sur laquelle nous reviendrons plus loin, dans « Le poète et le prote », p. 97.

12   Cité par Bernal, art. cité, p. 40, d'après Lair, « Le dossier René Martineau », p. 288. Houzé et Hérisson, *op. cit.*, p. 165, parlent de coquilles « plus ou moins voulues ».

DES ERRANCES DE LA PONCTUATION

Le lecteur est aussi dérouté par l'utilisation fantaisiste de la ponctuation (présence ou non du point d'exclamation, emploi ou non du tiret, de la majuscule après tiret ou point d'exclamation de fin de phrase, mésemplois divers) que par les inconséquences qui l'accompagnent[1]. On se demande ainsi, là où l'on a un *bon Dieu* dans *Idylle coupée* et *Le Douanier*, pourquoi l'on a *Bon-Dieu* dans *Saint Tupetu* et *La Rapsode foraine* tandis que Corbière hésite entre *Bon-Dieu* et *bon-dieu* dans *Un riche en Bretagne* où l'on peut du moins remarquer que la dernière occurrence se trouve dans un syntagme mis en italique : « De *la part du bon-dieu*. – Dieu doit être content : » (44) : cet exemple montre que la prise en compte d'expressions ou de tournures particulières peut inciter le poète-écrivain à des décrochements des normes d'usage. Mais quant au reste, on ne peut que souscrire au point de vue de Walzer qui parle d'une ponctuation « éminemment instable, accordée à l'humeur du moment » qui l'a incité à la solution sage de « s'en tenir rigoureusement au seul texte revu – mal revu – par Corbière », à quelques exceptions près[2]. La question de l'inflation de la ponctuation de ses textes empreints des marques de l'oralité témoigne de façon évidente d'une nature écorchée où la subjectivité trouve à s'exprimer par la multiplication de ces signes et la prolifération de l'italique et des capitales, mais il ne faut pas perdre de vue non plus que ce phénomène s'inscrit aussi dans une tradition dont peuvent témoigner les romantiques eux-mêmes. Voir ainsi les points d'exclamation cumulés dans ces vers de Lamartine qui, par ailleurs, recourt assez volontiers aux lignes de points[3] :

---

1   Sur le rapport de Corbière à la ponctuation, voir les réflexions générales de Lescane, « Écrire, peindre », p. 97-106.
2   Éd. citée, p. 691-692.
3   Voir en particulier la Cinquième époque. Passages extraits d'*Œuvres poétiques complètes*, éd. Guyard, p. 725 et 737. Sur la fonction des lignes de points chez Corbière, voir Mejjati, « Les lignes de points ».

> Esprit saint ! conduis-les, comme un autre Moïse,
> Par des chemins de paix à la terre promise !!!… (*Jocelyn*, Huit. ép.)

Il ne faut pas non plus surévaluer la question du nombre de points de suspension, variable à cette époque, en dépit de la fréquente limitation à trois (quatre ou cinq n'est pas rare[4]), ni même celle de leur position, comme on peut le constater dans ces vers de Banville, parus en 1842 chez Pilout[5] :

> Chaque pas, chaque souffle était un souvenir
> De ce bonheur enfui pour ne plus revenir :
> … Mais – au fait – je m'arrête à faire de l'églogue
> Tandis que mon héros emplit son catalogue.

Bernardelli a attiré l'attention sur la difficulté de discerner précisément la responsabilité du poète dans les errements typographiques du recueil, précisant[6] : « il faut, en somme, faire la part du hasard et de la méprise d'un côté, et celle de l'intention et de la fantaisie de l'autre : chose tout autre que facile, étant donné la masse notable et diversifiée des anomalies, et du caractère, disons-le ainsi, de continuité et de progression insensible qui existe entre les plus manifestes et les plus grossières d'un côté et les plus légères et bizarres de l'autre ». Toutefois, la fréquence élevée des mêmes erreurs n'incite guère à mettre sur le compte du prote des irrégularités que l'on peut du reste aussi observer dans les autographes du poète[7]. Parmi les observations qui ont pu être

---

4 Selon l'imprimeur H. Fournier, *Traité de la typographie*, 3ᵉ éd. p. 85 (la 1ʳᵉ éd. est de 1825) : « Plusieurs *points* consécutifs (trois au minimum) signalent une lacune ou une suspension dans le discours » ; selon J. Claye, *Manuel de l'apprenti compositeur*, 2ᵉ éd., p. 121 (la 1ʳᵉ éd. est de 1871) : « On indique une lacune ou une suspension dans le discours par un certain nombre de points consécutifs, trois ou cinq au moins, et quelquefois par une ou plusieurs lignes de points ». Pour un exemple parmi d'autres, voir *Les Mariages de fer* d'A. Vellaud, édité par A. Lacroix et Verboeckoven et Cⁱᵉ à Paris, et imprimé par Ernest Bourges.

5 Dans *Stéphen*, chant II, VII (*Les Cariatides*, p. 104-105).

6 « Il testo contumace », p. 36 : « *occcoreva insomma fare la parte del caso e della svista da un lato, e quella dell'intenzione e della fantasia dall'altro ; cosa tutt'altro che facile, per la massa notevole e diversificata delle anomalie, e per il carattere, diciamo così, di continuità e di insensibile progressione che esisteva tra le più vistose e grossolane da un lato e le più lievi e bizarre dall'altro* ».

7 Dansel, *Langage et modernité*, p. 35 et 38, relève ainsi *chiffonier* et *glâner* dans *Paris nocturne* (contre les réguliers *chiffonnier* et *glane* d'*Idylle coupée*). Voir aussi *infra*, p. 41 n. 4, notre inventaire des formes déviantes dans l'album Noir.

faites, en voici quelques-unes – avec des exemples souvent nouveaux, plus d'autres –, qui nous permettront de mettre en évidence quelques régularités derrière la fantaisie de cette ponctuation. L'emploi des majuscules est parfois contradictoire, avec des omissions injustifiées : « La Palisse » p. 141, mais « monsieur la Palisse » p. 169[8] ; on lit « *Jésus-christ* » p. 257, au v. 50 de *Matelots*, mais bien « *Jésus-Christ* » dans la note de bas de page : la bévue, dans ce genre de cas, est manifeste, sans que l'on puisse pour autant attribuer avec certitude la responsabilité à l'un ou l'autre, si ce n'est que Corbière oubliait parfois les majuscules aux noms propres[9]. On peut également évoquer « la Pipe d'un poète » dans un sonnet dont le titre, dans la table des matières, est *La Pipe au Poète*. Mais si l'on prend en considération que le prote ne travaille pas à proprement parler sur des poèmes mais, de façon linéaire, sur des successions de caractères, reproduisant aussi mécaniquement que possible ce qui lui a été confié, on peut raisonnablement penser que Corbière n'y est pas pour rien. L'usage – ici injustifié – des majuscules de phrases n'est pas plus assuré comme on peut le voir pour le pronom *il* après deux-points dans les vers suivants de *Décourageux*, ce qui indique chez Corbière une incertitude liée à la polyvalence de ce signe dont le rôle de frontière peut aussi bien être lié à l'introduction d'un discours direct qu'à celle d'un énoncé explicatif ou illustratif (1-3) :

> Ce fut un vrai poète : Il n'avait pas de chant.
> Mort, il aimait le jour et dédaigna de geindre.
> Peintre : il aimait son art – Il oublia de peindre…

(Nous parlerons dorénavant de « majuscule de mot » – normalement dévolue aux noms propres et aux antonomases – et de « majuscule de séquence » lorsque la majuscule porte sur une séquence quelconque, ce

---

8 Il n'y a pas de raison de suivre Dansel, *op. cit.*, p. 41, pour qui Corbière « a peut-être voulu évoquer *la Police*, d'autant que "la Palisse" rime avec "police" » ; la distinction est imposée par le parallélisme des images, fondé sur la paronomase (« Police des polices ! » / « Puits de vérité de monsieur la Palisse ! ») par ailleurs séparées de deux vers contenant d'autres images. Même distinction dans le parallélisme plus étroit encore de *Laisser-courre* : « J'ai laissé la police / Captive en liberté, / J'ai laissé La Palisse / Dire la vérité… ».

9 Voir ainsi à propos d'une de ses lettres de jeunesse Bernardelli, « Il testo contumace », p. 57, n. 26 ; ou encore « le vieux jumeau *tityre* » au f° 14r° de l'album Noir (fac-similé dans *ffocsoR*, éd. Houzé, transcription p. 26). La majuscule est semblablement omise dans « TUPETU », au v. 4 de *Saint Tupetu*.

qui, dans l'usage normatif, concerne les phrases ou les vers, mais que Corbière peut aussi employer pour des propositions ou des syntagmes détachés ou présentés par deux-points.)

Même hésitation avec les propositions introduites par un impératif dans *Sonnet posthume* (34) :

> Dors : on t'aimera bien – L'aimé c'est toujours l'Autre...
> Rêve : La plus aimée est toujours la plus loin...

Il ne sera pas possible d'avancer sur cette question si l'on ne cherche pas à comprendre le système sémiotique qui sous-tend cette fantaisie apparente. Prenons pour commencer ces deux vers, par ailleurs identiques, de *Litanie du sommeil* :

> SOMMEIL ! écoute-moi : je parlerai bien bas : (15)

> SOMMEIL – Écoute-moi, je parlerai bien bas : (84)

Corbière a de toute évidence choisi de donner une certaine autonomie à l'apostrophe[10]. La première fois l'apostrophe est suivie d'un point d'exclamation, la seconde fois d'un tiret ; *écoute-moi* commence la première fois par une minuscule, la seconde fois par une majuscule. En outre, pour introduire le même discours, l'impératif est suivi la première fois de deux-points, faisant de « je parlerai bien bas » – proposition incidente – un discours rapporté, introduisant lui-même le discours proprement dit, mais ce choix s'accompagne d'un enchâssement de la ponctuation par deux-points plutôt contraire aux usages ; la seconde fois, l'impératif est suivi d'une virgule qui fait de cette proposition un commentaire préalable au propos rapporté, relatif à la manière dont il sera rapporté. L'incohérence dans l'emploi des signes typographiques qui concerne l'articulation du propos à l'apostrophe se retrouve naturellement ailleurs dans ce poème, et un examen quelque peu attentif peut mettre en évidence des défaillances dans un système par ailleurs bien établi. Contentons-nous des énoncés qui accompagnent le thème de l'apostrophe d'une apposition variable sous la forme d'un SN constitué d'un substantif et d'un complément quelconque ; on rencontre cinq ou six présentations différentes :

---

10   Sinon, on aurait plutôt: « SOMMEIL, écoute-moi ! Je parlerai bien bas : ».

Sommeil – Ciel-de-lit de ceux qui n'en ont pas ! (16)

SOMMEIL ! – Oreiller blanc des vierges assez bêtes ! (19)

– SOMMEIL ! Voleur de nuit ! Folle-brise pâmée ! (29)

SOMMEIL Brise alizée ! Aurorale buée ! (36)

SOMMEIL auréolé ! féerique Apothéose, (46)

SOMMEIL ! Honnêteté des voleurs ! Clair de lune (65)

La forme de loin la plus fréquente (quinze cas) combine <point d'exclamation + tiret + majuscule> (ex. : 19) ; dans quatre cas, le tiret seul fait défaut (29, 46 et 65 ; voir aussi 110, avec la variante « SOMME ! »), et l'on ne peut écarter le fait que, au vers 29, son absence semble liée à la présence du tiret en tête de vers, présence qui ne se justifie en rien et qui semble résulter d'un déplacement[11] ; dans deux cas, le point d'exclamation seul (16, plus 72) ; dans un cas, le point d'exclamation et le tiret (36). L'absence de petites capitales au vers 16 (et 72) semble résulter d'un oubli : la présence du tiret comme la nature du prédicat (un SN) montre bien que l'on a affaire à la même structure <Thème + Prédicat> ; le tiret a visiblement été omis au vers 36 qui termine la troisième laisse, où l'emploi des petites capitales n'est pas lié à la servitude typographique qui l'impose après grande initiale[12] : ces exceptions suggèrent donc davantage une défaillance ponctuelle liée à l'inattention plutôt qu'à des choix de présentation alternatifs. Au vers 46 enfin, il manque le tiret, et le prédicat qui suit commence par une minuscule : cette situation semble liée au fait que c'est le seul cas où SOMMEIL est directement accompagné d'une épithète, avant le prédicat habituel. Toutefois, les petites capitales étant liées à la grande initiale de la laisse, un doute subsiste sur la fonction du syntagme qui se rapproche davantage d'une description que d'une apostrophe, comme dans le second hémistiche du vers 26 : « SOMMEIL ! – Loup-Garou gris ! Sommeil Noir

---

11   Le vers s'inscrit dans une succession de la même structure <Thème + Prédicat>, traversant de bout en bout le poème, avec le même thème, toujours en apostrophe. Le tiret toutefois se retrouve devant le substitut pronominal au v. 55. Le phénomène semble se répéter au sein du v. 67 : « […] Clair de lune / Des yeux crevés ! – SOMMEIL ! Roulette de fortune / De tout infortuné ! […] »

12   C'est l'artifice que l'on trouve au début de chaque poème du recueil. Nous reviendrons sur ce problème p. 104-110.

de fumée!». Mais que dire du second hémistiche du vers 118 dont la structure générale est identique à celle du premier, avec une virgule au lieu du point d'exclamation et l'absence de petites capitales : «SOMMEIL! Drame hagard! Sommeil, molle Langueur!»? Tout au long du poème en effet, hormis ce cas, le thème en fonction d'apostrophe est toujours présenté en petites capitales, y compris lorsqu'il est représenté par le pronom : «TOI[13]». Le parallélisme entre les seconds hémistiches des vers 26 et 118 tend en tout cas à suggérer qu'une virgule a été omise avant « Noir de fumée» qui pourrait être une apposition détachée. L'absence de petites capitales au thème se retrouve cependant en tête du vers 16 où la présence du tiret et de la majuscule suggère par contre que le recours aux minuscules peut résulter d'un défaut, vraisemblablement imputable au poète qui aurait pu ne pas la marquer d'une façon suffisamment nette[14], et l'on ne peut exclure qu'il en aille de même pour les seconds hémistiches évoqués.

Une question subsiste quant à la portée exacte de la majuscule dans le contexte précis de *Litanie du sommeil* : porte-t-elle sur *l'ensemble* du prédicat ou sur le seul substantif qui en est le noyau? Le second hémistiche du vers 36 et les vers suivants, où le prédicat commence sur un adjectif antéposé, laissent subsister un doute :

SOMMEIL! – Triste Araignée, étends sur moi ta toile!» (45)

SOMMEIL auréolé! féerique Apothéose, (46)

SOMMEIL! Drame hagard! Sommeil, molle Langueur! (118)

SOMMEIL! – Petite pluie abattant l'ouragan (125)

SOMMEIL! – Long corridor où plangore le vent! (127)

Dans les trois premiers en effet, le substantif porte bien une majuscule bien qu'il ne soit pas en tête du syntagme, et l'adjectif antéposé porte bien une majuscule dans le premier. Dans les deux derniers, l'adjectif prend la majuscule initiale tandis que le substantif postposé en est dépourvu, ce qui appuierait l'hypothèse que l'on a plutôt affaire,

---

13 *Cf. infra.*
14 Dans la première version que l'album Noir donne du seul début du poème (f⁰ 8r⁰), « Epicier » (« Ruminant » dans *Les Amours jaunes*) et « l'insomnie » du v. 2, tous deux en petites capitales plus une majuscule initiale à *insomnie* dans le recueil imprimé, figurent simplement en une plus grande taille (voir *infra*, p. 106).

dans ces contextes par ailleurs identiques, à une majuscule de séquence. On peut cependant noter que *petite* et *long* sont des adjectifs de grande fréquence, portant sur une caractéristique strictement formelle de l'objet considéré (taille, intensité), ce qui peut amener à considérer les syntagmes *Petite pluie* et *Long corridor* comme des variétés de « Pluie » et de « Corridor » pouvant justifier le report de la majuscule en tête de syntagme, mais cette explication ne vaut pas pour « Aurorale buée ! » (36). On remarquera par ailleurs que l'absence de majuscule à « féerique » semble directement liée à l'absence d'un tiret antérieur[15], comme si, dans ce contexte particulier, le tiret commandait l'usage de la majuscule, ce que corrobore « molle Langueur ! » après virgule au v. 118. Si l'on passe en revue les différents prédicats associés au sommeil, on peut vérifier que, le plus souvent, c'est bien le substantif qui porte la majuscule, l'épithète ne portant qu'une majuscule de séquence après tiret, comme nous l'avons vu ou, bien entendu, une majuscule de vers comme au v. 21 (« – Moelleux Matelas [...] »). Les syntagmes après conjonction confirment l'association de la majuscule au substantif : « et Rime du poète » (25), « et Baiser de l'Aimée [...] » (28), « et Torchon neuf [...] » (37), « Et Soupape à secret [...] » (20), « et nocturne Cilice » (80) *etc.* Le phénomène est plus évident encore dans les constructions parallélistiques avec un chiasme qui met un substantif en fonction tantôt d'élément régi, tantôt d'élément recteur :

> Nourrice du soldat et Soldat des nourrices ! (77)
>
> Somme ! Actif du passif et Passif de l'actif ! (110)

Les exceptions sont finalement peu nombreuses : outre les trois déjà cités, voir « muet blanc ! » (90 ; après point d'exclamation), « Grand fleuve » (103), « et corne du cornard ! » (104), « Banal four » (116), « De la femme rêvant pluriel masculin ! » (171) qu'on opposera à « Du jeune homme rêveur Singulier Féminin » (170), et l'on ne saurait négliger le fait que, dans ses autographes, Corbière omet parfois la majuscule, y compris en tête de vers, ce qui fait de ces exceptions davantage le fruit d'une négligence que d'une intention.

On a vu que des signes de ponctuation sont parfois omis ou employés mal à propos. Un examen plus approfondi met en évidence le lien que ce

---

15   Ce qui n'empêche pas d'avoir une minuscule dans « Aurorale buée ! » (36).

genre d'omissions peut avoir avec d'autres éléments de la ponctuation, tels qu'un tiret, qui entraîne fréquemment l'omission d'un point, parfois d'un point d'exclamation – comme dans les apostrophes au Sommeil –, exceptionnellement d'un point d'interrogation, comme dans « pour quoi – Pour le four !... » (« Donc, *la tramontane...* », 8). On a ainsi d'un côté, dans *Le Fils de Lamartine* (29-32) :

> Ces souvenirs sont loin... – Dors, va ! Dors sous les pierres
>   Que voit, n'importe où, l'étranger,
> Où fait paître ton Fils des familles entières
> – Citron prématuré de ta Fleur d'Oranger –

de l'autre (33-34) :

> Dors – l'Oranger fleurit encor [*sic*]... encor se fane ;
> Et la rosée et le soleil ont eu ses fleurs...

ou encore (37-39) :

> – Dors – L'Oranger fleurit encor [*sic*]... et la mémoire
> Des jeunes d'autrefois dont l'ombre est encor là,
> Qui ne t'ont pas pêchée au fond d'une écritoire...

Le premier quatrain est dépourvu de ponctuation de fin de phrase (on attendrait plus précisément un point d'exclamation dans cet énoncé à l'impératif) ; le tiret initial, introduisant le même impératif aux vers 29 et 37, fait défaut au v. 33, peut-être en liaison avec la présence du tiret fermant le vers précédent ; l'impératif *Dors* des vers 31, 33 et 37 est dépourvu de point d'exclamation, à ceci près que, pour la première occurrence au v. 29, la modalité porte sur *va*, et la proposition suivante commence par une minuscule au v. 33 en contradiction avec le v. 37 : toutes ces divergences ont lieu à proximité d'un tiret placé avant (emploi injustifié de la majuscule initiale) ou après (omission d'une ponctuation finale). Mais les choses ne sont pas non plus aussi simples. Ainsi, dans ces deux vers de *Féminin singulier* (9-11) :

> ... Ah tu ne comprends pas ?... – Moi non plus – Fais la belle
> Tourne : nous sommes soûls ! Et plats : Fais la cruelle !
> Cravache ton pacha, ton humble serviteur !

Il faudrait un point d'exclamation après *Ah* – ou du moins une virgule[16] –, un point simple ou d'exclamation après « Moi non plus », une virgule ou un point d'exclamation voire deux-points après « Fais la belle » : on peut du moins constater que, en présence d'une interjection, l'auteur peut se sentir dispensé d'ajouter le point d'exclamation, peut-être parce qu'il considère que le caractère exclamatif de l'énoncé suffit à l'en dispenser.

Si l'absence de ponctuation finale est souvent liée à la présence d'un séparateur, il arrive aussi qu'elle soit immotivée, comme dans ces vers du dernier quatrain du *Crapaud* :

> Vois-le, poète tondu, sans aile ?
> Rossignol de la boue... – Horreur ! –
>
> ... Il chante. – Horreur ! ! – Horreur pourquo[i]
> Vois-tu pas son œil de lumière...
> Non : il s'en va, froid, sous sa pierre.
> ....
> Bonsoir – ce crapaud-là c'est moi. (9-14)

Si la troisième occurrence de « Horreur » voit disparaître le point d'exclamation, c'est parce qu'elle perd la modalité que lui conférait son expression par ce qu'on comprend être la compagne du poète : le poète protagoniste reprend l'expression de son allocutaire pour s'interroger sur son bien-fondé, et l'on pourrait s'attendre, à une ponctuation – non indispensable cependant – tel qu'un point d'interrogation, comme on s'attend à ce que l'adverbe interrogatif soit suivi d'un point d'interrogation qui a peut-être disparu avec le *i* final et qu'introduisent les différents éditeurs depuis Martineau, de même que la proposition interrogative qui suit : « Horreur [?] pourquo[i ?]] / Vois-tu pas son œil de lumière [?][17]... ». Cette déficience d'indices suscite quelque doute herméneutique : on peut ainsi se demander si le mot interrogatif sert bien à interroger cette caractérisation : « pourquoi "Horreur" ? » ; ou, de façon certes moins probable, s'il ne porte pas plutôt sur le propos exprimé au vers suivant : « Horreur [?] pourquo[i] / Vois-tu pas son œil de lumière [?]... ». D'autres

---

16 Pour la première, préférable au point d'exclamation comme au v. 14 de *Ça ?* : « – Ah, vous avez couru l'Originalité ? ».

17 La plupart des éditeurs (pas Vanier) ajoutent simplement un point d'interrogation après « pourquoi ».

questions se posent quant au dernier vers : à qui s'adresse ce « Bonsoir » dont aucun signe n'introduit la réplique, pas plus que la négation du vers précédent apportée à l'interrogation du v. 12 ? Pourquoi la proposition finale est-elle dépourvue de majuscule alors que son articulation à la formule de congé est des plus lâches et succède au tiret qui la détache ?

La majuscule fait même parfois défaut en début de réplique comme au v. 25 de *La Goutte* : « – Ouf ! c'est fait [*on attendrait ici un point simple ou un point d'exclamation ou trois points de suspension*] – Toi, Lascar ! – moi [*on attendrait une majuscule dans cette réplique*], Lascar, capitaine ». Il arrive que des énoncés parallèles mettent en évidence la diversité des traitements, comme on peut l'observer dans les enchaînements « Sais-tu ?... Ne sais-tu pas [...] » (150) *vs* « Sais-tu ?... ne sais-tu pas [...] » (160) de *Litanie du sommeil*, où les points de suspension ont pu inconsciemment cautionner l'omission ou non de la majuscule, ceux-ci pouvant aussi bien conclure un énoncé que l'interrompre en une reformulation par épanorthose. Lorsqu'aucun enjeu d'interprétation ne se pose, on ne voit guère pourquoi maintenir ces bizarreries qui perturbent inutilement la lecture, alors qu'un minimum d'uniformisation, dans le sens des usages que Corbière se contente d'appliquer de façon inégale, paraît s'imposer, ce qui, naturellement, est tout le problème posé par la ponctuation des *Amours jaunes*. On peut du reste s'interroger sur la restitution d'une ponctuation finale manquante, sachant que le choix entre un point d'exclamation ou un simple point peut dans certains cas se discuter, ce qui cautionne de toute façon une certaine prudence dans l'établissement du texte.

Corbière n'est pas sûr de lui dans des situations de conflits entre signes de ponctuation, en particulier lorsque se télescopent différentes modalités :

> Pourquoi, Belle-de-nuit impure,
> Ce masque noir sur ta figure ?...
> – Pour intriguer les songes d'or ?...
> N'es-tu pas l'amour dans l'espace,
> Souffle de Messaline lasse,
> Mais pas rassasiée encor ! (*Insomnie*, 25-30)

Dans la dernière phrase, interrogative, le syntagme participial détaché en fin de phrase et portant la modalité exclamative promeut le point d'exclamation et occulte le point d'interrogation[18]. Dans la strophe suivante qui enchaîne trois propositions interrogatives, la suspension finale entraîne l'omission du point d'interrogation à la fin de la première (31), et le signe attendu à la fin de la troisième (36) se trouve remplacé par un simple point qui semble être induit par la relative détachée, de modalité assertive :

> Insomnie, es-tu l'Hystérie...
> Es-tu l'orgue de barbarie
> Qui moud l'*Hosannah* des Élus ?...
> – Ou n'es-tu pas l'éternel plectre,
> Sur les nerfs des damnés-de-lettre,
> Râclant [*sic*] leurs vers – qu'eux seuls ont lus. (*Insomnie*, 31-36)

On ne peut non plus s'empêcher de se laisser aller à s'interroger sur la pertinence de telle ou telle omission. Ainsi, à la fin du v. 31, les points de suspension invitent à une autre interprétation où la seconde interrogation (31-32) serait une reformulation, ou plutôt une correction de la première à peine esquissée. Une même situation peut se prêter à des choix différents de signes, même dans des vers proches, selon « l'humeur du moment » comme le dit Walzer[19] ; c'est ainsi que pour introduire un discours rapporté, Corbière recourt indifféremment aux deux-points ou aux tirets dans *Rapsodie du sourd* (v. 15-16), avec l'habituelle hésitation dans l'usage de la majuscule initiale :

> En me disant : vieux pot..., ou rien, en radouci ;
> Et je lui répondrai – Pas mal et vous, merci ! –

L'apodose peut de la même façon se trouver séparée de la protase de façon diverse, soit avec une virgule, soit avec deux-points, comme aux v. 17-18 du même *Rapsodie du sourd* :

> Si l'un me corne un mot, j'enrage de l'entendre ;
> Si quelqu'autre se tait : serait-ce par pitié ?...

Dans « Mon blason, – pas bégueule, / Est, comme moi, faquin » (*Bohême de chic*, 29-30), le détachement du prédicat par un tiret n'est

---

18 Comparer au v. 26 d'*Insomnie* où les points de suspension suivent le point d'interrogation.
19 Éd. citée, p. 696.

pas compréhensible sans tiret fermant. Corbière hésite dans un même contexte entre point d'exclamation et virgule après une interjection ; ainsi dans les appels des matelots au capitaine Bambine, mêmement construits : « – Ah ! commandant ! assez ! », « – Ah, capitaine ! grâce !... » (*Bambine*, 7 et 10), mais on peut dans de tels cas invoquer la différence prosodique qu'implique l'usage ordinaire de ces signes, avec une pause après le premier, un repos après le second, avec une intonation différente.

Le détachement de syntagmes entre tirets soulève le même genre de problème. C'est ainsi que l'adverbe de temps *toujours* commence inopinément par une majuscule de séquence après le tiret qui clôt la concessive dans *À la mémoire de Zulma* (15-19) :

> – Je la trouvai – bien des printemps,
> Bien des vingt ans, bien des vingt francs,
> Bien des trous et bien de la lune
> Après – Toujours Vierge et vingt ans,
> Et... colonelle à la Commune !

Le tiret ouvrant déclenche ainsi souvent – et nous l'avions déjà observé dans *Litanie du sommeil* – le recours à la majuscule, qu'on trouve jusque dans le détachement de l'apposition dans *Sonnet à sir Bob* :

> Et je serai *sir Bob* – Son seul amour fidèle ! (*Sonnet à Sir Bob*, 12)

Le tiret ouvrant seul sert normalement à construire le discours rapporté, mais Corbière peut le substituer à une virgule ou un point-virgule dans des cas de zeugme, tandis qu'il emploie les deux-points pour introduire l'apodose au lieu de la virgule initialement choisie :

> Si j'étais noble Faucon,
> Tournoîrais sur ton balcon...
> – Taureau : foncerais ta porte...
> – Vampire : te boirais morte... (*Chanson en 'si'*, 1-4)

Des structures enchâssées viennent parfois alourdir la lecture, comme l'usage des deux-points au v. 57 d'*Un jeune qui s'en va* :

> – Décès : Rolla : – l'Académie –
> Murger, Beaudelaire [*sic*] : – hôpital, –
> Lamartine : – en perdant la vie
> De sa fille, en strophes pas mal... (*Un jeune qui s'en va*, 57-60)

Avec cette strophe, on rencontre une autre difficulté avec le contre-emploi des tirets d'incise[20] qui viennent encadrer les prédicats. On se demande en outre, dans les deux premiers vers, pourquoi « l'Académie » n'est pas suivi d'une virgule devant le tiret fermant[21] contrairement à « hôpital » qui remplit une fonction semblable dans un contexte semblable. On mettra de côté la question du tiret initial dont la présence surprend. Ensuite, Corbière enchaîne plusieurs thèmes suivis de leurs prédicats après deux-points, encadré de deux tirets, le tiret fermant faisant défaut en fin de strophe où il serait redondant[22]. De façon inattendue, ce système se trouve ensuite bousculé. Tout d'abord, le tiret fait défaut pour l'évocation de Moreau, mais surtout, avec Escousse, c'est un autre dispositif qui prend la relève où les tirets, succédant à un point final, tiennent lieu de séparateurs entre l'évocation des différents personnages – Escousse, Gilbert, Lacenaire, Lord Byron, Hugo –, alors que rien à proprement parler, après Rolla, n'introduit le couple Murger – « Beaudelaire », Lamartine ou Moreau, dans des contextes pourtant tout-à-fait semblables. Les deux-points demeurent par contre devant le prédicat, sans les tirets encadrants précédents :

> – Escousse encor : mort en extase
> De lui ; mort phthisique d'orgueil.
> – Gilbert : phthisie[23] en paraphrase
> Rentrée, en se pleurant à l'œil. [...] (69-72)

Dans les strophes suivantes, les deux-points qui séparaient les prédicats des noms de personnages auxquels ils sont associés sont remplacés par une virgule pour Lacenaire et Lord Byron, comme cela, du reste, avait été le cas pour Moreau, parce qu'il s'agit d'une apposition et non plus d'un commentaire sur la façon dont sont morts les personnages :

> – Un autre incompris : Lacenaire,
> Faisant des vers en amateur [...] (73-74)
>
> – Lord Byron, gentleman-vampire, [...] (77)

---

20 Clonts, « Le tiret », p. 14, évoque à ce sujet un « agencement [...] perturbé ».
21 Rappelons, que, à l'époque de Corbière, la virgule (ou tout autre séparateur) précède toujours le tiret fermant.
22 Plus précisément, Lamartine introduit un prédicat composite qui s'étend sur la strophe suivante (sans enjambement).
23 Graphies d'époque, comme l'a noté Fongaro, « Sur le texte », p. 81.

L'emploi même du tiret – déclenchant souvent le choix inopiné de la majuscule de séquence – pour introduire l'apodose, en lieu et place d'une virgule, constitue une autre singularité, comme dans les vers suivants :

> Si nous en mourons – ce sera de rire… *(À une camarade*, 35)
>
> S'il faut payer – paye – Et fais tête
> Aux fouets qu'on te montrera. (*À mon chien Pope*, 15-16)
>
> Si ce n'était pas vrai – Que je crève ! (*Le Naufrageur*, 1) ;

La même substitution s'observe dans du discours direct avec des apostrophes ou l'introduction de propositions incidentes dépourvues de quelque caractère parenthétique que ce soit puisqu'elles ressortissent de la même fonction phatique :

> Mords – Chien – et nul ne te mordra. (*À mon chien Pope*, 12)
>
> – Ah ! c'est que moi – vois-tu – jamais je ne caresse, (*Sonnet à sir Bob*, 3)

Les tirets peuvent même se trouver substitués à d'éventuels guillemets – qui semblent dispenser l'auteur d'une ponctuation finale –, même lorsque l'emploi de l'italique (doublé de capitales dans notre exemple) les rendrait également superflus :

> – C'est au boulevard excentrique
> Au – *BON RETOUR DU CHAMP DU NORD* –
> Là : toujours vert le jus de trique,
> Rose le nez des Croque-mort… (*Idylle coupée*, 26)

Cette redondance de la ponctuation se retrouve après un déterminant avec les deux-points qui se voient attribuer une fonction semblable dans *À une demoiselle* (5-8)[24] :

> – Cauchemar de meunier, ta : *Rêverie agile !*
> – Grattage, ton : *Premier amour à quatre mains !*
> O femme transposée en *Morceau difficile*,
> Tes croches sans douleur n'ont pas d'accents humains !

La version de *La Vie parisienne* ignore les deux-points, que Corbière ait fourni au journal une version qui en était dépourvue ou que le prote

---

24   On a correctement « Depuis les *Tour de Nesle* / Et les *Château de Presle*, » dans *Gente dame*, 7-8.

ait pris l'initiative de gommer l'anomalie, comme il supprime les tirets de « *clef-de-sol* » et « *clef-de-Fa* » en mettant une majuscule à *sol* comme à *Fa*. C'est ainsi que les signes de ponctuation peuvent se voir investis de propriétés ou de fonctions nouvelles selon l'humeur du poète : le tiret ouvrant peut déclencher l'utilisation − par ailleurs immotivée − d'une majuscule de séquence[25], le tiret fermant dispenser de l'utilisation d'une ponctuation finale ; les tirets encadrants ou le tiret isolé peuvent servir à détacher le prédicat du thème ou l'apodose de la protase ; les tirets peuvent se substituer aux virgules pour détacher une apostrophe ou une proposition incidente ; les tirets ou deux-points peuvent servir à la mise en relief du nom d'un débit de boissons ou d'un titre quelconque en plus de l'italique.

Cette situation complexe et confuse pose, dans le cadre d'une édition critique, des problèmes de principe qui ne peuvent pas être résolus ou même être abordés de façon satisfaisante sans une étude approfondie du système sémiotique général et des éventuels sous-systèmes sur lesquels repose la représentation typographique de la prosodie, de la syntaxe et de l'organisation informationnelle des énoncés dans les vers des *Amours jaunes* et sans un examen des usages manuscrits de Corbière, mais aussi des usages contemporains dans l'imprimerie, à commencer par la maison Alcan-Lévy à laquelle ont fait appel les frères Glady, voire même les manuscrits des écrivains contemporains, seul moyen de distinguer ce qui relève d'une solution singulière mais dotée d'une certaine légitimité, de l'indécision, de la confusion ou de l'omission. C'est notamment en prenant en compte ce genre de considérations que l'on pourra peut-être envisager des réponses concrètes aux questions que soulève l'établissement du texte pour lequel il ne sera jamais de trop de méditer encore et encore les réflexions de G. Bernardelli selon qui[26]

> se pose le problème d'établir où s'arrête la responsabilité du prote et où commence celle de l'auteur ; il faut, en somme, faire la part du hasard et

---

25 Sur ce concept, voir *supra*, p. 27-28.
26 « Il testo contumace », p. 36 (trad. nôtre) : « si poneva il problema di stabilire dove terminasse la responsabilità del proto e dove cominciasse quella dell'autore ; occoreva insomma fare la parte del caso e della svista da un lato, e quella dell'intenzione e della fantasia dall'altro : cosa tutt'altro che facile, per la massa notevole e diversificata delle anomalie, e per il carattere, diciamo così, di continuità e di insensibile progressione che esisteva tra il più vistose e grossolane da un lato e le più lievi e bizzarre dall'altro. »

de la méprise d'un côté, et celle de l'intention et de la fantaisie de l'autre : chose tout autre que facile, étant donné la masse notable et diversifiée des anomalies, et du caractère, disons-le ainsi, de continuité et de progression insensible qui existe entre les plus manifestes et les plus grossières d'un côté et les plus légères et bizarres de l'autre.

UNE DÉSINVOLTURE CONGÉNITALE

Les négligences de Corbière dans *Les Amours jaunes* peuvent d'autant moins être mises sur le compte d'une volonté de choquer le lecteur qu'elles reflètent son usage personnel de la langue, comme on a pu l'évoquer à propos de sa correspondance[1] et des versions manuscrites de ses poésies[2]. On peut le constater aussi en feuilletant l'album Noir où Corbière mettait ses vers au propre[3], album qu'il ne destinait pas au grand public des lettrés : on relève en effet dans les 537 vers de ce recueil autographe plus d'une trentaine de fautes d'orthographe, dont la plupart, au demeurant, concernent l'emploi des accents[4] ; on y trouve des mésemplois (ou plus rarement des omissions du trait d'union : *là bas*, trois occurrences) semblables à ceux des *Amours jaunes* : outre le cas de lexies (*ange-gardien*, *débits-d'-tabac*, *batterie-de-cuisine*) ou toponymes (*l'Ile-de-Batz*) où Corbière adopte une union bien attestée dans des lexies comparables, on trouve des pseudo-lexies (*brave-homme*, *vieux-jumeaux*[5], *pomme-d'amour*, *vouloir-bien*), des locutions adverbiales (*de-temps-en-temps*, *quinze-jours*, *à-peu-près* [qualifiant *une vie*], *tout-d'-même*, *comme-quoi*) ou exclamatives (*Eh-bien*). Dans *c'est-assez*, le procédé se justifie comme évocation subliminale du « çétacé [*sic*] qui lave sa vaisselle », sous-titre du poème (*Le Bain de mer de Madame X****).

---

1   Sur cet aspect, voir notamment Walzer, éd. citée, p. 13 et 923 ; Dansel, *Langage et moder-nité*, p. 33-44 ; Bernardelli, « Il testo contumace », p. 40-41.
2   Voir Bernardelli, « Il testo contumace », p. 41-42.
3   Voir Houzé, « Corbière créateur d'objets », p. 29, qui n'entre cependant pas dans le détail.
4   Détail au fil du texte : fautes diverses relatives aux accents (dans *mendîrais*, *î* remplace conventionnellement *ie* en poésie) sur lesquelles nous reviendrons (voir *infra*, p. 88-89 à propos du circonflexe et 61 à propos de *và*) ; au trait d'union (voir *infra*) ; autres cas : *razoirs*, *calembourg*, *gabloux* (sing.), *cu* (en reprise de *cul*, mais le mot rime avec *vécu* : c'est ici *cul* qui est fautif au regard de la licence poétique), *s'emprumpte*, *brisans*, *artichaux* (plur.), *dégeulade*, *pous*, *razibus*, *boyeaux*, *geuzard*, *secour*, *capeyras*, *mercenairs*.
5   *Mes vieux-jumeaux*, titre qui sera modifié en *Frère et sœur jumeaux*. Dans la version imprimée, Corbière recourt dans le corps du poème aux majuscules, évoquant « Mes Vieux Jumeaux », procédé qui confère au syntagme une valeur dénominative. Sur les différentes versions du poème, voir Degott, « *Les Amours jaunes* à la lumière de l'album Noir », § 43-49.

Bernardelli a fort justement réfuté les appréciations de Dansel qui tendait à attribuer à Corbière une intention plus ou moins consciente, en allant jusqu'à des affirmations péremptoires : « tout nous prouve que Tristan Corbière s'appliquait à désapprendre l'orthographe », évoquant « ses inadvertances plus ou moins contrôlées[6] » et « [s]es velléités de simplification », « une attitude ostensiblement dédaigneuse » à l'égard des consonnes redoublées, alors même qu'il signalait que son père « commettait également des fautes de gémination[7] » ; il voyait même, à propos du mésemploi de l'accent circonflexe, « une volonté de provocation », ce qu'il tempérait en précisant[8] : « plutôt dans l'esprit que dans la forme ». Antoine Fongaro a plus justement conclu[9] : « L'extraordinaire caprice de la ponctuation, de l'accentuation, de l'emploi de l'italique, de l'orthographe enfin [...] ne saurait constituer, de la part de Tristan Corbière, une démarche voulue et révolutionnaire. » Laurent Lescane a parfaitement bien évoqué la problématique générale de la ponctuation au XIXe siècle, de l'opposition qui peut exister entre « ponctuation sous la plume et ponctuation imprimée » et de l'absence de règles bien définies dans le travail des imprimeurs[10]. Une citation qu'il donne de M.-D. Fertel – sans du reste en tirer de leçon particulière –, illustre à notre avis de façon très précise la situation dans laquelle nous nous trouvons dans le cas des *Amours jaunes*[11] :

> Il arrive très-souvent qu'un Auteur, qui a plûtôt en vûe l'ordre de son Ouvrage, que le soin de bien ponctuer les membres de ses periodes, met quelquefois, faute d'attention, des ponctuations toutes opposées à celles qui devroient y être ; & beaucoup de Compagnons n'en ayant point de connoissance, les mettent comme elles sont dans la copie, soit qu'elles soyent bien ou mal.

Cette situation que l'auteur décrit dans un ouvrage de 1723 garde toute sa valeur pour la situation concrète qui nous occupe, même si l'écriture s'était depuis davantage disciplinée, les imprimeurs eux-mêmes se constituant en la matière une sorte de doctrine nourrie de la longue expérience acquise dans le cadre de la profession qui leur faisait

---

6   Il y voit même une riposte « au dressage orthographique » (p. 44).
7   Sur cette question, voir *infra*, p. 67, 85 et 88.
8   Bernardelli, « Il testo contumace », p. 58, n. 38 ; Dansel, *Langage et modernité*, p. 33, 35, 36 et 39.
9   « Sur le texte », p. 77.
10 « Comment peut-on », p. 104-105.
11 *La Science pratique de l'imprimerie*, p. 219 (graphies d'origine).

aborder les manuscrits de leurs clients avec un mélange de rigueur et de pragmatisme. Lescane rapporte ainsi l'opinion de l'imprimeur limougeaud M. Chapoulard qui écrit en 1865[12] : « Seul l'imprimeur instruit et expérimenté est conséquent dans sa manière de ponctuer, et sur ce point, l'auteur doit s'en rapporter à lui ». Il est possible que, dans le cas des *Amours jaunes*, le prote ait préféré s'en tenir à la lettre et au signe de ponctuation devant un auteur fantaisiste et sans doute impossible à raisonner. Cependant, lorsqu'il confie ses textes à la rédaction de *La Vie parisienne*, on assiste à diverses modifications secondaires qui trahissent l'intervention du rédacteur confronté aux conceptions singulières du poète[13] : la ponctuation peut être allégée et amendée, l'usage des tirets rationalisé, des graphies obsolètes comme *fesant* et *fesaient* normalisées, bien que cette graphie ancienne, que Corbière n'emploie pas exclusivement[14], qu'on retrouve dans des autographes y compris tardifs[15], et qui correspond précisément à la phonie du mot, ne soit pas une simple fantaisie personnelle puisqu'elle est toujours usitée à son époque, y compris dans l'édition : c'est ainsi que l'on peut relever *fesaient* dans la première édition des *Exilés*[16]. Autre exemple chez Jean-Baptiste Brossard, notaire à Chatonnay, qui, dans une fable imprimée, évoque « le pré [...] Où notre rossignol fesait briller sa voix », défiant involontairement l'âne que cette « voix rachitique » exaspère au point de le décider de montrer ce dont il est capable[17] : « Fesons donc aujourd'hui briller notre savoir ; / L'honneur, nous en fait un devoir. » Le contexte peut naturellement donner à voir dans cet exemple un archaïsme, en hommage à La Fontaine, mais la condamnation par l'Académie de ce

---

12 Art. cité, p. 106.
13 Certaines interventions affectent l'interprétation, comme la position des deux-points au v. 39 du *Douanier* qui élargit plus ou moins l'énumération dans *La Vie parisienne* en incluant ce qui n'est qu'une apostrophe ou une apposition dans *Les Amours jaunes* : « – Tout se trouvait en toi, bonne femme cynique : / Brantôme, [*etc.*] » dans *AJ* devient « – Tout se trouvait en toi : bonne femme cynique, / Brantôme, [*etc.*] » dans *VP*.
14 Voir p. ex. *faisais* dans *Bonne fortune et fortune* ; *faisant* dans *Un jeune qui s'en va* ou *Le Poète contumace* ; *faisaient* dans *Duel aux camélias* ou *Le Poète contumace*, etc. Le fait est que Corbière ne mélange pas les formes au sein d'un même poème, celles en *fes-* étant cantonnées dans *Idylle coupée* (deux fois *fesant*), *La Pastorale de Conlie* (*fesant* et *fesaient*) et *Le Novice en partance* (*fesons*).
15 Voir ainsi, p. ex. *fesais* dans « Moi ton amour ?... » ajouté p. 40 dans son exemplaire personnel ; éd. Houzé, « Le dernier Corbière », p. 329.
16 Éd. 1867, p. 77 (mais *faisaient* p. 216).
17 Dans *L'Âne et le rossignol, fable*, [1866], n.p.

genre de formes qui sentaient encore leur Ancien Régime ne les avait pas éradiquées des usages, y compris littéraires, comme on peut s'en rendre compte en consultant Gallica. C'est sans doute de son propre père que notre poète tenait cette habitude, bien que ce dernier – à moins que l'imprimeur n'en soit responsable – emploie de préférence les formes régulières en *fais-*[18].

Les traits d'union d'*aires-de-vent* (*Le Douanier*), ceux de *tour-à-tour* (*Le Bossu Bitor*), celui, à la rime, de *Fornarine-*/*Graziella* (*Le Fils de Lamartine*) sont abandonnés ; le premier de *faux-turcs-espagnols* (*La Pastorale de Conlie*) de même, avec introduction des majuscules manquantes ; les deux premiers de *Cygne-de-Saint-Point* (*Le Fils de Lamartine*) de même, avec abandon de l'italique et de la majuscule initiale ; de même ceux de *Mois-noir*[19] et *Mois-plus-noir* (*La Pastorale de Conlie*) avec abandon de l'italique et des majuscules qui signalent par contre le calque d'expressions bretonnes – *miz du* et *miz kerzu* – pour désigner respectivement les mois de novembre et de décembre, comme indiqués en commentaire entre tirets. Accents : le circonflexe de *à crû* (*À une demoiselle*) est abandonné. Comment en effet ne pas attribuer à la rédaction de *La Vie parisienne* seule l'ensemble de ces interventions sur des usages aussi déroutants ? Bernardelli en vient quant à lui à évoquer « des habitudes rédactionnelles qui devaient être devenues chez lui une seconde nature[20] » :

> [...] il est difficile de penser que le névrotique, bizarre et un peu frénétique Tristan [...] pût avoir modifié et uniformisé dans cet unique cas [*de publication d'un recueil poétique*] des habitudes rédactionnelles qui devaient être devenues une seconde nature : d'autant plus si l'on tient compte de la patience, de la méticulosité et de l'attention que requiert une telle opération, toutes ces choses qui, assurément, ne sont pas comprises dans l'économie nerveuse de l'instable et faible « *Mazzzeppa* [*sic*] » Corbière ; [...][21]

---

18   Voir ainsi dans *Le Négrier* : *fesais* p. III et 412, *fesait* p. 11, 13, 35 *etc.*, *fesaient* p. 103, 115, *fesant* p. 353, *fesons* p. 161, *fesions* p. 236. Mais *faisais* p. IV *etc.*, *faisant*, p. XIV *etc.*, *faisait* p. 1 *etc.*, *faisaient* p. 6 *etc.*, *faisions* p. 22 *etc.*

19   Sans trait d'union (mais avec l'italique également) dans *Le Douanier*, 9.

20   « Il testo contumace », p. 43-44 (trad. nôtre) : « [...] *riesce difficile pensare che il nevrotico, bizzarro e un po' frenetico Tristan* [...] *possa aver modificato ed uniformato in quest'unico caso abitudini redazionali che dovevano essere diventate una seconda natura : tanto più se si tien conto della pazienza, dell'acribia e dell'attenzione che una simile operazione richiede, tutte cose, queste, di sicuro non comprese nella precaria economia nervosa dell'instabile e labile Mazzzeppa* [*sic*] Corbière ».

21   Sur l'allusion finale voir *infra*, p. 480.

Ces négligences ne doivent par conséquent pas être mises sur le compte d'une volonté de provocation qui a bien d'autres manières de se manifester, notamment par l'utilisation d'une langue empruntant à tous les registres et ne reculant pas même devant les solécismes. On peut du reste comprendre les restrictions des v. 19-20 d'*Épitaphe*, au moins en partie, comme une reconnaissance de ces maladresses qui affectent la qualité de ses vers : « Poète en dépit de ses vers ; / Artiste sans art… ».

Il suffit de comparer le recueil avec d'autres ouvrages issus du même éditeur[22] pour constater que le manque de soin accordé à l'édition des *Amours jaunes* est exceptionnel et vraisemblablement lié aux relations qu'entretenait le poète, manifestement insensible à ces aspects formels, avec son éditeur qui, vraisemblablement, se reposait entièrement sur ses auteurs pour la correction des épreuves, son imprimeur se gardant peut-être quant à lui de toute initiative sur le texte si peu conventionnel qui lui était confié[23]. Le volume des *Amours jaunes* s'inscrit dans la production des frères Glady que Bernardelli considère comme destinée à des amateurs et à des bibliophiles, caractérisée – notre recueil mis à part – par « una coretezza quasi assoluta[24] ». Les frères Glady n'ont en fait publié que très peu de poésie, dont un seul recueil antérieur aux *Amours jaunes*, soit *Læta mæsta* de P. Darasse, paru le 26 mai précédent sous la raison sociale « Librairie du XIXe siècle[25] », où l'auteur, dans sa préface, conseille à ses lecteurs peu portés à la mélancolie de s'en tenir aux *læta* afin de s'éviter de « choir en tristification », et, dans son poème final, s'interroge sur l'avenir des recueils poétiques, se demandant s'il n'aurait pas mieux fait de se noyer plutôt que d'affronter le public, non sans espérer que ses poèmes feront la conquête des dames, évitant ainsi à l'éditeur

---

22 Voir Bernardelli, « Il testo contumace », p. 39-40.

23 Walzer, éd. citée, p. 691 évoque « une édition très soignée du point de vue typographique, mais malheureusement corrigée par des novices ».

24 « Il testo contumace », p. 40. Voir sur le site Gallica les recueils suivants publiés en 1875 : *La Bohême sentimentale* de Maurice Montégut (mentionnée par Bernardelli ; « Typographie Georges Chamerot ») et *Coups de bâton* de Louis Verbrugghe (« Imprimé par J. Claye pour Glady frères, éditeurs »), où l'on trouve tout au plus quelques lignes orphelines qui n'affectent que la mise en page (et dont on peut relever près d'une quinzaine de cas dans les *Amours jaunes* ; voir p. 69, 74, 91 *etc.*).

25 Sur la production des frères Glady, voir Debauve, « Autour de la publication », p. 56-57, et les compléments apportés par L. Maunoury, signalés par Steinmetz, *Une vie à-peu-près*, p. 431, n. 1.

« de boire un funeste bouillon[26] ». Avec ses ornements, sa gravure en
page de titre présentant la devise de la maison – « NON GLADIO
GLADY » –, culs-de-lampe, vignettes, bandeaux, et initiales ornées
des poèmes liminaires, la variété et l'élégance des caractères choisis[27]
ainsi que l'insertion d'une eau-forte[28], le volume a en outre toutes
les caractéristiques d'une édition de luxe, en particulier dans les neuf
exemplaires tirés sur papier jonquille[29], qui font davantage ressortir
le désastre typographique qu'il offre au lecteur, ce qui vaut au livre la
description par Bernardelli d'un volume excellemment confectionné
pour un texte imprimé de façon désastreuse[30]. Comme le note l'un des
premiers recenseurs de l'ouvrage, Alexandre Piedagnel, dans la *Revue
de France* : « Au point de vue matériel, le livre est fort élégant : il fait
grand honneur aux éditeurs – qui ne s'en tiendront pas là ! », passant
toutefois sous silence la question de son inachèvement[31].

Cet aspect témoigne de l'attention que Corbière accordait à la mise en
page, ce qui rend d'autant plus frappant son désintérêt pour les questions
d'ordre typographique où l'on a pu également envisager la part qu'eût
pu y prendre le prote. Fongaro a ainsi évoqué avec quelque excès « la
responsabilité, certainement importante, du typographe dans toutes ces
anomalies[32] », mais on ne peut pas mettre au compte de l'imprimeur
sollicité pour ce recueil l'état désastreux du texte imprimé, même s'il
n'est pas question de le dédouaner d'éventuelles erreurs typographiques
ou coquilles[33] : comme le fait remarquer G. Bernardelli, s'il fallait l'en

---

26　L'ouvrage est imprimé par l'atelier de typographie Georges Chamerot, comme d'autres
　　ouvrages des frères Glady (*cf. supra* n. 24).
27　Voir parmi d'autres Bernardelli, « Il testo contumace », p. 31.
28　Pour la description externe du volume, voir Walzer, éd. citée, p. 1433-1434 ; Steinmetz,
　　Une vie à-peu-près, p. 403-404. Pour une description de l'eau-forte, voir en particulier
　　Houzé et Hérisson, *op. cit.*, p. 83-84.
29　Voir Houzé, « Corbière créateur d'objets », p. 29.
30　« Il testo contumace », p. 39 : « *Pubblicato il libro o meglio, per essere precisi, eccelentemente
　　confezionato il volume e disastrosamente stampato il testo, Corbière lo diffonde normalmente,
　　inviandone copie d'omaggio con dedica a parenti, amici e critici* » ; « Une fois le livre publié ou
　　mieux, pour être précis, une fois le texte confectionné de la meilleure des façons mais
　　imprimé de façon désastreuse, Corbière le diffuse normalement, envoyant des copies
　　d'hommage dédicacées à des parents, des amis et des critiques » (trad. nôtre).
31　*Revue de France*, III, 8 (oct. 1873), p. 233-234.
32　« Sur le texte », p. 77.
33　Voir ainsi l'oubli fréquent d'espaces avant tel ou tel tiret, point d'exclamation *etc.* ; les
　　rares défauts d'impression de tel ou tel caractère comme l'*i* de *pourquoi* terminant le v. 11

rendre responsable « il devait alors s'agir d'un prote dont l'incompétence et la distraction sortent de l'ordinaire pour laisser passer un nombre aussi élevé d'irrégularités ; le même prote, du reste, qui a supervisé avec tant de soin la composition des pages, la distribution des espaces et des lignes, le centrage exact des titres et le choix des caractères[34] » : le prote n'aura corrigé que les erreurs qui lui auront été signalées par l'auteur sur les épreuves à lui confiées. C'est en effet Alcan-Lévy, petit imprimeur certes – qualifié d'« imprimeur gastronome » par Monselet en raison de son activité ouverte aux demandes d'impressions de menus et autres faire-part[35] –, mais habitué des textes littéraires et plus précisément poétiques puisqu'il imprime également pour le compte d'Alphonse Lemerre les cinq numéros de *La Gazette rimée* (février-juin 1867), les neuf numéros de *La nouvelle Némésis* (août-octobre 1868) et certains numéros de *La Jeune France* et qui a déjà imprimé, pour le compte de Hetzel, d'Édouard Dentu ou Alphonse Lemerre comme pour son propre compte, des plaquettes ou recueils de poésie sans défauts apparents[36], recevant même compliments et récompenses, comme l'indique Y. Bernal qui s'est penché sur l'activité de l'imprimeur[37]. Ceci étant, il est frappant que la critique ait fermé les yeux sur cet état déplorable du texte, tout un chacun sachant, finalement, que, de toute façon, la poésie est ailleurs. L'un de ses premiers critiques, frappé par l'originalité du ton et

---

du *Crapaud* ; les nombreuses coquilles, diverses erreurs de style de caractères comme les deux-points en italique après une séquence en romain au premier vers de *Décourageux etc.*, le mélange du romain et de l'italique dans le titre « ÇA » dans la table des matières *etc.* (Bernal, « Corbière, les coquilles », p. 32-36, en liste l'essentiel).

34 « Il testo contumace », p. 35 (trad. nôtre) : « *doveva trattarsi di un proto dalla incompetenza e dalla distrazione fuori dell'ordinario, per lasciare passare un numero così alto di irregolarità : lo stesso proto del resto che con tanta cura sovrintendeva alla comppsizione degli spazi e dei fregi, alla esatta centratura dei titoli, alla scelta dei caratteri* ».

35 *L'Almanach gourmand*, pour l'année 1867, Paris, Librairie du Petit journal ; au 8 mars du « calendrier gastronomique ».

36 Voir p. ex., pour la période qui nous intéresse : *Sonnets à Ninon* de Winoc Jacquemin, Paris, Lemerre, 1867 ; *Angélique. Poème – Pensées* de Camille Delthil, Paris, Hetzel, 1869 ; *Premiers rayons et épines. Poésies* d'A. Caminat, Paris, Typographie Alcan-Lévy, 1870 ; *Poésies du Marquis Eugène de Lonlay*, Paris, chez Alcan-Lévy, 1970 ; *La Ronde des Courtisanes* de Georges, Paris, s.n., 1870 ; *Date lilia* d'Hector de Saint-Maur, Paris, Impr. Alcan-Lévy, 1872 ; *Le Repentir. Récit d'un Curé de campagne. Poème* d'Albert Delpit, Paris, E. Dentu, 1873 ; *Le Livre défendu* d'Ed. Allony [E. de Lonlay], Paris, E. Dentu, 1873.

37 « Corbière, les coquilles », p. 41-43 ; nous sélectionnons et complétons ici les indications données par cet auteur en nous concentrant sur la période qui nous intéresse. Voir aussi les précisions données par le même dans « Elzévirien à voir », p. 249-252.

manifestement sensible au renouveau que le poète apportait dans le cadre de l'académisme ambiant, considérait du reste comme négligeables « les bizarreries de style dont la fréquence fatigue plus qu'elle n'ennuie[38] ».

De fait, Corbière n'a pas de doctrine en matière de ponctuation : ses choix et ses oublis semblent obéir à de simples pulsions au gré de l'écriture, comme il le faisait au collège, sans réfléchir davantage « avant de [s]e laisser aller au caprice de [s]a plume ou au courant de ses idées » comme le lui reprochait son père[39], ponctuant selon l'inspiration du moment.

38 Exhumé par Houzé de *La Bibliographie contemporaine*, 1re année, 1er oct. 1873, p. 140-141.
39 Lettre citée par Bernardelli, « Il testo contumace », p. 42.

PONCTUATION ET INTERPRÉTATION

Parler comme Fongaro d'«étourderies conjuguées du poète et du prote» ou de «phénomènes tout à fait anodins et qui ne sauraient tirer à conséquence ni pour la langue ni pour la poésie» paraît quelque peu abusif lorsque l'on prend en compte leur quantité (si ce n'est leur qualité), ce que le critique reconnaît malgré tout en concédant que «le lecteur est plus d'une fois choqué par les contradictions qu'il rencontre dans le texte[1]». Les négligences et incohérences répétées du recueil ne doivent pas en effet être balayées d'un simple revers de main au motif que la poésie de Corbière est justement «ailleurs», car elles suscitent parfois des interrogations sur de possibles coquilles[2], ou même sur la construction et le sens voulus, les variations semblant aussi bien liées à des changements d'humeur qu'à de pures inconséquences[3]. Ainsi, le fonctionnement des tirets ouvrant/fermant censés isoler une unité syntagmatique du contexte pose souvent problème, non seulement pour l'apparition immotivée de majuscules et l'absence de ponctuation finale qu'ils peuvent engendrer, mais aussi pour des raisons liées à la structuration des énoncés comme au v. 2 de *Sonnet à sir Bob* :

> Beau chien, quand je te vois caresser ta maîtresse,
> Je grogne malgré moi – pourquoi ? – Tu n'en sais rien...

La minuscule de *pourquoi* semble rattacher l'interrogation à ce qui précède, que l'on y voie une interrogation sur l'énoncé ou l'expression

---

1 «Sur le texte», p. 77 et 83. On trouvera dans Houzé et Hérisson, *op. cit.*, p. 396-399 et 403-410, un précieux relevé commenté de diverses anomalies de ponctuation, dont certaines sont ici discutées. Dans la table des matières, «poète» prend la majuscule – comme «cigale» – dans le poème introductif mais pas dans le poème conclusif.
2 Voir en particulier *infra*, p. 219, notre remarque à propos du v. 17 de *Ça ?* ; p. 145-147, à propos de *cabré* dans un vers du *Douanier*.
3 Sur la question générale de l'expressivité de la ponctuation chez Corbière, voir Lescane, «Revoir la ponctuation des *Amours jaunes*».

même du grognement, alors qu'il s'agit plus vraisemblablement d'une phrase nouvelle, portant bien sur l'énoncé précédent, le tiret fermant semblant l'isoler de ce qui vient pourtant lui apporter réponse.

Examinons à présent les strophes suivantes de *Paria* (39-48) :

> Mon passé : c'est ce que j'oublie.
> 40   La seule chose qui me lie
> C'est ma main dans mon autre main.
> Mon souvenir – Rien – C'est ma trace.
> Mon présent, c'est tout ce qui passe
> 44   Mon avenir – Demain… demain
>
> Je ne connais pas mon semblable ;
> Moi, je suis ce que je me fais.
> – *Le Moi humain est haïssable…*
> 48   – Je ne m'aime ni ne me hais.

On se demande pourquoi le prédicat de « Mon passé » est introduit par deux-points, mais pas celui de « Mon souvenir » ni celui de « Mon présent » ou de « Mon avenir ». On se demande pourquoi « C'est ma trace » (42) commence par une majuscule, alors qu'un parallélisme semble le rapprocher de « c'est ce que j'oublie » et de « c'est tout ce qui passe », prédicats respectifs de « Mon passé » et « Mon présent » : la majuscule suggère qu'il s'agit au contraire d'une phrase nouvelle, avec une proposition indépendante, laissant « Mon souvenir » isolé ; à moins de voir en « Rien » – à la majuscule ambiguë – son prédicat qui serait ainsi le véritable pendant à « c'est ce que j'oublie », alors que les tirets semblent désigner ce pronom comme une apposition détachée. Quant à « Mon avenir », on se demande s'il est placé sur le même plan que « Mon passé », « Mon souvenir » et « Mon présent », puisqu'aucun signe de ponctuation ne vient clore l'énoncé précédent (« c'est tout ce qui passe »), invitant à voir en lui le COD de *passe* : « Mon présent, c'est tout ce qui passe / Mon avenir ». Mais si l'on défend l'idée qu'un point final a été omis à la fin du v. 43[4], on se demande alors si « Demain » avec une majuscule est le prédicat de « Mon avenir » comme « Rien » pourrait l'être par rapport à « Mon souvenir », ou s'il n'est pas plutôt

---

4   Comme le fait Bernardelli, « Il testo contumace », p. 50-51, qui défend aussi l'hypothèse de l'omission du point en fin de strophe (vers suivant) (nous sommes bien évidemment d'accord avec lui).

une apposition détachée (« Mon avenir – [qui est] Demain ») comme le suggère l'emploi du tiret mais que l'emploi de la majuscule vient contredire si l'on ne savait que le tiret déclenche souvent chez Corbière l'emploi inopiné d'une majuscule (sans parler d'une valeur générique que la majuscule permet parfois d'exprimer). Le problème se complique encore avec l'absence de point en fin de strophe qui peut inviter à voir en « demain » avec minuscule un CC de la proposition indépendante qui suit en ouverture de la strophe suivante, tandis que « Demain » avec une majuscule serait le même adverbe détaché en tête de phrase, auquel cas on attendrait un point après « Mon avenir » : « Demain... demain[,] / Je ne connais pas mon semblable ». Ce à quoi s'oppose, naturellement, la division en strophes (de longueur variable), dont l'unité est partout ailleurs définie par la disposition des rimes et par le sens. Du point de vue strictement sémantique, on ne peut manquer de relever que « Mon passé », « Mon avenir » et « Mon présent » s'inscrivent dans une même orientation chronologique, laissant « Mon souvenir » de côté comme un thème rattaché à « Mon passé », ce qui incite à comprendre le v. 42 comme "Mon souvenir n'est rien, sinon la trace que je laisse derrière moi". Pour autant, rien ne nous permet de penser que c'est à dessein que Corbière a aussi mal ponctué son texte, et c'est à nous qu'il appartient aujourd'hui de tenter de résoudre les problèmes herméneutiques que ces inconséquences peuvent nous poser, si tant est que l'on puisse trancher.

Ce qui distingue par conséquent Corbière des autres poètes, c'est le fait qu'il ne cherche pas à remédier dans son recueil poétique aux déficiences et aux ambiguïtés d'ordre typographique, ce qu'il ne fait pas par provocation mais par une certaine méconnaissance doublée d'une insouciance à l'égard des règles et du rituel des épreuves, son projet poétique n'incluant pas la perfection ni la cohérence linguistique et formelle dont se soucient les écrivains ordinaires : tout à fait conscient de sa singularité, Corbière se dit poète « en dépit de ses vers ». Comme il le dit en tentant vainement de caractériser son recueil : « Ce n'est poli ni repoli. [...] A peine est-ce français ! », ce qui suffit à expliquer les interventions, certainement discutables dans le détail[5], de la rédaction de *La Vie parisienne*[6]. Ces manquements innombrables d'une ponctuation

---

5   Voir notamment les observations de Bernardelli, « Il testo contumace », p. 42-43, et de Fongaro, « Sur le texte », p. 78.
6   Voir *supra*, p. 43-44.

incertaine qui suit les humeurs du poète écrivant sont peut-être l'une des clés susceptibles d'expliquer dans *Cris d'aveugle* le quasi-abandon de cette convention embarrassante que constituait pour lui ce système aux règles complexes destiné à la clarification du texte, dont il n'avait qu'une connaissance approximative[7].

Ce dédain de la ponctuation et de la typographie rend en tout cas d'autant plus significatif le respect scrupuleux de l'alignement relatif des vers de même mesure, ordonnés de façon à rendre compte de leur longueur, les alexandrins étant les plus proches de la marge gauche des pages conformément à l'usage traditionnel des recueils poétiques en vers (avant l'introduction du vers libre)[8] : ce dispositif peut du reste aider à résoudre certaines ambiguïtés comme « Aussi goélands que les goélands » (*Le Naufrageur*, 7) qui est un octosyllabe, non un taratantara, comme le prouve du reste le signe de synérèse adopté dans l'album Noir[9] ; et ce scrupule est bien utile pour repérer telle ou telle synérèse abusive comme certaines diérèses facultatives, ou pire encore fautives, à effectuer, non, parfois, sans quelque marge d'incertitude, comme dans « Chiens errants, vieux rats, fraudeurs et douaniers » (*Le Poète contumace*, 14), qui est un alexandrin, non un taratantara (5 + 5), la diérèse portant sur *chiens* ou *vieux* dans le premier hémistiche[10], sur *douaniers* dans le second[11]. On opposera par ailleurs les incertitudes et les hésitations dont le poète fait preuve dans l'emploi des accents à la sûreté avec laquelle il signale systématiquement par le circonflexe la présence d'*e* muets postvocaliques comme l'y incitait la tradition poétique, comme dans *oublîrai*[12].

---

7   Sur ce poème voir *infra*, p. 93-95.

8   Le principal problème concerne *Le Douanier* où octo- et heptasyllabes partagent le même alignement (Billy, « Corbière avant Tristan », p. 178 et 184). Ailleurs, les défauts d'alignement concernent un vers affecté d'une grande capitale initiale : un taratantara parmi des octosyllabes (*Épitaphe*, 8) ; un autre taratantara en tête d'un morceau hétérométrique, mêlant octosyllabes et alexandrins, aligné sur les octosyllabes (*Grand opéra*, IIIe acte, 1), sur lequel voir p. 237. Dans *Sonèto a Napoli*, le dernier vers – un pentasyllabe – est aligné sur les autres, de sept syllabes. Dans *Le Phare*, le v. 2 est décalé vers la droite (le décalage correspond à la largeur de la grande capitale). Restent de rares décalages fautifs, comme p. 249, aux v. 74 et 84.

9   Voir Billy, « Corbière avant Tristan », p. 190-192 (où l'on corrigera la coquille à « taratantatara »).

10   Plus vraisemblablement sur *vieux* qui vient en second.

11   Plus vraisemblablement sur *doua-* (ce que justifie l'étymologie) que sur *niers* (bien que Corbière traite en diérèse divers mots suffixés en *ier*).

12   Voir *infra*, p. 138.

ORTHOGRAPHE ET DYSORTHOGRAPHIE

Dansel a mis à plat de façon assez détaillée les questions touchant à l'orthographe dans les *Amours jaunes*, avec un classement certainement discutable[1] mais qui donne une bonne idée du problème. On peut regrouper les phénomènes sous les rubriques de la gémination, des accents, de l'*s/x* de flexion, de l'*s* adverbial, des substitutions de graphèmes, de l'abandon de lettres étymologiques, de l'emploi des majuscules et de celui du trait d'union, de la graphie des mots étrangers enfin. Fongaro a depuis apporté de nombreuses clés qui permettent d'apprécier correctement diverses irrégularités que l'on avait pu relever dans une certaine méconnaissance des usages de l'époque : il est même nécessaire de garder à l'esprit que les normes connaissaient des hésitations d'un dictionnaire à l'autre et qu'elles pouvaient même évoluer d'une édition à l'autre de ces ouvrages de référence. Toujours est-il que les anomalies observées doivent être mesurées à l'aune des normes mais aussi à celle des usages graphiques contemporains tant dans l'édition que dans l'écriture personnelle des écrivains[2]. Exemple parmi d'autres, pour nous en tenir aux poètes, Baudelaire, qui « était obsédé par la correction orthographique[3] », n'était pas toujours régulier dans ce domaine, écrivant *aumones, cloitres, hopital, pamoisons* ou même *pret* dans ses poèmes ; *abbréviation, appaiser, inapperçu, caraffe, chipper, cravatte, difammer, raffollent* ou *ribotte*, ou encore *acquiter, raccomoder, resuscitant, soumetrai etc.* dans sa correspondance. Mais il n'en était pas plus assuré lorsqu'il passait à la correction d'épreuves ou travaillait à la réédition des *Fleurs du Mal*, ressentant le besoin de faire part à Poulet-Malassis de ses incertitudes sur l'emploi des accents ou le redoublement de

---

1 *Langage et modernité*, p. 35-43. La catégorie « inadvertances » orthographiques est un fourre-tout.
2 Voir l'examen détaillé auquel se livre Fongaro, « Sur le texte », p. 79-81 et les remarques sur Baudelaire p. 83.
3 Selon l'expression de Nuiten, *Les Variantes*, p. 3.

consonnes[4], alors que la correction de son texte ne semble pas avoir particulièrement préoccupé Corbière.

Le désintérêt de notre poète pour ces questions se traduit du reste de façon négative au travers de l'*errata* où il ne trouve que deux vers à reprendre[5], ignorant par contre telle ou telle coquille (ou peut-être transcription littérale de *lapsus calami*)[6], à tel point que l'on peut effectivement se demander s'il a seulement revu les épreuves avec un tant soit peu d'attention, moins au vu de ses manquements à l'orthographe qui doivent être relativisés que des bévues typographiques et surtout de l'emploi irrégulier et incohérent de la ponctuation : l'attention du poète « pédicure[7] » semble s'être alors concentrée sur la question de la mesure, les deux vers repris dans l'*errata* fautant par un mot de trop ou de moins, ce qui ne l'empêche pas de ne pas remarquer des problèmes du même ordre affectant d'autres vers[8]. La présence même de l'*errata* comme l'état déplorable du texte tend même à indiquer que Corbière n'a vraisemblablement pas procédé à une lecture critique de son texte dans le temps qui lui était imparti pour la révision des épreuves, ces corrections étant intervenues *après* l'impression de l'ouvrage[9]. Comme l'a démontré Bernardelli, l'absence de corrections sur son propre exemplaire dont les marges et pages vierges sont par contre l'objet d'ajouts manuscrits de poèmes nouveaux et de ponctuels remaniements est particulièrement significatif du désintérêt de Corbière pour ces petites choses qu'il n'éprouve naturellement pas le besoin de corriger sur les exemplaires qu'il envoie à tel ou tel de ses parents, amis ou critiques[10]. Ces irrégularités, bévues et incohérences qui ont subsisté dans l'ouvrage

---

4   Voir les nombreux éléments rassemblés par Nuiten, *Les Variantes*, p. 3-15 et 33-37. Voir aussi la remarque de Fongaro, « Sur le texte », p. 81, sur l'emploi de *stygmate* et *alterre*.

5   *Errata* plus ou moins ignoré dans diverses réimpressions selon Walzer, éd. citée, p. 1338, note à p. 817.

6   Voir p. ex. « des souvenir [*sic*] de cœur » (p. 299), l'omission de l'accent dans « l'Antechrist » (p. 199), « plait » (p. 246), « citoyens-décreteurs » (p. 247) ; pour d'autres exemples, voir Bernardelli, « Il testo contumace », p. 31. On peut supposer que divers problèmes de ponctuation sont liés à l'inattention de Corbière ou/et du typographe comme l'absence de virgule après IMPRIMÉ, apposition détachée constitutive du v. 2 de *Le Poète et la Cigale* ; ou encore le point-virgule terminant le v. 32 de *Paria* (supprimé par Aragon et Bonnin, éd. citée, p. 11 et 302).

7   Selon l'expression de « Poète. – Après ?... Il faut *la chose*... », en suivant l'interprétation d'Aragon et Bonnin, éd. citée, p. 37, qui comprend « arrangeur de pieds [*syllabes*] ».

8   Cf. *infra*, p. 140.

9   Cf. *infra*, p. 120.

10 Voir Bernardelli, « Il testo contumace », p. 39.

imprimé sont à ce point fréquentes que le lecteur aventureux a dû se trouver pour le moins décontenancé quand le traitement provocateur de la langue même et ses « quolibets de commis-voyageur insupportable » ne suscitaient pas son rejet, ne voyant là que les travers si bien décrits par Huysmans, en s'arrêtant à son constat ainsi résumé : « C'était à peine français », sans en voir les fulgurances d'expression[11]. Que Corbière en fût conscient nous paraît évident au vu de son envoi manuscrit, l'exposant aux mauvais traitements matériels et correctifs des lecteurs[12] :

> Et toi, va mon Livre. Qu'une femme te corne, qu'un fesse-cahier te fesse, qu'un malade te sourie.
> Reste pire − <tes moyens te le permettent>[13] Dis à ceux du métier que tu es un monstre d'artiste[14]...
> Pour les autres : 7 f. 50.
> Va mon livre, & ne me reviens plus

S'il pouvait défier les professionnels de l'édition, n'était-ce pas par la combinaison de l'excellence formelle et de la négligence linguistique, là où le chapitre de la correction orthographique *sensu lato* préoccupait ses confrères soucieux de présenter à leurs lecteurs un ouvrage répondant à un certain idéal de perfection éditoriale ? D'autres penseront sans doute que la *monstruosité* que voyait Corbière dans son ouvrage résidait moins dans ces aspects dont tous ses autographes témoignent qu'il s'en désintéressait plutôt, que dans la nouveauté iconoclaste d'un discours poétique qui a dû frapper ses lecteurs, du moins ces « gens du monde, cette clientèle qui fait rarement emplète [*sic*] de poésie » dont parlera Pol Kalig, le cousin de Corbière, qui, « séduits par le titre bizarre », se seront heurtés à un objet poétique dont l'extravagance même ne pouvait que les choquer[15] :

---

11 *À rebours*, p. 248-249.
12 Levi, « New lights », p. 237, y voyait un poème ; Walzer, éd. citée, p. 1389, parle d'un « essai de préface abandonnée ». L'envoi − intitulé *Parade* − remplace en fait la préface « oubliée » que mentionne Corbière dans un premier temps. Voir Houzé, « Le dernier Corbière », p. 317 et 340 (fac-similé).
13 La phrase entre coins a été rajoutée après coup ; fac-similé dans Houzé, « Le dernier Corbière », p. 340, fig. 1.
14 À comprendre comme "un monstre commis par un artiste" ; *cf.* l'évocation dans la fable finale de « Son honteux monstre de livre ».
15 Cité par Martineau, *Tristan Corbière*, p. 93. Voir en particulier le témoignage du critique belge signant E.V. dans *L'Art universel* du 1er nov. 1873 cité par Debauve, « Autour de la publication », p. 72-76 (commentaire p. 66-67).

« Le côté leste, vigoureux et brutal, effroyablement vécu, leur éclata à la figure, les aveugla si bien qu'ils crièrent à l'abomination. » Rien en effet ne préparait le lecteur à la crudité de certains poèmes, même pas leur parution chez les frères Glady dont c'était là le premier ouvrage offrant un caractère scabreux comme l'ont démontré en leur temps Bernardelli et Debauve[16]. L'examen auquel a procédé A. Fongaro montre que les atteintes à l'orthographe sont beaucoup plus limitées qu'elles n'ont longtemps semblé. Un certain nombre de graphies anciennes étaient les formes d'usage du temps de Corbière, comme *phthisie*, *phthisique*, parfois en concurrence avec les formes modernes, comme *Norwégiens* et *syrènes*, mais Corbière peut également faire appel à des archaïsmes comme *huys* et *hyver*[17]. On peut apporter quelques précisions sur ces formes :

Norwégiens : selon Frantext, la forme est très minoritaire, avec quatre occurrences de 1800 à 1873, dont celle des *Amours jaunes*, les trois autres datant plus précisément de 1824 et 1827, contre trente-quatre de *norvégien(s)*, mais ces données ne nous semblent pas représentatives. Bescherelle, dont le grand dictionnaire date de 1843, n'a toujours qu'une entrée à *Norwégien* dans sa quatorzième édition (*DN* II, 656) tandis que Larousse retient « NORVÈGE ou NORWÈGE » comme entrée principale, usant de la forme « Norvégiens » dans l'article, avec une entrée secondaire à « NORWÈGE ou NORWÈGIEN » (*GDU* XI, 1098, 1100), témoignant ainsi de l'évolution des usages (Littré ignore le mot). Gautier, Sainte-Beuve et Vacquerie, mais aussi Banville et Mendès, usent généralement de l'ancienne forme. Rimbaud ne connaît que *Norwège(s)* et *norvégien*.

syrènes : Corbière emploie au dernier vers du *Bossu Bitor* cette forme antiquisante, alors qu'il recourt à la forme académique dans *Laisser-courre* (18). Si Littré et Larousse n'ont plus qu'une entrée à *sirène*, conformément à la tradition académique, Bescherelle en a une également à *syrène*, sans qu'aucun lien ne soit explicitement établi entre

---

16   Bernardelli, « Il testo contumace », p. 53-54, n. 2 ; Debauve, art. cité, p. 55-58. Voir aussi le commentaire de Murphy, « Langues jaunes et vertes », n. 6. L'ignorance de ces contributions indispensables égare encore aujourd'hui maints commentateurs sur la réputation « sulfureuse » des frères Glady qui ne viendra que plus tard.

17   Cette graphie se retrouve dans sa lettre de novembre 1870 à Christine Puyo, voir Houzé, « Traces de Tristan Corbière », p. 21. À noter qu'É. Corbière emploie *hyvernage* dans *Les Trois pirates*, I, p. 6.

les deux articles (*DLF* IV, 1334, 1416). De fait, cette dernière graphie connaît un usage minoritaire concurrent de la norme tout au long du XIXᵉ siècle, plus prisé semble-t-il dans les milieux de l'art. Nous n'avons pas trouvé *sirène* dans les romans d'Édouard Corbière que nous avons consultés, mais *syrène* se trouve dans *Les Trois pirates* (I, p. 305). Un autre poète, Gindre de Mancy, emploie également l'une et l'autre forme dans un même recueil, sans que l'on sache s'il s'agit bien d'une alternative d'auteur[18].

huys : Corbière ne connaît qu'*huys* (4 occurrences) mais l'*y* disparaît dans *huissier(s)* (5). Cette préférence d'ordre esthétique ne semble pas répondre à une réelle volonté d'archaïsme que les contextes, du reste, n'appellent pas (au contraire d'*eschôlier*). Frantext ne l'atteste que chez Corbière et Michelet.

Parmi les graphies anciennes des *Amours jaunes*, il en est une dont il ne semble pas que l'on se soit avisé, si l'on en croit la persévérance des éditeurs, de Walzer à J.-P. Bertrand, à la tenir pour un archaïsme : le singulier *rais* (deux occurrences), qu'on trouve chez Aloysius Bertrand, Balzac (en parlant d'une roue), Flaubert, Bourget, Henri de Régnier, Huysmans, Verlaine, et dont l'usage se perpétue chez Maurice Barrès, Léon Bloy, Claudel, Gide, Raymond Roussel *etc*. De fait, *rai* est alors exceptionnel, avec une seule occurrence dans Frantext, chez Alphonse Daudet. Les dictionnaires d'époque ne connaissent que *rais*, conformément à la tradition académique qui, dès 1694, entérine l'usage qui s'était imposé à la fin du moyen-âge, Bescherelle précisant « s. m. pl. » pour le sens ici concerné, réservant une entrée à part comme « s. m. » pour le sens technique de rayon de roue (*DN* II, 1075). Larousse n'a qu'une entrée, à *rais*, défini comme « s. m. », soit sans mention de nombre, avec la définition « Rayon », le seul exemple au singulier concernant l'acception technique (*GDU* XIII, 658), reflétant ainsi les données fournies par le dictionnaire de l'Académie qui, dans sa septième édition (1878), donne également une seule entrée *rais*, présenté comme « s. m. pl. », avec une définition au pluriel, accompagnée de quelques exemples dont deux, contradictoires, ont *rai* au singulier, pour la seule acception technique, exemples repris des éditions précédentes où il y avait encore

---

18 *Les Échos du Jura*, p. 157 et 475.

un *s* : « *Il y a un rais rompu à cette roue* [...] » (*DAF* II, 561). N. Catach
considère que l'Académie a ici « écouté » la remarque de Littré (*DHOF*
867) qui, quatre ans auparavant, regroupant quatre acceptions différentes
sous la même entrée *rais* donné cette fois comme « s. m. », avec une
définition au singulier, précisait : « On devrait écrire *rai* au singulier
comme on faisait autrefois ; l'*s* n'a aucune raison d'être » (*DLF* IV, 1454),
infléchissant ainsi l'usage des écrivains et gens de lettres qui reviendront
peu à peu à la forme ancienne que reconnaîtra seule l'Académie dans sa
huitième édition achevée en 1935, avec un exemple au singulier pour
trois acceptions.

Une fois écartés les cas de licence poétique, conformes aux conceptions
en usage[19], les cas de graphies anciennes dont on usait encore à l'époque
de Corbière et, naturellement, la question des mots étrangers pour lesquels
le poète n'avait pas de connaissances précises, il reste essentiellement
des problèmes de redoublement de consonnes et d'accents que le poète
semble avoir hérités de son père auquel il doit tant, de sa culture et de
son imaginaire maritimes à son antiromantisme[20], comme il lui doit
une certaine liberté, plus ou moins significative, dans l'emploi du trait
d'union ou des majuscules initiales. L'inventaire des fautes d'orthographe
proprement dites et de l'utilisation inappropriée du singulier ou du
pluriel se réduit alors de façon significative, d'autant que l'on peut
relever parmi les cas restants des graphies alternatives attestées chez de
grands écrivains du XIXe siècle. Dans la plupart des cas, le problème
posé est lié à l'existence de telles graphies dont la préférence ne tire pas
à conséquence, mais le mésemploi des accents peut par contre soulever
des problèmes d'interprétation lorsqu'ils sont susceptibles de remplir
une fonction diacritique dans la langue académique (*çà* vs *ça*, *crû* vs *cru*
etc.). Notre examen portera sur la liste des corrections apportées par
Walzer, plus divers compléments, en mettant pour l'instant de côté les
formes déviantes où l'on a pu suspecter des rimes pour l'œil[21] que nous
examinerons au chapitre suivant de même que les licences poétiques.

Les formes qu'on ne retrouve pas dans le corpus XIXe siècle de Frantext
sont manifestement des inadvertances, d'autant plus évidentes quand
elles s'accompagnent d'hésitations avec les formes correctes, avec cette

---

19   Voir *infra*, p. 79-80.
20   Voir notamment Roudaut, *Ce qui nous revient*, p. 295-320 (« Les deux Corbière »).
21   Sur ces dernières, voir *infra*, p. 85-90.

réserve toutefois que l'on ne peut, dans le détail, imputer avec certitude ces dernières au poète plutôt qu'au prote, une présomption générale incitant plutôt à mettre les cas déviants sur le compte du poète. Il serait en tout cas pour le moins excessif d'imputer au prote qui s'est occupé de la composition des *Amours jaunes* une quelconque « ignorance de l'orthographe » à moins d'établir la preuve de sa responsabilité à travers, notamment, d'autres productions de Calmann-Lévy sur lesquels le même prote aurait sévi[22]. Certaines de ces formes attirent quelques remarques, que ce soit sur la pertinence d'une correction ou sur la présence, justement, de formes régulières dans le recueil, ou encore sur des aspects stylistiques divers ou de l'attestation desdites formes chez le père du poète qui constitue clairement pour Corbière une référence et une autorité (l'astérisque signale les formes corrigées par Walzer) :

Çà*/*çà** pour *Ça/ça* et inversement (*) : lorsqu'il n'emploie pas les capitales (pour lesquelles l'imprimeur ne connaît pas les accents associés à la lettre *A*), Corbière emploie l'accent grave pour le démonstratif, aussi bien au v. 12 – où il est mis en relief par l'italique – que dans l'en-tête de la page 4 (« *Çà* »), pour désigner le recueil des *Amours jaunes* comme un objet non identifié, échappant à toute classification :

> … ÇA c'est naïvement une impudente *pose;*
> C'est, ou ce n'est pas *çà* : rien ou quelque chose[23]…
> – Un chef-d'œuvre ? – Il se peut : je n'en ai jamais fait.
> – Mais, est-ce du huron, du Gagne, ou du Musset ?

Il y a une différence fondamentale entre *ça* et *çà* dont la discrimination par l'accent ne semble, dans une première approche, rien devoir à l'orthographe. Le premier est employé en fonction de thème, désignant l'objet considéré ; le second, en fonction de prédicat, c'est-à-dire

---

22 Ce que fait imprudemment Steinmetz, *Une vie à-peu-près*, p. 403, qui précise : « ignorance […] aggravée encore par les exigences singulières de Corbière : nombreux mots écrits à l'ancienne ou avec des traits d'union inhabituels, ponctuation expressive surmultipliée criblant les fins de vers de points d'exclamation ou de suspension ».

23 On notera au passage l'emploi inconséquent de la virgule : absente après « ÇA », où le détachement l'impose, on la trouve dans « S'il vit, c'est par oubli », p. 14, « Mon bout de crayon, c'est ma lyre » (*Un jeune qui s'en va*, 7), « tout cela, c'est moi » (*Guitare*, 11) *etc.* ; les contre-exemples ne manquent pas cependant : « ce crapaud-là c'est moi » (*Le Crapaud*, 14), « ce Dieu c'est quelque chose » (*Déclin*, 10), « La passion c'est l'averse / Qui traverse ! » *Après la pluie*, 13-14), « Le reste c'est le bel ouvrage au chirurgien » (*Matelots*, 84).

ce qu'on dit à propos du thème, ce qui le caractérise : « ÇA, c'est ou ce n'est pas *çà* » ; il semble en effet bien difficile de voir ici l'adverbe de lieu. De caractère emphatique, l'accent revêtirait ainsi une fonction particulière lorsqu'une valeur substantivale est donnée au pronom, d'autant que, partout ailleurs où le démonstratif est concerné, Corbière écrit la forme correctement ; le pronom ne servirait plus simplement à désigner l'objet de l'attention : il constituerait une catégorisation de l'innommable, du « je-ne-sais-quoi », et cette catégorisation semble être portée par le titre même si l'on en croit la forme du titre courant[24] qui s'oppose également au titre proprement dit du poème – « ÇA *?* » – par l'absence du point d'interrogation : « *Çà* » (p. 4), absence qui se retrouve dans le titre de la section désignant vraisemblablement le contenu de l'objet que le lecteur tient en mains[25]. Cependant, force est de constater que Corbière ne connaît pas l'usage diacritique de l'accent dans l'écriture de l'adverbe qu'on trouve au v. 58 de l'Acte I de *Grand opéra* (– Ça : n'as-tu jamais arrêté ») ni

---

24   En effet, dans ce que l'on doit considérer comme la première section du recueil, les titres courants des poèmes suivants ne correspondent pas à celui de la section mais à celui du poème en cours, soit, successivement, *Paris* et *Épitaphe*. *Cf.* note suivante.

25   Dans Houzé et Hérisson, *op. cit.*, p. 168 et 170-171, Houzé évoque la complexité de la structure du recueil pour cette section qui, à la fois « cascade de préfaces » (*cf.* Laforgue, « Une étude sur Corbière », p. 2, pour qui *Ça* est le titre de la préface) et section propre, présente des signes contradictoires : 1°) le titre *ÇA* de pleine page, suggère que la première section englobe *Paris* et *Épitaphe* qui sont dépourvus d'une telle page liminaire, mais ces deux poèmes sont, tout comme *Ça ?*, dotés chacun d'un bandeau, au même titre que les seuls poèmes liminaires des autres sections ; 2°) supposé être une section puisque donné en pleine page, *ÇA*, a bien un titre courant, écrit en minuscules (sauf initiale) comme dans les autres sections, ce changement de casse faisant apparaître un accent grave : « *Çà* » ; 3°) par contre *Paris* et *Épitaphe* ont pour titre courant leur propre titre, ce qui, comme le bandeau liminaire, les érige au rang de sections, contredisant l'absence d'une page de titre de section ; 4°) alors que les autres sections du recueil se terminent toutes sur un cul de lampe (spécifique), ni *Ça ?* ni *Paris*, ni même *Épitaphe* ne se terminent ainsi, un simple fleuron marquant la fin de chaque poème au même titre que les autres poèmes du recueil (à l'exclusion de ceux qui terminent chaque section). Pour ajouter à la confusion, la table des matières détache les trois titres comme les six sections suivantes au moyen d'un fleuron identique, avec le même emploi de la capitale italique (au A près dans « ÇA ») ; mais « ÇA », comme « *PARIS* » et « *ÉPITAPHE* », se trouve aligné à gauche, avec, au bout d'une série de points de suite, le numéro de p. 3 aligné à droite à l'instar de chacun des poèmes des sections suivantes, numéro de page qui correspond en fait au début du poème *Ça ?*, non à celui de la section *ÇA* donné en entrée, titre qui occupe la p. 1. Le sous-titre seul est dépourvu d'équivoque, passant directement de « ÇA » à « LES AMOURS JAUNES », ce qui ramène implicitement *Paris* et *Épitaphe* au rang de poèmes.

dans l'intriguant composé « Ah-ça » v. 174 du *Bossu Bitor*. Il est en fait plus vraisemblable que la présence ou non de l'accent ne soit pas significative si l'on songe que Corbière faisait déjà la confusion dans sa jeunesse : il pouvait écrire « çà t'affligerait et ça ferait », comme il pouvait omettre l'accent dans l'adverbe *là* : « Voila », « si j'avais été la[26] ». La présence d'un accent parasite dans « Çà m'est égal » et sur l'impératif « và » dans l'album Noir (quatre occurrences)[27] vient lever le doute : sa présence dans *Les Amours jaunes* trahit là encore une inadvertance, directement reproduite du manuscrit qu'il aura soumis à l'éditeur, inadvertance que l'on retrouve avec le circonflexe dans l'interjection *Hâ !* au second acte de *Grand opéra*.

*Bohême** : dans « remontant le cours / De l'Élysée à la Bohême » (*Le Convoi du pauvre*, 20), il y a un jeu de mots où le nom propre est censé évoquer le nom commun (le quartier de la bohème) pour lequel Corbière a une orthographe hésitante ;

*bohême** : notre recueil préfère nettement *ê* (« C'est la bohême, enfant... » et *Bohême de chic*, *À une Camarade* : « un bohême ») à *è* (*Male-Fleurette* : « *la fleur de bohème* »). Murger notamment usait du circonflexe ; Pierre Larousse également dans son entrée, tout en indiquant que « L'Académie écrit dans ce sens *Bohême* par un *è* », en refusant ce distinguo dont la raison lui échappe (*GDU* II, 866). Dans une litanie dédiée à « Sainte Bohême » copiée sur une feuille de garde de son exemplaire personnel, Corbière emploie 14 fois le mot, toujours avec le circonflexe, tandis que dans un essai de prose écrit à la suite, on trouve deux fois le mot (au pluriel), dans les deux cas avec l'accent grave[28]. Rappelons que Baudelaire, dans des mots où, certes, la fonction diacritique n'était pas liée à la polysémie, laissait imprimer *blasphême*, *diadême*, *emblême* et *trève* en 1857[29] ;

*côtre** : Corbière ne varie pas sur les huit occurrences de ce mot ; la pertinence de la graphie – toute relative pour ce dérivé d'angl. *cutter* – est

---

26   Voir les transcriptions données par Houzé, « Deux lettres inédites », p. 276 et 279.

27   Houzé, *ffocsoR*, p. 28 (f° 24r° : « Jeune philosophe en dérive »), et 22 (f° 2r° : sans titre – à l'envers, en haut à gauche) et 29 (f° 26r° : *A mon Roscoff*) respectivement. *Và* se retrouve dans la 17ᵉ strophe d'*Une mort trop travaillée* ainsi que dans le 11ᵉ quatrain d'une ancienne version de *Rapsodie d'un sourd* ; voir les transcriptions qu'en donne Houzé, « Nouvelle édition », p. 266 et 271-272.

28   Houzé, « Le dernier Corbière », p. 313-316.

29   Nuiten, *Les Variantes*, p. 33-34.

relevée par Dansel[30] : elle est en effet analogique de celle des mots où *ô* correspond toujours à un [o] fermé, en liaison ou non avec l'amuïssement d'un *s* (*apôtre, côte, trône, tôt etc.*), phénomène qu'on observe aussi dans *arôme** bien attesté par contre chez d'autres écrivains[31], motivation qui fait que l'on ne peut pas la tenir pour une simple faute d'orthographe. Corbière tient sans doute la forme de son père qui l'emploie ainsi dans *Le Négrier*, contrairement à La Landelle ; *clignotte**, pour lequel Fongaro semble suggérer l'attraction de la rime précédente *calotte : pâlotte*. C'est la graphie qu'adopte Verlaine dans *Chevaux de bois* (hors rime). Voir toutefois *infra*, p. 87-88, à propos des rimes ; *crû** (pour *cru*), pour lequel le recueil hésite, dans l'expression *à cru*, entre l'ajout du circonflexe (*Bohême de chic, À une demoiselle*) ou non (*Le Bossu Bitor*), ainsi que dans l'adjectif : *crû(s)* (*Épitaphe, Idylle coupée*) ou *cru* (*Le Bossu Bitor*, en rime avec *chahut*) : on remarquera que l'usage n'est pas contradictoire au sein d'un même poème, avec l'absence d'accent dans les deux occurrences du *Bossu Bitor*. Si nous n'avons pas trouvé le mot dans le roman de son père, *Le Négrier*, nous ferons remarquer qu'on y trouve par contre *dûs*. Cette incertitude qui pèse sur l'emploi du circonflexe peut laisser planer des doutes sur les véritables intentions du poète pour autant qu'il en ait eues. C'est ainsi que Le Dantec hésite sur l'interprétation de *trop crû* dans *Épitaphe* (48 : « Trop crû, – parce qu'il fut trop cuit », mais avec, deux vers avant : « Ne croyant à rien, croyant tout. »)[32] ; *hâl-* dans *hâle** (3e pers., dans *La Rapsode foraine* ; impér. dans *Le Bossu Bitor*[33] et *Le Renégat*), *hâlent** (*Le Bossu Bitor* et *Le Novice en partance*) et *hâler* (*Le Bossu Bitor*), n'est pas une graphie personnelle : c'est celle de La Landelle qui fait dériver le verbe de l'interjection « hâ[34] ! » et Corbière l'a vraisemblablement héritée de son père qui, dans *Le Négrier*, l'emploie toujours ainsi[35]. Dans *La Rapsode foraine*,

---

30 *Langage et modernité*, p. 38.
31 Voir *infra*, p. 66-67.
32 Éd. citée, p. 241.
33 Curieusement, et comme dans « hâler son bitor de misère », Walzer maintient ici le circonflexe : « Hâle à toi... ».
34 *Le Langage des marins*, p. 64 et 164 ; *FEW* 16, 130 le rattache au germ. oriental **halon*.
35 Mais pratiquement pas dans *Les Folles brises*, p. ex., comme on le verra plus loin, ou dans *Les Îlots de Martin Vaz* : rappelons que la quatrième édition du *Négrier* est donnée comme revenant au manuscrit de l'auteur.

le circonflexe est sans doute de trop, car s'il peut s'agir de l'issue de
germ. *halon, pris au sens figuré, l'issue de *halare (*FEW* 4, 377),
qui a donné *inhaler, exhaler* et *haleter*, ne peut être tout à fait écartée, même si ce mot est connu comme un régionalisme étranger à
la Bretagne (209-211) :

> Elle hâle comme une plainte,
> Comme une plainte de la faim,
> Et, longue comme un jour sans pain,
> Lamentablement, sa complainte...

N'écrit-il pas « – Taureau : foncerais ta porte... » (*Chanson en 'Si'*,
3) ? On ne peut en effet manquer de rapprocher cet emploi de
l'expression *exhaler une plainte*, même si le COD, ici, est *sa complainte*.
On peut ici citer tel passage d'un roman d'Édouard Corbière, qui
présente la même ambiguïté quant au sens : « tu viens d'épeler ce
mot [*il s'agit de "l'arithmétique", que l'élève vient de reproduire après
son maître qui le lit à la grecque : "larusmétiqueu..."*], qui est un peu
dur à haler, presque aussi bien que moi, le diable m'élingue ! » (*Les
Folles brises*, II, p. 43), à rapprocher de tel autre passage : « mon
ami ne put s'empêcher de me dire tout bas en donnant un libre
cours à l'indignation qu'il avait besoin d'exhaler : [...] » (*op. cit.*, II,
p. 151), qui donne à voir dans *haler* de la citation précédente une
forme réduite d'*exhaler* par contamination des racines et du sens :
l'articulation du mot savant est aussi difficile à sortir de soi (*exhaler*) qu'à tirer de soi (*haler*). L'image de *La Rapsode foraine* n'est pas
sans faire écho à celle du vieux marin de l'*Anémone* « qui, accoudé
sur le bossoir d'avant, psalmodiait une ancienne complainte dont
les accents allaient se perdre avec le souffle fugitif des vents, ou se
confondre avec les soupirs mélancoliques des flots[36] ».

mâle-mort (*vs male-fleur* et *Male-Fleurette*) : le circonflexe est clairement
abusif au vers 10 de *Fleur d'art* (« la mâle-mort de l'amour ») ; de même
au vers 32 de *La Pastorale de Conlie*, même si ce sont les mobilisés
du Morbihan qui en sont menacés. Walzer y voit une « plaisanterie
orthographique » qui lui « semble [...] bien du goût de Corbière[37] ».

---

36 É. Corbière, *Les Îlots de Martin Vaz*, I, p. 33-34.
37 Éd. citée, p. 1285. Il attire l'attention, p. 1365, sur les méprises qui ont pu porter sur
    Male-Fleurette et *male-fleur*.

Le circonflexe peut cependant se rencontrer, même si c'est rarement : « Louis [...] fit mourir de mâle mort les chefs de la rébellion », « châtier les auteurs en les faisant mourir de mâle mort[38] ». Quant au tiret, son emploi se rencontre parfois, comme chez Gautier, dans *Le Capitaine Fracasse* (1863, II, p. 72) ou dans *Les Compagnons du roi* d'Albert Delpit (1874, p. 124).

*pêché** (*fleur de p.*) dans *Pudentiane*, contre *péché* dans *Le Fils de Lamartine* ; Corbière se plaît à des emplois ambigus du verbe qui viennent compliquer les choses :

> – Dors – L'Oranger fleurit encor [*sic*]… et la mémoire
> Des jeunes d'autrefois dont l'ombre est encor là,
> Qui ne t'ont pas pêchée au fond d'une écritoire…
> Et n'en pêchaient que mieux ! – dis, ô *picciola !* (*Le Fils de Lamartine*, 37-40)

> … Il faisait beau quand nous mettions en panne,
>   Vent-dedans vent-dessus ;
> Comme on pêchait !… Va : je suis dans la panne
>   Où l'on ne pêche plus. (*À mon côtre*, 37-40)

Il y a là en effet un jeu de mots évident, que l'on retrouve du reste dans *Paris nocturne* copié sur une page vierge de son recueil personnel au regard de *Steam-boat*[39] :

> Le long du ruisseau noir, les poëtes pervers
> Pêchent ; leur crâne creux leur sert de boîte à vers.

Il faudrait corriger *pêchaient* en *péchaient* dans *Le Fils de Lamartine* ; *À mon côtre* repose en partie sur une métaphore où la scène maritime évoque l'orgie à laquelle aspirent les marins embarqués, ce qui crée une ambiguïté plus ou moins occultée dans le recueil par la confusion occasionnelle des accents qui, paradoxalement, la favorise. De fait, Corbière n'a pas d'idée arrêtée sur la pertinence du circonflexe qu'il emploie librement, dans une situation que l'on peut comparer à celle des vers *haler* et *hâler*.

*rambranesque**, à opposer au correct « Rembrandt » de *Gente dame*. D'après les informations fournies par Gallica, le néologisme apparaît pour

---

38 *Mémoires de la Société d'agriculture, sciences, belles-lettres et arts d'Orléans*, 2ᵉ série, XVI, 1-2 (1874), p. 69 et 90 (article signé E. Bimbenet).
39 Voir la transcription qu'en donne Houzé, « Le dernier Corbière », p. 327.

la première fois dans un catalogue de tableaux[40] à propos de *La Présentation au temple* de Christian Dietrick où la mise en italique signale le néologisme dont ce n'est pas pour autant nécessairement le premier emploi : « son effet lumineux et *rembranesque* ». Arsène Houssaye, les frères Goncourt, Théophile Gautier et Champfleury l'emploient avant Flaubert (1869). Exceptionnelle, la forme en *ram-* apparaît à deux reprises (avec majuscule initiale) dans un compte rendu du Salon de 1837 dans *L'Indépendant*[41].

Autres formes « fautives » : *à fond perdu**, *Beaudelaire** – faute que commettront Gide, Proust, Barrès ou Mauriac –, *bien sur**, *crève**, *dégaînant**, *dégaîne** (s.), *dégaîne** (v.), *dégouté**, *dégoûtaî*, *mat-de-flèche**, *molissez**, *païssions**, *plait**, *rengaîne**, *sensées** (pour *censées*), *sursoît**, *veûles**, *vint** (pour *vînt*) : comme on le voit, il s'agit le plus souvent de problème d'accents, en particulier de l'usage du circonflexe. Lorsque le mot revient, la faute disparaît généralement : *sûr(e)*, *crève* (4 occurrences, plus *crèverai*), *dégoûté* (deux occurrences, plus *dégoût(s)*, *Dégoûteux*) ; on trouve par ailleurs *mât(s)*, *mâture* et *mâter*, *mollir*. Si l'on trouve *fonds* dans *Élizir d'Amor*, on trouve aussi *fond* dans un contexte qui peut paraître ambigu : dans *Idylle coupée*, Corbière évoque le fumier où le poète cherche la perle, détournant le vers de La Fontaine (« C'est le fonds qui manque le moins ») avant d'écrire : « C'est toujours un fond chaud qui fume, / Et, par le soleil, dardé d'or... » ; on a de la peine ici à imaginer qu'il s'agît d'un creux alors que l'on s'attend à un tas que le soleil a plus de chance d'atteindre, et la correction apportée par le vers suivant (« Le rapin nomme ça : bitume » c'est-à-dire 'trottoir') ne vient que confirmer la faute que l'enchaînement thématique et l'image associée dans la relative incitent à voir ici. Le flottement le plus important concerne *goéland* : on trouve aussi bien *goélands* (*Le Naufrageur*) que *goëlands* (*Le Poète contumace*, *A mon côtre*) ou *goëland* (*Le Douanier*), anomalie sur laquelle nous reviendrons[42].

Dans *Le Phare*, Walzer supprimait imprudemment le circonflexe de *se mâte* (« Il [*le phare*] se mâte et rit de sa rage » v. 9), sans commenter son choix. Bescherelle définit la construction pronominale du verbe

---

40 *Catalogue de tableaux du premier ordre et des trois écoles, réunis par M. de Lahante, dans la galerie Lebrun*, Paris, Impr. de Ballard.
41 Xe année, 27 avril 1837, p. 1.
42 *Cf. infra*, p. 90-91.

comme « Être mâté », et *mâté* correspond dans le cas qui nous occupe à « Dresser, mettre un objet debout » par extension de sens (*DN* I, 462)[43]. Corbière donne à voir le phare se dressant tel un mât, en une métaphore obscène que put relever M. Grundt, admonestant ainsi les éditeurs[44] : « S'il vous plaît, Messieurs les Correcteurs des *Amours Jaunes*, ne castrez pas Tristan quand, avec son *Phare, il se mâte* ». L'image est explicitement sollicitée dans le quatrain précédent :

> Debout, Priape d'ouragan,
> En vain le lèche
> La lame de rut écumant…
> – Il tient sa mèche.

Cet exemple montre en tout cas que l'usage corbiérien du circonflexe n'est pas une simple question d'usage graphique puisqu'il peut prêter à confusion, d'une manière différente ici de celle que nous avons vu pour le couple *pêcher/pécher* où l'ambiguïté est plus difficile à démêler.

Frantext ne fournit aucun renseignement sur le verbe *bramer* sur lequel Corbière hésite : *brame* (3e pers.) dans *À l'Éternel Madame, tu brâmes** (en rime avec *flammes*) dans *Le Poète contumace* ; sur *mules* que Corbière emploie avec l'accent circonflexe (*mûles*). Il s'agit ici, comme bien souvent dans l'emploi du circonflexe, d'inadvertances de la part du Corbière, tout comme dans *veûles*.

Voyons à présent, en écartant les cas où l'on a pu ou pourrait invoquer une rime pour l'œil[45], les cas de graphies alternatives qui se retrouvent dans Frantext chez d'autres écrivains du XIXe siècle, sachant que, dans certains d'entre eux, il peut aussi s'agir accidentellement, d'inadvertances ; nous mentionnerons la présence du mot chez les écrivains, qui sont le plus souvent des auteurs majeurs, à l'occasion chez des scientifiques faisant autorité (l'astérisque signale ici encore les formes corrigées par Walzer) :

*arôme** : son accentuation est attestée jusque dans certains dictionnaires, comme l'a indiqué Fongaro qui la relève chez Littré. De fait, Littré,

---

43   Voir l'occurrence qu'en donne Frantext chez Loti : « celui du carrosse doré se mâte tout debout sur ses pieds de derrière » (*Au Maroc*). La Landelle, *Le Langage des marins*, p. 66, ne connaît que *mâter*, « planter le mât ».

44   « Le Poète et la Cigale », p. 95. Ceci dit, l'auteur accorde à Corbière une confiance excessive dans sa maîtrise de l'orthographe.

45   Voir *infra*, p. 83-90.

qui prend *arome* pour entrée – comme du reste Pierre Larousse (*GDU* I, 679) –, se plie aux normes de l'Académie tout en s'interrogeant ainsi : « Pourquoi l'Académie, qui met un accent circonflexe à dôme, à cône, n'en met-elle pas à arome, dont la prononciation est la même, et où le mot grec a aussi un ω ? » (*DLF* I, 197). Bescherelle (*DN* I, 238), quant à lui, opte sans discussion pour *arôme*, avec des exemples à l'avenant. Fongaro signale la graphie chez Mallarmé[46]. Frantext en donne aussi des attestations chez Edgar Quinet, Leconte de Lisle, Maupassant, Zola, Huysmans et Alphonse Daudet. La graphie est en effet alors très courante : c'est elle que Baudelaire retenait en 1857[47], et nous l'avons également rencontrée chez Sainte-Beuve, Gautier, Banville, Sully Prudhomme, Heredia et Verlaine ;

*barcarole** se rencontre chez Balzac (qui connaît aussi le régulier *barcarolle*), Sainte-Beuve (au pluriel, en rime avec *paroles*) et Lamartine ;

*blasphêmez** : on trouve *blasphêmais* chez Baour-Lormian. En 1857, Baudelaire hésitait entre le circonflexe et le grave dans le substantif[48] ;

*carêner** (mais *carène* [s.] dans *Le Bossu Bitor* et *À mon côtre*) : Hugo met le circonflexe au substantif, de même Cuvier, et Georges Docquois dans *Bêtes et gens de lettres* (1895) ;

*chuchotte** se trouve chez Balzac, Victorien Sardou, Alphonse Daudet et Edmond Rostand, auxquels nous pourrions ajouter Silvestre (*Les Renaissances*, p. 99 : *chuchottent* ; mais *chuchotement*) ou Mallarmé (*Pages*, p. 165 ; mais *chuchoter, -ements*), Richepin ou Van Hasselt. Tristan semble tenir la gémination de son père (*Le Négrier*, p. 21 : *chuchottant*) ;

*gaîne** (s.) se trouve déjà chez Sainte-Beuve, Hugo, Gautier, George Sand et Leconte de Lisle, auxquels on peut ajouter Léon Dierx[49], et telles sont les entrées des dictionnaires de Bescherelle (*DN* II, 4), Larousse (*GDU* VIII, 927) et Littré (*DLF* II, 1816), conformément à la 6ᵉ édition (1835) de celui de l'Académie qui l'abandonnera pour *gaine* en 1878[50] : il s'agit donc ici d'une graphie parfaitement correcte en son temps, et l'on remarquera que Corbière, qui l'emploie deux fois,

---

46 Voir Fongaro, « Sur le texte », p. 78.
47 Nuiten, *Les Variantes*, p. 33.
48 Il employait le grave dans *Les Phares*, *De profundis clamavi* et *Lesbos*.
49 *Le Rêve de la mort*, dans *Les Lèvres closes*, p. 98 et 248.
50 Littré lui reprochait d'être inconséquente en n'employant pas le circonflexe dans les verbes dérivés (*dégainer etc.*)

met toujours le circonflexe, de même qu'il laisse imprimer *dégaîne* (deux occurrences), *dégaînant* et *rengaîne*. Édouard Corbière écrivait de même (*Le Négrier*, p. 15) ;

*grouins**, que Fongaro signale chez Michelet, est également attesté chez Cuvier, Hugo et Maxime du Camp, et correspond à la prononciation dissyllabique de l'époque reconnue par Bescherelle et Littré (voir *infra*, p. 180). Le père de notre poète ne l'écrit pas différemment dans *Le Négrier* (p. 52) ;

hosannah se rencontre chez Chateaubriand, Flaubert, Rimbaud, Verlaine et Villiers de L'Isle-Adam ;

indou, pour désigner la langue, se trouve chez Jules Verne, comme épithète chez Hugo (« mot indou ») et William Whitney (*La Vie du langage*, 1875)[51] ;

paroxisme, chez Maine de Biran, Stendhal, Leconte de Lisle et Ponson du Terrail, auxquels nous pouvons ajouter Murger, Banville et Silvestre ;

*popotte** (où l'italique signale l'origine populaire), chez Paul Bourget ;

*râclant** : le verbe est doté d'un circonflexe chez Champfleury, Barbey d'Aurevilly, Huysmans et Jules Verne ; *râcler* est l'entrée du dictionnaire de Bescherelle (*DN* II, 1069) ;

raffalé se rencontre chez Huysmans (de même que la forme normée *rafalé*). Tristan la tient sans doute de son père (*Le Négrier*, p. 187, 188)[52]. Dans *Le Langage des marins*, La Landelle voit dans le mot un dérivé d'*affalé*[53] :

> Un navire *affalé* sur une côte par le vent ou par le courant est poussé en *aval* ; on a dit dans l'origine *avalé*.
>
> Est-il doublement affalé, par le vent et par le courant ou par un *redoublement* de vent, il est *re-affalé*, *raffalé*, – qu'on écrit *rafalé* mais dont on ne se sert guère qu'au figuré dans le sens de misérable.

Le mot est étymologiquement rattaché à *rafale* dans *FEW* 10, 28 : « *rafalé* adj. "qui a subi une rafale (navire) ; qui vient de subir un revers de fortune" […] "dont l'extérieur annonce une misère complète" (1806 […]) » ; la gémination se rencontre encore à la fin du XIXe siècle chez Virmaître[54] ;

---

51   Frantext n'enregistre *hindou* au XIXe siècle que chez Châteaubriand.
52   Son père qui hésite par contre entre *raffale* et *rafale*.
53   *Le Langage des marins*, p. 167.
54   *Dictionnaire d'Argot*, p. 239 : « RAFFALÉS : Être dans la misère, emporté par la *raffale* [sic] de la *dèche* (Argot des voleurs) ».

râtissant* : le verbe est doté d'un circonflexe chez George Sand et
Flaubert ; l'attraction de *râteau* est ici évidente ;
relai*, chez Du Camp, Hugo et Victor Bréal ;
rengaîne* : le verbe est doté d'un circonflexe chez Pétrus Borel, George
Sand, Louis Reybaud, Flaubert, les frères Goncourt et Huysmans ; il
l'est également dans les dictionnaires de Bescherelle (*DN* II, 1149),
Larousse (*GDU* XIII, 958) et Littré (*DLF* IV, 1616).

On peut également rencontrer telle ou telle singularité de l'écriture
corbiérienne présentant une certaine justification. Il en va ainsi de « gardenational » (p. 63), agglutination que l'on peut rapprocher du moqueur
gendelettres de Banville (*Odes funambulesques*), tandis qu'il unit les deux
mots composants (« Garde-national ») dans la lettre que Corbière adresse
à sa tante Christine Puyo en novembre 1870 avant de contracter la forme
en « Garnationals » soulignant sa conception de l'expression comme
une lexie continue, tout comme il le fait dans « un homme *comifaut*[55] ».
   Certains points de morphosyntaxe ont été abusivement « corrigés ».
Walzer éprouve ainsi la peine de mettre au singulier le participe passé
dans « – Comme un songe passés, douanier, ces jours de fête ! » (*Le
Douanier*, 72), alors que l'on peut très bien comprendre cette construction
comme l'équivalent d'un ablatif absolu, avec une transposition forcée
permettant d'assurer la correction de la césure (au lieu de : « Ces jours
de fête passés comme un songe ! »), d'autant que le singulier *passé*
rendrait la construction elliptique pour ne pas dire obscure[56]. La graphie fautive *à pieds** est vraisemblablement une inadvertance puisque
l'expression est correctement écrite dans *Élizir d'Amor* (18) et dans
Déjeuner de soleil (36, certes à la rime avec *s'assied*) ; l'accord de l'adjectif
dans *des nouveaux-nés** qui se trouve aussi chez les frères Goncourt n'est
pas non plus rare dans l'usage[57]. Walzer amende en outre le genre de
l'article dans « un espèce de nom de dieu » (*Le Novice en partance*) où
il se demandait s'il s'agissait d'une coquille ou d'une ignorance[58] et

---

55   Voir Houzé, « Traces de Tristan Corbière », p. 19 (et n. 1), 20 et 21.
56   La leçon imprimée est défendue par Aragon et Bonnin, éd. citée, p. 413.
57   Voir p. ex., sur Gallica : *De la mortalité des nouveaux-nés dans la Charente-Inférieure*, par
     L. Merle, [La Rochelle, 1868] ; *Notice sur les soins à prendre à l'égard des nouveaux-nés etc.*,
     par Mlle A. Bertin, sage-femme et herboriste, Paris, impr. de Vve Renou, Maulde et Cock
     (Paris), [1873].
58   Éd. citée, p. 349.

où Aragon et Bonnin voient une « incorrection attribuable au parler populaire du novice[59] », bien que les discours rapportés de ce dernier ne présentent pas d'autres traits qui seraient significatifs d'un tel parler. L'accord avec le déterminé (en l'occurrence *nom*) est pourtant conforme à un usage bien établi, même s'il est marginal, dans la langue soignée, comme le relève M. Grevisse (*BU* § 588, n. 198), *espèce* ayant valeur d'épithète comme *diable*, de sorte qu'Hugo – qui n'est pourtant pas coutumier du fait avec l'article – peut évoquer « cet espèce de cirque » ou « cette diable de Vendée » dans *Quatre-Vingt-Treize*. On peut aussi relever dans Frantext « un espèce d'abrégé » chez Cuvier, « un espèce de confesseur » chez George Sand, « un espèce d'écriteau » ou « un espèce de col » chez Edmond de Goncourt, « un espèce de cône » chez Jules Verne *etc*. Il convient toutefois de faire observer que, dans ses romans, le père du poète semble avoir employé systématiquement *espèce de* au féminin : on ne peut donc exclure qu'il puisse s'agir là d'un simple bourdon, voire d'une correction spontanée du prote qui pouvait pratiquer l'accord avec le déterminé. C'est sans doute ainsi que s'explique chez le père de Corbière l'exception « un espèce de jury de vieillards » dans l'édition de 1855 « revue sur un nouveau Manuscrit de l'Auteur » du *Négrier* (p. 390), alors que la seconde édition (p. 57) que nous avons pu consulter sur la copie numérisée du site Gallica donne bien « une espèce… ». Le seul autre emploi significatif que nous connaissions du mot chez Tristan est « c't'espèce d'bric à brac » du *Panayoti* où les apostrophes renvoient en principe au féminin *cette*, dans un contexte marqué de langue populaire[60], mais l'incertitude demeure dans la mesure où Corbière écrit aussi « à c't'instant-là » comme il écrit « à c't'heure[61] ». Si la correction de Walzer est défendable, ce n'est donc certainement pas sur la base du critère normatif qu'il invoque mais sur celle de l'usage personnel probable du poète.

Les questions touchant à l'emploi du trait d'union, que l'on tend à considérer comme secondaires, ont leur importance du point de vue

---

59 Éd. citée, p. 389.
60 L'absence de redoublement du *t* n'est pas significatif : *cf.* « c'te patte-ci », « au milieu d'c'te bouillie ».
61 À noter toutefois que nous n'avons pas dépouillé la totalité des autographes du poète. Pour *Le Panayoti*, voir le fac-similé des f° 28r°-29r° de l'album Noir dans Houzé, *ffocsoR*, transcription p. 30.

linguistique et philologique, car le désordre occulte des régularités ou des traits symptomatiques de la conceptualisation et de l'utilisation du langage par Corbière. Mettons d'emblée de côté le cas de l'emprunt *farniente* (dans *Libertà*) – à opposer au *Farniente* de *Veder Napoli* –, absent de Frantext mais attesté chez un Banville[62] ou un Mérat, tandis qu'un Jacques Brasdor intitule *Le Far Niente* un recueil de poésies publié en 1869[63] ; c'est du reste la seule forme reconnue par Bescherelle (*DN* I, 1233), Larousse (*GDU* VIII, 113) et Littré (*DLF* II, 1621) tandis que l'Académie, qui intègre le mot à partir de sa 7ᵉ édition, adopte la forme agglutinée actuelle (*DAF* I, 725). Mettons également de côté le cas des locutions, telles que *à fleur-de-terre*, calqué sur *à fleur d'eau*, ou des lexies, telles que *cordes-à-boyau* ou *sacs-de-nuit* pour lesquelles Corbière étend un procédé traditionnel. Mettons aussi de côté son extension à des expressions diverses telles que *ici-bas*, analogique de *là-bas*, ou, plus inattendue, *ah-ça* sur lesquelles nous reviendrons[64]. Pour le reste, Bernardelli, qui hésite à les attribuer à Corbière ou au typographe, distingue implicitement procédé rhétorique, avec l'agglutination d'images de caractère paradoxal ou antithétique dans la juxtaposition de deux substantifs (*arlequin-ragoût, fiacre-corsaire, ermite-amateur etc.*), et procédé lexiurgique, avec des inventions lexicales comme *gentleman-vampire* ou *homme-ceci-tûra-cela* dérivé du titre d'un chapitre de *Notre-Dame de Paris*, qui procèdent de façon différente[65], auxquels on pourrait ajouter le cas particulier de « Ce lapin de gouttière : / *Vingt-ans* » (*Le Poète contumace*) : les quatre premiers exemples regroupent un thème et un prédicat, l'avant-dernier est une lexicalisation d'une proposition empruntée à Victor Hugo, le dernier, un âge. Les autres cas, qui seraient « privés de motivation et de fait contraires à l'usage courant » : *bouts-rimés, quart-d'heure, vent-de-bout, tête-de-turc, vert-sombre, rouge-fin, fait-divers, fil-de-fer, vierge-folle, à-peu-près, mardi-gras, sergent-de-ville, Bon-Dieu etc.*, sont là encore disparates, avec de véritables mots composés ou tout au moins des lexies dont le sémantisme a une certaine spécificité (un quart d'heure n'est

---

62   Dans *Stéphen*, I, II (retitré ensuite *Les Baisers de Pierre*) et *Le Songe d'une nuit d'hiver* (retitré ensuite *Songe d'hiver*) ; *Les Cariatides*, p. 74 et 165. La graphie sera reconduite tout au long des rééditions jusqu'à la fin du siècle.

63   Dans *La Ferme* (*Les Chimères*, p. 15).

64   Voir *infra*, p. 75.

65   « Il testo contumace », p. 32.

pas simplement le quart d'une heure, c'est aussi une unité de mesure)
– où l'usage est du reste parfois fluctuant –, des transferts de catégorie
(comme dans la «*Dame pleine de comme-il-faut*» de *La Rapsode foraine*)
et des combinaisons occasionnelles («*Dame-de-merci*», *ibid.*). Il faut par
ailleurs remarquer que le trait d'union sert quelquefois à rattacher à
un substantif tout un complément déterminatif, comme *un philosophe-
errant dans la campagne* pour qualifier le pauvre en Bretagne (*Un riche
en Bretagne*, 3), à moins, naturellement, de voir un CC autonome dans
le SN prépositionnel : les éléments du complément restent alors déliés.

Un examen des formes d'*À une Rose*[66] nous servira de base de réflexion.
Si l'on met de côté le cas des noms composés tels que *rose-thé, coup-de-
soleil, fil-de-fer* ou *faux-cols*, le trait d'union est essentiellement utilisé pour
associer un complément déterminatif (abrégé ci-dessous en COMP) à une
base nominale, associant éventuellement à la construction des jeux de
mots exploitant la polysémie de leurs composants[67] : substantif suivi d'un
complément de nom dans (*vent de*) *pastille-du-sérail, hanneton-d'or* ; d'un
nom apposé aussi bien dans *épine-postiche, papillon-coquelicot, Vénus-Coton*
que dans la lexie *rose-pompon* ; d'un adjectif épithète dans *rose-mousseuse*,
qui désigne une variété de roses et fait son entrée en poésie – sans le
trait d'union – chez Mérat et Valade[68] ; d'un nom propre dans la lexie
papier-Joseph ; la même démarche se retrouve dans l'agglutination d'un
adjectif antéposé au nom qu'il qualifie : *fausse-fleur, fausses-perles de rosée*.
Le trait d'union unit enfin deux noms dont il est difficile de prétendre
avec certitude que le second détermine le premier : *soir-matin*. Le tiret
a alors une fonction particulière qui nous donne à percevoir comme un
tout l'entité ainsi déterminée, et non comme une entité simple assortie
d'une caractérisation. Le poème lui-même procède à une resémantisa-
tion, voire une recatégorisation de certains de ces composés singuliers,

---

66 L'emploi de la majuscule se trouve dans la table des matières. Le seul emploi isolé du
    mot, dans l'apostrophe « ô rose » ou « ô rose / De couperose », selon l'interprétation (voir
    infra), est un nom commun, mais le contexte maintient l'ambiguïté : il s'agit bien de
    la fleur qui vient fleurir les faux-cols, mais tout autant de la femme, « gommeuse », qui
    vient fleurir les cœurs.

67 Sur ces aspects sémantiques, voir les commentaires au texte d'Aragon et Bonnin, éd. citée,
    p. 99-103.

68 Dans *La Conteuse* : « Daigne ouvrir ta bouche amoureuse / Au parfum de rose mousseuse »
    (Mérat et Valade, *Avril, Mai, Juin*, LXIX ; cité d'après Valade, *Poésies*, p. 139) ; Mérat dans
    le prologue de *Fleurs de Bohême* : « Se plaindra-t-on qu'il manque à la rose mousseuse /
    L'odeur des fleurs d'orange et de la tubéreuse [...] ? » (*Les Chimères*, p. 149).

en liaison avec le titre du poème : parfois, on ne sait plus tout à fait si *rose*-<COMP> est à interpréter comme doté d'une base nominale ou d'une base adjectivale. Au v. 1 où le composé se trouve détaché : « Rose, rose-d'amour vannée, », la présence de *vannée* amène à comprendre le composé comme de nature substantivale : « Rose » est métaphoriquement décrite comme une rose d'amour fatiguée, à moins qu'il ne faille comprendre une rose vannée par l'amour[69], mais on peut aussi comprendre que Rose est rosie d'un*e* amour fatiguée puisque Corbière emploie le mot au féminin – bien qu'au singulier – dans *Après la pluie*, dans une phrase à la syntaxe téméraire (43-45) : « Veux-tu d'une amour fidelle, / Éternelle ! / Nous adorer pour ce soir ?... ». Cet archaïsme – qui n'a subsisté qu'au pluriel – avait ces défenseurs dont Littré, comme le rappelle Ch. Lebaigue[70] :

> On a demandé aussi que le nom *amour* fût ramené à un seul genre, soit au singulier, soit au pluriel. Littré combat cette idée, et avec raison. « Une règle nouvelle ferait considérer par le gros des lecteurs comme des fautes les passages de nos auteurs où *amour* est féminin, grave dommage pour leur mémoire et pour notre plaisir. *Amour* était féminin dans l'ancienne langue, comme tous les noms formés du latin en *or* ; *douleur, peur*, de *dolor, pavor*, etc. C'est un archaïsme à conserver, quand il signifie la passion d'un sexe pour l'autre. »

Cet usage se rencontre ainsi chez Musset qui évoque les « façons d'une amour fidèle et bien gardée, / L'allure d'une amour défaillante et fardée », dans *Les Marrons du feu*, où l'adoption du féminin peut tout au plus répondre à la nécessité de l'alternance des genres de rimes ; voir aussi du même la strophe XXVII d'*Une bonne fortune* :

> Elle s'arrêterait là-bas, sous la tonnelle.
> Je ne lui dirais rien, j'irais tout simplement
> Me mettre à deux genoux par terre devant elle,
> Regarder dans ses yeux l'azur du firmament,
> Et pour toute faveur la prier seulement
> De se laisser aimer d'une amour immortelle.

---

69 *Cf.* les « plis *rose-d'amour* » du *Bossu Bitor* (79) ; mais voir aussi « Elle, c'était la rose / D'amour » du *Novice en partance* (61-62).
70 *La Réforme orthographique*, p. 74-75, n. 1. L'Académie rappelle encore en 1878 qu'« AMOUR, quand il signifie, La passion d'un sexe pour l'autre, est quelquefois féminin au singulier en poésie, et presque toujours féminin au pluriel, même en prose » (les exemples sont tous au pluriel).

Le choix du féminin permet ici d'assurer la rime, comme c'est le cas chez Hugo[71] :

> Hélas ! j'aime pourtant d'une amour bien profonde !
> Ne pleure pas ; mourons plutôt ! – Que n'ai-je un monde !
> Je te le donnerais ! [...]

L'usage du féminin se perpétue naturellement au-delà des premières générations romantiques, toujours avec une connotation archaïsante. Banville évoque ainsi « cette vaillante amour » dans *La Belle Aude*[72] ; Hervilly, « cette amour vulgaire[73] » ; et pour la rime, Silvestre, l'amour « suivie » de regrets ou « venue, / Comme les zéphyrs, sur l'eau », ou encore le « lent baiser par qui l'amour est soulagée » et son « amour première[74] » ; ou encore Gustave Pradelle, une « amour tout immatérielle[75] ». Il y a toutefois chez Corbière une dimension particulière car la graphie de *fidelle* contribue chez lui à souligner l'archaïsme voulu.

L'amour donne à Rose / la rose cette couleur de « rouge-fin » que la polysémie de *fin* rend du reste *a priori* indéfinissable. Si *rose thé* est ordinairement un adjectif de couleur, « rose-thé » du poète prend une valeur nominale avec le commentaire « Dans le grog, peut-être », interprétation qu'appuient les roses-thé de Gautier[76]. Le singulier *rose-mousseuse* désigne clairement, de par l'accord, sa base comme substantif, ce que confirme l'anaphore (« sur toi pousse / Souvent la mousse »). L'utilisation du trait d'union dans ces composés aide en tout cas à comprendre que le syntagme apparent de l'apostrophe dans « Va, gommeuse et gommée, ô rose / De couperose, fleurir [*etc.*] » au dernier quatrain est peut-être à comprendre autrement que comme « ô [toi qui est] rose de couperose », avec une possible inversion : « Va, ô rose, gommeuse et gommée de couperose, [*etc.*] », expression certes singulière mais bien en accord avec d'autres images insolites de ce poème, qui implique de postuler l'omission d'une virgule après *rose*, hypothèse que rend probable la désinvolture générale de Corbière à l'égard de la ponctuation.

---

71   *Hernani*, IV, v (texte de 1830).
72   *Les Exilés*, p. 136.
73   *Les Baisers*, p. 41.
74   *Rimes neuves et vieilles*, p. 111 et 119 ; *Les Renaissances*, p. 75 et 114.
75   *PC (1869)*, p. 294.
76   Voir *infra* p. 332, n. 6.

Aux cas de locutions du type *tour à tour* ou *bord sur bord*, où Corbière insère des traits d'union dans *Le Bossu Bitor* (63, 129)[77], il convient d'ajouter de plus curieux regroupements que l'on peut relever çà et là : « CI-GIT » (*Pudentiane*), « Ah-ça » pour *Ah çà !* (*Le Bossu Bitor*, 174)[78], « comme-ça » (*Le novice...*, 6)[79]. Dans de tels cas, Corbière effectue l'agglutination sur une interjection ou un connecteur en donnant à ces regroupements la valeur de composés illusoires. Il commettait déjà ce genre de fautes dans sa jeunesse dans le cadre de divers syntagmes ou locutions : on peut ainsi trouver *avec-ça, et-puis, vous-tous, après-lesquelles, autre-chose* dans des lettres de 1859-1860[80], et l'on peut trouver çà et là dans les imprimés de l'époque de possibles modèles tels que « non-seulement[81] ». On sait que, à l'opposé, Corbière omet parfois le trait d'union attendu : « là haut », « Notre Dame[82] ». Ce genre d'anomalies se rencontre dans sa correspondance ; ainsi, dans une lettre de novembre 1870 à sa tante, on peut relever d'un côté « Eh-bien », « halte-là », « dites-donc », de l'autre « elle même[83] ». On peut aussi y relever la connexion formelle des composants d'un syntagme nominal, comme dans « faux-air », ou dans des expressions figées : « pleine-de-grâce », « corps-et-biens », ce qui tend à écarter l'idée d'erreurs du prote[84]. Le tiret, qui s'explique comme le signe formel de l'unité syntagmatique de l'expression, revêt alors un caractère superfétatoire ou du moins contraire à la tradition orthographique.

L'emploi du trait d'union dans des composés occasionnels suscite d'autres questionnements. C'est ainsi que Corbière hésite dans l'emploi du tiret dans des constructions par ailleurs identiques et parallèles, soulignées par l'italique, comme dans :

> Ces *Galimard cherchant la ligne*,
> Et ces *Ducornet-né-sans-bras*, (*Idylle coupée*, 61-62)

---

77 Mais « bord sur bord » dans *Bambine*, 15.
78 Dans « Ah-ça : t'es porté sur la chose ? » » à rapprocher de « – Ça : n'as-tu jamais arrêté / Musset... musset pour sérénade ? » (*Grand opéra*, 58-59).
79 À noter que l'on trouve « c'est-là » dans la quatrième édition du *Négrier* d'Édouard Corbière (p. 289).
80 Voir les transcriptions données par Houzé, « Deux lettres inédites », p. 276, 277 et 280.
81 *Philosophie de l'esprit*, de Hegel, trad. Véra, I, p. C, n. 1, p. CI *etc.*
82 Bernardelli, « Il testo contumace », p. 32. Nous excluons *male heure* de sa liste.
83 Éd. Houzé, « Traces de Tristan Corbière », p. 17, 21 et 18 respectivement, ainsi que le fac-similé du début de la lettre donné sur planche non numérotée. Le cas de *tout-à fait*, p. 19, est de l'ordre du *lapsus*.
84 *Ibid.*, p. 19 et 21.

Fongaro a aussi attiré l'attention sur ces vers où l'usage contradictoire des traits d'union semble, selon lui, fait à contre-sens[85] :

> Faisant, d'un à-peu-près d'artiste,
> Un philosophe d'à peu près, (*Le Poète contumace*, 39-40)

Le premier emploi est pourtant clairement substantival (nom composé), ce qui justifie l'emploi du trait d'union, mais le second semble davantage relever d'un emploi adverbial d'une locution prépositionnelle, à laquelle la construction indirecte choisie confère une fonction épithétique (un philosophe approximatif ? ou approximativement un philosophe ?) On remarquera cependant que Corbière ne faisait pas la distinction dans *Une mort trop travaillée* dont ces vers dérivent[86] :

> C'était à-peu-près un artiste
> C'était un poëte à-peu-près, (1-2)

Le cas n'en est pas moins à rapprocher de celui qu'on observe dans *La Rapsode foraine* (179-180) où les traits d'union opposent un droit particulier d'ordre juridique à un droit divin :

> – Le droit-du-seigneur à leurs serres !...
> Le droit du Seigneur de céans ! – (*La Rapsode foraine*, 179-180)

Quant au tiret après apostrophe de *pudeur-d'-attentat* de *Pudentiane*, dont la mise en italique souligne la conception comme nom composé qui trouve sa pleine justification dans sa dérivation d'« attentat à la pudeur », il convient de signaler que cette particularité se retrouve dans l'album Noir avec *débits-d'-tabac* (f° 28r°) où la présence des tirets n'a par contre pas de justification[87], même si le second y apparaît sous une forme très abrégée, pratiquement réduite à un point, et surmontée de l'apostrophe qui semble venir rectifier la faute, ce qui a très bien pu être le cas dans *pudeur-d'-attentat*. On peut du reste relever également, dans le même poème, *tout-d'-même* et même *Tout'-d'-même*, où l'apostrophe

---

85   « Sur le texte », p. 78.
86   Transcription dans Houzé, « Nouvelle édition », p. 266.
87   On trouve « débit de tabac » dans le commentaire apporté au titre de *Petite pouësie* (f° 10r°). L'emploi du tiret est tout aussi peu justifié dans « poissons-rouges », au même vers du *Panayoti* qui adopte la langue populaire parlée « c'est pour les poissons-rouges dans les débits-d'-tabac ».

surmonte chaque fois le trait d'union. Il est donc peu probable que la faute incombe au prote qui se sera ici strictement conformé aux indications de sa copie. Toutefois, du point de vue des règles sous-jacentes à l'orthographe, si la présence du tiret ne peut se justifier devant voyelle du fait de l'élision (on devrait avoir *pudeur-d'attentat*), elle s'imposait devant consonne, où l'apostrophe note simplement l'apocope nécessaire à la bonne prononciation des composés artificiels concernés : *débit-de-tabac* en quatre syllabes ; *tout-de-même* en deux.

Ces différents éléments, en particulier le fait que le recueil ne fait que refléter les usages ordinaires du poète qui héritait en partie de ceux de son père, nous amènent à ne pas voir dans l'apparente fantaisie de Corbière vis-à-vis de l'orthographe une volonté de provoquer le lecteur. On peut du reste rapprocher le cas de Corbière de celui d'un Pétrus Borel. L'examen de *Rhapsodies*, publié en 1834, met en effet en évidence toutes sortes de graphies inattendues, voire aberrantes, avec des redoublements de lettres intempestifs ou omis[88] : *applanir*, attérer*, barbottant, béfroi*, chevrottante, cigarre*, creuzet*, hangard*, infidelle, japer, marre*, parangoner, raffolir, tremblottera* ; des lettres muettes ajoutées ou omises : *hangard*, lycantropie** ; des accents manquants : *chenevis, babord, s'enchasse**[89] ; des circonflexes ajoutés : *haîne** (au côté de *haine*), *gnôme, embrâsê** ; substitués ou modifiés : *anathême, blémir, thême* ; voir aussi *par fois** (au côté de *parfois*), *walse** (mais *Verther*), *dolmeins, stygmate, juri** (table) ; des traits-d'union insérés : *juxta-posé*. La seule différence est leur nombre, mais il faut tenir compte du fait que *Rhapsodies* contient près d'un tiers de moins de vers que *Les Amours jaunes*, en excluant les reprises de vers dont le nombre est relativement important.

---

88 L'astérisque signale les formes rectifiées dans la réédition posthume (1868).
89 Nous ne parlons pas de *ame*, commun à l'époque, graphie que Corbière n'ignore pas dans ses autographes.

RIME, MESURE ET ORTHOGRAPHE

Les règles traditionnelles de la versification ont développé une conception phonogrammatique de la rime qui la distingue nettement d'autres versifications, comme l'anglaise : les rimes françaises ne sont pas à proprement parler des rimes phonétiques, notamment parce qu'elles intègrent la dimension diachronique liée à l'histoire de la littérature versifiée savante, ce qui explique du reste l'acceptation de véritables cultismes tels que la rime normande que Verlaine s'interdira, comme *estafier : fier* (*Bohême de chic*), ou encore ces archaïsmes que l'on qualifie avec quelque approximation de « rimes pour l'œil[1] » telles que *fuseaux : Atropos*[2] (*Litanie du sommeil*), *Jésus : 'Vide latus'* (*La Rapsode foraine*), *paradis : 'De profundis'* (*Cris d'aveugle*), *sourds : les ours* (*Rondel*). Dans le cas de *bénit : granit* (*Cris d'aveugle*), il faut savoir que le mot connaissait une prononciation alternative, comme le note Littré[3], dont témoigne la rime *granits : infinis* du *Rolla* de Musset. Les poètes avaient ainsi développé une attention particulière à ce qui est abusivement considéré comme un caractère visuel de la rime, sans toutefois en faire une religion : leur attention repose en effet sur l'équivalence de graphèmes plutôt que de lettres[4], donnant lieu à des licences orthographiques diverses. Ce qui est frappant lorsqu'on a pris la mesure des critiques portées sur le traitement de l'orthographe dans *Les Amours jaunes*, même en les relativisant à la lumière des usages contemporains, c'est le respect scrupuleux de ces licences qui témoigne d'un attachement réel de Corbière aux conventions poétiques. C'est ainsi que l'on trouve

---

1   Plusieurs de ces rimes corbiériennes ne satisfont pas plus l'œil que l'oreille, mais le poète ne se distingue ici en rien de la tradition poétique dont témoignent, parmi tant d'autres, *luth : salut* chez Hugo, Banville ou Verlaine, *hélas : plats* ou *tous : genoux* chez Hugo, *lits : lis* (= *lys*) ou *Chaos : animaux* chez Baudelaire *etc.*

2   Il s'agit en fait d'une laisse impliquant d'autres mots-rime, en *aux, eaux* et *os.*

3   *DLF* II, 1918 : « gra-ni, ou, plus souvent, gra-nit' ».

4   Sur la structure – complexe – de la rime française et sa notation, voir Billy, *Les formes poétiques*, p. 443-444.

des formes archaïques préservées à ce titre : *je voi* : *roi* (*Bohême de chic*) et *pié* : *moitié* (*Idylle coupée*), *nud* : *Sainte-Anne-de-la-Palud* (*La Rapsode foraine*) ; que l'*s* de *remords* se voit supprimé pour rimer avec des mots en *ort* (*Litanie du sommeil*, *La Pastorale de Conlie*), tandis que l'on trouve *remords* en rime avec *dehors* dans *Litanie*. Corbière étend la licence à *à rebour*, en rime avec *sourd* (*Rapsodie du sourd*), ce qui, par contre, pèche contre la règle – plus relâchée, il est vrai, que l'interdiction de « rimer le singulier avec le pluriel[5] » – qui tend à proscrire les rimes d'un mot terminé sur une occlusive amuïe avec un autre qui en serait dépourvu, règle que les poètes s'autorisaient à enfreindre sous certaines conditions, avec généralement moins de liberté que Corbière que le style bas n'effrayait pas[6].

Dans les rimes en [e], pour se limiter aux aspects les plus élémentaires, les mots terminés en é (éventuellement *ai*) doivent rimer entre eux : nous noterons $|e|$ ce paradigme ; ceux terminés en *r* également : $|e^{\kappa}|$; de la même façon, les mots terminés en *és/ez* (exceptionnellement *ais* en [e] fermé) doivent rimer entre eux : $|e^{s}|$; ceux terminés en *rs* également : $|e^{\kappa s}|$. Cette discrimination de variétés de rimes phonétiques en [e] explique l'utilisation du doublet poétique *pié*, *pied* ne pouvant guère rimer qu'avec *assied*, *rassied* (ou des dérivés de *pied*), dans un nouveau paradigme que nous notons par $|e^{t}|$[7], et c'est ce que fait Corbière lorsqu'il rime *s'assied : à pied* dans *Déjeuner de soleil*, se gardant bien des dérisions d'un Verlaine tardif qui rimera *effrayé : s'assié*[8]. C'est cette règle complexe à l'origine de cinq paradigmes distincts qui explique aussi qu'un Musset use du doublet *pié* au pluriel pour l'associer à *oubliés* dans *Souvenir*, ce que tous les romantiques ne s'astreignaient pas à faire[9]. Si Baudelaire pouvait rimer *baisers : décomposés* ou *pensers : révulsés* qui mêlent les paradigmes $|e^{\kappa s}|$ et $|e^{s}|$, c'est parce que cette licence se justifiait à ses yeux pour des raisons stylistiques : l'obtention d'une rime riche ne pouvait en effet se faire qu'à ce prix, *baisers* et *pensers* étant les seuls mots en $|e^{\kappa s}|$ appuyés en [z] et [s] respectivement. La même licence qu'on observe dans ses

---

5   Voir *infra*, p. 152-161. Walzer, éd. citée, corrige la forme (ce qui nous avait induit en erreur dans notre article de 2000, *f* 8).

6   Voir *infra*, p. 81-83.

7   Rappelons que les occlusives finales aujourd'hui amuïes avaient une articulation sourde, indépendamment de la graphie : *d* comme *t* se prononçaient [t].

8   Dans *Sur la manie qu'ont les femmes actuelles de relever leurs robes* (*Invectives*, p. 97).

9   Avec p. ex. *noyés* (Hugo) ou *liés* (Vigny).

rimes léonines : *souliers* : *humiliés*[10] et *Boucher* : *débouché* – qui mêle les paradigmes |e^{ʀ}| et |e| –, ne s'explique pas autrement. Corbière quant à lui respecte scrupuleusement la règle dans presque tous les cas. Lorsqu'il s'en écarte, c'est avec une précaution. Dans *souliers* : *pieds* (*Laisser-courre*) et *troupiers* : *pieds* (*Matelots*), il utilise la forme graphique normale de *pieds*, les mots associés n'étant pas en *és/ez*, mais en *iers* : on peut peut-être y voir une extension du paradigme |e^{ʀs}| à |e$^{[consonne]s}$|. Cette situation jette quelque doute sur *clefs* : *voulez* dans *Le Bossu Bitor*, qui peut passer pour une inadvertance puisque le doublet commun *clés* aurait respecté la convention poétique en rattachant cette rime au paradigme en |e^s| (*clés* : *voulez*)[11]. Corbière se montrait par contre beaucoup plus libre dans l'album *Noir* où l'on trouve associés *contrarié* : *décharger* ou même *préservé* : *rochers* dans *Journal de bord*, mais il s'agit là du seul poème de Corbière à être écrit en vers libérés par le recours à la langue parlée qui le dispense de cette convention poétique parmi d'autres, autant qu'il s'en sentait affranchi dans *Le Panayoti*, long monologue en langue parlée, cette fois populaire[12].

L'exemple de Baudelaire montre que le problème posé par les limites combinatoires des différents paradigmes de rimes a pu amener un certain assouplissement du système dans le style élevé, tandis que le style bas qui fait volontiers appel à la langue parlée était par nature plus conciliant en ces matières. Considérons ainsi la règle imposant la présence des mêmes consonnes occlusives finales amuïes dans les mots-rime associés, avec les équivalences *t/d*, *k/g* et *p/b*. La Fontaine n'hésitait pas à rimer, sans l'excuse du moindre renforcement, *accourt* : *tour*, *perd* : *Jupiter*, *respect* : *bec*[13], *autant* : *camp*, *profond* : *long* etc., ce que jamais Racine ne se serait permis en dehors des *Plaideurs* où il se risque à rimer *donc* avec *pardon* ou *création*, accommodant par contre *hasar* en rime avec *car* comme *je*

---

10 Rappelons que l'imperfection de la rime reposant sur une équivalence voyelle/semi-voyelle, avec une rime mi-riche ([lje]) mi-léonine ([li-e]), est parfaitement assumée dans la tradition poétique savante. Racine rime ainsi *envier* : *payer* (*Iphigénie*), *grossier* : *justifier* (*Phèdre*), *premier* : *oublier* (*Britannicus*).

11 Ce genre de négligence est typique de Corbière. C'est ainsi qu'il écrit (à l'envers) dans l'album *Noir* : « J'ai trop vécu, / […] et je brise mes armes / sur ce vieux cul ! / Oui, sur ce vieux cu ! ! ! » (f° 7r°), négligeant dans un premier temps la licence classique avant d'y recourir dans le bis.

12 Sur ces poèmes et l'affranchissement des conventions poétiques, voir Billy, « Corbière et le vers libéré ».

13 *Respect* se prononçait [ʀɛspɛk].

voi avec *moi* et *Voi !* avec *liez-moi*, leçon que Corbière a parfaitement retenue. Mais, si au XVIIᵉ siècle, dans le style élevé, les consonnes amuïes étaient soigneusement restituées, au XIXᵉ siècle, lorsque la consonne avait cessé d'être articulée même dans ce style, la licence n'était tolérée que lorsqu'elle pouvait enrichir la rime (*sang : puissant*). En accord avec le registre choisi, Corbière enfreint volontiers la règle, aussi bien dans les rimes non appuyées : *peloton : plomb, aplomb : donjon, tambour : sourd, encor : mort, cauchemar : l'art etc.*, que dans les appuyées : *long : jalon, nuit : ennui, ouvert : hiver, moi : voit, éteint : sacristain, gardien : tient, sursoit : soi, peu : peut, capitan : autant, couteau : tantôt, ça : forçat, mort : Armor,* où la présence d'un appui commun, fût-il approximatif (*gardien : tient*), atténue la licence. Il revient toutefois en deux occasions à la règle ancienne pour le paradigme |ãᵏ|, rimant *blanc : flanc* dans « Donc, *la tramontane...* » et *blanc : banc* dans *Le Poète contumace* (69-70). Dans le premier cas, il est difficile de soutenir catégoriquement que la rime pour l'œil a été recherchée plutôt que l'appui qui lui est indissolublement lié, même s'il n'y a pas d'autre mot en |lãᵏ|. Certes, Corbière avait toute licence pour recourir à quelque forme en |lã| ou |lãᵗ|[14], mais la sémantique joue toujours un rôle non négligeable dans le choix d'une rime ; or, dans le cas présent, le choix de *flanc* trouvait une motivation directe dans l'évocation peu avant de la rate :

> Ravalant ta rate rentrée,
> Va, comme le pélican blanc,
>
> En écorchant le chant du cygne,
> Bec-jaune, te percer le flanc !...

Dans *Le Poète contumace*, le souci de la rime pour l'œil est également sujet à caution car Corbière joue sur les mots, transformant l'expression *en rupture de ban* pour l'adapter au banc d'huîtres auquel il compare la société dans laquelle évolue le poète[15] :

---

14   Le rimaire des *Amours jaunes* fournit à lui seul *l'an, brûlant, filant* et *goéland.*
15   Dans une herméneutique que l'on qualifiera de libérée, Bernal, « Corbière, les coquilles », p. 31-32, voit dans *coquille* un autre jeu de mots renvoyant à la substitution de *banc* à *ban*. Comment suivre l'auteur qui affirme : « ce *c* revient, cette fois doté de sa sonorité, dans la proclamation identitaire "c'est moi" » ? Comment souscrire à sa conclusion : « Cette strophe nous semble signifier à quel point Corbière adoube la coquille comme un des leitmotive de sa poétique, délibérément bancale » ?

Je rime, donc je vis... ne crains pas, c'est *à blanc.*
– Une coquille d'huître en rupture de banc ! –

Le jeu de mots se trouve déjà dans la lettre que le poète adresse en
novembre 1870 à sa tante où la rime ne saurait être en cause[16] :

Conscrit volontaire dans l'arrière-banc d'huîtres de la *landsturn*[17] roscovite,
il en suit *in petto* tous les exercices.
[*Note de B. Houzé* : « "d'huîtres" est ajouté dans l'interligne, au-dessous
d'"arrière-banc" ». *Corbière semble avoir d'abord écrit « arrière-ban » avant de
trouver son jeu de mot.*]

Du fait même des registres explorés, on n'est évidemment pas surpris
de voir Corbière faire place aux rimes pauvres les moins acceptables, avec
les rimes en [e], et plus précisément en |eˢ| (*sacrés : marqués*), |eʳ| (*prêter :
rimer* dans *Le Poète et la Cigale*, qui emprunte au genre familier de la
fable) et |eᵊ| (*idée : rimée, dégréée : marée*[18], *dorée : fardée*), ou, plus souvent
encore, en |ãᵗ| (21 cas sur 40 : *enfant : testament, souvent : cent, enfant : tant*
etc.) ou |ãˢ| (14 cas sur 36 : *dedans : francs, mourants : printemps, ouragans :
chats-huans* etc.)[19]. Seules des questions d'ordre statistique expliquent
que Corbière présente davantage de rimes pauvres en [ã] qu'en [e] : la
combinatoire est beaucoup plus grande dans le second paradigme, et,
par conséquent, la rime enrichie beaucoup plus facile à trouver.

Le problème des graphies fautives au regard des normes dictionnai-
riques offre plus souvent que l'on ne croit un leurre à la critique. On a
pu invoquer la possible recherche de rimes pour l'œil dans un certain
nombre de cas de gémination fautive. Sachant que ces problèmes de
gémination se présentent aussi hors rime, on est déjà moins disposé à
admettre une telle justification sans un examen aussi poussé que possible,
les mots impliqués étant souvent isolés dans l'œuvre de Corbière. Cela
semble ne pas faire de doute pour *fidelle*, en rime avec *éternelle* (dans *Après
la pluie*), « à la mode du XVIIIᵉ siècle » selon Le Dantec, « orthographe

---

16 Éd. Houzé, « Traces de Tristan Corbière », p. 19.
17 Pour *landsturm.*
18 On notera néanmoins l'affinité phonétique des terminaisons qui en fait une rime riche
    approximative : [ʁee]/[ʁe].
19 Sur notre façon de noter les rimes, voir Billy, *Les formes poétiques*, p. 443-444. Si l'infraction
    est plus courante avec les rimes en [ã], c'est uniquement en raison de ressources lexicales
    offrant des possibilités combinatoires plus limitées au regard de tel ou tel appui que dans
    les rimes en [e].

habituelle des chansons rococo » selon Walzer[20], mais plus justement
« à la mode ancienne », rien ne permettant de pointer précisément le
XVIIIe siècle : on ne trouve en effet ailleurs que *fidèle* (huit fois adj., une
fois subst.), le nom propre *Fidèle* et l'adj. *infidèle* (une occurrence), et
l'on ne manquera pas de relever que la rime pour l'œil ne peut être
invoquée dans *Sonnet à sir Bob* ou *Le Novice en partance* où *fidèle* rime
avec *Elle/elle*, pas plus que dans *fidèle : aile* (*Le Crapaud*), *vielle : Fidèle*
(*Le Poète contumace*), *fidèles : ailes* (*Guitare*), *chapelle : fidèle* (*Grand opéra*) ou
belle : fidèle (*Aurora*). De fait, si l'on veut bien prendre en considération
que l'adjectif qualifie le féminin *une amour*, c'est le syntagme tout entier
qui constitue un archaïsme délibéré, ce qui donne à penser que la rime
visuelle n'a vraisemblablement pas été recherchée pour elle-même et
qu'elle résulte plutôt d'une coïncidence[21].

Il convient de récuser le cas de *brisans*, en rime avec *trois cents ans* dans
Au vieux Roscoff[22] : la forme, inconnue dans Frantext pour le XIXe siècle,
se retrouve en rime avec *gens* dans *Le Naufrageur* mais le poète rime
(ou laisse imprimer) « brisants » avec *longtemps* dans *Le mousse*. Corbière
omet du reste également le *t* en dehors de la rime, dans *Le Naufrageur*
également et *À mon côtre*, comme il l'omet dans les deux occurrences de
l'album Noir, à savoir dans la *Barcarolle des Kerlouans naufrageurs*, ancienne
version du *Naufrageur* (« la bonne vierge des brisans »), et dans la prose
À mon Roscoff (« ta grande chandelle de l'île de Batz est là qui veille sur
les brisans là bas »)[23]. On peut penser que la graphie discutée n'est pas
sans rapport avec son emploi dans les romans d'Édouard Corbière dont
Tristan s'est abreuvé, où le romancier use encore en 1855 de *brisans*, dans
la quatrième édition du *Négrier* « revue sur un nouveau Manuscrit de
l'Auteur », en cohérence avec l'usage ancien qu'il avait appris et que
perpétuent divers éditeurs, bien après la réforme de l'Académie (1835) qui
imposa définitivement la restitution du *t* du singulier dans la formation

---

20 Éd. citée, p. 244 ; Walzer, éd. citée, p. 1274. La graphie est jusqu'en 1718 celle de l'Académie
qui la donne, en 1740, comme une graphie alternative aux côtés de *fidèle* retenu comme
entrée principale, avant de revenir à *fidelle* seul en 1762 pour ne plus retenir que *fidèle* à
partir de l'édition de 1798. À noter que, selon l'impression de son recueil, Borel rime
Infidelle ! avec *chancelle* dans *Le rendez-vous* (*Rhapsodies*, p. 22) bien qu'il écrivît ailleurs
fidèle, y compris en rime avec des mots en *elle*.

21 Voir *supra*, p. 73-74.

22 Graphie conforme à la version manuscrite donnée par J. de Trigon, *Tristan Corbière*, p. [93].

23 Fac-similé et transcription dans Houzé, *ffocsoR*, p. 27 (f° 20r°) et 29 (f° 26r°).

du pluriel des formes en *ant/ent*[24] : Édouard Corbière continuait ainsi
à écrire *enfans, militans, bâtimens, exigens etc.*, ses imprimeurs respectant
généralement son habitude. Cet archaïsme est en tout cas à rapprocher
de *tems*, d'usage courant dans les romans de son père aux côtés de *temps*,
que notre poète emploie à deux reprises dans le poème manuscrit *Une
mort trop travaillée*[25], en rime avec *vingt ans* puis *20 francs*, où l'on ne
peut invoquer la rime pour l'œil[26]. Cas restants (l'astérisque signalera
les formes corrigées par Walzer) :

bagoût : ragoût (*Le Bossu Bitor*) : résultant sans doute d'une analogie avec
goût, la forme fautive (également dans le texte de *La Vie parisienne*)
est inconnue de Frantext pour le XIXᵉ siècle, mais on peut y relever
quelques occurrences pour le siècle suivant, notamment dans la correspondance de Jacques Rivière avec Alain Fournier et chez Léon Daudet.
On la trouve déjà chez Édouard Corbière (*Les Folles brises*, II, p. 38).

*bricolle** (en rime avec *se recolle*) n'y est pas non plus attesté ; pour autant,
on ne peut savoir si la graphie est réellement motivée par la rime
pour l'œil, faute d'autres attestations chez Corbière ; *bricolle(s)* s'y
rencontre au siècle suivant (années 1920). Si l'on peut *a priori* invoquer ici la recherche d'une rime pour l'œil, force est de reconnaître
avec Fongaro que « l'explication ne vaut plus » pour *casserolles**, en
rime avec *castagnoles*, où la gémination est bien attestée dans Frantext
chez Frédéric Soulié (*Les Mémoires du diable*, 1837) et Zola ; ajoutons
que cette dernière forme est exclusivement employée dans le *Traité
de l'office : ouvrage indispensable aux maîtres d'hôtel, valets de chambre,
cuisiniers et cuisinières, et utile aux gens du monde* de T. Berthe (1844)
comme dans *Le cuisinier Durand : cuisine du Midi et du Nord*, 8ᵉ éd.
(1863) ; elle est majoritaire dans le *Petit dictionnaire de cuisine* par
Alexandre Dumas, publiée chez Alphonse Lemerre (1882).

*barbotte** (en rime avec *cocotte*) se rencontre chez Auguste Barbier et
Louis Reybaud[27]. Tristan semble tenir la gémination de son père
(*Le Négrier*, p. 58) ;

---

24 *Cf.* Lebaigue, *La Réforme orthographique*, p. 52-53 ; *DHOF* 78 et 1172.
25 Houzé, « Nouvelle édition », p. 266 et 269.
26 On trouve également *printems* dans le manuscrit *Vedere Napoli e morire* (en rime avec *dedans*) ; J. de Trigon, *Tristan Corbière*, p. [97].
27 Auteur du personnage de Jérôme Paturot.

*chats-huans** (en rime avec *ouragans*) : pourquoi cette graphie définitivement condamnée en 1835 par l'Académie dans sa remise à plat du pluriel des adjectifs et participes présents en *ant/ent*[28], alors que Corbière
connaît parfaitement le singulier (présent dans *Nature morte*) ? Seule
la rime pour l'œil *semble* pouvoir justifier cette graphie ancienne ;
*gifflent** (en rime avec *sifflent*) : on trouve *giffler* dans la correspondance
de Mallarmé, *gifflées* chez Verhaeren ; on trouve *giffle(s)* chez Balzac,
Hugo, George Sand, André Theuriet ; ajoutons *giffles* dans un roman
d'Édouard Corbière (*Tribord et bâbord*, I, p. 269) ;
noroî (en rime avec *quoi*) : la forme est ignorée de Bescherelle, Larousse
et Littré, mais ce dernier mentionne, sous l'entrée *nord-ouest* (III,
748) : « les marins et les gens de la côte disent : no-roûe » (au lieu
de « nor-douèst' »). Corbière prononçait « no-roua ». Dans les proses
de l'album Noir, il écrit *Noroi* sans *t* (et avec la majuscule)[29] : il n'y
a donc pas de raison de parler de rime pour l'œil (que le circonflexe,
au demeurant, tend plutôt à défigurer)[30].
*pelotte** (en rime avec *culotte*) se rencontre chez Du Camp, Champfleury,
Huysmans et les frères Goncourt ;
poudrain (en rime avec *grain*) : c'est l'orthographe – au lieu de l'académique
poudrin – dont use Corbière tant dans sa prose manuscrite *À mon Roscoff*[31]
que dans son récit *L'Américaine*[32]. Richepin ne connaît que cette graphie[33]. Il n'y a donc pas plus d'argument ici en faveur d'une rime pour
l'œil que dans *main : demain, malsain : gagne-pain, mains : humains etc.*
*printannière** (en rime avec *boutonnière*) : dans Frantext, uniquement chez
Joseph-François Michaud (*Le Printemps d'un proscrit*, 1803), pour le
XIXe siècle ; nous l'avons cependant trouvé également au masculin
chez Levavasseur[34] ;
rigolot (en rime avec *matelot* dans *Le Bossu Bitor*) est inconnu de Frantext
pour le XIXe siècle (mais présent dans la correspondance de Gide et

---

28 Voir *supra*, n. 114.
29 Éd. Houzé, *ffocsoR*, p. 25 (f° 13r°) et 29 (f° 26r°).
30 Comme le fait Bernal, « Corbière, les coquilles », p. 28, n. 38.
31 Éd. Houzé, *ffocsoR*, p. 29 (f° 26r°) : « un gros lezard [*sic*] invalide, avec sa croûte de fer
   grelée [*sic*] par la lune et le poudrain ».
32 *La Vie parisienne*, 12e année (1874), p. 663-667, à p. 666 (28 novembre) : « Ses cheveux
   mouillés […] étaient tout sales de poudrain ».
33 *La Mer* (1894) en contient ainsi quatre occurrences, plus *poudrainer*.
34 Levavasseur, Prarond et Argonne, *Vers*, p. 36.

Valéry) où l'on ne trouve que *rigolard*. Fongaro a attiré l'attention sur la relative légitimité que cette graphie pouvait trouver dans la formation du féminin ; la forme est à rapprocher de *saligot* (en rime avec *asticot* dans *Le Bossu Bitor*), qui est par contre attesté chez les frères Goncourt et Zola, et duquel Fongaro rapproche *saligoter*[35].

Pour les terminaisons en *otte* indues, Fongaro a indiqué que la gémination fautive se retrouvait également dans *chuchotte, popotte* (voir aussi *amatelotter* dans *Le Bossu Bitor*, 177) qui ne sont pourtant pas à la rime, attribuant le redoublement à un traitement généralisé des terminaisons *ote/otte*, ce qui vient par conséquent contredire l'hypothèse d'une gémination pour la rime dans le cas de *barbotte* et *pelotte*[36] ; on peut du reste noter au passage qu'on ne peut invoquer la rime pour l'œil dans le cas de *garotte* [*sic*] : *Iscariote* (*Sonnet de nuit*)[37] ou de *bottes : capotes* (*La Fin*). Rien n'interdit de penser qu'il en va de même pour les terminaisons en *olle* : Corbière rime bien *espagnole : molle* (*Pièce à carreaux*) ou *folles : espingoles* (*Au vieux Roscoff*), et l'on peut également relever la gémination constante de *p* dans *Mary-saloppe*, tant en rime avec *chope* ou *tope* que hors rime. Il est également bon de rappeler les observations de Nina Catach basées sur ses observations relatives à la normalisation de l'orthographe[38] :

> Le sens diminutif est beaucoup mieux ressenti, et le redoublement plus stable, pour *e* que pour *o*. En réalité, *olle* est assez rare [...], et *ote* fait partout concurrence à *otte* (*cf. échalote**, souvent écrit *échalotte*) : non seulement dans des mots sentis comme savants comme le masculin *ilote*, les féminins *matelote, capote, note, cote**, etc., mais également dans les dérivés des verbes en *oter* ou les diminutifs comme *petiote, fiérote*, etc. Cependant, 1564-1606 *manotes, menotes* devient *menottes***, sans doute en raison d'une expressivité diminutive particulière.

L'instabilité dont fait état cette spécialiste, liée à l'expressivité des mots concernés, a certainement pesé sur les usages individuels, et le

---

35 « Sur le texte », p. 80. Ceci dit, pour autant nul n'a jamais écrit *pianot* ou *tuyaut*.
36 *Ibid.*, p. 79 : « il se peut que Corbière, logique avec lui-même (un peu comme pour l'accent circonflexe) ait systématiquement doublé le *t* dans les finales en *ote* ». Il ne l'a pas en tout cas fait pour *capote(s), clapoter, dévotes*, sans parler de *note* ou *Iscariote*.
37 À noter que, dans Frantext (XIXᵉ), on trouve « le garote espagnol » dans *Le Capitaine Fracasse*, et « qu'on le garotte » dans *L'Amour-Trompette* de Daudet.
38 *DHOF* 1156.

cas de Corbière reflète très précisément cette tendance générale. On a pu constater que son père connaissait les mêmes problèmes pour autant que les mots concernés par ces soupçons de rimes pour l'œil se retrouvent dans son œuvre où l'on peut relever toutes sortes de géminations abusives, accidentelles (que l'on trouve chez Corbière en alternance avec la forme correcte)[39] ou récurrentes quand il ne s'agit pas de formes isolées : voir ainsi, dans la quatrième édition du *Négrier* que nous avons au moins partiellement dépouillée, celle de *t* dans *barbotter**, *charrettée**, *chuchottant**, *clapottant*[40], *cravatte***, *matelotte**, *rabotter** ; de *n* dans *rubannerie**, *timonnier* ; de *l* dans *dallots**, *imbécille***, *palliers**[41] ; de *p* dans *applatie, applatissans** (mais *aplati, aplatit*), *attrapper** (mais *attrapé*), *frippon** (mais *friponnerie*), *galoppant, galopper, tappe(s), tappant, tapperons, tappés, tappotant* (mais, exceptionnellement, *taper, tapes*) ; de *f* dans *échaffaudé* (mais *échafauder*), *muffle, renifflé** ; exceptionnellement de *c* dans *raccorni**. On peut à l'inverse constater des réductions diverses, parfois surprenantes : *assujétis**, *atelage, attérage(s), attérir, attérie, attérissent, attérissage, feuilletonée, nétoyer***, *pourissait**, *racrocher**, *tintamare*. Cette question du redoublement apparaît ainsi plus circonscrite, mieux contrôlée chez le fils que chez le père.

Pour ce qui est de la question du circonflexe, le problème est analogue : l'emploi de cet accent en des lieux où l'on ne l'attend pas en dehors de la rime, y compris dans les manuscrits de Corbière comme *crêches, flôt(s), grêve, lêcher, lêcherai, mêches, se répête, rôse, Bâtz* ou *Saint-Mâlo* dans l'album Noir (et son absence dans *ame* (4 occurrences), *grelée, hotesse* ou *pale* (adj.), tout comme est ignoré l'accent aigu dans *lezard, neant* ou *zephyr*) témoigne soit d'une négligence soit d'une certaine ignorance des règles ou/et d'un désintérêt pour la question comme le confirme sa correspondance où l'on peut trouver des « Nôtre » déterminant,

---

39   La forme est alors marquée de deux astérisques. Un seul astérisque signale que le lexème concerné est un *hapax* dans le roman : on ne peut par conséquent exclure qu'il ne s'agit alors de graphies accidentelles, mais l'ensemble fait sens.

40   Mais *clapoteuse*.

41   Le cas d'*imbécille*, p. 289, est à relativiser. Si la forme moderne se voyait adoptée par l'Académie dans sa 5ᵉ édition, la coupant ainsi de son dérivé *imbécillité* (DHOF 573), la forme ancienne concurrençait toujours dans l'usage. Toujours réticent aux innovations de l'Académie lorsqu'elles présentaient une quelconque inconséquence, Bescherelle donne comme entrée « IMBÉCILE ou mieux IMBÉCILLE » (*DN* II, 200). Hugo ne l'ignorait pas : Paul Berret, la signale ainsi dans son édition de *La Légende des siècles*, II, p. 524, 545 et 548.

« Hâvre », « batarde[42] » *etc.* Comme on le voit, si l'on excepte le cas de *chats-huans*, rien ne vient étayer la thèse de la rime pour l'œil que Corbière ne recherche pas lorsque l'homophonie est assurée : les formes que nous avons passées en revue sont souvent des *hapax* dans le recueil, voire dans les écrits conservés de Tristan, et leur graphie se retrouve souvent chez d'autres écrivains quand il ne les tient pas de son père. Elles sont vraisemblablement aussi peu significatives que la rime de *bête : se répête* dans l'album Noir, dans une pièce où riment en particulier *se cache à l'eau : cachalot, lame : se pâme, américain : requin, culotte : clapote*[43] dans lesquelles l'œil n'a rien à faire : tout au plus pourrait-on invoquer l'hypothèse d'une contamination. On remarquera pour finir que Corbière n'use pas de la variante *A()dieu-va !* qui eût rendu parfaite la rime pour l'œil dans *Noukahiva : Adieu-vat* [*sic*] (*Le Novice en partance*) ; de la même façon, ignorant la vedette des dictionnaires de l'époque, il préfère *grouins* à *groins* pour rimer avec *moins* ; il recourt ailleurs à la graphie pseudo-archaïsante *Abaylar* curieusement dépourvue du *d* étymologique pour rimer avec *liard* (*La Rapsode foraine*), en harmonie avec les références moyenâgeuses dans lesquelles elle s'inscrit (« L'*Istoyre de la Magdalayne,* / Du *Jvif-Errant* ou d'*Abaylar* »), au lieu d'*Abeilard* (alors en usage aux côtés d'*Abailard*) qu'il utilise à trois reprises[44], une fois à la rime, en écho à *l'art*, forme qu'il tenait sans doute de son père[45]. Ce n'est donc pas la rime pour l'œil que recherche Corbière, mais le respect de la convention

---

42 Lettre à C. Puyo, éd. Houzé, « Traces de Tristan Corbière », p. 18-19. Corbière semble toutefois plus attentif lorsqu'il écrit à sa tante que lorsqu'il écrit ses poèmes.
43 Dans *Le Bain de mer de Madame X****.
44 *Après la pluie*, 76, 78 ; *Élizir d'Amor*, 39.
45 Voir Tristan Corbière, *Élégies brésiliennes*, p. 13 ; rééd. dans *Brésiliennes*, p. 111. L'absence du *d* dans *Abaylar* pourrait au demeurant être une faute du prote, mais l'on pense davantage à une maladresse dans la recherche de l'archaïsme. *Abélard* n'apparaît que sporadiquement au XIXe siècle bien que, en 1858, Génin, *Récréations philologiques*, I, p. 435, la considérât comme « la forme la plus en usage » et qu'elle servit d'entrée à divers ouvrages de référence, tels que l'*Atlas étymologique et polyglotte des noms propres les plus répandus* de Philippe-Louis Bourdonné (1862) ou le *Dictionnaire abrégé de la langue française* de Michel Guérard et Antoine-Léandre Sardou (1864), contrairement à Larousse qui donne la priorité à *Abailard* (*GDUL* I, 19). Une recherche sur Gallica pour la période 1800-1873 et les seuls « livres » montre qu'elle représente moins de 3 % des occurrences collectées, les formes en *ai* et *ei* étant *grosso modo* équivalentes, tandis qu'une recherche sur les titres seuls, soit des ouvrages consacrés au moins en partie au personnage, donne huit fois la forme en *é*, quatre fois celle en *ai* et deux fois celle en *ei*. Pour la même période, Frantext donne 35 formes en *é*, 31 en *ai* et 27 en *ei*, résultat qu'il convient de lier aux critères de sélection de ce corpus essentiellement littéraire.

poétique, comme peut en témoigner plus éloquemment encore la rime d'*à rebour* avec *sourd*. Dans ces conditions, on pourrait se demander si la graphie de *chats-huans* n'est pas imputable au prote, mais les pratiques habituelles de Calmann-Lévy n'invitent pas à le penser. On ne trouve dans *Les Amours jaunes* que deux autres cas d'effacement du *t* devant l'*s* de pluriel : d'une part dans *brisans*, substantif obtenu par dérivation impropre d'un participe présent ; d'autre part dans *commençans*, adjectif d'origine semblable dans les « amoureux commençans ou finis » de l'épigraphe d'*Épitaphe*, dont Bertrand estime qu'il aurait été ainsi écrit « pour pasticher un pseudo-vocabulaire philosophique[46] ». C'est donc uniquement dans des formes grammaticalisées que Corbière recourt à ces graphies anciennes qui témoignent de son goût pour les graphies archaïsantes ou fantaisistes dont l'incidence à la rime est secondaire, et l'on peut observer un phénomène semblable dans les *lascifs bacchans* d'A. Houssaye[47].

Si à la rime, l'instabilité de l'orthographe s'expose à un certain contrôle, il semble que la mesure requît également une certaine régulation si l'on en juge d'après l'emploi de l'accent dans *goéland*, traité tantôt en diérèse, tantôt en synérèse. Le souci de Corbière quant à la façon de scander ce mot se manifeste en effet clairement dans l'album Noir où le poète use d'un signe de liaison suscrit pour signaler la synérèse dans un certain nombre de formes dont, précisément, « goelands[48] », ce qui implique qu'il considérait que la diérèse d'usage dans la langue poétique allait de soi pour ces mots. De façon plus précise, pour ce lexème, Corbière emploie dans *Les Amours jaunes* les trémas avec la diérèse (*Le Poète contumace*, *À mon côtre*), l'accent aigu avec la synérèse (*Le Naufrageur*). Dans *Le Douanier* cependant, le mot prend un accent circonflexe inattendu où l'on peut soupçonner une coquille, dans un contexte métriquement ambigu, le vers affecté pouvant aussi bien passer pour un octosyllabe (comme les vers précédents) que pour un heptasyllabe (comme les vers suivant le tétrasyllabe qui lui succède) selon le traitement de *goêland* que l'on décide d'appliquer :

---

46 Éd. citée, p. 71, n. 1. Il s'agit plus précisément d'un modèle hégélien (*cf. infra*, p. 115).

47 *Poésies complètes*, p. 133 ; en rime avec *provocants*.

48 Sauf dans *Le Panayoti* où il omet l'accent : « goeland » (en synérèse). Sur cette question, voir Billy, « Corbière avant Tristan », p. 173-177.

J'aime ton petit corps de garde
Haut perché comme un goêland
        Qui regarde
Dans les quatre aires-de-vent. (21-24)

Cette hésitation de lecture provient du contexte métrique ambiva-lent du poème, juxtaposant dans un même passage hepta- et octosyl-labes qui, contrairement à l'usage conventionnel suivi dans le reste du recueil, présentent le même alignement[49]. Malgré leur fluctuation, les variantes – que nous présentons dans l'ordre chronologique – semblent apporter un éclaircissement. Les deux premières versions du vers 22 sont heptasyllabiques en imposant la diérèse[50], celle de Levi ajoute un adverbe monosyllabique qui, logiquement, si l'on maintient la diérèse, devrait faire de ce vers un octosyllabe, comme les huit vers précédents de la strophe, si ce n'est que le vers 23 qui termine cette dernière n'a que sept syllabes[51] :

Bodros, 25	Perché comme un goëland	7 s.
Noir, 26	perché comme un goëland,	*id.*
Levi, 10	Haut perché comme un goëland	7 ou 8 s.
Vie par., 16	*idem*	
AJ, 22	Haut perché comme un goëland	*id.*

L'amphibologie voulue de ce poème au niveau métrique pourrait inciter à voir dans le circonflexe une volonté de souligner l'équivoque de la forme, laissant le lecteur seul devant l'incertitude de la mesure de ce vers. Il nous semble plus approprié d'envisager l'hypothèse que le prote ait pu se tromper en substituant un ê au ë probable de sa copie de travail[52]. Bien détaché par l'interposition d'un vers de trois syllabes, l'heptasyllabe qui clôt la strophe annonce quant à lui l'allure des strophes suivantes (quatorze heptasyllabes).

---

49 Sur cette unification, voir Billy, art. cité, p. 177-187, où nous ne nous appesantissons cependant pas sur ce passage précis.
50 Autrement, le vers serait le seul hexasyllabe du poème. L'absence de signe de synérèse dans l'album où Corbière prend soin de signaler les synérèses fautives à effectuer (y compris sur *goéland*) confirme cette lecture.
51 *Bodros*, manuscrit du docteur Bodros ; *Noir* : album Noir ; *Levi* : ms. inséré dans l'exemplaire personnel de Corbière (éd. Levi, « New light », p. 240-242) ; *Vie par.* : texte de *La Vie parisienne*.
52 Nous pensons davantage à une erreur antérieure dans le rangement des casses que le prote avait sous la main qu'à une erreur dans le choix de la casse au moment de la composition.

L'ABANDON DE LA PONCTUATION
DANS *CRIS D'AVEUGLE*

La raison pour laquelle Corbière renonce quasiment à la ponctuation dans *Cris d'aveugle* (à trois virgules près) nous échappera toujours : négligence ? acte précurseur ? « recherche d'"écriture naïve"[1] » ? Et pourquoi ce seul poème, du reste ? Le poète s'aventurait ici sur un terrain qui reste pratiquement inexploré avant Apollinaire. On ne peut toutefois ignorer qu'à l'été 1872 Rimbaud connaît une évolution comparable : si dans les premières versions conservées de *Larme*, *La Rivière de Cassis* et *Bonne pensée du matin*, datées de mai 1872, le poète introduit une ponctuation conforme à l'usage, dans les secondes versions – non titrées – qu'il en donne plus tard à Verlaine il l'abandonne purement et simplement si ce n'est quelques résidus dans *Larme*, versions dans lesquelles il abandonne par ailleurs l'usage conventionnel de la majuscule de vers, auquel il ne dérogeait pas jusqu'alors, au profit des seules majuscules en tête de strophes ou/et de phrases[2].

Il est par ailleurs troublant que le poème parût également dans *La Vie parisienne* (un mois environ après l'achevé d'imprimé des *Amours jaunes*) sans guère plus de ponctuation alors que la rédaction de la revue aurait pu d'elle-même lui donner une apparence plus conventionnelle en introduisant un minimum de signes[3]. On peut du moins remarquer que ce renoncement enlevait à Corbière l'embarras dont il témoigne habituellement dans l'emploi de la ponctuation. On peut également noter qu'il lui est arrivé de faire de même dans des poèmes de jeunesse, comme dans l'*Ode au chapeau*, bien que ce précédent paraisse trop lointain pour justifier ce retour à un tel

---

1 La dernière interprétation est suggérée par Houzé et Hérisson, *op. cit.*, p. 192.
2 *Œuvres complètes*, éd. Murphy, IV, *passim*.
3 *La Vie parisienne*, 1re année (1873), p. 603 (20 septembre). Outre les trois virgules présentes dans le recueil, on y trouve un point final à la fin de la première strophe, un autre après *De profundis* (34)

abandon[4]. Bernardelli a également signalé que l'épigraphe d'*Épitaphe*, cocasse élucubration sur le thème de la fin et du commencement, en est à peu près dépourvu[5], avec dans ce cas une évidente ironie rendant compte du caractère logorrhéique que peut prendre le discours hégélien. Il est toutefois un élément que, dans notre cas, il convient de prendre en compte, pointé par Lescane pour qui « [l]es valeurs rythmiques et expressives viendraient […] de ce chant[6] » : donné « Sur l'air bas-breton : *Ann hini goz* », le poème se rattache en effet à une tradition orale de *sonn* breton. On pourrait donc voir dans cet abandon un signe d'oralité, ce que vient conforter le fait que Corbière a déjà pratiqué cette écriture non ponctuée au sein de l'album Noir – qui se veut plus abouti que de simples brouillons – dans *Journal de bord*, pièce recopiée sur le contreplat droit de couverture de l'album Noir, dans laquelle il adopte précisément la langue parlée et ses apocopes caractéristiques sans même éprouver le besoin de substituer des apostrophes aux schwas effacés[7]. Le procédé n'est au demeurant pas sans écho avec la situation de l'aveugle auquel la ponctuation ne saurait être perceptible, repos et pauses éventuels qui sont en principe liés à la ponctuation étant de toute façon oblitérés par les exigences prosodiques de l'air indiqué qui nous invite à *chanter* le texte plutôt qu'à le lire[8].

Ann hini goz est le chant d'un amoureux qui compare à la vieille qu'il aime une jeune, à l'avantage de son aimée, avec un caractère allégorique par lequel s'affirme indirectement l'attachement des Bretons à la terre ancestrale justifiant pleinement qu'Édouard Corbière lui-même le qualifiât d'« air national du pays[9] ». Sa forme, d'après la transcription d'une version qu'en donne Narcisse Quellien, repose sur l'alternance d'un *diskan*, refrain hétérométrique non rimé, composé d'un heptasyllabe et d'un hexasyllabe, et de couplets constitués d'un

---

4   Walzer, éd. citée, p. 857-858.
5   « Il testo contumace », p. 33.
6   « Revoir la ponctuation », p. 9-10.
7   Houzé, *ffocsoR*, p. 15, 4ᵉ col.
8   On peut certes citer le cas d'*A mon côtre* qui présente une ponctuation normale, mais l'indication exacte n'y est pas « Sur l'air de *etc.* », mais « Vendu sur l'air de : *Adieu, mon beau navire !* », ce qui n'est pas une invitation à chanter, ou qui ne l'est qu'à titre indirect.
9   Et non de « chanson nationale du Finistère » : É. Corbière, *Cric-crac*, II, p. 85. Voir Betchaku, « À propos de la chanson bretonne *Ann hini goz* », p. 283 et 285-286.

distique d'octosyllabes monorimes[10], structure que Brizeux reproduit fidèlement dans *Barzonek pé Kanouen ar Vrétoned* (« Bardit ou Chant des Bretons »), composé sur cet air, si l'on excepte l'introduction de la rime dans le refrain[11]. Corbière a régularisé le *diskan*, transformé en un distique monorime d'hexasyllabes, et il en a modifié la fonction. Dans le *sonn*, le refrain est de prime abord lancé, sollicitant les participants, puis alternent couplets – chantés par le meneur éventuellement accompagné – et refrain, la dernière reprise rassemblant une dernière fois les participants pour clore le chant. Corbière n'en apporte pas moins des modifications structurales qui ne semblent pas avoir été commentées ou l'ont été de façon insuffisante. Dans *Cris d'aveugle*, chaque couplet se voit agglutiné le refrain en son début et en sa fin, se transformant ainsi en une sorte de sixain où se trouve gommée la distinction des voix avec la disparition du meneur, le poète s'emparant seul du refrain dont il renouvelle les paroles de sixain en sixain[12]. L'unité formelle de la pièce se trouve malgré tout préservée par la reprise d'une seule et même rime, en |ɔʁ*|[13] reconduite du début de la pièce à la fin. On notera en outre que, au sein de chaque sixain, la reprise du refrain subit généralement une variation quelconque, à l'exception du second couplet où le refrain est en outre dédoublé, ressassant l'invocation « *Deus misericors* ».

---

10 *Chansons et danses des Bretons*, p. 222-226 (partition p. 269).

11 *Œuvres complètes*, I, p. 300-304. Outre qu'il est rimé, le refrain voit son premier vers rompu par une rime interne en 4 + 3 syllabes. En outre, les reprises sont accolées aux couplets.

12 Il semblerait que ce soit telle(s) ou telle(s) de ces différences de structure que Lescane, « Revoir la ponctuation », p. 10, a plus ou moins confusément en tête lorsqu'il affirme avec sans doute trop d'assurance que « tel que le poème est écrit, il est bien difficile de faire coïncider les vers avec le rythme de la chanson » ; en effet, nous ne voyons pas qu'il y ait là une réelle difficulté, refrains et couplets étant syntaxiquement et musicalement autonomes, si ce n'est l'altération du refrain au regard de son modèle.

13 L'astérisque signifie ici que les mots-rime peuvent se terminer sur une consonne amuïe : *mort, misericors, sabord* etc.

LE POÈTE ET LE PROTE

Y. Bernal a récemment ouvert une voie de recherche nouvelle en levant le voile sur l'atelier d'imprimerie d'Alcan-Lévy et le rôle vraisemblable qu'a pu jouer le prote[1]. Son étude des coquilles des *Amours jaunes* – défini comme « un livre qui relève de la licence, se montre incorrigible » –, dans lequel Corbière pratiquerait « la coquille volontaire[2] », repose cependant sur une pétition de principe inversant les valeurs de la philologie en voyant dans les erreurs, non pas des indices dont l'étude est à même de contribuer à l'établissement du texte, mais des matériaux potentiellement authentiques dont il convient d'établir la légitimité herméneutique : toute erreur susceptible d'être justifiée par une interprétation *ad hoc* résulterait d'une recherche intentionnelle. Érigée en dogme, l'erreur se trouve ainsi sacralisée et signifiante *a priori*. Naturellement, cette démarche critique n'est pas dépourvue de tout fondement, s'appuyant sur les singularités de l'écriture de Corbière qui reflètent celles de son caractère. Mais rien ne ressemble plus à une preuve qu'une semblance de preuve ; à une réalité, qu'un désir de réalité ; à une vérité établie, qu'une fiction fondée sur un faisceau de vérités. Cette démarche trouve même dans l'édition de J.-P. Bertrand une sorte d'aboutissement avec un fétichisme de la coquille qui va jusqu'à la tentative de reproduire la moindre anomalie typographique du recueil, témoignant davantage d'un renoncement à toute critique textuelle que d'un progrès dans la connaissance du texte, fétichisme qui eût trouvé une bien meilleure et fidèle application dans un fac-similé de qualité[3].

---

1   « Corbière, les coquilles », p. 41-60.
2   Art. cité, p. 20 et 22.
3   Voir p. ex. l'omission des parenthèses fermantes au péritexte final de *La Pipe au soleil, Le Crapaud, Fleur d'art, À mon côtre* ; mais pourquoi l'ignorer dans *'I' Sonnet, Rapsodie du sourd*, à la fin de l'épigraphe du *Fils de Lamartine* ? Voir aussi les trois virgules égarées dans une ligne de points dans *Frère et sœur jumeaux* (35/36) où Mejjati, art. cité, voit une « fantaisie » de Corbière, bien que le phénomène se reproduise également dans les lignes de suite de la table des matières où l'on imagine mal que la fantaisie de Corbière ait pu s'exercer (une

Comme nous l'avons vu, l'examen détaillé des entorses à l'orthographe met en évidence des pratiques inspirées d'une certaine approximation dans la connaissance des règles et des normes en ce qui concerne l'emploi des accents – quand il ne s'agit pas de négligences – et le redoublement des consonnes ; quant au reste, le choix de telle ou telle forme reflète le plus souvent l'existence de graphies alternatives dans les usages de l'époque, certaines étant héritées de son père, de sorte que la question d'une correction dans l'établissement du texte ne doit pas plus se poser que pour les autres écrivains du XIXe siècle : la singularité poétique de Corbière s'affiche de bien d'autres manières pour que l'on s'encombre de simples bévues attribuables au manque d'intérêt général de Corbière pour ces détails, en dehors de cas spécifiques justifiant le maintien de la graphie déviante. Quant aux coquilles, la question qui est directement posée et celle de la correction des épreuves. Le fait, tout d'abord, qu'il n'en signale aucune sur son exemplaire personnel est à ce titre éloquent : Corbière ne les voit même pas, son attention étant concentrée ailleurs. Comme le relève Y. Bernal, lorsqu'il apporte une correction sur son exemplaire personnel, c'est une variante d'auteur qu'il introduit[4]. Il n'y en aurait que deux cas selon la critique[5], mais l'examen attentif des fac-similé donnés en annexe par B. Houzé[6] peut en révéler d'autres : c'est ainsi que, parmi les annotations que ce dernier inclut dans une ébauche de refonte du *Fils de Lamartine*, on trouve, p. 81, des éléments qui se rapportent de toute évidence à *Pauvre garçon* : « une cocotte enlevant un » a été inscrit juste au-dessus du titre, oblitérant une première inscription au crayon à l'exclusion de son dernier mot (« banquier ») qui doit être soustrait de la nouvelle inscription[7] ; il s'agit donc ici d'une intégration au titre : « une cocotte enlevant un / *PAUVRE GARÇON* ». S'il est difficile de comprendre de quelle façon les deux autres ajouts à

---

virgule, p. 345, au regard de « Le phare » ; voir aussi p. 343, l'« e » égaré dans la ligne de suite au regard de « Frère et sœur jumeaux ») ; mais pourquoi alors négliger celle qui se trouve entre les v. 34/35 de *La Goutte* ou celle qui se substitue au premier des trois points du v. 61 d'*Après la pluie* ? Bertrand respecte l'italique dans « *c'est* » au v. 2 d'*Un riche en Bretagne* ; mais pourquoi alors ne pas respecter l'italique pour les deux-points du v. 76 du *Bossu Bitor, etc.* ?

4   « Corbière, les coquilles », p. 21.
5   Houzé, « Le dernier Corbière », p. 336-337, n'en relève toujours que deux.
6   Art. cité, p. 340-341. La médiocrité des reproductions laisse planer des incertitudes.
7   Art. cité, p. 332 ; fac-similé p. 341 (fig. 4). L'inscription à l'encre inclut bien *un* contrairement à ce qui est dit n. 95.

la plume en marge des tercets de ce sonnet pourraient s'y intégrer[8], il est à remarquer que les annotations apportées au crayon en bas de page, « vous êtes drôle » et « en effet [*passage en blanc*] c'est un [*ou* mon *?*] rôle / Qu'il me récite là : mais après vous », font écho aux premiers vers du premier tercet de *Pauvre garçon*, qui se terminent sur « un garçon drôle » et « son rôle » respectivement. Mais si Corbière ne s'est pas intéressé aux coquilles, en dehors de l'exclamatif « O » du v. 64 de *Litanie du sommeil* noté dans l'*errata*, il est à remarquer que le prote ne s'y est pas davantage penché et qu'aucun correcteur professionnel ne s'est occupé de cet aspect de l'édition comme le montre le nombre considérable et inhabituel des fautes d'impression dues à des caractères mal calés sur les réglettes (lettres manquantes à l'impression), des défauts d'impression (jambages des *p* ou points sur les *i* ou *j* manquants, points manquants dans des séquences de points de suspension) ou à des erreurs de rangement dans les cassetins (substitution de *l* à *i*, de *I* à *l*, de *æ* à *œ*, de virgule au point[9], confusions de police et de corps), les irrégularités d'espacement, les défauts d'ajustement des caractères et surtout l'omission des paren-thèses fermantes, fréquente dans les péritextes, sans parler des virgules et autres égarées dans des lignes de points[10]. Les erreurs de rangement des caractères dans les cassetins n'étaient pas rares, ce que, dans notre recueil, on peut constater, par exemple, par la confusion entre guillemets anglais et guillemets français dont la concentration sur de rares pages est pour le moins suspecte[11].

Constatant après J.-L. Debauve qu'il s'est écoulé près de trois mois entre la mise sous presse (le 17 mai) et l'annonce au dépôt légal (le 13 août), à un moment où l'imprimerie Alcan-Lévy semble ne pas avoir été trop surchargée[12]. Mais alors, à quoi ce temps a-t-il bien pu être employé ?

---

8   Le second – « le somme qui délie » – semble échappé du v. 9 de *Petit coucher*, sonnet ajouté sur la page vierge (la 38ᵉ) au regard de *Pudentiane* ; transcription par Houzé, art. cité, p. 328.

9   *Cf. supra*, n. 3.

10   Pour des détails, voir Bernal, « Corbière, les coquilles », p. 34-40. Il faut détacher de son long examen divers aspects tels que les incohérences des notes de bas de page (37-38) ou les citations ou références approximatives (38-39) – qui ne sont du reste pas l'apanage du poète. On peut également trouver une séquence « ,.. » au lieu des trois points habituels, p. 44 (*Après la pluie*, 61)

11   Voir p. 7 et 45. Elle est isolée p. 93. Voir en outre les innombrables cas recensés par Bernal, art. cité, p. 34-36.

12   « Autour de la publication », p. 60. Cette hypothèse est fondée sur les déclarations d'imprimer, mais que savons-nous du personnel réellement mobilisé dans la période

Nous nous trouvons là dans le domaine de la spéculation, car tout est imaginable, jusqu'à l'absence d'un ouvrier pour maladie ou tout autre motif. Y. Bernal imagine que « c'est la présence de Corbière, typographe novice, ou auteur à la fois fantaisiste et sourcilleux, dans l'atelier, qui a allongé le temps d'impression[13] » qui aurait, selon lui, pût en partie être occupé par « l'ajout tardif de pièces pendant la composition et l'impression du volume[14] ». Mais on peut se demander si la présence même dans l'atelier, d'un auteur au tempérament aussi indiscipliné et exalté que Corbière, n'était pas plutôt une source de perturbation du travail des imprimeurs qu'une aide efficace. Nous refusons en tout cas pour notre part d'adopter l'hypothèse extrême qui voudrait que Corbière se soit ingénié à exiger du prote qu'il introduise des coquilles aussi contraires à son métier et mettant en cause tant son professionnalisme que sa dignité personnelle tout en engageant gravement sa réputation et celle de son employeur. Nous n'irions même pas jusqu'aux concessions d'Y Bernal[15] : « On le voit, certaines coquilles semblent voulues par Corbière pour corroder sa page et ce faisant corroborer sa poétique, comme un procédé aussi ludique qu'original, et même *inédit*, dont il exploite la richesse ». Conclusion qui, curieusement, vient juste après un paragraphe consacré à des « caprice[s] d'impression (donc d'origine mécanique et non humaine) » affectant les points suscrits des *i/j* ou le jambage de *p*. H. Fournier, auquel Y. Bernal se réfère volontiers, a particulièrement bien souligné l'importance du correcteur[16] :

> De toutes les attributions de la typographie, la lecture des épreuves est sans contredit celle qui exige les soins les plus attentifs ; aussi la correction qui en résulte constitue-t-elle au plus haut point, et dans le sens le plus sérieux, le mérite d'un livre. Ses autres qualités, celles qui ont rapport à sa composition et à son tirage, peuvent être soumises à la diversité des goûts et des appréciations ; mais la valeur qu'il tire de la pureté de son texte ne saurait lui être contestée, puisqu'elle repose sur des principes universellement reconnus. La composition et le tirage, plus ou moins satisfaisants, n'intéressent le livre

---

considérée (possibles défections pour maladie ou autres raisons) ? Il faudrait en outre tenir compte du train des travaux de ville pour la période considérée, sans doute impossible à déterminer avec quelque précision.

13   « Corbière, les coquilles », p. 50-51.
14   « Les trois enregistrements », p. 289-290.
15   « Corbière, les coquilles », p. 40.
16   *Traité de la typographie*, p. 259.

qu'au point de vue de la forme ; mais la correction est une question de fond, et la première de toutes. La meilleure édition est donc celle qui présente une entière conformité avec le modèle dont elle est la reproduction, et qu'en outre elle a su dégager des fautes évidentes qu'il pouvait contenir.

Et l'auteur de souligner que « l'imprimerie, ou, comme on dit aujourd'hui, la presse, se trouve dans des conditions qui ne laissent plus au correcteur le temps nécessaire pour une lecture sérieuse[17] ». On peut admettre qu'il y ait eu une première épreuve dans laquelle le correcteur l'aurait « collationn[ée] avec la copie pour voir si le compositeur s'y est exactement conformé[18] », mais rien ne permet d'envisager que le travail de révision du texte soit allé au-delà, du côté du prote, qui, censé « s'attacher scrupuleusement à l'observation de l'unité orthographique de la ponctuation, et des règles qui ont pu être spécialement adoptées quant à l'italique, aux grandes capitales *etc.*, dans l'ouvrage dont il suit la lecture », a négligé cette étape, s'assurant sans doute – plutôt convenablement – de la conformité du texte imprimé à la copie dont les manuscrits connus de Corbière indiquent qu'elle devait être fautive en bien des points, ce qui ressort plus particulièrement dans la fréquente omission de la parenthèse fermante dans les éventuelles indications finales de date et de lieu. Il y a par contre une claire défaillance dans la relecture de secondes épreuves[19] :

> C'est au correcteur de secondes qu'est dévolue la tâche plus importante et plus délicate de revoir les feuilles en dernier ressort ; sa lecture est définitive, et c'est d'elle que dépend, sous ce rapport si essentiel, la réputation de l'édition, et même celle de l'établissement […]. Il doit donc se pénétrer profondément des graves conséquences qui résulteraient de son inattention. Le correcteur de secondes est en position d'exercer avec une utilité très-réelle l'office de critique […]

On en est ici réduit à des hypothèses, mais il n'est pas difficile de comprendre que le prote, dérouté par un manuscrit aussi éloigné des règles ordinaires de l'orthographe, de la syntaxe et de la ponctuation avec maintes contradictions au fil de la lecture, a dû se laisser déborder par ce client si inhabituel et sans doute incontrôlable auquel il se trouvait

---

17 *Op. cit.*, p. 262.
18 Selon la description qu'en donne Fournier, *op. cit.*, p. 138.
19 Fournier, *op. cit.*, p. 265.

confronté. Selon Y. Bernal, ce prote serait ce Mr Saint-Léger auquel le poète dédicaça un exemplaire sous la forme ambiguë suivante, qui semble tenir de l'antiphrase[20] : « A M^r St-Léger, une de ses victimes ». Relevant à partir du 30 août 1873 sa signature à la fin d'une rubrique « Anecdotes et racontars » du *Journal amusant*, Y. Bernal suggère même que ce prote, qui s'était déjà illustré par un incident qui aurait pu lui coûter cher, aurait pu être congédié par Alcan-Lévy[21]. Quant à Corbière, la seule trace objective d'une révision de sa part réside dans l'*errata* succinct ajouté en fin d'ouvrage.

20   « Corbière, les coquilles », p. 53-60.
21   Art. cité, p. 58-59.

SERVITUDES TYPOGRAPHIQUES

Si le prote a scrupuleusement suivi le texte de la copie que lui avait confiée le poète, comme nous le pensons, il est des situations particulières où les conventions du métier l'ont emporté sur les probables indications du poète. Le cas le plus évident – et par conséquent le plus ignoré – concerne le traitement typographique des vers qui suivent de façon stricte la convention de commencer uniformément par une majuscule : tout laisse à penser en effet que la copie de travail dont disposait le prote était à cet égard approximative, à en juger par les poèmes autographes de Corbière. Il suffit de consulter la transcription que donne B. Houzé de l'album Noir pour constater que seules les majuscules de phrase sont systématiquement présentes en début de vers, les autres vers commençant presque toujours par une minuscule dans *Le Douanier de mer*, tandis que dans *Sonnet à Black* les vers 7 et 11 commencent par une minuscule ; dans les 36 vers d'*Histoire d'un apothicaire*, par contre, la majuscule est presque généralisée, l'avant-dernier vers faisant seul exception ; dans les 22 vers de *Petite pouësie*, la norme est suivie jusqu'au seizième vers, avant que Corbière ne relâche son attention, cinq des derniers vers faisant exception *etc.*, et ce manque de généralisation se retrouve dans les vers autographes dont il parsèmera son exemplaire imprimé[1]. Cette négligence des majuscules de vers n'est pas au demeurant une singularité de Corbière : on la retrouve, à des degrés divers, chez d'autres écrivains, y compris chez Hugo ou Baudelaire, la logique de la phrase pouvant, dans le flux de l'écriture, voire de la copie, occulter la convention typographique. Il arrivait même que les imprimeurs se conformassent à l'absence de cette convention en adoptant – vraisemblablement – des usages manuscrits, comme on peut le subodorer pour l'édition des *Adieux* (1844) ou celle des *Agrestes* (1845) d'Henri de Latouche, imprimées chez des éditeurs différents.

---

1   Voir les transcriptions qu'en donne Houzé, « Le dernier Corbière ».

Une autre caractéristique du recueil, également délaissée par la critique, retiendra plus spécialement notre attention : l'emploi des petites
capitales. C'est là en effet un domaine où le travail du prote interfère
avec les intentions du poète, posant aux éditeurs un problème qu'ils n'ont
pas toujours su affronter de façon correcte, faute d'avoir pu l'identifier
précisément : les mêmes petites capitales sont en effet employées d'une
part pour mettre en relief des mots, syntagmes ou phrases que Corbière
devait signaler d'une manière quelconque mais distincte des procédés
que le prote aura rendu par l'italique[2] ; d'autre part pour introduire
les poèmes (nous désignerons par A ce dispositif), mais toujours après
une grande initiale de deux points ou, de rares fois, une lettrine ornée[3]
(ci-dessous en gras), selon une convention typographique du métier
qui affecte invariablement la première suite continue de caractères, à
savoir le premier mot, quelle que soit sa catégorie grammaticale, éventuellement les deux ou trois premiers si ceux-ci sont séparés par une
apostrophe ou un trait d'union : ce peut donc être aussi bien un déterminant : « DES [essais] » (p. 3), « UN [chant] » (71) ; un pronom sujet :
« TU [ris] » (12), « CE [fut] » (153) ; un adverbe : « NE [m'offrez pas] »
(23), « PAS [d'éperon] » (143) ; une préposition : « EN [fumée] » (35) ; une
conjonction : « ET [vous] » (85), « QUE [me veux-tu] » (55), « COMME [il
était] » (83), « DONC, [la tramontane] » (11) ou une interjection : « OH »
(59), « EH [bien] » (327) ; que des mots pleins de nature diverse : « OUI »
(79), « MOI, [je fais] » (53), « BEAU [chien] » (33), « BATARD [de Créole] »
(5), « ATTOUCHEZ, [sans toucher] » (39) ou « EVOHÉ ! [fouaille] » (10).
Voici à présent des exemples de mots concaténés : « C'EST [la bohême] »
(9), « L'HOMME [de l'art] » (157), « QU'ILS » (209), « J'AIMAIS… [– Oh] »
(8), « J'AI [vu] » (77), « N'ENTENDS-TU [pas] » (125). Lorsque le premier
mot se réduit à une lettre isolée, le dispositif s'étend d'ordinaire au mot

---

2   Dans l'album Noir, l'écriture en script de la légende du portrait du capitaine Goulven
    marque nettement la distinction entre petites et grandes capitales (f° 13r°). Mais Corbière
    utilise plus souvent divers procédés de mise en relief : soulignement, changement
    d'inclinaison de l'écriture (ex. f° 5r°, 19r°) qui peuvent parfois se multiplier (au f° 9r°,
    on a deux strophes d'une écriture très nettement plus penchée que l'ordinaire, et, dans
    la dernière, Détresses se démarque par un redressement des caractères), combinaison des
    deux (26r°), adoption d'une taille supérieure (24r°), avec parfois deux ou trois degrés de
    variation (id. : « Point₁ perdu, mais un point₂ » ; cf. Lescane, « Écrire, peindre », p. 114),
    éventuellement combiné avec le soulignement (28r°, 29v°), renforcement d'initiales (9r°).
3   Cas des fabulettes ouvrant et clôturant le recueil ainsi que « Point n'ai fait un tas
    d'océans… », p. 253.

suivant : « O CROISÉE [ensommeillée] » (99), « O BELLE [hospitalière] »
(201) *vs* « O VÉNUS, [dans] » (115) *etc.* ; « A MOI, [grand chapelet !] »
(109) ; on rencontre cependant quelques exceptions « A [grands coups
d'avirons] » (149), « A [l'île de Procide] » (197)[4] *etc.* Le cas de « BUONA
VESPRE » fait exception, où la formule italienne a été considérée comme
un tout, comme le numéral « CENT VINGT » (279).

Ce procédé est également appliqué dans d'autres contextes. On doit
ici distinguer quatre cas, avec tout d'abord une extension du dispositif
A en tête de sections de poèmes : c'est le cas des actes de *Grand opéra*
et du « Cantique spirituel » enchâssé dans *La Rapsode foraine*, dont la
spécificité est soulignée par l'impression du texte en italique (B) ; en tête
de chaque groupe de vers d'*Épitaphe* (strophes) et des parties (introduction, conclusion) ou sous-parties (chacune des laisses) constitutives de
Litanie du sommeil (C) ; en tête du dernier vers de *Male-Fleurette*, refrain
ramenant le vers initial (D). Du point de vue fonctionnel, ces dispositifs
constituent de simples artifices de mise en page, contrairement à l'emploi
ordinaire des petites capitales qui sont alors le signe typographique d'une
propriété du texte même. Si le dispositif A, naturellement approuvé par
Corbière, est un procédé mécanique, contribuant à détacher les poèmes
les uns des autres pour en souligner l'individualité, il n'en va pas de
même des dispositifs B, C et D – qui interfèrent naturellement avec A
pour ce qui concerne le premier vers des pièces concernées – qui visent
à distinguer des parties ou sous-parties, de façon redondante dans le cas
de B où intervient un changement de style (passage à l'italique), et de
C où les parties sont déjà indiquées par le partitionnement en strophes
(*Épitaphe*) ou un autre artifice[5] : ces derniers marquages n'étant pas dans
la tradition de la typographie et de la mise en page, il faut qu'il y ait
eu là quelque indication dans la copie de travail, avec sans doute une
mise en relief particulière des initiales des passages concernés. C'est
ainsi que, dans l'album Noir, Corbière pouvait augmenter la taille des
caractères constitutifs du mot initial, soit de « grandes minuscules »
avec grande majuscule initiale[6] :

---

4   Voir aussi « O [corde-de-pendu] » (168) et « O [brun Amant] » (171) dans l'extension B
     du dispositif (voir ci-dessous).
5   Dans *Litanie du sommeil*, l'astérisque détache les parties et des interlignes, les laisses, qui
     sont, les unes et les autres, affectées par le dispositif.
6   Respectivement incipits du *Bain de mer de Madame X**** et du *Panayoti*.

Ah ! Madame HIX se déferle ! (f° 9r°)

Moi j'étais quartier-maître, quartier-maître et pilote (f° 28r°)

Les petites capitales simples étaient vraisemblablement rendues par le même procédé, comme au second vers du premier état brévissime (et sans titre) de *Litanie du sommeil* (f° 8r°), où l'on notera toutefois que l'augmentation de taille paraît moins ostentatoire que dans les cas précédents[7] :

> Vous qui ronflez auprès d'une femme endormie,
> Épicier, savez-vous ce que c'est l'insomnie ?

Passage qui, dans *Les Amours jaunes*, a pour correspondant[8] :

> Vous qui ronflez au coin d'une épouse endormie,
> Ruminant ! savez-vous ce soupir : l'Insomnie ?

Ce genre de dispositif soulève une première difficulté : ces petites capitales n'occultent-elles pas une volonté précise de mise en relief des mots concernés, *indépendamment de leur positionnement initial* ? On peut voir, dans l'exemple précédent, qu'il n'en est rien, le pronom initial n'étant pas mis en relief, du moins dans l'album Noir. L'examen, dans *Les Amours jaunes*, des catégories concernées par ce marquage, en dehors des dispositifs A, B, C et D, montre que le problème se limite aux substantifs, noms propres, pronoms personnels disjoints ou pronoms indéfinis[9] sans parler de groupes nominaux ou même de propositions entières correspondant à des vers entiers[10]. Tout le problème consiste d'une part à savoir si, dans tel ou tel cas, il n'y a pas un recoupement entre le dispositif ornemental de A qui s'inscrit dans la structure du recueil, celui de B ou D qui soulignent la structuration du poème ou celui purement redondant de C, et la mise en relief de mots ou d'expressions isolées ; d'autre part, dans le cas positif, à savoir comment la mise en relief éventuelle aurait

---

7 Le procédé se rencontre dans d'autres autographes : voir ainsi le cas de « *Railway di Pompeia* », p. 423-424.
8 À noter que le ms. ne met pas d'initiale majuscule à « insomnie ».
9 Mots qui peuvent naturellement avoir fonction de phrase, comme « Dors » dans *Sonnet posthume*, dont la récurrence aux v. 3 et 5 montre que le mot n'a pas à être mis en relief. Pour la mise en relief de pronoms, voir « Toi » dans *Litanie de sommeil* (55, 56) et « l'Autre » dans *Le Fils de Lamartine* (58) ; de noms propres : « Tupetu » (majuscule omise après deux-points).
10 Dans *Litanie du sommeil* (147) et *Le Fils de Lamartine* (12).

été rendue si les petites capitales ne l'avaient occultée : par des petites capitales ou par l'italique ? Les éditions qui reprennent le dispositif A, éventuellement B, C, D, éludent du même coup la difficulté, du moins pour autant que leurs auteurs en aient compris la logique et qu'ils se soient montrés scrupuleux. Le fait que sept pièces seulement soient concernées par la mise en relief *libre*, c'est-à-dire en dehors de ces dispositifs, donne à penser que le problème ne se pose généralement pas. On notera en outre que la plupart des cas se présentent dans *Litanie du sommeil* (22 cas), les six autres pièces se partageant onze autres cas[11]. On remarquera enfin que le procédé affecte fréquemment un substantif ou un pronom personnel en fonction d'apostrophe : outre SOMMEIL, SOMME, TOI et RUMINANT[12] dans *Litanie du sommeil*, c'est le cas de SEÑORA dans *Chanson en 'Si'* (123) et de CHÂSSE dans *Grand opéra* (128).

Aragon et Bonnin ainsi que Bertrand, dans la dernière édition en date du recueil qui a servi de base aux candidats à l'agrégation de Lettres modernes en 2020, reproduisent plus ou moins fidèlement ces dispositifs[13], choix éditorial qui tourne *de facto* le dos à une approche philologique du problème qui seule peut amener à progresser dans la critique textuelle et l'établissement du texte des *Amours jaunes*. Martineau et Le Goffic (1941) ne conservaient que le dispositif A, soit au seul début des pièces, recourant au bas de casse (après majuscule) pour son extension à d'autres situations (B, C, D). Se conformant aux normes de la collection « La Bibliothèque de la Pléiade » qui ignore le dispositif A, Walzer s'est trouvé directement confronté aux difficultés que nous avons identifiées, comme d'autres éditeurs après lui. Le problème apparaît principalement dans *Litanie du sommeil* où Walzer a confondu le dispositif C[14] avec des mises en relief libres, mises en relief qui ne concernent en fait que « SOMMEIL » et sa variante métrique « SOMME[15] » ainsi que « TOI » qui

---

11 Quatre dans *Saint Tupetu* (pour le même mot : *Tupetu*) ; trois dans *Le Fils de Lamartine*.

12 Sauf exceptions : « Sommeil » (16, 26 ?, 118) ; « Ruminant » (162).

13 Bertrand imprime ainsi (nous soulignons chaque fois l'élément fautif) « Un poète » (*Le poète et la cigale*), « N'ENTENDS-TU pas ? » (*Portes et fenêtres*) ; Aragon et Bonin, « A grands coups d'avirons » (*À un Juvénal de lait*), « O corde-de-pendu » et « O brun Amant » (*Litanie du sommeil*), « A l'île de Procide » (*Le Fils de Lamartine*).

14 Qu'il reproduit comme de juste pour le premier vers, contrairement à Lalanne.

15 Il y a cependant une exception au v. 16 (Corbière a fort bien pu négliger son soulignement), peut-être une autre au sein du v. 26 : « SOMMEIL ! – Loup-Garou gris ! Sommeil Noir de fumée ! » (*cf.* p. 29-30).

lui est coréférent, comme nous le verrons plus loin. Walzer n'en met pas moins en petites capitales maints substantifs qui doivent en être dépourvus (« Trop-plein » 37, « Voix » 51, « Fontaine » 54, « Surface » 76, « Soupirail » 82 *etc.*), mais aussi des adjectifs antéposés (« Grand » 62 et 103, « Sombre » 86, « Immense » 136) ainsi que, bizarrement, le déterminant « Du » (122), alors que les mots appartenant à ces catégories grammaticales, employés dans le même cadre prédicatif, sont toujours dépourvus de petites capitales[16]. Les éditeurs qui ont renoncé au dispositif C, comme Ch. Morice[17] (1926) et Le Goffic (1941), impriment ces mots en puisant à juste titre dans le bas de casse. Un doute subsiste quant à la restitution du substantif dans « SOMMEIL auréolé ! » (46) : assorti d'une épithète, le substantif se distingue des multiples « SOMMEIL ! » (en tête de laisse) (comme des « SOMMEIL ! », autres positions), pour se rapprocher de « féerique Apothéose ! » qui constitue le second hémistiche du même vers ou « Aurorale buée ! » (36) : l'abandon des petites capitales imposées par le dispositif C pourrait ici se justifier, le substantif n'étant plus focalisé par l'exclamation qui semble porter sur le prédicat dont il est le support, ou, de façon plus précise, sur la prédication dont il fait l'objet. Malgré tout, sa position initiale en tête d'une laisse de cinq vers (dont c'est la seule occurrence du mot) nous incite bien à y voir une nouvelle apostrophe au sommeil. Coréférent de SOMMEIL et dans la même fonction d'apostrophe, TOI suit le même traitement[18], comme le montre la mise en forme homogène de ces mots lorsqu'ils sont employés ailleurs qu'en tête de laisse ou de partie, ce que les éditeurs successifs ne semblent pas avoir compris, puisque l'ensemble ou presque des éditions que nous avons consultées renoncent aux petites capitales aux vers 55 et 56[19] (si ce n'est Bertrand, du seul fait de son parti-pris de reproduire les moindres singularités typographiques du recueil).

---

16 Il n'est qu'à comparer les deux hémistiches du v. 54 par lequel commence la huitième laisse : « FONTAINE de Jouvence et Borne de l'envie ! ».

17 C'est en effet le poète Charles Morice – dont le rôle est régulièrement occulté dans les notices et références bibliographiques – qui a établi le texte de l'édition « définitive » chez Messein, comme il apparaît dans l'avertissement donné après la préface, supprimé par la suite.

18 *Toi* est imprimé en bas de casse lorsqu'il est employé en d'autres fonctions : au v. 62, *toi* est CC ; au v. 148, bien qu'en apostrophe, il ne se réfère pas au sommeil mais au *ruminant* – l'homme en proie au sommeil –, comme le *vous* initial du poème (qui s'y réfère de façon collective plutôt que générique).

19 En plus des v. 17, 33 et 58 (soit en début de laisse) chez ceux qui ont renoncé au dispositif C.

Les petites capitales posent également un autre problème du fait que, contrairement aux majuscules, et pour autant que nous le sachions, elles n'existent pas en italique dans les casses d'Alcan-Lévy (comme chez tant d'autres imprimeurs[20]), comme on peut l'observer dès le poème liminaire, imprimé en italique : « UN *poète ayant rimé* ». De ce fait, l'abandon du dispositif d'apparat d'origine <Initiale de deux points OU lettrine + petites capitales> pour le(s) premier(s) mot(s) des poèmes pose non seulement le problème général de savoir s'il ne convient pas mieux de préférer l'italique au romain, qu'il faille ou non, par ailleurs, maintenir les petites capitales. Dans un certain nombre de cas, des parallélismes lèvent un doute éventuel : ainsi, la répétition de l'apostrophe à *Évohé* dans le sixième sonnet de *Paris* montre que le romain, norme typographique retenue pour ce poème, s'impose ici ; autre exemple : le romain s'impose pour l'« ETERNEL Féminin » par lequel commence *Féminin singulier*, d'autant qu'on peut le mettre en parallèle avec celui du second vers du poème précédent, À *l'Éternel Madame*. À l'opposé, par son parallélisme avec les formules semblables *Buona sera* et *Buona nocte*, le « BUONA VESPRE » qui commence *Do, l'enfant do...* doit être rendu par le romain *en contraste avec l'italique* utilisé comme norme typographique pour l'impression des rondels, en relation avec l'altérité linguistique de ces formules. Par contre, dans les quelques pièces où l'on trouve des mots en petites capitales en dehors des dispositifs A-D, la prudence s'impose d'emblée, prudence que n'ont pas toujours eu les éditeurs. Walzer ou Dansel se laissent ainsi piéger comme les éditeurs de Vanier et Messein et tant d'autres lorsqu'ils impriment « Voir *Naples et...* », traduction de l'expression italienne, en tête de *Veder Napoli poi mori*, ou « Pompeïa-station » en tête de *Vésuves et C*[ie], que Martineau rendait correctement par l'italique[21], en conformité avec le fait que, partout ailleurs dans le recueil, les mots ou syntagmes en langue étrangère sont généralement imprimés en italique, y compris la forme francisée *lazzarone* (et *Lazzarones*) dans *Veder Napoli*. Il en va de même dans le cantique spirituel de *La*

---

20 *Cf.* Fournier, *Traité de la typographie*, p. 61-62.

21 *Essai de biographie*, p. 106 et 107. Lalanne commet les mêmes erreurs que Walzer qui lui a sans doute servi de base. *Lazzarone* est cependant partout ailleurs traité en romain, jusqu'à son pluriel d'origine, soit aux p. 55 (*À une camarade*), 172 et 173 (*Litanie du sommeil*). Dans un autographe d'une version courte intitulée *Vedere Napoli e morire !* (où manque « lazzarone »), « Lazzarones » seul n'est pas souligné (Trigon, *Tristan Corbière*, p. [97]).

Rapsode foraine pour « MÈRE » (25) et « *l'*ENFANT » (56) où tous les éditeurs s'entendent à reproduire les deux substantifs en maintenant la rectitude originale des caractères alors que, pour le reste, le cantique est tout entier en italique : rien en effet ne peut nous donner à penser que Corbière ait voulu mettre le premier mot en relief ni le second doublement en relief, une édition correcte devant généraliser l'italique et imprimer respectivement « *Mère* » et « *l'*ENFANT[22] ».

---

22 On remarquera au passage que les cas de double mise en relief se font en combinant italique et grandes capitales, comme dans « *BON RETOUR DU CHAMP DU NORD* », de plus encadré de tirets (*Idylle coupée*), ou dans « *L'OCÉAN ! L'OCÉAN !! L'OCÉAN !!!* » (*Bambine*).

STRUCTURE ET ORNEMENTATION
DES *AMOURS JAUNES*

Corbière s'est davantage intéressé à la mise en page du recueil et à sa structure, jusqu'à intégrer après coup les poèmes liminaires dédiés *À Marcelle* : le premier cahier, et par conséquent la pagination marquée ou virtuelle (pages de titres, pages paires vierges, premières pages des poèmes), commence en effet avec la première section du recueil, soit le titre de *ÇA* sur une page propre. Cet ajout a posé le problème de l'intégration de la première pièce dans la pagination du recueil. Le poème est imprimé sur deux pages dont la seconde devrait être numérotée, ce qui n'est pas le cas, et cette particularité se retrouve dans la seconde page du poème final, ce qui plaide pour son ajout également après coup. Les deux pièces sont précédées de la même frise, là où le premier poème des différentes parties du recueil sont précédées d'un bandeau historié, à l'exception notable et sans doute significative de *Laisser-courre* par lequel commence *RACCROCS*, qui est la section centrale, où l'on retrouve précisément la frise de ces pièces périphériques. Dans la table des matières, c'est le chiffre « 0 » qui est indiqué, contrairement à tous les usages de l'édition, ce que l'on peut attribuer directement à la fantaisie de Corbière, et l'une et l'autre pièce sont précédées du titre « *A MARCELLE* », présenté exactement de la même manière que les titres de sections[1].

De la comparaison avec un volume de vers publié deux ans plus tard par les frères Glady, écrit par Louis Verbrugghe, poète influencé par Corbière à qui est justement dédié l'un de ses poèmes, deux autres l'étant à Monsieur le Comte et Madame la Comtesse de B. en lesquels Mortelette identifie Rodolphe de Battine et sa maîtresse qui l'auraient

---

[1] Majuscules et italique ; titre suivi d'un point et centré ; le second est précédé du même fleuron que les titres de sections (fleuron qui sépare également les titres de Ça, *Paris* et *Épitaphe* dans les mises en forme particulières décrites p. 60, n. 25).

accueilli à Douarnenez, « vraisemblablement au cours de l'été de 1874[2] »,
B. Houzé retire que l'édition des *Amours jaunes* met (paradoxalement) en
relief « le soin et la volonté de singularisation qui [la] caractérisent[3] »,
ce qui a dû nécessiter un investissement financier plus important, mais
il convient de ne pas perdre de vue le fait que le recueil de Verbrugghe
– publié en 1875 – ne sort pas des presses d'Alcan-Lévy mais de celles
de J. Claye. Outre la présence de lettres ornées, l'adjonction de bandeaux
et de culs-de-lampe, l'insertion d'une eau-forte gravée par l'auteur,
Les Amours jaunes se distinguerait ainsi des autres ouvrages publiés
par les frères Glady par le choix de l'elzévir, « cette police de titres
[*capitales italiques ornées*] aussi singulière, aussi ostensiblement archaïsante » qui, selon Y. Bernal, « entre en collision avec la modernité de
la poétique corbiérienne, qui s'écarte du ton élégiaque et autres poncifs
romantiques[4] ». On ne saurait naturellement contester que Corbière,
qui s'est montré si peu concerné par la correction de ses textes, se soit
par contre bien davantage intéressé à la bonne réalisation des signes de
prestige qui enjolivent son recueil, tous éléments dont la conception et
la réalisation soigneuse ont dû prendre un certain temps[5]. Pour autant,
nous ne pouvons que répéter que nous ne pensons pas qu'il entendît
sciemment provoquer le lecteur par sa négligence dans la révision de
son texte, cette négligence témoignant simplement de son désintérêt
pour ces aspects à ses yeux accessoires, sa poétique se situant sur un
tout autre terrain.

Si, en dehors des *Amours jaunes*, les frères Glady avaient fait appel à
Alcan-Lévy, c'était pour des brochures étrangères à la littérature, mais,
la même année que *Les Amours jaunes*, parut, sous le pseudonyme d'Ed.
Allony, une plaquette de 35 pages d'Eugène de Lonlay diffusée par la
librairie E. Dentu, issue des mêmes presses : *Le Livre défendu*, édition
princeps « ornée de vignettes et têtes de pages », composé de seize
poèmes plus un d'introduction[6]. Cette plaquette recourt également, en

---

2   Selon Mortelette, « Corbière, Hugo », p. 76-77, qui donne quelques informations sur les
     relations qu'ont pu avoir les deux poètes (en 1874), ce poème serait adressé à Corbière
     « parce que ce sonnet, qui est une profession d'athéisme, prend pour cible le poète des
     Contemplations ».
3   « Un hommage inconnu », p. 11.
4   « Elzévirien à voir », p. 254-255.
5   Debauve, « Autour de la publication » ; Houzé et Hérisson, *op. cit.*, p. 171.
6   https://gallica.bnf.fr/ark:/12148/bpt6k5610312z?rk=21459;2 (consulté le 17/09/2022).

tête de chaque poème et de la table, à des frises et des bandeaux parmi lesquels pas moins de six se retrouvent dans le recueil de Corbière : celui de *Ça ?* se retrouve p. 5 (*Le Livre défendu*); celui de *Paris*, p. 21 (*Le Trio*); celui d'*Épitaphe*, p. 19 (*Éloge de Lamartine*); celui de la section *LES AMOURS JAUNES*, p. 24 (*La Dernière Affection*) et p. 27 (*La Paysanne*); celui de *SÉRÉNADE DES SÉRÉNADES*, p. 36 (Table); celui de *GENS DE MER*, p. 9 (*L'Amour*) et 17 (*Christine Nilsson*). En tête d'un rondeau intitulé *Sarah Bernhardt*, p. 23, se trouve un bandeau de gravure sur bois, avec un motif floral, qui ne détonne pas moins que celui, analogue, de *RONDELS POUR APRÈS* dans *Les Amours jaunes*[7].

Que l'on retrouve les mêmes vignettes dans des ouvrages issus des mêmes presses n'a naturellement rien de surprenant, mais cela montre que le rôle d'Alcan-Lévy n'est pas des moindres dans l'originalité du recueil au regard de l'ensemble de la production des frères Glady, en apportant à la conception des *Amours jaunes* un savoir-faire volontiers salué par les critiques[8], sans le disparate qui entache *Le Livre défendu* dont les vignettes, de styles hétéroclites[9], se succèdent sans recherche d'harmonie. *Les Amours jaunes* affichent en effet une unité esthétique, comme l'a établi J.-L. Debauve, avec des « bandeaux et culs-de-lampe de la fonderie Deberny, inspirés de modèles du XVIe siècle, mis à la mode par la collection de la bibliothèque elzévirienne, mais de meilleur goût que les vignettes analogues utilisées par la maison Lemerre[10] ». Seule s'en détache la spécificité des vignettes de *RONDELS POUR APRÈS* sur lesquelles B. Houzé a attiré l'attention : le style, qu'il qualifie d'« archaïsant », du bandeau en tête de *Sonnet posthume* comme celui, très différent, du cul-de-lampe final composé de feuilles aldines[11] « contraste avec la finesse folâtre des autres ornements du recueil[12] », et l'on peut penser que le choix du bandeau a bien été effectué par Corbière, autant pour l'effet de rupture stylistique qu'il ne manquait pas de produire au

---

7 On y trouve également des frises et des culs-de-lampe dont le style moderne détonne tout autant.
8 Voir les témoignages rassemblés par Bernal, « Corbière, les coquilles », p. 42-43.
9 Les bandeaux alternent irrégulièrement avec des frises fantaisistes et cèdent même la place à une gravure en marge de la première strophe, composée de monosyllabes, de *Drame nocturne*, p. 29. Les culs-de-lampe sont également hétéroclites.
10 « Autour de la publication », p. 58.
11 Sur ce dernier, voir *infra*, p. 115-116.
12 Houzé et Hérisson, *op. cit.*, p. 171.

regard des autres bandeaux – ce qui signe sa volonté de détacher cette section du recueil – que pour un souci d'identification thématique de la section, avec un motif floral qui fait écho à l'évocation symbolique de diverses fleurs dans cette section.

B. Houzé va plus loin en évoquant la structure enchâssée du recueil articulé autour d'un centre traversant *Litanie du sommeil*, comme l'avait bien vu H. Laroche[13], au départage des laisses féminines et des laisses masculines, ce qui pourrait selon lui résulter d'un travail direct sur la distribution des pièces et des sections dans le recueil. L'interversion des parties *SÉRÉNADE DES SÉRÉNADES* et *RACCROCS* sur la page de titre pourrait du reste être un témoin résiduel de modifications intervenues lors du travail de composition. On peut ici évoquer deux aspects du recueil qui témoignent de pistes délaissées dans la réflexion qui a abouti à son organisation actuelle. Le bandeau de la section *RACCROCS*, donné en tête de *Laisser-courre*, est une simple frise, détonnant au regard des vignettes choisies pour les autres sections, et, comme nous l'avons dit, cette frise est identique à celle des pièces dédiées à Marcelle, ce qui suggère que ce poème, actuellement p. 139, a pu être conçu à un moment donné comme centre du recueil. Une autre particularité est le recours aux grandes majuscules ornées de filigranes : on ne les rencontre que trois fois dans le recueil ; elles marquent l'initiale des deux pièces liminaires ainsi que celle de « Point n'ai fait un tas d'océans… » en tête de la section *GENS DE MER*, actuellement p. 253. Ce poème, que B. Houzé désigne comme une préface qui « dispose [*GENS DE MER*] comme livre dans le livre[14] », est également le seul à être entièrement composé en italique et pourvu d'une lettrine ornée avec les pièces liminaires, si l'on met de côté les poèmes de *RONDELS POUR APRÈS* (moins la lettrine ornée initiale) – autre « livre dans le livre » si l'on veut –, ce qui désigne également *GENS DE MER* comme un centre possible du recueil à un moment ou à un autre dans la recherche du meilleur agencement des poèmes, avant que l'arrangement définitif ne situe « le centre paginal » au cœur même de *Litanie du sommeil* qui s'y prêtait particulièrement bien de par sa structure spéculaire[15].

---

13   *Les voix de la corbière*, p. 81, 173-174 et 192-199.
14   Houzé et Hérisson, *op. cit.*, p. 193.
15   Sur cette structure, voir *infra*, p. 153-154.

Évoquant une possible influence du *Parnassiculet contemporain* qui saluait ironiquement la parution du premier volume du *Parnasse contemporain*, B. Houzé a pu attirer l'attention sur le fait que « plusieurs bandeaux et culs-de-lampe de l'édition originale des *Amours jaunes* reprennent ceux de cet ouvrage[16] ». Il lui semble même que le sonnet *Panthéisme*, déjà présent dans la première édition, « consonne » avec l'épigraphe d'*Épitaphe*[17], mais le raisonnement absurde que Corbière y déploie apparaît bien davantage comme la parodie du raisonnement philosophique de Hegel sur la notion de système de pensée tel qu'en 1867 l'exposait Augusto Véra comme l'ont montré Aragon et Bonnin qui y ont relevé « de troublantes analogies[18] ». La plaquette satirique n'a pas été imprimée par Alcan-Lévy mais par l'imprimerie Jouaust, au 338 de la rue Saint-Honoré. De fait, il n'y a qu'une vignette en commun dans la première édition, mais elle est significative : le bandeau donné en-tête de l'« Avertissement » n'est en effet autre que celui de la première partie des *Amours jaunes*, donné en tête de *Ça ?*, pièce qui remplit également à sa manière la fonction d'un avertissement[19]. La seconde édition, augmentée de neuf pièces, qui paraît en 1872[20], soit quelques mois avant la déclaration d'imprimer des *Amours jaunes* (17 mai 1873)[21], reproduit ce bandeau au même endroit. Elle introduit en outre un bandeau en tête de son « anthologie », identique à celui qui commence la section de *SÉRÉNADE DES SÉRÉNADES*, en tête de *Sonnet de nuit*, et, pour conclure la collection primitive des poèmes – soit à la fin de la pièce *Bellérophon* –, arbore un cul-de-lampe constitué d'un empilement inversé de feuilles aldines très similaire à celui qui conclut le recueil de Corbière[22] : seul change (de peu) le nombre de

---

16 Houzé et Hérisson, *op. cit.*, p. 55 ; p. 180 est signalée la possible influence du début de *Panthéisme* sur l'épigraphe d'*Épitaphe*.

17 Houzé, « Un sonnet parodique ».

18 Voir la citation donnée par Aragon et Bonnin, éd. citée, p. 49, sans référence précise. Il s'agit en fait du premier volume de *Philosophie de l'esprit*, de Hegel, traduite et commentée par A. Véra, Paris, G. Baillière, p. xcv.

19 La pagination « 3 » donnée à la table des matières correspond au début du poème *Ça ?*, non à celui du titre « ÇA » qui figure en pleine page 1 comme s'il s'agissait d'un titre de section. Cette confusion est à relier au fait que ce poème métatextuel a pour sujet le recueil même dont il constitue une sorte de préface.

20 https://gallica.bnf.fr/ark:/12148/bpt6k1522317v?rk=21459;2 (consulté le 17/09/2022).

21 Lescane, « Trois enregistrements », p. 286-288.

22 D'aucuns objecteront que c'est la dernière section *Rondels pour après* que conclut le cul-de-lampe, mais on se souviendra que la fabulette conclusive a été ajoutée après coup (*cf. supra*, p. 111).

feuilles[23]. Le fait que le bandeau initial et le cul-de-lampe final[24], dont les styles sont pourtant bien différents, se retrouvent à l'ouverture de *Ça ?* et à la clôture de *RONDELS POUR APRÈS*, sections périphériques du recueil, semblent bien indiquer l'inspiration que Corbière aurait pu trouver dans la réédition du *Parnassiculet* : on se souvient que les poèmes *A Marcelle* n'ont été ajoutés qu'après coup et ne font par conséquent pas partie de l'économie générale du recueil auquel ils donnent une présentation humoristique. La probabilité de cette influence est d'une certaine manière renforcée par d'autres éléments. Une partie du tirage de la plaquette antiparnassienne (vingt des 500 exemplaires) a été effectuée « sur papiers de diverses couleurs », ce qui a pu inspirer à Corbière le choix d'une impression « sur Jonquille » de quelques-uns des 500 exemplaires (également) des *Amours jaunes*. De plus, l'opuscule se trouve orné d'une « très-étrange eau-forte », qui a également pu inspirer Corbière pour l'insertion de la sienne qu'il qualifie d'eau « très forte » dans une lettre à Camille Dufour[25]. Si cette hypothèse est juste, nous nous garderons bien, en ce qui nous concerne, d'en inférer que Corbière aurait voulu par là donner aux *Amours jaunes* une intention satirique dirigée contre l'école parnassienne qui devait être pour lui une découverte récente liée à sa montée dans la capitale, mais nous ne saurions pour autant douter que ce franc-tireur du Parnasse *sensu lato* aurait pu retrouver avec plaisir dans ces pastiches l'esprit et la liberté de ton qui l'avaient séduit dans *La Vie parisienne*. Il aurait du reste pu particulièrement goûter la remarque suivante de l'avertissement[26] :

> Les poëtes dont on lira tout à l'heure des pastiches, si heureux qu'ils pourraient faire partie de leur propre volume, sont des turcs attardés qui ont oublié, ou qui ne savent peut-être pas, que le Carnaval romantique est clos depuis trente ans.

---

23   Celui du *Parnassiculet* en présente un de plus, empilant 4 puis 2 puis 1 feuilles, là où *Les Amours jaunes* en empilent plus harmonieusement 3 puis 2 puis 1. Lescane, « Comment peut-on », p. 112, fait remarquer que ce nombre dans *Les Amours jaunes* correspond au nombre de rondels. Ajoutons que le bandeau qui ouvre la section de *Pièces inédites* – soit en tête de *Vaticination* – est identique à celui qui commence la section de *GENS DE MER*, en tête de « Point n'ai fait un tas d'océans ».

24   Final quant à la collection d'origine : les neuf pièces qui augmentent la première édition sont nettement détachées de la collection primitive avec la mention en belle page du faux titre « PIÈCES INÉDITES ».

25   Voir Walzer, éd. citée, p. 1061 ; Steinmetz, *Une vie à-peu-près*, p. 405.

26   *Le Parnassiculet*, 2ᵉ éd., p. 7.

Encore que le lecteur amateur et non partisan, étranger aux luttes d'influence et à la politique éditoriale des concepteurs du *Parnasse contemporain*, eût, pour des raisons diverses, matière à s'étonner en trouvant au sommaire du premier recueil la présence des frères Deschamps et de Vacquerie, voire, de Philoxène Boyer ; au sommaire du second, celle des frères Deschamps à nouveau, de Barbier, Laprade et Sainte-Beuve, sans parler, dans les deux recueils, de celle de Gautier, l'un des plus ardents acteurs des premiers combats dudit Carnaval. Il y avait néanmoins tant d'affinités entre l'art corbiérien – marqué par le débraillé linguistique, la désacralisation de la langue poétique, le goût immodéré pour le jeu de mots et le ton volontiers sarcastique – et la satire du *Parnassiculet* que le critique hostile de *L'Art universel* (« E.V. ») put voir dans *Les Amours jaunes* « un plaidoyer contre les exagérations de l'école moderne[27] » :

> Tous les vices des poëtes français d'aujourd'hui, esprit de mots, bizarreries grammaticales, néologismes malgré tout, versification fantaisiste, rime faisant naître l'idée, paradoxes, et que sais-je ? nous sont montrés, non pas à la loupe, mais au télescope. Ne serait-ce pas un avertissement, et serais-je loin de la vérité en voyant dans le livre de M. Corbière une dispute littéraire ?

---

27 *L'Art universel*, I, 18 (1er nov. 1873), p. 157.

CONCLUSION

L'un des problèmes qui continuent à se poser est la question fonda-mentale de l'établissement du texte corbiérien, ce qu'avait directement ciblé L. Lescane dans le titre de son article : « Comment peut-on publier Corbière ? » L'étude détaillée des particularités orthographiques et ponctuationnelles des *Amours jaunes*, particularités que l'on retrouve tant dans ses poèmes autographes que sa correspondance, mettent moins en évidence un « goût baroque des anomalies[1] » qu'une connaissance approximative de règles pas toujours clairement fixées et une certaine indifférence de l'auteur à l'égard de ces questions, là où la construction et la présentation de son recueil ont retenu toute son attention. Les rapports entre Corbière et ses éditeurs font penser à ceux du capitaine Gregg et de Mrs Muir que l'on peut illustrer par cet extrait d'un dialogue entre le fantôme du premier et son importune hôtesse à laquelle il a fini par s'attacher au point de lui dicter le récit de ses aventures, en se heurtant aux réactions académiques de sa secrétaire improvisée[2] :

> … Où en étais-je ?… Marseille n'est pas un port pareil que les autres…
> Lucy rectifia :
> – Pareil aux autres.
> – Pareil que, pareil aux, qu'est-ce que ça peut fichtre bien faire ? s'écria le capitaine. Nous ne faisons pas de la littérature, nous racontons sans fioritures, sans chichis, la vie d'un marin !
> – Je vous accorde, dit Lucy, que le récit est sans fioritures ni chichis.
> – Mettez-en si ça vous chante ! lança Gregg. Corrigez la grammaire tant qu'il vous plaira, je n'y vois pas d'inconvénient du moment que vous n'édulcorez pas le bouquin !

Et pourtant, là où l'on n'hésiterait pas à corriger l'auteur du *Négrier* dont l'orthographe est plus erratique encore, les éditeurs du fils y regardent

---

1   Lair, « Le dossier Martineau », p. 288.
2   R.A. Dick, *Le Fantôme de Mr Muir*, trad. L.-R. Dauven, Paris, Libretto, 2016, p. 140.

à deux fois quand ils ne sacralisent pas la moindre des singularités de son recueil. Mais Corbière se préoccupait-il tant de ce que pourraient en penser ceux qu'il qualifie plaisamment de « fesse-cahier », selon l'interprétation pertinente que Yann Bernal donne de l'expression[3] ? Pour autant qu'il s'en soit avisé, Corbière s'est-il jamais ému de voir ses textes « toilettés », de façon parfois excessive, par la rédaction de *La Vie parisienne* ? S'est-il seulement offusqué de constater que le prote avait systématiquement commencé chaque vers de son recueil par une majuscule alors que, dans ses manuscrits, il lui arrive souvent d'omettre cette spécificité française de l'impression de la poésie versifiée ? Il n'aurait certes pas consenti à ce que l'on remaniât la syntaxe de ses vers, mais son désintérêt pour la ponctuation, ou plutôt ses négligences et son absence de doctrine ou de modèle pleinement assuré qui l'amène souvent à tâtonner, essayant telle ou telle solution selon son humeur et les circonstances, montrent qu'il ne se serait pas opposé à ce qu'elle fût retouchée, au moins dans certaines limites qu'il conviendrait de définir, en usant de précautions qui ne peuvent s'appuyer que sur une étude philologique du texte imprimé et de ses manuscrits. On peut même considérer que ce que nous pouvons lire aujourd'hui est tout au plus le premier et unique jeu d'épreuves des *Amours jaunes*, non corrigé, plus un mince *errata* ajouté après coup.

En matière d'orthographe, il ne s'agit pas seulement de rectifier les coquilles, aspect qui fait naturellement consensus, à ceci près que des coquilles peuvent aboutir à des leçons fallacieuses, comme en témoigne « cabré » pour « cambré[4] », mais aussi les fautes proprement dites, à supposer que l'on ait fait la part des graphies régulières et des graphies alternatives encore en usage du temps de Corbière lorsque notre poète ne les a pas héritées de son père, fautes qui peuvent toutefois aboutir à des ambiguïtés gênantes comme c'est le cas dans l'emploi du circonflexe, lorsque la norme lui attribue une fonction diacritique. Il est cependant des graphies apparemment contradictoires qui semblent avoir quelque pertinence : ainsi en va-t-il de l'emploi de l'accent grave ou du tréma dans *goéland* où l'alternance remplit une fonction prosodique. Par contre – et contrairement à ce qu'on a pu soutenir –, l'emploi à la rime de graphies alternatives, ou du moins fautives, ne répond pas à un désir d'amélioration

---

3   « Corbière, les coquilles », p. 24.
4   Voir *infra*, p. 145-146.

visuelle de la rime par une altération consciente de l'orthographe : plus simplement, les compétences relativement limitées de Corbière en ces matières ou la simple inattention s'expriment à la rime comme ailleurs, en occasionnant des ambiguïtés du fait de l'association des mots-rime à d'autres, homophones, et par conséquent susceptibles d'homographies.

Mais le défi majeur auquel est confronté l'éditeur est certainement la définition du champ de son intervention dans le domaine de la ponctuation si personnelle de Corbière qui, malgré ses défauts, ses incohérences et ses oublis, tend souvent à infléchir la lecture et l'interprétation des mots et des phrases d'une manière inhabituelle, et même, parfois, dans un sens inhabituel, ses lacunes et ses ambiguïtés ouvrant parfois des voies nouvelles d'interprétation qui pourraient se voir condamnées par telle ou telle retouche qui semblerait s'imposer. Si l'amender sur une base normative desservirait ainsi souvent l'intention, peut-être inconsciente, du poète, il n'en est pas moins certain que la laisser en son état confus et lacunaire la dessert tout autant. Quant à la surponctuation et au manque de cohérence liés à l'application alternative ou simultanée de divers procédés, on ne saurait intervenir sans porter atteinte à leur fonction expressive par laquelle se manifeste le caractère instable et troublé du poète[5] : la conservation de ces divers dispositifs s'impose bien autrement que celui des omissions ou des lapsus par lesquels ce caractère pouvait également s'exprimer. Plus surprenant, dans ce contexte, l'abandon pur et simple – ou peu s'en faut – de la ponctuation dans *Cris d'aveugle* où l'on peut voir un souci de restituer la tradition orale du *sonn* breton dont s'inspire cette pièce ; encore que la logique voudrait que l'on supprimât les signes qui y subsistent comme subsistent ici ou là dans le recueil des *e* caducs donnant à tel ou tel vers une apparente hypermétrie que ne recherchait manifestement pas le poète. Si les leçons de la philologie incitent naturellement à la prudence dans l'établissement du texte et la justification des phénomènes déviants, elles offrent cependant encore à l'éditeur quelques marges et lui donnent toujours la possibilité d'enrichir encore et encore l'apparat critique qui doit l'accompagner.

L'incorrection orthographique et ponctuationnelle de Corbière n'est qu'un leurre, bien qu'on ne puisse l'amender sans discernement : sa poétique réside dans d'autres dimensions dont il convient à présent

---

5   Houzé et Hérisson, *op. cit.*, p. 58, évoquent le cas de Forneret dont le tempérament se traduisait par toutes sortes de bizarreries ou originalités typographiques.

d'explorer les aspects sans doute les moins connus, malgré les études qui ont pu leur être consacrées, à savoir dans le domaine de la versification et des formes poétiques, la dimension strictement littéraire des *Amours jaunes* ayant fait jusqu'ici l'essentiel des investigations en construisant l'image d'une personnalité poétique hors normes. C'est en effet également sur ce terrain formel que le poète se positionne dans le cadre de l'histoire littéraire comme au regard des poètes contemporains parmi lesquels il entend se faire une place.

DEUXIÈME PARTIE

LE VERS VÉREUX DES *AMOURS JAUNES*

– Ses vers faux furent ses seuls vrais.
Épitaphe.

S'il est un point où Corbière pouvait rejoindre Lamartine, c'est bien sur le plan de la versification. Le poète romantique faisait en effet trop souvent preuve de négligence après *Les Méditations poétiques*. Rappelons ainsi le jugement sévère que M. Souriau portait sur lui[1] :

> Rarement homme avait été aussi richement doué ; il a gâché son génie, comme sa fortune : il a jeté ses vers comme son argent, par la fenêtre. Il a atteint très vite son point de perfection relative, parce qu'il a cessé de travailler sérieusement, une fois ses premiers succès obtenus. [...] Il a eu trop vite horreur de l'effort. Malgré son prodigieux génie lyrique, malgré une facilité surprenante à rimer, Lamartine ne s'est approché de la perfection que dans les pièces qu'il a laissées longtemps sur le métier. [...] Ajoutons ceci : sans le labeur artistique, le poète le mieux doué est un faible versificateur. Tel est Lamartine.

Souriau souligne par ailleurs la conscience que le poète, qui se résumait dans la formule « Je ne suis pas assez artiste », se proclamant « amateur de poésie, plutôt que poète de métier[2] », avait de ses limites, révélant ainsi un aspect que l'on peut retrouver chez Corbière[3] :

> Du reste, il demandait grâce pour les incorrections de toute sorte qu'il reconnaissait avoir laissées dans ses vers, ne se croyant pas capable d'unir la correction et l'inspiration, espérant que « l'avenir » ne s'occuperait pas de lui pour décider
>
> Si l'hémistiche impie offensa la césure,
>
> dans ces chants qu'il appelle lui-même des *improvisations*.

Dès lors que l'on prend en compte la désinvolture de Corbière en matière de ponctuation et d'orthographe, on est en droit de se poser la

---

1   « La versification de Lamartine », p. 860.
2   *Ibid.*, p. 843 et 857.
3   *Ibid.*, p. 842-843.

question de savoir de quoi il retourne en matière de versification. Les innombrables défauts dans ce domaine que l'on peut relever dans les *Amours jaunes* se prêtent à une interprétation ambiguë dont témoigne l'histoire de la critique : dans quelle mesure et quand peut-on parler d'« un grand mépris de ce qu'on appelle les règles de la prosodie » comme Martineau[4], de « la profanation des règles académiques » comme Dansel[5], ou bien encore de simples négligences ? Ce serait en effet aller un peu vite en besogne que de considérer sans distinction que « Si Corbière est souvent incorrect, c'est *parce qu'il le veut* ainsi[6]... ». Dans son chapitre sur l'orthographe, M. Dansel se demande[7] : « n'était-il pas tout simplement le poète de l'imperfection par excellence ? » ; mais serait-ce pour cela que le critique – lui-même poète – se laisse aller à estropier tel ou tel vers de Corbière, ajoutant à celui-ci une syllabe, en en retranchant une autre dans celui-là[8] ? qu'il laisse imprimer *lapunars* ou *patelot*[9], comme en écho au *maletot* de Corbière[10] ? Toujours est-il que cette désinvolture du critique rend d'autant plus crédible l'idée que Corbière ait pu à l'occasion être lui-même victime de quelque déficit d'attention, voire de cécité d'inattention.

On a pu ainsi relever d'évidentes erreurs d'impression amputant certains vers d'une syllabe, comme le vers 6 de *À la mémoire de Zulma* où l'article indéfini est de toute évidence omis : « La lune a fait [un] trou dedans » (p. 51)[11], même si, pour obtenir la mesure requise par le contexte métrique, Corbière peut omettre délibérément un déterminant comme au vers 16 du *Renégat* : « Dans toutes langues c'est : Ignace ou

---

4   *Tristan Corbière*, p. 84.

5   *Langage et modernité*, p. 23.

6   J. Rousselot, *Poètes d'aujourd'hui*, p. 79, qui avait plus spécialement en vue la question de la diérèse et de la synérèse pour laquelle le jugement serait par contre fondé.

7   *Langage et modernité*, p. 33.

8   Dansel supprime ainsi *sur* dans « Le navire était soûl ; l'eau sur nous faisait nappe. » (p. 119 : *La Goutte*, 2) ; il ajoute par contre *de* après *hors* dans « Hors la terrestre croûte, » (p. 122 : *Libertà*, 61) ; il remplace « Serait-il » par « Est-il » dans « Serait-il mort *de chic*, de boire, ou de phthisie. » (p. 130 : *Pauvre garçon*, 13). Il supprime même le mot-rime dans « Métier ! se rimer finir ! » (p. 154 : *Un jeune qui s'en va*, 95).

9   *Ibid.*, p. 105 et 129.

10   Dans « Point n'est fait... », 13. La coquille a son défenseur dans Bernal, « Corbière, les coquilles », p. 33-34.

11   Un lecteur l'ajoute en marge dans l'exemplaire du dépôt légal digitalisé de Gallica (à noter que la p. 269 se trouve inopinément remplacée dans cette numérisation par un doublon de la p. 267).

Cydalyse » (p. 277). M. Dansel n'en a pas moins raison, en tête du chapitre qu'il consacre à la versification de Corbière, de comparer l'attitude
du poète à celle d'un flibustier[12] :

> Tristan Corbière s'est montré en versification le corsaire, ou mieux encore, le
> flibustier « voleur d'étincelles » qu'il n'a pu devenir en navigation. Dans sa
> démarche tout témoigne d'un souci de briser l'instrument, de défier la prosodie
> et le rythme, de transgresser avec hardiesse le code poétique.

Pour être apprécié à sa juste valeur, ce jugement doit toutefois être
précisé : Corbière respecte en effet scrupuleusement certaines règles,
parfois très pointues, voire, du point de vue moderne, dérisoires, et ce
scrupule est tantôt une soumission volontaire à des conventions poétiques qu'il ne songe pas à contester, tantôt une liberté qui n'est qu'une
commodité, tantôt enfin un respect forcé des règles pouvant prendre une
dimension parodique. Mais il lui arrive aussi de commettre des infractions
délibérées en introduisant dans ses vers des diérèses fautives qui, cette
fois, viennent saper les fondements mêmes de la versification savante.

---

12 *Op. cit.*, p. 53.

UNE CONTRAINTE IMPITOYABLE

Corbière est plus novateur par ses bizarreries de langage et son usage de l'argot, par sa syntaxe et ses images déroutantes qui reflètent les méandres de sa pensée et de ses sentiments, que par sa versification plutôt conforme à l'évolution des dernières générations poétiques avant l'essor du symbolisme, témoignant à tel point, selon le mot de Laforgue, le poète est « à l'étroit dans le vers[1] ». Cette syntaxe est en effet tourmentée, souvent elliptique[2], rompue par les anacoluthes, ouverte à des tours populaires et mâtinée de barbarismes, marquée par les figures de répétition, volontiers énumérative, fragmentée au point de suggérer à Y. Mortelette l'idée d'une « désagrégation de la phrase[3] », Corbière ne reculant pas devant d'improbables transpositions, comme l'antéposition d'*encor* dans les vers suivants (*Le Poète contumace*, 62-64) :

> [...] Et dans sa pauvre tête
> Déménagée, encor [*sic*] il sentait que les vers
> Hexamètres faisaient les cent pas de travers.

On ne peut toutefois ignorer que bien des tours forcés semblent résulter du seul besoin de surmonter quelque obstacle métrique, qu'il s'agisse d'assurer la césure comme dans l'exemple précédent, ou d'ajuster la mesure du vers (nous évoquerons plus tard la question des ellipses[4]) :

> – *Un mauvais chien toujours qu'un bon enfant parfois !* (*Matelots*, 54)

---

1   « Une étude sur Corbière », p. 6.
2   Évoquant le style télégraphique de Corbière, Dufau, « La modernité qui déchante », p. 165, cite le compte rendu qu'un chroniqueur de *L'Art universel*, I, 18 (1er nov. 1873), p. 156-157, donne des *Amours jaunes*, pointant précisément l'obscurité induite par « la diction très elliptique » du poète. Le critique y évoque en outre « des mots qui hurlent de se voir accouplés », qui « dansent une sarabande » entraînant le lecteur malgré lui.
3   « Le prédécadentisme », p. 147.
4   Voir *infra* p. 136 et 175-176..

> Ils ont tout rincé la frégate… (*Le Naufrageur*, 34)

Si elles sont dans l'ensemble redevables de sa personnalité tourmentée, les particularités de la langue de Corbière témoignent ainsi également d'une certaine difficulté à versifier, et nous aurons l'occasion d'évoquer plus précisément le cas de la gêne occasionnée par la question du schwa dans la gestation de ses poèmes ou le recours à diverses chevilles moyennant ellipses ou réductions de formes trop longues[5]. Dans l'énoncé sentencieux « A la botte vernie il faut robes à traînes ; » (*La Pastorale de Conlie*, 63), Corbière substitue un singulier douteux au pluriel générique (*A bottes vernies*) voire au pluriel réaliste (*Aux bottes vernies*) qui eussent contrevenu doublement aux règles de la versification par la perte d'une syllabe, à moins d'une articulation archaïsante de *vernies* en trois syllabes, avec une post-tonique à l'hémistiche. Dans *À la mémoire de Zulma*, au vers 17, le choix du singulier à l'allure curieusement partitive ne s'explique que par le gain d'une syllabe qui permet en outre de respecter le "nombre" de la rime[6] :

> Bien des trous et bien de la lune
> Après – Toujours vierge et vingt ans,
> Et… colonelle à la Commune ! (17-19)

Dans tel autre vers, le choix du singulier générique, bien qu'impropre au contexte, n'a d'autre justification que l'économie d'une syllabe (de même que la synérèse fautive sur *tué*) : « Il a tué toute *bête*, éreinté tous les coups » (*Le Renégat*, 27). Le cas est très différent des *grands bois de sapin* de *Poète contumace* (101) où ni la rime ni la mesure ne peuvent justifier le recours au singulier, vraisemblable résultat d'une étourderie du poète plus probablement que du prote. Corbière peut aussi procéder à de curieuses transpositions comme la mise en relief de l'adverbe *peut-être* dans « J'aimais… » qui lui permet une fois de plus de faire l'économie d'une syllabe, ou encore la postposition, pour la rime, d'un adjectif (ci-dessous *rouillée*) séparant un participe de son complément :

> Peut-être Elle pleure… – Eh bien : chante, (*Paris*, « J'aimais… », 8)

---

5   Voir *ibidem*.
6   Sur cette question, voir *infra*, p. 152-161.

Herse hérissant rouillée
Tes crocs où je pends et mords ! (*Sonnet de nuit*, 5-6)

Le procédé confine à l'hypallage dans « — Et je sens mon tuyau qu'il mord... » (*La Pipe au Poète*), comme dans la construction transitive de *braire* dans « Qu'un âne te braie ! » (*Fleur d'art*) qui permet une économie de syllabes. On pourrait encore évoquer les ruses affectant le lexique, les substitutions de mots aboutissant à des figures improbables comme dans le « monsieur en linge » de *Duel aux camélias*. Indépendamment de la question du sens que ces artifices mettent à mal en rendant son accès parfois laborieux, on observera que l'impact rythmique de ces expédients sur le vers est considérable du fait aussi de la multiplication des pauses et repos au sein du vers, souvent soulignée par une ponctuation envahissante, de l'utilisation — au demeurant limitée — d'enjambements et de rejets. Mais l'embarras du poète devant la contrainte métrique se manifeste également au travers de traits plus discrets, liés aux décalages entre code graphique et code phonétique, tels qu'en témoigne son traitement du schwa dans quelques rares cas d'hypermétrie apparente sur lesquels nous aurons à revenir[7]. On trouve même un cas d'épenthèse dans l'album Noir[8] :

Je mendîrais si bien !... Alors, peut-être qu'Elle
de sa main, metterait l'aumône dans ma main !

L'étendue de ces manifestations est tel que l'on en vient à se demander dans quelle mesure l'emploi fantaisiste de la synérèse et de la diérèse sur lesquels nous nous étendrons quelque peu n'est pas, du moins dans son fondement, une solution de facilité lorsque Corbière n'arrive pas à ajuster exactement sa pensée aux exigences de la mesure, ce dont témoignent également telle ou telle contraction forcée[9], ou encore la substitution inattendue de l'apostrophe « SOMME ! » à l'habituel « SOMMEIL ! » au vers 110 de *Litanie du sommeil*, ces mots n'étant pas synonymes.

---

7 Voir *infra*, p. 141-143.
8 Il est vrai que Baudelaire, par pure inadvertance, se laissa aller à écrire dans la prépublication du *Cygne* (titré *Causerie*) : « Eau, quand pleuveras-tu ? Quand tonneras-tu, foudre ? » (Nuiten, *Les Variantes*, p. 8).
9 Sur ces phénomènes qui ne se présentent pas toujours dans un contexte de langue parlée populaire, voir *infra*, p. 136 et 175-176.

Il n'est que de comparer ses vers à sa prose, que ce soit sa correspondance ou ses quelques textes en prose à caractère littéraire, pour constater le fossé formel qui les sépare : la contrainte a, chez Corbière, une véritable fonction heuristique en contribuant à l'élaboration d'une écriture poétique originale où la bizarrerie des tours d'une phrase « désécrite », selon le mot de Ch. Angelet[10], et les obscurités de l'expression n'ont pas manqué de frapper les lecteurs aux côtés de l'incongruité des images. Le poète était naturellement conscient de ses difficultés qu'il ne manquait pas de souligner à l'occasion : c'est naturellement lui le poète contumace dont « les vers / Hexamètres faisaient les cent pas de travers », s'interrogeant ironiquement dans son poème programmatique sur la nature de ses vers : « – Vers ?... vous avez flué des vers... – Non, c'est heurté. » (*Ça ?*, 13), concluant qu'il ne connaît pas l'Art, pas plus que l'Art ne le connaît. Par ces défauts, Corbière apparaît ainsi comme beaucoup plus embarrassé qu'un Lamartine dont Souriau a pourtant montré la difficulté à assujettir son verbe aux contraintes du mètre[11]. Les acrobaties qui en résultent viennent ajouter au désordre apparemment naturel de l'expression poétique de Corbière dont la phrase, selon Angelet, « découle, dans ses hésitations, ses chutes soudaines, ses brusques décharges, du besoin intense de restituer l'expérience de la vie jusqu'en ses discordances intimes[12] ». Il semble néanmoins que Corbière puisse retrouver l'aisance et la fluidité dont il fait preuve dans sa prose. C'est ainsi que le critique de *La bibliographie contemporaine* estime que le poète « se montre à son apogée » dans *RACCROCS*[13] : « Le poète n'a plus besoin, comme dans les *Amours jaunes*, de torturer la langue, de tordre le vers à sa fantaisie : sa poésie coule de source parce qu'elle est dictée plus par le cœur que par l'esprit. »

---

10   *La Poétique*, p. 103.
11   « La versification de Lamartine », p. 853-855.
12   *La Poétique*, p. 103.
13   *La Bibliographie contemporaine*, I, 1er octobre 1873, p. 141.

SCRUPULES

Aussi désinvolte soit-il quant à la qualité de son texte imprimé, Corbière n'en connaît pas moins parfaitement les conventions poétiques comme l'a bien vu Catulle Mendès qui, dans son rapport sur le mouvement poétique de 1867 à 1900 – récemment présenté par Armand Vareille –, voit en lui[1] :

> un Pierre Dupont à la fois plus et moins artiste, volontairement débraillé, chez qui les "négligences" proviennent de l'impertinence qui défie, non d'une candeur forte. En réalité, Tristan Corbière n'ignore rien de tout ce qu'il feint de ne pas savoir, envie tout ce qu'il donne l'air de dédaigner ou de mépriser ; son apparente simplesse est faite de malignité et d'impudence rageuse.

C'est ainsi que, contrairement au *Panayoti*, poème rédigé en langue parlée populaire que Corbière ne retient pas pour son recueil[2], il respecte dans les pièces des *Amours jaunes* l'interdiction d'hiatus qu'un Paul Stapfer considérait à l'époque comme « [l]a gêne la plus sotte » dont les poètes contemporains respectaient encore l'observation, louant Catulle Mendès pour avoir écrit dans *Le Consentement* : « *Va et* réclame-leur trente sicles d'argent » (qui apparaît deux fois dans le cours du poème)[3], ignorant que le poète amendera ce vers dans sa reprise en recueil en ajoutant un *s* euphonique[4] : « Vas, et réclame-leur [...] ». L'un des premiers comptes rendus des *Amours jaunes* n'en estime pas moins que Corbière s'adonne à la licence qu'il salue comme une liberté bien venue[5] :

---

1   « Tristan Corbière au miroir du *Rapport* », p. 76 (*Rapport*, p. 163).
2   Voir Billy, « Corbière et le vers libéré », p. 90-91, n. 19.
3   Voir l'extrait cité par Mortelette, *Le Parnasse*, p. 126 ; la citation vient de *PC (1869)*, p. 82 (où l'on a toutefois une virgule après « Va »).
4   *Les Poésies*, 1872, p. 100. Voir aussi « – Ils ont leur grâce, vas ! et, de plus, fais-leur rendre » (*Le Landgrave de fer*). Grammaticalement injustifié, cet *s* est de toute façon non fonctionnel du fait de la pause clairement marquée par la virgule. On remarquera au passage que, dans les versions manuscrites d'*À une mendiante rousse*, Baudelaire put user devant consonne – et donc sans motif – de cette forme licencieuse ; *cf.* Nuiten, *Les Variantes*, p. 8.
5   Signé E. V. ; *L'Art universel*, I, 18 (1er nov. 1873), p. 156.

M. Corbière ne redoute pas l'hiatus, et il a raison. Si l'hiatus n'existait pas dans le corps des mots, je comprendrais la règle qui l'interdit d'un mot à l'autre ; mais le génie de la langue française a rejeté la plupart des consonnes du latin, de manière à accumuler souvent les voyelles et à les heurter les unes contre les autres. Pourquoi respecter une règle illogique ?

Par convention, bien entendu, pourrait-on répondre. Et de fait, Corbière entend bien s'y soumettre ou, si l'on préfère, n'a pas idée de la remettre en cause. S'il accepte l'hiatus, c'est en fait, de façon exceptionnelle, dans le cadre d'expressions plus ou moins figées (*il y a*, dans *Le Bossu Bitor*, 183 ; « Le Moi humain », dans *Paria*, 47) et de mots-composés (*kyriè-éleison* [*sic*], dans *La Rapsode foraine*, 172) ainsi qu'au contact de mots de langue étrangère :

> – *Se habla español : Paraque… Raquando ?…* (*Chapelet*, 14)

> Inerte, ô Galilée ! et… *è pur si muove…* (*Veder Napoli*, 32)[6]

Dans « – Dernier *lazzarone* à moi le bon Dormir ! » (*ibid.*, 36), *dernier* fait la diérèse et la césure est élidée puisque, conformément à l'usage dans ce genre d'emprunts, Corbière élide systématiquement l'*e* de *lazzarone* comme à la césure de ce taratantara : « C'est un lazzarone enfin, un bohême » (*À une camarade*, 11) ; ou au sein de ce premier hémistiche d'alexandrin : « Lazzarone infini ! » (*Litanie du sommeil*, 128). Dans *Veder Napoli* : « — Dernier *lazzarone* à moi le bon Dormir ! », l'emploi de l'italique jette par contre un doute sur l'appartenance linguistique du mot, puisqu'il a la même forme en italien[7], alors que la forme francisée *Grazielle* (en rime avec *chandelle*) se distingue nettement de l'italien *Graziella* (en rime avec *voilà* ou *là*) dans *Le Fils de Lamartine* : une lecture « *lazzaroné* » (si ce n'est l'absence de l'accent aigu), ne peut alors être complètement écartée, avec un hiatus à la césure, mais sa pratique des diérèses fautives incite aussi bien à une lecture en trois syllabes de « Dernier ». L'italique est trompeur dans l'emploi adjectival de *Lazzarones* (en rime avec *trônes*), adaptation française d'it. *lazzaroni*, dans le même poème, forme qu'il emploie par contre sans italique dans *Litanie du sommeil* (en rime avec *fini*)[8].

---

6   Le *t* y étant purement résiduel (non liant), la tradition poétique interdit le contact de la conjonction avec une voyelle.

7   Gouvard, *Critique du vers*, p. 105, s'y laisse ainsi tromper.

8   Également dans *À une Camarade*.

Corbière n'est pas plus négligent que d'autres pour ce qui est des interjections. Si l'on peut ainsi relever « La mer moutonne !... Ho, mon troupeau ! » (*Le Naufrageur*), c'est à une confusion avec *oh* (ou une coquille) que l'on doit l'irrégularité[9]. Dans « Hurrah !... et le fossé derrière... » (*À ma jument Souris*), la pause neutralise l'hiatus, mais pas dans « Noyés ? – Eh allons donc ! Les noyés sont d'eau douce. » où l'*h* final marque du moins un coup de glotte. Hugo se relâchait parfois, comme à l'hémistiche de « Puis, elle frappe encore. "Hé ! voisine !" elle appelle. » dans *La Légende des siècles* (p.s., II, XIII, III, v).

Dans l'octosyllabe « Qu'on dirait qu'y en avait pas. » (*Novice en partance*, 2), où l'ellipse du pronom *il* et de la semi-négation, selon une convention courante, peut donner l'illusion d'un cas d'hypométrie ([kjã-na-vɛ-pa])[10], l'hiatus n'est qu'apparent, évité par un yod de transition : [ki] + [j] + [ã-na-vɛ-pa]. On pourrait aussi évoquer, à l'opposé, le *z* euphonique dans un discours rapporté en langue populaire : « *y a-z-un peu d'gomme* », [ja-zœ̃-pø-dgɔm] (*Bambine*, 4), si ce n'est qu'il s'agit là précisément d'un marqueur de la langue populaire. Le seul cas injustifiable d'hiatus, de plus du même au même – inadvertance ou négligence – se trouve à la césure, après une suspension qui en atténue cependant l'effet : « Apre à la vie *Ô Gué* !... et si doux en son rêve. » (*Déclin*, 2). C'est là bien peu de choses si l'on considère la fréquence de ce défaut chez Lamartine chez qui Souriau relève quelques cas, n'y voyant que l'effet d'une distraction et ayant même l'indulgence de considérer qu'il pourrait s'agir ici ou là d'une « faute d'impression » comme dans « En tout lieu, en tout temps » ou « De degré en degré » où l'adoption du pluriel réduirait l'hiatus[11] ; dans les cas irréductibles suivants, cependant, l'hiatus est atténué du fait qu'il intervient après une pause, ou du moins à l'hémistiche, entre le verbe et son complément :

---

9   *Cf.* « Oh le printemps ! » dans *Un jeune qui s'en va*. La faute se retrouve dans « Ho je vous sens encor » (*Cris d'aveugle*, 49).

10 Ainsi, « y en a plus » compte pour trois syllabes dans *Lettre du Mexique* (3). La forme réduite conserve naturellement son statut syllabique devant consonne : « qu'y prenne son soûl » (*Le Bossu Bitor*, 186) ; « Le saint homme y peut s'asseoir » (*Le Novice en partance*, 78). Comme on peut le voir dans le contexte des cas cités, s'il est associé à la langue populaire dans *Le Bossu Bitor*, ce marqueur de l'oralité se retrouve aussi dans la langue parlée ordinaire qu'utilise Corbière dans certains de ses poèmes.

11 « La versification de Lamartine », p. 844.

6

> Vous ? – Oui, moi. – Et comment ? – Je ne suis qu'un pauvre homme,
> (*Jocelyn*, Nouvel épilogue)
>
> Sa joie aurait rempli une nuit éternelle[12] (*La Chute d'un ange*, Quatorzième vision)

Autrement, Corbière préfère un barbarisme à l'infraction de l'interdit : « J'ai laissé dans l'Espagne » (*Laisser-courre*, 13), « Thermomètre à l'alcool, coucou droit à musique » (*Le Douanier*, 45) ; une ellipse dans une expression toute faite : « Philosophe, – à tort à travers. » (*Épitaphe*, 21) ; ou bien un archaïsme dont la seule raison d'être est d'ajuster la mesure tout en évitant l'hiatus : « Sans voir s'elle était blonde... Il adorait la lune ; » (*Décourageux*, 9) ; ou bien encore une crase absorbant la préposition *à* devant ou après un [a], évitant ainsi l'hiatus du même au même[13] :

> Quelquefois, vaguement, il se prenait attendre... (*Le Poète contumace*, v. 50)
>
> – Et, quand ç'a deux sous... ça les boit. (*La Rapsode foraine*, 220)
>
> [...] le hère
> Se reprenait hâler son bitor de misère... [...]
> – Ça t'y [*sic*] du vice !... Ah-ça [*sic*] : t'es porté sur la chose ?... (*Le Bossu Bitor*, 70, 174)

La préposition peut également se trouver absorbée après *là*[14] :

> J'ai, – quand il est là voir venir, –[15]
> Ton souvenir ! (*Steam-Boat*, v. 15-16)

---

12   M.-F. Suard, éd. citée, p. 1047, imprime « Son amour remplirait... » conformément au texte de 1838, sans mentionner en note la leçon critiquée par Souriau, présente dans l'édition de 1861.

13   Angelet, *La Poétique*, p. 113, pour qui la préposition est omise, ajoute le cas suivant où la présence d'un tiret (le tiret fermant est ignoré d'Angelet) et la majuscule qu'omet Angelet incitent à une tout autre interprétation, avec le commentaire de la proposition nominale initiale (*Décourageux*, v. 14-16) : « Mineur de la pensée : il touchait son front blême, / Pour gratter un bouton ou gratter le problème / Qui travaillait là – Faire rien. – ». En effet : ce n'est pas le décourageux qui travaillait là à ne rien faire. Le décourageux est un mineur de la pensée en ce qu'il touche et gratte, mais ce qu'il touche et gratte revient à ne rien faire devant le problème qui *le travaille*.

14   Angelet, *La Poétique*, p. 114, voit ici une « intention popularisante », ainsi que dans le cas précédent, mais si l'analyse est défendable dans *Le Bossu Bitor* où l'on a affaire à un discours rapporté de la maquerelle, dont la langue populaire est rendue avec un maximum d'authenticité, elle l'est beaucoup moins dans le cas de *Steam-Boat*.

15   Vers octosyllabique.

Corbière use naturellement des mêmes ruses que la tradition auto-
rise où l'interposition d'une quelconque consonne flottante suffit à
neutraliser l'hiatus au nom d'une possible liaison, fût-elle contraire
à la vraisemblance ou à l'euphonie. Ainsi, « Je mordrai les roquets,
elle me mordrait, Elle !... » (*Sonnet à sir Bob*, 13) en offre deux cas. Le
détachement du pronom *Elle* y est plus particulièrement révélateur du
poids des conventions, même si la pause est censée neutraliser l'hiatus :
pause ou non, les conventions poétiques qui s'inscrivent dans l'écriture
interdisent en effet la précession immédiate d'une voyelle pleine, ce qui
aurait été le cas avec le futur (« elle me mordra, Elle ! »). Deux exemples,
où la liaison, à la césure, paraîtrait forcée ou cacophonique : « – Va donc,
balancier soûl affolé dans ma tête ! » (*Rapsodie du sourd*, 47) ; « Ils allaient
devant eux essuyant les risées, » (*Frère et sœur jumeaux*, 5), où l'on conçoit
mal une liaison après *soûl* ou *eux*, problème il est vrai secondaire du
point de vue perceptif, la rupture de cohésion prosodique ne rendant
pas l'hiatus perceptible, la césure coïncidant dans les deux cas avec une
frontière syntagmatique. Autre exemple révélateur, où une pause rend
la liaison impossible : « Volait, rebondissait, roulait. Enfin la plainte »
(*Le Bossu Bitor*, 221).

Corbière respecte plus scrupuleusement encore l'interdiction des
séquences voyelle tonique + *e* muet devant consonne – qu'il lui arrivât
de pratiquer à titre de cultisme dans l'album Noir[16] – si ce n'est dans
un titre de journal où nécessité fait loi : « – Journal du soir : TEMPS,
SIÈCLE et REVUE DES DEUX MONDES ! » (*Litanie du sommeil*, 53)[17]. Dans
l'album Noir, une première version d'*Épitaphe* contient un vers fautif de
ce point de vue : « Gâcheur de vie hors de propos », mais c'est là une
faute que même Hugo et Leconte de Lisle pouvaient se laisser aller à
commettre[18]. Emporté par le « flot hexamètre » de *La Chute d'un ange*,
Lamartine présente de plus grandes négligences en oubliant la liaison
imposée lorsqu'il se laisse aller à écrire « une entaille / Que l'onde avait
creusée et qu'en changeant de lits / Sa chute avait laissée dans les rochers

---

16   Dans *Petite pouësie* (14) : « Affolées, prenant ses bandeaux pour leurs ailes. » Voir à ce sujet
        Billy, « Corbière avant Tristan », p. 172.
17   De même nature sont les cas de *remue-ménage* et *Baie des Trépassés* relevés par Grammont,
        Le Vers français, p. 466, chez Banville et Brizeux respectivement.
18   Pour le premier, voir ainsi p. 135 et « L'un a brûlé le Louvre. Hein ? Qu'est-ce que le
        Louvre ? » (*L'Année terrible, Mai*, IV) ; pour le second, M. Grammont, *Le Vers français*,
        p. 466, relève : « Le crucifix, le bloc, l'épée hors de la gaine ».

polis[19] », où l'*e* de *laissée* ne peut « s'élider[20] ». Souriau relève de son côté ce « vers de treize pieds » où « l'œil surtout est choqué » : « ces coupables clameurs / Qu'ont assez expiées mon exil et mes pleurs[21] ». Le fait que Corbière réduit scrupuleusement la séquence voyelle + *e* muet au sein des mots par l'adoption du circonflexe dans les futurs et conditionnels des verbes du premier groupe finit de nous convaincre de l'importance qu'il accorde à la convention poétique : *paîrai* (*Le Poète et la Cigale*, 12), *oublîrai* (« J'aimais... », 4), *paîront* (*A mon côtre*, 28), *tûra* (*Un jeune qui s'en va*, 82), *tournoîrais* (*Chanson en 'Si'*, 2)[22].

En matière de rimes, Corbière, nous l'avons vu, se montre également très scrupuleux du point de vue technique, en mettant de côté quelques rimes approximatives et les aspects proprement stylistiques (rimes pauvres, rimes dérivées, rime du même au même) pour lesquels les faiblesses rencontrées ressortissent du style bas adopté dans ce recueil dominé par l'ironie, la satire, l'humour noir et la dérision : c'est ainsi qu'il ne rime jamais des mots en *é* (*ai*) avec des mots en *er*, des mots en *ers* avec des mots en *és* (*ez*), comme on l'a vu de façon très précise dans un chapitre consacré en partie à la question des contraintes orthographiques qui pèsent sur la rime[23]. Il ne déroge pour ainsi dire jamais à l'interdiction de « rimer le singulier avec le pluriel », pour employer l'expression traditionnelle mais inexacte, fût-ce au moyen de ruses cocasses comme on le verra plus loin[24].

---

19 Éd. Guyard, p. 813.
20 Élision bien artificielle au demeurant, cet *e* étant devenu caduc, mais la règle impose cette fausse élision pour éviter des situations devenues problématiques au XVIᵉ siècle, où l'on eût prononcé [le-se-ə] en trois syllabes. Grammont, *Le Vers français*, p. 465-466, en signale d'autres cas chez Lamartine (*jetée*), mais aussi Musset (*aies, joues*), dont un gommé par une incorrection grammaticale (*l'avait trouvé gentille*), et Hugo (*aies*). Le cas de *aies* doit cependant être mis à part, car il est de même nature que les désinences de l'*imperfectum* en *(r)aient*.
21 « La versification de Lamartine », p. 843-844.
22 S'il écrit *dénoûment* dans le préambule en prose de *Saint Tupetu*, c'est en conformité avec un usage qu'entérine le dictionnaire de Bescherelle qui en fait son entrée principale, reléguant *dénouement* au rang de simple renvoi (*DN* I, 931 et 932) ; voir aussi Littré (*DLF* II, 1058).
23 Voir Iʳᵉ partie, chap. « Rime, mesure et orthographe », p. 80-81.
24 Voir *infra*, p. 152-161.

NÉGLIGENCES

Il est, dans *Les Amours jaunes*, une étourderie qui ne porte pas à conséquence, avec l'emploi inadéquat du doublet prosodique *encor* (une fois sur deux à la césure), forme dérogatoire dont l'emploi ne se justifie que devant consonne, lorsque la mesure requiert de maintenir sa prononciation dissyllabique – en parfaite conformité, au demeurant, avec l'usage de la langue parlée[1] –, comme dans « Garde-manger où l'*Ogre* encor va s'assouvir ! » (*Litanie du sommeil*, 93)[2] :

> Un livre ? – ... Un livre, encor[e], est une chose à lire !... (*Ça ?*, 6)
>
> Il lui restait encor[e] un hamac, une vielle, [...]
> Déménagée, encor[e] il sentait que les vers [...]
> – Eh bien ! non, viens encor[e] un peu me reconnaître ; (*Le Poète contumace*, 43, 63, 96)

Dans l'exemple suivant, la première occurrence seule est fautive : « Dors – l'Oranger fleurit encor[e]... encor se fane ; » (*Le Fils de Lamartine*, 33). On ne peut toutefois négliger le fait que Corbière écrit aussi parfois *encor* dans sa correspondance[3] où l'on trouve du reste d'autres apocopes après *r*[4]. Ces bévues mettent en évidence la désinvolture du poète qui ne pense pas à rétablir l'*e* d'*encor* devant voyelle mais tâche du moins,

---

1   C'est en effet la forme trisyllabique *encore* où même le schwa post-tonique est articulé qui est contraire à l'usage de la langue parlée, revêtant ainsi un marquage stylistique qui l'associe directement à la langue poétique. C'est ce qui explique que Corbière peut omettre le schwa final dans sa correspondance également (voir *infra*).

2   Nous ajoutons le *e* manquant entre crochets. On en trouve huit occurrences. Outre les exemples cités, voir *Le Convoi du pauvre*, 7 ; *Le Fils de Lamartine*, 37 ; *A mon côtre*, 61 et 69 (où l'adverbe se trouve à la césure).

3   *Cf.* Aragon et Bonnin, éd. citée, p. 206 : « ne m'a pas encor permis » (mais, p. 208, « je n'en ai pas encore compté »).

4   Éd. citée, p. 434 : « une pair ». Voir aussi Billy, « Corbière et le vers libéré », p. 91, n. 21, sur le cas du *Panayoti* ; dans l'album Noir également : « tient encor piquée là », f° 26r° (*À mon Roscoff*).

avec plus ou moins de bonheur, de remédier par l'apostrophe aux hyper-métries apparentes produites par une apocope spontanée dans l'emploi de la langue parlée[5]. Il ne faut pas croire pour autant que la faute ne se présente pas chez d'autres auteurs ; citons le cas de Verlaine qui, dans la première édition d'*Amour* (1888), laisse imprimer : « Et doux et digne encore de la Sainte Couronne[6] ». On se doute bien que de telles bévues doivent se présenter çà et là dans les éditions de poésie. Voir ainsi « Mais je suis libre encor, et je puis… je suis femme !… » dans *Rhapsodies* (1832) de Borel, « Crie au Seigneur : Encor, encor ! » ou « Qu'ici-bas de la vie enchaîne encore le poids, » dans *Harmonies poétiques* (1904), *etc.*

D'autres bévues viennent par contre affecter la mesure du vers, dont deux cas seulement sont amendés dans l'*errata* (*), les autres devant être corrigés par conjecture[7] :

O passagère [de] mon cœur, (*Steam-boat*, 11)

La lune a fait [un] trou dedans, (*À la mémoire de Zulma*, 6)

[O] Bain de voluptés ! Éventail de caresse ! (*Litanie du sommeil*, 64*)

Tel qu'une ~~la~~ vieille coque, au sec [et] dégréée (*Matelots*, 113*)[8]

Les indices de corruption sont clairs dans les deux premiers vers. Pour le « O » exclamatif du v. 64 de *Litanie du sommeil,* on remarquera qu'il s'agit non d'un oubli mais d'un défaut d'impression (l'espace correspondant est réservé) et on mettra le vers en parallèle avec « O Sourire forcé de la crise tuée ! » (35) ou « O brun Amant de l'ombre ! » (113) qui font bien apparaître la majuscule presque systématiquement associée aux substantifs noyaux de ces images descriptives du sommeil[9]. On peut

---

5   *Cf. infra*, p. 141-143.
6   *Lucien Létinois*, VI, p. 125.
7   Sur les premières, voir Bernardelli, « Il testo contumace », p. 31. Les corrections à apporter sont indiquées dans le texte : lacunes entre crochets, mot à supprimer barré. Houzé et Hérisson, *op. cit.*, p. 188-189 et 295, semblent accepter l'hypométrie de certains vers.
8   La présente erreur reflète sans doute une transcription littérale d'un passage de la copie de travail sur laquelle l'article défini ne devait pas être clairement biffé ; *cf.* la réfection du v. 8 de *Paris diurne* copié à la plume sur une page vierge de l'exemplaire personnel de Corbière : « ~~Un~~ Le marmiteux grelotte en attendant son tour » (transcription de Houzé, « Le dernier Corbière », p. 326).
9   Mais qui fait défaut dans « O corde-de-pendu de la Planète lourde ! » (68). Le problème rejoint celui que nous avons exposé *supra*, p. 30-31, dans d'autres vers du poème, après l'apostrophe au sommeil.

par contre relever quelques autres vers faux où la question de savoir s'ils sont ou non voulus comme tels s'impose. C'est ainsi que l'on trouve quelques vers hypermétriques où l'altération de la mesure est toujours liée à l'apocope incontrôlée d'un *e* post-tonique non élidable[10], inattention du poète qui apparaît en particulier au travers de l'étude génétique de ses textes : on peut en effet constater, en comparant les variantes de ses poèmes, que Corbière avait apporté des corrections à diverses négligences de ce genre ; ainsi, dans l'extrait donné dans la livraison du 13 septembre 1873 de *La Vie parisienne*, le vers 161 du *Bossu Bitor* présentait une syllabe de trop, le poète faisant sans doute l'apocope du schwa de *ceinture* : « A leur [*sic*] ceintures d'or, il faut ceinture dorée ! », hypermétrie rectifiée dans *Les Amours jaunes* par la suppression du pronom impersonnel : « A leurs ceintures d'or, faut ceinture dorée[11] ! ». On peut également relever dans un poème de jeunesse *Ay-Panneau !* écrit sur l'air d'*Ay Chiquita !*, une « correction » allant dans le même sens. Cette pièce applique en effet les conventions de la poésie savante dans le compte des syllabes, avec des couplets d'heptasyllabes ; au sixième, Corbière écrit d'abord « Il faut voir des médecins » avant de biffer les trois premiers mots pour les remplacer par « on consulte » dont l'apocope est bloquée par la « loi des trois consonnes », imposant la syncope dans *médecins*[12]. Ce genre d'erreurs subsiste dans *Les Amours jaunes*, y compris dans les discours rapportés en langue populaire parlée de *Bambine* et *Cap'taine Ledoux* (le schwa selon nous problématique est chaque fois signalé par des parenthèses)[13] :

> C'est pas pour mon plaisir, moi, v's'êt(e)s mon chargement : […]
> – A terr(e) ! q'vous avez dit ?… vous avez dit : à terre…
> A terr(e) ! pas dégoûtaî [*sic*] !… Moi z'aussi, foi d'mat'lot, […]

---

10 L'hypermétrie que Houzé et Hérisson, *op. cit.*, p. 295, attribuent au v. 46 de *Litanie du sommeil* est fausse : *féerique* n'a que trois syllabes, comme *féerie* n'en a que deux, la prononciation en quatre syllabes étant un fait d'usage étranger aux poètes du XIXᵉ siècle qui se conforment à la norme du français parlé (Bescherelle, *DN* I, 1239 ; Larousse, *GDU* VIII, 189 ; Littré, *DLF* II, 1635…).

11 La question se pose naturellement de savoir quelle version est antérieure à l'autre : ce serait celle de la revue si l'on se fie à la date, ce qui pourrait signifier que Corbière a fait la faute en recopiant ses vers. Pour d'autres cas, voir Billy, « Corbière et le vers libéré », p. 98-101.

12 Voir la transcription qu'en donne Houzé, « Naissances d'une œuvre », p. 357.

13 Nous complétons ici le relevé de Rannou, *De Corbière à Tristan*, p. 45, qui voit là « des étourderies […] qui ne lui sont peut-être pas imputables, les erreurs de typographie étant fréquentes à l'époque ».

Ne soulag' pas la coqu(e) : vous et moi, mes princesses [...]
– A terr(e)!... j'crâis f..tre ben! Les femm's!... pas dégoûté! (*Bambine*, 12,
22-23, 25, 28)

– Auguss! on se hiss' pas comm(e) ça desur les g'noux (*Cap'taine Ledoux*, 4)

Ce sont bien entendu des inadvertances liées à la notation des apocopes
et syncopes de la langue populaire qui s'observent du reste tout aussi bien
dans le long récit du *Panayoti*[14], mais il est, selon nous, d'autre cas où
Corbière n'a pas été conscient des apocopes qu'il pouvait spontanément
effectuer en composant ses vers lors de leur mise en écrit, comme dans
l'incipit, en principe octosyllabique, du *Naufrageur*, texte écrit dans une
langue plus conventionnelle : « Si ce n'était pas vrai – Que je crève ! » (*Le
Naufrageur*, 1). Walzer se demandait s'il ne fallait pas lire « Si c'n'était pas
vrai », mais on peut également suggérer de lire plutôt « Que j'crève ! »,
cet énoncé exclamatif nous ramenant directement au discours rapporté,
et donc à la langue orale. Ce genre d'étourderie se rencontre chez des
poètes censés être plus consciencieux. C'est ainsi que Baudelaire attira
un jour l'attention de son ami Prarond sur un vers faux, procédant en
fait d'une semblable apocope dans un passage dialogué de *La Question
d'Orient* : « Mon oncle, est-elle bien riche ? Aurons-nous de bon vin[15] ? »
Mendès commettra de la même façon un vers faussement hypermètre
dans la première édition de sa comédie-bouffe *Le Roman d'une Nuit*,
qu'il corrigera par la suite[16]. On peut encore relever l'inattention de
Verlaine qui publie l'alexandrin « Qui vous apprêtez à faire le tour de
ce monde, » (*À une dame qui partait pour la Colombie*), vers qui suppose
l'apocope du schwa de *faire*, parmi les additions de la seconde édition de
Dédicaces (1894) ainsi que, deux ans plus tard, dans *Chair* (sous le titre
À Madame***) où, sur son exemplaire, le poète corrigera l'hypermétrie
en substituant *du* à *de ce*[17].

L'apocope s'impose sans doute aussi pour ce vers d'*Aurora*, extrait
d'une chanson de marin (29) : « *Roul' ta bosse, tout est payé* », si l'on en

---

14 L'omission est déjà totale dans l'incipit : « Un requin dans ton lit, un(e) fill(e) dans mon
    hamac ! ».
15 Rapporté par Mouquet, Charles Baudelaire, *Vers retrouvés*, p. 43, qui précise en note que
    Prarond a biffé *bien* sur certains exemplaires afin de rétablir la mesure.
16 *La Revue fantaisiste*, II (1861), p. 5 (la correction consistera dans la suppression de *Cher*) :
    « [...] mais n‹importe, / Cher Lipard›, est-elle [*apocope*] morte au moins chrétiennement ? »
17 Sur Gallica, https://gallica.bnf.fr/ark:/12148/bpt6k72720f/f41.item (consulté le 10/09/2022).

croit l'exergue du poème dans l'album Noir (« Roul' ta boss' tout est payé »)[18]. Un autre cas se trouve occulté par l'emploi de chiffres dans *'I' Sonnet* : «– Je pose 4 et 4 = 8 ! Alors je procède, / En posant 3 et 3 ! […] ». Le signe égal ne peut être ici rendu que par un repos, avec une restitution textuelle « quatre et quatre huit » qui fait apparaître la violation de la convention commandant à la césure l'articulation du schwa post-tonique de *quatre* devant *h* aspiré. Il paraît beaucoup plus probable que Corbière usait ici du parler ordinaire, en procédant à l'apocope, avec un repos : « quat(r)' et quat(r)', huit ». Le problème n'apparaissait pourtant pas dans l'album Noir où le schwa du second « quatre » était bien articulé : « 1 2 3 4, et puis 4 : 8 – je procède / ensuite 3 par 3 –. […] ». On peut également relever une apocope dans *Chère* au troisième vers de *Vendetta*, où l'on attend un heptasyllabe : « Chère, tu me le payeras !… ». S'il avait réellement prononcé le schwa de *Chère*, Corbière aurait dû opter pour l'allomorphe *paîras* qui semble du reste lui avoir été plus naturelle puisque, pour le futur, il ne connaît ailleurs que la forme courte[19]. L'hypothèse qu'il ait écrit *payeras* pour *paîras* (comme Mendès se laissa aller à écrire *payement* pour *paîment*[20]) nous paraît moins vraisemblable.

La question des vers hypométriques du *Douanier* est plus délicate[21], mais tant le caractère de Corbière peu soucieux de perfectionnisme que ses efforts, certes inégaux, à corriger les apocopes qu'il commet en composant ses vers, ou encore la mise en œuvre massive de diérèses forcées et de synérèses non conventionnelles dont l'existence même

18 On n'y lit pas moins dans le poème « "hisse le grand foc, hisse le grand foc/"Roule ta bosse tout est payé », avant la reprise « "hiss' le grand foc ! ».

19 Soit *paîrai* (*Le Poète et la Cigale*, v. 12) et *paîront* (*A mon côtre*, v. 28). Aragon et Bonnin, éd. citée, p. 187, pensent qu'il convient aussi de comprendre – de façon subliminale – « Tu me le payeras cher », ce qui suppose une transposition, et l'on remarquera que, lu ainsi : « Cher tu me le payeras », la mesure se verrait rétablie. Si on lit « *paye* » monosyllabique devant consonne dans l'extrait du *Bossu Bitor* donné à *La Vie parisienne* : « Ça se paye du tonnage […] », c'est suite à une mauvaise transcription du manuscrit (non conservé) qui devait présenter « au tonnage » comme dans *Les Amours jaunes*.

20 Dans « Le payement de l'impôt sur le vin. // – Qu'on attende. » (*Contes épiques*, p. 48 ; *Poésies*, p. 142), vers dont il corrigera par la suite le défaut en adoptant *paîment*.

21 Nous n'évoquons que pour mémoire le cas de « Et l'amiral *** – Ce n'est pas matelot ! » (*Matelots*, 8) qui soulève un autre problème, à savoir l'identification du texte de deux syllabes suppléé par les trois astérisques. *Cf.* Billy, « Corbière et le vers libéré », p. 97. À noter qu'il ne compte pas dans « Quelques Mémoires sur *** – Essais de poésie… » de Musset (*Les Secrètes Pensées de Rafaël*).

repose sur un strict respect de la mesure au mépris des règles de scansion en usage[22], nous incitent à voir là encore des fautes d'inattention[23]. Seuls deux vers nécessitent des amendements pour présenter la mesure requise, amendements que nous intégrons ici entre crochets d'après des suggestions qui ont pu être faites[24] :

> Je te disais [tout] ce que je savais écrire... (58)

> Et sur ton front noir, tes lunettes vertes
> Sillonnaient d'éclairs ton [grand (?)] nez ca[m]bré... (66-67)

En ce qui concerne le premier, Walzer se demandait : « Pourquoi corriger à toute force le poète qui déclare de son recueil qu'il ne mérite pas le nom d'"ouvrage", parce que "Ce n'est poli ni repoli" (*Ça ?*, v. 10) », déclaration ambiguë de la part d'un éditeur qui n'hésite pas à apporter diverses corrections qui, selon lui, « s'imposent ». Le contexte métrique d'alexandrins autant que la structure métriquement irrégulière et isolée du vers (il n'existe pas de mètre césuré 4 + 7 dans la tradition poétique) signalent l'hypométrie, également présente dans la version de *La Vie parisienne* (livraison du 23 août 1873, p. 539), que Martineau a compensée par conjecture avec le pronom *tout*, qui, en réalité, est bel et bien présent dans la prépublication de *La Vie parisienne*[25]. L'édition Messein, préfacée par Charles Le Goffic, introduit par contre un pronom détaché : « Moi, je te disais ce que *etc.* », solution peu probable, car l'ignorance du pronom est d'autant plus malaisée qu'il fait l'objet d'une thématisation, alors que celle du codéterminant de la totalité est plus naturelle. La conjecture de Martineau se justifie du reste largement au regard du contexte, la phrase venant en réponse à la longue énumération qui court du vers 39 au vers 57 : « – Tout se trouvait en toi, bonne femme cynique : [...] / – Tout : [...] » ; puis l'énumération de son savoir : « Tu connaissais [...] », de façon métaphorique : « Tu reniflais [...] », et plus particulièrement ces vers « Tu savais tous les noms,

---

22   Pour les synérèses, voir *infra* le chap. « La tentation de la langue parlée », p. 168-172 ; pour les diérèses, « Le sabordage de la prosodie française ».

23   Sur la problématique des vers hypomètres, voir aussi Billy, « Corbière et le vers libéré », p. 94-96.

24   La correction de *cabré* est de nous ; voir *infra*, p. 145-146.

25   Contrairement à ce qu'affirme Walzer, éd. citée, p. 1357, qui rend Martineau responsable de l'ajout.

les cancans d'alentour, / Et de terre et de mer, et de nuit et de jour !... », longue période à laquelle semble justement pouvoir répondre le « *tout ce que* » restauré par lequel Corbière oppose à la mémoire du douanier son imaginaire de poète, concluant (59-61) :

> Et nous nous comprenions – tu ne savais pas lire –
> Mais ta philosophie était un puits profond
> Où j'aimais à cracher, rêveur... pour faire un rond.

Le vers 67 est par contre plus problématique bien que sa structure et son isolement signalent sans ambiguïté son irrégularité : il n'existe pas non plus de mètre césuré 5 + 4 dans la tradition poétique, et, du point de vue textuel, rien en soi ne signale une lacune, pas plus que la coquille concernant le *nez cabré* qui a trouvé ses défenseurs[26] mais qui est *cambré* dans les autographes conservés (album Noir, manuscrit Bodros[27]). Pis encore, les versions manuscrites du poème sont également hypométriques, avec une variante mineure (le verbe y est au singulier[28]). Connaissant la désinvolture de Corbière, l'omission de l'épithète *grand*, comme le supposait Le Goffic[29], paraît assez vraisemblable pour qualifier cet organe. Dans sa première édition de *Contes épiques*, Mendès omet semblablement l'épithète *bon* dans le second hémistiche de « Donc il est temps. Suspends, ô Dieu [bon], ta clémence ! », épithète qu'il rétablira par la suite[30]. Corbière qui s'avouait si laid (*Guitare*, 16) n'aurait-il pu affubler le douanier retraité d'un nez cambré semblable au sien, que Martineau qualifiait d'énorme[31] ? La silhouette de profil qu'il peint

---

26 Voir p. ex. Aragon et Bonnin, éd. citée, p. 413 : le mot évoquerait « à la fois une forme de nez et une attitude mentale » ; Cornulier, « Sur la valeur », p. 209, justifie « la dissonance rythmique » en associant l'hypométrie à l'« agressivité du nez » qui « casse[rait] le mètre ». En somme un nez busqué qui, tel un cheval, sans doute, se dresserait sur ses pattes de derrière... (*cf. DN* II, 504).

27 Pour le premier, voir Houzé, Tristan Corbière, *ffocsoR*, p. 22 (fac-similé fᵒ 3rᵒ) ; pour le second, voir Aragon et Bonnin, éd. citée, p. 469-471.

28 Le sujet était en effet *ta lunette verte*, singulier rejeté sans doute pour son impropriété du fait de sa spécialisation sémantique, nécessitant une modification du vers précédent, « ta plume grinçait dans ta main alerte » (terminé par une virgule dans l'album Noir), qui devient ainsi dans *Les Amours jaunes* « La plume crachait dans tes mains alertes ».

29 Correction approuvée par Le Dantec ; *cf.* Walzer, éd. citée, p. 1357. Voir aussi nos remarques dans « Corbière et le vers libéré », p. 94 et 96.

30 *Contes épiques*, p. 34 ; *Poésies*, p. 127. Le vers était complet dans *PC (1866)*, p. 91.

31 *Tristan Corbière*, p. 47.

en marge de sa copie, quasiment superposable à l'autoportrait tiré du registre de l'hôtel Pagano à Capri[32], le donne en effet à penser. Une telle caractérisation paraît en effet assez vraisemblable pour qualifier cet organe « immense », selon le mot de MacFarlane[33], tel qu'on le voit caricaturé dans les autoportraits du poète qui exagère à peine la réalité avec une cambrure héritée du nez paternel[34] – et auquel La Landelle donna un étirement hyperbolique[35] –, que, dans *Sonnet posthume*, lui-même imagine devoir être cassé « d'un bon coup d'encensoir[36] ». Son obsession cyranesque du nez, encore plus nette dans les visages donnés de face du carabinier Lantimèche et du « captaine » Dangu de l'album *Noir* (f° 5r°), du capitaine de la *Marie-Gratis* (f° 13r°) ou du « vieux soldat qui mendiait son pain » (f° 25r°) *etc.*, se manifeste de façon significative dans une lettre à un inconnu à qui il reproche le manque de charge du portrait qu'il a donné d'un mendiant, appelé « Le Nègle[37] » :

> Et puis ce nez… ce nez qui est à lui seul un long poème, vous en faites presque un nez bourgeois, presqu'un nez [*illisible* : humain (?)].
> Sondez ce nez dans la Nature, lisez-le, déchiffrez-le, décomposez-le, et croquez-le, tirez-en la quintessence pour humecter votre pinceau, polissez-le sans cesse et le repolissez […] Rêvez à ce nez [:] rien qu'à le voir il faut que l'âme devine qu'il pue des pieds […]

On pourrait aussi bien, il est vrai, suppléer par *long*, sans parler de *gros* qui est un autre candidat possible. Si la solution n'est pas univoque, l'hypométrie est selon nous bien réelle. Les cas d'allométrie par défaut

---

32 Album Noir, f° 3r° (éd. Houzé, *ffocsoR*, p. 22); autoportrait reproduit par Martineau, *Tristan Corbière*, 1925, p. 44.

33 *Tristan Corbière*, p. 34 : « Un nez immense et des lèvres sensuelles et charnues semblent absorber dans leur masse le reste du visage, creusant les joues et rapetissant les yeux […] on dirait plutôt une tête de chien ».

34 Voir, outre le portrait photographique en pied du poète reproduit notamment par Steinmetz, *Une vie à-peu-près*, dans le cahier iconographique inséré entre les p. 240/241, ou le médaillon gravé par David d'Angers dans Martineau, *Tristan Corbière*, planche entre p. 20/21.

35 Voir le cahier iconographique cité note précédente.

36 *Cf.* Billy, « Corbière et le vers libéré », p. 94 et 96. Voir en particulier le profil ajouté en marge de *Gente dame* dans son recueil personnel, reproduit dans Houzé, « Traces de Tristan Corbière », 2ᵉ planche. Voir aussi les planches III à IX données par Kutyla, *Une curiosité esthétique*, p. 35, 54, 55, 62, 65 et 67 ; la peinture « Un vieux marin de Roscoff », dans Houzé, « Tristan tous genres », p. 11.

37 Repérée et éditée par Houzé, « Traces de Tristan Corbière », p. 23-24, et « Tristan tous genres », p. 10.

d'attention ne sont pas une exclusivité corbiérienne comme on l'a vu pour Mendès. Il est ainsi plaisant de relever chez Lamartine lui-même une situation semblable ; dans *Jocelyn*[38], le poète romantique a en effet laissé amputé un vers dont le contexte d'alexandrins révèle clairement l'incomplétude :

> Vois qui la mène. – Eh bien ! – Eh bien, c'est lui, [– 2]
> Lui, le martyr d'hier et l'élu d'aujourd'hui.

M.-F. Guyard a suspecté ici avec grande vraisemblance l'omission du pronom *celui* devant le relatif[39]. Parmi les additions de la seconde édition de *Dédicaces*, Verlaine a publié deux alexandrins également amputés de deux syllabes : « Parfois – et puis nous dormirons, chair lasse. », au lieu de « Aussi parfois… » qui rétablit la mesure ; « Du mien bat en vos veines et le tout », au lieu de « Du mien, Sire, bat[40]… ». En feuilletant le premier recueil du *Parnasse contemporain*, on peut trouver une semblable bévue dans un vers d'Arsène Houssaye : « Il ne trouverait, en sortant du tombeau, » (*Molière*, p. 156), où il faut rétablir le préfixe (*[re]trouverait*) qui figure bel et bien dans les *Œuvres poétiques* de 1857. On trouve de la même façon ce qui est apparemment un décasyllabe commun (« Je n'en sais rien, mais un refus l'irrite ; ») au sein d'*Agarite* de Pétrus Borel, pièce dialoguée de 146 vers uniformément alignés à gauche, dont tous les autres ont les douze syllabes requises, laissant suspecter un autre cas d'inattention avec l'omission de quelque mot ou expression de deux syllabes (comme *du tout* p. ex.) dans le premier hémistiche[41].

Cette question des problèmes d'attention dans la transcription des vers ou/et la relecture des épreuves est plus fréquent qu'on ne le croit et peut tout aussi bien être une cause d'hypermétrie. On peut ainsi relever dans la même anthologie de 1866, chez le même Houssaye, le vers suivant, où le pronom du peintre est de trop, vers qu'on trouve du reste déjà tel quel dans ses *Poésies complètes* de 1850 et qui survivra jusque dans *Les*

---

38 *Huitième époque* (21 septembre 1800).
39 Lamartine, *Œuvres poétiques complètes*, p. 1877.
40 La correction est apportée dans l'édition Le Dantec et Borel des *Œuvres poétiques complètes*, p. 623, qui prétend donner le texte de 1894 mais n'indique pas d'où est tirée la correction que l'on trouve du moins dans l'édition de 1919 des *Œuvres complètes* par Messein, après retour à diverses sources, III, p. 189 et 197.
41 *Rhapsodies*, p. 76. La faute sera reproduite telle quelle dans la réédition posthume de 1868.

Poésies de 1877 malgré les divers remaniements que le texte y subit[42] : « Dans le pré de Paul Potter, à l'ombre du moulin » (p. 154). On peut encore citer le cas de Laprade laissant publier dans *Les Muses d'État*[43] :

> Chacun ses fonctions ; les Muses, quoi qu'on en die,
> Ont leur utilité, surtout la Comédie.

là où il faut lire « quoi qu'on die » (« comme dit Trissotin », dirait Banville), conformément à la première parution du poème dans *Le Correspondant* de 1861[44]. Le vers n'en sera pas moins repris sous cette nouvelle forme corrompue dans les *Œuvres poétiques* de 1878-1881, où l'on trouvera également non corrigé « Quand, certes, il aurait pu, la nuit et par surprise, » dans *Ce Gueux de Tacite*[45]. De la même façon, Verlaine commettra un impair parmi les additions de la seconde édition de *Dédicaces*, avec ce vers dans lequel il convient de supprimer l'épithète : « Le replias sur le petit cadavre avec des larmes, » (*Le Pinson d'E****, p. 96)[46]. Dans son *Quatorzain pour toutes*, Le Dantec croit nécessaire de rectifier un sixième vers hypermétrique « Comme aussi de l'alme maturité (que vicieuse [...] » en supprimant l'adverbe, bien que le vers se présente tel quel aussi bien dans la seule édition revue par l'auteur de *Dédicaces* que dans le seul autographe conservé, mais, la question de sa légitimité mise à part, cette solution n'est pas crédible si l'on prend en compte la régularité avec laquelle Verlaine respectait la diérèse poétique : ici encore, il convient de revenir à l'édition Messein de 1919 qui imprime : « Comme de la maturité (que vicieuse[47] ! ». Comment au vu de ces bévues ne pas penser que le tempérament naturel de Corbière

---

42 Dans *Voyages en Hollande*, II (p. 91). Nous n'avons pas eu accès à l'édition originale de *La Poésie dans les bois* qui devrait contenir le poème concerné.

43 *Poèmes civiques*, p. 107. L'hypermétrie échappe à Gouvard, *Critique du vers*, p. 183, qui situe la césure après *les*, ce qui implique une synérèse parfaitement inacceptable de la part de ce poète.

44 *Le Correspondant*, 54 (1861), p. 528.

45 *Œuvres poétiques*, III, p. 52. Le recours au doublet *certe* – que n'ignore pas Corbière (voir *infra*, p. 151) – s'imposait ici.

46 Voir le facsimilé de l'autographe conservé dans *L'Agonie de Paul Verlaine, 1890-1896*, Nᵒ 605 de la Bibliothèque Robert de Montesquiou, Maison du Bibliophile, s.d., p. 16 ; reproduit sur Gallica, https://gallica.bnf.fr/ark:/12148/bpt6k1525463c/f38.item (consulté le 10/09/2022).

47 *Œuvres complètes*, III, p. 122. Comme toujours dans cette édition collationnée sur diverses sources, aucune précision n'est donnée sur la provenance de la leçon corrigée.

ne pouvait que l'inciter à de telles négligences dont, finalement, deux seulement lui seront apparues dans sa révision tardive de son texte ? Plus répandu qu'on ne le croit, ce déficit d'attention se manifeste du reste tout aussi bien lorsqu'un poète s'avise à citer les vers d'un de ses confrères, et Corbière lui-même en aura fait les frais. C'est ainsi que, en recopiant le 8ᵉ vers d'*Épitaphe* pour ses *Poètes maudits*, Verlaine, grand pourfendeur du vers libre, donne une leçon hypométrique, avec deux erreurs de transcription dans le second hémistiche, l'une induite par la liaison qui ne nous intéresse pas ici mais dont dépend vraisemblablement l'autre (omission du discordantiel), fautes dont il ne s'avise ni au moment de corriger les épreuves ni dans l'édition augmentée de 1888 : « Mais sachant tout ; » au lieu de « Mais ne sachant où[48] ».

Corbière peut également prendre de grandes libertés avec la rime. Non seulement il commet quelques rimes pauvres en [e], comme cela arrivait à Musset qui savait heurter sur ce point les attentes de son public, mais il se permet jusqu'à des rimes approximatives, avec *plectre : damnés-de-lettre* (*Insomnie*), *vieille : Fidèle* (*Le Poète contumace*), *chatouiller : Amour-cavalier*[49] (*À la douce amie*) ou *aïeule : trèfle-quatre-feuille* (*La Rapsode foraine*)[50], ce qui est plutôt amusant si l'on songe qu'il arrivait à Lamartine de pêcher également en cela, rimant, dans *Jocelyn*, *découvre : trouve* (texte remanié plus tard pour amener la rime régulière *sache : cache*)[51], *à moduler ces hymnes : sur ces cimes* (changé ensuite en *à chanter ces retraites : sur ces crêtes*)[52] ou *épagneul : cercueil* (jamais remanié)[53]. Un cas d'un autre genre – appui pour l'œil si l'on veut – couvre une déficience de l'appui masquée par la graphie, dans *Paysage mauvais*, avec *bruit : nuit* dans le premier quatrain, mais *languit : fuit* dans le second[54]. On n'est guère surpris de trouver quelques rimes du simple et du dérivé,

---

48 Voir aussi p. 126, n. 8, les nombreuses fautes commises par Dansel.
49 On sait que l'appui est requis dans les rimes en [e] ; voir *infra*, p. 441.
50 Voir aussi *soleil : ciel* dans la version manuscrite de *Veder Napoli poi mori* dont J. de Trigon, *Tristan Corbière*, p. [97], donne un fac-similé.
51 *Cinquième épisode* (16 août 1794) ; voir éd. Guyard, p. 1876.
52 *Quatrième époque* (15 avril 1794).
53 *Neuvième épisode* (12 octobre 1800). Le poète récidive dans *La Chute d'un ange* avec *algue : vague*, rime corrigée dans la substitution de *rivage : image* (*Récit*). Musset rime semblablement *fièvre : rêve* dans *Confession d'un enfant de l'autre siècle*, mais la pièce n'a jamais été publiée par l'auteur.
54 Dans *Les Amours jaunes*, les rimes en |it| sont presque toujours appuyées, et la seule autre exception ne concerne pas /ɥ/, mais /ʁ/ et /v/ (*chérit : vit*). Le cas semblable en apparence

comme *plainte : complainte* (*La Rapsode foraine*), *s'égorge : gorge* (*Duel aux camélias*), *chanté : déchanté* (*La Cigale et le poète*), *passer : trépasser* (« Là : vivre à coups de fouet !... »), *cousu : décousu* (*Ça ?*)[55]. S'il ne s'interdit pas la rime identique, c'est dans des conditions particulières, dans les *bis* du deuxième couplet de *Cris d'aveugle*, n'usant jamais ailleurs que d'équivoques, comme *tiens* indicatif 1re ou 2e personne (*À ma jument Souris*), 1re personne ou impératif (*À la douce ami*e) ou *simples* adjectif ou substantif (*Un riche en Bretagne*).

---

de *tranquille : tuile* dans *Toit* n'est par contre pas *en soi* significatif du fait que les rimes en |il³| ne sont jamais appuyées dans *Les Amours jaunes*.

55   Naturellement, nous écartons les cas où l'effet de la dérivation se trouve gommé par une modification d'ordre sémantique de quelque importance : *Passion : compassion* (*Rapsodie du sourd*) ; éventuellement liée à un changement de catégorie : *partout : tout* (*Paria, Le Renégat*), *imprévu : vu* (*Paria*).

LICENCES, BRAVADES ET DÉFIS

Corbière nargue la tradition poétique en se moquant aussi bien de règles qui régissent la rime que de licences qui en assouplissent l'usage. Ainsi, s'il reprend scrupuleusement les licences de la « rime pour l'œil[1] », il abuse délibérément du procédé dans *La Rapsode foraine* où il rime [is] avec [il], là où la tradition n'accepte que la rime avec [i], comme le fait Corbière en rimant *amis : Quatre-bis* (*Libertà*) ou *profits : un fils* (*Le Fils de Lamartine*) :

> *Des croix profondes sont tes rides,*
> *Tes cheveux sont blancs comme fils...*
> *— Préserve des regards arides*
> *Le berceau de nos petits-fils !* (61-64)

Ce cas mis à part, Corbière adopte volontiers les licences ordinaires que lui concèdent les conventions poétiques, supprimant l'*s* non flexionnel de *certe* pour obtenir par élision le nombre de syllabes requis par la mesure : « – Certe, Elle n'est pas loin, celle après qui tu brâmes [*sic*], » (*Le Poète contumace*, 57). Là où il prend plus de libertés, c'est en étendant cette licence à des *pluralia tantum*, que ce soit pour la mesure ou pour la rime, comme *vêpres* ou *mâtines*, les mettant ainsi au même rang que les noms propres paroxytons terminés sur un *s* qui se prêtaient traditionnellement à cette réduction. Pour la mesure, relevons : « Seul, il se chante vêpre en berçant son ennui... » (*Un riche en Bretagne*, 27), licence qu'on peut rencontrer même chez les Parnassiens[2]. Bien qu'identique dans sa forme, le procédé se distingue de celui qu'affectionnait Lamartine, supprimant l'*s* dans *eux-mêmes* tant à l'intérieur du vers qu'à la rime en lui attribuant indirectement ainsi une valeur adverbiale, selon une

---

1   Voir *supra*, p. 79.
2   Voir ainsi Heredia : « Ce jour même, après vêpre, en tête du clergé, » dans *PC (1869)*, p. 383 ; Mallarmé : « Jadis selon vêpre et complie : » (*Sainte*). Pour la rime, voir *infra*, p. 156-157.

licence traditionnelle. C'est également pour respecter la mesure que Corbière utilise le singulier (générique) dans *gobe-mouche(s)* : « Gobe-mouche impuissant, mangé par un moustique, » (*Rapsodie du sourd*, 37).

L'attention que Corbière porte au respect de la règle du "nombre de la rime", conceptualisée dans les anciens traités comme l'interdiction de rimer le singulier avec le pluriel[3], n'est pas un simple scrupule comme le pensait Jules Laforgue[4], car il témoigne aussi à l'occasion, d'un caractère provocateur. Si, avant son voyage en Italie, il lui était arrivé de l'enfreindre, c'est dans des textes qui s'inscrivent dans le cadre de la poésie orale, étrangère à des titres divers à la poésie savante : soit dans des chansons qu'il avait écrites dans sa jeunesse « sur l'air de Fualdès », complainte populaire dont le texte présentait déjà ce genre de caracté-ristiques, tout comme le pastiche qu'en avait donné Musset[5] ; dans *Le Panayoti*, long monologue où Trémentin fait le récit du sabordage de la « balancelle[6] » ; enfin, dans le *Journal de bord* du capitaine Guiomard Théodore où Corbière s'essaya au vers libéré[7]. Micha Grin a par ailleurs cité des quatrains plus traditionnels et par leur langue (ordinaire) et par leur style où la règle est également ignorée, mais leur origine obs-cure n'est pas sans jeter quelque doute sur leur authenticité[8]. Dans *Les Amours jaunes*, le respect scrupuleux de cette règle se manifeste d'une façon singulière dans le cadre de *Litanie du sommeil* où les mots-rime dotés d'un *s* final sont soigneusement regroupés en début ou en fin de laisse, à l'exception d'une, masculine, en |aʁ*| où formes "plurielles" et formes "singulières" alternent (v. 103-107, entre accolades ci-dessous)[9] :

---

3   Sur ladite règle, voir Billy, « Le nombre de la rime » ; pour un premier inventaire des cas chez Corbière et leur discussion, voir Fongaro, « Sur le texte », p. 82, Billy, « Convention and parody », p. 348-353.

4   « Une étude sur Corbière », p. 7 : « cependant il n'osera jamais faire rimer un singulier avec un pluriel ». Il faut en excepter *Mort : corps* dans *Cris d'aveugle* où il ne s'agit cepen-dant pas d'un « pluriel » grammatical (sur ce cas, voir p. 158-159).

5   Sur cette question et ces textes, voir Billy, « Convention and parody », p. 347-351.

6   On y trouve : *Archi-Belle : d'moiselles : belle, Turcs : truc, l'eau : matlots, nerfs : mer* etc.

7   Sur ces deux derniers textes, copiés dans l'album Noir, voir Billy, « Corbière et le vers libéré ».

8   *À mon chien Tristan*, éd. Grin, « Un inédit » ; repris et commenté par Houzé, « Tristan tous genres », p. 13-16, qui les juge authentiques. Rimes fautives : *dégoût : matous, chien : mâtins, humains : main, vide : Danaïdes* ; voir aussi *percé : brûler* et *Liberté : caresser* qui pêchent contre une autre règle, de nature semblable.

9   Voir Billy, « Convention and parody », p. 346-347.

tempêtes · honnêtes · bêtes · faites	arête · tête · Proxénète · prophète · poète
fumée · embaumée · Aimée · pâmée	parfumées · *Traînées* · mort-nées[10] [...]
passe · grasse	espaces · traces · impasses
étoiles voiles (s.)	voile (s.) toile [...]
jocrisses · nourrices · polices	calice · Cilice · la Palisse [...]
{dards · cornard · lézards ·	homard · beaux-arts}
captifs · poussifs	actif · poncif · pensif
Langueur · blagueur	vainqueurs · longueurs [...]
éternité · Mont-de-Piété · déshérité ·	hallucinés · déplumés [...]
Léthé	

Cette discrimination est d'autant plus surprenante *a priori* que le poète, dans les laisses masculines, mêle indistinctement les mots-rime où la consonne flottante concerne un autre élément que l'*s* de flexion, comme en témoignent, p. ex., les séquences *jour · Amour · court · four · tour* ou *fringant · ouragan · revenant · vent*. Mais elle s'explique aisément du fait que la tradition poétique se montrait moins scrupuleuse pour les occlusives qui étaient presque toujours dépourvues de fonction morphologique[11] au contraire de *s* (et, dans une certaine mesure et pour une bien moindre fréquence, *x*) pour lequel il était beaucoup plus aisé d'éviter les rimes litigieuses[12]. Ce dispositif original vient souligner formellement la singularité de ce poème à la structure spéculaire, séparant radicalement laisses féminines et laisses masculines, qui occupe une position relativement centrale au sein du recueil[13] (comme de la section *RACCROCS*) et contient des clés d'interprétation importantes pour la poétique de Corbière[14]. Il entretient en outre des relations particulières avec *RONDELS POUR APRÈS* et ses invitations à l'ultime sommeil, tandis que son emploi récurrent des grandes majuscules en tête de strophe rappelle inévitablement celles des strophes d'*Épitaphe* : *Litanie du sommeil* apparaît ainsi comme la "césure" du recueil dont *RONDELS*

---

10 À noter que la distribution des formes au regard de l'appui se fait également par séries (*mée(s)* puis *nées*).

11 Les formes conjuguées des verbes faisant généralement exception, *t* correspondant généralement à une marque de 3ᵉ personne (dans *il sort*, p. ex., la marque morphologique est assimilée au *t* du radical).

12 Voir Billy, « Le nombre de la rime ».

13 Notamment au niveau de la pagination ; voir Laroche, « Sous le signe du sommeil », dans *Id., Les voix de la corbière*, p. 75-158. Voir aussi Houzé et Hérisson, *op. cit.*, p. 173-174.

14 Voir en particulier l'abondant commentaire de Houzé et Hérisson, *op. cit.*, p. 137-153.

POUR APRÈS apporterait la "rime", pour reprendre la métaphore de Corbière qualifiant le sommeil de « Césure du vers long et Rime du poète », aspects qui entrent parfaitement dans la structuration spéculaire du recueil mise en évidence par B. Houzé[15].

On peut observer une recherche similaire dans les quatrains de *Chapelet* (A) où la première rime présente le pluriel dans le premier (|ɛ̃tᵊˢ|), le singulier dans le second (|ɛ̃tᵊ|), comme Baudelaire l'avait fait en distinguant |ikᵊˢ| et |ikᵊ| dans *La Vie antérieure* (B), avec des rimes croisées différemment :

A.

plaintes	*Crucificcion*
Perfeccion	absinthe
Saintes	*Ascencion*
Circoncicion	complainte

B.

portiques	cieux
feux	mystique
majestueux	musique
basaltiques	mes yeux

Cette attitude scrupuleuse à l'égard du nombre de la rime est d'autant plus significative que Corbière n'enfreint pour ainsi dire jamais la contrainte, contrairement à Laforgue qui, dix ans après, l'abandonne dans ses *Complaintes*[16] : il continue bien la poésie savante sur le ton sarcastique qui est le sien, et le renouveau des codes de la versification n'est pas à son programme. C'est ainsi qu'il accepte les rares doublets de la tradition avec *remord* (*Litanie du sommeil*, *La Pastorale de Conlie*) ainsi que l'abandon de l's analogique des formes verbales conjuguées comme dans *je croi : moi* (*Vendetta*). Lorsqu'il rime *Battignole* avec *espagnole* (*Après la pluie*), c'est par fidélité à la tradition autorisant à retrancher les *s* finaux sans valeur morphologique des noms propres, aussi bien toponymes tels que *Athènes* mais aussi *Versailles, Naples, Londres, Bruxelles, Nîmes* etc., qu'anthroponymes tels que *Jules, Jean-Jacques, Charles* ou même *Hobbes* etc.[17]. Et s'il fait preuve de plus d'audace en appliquant la licence à la locution *à rebour*, pour rimer avec *sourd*, ce n'est pas non plus sans

---

15   Dans Houzé et Hérisson, *op. cit.*, p. 192-199.
16   S'il ne procède pas à cette discrimination dans *Véritable complainte d'Auguste Berthelon* et *La Complaincte morlaisienne*, c'est parce que ces deux pièces de jeunesse sont des « airs » dont l'oralité enlevait toute pertinence au procédé. Ce dernier ne prend en effet tout son sens que dans le cadre *littéraire* des *Amours jaunes* qui entend se définir par rapport à la poésie savante, précisément soumise à des conventions dont la raison d'être puise dans l'écriture.
17   *Hobbe : l'aube* dans *La Légende des siècles*, p.s., II, XIV, II. À noter que, à cette époque, la graphie sans *s* pour *Charles* peut également se rencontrer en prose.

précédents puisque Lamartine en usa de même avec *chamois* et *puits* avant de s'en repentir[18]. Les vers suivants de l'édition originale de *Jocelyn*, *Troisième époque* (25 septembre 1793) :

> Il vient de ses deux bras à mon cou se suspendre,
> Et, bondissant après comme un jeune chamoi,
> Me ramène à la grotte en courant devant moi » ;

seront ainsi remaniés moyennant la substitution d'un chevreuil[19]. Les vers suivants de *La Chute d'un ange* (1838), *Troisième vision*, conservés au moins jusqu'au t. V des *Œuvres complètes* de 1842 ici citées (p. 150) :

> Il fit signe à Cédar, en lui montrant le pui,
> De les faire descendre et boire devant lui,
> Afin qu'il pût de près les voir et les connaître.

seront finalement remaniés en remplaçant le second hémistiche du premier vers par « debout et sans appui[20] ». On peut ici constater que Lamartine allait plus loin que Corbière en supprimant même le *t* de *puits*, le second maintenant le *d* amuï de *sourd* qui contrevient à la règle générale sur les consonnes flottantes[21].

Mais à côté de ces situations plutôt conventionnelles, Corbière ne recule pas devant des licences surprenantes sinon cocasses, préférant le générique singulier au pluriel, en associant *un plat d'épinard* au *plat du hasard* (*Bohême de chic*, 40), *cueillir le champignon* à *un lumignon* (*Le Poète contumace*, 109), *la mettre en guenille* avec *une fille* (*Paria*, 51) ; ou encore, ignorant le pluriel existentiel après la préposition *sans*, en rimant *sans gant : bon vent !* (*Le Novice en partance*, 38) ou *doucement : sans dent* (*Laisser-courre*, 58). Il va jusqu'à déformer le nom de l'héroïne de Nodier, Inès de Las Sierras, pour le faire rimer avec *ce sera* et *rat* (*Le Poète contumace*, 143-145) :

> Apparais, un poignard dans le cœur ! – Ce sera,
> Tu sais bien, comme dans *Inès de La Sierra...*
> – On frappe... oh ! c'est quelqu'un...
>   Hélas ! oui, c'est un rat. »

18 Voir Billy, « Convention and parody », p. 349-350.
19 Avec pour pendant : « En courant devant moi m'entraîne à notre seuil » ; *Œuvres complètes*, IX, 1837, p. 176.
20 *Œuvres complètes*, XVI, 1861, p. 154. Sur ce cas, voir Billy, « Convention and parody », p. 350.
21 Sur la question des consonnes flottantes dans la formation des rimes, voir *supra*, p. 81-82.

Là encore, Corbière rejoignait Lamartine qui pouvait rimer *qu'il comptait par centaine* avec *au bord de la fontaine* (*La Chute d'un ange, Quatrième vision*), avant de renoncer à cette bizarrerie en rétablissant le pluriel, mais au prix d'une bizarrerie plus grande encore : « Ségor s'assit à l'ombre, aux marges des fontaines[22] ». On peut encore citer de lui ces vers de *Jocelyn* (16 décembre 1803) qui, par contre, ne recevront pas de correction[23] :

> J'avais monté longtemps ; mon front à large goutte
> Découlait de sueur dont je lavais ma route.

L'adjonction d'un *s* dans *les croque-morts* pour rimer avec *corps* de *Cris d'aveugle* substitue au singulier générique de la tradition orthographique – que l'on trouve dans *le nez des Croque-mort* en rime avec *Champ du nord* dans *Idylle coupée* – un pluriel qui produit un effet cocasse, puisqu'il peut être aussi bien compris comme existentiel que générique : « ceux qui croquent les morts », bien que l'hypothèse d'un pluriel non conventionnel du mot composé considéré comme une forme simple ne soit pas inconcevable[24]. Le parallélisme avec la variante du refrain rimant *la Mort : mon corps* (voir *infra*) laisse cependant subsister un doute sur la possible intention du poète.

L'abandon du pluriel s'observe dans des *pluralia tantum* tels que la locution adverbiale *à ténèbres* pour rimer avec *l'Angélus funèbre* (*Nature morte*, 2) ou dans *après vêpres*, pour rimer avec *lèpre* (*La Rapsode foraine*), ou de façon indirecte pour rimer l'épithète *dites* qui en dépend avec *bénite* (*Rapsodie du sourd*, 31-35) :

> Si j'étais un vieux bedeau,
> Mettrais un cierge au rideau…
> D'un goupillon d'eau bénite,
> L'éteindrais, la vespre dite,
> L'éteindrais !

---

22   Éd. Guyard, p. 892 (correction non signalée dans les notes et variantes). Pour d'autres cas, voir Billy, « Convention and parody », p. 350-351.

23   S'il se corrige en 1860, c'est uniquement pour supprimer l'incongruïté du second vers qui devient : « Ruisselait de sueur découlant sur la route » ; éd. Guyard, p. 776 et 1880.

24   Dans le même poème, la rime-refrain est en |ɔʁ*|, avec une consonne muette quelconque (marquée par l'astérisque), |ɔʁˢ| étant cantonné aux 2ᵉ, 3ᵉ (avec la licence signalée) et 8ᵉ couplets. Si la forme se retrouve dans *Petit mort pour rire*, ce n'est pas pour la rime : « Pour les croque-morts sont de simples jeux, ».

Si l'abandon de l's dans *après vêpre* (*La Rapsode foraine*) n'a aucune incidence dans l'oralité, ce n'est plus le cas dans *la vespre dite*[25] où le singulier
est directement perceptible au travers du déterminant féminin et du
participe, et par conséquent troublant. Dans *Le Bossu Bitor*, l'abandon se
fait de façon contradictoire avec *mâtines* mais pas avec *vêpres*, bien qu'ils
soient en rapport de coordination (63-65) :

> Morne, vers la cuisine
> Il piquait, droit, chantant ses vêpres ou matine,
> Et jetait en pleurant ses savates au feu…

Ce à quoi il convient toutefois de préciser qu'Hugo ne fera pas autrement
dans *Dieu*, pour préserver non pas la rime mais la mesure[26] :

> Ou bien est-ce le Dieu qui fait lugubrement
> Chanter, sous les rideaux de vêpre ou de matines,
> L'homme qui n'est plus homme aux chapelles sixtines,
> Et qui, lui créateur, se plaît à l'écouter ?

Corbière fait ainsi appel à des constructions asymétriques improbables, rimant *de murmure en murmures* avec *des rimes pures* (*Le Fils de
Lamartine*, 57) comme Lamartine rimait *sans nid et sans familles* (il est
question de la poule et du paon) pour rimer avec *leurs fécondes coquilles*
(*La Chute d'un ange, Deuxième vision*). Il adopte par contre un pluriel
distributif discutable lorsqu'il rime *guitares sans âmes* avec *ces dames* (*À
un Juvénal de lait*, 7) ou encore *robes à traînes* avec *des reines* (*La Pastorale
de Conlie*, 63) ; un pluriel à valeur fréquentative au singulier générique
pour rimer avec *compas* dans *Le Bossu Bitor* (57-58) :

> – Tiens : Bitor disparu. – C'est son jour de sabbats
> Il en a pour deux nuits : réglé comme un compas.

Mais il va plus loin dans *La Rapsode foraine* où il pèche délibérément
contre la grammaire, avec, de plus, une rime approximative (49-52) :

> – *Arche de Joachim ! Aïeule !*
> *Médaille de cuivre effacé !*

---

25 Le choix de la graphie ancienne semble gratuit.
26 *Le seuil du gouffre*, VI : *Une autre voix.*

> *Gui sacré! Trèfle-quatre-feuille!*
> *Mont d'Horeb! Souche de Jessé!*

Le cas le plus ingénieux concerne la troncation de *centimes* pour rimer avec *souvent* dans *À une Rose* (35-38) :

> Rose-mousseuse, sur toi pousse
> Souvent la mousse
> De l'Aï… Du BOCK plus souvent
> – À 30 Cent.

On voit que ce qui peut relever d'une certaine méprise sur les usages du pluriel et du singulier, méprise dont témoignent encore, en dehors de la rime, l'expression *à pieds* de *Hidalgo!* ou le *croque-morts* de *Petit mort pour rire*, trouve à se résoudre à la rime de façon à assurer à cette dernière sa régularité formelle. En respectant scrupuleusement l'interdiction de faire rimer « le singulier avec le pluriel », Corbière recourait ainsi aux facilités de Lamartine mais usait aussi de procédés plus radicaux par lesquels il pouvait défier les conventions poétiques. La seule exception selon A. Fongaro, où Corbière enfreint l'interdiction de « rimer le singulier avec le pluriel » concerne un *s* non flexionnel, dans *Cris d'aveugle* (17-18), dont on ne peut toutefois manquer de rappeler qu'il s'agit d'un « air » et relève donc à ce titre de l'oralité dans laquelle se neutralisent nécessairement convention et licence poétiques (« Sur l'air bas-breton : *Ann hini goz* »)[27] :

> Colombes de la Mort
> Soiffez après mon corps

Nous avons de la peine à imaginer que Corbière – comme le suggère Fongaro – avait écrit un *corp* licencieux que le prote aurait spontanément corrigé (encore qu'on ait le précédent du *pui* de Lamartine[28]), d'autant que, dans ce contexte où Corbière rime peu avant *croque-morts* avec *corps* auxquels ces vers font précisément écho[29], c'est bien le singulier *Mort* qui détonne. Sans prétendre y voir une quelconque influence, du moins rappellerons-nous que Musset se permit à deux reprises de rimer *corps*

---

27 « Sur le texte », p. 83. À noter que la rime fautive est déjà présente dans *La Vie parisienne*.
28 *Cf. supra*, p. 155.
29 Sur la structure de ce poème, voir *supra*, p. 94-95.

avec *encor*, une fois dans *Les Marrons du feu*[30], une autre fois dans des quatrains dédiés *À Julie*. Et l'on ne manquera pas de rapprocher cette incorrection de celle dont Lamartine se rendit coupable dans la première édition de *La Chute d'un ange* (Sixième vision)[31] :

> Et Daïdha, couvrant ses enfants de son corps,
> Sentit son cœur troublé par cet accent de mort.

Mais il y a également une autre exception, dans le dernier quatrain de *La Pastorale de Conlie* où il convient sans doute de voir une faute d'impression (p. 249) puisqu'elle est corrigée dans la version de *La Vie parisienne*[32] :

> La chair plaquée après nos blouses en guenille [*sic*]
> — Fumier tout seul rassemblé...
> — Ne mangez pas ce pain, mères et jeunes filles !
> L'*ergot* de mort est dans le blé.

Naturellement, la rime *fille : en guenille* de *Paria* peut, dans l'absolu, jeter quelque doute. Frantext n'atteste pour cette expression que le pluriel pour le XIXe siècle, si ce n'est un vers de Verlaine où l'on a affaire à une licence poétique destinée cette fois à légitimer l'absence de liaison conforme à la langue parlée : « Pauvre, presque en guenille et quasi prisonnier ! » (*Vive le Roy !*) : la rime du *Paria* constitue précisément une licence pour la rime. Pour autant, l'emploi du singulier ou du pluriel peut se discuter dans une certaine mesure, le premier pouvant prendre une valeur « collective », à moins qu'il ne s'agisse d'un vieux vêtement d'une seule pièce ; voir ainsi, dans *Cric-crac* d'Édouard Corbière (II, p. 270) : « Et tout cet orgueil misérable se carrant avec fatuité derrière la sale guenille qui le laissait voir dans toute sa difformité, n'était pas, je vous jure, ce qu'il y avait de moins dégoûtant et de moins digne de pitié à bord des pontons. » Pourtant, conformément à la pétition de principe qui sous-tend son article et le pousse à accorder *a priori* crédit à la moindre coquille, Y. Bernal voit dans ce singulier un « trait comique » qui « semble d'autant plus volontaire que Corbière respecte par ailleurs la "règle absolue de la versification classique" qui

---

30 Comme *vous êtes : je me jette, courez-vous : cou* ; *cf.* Billy, *Les Formes poétiques*, p. 351-352.
31 Corrigé l'année suivante en « veillant sur le couple qui dort » ; éd. Guyard, p. 913 et 1890.
32 Livraison du 24 mai 1873, p. 333.

veut qu'"un mot terminé par *s* ne peut pas rimer avec un mot qui ne se termine pas par *s*" » : *guenille* « sans son *s* final, apparaît donc lui-même déguenillé[33] ! ». Il peut au demeurant s'agir d'un défaut de composition comme celui qui affecte *pourquoi* dont le *i* a sauté à la fin du vers 11 du *Crapaud*. Les inadvertances plus ou moins semblables (*s* de pluriel ajoutés par mégarde) que l'on peut relever parmi les ajouts manuscrits introduits par Corbière sur son exemplaire personnel, dans des ébauches de refonte du *Fils de Lamartine*, sont par contre d'authentiques lapsus : « un flot hexamètre à la fleur d'orangers » en rime avec « un étranger » et « Conception trois fois immaculées » en rime avec « sa mère inoculée[34] », fautes naturellement absentes des *Amours jaunes* où ces vers sont également présents à peu de chose près.

Il n'est pas inintéressant de remarquer qu'en transcrivant le 41ᵉ vers de *La Fin* pour *Les Poètes maudits*, Verlaine commettra une faute qu'il ne corrigera pas, en transcrivant *sans cierges* sans l'*s* final, bien qu'en rime avec *dans les espaces vierges*[35] : le fait que Verlaine fut pour sa part lui aussi extrêmement scrupuleux quant au respect de l'interdiction de rimer « le singulier avec le pluriel[36] » montre à quel point ce scrupule prenait le pas sur le penchant naturel de Corbière à la négligence.

Si Corbière a manqué de rigueur sur cette question, ce n'est pas en effet dans *Les Amours jaunes*, ce qui ne peut que souligner l'importance qu'il accordait à la règle dans son œuvre imprimée. La version de *Veder Napoli poi mori* qu'il publie dans la livraison du 24 mai 1873 de *La Vie parisienne* présente un cas de rime « du singulier avec le pluriel » dans le premier quatrain[37] :

> Voir Naples et mourir. – Moi, j'en reviens. – Patrie
> D'Anglais vivants mal peints sur fond bleu-perruquier.
> Oh ! dans ce bleu, l'artiste en tous genres oublie
> De déclarer sa malle à l'azur des douaniers.

---

33   « Corbière, les coquilles », p. 28. La règle du nombre est ici mal formulée : un mot en *x* ou *z* amuï peut tout aussi bien faire l'affaire.

34   Transcriptions de Houzé, « Le dernier Corbière », p. 330 et 333.

35   Les deux vers sont séparés par un autre, de rime différente. C'est une situation semblable (avec en outre un interligne) qui explique dans « Une nuit que j'étais… » de Baudelaire la rime fautive *corps : sans effort* que certains critiques se sont efforcés de justifier ; *cf.* Billy, *Les Formes poétiques*, p. 347-353.

36   Sur les quelques infractions qu'il commet, voir Billy, « Le nombre de la rime », *f* 4-7.

37   *La Vie parisienne*, 11ᵉ année (1873), p. 335 (24 mai).

Cette faute est bien une faute d'auteur, absente de la version définitive où cette strophe, qui présente par ailleurs de notables remaniements, satisfait à la convention poétique (p. 187) :

Voir Naples et... – Fort bien, merci, j'en viens.

— Patrie

D'Anglais en vrai, mal peints sur fond bleu-perruquier !

Dans l'indigo l'artiste en tous genres oublie. [*sic*]

Ce *Ne-m'oubliez-pas* d'outremer : le douanier.

CORBIÈRE ET L'ALTERNANCE
DES GENRES

Mais à côté de ces licences plus ou moins tolérées, il est des conventions dont Corbière s'affranchit volontiers pour des raisons de commodité, sous certaines conditions toutefois. Le fait de souvent varier la forme des strophes au sein d'une même pièce est déjà l'indice d'une certaine indépendance d'esprit au regard de la tradition qui privilégie l'isomorphie au sein d'une même pièce, même si ladite tradition peut accepter, dans certains de ses courants, comme une pratique légitime des mélanges variés auxquels nous ne nous intéresserons pas ici[1]. On remarquera également qu'il lui arrive parfois de rompre occasionnellement l'isométrie souvent adoptée au départ. Il s'agit souvent d'un unique vers dans le corps du poème (*Décourageux, Veder Napoli, Mirliton*); du second vers dans les poèmes symétriques ouvrant et clôturant le recueil ainsi que dans *Le Renégat*; du dernier dans *Sonèto a Napoli*. Il y en a parfois davantage : voir *À mon chien Pope* (2 vers sur 20, dans la partie finale), *Rapsodie du sourd* (2 sur 58), *Le Fils de Lamartine* (4 sur 60), *La Fin* (7 sur 42); voir aussi un cas isolé dans le corps d'*Épitaphe*, constitué d'octosyllabes, après un exorde de trois alexandrins[2]. Mais c'est dans sa désinvolture à l'égard de l'alternance des genres[3] qu'il s'affranchit réellement des conventions dans le domaine bien réglé des formes poétiques : s'il respecte assez souvent la règle d'un bout à l'autre d'un même poème, ce n'est que six fois sur dix[4]. Lorsqu'il enfreint la règle, c'est davantage

---

1   C'est ainsi le cas des sizains variés qu'affectionnaient Musset ou Banville, là où Corbière adopte toujours des sizains homogènes pour une même pièce.

2   Dans *Aurora*, la rupture est liée à des citations de chansons; voir *infra*, p. 165-166.

3   Laforgue, « Une étude sur Corbière », p. 5, y voyait de simples oublis : « oublis, réels oublis, dans les alternances des féminines et des masculines » ; précisant non sans contradiction : « il les bouscule – par paresse », p. 7.

4   Sur les cent-une pièces du recueil, soixante-et-une sont de ce point de vue régulières, dont vingt-neuf strophiques, six à rimes suivies ou assimilées, les cinq rondels et vingt-et-un sonnets.

dans la succession des strophes qu'en leur sein, avec toutefois de notables exceptions : quatre cas dans des strophes d'*Épitaphe* et de *Rapsodie du sourd* dont trois quatrains sont à rimes exclusivement masculines ; deux cas dans *Le Poète contumace* ; un cas isolé dans *Ça ?* comme dans *Cap'taine Ledoux*. Cette distinction de traitement qui s'articule sur les divisions strophiques se retrouve dans le cadre des pièces optant plus ou moins systématiquement pour les rimes suivies : l'alternance fait en effet défaut plus souvent entre deux séquences contiguës de vers (*Épitaphe*, *Matelots*, *Le Bossu Bitor*, *Le Renégat*) qu'au sein d'une même séquence (*Épitaphe*, *Le Bossu Bitor*, *Aurora*)[5]. Il est plutôt exceptionnel que ces infractions à la règle soient liées à une solution de continuité typographiquement marquée, que ce soit par un astérisque (*Litanie du sommeil*) ou par une ligne de points (*Matelots*, *Le Bossu Bitor*, *Le Renégat*, *Le Douanier*). On verra dans la cinquième partie comment il en va des sonnets.

Dans les pièces en quatrains, le défaut d'alternance est souvent lié à une modification de l'arrangement des rimes préalablement choisi (*Un jeune qui s'en va*, *Frère et sœur jumeaux*, *Idylle coupée*, *La Rapsode foraine*) ou au choix arbitraire de commencer le quatrain sur une rime masculine ou féminine au mépris de ce qu'imposerait l'alternance (*Femme*, *Élizir d'Amor*, *Vendetta*, *Déjeuner de soleil*, *Le Phare*). Les deux phénomènes se rencontrent dans *Saint Tupetu de Tu-pe-tu*. C'est *Le Poète contumace* qui présente la plus grande concentration d'infractions, avec sept cas entre deux strophes et deux au sein d'une strophe, mais il s'agit également de la pièce la plus longue après *La Rapsode foraine*, avec 176 vers. La concentration est bien supérieure dans le poème programmatique *Ça ?*, avec sept cas pour 32 vers seulement : on ne peut oublier le caractère liminaire de ce poème qui suppose une écriture tardive (il est du reste daté du 20 mai 1873), ni son contenu puisqu'il s'agit d'une réflexion du poète sur la nature atypique du recueil qu'il soumet aux lecteurs. Tout se passe comme si, dans son incapacité à caractériser son recueil au moment où il va bien lui falloir affronter, au moins potentiellement, le lectorat habitué au respect de certaines conventions littéraires qu'il

---

5   Voir, à titre d'illustration, *Le Bossu Bitor*, 11-24 : *guerre · terre · démoli · Chili / port · s'endort · lourde · sourde · plaque · flaque / chaos · échos · mélancolique · musique* (la barre penchée signale un changement de séquence). Dans *Épitaphe*, 30-39, on trouve même une suite continue de trois rimes masculines : *pacotille · fille · rien · bien · enfant · testament · plat · plat / blême · lui-même*. Sur le cas d'*Aurora*, voir *infra*, p. 165-166.

sait mettre à mal, le poète forçait le trait plutôt que d'entrer sagement dans le moule.

Dans les quatrains de rimes embrassées, le maintien de la distribution des genres d'une strophe à l'autre entraîne automatiquement une rupture de l'alternance des genres de rimes, mais il arrivait que l'on préférât maintenir l'isomorphie des strophes au prix de ce défaut d'alternance. Corbière semble incapable de se conformer de bout en bout à ce genre de structures, mais on peut constater que c'est ainsi qu'il commence certains de ses poèmes : les trois premiers quatrains (sur huit) du *Convoi du pauvre*; les deux premiers de *Vésuves et Cie* (sur cinq), avant de mêler ces formes avec des quatrains de rimes alternées, accompagnées d'une atteinte non motivée au principe de l'alternance. Dans les autres pièces à strophes mêlées, l'alternance interstrophique n'est pas non plus toujours respectée (*La Pipe au poète, Le Poète contumace*, Ier acte de *Grand opéra, Rapsodie du sourd, Cap'taine Ledoux, Au vieux Roscoff*).

Sujettes à une isomorphie stricte liée à la structure mélodique sous-jacente, les pièces construites sur des airs de chansons peuvent naturellement ne pas se plier à la règle de l'alternance des genres (*Laisser-courre, Cris d'aveugle*), à moins que leur modèle ne s'y soumette pour une quelconque raison (*A mon côtre*). On remarquera cependant que *Chanson en 'Si'*, qui a toutes les caractéristiques d'une chanson bien qu'il n'y soit pas fait référence à un quelconque air, présente une anomalie dans les quatrième, sixième, neuvième et dixième strophes, où ce n'est plus la seconde rime des quintils (a7a7b7'b7'c3) qui est féminine mais la première (a7'a7'b7b7c3), ce qui trahit justement l'inattention portée dans l'écriture de ces strophes à la musique qui pourrait leur être associée[6].

Il arrive deux fois à Corbière de rendre l'alternance impossible par une disposition de rimes inadéquate pour embrasser trois rimes distinctes. Dans un cas, cette irrégularité est le fait d'une citation en deux temps d'un quatrain d'hexasyllabes à rimes embrassées tiré d'une chanson, un distique de rime plate s'interposant au beau milieu (*Aurora*, 13-20) :

Eux répondent en chœur, perchés dans les huniers,
Comme des colibris au haut des cocotiers :

6   *Au vieux Roscoff* qui se donne aussi comme chanson dans le sous-titre – « Berceuse en Nord-ouest mineur » – alterne en fait quatrains et sizains avant un huitain final, avec diverses irrégularités dans le genre des rimes comme dans leur arrangement.

« Jusqu'au revoir, la belle,
« Bientôt nous reviendrons… »

Ils ont bien passé là quatre nuits de liesse,
Moitié sous le comptoir et moitié sur l'hôtesse…
    « … Tâchez d'être fidèle,
    « Nous serons bons garçons… [»]

Les deux occurrences de la rime en |ɛlᵊ| sont séparées par le vers d'appel en |ɔ̃ˢ| suivi de deux vers en |ɛsᵊ| ; celles de la rime en |ɔ̃ˢ|, par la même rime en |ɛsᵊ| suivi du vers d'écho en |ɛlᵊ|. L'interposition de chansons ou vers cités (ou de proses) venant rompre la continuité de pièces par ailleurs métriquement homogènes n'est au demeurant pas une nouveauté[7].

Corbière n'en a pas moins été tenté par l'utilisation de l'homotonie avec l'emploi exclusif de rimes du même genre : c'est ainsi que *Sonèto a Napoli* est délibérément construit sur des rimes exclusivement masculines, et que le corps de *Litanie du sommeil* consiste en deux parties (chacune amorcée par un distique masculin similaire servant d'introduction), la première constituée de laisses féminines, la seconde de laisses masculines, sans que la pertinence du procédé ne soit évidente si ce n'est d'accentuer le caractère litanique du poème avec ses apostrophes répétées au sommeil. Cette disposition spéculaire rejoint en tout cas le goût du poète pour le parallélisme et l'opposition qui se manifeste plus particulièrement au travers de ses poèmes-jumeaux[8].

---

7   Voir p. ex. chez Musset la chanson de Cassius dans *Suzon* ou la prière de Ninon, rompant un vers à la césure, dans *À quoi rêvent les jeunes filles*.

8   À commencer par les poèmes symétriques ouvrant et fermant le recueil ; voir aussi *À l'Éternel Madame* et *Féminin singulier*, *À ma jument souris* et *À la douce amie*, sans parler de *Paris diurne* et *Paris nocturne* recopiés par le poète sur les pages vierges ou dans les marges des pages 32 à 35 de son exemplaire personnel ; *cf.* Levi, « New lights », p. 238-239. Pour d'autres aspects, voir *supra*, p. 153-154.

LA TENTATION DE LA LANGUE PARLÉE

Nous avons déjà évoqué l'influence inconsciente de la langue parlée sur la versification de Corbière à propos d'apocopes incontrôlées[1]. Cette tentation a même amené notre poète à l'utiliser de bout en bout dans la dernière pièce de l'album Noir, *Journal de bord* – expérience qu'il ne renouvellera pas –, avec même des rimes purement phonétiques telles que *port : Théodore* ou *année : navigué*[2]. Cette influence s'y traduit également par le recours relativement fréquent à la synérèse, rompant ainsi d'avec les conventions de la langue poétique en faisant place aux formes plus naturelles du discours quotidien.

On définira tout d'abord la synérèse comme la contraction d'une voyelle haute, soit [i], [y] ou [u], et d'une autre voyelle subséquente en une même syllabe, avec la palatalisation de la première, en [j], [ɥ] ou [w] respectivement. Cette licence repose donc sur un état préalable de la langue poétique où l'hiatus n'était pas encore réduit contrairement à son évolution dans la langue d'usage : ex. *passion*, [pa-si-ɔ̃] > [pa-sjɔ̃] (*Gente Dame*, 4). La langue poétique a toutefois subi d'innombrables évolutions, dont le détail importe peu ici, et la synérèse chez Corbière doit ainsi être mise en relation avec les usages poétiques contemporains pour savoir si l'on a affaire à une synérèse conventionnelle, à une synérèse facultative, plus ou moins acceptée, ou à une synérèse fautive, contraire auxdits usages.

La synérèse facultative permet aux poètes de procéder à un ajustement de la mesure, sans parler des mots rarement employés en poésie comme *biniou* où le poète jouissait d'une plus grande liberté[3]. Corbière adopte ainsi la synérèse dans *duel* (*Fleur d'art*), *miasmes* et *mouette* (*Steam-Boat*, 26), mots dont le traitement est variable au XIXe siècle, avec toutefois une

---

1   Voir *supra*, p. 141-143.
2   Sur la versification de cette pièce, voir Billy, « Corbière et le vers libéré », p. 97-101.
3   Synérétique chez Corbière comme chez Brizeux, elle fera la diérèse chez André Theuriet.

préférence pour la diérèse dans le cas de *duel* et de *mouette*. Dans certains mots, anciennement diérétiques, la synérèse avait fini par s'imposer, ce que Corbière respecte normalement dans *ancien, diable, fouet, jésuite, Juif-Errant* et *oui*, ainsi que dans *fouet, fouette, fouettée* auxquels on peut rattacher les plus marginaux *fouaillant* (*Le Poète contumace*) et *fouaillerais* (*Chanson en 'si'*), ou encore *lierre*. Mais il commet délibérément une faute lorsqu'il revient, occasionnellement, à la diérèse dans *chrétiens* (*La Rapsode foraine*, 94), *gardien* (*Grand opéra*, 30)[4], *ange-gardien* (*Litanie du sommeil*, 50), ou *fouet* (*À mon chien Pope*) et *fouetter* (*La Fin*), auxquels on rattachera *fouaille* dans l'incipit d'«Évohé! fouaille...» : il est en effet difficile de voir dans de tels cas des archaïsmes compte tenu de la fantaisie avec laquelle Corbière aborde la question de la diérèse[5]. Dans *viande* (*Le Bossu Bitor*, 153), le procédé revêt une valeur dépréciative pour désigner la chair marchandisée de la prostitution, comme elle servait à marquer l'excès dans la comparaison que Baudelaire faisait de Dieu dans *Le Reniement de Saint-Pierre*, insensible à «nos affreux blasphèmes» au point de s'endormir «Comme un tyran gorgé de viande et de vins[6]» :

> Et, quand on *largue tout*, il faut que la viande
> Tombe, comme un *hunier qui se déferle en bande!*

Il emploie *lierre* en diérèse dans *Le Poète contumace* (4 : «Au lierre râpé, venaient râper leurs dents») et *Le Douanier* (44), comme le fait occasionnellement Gautier, mais en synérèse dans *Saint Tupetu* (8 : «Beaucoup de foi... beaucoup de lierre...») selon l'usage ordinaire des poètes de son temps.

La synérèse fautive permet à Corbière d'éviter les ellipses maladroites, fût-ce au prix d'une faute de goût qui offensait toute la tradition poétique en recourant à une façon de parler qui, pour être celle de la langue d'usage, ne lui était pas moins étrangère, à l'exception de certains cas où la diérèse avait fini par rendre les mots «languissants» au point de pouvoir passer pour une disgrâce. La faute est d'autant plus saillante qu'elle est récurrente tout autant qu'imprévisible : la démarche de Corbière est aux antipodes de celle d'Armand Silvestre qui use à

---

4   On peut hésiter où faire porter la diérèse dans l'octosyllabe «– Dragon-gardien de la Vierge,» (*La Rapsode foraine*, 73) : *gardi-en* ou *Vi-erge*? Voir *infra*, p. 183.
5   Voir *infra*, p. 173-184.
6   *Le Bossu Bitor*, 153.

l'occasion du procédé, il est vrai de façon exceptionnelle[7], comme de celle de Gustave Rousselot, petit poète né quatre ans après Corbière, qui pratiquait assez systématiquement la synérèse dans un recueil paru un an après *Les Amours jaunes* où il confie au lecteur son sentiment sur ces pratiques que les poètes ne remettaient pas encore en cause[8] :

> Quelques-uns remarqueront, d'autres croiront devoir critiquer certaines inno-vations prosodiques que j'ai introduites dans ce poème. En effet, je trouve le moment venu de se séparer de la routine, de corriger ce qui est faux, et c'est pourquoi j'ai modifié le nombre ordinaire de syllabes accordé à tant de mots en dépit d'un juste usage, – surtout dans ces mots à terminaison en *ion* que tant s'obstinent à compter deux syllabes, tandis que la prononciation ne lui en donne qu'une. Pour moi, comme, pour la langue parlée, *lion*, *nation*, *ambition*, par exemple, sont des mots de une, deux et trois syllabes, et non de deux, trois et quatre, comme les rimeurs les comptent obstinément. Je ne parle pas de bien d'autres genres de mots encore dont j'ai modifié le nombre prosodique selon la parole, en ne me souciant pas de la routine. Mon idée est même que le poëte a le droit de compter ces mots en variant, au besoin, selon le hasard du vers, qui doit chercher la beauté et la vérité avant tout. Si quelques personnes craignent la confusion et l'inharmonie qui peuvent résulter d'une trop grande liberté prosodique, je ne partage pas leur opinion. Je suis persuadé qu'il ne peut en sortir que du bien, car, si ces règles soutiennent les faibles, elles gênent souvent les forts. La liberté poëtique et prosodique que je réclame dans toutes ses conséquences aura pour résultat de faire paraître les grands poètes plus grands encore, et les mauvais encore plus mauvais.

Corbière ne juge pas utile de faire une quelconque déclaration sur son utilisation, plus limitée, de la synérèse qu'il semble pratiquer comme une simple variable d'ajustement du vers, lorgnant du côté de la langue parlée, sans chercher sans doute à écorcher le bon goût prosodique. L'attraction de la langue quotidienne explique en effet pourquoi, dans un style poétique qui met si nettement en avant les tournures de la langue parlée, la synérèse n'est guère surprenante avec le suffixe *-ien*, le mouvement s'étant amorcé bien avant le Grand Siècle dans *chrétien*,

---

7   Voir ainsi *silencieusement* dans une de ses *Rimes neuves et vieilles* (*Triolets printaniers*, p. 97) ; *tuer* dans *Les Renaissances* (*Absag*, p. 97) ; *épanouissement* dans *La Gloire du souvenir* (IX, p. 25). À remarquer que, dans ce dernier cas, la syncope dans le suffixe *-ement* pourrait être envisagée comme alternative, mais les libertés que se permet le poète vont plutôt dans le sens de la synérèse ; voir ainsi, dans un mélodrame écrit en collaboration avec Hennequin, le cas de *niez, avouez, tuer* (*Aline*, p. 37, 41, 42).

8   Rousselot, *Le Poëme humain*, 1874.

gardien ou *ancien*[9], même si la haute poésie s'attache encore, au XIXe siècle, à perpétuer l'ancien usage en dehors de ces mots, du moins dans le fonds lexical cultivé par les poètes, et la contraction était d'autant plus naturelle que les mots concernés étaient soit exclus de, soit étrangers à, soit marginaux dans la langue poétique traditionnelle. On peut ainsi relever *tyrolienne* dans *Le Poète contumace*, en rime avec *éoli-enne*, régulièrement diérétique ; *parisien* et *pharmacien*, tous deux dans *Idylle coupée* ; *chirurgien* et *terriens* (deux occurrences) dans *Matelots*, mais dans *La Fin*, *terrien* au pluriel (imprimé erronément « *terriers*[10] ») fait l'objet d'une diérèse dans une apostrophe au dernier vers où le mot semble gagner un ton satirique : « – Laissez-les donc rouler, *terriers* [*sic*] parvenus ! » C'est également en diérèse qu'il traite *corsairiens* dans *Aurora*, mot étranger à la langue poétique. La synérèse qu'on observe dans *musicien* (*Épitaphe*) était déjà pratiquée par Scarron dans un registre burlesque, à l'encontre de la norme poétique, et les poètes du XIXe siècle employaient encore ce mot en diérèse à l'exception notable de Musset qui faisait de même avec *gordien*, *Hellespontien* ou *Pharisien* qui relèvent de la langue littéraire ou du moins cultivée, mais ne pouvait guère être accusé de licence lorsqu'il usait de cette même contraction dans les mots qu'il empruntait à la langue ordinaire, tels qu'*académicien*, *comédien*, *Égyptien*, *italien*, *patricien*, *Vénitien*, *Tyrolien*. Lamartine lui-même, qui ne s'aventurait qu'exceptionnellement hors de la langue poétique traditionnelle, faisait la synérèse dans *paroissien(s)*.

La synérèse ne surprend pas davantage dans d'autres mots étrangers à la langue poétique, à l'étymologie parfois obscure, ou empruntés, comme *assiette* ou *pioche* que les poètes qui les introduisent emploient généralement en synérèse, ni dans *gouapeur*, ni dans *fiacre* – déonomastique de *Fiacre*[11] – que les poètes du XIXe siècle, du moins Gautier, Prarond, Hugo et Sully Prudhomme, emploient également en synérèse, comme le faisait Voltaire, ni dans *marsouin* du scand. *marsvin* (*FEW* 16, 236), bien que Leconte de Lisle l'ait erronément traité en diérèse[12]. Elle est par contre plus discutable au regard des usages poétiques contemporains

---

9   La diérèse à laquelle recourt systématiquement Baudelaire est un archaïsme.
10   La coquille a ses défenseurs, de Walzer à Bernal (« Corbière, les coquilles », p. 35).
11   Le nom propre était traité en synérèse chez Eustache Deschamps avant de connaître, au XVe siècle, la diérèse.
12   Dans *Les Clairs de lune*, III (*Poëmes barbares*).

dans *chouette, girouette, goélands* ou *mouette*. Elle surprend bien davantage dans l'usage du suffixe *-ion* : *acclimatation* (*Lettre du Mexique*), *compassion* (*Rapsodie du sourd*), *conception* (*Le Fils de Lamartine*), *érection* (*Le Phare*), *passion* (*Gente Dame*), *Passion* (*Rapsodie du sourd*, *Le Bossu Bitor*), et, pour ce qui concerne les dérivés, *gardenational* [*sic*] (*Un jeune qui s'en va*) ; y compris dans les dérivés de l'italien : *gabion* (*Le Douanier*), *lampion* (*Le Phare*), bien que cela fût plus acceptable. On remarquera toutefois que Lamartine, qui ne transigeait pas avec le suffixe *-ion*, pouvait être plus relâché avec *million*[13]. Autres synérèses fautives avec yod[14] : *bestiaux, Diane, escient, extérieur, fiancée, harmonieux*, liesse, mariée, mendiant*, myope, myosotis, pieux, viatique* ; avec [ɥ] : *muet*, muette, remuer, sueur*, tué** ; avec [w] : *secoué*, louis*[15]. Corbière usait déjà occasionnellement de ce genre de synérèses dans l'album Noir[16]. On en relève également une dans une ancienne version de *Frère et sœur jumeaux*, alors intitulée *Les Vieux Jumeaux*, où le second hémistiche du vers 5, « et roides, sans pensées... », se présentait ainsi, après une virgule : « muets, comme sans pensée[17] ».

On peut relever un certain flottement dans l'utilisation des mots et des noms étrangers. C'est toutefois la forme non contractée d'origine qui est adoptée dans quatre occurrences sur cinq de *Graziella*, dans la forme francisée *Grazielle* et le dérivé *graziellant*, l'exception se situant dans un hémistiche où elle côtoie une synérèse fautive : « Graziella ! – Conception trois fois immaculée... » (45). Par contre, Corbière introduit systématiquement la diérèse dans les emprunts à l'espagnol de *Chapelet*, en contradiction avec la langue d'origine : « Avec tous les AVE de Sa *Perfeccion*, » *etc.* Il emploie indifféremment diérèse et synérèse dans *diamant* ou *violon*, mots où l'usage poétique est la diérèse, ainsi que dans *vielle*. Pour les mots de même racine que *violon* mais peu attestés en poésie, il emploie de façon contradictoire la synérèse avec *violoncelle*

---

13   M. Souriau, « La versification de Lamartine », p. 843, relève ainsi ce vers (de *Jocelyn*) : « Leur rayon vient à nous sur des millions d'années ! », auquel on peut ajouter : « Et j'entendis les voix d'un million de génies ». La synérèse se rencontre également chez Boulay-Paty, Brizeux, H. Moreau, Nerval à l'occasion, Soulary, une fois chez Rimbaud dans *La Comédie de la soif*, soit à un moment où il tourne le dos aux conventions poétiques.

14   L'astérisque signale l'emploi parallèle du mot en diérèse dans *Les Amours jaunes*.

15   Dans « – Cent louis !... – Eh, Eh ! Bibi... – Mon duc ?... » (*Déjeuner de soleil*) où il eût suffi de ne pas répéter l'interjection pour obtenir la prononciation correcte.

16   Voir Billy, « Corbière avant Tristan », p. 173-177.

17   Voir Martin, « Trois variantes », p. 55 et 57, qui qualifie le vers de « douteux » dans sa première version.

et la diérèse avec *violoncelliste* dans le même vers (*Litanie du sommeil*, 60 : «Du violoncelliste et de son violoncelle,»), la synérèse avec *viole*. Il fait encore la synérèse dans *douanier(s)* – sauf dans un vers du *Poète contumace*[18] –, *camélia* (*Duel aux camélias*) et *chouette* (*Nature morte*) contre l'usage, autant qu'il soit attesté ; *escouade* (*Le Bossu Bitor*), ce que ne contredit pas l'étymologie (lat. QUADRARE) ; *piaffe* (*À l'Éternel Madame*) et *gouine* (*Le Bossu Bitor*), tous deux synérétiques également chez Hugo (le premier chez Vigny également).

Là où la synérèse fautive est provocatrice, c'est dans le seul cas de *poète* (*Le Crapaud*) et *Poète-apothicaire* (*Le Fils de Lamartine*), où elle va à l'encontre et de la langue poétique et de la langue parlée, avec une intention clairement ironique. Il se distinguait en cela de Baudelaire qui avait tenté cette synérèse dans la première version de *Lesbos*, trouvant quelque prestige à cette forme cultivée par Mathurin Régnier qui n'était pour d'autres, à commencer par Agrippa d'Aubigné, qu'une forme prosodique alternative, avant de faire machine arrière devant le caractère irréductiblement cacophonique de ce cultisme précieux en se ralliant à l'usage ordinaire[19].

---

18   «Chiens errants, vieux rats, fraudeurs et douaniers.» (14) ; sur ce vers, voir *supra*, p. 52. Rimbaud l'emploiera en diérèse (*Les Douaniers*).

19   *Cf.* Billy, *Les Formes poétiques*, p. 15. Pour des exemples de cette synérèse on consultera Frantext ; voir aussi l'aperçu historique de Quicherat, *Traité de versification*, 2ᵉ éd., p. 307-309.

LE SABORDAGE DE LA PROSODIE
FRANÇAISE

Constatant que Corbière « compte arbitrairement le nombre des syllabes, qu'il allonge ou contracte suivant les besoins de la mesure », Le Dantec considérait que « C'est là une originalité de plus mais dont il n'est pas possible de savoir si elle était ou non volontaire, ni si Corbière la tenait de famille[1] ». Parlant de négligences, Martineau se demandait : « Quelle importance faut-il donc attacher à ces peccadilles et surtout quel intérêt y a-t-il à les discuter ? », ajoutant que « Un vrai poète, comme Tristan Corbière, laisse parler son âme et voilà tout[2] ». Or, ces pratiques déroutantes, générant d'innombrables cas d'hypométrie apparente dont « ces tas d'alexandrins qui, sans raison, par ci par là, n'ont que 11 syllabes » dont parlait Laforgue[3], constituent bel et bien une démarche volontaire dans le projet esthétique du poète tant elle est liée à l'élaboration même du recueil : leur absence dans les 527 vers de l'album Noir[4], constitué pour l'essentiel avant le voyage d'Italie (hiver 1869)[5], nous semble en effet significative, avec notamment d'anciennes versions du *Douanier* et de *Litanie du sommeil* (ce dernier il est vrai réduit à huit vers) qui ne laissent aucune place aux diérèses fautives qui, par contre, fleuriront dans *Les Amours jaunes* en sapant les fondements de la versification française. On peut aussi comparer l'incipit octosyllabique d'*Au vieux Roscoff* avec la version régulière de l'autographe conservé[6] :

---

1 Le Dantec, éd. citée, p. 17.
2 *Tristan Corbière* (1925), p. 25.
3 « Une étude sur Corbière », p. 5.
4 Le nombre exact dépend de la conception que l'on a du dernier texte, *Journal de bord*, où le poème proprement dit semble encadré d'éléments paratextuels aux allures de vers libre ; *cf.* Billy, « Corbière et le vers libéré », p. 85-86 et 89-90 (et fig. 1, p. 109).
5 Les pièces datées remontent toutes à 1867 et 1869 ; voir Houzé, *ffocsoR*, p. 8 (2ᵉ col.), 18, n. 10, et 32 (2ᵉ col.).
6 J. de Trigon, *Tristan Corbière*, p. [93].

AJ   Trou de flibustiers, vieux nid
Ms.   Trou de contrebandiers, vieux nid

Il ne s'agit par conséquent en aucun cas de ces hypercorrections qu'un apprenti poète peut commettre par méconnaissance des règles en ajustant librement la mesure des vers[7], mais d'une entreprise volontaire de provocation, et c'est précisément sur ce point que Corbière se distingue de G. Rousselot qui prônait la liberté du poète au regard de la seule diérèse poétique héritée de la tradition littéraire à laquelle il estimait que pouvaient être préférées les formes contractées de la langue parlée[8]. La version abrégée que donne *La Vie parisienne* de *La Pastorale de Conlie*, texte satirique amputé de sept quatrains mais introduit par deux nouveaux (adressés à Gambetta) et modifié en divers points, renonce à une diérèse fautive (*fumier*, 86) sur les trois de la version des *Amours jaunes*[9], mais en ajoute trois autres, sur *gibier*, peut-être *messieurs* mais plus vraisemblablement *chiens*, et *tiède* (70, 76 et 80), ce qui soulève le problème du rapport entre les deux versions, si celle de *La Vie parisienne*, donnée dans la livraison du 24 mai 1873[10], soit peu de temps après la déclaration d'imprimer du recueil (17 mai), n'a pas vu augmenter délibérément le nombre de diérèses fautives afin d'enchérir dans la charge, ou si Corbière n'a pas, pour son recueil, diminué l'agressivité de ses diérèses en en diminuant le nombre, ce qui nous surprendrait davantage :

AJ (70)   Ramas de vermine sans nom,
VP   Gibier de morgue sans nom,

AJ (76)   Des Français aboyaient – Bons chiens !
VP   Ces messieurs criaient : Bons chiens !

AJ (81)   – Va : toi qui n'es pas bue, ô fosse de Conlie !
VP   Et toi, tiède encore, ô fosse de Conlie,

---

7   Pour un cas ancien, voir Cornulier, « Corbière et la poésie comptable », p. 260-261, à propos de l'articulation trisyllabique de *puissent* dans un poème de jeunesse (*Ode au chapeau*).
8   Voir *supra* le plaidoyer du poète, cité p. 169.
9   Le vers – un octosyllabe – des *Amours jaunes* : « – Fumier tout seul rassemblé… », est modifié en : « Ce fumier tout seul rassemblé !… » Les diérèses fautives sur *paîssions* [sic] et *impuissants* (12 et 44) sont par contre maintenues.
10   Avec en sous-titre : « dédiée à maître Gambetta par un mobilisé du Morbihan », dans *La Vie parisienne*, 11ᵉ année (1873), p. 333 (24 mai).

S'il n'a pas accordé d'importance à l'artifice avant l'élaboration de son recueil, on ne saurait toutefois ignorer que, dans sa jeunesse, il en a usé de façon plutôt gratuite à moins d'un possible calembour (*sied* comme *scié?*), dans le sixième couplet de la *Véritable complaincte d'Auguste Berthelon* (heptasyllabes)[11] :

> seule la plante des pieds
> à son front serein sied

On remarquera au passage que ces diérèses déroutantes soulèvent quand même un problème général du fait de la présence de vers plus ou moins faux dans le recueil : le lecteur anonyme de l'exemplaire du dépôt légal numérisé sur Gallica introduit ainsi en marge une cheville aux vers 93 et 95 (il s'agit d'octosyllabes) de *Un jeune qui s'en va* (p. 64)[12] :

> [O] Métier ! Métier de mourir…
> Assez, j'ai fini mon étude,
> [O] Métier : se rimer finir !…
> C'est une affaire d'habitude.

Rien toutefois ne permet de repérer ou de suspecter sans préjugé parmi les innombrables vers concernés une quelconque lacune textuelle. On ne peut par ailleurs ignorer que la gestation de ces licences peut prendre naissance dans une certaine difficulté de Corbière à mouler spontanément son expression dans le carcan métrique, au point que Laforgue pouvait ressentir de la peine à le voir compter ses syllabes[13], ce dont témoigne les erreurs dans le compte des *e* caducs que l'on peut observer au travers de la genèse de ses poèmes telle qu'elle apparaît au travers des versions manuscrites conservées comme au travers de quelques vers dont l'hypermétrie n'est qu'apparente[14], mais aussi maintes chevilles telles les multiples ellipses (pronom sujet, semi-négation, article défini, conjonctions *et*, *que*, préposition *à*) ou réductions diverses (élision de *si*, *quel* pour *lequel*, aphérèse dans *foncerais* pour *j'enfoncerais*), ellipses et crases auxquelles il procède volontiers, sans que l'on puisse toujours

---

11 Transcription dans Houzé, « Naissances d'une œuvre », p. 366.
12 https://gallica.bnf.fr/ark:/12148/bpt6k10578489/f80.image (consulté le 10/09/2022).
13 « Une étude sur Corbière », p. 12.
14 Voir *supra*, p. 141-143.

invoquer le recours à un style volontairement marotique (comme dans *Chanson en 'si'*), telles que :

> – Quel a commencé ? – Pas moi, bon apôtre !
> Après, quel dira : c'est donc tout – voilà ! (*À une camarade*, 23-24)
>
> C'est drôle, est-ce pas : Les mourants (*Un jeune qui s'en va*, 2)
>
> – Taureau : foncerais ta porte... (*Chanson en 'Si'*, 3)
>
> – Moi : jamais n'ai chanté (*Libertà*, 14)
>
> La Vierge vous le rende. – Allons : au large ! ou : gare !... (*Hidalgo !*, 18)
>
> A leurs ceintures d'or, faut ceinture dorée[15] ! (*Le Bossu Bitor*, 161)
>
> Ah je te tiens ; on sait jouer Colin-maillard !... – (*Ibid.*, 191)
>
> Dans toutes langues c'est : Ignace ou Cydalyse, (*Le Renégat*, 16)
>
> – *Morts*... Merci : la *Camarde* a pas le pied marin ; (*La Fin*, 7)
>
> Ne fais pas le lourd : cercueils de poètes
> Pour les croque-morts sont de simples jeux, (*Petit mort pour rire*, 8-9)

Nous avons déjà vu que l'ellipse, la crase ou même une élision sortie de l'usage (*s'elle*) permettent parfois d'éviter un hiatus ; elles permettent aussi d'ajuster la mesure :

> Philosophe, – à tort à travers. (*Épitaphe*, 21)
>
> Quelquefois, vaguement, il se prenait attendre... (*Le Poète contumace*, 50)
>
> Sans voir s'elle était blonde... Il adorait la lune ; (*Décourageux*, 9)

Il convient toutefois de remarquer que l'ellipse de la semi-négation (le discordantiel) est courante chez les romantiques qui ne faisaient que per-pétuer une licence classique qui pouvait même passer pour une élégance. Voir ainsi dans *Hernani* telle réplique de Dona Sol : « Devions-nous pas dormir ensemble cette nuit ? ». Ce qui augmente les réserves sur cette question est le fait que cette ellipse, lorsqu'elle ne s'inscrit pas dans un style marotique, peut apparaître sans aucune motivation formelle, sa présence ou non ne changeant alors rien à la mesure comme dans les répliques suivantes des *Marrons du feu* de Musset :

---

15   Sur ce cas, voir *supra*, p. 141.

Ouf! – A-t-on pas trouvé là-bas une ou deux femmes
Dans la mer? [...] (Sc. I)

Holà! dites, marauds, – est-ce pas là que loge
La Camargo? [...] (Sc. III)

Dès lors, en l'absence de toute justification formelle, le procédé cesse d'être une simple licence pour devenir un marqueur de l'artificialité de la langue poétique, mais on peut penser, au vu des tendances générales de sa propre langue poétique, que Corbière était souvent bien loin de rechercher une afféterie de style alors qu'il semble si souvent à l'affût de facilités. De fait, si elle a bien constitué à l'origine une réponse à sa difficulté à ajuster sa pensée aux rigueurs du mètre, la diérèse fautive est devenue chez lui une véritable marque de provocation tant par la multiplication de son usage que par la manière sauvage dont le poète s'applique à la pratiquer. Si irrégulières soient-elles, les synérèses fautives ne sont en effet jamais qu'une concession à la langue parlée, et c'est surtout leur accumulation qui irrite le lecteur cultivé. Les diérèses fautives, par contre, ont un caractère autrement spectaculaire et provocateur tout en permettant d'accroître le vers d'une syllabe selon la mesure attendue : elles constituent alors de véritables caricatures de la diérèse poétique perpétuée par la tradition littéraire.

Le procédé intervient dans de multiples diphtongues ascendantes dans lesquels l'élément faible est dépalatalisé ou dévélarisé jusqu'à prendre une articulation stable, où la semi-voyelle se voit substituée la voyelle haute la plus proche : [i] remplace [j], [y] remplace [ɥ], [u] remplace [w]. Certaines diérèses apparentes n'en doivent pas moins être relativisées du fait de l'évolution phonétique des mots concernés. Ainsi, dans *suinter*, formé à partir de *suint* lui-même dérivé de *suer*, on a originellement affaire à la rencontre de deux voyelles. Mais, entérinant l'évolution du mot dans la langue d'usage, les poètes ont adopté la synérèse qui semble à peu près généralisée au XIXe siècle[16], à l'exception notable de Lamartine et de Gautier, de sorte que son emploi dans

---

16 Frantext en donne diverses attestations chez Hugo, Leconte de Lisle, Bouilhet et Léon Dierx, sans parler de Laforgue, auxquels on peut ajouter Laprade dans *Poèmes civiques* (*Des lanternes*), Verlaine dans *La Bonne Chanson* (XVI), Jean Aicard dans *Poëmes de Provence* (*Marseille*), Anatole France dans *Les Poëmes dorés* (*Le Chêne abandonné*), Mendès dans *Soirs moroses* (*Après la fin*) et *Hespérus*.

« Au lieu de suinter dans vos pommes de terre, » (*La Fin*, 29) n'a rien de fondamentalement surprenant, autant du fait de ses emplois chez des poètes alors prestigieux que par le retour à l'étymologie. Voici la liste des formes concernées par des diérèses proprement licencieuses, rangées par semi-consonnes puis diphtongues (l'astérisque signale les formes – souvent uniques – qui, dans le recueil, ne se présentent qu'avec la diérèse[17]) :

$$[j] > [i]$$

[ja] > [ia]	liard*
[je] > [ie]	*dernier, escalier*, fumier, hunier, métier, moitié, panier-à-salade* (mais *panier* syn.), *papiers, pied(s), râtelier, rosier,*
[jɛ] > [iɛ]	*altière, ciel, ciel-de-lit*, cierge, fière, fiers, fièvre, lierre, lièvre*, mièvre*, pièce, vieille,*
[jɛ̃] > [iɛ̃]	ange-gardien, *biens**, chien, *chiendent**, *chien-loup**, chrétiens, *far(-)niente**, gardien, *rien, vauriens, sieste, vieille*
[jø] > [iø]	*adieux, Dieu, milieu, vieux,*
[iœ]	*monsieur*[18],
[jɔ] > [iɔ]	*Dios*,*
[jɔ̃] > [iɔ̃]	paîssions* [*sic*],

$$[ɥ] > [y]$$

[ɥɑ̃] > [yɑ̃]	*don-juan*, Pur-Don-Juan-du-Commandeur*,*
[ɥi] > [yi]	*huile, huître, huys, impuissants, nuit(s), puits, Ver-luisant*,*

$$[w] > [u]$$

[wa] > [ua]	fouaille,
[we] > [oe]	*goéland(s),*
[wɛ] > [uɛ]	fouettant, fouets,
[wi] > [ui]	*ouïs* (pour *ois* ; voir commentaire *infra*),
[wɔ] > [uɔ]	*ruolze.*

---

17   Sans distinction du nombre éventuel ou autres variantes flexionnelles : Corbière emploie ainsi *impuissants* en diérèse, au contraire du singulier *impuissant*.

18   Dans *Un riche en Bretagne* : « Il eût été traduit par monsieur Delille, » (48). On peut hésiter entre l'absurde [møsiø] et la prononciation archaïsante [mɔ̃siœʁ].

La plupart de ces diérèses sont à la fois contraires à l'étymologie et à la tradition poétique. Certaines, pour être conformes à l'étymologie, sont malgré tout contraires à l'usage poétique du fait que la synérèse avait fini par s'imposer dans les mots concernés (en romain ci-dessus[19]). Rien toutefois ne permet, dans les contextes où s'observent ce genre de licences, de soupçonner Corbière d'une volonté d'archaïsme comme c'est clairement le cas chez Baudelaire dans l'emploi trisyllabique d'*ancien*. Rien non plus ne nous permet de songer à une négligence ou à une apparente ignorance des règles dans certains de ces détails comme celles dont témoignait Leconte de Lisle qui, dans la première édition de *Poëmes antiques* (1852), appliquait occasionnellement la figure à *bélier(s)* et aux désinences des première et seconde personnes du pluriel de l'imparfait (*parliez, caressiez, tombiez, retombions*)[20]. Un cas particulier concerne la 1re pers. de l'ind. pr. d'*ouïr* – qui fait depuis longtemps défection dans la conjugaison de ce verbe – où l'adoption de la graphie *ouïs* (pour *ois*), soulignée par le tréma, sert précisément à marquer la diérèse, bien que celle-ci soit très artificielle au regard de l'évolution phonétique de l'ancienne diphtongue – on devrait avoir [wɛ] > [wa] –, la prononciation [ui] adoptée correspondant par contre à la 2e pers. du prétérit. Seul le contexte permet d'interpréter correctement la forme :

> Du prêtre, sous l'autel, n'ouïs-tu pas les pas
> Et le mot qu'à l'Hostie il murmure tout bas ?... (*Grand opéra*, 15)

Il ne s'agit pas, selon nous, d'une énallage à proprement parler (après Le Dantec, Walzer parle d'une « inadvertance de temps »), mais bien d'une diérèse analogique, la conjugaison d'*ouïr* ([u-iʁ] en poésie) étant refaite sur le modèle de la 2e conjugaison telle que l'illustrent les verbes *fouir* ou *jouir*, où le barbarisme se conjugue à l'archaïsme, là où *entends*, qui a concurrencé *ois* avant de le supplanter, eût parfaitement convenu. À noter que le présent s'inscrit fort logiquement dans une série d'interrogations adressées à la Sainte Châsse, après « Portes-tu », « veille-t-elle », « font-ils » et « sais-tu », qui amènent la réponse finale :

> – Eh bien ! moi j'attendrai que sur ton oreiller,
> La trompette de Dieu vienne te réveiller !

---

19   Pour ces mots, voir *supra*, p. 168.
20   Il en corrigera certaines dans la reprise de ces poèmes en 1858 et 1874.

La diérèse dans *grouins* peut nous surprendre aujourd'hui, avec deux occurrences[21], mais, sans remonter au moyen âge, elle est conforme aux anciens usages puisqu'on la trouve attestée dès le XVIIIe siècle selon Frantext (chez Piron et le chevalier de Piis). Bien qu'ignorée du dictionnaire de l'Académie, la graphie « grouin » est bien attestée au XIXe siècle (y compris en prose)[22] ; elle a même une entrée, certes secondaire (renvoi), dans le dictionnaire de Bescherelle qui considère que le mot devrait s'écrire avec un tréma sur l'*i* (*DN* II, 75 et 77) : le mot était en effet devenu dissyllabique dans certains usages en dépit de son étymologie (lat. GRŬNIUM, *FEW* IV, 293b) comme l'indique Littré[23], vraisemblablement sous la même influence dissimilatrice qui avait fait apparaître à date plus ancienne la diérèse dans des mots tels qu'*ouvrier* ou *sanglier*, et il est particulièrement significatif que ce soit avec la diérèse qu'on retrouve ce mot dans *La Balancelle* bien que ce texte soit entièrement composé en langue populaire, ce qui exclut l'usage de la diérèse poétique[24] : « C'est comm' culots d' gargouss' gréés en grouins d' chiens ». Hugo ne l'emploie qu'en diérèse, aussi bien avec cette graphie qu'avec celle qui s'est finalement imposée[25] ; exemples :

Ces diacres ! ces bedeaux dont le groin renifle ! » (*Les Contemplations*, I, XIII)

Des grouins de pourceaux baisant des mufles d'ânes ! (*Toute la lyre*, II, IV, XVII)

Voir aussi chez Glatigny, avec la graphie moderne : « Leurs groins ont flairé les essences de roses » (*Le Fer rouge*, VII, 13). La diérèse dans *Juan* est à mettre à part dans la mesure où il s'agit d'un emprunt (et bien que l'espagnol fasse la synérèse). Musset l'adopte une fois (*Les Marrons du feu*), comme il le fait à l'occasion pour *Juana* dans *Don Paez*, et Edgar Quinet ne connaît qu'elle. Une diérèse qui surprend aujourd'hui[26] doit

---

21 Dans *Idylle coupée* (38) et *La Goutte* (32).
22 Fongaro, « Sur le texte », p. 81.
23 *DN* II, 75 : « Ce mot devrait s'écrire avec un tréma sur l'*i*, *groïn* » ; *DLF* II, 1941 : « aujourd'hui, il est de deux syllabes ».
24 *Viande, précaution, Lorient* et *chirurgien* y font ainsi la synérèse.
25 Il utilise la graphie alternative dans la première série des *Châtiments* (IV, XIII) : « Le porc Sénat fouillant l'ordure du grouin. ».
26 Walzer, éd. citée, p. 1349, la trouve « bizarre » ; Aragon et Bonnin, éd. citée, p. 389, la trouvent simplement « amusante ». Selon Aragon et Bonnin, éd. citée, p. 389, note au

être relativisée : *New-York* en trois syllabes, dans *Le Novice en partance*
(«– New-York… Saint-Malo… – Que partout Dieu vous garde !») où
Corbière devait prononcer [nø-i-ɔʁk], conformément – diérèse mise à
part – à l'usage signalé par Bescherelle (*DN* II, 635 : « neu-york ») et,
de façon indirecte, par Larousse qui, pour *newyorkais*, donne la prononciation figurée « neu-ior-kè » (*GDU* XI, 966). Les poètes qui ont usé
du mot lui donnaient plutôt deux syllabes, que ce soit Hugo, Musset
ou Banville[27], mais, dans sa tragédie *Les Enfants d'Édouard*, Casimir
Delavigne ne procédait pas autrement avec le nom de la vieille York,
prononcé [i-ɔʁk][28], et Hugo fera de même dans *L'Échafaud* (*Toute la
Lyre*, II, I, I)[29] :

> Richard d'York étouffe Édouard cinq ; Stramire
> Le Mauvais est mauvais, mais Jean le Bon est pire ;

La diérèse peut se trouver soulignée par son emploi à la rime, parfois
même de façon symétrique comme aux vers 5-8 de *Paysage mauvais* (5-8)[30] :

> – Calme de peste, où la fièvre
> Cuit… Le follet damné languit.
> – Herbe puante où le lièvre
> Est un sorcier poltron qui fuit…

Cette position permet de parfaire une rime léonine dans le troisième
sonnet de *Paris* :

> Poète. – Après ?… Il faut *la chose* :
> Le Parnasse en escalier,
> Les Dégoûteux, et la Chlorose,
> Les Bedeaux, les Fous à lier…

---

v. 77-78, elle renverrait à la langue populaire, mais ils ne donnent aucune indication sur
la prononciation qu'ils ont en vue.

27 Musset dans *Poésies nouvelles* (*Une Bonne Fortune*) ; Hugo dans *Les Châtiments* (*Le Parti du
crime*) ; Banville dans *Poésies complètes* de 1857 (*Le Palais de la mode*). Voir aussi, parmi les
poètes parnassiens, Hervilly dans *La Lanterne verte* (*Le Bas de jambe*) et Villemin dans
PC (1866), p. 247 (*Le Drame de Rachel*).

28 Signalé par Derême, *La Libellule violette*, p. 218.

29 Ici comme ailleurs, Hugo traite *Édouard* en diérèse (tout comme Delavigne et Vacquerie)
contrairement à Musset.

30 On retrouve cette même rime dans *Un jeune qui s'en va* (33-36). Voir aussi *mi-èvre : fi-èvre*
dans *Bonsoir*, *alti-ère : fi-ère* dans *La Rapsode foraine* où l'on trouve également *Gabri-el : ci-el*.

Corbière ne recule pas devant les emplois contradictoires d'un vers à l'autre, d'abord en diphtongue légitime, ensuite en diérèse plutôt que l'inverse (dans le premier exemple la diérèse se trouve même intégrée dans un groupe nominal que l'italique met en relief) :

« Reviens m'aider : Tes yeux dans ces yeux-là ! Ta lèvre
Sur cette lèvre !… Et, là, ne sens-tu pas ma fièvre
– Ma *fièvre de Toi* ?… – Sous l'orbe est-il passé
L'arc-en-ciel au charbon par nos nuits[31] laissé ? (*Le Poète contumace*, 87-90)

Vous ne me direz mot : je ne répondrai rien…
Et rien ne pourra dédorer l'entretien. (*Rapsodie du sourd*, 57-58)

Pour mouiller un pied d'ancre, Espérance propice !…
            Un pied d'ancre dans son cœur[32] ! (*Le Novice en partance*, 15-16)

parfois au sein d'un même vers (octosyllabes) :

Métier ! Métier de mourir…
Assez, j'ai fini mon étude,
Métier : se rimer finir !…
C'est une affaire d'habitude. (*Un jeune qui s'en va*, 93-96)

Sables de vieux os – Le flot râle
Des glas : crevant bruit sur bruit… (*Paysage mauvais*, 1-2)

On a déjà évoqué le traitement contradictoire de *violoncelliste* et de *violoncelle* dans *Litanie du sommeil* ; signalons encore celui de *piétinant* et de *pied* dans *Matelots* (71-73) :

– C'est plus qu'un homme aussi devant la mer géante,
Ce matelot entier !…
                        Piétinant sous la plante
De son pied marin le pont près de crouler :

Il n'est pas rare que la localisation d'une diérèse fautive fasse difficulté du fait que deux diphtongues ou plus pourraient s'y prêter, que ce soit sur les mêmes mots ou apparentées comme on l'a vu plus haut ou sur des mots différents. Dans les vers césurés, la question de l'hémistiche peut lever l'ambiguïté, mais dans les vers simples, seule l'étude systématique

---

31   Diérèse fautive sur *nuits* également.
32   Le v. 16 est un octosyllabe.

du phénomène chez Corbière permet alors de proposer une solution crédible[33]. Ainsi, dans « Du violoncelliste et de son violoncelle, », c'est la césure qui nous incite à faire la diérèse sur *violoncelliste*, la synérèse sur *violoncelle*. Dans « Charnier d'élus pour les cieux, » (*La Rapsode foraine*, 182), on peut constater que, si *cieux* est ailleurs toujours diphtongué (5 cas), *ciel* connaît quatre fois la diérèse[34] (sur vingt occurrences, dont un pluriel) ; *charnier* ne se trouve qu'une seule autre fois, employé correctement, mais on a vu que la diérèse est relativement courante dans *Les Amours jaunes* avec le suffixe *-ier* ; *charnier* venant en premier, on privilégiera cependant la diérèse sur *cieux*, d'autant plus que la coupe médiane est plus naturelle. En revanche, dans l'octosyllabe « – *Dragon-gardien de la Vierge,* » (*La Rapsode foraine*, 231), où l'on hésite entre *gardien* et *vierge*, le fait que pas une des dix-huit occurrences du substantif *vierge*[35] ne fasse la diérèse de façon certaine[36] fait plutôt pencher la balance en faveur de *gardien* – anciennement trisyllabique –, avec deux cas de diérèse assurés sur sept emplois. Dans « Bazar où rien n'est en pierre ; » (« Bâtard de Créole… », 3), il faut savoir que la diérèse (fautive) se rencontre neuf fois avec *rien* (pour un total de 48 occurrences), alors qu'elle n'apparaît jamais de façon assurée avec *pierre(s)* (huit autres occurrences). Naturellement, bien que Corbière procède également à des synérèses fautives, lorsque l'on a la concurrence d'une diérèse régulière la solution doit se plier à la règle. Ainsi, dans « – Et toi, Graziella… Toi, Lesbienne Vierge ! » (*Le Fils de Lamartine*), les règles privilégient la diérèse poétique dans *Lesbienne*.

La provocation se manifeste parfois de façon frontale, dès le premier vers. C'est ainsi que Corbière glisse une diérèse fautive dans l'incipit même de *La Goutte* : « Sous un seul hunier – le dernier – à la cape, », où la norme de la césure contraint à la faire porter sur *hunier* bien qu'il apparaisse le premier, plutôt que sur *dernier* et bien que par la suite ce mot soit employé très régulièrement dans ce poème, avec pas moins de quatre occurrences (4, 6 et 7), comme il l'est dans *Le Bossu Bitor* ou *Aurora* (une et deux occurrences). Même chose dans *Hidalgo*, poème en alexandrins qui débute par « Ils sont fiers ceux-là !… comme poux sur

---

33 Voir Billy, « Le sabordage de la prosodie française », § 2.6, p. 11-12.
34 En comptant *ciel-de-lit*.
35 Mais cela est vrai également des onze occurrences de l'adjectif et de *fil-de-la-vierge*.
36 Dans l'octosyllabe « *Gracia !* la Vierge vous garde ! » (*Grand Opéra*, 51) où la norme veut *Gracia* de trois syllabes.

la gale ! ». On peut par contre hésiter dans *Au vieux Roscoff*, constitué d'octosyllabes, avec deux sites possibles : « Trou de flibustiers, vieux nid » : si *flibustier* ne se retrouve ailleurs que dans *Saint Tupetu de Tupetu* où la diphtongue est respectée, on sait que la diérèse n'est pas rare avec le suffixe *-ier* ; cependant, *vieux* connaît deux fois la diérèse (dans *À l'Etna* et *Aurora*). L'ordre des mots incite cependant à faire porter la diérèse sur le second. Certains poèmes concentrent les diérèses fautives : les sonnets « Poète – Après ? … » et *Paysage mauvais* en contiennent respecti- vement quatre et trois ; *Hidalgo* en contient quatre, sur 24 vers ; *Le Poète contumace*, neuf, sur 176 vers ; *Litanie du sommeil*, sept, sur 163 vers ; *La Rapsode foraine*, sept également, mais sur 236 vers ; *Un jeune qui s'en va* en contient cinq, sur 104 vers ; *La Pastorale de Conlie*, trois sur 88 vers, et six, on l'a vu, sur les soixante de la prépublication.

Cette utilisation récurrente de diérèses déroutantes mettait à l'épreuve le lecteur de l'époque acculturé à l'usage de la diérèse poétique en le déstabilisant chaque fois qu'il se trouvait confronté inopinément à des vers dont la mesure lui semblait fausse, sans qu'il lui fût possible d'anticiper cet inconfort de lecture. La curieuse réaction de Laforgue face au vers 20 du *Bossu Bitor* (« Le ciel miroité semble une immense flaque. ») témoigne des troubles que cette façon de versifier pouvait causer chez le lecteur : il croit en effet que la diérèse porte sur *miroité* qui aurait ainsi quatre syllabes, ce qui est pour le moins surprenant ([miʀoate], sans doute comme le *moâ* des clowns), alors qu'elle doit porter sur *ciel*, comme dans les octosyllabes « Il a le ciel pour couronne » de *Paria* ou « L'innocent est près du ciel ! » de *La Rapsode foraine*. Corbière sapait ainsi sciemment l'un des fondements de la mesure des vers, ce qui a sans doute motivé, comme le pensent Rousselot et Bernardelli[37], cet aveu paradoxal[38] :

> Une tête ! – mais pas de tête ;
> Trop fou pour savoir être bête ;

---

37 Rousselot, *Poètes d'aujourd'hui*, p. 79, a plus particulièrement en tête la question de la diérèse et de la synérèse ; Bernardelli, « Il testo contumace », p. 36, vise plus globalement les « anomalies métriques abondantes » de ses vers.

38 Le v. 29 a naturellement donné lieu à d'autres interprétations ; Aragon et Bonnin, éd. citée, p. 53, y voient ainsi des « vers heurtant l'oreille accoutumée aux harmonies traditionnelles, classiques. Ou encore, le vers *sonne faux* parce qu'il trahit ce que Corbière lui-même nomme sa "pose" ».

Prenant un trait pour le mot *très*.
– Ses vers faux furent ses seuls vrais. (*Épitaphe*, 26-29)

On a du reste quelques témoignages montrant que la claire volonté de Corbière de se moquer de la convention poétique a bien été perçue par ses lecteurs. Le témoignage de l'un des premiers critiques à rendre compte de la publication d'une œuvre qu'il juge « violente, excessive, *énorme* (è normis), mais marquée au cachet de la force et d'une puissante originalité » – M. de Vaucelle – est à cet égard révélateur, évoquant « ce superbe dédain des conventions acceptées » où, toutefois, il voit surtout une facilité[39] :

> [...] l'auteur ne se gêne pas au besoin pour allonger ou raccourcir les mots à sa fantaisie, suivant qu'il faut à son vers une syllabe de plus ou de moins ; ce qui fait que le vers traité de cette façon peut bien avoir la mesure pour l'auteur, mais il ne l'a pas pour le lecteur exigeant qui voudrait bien avoir son compte ou rien que son compte de syllabes. Mais l'auteur se soucie bien de cela ; il en prend à son aise, avec la prosodie comme avec toute autre chose. Si les règles contrarient son inspiration ou sa fantaisie, ma foi, tant pis ; il fera plier les règles ou sautera par-dessus.

Dans la livraison du 1er novembre 1873 de *L'Art universel*, un autre signant E. V., aussi impitoyable que dépourvu de complaisance, s'exclame, après avoir relevé d'autres infractions aux règles prosodiques (hiatus – qu'il approuve –, réduction de *si* devant *elle*, abolition de la césure médiane)[40] :

> Et plus loin, je remarque des mots dont la valeur métrique se plie capricieusement aux besoins du vers ; que l'auteur trouve de grandes facilités dans cette licence, je le crois ; mais j'y trouve, moi, une énorme difficulté à la lecture, et ceux qui liront ces passages éprouveront le même ennui.

C'est justement cette pratique outrancière de la diérèse fautive qui déclenche la charge du critique qui donne à voir dans le texte corbiérien une entreprise dadaïste avant la lettre, comme si la seule évocation du procédé suffisait à le faire sortir de sa réserve. Citant à la suite les deux vers d'*Épitaphe* où Corbière définit le poète comme un artiste « sans art » et un philosophe « à tort à travers[41] », il ajoute :

---

39 Paru dans *L'Artiste*, XLIII, 1er nov. 1873, p. 300-301.
40 *L'Art universel* I, 18 (1er nov. 1873), p. 156.
41 Sans les tirets ni la virgule après *Philosophe*.

> C'est cela, rien n'est respecté ! Démolir et toujours démolir. Que nous importent les traditions ! Abattons ces fétiches usés du piédestal où nos gloires littéraires les ont élevés ; frappons aveuglément dans le passé ; langue, grammaire, syntaxe, prosodie, philosophie gisent sous nos pieds. Notre idéal, à nous, c'est l'incorrect, l'incohérent, l'incompréhensible. [...] nos poëtes ont été des cygnes et des rossignols, qu'ils deviennent des rats et des crapauds, « ces poëtes tondus ». Renversons le vieux, et nous trouverons le neuf ; ne laissons rien subsister : ni langue, ni règle ni bon sens.

L'auteur anonyme du compte rendu de *La Renaissance littéraire et artistique* (livraison du 26 octobre 1873), qui semble davantage y voir une négligence, considère que la forme des *Amours jaunes* – qu'il renonce à qualifier – « est digne des poètes burlesques antérieurs à Coquillart ; toutes les règles de la poésie, la rime et le rythme sont trop souvent mis de côté », se demandant[42] : « Pourquoi construire sur le sable un édifice que sa bizarrerie aurait rendu remarquable ? ». La raison d'être de ces violations délibérées des règles n'a jamais été si bien perçue que par Rousselot pour qui « les brisures de rythme qu'il provoque en comptant tantôt pour un pied, tantôt pour deux, des mots comme "cieux", "chien", "vieux", etc..., lui permettent de compléter sa silhouette de boiteux, d'accentuer le porte-à-faux où il se tient depuis qu'il est au monde, parce qu'il affirme ainsi sa rébellion contre tout ce qui est en ordre ». Ceci étant, il n'y a pas toujours chez Corbière l'expression d'une volonté de provocation nourrie de sa gêne à s'insérer dans l'histoire poétique : il peut aussi tirer de la diérèse des effets d'insistance, comme quand le poète qui ne voit *rien* venir répond à « Ma sœur Anne » (*Le Poète contumace*, 160-164) :

> *Ma sœur Anne, à la tour ; voyez-vous pas venir ?...*
>
> – Rien ! – je vois... je vois, dans ma froide chambrette,
> Mon lit capitonné de *satin de brouette* ;
> Et mon chien qui dort dessus – Pauvre animal –
> ... Et je ris... parce que ça me fait un peu mal.

Mais on ne peut en dire autant de *chien* qui vient deux vers après et qui, tout en faisant pendant à *rien*, produit par contre un effet cocasse où la cacophonie semble un rien teintée de scatologie. On peut retrouver

---

42   Cité par Steinmetz, *Une vie à-peu-près*, p. 426.

cette insistance dans la seconde apostrophe au chien Pope, avec une charge de mépris, en opposition avec la première où le mot est par contre traité conventionnellement (*À mon chien Pope*, 4-5 et 8-9) :

> N'être pas traité comme un chien,
> Chien ! tu le veux – et tu fais bien.
> [...] Ne jamais marcher sur les mains,
> Chien ! – c'est bon pour les humains.

CONCLUSION

De façon peut-être paradoxale, la versification des *Amours jaunes* révèle une connaissance approfondie des conventions poétiques avec une mise en œuvre souvent scrupuleuse : son respect de l'interdiction d'hiatus, de l'interdiction des séquences voyelle tonique + *e* muet devant consonne, Corbière s'appliquant même à recourir au circonflexe lorsque celles-ci se présentent au sein des mots. Son traitement de la rime témoigne là encore de sa fine connaissance de règles ou de traditions qu'il ne prétend pas remettre en cause, même lorsqu'il se permet des libertés qui sont courantes dans le style bas qui est souvent le sien. Corbière n'en apparaît pas moins comme embarrassé par le corset contraignant du mètre, recourant à toutes sortes d'artifices pour ajuster sa pensée aux exigences de la mesure, troquant ici un singulier générique à un pluriel existentiel ou l'inverse, recourant là à des ellipses manquant de naturel, là à des transpositions parfois acrobatiques, là encore à des contractions surprenantes, toutes pratiques significativement absentes de sa prose.

Pour autant, la désinvolture dont témoigne le poète à l'égard de la correction orthographique, ponctuationnelle et typographique de son recueil se manifeste quelques fois dans sa versification, comme le recours immotivé au doublet *encor* devant voyelle ou l'omission accidentelle de l'apostrophe dans quelques discours rapportés en langue populaire, donnant ainsi, ici ou là, l'apparence trompeuse d'une hypermétrie. Il recourt aux licences poétiques de la tradition telles que la possible chute des *s* finaux ne servant pas à l'expression du pluriel, et s'il se montre plus spécialement négligent à l'égard des règles, c'est surtout dans les libertés excessives qu'il prend au regard de l'alternance des genres de rimes.

Ce qui peut surprendre dans les pratiques versificatoires de Corbière est bien la manière dont il se retrouve avec Lamartine dans une poignée de rimes approximatives, dans d'apparentes hypométries dues à un déficit d'attention, dans l'excès de zèle et l'ironie dont il fait preuve dans sa manière de respecter la règle du nombre de la rime envers laquelle son anti-modèle se montrait quelque peu négligent. Mais ce qui est sans doute le plus frappant, c'est la liberté dont il use avec la synérèse, donnant souvent sa préférence aux contractions de la langue parlée, si ce n'est lorsqu'il l'applique par dérision à *poète* contre tous les usages, et plus encore la diérèse dont il abuse de façon provocatrice, laissant une empreinte personnelle, véritable signature d'auteur, de ce qui a pu n'être au départ qu'une manière facétieuse d'ajuster la mesure en esquivant ainsi les problèmes posés pas sa difficulté à versifier.

TROISIÈME PARTIE

UN TRAITEMENT POSTROMANTIQUE
DE LA CÉSURE

– Est-ce qu'il pouvait, Lui!... n'était-il
pas poète...
Immortel comme un autre?... Et dans
sa pauvre tête
Déménagée, encor [sic] il sentait que
les vers
Hexamètres faisaient les cent pas de
travers.
Le poète contumace.

Corbière utilise dans son recueil moins de vers césurés que de vers simples : près de 39 % sont des alexandrins (à peine plus que les octo-syllabes), et moins de 4 %, des taratantaras[1]. Dans son traitement de la césure, il adopte les formes de son temps, c'est-à-dire celles des romantiques où, « çà et là les poètes introduisaient, négligemment, des rythmes imprévus, fantaisistes, et que Victor Hugo lui-même a quali-fiés de "disloqués"[2] », car, comme l'écrit Martineau, « il sait la valeur de l'instrument qu'ils ont forgé[3] », adoptant à l'occasion les nouvelles formes affranchies par les Parnassiens de certaines contraintes, ce qui fait dire à M. Lindsay, pleinement conscient de ce respect général de la norme héritée, que son traitement de la césure semble se caractériser par un rejet délibéré mais non systématique des règles qui la gouvernent[4]. Son désintérêt pour les ternaires romantiques au sens de Rochette[5], c'est-à-dire fondé sur un parallélisme syntaxique strict à membres égaux ou inégaux, est toutefois remarquable, ce qui le rapproche davantage de la rythmique lamartinienne que de celle d'Hugo. Nous examinerons

---

1 D'après nos relevés (et nos interprétations), le recueil contient 4 095 vers dont 1 590 alexan-drins, 19 décasyllabes communs, 155 taratantaras (4 %), 1 505 ou 1 506 octosyllabes (37 %), 253 ou 254 heptasyllabes (6 %), 383 hexasyllabes (9 %), 8 pentasyllabes, 116 tétrasyllabes (3 %), 43 trisyllabes, 22 dissyllabes.
2 Boschot, « La réforme de la prosodie », p. 862.
3 *Tristan Corbière*, p. 87.
4 « The versification », p. 360.
5 C'est-à-dire fondés sur un parallélisme syntaxique (*cf.* Rochette, *L'alexandrin chez Victor Hugo*, en particulier p. 114-121).

dans la présente partie le traitement des vers césurés dans *Les Amours jaunes* : alexandrins syncopés, césures "pour l'œil", césures dans les mots composés et abolition de la césure médiane dans l'alexandrin, en terminant sur la pratique du taratantara.

Les quatrième et cinquième parties nous permettront par contre de mettre plus précisément l'alexandrin corbiérien en rapport avec celui du mouvement parnassien de façon à y déceler les possibles influences liant Corbière à ses confrères, ce qui nous permettra notamment d'établir plus précisément la modernité du poète.

ALEXANDRINS SYNCOPÉS

Sur le plan strictement métrique, l'alexandrin de Corbière est le plus souvent très régulièrement césuré, avec ce qu'il faut de déséquilibres rythmiques. Il n'ignore naturellement pas les artifices dont usaient à l'occasion les poètes romantiques pour assouplir le rythme ou le rompre occasionnellement en lui donnant ainsi plus de vie, sollicitant même l'attention du lecteur par une situation problématique que Martinon, qui y voit un défaut, a bien décrite[1] : « il ne faut pas que la césure sépare du mot qui précède un monosyllabe qui lui soit trop intimement uni par le sens, car en ce cas le monosyllabe tire à lui l'accent, et le rythme disparaît, si le lecteur ne fait pas un effort, parfois excessif, pour le conserver ». Dénonçant les lectures qu'en donnaient en son temps maints critiques, enseignants mais aussi acteurs, selon une habitude qu'il fait remonter à Becq de Fouquières (1881)[2], Martinon n'en considère pas moins que la scansion requise ne doit pas pour autant négliger la césure métrique, « *la césure*, dont on ne tient pas compte, sous prétexte qu'elle est très faible et qu'il n'y a point de "repos", mais sans laquelle pourtant le vers ne serait plus qu'une ligne de prose », Hugo imposant, selon lui, au lecteur des lectures aussi complaisantes que pénibles préservant l'accentuation de la sixième syllabe[3], ce qui est sans doute vrai dans une certaine mesure, c'est-à-dire dans l'idéal d'un modèle de diction plutôt que dans une pratique réelle où le poète lui-même devait bien, au moins dans certains contextes syntaxiques et certainement dans l'exécution de ses pièces, se laisser tenter par des dictions plus naturelles qui seules peuvent expliquer qu'il se soit parfois laissé aller à mettre un monosyllabe atone en 6e position, contrairement à ce que Martinon affirme

---

1   « Le trimètre » [1], p. 629.
2   *Ibid.*, p. 624.
3   « Le trimètre » [2], p. 40-42. Voir aussi [1], p. 629 : « tant que la sixième syllabe est accentuée, il y a une césure, il y a *la* césure ».

avec trop d'assurance[4]. Si l'exercice demandé semble en général plus ou moins praticable, il est en effet des cas où l'on ne voit pas comment il est réalisable en maintenant la compréhension de l'énoncé, comme dans :

> Si Corneille en trouvait un blotti dans son vers,
> Il le gardait [...] (*Réponse à un acte d'accusation*)

> [...] Et mon regard
> Errait ne voyant plus rien qu'à travers un voile, (*L'Échafaud*)

À en croire Martinon (à propos d'exemples qui nous paraissent pourtant moins problématiques), il faudrait admettre que « non seulement il nous fait mettre un accent sur une syllabe qui n'en devrait point garder [*ici*, trouvait *et* plus *respectivement*], mais il nous oblige parfois à l'ôter à la syllabe qui devrait l'avoir [*ici*, un[5] *et* rien], pour pouvoir l'attribuer à sa voisine ».

Corbière adopte à l'occasion ce procédé qui consiste à rejeter après l'hémistiche un monosyllabe ou un dissyllabe paroxyton. La césure sépare ainsi deux mots en étroite relation syntaxique (nom/adjectif, numéral/ nom, verbe/adverbe, verbe support/nom *etc.*), au sein d'un syntagme dont l'accent tombe en 7e position, donnant alors au vers une allure plus libre, voire prosaïque, en accord avec l'énoncé, à moins que l'on ne privilégiât la structure métrique en procédant au genre de diction artificielle dénoncé par Martinon, mais certainement facilité lorsque la tension prosodique entre les éléments placés de part et d'autre de la césure est plus lâche[6] :

> Sans compter un caban bleu qui, par habitude, (*Le Poète contumace*, 122)

> Peut-être elle sera veuve avant d'être épouse... (*Matelots*, 67)

> Le navire [...] s'endort
> Seul ; et le clapotis bas de l'eau morte et lourde,
> Chuchote [...] (*Le Bossu Bitor*, 17)

> – L'escouade d'un vaisseau russe, en grande tenue ; (*ibid.*, 146)

---

4   Voir la remarque *ibid.*, p. 44. Sur ce sujet voir *infra*, p. 308-314.
5   À noter ici la nécessité de la liaison qui souligne la solidarité prosodique du verbe et de son complément.
6   Dans « Jouant au bord de l'eau noire sous le beau temps, » (*Le Bossu Bitor*, 252), nous comprenons que l'eau apparaît noire sous le beau temps, non, bien entendu, que les gamins jouent sous le beau temps.

> T'es tortu, mais j'ai pas peur d'un tire-bouchon ! (*ibid.*, 188)
>
> Lisait le bordereau même de l'avenir ! (*Le Douanier*, 49)

Par analogie avec la musique, nous emploierons le terme de syncope pour évoquer l'effet de rupture rythmique produit par ce décalage de la division prosodique majeure du vers au regard de la césure qui, dans de telles situations syntaxiques, *peut* demeurer sensible grâce à une diction appropriée qui dépend au demeurant du degré de cohésion syntactico-prosodique entre le monosyllabe ou dissyllabe paroxyton rejeté et le syntagme qu'il introduit, au sein d'une structure descendante 7 + 5 clairement affichée. Le rejet interne est parfois renforcé par l'introduction d'une coupe immédiatement après, avec le détachement d'un thème : « – Oh, qu'elle s'en allait morne, la douce vie !... » (*La Pastorale de Conlie*, 29), ou encore d'une apposition ou d'une incidente qui peut atténuer l'effet en complétant le rejet :

> Il aime son pain noir sec – pas beurré de fiel... (*Un riche en Bretagne*, 4)
>
> Et tout ce qui vibrait là – je ne sais plus où – (*Rapsodie du sourd*, 53)

ou d'un complément quelconque :

> Nous : ceux-là qui restaient simples, à leur manière, (*La Pastorale de Conlie*, 67)
>
> L'administration meurt, faute de ballots !... (*Le Douanier*, 83)

Dans les cas que nous venons de voir, la coupe après la 7ᵉ position est dominante au sein du vers. Lorsqu'elle n'est que secondaire, le rejet interne n'en est pas moins saillant : « – Bon. Tu m'en conduiras une... et propre ! combien ?... » (*Le Bossu Bitor*, 117). Le rejet prend plus de relief dans les cas suivants, où, par extraction, le thème se trouve rejeté après la césure en fin de proposition :

> Un grain... est-ce la mort ça ? la basse voilure
> Battant à travers l'eau ! – Ça se dit *encombrer*... (*La Fin*, 11-12)

Corbière renouait ainsi avec ce « vers vague sans muselière » qu'évoquait Hugo dans *Quelques mots à un autre*[7]. Le procédé, en effet, n'était pas inconnu

---

7   « Tout est perdu ! le vers vague sans muselière ! » (*Les Contemplations*, I, XIII).

des romantiques : Vigny l'affectionnait de même que Musset, comme en témoigne ces vers de *Mardoche* où le poète tire des effets de prosaïsme[8] :

> – Mais la chose ne fait rien à notre héros. (v)

> [...] – Il était sobre
> D'habitude, et mangeait vite. – Son cuisinier
> Ne le gênait pas plus que son palefrenier. (x)

> Un dimanche (observez qu'un dimanche la rue
> Vivienne est tout à fait vide, et que la cohue
> Est aux Panoramas, ou bien au boulevard), [...] (xix)

> Ayant donc débarqué, notre héros fit mettre
> Sa voiture en un lieu sûr, qu'il pût reconnaître, [...] (xxii)

> La matinée était belle ; les alouettes
> Commençaient à chanter ; [...] (xxiv)

> Attendais que le temps vienne. – Et qu'en apprendrai-je ? (xxvi)

Corbière obtient un effet plus accusé encore en passant à la ligne dans ces vers de *Bambine* (18-19), où un rejet externe rompt le premier hémistiche après la deuxième syllabe :

> Bambine fait les cent pas.
>   Un ange, une femme
> Le prend : – C'est ennuyeux ça, conducteur ! cessez !

On peut opposer à ce cas l'alexandrin final de *Bonne fortune et fortune*, où la césure reste nettement marquée d'un repos, le second hémistiche étant simplement amorcé par une conjonction avant d'être interrompu par une suspension du discours qui rend la césure d'autant plus sensible que le membre suspendu se trouve rejeté à la ligne (10-12) :

> [...] mais Elle
> Me regarda tout bas, souriant en dessous,
> Et... me tendit sa main, et...
>   m'a donné deux sous.

Dans le vers suivant, le rejet interne s'inscrit dans une énumération qui découpe le vers en trois membres inégaux de 4 + 3 + 5 syllabes

---

8   Pour Vigny, voir Billy, « Innovation et déconstruction », p. 143, n. 1.

dont la syncope rythmique et la diérèse facultative occultent la structure sous-jacente : « Rose-des-vents, sacré gui, lierre bacchique [*sic*], » (*Le Douanier*, 44). Le déséquilibre de l'alexandrin est plus nettement renforcé lorsque le mot à la césure n'est pas un mot plein, sans être pour autant un proclitique ou une préposition monosyllabique[9], mais où un allongement ou une accentuation quelconque revêtirait un caractère artificiel, soit un auxiliaire, un forclusif ou le verbe-copule :

– Noblesse oblige. – Il est saint : à chaque foyer
Sa niche est là, tout près du grillon familier. (*Un riche en Bretagne*, 30-31)

– Matelots ! – Ce n'est pas vous, jeunes *mateluches*, (*Matelots*, 97)

Etarque à bloc ! – L'homme est libre et la mer est grande – (*Le Novice en partance*, 39)

On peut observer dans ces trois vers que la coupe principale se situe au sein du premier hémistiche, avec chaque fois une pause segmentant le vers en 4 + (3 + 5) ou 3 + (4 + 5) syllabes, mais le procédé donne bien la même impression d'un « déplacement » de la césure d'un rang vers l'avant, l'hémistiche n'offrant pas de coupe syntaxique au contraire de la frontière entre les 7e et 8e positions, à moins d'une diction forcée dont on imagine mal que Corbière se soit jamais senti obligé de marquer.

On remarquera que ces structures syncopées sont particulièrement concentrées dans *GENS DE MER*, avec onze cas répartis entre *Matelots* (2), *Le Bossu Bitor* (4), *Bambine* (2) et *Le Douanier* (3). Il arrive également, mais rarement, à Corbière de recourir à un contre-rejet, avec un monosyllabe accentué à la césure, pouvant même produire un effet de syncope ascendante marqué avec un rythme 5 + 7 :

Todos los santos… Mais il ne porte plus ça ; (*Le Renégat*, 17)

SOUPIRAIL d'en haut ! Rais de poussière impalpable, […] (*Litanie du sommeil*, 82)

---

9   C'est-à-dire ne pouvant être normalement détachés de leur base phonologique par l'interposition d'une apostrophe, d'une incise, d'une incidente, d'un adverbe ou d'un syntagme quelconque transposé (mais voir *infra* p. 211-212, n. 43). Sont donc exclus les monosyllabes métriques appartenant à des catégories grammaticales « grises » dont le comportement prosodique est variable : conjonctions, relatifs, déterminants indéfinis, adverbes d'intensité *etc.*

On ne peut plus soutenir dans ces deux cas que l'hémistiche, n'est pas marqué, même dans le cas de la conjonction *mais* dont la fonction argumentative s'ajoute à celle de connecteur, lui conférant une certaine force prosodique. Le contre-rejet interne, déterminant des structures rythmiques croissantes 5 + 7, est beaucoup moins représenté chez les romantiques comme chez Corbière. La raison principale en est d'ordre linguistique, les constituants syntaxiques commençant assez peu souvent par un mot fort ou du moins accentué réduit à une seule syllabe métrique. À cela, naturellement, s'ajoutaient des raisons d'ordre stylistiques qui, de façon générale, incitaient les poètes à éviter ce genre de situations, comme elles pouvaient au contraire, et paradoxalement, amener certains à y recourir, ce que pouvait favoriser le développement de l'enjambement dans le mouvement romantique. C'est ainsi que Musset peut écrire dans *Portia* :

> D'où partent ces accents ? et quelle voix s'élève
> Entre ces barreaux, douce et faible comme un rêve ? (II)

> – Quel homme fut jamais si grand, qu'il se pût croire
> Certain, ayant vécu, d'avoir une mémoire
> Où son souvenir, jeune et bravant le trépas,
> Pût revivre une vie, et ne s'éteindre pas ? (III)

Dans le vers suivant, la syncope s'inscrit dans un rythme ascendant différent (4' + 7) : « Ce sera drôle… Viens jouer à la misère, » (*Le Poète contumace*, 169).

LA NOTION DE CÉSURE
POUR L'ŒIL

La spécificité de la césure pour l'œil est de faillir à la fonction fonda-mentale de la césure qui est d'offrir un relief suffisant pour marquer la ligne générale du rythme, fût-ce par un simple accent de proéminence associé à une frontière de mots. Cette combinaison peut être jugée plus ou moins satisfaisante en fonction des époques, des registres et des poètes dont la tolérance est plus ou moins grande à l'égard de structures relâchées qui ne sont tolérées ou recherchées que pour des raisons stylistiques, dans des proportions toujours limitées. L'évolution de la sensibilité des poètes et de leurs goûts esthétiques qui accordent une place de plus en plus importante aux aspects rythmiques va s'accompagner chez les lec-teurs d'une évolution semblable, l'alexandrin allant progressivement vers un affranchissement longtemps occasionnel de la césure médiane, avec une limite que franchiront d'abord, de manière délibérée, Corbière et Verlaine comme nous le découvrirons progressivement dans les chapitres suivants et surtout dans la Ve partie, déterminant un déséquilibre de la structure du vers en déplaçant vers l'avant son axe métrique avant les bouleversements du Symbolisme[1]. C'est cette limite que Le Goffic et Thieulin mettent en évidence lorsqu'ils font remarquer[2] :

> [...] n'avons-nous point gardé, en lisant les trimètres romantiques, cette habitude de reposer un peu la voix à l'hémistiche ? Et n'est-ce point pour cela qu'une muette [« e » *post-tonique*] nous gêne et que nous tenons à voir à l'hémistiche un mot ou une fin de mot ?

Et, peut-on ajouter, n'est-ce point pour cela que des poètes novateurs vont user du procédé ? Loin d'abolir la césure, si ce n'est dans des

---

1   Voir V, chap. « L'abolition de la césure médiane chez les Parnassiens » et « Un précurseur du second Verlaine ».
2   Ch. Le Goffic et Thieulin, *Nouveau traité*, p. 84, n. 1.

contextes métriques particuliers qui ne se développeront qu'avec le
"second" Verlaine, la césure pour l'œil consiste en une occultation de
la césure médiane par un procédé que l'on peut assimiler à une forme
spécifique de rejet ou contre-rejet[3], ce qui semble apparaître justement
chez Verlaine lui-même lorsque, à propos du "premier" Rimbaud, il
fait le lien entre les deux procédés dans son constat[4] : « Peu de césures
libertines, moins encore de rejets ». Si le terme peut être contesté[5], la
notion n'en est pas moins pertinente. L'expression attire l'attention sur
le fait que la césure, pour être jugée satisfaisante, s'adresse avant tout
à l'oreille : si elle lui échappe, la césure n'en est pas moins présente,
que seul le lecteur est à même de situer. Mais on peut tout aussi bien
s'interroger sur le rôle de l'oreille, même si celle-ci est indéniablement
sollicitée (pour autant que le poète s'entendît toujours composer ses
vers) : lorsque, dans *Les Plaideurs*, Léandre s'exclame : « Tu porterais au
père un faux exploit ! » (I, v) – avant que L'Intimé ne grogne : « Hon !
hon ! » –, le spectateur peut-il vraiment affirmer avoir *perçu* la césure ?
Peut-il vraiment prétendre avoir saisi l'unité du premier hémistiche
lorsque, à l'ouverture de la scène II de l'acte III, Léandre déclare : « Je
me sers d'un étrange artifice [...] » (la scène précédente est conclue par
le souffleur s'exclamant : « Quel homme ! ») ? Peut-il vraiment affirmer
avoir perçu la césure lorsque Léandre déclare : « Allons à ce dessein
rêver ailleurs. » à la fin de la scène v de l'acte I ? Et quel peut bien être
le sens de *percevoir la césure* si l'on n'a pas perçu le vers en son entier ?

Ce que l'on entend communément par *césure* n'est jamais que la
manifestation superficielle des contraintes métriques qui s'exercent
dans le travail d'écriture poétique. Par sa fréquence élevée, c'est elle
qui assure la reconnaissance du mètre : l'hémistiche est en effet le lieu
ordinaire où se situe la coupe prosodique majeure du vers. Pour autant,
cette caractéristique macroprosodique n'est pas la plus significative (et les
classiques eux-mêmes admettaient la possibilité d'une certaine variation),
ce qui lui vaut d'être la cible privilégiée de certains poètes, tels que les
romantiques, désireux de rompre la monotonie de ce retour prévisible
de la coupe principale au mitan du vers et d'élargir l'inventaire limité

---

3   L'usage veut que ces notions soient appliquées dans un cadre syntaxique particulier
      maintenant un accent à la césure.
4   *Les Poètes maudits*, éd. Décaudin, p. 26.
5   Voir Cornulier, *Art poëtique*, p. 266-269.

de rythmes que celui-ci détermine. En dissociant coupe prosodique majeure et hémistiche, ces poètes maintenaient deux caractéristiques témoignant précisément de la nature exacte des contraintes métriques : l'accentuation de la 6e position et la présence d'une frontière de mots à l'hémistiche, entre cette position et la suivante. On peut ainsi identifier une *contrainte accentuelle* et une *contrainte morphologique*. La césure pour l'œil se manifeste précisément par la *neutralisation de la contrainte accentuelle* (non par sa violation), ce qui a pour conséquence l'occultation de la césure (non sa disparition)[6] : la 6e position peut être occupée par un monosyllabe atone mais pas par une syllabe post-tonique. En effet, seul le schwa post-tonique constitue une déficience de la chaîne acoustique, là où une voyelle pleine, stable par nature, accentuée ou non, présente une sonorité suffisante qui peut même, si le contexte le permet, lui valoir un accent de proéminence, comme on peut le constater déjà chez les classiques, tels que, chez Racine : « Attendons... Mais voici Polynice et la reine. » (*La Thébaïde*, II, II), « Et vous croyez qu'après une telle insolence » (*Alexandre*, I, III), « Pour lacérer ledit présent procès-verbal » (*Les Plaideurs*, II, IV) ou « Que lui dit-il ? Il est charmé de son esprit. » (*Ibid.*, II, VI)[7].

Ce cadre théorique est sous-jacent aux analyses des critiques les plus avertis du XIXe siècle, tel que Quicherat (1799-1884), théoricien du vers « représentant des théories classiques, ou plutôt pseudo-classiques » selon Souriau que son conservatisme irritait[8], qui bien avant la mode des césures pour l'œil se livrait déjà à des réflexions aussi approfondies que pertinentes sur le sujet. Ce grammairien était en effet alors le meilleur spécialiste des questions de versification, au point que son *Petit traité*, qui paraît en 1838, sera réédité tout au long du XIXe siècle, avec une

---

6   Sur cette conséquence, voir IV, « La réception de la césure pour l'œil ».
7   L'opposition pertinente n'est pas d'ordre binaire, entre syllabe accentuée *vs* non accentuée, mais d'ordre ternaire, entre tonique (marquée positivement)/atone (neutre)/post-tonique (marquée négativement), étant entendu que cette notion de tonique/atone/post-tonique réfère à la structure étymologique des mots, l'accentuation pouvant en français se réaliser autrement que par l'intensité lorsqu'elle ne s'est pas fortement atténuée (dissyllabes grammaticaux du type de *une*, *entre* etc.). La Grasserie (*Des principes scientifiques*, chap. XVII) opposait ainsi syllabe « tonique », syllabe « atone » et syllabe « muette », son aveu d'avoir traité de la seconde « implicitement, en même temps que de la syllabe tonique » (p. 304), soulignant l'interdépendance des deux premières catégories comme leur opposition à la troisième.
8   *L'Évolution du vers français*, p. 151 et 153.

cinquième édition en 1874 et une neuvième en 1886 (contrairement à la « deuxième » édition considérablement augmentée de 1850, jamais rééditée). Pour lui, qui n'était certes pas à l'avant-garde dans ses goûts poétiques mais dont le témoignage n'en est pas moins essentiel[9] :

> Le mot *césure* veut dire coupure. La césure d'un vers est l'endroit où il est coupé. [...] Dans l'alexandrin, il y a toujours une césure après la sixième syllabe : le vers se trouve ainsi partagé en deux hémistiches égaux [...]
> Quoique le vers alexandrin puisse se couper en différents endroits, et par conséquent avoir différentes *césures*, nous entendrons par ce mot la césure par excellence, c'est-à-dire celle de l'hémistiche [...] Pour les autres césures du grand vers, césures variables et arbitraires, nous nous servirons plus tard des mots *coupe, suspension*.

L'un des théoriciens de la versification préromantique, Louis Philipon de La Madelaine, qui distinguait pour sa part le *repos*, entendu comme catégorie métrique, de la *césure*, entendue comme catégorie syntactico-prosodique, mettait déjà en garde sur la nature du repos, affirmant que[10]

> ce serait une bien mauvaise manière de lire les vers, que de faire sentir continuellement ce repos ; ce serait les réciter en écolier, et détruire leur harmonie par une cadence monotone. Non, il n'est pas nécessaire que le lecteur s'arrête à ce repos ; il faut seulement qu'il s'y puisse arrêter.

En plein essor du romantisme, reprenant la définition de la césure comme une « coupure » dans laquelle il voit « un élément formel », emprunté à la versification latine, Quicherat évitait justement l'ambiguïté de la définition traditionnelle comme « repos[11] » Martinon apportera bien plus tard d'utiles précisions[12] :

> Il faut laisser cette expression de « repos à l'hémistiche » aux classiques, qui l'employaient faute de mieux, dans l'ignorance où ils étaient du rôle que l'accent joue dans le vers. Il y a des vers qui ont des repos, d'autres qui n'en ont point ; mais ce qu'on trouve partout, nous l'avons montré, ce sont des accents. [...] *La césure*, dans l'alexandrin, *est une division* (réelle ou formelle, peu importe) *qui détermine le rythme, et dont la place est marquée par l'accent qui est sur la sixième syllabe*. Et comme cet accent est fixe, la césure aussi est

---

9   *Traité de versification*, p. 11 (1838 et 1850).
10   *Dictionnaire portatif des rimes*, 3ᵉ éd., p. 26 et 28 (la 1ʳᵉ édition date de 1805).
11   *Traité de versification*, p. 11.
12   « Le trimètre » [1], p. 625-626 et 629.

fixe [[13]]. Si la césure coïncide avec la fin d'un élément syntaxique, ce qui est habituel, mais seulement habituel, chez les classiques, et beaucoup moins fréquent aujourd'hui, l'accent est très fort, et la césure aussi. S'il n'y a pas coïncidence entre la césure et la syntaxe, l'accent est faible et la césure aussi. Si enfin l'accent devient nul, la césure disparaît…

Et Martinon d'ajouter : « le vers aussi, car il n'y a pas de vers sans un rythme *déterminé*, et il n'y a pas de rythme *déterminé* sans césure » – où l'on peut songer, naturellement, au dodécasyllabe des derniers vers de Rimbaud. Mais il se montre ailleurs plus nuancé, écrivant à propos de vers dans lesquels un article ou une préposition d'une syllabe se trouve promu à la césure[14] : « Les Parnassiens ont encore affaibli la césure – cela semblait pourtant difficile, – mais ils ne l'ont pas supprimée complètement » : ce *pas complètement* correspond précisément au fait que la contrainte accentuelle a été simplement *neutralisée*. Quicherat lui-même évoque le rôle de l'accent tonique dont il ne perdait pas de vue la portée, aussi bien dans le cadre du mot phonologique (ex. *voyez-là*) que dans le cadre syntagmatique (*tous les hómmes*) ou intonationnel (*nous y serons tóus*), avant que ces concepts ne soient développés par la linguistique. Il définit une « règle générale » (RGC) selon laquelle la césure « doit toujours tomber sur une syllabe accentuée », avec élision d'un éventuel *e* post-tonique. S'il définit conventionnellement d'une manière trop large les situations qu'il convient d'exclure[15] : « On ne peut séparer par la césure des mots que la prononciation et la grammaire unissent, comme l'article ou l'adjectif possessif d'avec le substantif, la préposition d'avec son complément, les auxiliaires d'avec les participes, plusieurs mots formant une expression composée, comme *rendre raison*, *porter ombrage*, etc. », il prend la peine de nuancer, parlant de césure « trop faiblement marquée » après les auxiliaires, le verbe-copule, les verbes-supports (*demander raison*, *faire obstacle*, *faire connaissance*), de césure « insuffisante » lorsque le nom est séparé de l'épithète antéposée, ou lorsque l'épithète ou le complément de nom est rejeté sur le second hémistiche, critique dont il dispense les vers où le complément « remplit le vers », c'est-à-dire occupe tout le second hémistiche[16]. Ce qui retient

---

13   Étant sous-entendu que l'élision s'impose à l'hémistiche ; *cf.* RGC *infra*.
14   Art. cité, p. 45.
15   *Op. cit.*, p. 13-14.
16   *Op. cit.*, p. 14-17.

davantage l'attention dans son exposé préliminaire (LIM) et parmi les sept arguments (ARG) qu'il développe est sa position relative aux proclitiques et aux prépositions monosyllabiques où l'accent disparaît, la césure ne subsistant ainsi que pour l'œil[17] :

> [LIM] Dans toutes les langues, certains mots, surtout les monosyllabes, en particulier les pronoms et les prépositions, perdent leur accent dans la suite du discours, parce qu'ils se lient par la prononciation au mot suivant. Ainsi dans : Nous *sommes*, il *vient*, la *ville*, par *toi*, les monosyllabes *nous, il, la, par,* n'ont pas d'accent, et l'on prononce comme si les mots n'en faisaient qu'un.
>
> [ARG 2] Pour faire sentir la règle de l'hémistiche, Voltaire a fait à dessein ce mauvais vers :
>
> Adieu, je m'en vais *à* Paris pour mes affaires[18].
>
> [ARG 7] Nous avons vu combien était choquante la préposition *à* placée à la césure. Il en est de même des prépositions *pour, dans, sur, par, etc.* Mais les prépositions *après, devant, malgré,* et quelques autres également dissyllabes, sont tolérées à l'hémistiche[19].

ce que le théoricien illustre par des vers de Corneille, Boileau et Racine. C'est très précisément là que le mouvement parnassien, emboîtant le pas de Baudelaire, va procéder à un renouvellement de la pratique de l'alexandrin en usant de plus en plus volontiers de ces césures « choquantes », mais toujours avec une certaine parcimonie jusqu'à l'époque qui nous intéresse.

Ces remarques de Quicherat et d'autres de son exposé permettent de conceptualiser la notion de césure pour l'œil comme une césure qui ne satisfait pas l'oreille et n'entre pas dans le champ des licences que toléraient les poètes classiques et romantiques, déterminées par les conditions suivantes sur lesquelles des notes ajoutées à l'édition augmentée de 1850 apportent quelques précisions (N 2)[20] :

1. le mot à la césure n'est pas accentué (RGC, LIM), ce qui correspond à la neutralisation de la contrainte accentuelle ;

---

17 *Op. cit.*, p. 13, 15 et 17.
18 Voir *Encyclopédie ou Dictionnaire raisonné des sciences, des arts et des métiers*, art. « Césure ».
19 *Op. cit.*, p. 17-19.
20 *Op. cit.*, p. 322-332. Le premier point de cette note concerne la césure enjambante à l'italienne ; le troisième, la césure lyrique.

2. c'est un monosyllabe *métrique*, de nature grammaticale, autre qu'un auxiliaire ou un semi-auxiliaire, le cas échéant sous une forme élidée (ARG 1) : *et, un, sur etc.* (ARG 7) ou aussi bien *une, entre* (prép.) avec élision phonologique[21] ;

3. la septième position commence par un mot nouveau, comme l'impose notre contrainte morphologique (N 2.1) ;

4. il y a continuité de la chaîne phonologique par-delà la césure, un même syntagme et un même groupe accentuel se trouvant ainsi à cheval sur les deux hémistiches (en infraction à la règle d'ARG 2 et en lien direct avec les points 1° et 2°)

Il est d'autres situations que Quicherat aborde dans ses notes ou qu'il laisse même de côté (C-E) qu'il convient d'écarter de la qualification de « césure pour l'œil » mais qui ne constituent pas pour autant des césures admissibles ou du moins conventionnelles :

A. La 6ᵉ position ne peut pas être occupée par une syllabe « féminine », c.-à-d. une post-tonique d'origine ou un enclitique atone (RGC ; voir aussi N 2.3) ; est donc exclu un vers tel que : « Elle était belle, elle t'aimait, elle est passée » (Blanchecotte). Dans une telle situation, la contrainte accentuelle est violée et la césure abolie[22].

B. La septième position ne peut pas être occupée par une syllabe « féminine » (N 2.2) ; est donc exclu un vers tel que : « La pauvreté, squelette sombre aux yeux funestes » (Villers de l'Isle-Adam)[23]. Dans une telle situation, c'est la contrainte morphologique qui est violée et la césure est abolie[24].

C. Bien que succédant à un mot atone par nature, la césure est satisfaisante dès lors que la continuité phonologique est rompue par quelque artifice rhétorique (suspension, ellipse), syntaxique (incise, transposition) ou énonciative (discours haché[25]). La préservation de la césure est alors moins le fait d'une accentuation du mot

---

21 Quicherat n'évoque pas explicitement la question des dissyllabes à terminaison féminine.
22 Pour le cas particulier des césures lyriques, voir *infra* p. 255-256.
23 Sur ce vers, voir *infra* p. 365.
24 Pour le cas particulier des césures enjambantes à l'italienne, voir *infra* p. 255.
25 Ex. : « Puis donc, qu'on nous, permet, de prendre/Haleine, et que l'on nous[,] défend, de nous, étendre,/[...] » (Racine, *Les Plaideurs* ; éd. G. Forestier, p. 358) ; commenté par Gouvard, *Critique du vers*, p. 108.

grammatical, sujette à caution, que de la rupture prosodique qui s'ensuit ; ex[26]. :

> Pour la passante qui, d'un petit air vainqueur, (*Bonne fortune*, 2)
>
> Et ne trouvait pas, et… j'aimais le sentir bête, (*Pauvre garçon*, 3)
>
> Quelques Mémoires sur *** – Essai de poésie… (Musset, *Les secrètes pensées de Rafaël*)

D. Il n'y a pas élision *graphique* à la césure : *jusqu'*, *lorsqu'* ou *quoiqu'* sont ainsi exclus, ce qui rend suspect ce vers de Glatigny : « De la Villette jusqu'en ton sein, rue Aumaire[27] ! ». Hugo aurait écrit : « De paradis qui jusqu'en enfer se prolonge. » dans un poème posthume de *Toute la lyre*[28] ; cette graphie n'est toutefois pas de son fait et doit être imputée à l'éditeur de ses *Œuvres inédites*, son manuscrit portant bien lisiblement « jusque », l'*e* occultant une apostrophe inscrite dans un premier temps. Dans de telles situations, pour correspondre à une frontière de mots, la césure n'en est pas moins rendue « invisible » par l'agglutination des mots concernés dont seule l'apostrophe signale l'autonomie.

E. Il n'y a pas de trait d'union à la césure, ce qui exclut des vers tels que : « De meurt-de-faim, de va-nu-pieds, de rien qui vaille, » (L.-X. de Ricard)[29] ou « Mon pauvre homme, le Mont-de-Piété refuse » (Coppée)[30].

La rareté de l'apostrophe et du trait d'union à l'hémistiche ne signifie cependant pas que les vers interdits par la norme, qui relèvent de D et E, ne sont pas césurés : Ricard se refuse en effet de placer des polysyllabes à cheval sur l'hémistiche en dehors, précisément, de ce genre de cas qui respectent, dans une certaine mesure, la contrainte morphologique (la césure tombe entre deux composants) et la contrainte accentuelle (*va* et *Mont*, mots pleins constitutifs, sont accentués ou tout au moins

---

26 Bien que semblable, le cas de « "O lyre ! O délire ! O…" — Sonnet — Attention ! » (*I Sonnet*, 14) est différent, la particule exclamative portant un accent de durée et de hauteur, indépendamment de l'aposiopèse qui ne fait que le renforcer.

27 *Qu'est-il devenu ?* (*Gilles et Pasquins*, XIX).

28 Signalé par Gouvard, *Critique du vers*, p. 103, n. 40.

29 *L'Apologie du sire Pugnaire de Faucancourt*, dans *PC* (1876), p. 344.

30 *La Grève des Forgerons*, p. 10.

accentuables). On a pu penser que c'est l'exigence du blanc typographique qui aurait amené Hugo à user d'un subterfuge qui étonnait Martinon dans « Ils en sont à l'A, B, C, D, du cœur humain[31] ; » si ce n'est que cette manière d'écrire était une alternative graphique, comme le rapporte Littré, *s.v.* « ABC » (*DLF* I, 10 ; il précise sous une entrée à part que *ABCD* « Se dit quelquefois pour ABC ») : « L'Académie écrit A B C en séparant les lettres ; d'autres écrivent ABC en les joignant ; d'autres A, B, C, avec des virgules. » Hugo faisait partie de ces derniers, comme le confirme ce vers de *Cromwell* : « Au lieu d'A, B, C, dire : Aleph, Beth et Ghimel ! » ; et s'il publie parallèlement dans *Les Contemplations* (I, VII) : « Et le dévastateur du vieil A B C D ; », c'est avec là encore une dissociation des lettres constitutives du composé sans que la césure ne soit en rien concernée.

Ce point E devrait en principe exclure *très* lorsqu'il se trouve lié par un trait d'union à l'adjectif, au participe ou à l'adverbe qu'il modalise, si ce n'est que cette situation spécifique est un leurre[32]. Dans ce contexte, le trait d'union est en effet un usage typographique que l'écriture ne s'imposait généralement pas, qui perdure jusqu'aux années 1860 environ du fait de sa promotion par l'Académie jusqu'à la sixième édition de son dictionnaire et qui l'abandonnera en 1878, avant que la profession ne soit gagnée par l'usage moderne. Deux ans avant la publication de cette septième édition, Larousse continue à introduire le trait d'union tout en faisant le constat qu'« Un assez grand nombre d'écrivains semblent portés à rejeter cet usage » (*GDU* XV, 469). On assiste en effet dans ces années à un hiatus entre le texte publié et le manuscrit fourni par les auteurs, plus spécialement peut-être dans le domaine de la poésie. Le trait d'union s'immisce alors comme un corps étranger dans le système graphique original des poètes, vraisemblablement sinon certainement inséré par le prote :

Vous aimez mieux, c'est très-habile et j'applaudis, (Vacquerie)[33]

---

31   *Les Contemplations*, I, XIII. Martinon, « Le trimètre » [2], p. 52 : « il a cru sans doute que s'il eût écrit *abécédé*, le vers eût été complètement changé ! Idée bizarre ! Singulier respect de la forme extérieure ! ».

32   Indépendamment de l'aspect ici traité, l'adverbe fait partie de ces catégories grises dont l'acceptation est problématique. Son sens lui confère un caractère accentogène qui ne change rien à sa dépendance prosodique à l'égard du mot qu'il modifie.

33   *Souvent homme varie*, p. 38.

> Mes prophètes sont très-savants, et j'ai trois dieux
> Très-puissants, [...] (Leconte de Lisle)[34]

> Vu de trois quarts et très-ombré, suivant l'usage (Verlaine)[35]

> Le très-savant et très-miséricordieux (Heredia)[36]

Ce problème ne concerne toutefois pas *Les Amours jaunes*, d'une part parce que *très* ne s'y trouve jamais à la césure, d'autre part parce que l'imprimeur se conforme sans doute à l'usage de Corbière qui n'emploie généralement pas le trait d'union dans cette situation, à l'exception significative de *très-sensés* dans « les gens très-sensés » de *Male-Fleurette*, le syntagme adjectival perdant alors son caractère simplement évaluatif pour acquérir le statut d'un composé à fonction classifiante, comme dans le syntagme adverbial d'« un sacristain très-bien » (*Sonnet posthume*). Il procède de même dans les composés nominaux : « Ma très-chère » (*Vendetta*), « Très-haute devant le Très-haut » (*La Rapsode foraine*). Ceci étant, il convient de noter que Corbière construit *très* avec le trait d'union dans les seules deux occurrences de l'album Noir, dont une à la rime[37] :

> Dépareillé partout, très-bon, plus mauvais, très-
> fou, ne me souffrant pas... Encor si j'étais bête !

Sans ignorer que la question de l'accent est très discutée au XIXe siècle, le traité de Gustave Weigand publié en 1863 peut donner un aperçu de ce que les contemporains pouvaient percevoir comme des mots « naturellement inaccentués », sans prétendre, naturellement, que leur compétence linguistique se haussât toujours à la hauteur de vue de ce théoricien[38]. L'auteur classe ainsi divers mots grammaticaux d'une ou deux syllabes, pour autant que la seconde soit articulée sur un *e* caduc : 1°) les pronoms conjoints ; 2°) « Les petits mots de rapport et de détermination, savoir l'article, le nom numéral[39], le verbe auxiliaire, la préposition, la conjonction » ; 3°) les pronoms relatifs simples ; 4°) l'adjectif relatif *quel* ; 5°) « Quelques adverbes monosyllabes (*si*, *plus*, *trop*) qui s'appuient sur le

---

34   *La Vigne de Naboth* (*Poésies/Poèmes barbares*).
35   *César Borgia* (*Poëmes saturniens*).
36   *La détresse d'Atahualpa*, dans *PC* (1869), p. 391.
37   Au f° 24r°, dans « Jeune philosophe en dérive » ; éd. Houzé, *ffocsoR*, p. 28.
38   *Traité de versification*, p. 51-57.
39   Les exemples donnés montrent qu'il s'agit des adjectifs numéraux.

mot suivant » ; 6°) « la particule négative *ne*[40] ». Weigand n'ignore pas non plus les déplacements d'accents liés à l'enclise, ni la fonction jouée par le positionnement des mots d'où peut résulter la désaccentuation de formes intrinsèquement accentuées ou au contraire l'accentuation de formes intrinsèquement inaccentués[41].

Le développement d'un tel métadiscours implique de la part des poètes confrontés plus directement que d'autres aux propriétés formelles du langage une certaine compétence linguistique qui devait orienter leur travail de composition et leurs expériences rythmiques. Il est toutefois à noter que certains mots se pliaient plus difficilement à cette rationalisation de l'accentuation, pour lesquels nous parlerons de « catégories grises », tels que les déterminants indéfinis, les numéraux qui n'entrent pas dans la classe des déterminants[42], les adverbes d'intensité, l'adverbe *tout* ou les formes monosyllabiques des auxiliaires, qui, de par leur sémantisme, reçoivent une certaine force prosodique qui les distingue nettement des déterminants ou des pronoms conjoints et peuvent ainsi recevoir un accent d'insistance tout en entretenant une liaison forte avec le mot qui les régit. On peut même s'interroger sur le cas de l'interjection *ô* qui fait sans conteste l'objet d'une accentuation avec un allongement spécifique mais que, dans les corpus que nous avons dépouillés, nous n'avons rencontré à la césure que dans un vers de Verlaine, daté de 1873, aux accents nettement marqués en 4ᵉ et 8ᵉ positions : « En terreurs vaines, ô ma Reine. Je te dis [...] » (*La Grâce*).

De façon pratique, nous limitons délibérément ici la notion de césure pour l'œil aux alexandrins dont la 6ᵉ position est indifféremment occupée, dans les conditions ci-dessus énumérées, par un mot grammatical atone constitué d'une syllabe métrique (avec élision le cas échéant), définis par sa nature grammaticale et son degré de dépendance syntaxique ou prosodique au regard du mot qui le régit ou du groupe auquel il se rattache[43], à savoir : 1°) des proclitiques de premier ordre : articles

40 Weigand considère explicitement comme toniques les emplois pronominaux de *autre*, *tout* et *un* (num.), mais ne se prononce pas sur les adjectifs indéfinis ou les numéraux cardinaux.
41 *Op. cit.*, p. 54-57.
42 Même si les cardinaux peuvent, au moins en apparence, prendre la place des déterminants (ils rendent en fait souvent la détermination superflue).
43 Sauf artifice rhétorique tel qu'aposiopèse ou incise, comme chez Verlaine, dans « Et celle due à votre, hélas ! fidélité ! » (*Pour Marie****, dans *Dédicaces*, 2ᵉ éd., LXXIX). Une

(dont *une* devant voyelle), déterminants possessifs ou démonstratifs (dont *cette* devant voyelle), pronoms conjoints antéposés, semi-négation *ne* en 6ᵉ position ; 2°) des proclitiques de second ordre, qui s'appuient sur un groupe accentuel dont ils ne dépendent pas sur le plan syntaxique : pronoms personnels sujets, pronom *ce* introduisant une proposition relative[44] ; 3°) les prépositions métriquement monosyllabiques (ce qui inclut *contre* ou *entre* devant voyelle). Nous excluons les prépositions monosyllabiques terminant des locutions composées, telles que le *à* de *jusqu'à* ainsi que le dénominal *par* de *de par* dont l'entrée dans un processus de composition leur vaut un accent de proéminence, partageant ainsi le sort des prépositions ou locutions prépositionnelles polysyllabiques métriquement masculines (syllabe finale de pleine articulation) telles que *devant* ou *à travers*[45].

Nous n'en pensons pas moins que la notion de césure pour l'œil doit être étendue à divers mots ressortissant de catégories grises au regard de l'accent en fonction de leur contextualisation : les césures proprement parnassiennes ne se distinguent pas en effet exclusivement par la question de la déficience d'accent mais aussi par le degré de cohésion des formes que s'interdisent les romantiques avec les mots qui les suivent. De façon plus précise, nous considérons qu'entrent également dans le champ de la césure pour l'œil les conjonctions de coordination qui ne font office que de liaison (*et*, *ou*, *ni*)[46], les pronoms relatifs simples non précédés d'une préposition ou du démonstratif *ce* (ce qui exclut *à qui*,

---

transposition est en outre au demeurant possible (*cf.* « Et faux toupet avec, magistrale, une lippe » dans *Invectives*, XIX : *Autre magistrat*). Voir aussi nos précisions dans IV, « Présentation du corpus parnassien ».

44   Jusqu'ici, il s'agit des éléments ressortissant du « critère C » de Gouvard, *Critique du vers*, p. 87 (plutôt que de celui de Cornulier, *Théorie du vers*, p. 139, *Art poëtique*, p. 244-245, qui contient bizarrement des enclitiques). Toutefois, nous n'acceptons *ça* que lorsqu'il s'agit de l'ersatz populaire de *cela*, non d'un emploi clairement dépréciatif, auquel cas un minimum d'accentuation est requis, comme dans (pas d'exemple en 6ᵉ position) « Et ça fut jeté sur le quai, » (*Le Bossu Bitor*) *vs* « … Et je ris… parce que ça me fait un peu mal. » (*Le Poète contumace*, 164).

45   Leur degré d'acceptabilité est en effet supérieur, comme on peut le constater dans l'emploi par Hugo (mais semble-t-il pas avant 1852) du composé *jusqu'à* ; *cf.* Rochette, *L'alexandrin chez Victor Hugo*, p. 125-126, et Gouvard, *Critique du vers*, p. 100, qui donne pour *de par*, p. 94 (et 98), un argument étymologique non pertinent dans la mesure où l'expression est grammaticalisée.

46   Les autres conjonctions de coordination présentent en effet une moindre cohésion entre les termes coordonnés.

pour qui, ce qui/que, jusqu'où), les conjonctions de subordination simples (ce qui exclut *comme si, parce que, ne … que etc.*) sauf lorsque ces éléments sont suivis d'un repos ou d'un syntagme transposé. Le périmètre de la césure pour l'œil peut certainement être élargi à d'autres mots grammaticaux encore, d'une syllabe métrique, dès lors qu'ils sont suivis d'un monosyllabe métrique ou d'un dissyllabe féminin qui les régit, comme dans « Que le langage à nul être n'est interdit[47], ». Il serait selon nous excessif de l'étendre à ce genre de monosyllabes en dehors de ce contexte, bien que la plupart soient à peu près exclus de l'hémistiche tant dans la tradition classique que, en général, dans la romantique : pour présenter une cohésion relativement forte avec le mot suivant, de tels mots se prêtent à une accentuation secondaire, tels que les prédéterminants et déterminants indéfinis d'une syllabe, les numéraux ordinaux ou les adverbes d'intensité[48]. Nos commentaires relatifs aux *Amours jaunes* porteront également sur de telles particules.

---

47 Des Essarts, *Le Retour du fumiste*, p. 22. Pour des exemples chez Corbière, voir *infra* p. 220.
48 Dans « L'alexandrin de Victor Hugo », Gouvard apporte quelques lumières sur certaines classes de mots ou d'expressions dont l'acceptation à la césure est une marque de la pratique hugolienne du grand vers. Voir aussi, à propos de Verlaine, sa thèse *Recherches*, p. 272-334.

L'OCCULTATION DE LA CÉSURE
CHEZ CORBIÈRE

Dans *Les Amours jaunes*, Corbière admet plus volontiers que Baudelaire les césures pour l'œil. Comme les Parnassiens eux-mêmes, il ne cède pas au procédé dans tous les poèmes du recueil dont la composition s'est étalée sur plusieurs années, et on ne trouve généralement qu'un cas par poème concerné, à l'exception de *Litanie du sommeil* où il fait preuve du plus grand zèle (9 cas, soit 5,5 % des vers), dans *Le Poète contumace* (5), *Le navire en partance* (4), *Matelots* et *Le Bossu Bitor* (3 chacun). Il est assez frappant de constater que son acceptation du procédé parnassien ne s'accompagne guère de traitements semblables à la rime où l'on peut tout juste relever l'emploi de l'article contracté ou de l'indéfini[1] :

> « … Prendrais-tu pas quelque chose
>   « Qu'on arrose
> « Avec n'importe quoi… du
> « Jus de perles dans des coupes
>   « D'or ?… Tu coupes !…
> « Mais moi ? Mina, me prends-tu ? » (*Après la pluie*, 61-66)

> Elle était riche de vingt ans,
> Moi j'étais jeune de vingt francs,
> Et nous fîmes bourse commune,
> Placée, à fond-perdu [*sic*], dans une
> Infidèle nuit de printemps… (*À la mémoire de Zulma*, 1-5)

Son placement à la rime s'accompagne d'une mise en relief du morphème (et, par suspension, du syntagme qu'il introduit) contrairement à

---

1   En dehors des *Amours jaunes*, voir, dans *Le Panayoti* : « là, et c'est bleuf en double [*apocope*], qu'on navigue [*id.*] comm'sur une/Pancarte à Perruquier ; […] » (16-18) ; « Tout'-d'-même [*apocope*] j'étions gaillards tout le monde à bord par-ce [*sic*]/que [*id.*] j'attendins, pour l'bouquet d'la fin, la sacrée [*id.*] farce. (72-73).

ce qui se passe à l'hémistiche[2]. Corbière recourt au procédé dès l'album Noir, dans sa *Petite pouësie en vers passionnés de 12 pieds sur un air sensitive et sur Rosalba*, daté de 1867, où il en use même intensément, à raison de trois vers sur un total de vingt-deux, soit une proportion de un sur sept que le poète n'atteindra plus jamais :

L'oiseau, becquetant sa cerise souriante, (1)

Balance, illusée, en butinant ses deux seins, (4)

Redoublent d'azur en se mirant dans ses yeux. (12)

Ces vers ont en commun l'accentuation marquée de la 5e position, comme dans les formes syncopées romantiques qu'il a également pratiquées[3], mais ici, la présence d'un monosyllabe atone en 6e position accuse l'effet de rupture, faute de pouvoir offrir la marque accentuelle requise par la césure, avec une cohésion phonologique qui ne laisse pas la moindre place à un allongement qui pourrait la sauver. Un accent secondaire affecte la 8e ou la 9e position sans altérer pour autant l'effet recherché avec le déplacement de la coupe médiane dans la direction opposée, en deçà de la césure. Un autre accent, de rang variable, affecte la 2e ou la 3e position, trois fois avec une pause. Ces premiers emplois de la césure pour l'œil attirent d'autant plus l'attention qu'il s'agit uniquement de rythmes syncopés, formes plutôt marginales dans l'histoire de la césure pour l'œil. *Petite pouësie* apparaît ainsi comme un poème expérimental où Corbière s'essaie à un nouveau procédé affranchissant la syncope romantique de la contrainte accentuelle, procédé qu'il a bien dû trouver quelque part, ce que l'on tâchera d'éclaircir dans une autre partie[4].

Cette syncope rythmique qui déséquilibre la balance conventionnelle de l'alexandrin dans un mouvement ascendant (5 + 7), peut s'observer neuf fois dans *Les Amours jaunes*, trois fois avec une pause significative, et dans les trois cas devant la conjonction *et*, non suivie d'un repos. Une fois sur trois, on trouve un accent secondaire en 8e position[5] :

---

2   Nous reviendrons plus loin sur la distinction des deux procédés (voir p. 271).
3   Voir *supra*, le chap. « Alexandrins syncopés ».
4   Voir V, « L'influence de Banville ».
5   Dans une variante copiée sur la p. 83 de son exemplaire personnel (A), il déforme après coup le v. 47 du *Fils de Lamartine* (*AJ*) de façon à promouvoir une conjonction circonstancielle

Comme un sourd aveugle, et sa sœur dans un sillon[6], (*Frère et sœur jumeaux*, 22)

Grosse Nudité du chanoine en jupon court ! [...]
– Le Porc – rognonnant sa prière du matin ; (*Litanie du sommeil*, 115, 154)

L'équipage au diable, et Bitor...... toujours Bitor. [...]
Gardiens de la couleur, gardiens du pur contour... (*Le Bossu Bitor*, 72, 79)

Nous cherchions tous deux à nous dire quelque chose (*Le Novice en partance*, 63)

Dans les autres cas, l'accent secondaire tombe une fois sur la 7e, deux fois sur la 9e :

L'*Autre* n'est pas même à prendre avec des pincettes... (*Le Poète contumace*, 85)

Une bonne Vierge à la façon de Marseille : (*Le Novice en partance*, 83)

Un portrait de fille, et deux petites babouches, (*Lettre du Mexique*, 19)

Naturellement, l'effet de syncope est neutralisé par l'aposiopèse qui restitue à la césure visibilité et perceptibilité :

Ris ! montre tes dents ! mais... nous avons la police, (*Féminin singulier*, 7)

Et ne trouvait pas, et... j'aimais le sentir bête, (*Pauvre garçon*, 3)

À propos du vers 22 de *Frère et sœur jumeaux*, pour lequel il parle d'une « cadence dissymétrique 5-7 avec césure[7] forte après le cinquième pied », G. Martin a souligné l'importance particulière de ce rythme aux yeux du poète qui l'a conservé malgré un remaniement assez conséquent du texte[8]. On peut aussi relever un cas de syncope inversée où la coupe majeure est déplacée dans la direction opposée, au-delà de la césure, déterminant un rythme descendant (7 + 5), la présence d'un accent en 4e position n'altérant en rien la perception de la rupture de rythme : « Et

---

de temps à l'hémistiche ; deux pages plus loin (B), il introduit un pronom conjoint à la césure d'un vers nouveau (Houzé, « Le dernier Corbière », p. 333 et 334) : « Ce Fils avait vingt ans quand, Mère inoculée, » dans *AJ* devient « il avait vingt ans quand sa mère inoculée » dans A ; B : « Signor pouvez-vous me servir de cicerone » (p. 85).

6   La variante de l'album Noir introduit une virgule après *et*, ce qui change tout.

7   Au sens non métrique.

8   « Trois variantes », p. 59. Dans sa transcription de l'album Noir, Houzé, *ffocsoR*, p. 26, introduit après *et* une virgule que le fac-similé (f° 14r°) ne semble pas porter.

dans les siècles des siècles... ... Comme c'est long ! » (*Grand opéra*, 4).
Examinons à présent les quinze autres cas de césures pour l'œil. Sept
vers ont un rythme ternaire équiparti articulé sur deux accents majeurs
de niveau égal (dernier vers) ou non, l'accent dominant figurant alors
plus souvent en 4e qu'en 8e position (cas marqués d'un astérisque) :

> Prends mon sonnet, moi ta sonnette à faveur rose ; [...]
> La Mer roucoule sa *Berceuse pour naufrages ;* (*Sonnet à sir Bob*, 10, 114)

> Arche où le hère et le boa changent de peaux !* [...]
> Et les crins fous de ta Déesse ardente et blonde ?... (*Litanie du sommeil*, 137,
>   152)

> Et la rosée et le soleil ont eu ses fleurs...* (*Le Fils de Lamartine*, 34)

> – Le Cid... un cid par un *été* de carnaval : (*Hidalgo !*, 8)

> Filé son câble par le bout sans *fignolure...* (*Le Novice en partance*, 43)

Douze peuvent être ramenés à des rythmes ascendants 4-8 :

> – Son seul regret fut de n'être pas sa maîtresse. – (*Épitaphe*, 3)

> Pour mourir seul ou pour vivre par contumace... (*Le Poète contumace*, 38)

> Et qui t'assieds sur les casques-à-mèche honnêtes ! [...]
> Face-de-bois pour les créanciers et leur sorte ! [...]
> Conte de Fée où *le Roi* se laisse assoupir ! [...]
> Coup de rapière dans l'eau du fleuve Léthé ! (*Litanie du sommeil*, 18, 74, 91,
>   133)

> – Ils ont toujours, pour leur *bonne femme de mère*, [...]
> Riches de gloire et de trois cents francs de retraite, (*Matelots*, 59, 94)

> Lui, son navire et des cocotiers... au Chili. [...]
> – Va donc Paillasse ! Et le trousse-galant t'emporte ! (*Le Bossu Bitor*, 14, 101)

> – Je tremble aussi que vous n'oubliiez mes tendresses (*Le Novice*, 97)

> Rends ton gabion, rends tes *Procès-verbaux divers ;* (*Le Douanier*, 96)

Trois autres présentent un accent en 8e position mais pas sur la 4e ;
l'accent majeur se situe alors toujours sur la troisième, et dans deux cas,
on trouve en 4e ou 6e position la conjonction de comparaison *comme* qui
depuis Hugo et Baudelaire peut, à la rime ou à l'hémistiche (le second),
faire l'objet d'une mise en relief :

Crénelé comme la mâchoire d'une vieille, [...]
Tu sais bien, comme dans *Inès de La Sierra*... (*Le Poète contumace*, 8, 144)

Qui végète loin du vulgaire intelligent, (*Frère et sœur jumeaux*, 26)

Restent quatre vers, dans lesquels l'absence d'appuis en 4e ou/et 8e position confère au vers la liberté de la prose, ce qu'un Verlaine n'acceptera pas avant les années 1880 :

– Du *chic* pur ? – Eh qui me donnera des ficelles ! (*Ça*, 17)

Chat qui joue avec le peloton d'Atropos ! (*Litanie du sommeil*, 145)

Vous, vous n'êtes que des *pelletas* militaires... (*Matelots*, 102)

Par les crabes. Et ça fut jeté sur le quai, (*Le Bossu Bitor*, 248)

encore que le premier soit bien accentué aussi en 4e position, sur l'interjection, si l'on s'en tient au texte imprimé, l'absence de point d'exclamation laissant toutefois planer un doute sur la possibilité d'une coquille pour « Et », hypothèse que rend vraisemblable l'absence de virgule après l'interjection. Il est vrai que l'absence d'une quelconque ponctuation peut s'observer au v. 13 de *Fleur d'art* (« Si tu n'étais fausse, eh serais-tu vraie ?... »), ou encore au v. 20 d'*Insomnie*[9] :

Insomnie, es-tu donc pas belle ?...
Eh pourquoi, lubrique pucelle,
Nous étreindre entre tes genoux ?

On n'en est pas moins frappé par le fait que nos quatre vers sont accentués sur les positions 3 et 9[10]. Ce genre de vers prosaïques n'est pas absent du second recueil du *Parnasse contemporain*, où l'on relève :

Et vous, Nymphes qui dans les solitudes vastes [...]
Et des aigles qui, pour s'approcher du soleil, (Banville, *La Cithare*)

---

9   Voir aussi « Eh allons donc ! » (*La Fin*, 21). À noter que *ah* peut également se trouver dépourvu de point d'exclamation (ou de virgule) : voir p. ex. « Ah splendide ! » (« C'est la bohême... », 13), « Ah tu ne comprends pas ? » (*Féminin singulier*, 9) ; *oh* également : « Oh mon Dieu » (*Femme*, 3), « Oh le carcan ôté ! » (*Libertà*, 48) *etc.* Le même phénomène se rencontre dans les autographes du poète : on peut ainsi relever trois cas semblables de *ah* et autant de *oh* dans l'album *Noir*.

10   Dans le v. 102 de *Matelots*, l'accent dominant n'en est pas moins sur la 1re position du fait de la mise en relief du pronom.

> Trop tôt belle & que son innocence défend. (Cros, *Lento*)
>
> Descendre à travers ma rêverie en silence, (Mallarmé, *Poëme de Hérodiade*)

Le vers de Charles Cros comme le second de Banville reproduisent cette particularité des vers corbiériens accentués en 3ᵉ et 9ᵉ positions. En dehors des proclitiques, des prépositions monosyllabiques et de la conjonction *et*, on peut relever dans le recueil de Corbière deux autres cas de césures pour l'œil, après un auxiliaire ou le verbe-copule est immédiatement suivi en 7ᵉ position de la syllabe tonique de l'attribut dépourvu de complément[11] :

> – Noblesse oblige. – Il est saint : à chaque foyer (*Un riche en Bretagne*, 31)
>
> Étarque à bloc ! – L'homme est libre et la mer est grande – (*Le Novice en partance*, 39)

Dans les deux cas, la césure semble s'être déplacée d'un rang vers l'avant, mais l'accent principal tombe en quatrième position : on retrouve là encore le penchant de Corbière pour les rythmes ascendants 4-8. Deux autres vers retiennent l'attention, où Corbière place la césure après la conjonction *que*, introduisant une proposition ou un syntagme :

> … Et je ris… parce que ça me fait un peu mal. » (*Le Poète contumace*, 164)
>
> Tu n'étais vierge que de sa virginité ! (*Le Fils de Lamartine*, 24)

Ces cas doivent être relativisés. En effet, de par son statut syntaxique, cette conjonction a toujours bénéficié d'une certaine force prosodique qui la distingue de la plupart des mots grammaticaux, bien que la critique eût toujours peiné à lui reconnaître une quelconque particularité prosodique, d'autant que la particule entre ici dans des composés (*parce que*, *ne … que* restrictif) qui lui confère un accent de proéminence. C'est ainsi que Martinon s'étonnait de relever un tel emploi chez Laprade avec l'adverbe exclamatif[12] :

> C'est d'abord chez Laprade – on ne s'attendait guère à voir Laprade en cette affaire, – Laprade, lui qui repousse absolument la pratique du trimètre,

---

11 Au contraire de « Vous dont le métier est d'être toujours dorés » (*Veder Napoli*, 26), où le second hémistiche offre une cohésion prosodique qui affecte la structure rythmique du vers partagée entre 5-7 (diction naturelle) et 6-6 (diction « métrique » au demeurant forcée), selon le modèle d'exécution adopté.

12 Dans *La Samaritaine* (*Poèmes évangéliques*).

c'est Laprade, qui ose écrire ce vers; lequel n'était point indispensable pour respecter la parole sacrée :

« Donne, a-t-il dit, et *que* je boive. » Elle s'avance…

Mais, s'il s'agit sans doute du texte de la première édition (1852) – que nous n'avons pu consulter –, on lit dès la deuxième, parue l'année suivante, un alexandrin régularisé (1853, p. 161) :

« Donne, lui dit le Christ, j'ai soif. »

Elle s'avance, [...]

Si la correction montre bien la réticence de Laprade à l'accepter à la césure, le fait qu'un poète aussi classique dans sa pratique de l'alexandrin ait pu laisser passer ce vers témoigne de la réelle saillance prosodique de la conjonction. Pour notre part, nous ne trouvons l'emploi de cette particule à la césure qu'à partir de 1866, d'abord chez Verlaine (*Poëmes saturniens*), suivi de Jean Aicard (*Les Jeunes croyances*, 1867) et de Coppée (*Poëmes modernes*, 1869), soit chez des poètes qui sont déjà les plus ardents adeptes de la césure pour l'œil[13] :

Diaphanes, et que le clair de lune fait (Verlaine)

N'est pas heureux, c'est que son prochain ne veut pas. (Aicard)

D'avoir peur. Non. C'est que je serai dans une île (Coppée)

L'influence parnassienne apparaît donc dès l'album Noir, ce qui ne veut pas dire que Corbière a nécessairement été conquis dès cette époque par le procédé : sa version du *Douanier* est encore vierge de ce genre de césures, sans parler de *Litanie du sommeil* dont l'état est trop embryonnaire pour être significatif. Par contre, *Le Panayoti* en comporte deux, chaque fois avec *une*, apocopé :

l'tonnerrr' de Dieu n'est qu'une d'mi-foutaise à côté. (29)

ça n'fait qu'un pli, comme une dégeulade [*sic*] qui déborde. (87)

---

13   Respectivement dans les poèmes *Nuit du Walpurgis classique*, *Misère et Soleil*, *Angelus*.

LA CÉSURE DANS LES MOTS COMPOSÉS

Corbière ne va jamais jusqu'à s'attaquer au dernier verrou de l'alexandrin traditionnel qui interdit de placer une syllabe post-tonique en 6ᵉ position. Là où il se démarque plus particulièrement des poètes contemporains, c'est par son goût de mettre des mots composés, grammaticalisés ou non, à cheval sur les deux hémistiches – pour lesquels nous n'avons ici en vue que les cas où la composition est marquée par l'emploi de tirets –, indices montrant le plus souvent clairement la prégnance de la césure médiane dans ces écarts : *savoir-|mourir, Navaja-Dolorès-|y-Crucificcion, Mille-et-u|ne-nuits, extrait-|d'âge, philoso|phe-errant, rouler-|plat, pieds-|de-banc-de-cabaret, roi|de-soûls, tour-|à-tour, flambant-|neuf, Mary-|saloppe* (ces quatre vers dans *Le Bossu Bitor*), *Mary-|gratis, bon|ne-femme*[1]. Seul *Mille-et-u|ne-nuits*, sur lequel nous reviendrons, fait exception, mais dans tous les autres, l'accentuation de la 6ᵉ position est en effet maintenue, l'éventuelle post-tonique subséquente étant réduite par élision (*philoso|phe-errant*) ou articulée en 7ᵉ position (*roi|de-soûls* et *bon|ne-femme*). Il n'y a par conséquent pas abolition de la césure dans la plupart des vers concernés – qui ne s'accompagnent pas particulièrement d'appuis en 4ᵉ ou 8ᵉ positions –, si ce n'est dans *Mille-et-u|ne-nuits, roi|de-soûls* et *bon|ne-femme* qui présentent du moins un accent secondaire, sur lesquels nous reviendrons au chapitre suivant. Abstraction faite de ces cas, Corbière se plie à l'usage de ses contemporains lorsqu'ils admettent des mots composés enjambant la césure, ce qui est rare, comme on peut le voir déjà chez Hugo dans un registre satirique, avec *Napoléon-|le-Petit*, dans un alexandrin où la césure continue à jouer son rôle structurant en délimitant nettement les deux hémistiches, calque de formations telles qu'*Alexandre le Grand, Philippe le Magnanime etc.*, où l'introduction de traits d'union souligne ironiquement la caractérisation[2] :

---

1   Voir la liste dressée par Gouvard, *Critique du vers*, p. 212-214.
2   Pour une recension commentée des vers de ce type antérieurs aux *Amours jaunes*, voir Gouvard, *Critique du vers*, p. 204-212. Nous en écartons le cas de l'incipit de *Talaveyra*

« Sera Napoléon-le-Petit dans l'histoire » (*Les Châtiments*, 1953, II, VII). On pourrait en dire autant de tel vers de Musset (*La Loi sur la presse*, 1835), même si la 8ᵉ position (et la 4ᵉ également) y est accentuée, et de même d'un vers d'Auguste Vacquerie (*A un conquérant*, dans *L'Enfer de l'esprit*), avec des composés de nature différente :

> L'an de la quatre-vingt-cinquième olympiade, (Musset)
>
> O grand homme ! prétexte-à-déclamations ! (Vacquerie)

On sait que Baudelaire lui-même pratiqua – marginalement – la troncation d'un mot composé dans une pièce également satirique recueillie dans *Les Épaves*, où la césure continue malgré tout à jouer son rôle (*Sur les débuts d'Amina Boschetti*) :

> Je ne connais, en fait de nymphes bocagères,
> Que celle de Montagne-aux-Herbes-potagères

Chez Hugo, les traits d'union séparent les éléments d'un composé non grammaticalisé et par conséquent interprétables directement. Baudelaire procède de façon inverse avec un nom de rue, en réactivant le sens littéral de l'expression. Musset, que ce soit intentionnellement ou non, ne place pas la césure au sein de *quatre-vingt* dont le sens n'est pas réductible à l'addition du sens de ses composants, mais entre dizaines et unités. On ne peut bien entendu ignorer que ces composés ayant plus de six syllabes, leur intégration ne pouvait que se faire au détriment (apparent) de la césure, mais le phénomène se répète avec des composés plus courts, sans que le poète recherche un cadre rythmique particulier susceptible de rendre le procédé plus acceptable, comme on peut le remarquer même chez un Mérat, dans *Les Villes de marbre*, avec un authentique nom composé (et un rythme syncopé descendant) :

> Le regard bleu du lac d'Albano s'ouvrira,
> Joyeux des beaux lauriers-roses et des olives. (*Rome*, XI)

chez Ernest d'Hervilly, dans *La Lanterne en vers* (1868), avec un composé libre :

(*Toute la lyre*, I, I, II) car, dans l'édition originale (comme dans le manuscrit), le nom de la ville est dépourvu de traits d'union : « C'est à Talaveyra de la Reine, en Espagne. »

> [...] mais voici le cheval,
> Seigneur ! que le pur-sang-vélocipède imite ;

et dans *Les Baisers* (1872), aussi bien avec un composé libre – où la césure sépare deux syntagmes – qu'avec un nom propre :

> Je fouillais à deux-mains-trois-cœurs dans vos affaires, (*Puérilités*)
>
> Crépuscule, Jardin-des-Oliviers du cœur ! (*Affres d'amour*)

Lorsque Banville y recourt, en 1841, c'est dans un rythme descendant 8-4 (ce qui n'est pas en soi significatif)[3] :

> Encore, à l'Ambigu-Comique, ce serait
> Facile, on trouverait un passage secret
> Dans un mur féodal. [...]

On peut remarquer que Glatigny, dans *Gilles et Pasquins* (1872), recourt à ce procédé dans un rythme ternaire équiparti dont la structure, au demeurant, n'est pas soulignée par des pauses : « Ce n'est pas lui que Vrain-Lucas eût mis dedans. » (*Déjà nommé*) ; ou encore que Coppée, la même année, s'assure toujours d'un accent en 8ᵉ position dans *Les Humbles* (1872)[4] :

> Les habits d'opéra-comique qu'il fallait (p. 11)
>
> Dans le petit café-concert de la barrière, (p. 33)
>
> Et, bien que les après-midi soient étouffants, (p. 44)
>
> Chef-d'œuvre d'un tailleur-concierge de Montrouge, (p. 134)

Dans *La Grève des forgerons* (1869), il écrit un vers de la même veine : « Je pris mes deux petits-enfants sur mes genoux, » (p. 7), dans le suivant – qu'on rapprochera de celui de Baudelaire –, dépourvu d'accents en 4ᵉ et/ou 8ᵉ positions, et s'arrange du moins pour que la césure tombe après un mot fort, non une préposition : « Mon pauvre homme, le Mont-de-Piété refuse » (p. 10). Dans le seul vers de la sorte qu'il avait publié à cette époque, dans l'épilogue de *Poëmes saturniens* (« La Colombe, le

---

3   *Stéphen*, XLVIII (qui deviendra *Les Baisers de Pierre*) dans *Les Cariatides*, p. 97.
4   Voir les exemples relevés par Gouvard, *Critique du vers*, p. 210-212, qui en donne un commentaire stylistique.

Saint-Esprit, le saint Délire»), Verlaine recourt à un rythme ternaire asymétrique, accentué en 3ᵉ et 8ᵉ position[5]. La présence ou non d'un accent dominant en 8ᵉ position ne permet donc pas même de prétendre que, dépourvus de césure pour l'œil, ces vers ne sont pas césurés, même si l'on ne peut l'exclure *a priori* : une telle interprétation dépend en effet des pratiques versificatoires dont ces vers sont le fruit, avec une possible césure irrégulière ou non conventionnelle. Même Louis-Xavier de Ricard se laissera gagner par cette pratique, alors que ce poète reste toujours aussi insensible à la césure pour l'œil, dans un vers dont la structure ternaire équipartie étayée d'un parallélisme a pu favoriser l'apparente occultation de la césure médiane qui sépare le verbe-noyau de *va-|nu-pieds* de son complément[6]. L'emploi de mots composés à la césure apparaît ainsi le plus souvent comme une forme mineure de rejet interne.

La question de l'enclise n'est pas sans analogie avec la composition du fait de l'interdépendance des morphèmes en cause, du moins lorsqu'ils sont unis par un trait d'union, ce que les poètes évitent avec soin puisque la syllabe précédente y perd en principe son éventuel accent lexical. On peut du moins relever ces trois vers :

Puisqu'il est là, laissez-moi donc, par charité, (Des Essarts[7])

Or, quel parti vouliez-vous donc que nous prissions ? (Vermersch[8])

Brillez, éblouissez-moi ces Américains (Glatigny[9])

Le cas des deux premiers qui se moulent dans un rythme ternaire équiparti doivent être considérés à part du fait de l'adjonction de *donc* qui rebat les cartes au sein d'un mot phonologique étendu dont l'accent est reporté sur la 8ᵉ position au détriment de l'enclitique[10], la sixième pouvant faire l'objet d'un contre-accent, mais il nous paraît plus vraisemblable

5   Si le premier accent porte sur la 3ᵉ position, c'est au sein d'un groupe prosodique de quatre syllabes : il s'agit d'une forme particulière du ternaire équiparti, avec une première «coupe lyrique» ; *cf.* Martinon, «Le trimètre» [2], p. 51.
6   *Le retour du fumiste*, p. 208.
7   *Le retour du fumiste*, p. 26.
8   Dans «Caprices et variations sur des thèmes parnassiens», *La Caricature* (28 nov. 1869); *cf.* Murphy, *Le Premier Verlaine*, p. 208 (et 203, n. 126).
9   *Gilles et Pasquins*, XII : *Les Rois s'en vont*, p. 43.
10 Cette restructuration semble ne pas avoir lieu dans «[LE FUMISTE] Je dors./[LE CADI] Réveillez-vous donc pour écouter mon/Délibéré qu'aurait envié Salomon.» (Des Essarts, *ibid.*, p. 22), où l'enclitique peut porter un accent de hauteur.

qu'il y ait là un authentique déplacement de la césure[11]. Le troisième vers, avec son allure syncopée, est par contre surprenant pour l'époque. S'il peut être rapproché des *lauriers-roses* de Mérat, il ne s'en distingue pas moins du fait que l'accent lexical se perd dans l'enclise, alors qu'il peut se maintenir ou se transformer dans le mot composé en raison du polymorphisme de l'accentuation qui peut s'exprimer aussi bien par la hauteur ou la durée que par l'intensité. Pour autant, il peut être rapproché des suivants également tirés de *Gilles et Pasquins*, où le premier hémistiche se termine sur un mot grammatical relevant d'une catégorie grise (accentuable dans certains contextes), tout aussi forcés malgré l'absence de trait d'union, dont la structure rythmique syncopée descendante est tout aussi perceptible, avec plus de liberté que Corbière dans les vers que nous avons cités au chapitre précédent[12] :

(Qui d'ailleurs n'en est pas une) courir à l'aise, (XVII, p. 61)

Au théâtre ; j'aurais mis, plus que Darimon,
Une culotte courte ! [...] (XXX, p. 95)

rythmes que l'on rencontre également chez d'autres Parnassiens, mais plus rarement et avec une tension moindre entre les 6e et 7e positions, ce qui rapproche la versification de Corbière de celle de l'auteur de *Gilles et Pasquins* :

Ces poëmes sur deux rimes, en treize vers. (Mendès)[13]

Et ne sentent-ils plus rien en eux qui tressaille, (Dierx)[14]

Hélas ! — Et ce n'est plus même, quand vient le soir, (Dierx)[15]

A l'orient jamais plus de matins nouveaux ! (Dierx)[16]

Et que mon cœur n'est plus rien qu'une meurtrissure. (Silvestre)[17]

De sa légère peau morte l'insecte sort, (Aicard)[18]

---

11   Outre le chap. suivant, voir « L'abolition de la césure médiane chez les Parnassiens » et « Un précurseur du second Verlaine » dans la Ve partie.
12   Voir *supra*, p. 220.
13   *Canidie* (*Philoméla*, p. 74).
14   *Hellana* (*Poëmes et poésies*, XXXII, p. 193).
15   *Soleil couchant* (*Poëmes et poésies*, XXXIII, p. 241).
16   *Marche funèbre* (*Les Lèvres closes*, p. 149).
17   *Sonnets païens*, XIII (*Rimes neuves et vieilles*, p. 28).
18   *L'Âme du blé* (*Poëmes de Provence*, p. 145).

On n'est pas surpris de voir Corbière recourir à ce genre de césures lorsque le composé excède six syllabes, dans des vers dépourvus d'appui en 4ᵉ ou 8ᵉ positions, la perception auditive de la césure médiane n'étant alors pas occultée par l'enjambement qui en résulte, avec chaque fois un mot composant fort (dans des composés d'occasion) en 6ᵉ position et un monosyllabe grammatical en 7ᵉ :

> – Navaja-Dolorès-y-Crucificcion !... (*Chapelet*, 5).

> Sur ses jambes en pieds-de-banc-de-cabaret, (*Le Bossu Bitor*, 62)

La structure des mots composés concernés permet aux composants, lexicaux (*pieds, banc, cabaret* dans *pieds-de-banc-de-cabaret*) ou phonologiques (*de-banc, de-cabaret*), d'être perçus dans leur individualité, préservant ainsi la césure en dépit des apparences. Cette autonomie relative des composants apparaît plus particulièrement chez Musset lorsqu'il dispose les membres d'un numéral à cheval sur deux vers alors qu'il ne dispose jamais ainsi un mot simple :

> – Henri huit, révérend, dit Mardoche, fut veuf
> De sept reines, tua deux cardinaux, dix-neuf
> Évêques, treize abbés, cinq cents prieurs, soixante-
> Un chanoines, quatorze archidiacres, cinquante
> Docteurs, douze marquis, trois cent dix chevaliers,
> Vingt-neuf barons chrétiens, et six-vingts roturiers. (*Mardoche*, XXXVII)

Nous avons vu qu'il en allait de même avec les composés de taille inférieure :

> Et – manque de savoir-mourir – il écrivait : (*Le Poète contumace*, 66)

> Ou le réveil, extrait-d'âge de la catin ?... (*Litanie du sommeil*, 155)

> – Lui, c'est un philosophe-errant dans la campagne ; (*Un riche en Bretagne*, 3)

> Et, nous voyant rouler-plat sous les coups de crosse, (*La Pastorale de Conlie*, 75)

> Assis en deux, et, tour-à-tour[19] tirant au mur [...]
> Vêtus d'un frac flambant-neuf et d'un parapluie ; [...]
> Et regardant *Mary-saloppe* : – C'est pour toi, (*Le Bossu Bitor*, 129, 139, 235)

> À bord de la *Mary-gratis*, ont mis leur sac. (*Aurora*, 2)

---

19   Sur cet emploi abusif des traits d'union, voir *supra*, p. 75.

Deux seulement sont accentués à la fois sur les 4e et 8e positions, avec un rythme ascendant (5e vers) ou descendant (7e) ; trois autres ont un accent dominant en 8e position (1er, 3e et dernier vers) ; deux autres, en quatrième (2e et 4e vers) ; un enfin (le 6e), en septième. Corbière se distingue donc ici nettement de Coppée qui recherche toujours dans ce genre de vers une accentuation en 8e position. Il fait même place à trois formes syncopées où l'accent du mot composé tombe sur la septième, soit dans *Litanie du sommeil*, *La Pastorale de Conlie* et *Le Bossu Bitor* (139), ce qui le rapproche de Glatigny[20].

De plus, l'originalité de Corbière apparaît nettement du point de vue quantitatif. En effet, pas moins de dix vers voient la césure partager un mot composé, grammaticalisé ou non, là où les poètes parnassiens n'en présentent alors pas plus de deux par recueil : on n'en trouve qu'un chez Verlaine, dans *Poëmes saturniens*, en 1869 ; puis, trois ans plus tard, deux chez Coppée dans *La Grève des forgerons*, Glatigny dans *Gilles et Pasquins*, Hervilly dans *Les Baisers* et Vacquerie dans *Mes premières années de Paris*[21].

On peut par conséquent considérer que, dans ces emplois de mots composés, la contrainte morphologique n'a pas été violée, mais simplement neutralisée, de la même façon que nous avons considéré que, dans l'emploi de monosyllabes atones à l'hémistiche, la contrainte accentuelle est simplement neutralisée, ce que traduit l'absence d'incidences structurales clairement identifiables au-delà d'éventuelles préférences pour des formes rythmiques particulières : en effet, la frontière de mots requise fait place à une frontière séparant deux mots constitutifs d'un mot composé dont le premier ne se termine pas sur une syllabe post-tonique. Le tableau 1 nous permettra d'illustrer les différentes situations qui peuvent se présenter (en romain, les exemples tirés des *Amours jaunes* ; en italique et précédées d'un astérisque ceux qui ne sont pas actualisés chez Corbière ; « | » marque la frontière médiane) :

---

20 *Cf.* Gouvard, *Critique du vers*, p. 213-214, qui considère, p. 212, que les alexandrins de Corbière où la césure tombe après un trait d'union au sein d'un mot composé « ne répondent à aucun mètre de substitution particulier ».

21 Pour Verlaine, Coppée et Glatigny, voir Gouvard, *Critique du vers*, p. 210.

	Contr. Morph.	Contr. Acc.	Contr. Morph. et Acc.
Neutralisation	savoir-|mourir philoso|phe-errant	et | sa sœur et le | boa	*Mille-et-|une-nuits
Violation	tour-|à-tour roi|de-soûls *Mille-et-u|ne-nuits* *sau|vegarde*	entre | le mur	*sauve|garde*

TABL. 1 – Contraintes césurales.

Des situations plus complexes peuvent se présenter : ainsi, dans *sa\|voir-mourir* (ou *savoir-mou\|rir*), la contrainte morphologique serait violée mais l'accentuelle, simplement neutralisée ; dans *pêle-\|mêle* ou *quatre-\|vingts*, c'est la contrainte accentuelle qui serait violée mais la morphologique, simplement neutralisée. Dans les composés par agglutination, une frontière d'hémistiche après post-tonique d'origine (p. ex. *autre\|fois, sauve\|garde*) violerait l'une et l'autre contraintes.

Pour autant, il ne faut pas pécher par généralisation : il est tout à fait possible que, dans telle ou telle circonstance, tel ou tel poète ait traité ce genre de mots comme des mots simples, et que la présence du tiret à la césure ne soit pas véritablement significative dès lors que ces vers ont été écrits à une période où le poète acceptait des violations caractérisées des contraintes césurales. Ainsi, dans *Sagesse*, le seul vers de ce genre, « Car étant ton Dieu tout-puissant, je peux vouloir, » (II, IV, III) s'aligne vraisemblablement sur « D'oublier ton pauvre amour-propre et ton essence, » ou « Et que sonnent les angélus roses et noirs, » (II, IV, VII), tous accentués en 8e position[22]. Le même raisonnement pourrait du reste, au moins dans l'absolu, être soutenu pour tel ou tel cas de césures pour l'œil.

---

22   Voir V, « Un précurseur du second Verlaine ».

L'ABOLITION DE LA CÉSURE MÉDIANE

Contrairement aux Parnassiens qui ne la dépasseront qu'accidentellement voire involontairement, Corbière franchit à plusieurs reprises la seconde des quatre étapes définies par Dorchain dans l'affranchissement de la césure, étapes qui reposent sur un affaiblissement structural supposé progressif de l'alexandrin, avec le déficit d'un des signaux – accent ou frontière de mots – qui assurent sa reconnaissance[1]. Nous verrons plus loin qu'il n'y a en réalité que deux étapes à prendre en compte, celle des césures pour l'œil, qui a jusqu'ici retenu notre attention, et celle de l'abolition de la césure médiane qui peut se traduire de trois manières différentes[2].

Dans la première, des polysyllabes sont placés à cheval sur l'hémistiche de telle sorte que la tonique tombe au-delà, abolissant ainsi la césure médiane :

Qu'il *vîvait* [sic] *en concubinage avec des Muses !*... (*Le Poète contumace*, 28)

Tu régales, Limonadier de la Passion ? (*Le Bossu Bitor*, 203)

Commandaient et rossignolaient à l'unisson... (*Le Bossu Bitor*, 219)

– Regardez en appareillant, vers ma fenêtre : (*Le Novice en partance*, 107)

– Moi. – Toi, lascar ? – Je chantais ça, moi, capitaine. (*La Goutte*, 9)

L'un des premiers recenseurs du recueil mentionne – sans précision – « un vers que coupe l'hémistiche au milieu d'un mot », rompant ainsi « le principe de la poésie » (le rythme), ajoutant[3] : « si nous repoussons cette chaîne, écrivons en prose ». En réalité, dans ces cinq vers, l'abolition de la césure médiane se voit toujours accompagnée d'une accentuation de la 8e position. La seconde manière se caractérise par le placement de

---

1 Sur ces étapes, voir IV, « L'évolution de l'alexandrin selon Dorchain et Martinon », p. 252-254.
2 Étapes B, C et D de Dorchain (*infra*, p. 252).
3 *L'Art universel* I, 18 (1er nov. 1873), p. 157.

syllabes féminines (issues de post-toniques dans l'étymon ou d'enclise) en 7ᵉ position : l'accent d'hémistiche est bien respecté mais la division médiane ne l'est pas. Cette configuration recouvre en réalité des situations assez différentes dont certaines s'observent chez Corbière. Dans la première, c'est le premier mot lexical (ou la première lexie) d'un mot-composé qui se trouve à cheval sur l'hémistiche[4] :

> Conte des *Mille-et-une-nuits* doux à ouïr ! (*Litanie du sommeil*, 88)
>
> – Des Yankees longs, et roide-soûls par habitude, (*Le Bossu Bitor*, 128)
>
> Et *la petite bonne-femme en frac de mousse :* (*Le Novice en partance*, 103)

Ces vers présentent tous un rythme ternaire équiparti, d'allure ascendante ou descendante, y compris dans le premier où *Mille* porte un accent secondaire. Dans une autre manière, c'est la syllabe féminine finale de mots simples (ou le cas échéant composés) qui tombe en 7ᵉ position, irrégularité que, là encore, le poète ne se permet que dans le cadre de ternaires équipartis ou de rythmes descendants, où la 8ᵉ et, le cas échéant, la 4ᵉ position, prennent le pas sur l'hémistiche en jouant le rôle de pôles rythmiques : « – Pour toi : c'est ta seule œuvre mâle, ô Lamartine, » (*Le Fils de Lamartine*, 49). Il ne s'agit pas pour autant ici, à proprement parler, d'une « césure enjambante à l'italienne », qui constituerait une troisième manière[5] : dans ce vers en effet, la post-tonique ne conclut pas l'unité prosodique dans laquelle elle s'inscrit, le mot qui enjambe l'hémistiche s'intégrant dans un syntagme nominal dont l'accent final tombe sur la syllabe suivante (« ta seule œuvre mâle »), mettant une fois de plus en évidence la fonction structurale de la 8ᵉ position, soulignée par le détachement de l'apostrophe finale. Corbière écrira un autre vers de la sorte dans *Paris nocturne* sur une page vierge de son exemplaire personnel[6] : « – C'est la mort : La police gît – En haut, l'amour », où l'hémistiche se situe au sein d'un groupe intonatif.

---

4   Gouvard, *Critique du vers*, p. 214, rattache ces cas à celui de polysyllabes coupés par la césure en-deçà de la tonique, tels que « – Regardez en appareillant, vers ma fenêtre : » (*Le Novice en partance*, v. 107). Nous pensons que ce genre de cas représente l'étape C du parcours dessiné par Dorchain (cf. p. 252).

5   Voir *infra*, p. 255.

6   La transcription qu'en donne Houzé, « Le dernier Corbière », p. 327, diffère de la nôtre : « mort : – la police ». La majuscule est cependant nette et les deux-points ne sont pas rayés mais soulignés d'un trait qui ne se substitue pas à eux, selon le fac-similé qu'en

Une quatrième manière consiste à mettre une syllabe féminine en 6ᵉ position, violant ainsi la contrainte accentuelle, situation qui ne se rencontre qu'une fois dans le recueil, avec un mot grammatical : « Là, me pressant entre le mur et le garrot : » (*Hidalgo !*, 12). On a ici un ternaire équiparti d'allure ascendante, et donc, là encore, un accent en 8ᵉ position[7]. On ne trouve par contre pas chez Corbière de « césure lyrique » où une féminine en 6ᵉ position terminerait un groupe intonatif, soit une cinquième manière d'abolir la césure médiane traditionnelle[8].

Dans tous ces vers, quelle que soit la manière dont la césure médiane est abolie, l'émergence systématique d'un accent en 8ᵉ position met en évidence la mise en œuvre d'une contrainte métrique nouvelle s'exerçant au détriment des contraintes traditionnelles de l'alexandrin, et ceci avant même Verlaine et Mallarmé[9]. Cette constante attire l'attention sur des mots qui présentent une certaine ambiguïté prosodique tels que *quelque* ou *quoique* : sont-ce des mots métriquement masculins (syllabe finale de pleine articulation) ou féminins (syllabe finale d'articulation relâchée) ? Le problème se pose dans « On a toujours, puisque c'est dans notre nature, » (*Le Novice en partance*, 41). Ne peut-on aligner le cas de *puisque* sur celui de *entre* ? Il y a en fait une différence fondamentale entre les deux cas, redevable de l'étymologie : *entre* est l'issue d'un paroxyton latin (INTER) ; *puisque* est un composé dans lequel l'agglutination des composants n'est qu'une option parmi d'autres dans l'histoire de l'orthographe comme le montre le cas de *parce que* (*cf.* les oppositions *quoique vs bien que, lorsque vs alors que*, mais aussi le déterminant indéfini *quelque vs quel que*) qui a donné pour ce genre de formes la double possibilité d'une interprétation oxytone [kɛl'kœ] ou paroxytone ['kɛlk(ə)] : si *entre* se rattache à la même classe microprosodique que *une, cette* ou *autre, puisque* peut aussi bien se rattacher à celle de *certain* (dét.), *avec* ou *selon*[10]. C'est ce dernier traitement qui convient pour la lecture du vers

---

donnent Aragon et Bonnin, éd. citée, p. 56. On rapprochera en particulier ce vers du 5ᵉ et du 9ᵉ : « – C'est le Styx asséché : Le chiffonnier Diogène / – C'est le champ : Pour [H. : "pour"] glâner [*sic*] les impures charpies ».

7   Situation qui correspond à l'étape D de Dorchain (p. 252).

8   Sur ce type, voir p. 255-256.

9   Sur le premier, voir V, « Un précurseur du second Verlaine » ; sur le second, p. 369-370.

10   Cornulier, *Théorie du vers*, p. 134-141, a donné une théorisation inutilement compliquée de cette problématique, distinguant un « e masculin » et un « e féminin » y compris au sein des mots (voir Gouvard, *Critique du vers*, p. 231-245), là où il n'y a en réalité dans le

du *Novice en partance* qui, du reste, se distingue des précédents en ce qu'il n'est pas accentué sur la 8ᵉ position mais sur la 4ᵉ, particularité qui se retrouvera dix ans plus tard chez Leconte de Lisle, avec le déterminant *quelque* : « Serait-ce point quelque jugement sans merci[11] », accent qui fera également défaut avec *lorsque* chez Coppée : « Et la fièvre, lorsque tout à coup je remarque[12] ».

Notre conclusion va donc à l'encontre de celle de Gouvard qui dénie implicitement à notre poète ce caractère pionnier en affirmant à propos des vers qui présentent une 6ᵉ syllabe atone à voyelle pleine qu'ils « sont sans doute à lire comme se situant à la charnière d'une tradition moribonde, celle, conservatrice, qui attribuait depuis trois siècles la seule scansion 6-6 au vers de 12 syllabes, et celle, innovante, qui cherchait depuis le tournant des années 1850 de nouvelles formes pour de nouveaux vers[13] ». Le critique voit en effet dans certains de ces vers le « maintien d'une lecture 6-6 », avec des « effets de sens ponctuels », minimisant l'originalité de Corbière en lui prêtant des réticences : « les alexandrins M6 "purs" étant sentis comme véhiculant une configuration nouvelle par rapport à tout ce qui s'était fait depuis une vingtaine d'années, Corbière ressent le besoin, ponctuellement, de motiver l'infraction par un effet de sens, qui apporte en quelque sorte une compensation au phénomène ». Outre que les effets de sens relevés, pour le moins discutables, ne concernent que trois des neuf vers de sa liste, dont un vers ancien des *Pannoïdes*[14] où se vérifie du reste notre observation, on se demande pourquoi alors cette constante accentuation de la 8ᵉ position que nous retrouverons dans quasiment tous les vers de la période parnassienne, qui – de façon toujours sporadique – abolissent la césure médiane alors que Corbière adopte les rythmes d'accompagnement les plus variés dans son emploi de la césure pour l'œil[15] ? La réponse qui s'impose est d'ordre métrique :

---

système phonologique français qu'une unique voyelle – le schwa – et des conditionnements prosodiques distincts.

11   Dans *Le Lévrier de Magnus* (*Poèmes tragiques*), prépublié en 1883. Vingt ans auparavant, dans *Philoméla*, Mendès employait *quelque* à la césure dans un ternaire équiparti : « Il faut chercher quelque désert où ta douleur/Ait son affinité secrète qui l'apaise, [...] » (*L'Asile*).

12   Dans *Le Naufragé* (*Les Récits et les élégies*).

13   *Critique du vers*, p. 222. Les vers ici visés font exception du v. 49 de *Fils de Lamartine*, et du 12 d'*Hidalgo !*

14   « Tous les Panneau et Pariseau sont réunis ».

15   Voir V, « L'abolition de la césure médiane chez les Parnassiens ».

cette abolition de la césure se trouve systématiquement compensée par cette particularité dont la constance signale une contrainte spontanée, subie par le poète.

Il semble que ces formes novatrices soient toutes récentes dans la carrière du poète, le vers des *Pannoïdes* mis à part, si ce n'est qu'il est difficile de se prononcer sur les vers d'*Hidalgo !*, du *Bossu Bitor* et de *La Goutte*, faute d'informations sur la genèse de leur écriture : on les trouve en effet souvent dans des poèmes écrits ou développés tardivement (*Le Poète contumace, Le Novice en partance, Litanie du sommeil*), ce qui est sans doute également le cas du *Fils de Lamartine*, pièce certes inspirée du séjour du poète en Italie, en 1869-1870 (que Corbière n'a depuis cessé de remanier et qu'il remanie encore sans cesse après la parution de son recueil dans les marges de son exemplaire), mais dont les premières versions en sont dépourvues.

CORBIÈRE ET LE TARATANTARA

Corbière emploie le taratantara généralement en monométrie[1], soit dans des pièces entièrement monomètres (*A une camarade, Duel aux camélias, Fleurs d'art*, les cinq rondels), soit dans des passages monométriques (*Pudentiane, Le Douanier*[2], *Le Naufrageur*). Il l'emploie pour marquer la fin des quatrains et des tercets du sonnet *Heures* dont tous les autres vers sont des octosyllabes. Il l'emploie enfin deux fois isolément, avec une césure franche, d'une part au huitième vers d'*Épitaphe*, où il se trouve isolé dans un contexte de 56 octosyllabes, une pause venant souligner la césure[3] : « Du *je-ne-sais-quoi*. – Mais ne sachant où ; » ; d'autre part comme incipit du IIIe acte de *Grand opéra* : « Holà !... je vois poindre un fanal oblique », dans lequel Ploquin voit, non sans raison, un octosyllabe « auquel s'ajoute une exclamation », la suite étant constituée d'octosyllabes entrecoupés d'alexandrins[4]. La structure de ce genre de vers est généralement respectée, et Corbière ne va jamais jusqu'aux libertés que prendra Verlaine à partir de *Sagesse*, où, pour rivaliser avec « l'ambition du Vers Libre », il mêle « des rythmes d'un caractère non seulement différent mais opposé », « essay[ant] », selon ses propres termes, « d'émouvoir l'équilibre/D'un nombre ayant deux rythmes seulement[5] ». Les entorses les plus nombreuses à la division rythmique égale du vers

---

1 Leur distribution est rationnelle dans les sonnets polymétriques : ceux de *Pudentiane* sont cantonnés dans les tercets où ils sont employés sans mélange ; certes épars au milieu d'octosyllabes, les quatre d'*Heures* servent à clôturer les quatre parties du sonnet.
2 Avec toutefois un vers hypométrique : « Sillonnaient d'éclairs ton nez ca[m]bré... » ; *cf. supra*, p. 145-146.
3 Le poème commence par trois alexandrins.
4 « Étude », p. 75.
5 Dans un poème d'*Épigrammes* (II, ɪɪ) cité par Chevrier, *Le Décasyllabe à césure médiane*, p. 286-287. Verlaine n'usera de cette liberté que dans le cadre du décasyllabe, où, compte tenu de la mesure plus restreinte et de la concurrence de deux modèles métriques de dix syllabes, cette liberté apparaît souvent comme un mélange de formes différentes, individuellement légitimes mais incompatibles ; voir aussi Chaussivert, « Esthétique du taratantara verlainien ».

se trouvent dans *À une camarade*. Si la césure n'est jamais totalement occultée, on trouve quelques cas où la coupe prosodique majeure se trouve excentrée, rompant d'avec le rythme général de leurs congénères par un effet de syncope rythmique. Elle peut se déplacer vers l'avant, l'accent majeur tombant sur la 6e position :

> Mendiant, il a peur d'être écouté... [...]
> C'est possible : il est rare – et c'est son bien – [...]
> Et gardons à la pomme, jadis verte, (*À une camarade*, 10, 14, 19)
>
> J'ai vu le soleil dur contre les touffes (*Duel aux camélias*, 1)
>
> Sur les *noirs taureaux sourds, blanches cavales !* (*Le Naufrageur*, 26)

Dans deux de ces vers, la 5e position termine un substantif : *soleil*, *taureaux*, ménageant un repos possible à la césure, avec rejet d'une épithète monosyllabique ; dans les autres, elle est occupée par un auxiliaire ou verbe-copule monosyllabique, voire par une préposition ou un article défini où la voix ne peut s'arrêter sans artifice. Lorsqu'elle se déplace vers l'arrière, l'accent majeur tombe sur la quatrième, avec un rythme 4 + 6 nettement identifiable, ce qui ne lui donne pas pour autant le statut d'un décasyllabe commun compte tenu de son contexte métrique univoque, avec dans tous les cas une césure pour l'œil et un accent secondaire en 7e position :

> Bénitier où le serpent est caché ! (*Pudentiane*, 11)
>
> – Eh ! qu'il s'ôte de devant mon soleil ! (*À une camarade*, 8)
>
> Un cœur gravé dans ta manière noire, (*Fleur d'art*, 3)
>
> *Joyeuse, avec ses petites cymbales.* (*Mirliton*, 4)

On ne trouve par contre jamais de polysyllabes à cheval sur les deux hémistiches. Dans « CI-GIT ! La *pudeur-d'-attentat* [*sic*] *le hante...* » (*Pudentiane*, 13), la césure tombe entre deux constituants d'un mot composé, séparant le support de son complément. La contrainte morphologique est ainsi toujours respectée. Ceci étant, lorsque Corbière écrit ces poèmes (dont on ne peut dater précisément l'écriture), le taratantara n'a que timidement amorcé son évolution, la division médiane étant encore clairement la règle, mais sa pratique de la césure pour l'œil souligne la modernité du poète qui se montre à la pointe de l'évolution contemporaine, encore timide, du taratantara. On peut ainsi relever ces vers par lequel Léon Dierx commence *Portrait*, dont le premier laisse attendre une suite en décasyllabes communs[6] :

> Tes jeux sont beaux ; mes plus belles chansons
> Sont faites sur eux, ô ma bien aimée !

Dans *L'Oiseleur*, Louis Bouilhet écrit[7] :

> Toutes !… les voici toutes !… à la file !
> Hésitant un peu, n'osant approcher.

Dans *Musique orientale*, Mérat écrit[8] :

> Le désir blessé par un ciel fatal
> Monte épanoui, fleur des lèvres closes,
> Et le chant, comme un souffle sur des roses,
> Court avec des sons aigus de cristal.

Seul Verlaine allait plus loin, dans *Poëmes saturniens*, où il écrit : « Qui mélancoliquement coule auprès, » (*Le Rossignol*), vers qui doit cependant être mis en parallèle avec « Nuit mélancolique et lourde d'été[9], ».

---

6   *Poëmes et poésies*, XVII, p. 123-124.
7   *Dernières chansons*, XXVII, p. 179-180.
8   *Les Villes de marbre*, p. 7
9   *Poëmes saturniens*, VII, p. 61-62.

CONCLUSION

Dans son traitement de la césure, tant dans le taratantara que dans l'alexandrin qui, avec l'octosyllabe, est le mètre le plus représenté des *Amours jaunes*, Corbière recourt aux artifices les plus modernes. Il lui arrive d'accentuer davantage la septième position que la fin du premier hémistiche, procédé que pouvaient affectionner certains romantiques, en particulier dans la section *GENS DE MER*, avec un effet de syncope qui défie la césure. Il inverse rarement le déséquilibre en accentuant la cinquième position au détriment de la sixième. Mais là où Corbière se détache de la tradition romantique, c'est en introduisant des césures pour l'œil, y compris dans des structures syncopées, dans des proportions qui l'inscrivent clairement dans la modernité versificatoire de son temps à la pointe de laquelle le situe l'abolition occasionnelle de la césure médiane, procédé qui n'est à l'époque que très marginal et rarement assumé, dans des alexandrins où l'accentuation en huitième position vient alors prendre le relais de l'hémistiche. Cette liberté de la césure se retrouve dans le taratantara, avec plus de discrétion, ce qui est compréhensible si l'on tient compte du fait que ce mètre est dix fois moins représenté que l'alexandrin dans *Les Amours jaunes* : si l'on y rencontre des césures pour l'œil, il n'y a pas à proprement parler de vers dont la césure soit occultée.

La modernité de l'alexandrin de Corbière mérite donc une mise en contexte plus précise des *Amours jaunes*. Nous avons à cet effet entrepris de faire un état des lieux de la césure dans le cadre du mouvement parnassien afin de comprendre comment césures pour l'œil et vers occultant la césure médiane, pratiquement inconnus des romantiques, se sont développés au sein du mouvement.

QUATRIÈME PARTIE

L'ÉVOLUTION DE L'ALEXANDRIN
DE 1830 À 1873

Un écrivain assez connu, entre autres,
a dit que, pour lui, les vers, ce n'était
que ceci :
Ta ti, ta ti, ta ti ; ta ti, ta ti, ta ta.
[...] Il ne manque pas de vers qui sont
tels en effet, mais il y en a beaucoup
aussi auxquels ce reproche ne saurait être
adressé, et c'est une fâcheuse infirmité
de n'être pas capable de distinguer entre
les uns et les autres.
F. DE GRAMONT, *Le Vers français*, p. 4.

Corbière est naturellement un héritier de la versification romantique. C'est son rapport à la versification parnassienne qui doit
plus spécialement retenir notre attention, soit une évolution qui
concerne principalement la question de la « césure pour l'œil »,
notion aussi ambiguë que mal comprise que nous avons tenté de
préciser dans la partie précédente et qui recouvre un phénomène
stylistique initié par la publication des *Fleurs du Mal* avant que ne
se pose la question de l'abolition de la césure médiane qui ne se
concrétise véritablement que dans les années 1870. Nous arrêtons
notre enquête avant les développements variés du symbolisme repré-
sentés par Laforgue, Verhaeren et René Ghil, sans parler de *Mémoire*
et « Qu'est-ce pour nous, mon cœur... » de Rimbaud qui ne seront
pas publiés avant 1886/1895. En effet, la métrique de Corbière
témoigne d'un avant-gardisme bien réel qui le situe précisément
en-deçà de ces dernières évolutions. Situer Corbière dans le cadre de
la versification contemporaine présuppose toutefois que ce cadre soit
bien établi et que la théorie des mutations métriques et rythmiques
subies par l'alexandrin soit cohérente et bien comprise, ce qui est
malheureusement loin d'être le cas aujourd'hui, raison pour laquelle
nous nous attacherons tout d'abord à clarifier les choses en exposant
les théories qui ont été jusqu'à présent élaborées et en mettant leur
validité à l'épreuve des faits avant de dresser un tableau historique

de cette évolution. La présente partie porte plus spécialement sur l'histoire de la césure pour l'œil, la question de l'abolition de la césure médiane étant reportée à la suivante.

L'ALEXANDRIN ROMANTIQUE

Les romantiques ont ouvert la voie d'un certain assouplissement de la césure, promouvant « le vers vague sans muselière » enjambant plus ou moins librement d'un hémistiche sur l'autre comme d'un vers sur l'autre. C'est sur un mode lyrique que le programme en est ainsi fixé par Hugo, dans *Réponse à un acte d'accusation*[1] :

> [...] Le vers, qui, sur son front
> Jadis portait toujours douze plumes en rond,
> Et sans cesse sautait sur la double raquette
> Qu'on nomme prosodie et qu'on nomme étiquette,
> Rompt désormais la règle et trompe le ciseau,
> Et s'échappe, volant qui se change en oiseau,
> De la cage césure, et fuit vers la ravine,
> Et vole dans les cieux, alouette divine.

L'intention est on ne peut plus clair : c'est un appel à une libération de la syntaxe et de la prosodie du cadre métrique imposé, avec une valorisation des énoncés ainsi dégagés de la régularité classique et de la monotonie qu'elle pouvait engendrer. Mais en se focalisant sur les manifestations extérieures d'un phénomène proprement métrique qui ne saurait s'y réduire, cette démarche volontariste en est venu à faire perdre de vue l'essentiel, donnant à croire que la césure consiste en une division prosodique majeure du vers dont la localisation variable assurerait un renouvellement en profondeur de la pratique de l'alexandrin. L'avènement du mouvement parnassien n'a pas contribué à améliorer les choses, sans parler des développements nouveaux du symbolisme. C'est ainsi que, à la veille de la Première Guerre mondiale, G. Lote, qui s'arrêtait pourtant au tournant parnassien, pouvait constater[2] :

---

1   *Contemplations*, I, VII.
2   *L'alexandrin*, p. 568.

Les notions que nous avons aujourd'hui de la césure sont assez obscures, et les définitions que nous fournissent les traités sont généralement contradictoires. La cause en est les transformations qu'a subies depuis un siècle la technique du vers français [...]

Mais une chose est le métadiscours élaboré par les poètes ou construit par les grammairiens et les métriciens, une autre la réalité de la pratique des poètes. C'est ainsi que tout indique que, dans leur pratique de l'alexandrin, les romantiques, à commencer par leur chef de file, n'entendaient en aucun cas remettre en cause la césure médiane ; la libération prônée par Hugo s'inscrivait dans la seule dimension prosodique, promouvant dans le même temps un nouveau « modèle d'exécution » des vers (le *delivery design* de Roman Jakobson) qui jouera un rôle important dans l'histoire de la césure pour l'œil. Aussi assiste-t-on à un assouplissement des règles classiques avec une plus grande tolérance envers les prépositions polysyllabiques terminées sur une syllabe à voyelle pleine (*après, avec, parmi, selon*...), une acceptation à la césure des présentatifs voire des auxiliaires ou semi-auxiliaires de deux, plus rarement une syllabe, ce que les classiques ne toléraient qu'à titre d'exception, sous certaines conditions : ces formes faibles étaient en effet en mesure d'assurer une certaine accentuation « de proéminence » à défaut d'un accent lexical ou syntagmatique. Les romantiques font preuve de plus de licence encore en admettant des mots grammaticaux monosyllabiques autres que des proclitiques ou des prépositions, tels que des adverbes dans des locutions prépositionnelles comme *hors* ou *près* (*de*), le relatif *qui* (sans l'appui d'une préposition) ou le prédéterminant *tout*, ou même des locutions conjonctives ou prépositionnelles telles que *comme si* ou *de par*[3]. Avec Baudelaire, on assiste à l'emploi assumé à la césure de proclitiques ou autres monosyllabes centripètes atones ou faiblement accentués, marquant ainsi dans l'affaiblissement de la césure une nouvelle étape que même Hugo n'avait osé franchir, si ce n'est de façon sporadique[4]. *Les Fleurs*

---

3   Au-delà des observations bien connues relatives d'une part à la question générale de l'enjambement et du rejet, d'autre part à celle des ternaires et « trimètres » – dont la théorie n'est au demeurant pas des plus limpides, que ce soit du point de vue typologique ou fonctionnel –, on trouvera dans Gouvard, « L'alexandrin de Victor Hugo », la première étude sérieuse explorant de façon quelque peu précise les libertés prises par les romantiques en matière de césure au regard du modèle classique.

4   Voir *infra* notre chap. « La réception de la césure pour l'œil », p. 308-312.

du Mal ne donnent plus à voir dans les césures atones le simple fruit d'une étourderie mais bien un choix esthétique qui va conditionner le développement des césures parnassiennes[5].

---

5   Pour le détail, voir *infra* notre chap. « La résistible ascension de la césure pour l'œil ».

L'ÉVOLUTION DE L'ALEXANDRIN
SELON DORCHAIN ET MARTINON

En limitant son propos au cadre du ternaire équiparti (« à divisions égales »), et bien qu'il n'ignore pas que le problème excède ce cadre emblématique, A. Dorchain a décrit l'évolution de l'alexandrin comme une évolution conjointe des pratiques versificatoires et des sensibilités du public[1] :

> Chez Victor Hugo, les ternaires ne seront pas seulement beaucoup plus nombreux [*que chez les classiques*], ils seront beaucoup plus rarement réductibles à la coupe 6 + 6 ; et dans ce vers :
>
> > On s'adorait | d'un bout à l'au|tre de la vie...
>
> aucun procédé de diction ne permettra plus d'introduire un semblant de césure après le mot « bout ». Pourtant, ce mot reste une syllabe sonore ; et ainsi le poète a ménagé une transition nouvelle entre ce ternaire encore un peu honteux, qui n'ose s'avouer tel qu'il se présente, et le ternaire franc qui conviendra que sa double césure est l'équivalent de la césure centrale, dont le souvenir pourra, en conséquence, être effacé. Mais déjà l'oreille *n'entend plus* la mesure 6 + 6 à travers l'autre, et pourtant elle jouit aussi pleinement du vers que s'il avait la césure médiane ; le ternaire est désormais goûté pour sa propre cadence, et il ne reste plus qu'à achever son affranchissement par toutes les concessions légitimes, c'est-à-dire par celles qui n'affaibliront point les deux soutiens nouveaux du rythme, les deux césures mobiles[2].

C'est ainsi que le signal phonologique traditionnellement le plus saillant de la césure, soit le relâchement prosodique lié à la frontière prosodique majeure du vers, s'est vu peu à peu compromis par

---

1   *L'Art des vers*, p. 239-241.
2   Naturellement, l'épithète est discutable, Dorchain ayant en vue des coupes syntaxiques alternatives situées en des positions prédéfinies : la notion de mobilité se définit ici génériquement par opposition à la césure métrique dont le positionnement médian n'est pas encore remis en cause.

l'admission d'enjambements internes, sans pour autant compromettre, dans un premier temps, les signaux accentuel et morphologique qui ne commenceront à être affectés qu'avec l'essor de la poésie parnassienne. Voici comment le poète théoricien décrit les quatre étapes qui, selon lui, jalonnent cet affranchissement (nous les ordonnons entre crochets) :

> On arrivera ainsi, d'abord à permettre de simples enclitiques [*sic*] à la sixième syllabe [A] :
>
>> Où l'on jouait | sous la charrette | abandonnée.
>>   (FRANÇOIS COPPÉE, Olivier.)
>
> Puis, ces enclitiques étant des syllabes atones, il n'y aura plus de raison pour exiger qu'on mette à l'hémistiche une fin de mot ; on pourra tout aussi bien y placer une syllabe intérieure [B] :
>
>> Serait allée | en Palesti|ne, les pieds nus.
>>   (JEAN AICARD, Othello.)
>
> Autre corollaire : puisqu'il n'y a plus, à la sixième syllabe, cette césure qui n'avait pas le droit d'être enjambante, la septième pourra désormais être une muette non élidée [C] :
>
>> Mais n'ayant plus | de branches ver|tes pour grandir.
>>   (CHARLES DE POMAIROLS, Pour l'Enfant.)
>
> Enfin, la sixième syllabe elle-même pourra être une muette, aucune trace de césure n'étant plus reconnue nécessaire à cette place [D] :
>
>> Et tout à coup | l'ombre des feuil|les remuées.
>>   (JEAN MORÉAS, Cantilènes.)
>
> Et l'évolution du ternaire est ainsi terminée par son affranchissement complet d'avec le binaire à césure médiane.

L'évolution que dessine Dorchain apparaît ainsi comme un véritable parcours cognitif qui a pour point de départ le ternaire romantique comme cadre d'émancipation progressive de la césure médiane, reflétant très précisément l'interaction et la hiérarchie des contraintes dont la césure est la résultante, avec, d'une part, une contrainte accentuelle (CA) qui produit un signal acoustique (accent), d'autre part une contrainte morphologique (CM) qui produit un signal d'ordre cognitif (frontière de mots) en imposant le cas échéant l'élision[3]. Dans A (césure pour l'œil), il y a occultation de la césure : la contrainte accentuelle est neutralisée, le signal acoustique faisant défaut ; dans B-D, la césure est abolie. Dans B, à la neutralisation de la contrainte accentuelle s'ajoute l'absence du signal cognitif ; ce dernier fait également défaut dans C où apparaît en outre un signal acoustique contradictoire entraînant une perturbation de la perception du mètre, malgré l'accentuation de la 6ᵉ position, la suivante étant occupée par une syllabe post-tonique, de sorte que le lecteur se trouve face à une dépression prosodique en tête du second hémistiche putatif ; dans D, le signal acoustique est directement perturbé par la présence d'une syllabe post-tonique en 6ᵉ position, là même où l'on attend une syllabe accentuée, et où un monosyllabe atone (à voyelle pleine) eût du moins offert un support suffisant à la voix (*cf.* A)[4]. Notre corpus parnassien permet d'établir la chronologie suivante, à partir des premières attestations relevées (datation des recueils, non de l'écriture des poèmes concernés), où l'on voit que les quatre types apparaissent dans la même période, sachant que B, C et D sont exceptionnels avant *Les Amours jaunes*, recueil à partir duquel ils resteront toutefois marginaux :

A.   1857 : Et fait surgir plus d'un portique fabuleux (Baudelaire)
B.   1861 : J'aimais l'azur étincelant des cieux ! J'aimais (Blanchecotte)
C.   1859 : La Pauvreté, squelette sombre aux yeux funestes (Villiers)
D.   1861 : Elle était belle, elle t'aimait, elle est passée, (Blanchecotte)

Dorchain explique ensuite qu'il aurait pu « montrer la même évolution dans n'importe quelle formule trimétrique à divisions inégales », donnant pour exemple « le ternaire en 3 + 5 + 4 » doté d'un accent en 3ᵉ et 8ᵉ positions. Sans discuter cette notion de « ternaire » qui peut s'appliquer à des membres entretenant des rapports plus ou moins équilibrés, on peut en effet constater la pertinence de cette remarque en relevant la date de parution en recueil des premiers vers de ce type de notre corpus parnassien[5] :

---

3   Voir Billy, « Théorie et description » et « La Complainte de Geneviève ». Au contraire du signal acoustique, ce signal n'est pas *perçu* mais *conçu* en raison de la compétence linguistique du versificateur, du lecteur ou de l'auditeur.
4   Voir *infra*, p. 295-296 (et tabl. 1), le tableau récapitulatif des dysfonctionnements de la césure.
5   Dans les seconds exemples (nous n'en avons pas trouvé pour D parmi les recueils que nous avons dépouillés), la 4ᵉ position est occupée par une post-tonique.

A.   1866 : Tous vos chants et tous vos caprices de couleurs, (Mérat)
      1862 : Je me lève dans la fureur qui me consume : (Leconte)
B.   1868 : Et l'ennui des éternités déjà passées. (Cazalis)
      1871 : Et j'aspire ton souvenir avec paresse. (Aicard)
C.   1888 : Ou plutôt, je puis dire tout, vraiment chrétien. (Verlaine)[6]
      1888 : Dans les cages plus d'une cloche encor bruit, (*idem*)
D.   1893 : D'être grâce à votre talent de femme exquise-
      Ment amusante, [...] (Verlaine, pré-orig.)

Comme on peut le voir, C et D ne se trouvent cette fois illustrés que tardivement, à partir de la fin des années 1880, avec un décalage d'une vingtaine d'années qu'il convient de minimiser pour deux raisons : 1°) les rythmes 3-5-4 ont une fréquence très nettement inférieure à 4-4-4 ; 2°) quel que soit le cadre rythmique considéré, les types C et D ont une fréquence très inférieure au type B, lui-même, nous l'avons dit, exceptionnel avant *Les Amours jaunes*. Par ailleurs, Dorchain a confondu ici deux choses bien distinctes : d'une part la question de la structure *microprosodique* au niveau de l'articulation médiane des 6e et 7e positions, d'autre part la structure *macroprosodique* du vers. En effet, les exemples donnés, comme la définition du cadre retenu (des structures ternaires dont le second membre embrasse l'articulation médiane) montrent que les particularités prosodiques ne sont pas envisagées autrement qu'*au sein d'un groupe accentuel* constitué d'un syntagme propre qui correspond très précisément au second membre des ternaires considérés. Dans un tel contexte, il semble douteux qu'il puisse y avoir une évolution différenciée dans B, C et D où la césure médiane se trouve abolie purement et simplement du fait de la violation de l'une des contraintes métriques censées la déterminer, contrairement à ce qui se passe dans le cas de la césure pour l'œil (A). Si, pour « le ternaire en 3 + 5 + 4 », les dates d'apparition relevées chez les Parnassiens peuvent malgré tout en donner l'illusion, ce n'est en effet pas le cas pour les ternaires équipartis pour lesquels les quatre types sont apparus avant 1862.

Les configurations microprosodiques de l'hémistiche décrites pour les types B, C et D pourront par contre se présenter, à partir des années 1880, *entre deux groupes intonatifs*, avec des effets fondamentalement

---

6   Dans un poème de 1885. Dans les marges de son exemplaire des *Amours jaunes*, Corbière
     a alors déjà écrit : « – C'est la mort : La police gît. – En haut, l'amour ».

différents, la césure médiane n'y étant pas à proprement parler *abolie* mais plus exactement *altérée*. Dorchain s'arrête en effet aux évolutions parnassiennes de l'alexandrin, ne prenant pas en compte les évolutions à venir du symbolisme qui peut renouer avec des procédés anciens qui s'étaient jadis pratiqués dans le cadre du décasyllabe commun, avec des césures médianes tranchées mais bancales qui ne satisfaisaient qu'une des deux contraintes fondamentales, qu'elles privilégiassent la contrainte accentuelle (césure accentuelle à l'italienne 4' + 5) ou la morphologique (césure lyrique 3' + 6'). Laforgue, dont l'alexandrin connaît au demeurant des modifications structurales plus complexes, aura ainsi une inclination marquée pour la première et Verhaeren pour la seconde. Voici deux exemples consécutifs tirés des *Complaintes*, avec des effets différents[8] :

> Et buvant les étoiles à même : « ô Mystère !
> « Quel calme chez les astres ! ce train-train sur terre !

Dans le premier vers, la continuité prosodique atténue l'effet de la césure lyrique par l'adjonction d'un syntagme adverbial, avec un rythme régulier ponctué par l'accentuation de trois en trois syllabes ; une pause l'exalte au contraire dans le second. Et à présent deux exemples, également consécutifs, de césure après post-tonique chez Verhaeren, dont seul le second présente une frontière syntagmatique offrant la détente nécessaire à la constitution d'une césure lyrique, vers datés de 1886[9] :

> Et le cerveau, certes morne et lassé, soudain
> S'éveille en ces heures de fastueux silence

Avant Verhaeren, ces dernières formes ne se rencontrent jamais que de façon accidentelle en des expériences isolées, comme chez Verlaine, en

---

7   L'exemple précoce dans *Les Poèmes de l'amour* d'A. Renaud (1860), p. 110, résulte de toute évidence d'une coquille : « Rêvant à sa ville dont les bains embaumaient. » (composition fautive pour *villa*). La même méprise a, jusqu'à la fin du dernier siècle, affecté le vers « Forêts, soleils, rios, savanes ! – Il s'aidait / De journaux illustrés […] » de Rimbaud (*Les Poètes de sept ans*), où, depuis 1891 (*Reliquaire*), on ne cessait d'éditer « rives », faute de revenir sérieusement au seul autographe conservé ; *cf.* éd. Murphy, I, p. 419 et 422.

8   *Préludes autobiographiques*, v. 29-30.

9   *Vénus ardente*, 9-10 (*Les Bords de la route*, p. 17). Dominicy, « La césure lyrique », adopte un autre point de vue sur la question, sur la base de présupposés théoriques qui lui sont propres.

1887 : « Telles qu'au prix d'elles les amours dans le rang » (*Ces passions*, recueilli dans *Parallèlement*).

Un autre aspect de l'analyse de Dorchain retient l'attention : on ne sait pas dans quelle mesure il est ou non significatif que ses exemples s'en tiennent à des vers où la 8ᵉ position est accentuée, ou si son allusion à « n'importe quelle formule trimétrique à divisions inégales » irait jusqu'à admettre des formes telles que $4 + 3 + 5$ ou $3 + 4 + 5$. Ce point est particulièrement important comme l'a montré Martinon dans une analyse aussi décisive que négligée par la critique bien qu'elle remonte à plus d'un siècle, une dizaine d'années avant Dorchain, dans laquelle il s'est attaché à mettre à jour ce qu'il appelle « les lois » du « vrai trimètre[10] » : « Et d'abord, la césure classique disparaissant, y en a-t-il une autre, et où est-elle ? ou y en a-t-il deux ? » Établissant un parallèle avec l'hexamètre, Martinon considère que c'est l'accentuation en 8ᵉ position qui est déterminante :

> Le trimètre a aussi une césure, *la* césure, qui se met dans la seconde moitié du vers et non dans la première [...] La place de cette césure sera donc marquée par un accent fort sur la huitième syllabe. Mais, en même temps, et par un procédé analogue à celui du latin, une césure de soutien aura sa place marquée le plus souvent par un accent fort sur la quatrième syllabe.

Ainsi, à la césure « principale » associée à l'accent de 8ᵉ position, s'ajoute une césure « subsidiaire » ou « de soutien » qui serait marquée par l'accentuation de la 4ᵉ ou de la 3ᵉ position, la première pouvant prendre la forme d'une césure lyrique :

> L'heure passe, comme une femme sous un voile (Samain)
>
> Qui ridaient en s'élargissant l'eau solitaire (Gregh)

Il considère enfin que le trimètre s'est par la suite assoupli jusqu'à ce que la « césure de soutien » soit remplacée « par un accent quelconque », avec des exemples de Gregh : « On a ainsi en quelque sorte un vers de huit syllabes aux accents mobiles suivi d'un élément de quatre ». Martinon laisse toutefois subsister une incertitude, ou à tout le moins

---

10   Martinon, « Le trimètre » [2], p. 49-53. Dans son exposé, l'auteur ne perd jamais de vue les formes qui préludent à cette évolution, des césures faibles romantiques aux césures pour l'œil des Parnassiens.

une ambiguïté, en parlant de « césure » aussi bien pour la principale qui se caractérise par sa relative fixité (elle dépend d'un accent en 8e position, qu'elle tombe juste après elle ou en neuvième, après une post-tonique[11]) que pour la subsidiaire qui est mobile : seule la première a une fonction métrique, fonction que remplit la césure médiane dans le cadre de l'alexandrin traditionnel.

---

11   Nous parlons de césure « flottante » dans « Le flottement de la césure ».

LE MODÈLE DE *THÉORIE DU VERS*

Selon les tenants de la métricométrie l'effacement progressif de la césure médiane s'effectuerait dans le seul cadre des ternaires équipartis et des rythmes 8-4 et 4-8 – qu'ils désignent sous l'appellation captieuse et orientée de « semi-ternaires » – qui correspondent en réalité à des ternaires à membres inégaux tels que ceux « en 3 + 5 + 4 » ou « 4 + 5 + 3[1] », tous rythmes définis comme « mètres de substitution », notion étrangère à Dorchain mais sous-jacente chez Martinon. Dans son analyse, qui porte sur l'œuvre poétique de Rimbaud, Verlaine et Mallarmé, B. de Cornulier identifie quatre « systèmes [...] hiérarchis[és] en fonction de leur complexité et de leur ordre d'apparition[2] ». Après un premier qui correspond aux formes traditionnelles, l'évolution de l'alexandrin postromantique passerait ainsi par trois autres dont l'acquisition serait progressive[3] :

(S1) « système 1 » à césure médiane : « égalité naturelle 6-6 égale 6-6 » ;
(S2) « système 2 » : « égalité acquise 4-4-4 égale 6-6 » (p. 174) ; « tout vers qui n'a pas une coupe 6e (6-6) a une coupe 4e et une coupe 8e (4-4-4) » (p. 163) ; aux vers notés « 6-6 » [T1] s'ajoutent par conséquent les vers notés « 4-4-4[4] » [T2]
(S3) « système 3 » : « égalité acquise 8-4 égale 6-6 » (p. 174) ; « tout vers non mesurable en 6 + 6 ou 4-4-4 a du moins une coupe 8e » (p. 169) ; à T1 et T2 s'ajoutent donc les vers notés « 8-4 » [T3]

---

1 Sur cette notion, voir *infra*, p. 287.
2 *Théorie du vers*, p. 271.
3 *Op. cit.*, p. 156-174 : « L'interprétation métrique suppose simplement, au départ, l'exploitation de l'égalité naturelle 6-6 égale 6-6 ; puis l'incorporation de l'égalité 4-4-4 égale 6-6 ; puis, de nouveau l'acquisition de l'égalité 8-4 égale 6-6 ; progrès de l'apprentissage ». Les désignations par S1 *etc.* sont de nous.
4 Comme nous le verrons bientôt, dans cette théorie, les notations « 6-6 », « 4-4-4 » *etc.* ne signifient pas que les vers sont accentués sur les 6e (premier cas), 4e et 8e (second cas) *etc.* positions, mais que lesdites positions ne sont pas marquées C, P, F ou M (voir *infra*).

(S4) « système 4 » : égalité acquise 4-8 égale 8-4 égale 6-6 ; tout 12-syl-labe étranger aux précédents systèmes a du moins une coupe 4e (*cf.* p. 230, 235 et 271) ; aux précédents s'ajoutent donc les vers notés « 4-8 » [T4].

Cette progressivité se vérifierait chez les trois poètes étudiés (et quelques autres), chez qui « la mesure 4-8 ne va pas sans la mesure 8-4, qui elle-même ne va pas sans la mesure 4-4-4, alors que des poètes [*sans précision*] peuvent utiliser le 4-4-4 sans utiliser le 8-4, ou le 8-4 sans utiliser le 4-8[5] ».

L'application de ces filtres successifs laisse un reliquat de vers hors-systèmes (HS) qui ne répondent à aucune de ces conditions, soit, dirons-nous en reprenant la terminologie de l'auteur, *tout vers non mesurable en 6 + 6 et dépourvu de coupe 8e ou 4e*. Les quatre types reconnus comme systémiques sont souvent évoqués comme « rythmes[6] » ; les vers relevant des types T2, T3 et T4 sont définis comme des « vers d'accompagnement », ceux qui relèvent du type T1, comme « vers fondamentaux », leur équivalence métrique étant supposée faire l'objet d'un apprentissage progressif[7]. Cette détermination de rythmes considérés comme pertinents n'a rien de la nouveauté que l'on a pu y voir, car ce modèle recoupe en bonne partie les positions anciennes d'un Edmond Porcher qui, en 1914, considérait que l'alexandrin a longtemps « conservé intact son dessin rythmique 6 + 6 avec, à la césure, la dernière syllabe accentuée d'un mot » avant de connaître *dans le cadre de la poésie symboliste* une « modification durable » où la « base rythmique de tout le système [*on reconnaît ici S1*], a subi une atteinte exceptionnelle par la création du vers ternaire 4 + 4 + 4 [*soit l'équivalent de S2*], sans césure et sans arrêt à la sixième syllabe » par des poètes qui, outrepassant les libertés introduites par Hugo, « ont brisé la frêle passerelle de la césure » avec ce rythme dont la « cadence […] est aisément perçue par les auditeurs sans éducation spéciale de l'oreille », apportant, lorsqu'il est utilisé avec économie et discernement, « un effet nouveau, très accentué, et facilement perceptible par

---

5   *Op. cit.*, p. 271. L'italique est censé indiquer la présence d'un accent secondaire dans le membre de huit syllabes à l'exclusion de la quatrième ; en pratique, Cornulier ne fait référence qu'à la 3e ou la 5e.

6   Voir p. ex. p. 106.

7   Sur la notion, voir *op. cit.*, p. 98-110. Les types eux-mêmes sont respectivement définis comme « mesures d'accompagnement » et « mesure fondamentale » (p. 116 et *passim*).

tous », proposant également « [b]ien d'autres modifications rythmiques », adoptant « notamment, un vers 4 + 8 [*on reconnaît le type T4*] ou 8 + 4 [*ici, le type T3*], sans césure à la sixième syllabe » (vers auquel Porcher reproche de « n'apporte[r] aucune cadence appréciable à la place de la cadence 6 + 6 qu'il brise »), rejetant globalement les autres combinaisons (soit l'équivalent des vers HS) qu'il qualifie d'« excentriques[8] ». Une différence essentielle distingue cependant la théorie de Porcher de celle de Cornulier : le premier a en vue l'oblitération de la césure médiane, seule à pouvoir fonder une structure alternative, là où le second accepte tout aussi bien l'emploi de monosyllabes atones à l'hémistiche, soit des cas de "césures pour l'œil" selon la terminologie ancienne où la césure médiane n'est pas à proprement parler abolie, cas sur lesquels Porcher ne se prononce pas. Sa présentation des faits suggère cependant qu'il voyait dans le mouvement parnassien un prolongement des recherches rythmiques hugoliennes à une époque où la césure médiane n'était pas encore mise radicalement en cause.

La détermination des différents rythmes s'appuie sur une méthode *ad hoc*, consistant à caractériser « les positions syllabiques qui n'excluent pas une coupe métrique subséquente », selon la caractérisation de Gouvard[9], en marquant une bonne partie des positions non accentuées, à savoir celles qui contiennent des monosyllabes atones (C : articles et pronoms conjoints antéposés, semi-négation ; P : prépositions monosyllabiques), des syllabes antérieures à la tonique dans les polysyllabes (M) ou des syllabes post-toniques (F)[10]. L'application qui est faite de cette méthode implique que toute autre position est éligible à la césure, ce qui n'est pas exact comme on peut le voir dans des vers tels que « Un parfum, – et c'est le déluge qui consomme » (*Sagesse*), ou « Car ses yeux si francs, car sa bouche qui sourit, » (*La Bonne Chanson*) qui, par leur absence de marquage CPMF en 4e position relèvent de T2, bien que les accents internes soient en 3e et 8e position dans le premier, en 3e, 5e et 8e dans le second ; même chose pour « De tes péchés, et mes mains ! Et tu vois la croix, » (*Sagesse*) dépourvu de marquage CPMF en 8e position, malgré ses accents en 4e,

---

8   « L'alexandrin et le vers libre », p. 83-89. Porcher vise plus précisément la période symboliste.
9   *Critique du vers*, p. 85. À noter que si elles ne l'excluent pas, c'est qu'elles ne l'impliquent pas automatiquement.
10   Dans les perspectives données en lieu et place des conclusions de *Critique du vers*, p. 257-258, Gouvard évoque l'intérêt qu'il y aurait à élargir les critères de la métricométrie.

7ᵉ et 10ᵉ positions. Autre exemple, « Son espoir et dans tout son remords, que l'extase » de Verlaine (*Sagesse*) est classé T4 bien qu'il soit dépourvu d'accent en 4ᵉ et 8ᵉ positions. Ce « bruit » informationnel qui n'est pris en compte que de façon occasionnelle[11] est loin d'être négligeable : une analyse des 102 alexandrins du *Prologue* de *Poëmes saturniens* établit ainsi que 46 % des syllabes non marquées dans ce que nous appellerons la *zone métriquement contrainte*[12] se retrouvent *de facto* dans le champ des syllabes aptes à porter un accent significatif susceptible de leur voir conférer une fonction métrique. Et pourtant, 7 % d'entre elles ne présentent pas d'accent de groupe accentuel ou de mot lexical, avec diverses sortes de monosyllabes ou dissyllabes féminins appartenant à des catégories grises dont la plupart sont traditionnellement bannies de l'hémistiche : conjonctions de coordination (*et, ou*) ou de subordination (*que*), relatifs simples (*qui, que, où*), particule exclamative, adverbe d'intensité (*plus*), auxiliaire (*ont*), présentatif (*c'est*), autres mots grammaticaux (*jusqu', deux, avec*). Si ce pourcentage est dérisoire pour la 8ᵉ position (1 %), il monte à 8 % pour la 4ᵉ (avec en pratique *et, que* conjonction ou relatif, *ont* devant son participe). Or, si l'on peut aisément comprendre que la vogue des césures pour l'œil se soit accompagnée d'une extension des césures faibles à des catégories de mots jusque là exclues[13], on peut douter que ce genre de mots constituassent les articulations d'une « métrique de substitution » qui, pour être efficaces, devraient reposer sur des positions *nettement accentuées*, rendant ainsi chaque membre aisément « reconnaissable ». Et de fait, lorsque, dans *Critique du vers*, Gouvard analysera les vers de Coppée en y recherchant des « mètres de substitution », il rattachera en quelques occasions – et donc sans systématicité – d'autres formes (ci-dessous soulignées) aux catégories marquées CPMF dans la théorie, comme dans ces ternaires à membres inégaux[14] :

---

11   Voir p. ex. p. 166 de *Théorie du vers*, à propos de « Je courus ! Et les Péninsules démarrées ».

12   Nous entendons par là la zone allant de la 4ᵉ à la 8ᵉ position, où les contraintes de la césure sont susceptibles de s'exercer dans un vers de douze syllabes (*cf. infra*, p. 299). Sur ces cinq positions qui totalisent 510 syllabes, nous comptons 275 marquages CPFM (dont quatre seulement sur la 6ᵉ), dont 65 sur la 4ᵉ et 40 sur la 8ᵉ.

13   C'est ainsi que Gouvard, p. 94-97, donne des arguments pour écarter les adverbes monosyllabiques *près* et *hors* suivis de la préposition *de* du champ des césures problématiques au motif qu'Hugo les admet à la césure (ce qui n'en fait pas pour autant des fins de groupe accentuel).

14   Il va plus loin dans « De la sémantique », p. 145-147, en admettant comme « 4-4-4 » dans les années 1890 (qui ne nous concernent pas ici) des vers présentant des conjonctions (de

Un des leurs, <u>un</u> de ces mal contents[15] à front gris, (p. 198)

Pour la femme <u>et</u> pour les petiots[16], mes bons amis ! (p. 200)

Et plus rien ! <u>Mais</u> pour ces vieillards le sort complice (p. 201)

Le rejet de ce genre de formes, mises au même rang que les proclitiques, met clairement en évidence que ce qui le motive n'est pas nécessairement une question d'accentuation, car celle-ci est incontestable tant au premier vers (pronom tête de syntagme) qu'au troisième où la conjonction *mais*, qui introduit une proposition, se trouve mise en relief par l'antéposition du CC. Dans les deux cas, c'est le repos après la 3ᵉ position qui aura décidé de leur rejet, lié au seul fait qu'ils ne constituent pas le terme d'un groupe accentuel. Si le rejet du second est pleinement justifié, on s'étonnera que d'autres vers, certes rares, non marqués en 4ᵉ ou/et 8ᵉ positions comme « Tous vos chants et tous vos caprices de couleurs, » (Mérat) ou même « Sur un lit, comme l'on se penche sur un livre. » (Verlaine) n'aient pas bénéficié de cette juste réserve[17]. La méthode fait en outre abstraction de la hiérarchie accentuelle[18], de telle sorte que dans « Tu fermeras l'œil, pour ne point voir, par la glace, » de Rimbaud (*Rêvé pour l'hiver*) dont les accents dominants figurent en 5ᵉ et 9ᵉ positions se trouverait également classé comme T2. Il convient cependant de considérer que ces cas, comme les précédents, ne représentent pas un poids statistique suffisant pour remettre en cause les résultats.

Un autre aspect problématique concerne l'analyse « distributionnelle » telle que l'effectuent les tenants de la métricométrie. Celle-ci s'effectue en effet en quatre étapes *précisément calquées sur le postulat de l'apprentissage progressif des nouveaux « systèmes »* : dans un premier temps, l'examen porte sur la seule 6ᵉ position qui permet d'inventorier les vers CPMF6 ; dans un second temps, l'examen de ce premier inventaire porte sur la huitième, ce qui permet d'inventorier les vers CPMF6 non CPMF8, soit des vers en principe non accentués sur la 6ᵉ position mais accentués sur

---

coordination ou de subordination), des relatifs ou des adverbes monosyllabiques en 4ᵉ ou 8ᵉ position.

15 « malcontents » dans l'édition originale (1866).

16 « enfants » dans l'édition originale (1869).

17 *Op. cit.*, p. 190 et 194.

18 Si l'on met de côté le premier des trois vers de Coppée précédemment commentés (« Un des leurs, [...] »).

la 8ᵉ ; dans un troisième temps, l'examen du reliquat de cette sélection porte sur la 4ᵉ position, ce qui permet d'inventorier les vers CPMF6 et CPMF8 non CPMF4, soit des vers en principe non accentués sur la 6ᵉ ni sur la 8ᵉ position mais accentués sur la quatrième. Cette démarche fait ainsi l'impasse sur les particularités qui affectent les positions impaires 5 et 7 (entre autres), de sorte que la présence – loin d'être négligeable – de rythmes 5-7, se trouve purement et simplement ignorée alors même que ceux-ci jouent un rôle significatif chez Mallarmé et Rimbaud avant 1872 (de même que chez Banville, Glatigny ou, comme nous l'avons vu, Corbière[19]). Si, avant Laforgue, ces formes se trouvent systématiquement associées à une césure pour l'œil (quand ce n'est pas à une césure plus conventionnelle), c'est au même titre que la plupart des rythmes retenus au travers des phases successives de l'analyse distributionnelle effectuée par Cornulier, rythmes qui reposent sur l'accentuation des 4ᵉ ou/et 8ᵉ positions chez ces différents poètes. Dans son traité de versification, Gouvard évoquera les rythmes 5-7 et 7-5 à propos de Laforgue (et de Queneau) chez qui la césure médiane se trouve alors souvent occultée : il les présente comme des « mètres de substitution » qu'il considère comme des « scansions apparentées et aisément identifiables comme telles », nuançant en parlant de « formes métriques » qui « n'avaient pas le statut de "mètre" à part entière[20] », sans éprouver le besoin de justifier cette restriction, alors que, dans les vers en question, la césure médiane se trouve souvent bel et bien abolie contrairement à ce qui se passe – sauf exception – chez les Parnassiens[21]. De fait, lorsque, dans les alexandrins de Laforgue, la césure médiane se trouve abolie, l'accent dominant peut tomber n'importe où.

Cornulier considère par ailleurs que, dans le cadre de S2 et S3, il y a une « ambivalence métrique dans les vers C6[22] » : « Je n'exclus pas [...] que dans tous ces vers [C6] le rythme ternaire [T2] ou à coupe 8ᵉ [T3] ne puisse avoir une fonction métrique, c'est-à-dire compléter l'isométrie 6-6 *égale* 6-6 par l'isométrie éventuellement acquise 4-4-4 *égale* 6-6 ou 8-4 (3-5-4 ?) *égale* 6-6[23] ». Ce qui revient à dire que, dans les vers

---

19   Pour les premiers, voir p. 271, 323-324, 341-342 et 347 ; pour le dernier, p. 196-200.

20   *La Versification*, p. 139 et 138 respectivement.

21   Son étude de 1992, « Les mètres de Jules Laforgue », n'apporte pas plus d'éclairage sur ce point.

22   On ignore pourquoi le raisonnement n'inclut pas les vers « P6 ».

23   *Op. cit.*, p. 178 ; le verbe « compléter » employé laisse curieusement entendre que l'isométrie classique n'était pas complète. Les précisions entre crochets sont de nous.

considérés, les positions 6e et 8e (S3) plus le cas échéant la 4e (S2), soit des positions qui ne sont séparées les unes des autres que par une seule syllabe, *peuvent toutes avoir simultanément une fonction métrique*, ce qui va à l'encontre de ce que nous apprend l'histoire des mètres dans la versification française : à notre connaissance, les seules contraintes métriques qui s'exercent dans les vers considérés ne sont autres que celles de la césure médiane, si ce n'est qu'elles sont appliquées avec moins de force que dans la versification classique et romantique, avec un relâchement accentuel en 6e position ; quant aux 4e et 8e positions, leur accentuation ressortit de choix stylistiques qui varient au gré des poètes et de leur évolution artistique, choix qui relèvent de la rythmique, non de la métrique, ce que nous nous attacherons à démontrer en mettant à l'épreuve des faits la théorie des quatre systèmes. Plus récemment, confondant métrique et rythmique, le métricométricien a du reste soutenu le contraire à propos des vers déviants de *Poëmes saturniens* (« l'hypothèse 6+6 sans exception paraît favorable »), avec un argument tout aussi discutable, le critique considérant ainsi que, dans « De mes ennuis, de mes dégoûts, de mes détresses ! » ou encore « De la douceur, de la douceur, de la douceur ! », « un lettré pouvait ressentir encore le mètre 6+6, suspendant à la césure, après l'article (proclitique), le mot "dégoûts" ou "douceur" », évoquant cette fois confusément une « ambivalence (double valeur) rythmique, le 444 se superposant au 66 syntaxiquement entravé[24] ». On se souvient comment, à propos de tels vers, le lettré Sainte-Beuve exprimait son désarroi, reprochant précisément à ces vers de dérouter l'oreille[25].

La question plus radicale que l'on doit en effet se poser est celle de savoir ce qui, dans ces « systèmes », fait véritablement *système*, en mettant de côté le cas de S1 dont la poésie classique est la première et la meilleure illustration, et dont la poésie romantique constitue la prolongation. Pour cela, on peut s'interroger sur la place accordée par T2, T3 et T4 au sein d'un même recueil : en effet, pour qu'un « système » quelconque puisse s'imposer en tant que tel, il faut que sa place soit exclusive (ou du moins proche de l'exclusivité), assurant l'émergence régulière d'un signal clair distinguant ces formes des alexandrins ordinaires, seule cette stabilité étant susceptible de justifier et le concept de « système » et celui de

---

24   « Sur la métrique de Verlaine », p. 61.
25   Sur son témoignage et d'autres, voir *infra* notre chap. « La réception de la césure pour l'œil ».

« substitution ». Or, que ce soit chez Mallarmé, Rimbaud ou Verlaine, le critique n'a pas établi de telles situations, à aucun moment de leur carrière. En réalité, ces « systèmes » censés reposer sur les observations faites par le promoteur de la métricométrie s'accommodent dans la pratique de bien des formes qui leur sont étrangères, dans les proportions les plus variées, et ceci de façon systématique dès lors que le recueil contient plus de six vers déviants, ce qui en ruine le fondement.

Qu'en est-il en effet des œuvres de Rimbaud, Verlaine et Mallarmé qui constituent le corpus même de *Théorie du vers* ? En nous limitant ici aux cas de césures sur monosyllabe atone (CP6) dans les pièces publiées jusqu'à *Sagesse*, soit dans des recueils personnels (Verlaine), soit dans les deux premiers recueils du *Parnasse contemporain* (Mallarmé), plus l'œuvre encore inédite de Rimbaud avant 1872 (sans les *marginalia*[26]), on obtient la distribution suivante (nous ajoutons pour comparaison les données relatives aux deux premières éditions des *Fleurs du Mal* ainsi qu'aux *Amours jaunes*; entre parenthèses sont données les proportions sur dix)[27] :

	T2 « 4-4-4 »	T3 « 8-4 »	T4 « 4-8 »	HS	Total
Baudelaire 1857, 1861	10 (6,3)	–	4 (2,9)	–	14
Mallarmé 1866, 1871	3 (3,3)	2 (2,2)	1 (1,1)	3 (3,3)	9
Rimbaud 1870-1871	17 (3,3)	11 (2,2)	10 (2)	13 (2,5)	51
Verlaine 1866	22 (7,9)	1 (0,4)	4 (1,4)	1 (0,4)	28
Verlaine 1868-1870	11 (6,9)	3 (1,9)	1 (0,6)	1 (0,6)	16
Verlaine 1881[28]	27 (5,4)	13 (2,6)	6 (1,2)	4 (0,8)	50
Corbière 1873	9 (2,7)	5 (1,5)	15 (4,5)	4 (1,2)	33

TABL. 2 – Répartition des césures sur proclitique ou préposition monosyllabique chez Mallarmé, Rimbaud et Verlaine (plus Baudelaire et Corbière pour comparaison) dans les « systèmes » de Cornulier.

---

26 Soit les vers de collège, pièces de circonstance, bribes, *stupra* et *Album zutique* de l'éd. Rolland de Renéville et Mouquet.

27 Nous appliquons l'analyse métricométrique sans correctif, sur la seule base des critères CPMF6 (ce qui ne peut aller qu'en faveur de la théorie).

28 Sur *Sagesse* qui contient un nombre élevé de vers « M6 », « F6 » ou « F7 » contrairement aux précédents qui en sont généralement dépourvus, voir V, chap. « Un précurseur du second Verlaine ».

Nos trois poètes mêlent tous les types de vers dans les recueils ou ensembles concernés, quelle qu'en soit leur date, de 1866 à 1873. Mallarmé et Rimbaud les mêlent dans les mêmes proportions, T2 étant deux fois moins représenté chez eux que chez Baudelaire ou Verlaine, avec une proportion élevée de formes HS, d'un quart chez le second, d'un tiers chez le premier. On remarquera au passage que Corbière ne se distingue de Mallarmé et Rimbaud que par l'importance qu'il accorde à T4 au détriment de HS. Si l'on entre maintenant dans la chronologie des œuvres, on remarquera que, dès *Le Parnasse contemporain* de 1866, Mallarmé donne trois vers dotés d'un monosyllabe atone en 6ᵉ position dont le premier relève de T2, le second de T3 et le troisième est HS :

> Se traîne et va, moins pour chauffer sa pourriture (*Les Fenêtres*)
>
> Monte, comme dans un jardin mélancolique, (*Soupir*)
>
> Lève l'ancre pour une exotique nature ! (*Brise marine*)

Dans cette première sélection de son œuvre, Mallarmé serait donc déjà sorti du cadre défini dans *Théorie du vers*. Dans *Critique du vers*, Gouvard répartit les vers de Mallarmé en trois périodes distinctes, avec un fossé entre 1868 et 1875[29], soit la distribution suivante (rapport sur dix entre parenthèses) :

	T2 « 4-4-4 »	T3 « 8-4 »	T4 « 4-8 »	HS	Total
1861-1863	5 (10)	-	-	-	5
1864-1868	3 (1,4)	5 (2,3)	6 (2,7)	8 (3,6)	22
1875-1894	7 (2,3)	5 (1,7)	9 (3)	9 (3)	30

TABL. 3 – Même chose chez Mallarmé, en trois périodes.

Jusqu'à 1863, Mallarmé n'a cultivé que des formes s'inscrivant dans S2 : si S2 a une quelconque réalité dans le corpus de *Théorie du vers*, ce serait donc uniquement pour cinq vers écrits durant cette courte période, spécificité qui, soulignons-le, est totalement occultée dans l'essai de Cornulier. Du reste, la faiblesse des effectifs est telle que Gouvard

---

29   *Op. cit.*, p. 178-179 et 185-186.

emploie prudemment le conditionnel pour avancer que leur structure « pourrait refléter un mètre 4-4-4[30] ». À partir de 1864, Mallarmé varie les types de vers : dès cette année-là, des trois vers à césure sur monosyllabe atone qu'il écrit, l'un est de type T3, un autre de type T4, le dernier HS[31]. Constatant qu'à partir de cette date Mallarmé multiplie les formes HS – selon lui censés caractériser une phase préliminaire –, le disciple de Cornulier considère que désormais, aux yeux du poète, ce type de vers « ne diffère du 12-syllabe classique que par la morphologie de sa 6e position, et non pour son mètre, lequel demeure inchangé[32] », assertion qui, pour autant, ne modifie en rien leur non-conformité à S1 et revient à reconnaître implicitement la réalité métrique de la césure pour l'œil à ces vers tout en la déniant à ceux des types T2, T3 ou T4[33]. Ainsi donc, les premiers vers déviants de ce poète relèveraient de S2, mais à partir de 1864, si le type T2 est bien en forte régression, on ne peut soutenir sérieusement l'idée que l'on est passé de S2 à S3 alors que T4 et plus encore HS s'y trouvent déjà surreprésentés (à raison de 6 sur 10 en total cumulé). Le fait que les trois vers T2 de 1864-1868 sont tous datés de la fin de cette période et que quatre des six T4 – soit autant que de T3 avant cette date – datent au contraire du début (1864-1866) va également à l'encontre de l'idée d'un « apprentissage progressif » permettant de passer d'un « système » à l'autre.

L'hypothèse d'un apprentissage progressif, ici clairement contredit par la chronologie, est d'autant moins défendable que Mallarmé n'ignore rien du précédent de Baudelaire ni de celui de Banville dont nous évoquons plus bas la singularité[34] : l'apprentissage supposé d'une libération progressive de la césure médiane ne peut être réduite à une expérience personnelle chez des poètes sensibles à l'influence de leurs aînés encore couronnés du prestige de l'innovation ainsi qu'à l'émulation entretenue dans les cercles poétiques qu'ils fréquentent. Suivant sa voie personnelle, après une période d'expérience d'un ternaire assoupli, Mallarmé cultivait la césure pour l'œil pour ce qu'elle était : non pas une abolition de la

---

30 *Critique du vers*, p. 202.
31 Voir la liste (61b) donnée par Gouvard, *op. cit.*, p. 179.
32 *Critique du vers*, p. 179.
33 Ce que Gouvard, *op. cit.*, p. 178-179, reconnaît à sa façon en voyant dans ces vers des alexandrins « CP6 6-6 » qui ne diffèrent des formes classiques que par l'admission à l'hémistiche de formes grammaticales interdites par la tradition classique (et romantique).
34 Voir *infra*, p. 323-324.

césure mais une libération des contraintes rythmiques que cette dernière imposait, sans pour autant s'astreindre à de nouvelles contraintes, en explorant librement diverses formes rythmiques, dans un premier temps dans la foulée des ternaires romantiques avant de délaisser ces formes qui tendaient à détourner l'attention de la césure pour l'œil sur laquelle, par la suite, il attirera au contraire l'attention. Si l'on se penche sur le détail des variantes, on constate même que, dans *L'après-midi d'un faune*, à dix ans de distance, Mallarmé renonce en deux occasions au type T3, censé plus avancé, pour le type T2, là où la théorie développée dans *Théorie du vers* laisserait attendre l'évolution inverse :

1866   Par ma lèvre. Quand sur l'or glauque des lointaines

1876   Par le talent ; quand, sur l'or glauque de lointaines

1866   Dans les cygnes et les frissons, ô pierreries !

1876   Dans les clartés et les frissons ; ô pierreries !

Quant à Verlaine, c'est un des seize vers concernés de *Poëmes saturniens* et un des deux des *Amies* (1868) qui sont déjà hors systèmes (HS) ; pas moins de quatre vers de *Poëmes saturniens* sont déjà de type T4, contre un seul des recueils de 1868-1870 (Tabl. 2) : Verlaine aurait-il ainsi régressé avant de revenir à ces formes dans *Sagesse* (1881) ? Ajoutons que, dans *Poëmes saturniens*, on trouve trois fois plus de vers de type T4 que de type T3, ce qui ne va pas non plus dans le sens d'une progression d'un « système » au suivant, et nous doutons que la prise en compte des dates d'écriture établirait le contraire, comme on le verra plus loin[35]. La proportion de T2 aura certes progressivement diminué de 1866 à 1881 au profit principal de T3, mais il faut aussi remarquer que *Sagesse* se distingue des précédents recueils comme de ceux des confrères du poète par l'ouverture à des formes jusque là exceptionnelles sinon inconnues dans lesquelles les contraintes césurales de l'hémistiche sont violées (F6 ou M6), témoignant d'un tournant radical dans l'esthétique du poète[36].

La situation est encore plus frappante chez le Rimbaud d'avant les « derniers vers » : ce sont treize vers sur les cinquante concernés, soit

---

35   Voir *infra*, p. 353-355.
36   Le cas de *Sagesse* sera plus spécialement abordé dans V, « Un précurseur du second Verlaine ».

le quart, qui ne s'y plient à aucun « système », et T4 ne concerne pas moins d'un vers sur cinq : écrits pour l'essentiel en 1870-1871, ces vers témoignent éloquemment de ce que rien n'est alors acquis mais tout à conquérir, chaque poète explorant les ressources ouvertes par la césure pour l'œil selon ses goûts personnels qui ne sont pas encore assujettis à de nouvelles contraintes métriques mais ressortissent plutôt de choix stylistiques. Cornulier n'en a pas moins depuis soutenu que, « de *L'Homme juste* [...] jusqu'à environ le printemps 1872, les vers de Rimbaud sont conformes *au moins* au système 3[37] », ce qui revient à dire que le jeune poète serait passé directement de S1 à S3, faisant par conséquent l'économie de l'étape intermédiaire. Qu'en est-il en réalité ? Si l'on examine les pièces auxquelles une année est assignable entre 1870 et 1871[38] et celles de l'album zutique datables depuis la mi-septembre 1871 (Z), plus le dizain tardif « L'enfant qui ramassa les balles... » de l'album Régamey (R), on obtient la distribution suivante (rapport sur dix entre parenthèses)[39] :

	T2 « 4-4-4 »	T3 « 8-4 »	T4 « 4-8 »	HS	Total
1870	4 (3,1)	-	1 (0,8)	8 (6,2)	13
1871	14 (3,6)	11 (2,8)	9 (2,3)	5 (1,3)	39
Z + R	3 (2,1)	1 (0,7)	9 (6,4)	1 (0,7)	14

TABL. 4 – Même chose chez Rimbaud, en trois périodes.

Six vers sur dix sont hors systèmes en 1870, un sur dix l'année suivante avant de quasiment disparaître. Suivant l'exemple de Gouvard, Cornulier règle la question de ces vers HS en soutenant que, « jusqu'à la Commune, les 12v connus de Rimbaud sont conformes au Système 1 », ce qui est à tout le moins inexact puisque S1, tel qu'il le définit lui-même, suppose précisément l'absence de marquage CPMF6. Allant jusqu'à parler de

---

37   Dans *De la métrique à l'interprétation*, p. 335.
38   Année à laquelle nous rattachons *Les Assis, Le Bateau ivre, L'Homme juste, Les Poëtes de sept ans, Les Premières Communions, Oraison du soir* et *Voyelles*. Pour une discussion des datations, voir l'éd. Murphy, I, *passim*.
39   Le lecteur intéressé par les matériaux tels que les a rassemblés l'auteur consultera les listes données en appendice à *Théorie du vers*, p. 302-303 (vers non datés).

« détachement » du proclitique, il soutient que l'« on doit probablement scander, par exemple, [...] Ouvrant lentement leurs + omoplates, ô rage » ou « Fileur éternel des + immobilités bleues[40] », soit en faisant ressortir la sixième syllabe comme un temps fort (puisque tel est le sens de *scander*), ce qui va à l'encontre et du bon sens et de la scansion effectuée par des générations de lecteurs et du témoignage des poètes eux-mêmes[41]. L'attrait que Rimbaud témoigne pour les formes syncopées ascendantes dès 1870 – sous l'influence directe de Banville[42] –, indique clairement que le poète recherchait les propriétés rythmiques discordantes de la syncope plutôt que d'infliger la muselière du classicisme à des vers qui s'y dérobent aussi ostensiblement et dont l'existence même se justifie par la volonté de s'en affranchir. On remarquera par ailleurs que le parallélisme établi par l'auteur avec la promotion de monosyllabes atones à la rime[43] est fallacieux, parce que *la rime appelle précisément la mise en relief du proclitique*, contrairement à la césure. Ainsi, Musset qui ignore la césure pour l'œil pouvait-il écrire, dans *Les Marrons du feu*[44] :

> Il est large à peu près comme un quartier de lune, –
> Cousu d'or comme un paon, – frais et joyeux comme une
> Aile de papillon, – incertain et changeant
> Comme une femme. [...]

Si Hugo pratiquait les deux procédés dans *Marion de Lorme*, à l'inverse, ceux qu'on doit malgré tout tenir pour les premiers promoteurs de la rime pour l'œil, Baudelaire et Leconte de Lisle, ignorent cette acrobatie verbale dans les pièces qu'ils destinent à la postérité : pour reposer sur le même type de discordances, il n'en s'agit pas moins de procédés distincts répondant à des intentions ou des motivations différentes, et c'est précisément parce qu'ils ne devaient pas s'accompagner d'une suspension à l'hémistiche que l'emploi des monosyllabes atones déroutaient tant les contemporains tout en faisant le délice des poètes qui en usaient.

---

40 *De la métrique à l'interprétation*, p. 335-337.
41 Sur ces derniers, voir *infra* notre chap. « La réception de la césure pour l'œil ».
42 *Cf. infra*, p. 342. Il sera toujours intéressé par ces formes durant sa période « métrique » (*cf.* Billy, « Innovation et déconstruction », p. 129-141).
43 *Op. cit.*, p. 337-338.
44 Ignorant ces différences stylistiques, Ducoffre, « Verlaine et le romantisme », p. 11, voit dans « Chacun plantant, comme un outil, son bec impur » de *Voyage à Cythère* un « décalque » de ces vers de Musset.

Censés apparaître l'un après l'autre, T3 et T4 se développent *simulta-nément* chez Rimbaud en 1871, et ceci dès le mois de mai pour les pièces datées avec quelque précision, à savoir *Accroupissements* (deux et un des trois vers déviants respectivement) et *Les Poëtes de sept ans* (un et deux sur cinq déviants). On peut par ailleurs observer que la proportion de vers relevant de T2 est à peu près constante en dehors des pièces du dernier groupe. D'environ 3 à 3,5 sur dix, elle baisse en effet de 1,5 point dans la dernière série, régression qu'il convient de lier au fait que la propor-tion de vers relevant de T4 prend alors une importance considérable, anticipant de peu dans le registre parodique ou satirique qui est le leur un mouvement que l'on peut observer dans deux recueils parnassiens sérieux de 1872, à savoir dans l'apport de *Poèmes barbares* de Leconte de Lisle et *Les Humbles* de Coppée, ce qui est du reste aussi le cas des *Amours jaunes*[45]. Il est cependant significatif que ce soit dans *Intimités* (1868) et *Poëmes modernes* (1869)[46] que l'on voit ce mouvement amorcé, Coppée étant précisément la cible préférée des pastiches de Rimbaud[47].

Tant chez Mallarmé que chez Verlaine ou Rimbaud sur lesquels Cornulier a fondé son étude, il est donc impossible de soutenir l'hypothèse d'un apprentissage progressif, pas plus que celle des quatre « systèmes » qu'il a imaginés, si ce n'est dans les cinq premiers vers déviants que Mallarmé écrivit avant 1864.

---

45 Chez le premier, 6 sur 13 cas de césure pour l'œil que nous retenons sont de type T4 ; 5 sur 8 chez le second ; 13 sur 33 chez le dernier.

46 À raison d'un quart des cas de césures pour l'œil dans chacun de ces recueils.

47 Pour les dénombrements (et les proportions qui en découlent), voir *infra* Tabl. 6, p. 301-303.

LE MODÈLE
DE *CRITIQUE DU VERS*

La théorie métricométrique s'est vue révisée par J.-M. Gouvard sur la base d'un vaste corpus portant sur des poètes de la seconde moitié du XIXe siècle. Le disciple de Cornulier ignore les « systèmes » de son maître, mais il définit à la place trois étapes qualifiées de « modalités de passage d'une scansion 6-6 vers une ou des structurations propres aux alexandrins CP6[1] », à chacune desquelles il consacre un chapitre ou sous-chapitre[2] :

(M1) la première verrait l'essor d'alexandrins « CP6 6-6 » dans lesquels l'accentuation des 4e ou/et 8e positions ne serait pas recherchée, avec la prédominance de vers HS ; cette phase aboutirait à la « naissance du [mètre] ternaire par le rythme[3] » ;

(M2) la seconde verrait l'essor de mètres de substitutions ternaires avec des alexandrins « CP6 4-4-4 » (soit T2) ;

(M3) la troisième verrait la cohabitation du « mètre ternaire » (T2) et des « mètres semi-ternaires » (T3 et T4).

La théorie ainsi revisitée se distingue par conséquent de la précédente par le rattachement des vers HS à une phase située entre S1 et S2 et par la fusion de S3 et S4 (M3). D'un point de vue strictement théorique, ce postulat de trois modalités se trouve cependant contredit par une remarque de l'auteur qui soutient que l'essor du rythme ternaire

---

1   *Op. cit.*, p. 172.

2   *Critique du vers*, § 3.2 (le corpus considéré est défini aux p. 134-137) : « Alexandrins CP6 6-6 », p. 176-189 (M1) ; § 3.3.1 : « Alexandrins CP6 4-4-4 », p. 189-194 (M2) ; § 3.3.2 : « Mètre ternaire et mètres semi-ternaires », p. 194-202 (T3 et T4). Les désignations par M1 *etc.* sont de nous. Nous ne rectifions pas les éventuelles erreurs d'analyse ou d'interprétation.

3   *Op. cit.*, p. 173.

comme « scansion métrique » « aurait eu du mal à s'imposer s'il n'avait reçu le précieux secours de deux autres configurations, le 4-8 et le 8-4, lesquelles apparaissent concomitamment au 4-4-4 chez tous les auteurs des années 1860, dès que le nombre de CP6 dépasse la dizaine[4] ». Ces considérations reviennent à dire qu'il n'y a pas de passage de M2 à M3, ces « modalités » étant reconnues comme concomitantes, ce dont il eût logiquement convenu de conclure 1°) à l'existence de deux « modalités » seulement, la seconde (M2) absorbant M3 ; 2°) à l'existence d'un unique « mètre de substitution » (sans préjuger de la pertinence de l'expression que nous discuterons dans le prochain chapitre) qui se caractériserait par l'exercice d'une contrainte métrique portant sur la 4e ou/et la 8e position(s) dès lors que la césure médiane intervient après un monosyllabe atone, avec trois instanciations possibles : 4-4-4, 8-4 et 4-8. Il convient donc de se pencher sur les données présentées par l'auteur pour voir ce qu'il en est précisément de ce modèle interprétatif de l'histoire de la césure pour l'œil.

Le dénombrement, selon leur type, des vers présentés par l'auteur dans le cadre de chacune des trois « modalités » permet d'établir la fig. 1, page suivante, basée sur les pourcentages (les effectifs sont indiqués dans chaque tronçon d'histogramme, les totaux entre parenthèses).

Dans M1, près de la moitié des vers (46 %) sont pourvus d'un accent en 4e ou 8e positions, mais c'est la proportion relativement élevée de vers HS (25 %) qui sert ici de marqueur. Dans M2, la proportion des rythmes ternaires équipartis n'est pas éloignée de neuf vers sur dix. Dans M3, un vers sur deux est accentué sur la 4e ou la 8e position soit un peu plus qu'en M1, les vers accentués sur les deux s'accroissant par contre considérablement : de 29 % dans M1, ils représentent à présent 44 % ; si cette modalité se distingue de la première, c'est en fait par la marginalisation des formes HS. Si la distinction des trois « modalités » peut paraître convaincante au regard de cette figure, une étude plus poussée montre qu'elles n'obéissent en fait à aucune chronologie claire et spécifique, et que les types de formes se distribuent avec une liberté considérable au

---

4   *Op. cit.*, p. 194. Et dans la foulée d'annoncer qu'il va « dégage[r] [...] des observations en favveur d'une structuration complémentaire 8-4 / 4-8 ». Voir aussi « De la sémantique », p. 143, où il considère que « le 4-4-4 » est un « mètre très répandu » à l'époque de *Poëmes saturniens*.

sein de chaque ensemble. Les données présentées pour M1 s'étendent ainsi de 1859 à 1893 ; celles de M2, de 1864 à 1881 ; celles de M3, de 1860 à 1875.

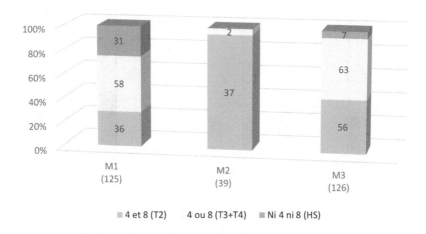

FIG. 1 – Proportion des types rythmiques associés à la césure sur monosyllabe atone par étapes, selon le cadre défini par Gouvard.

Pour ce qui est de la variation, nous nous limiterons à l'examen des sous-corpus présentés pour M1[5] dont voici la distribution exprimée en pourcentages, avec pour chaque tranche l'indication des effectifs (pour chaque sous-corpus, le nombre total de vers concernés est indiqué entre parenthèses)[6] :

---

5   *Critique du vers*, p. 176-189.
6   Nous ne discutons par contre pas la question des datations qui sont de la responsabilité de l'auteur. Nous avons exclu le cas de Laprade : des trois vers cités (p. 183), le premier doit être rejeté (*cf. supra*, p. 148) ; le troisième, « Marquant la place où, dans les vapeurs du matin, » (*Pernette*, 1868), sera quant à lui réécrit en 1870 de façon à restaurer la césure (« Rougissent à travers les vapeurs du matin. »)

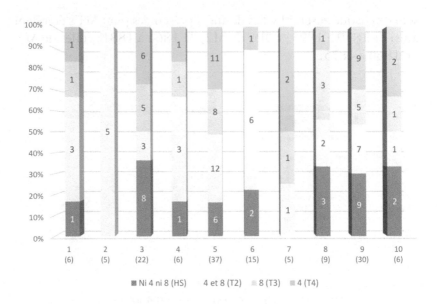

1. Baudelaire à partir de 1860 ; 2. Mallarmé 1861-1863 ; 3. Mallarmé 1864-1870 ;
4. Villiers ; 5. Glatigny ; 6. Mérat (*Les Chimères*, 1866) ; 7. Dierx 1864-1872 ; 8. Mendès
(*Soirs moroses*, 1876) ; 9. Mallarmé après 1871 ; 10. Heredia, des débuts à 1885.

FIG. 2 – Variation dans la première étape définie par Gouvard.

La présence de Mallarmé 1861-1863 (2) dont l'alexandrin « pourrait
refléter un mètre 4-4-4 » (cinq vers), n'a bien évidemment pas sa place
ici mais au chapitre suivant consacré aux « alexandrins CP6 4-4-4[7] » :
Gouvard ne l'évoque que pour mettre en évidence l'évolution des formes
chez ce poète. Nous avons complété les données fournies par Gouvard
lorsqu'elles se limitent à une sélection *ad hoc* de tel ou tel recueil :

> (4) Le corpus défini pour Villiers est d'autant moins significatif qu'il est
> chronologiquement disparate, avec six vers distribués sur vingt ans, le critique
> n'en jugeant pas moins pertinent de distinguer deux périodes, la première
> d'une seule année (1859) avec « de possibles 4-4-4 », qui ne concernerait que
> deux vers ; la seconde qui concernerait les quatre autres dont la composition
> se disperse sur vingt ans tout en empiétant sur la première : l'un (de type
> T3) est en effet daté de 1859, deux de 1866, le dernier de 1879.

_____

7   Nous ne l'avons pas pris en compte pour l'élaboration de la Fig. 1 (M1).

(6) La définition du corpus de Mérat est en outre des plus fragiles : centré sur « la partie des *Chimères* écrite en 1864 » (4 vers), il correspond en fait à la section *Fleurs de Bohême* dont le poète lui-même situe plus précisément l'écriture en 1863-1864, avec deux vers HS contre un T2 et un T4, tandis qu'il date la suivante (*Tableaux de voyage*), de 1864-1865, avec cinq alexandrins CP6 (tous T2)[8] : ce qui relève *précisément* de l'année 1864 est par conséquent pour le moins incertain, d'où notre décision d'étendre le corpus retenu par Gouvard au recueil entier.

(7) À la liste des vers que Dierx publia entre 1864 et 1872, nous avons ajouté le vers T4 omis « Longtemps il lutte, sans que son âme lassée » (*Poëmes et poésies*, XXII, p. 153).

(8) Nous tenons compte de tous les vers déviants de *Soirs moroses* de Mendès dont seuls les trois vers retenus par Gouvard (p. 184-185) ressortiraient de M1 : cet ensemble est en effet chronologiquement cohérent du point de vue de sa conception comme de son écriture.

Ces mises au point étant faites, une fois éliminé le second histogramme, on peut se pencher sur les neuf autres où l'on peut observer une variation phénoménale, naturellement amplifiée lorsque les effectifs sont faibles, qui ruine la cohésion apparente des données cumulées dans la fig. 1 : le type T2 présente ainsi des écarts extrêmes, allant de 1,4 (3) à 6,7 sur dix (6) ; T4 oscille entre 1,1 (6) et cinq sur dix (7) ; la plus petite variation qui concerne T3 est de 3,3/10. Le type HS – ni 4 ni 8 – censé caractériser une phase intermédiaire entre l'alexandrin romantique et les « mètres de substitution » atteint trois vers sur dix chez Mallarmé, tant en début (3) qu'en fin de carrière (9), et s'observe également chez Mendès (8) et Heredia (10) à 18 ans de distance, le seul vers concerné du premier datant de 1868, les deux du second, de 1885, selon les indications de l'auteur[9] ; il n'est plus que d'environ deux sur dix chez Baudelaire (1), Mérat (6) et Villiers (4) mais aussi chez Glatigny (5). Mais ce qui retient davantage l'attention est l'importance parfois considérable prise par les marqueurs de M2 (T2) et de M3 (outre T2, T3 et T4) : les deux cumulés atteignent huit à neuf sur dix chez Baudelaire (1), Villiers (4) et Glatigny (5) et les quatre vers de Dierx (7) qui n'illustre pas une seule fois le marqueur de M1. Force est de conclure de ces observations sur les corpora retenus par l'auteur pour illustrer ce qu'il appelle des

---

8   Voir la liste donnée par l'auteur p. 190, avec cinq vers présentés comme « des alexandrins potentiellement ternaires ».

9   *Op. cit.*, p. 194.

« alexandrins CP6 6-6 », que l'existence de M1 ne repose sur rien de tangible, d'autant que tous intègrent des vers de type T3 (sauf Mérat) et T4 censés renvoyer à la troisième étape M3.

On pourrait procéder de la même façon pour la modalité M2 dont Gouvard situe l'essor dans les années 1860[10]. Dans le chapitre dédié aux « alexandrins CP6 4-4-4 », le corpus Mérat fait ainsi apparaître deux vers T3[11] ; celui de *Melancholia* de Cazalis illustrerait bien M2 si les cinq vers présentés par Gouvard ne pouvaient faire oublier « Et l'ennui des éternités déjà passées. » où la césure est occultée, sans accent sur la 4e position ; celui de *Poëmes saturniens* également, s'il ne fallait ajouter aux douze vers qu'il recense quatre de type T4 et un de type T3, selon les données, par ailleurs incomplètes, qu'il fournit[12], ce que l'auteur, nous l'avons vu, reconnaissait en notant que T3 et T4 « apparaissent concomitamment au 4-4-4 chez tous les auteurs des années 1860 ». Seul *Les Paysans de l'Argonne* de Theuriet, dont on n'oubliera pas que l'écriture date de 1870, serait susceptible de représenter M2 si le nombre de vers concerné n'était si faible (trois) qu'il en est dépourvu de signification.

Examinons à présent de façon globale la dimension chronologique impliquée par la notion de « modalité » que l'auteur met en avant, à partir des dates d'écriture que lui-même avance pour les illustrer[13]. Dans la figure suivante en aires empilées, nous indiquons les valeurs pour les quatre types de vers par paires d'années, de 1859 à 1876 (les effectifs sont indiqués dans chaque tranche, le total sous chaque période)[14] :

---

10   *Op. cit.*, p. 184 et 187. Le critique ne relève cependant pour Mendès qu'un cas auquel il attribue la date de 1868 sans préciser d'où il la tient : son édition de référence (*Poésies*, 1876) ne donne en effet aucun élément de datation, et le premier volume de *Poésies* de 1892 donne cette édition comme sa première parution en recueil, sans précision de date d'écriture ou d'éventuelle prépublication des poèmes. *Soirs moroses* contient au demeurant un autre vers du même genre : « Aux reptiles et pour me gorger de soleil » (IV, *Spleen d'été*, p. 47).

11   En réalité il y en a trois ; *cf. infra*, p. 281, n. 17, à propos de « Tous vos chants et *etc.* ».

12   Aux douze vers T2 recensés p. 194, il faut en effet ajouter le T3 et les quatre T4 listés au chapitre suivant, p. 195, plus le T2 cité p. 227 (45). Mais il en reste une dizaine d'autres, tous T2 sauf un, HS (« Tu consoles et tu berces, et le chagrin », *Il Bacio*).

13   Nous tenons compte ici des reclassements ponctuellement effectués par l'auteur sur les résultats des tests « CP6 », corrections qui ne concernent au demeurant que quatre vers, pour les années 1866 (un T4 reclassé en T1, p. 198), 1869 (deux T2 en T3, p. 200 et 201), et 1873 (un T4 en T1, p. 195).

14   Nous laissons donc de côté les vers ultérieurs que présentent Gouvard, dont la distribution est au demeurant discontinue. Les vers des *Chimères* que Mérat date de « 1864-1865 »

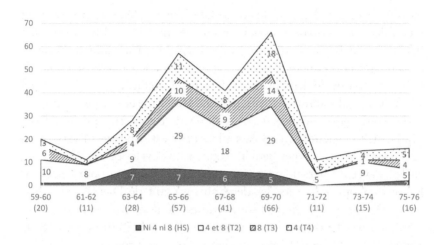

FIG. 3 – Tendances évolutives dans la distribution des types rythmiques associés à la césure sur proclitique ou préposition monosyllabique chez les Parnassiens.

Aucun type ne présente une progression ou une régression continue à même de soutenir le postulat de « modalités de passage ». La proportion de vers ternaires équipartis (T2) oscille en général entre 4 et 5 vers sur 10, si ce n'est deux pics : un de 7/10 en 1861-1862 (dont la moitié des huit cas sont du jeune Mallarmé) et un autre de 6/10 en 1873-1874 (dont six des neuf cas sont de Leconte de Lisle, les trois autres de Coppée), avec une baisse à 3/10 en 1863-1864 (dont cinq des neuf cas sont de Glatigny). Cependant, ce dernier cas mis à part, les extrêmes concernent des effectifs réduits, de onze à seize vers. Les vers HS ne sont que deux de 1859 à 1862 mais ils culminent à un vers sur quatre la paire d'années suivantes. Ils représentent 12 puis 14 % en 1865-1868 avant de diminuer de moitié puis de disparaître en 1871-1872 sans que l'on puisse prétendre y voir un phénomène significatif compte tenu des effectifs réduits sur ces années (deux et neuf vers respectivement). Si l'on examine le détail année par année (occulté dans la Fig. 3), il apparaît que c'est en 1864 que leur proportion est la plus forte avec trois vers sur dix (il n'y en a pas

---

sont ici rattachés à l'année 1865. Nous avons par contre retranché un vers de la liste (63), p. 181, car il y a aposiopèse (« S'il faut causer de ton… machin parlementaire, »), situation justement écartée par l'auteur dans ses mises au point méthodologiques (p. 107 et 109).

en 1863[15]), essentiellement du fait de Glatigny et Mérat (respectivement 3 et 2 des sept vers concernés), mais elle oscille ailleurs librement entre 0,5 et 1,5 sur 10, sans qu'une évolution régulière n'apparaisse. Supposé caractériser la première phase, ce type de vers ne caractérise en fait la versification que de deux poètes, Glatigny et Mérat. En 1865 et surtout 1866 (6 vers), il intéresse essentiellement Mallarmé et Coppée (3 et 2 des 7 vers concernés) ; en 1868 (rien en 1867), il ne concerne que Mendès et Mallarmé (3 chacun) ; en 1869, seul Coppée est concerné (4 vers). Pour ce qui est des autres types, seul T4 connaît un développement important en 1872 avec un tiers des vers (aucun en 1871), qui sont pour l'essentiel le fait de Coppée (4 vers, les deux autres étant de Dierx), mais cette année-là encore, les effectifs sont réduits (neuf vers) ; absent en 1861-1862, le type T3 disparaît à nouveau de 1871 à 1873 (un cas en 1874), années qui totalisent 17 vers déviants. Aucune progression régulière n'est par conséquent observable pour quelque type que ce soit, chaque poète procédant dans ses recherches rythmiques selon sa personnalité. Les variations de quelque importance que nous avons relevées sont le plus souvent liées à la faiblesse des effectifs, et l'on remarquera que la répartition des quatre types est relativement stabilisée dès lors que les effectifs dépassent quarante vers, soit de 1865 à 1870.

La théorie métricométrique soulève par ailleurs le problème de la *métricité* des structures identifiées au travers des vers déviants considérés. Ainsi, constatant qu'un Albert Mérat accompagne volontiers ce genre de vers d'une recherche d'accent sur les 4e et 8e positions, Gouvard en vient à évoquer l'émergence d'un « système où le 4-4-4 acquiert le statut de mètre de substitution », affirmant p. ex. que les onze vers concernés des *Villes de marbre* (datés de 1869)[16] : « répondent à un mètre 4-4-4 ou, pour le moins, 8-4, qui sera appelé "mètre de substitution", dans la mesure où il n'apparaît que pour pallier l'affaiblissement voire la suppression de la coupe médiane, de telle sorte qu'il semble se "substituer" au mètre 6-6 ». Seuls deux vers en effet de ce recueil ne sont pas des ternaires équipartis mais des ternaires à membres inégaux – à quoi il convient de préciser qu'ils présentent l'un et l'autre une post-tonique en 4e position (3'-5-4) –, alors que, dans les *Chimères* (1866), sur les neuf vers concernés, six sont

---

15 Pas plus du reste qu'en 1859, 1862, 1867 ou 1874.
16 *Op. cit.*, p. 191.

accentués en 4e et 8e positions, un en 4e et deux en d'autres positions (HS)[17]. De cette situation, Gouvard voit chez ce poète la plus claire illustration de sa deuxième modalité : dès lors qu'il accepte des monosyllabes atones à la césure, Mérat adopte presque systématiquement un rythme ternaire équiparti dans ce recueil. Qu'il s'agît d'une préférence esthétique ne fait aucun doute, mais qu'il s'agît d'un *mètre* est autre chose. Parmi les recueils parnassiens des années 1858-1873 que nous avons examinés, seuls quatre recueils vont dans un tel sens, où la césure pour l'œil est systématiquement associée au type T2, mais avec des effectifs généralement bien plus réduits. Ces recueils sont par ailleurs dispersés dans le temps, sur une période de treize ans : *Poésies complètes* de 1858 de Leconte de Lisle (2 occurrences), *Melancholia* de Cazalis (1868) et *Les Paysans de l'Argonne* de Theuriet (1870) pour cinq occurrences chacun, *Poëmes de Provence* d'Aicard (1873), pour huit occurrences. Si l'on se penche sur les recueils présentant, comme *Les Villes de marbre*, une combinaison exclusive de T2 et de T3, on se trouve amené aux mêmes conclusions, ces recueils étant disséminés de 1859 (*Premières poésies* de Villiers de L'Isle-Adam) à 1870 (*La Bonne chanson*), le plus souvent avec des effectifs infimes allant de deux à quatre césures sur monosyllabe atone, et n'excédant jamais sept[18]. Il est par contre tout à fait remarquable que, dans tous les vers T3 qu'ils contiennent, la 4e position soit occupée par une syllabe post-tonique : il y a bien là une unité structurale dans ces ensembles qui se caractérisent certes par l'accentuation mais également par la priorité sur l'accent accordée à la frontière syntagmatique entre les 4e et 5e positions. Ces formes constituent une particularité qui se présente déjà dans les ternaires romantiques par ailleurs régulièrement césurés. Ainsi, dans la liste des ternaires irréguliers de Hugo que dresse Rochette (tous basés sur un parallélisme), répondant selon lui à la formule qu'il note « 3+5+4 »,

---

17 Gouvard analyse en deux endroits bien distincts les vers concernés du recueil : p. 183 (vers de 1864) et 190 (autres). Dans la section *Tableaux de voyage* datée de 1864-1865, « Tous vos chants et tous vos caprices de couleurs, » (*La Trompe des Alpes*) que Gouvard qualifie d'alexandrin « potentiellement ternaire » doit être rejeté de ce classement arbitraire, la conjonction *et* sans pause ne pouvant être sérieusement tenue pour un support accentuel valable dans une métrique quelconque (ce qu'il fait du reste pour un vers de Coppée, p. 200) à moins, peut-être, d'être séparé du constituant conjoint par une transposition, ce qui n'est pas ici le cas.

18 Voir ainsi en 1865 *Les Pensées tristes* de Renaud (quatre T2 et deux T3), *La Bonne chanson* (6 et 1) et *Fêtes galantes* (4 et 1).

dix-sept sont de forme 3'-4-4 contre un 3-5-4 seulement[19] ; parmi ceux notés « 3+4+5 », six sont de forme 3'-3'-5 contre un seul 3-4'-4 ; le seul noté « 3+6+3 » est de forme 3'-5-3[20].

Au-delà de la notion pour le moins discutable de « modalité », dont la chronologie établit de toute façon l'inexistence, c'est la notion même de *mètre de substitution* qui fait en effet problème : ces vers de type T2 et T3 n'ont-ils pas tous en commun avec ceux de type T4 ou HS de présenter un monosyllabe atone à l'hémistiche, ce qui caractérise précisément la césure pour l'œil ? Comment donc les mètres alternatifs supposés pourraient-ils *se substituer* à une structure à césure médiane si celle-ci n'est pas complètement occultée mais maintenue avec une telle obstination, les contraintes morphophonologiques qui la déterminent continuant à s'y exercer, de façon, certes, atténuée, avec le refus d'une post-tonique en 6e position et le maintien d'une frontière de mots ? La formulation au mieux prudente de « semble se substituer » ne fait qu'ajouter à la confusion. La réalité des « mètres de substitution » reste, pour cette raison même, pour la diversité des pratiques et pour des raisons d'ordre probabilistique que nous verrons plus loin[21], une hypothèse dont les fondements sont des plus incertains avant les années 1870. Étudiant les cinq alexandrins « CP6 » de Cazalis dans *Melancholia* (1868) – tous ternaires équipartis –, l'auteur n'hésite pourtant pas à affirmer « qu'il ne s'agit plus, contrairement aux années 1850, d'un simple rythme de compensation à une mesure binaire affaiblie, mais bien d'un mètre nouveau, qui se substitue systématiquement au 6-6 lorsque l'actualisation de celui-ci est fortement compromis[22] », oubliant que le recueil contient un autre vers où la césure est cette fois incontestablement occultée par la présence d'un polysyllabe sur les positions 5 à 8, mais où la 4e est occupée par un article contracté, avec un rythme 3-5-4 : « Et l'ennui des éternités déjà passées. » Cette particularité tend à indiquer deux choses : d'une part, le rythme ternaire équiparti est un rythme d'appui qu'affectionne Cazalis, sans que l'on puisse pour autant lui attribuer

---

19   Plus un 3-5'-3 égaré dans la liste (le tiret signale une frontière de mots moyennant une éventuelle élision ; l'apostrophe, un schwa final non élidé).

20   *L'Alexandrin chez Hugo*, p. 115-116.

21   Voir *infra*, p. 291-292.

22   *Critique du vers*, p. 192. *Cf.* p. 189 : « Si le rythme ternaire ne traduisait pas nécessairement un mètre 4-4-4 pendant les années 1850, il indiquait, en la martelant, une voie nouvelle qui commence d'acquérir statut métrique au cours des années 1860. »

une fonction métrique autrement que de façon arbitraire ; d'autre part, comme on le verra plus tard, la structure rythmique de son unique vers non césuré s'inscrit parfaitement dans le cadre historique des vers dépourvus de césure médiane qui commencent à faire sporadiquement leur apparition chez les Parnassiens qui (Mallarmé et Verlaine mis à part) les commettent alors davantage par inattention que par intention[23].

Gouvard pointe en outre un aspect particulier de la démarche de Mallarmé qui, selon lui, par sa multiplication des vers accentués en 3e et 9e positions, « traduit [...] un état intermédiaire entre le 12-syllabe classique et un 12-syllabe qui serait réellement libéré de la scansion 6-6[24] ». Il convient tout d'abord de souligner que ces vers ne participent pas davantage de cet état de choses que les césures pour l'œil de ses confrères des années 1860/1870. Ensuite, il faut reconnaître à la démarche de Mallarmé une originalité par rapport à ses confrères qui n'est pas sans lien avec sa pratique d'une syntaxe acrobatique défiant la tradition grammaticale, le procédé permettant une certaine mise en relief du monosyllabe atone tant par la distance qui sépare les toniques les plus proches, favorable à l'émergence d'un simple accent de proéminence, que par des constructions singulières qui rompent la cohésion du clitique en le séparant de sa base par une transposition forcée, comme dans *Le Pitre châtié* : « Mille sépulcres pour y vierge disparaître. » Là où ses confrères s'attachent davantage à cacher la césure au profit de rythmes souvent variés, Mallarmé peut ainsi recourir à un procédé analogue à celui dont il peut user à la rime, sans, naturellement, les effets particuliers de la rime, avec une sorte de contre-rejet qui tient plus de la rupture de rythme que de la mise en relief. Mais à vrai dire Mallarmé va plus loin à partir de 1866 en rendant cette structure binaire méconnaissable dans quelques vers où l'accentuation, même artificielle, de la 6e position n'est pas sérieusement défendable, la tête de syntagme, monosyllabique, se trouvant directement introduite par le mot grammatical :

Aux ivresses de sa sève ? Serais-je pur ? (*Brise marine*)

Sans un murmure et sans dire que s'envola (*L'Après-midi d'un faune*, 2e vers.)

Loin du lit vide qu'un cierge soufflé cachait, (*Hérodiade*)

---

23   Voir *infra* p. 361-364.
24   *Op. cit.*, p. 182.

ce que, au demeurant, Baudelaire avait déjà fait dans *Le Voyage* («O mon semblable, ô mon maître, je te maudis!»), Verlaine dans *Poëmes saturniens* («Et le vieux tremble sa plainte sempiternelle.»), Mérat dans *Les Villes de marbre* («Si vous faites de nos grâces peu langoureuses», *Marmorea*), et quelques autres, Glatigny semblant affectionner cette syncope sous les formes le plus diverses, et ceci dès son recueil de 1864 *Les Flèches d'or* : «Dans sa force, dans son calme, dans sa grandeur.» (*Méduse*)[25]. La césure médiane est également tout aussi méconnaissable lorsque le mot grammatical suit directement une syllabe forte en 5e position comme dans ces trois vers du *Poëme de Hérodiade* (1868), dans une démarche visiblement inspirée de l'exemple de Banville dans *Le Festin des dieux* («Nous flottions, errants, dans le frisson des nuées» *etc.*) dont Corbière lui-même s'est sans doute inspiré[26] :

> Descendre à travers ma rêverie en silence, [...]
> Mais horreur! des soirs, dans ta sévère fontaine, [...]
> Métaux qui donnez à ma jeune chevelure [...]

Là encore, Glatigny n'est pas de reste, comme dans *Le Revenant* daté de 1861 mais publié onze ans plus tard dans *Gilles et Pasquins* : «Il se replongeait dans son canard à trois sous.» Si l'on veut bien croire qu'un Laprade, pour qui la poésie n'était jamais qu'une modalité d'écriture et non un art, pouvait se laisser par exception aller à des césures «semi-mécaniques[27]», il paraît bien difficile d'adopter ce point de vue pour un esthète tel que Mallarmé ou un homme de théâtre tel que Glatigny que ces rythmes scabreux, taquinant la césure à l'extrême, avaient de quoi séduire. Tout ce qu'on peut dire, c'est que, selon leur personnalité, encline à l'imitation ou à l'innovation, les poètes parnassiens se sont lancés dans une exploration des potentialités stylistiques de la césure pour l'œil dans le cadre et hors du cadre des ternaires, selon leur per-sonnalité et leurs dilections.

---

25 On aura noté que la 8e est occupée par une post-tonique dans tous les exemples cités, particularité qui renforce l'effet de syncope rythmique.
26 *Cf. infra*, p. 341-342. Dans le premier toutefois, où l'accent dominant porte sur la 2e posi-tion, la 5e porte un accent de proéminence à la manière de Verlaine dans *Sur le balcon* : «Emphatique comme un trône de mélodrame» (*Les Amies*).
27 *Cf. infra*, p. 363-364.

LA NOTION DE MÈTRE
CHEZ LES MÉTRICOMÉTRICIENS

Une dernière question, liée à la précédente, se pose à propos de la notion même de métricité dans le cadre de la théorie métricométrique : en effet, selon son fondateur, le concept de *mètre* se confond avec celui de *mesure* quand Cornulier n'emploie pas le terme comme un synonyme de *forme* déterminée par l'articulation de plusieurs mesures[1]. Cette formulation renoue en fait avec la conception classique du vers dont Gouvard a fourni divers témoignages[2], à commencer par celui de Port-Royal pour qui « sa structure ne consiste qu'en un certain nombre de syllabes », Marmontel invitant toutefois à dissocier *nombre* et *mesure* par la prise en compte de « la finale muette », les syllabes qui comptent devant être « sensibles à l'oreille[3] ». Cornulier définit « l'alexandrin 6+6 » comme « la *mesure fondamentale* » pouvant « [être] relayée par une *mesure d'accompagnement* » notée « 4-4-4 », avec chaque fois un astérisque qui renvoie à un glossaire où ces termes n'apparaissent pas, mais où l'on trouve une entrée « mètre fondamental / d'accompagnement » où se trouve rajoutée une « forme » (ou « rythme ») « 3-5-4[4] » (rejoignant ainsi Dorchain) ; ailleurs, il parle de « coupes[5] » ; ailleurs encore, de

---

1 Voir le « glossaire » proposé dans *Art poëtique*, p. 261, aux entrées « mesure, mètre », « mètre de base / contrastif », « mètre fondamental / d'accompagnement ». Ces définitions ne font pas état du principe d'équivalence « naturelle » (qui n'est autre au demeurant que la *paritas sillabarum* du moyen âge) pourtant inhérent à la métricométrie (*Théorie du vers*, p. 100-101), ni, du reste, de la question de l'accent sans lesquels « mètres » et « mesures » ne peuvent être reconnus.

2 *Critique du vers*, p. 10-12.

3 L'idée semble rejoindre celle d'A. Boyer que cite l'auteur à la page précédente, distinguant le *poids* qu'il identifie à une « valeur » (sans précision) et le *nombre* qui fait l'objet d'un compte : seule la terminologie change, avec l'ambiguïté induite par la polysémie de *nombre*.

4 *Art poëtique*, p. 86-90 et 261.

5 Lorsqu'il évoque, *op. cit.*, p. 90, « la forme 444, ou 354, mais d'autres encore », précisant : « La valeur de substitution de ces coupes n'est pas naturelle, mais semble reposer sur un apprentissage progressif ».

« périodicité compensatoire 444^6 » ; ailleurs encore, il évoque indifféremment des « rythmes » ou « mesures » qualifiés de « compensatoires ou de substitution », en apportant des précisions à la fois confuses, hésitantes et incertaines, en faisant un bref bilan des observations alors faites « chez certains poètes », qui « font apparaître une tendance générale au relâchement des mètres traditionnels, compensables, puis sporadiquement substituables par des rythmes compensatoires ou de substitution, rythmes précis tant qu'ils ne sont pas trop variés (et qu'à ce titre on peut encore reconnaître comme des mètres subsidiaires), d'abord, je crois, 4-4-4 puis 3-5-4, puis d'autres rythmes à 4v final (coupe 8e) [...] puis, je crois (car il y a débat sur le détail de cette évolution), des rythmes à 4v initial sinon terminal (coupe 4e sinon 8e)^7 ». Le simple fait d'admettre que 3-5-4 ou « d'autres rythmes à 4v final » ou « initial » puissent avoir statut de mètre témoigne d'une mécompréhension totale des lois qui régissent la métrique romane comme on le verra au chapitre suivant. Tout deviendrait ainsi matière à « mètre de substitution », pourvu, finalement, que les positions 4 et 8 s'y trouvent l'une ou/et l'autre sollicitée(s)^8. Gouvard considère par contre que « ces "mesures" 4-3-5, 4-5-3, 3-4-5 etc. sont caractéristiques de notre langue et non pas du mètre du vers^9 », ouvrant ainsi un nouveau fossé critique. En effet, puisque le maître et le disciple accordent un statut métrique à 8-4 et 4-8, le désaccord concerne uniquement les séquences 3-5 et 5-3 ; mais pourquoi ces séquences relèveraient-elles davantage de la langue que 4-4, alors que les trois cas se rencontrent fréquemment dans le cadre de l'octosyllabe ? Ce qui laisse pour le moins peser un doute sur l'interprétation de la « mesure » 4-4-4 dans laquelle il est fréquent que les accents de 4e et 8e positions n'occupent pas le même rang, l'un étant l'accent majeur du vers : tel est le cas du 8e dans « De ceux qui s'aiment sans mélange, n'est-ce pas ? » qui pourrait prétendre à la « mesure » 8-4 au même titre que « D'une joie extraordinaire : votre voix ».

Chez Cornulier, substitution et subsidiarité sont confondues^{10} lorsqu'il ne s'agit pas de compensation ; mètre, mesure, rythme, forme, coupe,

---

6   *Op. cit.*, p. 87.
7   *Op. cit.*, p. 46.
8   « Pour une approche », p. 46.
9   « De la sémantique », p. 144.
10   La notion de césure « subsidiaire » est sans aucun doute empruntée à Martinon, « Le trimètre » [2], p. 50, qui entendait par là tout autre chose (*cf.* p. 256).

périodicité, c'est tout un. Une question ne manque pas de se poser : si *le mètre* est une mesure, et si la mesure de l'alexandrin est double (6-6), pourquoi alors ne pas définir ce dernier comme « dimètre » ? Pourquoi ne pas parler de « dimètres de substitution » dans le cas de 8-4 et 4-8 plutôt que de « semi-ternaires » qui est une expression aussi contradictoire que tendancieuse, orientée dans une inféodation plus ou moins assumée au « trimètre » romantique, selon l'expression promue par Martinon ? Et justement, pourquoi parler de « ternaires » au lieu de « trimètres » là où il y a trois « mesures » (4-4-4) ? Le *distinguo* semble reposer sur une distinction subtile entre *mesure* et *nombre*[11] : « Une mesure de vers, ou *mètre*, est donc une suite d'un [*sic*] ou plusieurs nombres (un nombre, 8, pour le 8-syllabe, deux nombres, 6-6, pour l'alexandrin), chacun de ces nombres devant être inférieur à 9 pour être aisément reconnaissable ». La distinction est si subtile que l'auteur s'y perd lui-même dans un « glossaire » censé éclaircir les choses : s'il évoque la possibilité de parler de *sous-mesures* pour désigner ce qui est appelé *nombres* dans cette définition, c'est en les désignant comme les « mesures constitutives d'une mesure complexe », tandis que *mesure* ou *mètre* se dirait « d'une forme métriquement pertinente de vers ou de <u>partie de vers</u>, qui est généralement [...] une longueur caractérisée simplement en nombre de voyelles[12] ». Pour ajouter à la confusion, dans un article récent, le théoricien nous apprend, que la notion même de *mesure* qu'il a si longtemps défendue n'est en fait pas pertinente (contrairement à celle d'« équivalence métrique »)[13]. Soutenir que « l'hypothèse suivant laquelle, vers les années 1850 à 1870, certains 12-syllabes ont simultanément une césure classique *et* une forme ternaire, c'est-à-dire sont des 6+6 tout en étant rythmables en 4-4-4 (voire 3-5-4, ou 8-4, *etc.*) est très vraisemblable », est par ailleurs un déni implicite de la thèse d'une métrique de substitution sur cette période où les poètes veillent scrupuleusement à maintenir l'apparence d'une césure médiane avec la neutralisation de la contrainte accentuelle[14].

---

11 *Théorie du vers*, p. 88. Aucune limite n'étant fixée au nombre de *nombres* possible ni aucun minimum à ces *nombres*, la définition rend envisageable que, p. ex., 2-1-8-3-5 soit un mètre.

12 *Art poëtique*, p. 261. Le soulignement est nôtre.

13 « Si le mètre m'était compté ». L'idée que « le nombre n'est pas un mètre » est déjà formulée dans *Art poëtique*, p. 26-30, en contradiction avec le fait que, selon la définition paradoxale citée *supra*, un mètre puisse être « une suite » d'un seul nombre.

14 *Art poëtique*, p. 96.

Tant le flou des définitions et l'inconstance de la terminologie que les glissements de l'argumentation au gré des années témoignent de l'embarras des tenants de la métricométrie à conceptualiser l'évolution de l'alexandrin durant la période où le mouvement parnassien se développe jusqu'à l'émergence de courants nouveaux, principalement illustrés par l'essor du symbolisme. Si, dans *Critique du vers*, Gouvard limite comme Cornulier les mètres de substitution à des vers déviants accentués en 4ᵉ ou/et 8ᵉ positions (T2, T3 et T4), on a vu qu'il a depuis envisagé que ceux accentués en 5ᵉ ou 7ᵉ positions soient également plus ou moins concernés, et Cornulier n'hésitait pas à élargir la notion de « mètres subsidiaires » à des ternaires à membres inégaux[15], ce qui revient à déguiser des "césures mobiles", au sens voltairien (frontières syntagmatiques) avec les oripeaux du mètre.

Une question essentielle que les métricométriciens ne se sont pas posée est de savoir si ces « mètres de substitution » ne renvoient pas à quelque mètre historique réel susceptible de leur donner une certaine légitimité. Les types T2, T3 et T4 peuvent rappeler des formes qui n'ont connu au mieux qu'une fortune isolée dans la poésie lyrique médiévale dont le souvenir s'est souvent depuis longtemps perdu. Ainsi, T2 rappelle un mètre en ancien occitan sur lequel nous reviendrons[16] ; T3 en rappelle un autre, ‹8ᵐ-4ᵐ›, en anglo-normand[17] ; le type T4 a des antécédents dans la chanson populaire (p. ex. ‹4-8›)[18]. Le seul parallèle contemporain que l'on puisse établir concerne T2, précisément dans la seconde moitié du xixᵉ siècle, avec quelques essais expérimentaux ouverts par l'essor emblématique du ternaire romantique équiparti (‹4-4-4›)[19]. Ces mètres se définissaient naturellement par leur systématicité et ne se mêlaient ainsi jamais entre eux comme ils ne se mêlaient pas à l'alexandrin : l'idée que ces structures anciennes, exotiques, marginales ou liées à des

---

15   Voir *supra*, p. 285-286.
16   Voir *infra*, p. 294-295.
17   Chaque membre a une terminaison masculine (notée ᵐ) ; les crochets signifient que l'on a en vue les mètres eux-mêmes et les contraintes structurales qui les constituent. Sur ces mètres, voir Billy, « L'analyse distributionnelle », p. 816-818.
18   Voir p. ex. la chanson du *Comte Orry*, analysée succinctement – mais correctement – par F. de Gramont, *Les Vers français*, p. 89-90, qui n'en cite que deux vers. Voir la version qu'en donne l'adresse URL https://www.partitions-domaine-public.fr/pdf/10844/Traditionnel-Le-Comte-Orry.html (consulté le 10/09/2022).
19   Sur ces essais, voir *infra*, p. 378-383.

rythmes musicaux puissent tout à coup entrer en concurrence comme « mètres de substitution », en affectant rarement plus d'un pour cent des vers d'une même composition, est dépourvue de toute crédibilité.

La théorie développée par les métricométriciens, tant dans sa version primitive que dans sa forme révisée, doit par conséquent être abandonnée : la progression qu'ils décrivent et l'apprentissage qu'elle sous-tend sont des fictions dépourvues de fondement. L'empilement de « mètres » qui se substitueraient les uns aux autres pour compenser leur défaillance est une vue de l'esprit, d'autant que, dans plus de 95 % des cas, les contraintes proprement métriques qui sous-tendent la césure médiane se trouvent obstinément maintenues. Si seule l'une des trois mutations métriques qu'ils pensent avoir identifiés (à savoir T3) se trouve fondée, ce n'est pas dans le cadre de la césure pour l'œil qu'ils ont essentiellement en vue bien qu'ils en contestent la réalité, et cette mutation ne se met véritablement en place qu'à une date déjà avancée de leur chronologie, chez de rares poètes[20]. L'histoire de l'alexandrin qu'ils brossent ainsi pour la seconde moitié du XIXe siècle est une pure invention, relevant au mieux de l'uchronie métrique. La seule conclusion qui ait quelque pertinence se trouve au détour d'une démonstration contradictoire de Gouvard selon lequel « c'est [...] bien plutôt une diversification des pratiques qu'un ensemble d'usages concertés et cohérents, qui tendraient tous à imposer, par exemple, le mètre ternaire 4-4-4[21] », conclusion qui, au demeurant, ne fait que revenir au constat que Paul Stapfer faisait l'année même de la publication des *Amours jaunes*[22] : « Il s'est formé autour de M. Théodore de Banville un laboratoire de poésie où tous les rythmes possibles ont été curieusement essayés. » Sauf que, là encore, Gouvard fait référence à un mètre ternaire qui n'est pas plus défendable que dans le cadre de l'alexandrin romantique, car, dans la quasi-totalité des vers concernés antérieurs à la mort de Corbière, vers répondant aux critères CP6, une frontière de mots après syllabe pleine se présente systématiquement à l'exact milieu du vers, comme il en allait des vers romantiques les plus audacieux dont Ténint en des temps plus anciens, face aux libertés

---

20 Voir les éléments que nous rassemblons et discutons dans III, « L'occultation de la césure chez Corbière », et V, « L'abolition de la césure médiane chez les Parnassiens » et « Un précurseur du second Verlaine ».

21 *Critique du vers*, p. 176-177.

22 « La poésie française contemporaine » (28 mars), p. 2.

syntaxiques que promouvaient leurs auteurs en prêchant d'exemple sous la bannière équivoque des « césures mobiles », pouvait constater, non sans maladresse[23] :

> La césure [*entendue comme phénomène prosodique*] peut donc se déplacer, mais l'hémistiche classique, tout en se soudant au milieu du vers à l'autre hémistiche, doit avoir toutes ses syllabes pleines.

C'est même l'insistance que Ténint mit à attirer sur elle l'attention du lecteur que cette autre innovation du romantisme qu'est le ternaire équiparti, ce « vers à part » qu'il avait décrit sous le nom de « vers trimètre ou de trois fois quatre pieds[24] », que cette forme, donc, devenue caractéristique de la nouvelle école a pu constituer un cadre rythmique particulièrement favorable à l'occultation occasionnelle de la césure médiane, avec l'admission de monosyllabes atones qui permettait aux Parnassiens de se démarquer plus radicalement de leurs aînés en affichant ainsi insolemment leur modernité au regard de ce « poncif de coupe » que dénoncera Banville dans son *Petit traité* et que vise Sainte-Beuve dans les « Jugements divers et témoignages » qu'il ajoute en 1861 à *Vie, poésies et pensées de Joseph Delorme*, évoquant « tel passage où l'abus de la césure mobile ramène presque la monotonie qu'elle était destinée à prévenir[25] ».

---

23 *Prosodie*, p. 77. Ténint n'ignore pas la nécessité d'une frontière de mots, la *soudure* en question étant une manière de rendre compte de l'absence d'une frontière de syntagmes. D'une façon différente mais tout aussi maladroite, Mendès, *Rapport*, p. 160, dira que « la césure, sans être supprimée tout-à-fait, se déplace ».
24 *Prosodie*, p. 60 et 74.
25 Sur les poncifs dénoncés par Banville, voir *infra*, p. 318-319.

POUR UNE APPROCHE DESCRIPTIVE

Une interprétation satisfaisante des licences que peut prendre Corbière au regard de la césure ne peut s'accommoder d'un cadre théorique et d'une méthodologie aussi problématiques que ceux de la métricométrie. La première question que l'on doit se poser est la suivante : si, pour une raison quelconque, l'accent métrique du vers (accent dominant ou non) n'est plus en 6ᵉ position, où pourrait-il bien être ? L'histoire et la systématique des vers césurés établissant que la longueur des membres métriques varie de 4 à 8 syllabes[1], il faut nécessairement qu'un accent majeur tombe sur la 4ᵉ, la 5ᵉ, la 7ᵉ ou la 8ᵉ position, divisant le vers en deux membres de quatre, cinq, sept ou huit syllabes, ou sur les 4ᵉ *et* 8ᵉ positions, divisant le vers en trois membres. Si l'on tient compte du fait que les poètes évitent les accents en 5ᵉ ou 7ᵉ positions insuffisamment éloignées de l'hémistiche – à moins, justement, de rechercher un effet particulier en renouvelant les syncopes romantiques –, il ne reste que les 4ᵉ et 8ᵉ positions. Il ne faut par ailleurs pas oublier que dans son désir d'affranchissement de la tradition classique, le romantisme a fortement modifié au sein de l'alexandrin l'économie générale des rythmes au profit des formes axées sur les positions paires, et plus particulièrement la 4ᵉ et la 8ᵉ, là où la tradition privilégiait la 3ᵉ et la 9ᵉ positions[2]. Si l'on tient en outre compte du fait que, dans les poèmes hétérométriques, c'est l'octosyllabe que les poètes combinent le plus volontiers avec l'alexandrin, jamais le pentasyllabe dont la combinaison avec l'heptasyllabe reste rarissime[3], on ne sera plus guère étonné de voir les vers déviants présenter un accent majeur sur la 4ᵉ ou la 8ᵉ position plus souvent qu'ailleurs. Naturellement, augmentant la taille d'un des membres du vers ainsi constitués, le déplacement de l'accent médian

---

1 Billy, « L'analyse distributionnelle », p. 811-819.
2 *Cf. infra*, p. 371-373.
3 Baudelaire en donne un exemple dans *Le Poison*.

ouvrait la possibilité d'avoir un accent de même rang, ou du moins de rang proche au sein du membre long, avec les divisions habituelles de l'octosyllabe, soit, pour l'essentiel : 3-5, 4-4 et 5-3, et une préférence marquée pour les rythmes 3-5-4 et 4-5-3 (accents divisionnaires en 3e ou 9e positions) au détriment de 5-3-4 et 4-3-5 qui présentent des accents divisionnaires en 5e ou 7e positions.

Ceci étant, on peut constater une différence de traitement entre les monosyllabes atones et les monosyllabes centripètes divers qui relèvent de catégories grammaticales grises, alors même que leur admission à la césure semble concomitante de celle des proclitiques et prépositions monosyllabiques, dans des proportions au demeurant plus limitées : déterminants indéfinis, interrogatifs ou exclamatifs, adverbes d'intensité, conjonctions simples non suivies d'une pause ou d'un syntagme transposé, pronoms relatifs non appuyés d'une préposition *etc.* On doit toutefois relativiser les différences observables entre catégories grises et monosyllabes atones de statut au demeurant varié, car les uns et les autres n'occupent généralement pas les mêmes positions dans la structure comme dans la chaîne syntaxique. Pour prendre un exemple simple : dans *et que sur cet ennui*, le déterminant occupe le premier rang avant le substantif, la préposition le second, la conjonction de subordination le troisième et la conjonction de coordination le quatrième : *ennui* peut alors figurer sur la 8e, la 9e, la 10e ou la 11e position selon le mot grammatical que l'on promeut à l'hémistiche.

Mettons de côté cette question qui ne peut être abordée sans une étude circonstanciée pour nous pencher sur une question plus essentielle : dans quelle mesure la pratique de la césure pour l'œil est-elle liée à l'émergence d'un accent en 8e position ? Il suffit pour cela d'étudier la position du premier accent lexical après l'hémistiche dans les vers présentant une séquence constituée d'une préposition suivie d'un déterminant (article, démonstratif ou possessif) occupant l'un et l'autre une seule position métrique, dont l'un à l'hémistiche, pour constater que l'accent en 8e position n'est pas systématiquement recherché pour lui-même. Voici les fréquences des premiers accents rencontrés dans les différentes positions concernées, relevées chez Banville dans la première édition des *Exilés*, dans *Les Amours jaunes*, chez Mallarmé[4], le Rimbaud

---

4   Constituées à partir de la liste dressée par Gouvard, *Critique du vers*, p. 179, pour les années 1864-1870.

des « premières poésies » et Verlaine pour les recueils publiés avant *Sagesse*. Nous ajoutons les recueils lyriques de Glatigny jusqu'à 1872 en raison des affinités que son œuvre présente avec celles de Corbière[5] :

		P7	P8	P9	P10	Moy.	Diff.
Banville	prép | dét		5	4		8,4	
	prép dét |	2	6			7,8	0,6
Corbière	prép | dét		2	2		8,5	
	prép dét |	2	2			7,5	0,9
Mallarmé	prép | dét		3	3	1	8,7	
	prép dét |	1	2	2		8,2	0,5
Rimbaud	prép | dét		4	7	2	8,8	
	prép dét |	1	6	3	2	8,5	0,3
Verlaine	prép | dét		5	1		8,2	
	prép dét |		8			8	0,2
Glatigny	prép | dét			4		9	
	prép dét |	4	9	1	1	7,9	1,1

\| indique le lieu de l'hémistiche ; « Moy. » : position moyenne approchée ; Pn : n-ième position ; « Diff. » : écart entre les deux moyennes calculées pour chaque poète.

TABL. 5 – Le tropisme accentuel de la 8ᵉ position.

Si la 8ᵉ position jouait un rôle *métrique*, on s'attendrait à ce que son accentuation soit recherchée *indépendamment* du contexte syntaxique, et, par conséquent, lorsque la préposition est reculée d'un rang (en P5), à ce que le premier accent lexical rencontré[6] recule d'autant. Si ce

---

5   Voir V et VII, les chap. « L'influence de Glatigny ».

6   Ainsi celui de *bonne* dans *pour leur \| bonne femme*. Dans les rencontres accentuelles en fin de syntagme, nous faisons abstraction du pénultième (un seul cas : *beau* dans « Néfaste incite pour son beau cadre une rixe ») ; ce choix étant posé, il ne faut pas négliger que l'accentuation est un phénomène complexe : aussi bien *beau* que *cadre* peuvent être accentués, pourvu que cette accentuation s'appuyât sur des paramètres distincts, intensité, longueur ou hauteur). Dans les (rares) cas de mots composés, c'est le premier accent lexical qui est pris en compte lorsqu'il n'est pas suivi du dernier (ex. *casques* dans *sur les \| casques-à-mèche*).

n'est pas le cas, on s'attendrait à ce que la différence entre {prép | dét} et {prép dét |} soit d'un point, ce qui est quasiment le cas chez Corbière et Glatigny, mais elle est de 0,7 chez Banville et n'est plus que d'un demi-point chez Mallarmé ; elle est moindre encore chez Rimbaud (0,3) et Verlaine (0,2), ce qui implique que la 8e position exerce bien un tropisme, variable mais certain, chez ces poètes. Cependant, il semble que ce tropisme, est en bonne partie lié à la dilection, au demeurant variable de ces poètes, et plus spécialement Verlaine, pour les rythmes ternaires équipartis que le mouvement romantique leur avait légués. Chez Mallarmé et Rimbaud, dans le même contexte {prép dét |}, la position de l'accent varie de la 7e position à la 9e chez le premier ou la 10e chez le second (pour six et douze vers respectivement), là où Verlaine accentue systématiquement la huitième. On en conclura qu'une contrainte rythmique existe bien dans le cadre de la césure pour l'œil, s'exerçant avec plus ou moins d'intensité selon les poètes, mais que cette contrainte d'une part n'est pas pour autant un substitut de la césure médiane qui, à de rares exceptions près, ne subit pas encore les violations apportées dans *Sagesse*[7], d'autre part qu'elle s'exerce avec une intensité variable chez les uns et les autres. Corbière semble quant à lui insensible à l'attraction de la 8e position dans sa pratique de la césure pour l'œil.

Pour combattre l'inertie du rythme 6-6, largement dominant chez les Parnassiens (jusque chez Coppée et Verlaine), seuls des rythmes simples et nets, appuyés sur les accents majeurs du vers, pouvaient rivaliser et prétendre remplir une quelconque fonction de compensation. Dans ses recherches rythmiques, A. Ducondut considérait que, dans un vers de douze syllabes, seuls le rythme 4-4-4 pouvait prétendre à une fonction métrique en lieu et place des formes classiques[8]. A. Thomas a pu identifier au moyen âge un texte didactique isolé, en ancien occitan, contenant environ 1 530 dodécasyllabes – tous masculins – où rares sont les exceptions affectant l'une des deux positions, le philologue parlant d'un mètre caractérisé par une césure masculine, facultativement à la 4e ou à la 8e syllabe, avec une dominante de la forme descendante (8-4), et une tendance très nettement marquée à la division du plus

---

7   Sur *Sagesse*, voir V, « Un précurseur du second Verlaine ».
8   Voir *infra*, p. 379.

grand membre en deux segments égaux conformément à la structure des plus anciens octosyllabes[9]. Si nous avons récusé le concept de « mètre de substitution » dans le cas des césures parnassiennes où la notion de césure pour l'œil prend toute sa pertinence, les poètes s'appliquant soigneusement à éviter par ce biais une rupture radicale d'avec le modèle hérité de la césure médiane dont – à de rares exceptions près – ils préservent scrupuleusement le vestige, il n'en est pas moins certain que les rythmes structurés par l'accentuation des 4e ou/et 8e position(s) ont joué un rôle déterminant dans l'émergence et le développement du phénomène, comme en témoigne à la fois leur relative surreprésentation dans ce genre de vers chez certains poètes et les ratés qui s'observent çà et là, y compris chez Leconte de Lisle et Banville qui ont pu se laisser aller à s'affranchir de la césure médiane dans de rarissimes vers qu'ils ont corrigés par la suite[10]. On peut donc tout au plus, pour désigner ce genre de rythmes favorables à l'essor de la césure pour l'œil, parler de *structures (rythmiques) d'appui*[11].

L'évolution de l'alexandrin depuis l'époque classique jusqu'à Corbière peut être décrite en trois étapes, avec pour point de départ l'alexandrin romantique, étapes que nous hiérarchiserons de la façon suivante, en fonction des manifestations phonologiques résultant du jeu des contraintes accentuelle (CA) et morphologique (CM) pesant sur la césure ; nous indiquons entre crochets les quatre étapes du parcours cognitif esquissé par A. Dorchain pour l'alexandrin postromantique[12] :

1. CA et CM respectées : affaiblissement progressif de la 6e position par le développement des enjambements internes et émergence des rythmes ternaires parmi lesquels les formes équiparties jouent un rôle prépondérant bien que non exclusif avec un effet amplifié au regard de leur importance statistique réelle ;

---

9   « La versification de la *Chirurgie provençale* ». Il va de soi que les conditions de réalisation de ce mètre diffèrent des formes modernes du fait des spécificités prosodiques de la langue médiévale. Nous ne citons que pour mémoire les essais analogues de Baïf qui s'inscrivaient dans une toute autre perspective, ce poète explorant les potentialités ouvertes par la métrique gréco-latine autant que celles des structures musicales.

10   Voir *infra*, p. 361-362.

11   Voir aussi V, « Contraintes choisies et contraintes subies ».

12   Voir *supra*, p. 252. Le cas de la neutralisation de la CM – ignoré de Dorchain – a été plus spécialement abordé dans III, « La césure dans les mots composés ».

2. CA neutralisée / CM respectée [A] : *occultation de la césure* (césure
    pour l'œil) dont nous préciserons plus loin les circonstances[13] ;
3. CA ou CM violée : *restructuration de l'alexandrin* sur une 8e position
    accentuée, conformément à l'intuition de Martinon (mais dans des
    conditions plus restreintes)[14] :
    – CM violée / CA neutralisée : abolition de la césure médiane par
      l'emploi de polysyllabes à cheval sur l'hémistiche [B] ;
    – CM violée / CA respectée : emploi d'une post-tonique en 7e posi-
      tion [C] ;
    – CA violée / CM respectée : emploi d'une post-tonique en 6e posi-
      tion [D].

Nous n'en sommes pas encore aux remises en cause radicales de
Rimbaud ni aux innovations de Laforgue : le premier renoncera librement
à toute césure métrique tandis que le second adoptera des rythmes encore
inouïs, violentant par à-coups le mètre de toutes les façons possibles[15].

---

13 Voir *infra*, « La résistible ascension de la césure pour l'œil », p. 321-326.
14 Voir *supra*, p. 256-257, et les preuves que nous réunissons dans III, « L'occultation de la
    césure chez Corbière », et V, « L'abolition de la césure médiane chez les Parnassiens » et
    « Un précurseur du second Verlaine ».
15 Sur cette dernière évolution, voir *supra*, p. 264.

PRÉSENTATION DU CORPUS PARNASSIEN

L'histoire de la césure pour l'œil mérite donc d'être questionnée avec quelque recul, mais aussi avec quelque détail si l'on veut préciser l'influence du Parnasse sur Corbière. Nous nous intéresserons plus particulièrement à la variété des formes rythmiques associées au procédé. Pour cela, nous nous en tiendrons encore à la seule question des proclitiques et des prépositions monosyllabiques[1] dans les recueils et plaquettes de poésie antérieurs à 1874 présentant au moins un cas de cette sorte. Nos dénombrements excluent la poésie dramatique lorsqu'elle est publiée à part, dans des livrets ou des périodiques[2], comme c'est le cas des vers burlesques de *Qui veut des merveilles ?* écrits l'année de parution des *Exilés* et publiés l'année suivante dans *Le Hanneton*, où Verlaine et Coppée malmènent allègrement la césure[3]. Mallarmé se trouve par contre exclu de ce corpus, ses vers ne paraissant pas avant 1876 dans des publications personnelles.

Si la question des césures pour l'œil témoigne bien globalement de la volonté de leurs auteurs d'inscrire ces formes nouvelles dans le cadre métrique traditionnel de l'alexandrin, la question au cas par cas peut

---

1 En excluant le cas des locutions telles que *jusqu'à* ou *de par* (*cf. supra*, p. 212).

2 Nous écartons ainsi *Souvent homme varie* de Vacquerie (1859), mais nous retenons par contre, p. ex., *Hans et Marie* ou *Arabelle* que le poète recueille dans *Mes premières années de Paris*. Nous puiserons le cas échéant dans ce corpus complémentaire qui contient 74 cas de proclitiques ou prépositions monosyllabiques à la césure.

3 Sur ces vers, voir Gouvard, *Critique du vers*, p. 223-224 et 234-236. C'est à Gouvard que l'on doit la première recension des formes ici discutées, que nous complétons, corrigeons ou précisons le cas échéant. Gouvard, qui ne donne pas de tableau général sur l'histoire du phénomène, ne s'appuie pas toujours sur les éditions originales et n'indique pas les proportions de vers affectés. Son « corpus général » – par ailleurs plus large que le nôtre par la prise en compte de poètes de toutes tendances (mais tous les recueils qui s'y trouvent recensés ne contiennent pas de césures pour l'œil) – n'inclut pas la production d'Hervilly, Marc, Renaud ou Silvestre, et porte aussi bien sur des rééditions ou des recueils composites que sur des éditions originales.

toujours se poser, divers repentirs témoignant clairement que ces formes n'ont pas toujours été maîtrisées mais ont pu, en quelque sorte, été portées par un rythme particulier, généralement dérivé du ternaire romantique équiparti[4]. De cette situation, il résulte que l'on doit s'interroger sur la seule *possibilité* de structures métriques alternatives, à condition de poser le problème correctement, avec pour but d'identifier les accents remplissant une fonction structurante (éventuellement métrique) dans le rythme des vers considérés. La métrique historique établissant que les membres métriquement viables n'ont pas moins de quatre et pas plus de huit syllabes, nous avons cinq possibilités de telles structures, déterminées par l'accentuation des positions métriques suivantes : soit 4e et 8e, soit 4e seule, soit 5e seule, soit 7e seule, soit 8e seule. Une question plus délicate est de savoir si, dans ces structures, il y aurait une quelconque obligation d'élision d'une éventuelle post-tonique devant la syllabe subséquente pour qu'elles puissent prétendre à un statut métrique. En pratique, dans les mètres correspondant historiquement attestés[5], une telle obligation n'existe pas à la fin (césure lyrique) ni au début (césure enjambante) d'un membre métrique de quatre syllabes, soit dans notre cas ‹4-4-4›, ‹4-8›, ‹8-4› et ‹7-4›[6] ; par contre, dans le rare dodécasyllabe symétrique ‹7-5›, attesté chez les trouvères, on avait le cas échéant une césure épique : on s'attendrait donc à ce que ce mètre subît la même évolution que l'alexandrin dont les formes primitives présentaient le même traitement épique avant que l'obligation d'élision ne s'y imposât. Le fait que, dans les rares formes similaires qui apparaîtront çà et là l'élision soit facultative suffirait à montrer que, dans notre corpus, elles ne résultent pas de contraintes proprement métriques, comme en témoignent les deux vers non césurés suivants (rythmés 3-4'-4 et 4-3'-4) que, avant Laforgue, Verlaine commettra dans *Madrigal*, douzain satirique qui conclut le premier cycle de *Jadis et Naguère* :

> Du bout fin de la quenotte de ton souris, (v. 4)
> T'y jeter, palme ! et d'avance mon repentir (v. 11)

---

4   Voir *infra*, p. 307-314, à propos de Hugo.
5   Voir *supra*, p. 288.
6   Nous avons eu l'occasion de montrer l'existence de rythmes 3'-4-4 (p. 281-282 ; voir aussi p. 383 et 351-352) ; exemples de rythmes 3'-8 (sans accent dans la z.m.c. – voir *infra*) : « A tes mousses, à tes frondaisons incertaines, » (Glatigny, *Les Flèches d'or*, XXXIV) ; « Euménides ! qui sur vos beaux fronts secouez » (Banville, *La Cithare*).

Il serait naturellement vain de s'intéresser aux moindres détails de la structure accentuelle des 367 vers déviants considérés de notre corpus, aussi, seules les tensions rythmiques qui s'exercent dans la *zone métriquement contrainte* (z.m.c.), soit sur les positions 4 à 8, retiendront notre attention. Les accents présents en dehors de cette zone – liés ou non à des rejets ou contre-rejets –, fussent-ils de rang supérieur, ne sont par conséquent pas pris en compte. Pour la détermination de la hiérarchie accentuelle, nous privilégions le critère syntaxique ; ainsi, dans les constructions de type « X, Y et Z », nous considérons que les accents affectant X et Y (et Z) sont de même rang, bien que le repos après X détache nettement le premier groupe accentuel. Nous distribuons ces vers déviants en quatre classes ({...}) en fonction des mètres alternatifs *potentiels* (‹...›) auxquels renvoie la structure accentuelle de la z.m.c. Les éventuels problèmes d'interprétation sont abordés en introduction de chaque classe ou dans des remarques spécifiques. Les vers donnés en exemples seront de préférence tirés des *Amours jaunes*. Nous mettons en marge, en regard de chaque type, le nombre de vers concernés et leur pourcentage (entre parenthèses) :

Classes et types de rythmes

{4 et 8}

Les structures rythmiques équiparties pourraient aussi bien renvoyer à un mètre « bicésuré » ‹4-4-4› (en particulier 1°) qu'à des mètres simples ‹4-8› (en particulier 2°) ou ‹8-4› (en particulier 3°). On distinguera trois variantes rythmiques :

1°) deux accents dominants de même rang (syntaxique) en 4e et 8e positions (4=8) ; ex. : « Filé son câble par le bout sans *fignolure*... » (*Le Novice en partance*) ;   43 (11,7)

2°) deux accents dominants en 4e et 8e positions, dont le premier est de rang (syntaxique) supérieur (4>8) ; ex.: « Et les crins fous de ta Déesse ardente et blonde ?... » (*Litanie*)   119 (32,4)

3°) deux accents dominants en 4e et 8e positions, dont le second est de rang (syntaxique) supérieur (8>4) ; ex. : « Et la rosée et le soleil ont eu ses fleurs... » (*Le Fils de Lamartine*) ;   31 (8,4)

Rem. Il arrive que des positions hors z.m.c. présentent un accent de rang supérieur lié ou non à un rejet ; ex. : « – Le Cid... un cid par un *été* de carnaval : » (*Hidalgo !*)

{4 ou 8}	
1°) l'accent dominant de la z.m.c. est en 4e position (‹4-8›) et la 8e n'est pas accentuée ;	74 (20,2)
2°) l'accent dominant de la z.m.c. est en 8e position (‹8-4›) et la 4e n'est pas accentuée ;	61 (16,6)

Rem. Dans les deux cas, l'accent dominant du vers peut se situer en dehors de la z.m.c. ; ex. ‹8-4› : « Tu sais bien, comme dans *Inès de la Sierra…* » (*Le Poète contumace*)[7].

{5 ou 7}	
1°) ‹5-7› : l'accent dominant de la z.m.c. est en 5e position ;	20 (5,4)
2°) ‹7-5› : l'accent dominant de la z.m.c. est en 7e position ;	5 (1,4)

Rem. 1. Il arrive que la z.m.c. comporte un accent secondaire, éventuellement en 8e ou, respectivement, 4e position ; ex. : « – Le Porc – rognonnant sa prière du matin ; » (*Litanie du sommeil*) ; « Et dans les siècles des siècles… Comme c'est long ! » (*Grand opéra*)[8].
Rem. 2. Les (rares) vers présentant deux accents dominants de même ordre au sein de la z.m.c. dont un sur la 5e ou la 7e position sont rejetés dans **Autres** (1°) du fait de leur ambivalence.
Rem. 3. L'accent dominant du vers peut naturellement se situer en dehors de la z.m.c., lié ou non à un rejet ; ex. : « Couleur […] trop tôt devenue/ *Merdoie…* excepté dans les plis rose-d'amour, » (*Le Bossu Bitor*), accent de troisième rang en 8e position.

Autres	
1°) Équ. : configurations équivoques : la z.m.c. comporte deux accents de même rang, dont un au moins n'est pas en 4e ou 8e positions, comme dans les ternaires asymétriques.	4 (1,1)

7   En ce qui concerne l'accentuation de *comme* (d'un rang inférieur à celle d'*Inès*), rappelons que nous accordons la priorité aux classes lexicales sur les catégories grises, même si cela pourrait se discuter du fait des rééquilibrages éventuellement apportés dans la structuration prosodique des énoncés : ainsi, une conjonction même élémentaire peut fort bien être accentuée comme en témoigne éloquemment le vers suivant d'Aicard : « […] si l'homme ici bas/N'est pas heureux, c'est que son prochain ne veut pas. » (*Les Jeunes croyances*, p. 108), dans son premier recueil qui contient des poèmes écrits de 1863 à 1866, par ailleurs dépourvus de césures sur proclitique ou préposition monosyllabique, mais où l'on trouve à l'hémistiche deux emplois du déterminant indéfini *nul(le)*. Le poète ne se ralliera en effet au mouvement qu'à la faveur, semble-t-il, de la « seconde bataille d'Hernani » (*cf.* Mortelette, *Histoire du* Parnasse, p. 225-231).

8   Aveugle sur ce qui se passe au niveau des positions autres que la 4e et la 8e, les métrico-métriciens classent inévitablement ces vers en S3 et S4 respectivement (Cornulier) ou en M3 (Gouvard).

Ainsi, de rythme 4-3'-4 « O mon semblable, ô mon maître, je te maudis ! » (Baudelaire) peut être rattaché aussi bien à ‹4-8› qu'à ‹7-5›.

2°) {–} : la z.m.c. ne présente aucun accent ; ex. : « Vous, vous n'êtes que des *pelletas* militaires… » (*Matelots*), accentué en 1re, 3e et 9e positions.   10 (2,7)

Rem. (2°) Naturellement, la séquence atone qui s'étend ainsi sur au moins cinq syllabes se prête à une accentuation de second rang, purement rythmique (accent de proéminence), qui peut coïncider avec l'hémistiche. Dans le cas de l'exemple cité, un accent d'insistance tombe sur le *que* restrictif.

Le tableau ci-dessous donne une vue synoptique de l'importance relative des grands types rythmiques, par ordre de publication des différents recueils, les rééditions augmentées figurant à la suite des titres originaux (Baudelaire et Leconte de Lisle). Dans ces dernières, le décompte porte sur les seuls ajouts. Les recueils (ou apports) présentant un seul cas de monosyllabe atone à la césure sont exclus du tableau qui porte ainsi sur 42 recueils (sur un total de 55), auxquels nous ajoutons, à fin de comparaison, *Les Amours jaunes* ; lorsque le nombre d'alexandrins du recueil (Eff.) ne dépasse pas 150[9], nous mettons la proportion (‰) entre parenthèses ; l'astérisque qui suit le pour-mille indique que le recueil considéré contient également un alexandrin dépourvu de césure médiane[10] :

	{4 et 8}	{4 ou 8}	{5 ou 7}	{–}	Équ.	Eff.	‰
Baudelaire, *Les Fleurs du Mal* 1857	3	1|-				1824	2,2
[apport] 1861	6	2|-		1		808	11,1
[apport] 1868	1	-|1				306	6,5
Leconte, *Poésies complètes* 1858	2					7262	0,3
[apport] *Poésies barb.* 1862	9	3|3				4212	3,6
[apport] *Poèmes barb.* 1872	4	6|3				766	17

---

9   Au-delà, les effectifs passent à 228 (Coppée, 1869) puis 277 (Marc, 1869) et plus. Les valeurs nulles ne sont pas exprimées, si ce n'est dans les 2e et 3e colonnes, par un tiret.

10   Dans la formule « x|y » des colonnes {4 ou 8} et {5 ou 7}, x désigne 4 ou 5 respectivement ; y, 8 ou 7. Eff[ectifs] : nombre d'alexandrins du recueil (ou de son apport relatif à une édition antérieure).

Villiers, *Premières poésies* 1859	2	-|1				1859	1,6*
Glatigny, *Les Vignes folles* 1860		-|1		1		1005	2
Renaud, *Les Poèmes de l'amour* 1860	2	1|-				2264	1,3
Des Essarts, *Les Élévations* 1864	2	-|2				1698	2,4
Dierx, *Poëmes et poésies* 1864		2|-				1842	1,6
Glatigny, *Les Flèches d'or* 1864	3	-|1	-|1	1		1099	5,5
Renaud, *Caprices du boudoir* 1864	1	-|1				437	4,6
Renaud, *Les Pensées tristes* 1865	4	-|2			1	2102	3,3
Coppée, *Le Reliquaire* 1866	11	5|4	2|-			802	27,4
Mérat, *Les Chimères* 1866	5	1|1	-|1	1		1890	4,8
Silvestre, *Rimes neuves et vieilles* 1866	1	-|1				728	2,7
Verlaine, *Poëmes sat.* 1866	20	5|2	-|1			768	36,5
Banville, *Les Exilés* 1867	13	1|5	7|-	2		2637	10,6*
Dierx, *Les Lèvres closes* 1867	1	-|1				1596	1,3
Cazalis, *Melancholia* 1868	5					727	6,9*
Coppée, *Intimités* 1868	4	4|5				383	33,9
Verlaine, *Les Amies* 1868	1		-|1			28	(71,4)
Coppée, *La Grève des forg.* 1869	1	-|1				228	8,8
Coppée, *Poëmes modernes* 1869	10	5|5	2|-	2	1	1353	18,5
Marc, *La Gloire de Lamartine* 1869	1	-|1				277	7,2
Mérat, *L'Idole* 1869	2	1|-				280	10,7
Verlaine, *Fêtes galantes* 1869	4	-|1	-|1			74	(81,1)*

Glatigny, *Le Fer rouge* 1870		1|-	1|-			683	2,9
Silvestre, *Les Renaissances* 1870	1	1|-		1		1309	2,3
Theuriet, *Les Paysans de l'Argonne* 1870	3					150	(20)
Verlaine, *La Bonne Chans.* 1870	6	-|1	1|-			145	(55,2)
Aicard, *Les Rébellions* 1871	17	6|6		1	1	1468	21,1
Coppée, *Les Humbles* 1872	3	5|-				1640	4,9
Glatigny, *Gilles et Pasquins* 1872	7	9|1	7|-			1695	14,2
Luzarche, *Les Excommuniés* 1872	2	3|-				492	10,2
Mendès, *Hespérus* 1872	2	3|1				986	6,1
Mendès, *Contes épiques* 1872	4	2|1				688	10,2
Mérat, *Les Souvenirs* 1872	2	-|3				644	7,8
Vacquerie, *Mes Premières années* 1872	4	2|3		1		3004	3,3
Aicard, *Poëmes de Prov.* 1873	8					2577	3,1
Mérat, *Les Villes de marbre* 1873	9	-|2				1104	10
Corbière, *Les Amours jaunes* 1873	7	13|2	7|1	3		1590	20,8*

TABL. 6 – Vue synoptique des grands types rythmiques
dans la poésie parnassienne.

Penchons-nous tout d'abord sur la question préalablement posée de *la possibilité de structures métriques alternatives*. Les données réunies recueil par recueil n'infirment en rien nos conclusions sur les thèses métrico-métriques : dès le début, la plupart des recueils mêlent au moins deux classes de rythmes, et lorsqu'il ne s'y présente qu'une, c'est pour des effectifs réduits qui ne dépassent pas huit cas (Aicard, 1873). Ajoutons que, les césures pour l'œil étant le plus souvent disséminées, il n'y a en général aucun effet d'isométrie perceptible entre les vers déviants de même type, ce qui rend ininterprétable le rythme 4-4-4 qui pourrait aussi bien évoquer le mètre ‹4-4-4› que ‹4-8› ou ‹8-4› dont il constitue une possible actualisation. Du point de vue de la seule oreille, l'isorythmie de tels vers avec les ternaires romantiques toujours pratiqués a plus de chance d'apparaître à l'auditeur, nonobstant leur anomalie.

Cette question de fond mise de côté, la première chose qui frappe quand on se penche sur le détail de notre tableau est que *Les Amours jaunes*, qui fait partie des huit recueils présentant au moins 2 % de vers déviants, est celui qui rassemble le nombre le plus élevé de ce genre de vers, soit 33, juste avant *Les Rébellions et les Apaisements* (1871) d'Aicard (31 vers), puis *Poëmes saturniens* (1866) et *Les Exilés* (1867) (28 vers chacun). Il n'atteint toutefois pas en proportion les scores de sept autres recueils, principalement de Verlaine et de Coppée, sans parler des *Amies* et de *Fêtes galantes* – parus six et cinq ans plus tôt – des 7 ou 8 % desquels il se trouve bien en deçà, mais le nombre total d'alexandrins de ces recueils est beaucoup trop réduit pour que la remarque soit pertinente, d'autant que leur homogénéité les distingue nettement du recueil de Corbière, à l'inspiration éclectique, incluant des poèmes antérieurs à son séjour parisien :

	Date du recueil	N^bre alex[11].	%
Les Amours jaunes	1873	33/1590	2,1
Les Rébellions (Aicard)	1871	31/1468	2,1
Le Reliquaire (Coppée)	1866	22/802	2,7
Intimités (Coppée)	1868	13/383	3,4
Poëmes saturniens	1866	28/768	3,6
La Bonne Chanson	1870	8/145	(5,5)
Les Amies	1868	2/28	(7,1)
Fêtes galantes	1869	6/74	(8,1)

TABL. 7 – Recueils parnassiens où la fréquence des césures sur proclitique ou préposition monosyllabique est la plus élevée, comparés aux *Amours jaunes*.

---

11 Dans x/y, x est le nombre de vers déviants ici considérés, y le nombre total d'alexandrins du recueil.

On remarquera que seuls les deux premiers recueils sont véritablement comparables, avec dans l'un et l'autre cas un total approchant 1500 vers, les autres ne dépassant guère la moitié de ces effectifs (*Le Reliquaire* et *Poëmes saturniens*), sinon le quart (*Intimités*), et moins du dixième pour les trois derniers. Le recueil de Corbière s'inscrit donc bien dans ce courant novateur des partisans de la césure pour l'œil.

Afin de suivre l'évolution des césures sur monosyllabes atones dans le corpus parnassien, nous découperons la période considérée – qui court de 1857 à 1873 – en trois tranches, deux de six années plus une de cinq[12]. Nos dénombrements se limitent aux césures sur proclitiques ou prépositions monosyllabiques (c.p.o.). Le nombre total de cas s'élève à 40, puis 130, pour atteindre enfin 210, pour un nombre de recueils (rec.) croissant mais un nombre d'alexandrins relativement proche[13] :

	N^{bre} rec.*	N^{bre} alex.	N^{bre} c.p.o.	‰
1857-1862	9 (6)	19765	38	1,9
1863-1868	15 (12)	15089	124	8,2
1869-1873	24 (15)	22547	179	7,9

* Entre parenthèses, nombre de poètes concernés.

TABL. 8 – Évolution de la pratique de la césure sur proclitique ou préposition monosyllabique chez les Parnassiens, en trois périodes.

Le nombre de formes déviantes augmente régulièrement d'une période à l'autre, dans des proportions importantes. Leur proportion passe de 2 à 8 ‰ en moyenne dès la seconde période qui voit l'entrée de Coppée et de Verlaine sur la scène poétique, mais reste ensuite stable. On peut suivre plus précisément l'évolution dans le temps, de 1857 à 1873, avec, naturellement, un nombre de recueils variable selon les années (leur nombre figure entre parenthèses au-dessous de chaque année)[14] :

---

12 Le pour-mille donné pour chaque période indique la proportion de césures pour l'œil calculée sur le total d'alexandrins de la période considérée.
13 Le nombre d'alexandrins diffère dans un rapport de 1,2 de la première à la dernière période.
14 Nous indiquons sous le tableau les valeurs non nulles du rapport pour mille année par année.

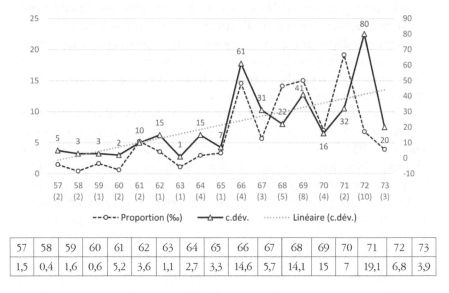

57	58	59	60	61	62	63	64	65	66	67	68	69	70	71	72	73
1,5	0,4	1,6	0,6	5,2	3,6	1,1	2,7	3,3	14,6	5,7	14,1	15	7	19,1	6,8	3,9

FIG. 4 – Fréquence des césures sur proclitique ou préposition monosyllabique chez les Parnassiens de 1857 à 1873.

On retrouve ici l'importance de l'année 1866 avec *Intimités* de Coppée et *Poëmes saturniens* qui totalisent à eux deux 50 des 61 vers déviants publiés cette année-là (quatre recueils). Si 1869 voit doubler le nombre de recueils, c'est encore Coppée qui, avec *Poëmes modernes* (et, accessoirement, *La Grève des forgerons*), apporte la plus importante contribution, avec deux tiers des vers déviants (27/41). On retrouve Coppée en 1872 où paraissent le maximum de dix recueils ou plaquettes, avec une contribution toutefois moins importante, dans *Les Humbles* (8 cas), l'apport principal étant cette fois fourni par Glatigny dans *Gilles et Pasquins* (24 cas), Leconte de Lisle dans les nouvelles pièces de *Poëmes barbares* (13 cas) et Vacquerie dans *Mes premières années de Paris* (10 cas). La proportion la plus élevée (19 ‰) est atteinte en 1871, essentiellement grâce au recueil de Jean Aicard, *Les Rébellions et les Apaisements*. Cependant, si l'on se penche sur le détail du corpus (tabl. 6), on constate que trois autres recueils, publiés en 1866, 1868 et 1870, dépassent ce score, à savoir, par ordre croissant : *Le Reliquaire* et *Intimités* de Coppée avec 27 et 34 ‰, sans parler de *La Bonne chanson* et de *Fêtes galantes* dont les scores élevés doivent être, on l'a vu, relativisés compte tenu de leurs effectifs réduits).

LA RÉCEPTION DE LA CÉSURE
POUR L'ŒIL

L'histoire des recueils individuels mérite d'autant plus d'être questionnée qu'il est probable, sinon certain, que Corbière a connu certains
d'entre eux. Ils jouent un rôle important dans la promotion du procédé
qui suscitait l'incompréhension de la critique tout autant que celle des
poètes romantiques pour lesquels la dislocation de l'alexandrin devait
porter sur la seule dimension rythmique, par le biais de l'enjambement
et du rejet, ou encore par la multiplication des repos ou des pauses, non
par la remise en cause de l'hémistiche, l'objectif de ces divers artifices
étant d'affaiblir le rôle des frontières métriques dans la perception du
lecteur ou de l'auditeur. Si Hugo a pu négliger la césure, c'est le plus
souvent de façon accidentelle, dans des vers perdus dans sa production,
voire dans les marges de sa production. Dorchain rapporte même que,
selon Émile Deschanel[1],

> son attachement aux habitudes classiques était tel qu'il s'indignait [...] quand
> on lui citait des vers de l'école parnassienne où un pronom possessif ou un
> article tombait à l'hémistiche. Il exigeait qu'il y eût toujours, à cet endroit
> du ternaire, un mot qui, dans un vers à césure médiane, eût été capable de
> déterminer la césure.

R. Lesclide raconte de façon romancée comment il avait attiré
l'attention du poète qui était, selon lui, « peu partisan des hardiesses
et des innovations qui se sont introduites en ces derniers temps dans
la prosodie », sur un vers à peu près ainsi rédigé : « Dans les palais,
dans les châteaux, dans les chaumières », suscitant en lui « une sorte
d'épouvante » qui l'amena à le récrire[2]. Cette anecdote montre en même
temps comment il était possible de trouver dans le rythme ternaire l'oubli

---

1   *L'Art des vers*, p. 238.
2   *Propos de table*, 3ᵉ éd. p. 224-225. Ce vers semble une invention de Lesclide.

relatif de la césure mais aussi l'importance qu'il y avait alors de ne pas l'abolir, ce qui suscitera l'étonnement rétrospectif d'un Martinon[3] :

> Mais pourquoi la respecte-t-il ? Pour la forme, sans plus, et, il faut oser le dire, par timidité ! Il crée un rythme nouveau, mais il n'ose pas aller jusqu'au terme logique de sa réforme. Il s'entête à vouloir sauver les apparences.

Il pouvait ainsi arriver au poète d'être victime de « cette espèce de duperie acoustique » dont parlera Rochette, « substituant peu à peu le sentiment d'une mesure à une autre, sous l'influence des contours de la syntaxe[4] ». Il serait toutefois inexact de considérer que le procédé lui fut à ce point étranger, mais il en use rarement, non sans excuses ou atténuations[5]. Il apparaît d'abord dans des textes destinés à la scène, apportant une réponse extrême à la volonté de renouveler l'alexandrin et à l'attraction de l'oralité requise par le jeu dramatique qui se trouvent affichées dans la préface programmatique de *Cromwell*, avec la quête affichée d'un vers « libre, franc, loyal, [...] sachant briser à propos et déplacer la césure pour déguiser sa monotonie d'alexandrin ; plus ami de l'enjambement qui l'allonge que de l'inversion qui l'embrouille » : c'est ainsi que l'on trouve des prépositions monosyllabiques (*pour, par*) promues à la césure dans *Cromwell* et dans *Marion de Lorme* où l'on trouve également l'article défini dans un vers dont la fragmentation par les répliques tend à occulter l'anomalie (IV, IV)[6] :

> LE DUC DE BELLEGARDE, *éclatant de rire.*
> Allons ! faites venir le Roi.
> Comme elle y va !
>
> MARION.
> C'est un refus ?
>
> LE DUC DE BELLEGARDE.
> Mais je suis vôtre !

---

3   « Le trimètre » [2], p. 45. Sur les rares exceptions du corpus, voir *infra*.
4   *L'alexandrin chez Victor Hugo*, p. 121. Voir aussi le commentaire de Martinon, « Le trimètre » [2], p. 47.
5   Naturellement, ce genre de vers a déjà fait l'objet de commentaires. Voir p. ex. Cornulier, *Art poëtique*, p. 84-85 (vers non-posthumes, depuis 1870) ; Gouvard, *Critique du vers*, p. 100-101 et 110-111.
6   Ducoffre, « Verlaine et le romantisme », p. 11, voit dans ce vers la matrice de « Vivre est un mal. C'est un secret de tous connu, » (*Semper eadem*).

Mais ce n'est sans doute pas non plus sans raison que c'est dans cette même pièce qu'Hugo se permet une semblable audace à la rime, témoignant d'une volonté exploratoire qui n'aura pas de véritables prolongements (II, III) :

BRICHANTEAU, *sautant de joie.*

Un bon duel ! c'est charmant !

SAVERNY, *à Didier.*

Mais où nous mettre ?

DIDIER.

Sous

Ce réverbère.

GASSÉ.

Allons, Messieurs, êtes-vous fous ?

On n'y voit pas. Ils vont s'éborgner, par Saint-George !

Pour être anecdotiques et noyées dans le drame, ces audaces n'en ont pas moins fait suffisamment impression pour que le procédé se voie moqué à diverses reprises dans des imitations irrévérencieuses. G. Lote a évoqué un exemple dans *Harnali* et trois dans *Oh ! qu'nenni*[7]. Évoquons en complément le cas de Carmouche, De Courcy et Dupeuty dans leur « amphigouri-romantique » *N, i, Ni* que Lote aborde sous un angle stylistique. Comme dans les deux premières parodies, l'interposition d'un tiret médian y met en évidence la neutralisation de la règle en un rappel ostentatoire du modèle de scansion classique *1-2-3-4-5-6 (bis)*, avec cette "césure semi-mécanique" dont parlera J. Mazaleyrat[8] :

De plus, j'ai vendu des – chaînes de sûreté. (p. 32)

Lorsque dans mes mains tu – remis cet instrument, (p. 37)

Dans les vers suivants, le recours à l'aposiopèse recouvre une intention semblable :

---

7   Lote, *En préface à Hernani*, p. 91. Brazier et Carmouche, *Oh qu'nenni*, p. 13 et 24. Dans les trois derniers, la césure métrique tombe au sein des syntagmes suivants : *de | ces jeunes gens, ni de | parasol, le | vrai bonheur.*

8   Voir aussi Gouvard, *Critique du vers*, p. 112, qui cite ces vers sans le tiret pourtant essentiel. Il mentionne ailleurs l'expression de Mazaleyrat, Éléments de métrique française, p. 164, à propos « d'une métrique de l'alexandrin où s'actualiserait un marquage de type CP6, et où se maintiendrait une scansion binaire classique » (p. 188).

J'ai fait deux cents fois le… *Siège de Sarragosse* [*sic*]*!*… (p. 32)

O ciel ! elle a pris ces… pillules [*sic*] mortifères. (p. 39)

Lote cite un autre vers de *N,i, Ni* qui témoigne de la même pesanteur de la césure médiane en formant un calembour que seul fait ressortir la scansion classique : « Tu seras le daim dont mes pieds suivront la trace » (I, VII). Dans un vers d'*Harnali*, ostensiblement signalée par le cadratin, la césure traverse même un polysyllabe où elle met en relief un accent d'ironie[9] :

> Quoi ! remettre à deux mains ! Tu voudrais donc que j'eusse
> Trompetté [*sic*] pour sa ma—jesté le roi de Prusse ?

Il est à noter que ces critiques de la césure hugolienne – qui insistent d'autant plus lourdement sur l'hémistiche qu'Hugo et ses acteurs devaient l'éclipser – sont au demeurant plus larges, affectant aussi bien la séparation du nom de l'épithète antéposée, brisant le vers qu'un vitrier se proposera de réparer (« Il vient pour tous les *vers* brisés »), avec un accent d'ironie sur *grand* :

> DON PATHOS, *à gauche.*
>
> Qu'es-tu ?
>
> LE VITRIER, *au milieu.*
> Je suis le grand – vitrier de Bohême. (p. 31)

Ces moqueries n'impliquent pas pour autant que l'exécution des vers critiqués laissât de quelque façon ressortir leur conformité métrique. Selon Gouvard, « la diction relativement libre des comédiens devait atténuer voire, dans une moindre mesure, légitimer » ces infractions[10] : mais que peut bien signifier cette assertion face au tollé général que suscitèrent ces vers dits à la scène qui ne purent être véritablement compris qu'à la lecture des livrets où la continuité du vers rompu par les répliques pouvait être pleinement reconstituée, tout allant dans le sens d'une abolition de la césure médiane en tant que phénomène sensible[11] ?

---

9   Lauzanne, *Harnali*, p. 778.
10 *Critique du vers*, p. 111.
11 Les éléments et les témoignages présentés par Rosa, « Hugo et l'alexandrin de théâtre », p. 312-319, ne mettent guère en évidence une prosodie révolutionnaire en dehors de

Comment imaginer que Mme Dorval enchaînât immédiatement « C'est un » après l'exclamation de Valter, qu'elle ménageât un repos sensible après l'article avant d'énoncer « refus ? », à moins d'introduire une suspension qu'Hugo ne voulait pas comme l'y signifie l'absence de points de suspension ? C'est dans le cadre de la poésie militante d'Hugo que l'on retrouve, de façon anecdotique et marginale, ce procédé que pouvait d'abord justifier l'écriture dramatique du poète qui se devait de donner une représentation stylisée de l'oralité. Une réticence certaine s'y manifeste d'ailleurs, comme dans *Les Châtiments* (1853) où l'on relève tout au plus l'emploi de *jusqu'à*, locution prépositionnelle qui, de par son déploiement sur deux syllabes, fonctionne comme les prépositions polysyllabiques (métriquement masculines : *avec, selon etc.*), mettant en relief le caractère extrême de ce qui est ainsi exprimé, comme dans : « On va même jusqu'à chuchoter à voix basse, » (*Eviradnus*)[12]. On la retrouve deux fois en 1859 dans la première série de *La Légende des siècles* (1859) où l'on trouve aussi un cas de *sans*. Quatorze ans plus tard, alors que le procédé s'est déjà bien établi chez divers poètes du Parnasse, on trouve dans *L'Année terrible* (1872) un cas de *aux* et un de *l'on*. L'examen de ces rares vers vraiment problématiques (monosyllabe atone en 6ᵉ position) publiés avant *Les Amours jaunes*, met en évidence diverses caractéristiques[13] :

> [DP] Je t'approuve. [B] Il faut, pour ne rien faire à demi, (*Cromwell*, I, IX)
>
> Entre les côtes, par le poumon, jusqu'au foie (*Marion de Lorme*, III.I)
>
> Sans m'arrêter et sans me reposer, je puis (*Légende des siècles* p.s., IV, II)
>
> On me lapide et l'on m'exile. C'est bien fait. [...]
> Même aux brigands, même aux bandits, c'est en être un ! (*L'Année terrible*)

Le premier, segmenté en deux répliques, présente une structure syncopée qui se prêtait bien difficilement à la « duperie acoustique » dont parlait Rochette. Trois autres sont accentués en 4ᵉ et 8ᵉ position, dont celui, morcelé, de *Marion de Lorme* précédemment cité plus les deux de

---

la question du vers brisé, mais on peut légitimement penser que, dans un tel cadre, la question de la césure pouvait passer au second plan tant au niveau de son exécution que de sa perception.

12 *Cf.* Gouvard, *Critique du vers*, p. 100-101.

13 DP : Le Député Plinlimmon ; B : Barebone.

L'Année terrible; le second est un ternaire asymétrique accentués en 4ᵉ et 9ᵉ position et le troisième porte deux accents, en 4ᵉ et 10ᵉ position, dont le second est suivi d'un repos en lien avec un contre-rejet. *L'Année terrible* fait par ailleurs place à une innovation d'une autre nature avec la mise en relief de la conjonction adversative *mais* (cinq cas), procédé moins rude rappelant l'emploi que Baudelaire faisait en son temps de *comme*, innovation prosodique dont Gouvard et Murphy ont justement conclu qu'elle ne s'inscrit pas exactement dans la même démarche que l'admission de monosyllabes atones à l'hémistiche[14]. Innovation relative puisque Banville avait déjà eu l'occasion de la mettre en œuvre dans *Les Exilés* (quatre occurrences) après un précédent de Baudelaire (*Les Petites Vieilles*, 41) et dont Corbière usera dans *Le Renégat* (17). Il faudra ensuite attendre la nouvelle série de *La Légende des siècles* (1877) pour retrouver le procédé, souvent avec des précautions qui témoignent de la timidité d'Hugo en la matière pour ne pas parler d'une réticence certaine, avec *chez, dans, par*, sans parler des locutions prépositionnelles moins problématiques *de chez* et *de par* ou le déterminant *pas une* dont le bisyllabisme atténue tout autant l'effet que dans *jusqu'*à, de même sans doute que dans *comme s'ils* (deux occurrences), dont le fonctionnement prosodique a été comparé à la locution *comme si* qu'Hugo avait mise à la césure dans *Odes et Ballades* et *Les Contemplations*[15]. Comme on le voit, ces quelques vers se perdent dans la masse de la production hugolienne[16]. On a mis du temps à considérer de façon confuse et pour le moins équivoque que, comme chez les classiques, « la scansion 4 + 4 + 4 est un contre-sens historique et rythmique », Hugo ayant « construit tous ses alexandrins, sans exception, sur la mesure métronomique 6 + 6 qui battait immuablement dans son cerveau[17] ». Rochette écrit ainsi, à propos de la césure médiane, que « si ce point de repère demeure essentiellement et

---

14   Gouvard, *Critique du vers*, p. 146-148 ; Murphy, « Quelques excentricités », p. 271-277.

15   *Cf.* Gouvard, *Critique du vers*, p. 148-149. On fera remarquer que la tradition orthographique qui a privilégié l'élision contredit la construction au féminin (*comme si elle*), alors que la forme élidée correspondante (*comme s'elle*) n'a pas survécu au moyen âge : il faut plutôt y voir une contraction, avec la réduction du pronom à sa seule consonne (*comme si·l*) : c'est ainsi la conjonction qui se trouve à la césure plutôt que le pronom. Sur l'ensemble des césures sur monosyllabe atone d'Hugo, voir Cornulier, *Art poëtique*, p. 80-86.

16   On peut aussi en relever dans les vers qu'il laisse de côté, comme : « Une savante ! ça trouble mes conjectures. » de Hugo (*Esca*, I, ı).

17   Porcher, « L'alexandrin et le vers libre », p. 84-85.

invariablement dans les vers de Hugo, c'est que le rythme, qui l'aurait le plus souvent effacé, n'a jamais chanté dans l'âme du poète », concluant que « le ternaire de V. Hugo ne relève point du rythme [*sous-entendu : métrique*] mais *de la syntaxe*¹⁸ » :

> Que le point de repère soit faible, qu'il soit légèrement atténué par le mouvement naturel de la phrase, par le voisinage de coupes ou d'accents plus fortement marqués, il n'importe. L'auteur l'a ainsi voulu.

Cette analyse repose en fait sur une perspective particulière, qui confond modèle d'exécution et modèle de vers, comme le montre l'invocation du mot de Brunetière selon lequel « l'artiste, en tant que tel, a le droit de n'être jugé que par rapport à ses intentions ». On ne peut de ce point de vue oublier l'analyse de Ténint qui donne en préambule à son petit traité une lettre dans laquelle Hugo ne tarit pas d'éloges sur son travail dans lequel se trouverait « expliqu[é] à tous ce que c'est que le vers moderne, ce fameux *vers brisé*, qu'on a pris pour la négation de l'art, et qui en est au contraire le complément », éloges qui certes relèvent davantage de la rhétorique que de l'analyse critique mais que le poète n'était en rien obligé d'honorer cet ouvrage d'un amateur dévoué. Le théoricien, qui n'envisageait pas même ces situations extrêmes de monosyllabes atones, considère que¹⁹

> Dans le vers parlé, la césure du milieu, césure classique, [...] est [...] très-souvent supprimée, mais il en reste toujours quelque chose, ou du moins il faut que le premier hémistiche se termine par un son plein [*c.-à-d. une syllabe non post-tonique*]. [...] Lors même qu'on le brise et qu'on y déplace la césure, on tient encore compte de sa césure primitive, on l'indique imperceptiblement, et c'est là une règle qu'il n'est pas loisible de violer.

L'adverbe *imperceptiblement* attire l'attention sur le fait que la diction du vers tend souvent à affaiblir la césure médiane dès lors que d'autres coupes prennent le pas sur elle, au point qu'elle peut passer inaperçue, ce qui est aisé à comprendre dans le cadre de la déclamation au théâtre plus encore que dans la lecture de salon. Si l'intention de la *marquer* est bien réelle et qu'un simple accent de proéminence peut sans doute faire l'affaire dans les vers romantiques typiques, l'emploi de monosyllabes

---

18   « L'alexandrin chez Victor Hugo », p. 120 ; la citation suivante se trouve p. 117.
19   *Prosodie*, p. 76-78.

atones qui respecte la contrainte morphologique tout en neutralisant la
contrainte accentuelle s'y oppose bel et bien, ce qui explique leur rareté
dans l'œuvre océanique d'Hugo comme leur inexistence chez ses partisans et imitateurs. La question de la diction des vers est naturellement
le fond du problème, de même que la question de la perception de la
césure, quoi qu'on en dise. Les repentirs dont le poète fait preuve sont
à cet égard significatifs ; outre celui plus ou moins authentique signalé
par Lesclide, on peut mentionner tel vers d'*Esca*, drame écrit en 1869
qui ne paraîtra pas avant 1881 dans *Les Quatre Vents de l'Esprit*, qui
n'est pas même un ternaire équiparti : « Moi pas. Par exemple, il faudra
travailler ferme… », raturé par le dramaturge qui, se ravisant, renonce à
l'adverbe (et à la rime) dont il compense l'absence par l'insertion d'une
interjection : « Moi pas. Ah ! Par exemple, il faudra travailler… » en rime
avec *s'éveiller*[20]. Si Hugo avait bien, à son habitude, respecté *la mesure
métronomique* tout en restant sensible à la contrainte morphologique, à
qui ce vers pouvait-il poser problème sinon à l'interprète destinataire ?

Après les premières expériences militantes d'Hugo au théâtre, les pro-
testations suscitées par l'emploi de monosyllabes atones à l'hémistiche ne
se développent qu'avec l'essor du mouvement parnassien qui en banalise
l'usage, bien que dans des proportions encore très marginales. S'appuyant
sur l'anthologie de Mortelette, Murphy rappelle ainsi la réaction de Sainte-
Beuve à l'envoi de *Poëmes saturniens*, en 1866, reprochant à Verlaine de
tels vers : « l'oreille la plus exercée à la poésie s'y déroute et ne peut s'y
reconnaître » ; ainsi que celle d'Anatole France, tout aussi choqué à la
parution du même recueil, tout en évoquant la réaction, plus ouverte, on
s'en doute, de Mendès pour qui « ces audaces » et « ces étrangetés volon-
taires » n'empêchaient pas le lecteur d'y trouver une certaine séduction[21].
Il est aussi de ces critiques indisposés qui sauront reconnaître les vertus
du procédé. L'année même de la parution des *Amours jaunes*, faisant état,
d'« une certaine affectation de négligence dans la coupe de l'alexandrin »
dans ce qu'il appelle « la jeune école », Paul Stapfer, citant quelques vers
où ne subsiste de la césure qu'une simple apparence[22], considère dans la

---

20 Signalé par P. et V. Glachant, *Essai critique*, p. 451 (*cf.* ms. BnF, Fr. nouv. acq. 24762,
    f° 227r°).
21 Murphy, « Versifications », p. 76 et 78.
22 Dans « La poésie française contemporaine » ; voir l'extrait publié par Mortelette, *Le
    Parnasse*, p. 125.

livraison du *Temps* du 28 mars que tel vers de Ménard « est bon » mais que tels autres de Coppée (qu'il ne nomme pas) sont mauvais[23], car « il n'y a plus d'art ni de vers », ajoutant : « c'est de l'incurie toute pure et il ne reste pas même un pas à faire pour dire avec un versificateur excentrique du jour:/Je me peigne nonchalamment à mon miroir[24] ». Mais, quatorze ans plus tard, dans son étude sur Racine et Hugo, le critique se montrera plus ouvert. Certes, il dit de ces vers que la « loi essentielle, qu'on ne peut enfreindre sans que le vers s'écroule et se fonde en prose », c'est « qu'il doit être toujours facile à la première audition de vérifier la mesure de l'alexandrin, et, pour cela, de le diviser instantanément en deux groupes de six syllabes, quelles que soient d'ailleurs les autres césures [*entendez : coupes syntaxiques*] que l'art du poète ait pu vouloir accuser[25] » :

> Les vers où ce point de repère se dérobe entièrement, où l'esprit ne distingue d'abord nulle mesure, ne sont point des vers. [...] Quand le vers en est là, sa ruine étant complète, la prétention serait un peu forte de vouloir le régler, le maintenir, et d'empêcher, par exemple, le même mot d'occuper à la fois l'un et l'autre hémistiche, comme dans le distique suivant :
>
> > Le train parti de Versailles pour Saint-Lazare,
> > Étant omnibus, s'arrêtait à chaque gare[26].

Toutefois, il reconnaît qu'une structure ternaire équipartie comme celle de « Chacun plantant comme un outil son bec impur » (Baudelaire) peut suppléer la division médiane[27]. Il n'est au demeurant pas impossible que ce soit la structure comparative de Baudelaire qui ait motivé, dans son article de 1873, sa clémence envers Ménard dont le vers ne présente aucun appui rythmique secondaire au niveau des 4e et 8e positions[28],

---

23 La césure ménagée pour l'œil seul sépare *de la | haute philosophie, sur le | front, et | chasser* (voir aussi *quel\que autre bête*).

24 Déformation du vers bien connu du *Poëme de Hérodiade* alors paru dans *PC (1869)* : « Aide-moi, puisqu'ainsi tu n'oses plus me voir, / A me peigner nonchalamment dans un miroir. »

25 Stapfer, *Racine et Victor Hugo*, p. 287-289.

26 Citation arrangée de vers explicitement tirés d'une charge de Jules Lemaître.

27 Ce qui ne l'empêche pas de rejeter un vers semblable de Coppée : « Lui qui vécut dans les murs froids d'une mansarde ».

28 Ce qui mérite d'être noté cependant, c'est, d'une part, que la comparaison ne s'arrête pas comme chez Baudelaire au beau milieu du second hémistiche, d'autre part, qu'elle a toutes les apparences d'un parfait octosyllabe.

mais où, pourtant, il considérait que « la suppression de la césure est un effet de l'art » bien « qu'il n'y ait point de césure du tout[29] » :

> [...] La sirène
> Les attire comme un irrésistible aimant

L'enjambement qui détache la comparaison déployée sur huit syllabes n'est peut-être pas non plus étranger à cette appréciation positive. De façon semblable, Stapfer exclut de sa condamnation « Les clairs feuillages sous les rayons semblaient rire » (Banville) « parce qu'il y a un *effet* qui peut justifier très exceptionnellement l'excessive irrégularité de la coupe[30] ».

Pour bien comprendre le succès de ces césures qui se dérobent à la lecture, il ne faut pas oublier non plus que le romantisme a modifié très sensiblement la diction des vers, et qu'elle tend en particulier à occulter ce repos trop évident dans la tradition classique, comme l'a noté G. Lote dans l'article qu'il a consacré au vers romantique, qu'il conclut ainsi[31] : « Bien que toujours identique à lui-même pour l'œil, il [*l'ancien vers français*] perd souvent, en passant par la bouche de ceux qui le récitent, cette césure qui conditionnait jadis son uniforme mélodie ». Certes, Lote écrivait bien après l'extinction du romantisme et du Parnasse, mais on peut relever maints indices d'époque qui n'ont pas toujours été compris par la critique mais allant précisément dans ce sens. Rappelons-nous comment, en 1865, à propos de tels vers de Baudelaire, Verlaine évoquait le procédé[32] :

> jeux d'artiste destinés, suivant les occurrences, soit à imprimer au vers une allure plus rapide, soit à reposer l'oreille bientôt lasse d'une césure [*il faut comprendre : syntaxique*] par trop uniforme, soit tout simplement à contrarier un peu le lecteur, chose toujours voluptueuse.

Marquerait-on la césure par le moindre repos, la moindre suspension ou la moindre accentuation contre nature qu'aucun effet d'accélération

---

29 Stapfer arrange la citation tirée de *La Sirène* d'abord paru dans *PC (1866)*, p. 35, et qui sera recueilli dans *Rêveries d'un païen mystique* (1876), où le vers précédent se lit ainsi : « Mais la molle sirène, à la voix caressante, ».
30 *Racine et Victor Hugo*, p. 289, n. 1.
31 « Le vers romantique », p. 480.
32 *L'Art*, 1re année, 8 (23 déc. 1865), p. 3. Murphy qui le cite dans son édition de *Poëmes saturniens*, p. 314, n'en voit pas moins (p. 315) dans « Pour entendre un de ces concerts, riches de cuivre, » (*Les Petites Vielles*) – qui ne concerne au demeurant qu'un numéral – « un effet suspensif exprimant le ravissement d'une de ces vieilles dames ».

ne pourrait être obtenu et que le repos de l'oreille envisagé ne s'y manifesterait point[33]. Quant au lecteur contrarié, n'est-ce pas celui qui, comme Sainte-Beuve, se sent obligé d'accentuer un monosyllabe atone qui, précisément, se dérobe à ce traitement contraire à sa nature ? Et n'est-ce pas précisément en le détachant lourdement au moyen du tiret cadratin que les parodistes du théâtre du jeune Hugo se gaussaient de ces innovations rythmiques en dénonçant ainsi les atteintes qu'elles apportaient à la tradition ? Un satiriste des années 1870 qui signe « Claude » nous donne ici une indication très nette dans « La dernière scène de Marion Delorme », où Didier « parcourt le théâtre à grands pas avec une explosion de cris de rage[34] » :

> J'aurais – pu – comme un autre – aller à vous – un jour
> Un jour de printemps – pour acheter – de l'amour…

Le placement des tirets implique ici le gommage de la césure médiane. Soutenir l'idée que le proclitique devait être détaché revient à projeter sur le « modèle d'exécution » (*verse delivery* de Jakobson) – modèle dont les préconisations peuvent au demeurant être à tout moment remises en question par l'exécutant – ce qui relève du « modèle de vers » (*verse design*), avec l'idée que la métricité du vers doit nécessairement se traduire par une manifestation acoustique, alors qu'elle s'exprime avant toutes choses dans la *conformation* même du vers au moment de sa genèse sous l'effet de l'exercice des contraintes métriques[35]. On retrouve ici l'idée maladroitement formulée par Mendès du maintien d'une « halte "possible" », ce que nous comprenons comme une pure virtualité, un arrêt que l'on pourrait marquer mais qu'on ne marque pas[36]. Comme l'a souligné Verluyten, structure métrique et structure prosodique sont

---

33 Dans « De la sémantique », p. 135, Gouvard semble se rallier à cette analyse : « l'oreille se repose de ne plus entendre aussi nettement le martèlement de la cadence 6-6 ; l'allure s'accélère pour n'avoir pas été freinée suffisamment à la fin du premier hémistiche ». Bobillot, « Et la tigresse », p. 286, voit dans ce passage la preuve que la césure médiane était bien attendue du lecteur et que son défaut le contrariait.

34 *La Vie parisienne*, 11e année (1873), p. 157-158 (8 mars).

35 Le modèle d'exécution peut naturellement mettre l'accent sur les spécificités requises par le modèle de vers, en exagérant même, selon le bon vouloir du lecteur ou du diseur, les manifestations, mais il ne faut pas perdre de vue qu'il ne s'agit jamais que d'un modèle dont la rigueur se trouvera souvent prise en défaut par les aléas de l'exécution.

36 *Le mouvement poétique français*, p. 195-196.

« deux structures *abstraites*, qui ne doivent pas nécessairement être réalisées telles quelles : il faut, tout simplement, distinguer la phonétique de la phonologie[37] ».

Les transcriptions que Lubarsch a donné de déclamations de Banville[38] montre à quel point ce poète, bien que respectueux de la diérèse poétique, se souciait peu de la mesure de ses propres vers, apocopant à l'envie tel ou tel schwa : on voit mal comment, dans ces conditions, le poète, qui est sans doute celui qui a le plus contribué à la diffusion de la césure pour l'œil, se serait laissé aller à des scansions métriques aberrantes censées sauver la césure comme phénomène sensible, là où les apocopes ruinaient la perception de la mesure et du mètre. S'il paraît, dans son *Petit traité*, des plus conventionnels dans ses évocations de la césure (qu'il confond avec un repos), le poète–théoricien n'en approuve pas moins la « remarquable prosodie » de Ténint et ses « douze combinaisons différentes, en partant du vers qui a sa césure [*entendue comme coupe syntaxique majeure*] après la première syllabe pour arriver au vers qui a sa césure après la onzième syllabe », ce qui « revient à dire qu'en réalité la césure peut être placée après n'importe quelle syllabe du vers alexandrin », tombant même dans la surenchère[39] : « Faisons plus : osons proclamer la liberté complète et dire qu'en ces questions complexes l'oreille décide seule. » Lorsqu'il rend hommage à Hugo pour avoir trouvé « la formule moderne » du grand vers, c'est pour se désoler qu'il « n'ait pas été un révolutionnaire tout à fait », lui qui « pouvait [...] briser tous les liens dans lesquels le vers est enfermé, et nous le rendre absolument libre, mâchant seulement dans sa bouche écumante le frein d'or de la Rime ! », révolution inachevée qu'il considère indépassée. Selon lui, « les nouveaux poëtes copièrent et imitèrent à l'envi les formes, les combinaisons et les coupes les plus inhabituelles de Hugo, au lieu de s'efforcer d'en trouver de nouvelles », conseillant lui-même à ses lecteurs, en bon pédagogue, cette imitation qui les rendrait aptes à faire « des vers qui seront EN APPARENCE libres et variés » tout en les condamnant à se perdre dans des « PONCIFS ROMANTIQUES, poncifs de coupes, poncifs de phrases, poncifs de rimes », ajoutant : « et le poncif, c'est-à-dire le lieu commun passé à l'état chronique, en poésie comme en toute autre chose, c'est

---

37   Verluyten, « L'analyse de l'alexandrin », p. 52.
38   *Über Deklamation*, p. 22-23, 26-27.
39   *Op. cit.*, p. 12-13, 21 et 96-97.

la Mort[40] ». Quant à son apport personnel comme à sa pratique de la césure pour l'œil, le poète reste désespérément muet, et lorsqu'il affiche son rêve de libération, c'est pour anticiper gaillardement l'avènement du vers libre[41] :

> j'aurais voulu qu'il pût s'élever assez haut dans l'air libre pour ne plus rencontrer ni barrières ni obstacles pour ses ailes. J'aurais voulu que le poëte, délivré de toutes les conventions empiriques, n'eût d'autre maître que son oreille délicate, subtilisée par les plus douces caresses de la musique. En un mot, j'aurais voulu substituer la Science, l'Inspiration, la Vie toujours renouvelée et variée à une Loi mécanique et immobile [...]

Décevant certainement par son manque de rigueur et son esprit cabotin, le *Petit traité* laisse du moins entendre que le poète a bien dépassé le modèle hugolien sans oser franchir le pas formel de la césure médiane, comme en témoigne son utilisation généreuse et exploratoire de la césure pour l'œil dans *Les Exilés*, même s'il s'est une fois aventuré au-delà, dans un vers – dont on soulignera la tonalité présymboliste – de *La Reine d'Omphale*, vers qu'il finira par amender[42]. Et quel progrès pouvait apporter ce pas au regard de la tradition romantique sinon de dérouter lecteurs et auditeurs en rendant *non perceptible* l'articulation médiane du vers ?

---

40 *Op. cit.*, p. 95-98.
41 *Op. cit.*, p. 96. Voir le commentaire solidement argumenté d'Edwards, *Le 'Petit Traité'*, p. 96-98, pour lequel Banville « fut tout simplement incapable de concevoir une poésie en vers libres modernes ». S'il ne l'a pas conçue, du moins l'aura-t-il rêvée.
42 Sur ce vers, voir *infra* p. 361.

LA RÉSISTIBLE ASCENSION
DE LA CÉSURE POUR L'ŒIL

L'histoire de la césure pour l'œil (comme celle de l'abandon de la césure) peut s'observer à différents niveaux, tout d'abord au travers de l'écriture ou la réécriture des poèmes ; ensuite au niveau de la diffusion dans les cercles poétiques ; enfin au niveau de la réception. La question de la diffusion du procédé au sein de l'école parnassienne, dont les membres échangeaient constamment au gré de rencontres et d'échanges, serait naturellement plus précise si l'on se penchait, sur les prépublications en revues, et au-delà, sur la correspondance des poètes et les différentes chroniques, recensions et mémoires qu'ils ont pu donner. Ainsi, l'influence du jeune Baudelaire comme celle de Mallarmé, de Rimbaud ou d'Heredia s'est manifestée bien avant la parution en recueil de leurs œuvres. Mais, dans la mesure où c'est Corbière qui nous intéresse, c'est à travers les recueils poétiques que nous avons choisi d'aborder le phénomène, en écartant par conséquent la question des prépublications, sachant que le poète n'avait certainement pas accès à tous les périodiques accueillant les vers des poètes et que nous ne savons pas précisément qu'elles ont été ses lectures dans ce domaine.

C'est véritablement Baudelaire qui donne l'envoi avec la première édition des *Fleurs du Mal* où l'on trouve quatre cas de césures sur proclitique ou préposition monosyllabique (mais aussi quatre cas de *comme*, deux de *quel* et un de *dont*, catégories grises que nous ne prenons pas ici en compte) qui suscite l'émulation de Villiers et de Vacquerie en 1859, avec trois cas pour le premier (*Premières poésies*) et quatre pour le second, dans une comédie (*Souvent homme varie*), puis Glatigny l'année suivante avec deux cas (*Les Vignes folles*). La seconde édition en 1861 avec neuf nouveaux cas relancera l'intérêt pour ces formes[1]. En 1862,

---

1   Sur ces vers de Baudelaire, voir Murphy, « Effets et motivations » ; sur ceux de Villiers et Glatigny, Gouvard, *Critique du vers*, p. 180.

Des Essarts donnera pas moins de sept cas dans sa tragi-comédie *Le Retour du fumiste*. Le cas de Leconte de Lisle est révélateur. Si, dans *Poëmes antiques* de 1852, on trouve une fois, parmi des vers de facture très classique où même les auxiliaires sont bannis de la césure, la conjonction *si* à l'hémistiche[2] (« Aux vents d'orage, si j'écoute ta prière. »), il faut attendre 1858 pour trouver chez lui une préposition monosyllabique (*sous*) à la césure[3]. *Poésies barbares* apporte par contre quinze nouveaux cas dans des poèmes de 1862, soit un an après la seconde édition des *Fleurs du Mal*, le plus souvent avec des accents dominants en 4e et 8e positions, ou à défaut, un accent dominant en 4e ou 8e position, les vers suivants faisant exception :

> Le jour tombe. Que mon Seigneur se lève et mange. [...]
> « Je me lève dans la fureur qui me consume : (*La Vigne de Naboth*, p. 10, 20)
>
> Et son ombre, dans sa chaleur et sa poussière, (*Le Corbeau*, p. 45)

Un autre vers, où la césure est plus acceptable du fait de l'emploi d'une locution prépositionnelle que son bisyllabisme rapproche des prépositions de deux syllabes[4], accuse une singularité rythmique tout-à-fait remarquable par son caractère déroutant : « Jusqu'aux astres, jusqu'aux Anges, jusques à Dieu ! » (*Les Deux Glaives*, p. 229), forme que Martinon qualifie de ternaire « à coupes lyriques[5] », c'est-à-dire dont les deux coupes tombent après une post-tonique suivie d'un repos sensible[6]. Leconte renchérissait ainsi sur un modèle rythmique hugolien de la première série de *La Légende des siècles* (1859), en supprimant l'accent d'hémistiche dans ce genre de structures[7] : « Cela vogue, cela nage, cela chavire ; »

---

2   Dans *Hélène*, *Poëmes antiques*, p. 95.
3   Deux cas, dans Çunacépa et *Les Hurleurs* (*Poésies complètes*, p. 223 et 249).
4   Rappelons que ce genre de cas n'entre pas dans nos décomptes.
5   C'est la présence d'une pause qui détermine la "coupe lyrique", ce qui n'est pas le cas dans le second vers cité. Martinon, « Le trimètre » [2], p. 51, en donne cinq illustrations tirées de *La Légende des siècles*, p.s., dont : « Heureux d'être, joyeux d'aimer, ivres de voir. » (*Le Sacre de la femme*) ; « Les ours au crâne plat, les chacals convulsifs / Sont féroces ; l'hyène infâme est implacable » (*Le Parricide*).
6   Le critique écrit, p. 53 : « On ne sait pas trop [...] comment scander » à propos d'un cas analogue tiré du *Lévrier de Magnus* : « Le temps passe. Dans la pourpre de l'Occident » (*Poèmes tragiques*).
7   On se rappelle ce vers de Baudelaire : « Dans quel philtre, dans quel vin, dans quelle tisane, » et sa variante interrogative (*L'Irréparable*).

(XV, I). Si l'on peut naturellement parler ici de rejet interne, ce n'est plus que de façon artificielle dans le vers suivant de *Booz endormi* (I, VI), tant l'auxiliaire en position prétonique se lie au participe[8] : « Près des meules, qu'on eût prises pour des décombres, » (I, VI). Si la figure métrique est inexistante dans *Les Poésies* et exceptionnelle dans *Odes funambulesques*[9] que Banville publie coup sur coup en 1857, la césure pour l'œil se trouve singulièrement cultivée neuf ans après dans *Les Exilés*, avec pas moins de 28 cas distribués dans des poèmes écrits de 1860 à 1866[10], et dont l'essentiel est concentré dans *L'Éducation de l'Amour* (1864) et (surtout) *Le Festin des Dieux* (1866), avec respectivement cinq et douze cas[11]. La césure pour l'œil y est deux fois sur trois associée à un accent dominant en 4e et/ou 8e positions, et les vers suivants, pour avoir une coupe après une quatrième occupée par une post-tonique souvent suivie d'un repos, présentent bien un accent en 8e position, exactement comme ceux de *La Vigne de Naboth* et du *Corbeau* présentés plus haut, si ce n'est que dans deux cas le repos conclut un enjambement :

> Aux racines traînant leurs cheveux, sont mêlés
> Des reptiles ; dans les rameaux échevelés
> Volent de grands oiseaux peints d'azur et de soufre ; (*L'Education de l'amour*,
>   p. 74)

> Nous flottions, errants, dans le frisson des nuées
> Et des fleuves, dans les forêts et sur les monts
> Sourcilleux ; [...] (*Le Festin des dieux*, p. 217)

Dans un autre vers, la « coupe lyrique » s'inscrit dans un parallélisme ternaire : « Tous les pauvres, tous les rêveurs, tous les maudits » (*L'Âme de Célio*, p. 210). Pas moins de huit vers se distinguent d'une autre manière par leur rythme syncopé ascendant 5 + 7 dont nous montrerons qu'ils

---

8   Particularité que l'on retrouve dans cet autre vers du recueil : « Une poudre qu'il a prise dans les tombeaux » (VI, I).

9   Dans la première scène des *Folies nouvelles*, prologue donné pour la réouverture des anciennes *Folies concertantes*, le 21 oct. 1854 : « Au meurtre ! épargnez un bourgeois ! [*ici, didascalie*] J'ai donné contre / Un mur [...] ».

10   Voire 1858, pour la conjonction *mais* : « Semble immobile ; mais je le sens tournoyer. » (*L'Attrait du gouffre*, p. 147).

11   Ces deux pièces sont respectivement composées de 347 et 204 alexandrins. Les autres cas ne se présentent qu'à raison d'un ou tout au plus deux (*La Reine Omphale*, 1861) par poème, pour un nombre variable d'alexandrins.

ont vraisemblablement inspiré Corbière[12]. Un autre vers du *Festin des dieux* présente un rythme plus complexe et moins conventionnel, avec deux accents internes, en 3e et 9e positions plus un, secondaire, en septième : « Dans leur gloire sur leurs trônes d'or, ou debout, (p. 215) ». Une autre innovation de Banville retient l'attention : là où Leconte de Lisle prend soin d'employer la césure pour l'œil au compte-goutte, l'ami de Baudelaire en fait un usage nettement plus offensif. Non seulement il les multiplie, en particulier dans *L'Éducation de l'amour* (2 %) et *Le Festin des dieux* (6 %), mais il lui arrive aussi d'y recourir dans deux ou même trois vers d'affilée comme on peut le constater dans l'exemple précédemment cité tiré du second, ou les passages suivants[13] :

> Mais, afin que je sois à jamais célébrée
> Par les chanteurs épars sous la voûte azurée,
> Et que cette quenouille, où seule j'ai filé
> La blanche laine en mon asile inviolé,
> A jamais parmi les mortels surpasse en gloire
> Le foudre ailé du roi Zeus et la lance noire
> D'Athènè, qui frémit sur son bras inhumain,
> Daigne [...] (*La Reine Omphale*, p. 37-38)

> [...] et je les vis, assises
> Dans leur gloire sur leurs trônes d'or, ou debout,
> Reines de clarté, dans la clarté. Mais surtout
> Je la vis, celle dont la mer avec ses îles
> Riantes réfléchit les doux regards mobiles, (*Le Festin des dieux*, p. 215, 217)

Ce volontarisme affiché par Banville suscita l'émulation des poètes de la mouvance parnassienne, sachant que certains resteront insensibles à cette nouvelle esthétique, comme Sully Prudhomme – pourtant plus jeune que lui de seize ans – ou André Lemoyne qui se laissera toutefois aller à écrire, dans *Légende des bois et chansons marines* (1878), ce vers dont le rythme ternaire équiparti (mais de structure ascendante) semble avoir distrait son attention : « Les deux veilleurs, par une étroite meurtrière, » (*Nuit en mer*). Certains poètes ne se laissent tenter par le procédé que de façon épisodique, comme Auguste Lacaussade chez qui l'on relève de

---

12 Voir *infra* p. 341-342.
13 Nos pourcentages ne tiennent compte que de l'emploi de proclitiques ou prépositions monosyllabiques à la césure, mais on pourrait y ajouter des relatifs (voir *dont* dans le second extrait, 4e vers cité) et des conjonctions.

rares écarts[14] ou encore Léon Dierx avec trois cas dans *Poëmes et poésies* de 1864 et deux dans *Les Lèvres closes* de 1867. Ménard ne l'adoptera que tardivement et de façon exceptionnelle dans *Rêveries d'un païen mystique* (1876) avec un tour baudelairien, dans une intention bien réfléchie, le poète, par le déséquilibre radical de l'alexandrin, donnant à sentir la force d'attraction irrésistible de l'aimant :

> Mais la molle sirène, à la voix caressante,
> Les attire comme un irrésistible aimant. (*La Sirène*)

D'abord peu sensible au procédé qu'il semble pratiquer comme une concession faite à la mode dans *Le Vénusberg*, Anatole France réécrira deux vers de *Poëmes dorés* pour leur donner ce vernis[15] esthétique. Parmi les poètes tôt conquis par le procédé, on peut signaler le cas d'Armand Renaud qui en donne deux en 1864, dans *Caprices de boudoir*, puis sept l'année suivante, dans *Les Pensées tristes*. Coppée adopte également le nouveau style dès ses débuts, avec pas moins de vingt-cinq cas dans *Le Reliquaire* de 1866 – la plupart dans *Le Justicier* qui clôt le recueil, précisément dédicacé à Banville –, et son ami Verlaine en fait autant avec trente cas. Si, la même année, Albert Mérat ne présente que quatre vers de ce genre dans *Les Chimères* (poèmes écrits en 1864-1865), il en donne onze dans *Les Villes de marbre*, poèmes publiés en 1873 mais datés de 1869, et six dans *Les Souvenirs* de 1872. Fervent admirateur de Banville, Glatigny retient l'attention : si l'on ne trouve que deux cas de monosyllabes atones en 6ᵉ position dans *Les Vignes folles* de 1860, on en trouve sept en 1864 dans *Les Flèches d'or*, quatre en 1870 dans *Le Fer rouge* puis vingt-quatre en 1872 dans *Gilles et Pasquins* (poèmes écrits en 1870), dont seize seulement présentent un accent majeur en 4ᵉ et/ou 8ᵉ positions. Le cas d'Auguste Vacquerie – auquel *Le Fer rouge* est dédié –, dont Banville avait publié quelques stances en tête de la deuxième édition d'*Odes funambulesques*, est également significatif : après une production de facture très conventionnelle, conçue de 1838 à 1845, le poète revient à la poésie deux ans après la première édition des *Fleurs du Mal* dans des

---

14   Gouvard, *Critique du vers*, p. 193 et 219.
15   Ainsi dans *Les Affinités* : « Elle laisse flotter ses yeux couleur de mer. » (p. 49) réécrit en « Elle laisse errer son regard couleur de mer. » (*Poésies*, 1896, p. 44) ; dans *Homâï*, « L'eau des saphirs tremblait, stagnante, sur son flanc ; » (p. 87) en « Les gouttes froides des saphirs mouillaient son flanc ; » (1896, p. 73).

textes destinés à la scène, plus tard dans un recueil lyrique. Nous avons vu que sa comédie *Souvent homme varie*, donnée en 1859, en présentait quatre[16] ; treize ans après, il en donne dix dans son recueil de souvenirs en vers, *Mes premières années de Paris* (1872). En 1874, il reprendra son drame burlesque de 1848, *Tragaldabas*, en renouvelant profondément le texte primitif, en y introduisant sept cas de césures pour l'œil. Si Léon Valade n'en donne aucun en 1863 dans *Avril, Mai, Juin*, la traduction en vers d'un poème de Henri Heine – *Intermezzo* – qu'il donne en 1868 avec Mérat en contient un[17], dans lequel aucun appui compensatoire n'est recherché en 4ᵉ et/ou 8ᵉ positions, alors que son recueil de 1874, *A mi-côte*, en contiendra quinze, dont dix ont un appui dominant sur l'une ou/et l'autre de ces positions. C'est donc précisément dans cette période de 1866 à 1872 que la rime pour l'œil devient un marqueur de la nouvelle école, du moins chez une grande partie de ses affiliés, et c'est précisément la période où, à partir de l'album Noir (1867-1869), Corbière va cultiver le procédé.

---

16   Notre source est l'édition de son *Théâtre complet* en 2 vol., en 1879.
17   Le dernier de XXIV, p. 33, dont on soulignera qu'il sert de clôture : « La route par où l'on se retrouve est fermée. » Il n'est pas assuré que les pronoms sujets, qui ne sont pas des proclitiques au sens étroit du terme dans la mesure où ils ne se rattachent pas à des mots qui les régissent, et en particulier *l'on* qui est un syntagme nominal d'origine, présentent le même degré de cohésion que les formes pronominales régimes.

CONCLUSION

L'activité poétique de Corbière se situe pour l'essentiel au moment même où la césure pour l'œil connaît son plus grand essor. Bien après les césures militantes du jeune Hugo, une dizaine d'années après que Baudelaire lui eût donné ses lettres de noblesse, alors même que Coppée, Verlaine et Banville, de même que Mallarmé dans des publications collectives, en explorent librement les potentialités esthétiques au travers de rythmes plus ou moins réguliers, variant dans diverses proportions en fonction de leur sensibilité propre, Corbière consigne seize poèmes dans l'album Noir, parmi lesquels *Petite pouësie* en particulier témoigne de sa première recherche dans ce domaine, dont nous allons bientôt montrer que l'exemple de Banville dans *Les Exilés* l'a sans doute inspiré. *Les Amours jaunes* marquent en effet un tournant significatif avec une exploration particulièrement variée des ressources rythmiques du procédé quand il n'occulte pas la césure médiane avec une insistance inhabituelle, ce qui nécessite une confrontation systématique de ses pratiques personnelles avec la production parnassienne de l'époque.

CINQUIÈME PARTIE

CORBIÈRE ET LE MOUVEMENT PARNASSIEN

Sur le *railway* du Pinde est la ligne, la
forme ;
I Sonnet.

Jules Laforgue, qui considérait que Corbière « a une influence
romantique, picaresque dans sa jeunesse », ajoutait : « pour le reste
dans son volume pas la moindre trace de *parnassien*, de *Baudelairien* »,
ce qu'il faut prendre garde de ne pas mésinterpréter, l'auteur voulant
de toute évidence mettre en relief les seuls choix poétologiques qui
sont propres à l'auteur des *Amours jaunes*, différant radicalement de
ceux des tenants de l'art pour l'art et des courants contemporains[1].
C'est en effet à Baudelaire que la poésie d'expression personnelle doit
l'adoption de la césure pour l'œil comme d'un outil légitime permettant
de renouveler l'expressivité de l'alexandrin, ce qui est d'autant plus
important pour notre propos que *Les Fleurs du Mal* font précisément
partie des lectures qui ont le plus inspiré Corbière. Mais qu'en est-il de
l'influence des Parnassiens sur ce poète qui ne fait jamais explicitement
référence à leur école ?

Lindsay voyait dans le fameux vers-devise concluant *Épitaphe* – « L'Art
ne me connaît pas. Je ne connais pas l'Art. » – une double critique
visant « la boursouflure et la sentimentalité des poètes romantiques et
la perfection technique des Parnassiens » ; dans le *pédicure* de « Poète.
– Après ?... Il faut *la chose...* », « évidemment une allusion ironique aux
Parnassiens » ; dans *'I' Sonnet*, une critique de « la monotonie, la symétrie
et la mathématique enfin de la poésie Parnassienne[2] », et nombreux
sont les critiques à partager cette analyse[3]. Ces positions semblent mal
s'accommoder de l'ignorance dans laquelle Corbière tient les poètes
de cette école. Yann Mortelette a cependant récemment avancé qu'il
convient de remettre en cause l'idée que Corbière aurait pu ignorer les

---

1   « Une étude sur Corbière », p. 6.
2   « Une édition critique », p. 493 et 495.
3   Nous y reviendrons dans VI, « Sonnet sur le sonnet ».

Parnassiens et leur éditeur attitré[4], mais il faut bien reconnaître que les faits objectifs qu'il mentionne quant aux liens – pour le moins distants – qui ont pu se tisser entre Corbière et des poètes liés au mouvement concernent les dernières années du poète, après la parution des *Amours jaunes*[5]. Les réminiscences qu'il met en avant établissent davantage le rapport de Corbière aux romantiques, en particulier à Hugo et au Gautier d'*Émaux et camées*[6]. Ceci étant, il fait état dans le « gâteux revenant » du *Poète contumace* d'une possible réminiscence du *Dernier souvenir* de Leconte de Lisle, poème recueilli dans *Poèmes barbares* « sortis en librairie le 21 novembre 1871 » ; une autre de Coppée, en raison d'un « air de famille » qui rapprocherait *Lettre du Mexique* de *Lettre d'un mobile breton*, paru en plaquette avec un achevé d'imprimer du 5 novembre 1870. Le lien qu'il voit dans les vieux duo de *Frère et sœur jumeaux* avec le vieil abbé et la vieille dévote à l'amour inavoué d'*En province* que Coppée publie en 1872 dans *Les Humbles* est beaucoup moins convaincant, d'autant qu'une première version du poème de Corbière se trouve déjà dans l'album Noir, antérieur à l'hiver 1869-1870, alors qu'*En province* ne paraîtrait pas avant février 1872[7]. À ce propos, nous ferons remarquer que le thème du vieux couple se retrouve par contre de façon beaucoup plus fidèle et suggestive dans un poème d'Eugène Manuel intitulé *La Promenade*, daté de 1868, qui ne paraîtra également en recueil qu'en 1872 et ne peut par conséquent avoir inspiré Corbière ; en voici la fin[8] :

---

4   « Corbière, Hugo », p. 73-74.
5   Le souvenir qu'évoque Frédéric Plessis de ces vacances passées à Douarnenez, où Heredia qu'il y retrouvait lui avait témoigné de sa connaissance de l'œuvre de Corbière, est selon toute vraisemblance postérieur à la publication des *Amours jaunes*, mises en librairie le 13 août, comme le montre les faits rassemblés par Mortelette, art. cité, p. 74-75, qui date le séjour d'Heredia du 15 juillet au 22 octobre. La rencontre entre les deux poètes, située en septembre 1866, est purement spéculative.
6   Mortelette, art. cité, p. 79-80, voit dans *À une rose* des réminiscences de *La Rose-Thé* de la 4ᵉ édition d'*Émaux et camées* (1863). La rose-thé de Corbière peut tout aussi bien renvoyer au poème *À une robe rose* au titre proche, présent dès la première édition, où « cette robe étrange / qui semble faite de ta chair » et « Sa trame vivante qui mélange / Avec ta peau son rose clair », ne sont pas moins évocateurs que « Son tissu rose et diaphane / De la chair a le velouté » de *La Rose-thé*. Le *papillon-coquelicot* de Corbière, qui « palpite à la colle / De la corolle », peut tout aussi bien être rapproché de la comparaison par Gautier du tissu, « Frais comme un cœur de rose-thé », à une aile d'abeille qui « Voltige autour de ta beauté ».
7   Mortelette, art. cité, p. 78-79 et 81.
8   Manuel, *Poëmes populaires*, XXXIII, p. 167-169 (40 alexandrins à rimes suivies). Signalons aussi le long poème, d'une toute autre tonalité, *Vieux Époux* de Lafenestre, qui aurait

> Le long du sentier vert je les suivis des yeux.
> Et, tandis qu'ils allaient au soleil, tout joyeux,
> A voir ainsi survivre au temps la vieille flamme,
> Dans ces vivants débris ne voyant plus que l'âme,
> Je partageai l'espoir des tendresses sans fin,
> Et je compris, amour, ton mystère divin !

Dans les deux cas, dans un format similaire, le poète s'émeut devant le spectacle d'un vieux couple, jumeaux ou époux, se témoignant d'affectueuses attentions. Quoi qu'il en soit, Mortelette aura ouvert la voie de recherches prometteuses. Dans son chapitre « Un lecteur méconnu du Parnasse », B. Houzé évoque ainsi la connaissance que Corbière pouvait avoir des Parnassiens, pointant plus particulièrement l'influence de Banville dont *Le Saut du tremplin* se trouverait récupéré dans la chute du *Bossu Bitor*, et celle de Gautier dont les « gardiens du contour pur » (*Le Bossu Bitor*, 80) du poème intitulé *L'Art* font l'objet d'une allusion moqueuse dans le même poème[9] mais où il nous paraît difficile de voir une portée polémique. Pour provenir de ce qu'on appelle l'école parnassienne, ces influences n'en renvoient pas moins à des œuvres antérieures à la constitution du mouvement : *Le Saut du tremplin* paraît d'abord en 1857, dans la première édition d'*Odes funambulesques*, tandis que *L'Art* paraît pour la première fois dans la seconde édition d'*Émaux et camées*, en 1858. B. Houzé estime par contre probable que le poète ait eu accès aux deux premiers recueils du *Parnasse contemporain*. Il évoque de façon précise et argumentée l'influence d'Albert Glatigny sur *RONDELS POUR APRÈS*[10]. L'approche de l'œuvre de Corbière sous l'angle métrique nous permettra de mettre en évidence cette influence des poètes parnassiens, déjà évoquée à propos de *Petite pouësie* sur laquelle nous allons revenir, par l'adoption de certains procédés métriques par lesquels ils se sont démarqués de la versification romantique, à commencer par la césure pour l'œil qu'ils avaient mise à la mode.

été composé dans la période 1864-1870 mais ne paraîtra en recueil qu'en 1874 (*Idylles et chansons*, p. 33-37).

9 Dans Houzé et Hérisson, *op. cit.*, p. 63-64. La reprise de Banville se limite à la rime finale *tambour : amour* – position naturellement significative –, mais la rime est déjà présente chez Baudelaire dans *Le Vin du chiffonier*. Houzé et Hérisson, p. 59, procèdent également à quelques rapprochements entre « le Gautier romantique » et *Les Amours jaunes*.

10 Nous reviendrons sur cette influence dans la partie que nous consacrons à ce poème composite, mais nous montrerons ici même qu'elle se ressent aussi dans le traitement que Corbière fait de la césure.

L'INFLUENCE DE BANVILLE

Situer la prosodie de Corbière dans l'histoire de la versification du XIXe siècle ne va donc pas sans soulever quelque difficulté, d'une part parce que les références littéraires explicites de Corbière se limitent aux romantiques et à Baudelaire, d'autre part parce que la versification parnassienne est entretemps venue prolonger la versification romantique. Steve Murphy a ainsi fait le point quant au second aspect[1] :

> Pour tout dire, la « versification parnassienne » est une expression assez futile si l'on songe par là à opposer cette versification à la versification romantique, dont elle procède sans solution de continuité. D'une part, beaucoup des auteurs du Parnasse n'iront pas plus loin que la versification des années 1830 ; d'autre part, la plupart des formes de vers que les recenseurs allaient incriminer se trouvaient déjà dans la poésie de Baudelaire, Villiers de l'Isle-Adam, Glatigny ou Leconte de Lisle avant la naissance du *Parnasse contemporain* voire, sporadiquement, dans l'œuvre de Hugo ou de Musset, principalement dans la poésie satirique ou dans des vers de théâtre ; l'enjeu sera surtout l'augmentation de fréquence de tels vers […]

On peut apporter quelque nuance à cet avis peut-être excessif : tout d'abord, bien que contemporain des romantiques et indéniablement sujet à leur influence, Baudelaire n'a pas échappé aux tentations du Parnasse de l'annexer à leur école dont l'éloignaient autant ses goûts, ses idées et son esthétique que son indépendance d'esprit et ses fréquentations qui le rapprochaient davantage de Borel et d'O'Neddy pour une partie importante de son œuvre, ses liens d'amitié avec Gautier ou Banville n'allant pas jusqu'à partager leur esthétique ; ensuite, le mouvement parnassien se met en branle bien avant la naissance du *Parnasse contemporain* qui n'est qu'une vitrine équivoque du mouvement et dont la contribution à la mode des formes parnassiennes les plus singulières est certainement moindre que celle des recueils publiés à

---

1   « Versifications », p. 82.

partir de 1866 par certains de ses meneurs, en particulier par Coppée – qui n'est du reste pas représenté dans le premier volume collectif – et Verlaine, respectivement dans *Le Reliquaire* et *Poëmes saturniens* ; enfin, la question de fréquence ne peut être réduite à la seule dimension statistique : il s'agit certes de prendre la mesure de l'accroissement des formes critiquées dans l'histoire du mouvement, mais il ne faut pas non plus négliger que ce qui résulte d'une intention stylistique incontestable et encore personnelle chez un Baudelaire – imité par Villiers de L'Isle-Adam[2] – a pu résulter chez d'autres d'une provocation (ce fut le cas du jeune Hugo), d'une négligence (le Hugo de *La Légende des siècles*, p.s.) parfois assumée (ce fut le cas de Musset), d'un prosaïsme ou d'une facilité, de façon souvent exceptionnelle. S'il y a une spécificité à la versification parnassienne, c'est bien, chez un certain nombre de ses acteurs, l'adoption de la césure pour l'œil qui trouve véritablement sa source chez Baudelaire pour lequel il s'agissait d'un moyen parmi d'autres d'afficher son originalité, voire sa singularité poétique, moyen dont les poètes qui lui emboîteront le pas feront un insigne formel par lequel afficher son appartenance ou son adhésion à un mouvement poétique nouveau en revendiquant une modernité qui rompait ostensiblement d'avec la tradition romantique.

Gouvard a pu évoquer « la quinzaine d'années au cours de laquelle non seulement s'installent les mètres de substitution [*en réalité : les césures pour l'œil*[3]], mais aussi où la césure médiane de l'alexandrin subira tous les outrages, soit de 1860 à 1875[4] », et c'est très précisément à partir du milieu de ces années que Corbière écrit la plupart des poèmes des *Amours jaunes*, multipliant les formes déviantes, tant par l'occultation de la césure médiane que par sa suppression. Comment ne pas penser que

---

2   L'imitation est flagrante dans deux des trois vers concernés de ses *Premières poésies*, p. 41, 143 et 169, avec un comparant cantonné ou rejeté au second hémistiche : « Elle était là, comme un fantôme de la Vie : » (*Hermosa*) ; « Sur la colline, où les trois croix étaient plantées, » (*Chant du Calvaire*) ; « Quelque chose comme un cadavre était gisant. » (*ibid.*). Le premier et le dernier vers rappellent en effet : « Chacun plantant, comme un outil, son bec impur » (*Voyage à Cythère*) ; « Exaspéré comme un ivrogne qui voit double, » (*Les Sept Vieillards*) ; « Qu'il s'infiltre comme une extase dans tous ceux […] » (*L'Imprévu*).

3   Rappelons que les « mètres de substitution » de la métricométrie ne sont tout au plus que des structures rythmiques d'appui, la *césure métrique* subsistant au travers du maintien de la contrainte morphologique et de la simple neutralisation de la contrainte accentuelle ; *cf.* p. 202-203 et 252-253.

4   *Critique du vers*, p. 195.

Corbière, lui aussi, a pu être influencé par l'évolution de la versification dont les Parnassiens donnaient tant de témoignages ? Cette évolution que l'autorité de Baudelaire pouvait créditer peut s'observer justement dans les deux premiers recueils du *Parnasse contemporain* dont Corbière aurait pu lire des pièces[5] et dont les premières livraisons ont pu attirer le reproche d'un Pierre Denis – au demeurant hermétique à toute poésie – dénonçant le « poétereau » qui « en corrigeant ses épreuves songe à l'étonnement et à l'admiration universels qui vont accueillir [...] telle ou telle césure audacieuse[6] ».

Dans le premier, on peut relever vingt-six vers présentant un proclitique ou une préposition monosyllabique à la césure, répartis entre quatorze auteurs, dont seuls Louis-Xavier de Ricard en donne jusqu'à cinq, Verlaine en donnant quatre[7], Leconte de Lisle et Mallarmé, trois chacun. Si l'apport de ce premier recueil peut avoir valeur de manifeste tant la figure métrique est étrangère à la manière de versifier de celui qui assure aux côtés de Mendès la codirection de la publication, lui qui ignore toujours le procédé dans son dernier recueil, *Ciel, rue et foyer,* paru la même année[8], il paraît peu probable que Corbière s'en fût inspiré, d'autant qu'il a davantage eu l'occasion de découvrir le second à l'occasion de ses séjours parisiens à l'automne 1871 et durant l'hiver 1872-1873. Dans le recueil de 1871, le nombre de ces césures déviantes a doublé, avec cinquante vers répartis entre treize auteurs, dont le tiers est de Banville (dix-sept, dont seize dans *La Cithare* qui sera par la suite recueilli dans la seconde édition des *Exilés*), six de Leconte de Lisle (*Kaïn*), six autres de Mallarmé (*Poëme de Hérodiade*) qui présente en outre un cas de polysyllabe à cheval sur les deux hémistiches, cinq de Mendès : tant la quantité des vers concernés, avec une concentration significative chez le premier[9], que la personnalité de leurs auteurs et leur position dans le recueil font de

---

5   Telle est l'opinion de Houzé dans Houzé et Hérisson, *op. cit.*, p. 64.

6   Voir Murphy, « Versifications », p. 72-74, qui attire l'attention sur cette critique du « parnassisme » ; pour l'article lui-même, paru dans *Le Nain jaune*, IVe année, n° 261 (10 mars 1866), p. 4-5, voir Mortelette (éd.), *Le Parnasse*, p. 41-45.

7   La proportion est très différente chez l'un et chez l'autre, atteignant 1,7 % seulement chez Ricard contre 4,9 % chez Verlaine.

8   Si ce n'est avec la conjonction *quand* dans *En passant*, daté de 1864 : « La foudre est en lui ! — Quand elle semble assoupie, » (p. 63). Dans *PC (1866)*, il emploie également (une fois chacun) *comme* et *dont* non suivi d'un repos.

9   Elle atteint 4,4 % des alexandrins que comptent la contribution de Banville (près de 4,5 % chez Mallarmé), contre 1,2 % pour Leconte de Lisle (1,9 % chez Mendès).

Kaïn et *La Cithare* de véritables vitrines de la césure pour l'œil que les lecteurs pouvaient déjà découvrir dans les deux premières livraisons de 1869[10]. Ce nombre chutera toutefois en 1876, avec seize cas seulement, répartis entre neuf auteurs, à raison d'un ou deux vers chacun, sauf trois chez Leconte de L'Isle (dans *Hiéronymus*) et trois autres chez Ricard (*L'Apologie du sire Pugnaire de Faucancourt*). L'histoire de la césure pour l'œil au travers des trois recueils du *Parnasse contemporain* met ainsi en évidence un *culmen* en 1871, soit dans la période la plus prolifique de Corbière : la proportion d'alexandrins déviants ici considérés passe en effet de 0,5 à 0,9 % avant de décroître à 0,3, régression qu'il convient de relier à l'ouverture du recueil à de nombreux poètes éloignés, voire étrangers au mouvement.

C'est donc au moment où la mode des césures pour l'œil reçoit le plus de publicité dans l'histoire du *Parnasse contemporain* que Corbière écrit l'essentiel des poèmes des *Amours jaunes*. Nous nous pencherons ici sur le recueil de 1871, plus susceptible d'avoir attiré son attention. Des six vers innovants de Leconte de Lisle, trois sont accentués sur les 4e et 8e position ; seul un vers est un pur ternaire souligné par la ponctuation (p. 5), les cinq autres ont un rythme ascendant, avec l'accent principal en 4e position ou, dans un cas, sur la troisième. Ils prolongent ainsi de diverses façons la tradition romantique au-delà de l'effacement des signes sensibles de la césure (en marge, les accents principaux, le moins proéminent figurant entre parenthèses) :

Et les taureaux, & les dromadaires aussi, (p. 2)	4e (9e)
Ils s'en venaient de la montagne & de la plaine, (p. 4)	4e (8e)
Car il connut, dans son esprit, que c'était là (p. 5)	4e 8e
Ni les aigles, ni les vautours ne mangeront (p. 6)	3e (8e)
Un Cavalier, sur un furieux étalon, (p. 7)	4e (9e)
De jour en jour, en cet adorable berceau, (p. 12)	4e (9e)

Dans le même recueil, Banville et Mallarmé font par contre parfois appel à d'autres configurations qui rompent localement d'avec la tradition que prolonge Leconte de Lisle et sont parfois irréductibles à des schémas plus communs[11] :

---

10   *Kaïn* ouvre la série dont il constitue le premier fascicule, paru le 20 octobre 1869 ; *La Cithare* constitue le second, paru le 5 novembre suivant.
11   Les vers suivants sont tirés de *La Cithare* et de *Poëme de Hérodiade* respectivement.

Et vous, Nymphes qui dans les solitudes vastes (Banv., p. 36)   2ᵉ (3ᵉ (10ᵉ))
Descendre à travers ma rêverie en silence, (Mall., p. 332)   2ᵉ (5ᵉ) 9ᵉ

Mais c'est surtout leur utilisation de formes syncopées affranchies de la contrainte accentuelle de la césure médiane qui retient l'attention. On n'en trouve pas moins de cinq dans *La Cithare* de Banville (272 alexandrins) et deux dans *Poëme de Hérodiade* de Mallarmé[12] ; Léon Cladel (*En Quercy, l'été*) et Ernest Hervilly (*A la Louisiane*) suivent le mouvement avec, respectivement, deux (consécutifs) et un vers[13] :

> Vivaient en exil dans l'univers infini, […]
> Il s'est éveillé dans les flancs de la Cithare […]
> De colliers brillants dont la splendeur environne […]
> Et des aigles qui, pour s'approcher du soleil, […]
> Douloureusement sur la cithare sonore. (Banv., p. 40-45)

> Elle voit son Davis […]
> Qui fume, accoudé sur l'habitacle poli,
>   En casquette à longue visière ; (Herv., p. 120)

> […] les blés
> Jaunis succombaient sous leurs épis d'or brûlés ;
> Il faisait un août à racornir les arbres, (Clad., p. 153)
> Mais, horreur ! des soirs, dans ta sévère fontaine, (Mall., p. 333)
> Métaux qui donnez à ma jeune chevelure (Mall., p. 336)

Nous avons vu, dans une pièce de l'album *Noir*, que Corbière avait singulièrement pris goût pour ce genre de formes dans un essai sans lendemain, que notre poète date du 15 juillet 1867. Le zèle dont il y fait preuve témoigne d'une volonté d'expérimentation d'un procédé sans doute fraîchement découvert[14]. Ce qui est plus particulièrement remarquable, c'est en effet que, des vingt-deux vers de ce poème (*Petite pouësie*), ce sont les seules césures pour l'œil qui s'y rencontrent, dans une proportion inédite (1,3/10), alors que, dans *La Cithare*, les cinq vers syncopés ne constituent qu'un quart des vers de cette sorte (dix-neuf au total, soit 0,5/10) que comporte ce poème de 372 alexandrins. Comment Corbière aurait-il pu ainsi devancer Banville alors que rien dans les vers qu'il avait jusqu'alors écrits ne laissaient présager une telle évolution ?

---

12   Pour ceux-ci, voir *supra*, p. 284.
13   On remarquera que la coupe majeure est décalée par un rejet chez d'Hervilly.
14   Voir *supra*, p. 216.

Le premier recueil du *Parnasse contemporain* ne pouvait pas lui donner matière à une telle expérimentation : seuls sept vers y présentent ce genre de syncopes, disséminés dans le recueil, dont un isolé dans *L'Exil des dieux* de Banville (sur un total de 204 alexandrins) : « Les grands dieux en pleurs dans la brume évanouis, », poème où l'on relève cependant quelques césures particulièrement faibles :

> Que leur flot pleure, et quand la Reine auguste penche [...]
> Du sein de l'Erèbe, où dormaient tes ailes noires, [...]
> Et ne peut dire : c'est l'homme. Je le connais. [...]
> [...] Les dieux enivrés d'ambroisie
> S'en vont et meurent, mais tu vas agoniser.

Mais ce n'est pas uniquement par cette particularité métrique que *Petite pouësie* retient l'attention : ce poème présente en outre des caractéristiques stylistiques et rhétoriques qui le détachent nettement du reste de son œuvre par leur préciosité. Selon Cornulier – qui ne donne aucune précision –, ces vers « donnent presque sans cesse l'impression de parodier ou carrément citer des clichés et formules poétiques passées de mode[15] ». L'image de « ces hanaps d'albâtre / Où la rosée épanche un bouton » peuvent ainsi évoquer la « Julie, au sein étincelant, / Au sein plus que l'albâtre et solide et brillant » de Chénier. Mais il paraît plus douteux que Corbière se soit jamais intéressé au pâle Millevoye alors que, dans ses *Élégies brésiliennes*, son père s'était lui-même essayé au style élégiaque dans la tradition néo-classique du XVIIIe siècle qui a perduré jusqu'à l'avènement du romantisme[16]. C'est ainsi qu'il a pu lire, par exemple,

> Si l'aimable métempsycose
> Fait un jour, selon mon désir,
> Passer votre dernier soupir
> Dans le sein d'un bouton de rose,
> Lise, je deviendrai Zéphir ;
> Mais non pas ce Zéphir volage
> Qui, sous l'aile d'un papillon,
> De toutes les fleurs du bocage
> Baise le tendre vermillon.

---

15   « Corbière pouëte précieux », p. 204, avec une allusion à Millevoye.
16   *Élégies brésiliennes*, p. 18 ; rééd. dans *Brésiliennes*, p. 100.

> Pour vous seule, aux bosquets de Gnide,
> M'échappant avec le matin,
> J'irai, Lise, dans votre sein
> Épancher mon haleine humide.

Rien que du point de vue lexical, ce passage n'a pas moins de huit mots en commun avec *Petite pouësie* où l'on trouve successivement : *seins, épanche, bouton, rôse, papillon, ailes, zephir, haleine*. Cette préciosité est du reste loin d'être absente de *La Cithare* de Banville, dont nous citerons ce passage évoquant l'apparition de Vénus dont le regard fait cligner Phœbus, où l'on peut trouver quelque écho aux vers du poète chantant sur un ton satirique Rosalba aux trente-deux perles d'Orient :

> Et les Heures alors, filles du Roi des cieux,
> Parèrent sa poitrine & son cou gracieux
> De colliers brillants dont la splendeur environne
> Sa chair de neige, puis ornant d'une couronne
> Son front ambroisien, s'empressèrent encor
> Pour attacher à ses oreilles des fleurs d'or !

Les préciosités de Corbière semblent en effet parodier les images de Banville, sa « Cypris nocturne », avec des roses sur sa lèvre, et ses vierges qui secouent des opales de leurs cheveux, si ce n'est que Corbière ne pouvait pas connaître ce poème où l'on trouve pas moins de dix-sept césures pour l'œil, dont une proportion singulièrement élevée est associée à un rythme syncopé (sept cas), car il paraît pour la première fois dans la livraison du 5 novembre 1869 de la seconde série du *Parnasse contemporain*, soit bien après *Petite pouësie* datée du 15 juillet 1867. Il aurait par contre déjà pu trouver chez lui de tels éléments, plus diffus, peut-être, dans ses premiers recueils, comme la « bouche folle aux perles inconnues » du *Stigmate* (*Les Cariatides*, 1842)[17]. La première édition des *Exilés* – qui reprend du reste *L'Exil des dieux* –, publiée en 1867 mais dont l'achevé d'imprimer est du 20 novembre 1866, a par contre de quoi retenir notre attention, car c'est au sein de ce recueil, dans *Le Festin des Dieux*, que l'on trouve pratiqués pour la première fois de façon intensive des rythmes syncopés postromantiques, avec six des sept cas

---

17   On se souvient au passage de ces vers d'*Odes funambulesques* (1857, p. 77) : « […] la mienne [*jeune odalisque*] a ses trente-deux dents, / L'œil vif, le jarret souple : elle est blanche, elle est nue, / Charmante, bonne fille, et de plus inconnue. »

que contient le recueil (marqués ci-dessous d'un astérisque), innovation technique suffisamment frappante dans le contexte de l'époque pour susciter chez Corbière le remarquable engouement dont font preuve les rythmes semblablement syncopés de *Petite pouësie*[18] :

> Je les vis, et près d'eux, sereines dans leurs belles
> Demeures, je vis les déesses immortelles !* (83-84)
> [...] et je les vis, assises
> Dans leur gloire sur leurs trônes d'or, ou debout,
> Reines de clarté, dans la clarté. Mais surtout*
> Je la vis, celle dont la mer avec ses îles [...] (96-99)
> Ce n'était pas assez d'être pareils à toi
> Par le rhythme ailé, par le chant qui t'a fait roi,* [...] (129-130)
> Nous flottions, errants, dans le frisson des nuées*
> Et des fleuves, dans les forêts et sur les monts
> Sourcilleux ; [...] (152-154)
> Et tu n'es plus seul ! dans nos palais grandioses* [...] (175)
> La grande Aphroditè, caressante et laissant
> Courir sur son dos sa chevelure embaumée.* (189-191)

On notera toutefois que ces six vers sont quelque peu dispersés dans cette pièce de 204 alexandrins qui contient plus de neuf autres cas de césures pour l'œil dont certains leur sont du reste juxtaposés (ainsi 97, 153 ; voir le relatif au vers 99), mais le rapport n'en est pas moins le double de celui que présente *La Cithare*. À noter que le procédé s'accommode à l'occasion d'enjambements (84, 98). Il est frappant de constater que les premiers vers à césures pour l'œil de Rimbaud, écrits avant l'été 1870, ont également tous un rythme syncopé ascendant, parmi lesquels ceux de *Soleil et Chair* qui fait précisément écho à *L'Exil des dieux* de Banville[19] : Corbière et Rimbaud se retrouvent ainsi sur ce terrain[20].

On peut naturellement s'interroger sur le prénom de la femme au portrait. Dans son édition de l'album Noir, B. Houzé a pointé dans une comédie de Mme de Staël un personnage tout à fait respectable, une jeune Malouine de seize ans courtisée par un jeune rentier qui

---

18 Le septième se trouve dans *L'Exil des dieux*. Voir aussi : « Il est sérieux, mais avec un air de fête. » (*Le Pantin de la Petite Jeanne*), « Du sein de l'Erèbe, où dormaient tes ailes noires, » (*L'Exil des dieux*), « Dans la nuit brûlante où la plainte continue » (*Cléopâtre*).

19 Les deux autres dans *A la musique* et *Le Châtiment de Tartuffe* ; voir aussi « – Ah ! quel beau matin, que ce matin des étrennes ! » (*Les Étrennes des orphelins*).

20 À noter qu'Ischi, « Corbière et Rimbaud », a pu établir des analogies troublantes entre leurs œuvres.

l'agrée, cultivant la littérature dramatique, que son père, le capitaine Kernadec, traite de « faiseur de madrigaux » étranger à la carrière militaire, qu'il ne saurait accepter comme gendre[21]. Selon Cornulier qui évoque un personnage de Barbey d'Aurevilly, Rosalba la Pudique, maîtresse d'un officier, décrite comme un « monstre d'impudicité », le nom ne déparerait pas dans l'onomastique des prostituées. De fait, bien avant *Les Diaboliques*, paru en 1874, le prénom apparaît dans la littérature contemporaine pour désigner des femmes de petite vertu au statut variable, allant de la grisette à la demi-mondaine. Dans *Le Grand et le petit trottoir* d'Alfred Delvau, par ailleurs auteur d'un essai sur *Henry Murger et la Bohême* paru la même année, en 1866, c'est une grisette qui porte ce nom, jouant un rôle bien secondaire parmi ses consœurs, Chiffonnette, Trépignette, Héloïse et la Borgnotte. Aurélien Scholl fait une allusion furtive à « une marquise de *quinze onces* » dans *L'Outrage*, paru l'année suivante. Plus près de Corbière, Rosalba est aussi le nom d'un personnage de vaudeville : ainsi se prénomme la femme à barbe d'Élie Frébault dans une pièce représentée en mars 1866 au Théâtre des Délassements Comiques, que le boniment décrit comme « la jeune et belle femme à barbe, la seule de son espèce et de son sexe, âgée de 17 ans 3 mois et 10 jours, née native de la Venise du nord, d'Amsterdam en n'Hollande » (sc. IV), qu'Athanase tente d'approcher en soudoyant de trois francs, plus trois encore, plus la promesse de trois autres, Gaspard, un collègue de Rosalba, qui, « jaloux de ces hommes qui la regardent pour deux sous ! », nourrit pour son compte un béguin à son endroit (sc. III)[22]. En 1869, dans *Le Far Niente*, Jacques Brasdor évoque le sort de quelques « étoiles filantes », dont une Rosalba[23] :

Rosalba, la comtesse altière,
A vieilli sans perdre son nom ;
Mais d'un crochet de chiffonnière
Elle a barré son écusson.

21 *Le Capitaine Kernadec* ; Houzé, *ffocsoR*, p. 34 (f° 10r°).
22 *La Femme à barbe*. On pourrait multiplier les notations comptables de la pièce, à l'instar de Cornulier pour le poème de Corbière : Rosalba reproche ainsi à Gaspard de lui avoir « cassé un pavé de trente centimètres sur 25… sur l'estomac… » (sc. III) ; elle évoque dans sa chanson un p'tit gars du village, Lucas : « En un jour il fait plus d'ouvrage / Qu'un aut' n'en fait en huit ou neuf !.. » ; le spectacle de Rosalba rapporte une recette de « Vingt-sept sous… et deux boutons de guêtres… » plus le billet… doux d'Athanase *etc.*
23 *Le Far Niente*, p. 57.

En 1870, dans *Les Courtisanes du monde*, Arsène Houssaye évoquera dans les termes suivants l'inspiratrice d'une vocation[24] : « elle jura qu'elle serait, elle aussi, une Rosalba, "le miracle des Grâces" ». De tout ceci il ressort que Rosalba est un nom plaisant à la mode, susceptible de convenir à de tels personnages, mais on ne comprend pas vraiment pourquoi la dame du débit de tabac de Saint-Pierre-Quilbignon qui retient l'attention de Corbière serait intentionnellement affublée d'un prénom ainsi connoté. Il n'est par contre pas sans intérêt de rappeler que, dans sa jeunesse, Corbière « trouss[ait] des poèmes polissons contre des Morlaisiens pittoresques[25] », s'en prenant au greffier Panneau mais aussi à un cordonnier, à l'occasion de son départ pour la retraite, dans *La Véritable complaincte d'Auguste Berthelon mort à l'art, fin courant – sur l'air de Fualdès – dans sa villa San Crepina (route de Paris)*[26], et ce penchant pour cette même veine fantaisiste se retrouve dans l'album Noir où le poète consacre des couplets à narrer l'histoire burlesque de l'apothicaire Danet[27]. *Petite pouësie* relève de la même fantaisie, tournée cette fois vers la tenancière ou employée du bureau de tabac de Saint-Pierre-Quilbignon, dont rien ne dit qu'elle fût de petite vertu mais dont tout semble indiquer qu'elle s'acquittât efficacement de sa fonction comme le suggère le soigneux décompte des vingt-deux vers du poème. Ceci étant, bien que relevant de la même veine comique, ce poème se distingue par sa forme (rimes plates) des précédents, tous écrits sur un air à la mode, et où domine la recherche du calembour.

Mais il est à l'époque une autre Rosalba, historique cette fois, qui fait son retour : Rosalba Giovanna Carriera, peintre vénitienne de la première moitié du XVIIIᵉ siècle réputée pour avoir lancé en France la mode du pastel, artiste dont une traduction en français du journal dans lequel elle relate son séjour à Paris fut publié en 1865, renouvelant ainsi l'intérêt du public pour son œuvre[28]. On pourrait ainsi penser que la Rosalba de l'album Noir usât à ce point des fards que son visage eût l'allure d'un pastel.

---

24 *Les Courtisanes du monde*, III, p. 157.
25 Walzer, éd. citée, p. 665.
26 Walzer, éd. citée, p. 859-861 ; Houzé, « Naissances d'une œuvre », p. 364-368 (avec fac-similé). S'il y verse davantage dans le calembour, on y trouve ce vers à la syntaxe précieuse : « Plus n'iront filles mutines ».
27 Éd. Houzé, *ffocsoR*, p. 42 (fᵒ 7rᵒ) : *Histoire d'un apothicaire*.
28 *Journal de Rosalba Carriera pendant son séjour à Paris en 1720 et 1731*, trad. par Alfred Sensier, Paris, J. Techener, 1865.

On relève dans un catalogue de vente un « Portrait de l'artiste peint par elle-même tête nue, une légère dentelle mêlée à ses cheveux (poudrés et coupés) des pendants d'oreille en perles » où l'artiste a « le front large » et « la bouche serrée » ; dans un autre, un « Buste de femme avec un collier de perles, robe bleue, bouquet de fleurs[29] » : si le bouquet fait défaut dans l'aquarelle de Corbière, on trouve une rose dans ses cheveux. Voici comment, dans *Le Parnasse contemporain* de 1871, Gautier fera référence aux portraits de l'artiste dans les tercets d'un sonnet daté de 1870[30] :

> L'amour de mon marbre a fait un pastel,
> Les yeux blancs ont pris des tons de turquoise,
> La lèvre a rougi comme une framboise,
>
> Et mon rêve grec dans l'or d'un cartel
> Ressemble aux portraits de rose & de plâtre
> Où la Rosalba met sa fleur bleuâtre.

On remarquera que le début même de la *Petite pouësie* ressortit d'une inspiration analogue à l'image fruitière du premier tercet :

> L'oiseau, becquetant sa cerise souriante,
> Rencontre pour noyaux, (O trop douce erreur !) trente-
> Deux perles d'Orient. [...]

tandis que la métaphore par laquelle le poète évoque la dentition de son personnage rappelle la « bouche folle aux perles inconnues » que Banville évoquait ailleurs, dans *Le Stigmate* que Corbière aurait pu lire[31], ou encore la lèvre qui « a le parfum d'Orient / Où l'aurore a caché ses perles en riant » d'*Évohé*, Satire sixième[32]. La chronologie, certes, interdit de voir une quelconque influence du sonnet de Gautier sur *Petite pouësie*, mais ces rapprochements témoignent d'une semblable sensibilité au-delà de la dimension parodique du poème. On peut également remarquer que le portrait aquarellé de la Rosalba dont Corbière accompagne le poème dans l'album n'est pas sans évoquer, certes, de façon très générale, le poème ancien *Pastel* (1835) du même Gautier, en particulier ses deux premiers quatrains :

---

29 *Journal de Rosalba*, p. 477 et 539.
30 Dans le sonnet « J'aimais autrefois la forme païenne », p. 262.
31 *Les Poésies* (1856), p. 156 ; repris dans *Les Cariatides* de 1864, même page.
32 *Odes funambulesques*, 1re éd., p. 129.

> J'aime à vous voir en vos cadres ovales,
> Portraits jaunis des belles du vieux temps,
> Tenant en main des roses un peu pâles,
> Comme il convient à des fleurs de cent ans.
>
> Le vent d'hiver, en vous touchant la joue,
> A fait mourir vos œillets et vos lis,
> Vous n'avez plus que des mouches de boue
> Et sur les quais vous gisez tout salis.

Les rapprochements avec Banville prennent en tout cas davantage d'éclat si l'on tient compte de l'envoi, au demeurant trivial et impersonnel, qui accompagne un exemplaire des *Amours jaunes* récemment repéré par P. E. Richard[33]. Ceci étant, il est à noter que Corbière semble parfois anticiper l'évolution de la poésie, comme il anticipe des thèmes, images et expressions de Rimbaud[34], et ceci jusqu'en certaines des caractéristiques linguistiques et prosodiques de *Petite pouësie* auxquelles des poètes symbolistes pourront se complaire, comme l'archaïsme *illusée* (*DALF* IV, 543) ou l'articulation en quatre syllabes de *affolées*, avec un hiatus qui fera les délices d'un Moréas ou d'un René Ghil.

---

33   « Deux nouveaux envois », p. 303-304, et Fig. 4.
34   Voir Ischi, « Corbière et Rimbaud », pour des recoupements précis entre l'œuvre des deux poètes.

L'INFLUENCE DE GLATIGNY

Si le nombre de volumes s'accroît d'une période à l'autre, l'équilibre des grands types rythmiques est à peu près respecté, si ce n'est une légère régression des rythmes ternaires équipartis ({4 et 8}) qui passent de 61 % dans la première période à 54 puis 52 %, et une augmentation significative des formes autres dans la seconde période, qui passent de 5 % à 14 % avant de redescendre à 8 %, comme le montre la fig. 5 (les valeurs absolues sont indiquées au sein de chaque colonne) :

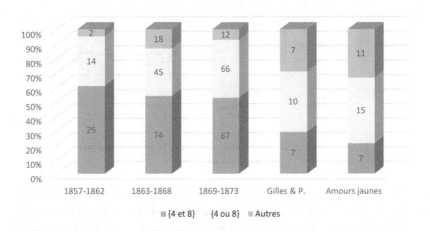

FIG. 5 – Évolution des grands types rythmiques associés à la césure sur proclitique ou préposition monosyllabique chez les Parnassiens et dans *Les Amours jaunes*.

Le pic relatif atteint pour les formes autres dans la seconde période est dû à l'expérimentation de formes syncopées par Banville dans *Les Exilés* (7 vers). Dans cette figure, nous avons délibérément retranché de la troisième période les 24 cas de *Gilles et Pasquins* du fait que Glatigny

n'y respecte pas les proportions observables sur le reste du corpus parnassien où les rythmes ternaires équipartis sont majoritaires : dans ce
recueil, la proportion des ternaires équipartis ne dépasse pas un vers
sur trois, ce qui le rapproche des *Amours jaunes* (un sur cinq), similarité
que nous examinerons plus finement.

Voici à présent, en pourcentages, le détail de la répartition des vers
déviants par types rythmiques, donné en proportions relatives, en
excluant de la figure (mais non des commentaires) *Gilles et Pasquins* :

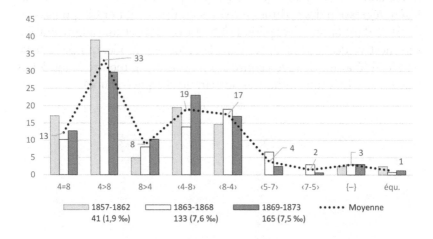

FIG. 6 – Évolution des différents rythmes chez les Parnassiens,
en trois périodes.

Ce qui frappe tout d'abord est l'absence d'une évolution tranchée
d'une période à l'autre des différents types dont la variation reste toujours
proche de la moyenne. Si l'on se penche sur les structures ternaires qui
sont les plus fréquentes (près de 53 % des césures pour l'œil prises en
considération, soit un vers sur deux), ce qui ressort est la proportion
relativement réduite des ternaires équipartis équilibrés (4=8), les formes
ascendantes (4>8 : accent dominant en 4ᵉ position) dominant largement,
malgré leur régression progressive de neuf points (de 39 à 29,7 %), au
profit principal des formes descendantes (8>4 : accent dominant en
8ᵉ position). Pour ce qui est du détail des recueils (Tabl. 6), et sans perdre
de vue que les quantités sont souvent trop faibles pour tirer toujours

des conclusions tranchées[1], on doit noter une assez grande variation. À titre d'exemple, les cinq vers concernés de *Melancholia* de Cazalis (1868) et les huit de *Poëmes de Provence* d'Aicard (1873) présentent un rythme ternaire équiparti[2], contre les trois quarts dans *Les Fleurs du Mal* (dès 1857) et *La Bonne Chanson* de Verlaine (1870), un peu plus dans *Les Villes de marbre* de Mérat (1873), un peu moins dans *Poëmes saturniens*; la proportion est de deux tiers dans *Fêtes galantes* (1869); elle n'est plus que de moitié dans l'apport de *Poésies barbares* de Leconte de Lisle (1862), *Le Reliquaire* de Coppée et *Les Chimères* de Mérat (1866) comme dans *Les Rébellions* d'Aicard (1871); elle tombe à moins d'un tiers dans *Intimités* de Coppée (1868), *Les Renaissances* de Silvestre (1870) et *Poëmes barbares* (1872), et en dessous dans *Intimités* de Coppée (1868), comme, du reste, dans *Gilles et Pasquins* de Glatigny (1872). Dans *Les Amours jaunes*, elle tombe à un cinquième.

Que la 4e position tienne une place prépondérante dans les ternaires est particulièrement remarquable. Sur l'ensemble du corpus, les ternaires équipartis se distribuent en effet selon les proportions suivantes (exemples tirés de la première édition des *Exilés*) :

1. six fois sur dix (62 %), la quatrième position est dominante (rythme ascendant $4>8$)[3] : « La blanche laine en mon asile inviolé, » (*La Reine Omphale*)
2. deux fois sur dix (22 %), les deux accents sont de même rang ($4=8$) : « Où la caresse, les aveux, les doux refus » (*L'Éducation de l'amour*)
3. deux fois sur dix (16 %), la huitième est dominante (rythme descendant $8>4$) : « Toute pareille à son désir, naquit dans l'herbe » (*La Rose*).

Ce déséquilibre que l'on a pu observer chez Leconte de Lisle et Coppée[4] peut s'expliquer par le fait que, dans le dernier cas, la structure s'apparente à un rejet, dans le premier, à un contre-rejet (atone).

1 Dans les relevés qui suivent, seuls les recueils contenant au moins 8 vers déviants selon les critères retenus sont pris en considération, *Melancholia* mis à part.
2 Les autres recueils ne présentant que des ternaires équipartis ne contiennent qu'un ou deux vers déviants.
3 À noter que les proportions extrêmes culminent ici à 66 % des vers {4 et 8} en 1863-1868 et descendent à 56 % en 1869-1873.
4 Gouvard, *Critique du vers*, p. 196-202

Cette primauté de l'accent de 4ᵉ position dans la hiérarchie syntaxique rejoint une particularité de l'alexandrin des classiques qui, nous dit Martinon[5], « mettaient l'accent prépondérant du vers dans le premier hémistiche, quand il n'était pas à la césure, mais presque jamais dans le second », ce qui correspond précisément au précepte classique que Mourgues, dans la VIIᵉ règle du chapitre qu'il consacrait à la césure, formulait de la façon suivante, assortissant la règle d'une explication particulièrement pertinente[6] :

> On doit éviter *d'enjamber* du premier Hemistiche au second : je veux dire, que si on porte un sens au-delà de la moitié du vers, il ne faut pas l'interrompre avant la fin : parce qu'alors le vers sembleroit avoir deux Cesures, ce qui seroit desagreable.

Le théoricien n'avait toutefois pas ici en vue ce qui deviendra le ternaire romantique – à membres égaux ou inégaux –, dont on a signalé divers prodromes chez les classiques : c'est en effet dans le cadre du décasyllabe commun qu'il prend son exemple où, à la césure métrique, s'ajoute une coupe après une septième post-tonique : « Et s'habillant – en homme, – sous le linge ». Mais il précise dans la VIᵉ règle, à propos de la nécessité de ne pas séparer le substantif de son génitif ou de son épithète ni le verbe de son régime : « Si pourtant ce qu'on a reservé pour le second Hemistiche, le remplit tout entier, avec le secours de quelque Epithete, ou Attribut, toutes ces separations sont permises, & receuës » ; s'il affirme qu'on ne peut séparer deux épithètes dépendant d'un même substantif, c'est avec la réserve suivante : « à moins que le dernier Attribut ne fasse tout seul la moitié du vers » ; avec, dans les deux cas, des exemples d'alexandrins.

Les structures cumulées {4 et 8} et {4 ou 8} sont seules représentées dans la plupart des recueils contenant jusqu'à cinq vers déviants, des *Fleurs du Mal* de 1857 (4 cas) aux *Excommuniés* de Luzarche (1872) en passant par *Melancholia* de Cazalis (1868). Font exception *Les Vignes folles* et *Le Fer rouge* de Glatigny, *Les Amies* de Verlaine et *Les Renaissances* de Silvestre. Mais

---

5   « Le trimètre » [2], p. 49, n. 1.
6   *Traité de la poesie françoise*, p. 115. Pour un point de vue complémentaire à propos de la tendance à renforcer davantage l'accent de 4ᵉ position que celui de 8ᵉ par une pause ou un repos consécutif, voir Gouvard, *Critique du vers*, p. 194-202 (qui ne fait aucune mention de ce précepte).

au-delà de cinq, elles ne sont exclusives que dans *Les Humbles* de Coppée (1872, huit c.p.o.), *Poëmes de Provence* d'Aicard (1873, huit) et *Hespérus* de Mendès (1872, six). Dans les recueils d'au moins dix vers déviants, tous les vers sont concernés dans *Poésies barbares* (1862, quinze c.p.o.) ainsi que dans l'apport de *Poèmes barbares* (1872, treize), dans *Intimités* de Coppée (1868, treize) et *Les Villes de marbre* de Mérat (1873, onze), soit à des dates avancées dans la période de l'histoire de la césure pour l'œil qui nous concerne. Pour le reste, la proportion est de 9/10 dans *Les Fleurs du Mal* (1957, neuf c.p.o.), *Poëmes saturniens* (1866, 28)[7] et *La Bonne Chanson* de Verlaine (1870, huit), *Les Rébellions* d'Aicard (1871, 31), *Le Reliquaire* de Coppée (1866, 22) et *Mes premières années à Paris* de Vacquerie (1872, dix); de 8/10 dans *Les Chimères* de Mérat (1866, neuf), *Poëmes modernes* de Coppée (1969, 25) et *Fêtes galantes* (1869, six); de 7/10 dans *Les Exilés* de Banville (1867, 28), *Les Flèches d'or* (1864, six) et *Gilles et Pasquins* (1872, 24), proportion qui est également celle des *Amours jaunes*.

Les structures autres demeurent minoritaires, mais atteignent en tout 14 % dans la seconde période, en lien, comme nous l'avons déjà dit, avec les formes syncopées dans *Les Exilés*. Les structures déviantes que cultivera Mallarmé, sans accent dans la zone métriquement contrainte ({–}) – dont *Les Amours jaunes* présentent trois cas[8] –, représentent une proportion non négligeable, à raison de 3 % environ, et ceci dès le début :

Ont d'orage dans leurs sérénités divines, (Glatigny, *Les Vignes folles* 1860)

A tes mousses, à tes frondaisons incertaines, (*Id.*, *Les Flèches d'or* 1864)

Frais et blanc, avec un balancement coquet; (Mérat, *Les Chimères* 1866)

Dans leur gloire sur leurs trônes d'or, ou debout, [...]
Et, miracle! sur son doux visage, le dieu, (Banville, *Les Exilés* 1867)

Elle ordonne, dans son immuable dessein, [...]
Et l'or pâle de ta chevelure pareil (Coppée, *Poëmes modernes* 1869)

---

7   Une seule exception sur les 28 vers concernés : « Tu consoles et tu berces, et le chagrin » d'*Il Bacio*, qui a la même structure accentuelle que « Si vous faites de nos grâces peu langoureuses » de Mérat paru la même année (*Les Chimères*, p. 176). L'accent dominant et la ponctuation y détermine cependant avec netteté un rythme syncopé descendant. Quelques années plus tôt, Mendès donnait, avec un numéral : « Ces poèmes sur deux rimes, en treize vers. » de Mendès (*Philoméla*, p. 74). Pour des précédents romantiques, voir *supra* p. 283-284 (et 197-198).

8   Voir *supra*, p. 219-220.

Et la pourpre qui sur ton épaule descend (Silvestre, *Les Renaissances* 1870)

Soleil, centre de la création profonde, (Aicard, *Les Rébellions* 1871)

Et tu cites à tes contradicteurs vaincus (Vacquerie, *Mes Premières années* 1872)

L'examen des tendances observables chez les principaux adeptes de la césure pour l'œil permet d'apporter un éclairage complémentaire. Le tableau 9 réunit ainsi les données concernant les recueils (ou apports nouveaux) comportant au moins huit vers présentant une césure sur proclitique ou préposition atone, en valeur absolue pour le nombre de vers déviants (Tot.), en valeur relative (arrondi sur dix, en italique[9]) pour la proportion des diverses structures considérées[10] :

	Date	Tot.	{4 et 8}	{4 ou 8}	{5 ou 7}	Autres
Les Fleurs du Mal	1861	13	7	3		1*
Leconte, *Poésies barb*	1862	15	6	4		
Coppée, *Le Reliquaire*	1866	22	5	4	1	
Mérat, *Les Chimères*	–	9	6	2	1	1
Verlaine, *Poëmes saturniens*	–	28	7	3		
Banville, *Les Exilés*	1867	28	5	2	3	1
Coppée, *Intimités*	1868	13	3	7		
Coppée, *Poëmes modernes*	1869	25	4	4	1	1*
Verlaine, *La Bonne Chans*	1870	8	8	1	1	
Aicard, *Les Rébellions*	1871	31	5	4		1*
Coppée, *Les Humbles*	1872	8	4	6		

---

9   L'arrondi peut faire que les totaux soient à un point près (Baudelaire 1861, Banville, 1867).

10   Dans {4 ou 8}, seul l'accent dominant au sein de la z.m.c. est pris en considération, ce qui implique qu'un vers tel que « Nous cherchions tous deux à nous dire quelque chose » (*Le Novice*) dont l'accent dominant est en 5ᵉ position n'est pas classé en {4 ou 8}. La classe « Autres » comporte des vers dépourvus d'accent dans la z.m.c. mais aussi des vers de structure équivoque (*cf.* p. 300-301), signalés par l'astérisque).

Glatigny, *Gilles et Pasquins*	–	24	3	4	3	
Leconte, *Poèmes barb.* [apport]	–	13	3	7		
Vacquerie, *Mes Premières années*	–	10	4	5		1
Aicard, *Poëmes de Prov.*	1873	8	10			
Corbière, *Les Amours jaunes*	–	30	2	5	2	1
Mérat, *Les Villes de marbre*	–	11	8	2		

TABL. 9 – Distribution des rythmes associés à la césure
sur proclitique ou préposition monosyllabique chez Corbière
et les principaux adeptes parnassiens de la césure pour l'œil.

Seul Aicard généralise les rythmes ternaires équipartis, et ceci seulement en 1873. C'est Mérat qui, la même année, occupe le second rang, avec un score de 8, et Verlaine, dans *La Bonne Chanson*, en 1870 (plus précisément, trois vers sur quatre). Après eux, Verlaine encore, dans *Poëmes saturniens*, et Baudelaire en 1861 atteignent ou approchent 7 vers sur 10. C'est donc davantage dans les années 1870 que l'attention portée à ce genre de rythmes est la plus grande (et non au début des années 1860)[11]. *Les Amours jaunes* est le recueil qui présente le moins de rythmes ternaires (deux vers sur dix); suivent *Gilles et Pasquins* de Glatigny (1872), *Intimités* de Coppée (1868) et l'apport de *Poëmes barbares* de Leconte de Lisle (1872), à raison de trois vers sur dix. Si l'on se penche à présent sur la chronologie des recueils d'un même poète contenant au moins trois vers déviants de notre inventaire, on peut constater qu'il n'y a pas d'évolution significative témoignant au début de l'œuvre de chaque poète d'une plus grande présence des rythmes ternaires équipartis, ce que nous avions déjà pu constater pour Baudelaire (sur la base des dates d'écriture estimées de ses poèmes, ce qui est une autre

---

11 Rappelons que, selon Gouvard, *Critique du vers*, au-delà de la variation propre à chaque poète, les rythmes ternaires ({4 et 8}) seraient majoritaires au début des années 1860 avant de céder du terrain devant les «semi-ternaires» ({4 ou 8}), voire d'autres formes.

perspective que celle des recueils qui touche à la réception de l'œuvre du poète telle que Corbière a pu la connaître[12]), et tout aussi bien chez Mallarmé et Rimbaud[13] :

		Date	Tot.	{4 et 8}	{4 ou 8}	{5 ou 7}	Autre
Aicard	*Les Rébellions*	1871	31	5	4		1*
–	*Poëmes de Prov.*	1873	8	10			
Baudelaire	*Les Fleurs du Mal*	1857	4	8	3		
–	[apport]	1861	9	7	2		1*
Coppée	*Le Reliquaire*	1866	22	5	4	1	
–	*Intimités*	1868	13	3	7		
–	*Poëmes modernes*	1869	25	4	4	1	1*
–	*Les Humbles*	1872	8	4	6		
Glatigny	*Les Flèches d'or*	1864	6	5	2	2	2
–	*Gilles et Pasquins*	1872	24	3	4	3	
Leconte	*Poésies barbares*	1862	15	6	4		
–	*Poèmes barb.* [app.]	1872	13	3	7		
Mérat	*Les Chimères*	1866	9	6	2	1	1
–	*L'Idole*	1869	3	7	3		
–	*Les Souvenirs*	1872	5	4	6		
–	*Les Villes de marbre*	1873	11	8	2		
Verlaine	*Poëmes saturniens*	1866	28	7	3		
–	*Fêtes galantes*	1869	6	7	2	2	
–	*La Bonne Chans*	1870	8	8	1	1	

TABL. 10 – Évolution dans le temps de cette distribution chez les principaux d'entre eux.

Seuls Leconte de Lisle et Glatigny privilégient dans un premier temps – au demeurant sans excès – les rythmes ternaires équipartis ({4 et 8}) avant de leur préférer les formes binaires {4 ou 8}, alors que

12 L'édition de 1868 qu'a vraisemblablement utilisée Corbière n'ajoute que deux occurrences, avec un vers accentué sur les 4e et 8e, un autre sur les 3e et 8e positions.
13 Voir *supra*, p. 267-270.

l'évolution est très nettement inversée chez Jean Aicard et se fait en dents de scie chez Mérat. Il n'y a pas d'évolution tranchée chez Baudelaire, Coppée et Verlaine. Ces résultats vont donc également à l'encontre du principe de progression défini par les tenants de la métricométrie[14] : chaque poète explore à sa convenance les libertés offertes par la césure pour l'œil, s'accordant du moins, en général, à éviter l'accentuation des 5e ou 7e position que seuls Banville et son disciple affiché Glatigny – mais aussi Mallarmé et Rimbaud, absents du tabl. 10 – se sont plus à rechercher, à l'occasion de tel ou tel poème, à un moment ou l'autre de leur carrière, comme le premier, ou de façon plus constante, selon la pertinence du rythme au gré de la composition.

Les relevés de Gouvard, basés sur un corpus assez représentatif de la poésie du troisième quart du XIXe siècle, tendent à montrer que le phénomène de la césure pour l'œil déborde rarement le mouvement parnassien. Il convient cependant de montrer que, en dehors de la poésie littéraire qui était l'objet de sa thèse, la césure pour l'œil a pu gagner des versificateurs qui n'avaient pas véritablement de vocation proprement poétique. On peut ainsi s'intéresser à la presse qui accueille volontiers une production satirique de la part d'amateurs qui ont pu être gagnés par la nouvelle mode. Le cas de la poésie parodique et satirique est d'autant plus intéressant, que la poésie des *Amours jaunes* en a indéniablement le caractère. Toutefois, la question se pose de savoir s'il s'agit là d'une liberté prise avec les règles en liaison avec le registre bas adopté ou s'il s'agit d'une influence des courants les plus novateurs voire d'une critique indirecte de ces libertés ; le cas de Vacquerie qui laisse passer quelques césures pour l'œil dès 1859 dans sa comédie *Souvent homme varie* est à cet égard significatif d'une influence directe, qu'il s'agisse d'une manière d'afficher une certaine modernité ou de bénéficier de cet assouplissement autorisé par l'exemple de Baudelaire. Murphy qui relève le phénomène dans *Le Parnassiculet contemporain* (1867) et d'autres textes parodiques de la même époque, rappelle ainsi le relâchement plus ou moins semblable qui s'observe sporadiquement dans la poésie satirique ou dramatique de Victor Hugo et de Musset chez lesquels on peut douter que le phénomène soit en quoi que ce soit déterminé par le caractère proprement satirique des

---

14 Voir *supra*, p. 259-260 et 273.

pièces concernées[15]. Cependant, dans le *Parnassiculet*, ces libertés, que les poètes parnassiens ne s'autorisaient pas tous de la même façon ni avec le même allant[16], sont des parodies et non le résultat d'une facilité que pouvait autoriser le style bas. En effet, si quatre alexandrins seulement y présentent un déterminant en 6ᵉ position, c'est avec une relative concentration qui attire l'attention ; le sonnet *Avatar* en contient deux, à la suite l'un de l'autre, avec un accent dominant sur la 4ᵉ ou la 8ᵉ position[17] et le premier quatrain de *Gaël'Imar au grand pied*, parodie du *Cœur de Hialmar*[18], juxtapose également deux vers de ce genre, dont le second seul a un rythme ternaire équiparti[19] :

[…] – J'ai forcé des couvents
Et des nonnes, sous une armure sarrasine, […]
Et, le cœur plein de ces femmes qui furent miennes, (*Avatar*, 7-8, 13)

Dans un grand lit sculpté, sur deux larges peaux d'ours,
L'écuyer Gaël'Imar près de la reine Edwige
Repose ; – Ainsi que la loi danoise l'exige,
Ils ont entre eux, veuf de sa gaîne de velours,
L'acier d'un glaive nu qui les tient à distance. (*Gaël'Imar*, 1-5)

Que Glatigny cultive ce genre de vers plus que d'autres[20] n'en est pas moins particulièrement significatif, étant donné le caractère précisément satirique de son œuvre poétique, d'autant plus que Corbière semble avoir lu son recueil *Gilles et Pasquins*[21], mais on ne peut simplement

---

15   « Versifications », p. 77 et 82. Rappelons que Musset n'est concerné que pour un vers de *Mardoche* et que les cas hugoliens (*voir supra*, p. 311), à l'époque qui nous occupe, sont rares et perdus dans la masse.

16   Murphy, art. cité, p. 82 : « beaucoup des auteurs du Parnasse n'iront pas plus loin que la versification des années 1830 ».

17   Au v. 8 ; nous mettons de côté l'accent de 3ᵉ position bien qu'il soit d'un rang supérieur à celui de 8ᵉ, parce qu'il porte sur un enjambement, soit un prolongement syntaxique du vers précédent, calé en deçà de la 4ᵉ position.

18   Dont les neuf quatrains, au demeurant, n'en contiennent qu'un : « Comme des merles dans l'épaisseur des buissons ? » (*Gaël'Imar* est constitué de huit quatrains).

19   Ici encore, nous ne prenons pas en considération le rejet en tête du v. 3.

20   Gouvard, *Critique du vers*, p. 180-182, donne une liste commentée des vers concernés, de 1860 à 1871 (dont six vers – arbitrairement datés de « 1864 » – qui n'ont rien à y faire car ils appartiennent à *Une Exécution*, ajout des *Poésies complètes* de 1879). Il convient toutefois de souligner que *Les Vignes folles* (1860) ne contiennent que deux vers de ce genre, alors que, douze ans après, *Gilles et Pasquins* en contiendront 24.

21   Sur cette probable lecture, voir *infra*, p. 477-481.

mettre au compte d'un quelconque laisser-aller ces nouvelles pratiques
que Glatigny n'a adoptées que progressivement : on ne trouve chez lui
que deux vers promouvant un monosyllabe atone à la césure dans *Les
Vignes folles* de 1860 ; quatre ans après, on en trouve six dans *Les Flèches
d'or*, douze ans après, vingt-quatre dans *Gilles et Pasquins*, soit une
progression qui suit l'évolution générale des poètes parnassiens. Cette
expansion est chez lui le signe d'une option esthétique bien plutôt que
d'une négligence, à une époque où ce genre de césures est dans l'air du
temps, comme on peut le constater chez des versificateurs d'occasion.
On peut ainsi signaler tels pastiches de Hugo et Musset, tous signés
« Claude », parus dans *La Vie parisienne* l'année même où Corbière place
dans cette revue quelques vers[22] :

> Thiers sommeillait dans un salon très-bien meublé. [...]
> Semblait pénible et l'on entendait des paroles [...]
> C'est qu'il rêvait et qu'il voyait un très-vieux chêne [...]
> La présidence est un pouvoir très-admissible. (*Thiers endormi*)[23]
>
> Ce n'est pas vrai que tu vas mourir. – Je t'en prie, (*La dernière scène*)[24]
>
> Et sentant que c'est sa suprême signature, (*La Nuit de Mars*)[25]

On observe toutefois ici moins de variété et de liberté que chez
Corbière ou Glatigny, l'auteur de ces vers s'appuyant assez volontiers
sur les 4ᵉ ou/et 8ᵉ positions. La versification de Corbière nous paraît
toutefois devoir être évaluée à l'aune de la poésie proprement littéraire
au vu des connaissances que l'on a sur la culture du poète et l'ambition
qu'il affiche dans son recueil. Les données que nous avons pu accumuler
sur les poètes du mouvement parnassien sont à cet égard éloquentes, car
leur comparaison montre que l'usage de la césure pour l'œil par Corbière
se rapproche très significativement de celui de *Gilles et Pasquins*, tant
en nombre (respectivement 33 et 24 cas) – mais avec une proportion
supérieure (2 contre 1,4 %) –, que dans certaines tendances comme on
peut le voir au travers de la figure suivante (pourcentages) :

---

22 Voir aussi le vers cité p. 317.
23 *La Vie parisienne*, 11ᵉ année (1873), p. 37 (11 janvier).
24 *La Dernière Scène de Marion de Lorme, La Vie parisienne*, 11ᵉ année (1873), p. 157-158
    (8 mars).
25 *La Vie parisienne*, 11ᵉ année (1873), p. 203 (29 mars).

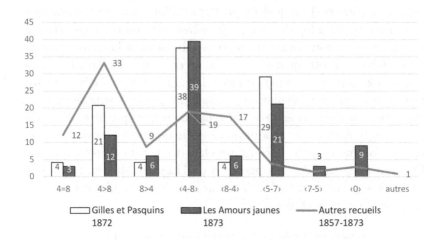

Fɪɢ. 7 – Distribution comparative des rythmes associés
à la césure sur proclitique ou préposition monosyllabique
dans *Les Amours jaunes* et *Gilles et Pasquins* de Glatigny.

Là où la tendance générale privilégie les rythmes ternaires équipartis,
en particulier ceux qui ont un mouvement ascendant (4>8), Corbière
privilégie les rythmes binaires ascendants, dépourvus d'accent secondaire
en 8ᵉ position («4-8»), comme Glatigny qui accepte par contre plus facilement les ternaires équipartis ascendants, dans des proportions cependant
modestes. Comme Glatigny, Corbière se distingue par l'importance
relative qu'il accorde aux structures syncopées ascendantes, avec un
accent dominant sur la 5ᵉ position («5-7»), même s'il y fait preuve de
moins d'insistance. S'il manifeste un certain intérêt pour la structure
inverse («7-5»), que nous avons relevée dans *Grand opéra* (« Et dans les
siècles des siècles… Comme c'est long ! ») ainsi que dans *La Pastorale
de Conlie* (75) et *Le Bossu Bitor* (139)[26], on peut du moins relever un ou
deux vers dans *Gilles et Pasquins* qui vont dans ce sens[27] :

> Brillez, éblouissez-moi ces Américains (XII)

> Car le fameux dompteur Mirecourt, qui les a
> Élevés, m'a dit que Wolff un jour le laissa (XXXIV)

---

26 Voir *supra* p. 217-218 et 228.
27 *Gilles et Pasquins*, p. 43 et 107.

Il est bien peu probable que Corbière ait été influencé par Mallarmé qui publiait dans le premier recueil du *Parnasse contemporain* : « Aux ivresses de sa sève ? Serais-je pur ? » (*Brise marine*), ou même par le Verlaine des *Poëmes parnassiens* et de *Fêtes galantes* dont rien n'indique qu'il les ait jamais lu[28]. Il faut également écarter un vers affine de Mérat qui ne paraît en recueil qu'en 1873[29] : « Joyeux des beaux lauriers-roses et des olives.» (*Rome*, XI). Nous n'irions pas jusqu'à soutenir que Corbière se soit laissé imprégner par la rythmique du vers glatinien dont l'originalité et l'audace avaient certainement de quoi le séduire, bien que les preuves ne manquent pas de sa connaissance de l'œuvre de Glatigny, comme cela apparaît de façon particulièrement nette dans sa pratique du rondel[30]. Il nous paraît plus défendable de parler d'une sensibilité métrique commune qui les rapproche en les démarquant semblablement du mouvement contemporain.

---

28 Voir cependant p. 443.
29 Voir aussi « La tâche pourtant plus rude que nourricière ; » (*Rome*, VIII) où l'accent dominant (selon la hiérarchie syntaxique) est cependant en 2e position, avec en 5e un accent de saillance comparable. *Les Villes de marbre*, p. 56 et 63.
30 Voir VII, « L'influence de Glatigny ».

L'ABOLITION DE LA CÉSURE MÉDIANE
CHEZ LES PARNASSIENS

Nous avons déjà évoqué la réaction de Paul Stapfer devant un vers non césuré du *Poëme d'Hérodiade* de Mallarmé[1]. C'est aussi à propos d'un autre vers du poète : « Accable, belle indolemment comme les fleurs[2] », que cette abolition de la césure suscite en 1867 le rejet d'un Victor Fournel qui considère déjà le poète comme « une des colonnes du cénacle[3] » : « il s'est même trouvé un *enragé* qui a poussé le zèle jusqu'à placer l'hémistiche au milieu d'un mot ». Même les poètes de l'époque avaient de la difficulté à accepter cet abandon de la césure que facilitait certes l'essor du ternaire romantique qui avait familiarisé les lecteurs avec des formes rythmiques alternatives aux formes classiques, parce que la césure exerçait encore une attraction telle qu'il convenait d'en donner au moins l'illusion. C'est ainsi que Banville, qui s'était laissé aller à commettre un tel vers dans *La Reine Omphale*, d'abord publié en juin 1861 dans la *Revue fantaisiste*, dut faire machine arrière après la première édition des *Exilés* (1867) – où le vers est encore repris tel quel –, le régularisant dans les éditions suivantes, soit à partir de 1878, alors que Mallarmé avait déjà bien assis et sa réputation et son esthétique du vers dépourvu de césure médiane[4] :

Où je filais pensivement la blanche laine ; (1861, 1867)

Où je filais d'un doigt pensif la blanche laine, (1878 et *sq.*)

---

1   Voir *supra*, p. 315.
2   Nettement accentué sur les 4e et 8e positions, après le rejet « Accable ».
3   Voir l'extrait publié par Mortelette, *Le Parnasse*, p. 75.
4   Gouvard, *Critique du vers*, p. 216, soutient que la première version « est un 6-6 puisque la variante [*qui est, soulignons-le, une correction*] (…) écarte toute possibilité d'une autre scansion » : c'est précisément parce que la première version ne ménageait pas l'illusion de la césure médiane requise par la tradition poétique que Banville l'a corrigée.

Changement d'époque et de sensibilité, en 1892, l'un des tenants de l'orthodoxie métrique classico-romantique, Sully Prudhomme, n'aura aucune peine à ignorer la césure médiane dans la première leçon, évoquant un « rejet [...] très heureux[5] », témoignant ainsi d'une évolution des sensibilités dans la perception de l'hémistiche. Dans son recueil de 1873, Corbière fait quant à lui preuve d'une maturité précoce en multipliant ces vers, dans des proportions encore modestes mais significatives, affirmant ainsi spontanément sa singularité provocatrice.

L'abolition de la césure médiane ne se réduit toutefois pas à ce genre de cas où un polysyllabe vient souder les hémistiches : elle se manifeste chaque fois que la contrainte morphologique cesse de s'exercer, ce qui peut aussi se traduire par une post-tonique en 7e position, ou lorsque la contrainte accentuelle est violée par l'emploi d'une post-tonique en 6e position, configurations qui, avant *Les Exilés*, ne se manifestent que de façon sporadique, témoignant de ce que l'ignorance de l'hémistiche résulte davantage d'une inadvertance que d'une recherche, dont nous allons montrer qu'elle résulte d'une restructuration métrique accidentelle. Leconte de Lisle lui-même écrivait dans la première version de *Kaïn* (*Qaïn*), donnée dans la livraison du 20 octobre 1869 du *Parnasse contemporain*[6] :

[...] & voilà,
Plus haut que ce tumulte vain, comme il parla
D'une voix lente & grave & semblable au tonnerre, [...]

Le poète s'était ainsi laissé distraire par le « déplacement de la césure[7] » – si l'on veut bien accorder crédit à cette notion qui retenait l'attention des lecteurs et critiques au XIXe siècle –, adoptant un rythme descendant tel qu'il en use parfois ailleurs dans ce poème dans le plus grand respect de la césure métrique, comme aux vers suivants :

Tantôt, comme des blocs d'airain, pendaient dans l'air ; (38)

---

5   *Réflexions sur l'art des vers*, p. 82. Martinon, « Le trimètre » [2], p. 45, considère à ce propos que, en y voyant simplement un « enjambement du premier hémistiche sur le second », Sully Prudhomme n'avait pas eu « la pleine notion du trimètre ».
6   *PC (1869)*, p. 10.
7   Sur cette conception, voir *infra*. Cornulier, *Art poétique*, p. 89-90, estime que la césure médiane est ici maintenue sous une forme enjambante (soit 6'-5). Il évoque le souvenir d'Heredia selon qui son maître aurait corrigé son vers après qu'il lui eût « fait remarquer que la césure se trouvait au milieu d'un mot », ce qui n'était jamais qu'une façon de parler.

Avec leur bouche épaisse & rouge, & pleins de faim. (65)

Il dit à sa famille errante : – Bâtissez (107)

Rugir, liés de marche en marche, &, sous tes porches (144)

Cette distraction témoigne clairement de l'effacement de la césure médiane et de la fonction métrique qui pouvait ainsi être *accidentellement* associée aux rythmes ternaires équipartis et, plus précisément, à l'accentuation dominante de la 8ᵉ position chez les poètes parnassiens, dans ce qui n'est, à la base, que des variantes rythmiques de l'alexandrin tirant partie de la mobilité des accents au sein des hémistiches, devenant des structures alternatives prêtes à prendre le relais de la césure à l'hémistiche. Ce n'est qu'après coup que le poète s'aperçut de sa bévue et remplaça *vain* par *entier* dans la reprise en recueil du poème en 1872, dans *Poëmes barbares*, restaurant ainsi la césure déficiente avec l'intégrité du second hémistiche grâce à l'élision du « e caduc » problématique. Victor de Laprade, qui n'était pas parnassien – bien que *Le Parnasse contemporain* retînt deux pièces de lui pour son dernier recueil –, et que la mode des césures pour l'œil n'a pas véritablement touché[8], commit la même année (1869) une bévue semblable dans son éloge de la désobéissance civile, intitulé *Pernette*, deux fois réédité au cours de la même année[9] :

Eux, sans rien voir et comme seuls dans l'univers,
S'étreignaient, s'appelaient de mille noms divers.

Prenant soudain conscience de son étourderie, le poète amenda son vers en normalisant la coupe problématique à partir de l'édition illustrée de 1870 : « Eux, sans rien voir, perdus et seuls dans l'univers, ». Il est du reste significatif que, s'il laisse échapper une césure pour l'œil dans ce récit en vers[10] :

Le regard du songeur descend avec l'aurore
Vers un petit clocher dont la flèche se dore,
Marquant la place où, dans les vapeurs du matin,
Cache ses rouges toits un village lointain.

---

8   *Cf.* p. 220-221.
9   Ici cité le texte de la 2ᵉ édition (1869), p. 230.
10   *Pernette*, 2ᵉ éd., p. 88.

c'est également par négligence, comme le montre sa correction dans la même édition illustrée[11] :

> [...] dont la flèche se dore ;
> Et les toits entrevus d'un village lointain
> Rougissent à travers les vapeurs du matin.

Il est donc frappant que cette abolition de la césure médiane n'apparaisse pas chez Banville et Leconte de Lisle, tout comme chez Laprade, comme un aboutissement d'une dégradation progressive de la césure, qui marquerait en quelque sorte la stabilisation d'un authentique mètre de substitution, mais comme une manifestation épisodique, où la prégnance du rythme ternaire ou l'accentuation dominante de la 8e position a pu amener le poète à l'ignorer. Pour le dire autrement, ces atteintes à la césure médiane comme les repentirs qui s'ensuivent montrent qu'en composant ces vers, les poètes n'avaient pas en tête l'impulsion métronomique de la tradition classique : 1-2-3-4-5-6 (bis), mais bien une autre, que les poètes romantiques avaient ainsi réglée sans pour autant l'occulter complètement : 1-2-3-4 (ter), si ce n'est 1-2-3-4-5-6-7-8/1-2-3-4 apte à leur faire négliger complètement la césure médiane dont ils préservaient pourtant partout ailleurs le souvenir en se maintenant dans la tradition encore prestigieuse de l'alexandrin classique. Comme l'exprimait Rochette pour qui ces deux impulsions, comme nous les nommons, ne sont pas en rapport d'exclusion, la syntaxe s'accommodant de la contrainte métrique[12] : « Il y a là comme deux forces qui se tiennent en échec et se neutralisent ; mais on sent bien que l'équilibre est instable et que peu à peu la formule grammaticale finira par s'imposer à l'oreille et lui donner le change. »

C'est très précisément là qu'intervient la réorganisation métrique dont ces diverses défaillances de la césure médiane sont la manifestation. Le fait que les 4e et 8e positions y jouent un rôle déterminant doit être mis en relation avec ce que nous enseigne l'histoire des mètres dans la poésie française dont hérite le XIXe siècle : d'une part le plus petit membre viable déterminé par les contraintes métriques est en effet précisément de quatre syllabes ; d'autre part, les contraintes métriques

---

11   *Pernette*, éd. ill., p. 92-93.
12   *L'alexandrin chez Victor Hugo*, p. 114-121, à propos de la distinction entre « alexandrin ternaire » et « rythme ternaire ».

ne s'exercent au sein du vers qu'au-delà de huit syllabes[13]. Ces particularités métriques de la versification rendent tout aussi bien compte
du fait que les structures syncopées du romantisme articulées sur la 5e
ou la 7e position ont pu à leur tour faciliter l'émergence des syncopes
parnassiennes auxquelles Corbière s'est d'abord essayé dans *Petite pouësie*, formes qui trouveront leur aboutissement chez Jules Laforgue avec
l'affranchissement de la césure médiane. Les rythmes 4-4-4 et 8-4 vont
dès lors pouvoir servir de structures d'appui favorisant l'effacement
occasionnel de la césure que les poètes pourront ou non assumer selon
leurs options esthétiques, voire stratégiques dans leur carrière poétique.
Ainsi, si Mallarmé se montre moins scrupuleux que ses prédécesseurs,
c'est parce que cet affranchissement même, au demeurant pratiqué
avec une grande économie, le séduit. Il assume l'abolition de la césure
médiane dès le premier recueil du *Parnasse contemporain*, dans le second
vers de *L'Azur* critiqué par Fournel qu'il ne modifiera pas plus que le
vers déjà évoqué d'*Hérodiade* épinglé par Stapfer, vers où l'on peut encore
observer le relais rythmique assuré par l'accentuation des positions 4
et 8 qui imprime à ces vers une structure ternaire régulière. Le phénomène apparaît en fait dès 1859 dans les *Premières poésies* de Villiers de
L'Isle-Adam, recueil qui ne contient que trois cas de césures pour l'œil
pour un total de 1859 alexandrins composés dans les années 1856-1858,
au début d'une strophe[14] :

> La Pauvreté, squelette sombre aux yeux funestes
> Qui, le soir, foule aux pieds les couronnes célestes
> Des vierges de seize ans, allait te consumer ; (*Hermosa*, II, CVIII)

En 1861 paraissent trois nouveaux vers de ce genre dans *Nouvelles poésies*
de Blanchecotte, poétesse à la versification par ailleurs très conventionnelle
qui ne cède qu'une fois à la nouvelle mode des césures pour l'œil sur le

---

13   Billy, « L'analyse distributionnelle », p. 818.
14   D'après les relevés de Gouvard, *Critique du vers*, p. 180. A. Villiers de L'Isle-Adam, *Premières
     poésies*, p. 88. Martinon, « Le trimètre » [2], p. 47, considère qu'« il n'est pas sûr que, dans
     la pensée de l'auteur, ce fût un trimètre » : « il pouvait y avoir là simplement une césure
     à l'italienne, ou qu'on appelle quelquefois une césure enjambante, où la syllabe muette
     non élidée compte dans le second hémistiche ». La postposition de l'épithète montre qu'il
     s'agit bien d'une structure ternaire étayée sur trois constituants syntaxiques distincts,
     d'autant que les césures « enjambantes » *stricto sensu* attendront les poètes symbolistes
     pour se faire une place assumée dans la prosodie de l'alexandrin.

millier d'alexandrins du recueil, vers dont la structure ternaire équipartie (une fois étayée d'un parallélisme syntaxique) a pu tromper la
vigilance de l'auteur en occultant la césure médiane[15] :

> Il me faut le soleil vivant pour m'éclairer.
> Il me faut l'air et l'infini, le libre espace. (*Deux sœurs*)
>
> J'aimais l'azur étincelant des cieux ! J'aimais
> Ce que je ne vois plus ni n'entendrai jamais, [...] (*La Vision de la mort*)
>
> Elle était belle, elle t'aimait, elle est passée,
> Répandant la lumière en ton cœur ébloui ; (*A ****)

En 1863, Mendès donne un nouveau vers de ce genre dans *Philoméla*
qui ne contient que deux cas de césures pour l'œil sur un total d'environ
900 alexandrins[16] :

> Et quand l'aurore a terrassé la messe noire,
> L'infâme dans mon cœur saignant, saignant toujours,
> Afin de compléter le rit blasphématoire,
> Trempe son ongle rose et se signe à rebours. (*Le Bénitier*)

En 1866, Armand Silvestre en présente un dans un rondeau de *Rimes
neuves et vieilles*[17], recueil qui ne contient que deux cas de césure pour
l'œil (significativement cantonnés dans un seul et même court poème
de neuf vers[18]) :

> Le temps viendra du rêve et des choses voilées
> Qu'au-dessous du linceul les trépassés verront,
> Et des splendeurs sous d'autres formes révélées,
> Et de la liberté que nuls ne troubleront,
> Le temps viendra !

Dans tous ces vers, l'accentuation des 4e et 8e positions est récurrente. Ce n'est pas le cas chez Cazalis qui n'accentue pas la 4e position

---

15 *Nouvelles poésies*, p. 84, 114 et 117. Gouvard, *Critique du vers*, p. 174-175, mentionne trois
cas de césures pour l'œil (dans des ternaires équipartis) qu'il dit avoir été « composés
entre 1850 et 1861 » mais qui sont tirés des *Nouvelles poésies* de 1861 où aucune indication
de date n'est donnée (à noter que *Rêves et réalités* de 1855 n'en comporte aucun).
16 La graphie *rit* est courante à l'époque.
17 Dans « Le temps viendra... », p. 153.
18 *Rimes tierces*, p. 66-67.

dans le dernier vers de la pièce intitulée *Le Poëme*, publiée en 1868, où le « déplacement de la césure » participe directement de la mise en relief du mot *éternités* avec un effet sensible d'harmonie imitative[19] :

> [...] la création entière est mon poëme,
>
> Est un poëme étrange où se mêlent des pleurs,
> Et dont vous, ô mortels, vous êtes les pensées,
> O vous qui partagez ma joie et mes douleurs
> Et l'ennui des éternités déjà passées.

On peut également signaler, dans le cadre de la poésie dramatique dont on connaît la plus grande liberté potentielle, outre les deux vers de *Qui veut des merveilles ?* (1868) de Verlaine et Coppée cités par Gouvard[20], ce vers d'*Aline*, drame d'Hennequin et Silvestre représenté pour la première fois le 22 septembre 1873, soit un mois et demi après l'achevé d'imprimer des *Amours jaunes*, où l'accent dominant de 3ᵉ position, hors zone métriquement contrainte, n'enlève rien au rôle d'appui métrique de l'accent secondaire en 8ᵉ position : « – C'est le seul que la pauvreté ne m'ait pas pris. » (p. 18). Citons encore dans *La Part du Roi* de Mendès, comédie représentée pour la première fois le 20 juin 1872[21] :

> Mais mon remords est assez grand de vos douleurs
> Sans qu'il faille ajouter votre sang à vos pleurs.

Un tableau synoptique nous aidera ici à suivre cette évolution au travers des recueils publiés et à mettre en évidence l'originalité de Corbière, en classant les vers en relation avec les « étapes » envisagées par Dorchain (CA : contrainte accentuelle, CM : contrainte morphologique ; + : respectée ; ⁻ : violée ; 0 : neutralisée)[22] :

---

19   *Melancholia*, p. 80.
20   *Critique du vers*, p. 224.
21   *Théâtre en vers*, p. 96. Nous n'avons pu vérifier la conformité de l'édition à l'originale.
22   Sur Dorchain, voir p. 252. Les crochets signalent les cas qui ont par la suite fait l'objet d'une rectification de la césure.

	Dorchain B CM⁻ (CA⁰)	Dorchain C CM⁻ (CA⁺ ᵒᵘ ⁰) 7ᵉ post-tonique	Dorchain D CA⁻ (CM⁺) 6ᵉ post-tonique
1859, Villiers de L'Isle-Adam		squelet|te sombre	
1861, Blanchecotte	et l'in|fini, étin|celant		elle | t'aimait
1863, Mendès	a ter|rassé		
1866, Silvestre		d'au|tres formes	
1867, Banville	pensi|vement		
1868, Cazalis	des éter|nités*		
1868, Verlaine/ Coppée	cosmo|polite, galvano|plastie*		
1869, Laprade		[com|me seuls]	
1869, Leconte de Lisle		[ce tumul|te vain]*	
1869, Mallarmé	noncha|lamment		
1869, Verlaine	épou|vantable		
1871, Lacaussade	la Ré|publique		
1872, Mendès	as|sez grand		
1873, *Les Amours jaunes*	en concu|binage*, Limo|nadier**, rossi|gnolaient*, en appa|reillant*, Je chan|tais ça	Mille-et-u|ne-nuits, ta seule œu|vre mâle*, roi|de-soûls, bon-|ne-femme	entre | le mur
1873, Hennequin/ Silvestre	la pau|vreté*		
1874, Lafenestre	l'in|terminable		
1875, Blanchecotte	*Aujour|dhui* meurt*		

L'astérisque signale l'absence d'accent en 4ᵉ position ; le soulignement, celle en 4ᵉ et 8ᵉ positions ; deux astérisques, une 4ᵉ post-tonique. « | » désigne la frontière médiane.

Tabl. 11 – L'abolition de la césure médiane chez Corbière et les Parnassiens.

Comme on peut le constater, dans les 29 cas recensés jusqu'à *Sagesse* inclus, le vers de Lafenestre excepté[23], la 8e position se trouve accentuée alors que la 4e ne l'est pas une fois sur trois, et son accentuation correspond souvent à une fin de syntagme. Ces proportions ne permettent guère de soutenir que c'est la routine du ternaire romantique, l'un de ces « poncifs de coupe » auquel pensait Banville[24], qui a permis l'émergence de ces vers dépourvus de césure médiane, si ce n'est dans une proportion indéterminée de cas impossibles à désigner dans le détail si ce n'est dans le cas de Blanchecotte dont le peu de vers déviants, césures pour l'œil comprises, sont tous des ternaires équipartis. Nous avions déjà relevé cette constante chez Corbière, chez qui c'est un vers sur deux qui ne présente pas d'accent sur la quatrième. La rareté des cas où une post-tonique occupe la 6e position (Dorchain D) ne signifie rien de particulier. En effet, l'examen des 98 vers du *Prologue* de *Poëmes saturniens* présentant une césure traditionnelle établit qu'un sur dix seulement comporte une post-tonique deux syllabes avant l'hémistiche (soit en 4e position) : dans notre tableau 11, la proportion de vers comportant une post-tonique deux syllabes avant la huitième est de 0,7/10 (2 cas sur un total de 29). Dans les pièces que Verlaine écrira dans les années 1873-1875, cette proportion passe à 1,2[25]. La quasi-constance de l'accentuation en 8e position des vers violant les contraintes césurales de l'hémistiche se vérifie dans les vers analogues de Rimbaud d'avant les « derniers vers[26] » :

Je courus ! Et les péninsules démarrées (*Le Bateau ivre*)

[...] des N d'or et de neige [...]
Eclatent, tricolorement enrubannés. » (*Ressouvenir*[27]).

Le seul vers – beaucoup plus tardif – de Mallarmé à présenter une post-tonique en 6e position présente du reste cette particularité : « Nubiles plis l'astre mûri des lendemains » dans le *Tombeau* de Verlaine (1897).

---

23 Sur ce vers, voir p. 385.
24 *Cf. supra*, p. 318-319.
25 Cinq cas sur un total de 43 vers dépourvus de césure médiane ; voir tabl. 12, p. 392-393.
26 Il n'en a pas moins été soutenu que, dans le premier cas cité, « la césure » interviendrait après une frontière de morphèmes, la forme étant mise en parallèle avec *presqu'île* (Cornulier, « Pour une approche », p. 43 ; *cf.* M. Murat, *L'Art de Rimbaud*, p. 50-51), ce qui est faux, l'hémistiche tombant *au sein* du premier morphème (*pé|n*).
27 Dans l'*Album zutique*.

Il paraît assez révélateur que son seul vers qui échappe à cette analyse
(« Peut-être que cette profondeur du désastre »), également avec une
post-tonique sur la 6ᵉ position, se trouve dans un brouillon et se verra
corrigé de façon à s'y plier : « Peut-être que cet[te] attirance du désastre »
(*Finale*)²⁸. Ceux de Germain Nouveau entrent également dans le cadre
de cette restructuration de l'alexandrin²⁹.

On ne peut naturellement écarter l'hypothèse que, *dans des cas
spécifiques*, ce ne sont pas les contraintes du mètre alternatif qui auront
joué mais bien celles de l'alexandrin coutumier : ce n'est ainsi sans
doute pas un hasard si, dans les deux seuls cas de *Qui veut des mer-
veilles ?* – publié, rappelons-le, en 1868 –, *cosmo|polite* et *galvano|plastie*,
la frontière médiane sépare les composants d'un composé savant et
que l'on y trouve à la rime le même genre de structures avec *galvano-/
plastie* et *Hispano-/Américain*³⁰, rapprochant ces vers des cas de mots
composés examinés au chapitre « La césure dans les mots composés »
(IIIᵉ partie). On peut porter le même soupçon à propos de « Et la tigresse
épouvantable d'Hyrcanie » de *Fêtes galantes* : en effet, la 6ᵉ position
s'y prête à un accent d'insistance qui en fait toute l'expressivité, vers
qui ne peut être le fruit d'une simple inadvertance dans un poème
(*Dans la grotte*) qui ne comporte que trois alexandrins, dispersés au
sein des trois quatrains qui le constituent, vers dont la conception n'a
du reste pas été immédiate, puisqu'il a été précédé d'une première
version plus conventionnelle dans le contexte de l'époque : « Et les
tigresses, – ô Clymène, – d'Hyrcanie », dans le même cadre rythmique
de ternaire équiparti. La modification du vers a du reste sans doute
était favorisée par le fait, relevé par J.-P. Bobillot, que les trois autres
vers du quatrain sont des octosyllabes uniformément accentués sur la
4ᵉ position (contrairement à ceux des autres couplets), imposant une
scansion 4-4 qui entre en écho avec la structure rythmique 4-4-4 de
cet alexandrin licencieux³¹. Il en ira de même des césures provocatrices
aux syllabes inconvenantes de *Madrigal* : « Du bout fin de la quenotte
de ton souris » (1871) ou de *Ces passions* : « Avec des particularités

---

28   *Cf.* Gouvard, « L'alexandrin d'*Hérodiade* (1866-1898) », https://www.academia.edu/35526019/
     LAlexandrin_dH%C3%A9rodiade_1866_1898 (consulté le 10/09/2022), p. 16.
29   Voir la liste dressée par Gouvard, *op. cit.*, p. 215.
30   *Cf. Théorie du vers*, p. 166-167.
31   Bobillot, « Et la tigresse », p. 283-284.

curieuses » (1889) où l'accent le plus proche tombe respectivement sur la 7e ou 9e position[32].

Ce qui est particulièrement notable, c'est que, chez tous ces poètes, ces déviations sont toujours des phénomènes isolés, à l'exception de Corbière qui affiche ainsi sa modernité, en particulier dans *Le Bossu Bitor* et *Le Novice en partance* qui contiennent l'un et l'autre trois cas, poèmes rattachés à la même section *GENS DE MER*, comme l'a fort bien remarqué B. Houzé qui, sans entrer dans les détails, concluait de la multiplication de ce qu'il appelle « des césures au milieu d'un mot[33] » : « Du moins peut-on dire que *Les Amours jaunes* participent ici pleinement au mouvement de subversion métrique induit par les publications les plus remarquables sur ce plan à son époque. »

La particularité structurale que nous avons mise en évidence n'avait pas échappé à Martinon qui, au début du dernier siècle, considérait que, lorsque la césure médiane s'efface, il y aurait une césure « marquée par un accent fort sur la huitième syllabe », et en même temps « une césure de soutien [...] marquée le plus souvent par un accent fort sur la quatrième syllabe[34] », posant « en principe que *quand la sixième syllabe du vers n'est pas accentuée, il est à peu près indispensable que la huitième le soit*[35] », ce qui se verra vérifié dans les faits jusqu'au début des années 1880, avec le développement du symbolisme, sans parler du cas particulier de Rimbaud en 1872. Il en venait ainsi à évoquer « un vers de huit syllabes aux accents mobiles suivi d'un élément de quatre », en insistant toutefois sur la tendance à diviser en deux parties égales le membre long, tendance qui l'amenait à parler d'une « césure subsidiaire[36] » dont le caractère facultatif ne doit pas nous leurrer : seule la « césure principale » répond à une fonction métrique, la césure facultative ressortissant du rythme du vers.

La nouvelle étape que signe le mètre alternatif ‹8-4› dans l'histoire de l'alexandrin reflète par ailleurs très précisément le trait le plus

---

32 Sur ces deux vers, voir Cornulier, *Théorie du vers*, p. 235-236 et 241.

33 Dans Houzé et Hérisson, *op. cit.*, p. 191, où il rectifie un jugement timoré que nous avions porté dans une étude ancienne de 2005 (remaniée en 2014).

34 « Le trimètre » [2], p. 49. En fait, le critique s'exprime ainsi : « lorsque la césure classique disparaît » ; mais le choix de ses exemples montre qu'il a aussi bien en vue l'affaiblissement de la césure médiane (la coupe syntaxique dominante ne correspond pas avec l'hémistiche) que son occultation (césure pour l'œil) ou son abolition *proprio sensu*.

35 Art. cité, p. 54. Sur l'analyse de Martinon, voir aussi p. 256-257.

36 *Ibidem.*

significatif de l'évolution du grand mètre que les romantiques ont impulsée en rompant d'avec la relative rigidité héritée de la tradition classique. Une étude comparative de l'alexandrin à l'époque classique et à l'époque romantique, menée par J.-M. Gouvard, a ainsi mis en évidence l'importance accrue de la 8e position qui constitue volontiers chez les romantiques une fin de mot lexical, endossant le rôle que les classiques faisait jouer à la 9e, évolution qui n'a pas d'équivalent au sein du premier hémistiche, comme on peut le voir au travers de la figure suivante où est représentée la distribution en pourcentage des marquages M et F sur les douze positions métriques du vers[37] (« Pn » : n-ième position) :

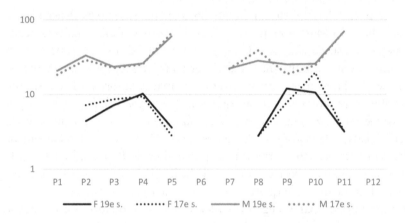

FIG. 8 – Distribution comparative des marquages M et F sur les douze positions métriques du vers au XVIIe et au XIXe siècle.

Si la distribution du critère M ne varie pas de manière significative sur le premier hémistiche, il n'en est pas de même de F dont la diminution est importante en 2e position, ce qui à vrai dire n'a pas ici de signification

---

37 *Critique du vers*, p. 115-127, en particulier p. 124-125 à propos des critères F et M qui correspondent respectivement aux syllabes post-toniques et, pour l'essentiel, aux syllabes atones au sein de mots polysyllabiques. Les valeurs associées aux courbes de Gouvard sont les pourcentages indiqués par l'auteur dans sa thèse (*Recherches*, p. 185). Le critère F (maximum estimé de 19,6 % en P10) étant nettement moins représenté que M (max. 69,8 % en P11), nous avons adopté une échelle logarithmique.

particulière[38]. Quant au second hémistiche, la régression du critère M en 8ᵉ position comme l'augmentation du critère F sur la 9ᵉ correspond en grande partie à l'accroissement des fins de groupes accentuels ou de syntagmes accentués sur la 8ᵉ. La régression de F au niveau de la 10ᵉ position comme l'augmentation de M au niveau de la 9ᵉ signalent pour leur part un changement dans la structure rythmique de l'alexandrin dont les formes classiques privilégiaient l'accentuation de la neuvième. L'émergence du mètre alternatif ‹8-4› apparaît ainsi comme l'aboutissement des mutations qui affectent l'équilibre rythmique du grand vers ‹6-6› à l'époque romantique, après que l'essor de la césure pour l'œil eut ouvert la porte à l'oblitération de l'hémistiche et à la ruine de la césure médiane. Ces observations n'ont du reste pas échappé à Martinon qui, s'appuyant « sur des statistiques précises », a pu affirmer à propos du « faux trimètre » hugolien (ternaires égaux aussi bien qu'inégaux) que[39]

> le type 3-3, employé au second hémistiche avec une prédilection marquée chez Racine et les classiques, cède la place dans V. Hugo au type 2-4, qui, à cette place, facilite singulièrement le trimètre. En second lieu, si le déplacement de l'accent prépondérant atteignait 20 % dans *Britannicus*, dans V. Hugo il atteint et dépasse le double : près de 45 % dans *les Chevaliers errants*. Enfin les modernes ne répugnent plus, comme Racine, à mettre l'accent prépondérant au second hémistiche aussi bien qu'au premier.

Le rapprochement avec le cas du décasyllabe commun est à cet égard édifiant car ce mètre a connu une altération de même nature chez Voltaire qui, dans *Nanine*, se laissait aller à écrire, de loin en loin, souvent pour conclure des tirades, des vers tels que les trois premiers suivants, ou même le dernier, qui, dans un tel contexte, n'est pas une césure pour l'œil[40] :

---

38 Gouvard, *op. cit.*, p. 125, considère que « le profil du premier hémistiche [...] demeure inchangé des années 1630 à 1840 », bien que, selon le tableau de synthèse qu'il donne dans *Recherches*, p. 185, l'écart au niveau de la 4ᵉ position soit loin d'être négligeable, passant de 67 % au XVIIᵉ siècle à 58 % au XIXᵉ (l'écart est plus précisément de 8,8 points alors qu'il ne dépasse pas 3,4 sur les autres positions). Plus significative est la nette régression des monosyllabes atones sur la même 4ᵉ position, avec une baisse qui n'est pas éloignée du quart pour le critère C et supérieure au tiers pour le critère P (voir les courbes données par l'auteur p. 123 et 124).

39 Art. cité, [2], p. 40.

40 Pour le détail, on se reportera à l'excellent mémoire malheureusement inédit de Jean-Luc Guilbaud (Université de Nantes, 1994). LC : Le Comte ; N : Nadine ; M : Marin.

CA violée :	Vous en ê<u>tes</u> la preuve… ah çà, Nanine, (I, VII)
CM violée :	[LC] Qui ? Vous, obscu<u>re</u> ! Vous ! [N] Quoi que je fasse. (*ibid.*)
CM violée et CA	Vous porterez cette somme complète
neutralisée :	De trois cents <u>lou</u>is d'or ; n'y manquez pas : (I, IX)
CA neutralisée :	[LC] Crève tous <u>les</u> chevaux. [M] Vous voilà pris. (I, I)

Dans cette pièce, le mètre traditionnel ‹4-6› cède ainsi épisodiquement la place à un mètre alternatif ‹6-4›, renversant l'allure rythmique du vers qui, ascendante d'ordinaire, devient descendante. On aura remarqué qu'ici, comme dans l'alexandrin, la césure se trouve décalée de deux syllabes vers l'avant avec un second membre métrique de quatre syllabes et une césure flottante liée au caractère facultatif de l'élision.

CONTRAINTES CHOISIES
ET CONTRAINTES SUBIES

L'abolition de la césure médiane s'accompagne ainsi d'une restructuration métrique par l'exercice d'une contrainte alternative déterminant un accent en 8ᵉ position. Cette contrainte subie par le poète peut être comparée aux contraintes que se sont choisies certains poètes soucieux de trouver une alternative métrique à l'alexandrin dans le même cadre formel de douze syllabes. Ce désir de nouveauté était naturellement lié à l'hégémonie du grand vers et à la lassitude que sa pratique pouvait entraîner : de la même façon que les romantiques avaient entrepris une première remise en cause en exploitant les ressources stylistiques de la discordance entre mètre et syntaxe, les nouvelles générations de poètes recherchaient des voies nouvelles dont la césure pour l'œil était encore un compromis qui fragilisait certes la structure du grand vers mais ne la remettait pas en cause. Pour comprendre l'essor de ces nouveaux mètres, il nous paraît utile de reprendre la discussion du concept de césure et de sa perception au cours du XIXᵉ siècle.

Il ne fait pas de doute que, jusqu'aux romantiques au moins, l'alexandrin est *dans son essence même* conçu comme ayant un "accent fixe" (ou un "repos") sur la sixième position, la polémique portant sur la présence des accents « mobiles » et sur leurs rapports hiérarchiques avec l'accent fixe dont la saillance était variable[1]. Mais on négligeait souvent la finalité ou la raison d'être de la césure – qui, selon P. Larousse, serait de « régler la cadence » du vers en intervenant en un lieu prévisible – pour y voir une simple coupe syntaxique. C'est cette focalisation sur les manifestations extérieures de la contrainte métrique inhérente à l'alexandrin qui a pu donner naissance au concept contradictoire de « césure mobile » par lequel on constate que le signal ou les signaux

---

1   Voir notamment Ackermann, *Traité de l'accent*, chap. XI, p. 66-72.

attendus de la césure s'y trouvent éclipsés par la présence de signaux
de même nature plus saillants en quelque autre endroit du vers, au sein
des hémistiches, ce qu'accusait encore la mode de l'enjambement et du
rejet qui permettaient de s'affranchir occasionnellement – à condition de
respecter la contrainte morphologique – tant des frontières d'hémistiches
que des frontières de vers. Ce signal, d'ordre macroprosodique (frontière
de groupes intonatifs) éclipsait ainsi les signaux microprosodiques
pourtant spécifiques et caractéristiques de la césure médiane, seule
pertinente du point de vue métrique, avec l'obligation d'élider les
éventuelles syllabes post-toniques à l'hémistiche. Le concept métrique
de césure s'effaçait ainsi au regard des critiques devant la concurrence de
signaux de même nature au sein du vers. Cette prééminence accordée à
la coupe syntaxique majeure qui constituait le marqueur le plus significatif de l'articulation métrique interne de l'alexandrin dans la tradition
classique ouvrait ainsi la voie à une ambiguïté terminologique qui n'a
cessé de peser sur les débats de l'époque. Le commentaire qu'en donnera
Larousse en revenant à la distinction voltairienne (qui se démarquait des
conceptions de Port-Royal[2]) entre « hémistiche » (césure métrique) et
"césure" (coupe syntaxique) – termes auxquels le lexicographe substitue,
dans le reste de son article, ceux de "césure" et "coupe" respectivement,
comme le faisait Quicherat –, rend parfaitement compte du flou qui a
pesé sur ces notions[3] :

> Plusieurs dictionnaires enseignent que l'hémistiche est la même chose que la
> césure ; mais il y a une grande différence, dit Voltaire, et il ajoute : "L'hémistiche
> est toujours à la moitié du vers : la césure, qui rompt le vers, est partout où
> elle coupe la phrase [...]".

Cette doctrine est répandue à l'époque romantique qui désigne généralement par « césure » une coupe syntaxique quelconque, pouvant ou
non coïncider avec l'hémistiche. Comme le dit sentencieusement Victor
Bernard en 1850[4] :

---

2   « Breve instruction », p. 635 : « La *Cesure* est un repos qui coupe le vers en deux parties,
     dont chacune s'appelle *hemistiche*, c'est-à-dire, demy vers ». Voltaire prend *hémistiche* au
     pied de la lettre.
3   *GDU* III, 819. *Cf.* les remarques de Gouvard, « Le vers de Pierre Larousse », p. 58-62. Ce
     commentaire sera repris à peu près tel quel par Littré, à l'article « Hémistiche » (*DLF*
     II, 2004).
4   *Code poétique*, p. 7-8.

L'hémistiche en son lieu — prend sa place de droit.
La césure n'adopte = elle = jamais d'endroit ;
Plus libre en son allure = elle tranche = divise,
Coupe = en deux ou trois parts = selon qu'elle s'avise,
Le vers = à tel endroit qu'il lui plaît de choisir,
Ou plane sur plusieurs suivant son bon plaisir.

C'est elle qui explique l'expression de "césure mobile" que l'on trouve déjà dans *Vie, poésies et pensées de Joseph Delorme*, dès sa première édition[5], où Sainte-Beuve, affirme son peu de goût pour « l'alexandrin à césure fixe » ou « invariable » de Boileau[6]. En 1868, Gautier, qui lie l'essor de la "césure mobile" à l'imitation de l'hexamètre grec par Chénier, avec « les variétés de coupes, les suspensions, les rejets, toute cette secrète harmonie et ce rhythme intérieur retrouvés par le chantre du *Jeune Malade*, du *Mendiant* et de *l'Oarystis* », évoque semblablement « la mobilité facultative de la césure » dans sa préface à la première édition des œuvres complètes de Baudelaire. Et l'un comme l'autre montrent, par leur production poétique même, qu'ils n'ont pas perdu de vue la nécessité de la frontière d'hémistiche et des obligations microprosodiques que le mètre lui associe sans faillir[7]. En effet, ce décentrement de la coupe prosodique majeure du vers n'affectait en rien la manifestation des autres marques, morphologique et accentuelle, de la césure *stricto sensu*, si ce n'est l'affaiblissement parfois extrême de l'accent médian. Ce conflit entre mètre et syntaxe que semble occulter la terminologie avait entretemps était conceptualisé par le théoricien de la versification romantique, W. Ténint, dans une formulation inexacte et ambiguë, affirmant d'un côté que « [l]a césure peut […] se déplacer », d'un autre que « Dans le vers parlé, la césure du milieu […] est […] très-souvent supprimée, mais il en reste toujours quelque chose, ou du moins il faut que le premier hémistiche se termine par un son plein [*soit une syllabe non post-tonique*] », avec un premier hémistiche « complet comme son, sinon comme sens », pour évoquer *a minima* l'obligation d'élision et la nécessité d'une frontière de mots[8].

---

5   Éd. 1829, p. 210.
6   Éd. 1863, p. 148, 292 et 298 (nous n'avons pu consulter l'édition de 1861 de Poulet-Malassis et De Broise reprise par Charpentier).
7   Baudelaire, *Œuvres complètes*, t. I, p. 42.
8   *Prosodie*, p. 76-77 (*cf.* p. 313). Murphy, « Versifications », p. 77-78, s'y laisse ainsi prendre en affirmant que « la poésie de l'époque apporte un démenti catégorique » à Ténint,

L'émergence d'un alexandrin renouvelé se trouve déjà envisagée dix ans avant *Les Amours jaunes*, de façon certes schématique, par un théoricien du vers, Abel Ducondut, dans son *Examen critique de la versification française classique et romantique* de 1863. Cet auteur n'avait pas manqué de constater que les romantiques, qui se piquaient d'avoir libéré le vers de « la cage césure », s'arrêtaient à mi-chemin[9] :

> La règle de la césure à la sixième syllabe étant acceptée, depuis quelque trois cents ans que l'E muet perdit de sa sonorité, ce fut une règle dérivée de la première, et incontestée, que la sixième syllabe devait être accentuée et séparée de la septième ; partout ailleurs un E muet peut trouver sa place.
>
> La suppression de la règle-mère entraîne fatalement la suppression de celle qui en dérive. Ne voulant pas de césure après la sixième syllabe, les romantiques ne devraient plus exiger que cette syllabe soit toujours, quand même, accentuée et séparée de la septième ; l'E muet devrait y trouver sa place comme en toute autre partie du vers.

Et de préciser que, parmi les millions de vers publiés par les poètes dramatiques des trente dernières années, pas un seul ne s'y trouve « dans lequel la sixième syllabe soit un E muet, [...] Ou la pénultième d'un mot masculin, [...] Où la septième soit une terminaison féminine non élidée[10] » – soit les configurations étudiées dans nos chapitres « L'abolition de la césure médiane » (chez Corbière) et « L'abolition de la césure médiane chez les Parnassiens » –, ajoutant[11] :

> Pour ce qui regarde la césure mobile, nous défions encore qu'on puisse trouver dans les œuvres romantiques un vers semblable à ceux-ci :
>
> Devant ton seuil, — au souffle noir — de la tempête.
> ....
> Et Pénélope — aux poursuivants — toujours cruelle.
>
> vers faux par rapport à la césure classique, mais très-justes par la double césure, après la quatrième et la huitième syllabe.

---

et, s'il exonère Banville qui « semble [lui] emboîter le pas », c'est en raison de ses vers qui prouvent « qu'il faisait bien une distinction entre césures et coupes rythmiques », négligeant le fait que Ténint n'y aurait pas dérogé s'il avait bien voulu versifier. Pour une discussion plus générale et formalisée des conceptions de la césure et de la discordance, voir en particulier Verluyten, « L'analyse de l'alexandrin », p. 38-51 (p. 42-43 sur Ténint).
9   *Examen critique*, p. 75.
10   Nous corrigeons l'impression fautive du typographe (« édiflée »).
11   *Op. cit.*, p. 76.

C'est ce respect scrupuleux d'une frontière morphologique entre les 6ᵉ et 7ᵉ positions des alexandrins romantiques, associé au refus de post-tonique en 6ᵉ (ou 7ᵉ) position, qui fonde la notion de césure pour l'œil en lui conférant une pleine légitimité, et les Parnassiens ne chercheront pas à remettre ce principe en cause avant Verlaine, après que le mouvement l'eut mis sur la touche[12]. Ceci dit, chez Ducondut, la notion revisitée de "césure mobile" désigne le déplacement occasionnel de la césure médiane *en des positions* déterminées du vers, toujours les mêmes, et c'est cette *détermination* même qui garantit leur métricité[13] :

> Le mot *césure mobile*, si on l'adoptait, signifierait le mélange régulier ou irrégulier des deux coupes [*soit ‹6-6› et ‹4-4-4›*]. Cette combinaison serait-elle harmonieuse ? Peut-être. Dans certains cas, il nous semble qu'on en pourrait tirer un parti avantageux.

Cette anticipation d'un mètre bi-césuré qui trouvera quelques illustrations s'appuie sur une théorie simple, que l'auteur expose de la façon suivante[14] :

> On a parlé de « césure mobile ». — Sous peine de cesser d'être harmonieux, c'est-à-dire de cesser d'être un vers, l'alexandrin, trop long pour une seule mesure, doit se soumettre à cette loi de se diviser en parties ayant entre elles un rapport musical. Douze syllabes, pour obtenir ce résultat, ne peuvent se diviser que de six en six, césure classique ; de trois en trois, ce qui donne le même résultat ; ou de quatre en quatre. On aurait pu demander le droit de pratiquer cette dernière méthode.

Dans les années 1850-1860, André Van Hasselt, qui se réclamait autant des théories de Scoppa que de l'exemple du père même de Ducondut, publiait ses premières études rythmiques ou « compositions rythmées d'après des formules musicales[15] », parmi lesquelles on trouve des illustrations de la solution envisagée d'une division de trois en trois

---

12   Voir chapitre suivant.
13   *Op. cit.*, p. 78. Voir aussi, p. 72 : « L'emploi à volonté des vers à césure simple et à césure double pouvait seul constituer ce qu'on aurait pu nommer la césure mobile. Ce n'est pas là ce qu'ont fait les romantiques ».
14   *Op. cit.*, p. 70-71. En 1911, Rochette, *L'alexandrin chez Victor Hugo*, p. 49-50, estimera lui aussi que « le vers de douze syllabes » pouvait « être pensé » sur l'un ou l'autre de ces « rythmes », parce qu'ils « réunissent les conditions de symétrie qui satisfont et enchantent l'oreille », déterminant « des vers différents, irréductibles, et non pas deux variétés d'un même type ».
15   Voir le chap. VIII que Louis Alvin consacre à ces recherches dans *André Van Hasselt, sa vie et ses travaux*, p. 239-278. Sur les théories de Scoppa, voir Gouvard, « Le vers français ».

(‹3-3-3-3›), telles que les vers impairs de *Dans la forêt*, daté de 1857 (en alternance avec des ennéasyllabes ‹3-3-3›)[16] :

> Oh ! la verte forêt, oh ! la verte forêt,
>> Qu'il est doux, qu'il est doux ton silence !
> N'es-tu pas pour l'esprit un asile secret ?
>> Un refuge où notre âme s'élance ?

Dans cet exemple, on observe un regroupement syntagmatique en 6-6 (et 3-6[17]). Hugo lui-même trouva le moyen de recourir à ce mètre pour intégrer une chanson forgée de toute pièce, composée de trisyllabes masculins rimés, dans la forme alexandrine de sa tragédie *Esca* (I), qui sera recueillie dans *Les Quatre Vents de l'Esprit* :

> LISON, *reculant.*
>> [...] Le diable !
> Je comprends.

> *On entend une musique sous les arbres et une vague chanson murmurée qui semble chantée au loin par des passants invisibles.*

> CHANSON.
> — Les lutins — dans les thyms — les hautbois —
> dans les bois — les roseaux — dans les eaux — ont des voix. —
> donc faisons — des chansons — et dansons. — l'aube achève —
> notre rêve — et l'amour — c'est le jour. —

> LISON, *pâmée et fascinée.*
>> Je suis Ève !

On remarquera que, pour *réguler* le mètre, la division procède dans nos deux exemples par la disposition séquentielle de modules rythmiques (des groupes accentuels), dépourvue de césures proprement dites, là où le mètre ‹4-4-4› imaginé par Ducondut repose sur une organisation syntagmatique, nonobstant d'éventuels rejets, chaque membre pouvant présenter plusieurs accents, comme le montrent les essais rythmiques de son père (publiés en 1856) qu'il donne en exemple[18] :

> Dans un volume publié il y a quelques années, mon père a proposé cette double césure pour les vers destinés à s'allier à la musique.

---

16 *Nouvelles poésies*, p. 291-292.
17 On peut aussi avoir 6-3, p. ex. : « Le poète songeur, tu l'accueilles. »
18 *Op. cit.*, p. 71.

Cœur de quinze ans, – il faut aimer – dès qu'on sait plaire
Plus tard, hélas ! – il est trop tard – pour s'enflammer.

L'exemple de ces deux vers n'est certes pas très heureux puisqu'un lecteur non averti n'y verra rien de différent du « trimètre » romantique, mais il suffit de se reporter au poème dont ils sont tirés – *Le Temps fuit* –, poème constitué de trois quatrains isométriques dont l'auteur décrit les vers comme étant composés de « péons 4[es19] », pour constater que la sixième position peut indifféremment se trouver aussi bien occupée par un mot grammatical atone (pronoms conjoints *se, nous*) que par une syllabe "féminine" (*el'le[6] vous[7] dit[8]*). Dans le poème suivant, intitulé *Le Roman* (36 vers), composé dans le même mètre, il n'est plus possible de se laisser leurrer, comme le montre plus spécialement le second sizain :

Sage qui sait mettre des bornes à ses vœux !
Qui sans mesure, âpre, désire, est-il heureux ?
Le jour présent se sacrifie à l'avenir,
Comme si l'heure ne devait jamais finir !
Puis, lorsqu'enfin rate le drame, au dénoûment,
Vient le réel, pour l'idéal du beau roman.

Ce « rythme à 3 périodes de 4 temps » dont il réfutait l'existence, fût-ce à titre alternatif, chez Hugo, se retrouve chez Van Hasselt qui écrit, par exemple, en 1851[20] :

Sur le rocher de l'épopée et de l'histoire,
Conseil béni,
Vous habitez vos larges tentes de victoire
Dans l'infini.

Plus tard popularisé par Rostand dans les stances de Photine (*La Samaritaine*, 1897), ce mètre sera qualifié de « bicésuré » par Claudius Popelin dans un sonnet, *Au clair de la lune* (1888), dont les vers 5, 7, 10 et 13 n'offrent effectivement pas même l'apparence d'une césure médiane pour l'œil, au contraire des vers 3, 6 et 14[21] :

---

19 J.-A. Ducondut, *Essai de rhythmique française*, p. 220.
20 *Poëmes, paraboles*, p. 217.
21 Au contraire des v. 3, 6 et 14. Popelin, *Un livre de sonnets*, p. 170. Pour une description de ce mètre, voir les remarques de Dorchain, *L'Art des vers*, p. 244-245, qui considère toutefois qu'il ne devrait pas être employé sans mélange, l'alexandrin à césure médiane

Sur l'étang bleu que vient rider le vent des soirs
Séléné penche, avec amour, sa face blonde,
Et sa clarté, qui se reflète au ras de l'onde,
Met un point d'or au front mouvant des roseaux noirs.

Déjà la flore a <u>refermé</u> ses encensoirs.
L'oiseau se tait et le sommeil étreint le monde
Écoute bien, tu <u>n'entendras</u> rien à la ronde
Que palpiter mon cœur gonflé d'ardents espoirs.

Dans une main je tiens ta main mignonne et blanche,
Mon bras te ceint, mon <u>autre</u> main est sur ta hanche,
Je sens ton corps, ton corps charmant tout contre moi.

Ta lèvre s'ouvre, un mot divin sur elle expire,
Mais ton regard qui <u>laisse</u> voir ton doux émoi,
Avant ta lèvre à mon regard a su le dire.

Cependant ce mètre se trouve utilisé régulièrement bien avant cette époque tardive, aux côtés de l'alexandrin *proprio sensu* dans des poèmes des années 1860, où ces mètres ont une distribution distincte, ce qui correspond précisément à l'idée que Ducondut se faisait du concept de "césure mobile", à savoir « le mélange régulier ou irrégulier » de l'alexandrin traditionnel et du ternaire ‹4-4-4›. *Confidence* d'Auguste Châtillon, sur lequel Gouvard a pu attirer l'attention, pièce dialoguée publiée en 1860, reprise en 1866, offre ainsi trois quatrains d'alexandrins (2ᵉ, 3ᵉ et 5ᵉ) et deux de dodécasyllabes accentués sur les positions 4 et 8, sans le moindre souci d'une césure médiane (1ᵉʳ et 4ᵉ quatrains), dont les doubles coupes sont toujours ou masculines ou élidées[22]. Le mélange n'y est toutefois pas une simple convenance puisqu'il sert une intention rhétorique, l'alexandrin bicésuré correspondant toujours à un discours de l'amoureuse[23]. On peut également signaler le poème suivant, daté de 1868 (publié en 1871), où Jean Aicard recourt cette fois à la double césure pour conclure chacun des quatrains dont tous les autres vers sont des alexandrins *stricto sensu*[24] :

---

restant la forme esthétique de référence à laquelle l'oreille se plaît à revenir, ce qui était le point de vue de Ducondut fils.

22 Dans *A la Grand'Pinte*, p. 127 ; repris dans *Poésies*, p. 300. Voir Gouvard, *Critique du vers*, p. 235-236 ; pour l'analyse métrique, voir Cornulier, *Art poëtique*, p. 93-94.

23 Cependant, celle-ci s'exprime aussi en alexandrins dans les 2ᵉ et 3ᵉ quatrains dont elle partage les vers ou les hémistiches avec sa confidente de sœur.

24 *Les Rébellions et les Apaisements*, XXVI, p. 157-158.

Je t'aime doucement, comme j'aime les fleurs ;
Je suis sans passion ; je suis plein de tendresse ;
Quand je suis loin de toi, mes yeux n'ont pas de pleurs,
Et j'aspire ton souvenir avec paresse.

Je t'aime doucement, & mon cœur ne bat pas
Plus vite quand je vois ta beauté m'apparaître,
Et que tu sois très-proche, ou que tu sois là-bas,
Le même calme inaltérable est dans mon être.

Je t'aime doucement ; je t'aime sans désir ;
Je rêve sans frissons au baiser de ta lèvre :
Je n'ai ni vif chagrin par toi, ni vif plaisir,
Et mon amour est la langueur, & non la fièvre.

Or si je suis ainsi, tu connais bien pourquoi :
La résignation m'a fait cette attitude ;
Certain de ne pouvoir jamais atteindre à toi,
Je me suis fait du désespoir une habitude.

Dans ce contexte, le vers 12 qui porte un proclitique en 6ᵉ position n'a que l'apparence des césures déviantes proprement parnassiennes : il s'agit bien d'un dodécasyllabe bicésuré et non d'un *alexandrin* à césure pour l'œil. Le quatrième vers dévie quelque peu du dimètre décrit par Ducondut, avec une post-tonique en 4ᵉ position, témoignant clairement du rôle déterminant de la huitième : le mètre semble ici pouvoir s'instancier en 4-4-4 ou 8-4, voire peut-être en 4-4-4 et 3'-4-4 à coupe lyrique[25].

Indépendamment de ces poèmes de Châtillon et d'Aicard, l'examen des alexandrins parnassiens dépourvus de césure médiane est révélateur en ce qu'un tiers des vers concernés avant 1873 – examinés au chapitre précédent – sont accentués en 8ᵉ position mais pas en quatrième, mettant ainsi en évidence le rôle déterminant de la huitième. L'invention du bicésuré semble ainsi, sous une forme construite et planifiée rappelant le « trimètre » de Ténint, faire écho à l'émergence naturelle des alexandrins licencieux de l'époque, ce qui n'est pas sans analogie avec la situation de l'ennéasyllabe ternaire issu de la poésie

---

25   Ainsi isolé, le v. 4 laisse en effet d'une certaine manière subsister une incertitude sur son premier membre puisqu'on pourrait défendre l'idée qu'une frontière de mots est requise entre les 4ᵉ et 5ᵉ positions et que la contrainte accentuelle peut ne pas s'y exercer (coupe lyrique). Cette analyse pourrait tout aussi bien se défendre pour les ternaires romantiques 3'-4-4 ou les rythmes parnassiens à césure pour l'œil semblables, en particulier lorsqu'un repos se présente après la post-tonique.

assujettie au chant où les 3ᵉ et 6ᵉ positions sont normalement accentuées si ce n'est que l'accentuation peut faire défaut sur la 6ᵉ comme dans la fameuse chanson de Malherbe, « Sus, debout la merveille des belles[26] ». La syntaxe y divise le plus souvent le vers en deux segments inégaux ordonnés, de trois et six syllabes, structure qui se retrouve dans la romance du *Secret* de François-Benoît Hoffman (1796), mentionnée par Gribenski[27], chez qui la 6ᵉ position est par contre systématiquement accentuée (« Je te perds, fugitive espérance ! »). Si la structure de ces ennéasyllabes a nécessairement un caractère "métrique", il ne faut pas perdre de vue que l'on entre là dans la *parodie* musicale et non dans la métrique naturelle du langage, affranchie de la musique, comme le fait remarquer Gribenski et comme les concevait Ducondut père : la contrainte porte directement *sur le rythme du vers* ; dans l'alexandrin bicésuré, elle porte à un niveau supérieur, sur l'articulation du vers en trois membres métriques, en laissant une grande liberté à l'organisation rythmique interne des hémistiches.

Si, dans les alexandrins parnassiens dépourvus de césure médiane, un tiers n'est pas accentué en 4ᵉ position, dans les dix concernés des *Amours jaunes*, c'est la moitié qui n'est pas accentuée sur cette position, ce qui est beaucoup trop pour que l'on puisse parler de contrainte métrique puisqu'on peut observer le même phénomène dans l'octosyllabe, p. ex. dans *À la mémoire de Zulma*, *Idylle coupée* ou *L'Etna*, et où l'on peut du reste rencontrer des scores plus élevés encore comme dans *Vénerie*, *Portes et fenêtres* ou *Le Mousse* avec six vers sur dix[28]. Il y a par conséquent une distinction claire à établir entre le mètre bicésuré aux contraintes *choisies* qui résulte d'une recherche délibérée et le mètre nouveau aux contraintes *subies*, déterminé par une simple contrainte sur la 8ᵉ position que nous avons vu apparaître sporadiquement dans la pratique de l'alexandrin dès les années 1860.

Il faudra attendre 1874 pour trouver chez un poète des plus inattendus, George Lafenestre, un alexandrin isolé irréductible à ces nouvelles

---

26 Voir ainsi « Tous les vents tiennent leurs bouches closes, » ; la 6ᵉ y est accentuée dans sept vers sur vingt, ce qui ne témoigne pas dans cette pièce de l'existence d'une contrainte particulière sur cette position.

27 « Vers impairs », § 3.

28 Mais aussi des scores bien inférieurs, de deux sur dix, dans *À ma jument Souris* ou *Nature morte*.

structures, en tête d'un quatrain qui fait partie de la description d'un cortège funèbre[29] :

> Pas un arbre dans l'interminable poussière
> D'où s'étende un lambeau d'ombre sur les piétons.
> Deux vieillards essoufflés, qui traînent en arrière,
> Trébuchent ; leurs doigts chauds glissent sur leurs bâtons.

L'étrangeté de ce vers – écrit dans la période 1864-1870 – de l'un des Parnassiens les plus rétifs à la césure pour l'œil, est soulignée par l'enchaînement avec un vers dont le rythme syncopé est également inhabituel, et, qu'il soit ou non le résultat d'une recherche consciente (mais peut-il avoir échappé à la conscience d'un versificateur aussi méticuleux que Lafenestre ?), l'effet stylistique en est frappant, avec dans les deux cas l'étirement de l'expression par-delà l'hémistiche où l'on retrouve la recherche de Cazalis dans ses *éternités déjà passées*[30]. Que le mot enjambant l'hémistiche soit précisément l'épithète *interminable* joint à l'effet saisissant une motivation stylistique tout aussi frappante, d'autant plus qu'un possible accent d'insistance tomberait sur la seconde syllabe, soit en 7e position, soit le début du second hémistiche putatif. Ce cas mis à part, la régularité de l'accent en 8e position est donc une constante dans les vers violant la contrainte morphologique ou l'accentuelle, aussi bien chez Corbière que chez les Parnassiens. Rappelons qu'elle ne se retrouve par contre pas parmi les vers où la césure tombe au sein d'un mot composé, après un trait d'union, situation dont nous avons déjà souligné l'ambiguïté chez divers poètes de l'époque, le trait d'union n'étant pas incompatible avec la césure traditionnelle de l'alexandrin puisqu'il respecte d'une certaine façon la contrainte morphologique en séparant précisément les mots composants d'un mot ou d'une expression composée dans les mêmes conditions microprosodiques[31].

---

29 *Survivants*, dans *Idylles et chansons*, p. 154.
30 *Cf.* p. 367.
31 Voir *supra*, p. 208-210 et 229-230.

UN PRÉCURSEUR DU SECOND VERLAINE

Nous avons vu que Corbière, sur divers points, est en avance sur Verlaine. Dans l'article qu'il consacre à ce dernier en 1884 dans *La Revue indépendante*, Louis Desprez relève à propos de *Sagesse* (1881) qui témoignait d'un renouvellement profond de son art « une bien plus grande liberté de césure que dans la plupart des poètes parnassiens eux-mêmes ; et, grâce à cette liberté, des effets inattendus[1] ». On peut ici s'interroger sur les particularités que vise plus spécialement le critique, mais ce qui retiendra notre attention est le parallélisme que l'on peut établir dans l'évolution de la technique de l'alexandrin chez Corbière et chez Verlaine à qui Charles Morice et Léo Trézenik firent découvrir durant l'hiver 1882-1883 *Les Amours jaunes* qu'il n'aurait lu qu'en avril 1884[2], ce que nous ferons en tâchant de faire la part de l'influence de Rimbaud sur le second.

La versification de Rimbaud a connu, comme on sait, deux périodes bien distinctes : la première, qui se développe dans les années 1869-1871, présente, selon le témoignage même de Verlaine, « [p]eu de césures libertines ». Dans la seconde, Rimbaud introduit des "vers faux" dans des poèmes par ailleurs isométriques dont la mesure fondamentale repose sur un mètre simple (non césuré) et procède, dans « Qu'est-ce pour nous mon cœur... » et *Mémoire*, selon des modalités différentes, à la déstructuration de l'alexandrin, ce qu'on ne peut ramener à un emploi traditionnel du grand mètre où apparaîtraient ponctuellement des "césures libertines" : la césure du mètre ancien est purement et simplement abandonnée, avec des coupes prosodiques dont le positionnement et la nature (masculine ou féminine, élidée ou enjambante) sont imprévisibles, hormis des retours passagers à l'isométrie classique[3]. En effet, si l'on peut y rencontrer des

---

1   « Verlaine », p. 227.
2   Voir Loubier, « Deux flâneurs », p. 96-98.
3   Sur la versification de Rimbaud, voir Roubaud, *La Vieillesse d'Alexandre*, p. 19-33, et Cornulier, *De la métrique à l'interprétation*. Sur la question particulière du dodécasyllabe des derniers vers, voir aussi Billy, « Innovation et déconstruction », p. 151-181. Le cas de

césures "parnassiennes", on peut tout aussi bien y trouver des infractions qui ne laissent pas même subsister l'explication par la césure pour l'œil, que ce soit en affectant la contrainte prosodique avec des schwas post-toniques en 6ᵉ position, ou même la contrainte morphologique, avec des polysyllabes à cheval sur les hémistiches putatifs, certains avec une post-tonique sur la 7ᵉ position, abolissant dans tous les cas purement et simplement la césure.

À la même époque, Verlaine écrit les poèmes de *Romances sans paroles* : des expériences de Rimbaud, Verlaine retient alors l'emploi de mètres courts associés à ces « espèces de romances » qui l'enchantaient, sans toutefois y introduire de vers faux. Son emploi du décasyllabe commun est encore conventionnel (*Ariettes oubliées*, V) ; s'il emploie l'ennéasyllabe et l'hendécasyllabe, c'est soit avec une césure régulière, coupant ces vers en 4 + 5 (*Chevaux de bois*) ou 5 + 6 (*Ariettes oubliées*, IV), soit sous une forme rythmique particulière qui accentue la 3ᵉ et, souvent, la 6ᵉ position de l'ennéasyllabe (*Ariettes oubliées*, II), conformément à la tradition de ce mètre lyrique[4]. Ce qui frappe donc dans cette réhabilitation de formes anciennes ou du moins étrangères à la poésie savante, c'est la régularité métrique des structures employées. *Sagesse*, dont les poèmes sont pour la plupart écrits durant l'incarcération du poète à Bruxelles de 1873 à 1875, avec des additions écrites jusqu'en 1880, témoigne de nombreuses mutations intimement liées à la rupture d'avec Rimbaud et ses conséquences matérielles, psychologiques et spirituelles. Ce recueil voit tout d'abord augmenter considérablement le nombre d'alexandrins non conformes à la doctrine romantique dans des pièces écrites de septembre 1874 – ou peu avant – à 1879, la plupart avant novembre 1875, soit deux ou trois ans après la parution des *Amours jaunes* : on y trouve en effet 51 vers déviants dont 42 avant cette date parmi lesquels les quinze du recueil qui ne sont pas conformes à la mode parnassienne. Dans *Romances sans paroles*, dont les poèmes ont été écrits avant la fuite en Belgique de mai à avril 1873, recueil certes pauvre en alexandrins (126 vers), seuls deux étaient contraires à la doctrine romantique mais conformes à la mode parnassienne :

Mémoire est particulier, avec des passages où Rimbaud revient à l'alexandrin, soit dans les six premiers vers de l'avant-dernier huitain – bousculés par trois contre-rejets – et les trois derniers vers.

4   *Cf.* p. 383-384. Seuls le v. 3 échappe à ce rythme : « Et dans les lueurs musiciennes ».

L'ombre des arbres dans la rivière embrumée (*Ariettes oubliées*, IX)

Et vous bêlâtes vers votre mère – ô douleur ! – (*Child Wife*)

Plus remarquable encore est la concentration singulière des vers déviants en « un dosage inquiétant de discordances[5] », que l'on peut relever dans divers sonnets de *Sagesse* écrits en prison, les uns datés d'avant le 8 septembre 1874 (II, IV), les autres d'août à octobre 1875 (I, III-IX), soit alors même que le poète se voit rejeté des cercles parnassiens : trois cas dans « Beauté des femmes… » (I, V) et « Sagesse d'un Louis Racine… » (I, IX), et 25 répartis dans neuf des dix sonnets du long poème composite II, IV, dont pas moins de six dans « Et pour récompenser… » (II, IV.VII [c]), concentrés dans les vers 8 à 14, conférant à ce sonnet une allure inhabituelle que les rejets du second quatrain accusaient encore et qui avait de quoi dérouter les lecteurs les plus aguerris aux innovations parnassiennes (nous indiquons en marge les accents dominants sur deux niveaux, niveaux distingués par le parenthésage, les éventuels rejets étant démarqués par un crochet fermant) :

Et pour récompenser ton zèle en ces devoirs	(6e) 8e
Si doux qu'ils sont encor d'ineffables délices,	2e (6e)
Je te ferai goûter sur terre mes prémices,	4e (6e) 8e
La paix du cœur, l'amour d'être pauvre, et mes soirs	4e (6e) 8e
Mystiques, quand l'esprit s'ouvre aux calmes espoirs	2e] 6e (7e)
Et croit boire, suivant ma promesse, au Calice	3e (6e) 9e
Éternel, et qu'au ciel pieux la lune glisse,	3e] (6e) 8e
Et que sonnent les angélus roses et noirs,	3e (8e)
En attendant l'assomption dans ma lumière,	4e 8e
L'éveil sans fin dans ma charité coutumière,	4e (9e)
La musique de mes louanges à jamais,	(3e) 8e
Et l'extase perpétuelle et la science,	(3e) 8e
Et d'être en moi parmi l'aimable irradiance	4e ((6e) 8e)
De tes souffrances, enfin miennes, que j'aimais !	4e 8e

Le lecteur n'est dérouté qu'à partir du second quatrain, avec, pour commencer, un rejet, mais c'est à partir du vers 8 que la césure fait

---

5   Murphy, « Versifications », p. 82.

structurellement défaut, et ceci de façon continue, l'avant-dernier vers excepté[6]. L'allure du poème ne prend toutefois jamais l'apparence erratique de « Qu'est-ce pour nous mon cœur » ou de la plus grande partie de *Mémoire*, car les 4e et 8e positions prennent le relais pour assurer une certaine stabilité rythmique, dix vers présentant au moins un accent secondaire sur la 8e, quatre étant accentués sur les deux. Ce n'est pas que Verlaine n'ait pas déjà tenté ce genre d'expérience : dans *Poëmes saturniens*, le sonnet *À une femme* ne présentait pas moins de cinq cas de césures pour l'œil plus une fois *comme* à l'hémistiche[7]. Mais c'est davantage sur l'aspect qualitatif que Desprez fondait son appréciation, en visant des audaces que n'avaient pas les autres Parnassiens (au contraire de Corbière). Verlaine accepte ainsi aussi bien en 6e qu'en 7e position des syllabes "féminines", avec le schwa final de mots grammaticaux de deux syllabes dans les vers suivants qui, toutefois, sont tous accentués sur les 4e (souvent dominante) et 8e positions[8] :

> Une candeur d'une fraîcheur délicieuse… (*Sagesse*, I, VI, 11)

> Ô, va prier contre l'orage, va prier. (I, VII, 14)

> En louant Dieu, comme Garo, de toutes choses ! (I, IX, 14)

> Dans votre sein, sur votre cœur qui fut le nôtre, (II, IV, VI, 13)

> Brouille l'espoir que votre voix me révéla, (II, IV, VII [d], 13)

Autre forme innovante, inconnue de Corbière[9], Verlaine admet également en 7e position un enclitique : « Bonté, respect ! Car, qu'est-ce qui nous accompagne, » (I, V, 13). Dans ce vers – où l'accent dominant tombe également sur la 4e position –, l'accent d'hémistiche est malgré tout respecté, et l'on remarquera que la locution focalisante qui commence avec lui, *qu'est-ce qui*, se clôt sur la 8e position, avec une accentuation secondaire. Tout laisse supposer que Desprez avait en vue ce genre de cas qui participent de l'abolition de la césure médiane, autant que

---

6   Sur cet effet dû à la multiplication des césures déviantes, effet que peut renforcer l'utilisation d'enjambements et la fragmentation des vers, voir A. Dorchain, *L'Art des vers*, p. 247, à propos d'un passage de *Caprice* de Verlaine.

7   *Cf. Poëmes saturniens*, éd. Murphy, p. 319.

8   C'est également le cas dans cinq des vers de ce genre des *Amours jaunes*, dont l'un est dépourvu d'accent sur la 4e position. Voir *supra*, p. 232-233.

9   Mais équivalente aux vers examinés p. 232.

l'emploi d'un polysyllabe à cheval sur les 6e et 7e positions que l'on peut relever dans neuf vers :

Avec du sang déshonoré d'encre à leurs mains. (I, III, 16)	(4e (8e)) 9^e
Ce n'est pas la méchanceté, c'est la bonté. (I, III, 68)	(3e) 8^e
Puis franchement et simplement viens à ma Table (II, IV, VII [a], 9)	(4e) 8^e
D'oublier ton pauvre amour-propre et ton essence, (II, IV, VII [b], 10)	3e (8e)
Et que sonnent les angélus roses et noirs, (II, IV, VII [c], 8)	3e (8e)
En attendant l'assomption dans ma lumière, (II, IV, VII [c], 9)	4e (8e)
Et l'extase perpétuelle et la science, (II, IV, VII [c], 12)	(3e) 8^e
De tes souffrances, enfin miennes, que j'aimais ! (II, IV, VII [c], 14)	4e 8^e
D'une joie extraordinaire : votre voix (II, IV, VII [d], 2)	(3e) 8^e

Dans cinq de ces vers, l'accentuation de la 8e position est nettement mise en avant, et dans les autres, cette position est également accentuée même lorsque l'accent dominant se trouve ailleurs (sur la 3e ou la 4e), ce qui rejoint la pratique de Corbière à qui l'on doit cette innovation que Verlaine explore à son compte, tandis que Mallarmé, qui est beaucoup plus avare de ce genre de vers, recourt plus volontiers à des structures ternaires épaulées sur les 4e et 8e positions[10]. Dans le premier vers où l'accent principal tombe sur la neuvième, il ne faut pas perdre de vue qu'il y a là une transposition forcée puisque ce qui est déshonoré est *du sang d'encre*, non simplement *du sang* : il ne s'agit pas d'un sang que l'encre déshonorerait. La raison de cette transposition est au demeurant d'ordre structurel, car sans elle, le vers eût été faux tant en ce qui concerne la césure que sa mesure : *Avec du sang d'encre déshonoré à leurs mains.* Gouvard attire l'attention sur le fait que, dans une version manuscrite, Verlaine avait annoté en marge « césure à changer », comme pour *contre | l'orage*, mais tout aussi bien au regard de « N'être pas né dans le grand siècle à son déclin, » (I, IX) où la césure médiane n'est pas véritablement abolie, en déduisant que, dans les trois cas, Verlaine considérait que ces vers étaient césurés à l'hémistiche. L'expression de Verlaine ne nous semble cependant qu'une façon de parler

---

10 Sur les douze vers concernés (voir listes dans Gouvard, *Critique du vers*, p. 217 et 218), seuls deux font exception, dont l'un est accentué en 8e position : « Un selon de chers pressentiments inouï » (*Finale de Hérodiade*) ; « D'une enfance qui s'enfuyait avec de longs [...] » (*Le Faune*, fragment). Dans le premier, le poète a peut-être voulu mettre en relief la syllabe initiale de *pressentiments* parce qu'elle est le support potentiel d'un accent d'insistance. L'anomalie de ce vers fait d'une certaine façon écho à la diérèse fautive dans *espalier* au vers précédent (*Œuvres complètes*, éd. Marchal, p. 151).

pour signaler *la défectuosité* de la césure attendue, telle que la « forte licence »
que Rimbaud signalait à Izambard à propos de la tigresse *épouvantable*,
témoignant du fait que « le poète a parfaitement conscience de ses audaces
et hésite, aux alentours de 1880, à innover[11] », audaces où la césure médiane
brillait par son insuffisance ou son absence.

C'est donc précisément à l'époque où il s'est détaché du Parnasse[12],
et plus précisément de septembre 1874 à novembre 1875, date après
laquelle les poèmes de *Sagesse* ne présentent plus d'alexandrins déviants
qu'avec des césures pour l'œil, que Verlaine témoigne de ce goût immodéré pour l'abolition de la césure médiane, longtemps après son essai
des *Fêtes galantes* et deux ans après son pastiche de Banville, *La Princesse
Bérénice* (« Et dans la plainte langoureuse des fontaines, »)[13], dans diverses
pièces dont la plupart ne paraîtront en recueil que dans les années 1880,
la plupart dans *Sagesse* et *Jadis et Naguère*, deux plus tard encore dans
Invectives, quelques-unes restant inédites à la mort du poète. L'examen
de l'articulation médiane des 43 vers post-parnassiens qu'on y rencontre
est éloquente :

	Dorchain B CM⁻ (CA⁰)	Dorchain C CM⁻ (CA⁺ ᵒᵘ ⁰) 7ᵉ post-tonique	Dorchain D CA⁻ (CM⁺) 6ᵉ post-tonique
1881, *Sagesse*	du sang désho|noré d'encre[14], la méchan|ceté*, sim|plement, ton pauvre a|mour-propre*, extraor|dinaire*, les an|gélus*, l'assom|ption, perpé|tuelle*, en|fin miennes	qu'est-|ce qui, sur vo|tre cœur, vo|tre voix	d'une | fraîcheur, contre | l'orage, comme | Garo

---

11   Dans « De la sémantique », p. 129-130. Gouvard évoque également des corrections apportées
      à d'autres alexandrins du recueil, éliminant les déviations *méchan\|ceté*, *comme | Garo*.
12   *Cf.* Murphy, éd. *Poèmes saturniens*, chap. « Verlaine parnassien : définitions, filiations,
      nuances », p. 203-256.
13   Ce n'est sans doute pas un hasard si ce vers rappelle celui de *La Reine Omphale*, ce poème
      étant repris dans *Les Exilés* où se trouve recueilli le cycle de sonnets des *Princesses*, dont
      l'un intitulé *Omphale*.
14   Pour ce vers, où l'accent dominant tombe sur la 9ᵉ position, voir *supra*, p. 391.

1884, *Jadis et Naguère* Pièces de 1871-1874[15]	des li|bertins*, lan|goureuse, dévir|giné, languis|samment*, dans les Assomp|tions*, d'éton|namment*, par ex|cellence, vous ne sa|vez pas*, en ren|fonçant	d'u|ne Vierge, cet|te fille, u|ne forme, consis|te-t-il, d'au|tre vie, excla|me-t-elle	Elle | ne put
1896, *Invectives* Pièces de 1874[16]	anté|rieurs*, épou|vantable		
Poèmes posthumes contemporains de *Sagesse*[17]	l'emmer|dement*, En gé|néral, la sous-ven|trière*, à l'é|tranger, vo|yagé(*), les a|vant-goûts(*), pas sé|rillieux(*), Jusqu'à nou|vel ord'*		
Variantes abandonnées[18]	pour com|patir		votre | berger

* signale l'absence d'accent syntagmatique en 4ᵉ position ; (*) même chose, mais avec un mot de catégorie grise néanmoins accentuable.

TABL. 12 – L'abolition de la césure médiane dans les vers écrits en prison.

Comme pour les cas semblables étudiés au chapitre « L'abolition de la césure médiane chez les Parnassiens », pas un seul de ces vers ne déroge à l'accentuation de la 8ᵉ position, avec souvent une fin de syntagme, ce qui n'a pas empêché des critiques tels que Verluyten de prétendre que la césure médiane serait maintenue là où l'hémistiche est enjambé par un polysyllabe accentué sur la 8ᵉ position[19], ou Gouvard

---

15 Pièces concernées : *Luxures* (1873), *La Princesse Bérénice* (1871), *Le Poète et la Muse* (1874), *La Grâce* (1873), *L'Impénitence finale* (1873) et *Amoureuse du Diable* (1874).
16 Pièces concernées : *Opportunistes* (1874), *Souvenirs de prison* (*Mars 1874*).
17 Pièces concernées : « Ah merde alors… », « La sale bête !… », « N. de D. !… » et *Ultissima verba*.
18 Pièces concernées : I, V et III, XII. *Cf.* Gouvard, « De la sémantique », p. 132 et 134.
19 Dans « L'analyse de l'alexandrin », p. 59 et 64-66, Verluyten considère que la césure médiane n'a pas disparu parce que ce qu'il appelle la « contrainte sur la DE [*discordance d'étiquetage*] de proéminence » s'y trouverait respectée, au motif (infondé) que la versification française intégrerait les contre-accents (accentuation secondaire de l'antépénultième) dans l'actualisation du mètre.

de ne pas voir simplement dans maints d'entre eux la « scansion de substitution 8-4, voire 4-4-4 » qu'il attribue aux autres, du fait que les vers ainsi écartés ne « répondraient » pas « à une métrique de substitution standard » en raison de l'absence de « 4-8 » (mais n'est-ce pas le cas également de tous les vers M6 jusqu'au milieu des années 1880, comme de la plupart au-delà ?). Le critique met en effet à part les vers où l'hémistiche coïnciderait (selon des analyses tout-à-fait contestables[20]) avec une frontière de morphèmes, dans lesquels il voit « des vers "ambivalents", c'est-à-dire qui admettent à la fois une mesure (4-4)-4 et une mesure 6-6 », voire même des vers « qui ne sont pas des 8-4 mais des 6-6 "modernes" ou "post-classiques", tout comme les CP6 6-6 composés par toute une génération de poètes[21] », laissant sans réponse les questions que le lecteur ne peut s'empêcher de se poser : mais que signifie précisément « mesure » ? que sont ces mesures au regard de la structure *proprement métrique* de ces vers, de la réalité de leur diction, de leur lecture ou même de leur composition ? Cette recherche obstinée de l'hémistiche là même où il a disparu n'a d'égal que l'obstination du métricométricien à l'ignorer dans les cas de césures pour l'œil, où sa présence est pourtant délibérément et ostensiblement maintenue par les poètes.

La liberté de l'accentuation de la 4ᵉ position – qui concerne six à sept vers sur dix (17 à 20[22]) – ne saurait en rien répondre à une quelconque contrainte métrique : la division du premier membre par un accent médian est certes supérieure à ce que l'on observe généralement dans l'octosyllabe mais elle n'est pas pour autant exigée (7/10). Ainsi,

---

20   Ses découpages *ad hoc* mettent en effet clairement en évidence le caractère artificiel de son interprétation, allant à l'encontre et des contraintes articulatoires et des structures lexicologiques et dérivationnelles. C'est ainsi qu'il met sur le même plan les séquences morphémiques (rebaptisées « suffixes ») en *-ement, -émeent, -amment* et *-emment* des adverbes déadjectivaux, avec des formes dont la « frontière "base + suffixe" » coïnciderait avec ce qu'il identifie comme la frontière médiane (symbolisée par un trait d'union), telles que *languis-sament, indiffér-emment, cordial-ement* ou *aggrav-ément*, ce qui est doublement faux : la seconde se situe entre *indiffé-* et *-remment, cordia-* et *-lement, aggravé-* et *-ment*; la frontière morphémique commune, entre *indifférem-, cordiale-, aggravé-* et *-ment*. La note 25 de « Frontières de mot », p. 58, établit clairement le caractère arbitraire de ces découpages aberrants : « Distinguer les adverbes formés sur les adjectifs féminins [...], en -ent ou ant [...] ou des participes passés adjectivés [...] n'a aucun intérêt puisque c'est la frontière base/morphème qui nous intéresse ».
21   *Critique du vers*, p. 229-230, à propos de vers étiquetés « Morph6 ».
22   Selon que l'on inclut ou non les vers notés « (*) ».

comme chez Corbière[23], et sous réserve d'une étude systématique, si la proportion, chez Verlaine, est généralement inférieure à 4/10, elle peut être nettement supérieure comme on peut le vérifier en examinant telle ou telle pièce de *Poëmes saturniens* : dans *Grotesques*, ce sont 14 vers sur 40 (3,5/10) qui présentent un accent sur la 4ᵉ position ; dans *Femme et Chatte*, 5 sur 14 (3,6) ; dans *Les Renards*, 15 sur 40 (3,8), dans *Vœu final*, 8 sur 20 (4) ; mais dans *Malines*, ce sont 11 vers sur 20 (5,5) ; dans « Les chères mains qui furent miennes », 12 sur 20 (6). Le score élevé que l'on observe dans les vers post-parnassiens reflète l'attrait général de Verlaine pour les rythmes ternaires équipartis : lorsqu'il adopte les césures pour l'œil, des *Poëmes saturniens* à *La Bonne Chanson*, c'est justement sept fois sur dix dans le cadre de telles structures[24]. Dans ces effacements de la césure médiane, Verlaine s'en prenait au principal « poncif de coupe » du romantisme, mais, dans *Sagesse*, la proportion n'est plus que de trois à quatre vers sur dix (3,4), ce dont on peut conclure que, dans ce nouveau recueil, Verlaine se sent plus libre d'explorer une diversité de rythmes avec la césure pour l'œil, mais pas lorsqu'il se met à explorer les formes dans lesquelles la césure médiane est occultée (6 à 7/10), contrairement à Corbière (4,4).

On se trouve ainsi face à une nouvelle structuration métrique de l'alexandrin, articulée sur la 8ᵉ position, avec une césure flottante susceptible de tomber entre les 8ᵉ/9ᵉ (masculine ou élidée) ou les 9ᵉ/10ᵉ (féminine non élidée) positions, et c'est bien Corbière qui a ici la priorité sur ses confrères qui n'en avaient jusque là usé que par inadvertance ou à titre d'exception, avant que Verlaine ne l'adopte de septembre 1874 à novembre 1875. Comme on ne peut cependant douter que ces poètes n'ont pas songé un seul instant à écrire autre chose que des alexandrins (contrairement à un Châtillon qui changeait délibérément la structure du vers dans *Confidence*), force est de constater qu'il y a là bel et bien un *déplacement de la césure* métrique. Ce déplacement est en effet ici systématiquement cadré par l'exercice d'une contrainte subie et consentie, ce qui lui confère une signification métrique avec une modification structurelle du vers, ce qui cessera d'être le cas chez Laforgue où la libération des contraintes césurales de la tradition donnera lieu à toutes les formes

---

23 Voir *supra*, p. 384.
24 *Cf. supra* Tabl. 2, p. 266.

possibles. Ainsi, dans les 721 alexandrins de *Complaintes* – dont 10 % présentent une césure pour l'œil –, près de 18 % violent l'une ou l'autre des contraintes césurales de l'hémistiche. Des 127 vers concernés, seuls 40 présentent une tonique en 8ᵉ position, qu'elle soit dominante ou de second rang : ce sont donc deux vers sur trois qui échappent au cadre illustré par Corbière et Verlaine, avec toutes les formes rythmiques possibles, accents et coupes étant distribués librement[25]. On ne peut par conséquent invoquer dans les *Complaintes* un changement de structure, mais un abandon épisodique des contraintes césurales.

Si l'on se tourne à présent vers les poètes romantiques qui ont écrit avant l'avènement du Parnasse, on peut relever chez Hugo un cas très particulier d'aposiopèse dans *Esca* (I, II), pièce qui certes ne paraîtra que beaucoup plus tard, où l'on ne peut assurer que l'interruption n'est pas du seul fait de l'allocutaire plutôt que le comblement d'une hésitation de l'énonciateur, cas qui, pour s'inscrire dans le cadre du ternaire romantique équiparti, n'entre pas moins dans celui que nous avons défini[26] :

GALLUS
Va, je suis impénétrable.

Inaccessible, inex…

GUNICH
Pugnable.

Souriant et saluant.
Et vulnérable.

Mais si l'on remonte aux débuts du romantisme, on a la surprise de découvrir chez un Pétrus Borel deux vers aberrants qui échappent aussi bien à l'ancien canon métrique qu'au nouveau, alors inconnu, vers que l'on peut qualifier d'antimétriques, dans lesquels les signaux prosodiques attendus à l'hémistiche semblent se dérober en se déportant d'une syllabe vers l'avant (le second est fragmenté en quatre membres par les répliques)[27] :

---

25   Cette liberté n'est pas l'expression d'une distribution aléatoire : le poète peut avoir des préférences. On peut ainsi noter que, dans une quarantaine de ces vers, l'accent dominant est en 4ᵉ, dans une quarantaine d'autres, en 7ᵉ.

26   *Les Quatre Vents de l'Esprit*, dans *Œuvres complètes*, *Poésie*, XV, p. 300.

27   À noter que le second comporte un accent majeur en 8ᵉ position (correspondant à un mot-phrase) contrairement au premier.

Adrien, que je redise encore à toi-même, (*Rhapsodies*, p. 77)

> ORLANDO
>
> Fervente
>
> La prière ! on prononçait...
>
> AGARITE
>
> Quoi ?
>
> ORLANDO
>
> Mon nom !
>
> AGARITE, *d'un air mignard.*
>
> Jaloux,
>
> Je vous nommais à Dieu, car je priais pour vous. (*Id.*, p. 80)

Il est possible que la transcription fautive de quelque manuscrit soit en cause dans le premier cas, où le déplacement de l'apostrophe suffirait à rétablir la césure (« Que je redise encore, Adrien, à toi-même, »)[28], mais force est de ne voir aucune cause raisonnable à l'irrégularité du second. Mais revenons à *Sagesse* : si un nouveau modèle métrique articulé sur la 8ᵉ position se substitue occasionnellement à l'alexandrin symétrique dans lequel l'hémistiche définit les domaines sur lesquels s'exercent les contraintes traditionnelles de la versification française, on peut se demander dans quelle mesure ce qui a l'apparence d'une césure pour l'œil ne s'inscrit pas en réalité dans le cadre de ce mètre alternatif à césure flottante ‹8-4› plutôt que dans le traditionnel ‹6-6› : on devrait en effet s'attendre à ce que, dans ce recueil, les vers déviants dotés d'un proclitique ou d'une préposition monosyllabique à l'hémistiche présentent plus souvent un accent en 8ᵉ position que dans les recueils précédents. Voici, recueil par recueil, les données favorables à un possible rattachement au mètre ‹8-4› et celles qui le sont moins (x>8 : l'accent dominant n'est pas celui de 8ᵉ position[29]) ou pas du tout (non 8 : pas d'accent en 8ᵉ position) :

---

28 Nous avons pu ainsi signaler, p. 147, un cas d'hypométrie visiblement dû à une mauvaise transcription.

29 x = 4, 5 ou 7.

	4=4 et 8>4	8 et non 4	x>8	non 8	Total
Poëmes sat.	9	2	12	5	28
Les Amies	-	-	1	1	2
Fêtes galantes	3	1	1	1	6
La Bonne Chans.	3	1	4	-	8
Sagesse	6	9	7	13	35

TABL. 13 – Accentuation de la 8ᵉ position des vers présentant un proclitique ou une préposition monosyllabique dans les recueils de Verlaine, jusqu'à *Sagesse* inclus.

Les proportions ne sont significatives que pour la trentaine de vers de *Poëmes saturniens* et de *Sagesse* qui présentent des effectifs suffisants, avec dans les deux cas quatre vers sur dix favorables à un tel rattachement[30]. Les données ne semblent donc pas nettement favorables à l'hypothèse d'une réelle incidence. On peut même constater que la proportion de vers déviants défavorables à ce rattachement (non 8) passe du simple au double de *Poëmes saturniens* (1,8/10) à *Sagesse* (3,7). Toutefois, dans les seules pièces de *Sagesse* contenant des vers dans lesquels la césure médiane est occultée (Pièces CMO)[31], les résultats sont nettement significatifs. Les 35 vers du recueil présentant un monosyllabe atone en 6ᵉ position y sont en effet ainsi répartis :

	4=4 et 8>4	8 et non 4	x>8	non 8	Total
Pièces CMO	4	6	1	3	14 (sur 194)
Autres pièces	2	3	6	10	21 (sur 360)

TABL. 14 – Même chose dans les pièces CMO.

La proportion des vers favorables à l'hypothèse d'une incidence du mètre alternatif augmente en effet considérablement, avec dix des quatorze vers concernés (7,1/10), contre cinq sur vingt-et-un (2,4/10) dans les autres pièces. Naturellement, il est impossible de savoir pour tel ou tel des dix vers concernés si c'est bien le mètre ‹8-4› qui l'a emporté

30 3,9/10 dans le premier, 4,3 dans le second.
31 Soit les pièces I, III ; I, V-VII ; I, IX ; II, IV.VI-IX.

plutôt que le ‹6-6›[32] : dans un tel contexte, ces structures sont au cas par cas irrémédiablement ambiguës et leur interprétation indécidable. De la même façon, la même question se pose pour les césures médianes (putatives) sur traits d'union (CA⁺, CM⁰), et il n'est ainsi *peut-être* pas fortuit que le seul cas concerné ici présente un accent en 8ᵉ position, dans une pièce qui, pour ne pas contenir de vers dépourvus de césure médiane, n'en est pas moins de la même époque que les pièces CMO : « Car étant ton Dieu tout-puissant, je peux vouloir, » (II, IV.III).

Le même raisonnement pourrait bien évidemment être tenu pour les vers de ce genre dans *Les Amours jaunes*, mais leur étude montre qu'il n'en est rien : près de la moitié seulement des vers présentant un proclitique ou une préposition monosyllabique en 6ᵉ position (10/22) dans les sept pièces CMO du recueil[33] *pourraient* avoir été conformés par le mètre alternatif ‹8-4›. Cette absence d'incidence doit être mise en relation avec la dispersion des vers dépourvus de césure médiane dans les pièces CMO considérées, soit un vers sur cent contre sept sur cent pour Verlaine[34]. Pour être plus précis, en poussant plus loin l'analyse des pièces CMO de *Sagesse*, on s'aperçoit que l'on a en fait affaire à deux ensembles bien distincts : « Qu'en dis-tu, voyageur… » (I, III) est une longue pièce constituée de 68 alexandrins, regroupés en quatrains, parmi lesquels les deux vers ignorant la césure médiane tendent à se perdre[35], avec un unique cas de monosyllabe atone à l'hémistiche, dont la 8ᵉ position est accentuée (« Si le même dans cette extrême décadence ! »)[36]. Les pièces restantes sont par contre toutes des sonnets, formes relativement brèves et fortement structurées dans lesquelles l'effet de toute anomalie se trouve amplifié : dans celles-ci, c'est au moins un vers sur dix (1,4) qui connaît l'abolition de la césure médiane et sept à huit sur dix des vers présentant un monosyllabe atone à l'hémistiche (dix sur treize) sont accentués en 8ᵉ position. C'est cette différence de proportion dans la

---

32 Si tel était le cas, l'on ne pourrait parler de « césure [*sous-entendu* médiane] pour l'œil ».

33 Soit *Le Poète contumace*, *Litanie du sommeil*, *Le Fils de Lamartine*, *Hidalgo*, *Le Bossu Bitor* (3 cas), *Le Novice en partance* (2 cas) et *La Goutte*.

34 Respectivement, dix vers sur un total cumulé de 740 alexandrins, et quatorze sur 194.

35 Même si le second (« Ce n'est pas la méchanceté, c'est la bonté. ») est stylistiquement valorisé par sa position terminale qui lui permet de conclure le poème. Il convient de noter que le premier (v. 16) sert quant à lui à conclure un autre quatrain (le quatrième).

36 Il s'agit du v. 37. À noter que le v. 23 présente également une césure pour l'œil : « Qui les a bus ? Et quelle âme qui les recense », sans accent sur la 8ᵉ.

répartition des formes nouvelles au milieu des anciennes qui permet de comprendre comment les contraintes du mètre alternatif peuvent être renforcées au détriment des contraintes traditionnelles chez Verlaine, alors qu'elles tendent à se diluer chez Corbière.

Avant *Sagesse*, seul Corbière présente un nombre important de vers dépourvus de césure médiane, relevant de l'une ou l'autre des trois classes de violations que nous avons identifiées. Le rapprochement avec Verlaine est d'autant plus frappant si l'on fait état du fait que, parmi les sept poèmes de *Sagesse* écrits *après 1875* contenant des alexandrins (150), aucun ne contient de tels vers, alors que l'on peut y relever huit cas de césures pour l'œil[37], soit dans la même proportion que dans les poèmes antérieurs (5,3 %), comme si le poète s'était alors désintéressé de ces nouvelles formes après en avoir fait l'expérimentation[38]. On pourrait dès lors se demander si Verlaine ne venait pas par quelque biais de découvrir l'œuvre de Corbière, au moins tels de ses poèmes présentant ce genre d'abolition de la césure médiane. Iris Gérault date de 1878 les premières références d'écrivains à l'œuvre de Corbière, avec une lettre d'Huysmans du 10 avril à Théodore Hannon, à propos de certains de ses vers auxquels il trouve des accents corbiériens[39]. Mais Yann Mortelette cite un témoignage plus ancien de Frédéric Plessis selon lequel Heredia, lors d'un séjour à Douarnenez durant l'été 1873 avec Mallarmé, lui présentait Corbière comme « un poète qui fait des vers bizarres mais non sans talent[40] ». Le séjour de Verlaine en prison ne lui interdisait pas visites et correspondance, mais on ne trouve nulle trace de référence à l'œuvre de Corbière avant le projet des *Poètes maudits*, et plus précisément avant la seconde semaine d'avril 1884 où il fait part de la réception des *Amours jaunes* à Charles Morice et à Vannier qui le lui avaient fait parvenir[41], ce qui laisse peser de sérieux doutes sur la déclaration liminaire qu'il donne dans l'avertissement de 1884 (non repris en 1888), par laquelle il prétend confusément que son portrait de Corbière « remonte à 1875, année même de la publication des *Amours*

---

37   Dans I, xv, II, iii, III, xvi et xx de la première édition.
38   Cet intérêt pour ce genre de formes ne reviendra vraiment qu'à partir du milieu des années 1880, mais toujours de façon exceptionnelle, et c'est en juillet 1885 que paraissent *Les Complaintes* de Laforgue.
39   « Corbière face à la critique », p. 108-109.
40   « Corbière, Hugo », p. 74-75.
41   *Correspondance générale*, I, p. 855 et 856.

jaunes, et de sa mort[42] », ce qui nous situe de toute façon après ses essais des années 1871-1874. Tout tend donc à indiquer que l'évolution métrique de ces années traduit simplement le développement spontané d'un penchant naturel de Verlaine dont les prémisses se manifestent dès l'essai de *Fêtes galantes*[43].

---

42 La date indiquée, bien qu'exacte en ce qui concerne la mort du poète, résulte sans doute d'une erreur de lecture du prote puisque, p. 10, Verlaine donne la date correcte de l'édition.

43 Nous avons en effet émis des réserves (p. 370) quant aux vers issus de sa collaboration avec Coppée.

CONCLUSION

La versification des *Amours jaunes* s'inscrit ainsi clairement dans son époque. S'il continue les formes romantiques, Corbière ouvre la porte aux procédés que, depuis une dizaine d'années, des poètes parnassiens de premier rang, qui les empruntaient à Baudelaire, avaient mis à la mode, à commencer par Leconte de Lisle, suivi de Banville, puis de Coppée et Verlaine dont les recueils imprimés en 1866 marquent une étape décisive dans l'histoire de la césure pour l'œil dont le succès trouve cinq ans plus tard un témoignage collectif avec le second recueil du *Parnasse contemporain*. Si sa connaissance des *Fleurs du Mal*, vraisemblablement dans sa troisième édition, ne fait aucun doute, on a pu s'interroger sur les lectures parnassiennes de Corbière, des deux premiers recueils du *Parnasse contemporain* à *Gilles et Pasquins* de Glatigny, recueil dont une étude métrique circonstanciée met en évidence les affinités avec la versification corbiérienne. L'adoption de rythmes syncopés ascendants, sans accentuation possible de la sixième position, d'abord expérimentés en 1867 dans *Petite pouësie sur Rosalba*, semble s'inspirer des pratiques d'un Banville dans la récente édition des *Exilés* dont il semble en outre parodier le style.

S'il « joue » bien « de l'éternel crin-crin » comme le lui reproche Laforgue, Corbière en use avec une liberté nouvelle qui ne se limite pas à celle des Parnassiens. Toutefois, jamais Corbière n'en vient à s'affranchir du besoin de la césure : les rares fois où il l'abolit à l'hémistiche, c'est toujours en s'appuyant sur l'accentuation de la 8e position, témoignant par là d'une évolution métrique dans l'histoire du grand vers avec l'émergence d'une contrainte nouvelle prenant occasionnellement le pas sur les contraintes classiques, un nouveau mètre ‹8-4› prenant ainsi le relais structurel du ‹6-6› défaillant de la tradition. Sur ce point particulier, en préfigurant les mutations structurales dont témoigneront plus éloquemment les poèmes de *Sagesse* écrits en 1874 et 1875, la versification des *Amours jaunes* se situe à l'avant-garde de l'évolution métrique de l'alexandrin avant que les développements symbolistes de Laforgue, Verhaeren et René Ghil ne rebattent les cartes[1].

---

1   Nous mettons naturellement de côté les derniers poèmes en alexandrins de Rimbaud qui ne paraîtront pas avant 1886 (« Qu'est-ce pour nous, mon cœur... », dans *La Vogue*).

SIXIÈME PARTIE

LE SONNET DANS *LES AMOURS JAUNES*

Quatorze vers, grand Dieu ! le moyen
de les faire !
Régnier DESMARAIS, d'après Lope
DE VEGA[1].

Le mélange d'insoumission et de convention qui est consubstantiel
à l'activité versificatoire de Corbière se retrouve dans sa pratique des
formes fixes auxquelles il accorde une importance significative : *Paris*
est en effet une suite homogène de huit sonnets dont l'unité thématique est soulignée par l'emploi commun de l'octosyllabe, suite qui
constitue le cœur de la première section, centrée sur la montée du poète
à Paris, précédée de *Ça ?*, pièce introductive où le poète s'interroge
sur la nature de son recueil, et *Épitaphe* qui lui fait pendant par son
caractère conclusif, où Corbière s'attache à dresser son portrait tout en
donnant un prolongement au dernier sonnet au cinquième vers duquel
il fait écho : « Fais de toi ton œuvre posthume ». Nous avons vu, dans
l'introduction, comment la dernière section, *RONDELS POUR APRÈS*,
faisait pendant à la première, avec un sonnet, donné en préambule
(*Sonnet posthume*) qui entre en résonance tant avec le dernier sonnet de
Paris qu'avec *Épitaphe*. Un parallélisme plus étroit s'établit entre *Paris*
et *RONDELS POUR APRÈS* qui ont la particularité de se présenter
comme des poèmes composites et homogènes, dans les deux cas à "forme
fixe", l'un une suite de huit sonnets, l'autre une suite de cinq rondels,
dont la cohésion interne est chaque fois soulignée par l'unité métrique
et thématique de l'une et l'autre série, parcourue de multiples échos
internes[2]. D'autres pièces témoignent de l'importance du genre pour le
poète au travers d'approximations de la forme fixe[3], approximations que

---

1   *Les Cariatides*, IX, I.
2   Le seul autre poème partitionné est *Grand opéra*, divisé en trois « actes ».
3   Voir en particulier Lescane, « Comment peut-on », p. 119-120, à propos des v. 54-81 de
     Litanie du sommeil (à noter que le dernier sizain n'est pas exactement monorime, se divisant
     en deux tercets, le premier en |is^{ɔs}|, le second en |is^{ɔ}|, dont l'autonomie est soulignée par

l'on peut du reste retrouver pour le rondel, malgré son emploi beaucoup plus limité, dans les vingt-trois octosyllabes sur deux rimes de *À la mémoire de Zulma* dont les quintils et quatrains[4] présentent des reprises informelles, ou dans les deux dernières strophes sur deux rimes (un sizain et un quatrain) du *Naufrageur* avec les reprises de *saltin, morgate* et *frégate*, et leurs retours d'expressions à la rime évoquant des refrains informels. On ne trouve par contre pas dans la dernière section cette attitude provocatrice que Corbière affectionne dans *Paris*, à la tonalité amère et sarcastique. Les libertés qu'il prend avec le sonnet s'appuient autant sur l'autorité de Baudelaire que sur ses habitudes personnelles en matière de versification, avec en particulier diverses infractions à la règle de l'alternance des genres de rimes.

---

diverses particularités syntaxiques, rhétoriques et typographiques); 121-122, à propos de *La Pipe au poète*. Mortelette, « Le prédécadentisme », p. 149-150, à propos de *La Pipe au Poète, A la douce amie, Paria* et du début du *Bossu Bitor*, exemple moins convaincant puisque le supposé sizain initial est une suite de rimes plates. Voir aussi nos remarques à propos de *Vénerie*, p. 431. Nous nous bornerons ici aux sonnets *proprio sensu*.

4   5 + 4 + 5 + 4 (aa*bb*a aa*bb* aa*bbb* aa*bab* aa*bb*).

LE CONTEXTE PARNASSIEN

Quoiqu'il raille la Muse d'Archimède, Corbière n'est pas le moins du monde insensible à la « beauté pythagorique » du sonnet, à sa « forme géométriquement arrêtée[1] ». Sur les 94 poèmes des *Amours jaunes*, on trouve pas moins de 31 sonnets, soit une pièce sur trois[2], et Corbière n'en ajoutera pas moins de trois nouveaux dans les marges de son exemplaire personnel[3]. L'importance du sonnet est telle au XIXᵉ siècle qu'il nous semble essentiel de porter une attention particulière à la manière dont Corbière l'utilise dans le cadre des *Amours jaunes*, moins sur le plan des thèmes et des aspects littéraires qui retiennent habituellement l'attention – au même titre que les autres compositions de Corbière –, que sur le plan formel qui fait très précisément la spécificité du genre[4]. Comme Baudelaire, mais de façon différente, il n'entend pas se soumettre aux conventions du genre tout en respectant le dogme de la division en deux quatrains plus deux tercets, si ce n'est qu'il en inverse l'ordre dans *Le Crapaud*. Par contre, il applique volontiers à la forme sonnet (mais c'est aussi le cas du rondel) des procédés dont on use ordinairement, quand cela arrive, dans des poèmes qui ne relèvent pas des formes fixes, plus rarement dans des formes strophiques : il peut rompre la linéarité du vers en passant à la ligne[5], ou la continuité du quatrain ou du tercet en insérant une ligne de points[6].

---

1   Lettre à Armand Fraisse du 18 février 1860, *Correspondances*, I, p. 676 ; Gautier, préface à la 3ᵉ édition des *Fleurs du Mal*, p. 44.
2   Seul celui de *Grand opéra* ne constitue pas une pièce indépendante ; du moins est-elle isolée pour constituer le « second acte ». Nous comptons les poèmes constitutifs de *Paris* ou de *RONDELS POUR APRÈS* comme des pièces à part entière, indépendamment de leur intégration dans une collection significative.
3   Soit *Paris diurne, Petit coucher* et « Moi ton amour ?... ». Voir la transcription qu'en donne Houzé, « Le dernier Corbière », p. 325-326 et 328-329.
4   Durand, « Avatars de la forme sonnet », p. 268-271, se contente de quelques remarques relatives au sonnet inversé (*Le Crapaud*) et aux deux versions connues d'*'I' Sonnet*. Il ignore de toute évidence, de même que Gleize, au demeurant, le sonnet intégré dans *Grand opéra*.
5   « Tu ris. – Bien !... », *Bonne fortune*.
6   *Le Crapaud, Pauvre garçon, Toit*, IIᵉ acte de *Grand opéra*.

J.-M. Gleize affirmait que le sonnet représente pour Corbière « la forme achevée de la poésie ». On peut supposer que, sur ce point, le critique avait en vue *'l' Sonnet* qui présente cette forme poétique comme une structure obéissant à des lois rigoureuses. L'importance du sonnet pour Corbière ne saurait de toute façon faire de doute, avec un position-nement souvent valorisant : outre le cas particulier de *Paris*, quatre des sept sections commencent par un ou deux sonnets. La deuxième section *Amours jaunes*, qui en contient onze, commence par deux sonnets appa-riés (*À l'Éternel Madame* et *Féminin singulier*) ; la troisième, *SÉRÉNADE DES SÉRÉNADES*, qui en contient six, commence par *Sonnet de nuit* ; la cinquième, *ARMOR*, par un sonnet également, le seul de la section (*Paysage mauvais*) ; la septième et dernière enfin, qui regroupe les rondels, par *Sonnet posthume. RACCROCS* en compte trois, *GENS DE MER* un seul. Selon Gleize[7] :

> [...] l'intervention sur le sonnet se caractérise par une certaine ambivalence : d'une part le sonnet, en tant qu'il représente pour Corbière la forme achevée de la poésie, la « perfection » formelle, la mécanique poétique fonctionnant à son meilleur régime, est l'objet de la critique. De cette perception fixée et fixiste, le sonnet parnassien est, bien entendu, le meilleur exemple, et c'est lui qui est directement attaqué par Corbière, à la fois comme forme dominante de la poésie « objective » (réduisant la poésie à l'objet, à l'objet d'« art »), et comme forme de la poésie dominante, académique, « française ». Ce sonnet, Corbière va donc le triturer, en faisant de la forme « fixe » une forme plurielle, malléable, en préférant le vers court (pour libérer le sonnet de l'alexandrin), en faisant jouer les structures internes, la syntaxe contre la grille taxique, en le coupant, l'inversant, etc.

C'est ainsi que le critique développe une thèse singulière, voyant dans le recueil de Corbière « [u]ne traversée opérative de la poésie française, de Ronsard, comme le titre semble l'indiquer, au Parnasse ("O Muse d'Archimède !") ». Mais que savait Corbière du mouvement parnassien dont on connaît bien l'hétérogénéité[8], et surtout du sonnet parnassien qui reflétait cette hétérogénéité, et qu'en pensait-il exactement ? Que fait-on des références omniprésentes aux poètes romantiques dans son œuvre, qui témoignent d'une préoccupation obsessionnelle semblant ne faire aucune place au mouvement parnassien ni à ses représentants si ce

---

7   *Poésie et figuration*, p. 104-115, citation p. 107.
8   Voir en particulier Murphy, « Versifications », p. 67-69.

n'est à Baudelaire qui ne s'y est retrouvé rattaché que sur l'insistance de Mendès qui réunira notamment *Les Nouvelles Fleurs du Mal* dans le second recueil du *Parnasse contemporain*[9], et dont les nombreux sonnets libertins révoltaient Gautier et suscitaient l'incompréhension de Banville[10] ? Rendant compte dans la *Revue des Deux Mondes* de l'état de la poésie contemporaine en 1866, Constant Martha pouvait certes s'interroger sur « la manie des sonnets » qui serait devenue « le genre à la mode » et donnerait à voir « combien nos poètes sont heureux de porter des chaînes inutiles[11] » :

> Mais comment ne sent-on pas que cette musique est de la plus agaçante uniformité ? On veut que nos oreilles et notre esprit entendent toujours des pièces de quatorze vers dont les rimes sont croisées de la même manière, et qui se terminent invariablement (c'est une loi du genre) par un mot qui a la prétention d'être piquant ou sublime. Il faut rire, il faut pleurer en quatorze vers, ni plus ni moins, et au bout de ces quatorze vers on est tenu de s'étonner. Que la pensée soit grande ou petite, elle n'a qu'à s'arranger de cette mesure imposée par Apollon voulant pousser à bout tous les rimeurs françois. Si elle est trop grande, on la fera rentrer en elle-même ; si elle est trop courte, on l'étirera sur ce lit orthopédique.

Jasinski, qui n'oubliait pas les précédents de Baudelaire et de Banville ni les premiers recueils parnassiens des années 1860, a affirmé à propos du même recueil de 1866 que, outre « la recherche de la forme parfaite, du terme exact et de la rime riche [...] ce que le Parnasse apportait [...] de nouveau, c'était l'éclatante réhabilitation du sonnet », insistant sur l'importance que revêtait son caractère collectif[12]. Et le fait est que l'on n'y trouve pas moins de 80 sonnets représentant 40 % des pièces qu'il contient. Mais que représente réellement alors le sonnet chez les principaux maîtres parnassiens avant 1873 ? Pas grand-chose au regard des *Fleurs du Mal* dont une pièce sur deux relève de ce genre (contre une sur trois dans *Les Amours jaunes*) et dont nous savons que Corbière l'avait certainement lu : le genre occupe une place anecdotique

---

9   Voir M.-Ch. Natta, *Baudelaire*, p. 710-711.
10 Voir Billy, *Les Formes poétiques*, p. 264-274. Sur les réticences idéologiques du poète à l'égard du mouvement parnassien, voir John Charpentier, « La réaction parnassienne et le renouveau de la fantaisie » (1925), dans Mortelette (éd.), *Le Parnasse*, p. 349-354.
11 « La Poésie du jour », p. 1027-1028.
12 *Histoire du sonnet*, p. 213.

dans l'œuvre de Leconte de Lisle et nulle chez Coppée ; les poèmes de jeunesse que Banville réunit en 1857 ne contiennent que dix-huit sonnets, et il lui faudra attendre 1874 pour publier une collection conséquente et homogène de 23 sonnets avec *Les Princesses*[13] dont dix, certes, paraissaient dès 1867 dans *Les Exilés* ; la plupart des sonnets de Gautier ont été composés aux grandes heures du romantisme. Les sonnets de Heredia sont diffusés dans des revues ou recueils collectifs en attendant leur parution tardive en recueil (1893), avec des formes plus libres à ses débuts[14] : il en donne cinq plus ou moins réguliers dans le premier recueil du *Parnasse contemporain*[15], aucun dans celui de 1871 dont il clôture la série en un long "poème tragique" (*La Détresse d'Atahuallpa*) par lequel il tourne ostensiblement le dos à la forme fixe, et vingt-cinq en 1876. Les sonnettistes parnassiens les plus en vue sont alors Mendès, avec 21 sonnets dans *Philoméla* en 1863, et surtout Albert Mérat, avec 37 sonnets dans *Les Chimères* en 1866, vingt autres en 1869 dans *L'Idole* et 46 en 1872 dans *Les Souvenirs* qui ne contiennent que des sonnets ; Sully Prudhomme, avec les 61 sonnets des *Épreuves* (1866) ; Armand Silvestre, avec les 40 de *Rimes neuves et vieilles* (1866) – dont les 23 *Sonnets payens* – et les 52 des *Renaissances* (1870), souvent organisés en séries. On ne peut oublier non plus le recueil non signé de 105 sonnets que Mérat et Valade publient en 1863 : *Avril, mai, juin*. Mais Corbière avait-il une connaissance aussi globale et précise, et une vision aussi nette d'un mouvement qui pouvait être abordé sous bien des angles différents compte tenu des différents courants qui le composaient ?

Le Parnasse contemporain de 1866 pouvait certes avoir fourni à Corbière matière à méditer : c'est ainsi – pour s'en tenir aux principales figures du mouvement – que dans sa première livraison, on trouve cinq sonnets d'Heredia, cinq autres de Ménard dans la deuxième et six de Baudelaire dans la cinquième, tandis que la dix-huitième et dernière livraison constituait ce que Mortelette décrit comme un « raccourci du *Parnasse* en dix-sept sonnets » signés d'autant de poètes parmi les plus représentatifs du mouvement si l'on en excepte Antoni Deschamps[16]. Mais a-t-il

---

13   Voir Killick, « Banville et le sonnet », 87-88 et 107.
14   Killick, art. cité, p. 114-115.
15   Voir *infra*.
16   *Histoire du Parnasse*, p. 180.

seulement consulté ce premier recueil boudé par le public[17] alors qu'il ne montera à Paris qu'en 1872 où il pouvait par contre aisément trouver le second ? Si le sonnet occupe une place relativement importante dans les trois recueils du *Parnasse contemporain*, c'est sans doute moins pour l'intérêt particulier que leurs éditeurs auraient porté à la forme fixe que pour de simples raisons d'ordre économique, la brièveté du genre augmentant considérablement les capacités d'accueil de ces anthologies comme elle lui valait une bonne représentation dans la presse, mais il est certain que la collection qui termine le premier recueil, les sept *Sonnets mystiques* de Ménard[18], ceux de Silvestre et les huit de Popelin dans le second recueil contribuent à donner de l'importance à ce genre dont la pratique, particulièrement appréciée dans les salons et les albums, n'en doit pas moins être relativisée. En 1869, les 42 sonnets d'autant de poètes différents de *Sonnets et eaux-fortes* – dont on ne manquera pas de souligner au passage le caractère élitiste qui l'a vraisemblablement tenu éloigné des lectures de Corbière – témoignera éloquemment du statut particulier dont la forme pouvait malgré tout jouir dans la nouvelle école. Comme on le voit, l'évolution de l'école parnassienne ne pouvait que confirmer Martha dans son jugement, lui qui concluait de façon radicale[19] :

> C'était bien la peine de faire une révolution littéraire, de renverser toutes les barrières établies, d'insulter les grands hommes du passé, tout cela pour aboutir à ne refaire que des sonnets,
>
> > Et pour qu'en deux quatrains de mesure pareille
> > La rime avec deux sons frappât huit fois l'oreille,
> > Et qu'ensuite six vers artistement rangés
> > Fussent en deux tercets par le sens partagés.

Soit très précisément ce que Corbière décrit par sa formule « Je pose 4 et 4 *etc.* ». Mais cette convergence ne saurait nous amener à penser que le poète, dont l'intérêt porté au genre ne s'est jamais démenti, ait pu en quelque façon partager les jugements à l'emporte-pièce du

---

17 Sur l'insuccès du recueil, voir notamment les remarques de Valazza, *La Poésie délivrée*, p. 51-52.

18 Il y paraît en outre quatre sonnets de Gabriel Marc dans la 6ᵉ livraison, trois de Louisa Siefert en plus de ceux de Mérat dans la 7ᵉ, trois de Gautier dans la 9ᵉ, ceux de Ménard et de Popelin dans la 11ᵉ.

19 « La Poésie du jour », p. 1028.

critique et qu'il ait pu voir à travers '*I' Sonnet* l'occasion de pourfendre le culte de la forme attribué aux Parnassiens. D'autant qu'on ne saurait oublier que le sonnet n'avait pas attendu la nouvelle école pour se tailler une place de choix. Sainte-Beuve pouvait écrire dans sa chronique du 9 février 1852[20] : « Dans un tableau complet de la poésie en 1852, il y aurait, comme au temps de Guillaume Colletet, un chapitre essentiel à écrire : *Du Sonnet* ». Le genre était en effet si bien ancré dans les usages poétiques que nombre de poètes s'essayaient volontiers à la forme, le plus difficile n'étant jamais que de trouver un sujet, comme s'en amuse Hector Berge en 1863, interpellant ainsi sa muse pour lui demander ce qu'il pourrait bien chanter pour plaire à son lecteur[21]. Le sonnet est en effet alors toujours d'une pratique courante comme en atteste le répertoire dressé par L. de Veyrières pour les années 1801-1869, où, sur la période qui nous intéresse, l'on peut relever des poètes d'importance diverse, d'âge divers, d'où se détachent les noms de Joséphin Soulary, Gustave Le Vavasseur et Louis Veuillot, sans parler de poètes bien oubliés tels que François Fertiault qui se trouve du reste associé au *Parnasse contemporain* de 1866 ou d'autres plus obscurs, d'Edmond Arnould dont les *Sonnets et Poëmes* sont publiés par son fils en 1861 (l'année de sa mort), Louis Goujon et les 250 sonnets de ses *Inspirations de voyage* (1866), ou encore Louis Salles qui publie 118 sonnets dans ses *Amours de Pierre et de Léa* (1870), pour s'en tenir aux productions de quelque importance[22], sans parler des soixante *Sonnets à Ninon* de Winoc Jacquemin (1867). On peut par ailleurs se montrer surpris de ce que, lorsqu'il contribue au second *Parnasse contemporain*, Soulary, selon Gautier « [e]ntre tous ceux qui aujourd'hui *sonnent le sonnet* [...] le plus fin joaillier, le plus habile ciseleur de ce bijou rhythmique[23] », ne donne pas une seule pièce du genre alors que, dans cette vitrine de l'art parnassien, il eût pu si aisément faire montre de son habileté en ce domaine[24]. Au demeurant, *Le Parnassiculet contemporain*, paru en 1867, qui est un bon reflet de la réception du recueil, n'accorde qu'une importance limitée au genre puisqu'il n'en contient jamais que trois

---

20 *Causeries du lundi*, t. V, p. 307.
21 *Les Guirlandes*, p. 147-148.
22 *Monographie du sonnet*, II, p. 107-202.
23 « Rapport », p. 103.
24 Il se rattrapera par contre pour le recueil suivant où il ne donnera que des sonnets (six).

– tous avec des quatrains hétéromorphes[25] – sur les dix pièces qu'il comporte, dont l'un ouvre son anthologie satirique et où *L'Automate* présenté comme un « rondeau estrambote » fait allusion aux sonnets estrambotes de Louis-Xavier de Ricard, parus dans la première série du *Parnasse contemporain*, l'appendice de neuf pièces de la réédition de 1872 n'en ajoutant que deux : cette place est relativement modeste, d'autant plus que le format du pamphlet se prêtait à voir surreprésenté ce petit genre.

Quant à la prétendue régularité parnassienne qui aura certainement échappé à Corbière, on se souviendra que, en 1868, Gautier déplorait que « la jeune école se perm[î]t un grand nombre de sonnets libertins[26] ». Apportons quelques précisions : dans le recueil collectif de 1866, Heredia publie trois sonnets aux quatrains hétéromorphes[27], Valade également[28] ainsi qu'Eugène Lefébure qui les construit en outre sur quatre rimes[29]. Des six de Baudelaire, la moitié n'avait rien de régulier, *Le Rebelle* étant même sur sept rimes, *L'Avertisseur* et *Bien loin d'ici* des sonnets inversés. Dans le recueil de 1871, on trouve des quatrains hétéromorphes chez Louise Colet (deux pièces), Ernest d'Hervilly, Henry Rey et Armand Silvestre (trois pièces[30]). Dans *Les Chimères* (1866), Mérat publie un sonnet cumulant les mêmes "irrégularités" que celui de Lefébure, ainsi qu'un autre sur sept rimes suivies (comme *Sur "Le Tasse en prison"* de Baudelaire), ce qui n'a pas empêché son recueil de recevoir les suffrages des membres de l'Académie française qui, il est vrai, n'ont jamais pris position sur les règles du genre[31]. Le dogme banvillien, qui ne sera quant à lui promulgué qu'en 1872, ne parviendra jamais à s'imposer tout-à-fait aux poètes parnassiens : en 1866, un sur dix suit la forme promue par Banville ; en 1871, deux sur dix ; en 1876, quatre sur dix. Si l'on se reporte aux recueils des principaux poètes concernés, on s'aperçoit que Silvestre est très laxiste dans sa pratique du genre : il construit ainsi volontiers

---

25   Tous ont des quatrains hétéromorphes (a*bb*a a*bab* ou a*bab* b*aa*b).
26   Préface à la 3ᵉ édition des *Fleurs du Mal*, p. 44. Il est vrai qu'il avait en vue le seul Baudelaire.
27   Voir *infra*, p. 434.
28   *Rêve d'été* (a*bab* a*bb*a).
29   *Couchant* (a*bab* c*dd*c eef ggf).
30   *Nouveaux sonnets païens*, I (a*bab* a*bb*a) et IV (a*bab* b*aa*b) et *Souvenir des Girondins* (a*bb*a a*bab*).
31   Dans *Les Chimères*, qui contient 48 sonnets, *Trumeau*, p. 22 : 12 a*bab* c*dd*c efe fgg ; *L'Idole*, p. 31 : 12 a*a*bb c*c*dd eef fgg.

ses quatrains sur des arrangements de rimes différents, quelquefois sur trois ou quatre rimes, réutilise à l'occasion des rimes déjà employées *etc.*

Nous voyons par conséquent mal, dans ces conditions, comment Corbière, lui-même adepte du sonnet et dont tout montre par ailleurs qu'il se désintéresse du mouvement parnassien, pourrait utiliser son modeste sonnet sur le sonnet pour critiquer son formalisme. La connaissance avérée que Corbière avait de *Gilles et Pasquins* de Glatigny[32] nous invite par contre à nous pencher sur ce recueil où l'on trouve neuf sonnets, de formes variées, aussi bien dans les tercets (quatre arrangements différents) que dans les quatrains (même chose, dont un sur quatre rimes disposées librement)[33]. Mais elle nous incite aussi à nous demander s'il n'avait pas lu d'autres recueils de ce poète. C'est ainsi que ses sonnets de *Paris* qui, rappelons-le, n'ont pas été écrits avant son séjour parisien d'avril 1872, ne sont pas sans écho dans le long poème *Les Antres malsains* qui clôt *Les Vignes folles*, dont on citera les trois quatrains suivants[34] :

> Sans craindre que le vent nauséabond altère,
> Muse, avec tes rosiers la neige de tes seins,
> Tu peux, fille robuste à la parole austère,
> Pénétrer avec moi dans les Antres malsains,
>
> Dans les gouffres du rire et des pleurs lamentables,
> Des haillons que le vin a rougis tristement,
> Où, harassé d'ennui, les coudes sur les tables,
> Se vautre le bétail de l'abrutissement. [...]
>
> C'est là que le jeune homme, avide de connaître
> Le plaisir qui l'appelle avec un air moqueur.
> S'en vient assassiner, à tout jamais peut-être !
> L'idéal florissant qu'il porte dans son cœur.

On y retrouve la queue du premier sonnet, avec le planton qui « pousse à la chaîne », l'« incendie éteint », la « pauvre Muse pucelle » – selon l'expression que le poète emprunte à Hégésippe Moreau[35] – qui « [f]it le

---

32 Voir *infra*, p. 477-480, à propos de *RONDELS POUR APRÈS* ; voir aussi *supra*, p. 347-359, à propos du traitement de la césure.

33 Pièces XXII, XXV-XXVII (deux sonnets), XXXV, XXXVIII-XL.

34 *Les Vignes folles*, p. 163-174 ; nous citons les deux premières strophes ainsi que la cinquième.

35 Dans *Les Jeux de l'amour et du hasard* : « Il n'est plus de muse pucelle, / Et les bois du Pinde, malsains, / Mènent tout droit aux Capucins » (*Le Myosotis*, nouv. éd., p. 80). Moreau se souvenait sans doute ici des bouts-rimés de La Motte sur les lois du sonnet : « Le Lecteur

trottoir en *demoiselle*[36] » ; le « paradis [d]es mahomets et des houris, [d]es dieux souteneurs qui se gifflent [*sic*] » du second ; le « Naïf » qui « *voudrait que la rose, / Dondé ! fût encore au rosier !* » du troisième ; l'évocation des orgies dans les quatrième et sixième sonnets ; le reniement de son passé provincial dans le cinquième : soit plus d'éléments objectifs qu'il n'y en a entre *Bonne fortune et fortune* et *À une passante* que l'on a coutume de donner comme son modèle[37] bien que leur lien concret se limitât au personnage de la passante, comme si, depuis *Les Fleurs du Mal*, la passante n'était pas une expérience et un fantasme assez largement partagé, et que son apparition dans un poème ne pouvait se faire sans convoquer *ipso facto* ce précédent, ce qui est sans doute vrai de maint lecteur mais, à notre avis, plus discutable en ce qui concerne l'auteur[38]. Le thème se retrouve du reste dans *Gilles et Pasquins*, traité de façon différente encore, dans le sonnet intitulé *Dans la rue* daté de mars 1869, où l'influence de Baudelaire ne saute pas non plus aux yeux (**XXXIX**) :

> Hé, là-bas ! hé ! la jupe au vent !
> Ohé ! la petite personne,
> Arrêtez-vous. Mon cœur frissonne
> En proie à l'espoir décevant.
>
> Oh ! le beau corsage mouvant !
> Et comme l'amour déraisonne
> Devant ces grands yeux d'amazone
> Plus clairs que nul soleil levant !
>
> Arrêtez-vous donc ! Elle trotte
> Sans répondre, et gardant ses bas
> Immaculés, vierges de crotte.
>
> Je reviens, mes projets à bas,
> Mais content, car c'est gai la rue
> Quand Rose vous est apparue !

---

chaste y veut une Muse pucelle » (sur ce sonnet, voir *infra*, p. 426). André Gill et Louis de Gramont évoqueront plus tard de façon semblable la muse romantique : « O Muse ! vous qu'on dit pucelle, / Depuis Homère aux nobles chants, / Vous avez eu, ma chère belle, / Une rude liste d'amants. » (cité par Valazza, *La Poésie délivrée*, p. 107).

36   Sur la muse vénale de Glatigny, voir Valazza, *La Poésie délivrée*, p. 69-75, et son chapitre « La Muse dépouillée », p. 103-110, qui évoque le traitement du thème, des *Jeunes-France* de Gautier aux Hydropathes.

37   Voir encore dernièrement Mortelette, « Le prédécadentisme », p. 150-151, qui parle d'une « réécriture burlesque ».

38   Nous reviendrons sur cette rencontre textuelle p. 432.

SONNET SUR LE SONNET

Le sonnet a toujours constitué une tentation métapoétique pour les poètes, et l'on peut se demander si dans *Heures*, Corbière, annonçant avoir « compté plus de quatorze heures », ne fait pas précisément allusion à sa forme finie, sur le chemin de « la male heure » qui l'appelle ; de façon semblable, « un glas... deux glas » qui conclut le premier tercet où le poète dit « entend[re] comme un bruit de crécelle » vient ponctuer les rimes couées qu'il affectionne avec le retour de la rime en fin de poème : « Ne compte pas. » Mais c'est dans *'I' Sonnet* que le poète cède pleinement à la tentation. Tout en considérant que « le contact avec le milieu parnassien reste [...] un fait de biographie plutôt que de poétique », à la suite d'une communication alors récente de Y. Mortelette[1], B. Houzé considère que ce poème « conçu à l'époque de l'album, montre une vision caricaturale du Parnasse et correspond bien à l'esthétique "relâchée", en termes prosodiques et métriques, de *ffocsoR* » (l'album Noir), précisant[2] :

> « I Sonnet » renvoie sans doute au Parnasse, mais comme à un repoussoir :
> sa caricature d'une poétique respectant scolairement les formes fixes suggère
> une lecture de seconde main plutôt qu'une attention aux meilleures œuvres
> de ce groupe, et certainement pas une influence de celles-ci sur Corbière. Il
> est également envisageable que Corbière ait visé Heredia en particulier, dont
> il avait pu entendre des conseils de composition poétique.

B. Houzé pense à l'évocation que Louis Tiercelin (poète né à Rennes en 1846) a faite d'une rencontre où Heredia lui apprenait à écrire ses sonnets sur du papier quadrillé pour éviter des reprises trop rapprochées d'un même son, hypothèse qui implique à tout le moins que Tiercelin

---

1   Depuis publiée sous le titre de « Corbière, Hugo ». Comme nous l'avons dit, les contacts qui se seraient noués, pour autant qu'ils soient attestés, sont postérieurs à la parution des *Amours jaunes*.

2   « Corbière lecteur de Verlaine », p. 303-304 (dont n. 14) et 315. On prendra note de ce que, n. 13, il considère que *'I' Sonnet* « ne reprend aucune "manière" critique du Parnassiculet ».

l'aurait rapportée à Tristan avant l'hiver 1869-1870 puisque l'album Noir donne une première version d'*'I' Sonnet*[3], alors que nous ne connaissons rien des rapports que les deux poètes auraient pu entretenir[4]. L'injonction liminaire « *Réglons notre papier et formons bien nos lettres* » pourrait en effet faire allusion au propos d'Heredia, mais on ne saurait négliger le fait que cet exergue, emprunté à l'univers scolaire[5], ajouté lors de la réécriture du poème, est en fait emprunté aux vers 3-4 de la version de l'album Noir qui en était dépourvu :

> Sur du papier réglé, pour conserver la forme
> Je sais ranger les vers et les soldats de plomb.

vers ainsi modifiés dans le recueil :

> Qu'en marquant la césure, un des quatre s'endorme...
> Ça peut dormir debout comme soldats de plomb.

Si nous admettons que Corbière a connu l'anecdote, on comprendrait que cela ait pu l'inciter à mettre l'idée en exergue. Suivant l'opinion de Lindsay et l'exégèse qu'Angelet a donné du troisième poème de *Paris*[6], Mortelette considère que, « Comme ce sonnet fait allusion aux grandes tendances poétiques contemporaines, il y a de fortes chances pour que "Le Parnasse en escalier" vise les Parnassiens[7] », bien que le poète n'y fasse pas particulièrement allusion à ces derniers puisque, comme le critique le rappelle, selon Angelet, les Dégoûteux, les Bedeaux, la Chlorose et l'Incompris du poème feraient respectivement référence aux poètes du spleen, aux poètes lamartiniens, à ceux de la bohème romantique et à Victor Hugo. Quant à l'expression « le Parnasse en escalier » qui viserait les Parnassiens, de même que l'endroit où Corbière nous dit avoir écrit son poème (au Pic de la Maladetta[8]) pourrait être une manière

---

3   Voir le fac-similé du poème, f° 22r°, dans *ffocsoR*, éd. Houzé, transcription p. 27 et n. 1, p. 36. Sur la datation de l'album, voir *ibid.*, p. 8, col. 2.
4   « Corbière lecteur de Verlaine », n. 14. Rien ne vient préciser ce que le poète parnassien avait en vue.
5   Sur cet aspect, voir Cornulier, « Corbière et la poésie comptable », p. 240-250.
6   Angelet, éd. citée, p. 38-39 ; pour Lindsay, voir p. 331.
7   « Corbière, Hugo », p. 77-78.
8   Sur cette mention (« *Pic de la Maladetta. – Août.* »), voir la note de Walzer mentionnée *infra*, p. 422, n. 16, et Cornulier, « Corbière et la poésie comptable », p. 246-247, qui évoque une possible réminiscence de Gautier.

de « se moquer de la fidélité des Parnassiens au Mont Parnasse » selon Lindsay[9], comment ne pas y voir une simple adaptation du *Gradus ad Parnassum* que, dans un sonnet intitulé *Puérilités*, de même intention moqueuse, le Parnassien Ernest d'Hervilly dont nous n'avons pas de raison de penser qu'il se moquât de ses amis évoquera ainsi littéralement[10] :

> O polkas ! – Je devins son esclave ordinaire
> Un soir de « sauterie : » *Amo*, dis-je, *ergo sum !*
> Depuis lors, en l'honneur de cette pensionnaire,
> Tu fus fleuri de vers, *Gradus-ad-Parnassum !*

Rien en effet ne vient objectivement conforter une lecture au second degré contrairement à l'expression « Ceux-là du Mont-*Parnassien* » d'un Auguste Châtillon où le démonstratif et l'emploi de l'italique désignent la cible sans ambiguïté[11]. Nous n'y voyons pour notre part que « ce vieux nom ridicule et qu'entre romantiques nous avons assez sifflé » dont parle Barbey d'Aurevilly en 1866[12], le métaphorique mont d'Apollon que gravit l'apprenti poète en marchant sur les traces des romantiques, au même titre que le Pinde que l'énonciateur d'*'I' Sonnet* entend gravir en suivant le chemin tracé par la ligne du *railway* qui n'est jamais qu'un escalier mécanique, dont Laprade faisait descendre les Muses stipendiées dans sa satire contre « les Muses d'État », en décembre 1861[13] :

> O groupe des Neuf Sœurs, si vieux et si novice,
> Qui descendez du Pinde en rêvant d'un héros…
> Allez chez l'inspecteur prendre vos numéros.

On notera au passage que *Le Parnasse breton contemporain*, coédité en 1889 par Tiercelin et Guy Ropartz, ne représente pas l'activité poétique d'une école particulière mais la production poétique bretonne contemporaine que les éditeurs avaient pu trouver à illustrer[14] : cet emploi de *Parnasse* montre bien le caractère ambigu du terme qui, à cette époque, ne doit pas être systématiquement associé au mouvement

---

9 « Une édition critique », p. 495.
10 *Les Baisers*, p. 11.
11 Dans *Les Pierrots*, Châtillon, *Poésies*, p. 72.
12 « Le Parnasse contemporain » ; cité par Mortelette dans *Le Parnasse*, p. 61-67, à p. 62.
13 Laprade, *Poèmes civiques*, V, p. 108.
14 Voir Mortelette, *Histoire du Parnasse*, p. 407-408.

parnassien comme l'avait fait d'emblée un Barbey d'Aurevilly offensé de voir fermer les portes du recueil à son ami Amédée Pommier, entraînant derrière lui la critique[15] : rien dans son intitulé ne justifie sa perception comme un symbole univoque qui aurait cessé de renvoyer au mont d'Apollon[16], et le choix même de ce titre renvoyait à une tradition d'anthologies bien établie, renouvelée en 1864 par le *Parnasse satyrique du dix-neuvième siècle*[17]. S'il en était besoin, que l'on songe au projet de revue poétique présenté par G. Duportal dans *Le Parnasse français contemporain*, présenté en 1869, dont le titre ne doit pas faire illusion, le promoteur du projet ne faisant pas la moindre référence à l'entreprise de l'école « parnassienne[18] ». Accueillant dès le début des poètes d'autres courants plus conservateurs[19], l'évolution du *Parnasse contemporain*, de plus en plus ouvert aux collaborations extérieures au mouvement, montre du reste combien une lecture purement identitaire du titre serait erronée, même si les Parnassiens entendaient bien y jouer les premiers rôles[20]. Pour autant l'on ne saurait négliger que c'est bel et bien le recueil de 1866 qui donne au mouvement une identité que la critique est la première à consacrer en donnant un sens restreint à l'ancien nom de *parnassiens* par lequel on désigna longtemps les poètes. Mais quel était l'impact de la critique littéraire sur Corbière ?

S'il a bien montré la distinction qu'il y avait à faire entre les deux versions connues d'*'I' Sonnet*, B. Dufau rejoint B. Houzé et Mortelette[21] : « la version des *Amours jaunes*, dans un contexte qui voit les Parnassiens à l'avant-garde de la poésie, prend un tour qui transforme la blague potache d'un album non destiné à la publication en véritable prise de position au sein du champ poétique : en remaniant "I Sonnet", Corbière

---

15   Mortelette, *op. cit.*, p. 206-208.
16   Nous rejoignons par conséquent Walzer qui, à propos du « Pic de la Maladetta » où Corbière situe l'écriture de son poème, éd. citée, p. 1271, estime que le poète « semble plutôt considérer ici ce sommet comme une espèce de mont Parnasse hanté des Muses métriciennes ».
17   Mortelette, *Histoire du Parnasse*, p. 172-173.
18   Mortelette, *op. cit.*, p. 405-406, signale cependant quelques liens avec la nouvelle école, mais le projet de Duportal a bien l'ambition d'être ouvert aux « poètes contemporains » sans pour autant afficher une quelconque modernité conquérante (et encore moins un programme régionaliste).
19   Voir p. 117, 147, 363 et 414.
20   C'est ainsi que Mortelette, *Histoire du Parnasse*, p. 182, peut écrire que le premier recueil « ressemble à une galerie de la poésie en 1866 ».
21   Dufau, « La modernité qui déchante », p. 151.

fait d'une pierre deux coups en visant à la fois l'école et le Parnasse ».
Commentant le mélange de modernité et d'antiquité dans le remaniement apporté dans la version des *Amours jaunes*, il montre que ce
« télescopage de l'antique et du moderne » s'inscrit plus généralement
dans le cadre du « néo-burlesque Second Empire » – qui n'avait rien
en soi d'antiparnassien[22] –, rejoignant ainsi l'analyse de R. L. Mitchell
selon lequel, « *contrary to the usual mode of parody, Corbière's criticism of
Parnassian poetry is expressed* on his own terms », insistant toutefois sur le
fait que « *his parodic treatment of an alien "school" of poetry hides the indirect
statement* [...] *of his own method of writing*[23] » : que Corbière tourne ainsi le
dos aux procédés habituels de la parodie – dont il use précisément avec
les romantiques – n'amène ni l'un ni l'autre à douter qu'il y ait, précisément, parodie, assurés qu'ils sont d'une cible que Corbière, pourtant,
ne pointe pas. En mettant l'accent sur un mélange « néo-burlesque »
dont J.-L. Steinmetz relève la présence en d'autres endroits du recueil[24],
Dufau fait aussi peu de cas que Mitchell des courants fantaisiste et
satirique du mouvement. Il n'est pas sans intérêt de remarquer que
cette intrusion de la modernité commence avec « le railway du Pinde »
avant de se poursuivre avec le chloroforme[25] (en rime avec *forme*), puis
la comparaison des vers aux fils du télégraphe et celle du poème à un
télégramme « sacré ». La première évocation trahit surtout l'influence
du (probablement second) voyage en Italie et de l'ascension du Vésuve
qui auront inspiré à Corbière un plus ample remaniement du poème,
l'amenant notamment à renoncer au caractère quelque peu rudimen-
taire de l'anaphore liant quatrains et sizain : « Je vais (*var.* sais) faire
un sonnet », formule répétée qui est à l'origine du titre retenu pour les
Amours jaunes, '*I*' *Sonnet*, avec le chiffre romain pour le numéral, mis
en relief, comme de la parenthèse empruntée à Oronte qu'il introduit
au vers 9 (« Sonnet – c'est un sonnet – »)[26] : elle fait en effet écho au
syntagme hors phrase « *Railway di Pompeia* » par lequel commencent
deux versions anciennes de *Vésuves et C*[ie], intitulées *Au Vésuve*, qui a pour

---

22　Dufau, art. cité, p. 152-156 ; Steinmetz, *Tristan Corbière*, p. 240-242.
23　« Tristan Corbière's "I Sonnet" », p. 37.
24　*Tristan Corbière*, p. 240-242.
25　Qui, notons-le, fait écho à la réécriture du v. 3 : « Qu'en marquant la césure, un des
　　quatre s'endorme... ».
26　Le titre originel est simplement *Sonnet*. On a « I SONNET » p. 31, mais « I [*petite majuscule*]
　　Sonnet » dans la table.

fonction de situer le cadre du poème[27]. Le télégraphe ne peut quant à lui être dissocié de son utilisation dans *À une demoiselle* où le poète voit dans le clavecin un « [t]élégraphe à musique » apte à traduire l'« accord de sa lyre », dont toute référence au Parnasse semble exclue.

Faisant plus spécialement référence à la reprise de l'annonce d'Oronte désireux de déclamer son poème, David Scott considérait que, « *By picking up this ironic motif and blending into his own sonnet, Corbière takes irony to the verge of self-parody* », relevant au passage que le poète s'y montre « *meticulously, even ingeniously, obeying the rules he is satirizing*[28] » ; s'il évoque une critique du formalisme parnassien, c'est uniquement au travers de la pratique du poète qui parodierait ses propres « tendances parnassiennes[29] » :

> *Self-conscious on both formal and thematic levels, the Corbière of* Sonnet à Sir Bob *and* Le Crapaud *is a Romantic who uses the sonnet to burlesque his own romanticism whilst the Corbière of* I Sonnet *is a skillful formalist who uses the sonnet to parody his own Parnassian tendencies.*

On peut à vrai dire se demander s'il ne s'agit pas d'un poème ancien, comme le suggère précisément le ton potachique de ce sonnet, et l'on ne doit pas négliger le fait que l'élève Corbière devait volontiers écrire des vers sur ses cahiers d'écolier. Même s'il estime que ce texte « relève d'une haute virtuosité » au point de considérer qu'« il ne semble pas que Corbière ait été capable d'un tel tour de force alors qu'il n'avait que dix-sept ans », estimant qu'« il serait aventureux [...] de penser qu'à cette époque, poète prématuré, il ait été en mesure de confectionner une telle réussite », Steinmetz y voit du moins la possibilité d'un « très allusif souvenir » au séjour que Tristan passa durant l'été 1862 à Luchon avec sa mère, que la mention finale du poème – absente de la version ancienne – (« Pic de la Maladetta. – Août. ») semble rappeler[30]. Nous ne contestons pas que ce que nous supposons être une fantaisie de jeunesse relevant

---

27 Textes dans Walzer, éd. citée, p. 1313 ; Aragon et Bonnin, éd. citée, p. 462-463. La transcription que Jean de Trigon, *Tristan* Corbière, p. 88, donne de la seconde version ne fait pas apparaître la mise en relief du syntagme, contrairement au fac-similé : lettres déliées de plus gros corps (que pourrait rendre l'emploi des petits capitales) et souligne- ment (correspondant à l'italique).

28 *Sonnet Theory and Practice*, p. 80-81.

29 *Ibid.*, p. 82.

30 *Tristan Corbière*, p. 113-114 (et 112 pour la lettre du 25 juillet).

de l'exercice de style puisse parfaitement entrer en résonnance avec les critiques adressées en 1866 par un Alcide Dusolier au « formisme » des Parnassiens[31] : « rien ne se ressemble comme deux *formistes*, et cela par la raison toute simple que la forme est chose artificielle et convenue qui s'apprend comme l'orthographe ou le trapèze ». Pour autant, comme l'a avancé B. de Cornulier en évoquant les formules arithmétiques de l'*Art poétique*[32], les préceptes d'*'I' Sonnet* peuvent tout aussi bien être rapprochés des « rigoureuses lois » que, selon Boileau dont le goût personnel pour le genre était des plus limités[33], Apollon inventa pour éprouver les rimeurs. Il ne faut pas oublier non plus que la forme d'*'I' Sonnet* ne correspond à aucun sonnet-type de l'époque, avec ses rimes alternées dans les quatrains et ses tercets sur deux rimes, mais ce qui retient en fait l'attention est que Corbière, qui pointe le caractère concentré de ce genre de poèmes avec un numéral, mâtiné d'un jeu de mots, qui renvoie aux contraintes liées aux tarifs postaux (« Télégramme sacré – 20 mots » : *vains* mots[34]), décrit au moyen d'une formulation arithmétique la division stricte du sonnet en quatre parties ordonnées, posant « $4 + 4 = 8$ » puis « $3 + 3$ » là où Boileau pointait à peine différemment dans une description reposant sur la formule sous-jacente $2 \times 4 = 8$ puis $2 \times 3 = 6$[35] : dans la première version, Corbière présente cette addition comme l'âme même du sonnet ; dans les *Amours jaunes*, elle en devient « la preuve », cette formule étant la signature formelle du genre qui rend le sonnet immédiatement recon- naissable, s'accommodant des irrégularités les plus variées que lui-même ne manque pas de mettre en application, rendant ainsi compte de façon radicale de cette beauté « pythagorique » que Baudelaire, qui n'avait pas la religion de la quadruple rime, voyait en lui, son apostrophe à la « Muse

---

31 « Les Impassibles », col. 3. Cité par Mortelette, *Le Parnasse*, p. 51. L'article porte sur l'école qu'il désigne sous le nom de « groupe des IMPASSIBLES », sans référence explicite aux huit premières livraisons du *Parnasse contemporain* (son article paraît dans le *Figaro* du 29 avril) qui sont très largement dominées par ses acteurs (seuls Vacquerie et Antoni Deschamps font exception).

32 « Corbière et la poésie comptable », p. 249-250.

33 On ne connaît de lui que deux sonnets complets (sur le modèle que Banville érigera en règle) et un autre fragmentaire (il n'en publia qu'un seul). *Cf.* E.W. Olmsted, *The Sonnet in French Literature*, p. 172-175.

34 *Cf.* Aragon et Bonnin, éd. citée, p. 79. Sur la raison du nombre 20, nombre maximal forfaitaire des services télégraphiques, voir Cornulier, « Corbière et la poésie comptable », p. 247-248.

35 *Cf. supra*, p. 413.

d'Archimède » semblant même rendre hommage à son prédécesseur. Que l'on compare avec la façon dont Eugène de Lonlay reprend en 1870 les préceptes de l'*Art poétique* dans son propre sonnet sur le sonnet, cité par Y. Bernal, où le poète fait toutefois valoir, à l'instar de Boileau, le principe de la quadruple rime (que Corbière passe sous silence tout en le respectant scrupuleusement dans son poème)[36] :

> D'un quatrain redoublé qui marche sur deux rimes,
> Et de six autres vers bons, s'ils ne sont sublimes,
> Ce petit poème est d'un seul jet composé.

Mais l'ignorance dans laquelle Corbière tient la précision de Boileau[37] se rencontrait déjà au XVIIIe siècle lorsque Antoine de La Motte, énonçant les lois du genre, n'évoquait pour la forme que : « Deux quatrains, deux Tercets ; qu'on se repose là[38] ». Il ne s'agit donc pas de dénigrer l'usage que « les Parnassiens », pour autant que l'on s'entende sur ceux que l'on désigne ainsi, ont pu faire de la forme fixe et du caractère, élitiste au mieux, académique au pire, que l'on ne manque pas de leur associer abusivement en négligeant le courant fantaisiste qui accompagna le mouvement. On n'en remarquera pas moins que l'image militaire des vers des quatrains :

> Vers filés à la main et d'un pied uniforme,
> Emboîtant bien le pas, par quatre en peloton ;
> Qu'en marquant la césure, un des quatre s'endorme...
> Ça peut dormir debout comme soldats de plomb.

trouve des échos dans le sonnet sur le sonnet de Gautier, daté du 14 juillet 1870, dédié « [à] maître Claudius Popelin, émailleur et poète », qui ne paraîtra semble-t-il qu'en 1875, avant l'édition posthume des *Poésies complètes* de 1876[39] :

---

36 *Recueil complet*, p. 18 ; voir Bernal, « Corbière, les coquilles », p. 254, n. 66.
37 « On dit [...] qu'un jour ce dieu bizarre / Voulut qu'en deux quatrains de mesure pareille / La rime avec deux sons frappât huit fois l'oreille ».
38 La Motte, *Lettres*, p. 215. Il est vrai que François Maynard était passé par là.
39 *Cinq octaves de sonnets*, p. 50-51 (nous corrigeons le « Crétés » du texte de Popelin que nous citons) ; Gautier, *Poésies complètes* (1875), II, selon la notice 2368 de De Spoelberch de Lovenjoul, *Histoire des œuvres de Théophile Gautier*, II, p. 481-482. Jasinski, *Poésies complètes*, III, p. 204, renvoie à la réédition des *Poésies complètes* de 1889. Sur ce sonnet, voir le commentaire de Scott, *Sonnet Theory*, p. 31-32.

> Les quatrains du sonnet sont de bons chevaliers
> Crêtés de lambrequins, plastronnés d'armoiries,
> Marchant à pas égaux le long des galeries,
> Ou veillant, lance au poing, droits contre les piliers.

Corbière introduit simplement dans la version des *Amours jaunes* une autre dimension en attribuant plaisamment des vertus soporifiques à la régularité des vers et des césures comme à la rime multiple que l'exemple donné – « *chloroforme* » – vient concrètement compléter dans son poème. Nul ne soupçonnera Gautier de faire ici une charge anti-parnassienne, d'autant que ce genre d'images, sous des formes variées, est ancienne et ne concerne pas seulement le sonnet. Qu'on se rappelle ces vers de *Namouna* (I, XLIX) où l'on ne peut guère voir une condamnation des rimes suivies de la poésie classique au motif que Musset, quant à lui, use librement du rejet et de l'enjambement, mais plutôt la défense d'un renouvellement nécessaire des rythmes poétiques pour l'usage des nouvelles générations de poètes :

> L'âme et le corps, hélas ! ils iront deux à deux,
> Tant que le monde ira, – pas à pas, côte à côte, –
> Comme s'en vont les vers classiques et les bœufs.

Semblablement, Boulay-Paty avait pu filer la métaphore des « bataillons d'alexandrins carrés » sur lesquels Hugo entendait faire « souffler un vent révolutionnaire » dans *Réponse à un acte d'accusation*, comparant, dans un sonnet justement, les vers du maître, « ce Napoléon de notre poésie », à une armée en ordre de marche, dans un poème que Gautier n'avait pas oublié[40]. C'est cette inertie même du mètre dans l'alexandrin, que l'abbé Delille et Chénier avaient déjà mise à mal, que les romantiques, Hugo en tête, entreprirent de combattre en prônant l'enjambement et d'autres procédés de segmentation du vers dont ils firent, du reste, un usage inégal. Un autre sonnet d'Hervilly, *Trahison*, publié en 1868, que le poète insère à la fin d'un autre poème en sollicitant la permission de ses amis, porte en exergue le « Sonnet, c'est un sonnet » d'Oronte que Corbière cite entre parenthèses au v. 10 de sa nouvelle version d'*'I' Sonnet*[41].

---

40 Boulay-Paty, *Sonnets*, p. 84. Gautier cite en effet le sonnet entier dans le compte rendu qu'il donne de ce recueil dans *La Presse* du 28 juillet 1851.
41 *La Lanterne en vers de couleur*, p. 10.

Comme on le voit, le courant fantaisiste ouvrait des voies que Corbière empruntait, et l'on n'est pas peu surpris de trouver dans le dernier tercet d'un autre sonnet d'Hervilly, intitulé *Tima*, l'expression des tendances masochistes que Corbière représente volontiers au travers de la figure du chien soumis mendiant les faveurs de sa maîtresse fantasmée, celle d'Hervilly étant toutefois dépourvue de cruauté[42] :

> Et lorsque, fils-de-chien, de mes lèvres voraces
> Je baisai son pied nain, pour la première fois,
> Tima rit largement, une dragée aux doigts...

Rien par ailleurs ne justifie particulièrement l'hypothèse d'Aragon et Bonnin selon lesquels Corbière pourrait viser, au-delà de l'école parnassienne, «une poésie asservie aux codes et moules littéraires[43]». Il s'amuse bien plutôt de la contrainte, comme lorsqu'il écrit, dans *À l'Éternel Madame*[44] :

> Sois femelle de l'homme, et sers de Muse, ô femme,
> Quand le poète brame en Ame, en Lame, en Flamme !

vers qui rappellent les « rimes à sonnet » du librettiste Henri Meilhac[45] :

> Un sonnet, dites-vous ? Savez-vous bien Madame,
> Qu'il me faudra trouver trois rimes à sonnet ?
> Madame, heureusement, rime avec âme et flamme,
> Et le premier quatrain me semble assez complet.

Même si sa versification n'a rien d'impeccable, son goût pour le sonnet comme pour le rondel, le fait qu'il y mette moins d'irrégularité qu'on ne le croie, la régularité formelle de nombreuses pièces des *Amours jaunes* indiquent que les exigences formelles de la tradition poétique avaient bien son assentiment malgré une certaine difficulté à se soumettre à ses règles. Le fait qu'il emploie ici la quadruple rime est à relativiser au regard du fait qu'un sonnet sur deux des *Amours jaunes* est dans le même cas, le fait que les quatrains présentent le même arrangement également

---

42   *Les Baisers*, p. 23-24.
43   Éd. citée, p. 77.
44   Voir le commentaire que Scott, *Sonnet Theory*, p. 81, fait de ces vers.
45   Ce sonnet est souvent cité à partir de la fin des années 1880. Voir p. ex. *La Grande Revue*, 1ʳᵉ année (1888), p. 228 (les autres mots-rime sont *entame* et *âme*).

(seuls trois sonnets font exception), mais le choix de deux rimes pour les tercets indique, joint à ces caractéristiques, que Corbière s'est particulièrement appliqué dans l'écriture de cette pièce, ce qui ne suffit pas à conclure, comme le font les éditeurs cités, que le poète « utilise la forme canonique [*ce qui est inexact*] du sonnet en alexandrins pour la tourner en dérision ». Tous ces éléments nous incitent à voir dans 'I' *Sonnet* un divertissement plutôt qu'un poème polémique, s'inscrivant dans une démarche plus générale que Jules Laforgue n'a pas manqué de pointer[46] :

> — à chaque sortie il avertit : vous savez ! me prenez pas au sérieux. tout ça, c'est fait de chic, je pose. Je vais même vous expliquer comment ça se fabrique.

---

46 « Une étude sur Corbière », p. *2*.

LES QUATRAINS

Corbière a une pratique assez particulière du sonnet. Il semble en effet traiter la forme avec autant de liberté que Baudelaire : 60 sonnets des *Fleurs du Mal* suivent 28 modèles différents ; les *Amours jaunes* réunissent quant à eux 31 sonnets sur 14 modèles distincts. On ne peut par conséquent pas écarter l'idée que c'est la liberté formelle de son aîné qui a inspiré Corbière dans sa pratique du genre, d'autant qu'il partage avec lui quelques singularités. Il lui arrive par ailleurs d'entreprendre ce qui semble un mauvais sonnet avec deux quatrains hétéromorphes sur les mêmes rimes avant de poursuivre avec deux autres quatrains (*Vénerie*)[1] :

Vénerie	sourie	voici	j'aboyais
fois	voix	rue	relaie
écurie	bois	aussi	laie
Abois	*varie*	pied-de-grue	croyais

Deux traits caractéristiques des sonnets des *Amours jaunes* tendent en effet à montrer l'influence de la lecture des *Fleurs du Mal* – vraisemblablement dans la troisième édition parue quelques années auparavant (1868) –, comme on le verra bientôt. De cette lecture, faite semble-t-il tardivement puisque les poèmes de jeunesse et l'album Noir en sont exempts[2], témoignent les réminiscences de *La Pipe* dans *La Pipe au Poète* ou de *Duellum* dans *Duel aux camélias*, l'évocation des albatros « gauches et veûles [*sic*] (…) mal culottés comme leurs brûle-gueules » dans *Matelots* où l'oiseau sert cette fois de métaphore aux matelots[3], possiblement la « Muse malade » d'*Idylle coupée*, de façon plus discutable un

---

1   Nous ne saurions prétendre que l'alternance de rimes alternées et de rimes embrassées ait été délibérément recherchée.
2   Remarque faite par Houzé, « Corbière lecteur de Verlaine ? », p. 303.
3   Voir Laroche, *Les voix de la corbière*, p. 32.

écho d'*À une passante* dans *Bonne fortune et fortune*[4]. Les indices objectifs
d'imitation font en effet plutôt défaut dans ce dernier cas bien que le
parallélisme entre les deux poèmes soit suggestif[5], même si Corbière
n'ignorait vraisemblablement pas le poème de Baudelaire : l'expérience
des passantes est le lot commun du provincial égaré dans Paris[6] ; en
effet, pour autant qu'elle soit avérée, l'imitation ne saute pas aux yeux,
le point commun se limitant au thème de la passante, tandis que, dans
La Pipe au Poète, elle est clairement marquée par des reprises textuelles
plus littérales que ne le pense Laroche qui évoque simplement la reprise
du titre et du sujet[7] : outre le titre (et le mètre commun), l'incipit « Je
suis la Pipe d'un poète » adapte celui de Baudelaire (« Je suis la pipe
d'un auteur »). Le second couplet commence avec un calque syntaxique
évident, soit une proposition temporelle initiée par *quand* suivie de la
proposition principale dont Corbière reprend le sujet et le verbe : « Quand
ses chimères éborgnées / Viennent se heurter à son front, / Je fume... »
reprend en effet « Quand il est comblé de douleur, / Je fume comme la
chaumine / [...] ». Moins évident sans doute, l'évocation des « cliquetis du
fer » de *Duellum* se retrouve bien dans les « parades bouffes » des « deux
fers soleill[ant] ». On remarquera surtout que *Bonne fortune et fortune* se
donne d'emblée comme un parallèle au poème qui le précède dans le
recueil, *À la mémoire de Zulma*, opposant son incipit (« Moi, je fais mon
trottoir, quand la nature est belle, / Pour la passante ») à Zulma et sa
« chasse aux passants », le titre *Bonne fortune et fortune* faisant écho à la
« bourse commune » du couple formé par le poète et Zulma.

D'une part, l'abandon de la rime quadruple qui concerne près de six
pièces sur dix dans *Les Fleurs du Mal*[8], peut s'observer dans pas moins

---

4   Voir notamment Houzé et Hérisson, *op. cit.*, p. 61-63. Selon Houzé, le titre de *Male-Fleurette*
    renverrait à celui du recueil de Baudelaire, ce dont nous nous permettons de douter, cette
    construction archaïque – où *male* est un adjectif – s'inscrivant dans un contexte qui n'offre
    pas de rapprochement évident avec le thème des « fleurs du mal ». Ajoutons que Balcou,
    « De Baudelaire à Corbière », voit une influence de *Tableaux parisiens* sur *Paris*.
5   Voir notamment Mortelette, « Le prédécadentisme », p. 150-151.
6   Laroche, *Les voix de la corbière*, p. 32, voit précisément dans l'emploi de la majuscule un
    indice : « La Passante avec majuscule, c'est-à-dire celle de Baudelaire, bien entendu ».
    Cependant, les conditions d'emploi de la majuscule dans *Les Amours jaunes* n'autorisent
    pas pleinement cette conclusion, pour séduisante qu'elle soit.
7   Laroche, *ibid.*
8   Dans sept sonnets des *Fleurs du Mal*, les quatrains sont sur 3 rimes ; dans 14 autres, sur
    4 rimes.

de treize pièces des *Amours jaunes*, soit quatre sur dix[9] ; d'autre part le choix de quatrains de rimes plates auquel Baudelaire recourt une fois sur dix s'observe dans quatre pièces, où il est du reste associé à l'abandon de la quadruple rime (*Déclin, Bonsoir, Litanie, Sonèto a Napoli*)[10]. Les quatrains de rimes plates dont l'invention remonte à Évariste Boulay-Paty, ne reçoivent véritablement la reconnaissance des poètes qu'avec la parution des *Fleurs du Mal*[11], et l'on remarquera au passage que seul ce genre de formes est absent des deux premières éditions du *Parnasse contemporain*. C'est en outre Baudelaire qui crédite de son autorité le renouvellement des rimes dans les quatrains qui a longtemps suscité l'incompréhension des puristes, en particulier celle de Gautier, et qu'il avait vraisemblablement emprunté à François Maynard[12]. Son influence se manifeste du reste déjà dans les deux premiers recueils du *Parnasse contemporain* (et plus spécialement dans le premier), avec pas moins de huit pièces, trois autres ayant des quatrains sur trois rimes, ce qui représente pas moins de 7 % des 151 sonnets qui s'y trouvent : dans le recueil de 1866, on trouve, outre *Le Rebelle* de Baudelaire, *Le Dernier Mot de l'amour* d'Arsène Houssaye, *À celle qui est tranquille* et *Vere novo* de Mallarmé, *À ma fenêtre*, *Couchant* et *Le Pingouin* d'Eugène Lefébure. Comme on le voit, Corbière ne révolutionnait pas le genre, mais il y mettait un zèle inhabituel puisqu'il recourt à ce genre de formes plus de quatre fois sur dix.

Ceci étant, le poète des *Fleurs du Mal* respectait certains principes pour lesquels l'auteur des *Amours jaunes* n'a guère d'égards, comme la règle d'isomorphie des quatrains qui puise ses racines dans les origines du genre, bien que l'histoire du sonnet ait sur ce point été occasion-nellement marquée de ruptures pour des raisons diverses (négligence, convenance personnelle, recherche délibérée d'un contraste), tandis que

---

9   Dans *Les Amours jaunes*, deux sonnets ont leurs quatrains sur trois rimes (*Fleur d'art* et *Paysage mauvais* ; c'est également le cas de « Moi ton amour ?... » que Corbière transcrit en marge de la p. 40 de son exemplaire, éd. Houzé, « Le dernier Corbière », p. 329) ; douze, sur quatre rimes : « Donc, *la tramontane...* », *Duel aux camélias*, *Déclin* et *Bonsoir* (contigus), *Toit* et *Litanie* (contigus), *Heures*, *Grand opéra* (acte II), *À une demoiselle*, *Sonèto a Napoli*, *Sonnet posthume* plus *Le Crapaud*.

10   Ces deux licences se présentent simultanément dans deux pièces des *Fleurs du Mal* : *Le Revenant* et *Le Vin des amants* (quatrains sur trois rimes, sur quatre si l'on tient compte de l'appui).

11   Voir Billy, « Des lectures occultées ».

12   Voir Billy, *Les Formes poétiques*, p. 328-335.

Corbière, dans deux sonnets aux quatrains sur quatre rimes, varie la disposition des rimes : *Sonnet posthume* commence ainsi avec des rimes alternées suivies de rimes embrassées ; *Heures*, avec des rimes embrassées suivies de rimes plates, ce qui est plus rare, mais se rencontre déjà chez Musset, arrangement notablement absent de l'œuvre de Soulary : l'auteur de *Sonnets humouristiques* n'évitait guère en effet, depuis la troisième série d'*Éphémères* (1857), l'hétéromorphie des quatrains dont il appréciait sans doute la variété, mais il s'astreignait du moins à croiser les rimes, en les embrassant ou les alternant librement. Un seul des trois sonnets ajoutés à la main sur son exemplaire personnel, *Paris diurne*, présente des quatrains hétéromorphes (sur les mêmes rimes), avec des rimes plates puis embrassées selon un arrangement qui, en outre, enchaîne trois vers homorimes (*aa*bb b*aa*b). Même les Parnassiens ne reculaient pas devant de telles asymétries dont témoignent divers exemples dans les recueils du *Parnasse contemporain*, à commencer par Heredia dont trois des cinq sonnets qu'il donne en 1866 présentent cette irrégularité[13] :

Fleurs de feu (p. 13)	12 a*bb*a b*ab*a ccd eed
Artémis (p. 14-15)	12 a*bb*a b*ab*a ccd eed
Prométhée (p. 16)	12 a*ba*b a*bb*a ccd eed

Les deux premières éditions du *Parnasse contemporain* ne recueillent ainsi pas moins de douze pièces de ce genre (en croisant toujours les rimes, comme Soulary et Heredia), soit 8 % des sonnets qui s'y trouvent, et la proportion s'accroît même de la première à la deuxième, en passant de cinq (sur 80) à sept (sur 72) : les deux uniques sonnets concernés sur les 31 des *Amours jaunes* représentent quant à eux une proportion bien moindre (6,5 %), ce qui témoigne, sur ce point, d'un esprit plus conventionnel chez Corbière que chez les Parnassiens.

---

13   Les 31 sonnets qu'il donnera en 1876 ont par contre des quatrains homogènes (de rimes embrassées uniquement).

LES TERCETS

Pour ce qui est des tercets, là où Baudelaire fait preuve d'un grand éclectisme[1], Corbière se montre conventionnel, avec une préférence très fortement marquée pour les rimes couées du sonnet français primitif, celui de Marot, formation qui reste majoritaire tout au long du XVIe siècle (67,5 % du corpus d'Olmsted[2]) et redevient majoritaire au XIXe jusqu'à la période qui nous occupe[3] : quatre sonnets seulement des *Amours jaunes* suivent d'autres schémas, alors que même *Le Crapaud* qui intervertit l'ordre des quatrains et des tercets, comme le fameux sonnet sur le sonnet, recourt aux rimes couées. Les sonnettistes du *Parnasse contemporain* font là preuve d'une bien plus grande variété, en particulier dans le recueil de 1866 qui offre dix arrangements différents et dont un sonnet sur deux seulement recourt aux rimes couées dans les tercets, 17,5 % répondant au type ccd ede que promouvra Banville (avec les quatrains de rimes embrassées). Proportion qui diminue nettement en 1869 (38 %) au profit des tercets (et plus généralement de la forme) banvilliens (28 %).

La distribution des rimes couées chez Corbière s'accompagne presque toujours d'une organisation textuelle qui épouse la division en tercets, seul *Paysage mauvais* s'en détachant quelque peu par un contre-enjambement :

> – La Lavandière blanche étale
> Des trépassés le linge sale,
> Au soleil des loups... – Les crapauds,
>
> Petits chantres mélancoliques
> Empoisonnent de leurs coliques,
> Les champignons, leurs escabeaux.

Cette concordance entre texte et organisation par les rimes se retrouve dans les trois sonnets écrits sur des pages vierges de son exemplaire anonyme,

---

1   Voir Billy, *op. cit.*, p. 357-359.
2   *The Sonnet in French Literature.*
3   60 % environ selon nos observations personnelles.

Paris diurne, qui est un sonnet caudaté (prolongé d'un vers-commentaire reprenant la rime finale), *Petit coucher* et « Moi ton amour ?… » Elle est rompue dans trois pièces du recueil où le texte des tercets s'organise en quatre vers plus deux (*Duel aux camélias* et *Sonnet de nuit*) ou en deux plus quatre (*'I' Sonnet*).

La forme réputée banvillienne des tercets[4] ne se trouve que dans « Donc, *la tramontane…* », par ailleurs irrégulier avec ses sept rimes, et ses quatrains ont des rimes alternées. Les tercets de « Tu ris. – Bien !… » sont à rimes plates ; ceux de *Sonnet posthume*, sur deux rimes alternées. Les tercets de *Fleur d'art* ont une structure anomale (aba ccb) qui interdit l'alternance des genres de rimes, avec la séquence *armoire · braie* :

> Allons, pas de pleurs à notre mémoire !
> – C'est la mâle-mort de l'amour ici –
> Foin du myosotis, vieux sachet d'armoire !
>
> Double femme, va !… Qu'un âne te braie !
> Si tu n'étais fausse, eh serais-tu vraie ?…
> L'amour est un duel : – Bien touché ! Merci.

On ne peut manquer de rapprocher ce cas de celui qui s'observe dans *Le Cadre* de Baudelaire, où la correction était facile à apporter, mais où nous voyons un cultisme référant aux pratiques anciennes du sonnet telles que les illustrait encore Du Bellay[5], explication que nous ne défendrions pas pour Corbière dont les choix esthétiques étaient si fondamentalement différents. Cette structure est d'autant plus étonnante dans *Fleur d'art* qu'une interversion des vers 10 et 11 paraît naturelle, d'autant qu'elle s'intégrerait parfaitement dans des rimes couées appuyées par la division textuelle des tercets. L'absence de variante n'empêche pas de spéculer sur une cause possible de cette irrégularité qui pourrait être liée à une disposition particulière du poème dans l'autographe à partir duquel le prote a composé le texte, avec, p. ex., une première version du dixième vers barrée et la nouvelle version imprimée notée en quelque lieu prêtant à confusion.

---

4   Dont on n'oubliera pas qu'elles sont liées à l'emploi de rimes embrassées dans les quatrains ; les rares fois où Banville y use de rimes alternées, les quatre vers finaux du poème adoptent les rimes embrassées.

5   Sur cette question, voir Billy, *Les Formes poétiques*, p. 294-296.

MÈTRE ET GENRE DES RIMES

Les sonnets des *Amours jaunes* sont majoritairement monométriques, avec l'octosyllabe dans treize pièces[1] et l'alexandrin dans onze. Son goût pour l'octosyllabe pouvait s'appuyer sur *Les Fleurs du Mal*, mais il y montre plus d'application que Baudelaire qui ne l'y emploie que neuf fois, lui trouvant sans doute moins de lourdeur qu'à l'alexandrin dont il craignait « [q]u'en marquant la césure, un des quatre s'endorme... ». Il eût pu dire avec Louis Veuillot[2] :

> Les douze pieds, c'est la charrette,
> Pégase regimbe, il s'arrête,
> Voyant qu'il faut prendre le pas.
>
> Libre de cette peur fatale,
> Sur huit pieds, fringant il détale,
> Et s'il crève il ne traîne pas.

Plus original est l'emploi de l'heptasyllabe dans *Sonnet de nuit* et celui du décasyllabe à césure médiane dans *Duel aux camélias* et *Fleur d'art* qui se succèdent dans le recueil au sein de la section des *AMOURS JAUNES*. En monométrie, l'heptasyllabe ne se retrouve ailleurs que dans *Élizir d'Amor* et *Vendetta*, alors que le taratantara, dont Baudelaire avait usé dans *La Mort des amants*, se retrouve dans les rondels uniquement. Dans ses sonnets polymétriques, Corbière recourt normalement à des structures rationnelles au niveau de la distribution des mètres,

---

1   Lescane, « Comment peut-on », p. 120, considère l'emploi de l'octosyllabe comme contrevenant aux règles du genre, en référence aux poètes de la Pléiade qui ne l'utilisaient pratiquement pas. Ce mètre, souvent – mais non systématiquement – attaché à un ton badin, volontiers satirique, n'en est pas moins bien ancré dans la pratique de certains poètes tels que Maynard, Scarron ou Benserade pour la période classique, Boulay-Paty, Burdet, Baudelaire, Soulary, Glatigny ou Veuillot au XIXe siècle, avant Corbière. Que Maynard, Baudelaire ou Soulary puissent par ailleurs s'écarter à l'occasion des canons du genre ne change rien à l'affaire.
2   *Le Sonnet*, dans *Les Couleuvres*, p. 94.

avec généralement un mètre dominant et un mètre secondaire plus court. Dans *Toit*, le mètre dominant est l'heptasyllabe, le pentasyllabe se trouvant aux vers pairs des quatrains et au troisième vers des deux tercets. Dans *Heures*, Corbière recourt à une combinaison originale avec l'octosyllabe comme mètre dominant et le taratantara comme mètre secondaire pour conclure chacune des quatre parties du sonnet : la mesure particulière du taratantara, composé d'hémistiches de cinq syllabes, offre un contraste fort avec le vers pair dominant. La formule qu'il adopte pour *Pudentiane* qui fait appel à trois mètres différents est plus remarquable encore : les quatrains alternent alexandrin et octosyllabe, dans une alternance tout à fait classique remontant à Desportes[3], tandis que les tercets sont uniformément faits de décasyllabes à césure médiane, offrant ainsi un contraste encore plus marqué au regard des quatrains puisque les hémistiches du taratantara ne diffèrent que d'une syllabe de ceux de l'alexandrin. Seul *Sonèto a Napoli* se détache du lot : il est en effet constitué d'heptasyllabes à l'exception du dernier vers, de cinq syllabes, qui est un syntagme tout fait, « con Pulcinella », repris de l'exergue qui associe ce personnage de carnaval à toutes sortes de moments festifs[4]. L'alexandrin se retrouve dans les sonnets que Corbière ajoute sur des pages vierges de son exemplaire personnel, en alternance avec l'octosyllabe dans *Petit coucher*.

Si l'on met de côté le cas de *Sonèto a Napoli*[5], Corbière respecte généralement l'alternance des genres au sein des sonnets : vingt-et-un d'entre eux sont sur ce point réguliers, soit deux sonnets sur trois. Mais il lui arrive aussi de commettre des infractions à la règle comme il le fait parfois dans ses poésies strophiques ou en rimes suivies : c'est du reste là qu'il se montre le plus irrespectueux à l'égard de la tradition poétique, même s'il respecte habituellement la règle, et qu'il tourne le dos à la rigueur d'un Baudelaire. Le défaut d'alternance se présente toutefois uniquement dans la transition entre deux parties constitutives du sonnet, jamais au sein d'un quatrain ou d'un tercet : on le trouve quatre fois dans la transition des quatrains aux tercets, dans « Là : vivre à coups de fouet !… », « J'aimais… – Oh, ça n'est plus… », *Chapelet* et

---

3   Dans la paraphrase du psaume LXII ; *cf.* Martinon, *Les Strophes*, p. 141-142.
4   Il reproduit même dans la reprise les caractéristiques typographiques de l'exergue : tirets encadrant le syntagme et capitales.
5   Sauf le dernier vers, un pentasyllabe, comme on l'a dit *supra*.

Sonnet posthume; deux fois entre les quatrains (*Heures, Le Crapaud*); une fois entre les tercets, dans *Fleur d'art*, discuté plus haut; une fois enfin en deux endroits, à la fois entre les deux quatrains et entre quatrains et tercets (*Grand opéra*, IIᵉ acte).

NÉGLIGENCES DANS LE CHOIX
DES RIMES

Là où Baudelaire diversifiait ses rimes, Corbière peut, dans les tercets, réemployer des rimes déjà présentes dans les quatrains. Dans « Donc, *la tramontane*... », l'effet est atténué, voire neutralisé, dans la mesure où il s'agit d'une rime de haute fréquence – en |e³| – dans laquelle l'appui exigé par la tradition est distingué, bien que Corbière ne respecte pas toujours cette règle dans son recueil, du fait qu'il adopte généralement un registre bas[1] : les quatrains commencent avec *montée : Prométhée*, les tercets, avec *curée : rentrée*. La tradition considère en effet que l'appui est nécessaire à l'identité de ce genre de rimes. On trouve du reste dans le premier recueil du *Parnasse contemporain* deux cas semblables : *Réminiscence* de Léon Valade a sa deuxième rime en |ʁe³| (*ignorée : respirée*) et la troisième en |se³| (*effacée : pensée*) ; « Parfois une Vénus, de notre sol barbare » de Gautier a sa deuxième rime en |te| (*respecté : beauté :: argenté : nudité*) et la troisième en |me| (*fermé : surmé : parfumé*)[2]. Dans le recueil de 1869, *Le Désir* d'Albert Mérat a sa première rime en |ye³ˢ| (*buées : continuées*), la troisième en |ine³ˢ| (*matinées : terminées*)[3] : comme on le voit, le sonnet de Corbière ne s'éloigne guère des pratiques parnassiennes sur ce point particulier. On se souvient du parti que Baudelaire a pu tirer de cette propriété dans son sonnet inversé *Bien loin d'ici*, opposant |te³| (*Dorothée : heurtée*) à |ʁe³| (*sacrée : parée : préparée*)[4].

Cette reprise en tête des tercets de la rime initiale du sonnet semble résulter chez Corbière d'une recherche plus ou moins consciente puisqu'on la retrouve dans *Fleur d'art*, avec une rime en |waʁ³| (*histoire : noire*,

---

1   *Cf.* p. 83. Les approximations phémiques étaient traditionnellement acceptées, comme dans *posée : blessée* (*Steam-boat*), *croisés : cassés* (*Pièce à carreaux*), *risées : pensées* (*Frère et sœur jumeaux*), *passés : pavoisés* (*Matelots*) ou *bordé : dégoûté* (*Bambine*).
2   *PC (1866)*, p. 158 et 273.
3   *PC (1869)*, p. 205.
4   *Cf.* Billy, « *Bien loin d'ici* ».

puis *mémoire : armoire*), et dans *Paysage mauvais* avec une rime en |alˠ| (*râle : avale*, puis *étale : sale*). Ce phénomène s'observe d'ailleurs aussi chez certains poètes du *Parnasse contemporain*[5] : ainsi, dans le recueil de 1866, *Devant la Mélencolia d'Albert Durer* de Cazalis a sa première rime (*pierre : terre :: monastère : poussière*) et sa troisième (*mystère : cimetière*) en |ɛʁˠ|. La recherche y devient évidente dans un autre sonnet de Cazalis, *À l'enfant blonde*, dont le vers 9 reprend ni plus ni moins l'incipit et la rime qui l'accompagne[6]. Corbière recourt à des reprises plus libres dans d'autres sonnets : ainsi, dans *Sonnet posthume*, les tercets sur deux rimes (*voile : poêle : moelle, voir : encensoir : éteignoir*) reprennent peu ou prou les rimes du second quatrain (*étoiles : toiles, noir : soir*). Dans *Sonèto a Napoli*, la seconde rime est en |ɑ̃ᵗ|, sans appui contrairement à l'usage (*soleillant : amant*), la première des tercets également mais avec un appui distinctif (*filant : brûlant*). Dans « C'est la bohême, enfant... », on n'est pas loin d'un sonnet sur deux rimes, n'est-ce la rime en |idˠ| du second tercet (*candide : splendide*) : les deux rimes des quatrains, en |iˠ| et |uʁ| sont en effet reprises dans les tercets, la première avec un changement d'appui : *renie : colonie :: finie : calomnie* puis *remplie : lie* ; la seconde sans appui du tout : *à jour : tambour :: jour : amour* puis *tour : plus court*. Dans ce genre de reprises, les poètes du *Parnasse contemporain* semblent rechercher systématiquement une démarcation des rimes impliquées par des appuis spécifiques : ainsi, dans *À ma fenêtre* d'Eugène Lefébure – sonnet sur sept rimes –, la seconde rime est en |mɑ̃ᵗ| (*obliquement : sautillement*, la dernière en |pɑ̃ᵗ| (*répand : serpent*), se conformant au demeurant à l'exigence d'appui pour ce genre de rimes[7].

---

5   Et l'on peut y joindre les cas de rimes en [e] dans les sonnets de Valade et de Mérat mentionnés ci-dessus.
6   *PC (1866)*, p. 171. Dans *Cave amorem*, Claudius Popelin commence et termine sur la même rime en |ʁeˢ| : *dorés : diaprés :: enivrés : sacrés* dans les quatrains, *déchirés : enamourés* dans les tercets, *PC (1869)*, p. 349.
7   *PC (1866)*, p. 216.

LE CRAPAUD

Le cas du sonnet inversé *Le Crapaud* est particulier : Corbière ne semble pas avoir emprunté cette forme au poète des *Fleurs du Mal* dont le seul sonnet de ce genre, *Bien loin d'ici*, introduit dans la troisième édition de 1868, présente des caractéristiques formelles très éloignées de la forme adoptée par Corbière si ce n'est l'emploi commun de l'octosyllabe[1]. B. Houzé a mis l'accent sur la troublante similarité de l'image des vers 2-3 (« – La lune plaque en métal clair / Les découpures du vert sombre. ») du *Crapaud* avec celle par laquelle commence *Croquis parisien* (« La lune plaquait ses teintes de zinc / Par angles obtus »)[2]. Il n'a pas manqué de relever que le recueil de Verlaine contenait précisément un sonnet inversé – c'est même la première pièce du recueil après le prologue –, *Résignation*, dont la forme s'écarte à vrai dire sur bien des points de celle de Corbière, tant par son mètre – le taratantara – que par la disposition des tercets (a*bb* a*cc*) et l'homogénéité des quatrains (c*ddc* c*ddc*).

On peut douter que notre poète se soit jamais intéressé à la poésie du lorientais Brizeux qui est à l'origine du sonnet inversé[3], dont l'œuvre diverge tant de la sienne par le style, l'inspiration et la sensibilité, et dont la vie et la philosophie étaient aux antipodes des siennes. Toutefois, d'un point de vue purement objectif, Corbière aurait pu, par curiosité, parcourir ses *Œuvres complètes*, réunies en 1860, où se trouvent rassemblées avec quelques autres poèmes les sonnets du poète dans la deuxième partie de *Cycle*[4]. La forme du *Crapaud* repose sur

---

1   Voir Billy, « *Bien loin d'ici* ».
2   « Corbière lecteur de Verlaine », p. 308-312.
3   Nous mettons de côté un premier essai de Louis Ayma bien qu'il commence, comme *Le Crapaud*, par des rimes couées (a*a*b c*c*b d*d*ee d*d*ff) ; voir A. Chevrier, « Iconicité et symétrie », p. 332. Il est en effet fort peu probable que Corbière ait jamais eu accès à l'œuvre du poète périgourdin.
4   *Œuvres complètes*, II, p. 409-432.

une commutation des tercets et des quatrains : il commence en effet
par des rimes couées comme il le fait généralement dans ses sonnets
« à l'endroit » : aa*b* cc*b* d*ee*d f*gg*f. La démarche de Brizeux est très
différente : l'inversion que ce poète entend mettre en place consiste
à remonter du 14e vers au premier, ce que l'on peut moins établir
d'après l'observation de la structure des tercets – très variable chez
ce poète – que d'après celle des formules métriques intégrales des
sonnets symétriques de *Symboles,* dont le premier, inversé, commence
sur un octosyllabe, et dont le second, à l'endroit, se termine de la
même façon[5]. Ce qui incite à voir chez Brizeux une inversion plus
systématique est le programme présenté dans *Formes et Pensées* où le
poète compare le sonnet à une forme pyramidale que la tradition aurait
« posé sur la pointe », et que lui, entend remettre à l'endroit, ce dont
témoigne également la structure rhopalique du sonnet inversé *Le Hêtre*
dont la mesure progresse du premier tercet aux quatrains, en passant
de l'octosyllabe (1er tercet) au décasyllabe commun (2d tercet) puis à
l'alexandrin (quatrains).

On ne peut écarter l'idée que Corbière ait eu connaissance des
sonnets du poète lyonnais Joséphin Soulary, plus vraisemblablement
dans la dernière édition parue en 1872 chez Alphonse Lemerre que sa
diffusion rendait plus accessible[6] que l'édition par souscription *Sonnets,*
poèmes et poésies imprimée à Lyon par L. Perrin en 1864 ou l'une des
deux éditions de *Sonnets humouristiques,* parues en 1858 et 1859, chez
N. Scheuring qui recourait aux services du même imprimeur[7] : ses
relations avec le peintre lyonnais Paul Chenavard avec lequel il fit le
voyage en Italie et celles, plus épisodiques et obscures, avec le poète
également lyonnais Gustave Mathieu (deux personnalités que côtoya
Baudelaire) indiquent une voie qui aurait pu l'amener à s'intéresser à
Soulary dont l'humour avait de quoi l'attirer[8]. À supposer qu'il ait lu ses
poèmes et que ce soit par le recueil Lemerre, cela situerait l'écriture du
Crapaud vers la fin de la carrière de Corbière. La structure de ce poème

---

5   Formule : a^{8}b^{8}a^8 b^{10}c^{10}c^{10} d^{12}e^{12}e^{12}d^{12} d^{12}e^{12}e^{12}d^{12}.

6   Dans le premier volume : *Sonnets (1847-1871).* Voir aussi l'édition de Schellino, basée sur
     celle de Lemerre.

7   Sur la chronologie de ces éditions et leur préhistoire, voir Billy « *Bien loin d'ici* », p. 202,
     n. 63.

8   Steinmetz, *Tristan Corbière,* p. 317-319 et 222 sur Chenavard, 423 sur Mathieu, 436 sur
     les deux.

est en effet proche de celle des sonnets inversés du poète lyonnais avec lesquels il partage les tercets de rimes couées, et plus proche encore de l'un d'entre eux, *Le Sonneur*[9] :

Abîme pour abîme (LXXXIX)	12	aa*b* cc*b* de*d*e de*e*d
Le Phrénologue (XC)	12	aa*b* cc*b* de*d*e e*d*ed
Le Sonneur (CLII)	8	*a*a*b* cc*b* de*e*d de*e*d
Idylle (CXLI)	5+5	*a*a*b* cc*b* de*d*e de*d*e

Les quatrains du *Crapaud* sont à rimes embrassées, comme ceux du *Sonneur*, mais ces rimes sont renouvelées d'un quatrain à l'autre selon un procédé apprécié de Corbière. Comme *Le Sonneur* encore, *Le Crapaud* recourt à l'octosyllabe. Quoi qu'il en soit de ces convergences, il convient d'être prudent, car on ne peut pas non plus exclure absolument que Corbière soit directement parti de *Bien loin d'ici*, ou même des sonnets inversés de Brizeux, voire de *Résignation* pour construire un poème à son idée, recourant dans les tercets aux rimes couées dont il était coutumier et multipliant les rimes dans les quatrains pour les libertés d'expression que lui permettait ce procédé qu'il affectionnait.

Selon une note de l'article qu'il a consacré à un autre *Crapaud*, Fongaro estime qu'Apollinaire aurait pu lire celui de Louis Bouilhet, sans se demander si ce dernier n'avait pas pu inspirer Corbière[10]. Parue en 1859 dans *Festons et astragales* que Corbière a fort bien pu lire, peut-être même en le prenant dans la bibliothèque de son père, la pièce de Bouilhet est certes constituée de six quatrains de rimes alternées, mais elle recourt également à l'octosyllabe – ce qui n'est certes pas en soi déterminant – et commence sur le même ton bucolique et le même thème que le sonnet de Tristan. Et surtout, s'il ne s'identifie pas à la bête qu'il interpelle toutefois comme son « pauvre ami », du moins son auteur la compare-t-il à Roméo auquel peut faire écho le *rossignol de la boue* de Corbière. La structure dialoguée du poème de Corbière va du reste dans ce sens en mettant en scène le poète énonciateur et ce qu'on estime être sa compagne, faisant écho à l'interpellation, sur deux quatrains, du crapaud dans la pièce de Bouilhet[11] :

9 Numérotation de l'édition Lemerre.
10 « Le Poète et le Crapaud », p. 124, n. 13.
11 *Festons et Astragales*, p. 153-154.

L.B.[12]	T.C.
L'ombre descend, la terre est brune,	Un chant dans une nuit sans air…
Tous les bruits meurent à la fois ;	– La lune plaque en métal clair
Seul, les yeux fixés sur la lune,	Les découpures du vert sombre. (1-3)
Le crapaud chante au bord du bois.	
Du vieux tronc qu'un lierre festonne	… Un chant ; comme un écho, tout vif,
Il sort ainsi, quand vient le soir ;	Enterré, là, sous le massif…
Comme une flûte monotone,	– Ça se tait : Viens, c'est là, dans l'ombre…
Sa voix monte sous le ciel noir.	(4-6)
Ah ! pauvre ami, vieux camarade !	
Que dit-elle à l'astre argenté,	
Ta longue et morne sérénade	
Qui pleure dans les nuits d'été ?	
Crois-tu qu'enfin lasse et charmée	
Par tes tristesses d'opéra,	
Au long d'une échelle enflammée,	
Ta Juliette descendra ?…	
Tant que l'ombre étale ses voiles,	
Il reste là, s'évertuant,	
Sous le balcon d'or des étoiles,	– Un crapaud ! – Pourquoi cette peur, (7)
Roméo sinistre et gluant.	Vois-le, poète tondu, sans aile,
	Rossignol de la boue… – Horreur ! – (9-10)
Puis il retourne vers son antre,	Non : il s'en va, froid, sous sa pierre. (13)
Au premier sourire du jour,	
Traînant, dans l'herbe, son gros ventre,	
Plein de poisons et plein d'amour.	

Ces deux quatrains mis à part, seuls deux vers de Corbière n'ont pas d'écho direct dans ceux de Bouilhet : d'une part « Près de moi, ton soldat fidèle ! » (v. 8) qui explicite la présence de la compagne du poète, encore que l'évocation de la « Juliette » du crapaud établisse chez Bouilhet un parallèle éclairant ; d'autre part le dernier vers qui établit le lien métaphorique entre le poète et le crapaud : « Bonsoir – ce crapaud-là c'est moi », encore que, là encore, l'apostrophe au « pauvre ami, vieux camarade » suggère chez Bouilhet une certaine identification du

---

12   Quatrains 1-2 et 5-6.

poète au crapaud. Si donc on met de côté les deux quatrains centraux de Bouilhet qui constituent un développement en modifiant le point de vue – le poète y interpelant le crapaud en interrogations rhétoriques –, les points de rencontre entre les deux poèmes, dans des moules divers mais de même mètre et de dimension comparable, sont à ce point nombreux que la possible influence du poème de 164 alexandrins à rimes suivies d'Hugo paraît en comparaison bien ténue[13] : la miséricorde qui joue un rôle central chez Hugo n'a point de place ni chez Bouilhet ni chez Corbière, pas plus que le martyre dont la bête fait l'objet ; son crapaud ne chante pas, sa laideur et sa misère sont mises en avant, ce qui n'est le cas chez Corbière que dans le regard de la compagne du poète. Chez Hugo, la scène se passe au couchant, ce qui n'est déjà plus le cas chez Bouilhet où la lune a pris le relais comme chez Corbière ; elle se situe autour d'une ornière, là où Corbière prend pour cadre des arbres et des buissons, ce qui le rapproche par contre de la scène de Bouilhet qui se situe à la lisière d'un bois, au pied d'un vieux tronc. Seule l'évocation de l'horreur et la lumière qui luit dans l'œil du crapaud rappellent le grand poème hugolien :

> Un crapaud regardait le ciel, bête éblouie ;
> Grave, il songeait ; l'horreur contemplait la splendeur.
> [...]
> Pas de bête qui n'ait un reflet d'infini ;
> Pas de prunelle abjecte et vile que ne touche
> L'éclair d'en haut, parfois tendre et parfois farouche ;
> Pas de monstre chétif, louche, impur, chassieux,
> Qui n'ait l'immensité des astres dans les yeux.

Que « son œil de lumière » nous rappelle tout cela ne peut certes être écarté – pas plus qu'on ne peut douter que Corbière ait lu le poème de Hugo –, mais c'est bien peu au regard des points de rencontre avec le poème de Bouilhet.

---

13 Sur les analogies avec le poème d'Hugo, voir notamment Mortelette, « Corbière, Hugo », p. 82-83.

CONCLUSION

Corbière pratique le sonnet aussi bien comme pièce indépendante, disséminée dans différentes parties du recueil, que comme élément constitutif d'une série homogène, dans *Paris*. Le genre y occupe une place relativement importante puisqu'il concerne une pièce sur trois. Dans son sonnet sur le sonnet, il décrit plaisamment les contraintes induites par ce genre, sans que l'on puisse y voir une charge antiparnassienne comme on le prétend souvent, autant parce que le sonnet n'est pas l'apanage des Parnassiens que parce qu'il occupe une place très variable dans l'œuvre des différents acteurs du mouvement, avec un respect des règles (mais quelles règles ?) tout à fait discutable, loin de la rigueur qu'on lui suppose. S'il témoigne d'une grande liberté dans les formes qu'il adopte, c'est à peu près exclusivement dans les quatrains où il varie l'arrangement des rimes, abandonnant le cas échéant la reprise des mêmes rimes, recourant le plus souvent aux rimes couées dans ses tercets, respectant le plus souvent la concordance de la syntaxe et des structures rimiques. L'influence de Baudelaire, vraisemblablement au travers de la troisième édition des *Fleurs du Mal*, se fait sentir dans cette liberté, comme, sans doute, dans le choix du sonnet inversé pour *Le Crapaud* dont l'inspiration semble par ailleurs très proche de celle du *Crapaud* de Bouilhet, mais il fait preuve également de libertés que Baudelaire ne se permettait pas, que ce soit dans l'adoption de quatrains hétérogènes, d'asymétries dans l'emploi de la polymétrie, dans les défauts d'alternance des genres ou les négligences apportées dans le choix des rimes, avec, parfois, des reprises qui lui servent à souligner la bipartition du sonnet en quatrains et tercets.

SEPTIÈME PARTIE

RONDELS POUR APRÈS

> Un jour la pâle Mort vint frapper à sa porte ;
> Il la fit rafraîchir, rajusta son bonnet,
> Et la complimenta, si bien qu'il fit en sorte
> De pouvoir achever sa pipe et son sonnet.
> BANVILLE, *Ceux qui meurent*[1].

Le traitement du rondel par Corbière est bien connu pour son approximation. Il attire d'autant plus l'attention qu'il est au cœur même d'une section spécifique qui se distingue par son organisation en continu, soulignée par l'emploi uniforme de l'italique, ce qui lui a valu la qualification de « poème de poèmes[2] ». Par cet aspect, cette section fait pendant à la suite de sonnets intitulée *Paris*[3] qui peut du reste passer pour une sorte de section du recueil comme le suggère l'emploi d'un titre courant spécifique et la présentation de la table des matières qui imprime en capitales les titres de *Ça ?* (sans le point d'interrogation), *Paris* et *Épitaphe* suivi d'un fleuron identique à celui qui délimite les sections proprement dites, de *LES AMOURS JAUNES* à *RONDELS POUR APRÈS*[4]. En outre, *Paris* est suivi d'*Épitaphe* qui porte sur la personnalité du poète alors que la section *RONDELS POUR APRÈS* est introduite par *Sonnet posthume* qui fait justement écho à *Épitaphe*. Le poète a même orné de collages les six pages de cette section dans son recueil personnel, aspect particulièrement bien étudié par B. Houzé[5]. Ce qui a été moins exploré, c'est l'insertion des rondels de Corbière dans l'histoire de la forme, si ce n'est un point essentiel, également mis en évidence par Houzé : l'influence de Glatigny au détriment de Banville,

---

1   *Les Cariatides*, IX, I.
2   Houzé, « Corbière créateur d'objets », p. 29.
3   Houzé, *ibid.* et Houzé et Hérisson, *op. cit.*, p. 171-172.
4   La seule différence est que ces titres sont alignés à gauche et non centrés. Sur les ambiguïtés de la construction du recueil et les particularités des sections d'ouverture et de clôture, voir Houzé et Hérisson, *op. cit.*, p. 168-172, ainsi que nos remarques p. 60 n. 25.
5   « Traces de Tristan Corbière », p. 24-26 et planches non paginées. Sur ce parallélisme, voir Houzé et Hérisson, *op. cit.*, p. 171-172.

aspect que nous entendons approfondir ici en examinant la manière dont le genre a été remis à la mode au XIXe siècle et en mettant en lumière d'autres lieux de rencontre entre *RONDELS POUR APRÈS* et certains poèmes de Glatigny. Nous évoquerons pour terminer l'influence possible de Louis Bouilhet dans l'inspiration de la section, inspiration que nous avons déjà relevée dans *Le Crapaud*.

UN RONDEL À *PEU PRÈS*

Le choix du rondel offrait au poète les ressources du retour des mêmes rimes et de sa ritournelle, répétitions propices à l'atmosphère rêveuse de ces poèmes. On a fait remarquer que la structure de base n'est ni celle de 14 vers ni celle de 13 vers, formes que Banville prônera successivement[1]. Le choix d'employer le taratantara de façon exclusive est frappant, mètre dont Chevrier dit[2] : « Ce vers est celui de la romance. Il contribue au rythme berceur du poème, amplifié par les refrains ou les reprises ("Dors" dans les trois premiers rondeaux) ». Dans *Au vieux Roscoff*, « Berceuse en Nord-ouest mineur », Corbière emploie l'octosyllabe (en quatrains). Si l'on sait que le pentasyllabe est un mètre parfois utilisé dans les berceuses, dont témoigne, combiné à l'heptasyllabe, jusqu'au modèle de *L'Invitation au voyage* de Baudelaire[3], ce n'est pas, à notre connaissance, le cas du taratantara qui était alors à la mode dans le cadre de la poésie savante. Baudelaire l'avait déjà associé à un thème funèbre dans *La Mort des amants* ; en 1860, Armand Renaud publie *Le Palanquin* où il chante la mort du porcelainier et de son amante[4]. C'est semble-t-il dans cette décennie que, dans la poésie littéraire du moins, le mètre se voit associées des références au genre de la berceuse avec, de plus, une thématique funèbre, comme dans *La Plainte du bûcheron* d'André Theuriet, publiée en 1867[5]. Voici le début (premier couplet plus le premier vers du suivant) de cette pièce qui met en scène un vieux

---

1   Ce fait est ignoré par la critique qui recourt indifféremment à l'une ou l'autre édition en en méconnaissant les différences. Bellati, *Formes fixes et modernité*, p. 58, et Chevrier, *Le Décasyllabe à césure médiane*, p. 308, ont en vue le modèle de 13 vers ; Houzé, « Corbière lecteur de Verlaine ? », p. 304-307, celui de 14 vers. On trouvera un excellent commentaire littéraire de cette section, particulièrement étudiée, dans Houzé, *Les Amours jaunes*, p. 135-153.

2   *Le Décasyllabe à césure médiane*, p. 308.

3   À savoir *Berceuse* de Châtillon ; voir Robb, *La Poésie de Baudelaire*, p. 262-263, et Billy, *Les Formes poétiques*, p. 230-231.

4   *Les Poèmes de l'amour*, p. 39-46.

5   *Le Chemin des bois*, p. 31-34.

bûcheron racontant à son petit-fils orphelin comment son père, qu'il berça jadis de la même façon que lui, s'est retrouvé en prison pour avoir braconné afin de nourrir les siens :

> Dodo, l'enfant do! – La forêt sommeille ;
> Assis près d'un feu clair et réchauffant,
> Un vieux bûcheron endort un enfant.
> L'enfant a l'œil bleu, la lèvre vermeille ;
> Le vieux est courbé, ridé, grisonnant...
> « Dors, mon doux mignon, la forêt sommeille.
> Dors, le plus beau temps est l'âge où l'on dort ! » [...]

La même année, Léon Dierx l'emploie dans un poème des *Lèvres closes*, associant également ce mètre à une berceuse funèbre dans *La Chanson de Mahâl* où l'on assiste au spectacle de la pauvre Gemma déplorant son veuvage, tandis que la vieille Mahâl chantonne dans son coin, à demi-endormie devant son rouet, la plainte que voici dont les couplets émaillent le récit du poète et où le thème de la fleur funeste se présente déjà, bien qu'utilisé d'autre façon que chez Corbière[6] :

> La pluie aux grains froids là-haut tombe à verse.
> Mon cher enfant dort, et moi je le berce,
> Dans son berceau fait de chêne et de plomb.
> J'entends un bruit sec qui gratte et qui perce.
> Tu dors, mon enfant, d'un sommeil bien long !
> — Mon enfant s'agite en ses draps de plomb. [...]
>
> Un lourd cauchemar, mon enfant, t'agite.
> Ton berceau de chêne est un mauvais gîte.
> — Mon âme est partie, et vide est mon corps.
> Si je vis ou rêve, hélas ! moi j'hésite.
> J'appartiens souvent aux âmes des morts ;
> Mon enfant, ton âme agite mon corps. [...]
>
> Dans l'œil des enfants lisent leurs nourrices.
> Les morts ont aussi parfois leurs caprices.
> Lorsque tu souffrais, je sais une fleur
> Que je te donnais pour que tu guérisses ;
> Son baiser rendait ton sommeil meilleur.
> — Mon enfant demande une étrange fleur ! [...]

---

6   *Les Lèvres closes*, p. 121-133. La pièce est composée de cinq sizains rimés *aababb*, avec un mot-refrain à la rime des v. 3 et 6, renouvelé d'une strophe à l'autre.

Il sait des secrets plus vieux que la tombe !
— La pluie aux grains froids sur mes membres tombe.
Oh ! rouge est la fleur ! mortel son poison !
Pourquoi la veut-il ? pour quelle hécatombe ?
— Moi, dans la forêt, je cours sans raison !...
Un mort veut baiser, ô fleur ! ton poison !

Hier, j'ai frotté de poison sa bouche.
Dans son cadre il dort : que nul ne le touche[7] ! [...]

A travers un cadre il tendait la bouche,
J'ai frotté la fleur. Que nul ne le touche !
— Le désir des morts dompte les vivants.
Ainsi qu'un portrait, dans un cadre il couche !
— Dans mon vieux corps vide et branlant aux vents,
Les âmes des morts veillent les vivants !

Cette association du taratantara à l'évocation de la mort se retrouve l'année suivante dans la danse macabre de Cazalis (*Égalité, Fraternité*), d'où, par contre, toute référence aux berceuses disparaît[8] :

Zig et zig et zig, la Mort en cadence
Frappant une tombe avec son talon,
La Mort à minuit joue un air de danse,
Zig et zig et zag, sur son violon.

Ce qui frappe dans la forme des rondels de Corbière, généralement décomposés en trois groupes de quatre, trois et cinq vers respectivement, structurellement justifiés, c'est autant leur similitude que leurs divergences qui font penser à des variations autour d'un canevas bien précis[9] :

Titre	Forme										
Rondel	A b a b b a A b a b a A
	10' 10 10' 10 10 10' 10' 10 10' 10 10' 10'
Do, l'enfant, do...	A b b a a b A a b a b A
	10' 10 10 10' 10' 10 10' 10' 10 10' 10 10'

---

7   Ces deux vers suscitent une réaction intériorisée de la part de Gemma avant que Mâhall ne les remanie pour répondre à ses attentes informulées.
8   *Melancholia*, p. 137-139.
9   Voir notamment Bellati, *Formes fixes et modernité*, p. 58-62 ; repris dans *Ead.*, « Le renouveau du rondeau ».

Mirliton	A	b	b	a	a	b	A	a	b	b	a	A
	10'	10	10	10'	10'	10	10'	12'	10	10'	10	10'
Petit mort pour rire	A	b	b	a	a	b	a	a	b	b	a	A
	10'	10	10	10'	10'	10	10'	10'	10	10	10'	10'
Male-Fleurette	A	b	b	a	a	b	A	a	b	b	a	a	A
	10'	10	10	10'	10'	10	10'	10'	10	10	10'	10'	10'

TABL. 15 – Structure des rondels de Corbière.

Même les reprises se prêtent à diverses variations : variation initiale dans *Do, l'enfant, do...* portant sur le vœu en italien marquant une progression temporelle de *Buona vespre* à *Buona notte* en passant par *Buona sera* ; abandon de la première reprise dans *Petit mort pour rire* ; variante interprétative dans *Male-Fleurette*, renouant avec le titre de la pièce, avant le rappel final de l'incipit. Du point de vue syntaxique, on remarquera que le premier vers est le plus souvent une proposition indépendante, qui revient en l'état. Dans *Male-Fleurette*, il se présente comme une proposition principale prolongée par une relative au deuxième vers. Seul *Do, l'enfant do...* se détache avec une structure tronquée par l'aposiopèse qui rend sa reprise quelque peu énigmatique, avec l'attente d'un prédicat qui ne vient pas : « *Buona vespre !* Dors : Ton bout de cierge... ». Si, au début, l'attente trouve à se satisfaire, c'est par le biais d'une proposition indépendante qui nous apprend que le cierge est resté, planté là par ceux qui ont mis l'enfant au lit : « On l'a posé là, puis on est parti. » Dès lors, les reprises resituent la scène, avec l'enfant confronté au cierge abandonné témoignant encore d'une présence déjà passée, si ce n'est à la première reprise où le couplet final commence par l'hyperbate : « Est mort ».

Ce qui a plus particulièrement séduit Corbière dans la formule à 12 vers est le caractère cyclique du poème comme en témoignent les figures d'ouroboros dont il a orné *Petit mort pour rire* sur son exemplaire personnel[10], caractère accentué dans la dernière pièce par le détachement de la dernière reprise qui reproduit les caractéristiques typographiques du début de poème (initiale de deux points et premier mot en petites capitales *Ici*), comme s'il s'agissait d'une inscription votive. L'emploi

---

10 Houzé, « Traces de Tristan Corbière », planche en regard de la p. 25. Sur le recours à des constructions cycliques dans le recueil, voir Ozawa, « "Rondels pour après" », p. 212-213, et Houzé et Hérisson, *op. cit.*, p. 177.

presque exclusif du taratantara, renforce l'unité de la section dont l'inspiration, tournée vers les funérailles du poète – pour reprendre le titre de l'abondant commentaire de Giuseppe Bernardelli[11] –, est commune aux cinq rondels que résume d'une certaine façon le sonnet introductif, écrit par contre en alexandrins. *Mirliton* fait toutefois exception avec un alexandrin en tête du quintil, strophe qui se trouve justement décomposée de manière à détacher ce vers allomètre qui renoue avec celui de *Sonnet posthume* pour évoquer le chœur des rafales, « [p]leureuses en troupeau ». Dans *Male-Fleurette* où la reprise finale se voit détachée en une phrase isolée, le quintil ainsi estropié se trouve reconstitué par l'adjonction d'un vers. La disposition des rimes de la matrice (rimes embrassées) se trouve modifiée dans *Rondel* qui, pour maintenir les rimes alternées, n'en modifie pas moins leur ordre relatif dans le tercet et le quintil. Cet ordre est également altéré dans le quintil de *Do, l'enfant, do...*, après la commutation des rimes dans le tercet. Mais si l'on examine ce que ces rondels ont en commun, une structure bien déterminée de douze vers se dégage qui, dans le détail, n'est véritablement actualisée dans aucun des cinq poèmes (x signale telle ou telle divergence) :

Points communs aux cinq rondels	A b x x 10' 10 10 10'	x x A 10' 10 10'	x x b a a x 10 10 10' 10'
P.c. partagés par deux à quatre rondels[12]	A b b a 10' 10 10 10'	a b A 10' 10 10'	a b b a A 10' 10 10 10' 10'

TABL. 16 – Points communs aux cinq rondels.

Cette forme de douze vers est à ce point exceptionnelle dans la façon d'éditer les rondeaux-quatrains anciens qu'il est peu vraisemblable que Corbière y ait trouvé son inspiration. Nous donnerons tout d'abord un aperçu historique du rondeau qui permettra d'apporter quelques lumières sur le genre, en particulier sur sa restauration au XIXᵉ siècle, encore mal connue[13].

---

11 « Le esequie del poetino ».
12 Le quatrain dans quatre ; le tercet dans trois ; le quintil dans deux.
13 Pour un historique quelque peu détaillé du genre, voir Raynaud, *Rondeaux et autres poésies*, p. XXXV-LI.

UNE ANTIQUITÉ

Sébillet témoignait encore, au milieu du XVIe siècle, de la concurrence du rondeau à refrain – dont le *triolet* est alors le meilleur représentant – et du rondeau « à rentrements », dans une définition du genre (qui exclut en fait le triolet)[1] : « Car tout ainsi que au cercle (que le Français appelle Rondeau) après avoir discouru toute la circonférence, on rentre toujours au premier point duquel le discours avoit esté commencé : ainsi au Poème dit Rondeau, après tout dit, on retourne toujours au premier carme [*comprendre : "vers"*] ou hémistiche pris en son commencement. » Ce en quoi il marque un tournant dans la tradition est sa définition du « rondeau simple », basé sur un quatrain[2] :

> Le Rondeau simple a quatrain en premier couplet [*nous parlerons ici de « matrice »*], et quatrain en dernier [*notre « couplet »*], unisones [*sur les mêmes rimes*], dont les premiers et derniers vers symbolisent [*riment ensemble*], et les deux du milieu demeurent en rime plate [*soit des rimes embrassées*]. Le second couplet [*notre « demi-couplet »*] n'a que deux vers ressemblant en rime les deux premiers du premier couplet : et reprend-on après le second couplet, et en la fin du tiers [*notre « couplet »*] le premier vers du premier [*c'est alors un refrain*], ou seulement l'hémistiche [*un rentrement*].

Pour Sébillet, le *rondeau simple* est donc un rondeau-quatrain dont les reprises peuvent aussi bien porter sur le vers initial seul (refrain) que

---

1   Cité d'après Goyet, *Traités de poétique*, p. 109. Dans le triolet, c'est ce que Sébillet appelle le premier « couplet » en entier qui est repris à la fin, non le premier « carme », terme synonyme de *vers* ; le triolet se trouve par contre inclus dans la qualification de « parfait » (voir citation *infra*, p. 462). Le théoricien identifiait quatre « sortes » de rondeaux : le *triolet*, le *rondeau simple* (matrice de quatre vers), le *rondeau double* (matrice de cinq vers) et le *rondeau redoublé ou parfait* qui n'entre pas ici en considération. On notera au passage que, bien que qualifiant une sorte particulière de rondeau, la dernière épithète n'a ici que son sens général, la perfection d'un rondeau pouvant aussi bien porter sur le fait de reprendre le premier vers en entier (dans le *rondeau simple*) que la reprise progressive de quatre vers du « couplet initial » (dans le *rondeau redoublé*).

2   Éd. citée, p. 110-111 ; il nous arrive exceptionnellement de retoucher la ponctuation.

sur ses premiers mots (rentrement) ; soit, pour un quatrain de rimes embrassées (r = rentrement) :

(1) Abba abA abbaA
(2) abba abr abbar

Suivent deux exemples empruntés à Clément Marot. Le premier est du second type (« On le m'a dit, dague à ruëlle », reprise : « On le m'a dit ») ; le second, dont il ne cite que le premier vers, serait du premier type qui aurait pu servir de modèle à Corbière (« Qu'on mène aux champs ce coquardeau »). Toutefois, les éditeurs de Marot, tels qu'Héricault en 1867, limitent la seconde reprise à un rentrement (les quatre premières syllabes)[3]. Par ailleurs, Sébillet ajoute ceci : « Et pour entendre cette différence de reprise ou répétition, tu dois noter que le Rondeau simple est lors parfait, quand à la fin du second couplet on répète les deux premiers vers du premier ; et à la fin du tiers on reprend tout le premier entier. » Sébillet fait ainsi place à une formule de treize vers, qu'il considère comme vieillie[4] :

(3) ABba abAB abbaA

Sébillet reconnaît en effet que les modernes ont renoncé à cette dernière forme « pour ce que se fâchant de tant longue redite, [ils] ont avisé[5] pour le plus court et pour le meilleur de ne reprendre que le vers premier aux Rondeaux doubles et simples, ou deux ou trois mots premiers comme porte la sentence ».

C'est dans une certaine confusion que, au XIXe siècle, les lettrés renouent avec ce genre ancien, comme en témoignent aussi bien l'état de la lexicographie que l'édition des rondeaux anciens où l'on hésite sur l'extension à donner aux reprises là où les manuscrits ne donnent en général que leur amorce. Émile Littré semble ainsi réduire le rondeau de Charles d'Orléans au triolet dans une définition ambiguë et imprécise (*DLF* IV, 1)[6] :

---

3   Éd. citée, p. 188.
4   « [D]e quelle sorte tu en trouveras encore chez les vieux Poètes, et en Moralités et farces ».
5   Et non « osé » édité à tort par Goyet.
6   *DLF* IV, 1756.

Petit poëme nommé aussi triolet, où le premier ou les premiers vers reviennent au milieu et à la fin de la pièce. On a de ces rondeaux de Froissart et de Charles d'Orléans.

La définition qu'il donne du triolet proprement dit est pourtant dépourvue d'ambiguïté : « Nom d'une petite pièce de poésie française, qui consiste en un couplet de huit vers, dont le premier se répète après le troisième, et le premier et le second après le sixième » (*DLF* IV, 2348). N'évoquant que les formes à rentrements, Larousse donne tout d'abord une définition à la fois vague, imprécise et réductrice (*GDU* XIII, 1366) : « Pièce de huit, treize ou vingt-quatre vers sur deux rimes, avec certaines répétitions obligées ». Il définit ensuite deux variétés, le *rondeau simple* qui est pour lui une forme à rentrements et le *rondeau redoublé*, forme apparentée à la glose espagnole qui ne nous intéresse pas ici : il ignore par conséquent purement et simplement le rondeau à refrain pratiqué par Corbière, dans la droite ligne de la tradition poétologique classique qui ne connaissait que la forme moderne à rentrements. Il consacre au triolet une entrée spécifique, comme Littré, et comme le faisait déjà Carpentier dans son *Gradus français* en 1822[7]. Dans son *Dictionnaire universel des littératures* paru en 1876, Gustave Vapereau, qui a une bien meilleure connaissance du sujet, nous explique tout d'abord que, au XIVᵉ siècle, le rondeau – « anciennement RONDEL » – se composait « sans distinction de stances ou de couplets, de huit vers seulement, dont le premier est répété au milieu et les deux premiers repris à la fin », avec un exemple de Guillaume de Machaut qui ne se distingue du triolet que par l'emploi du décasyllabe[8]. Et de donner l'aperçu historique suivant[9] :

Dès ce temps et surtout au XVᵉ siècle, le rondeau se fixe et prend un rhythme plus marqué. Il consiste essentiellement en trois groupes de vers ou couplets, dont le second et le troisième se terminent, en guise de refrain, par la répétition du premier ou des deux premiers vers de la pièce. Le premier groupe est toujours un quatrain, le second est *un tercet ou un quatrain*, et le troisième *compte cinq ou six vers*, suivant que l'on répète, en le terminant, un ou deux vers du commencement. *Le nombre total des vers variera ainsi de douze à quatorze vers*. La pièce entière roule sur deux rimes.

---

7   *Gradus français*, p. 1021-1022.
8   Vapereau, *Dictionnaire universel des littératures*, p. 1763.
9   Le soulignement par l'italique est nôtre.

Vapereau simplifiait ainsi la situation au Moyen Âge en considérant uniquement le cas du rondeau-quatrain, simplification qui pouvait au moins en partie s'étayer sur la présentation ancienne de Sébillet et rendait compte de l'usage dominant dans la pratique du genre au XVᵉ siècle qu'un renouveau de l'intérêt pour l'œuvre de Charles d'Orléans depuis les romantiques pouvait mettre en évidence. C'est ainsi que, dans son *Tableau historique et critique de la poésie française*, Sainte-Beuve évoquait « cet enchaînement régulier de rimes féminines et masculines qui a été une élégance de style avant d'être une règle de versification » en donnant pour exemple trois rondeaux-quatrains déployés sur 13 vers (divisés en 4 + 4 + 5)[10], introduisant ainsi une sorte de règle qui, pour n'avoir rien de déterminant dans la pratique médiévale dont celle du prince, frappera suffisamment Banville dans un premier temps[11]. La description de Vapereau permet de définir quatre formules possibles, soit, pour une matrice faite d'un quatrain de rimes embrassées, les suivantes, où (0) rappelle la structure primitive[12] :

	Matrice	Demi-couplet + reprise médiane	Couplet + reprise finale
(0) 16 v.	*A B B A*	*a b A B*	*a b b a A B B A*
(1) 14 v.	A B B b a	a b A B	a b b a A B
(2a) 13 v.	A B B b a	a b A B	a b b a A
(2b) 13 v.	A B B b a	a b A	a b b a A B
(3) 12 v.	A b b a	a b A	a b b a A

TABL. 17 – Typologie des restitutions de rondels anciens.

10 Sainte-Beuve, *Tableau historique*, p. 5-7. Type (2a) ci-dessous. Le premier en décasyllabes communs, les deux autres en octosyllabes. Le quatrain qui sert de matrice est chaque fois de rimes embrassées, la première masculine, la seconde féminine.

11 Villemain, *Cours de littérature*, p. 236-237, auquel renvoie Sainte-Beuve, avait bien remarqué que Charles d'Orléans « observe rarement le mélange alternatif des rimes masculines et féminines », mais il en excepte curieusement les rondeaux : « Cette règle n'était encore suivie que dans les rondeaux et dans quelques pièces en vers d'inégale mesure », pour se contredire en citant peu après « Les fourriers d'été sont venus », tout en rimes masculines. À noter qu'il cite aussi « Le temps a laissié son manteau » ; les rondeaux qu'il donne ont 13 vers, disposés en 4 + 4 + 4 + 1.

12 Nous ne connaissons pas d'attestation de (2b), à laquelle il est tout à fait possible que Vapereau ne songeât point.

Vapereau citait à l'appui « Le Temps a laissié son manteau » sous la forme de 12 vers (3) que Sébillet met en avant dans son second exemple[13], avec le rappel, dans les deux reprises, du seul premier vers du refrain[14]. Ce poème, pour lequel le recueil autographe du poète donne des amorces limitées aux deux premiers mots (« Le temps *etc.* »), a en fait connu toutes sortes de restitutions au XIXe siècle. Pour ce qui est des éditeurs de Charles d'Orléans, au début du siècle P.-V. Chalvet le publie en 13 vers et trois parties (4 + 4 + 5)[15] ; en 1842, J.-M. Guichard reproduit le texte en donnant les amorces (deux mots) des deux premiers vers pour la première reprise, celle du premier seul pour la seconde, avec une division du poème après la première reprise, ce qui suggère la même forme de 13 vers, mais en deux parties (8 + 5)[16] ; la même année, Aimé Champollion-Figeac la publie en 12 vers et trois parties (4 + 3 + 5)[17]. Le premier tome de l'anthologie dirigée par Eugène Crépet, paru en 1861, reprend le texte de Champollion-Figeac avec des retouches que reproduira Vapereau[18]. Dans son *Encyclopédie du dix-neuvième siècle*, d'abord publiée en 1836-1853 (une quatrième édition paraîtra en 1877), Ange de Saint-Priest, sur lequel nous reviendrons, cite par contre la pièce en 14 vers (8 + 6) avec la reprise des deux premiers vers du refrain tant à la fin qu'au milieu[19]. Un même éditeur n'est pas pour autant cohérent d'un rondeau à l'autre[20] : si Chalvet applique le même canevas de 13 vers pour la totalité des rondeaux-quatrains, avec deux amorces pour la première reprise et une pour la dernière, Champollion-Figeac donne généralement 13 vers (4 + 4 + 5), quelquefois 12 (4 + 3 + 5), exceptionnellement 14 (4 + 4 + 6)[21]. Guichard généralise l'emploi d'amorces suggérant une

---

13 Voir *supra*, p. 462.
14 Vapereau, *op. cit.*, p. 1991. Il reprend le texte de Champollion-Figeac comme le montre l'adoption de *Goultes* (il substitue par contre *riant* au *raiant* de son modèle).
15 Éd. Chalvet, p. 257.
16 Éd. Guichard, p. 423. Banville s'appuiera sur ce texte pour la première version de son *Petit traité*, mais avec 14 vers (voir *infra*).
17 Éd. citée, p. 136-137 (édition basée sur le manuscrit de Grenoble).
18 Crépet, *Les Poëtes français*, t. I, p. 415-420 ; texte repris avec deux retouches : *raiant* > *riant, Qui en* > *Qu'en*) ; la notice et le choix des textes sont d'Anatole de Montaiglon qui, sous le titre « Rondeaux », regroupe huit pièces de 13 vers et deux de 12, disposés en trois strophes.
19 Voir p. 467-468.
20 Voir aussi Cocking, « The 'invention' of the rondel », p. 53.
21 Éd. citée, p. 269-270, Rondel XLV.

résolution en 13 vers disposés en deux groupes (8 + 5), dispositif qui se rencontre dans le premier noyau constitutif de la collection de rondeaux recueillis dans le manuscrit autographe de Charles d'Orléans sous la désignation de « chansons », partie présentant des réserves pour la copie des mélodies qui devaient leur être associés[22].

---

22 Avec les amorces des deux premiers vers à la suite du demi-couplet, celle du seul premier à la fin.

BANVILLE ET LA RESTAURATION
DU GENRE

Si Vapereau emploie « rondeau » pour désigner toutes les variétés de la forme, Banville, dans son *Petit traité de poésie française*, procède à la spécialisation des doublets, « rondel » lui servant à désigner la forme orléanesque tandis que, selon l'usage toujours en cours, il réserve « rondeau » au rondeau à rentrements. Le terme de « triolet » – apparu au début du XVIe siècle – est naturellement réservé pour désigner la restauration de la petite forme de huit vers primitive à laquelle sera désormais associé le seul octosyllabe. Banville a en fait évolué tant dans sa pratique du rondeau à refrain que dans la présentation qu'il en donne dans son traité où, dans un premier temps, il suit et promeut le modèle retenu par A. de Saint-Priest dans son *Encyclopédie du dix-neuvième siècle*, dont il est bon de rappeler qu'elle est rééditée en 1870-1872 (3e édition). Voici comment le genre s'y trouvait décrit, de façon équivoque, mais très précisément sous la désignation ancienne que retiendra le poète parnassien[1] :

> La forme qui se rapproche le plus du rondeau musical est le rondel dont aucune poétique ne parle[2] mais dont on trouve de nombreux exemples dans nos vieux poètes. Le rondel se compose de deux couplets, de quatre vers et d'un refrain de deux vers ; ce refrain commence le rondel ; il se trouve ainsi répété trois fois, au commencement, au milieu et à la fin du poëme.

---

1   *Encyclopédie du dix-neuvième siècle*, t. 20 (1872), p. 525 ; texte inchangé par rapport à la première édition, t. 21 (1846), p. 525. Il consacre la désignation de « rondeau » aux seules formes à rentrements comme Banville et Gaudin, bien qu'il emploie le terme de façon générique comme entrée (le « rondeau poétique »), distinguant quatre variétés : *rondel, rondeau double, rondeau simple* et *rondeau redoublé*, ce qui ne correspond qu'en apparence à la nomenclature de Sébillet : son rondeau « double ou ordinaire » est le rondeau-cinquain moderne à rentrements ; son rondeau « simple », semble-t-il, un rondeau-quatrain à rentrements.

2   Ce qui est inexact puisque Sébillet en fait état au XVIe siècle (voir *supra* p. 461-462), mais l'auteur a vraisemblablement en vue les traités du XIXe, à commencer par le *Gradus français* de Carpentier qui l'ignore.

D'après la disposition du refrain, il est évident que le rondel est tout entier sur deux rimes.

Cette description est suivie de l'exemple du *Renouveau*, titre souvent donné au poème de Charles d'Orléans déjà évoqué « Le Temps a laissié son manteau », déployé sur 14 vers disposés en deux groupes de 8 et 6 vers (8 A B *b* a a *b* A B a *b b* a A B), le tout pouvant en effet se décomposer en R + 4 + R + 4 + R. Si nous ne savons pas à qui Saint-Priest doit cette restitution dont il est peut-être directement responsable, du moins peut-on observer qu'il rejoint ici W. Ténint qui, dans son traité, n'évoquant ce genre de formes que comme des étapes préludant à l'émergence de la forme moderne (à rentrements), citait dans le même format de 14 vers un autre rondel de Charles d'Orléans (« Allez vous-en, allez, allez ») que le théoricien du romantisme donnait toutefois en un seul bloc indivis[3]. C'est précisément ce format que Banville, dans un premier temps, adopte pour modèle dans une série de six pièces publiée en 1858 dans la *Revue française* sous le titre générique *Rondels* : ces pièces sont toutes en octosyllabes et commencent uniformément sur une rime masculine, les vers étant cette fois répartis en trois strophes de 4 + 4 + 6 vers[4].

C'est encore cette forme qu'il donne pour modèle du genre en 1872 dans la première édition de son *Petit traité*[5], fondant justement sa description sur l'exemple de « Le temps a laissié son manteau » dans le texte de Guichard[6] dont il développe les amorces de la même façon que Saint-Priest (qui reproduisait le même texte, disposé par contre en 8 + 6 vers, en le modernisant le plus souvent)[7] ; voici comment Banville,

---

3   Ténint, *Prosodie*, p. 167-168.

4   *Revue française* IV, XII (1858), p. 486-489 : *Ma mie, Les Nymphes, Le Dieu Caprice, La Petite Véronique, Le Vin de Nuits, Le Laurier*. La série se conclut sur huit quatrains dédiés à Émile Deschamps « qui, le 5 janvier, m'a envoyé un ruban de la Légion d'Honneur qu'il avait porté ».

5   Après une parution en feuilleton en 1871-1872 dans l'*Écho de la Sorbonne, Moniteur de l'Enseignement secondaire des jeunes filles*.

6   Qui se serait fondé sur le manuscrit autographe (Paris, *Bnf*, fr. 25458 : *O* selon la siglaison de Champion) (voir p. XIX), mais s'est en réalité basé sur BnF, fr. 1104 (*O²*) qu'il a également consulté pour ordonner les pièces : la reprise médiane n'a qu'une seule amorce dans *O*, et la préférence de *souleil luisant* de *O²* au *soleil luyant* de *O* va dans le même sens.

7   Vapereau suit par contre le texte de Champollion-Figeac. Pour Cocking, « The 'invention' of the rondel », p. 53 et 54, qui n'ignore pas qu'il s'est appuyé sur l'édition Guichard, « *Banville must have failed to realize that the last 'etc.'* [dans la dernière amorce : "Le temps etc."] *indicated the repetition of one line only, for he added:* / De vent, de froidure et de pluye ».

qui considère comme Sainte-Beuve que le genre est soumis à l'alternance des genres, après en avoir décrit les deux premiers quatrains, y décrit la partie finale d'un « Rondel commençant par un vers masculin[8] » :

> Nous avons ensuite une troisième strophe de *six vers*, composée d'abord d'un quatrain où les rimes masculines sont au premier et au quatrième vers, et où les rimes féminines sont au second et au troisième vers, – puis *des deux* vers *formant refrain*, ramenés une troisième fois.

Mais Banville renoncera quelques années plus tard à cette première conception[9]. En 1875, il publie vingt-quatre *Rondels composés à la manière de Charles d'Orléans*[10] dans lesquels il revient à la forme de 13 vers (8 Abba abAB abbaA) que Sainte-Beuve présentait dans son *Tableau historique et critique de la poésie française* dont une nouvelle réédition avait été donnée en 1869, où la seconde reprise se limite au premier vers. Ces poèmes introduisent une certaine variété et quelques libertés : si la plupart d'entre eux sont toujours en octosyllabes, deux sont écrits en des mètres plus courts[11] ; ils commencent indifféremment par une rime masculine ou une féminine, mais il arrive aussi que les deux rimes soient homotones[12]. Dans son adresse à Armand Silvestre, rédigée le 10 juillet 1875, Banville qui évoque le poète au cri « mélancolique » de « Je suis cellui au cueur vestu de noir » présente sa tentative comme nouvelle, sans référence apparente à son propre essai de 1858[13] :

> J'essaie encore une fois de ressusciter, après le *Triolet* et la *Ballade*, un de nos vieux rhythmes français, dont l'harmonie et dont la symétrie sont charmantes. Des rhythmes, n'en invente pas qui veut ; mais c'est quelque chose peut-être que de tirer de l'oubli quelques-uns de ceux que nos aïeux nous ont laissés en bloc, comme un tas de pierreries enfermées dans un coffre, que le féroce XVIIe siècle a failli jeter à l'eau avec tout ce qui était dedans, sans autre forme de procès.

---

8 Banville, *Petit traité*, éd. 1872, p. 163-165. L'italique est de nous, afin de mettre en évidence les spécificités de cette première édition.

9 Nous n'avons pas consulté l'édition de 1875 à la Librairie de l'Écho de la Sorbonne.

10 Banville, *Poésies. Occidentales*. Voir aussi l'édition annotée par Sorrell et la présentation qui l'accompagne. Sorrell ne connaît que l'édition Charpentier du *Petit traité* qui adopte la nouvelle conception (il renvoie plus précisément à la réédition tardive de 1891).

11 *La Terre* est en tétrasyllabes, *L'Air* en hexasyllabes.

12 Masculines dans *Le Feu*, *La Paix* ; féminines dans *L'Air*, *La Lune*, *La Guerre*.

13 Cité d'après Banville, *Poésies complètes* (1878), t. II, p. 299.

Ces pièces sont composées sur des thèmes complémentaires (*Le Jour, La Nuit ; La Pêche, La Chasse ; Les Étoiles, La Lune ; La Paix, La Guerre ; Les Métaux, Les Pierreries*) ou sériels (les quatre saisons ; les quatre éléments ; les grands moments de la journée : *Le Matin, Le Midi, Le Soir* ; trois boissons : *Le Thé, Le Café, Le Vin*). Elles seront reprises l'année suivante dans le troisième recueil du *Parnasse contemporain* (sans l'adresse à Silvestre)[14] avant d'être recueillies dans les *Œuvres complètes* de 1878. Ce retour au modèle de Sainte-Beuve amènera Banville à modifier en conséquence sa présentation du genre à partir de 1881 dans les rééditions de son traité chez Charpentier qui visent alors le « public lettré[15] », amputant, pour commencer, de son quatorzième vers l'exemple de Charles d'Orléans qu'il accompagne de son commentaire ainsi modifié[16] :

> Nous avons ensuite une troisième strophe de *cinq vers*, composée d'abord d'un quatrain où les rimes masculines sont au premier et au quatrième vers, et où les rimes féminines sont au second et au troisième vers, – puis *du* vers *qui commence le Rondel*, ramené une troisième fois.

On remarquera au passage que son exposé reprend quant au reste celui de 1872, avec par conséquent le principe de l'alternance des genres de rimes qu'il lui arrivait pourtant d'ignorer dans ses *Rondels* de 1875. Que s'est-il passé avant ce revirement ? Banville aurait-il enfin lu l'étude que Paul Gaudin a consacrée au genre, parue deux ans avant la première édition du *Petit Traité* ? Gaudin explique en effet comment, selon lui, le genre a évolué, du rondeau primitif (dont dérive le triolet) au rondeau simple de Charles d'Orléans[17] :

> D'abord, semble-t-il, pas d'autre règle que le caprice de chacun : tel rondeau de ce temps n'a pas moins de dix-huit vers. Puis on pose une limite, un nombre fixe est adopté : treize vers ; et les poëtes emploient, concurremment avec l'ancien rhythme, cette coupe nouvelle, qui ne diffère du type aujourd'hui en usage [*Gaudin a ici en vue le rondeau à rentrements*] que par la longueur du refrain.

---

14 *PC (1876)*, p. 9-32. Sur ces pièces de Banville, voir Bellati, *Formes fixes et modernité*, p. 21-24 (qui ne parle que de la reprise en recueil de 1875).

15 Edwards, *Le 'Petit Traité'*, p. 92.

16 Sur ce revirement, voir Cocking, « The 'invention' of the rondel », p. 53-54. *Petit traité*, éd. 1881, p. 185-188 (l'italique est nôtre).

17 *Du rondeau, du triolet, du sonnet*, p. 15. Voir aussi p. 10-14 une esquisse de l'évolution générale du genre.

Il donne l'exemple d'un autre rondeau de Charles d'Orléans, « Gardez le trait de la fenestre », illustrant la variété de treize vers (4 + 4 + 5)[18]. Il convient de remarquer que Paul Gaudin donnait également un autre exemple de rondeau simple, mais déployé sur 12 vers seulement, d'Octovien de Saint-Gelais (« Pour reverdir je l'ay plantée »), dans lequel la reprise tant médiane que finale est limitée au premier vers du refrain (8 Abba abA abbaA)[19], ce qui est précisément la forme de base retenue par Corbière, jusque dans la distribution du genre des rimes. Il semble toutefois beaucoup plus probable, comme le pense J. M. Cocking[20], que ce soit la publication chez Alphonse Lemerre en 1874 d'une nouvelle édition des poésies de Charles d'Orléans qui a déterminé ce changement, son éditeur, Charles d'Héricault, qui revient cette fois directement au manuscrit autographe de Charles d'Orléans, adoptant systématiquement le format triparti de 13 vers[21]. En effet, gommant toute référence à l'édition Guichard (mais sans modifier pour le reste son texte), Banville renvoie cette fois à celles de Champollion-Figeac et Héricault dont le texte au demeurant diffère entre eux autant que de celui de Guichard, chacun s'étant basé sur un manuscrit différent[22]. Selon Henri Morier, cette modification formelle confère à la pièce « une nuance d'une finesse exquise[23] » :

> À la fin de la seconde strophe, le refrain complet, constitué de deux vers, s'est fait deux fois entendre. On l'a déjà dans l'oreille. Or, à la fin du rondel, il fait mine de réapparaître : l'entendrons-nous en entier ? Ne suffit-il pas d'une indication ? La syntaxe doit permettre de relire seul le premier vers du refrain ; à lui seul, il doit recréer l'ambiance ; il sera d'autant plus suggestif que le second vers chantera dans la mémoire.

Empruntée à Héricault, cette refonte du parangon banvillien caractérisée par l'asymétrie des répliques connaîtra une bien meilleure fortune

---

18 8 ABba abAB abbaA ; op. cit., p. 13-14. À noter que le premier tome de l'anthologie dirigée par E. Crépet, paru en 1861 (Les Poëtes français, t. I, p. 416-417), donne à ce poème un vers de moins (4 + 3 + 5)

19 Op. cit., p. 23.

20 Selon Cocking, « The 'invention' of the rondel », p. 54, c'est à l'occasion de cette parution qu'il aurait compris son erreur d'avoir donné 14 vers au poème de Charles d'Orléans.

21 Éd. Héricault, t. II, p. 115. Il transcrit en effet correctement *soleil luyant*, là où Guichard donne *souleil luisant*.

22 Héricault utilise O ; Guichard, O² ; Champollion-Figeac, le manuscrit de Grenoble.

23 Morier, *Dictionnaire de poétique*, p. 1050. Toute la démonstration du poéticien est à relire.

que son essai de 1858 – théorisé en 1872 –, qui semble n'avoir guère eu d'écho en dehors d'un poème que Glatigny publiait deux ans plus tard dans *Les Vignes folles*, recueil précisément dédié à son « cher et bien-aimé maître Théodore de Banville[24] ». Aussitôt promue dans sa réédition du *Petit traité*, la nouvelle forme de 13 vers trouve en effet à s'illustrer par divers poètes de 1880 à 1885 : Robert Caze, Jules Lemaître et Georges Nardin en 1880, Narzale Jobert en 1881, Georges Leygues en 1882, Maurice Rollinat en 1882 et 1883, Emile Maze en 1885[25]. Le rondel des *Amours jaunes* tourne quant à lui le dos aux deux voies ouvertes par Banville, Corbière recourant à un simple refrain d'un seul vers.

---

24 Glatigny, *Les Vignes folles*, p. 27-28 ; titré *Rondel*, son poème est un hommage à « Mademoiselle Valentine » : « Le rondeau, le sonnet galant, / Semblent croître sous sa bottine ». La première rime est féminine, la seconde, masculine. Le poème sera réédité dans le recueil *Poésies* de 1870 (achevé d'imprimé du 30 octobre 1869).

25 On trouvera leurs recueils numérisés sur le site de Gallica.

LE REGARD DU COMTE DE GRAMONT

Trois ans après *Les Amours jaunes*, la forme de 12 vers sera reconnue comme l'aboutissement du genre par le comte de Gramont[1]. Formé en marge du romantisme dans les années 1830, ce poète s'est notamment illustré par la reprise de formes anciennes, associant volontiers le pastiche linguistique à sa pratique du rondeau à rentrements et de la ballade. Cultivant volontiers le genre difficile de la sextine qu'il renouvelle par l'introduction de la rime, sonnettiste convaincu ouvrant à l'occasion le genre à des thèmes d'actualité, le comte de Gramont est aussi un théoricien averti. Il a plus particulièrement publié, en 1876 – selon les indications de la *BnF* –, un traité de versification qui fait nettement concurrence à celui de Banville puisqu'il paraît dans la « Bibliothèque d'éducation et de récréation » de l'éditeur Hetzel quand Banville publiait d'abord son *Petit traité* dans *L'Écho de la Sorbonne,* « Moniteur de l'Enseignement secondaire des jeunes filles ». Si le *Petit traité* a rencontré le plus grand succès, cela tient bien davantage à l'aura de son auteur qu'à ses qualités propres, l'auteur s'y laissant volontiers aller à des facilités, pirouettes et naïvetés sans pouvoir rivaliser avec l'exposé savant, aussi sérieusement documenté qu'il était possible à l'époque, de Gramont qui ne fait référence au traité du poète parnassien que de façon allusive, lorsqu'il évoque, à propos du sonnet, « une opinion accréditée aujourd'hui », voulant qu'il n'y ait de forme régulière que celle, précisément, que promouvait Banville[2]. Du moins ne néglige-t-il pas le rôle du poète dans la réhabilitation du pantoum – reconnaissant au passage le rôle d'Asselineau –, le comptant au nombre de ces « très-rares adeptes parmi lesquels [il] est celui qui en a le mieux fait sentir la délicatesse et la valeur harmonique[3] ».

---

1 *Le vers français*, p. 273-274.
2 *Op. cit.*, p. 255.
3 *Op. cit.*, p. 313 ; sur Asselineau, voir aussi Billy, « *Harmonie du soir* », p. 81-82.

Sa présentation du genre prend un tour historique, comme chez Vapereau, avec toutefois des références différentes[4]. Déjà esquissée par Saint-Priest une trentaine d'années auparavant[5], l'interprétation structurale qu'il donne de la forme à 14 vers – que promouvait Banville en 1872 – est des plus originales, tout en se trouvant contredite par la disposition qu'il donne à l'exemple qu'il emprunte également à Charles d'Orléans (« Allez-vous en, allez, allez... »)[6] :

> Ce sont toujours maintenant deux quatrains sur deux rimes, l'une masculine l'autre féminine invariablement, ce qui est à noter, comme une preuve que ces petites pièces étaient bien en effet destinées à être chantées. Les deux quatrains sont à rimes embrassées, mais en ordre inverse, c'est-à-dire que si dans le premier, le premier et le quatrième vers sont sur la rime masculine, ils sont, dans le second, sur la rime féminine, et réciproquement. En dehors des deux quatrains se trouvent deux vers, un de chaque rime, lesquels commencent la pièce et y reviennent en refrain à la fin de chaque couplet.

Il dispose en fait son exemple comme Saint-Priest, en un huitain plus un sizain (soit ABbaabAB abbaAB) que son analyse divise en une alternance de distiques (le refrain) et de quatrains : AB baab AB abba AB, les formes canoniques du genre se transformant ainsi en une sorte de chanson alternant refrain et couplets, ouvrant ainsi une voie nouvelle qu'empruntera la poétesse Amélie Gex dans ses *Poésies* de 1879 d'où nous tirons l'exemple suivant, intitulé simplement « Rondel[7] » :

> Mon pauvre cœur laisse dormir ta peine,
> Ton grand amour il le faut oublier !
>
> A tous les vents, pourquoi le publier ?
> Pourquoi le dire aux bois, à la fontaine ?
> Pourquoi vouloir qu'au nom de Madeleine,
> L'écho du val puisse encor s'éveiller ?

---

4   Gramont évoque Froissart et Eustache Deschamps pour l'époque ancienne ; Vapereau, Machault.

5   *Cf.* p. 467-468. Le t. XXI paraît en 1846.

6   *Op. cit.*, p. 272-273. On remarquera que, comme Sainte-Beuve, il considère que l'alternance des masculines et des féminines était de rigueur, ignorant que la tradition ancienne du rondeau ne s'en est jamais souciée.

7   *Poésies*, p. 136. Elle en donne un autre p. 138. Elle distingue ainsi le *rondel* du *rondeau* dont elle donne quelques illustrations, dans tous les cas des rondeaux-cinquains à rentrements.

> Non, non ! Mon cœur, laisse dormir ta peine
> Ton grand amour il le faut oublier !…
>
> Ne sais-tu pas que toute plainte est vaine !
> Que de tes pleurs on pourrait te railler ;
> Ne sais-tu pas que le temps fait rouiller
> Tous les anneaux de la plus forte chaîne ?…
>
> Mon pauvre cœur, laisse dormir ta peine,
> Ton grand amour il le faut oublier !

Après avoir rappelé que la forme s'est régularisée chez Charles d'Orléans, Gramont nous explique que, libérée de la musique, « la modification s'accentue » chez Octovien de Saint-Gelais, le genre des rimes devenant – selon lui – indifférent[8] :

> il n'y a de répété que le premier vers seul et non plus les deux ; parfois même ce refrain ne se compose que des premiers mots de ce vers. Enfin la pièce est formellement divisée en trois parties, savoir deux quatrains à rimes embrassées et disposées de même, entre lesquels s'intercale un distique sur les deux rimes ; après ce distique et à la fin du second quatrain se trouve répété le premier vers de la pièce, lequel, loin de former un sens entier, est toujours lié intimement, dans ces répétitions, avec les vers qui le précèdent.

Suit l'exemple suivant, où l'on reconnaît très précisément la forme de base sous-jacente aux rondels de Corbière, si ce n'est que le mètre employé est le décasyllabe commun :

> De ce qui est au pouvoir de Fortune
> Nul ne se doit vanter ny tenir fort :
> Car ung jour sert de plaisir et confort,
> Et l'autre apres, de courroux et rancune.
>
> Aux ungs est bonne, aux autres importune,
> Estrange à tous, car nuls n'entent le sort
> De ce qui est au pouvoir de Fortune.
>
> Les ungs ont d'elle honneur, sçavoir, pecune ;
> Les autres n'ont que pitié et remort,
> Et povreté, qu'est pire que la mort.
> Est-il aucun qui soit seur soubz la lune
> De ce qui est au pouvoir de Fortune ?

---

8   *Op. cit.*, p. 273-274. Curieusement, il lie l'indifférence à l'alternance des genres de rimes à l'abandon de la musique, bien que la musique n'ait jamais imposé une telle règle.

Et le théoricien de commenter ainsi l'intérêt de ce nouveau dispositif, en faisant la transition avec le rondeau à rentrements :

> On voit que le vers répété ne figure plus là en qualité de motif donné, mais simplement comme un refrain, que l'art du poëte doit ramener naturellement, sans nulle contrainte, aux endroits voulus[9].

Mallarmé sera sensible aux vertus de cette forme. Si nous n'avons pu identifier la source de Gramont, nous ferons remarquer que, dans l'édition que donne Gellibert des Seguins de la biographie que Guillaume Colletet consacre à Saint-Gelais se voient cités quelques « rondels », soit en des formes à rentrements, soit avec le rappel du seul premier vers entier dans le format de 12 vers adopté par Gramont[10]. Quoi qu'il en soit, ce n'est qu'en 1876 que la forme dont s'inspirent les rondels de Corbière trouve sa pleine reconnaissance, soit quatre ans après la publication de *Gilles et Pasquins* où Albert Glatigny en donnait les premières illustrations modernes.

---

9   Il ajoute que l'effet est renforcé dans les formes à rentrements : « Le changement est encore mieux appréciable quand les premiers mots seulement du vers forment le refrain qui reste par suite hors de rime. »
10   *Vies d'Octovien*, p. 54-57, note (cinq cas).

L'INFLUENCE DE GLATIGNY

S'il avait imité le premier Banville dans sa jeunesse (il avait 22 ans à la parution de *Vignes folles*), en novembre 1867, à l'occasion d'une tournée qui l'avait conduit à Bayonne, Glatigny emprunta une autre voie dans une série de six pièces que le poète comédien publiera l'année même de la parution du *Petit traité de poésie française*, soit un an avant la parution des *Amours jaunes*, dans *Gilles et Pasquins*, sous le titre générique de *Rondels*[1]. Ce rapprochement, qui avait été fait par A. Chevrier, a depuis été approfondi par B. Houzé qui leur trouve de « nombreuses analogies[2] » : la limitation au seul vers initial dans la première reprise du refrain est en effet une caractéristique des rondels de Corbière (exception faite de *Petit mort pour rire* où la reprise est remplacée par un vers nouveau) comme de ceux de Glatigny, avec également − sauf altérations locales − des quatrains de rimes embrassées, la différence essentielle résidant dans la substitution par le poète des *Amours jaunes* du taratantara à l'octosyllabe de son probable modèle. Même les titres se font écho, *RONDELS POUR APRÈS* répondant, d'une certaine manière au simple *Rondels* de Glatigny. L'unité thématique qui parcourt la série des *Amours jaunes* ne se retrouve cependant pas dans celle de *Gilles et Pasquins* dont l'unité est toute circonstancielle. Et de fait, Corbière a tout à fait eu le temps de lire le recueil de Glatigny, même si sa parution prévue pour octobre 1870 avait été ajournée du fait des « événements qui ont précédé et suivi la chute de la Commune » : *La Renaissance littéraire et artistique* en donne ainsi un compte rendu dans sa livraison du 29 juin 1872[3],

---

1   *Gilles et Pasquins*, p. 14-18.
2   Chevrier, *Le Décasyllabe à césure médiane*, p. 308 ; Houzé, « Corbière lecteur de Verlaine ? », p. 304-307. La forme en est systématiquement 8 A*bba ab*A *abb*aA. Les cinq premiers sont respectivement intitulés *Pour la bonne Amie, Sur Thérèse, La Route à suivre, Les Moineaux, Dans la Coulisse* ; le dernier (« Vive la Muse et les rimeurs ! ») est un envoi à Valéry Vernier.
3   Apparemment sous la signature de Gustave Morel qui apparaît après la recension suivante des *Destins* de Sully Prudhomme (p. 79-80). Le préambule de l'auteur est daté du 15 juin 1871.

et l'on peut penser que Corbière aura écrit ses rondels dans l'intervalle précédant la mise au net de son recueil, ce qui aurait pu leur valoir sans doute, autant que leur caractère funéraire, d'en constituer la dernière section. Si l'on tient compte du fait que le sixième rondel de Glatigny se détache de la série en ce qu'il se définit comme « envoi », on constatera que les cinq *RONDELS POUR APRÈS* s'inscrivent dans le même calibre, et l'on peut peut-être se demander si le choix du taratantara (5 + 5) ne s'appuie pas d'une certaine manière sur ce nombre[4]. Autre différence d'avec son vraisemblable modèle, Corbière commence toujours sur une féminine, là où Glatigny commence uniformément sur une masculine (8 A*bb*a a*b*A a*bb*aA).

Pour être un poète volontiers ironique, amateur de burlesque, Glatigny n'a pas l'amertume de Corbière ni son style échevelé, mais B. Houzé n'en relève pas moins des analogies frappantes. C'est ainsi que son « envoi » à Valéry Vernier évoque les poètes comme « les gentils écumeurs / De lys, d'étoiles, de feuillages » et que deux autres pièces du recueil recourent à l'expression rare de « ferreurs de cigales[5] ». Cette piste s'avère plus fructueuse encore si l'on se reporte aux textes, puisque Glatigny applique l'expression figurée aux poètes. Si, dans *La Presse nouvelle*, il évoque en heptasyllabes « Le gai ferreur de cigales / Battant sous les astragales / Du pampre aux coteaux d'Aï, / Une folle pretantaine[6] », dans *Carte de visite* qui daterait de 1866[7], l'expression évoque la vie fantaisiste du poète en des quatrains utilisant, comme les rondels de Corbière, le taratantara, qui rappellent parfois singulièrement les vers de Tristan. Voici pour commencer le deuxième et le troisième quatrain de la première partie :

> Les heures passaient, folles, inégales,
> Mais sonnant la joie et chantant l'espoir.
> Étions-nous heureux, ferreurs de cigales,
> De vivre en plein jour les rêves du soir !

---

4 Houzé, « Corbière lecteur de Verlaine ? », p. 305, considère *Male-Fleurette* comme « partageant avec l'envoi de Glatigny d'être une défense et illustration de la poésie contre la "prose" (Glatigny) ou les "cucurbitacées" (Corbière) ».

5 Houzé, *loc. cit.*, p. 306-307.

6 *Gilles et Pasquins*, p. 153. Le poème paraît la même année à part, chez le même Lemerre, dans une plaquette de douze pages.

7 *Op. cit.*, p. 121-125.

O jours bourdonnants tout remplis d'abeilles
Comme l'air flambait! Comme l'horizon
Foisonnait de fleurs aux astres pareilles...
Et l'amour chantait si haut sa chanson!

Ce sont précisément ces vers que Jules Claretie choisira en évoquant la mort de Glatigny à 35 ans, quelque deux mois avant l'achevé d'imprimer des *Amours jaunes*[8], dans le cadre d'une conférence consacrée aux voyages de Molière, à propos de la vie misérable et exaltante du jeune comédien[9]. La quatrième partie du poème se termine sur ces vers où le poète évoque sa fin, thème précisément choisi par Corbière dans *Mirliton* :

Si! nous cueillerons encor des étoiles
Dans les vastes cieux frissonnants et clairs,
Nous verrons encor, terrible, sans voiles,
La grande Vénus aux yeux pleins d'éclairs!

On retrouve là le thème corbiérien du « beau décrocheur d'étoiles » sur lequel nous reviendrons. Le poète enchaîne avec les trois quatrains suivants qui concluent la cinquième et dernière partie du poème :

Donc, adieu, mon pauvre enterré! Sois sage,
Puisque la sagesse, à ce qu'il paraît,
Consiste à cloîtrer l'oiseau de passage
Qu'effrayait le vent froid de la forêt.

Pour moi, dont la peau tannée et roussie
Par tous les soleils ne redoute rien,
Je suis ma chimère et ma fantaisie,
Poëte lyrique et comédien!

Et quand j'atteindrai le bout de la voie,
Enivré d'espace et plein d'univers,
Je mourrai, le cœur débordant de joie,
Murmurant encore une fin de vers.

Naturellement, le poème de Corbière est d'une tout autre tonalité, plus sombre et mélancolique, mais l'idée est la même, avec cette conclusion si proche :

---

8   Le 16 avril 1873.
9   *La Renaissance littéraire et artistique*, II, n° 16 (24 mai 1873), p. 123.

> La Muse camarde ici posera,
> Sur ta bouche noire encore elle aura
> Ces rimes qui vont aux moelles des pâles...
> Dors d'amour ; méchant ferreur de cigales.

Ces éléments sont en tout cas suffisamment convergents pour nous faire accepter l'idée que Corbière a bien lu Glatigny, comme le suggère également la liberté dont il use avec la césure. Lorsqu'en Italie, il se fait imprimer une carte de visite au nom de « Mazzzeppa Corbière[10] » où son identification à ce personnage fait clairement allusion au Mazeppa des *Orientales* dont il cite la chute (« Il court, il vole, il tombe et se relève roi ! »), il connaissait peut-être déjà *La Course* que Glatigny avait publié dans *Les Vignes folles* en 1860 et redonnera en 1870 dans la réédition de ses premiers recueils, où l'on trouve ce portrait du poète en héros masochiste[11] :

> J'appartiens à jamais au farouche Idéal
> De la Beauté physique et de l'Amour sans bornes,
> Et je vais, sur le monstre au vol lourd et brutal,
> A travers les Édens et les horizons mornes.
>
> Je sais bien que la mort est au bout du chemin,
> Qu'il me faudra cracher mes poumons, que l'espace
> S'écroule, que je n'ai bientôt plus rien d'humain,
> Et que l'herbe se fane aux endroits où je passe.
>
> Mais qu'importe ? je vais, et toujours dans ma chair
> Chaque lien imprime une rouge morsure ;
> Qu'importe ? laissez-moi, mon supplice m'est cher,
> J'aime à sentir le froid aigu de la blessure ! [...]

En écrivant son poème, Glatigny ne devait pas quant à lui avoir oublié ces vers que Vacquerie adressait un quart de siècle plus tôt à Louis Bouilhet en usant de la métaphore pour évoquer le sens critique de l'artiste et son indépendance[12], sens dont Corbière, n'était pas dépourvu :

---

10   Voir Bernardelli, p. 58, n. 37 ; Walzer, éd. citée, p. 689-690.
11   *Les Vignes folles*, p. 129-132 ; *Poésies*, même pagination.
12   *Demi-teintes*, p. 33-34 (IX). Bouilhet n'avait pas encore publié de recueils à cette époque, mais Louise Colet, *Ce qu'on rêve en aimant*, p. 42, lui fera dire, en 1854 : « Le vrai poëte, / Prêtre austère, fier prophète, / N'aime que le Dieu qu'il sert ; / Et, dédaigneux de la gloire, / Monte sur sa tour d'ivoire, / Et chante dans le désert ! »

Que t'importe ? — Pour toi, rare et sévère artiste,
Qui loges dans ton œuvre, et, comme l'alchimiste,
Vis éternellement penché sur ton charbon,
Le journal t'est égal et le doute t'est bon !
L'alchimiste, de qui le feu brûle la bouche,
Sent-il à ses talons l'ordure d'une mouche ?
Comment t'enquerrais-tu des journaux ? — Et pourquoi ?
Ah ! le meilleur de tous tes critiques, c'est toi !
Ton doute, lorsqu'il entre avec sa face blême,
Et réclame, et querelle, et sur Mazeppa même
Se jette, et se fait loup aux jambes du cheval,
Hurle tout aussi bien que le plus grand journal !

La métaphore « ferreur de cigales » nous renvoye, d'une certaine façon, à la cigale des parodies de la fable de La Fontaine qui clôturent le recueil des *Amours jaunes* en l'ouvrant et le fermant, bien qu'il ne s'agît plus ici de la Cigale métaphorique de La Fontaine mais bien du genre entomologique, la métaphore se déplaçant sur *ferreur*. Ce changement notable est l'indice d'un renouveau de l'inspiration de Corbière que la critique n'a pas manqué d'observer dans la tonalité de la dernière section des *Amours jaunes* que l'on peut maintenant dater approximativement en la situant dans la dernière phase de la création poétique du poète « au cœur vêtu de jaune ».

Mais si Corbière tient bien son modèle de Glatigny, à qui ce dernier a-t-il emprunté ce format de douze vers si marginal dans la restitution des rondels-quatrains du moyen-âge ? Son biographe Job-Lazare nous apprend qu'en janvier 1868, soit quelques mois après avoir écrit sa série de rondels, de nouveau à Bayonne, le poète projetait avec lui de créer un journal littéraire – ce sera *Le Falot cosmopolite* dont ne paraîtront que onze numéros durant l'été 1868[13]. Le 12 juillet, il lui envoyait le début d'un pastiche du *Testament* de Villon, dédié à Charles Monselet[14]. Une question se pose ici : dans quelle édition Glatigny a-t-il lu Villon dont, toujours selon Job-Lazare, « il a contribué dans une large proportion à remettre à la mode les tournures élégantes et les mesures sonores[15] » ? Villon ne nous a certes laissé que deux ou trois rondeaux que la tradition

---

13 *Glatigny, sa vie, son œuvre*, p. 71-74.
14 *Op. cit.*, p. 75-84. Pour des précisions sur ce poème, absentes de la biographie de Job-Lazare, voir Roussel, « Lettres de Glatigny », p. 20-21.
15 *Op. cit.*, p. 145.

présente avec des rentrements, mais la biographie, parue en 1859, que lui consacre Antoine Campaux contient un long appendice sur l'« école de Villon » contenant quinze rondeaux-quatrains – dont quatorze d'octosyllabes – tirés du *Jardin de Plaisance et Fleur de Rethoricque* au travers des transcriptions qu'en avait données Lenglet Dufresnoy dans une étude inédite[16], dont pas moins de douze sont présentés dans un format de douze vers distribués en deux ou trois parties, cinq étant coupées 7 + 5, sept, 4 + 3 + 5[17]. On peut penser que, lorsqu'il écrivit son premier rondel sur un format de quatorze vers, publié l'année suivante dans *Les Vignes folles*, Glatigny n'avait sans doute pas encore lu ce livre (si tant est qu'il le lût jamais), ou du moins qu'il n'avait pas encore compris le parti qu'il pourrait tirer du format court. Cette disposition se retrouvera par contre en 1867 dans la seconde édition des *Œuvres complètes* de Villon préparée par Bernard de La Monnoye et mise à jour par Pierre Jannet, qui intègre certaines des pièces que Campaux attribue à son « école[18] ». Le poète, à même de pasticher brillamment le *Testament*, pouvait naturellement se désintéresser de cette nouvelle édition d'une œuvre qui lui était si familière, mais le fait que les rondels de *Gilles et Pasquins* sont datés de novembre 1867, l'année même où paraît le livre de Jannet, montre qu'il a pu la consulter, car l'ouvrage est annoncé comme étant en vente dans le numéro du 15 avril de *L'Illustrateur de l'exposition universelle* qui eût lieu cette année-là.

---

16   Campaux a en effet utilisé l'édition – conservée à la Bibliothèque de l'Arsenal – que cet érudit du XVIIIe siècle avait consacrée à Villon, retenant 39 pièces du *Jardin de Plaisance* des 45 qu'elle contient.

17   *Op. cit.*, p. 336-356 ; les trois autres, p. 337-338, 341 (n.) et 349 sont présentés comme des rondeaux à rentrements. Dans *Le Jardin de Plaisance*, les reprises sont presque toujours signalées par la simple amorce des premiers mots.

18   *Œuvres complètes*, p. 133-149. Jannet reprend six rondeaux-quatrains dont cinq ont le format glatinien (pièces I, VII, VIII, XI et XV), un seul se présentant avec des rentrements (XII). Lemerre récupérera les invendus qu'il donnera comme « troisième édition » en 1873, trois ans après la mort de Jannet.

UNE INFLUENCE DE LOUIS BOUILHET ?

On peut s'interroger sur l'origine de l'une des plus belles images de *RONDELS POUR APRÈS*, « décrocheur d'étoiles », dans *Sonnet posthume*, thème qui réapparaît avec le « voleur d'étincelles » du premier rondel, puis, sous la forme d'une variante, dans *Petit mort pour rire*, avec le « léger peigneur de comètes », expressions qui désignent métaphoriquement l'activité du poète comme tout aussi inutile et impossible que celle du « méchant ferreur de cigales » de *Mirliton*. B. Houzé voit dans un poème de Banville, *La Sainte Bohême* (et l'on se souvient que « la male-fleur » est « la fleur de bohème »), la source du « décrocheur d'étoiles[1] » :

> Si nous manquons de pierreries
> Pour parer de flammes fleuries
> Ces flots couleur d'or et de miel,
> Nous irons, voyageurs étranges,
> Jusque sous les talons des anges
> Décrocher les astres du ciel !

Toutefois, ce n'est pas, comme Banville, pour orner les tresses de ses amoureuses que Corbière envisage de décrocher les étoiles, mais il convoque l'image entre l'évocation de l'amoureuse lointaine et celle du baiser qui l'attend sous le voile, sa quête prenant une allure d'absolu :

> *Dors : on t'appellera beau décrocheur d'étoiles !*
> *Chevaucheur de rayons !... quand il fera bien noir ;*
> *Et l'ange du plafond, maigre araignée, au soir,*
> *– Espoir – sur ton front vide ira filer ses toiles.*

La Sainte Bohême, pièce insérée dans la deuxième édition d'*Odes funambulesques* (1859), était beaucoup plus optimiste que les pièces de

---

1   Voir Houzé et Hérisson, *op. cit.*, p. 147.

RONDELS POUR APRÈS. Le poète y est conquérant et triomphant, ne craignant ni Dieu ni la mort par laquelle il irriguera la vie :

> Nous mourrons ! mais, ô souveraine !
> O mère ! ô nature sereine !
> Que glorifiaient tous nos sens,
> Tu prendras nos cendres inertes
> Pour en faire des forêts vertes
> Et des bouquets resplendissants !

Si l'expression semble bien dérivée de celle de Banville, on peut trouver chez Louis Bouilhet, « poète curieux seulement de métaphores, de comparaisons, d'images » selon G. Flaubert[2], une possible source d'inspiration complémentaire. Sous-titré « Légende », *Le Poëte aux étoiles*, publié dans *Festons et astragales* la même année que la deuxième édition d'*Odes funambulesques*, raconte comment, rejeté des « bourgeois honnêtes » – et l'on se souvient des « bêtes bourgeois » de *Petit mort pour rire* comme des « Cucurbitacés » de *Male-Fleurette* –, le poète se retire, « Prêt pour la dernière épreuve, / Loin du monde » pour chanter une dernière fois « les longs tourments / De l'amour et de la gloire » jusqu'à faire « tressaillir l'eau noire » du fleuve au bord duquel il s'est installé[3] :

> Soudain, par l'ordre d'un Dieu,
> Les étoiles attendries
> S'arrêtèrent, au milieu
> De leurs blanches théories…
>
> Puis il les vit sans effort
> Glissant des voûtes profondes,
> Comme de grands sequins d'or,
> Trembler, dans l'eau, toutes rondes.
>
> Il y plonge, il veut savoir…
> O prodige !… il en prend une,
> Puis deux, puis quatre… et bonsoir
> Les soucis de l'infortune !

Il revient alors « tout radieux / Vers les villes où nous sommes » pour tenter de monnayer ses étoiles :

---

2   Dans sa préface à Bouilhet, *Dernières chansons*, p. 12.
3   Bouilhet, *Festons et astragales*, p. 213-217.

> Son frac noir, aujourd'hui roux,
> Fort peu payé, sans reproches,
> Semblait, à travers les trous,
> Porter le ciel dans ses poches.

Mais auprès du boulanger, du tavernier, du marchand de toiles et des savants de l'Institut, à travers lesquels on peut reconnaître les « gens très-sensés » de *Male-Fleurette*, il n'essuie que refus, si bien que :

> Il mourut, le lendemain,
> Aiglon né chez les reptiles,
> Maigre et serrant dans sa main
> Ses étoiles inutiles !…

Le narrateur raconte alors comment le hasard l'amena à croiser le convoi funèbre, suscitant sa compassion, avec la même anaphore qui traverse *RONDELS POUR APRÈS*, de *Sonnet posthume* à *Mirliton* :

> Dors, poëte, on frappe en vain
> A nos tavernes immondes ;
> Dors, ô mendiant divin
> Qui payais avec des mondes !
>
> Quelque jour, les fossoyeurs
> Verront, tombant en prière,
> Des soleils intérieurs
> Luire aux fentes de ta bière,
>
> Et, sous leur pic effaré,
> Brisant la planche sonore,
> Feront du tombeau sacré
> Jaillir une grande aurore !

Dans *Petit mort pour rire*, Corbière ne donne pas même cet espoir à ses fossoyeurs blasés qui ne voient plus qu'un mort, mais l'œuvre du poète lui survit également, comme si sa mort était nécessaire à son épanouissement :

> *Ne fais pas le lourd : cercueils de poètes*
> *Pour les croque-morts sont de simples jeux,*
> *Boîtes à violon qui sonnent le creux…*
> *Ils te croiront mort – Les bourgeois sont bêtes –*
> *Va vite, léger peigneur de comètes !*

Nous avons montré que *Le Crapaud* de Corbière était vraisembla-blement redevable de celui de Bouilhet, tiré du même recueil, *Festons et astragales*, que Corbière aurait pu trouver dans la bibliothèque de son père.

CONCLUSION

L'histoire du rondel qui trouve un certain regain d'intérêt dans la seconde moitié du XIXᵉ siècle met en évidence la dette de Corbière à l'égard de Glatigny auquel par ailleurs il reprend des expressions significatives. Il tourne ainsi le dos aux deux formes de quatorze puis treize vers successivement promues par Banville, la première fois en 1872 dans son *Petit traité* que notre poète, vraisemblablement, ignorait, avant de changer d'avis dans sa réédition quelques années plus tard chez Charpentier. La forme plus courte et moins pesante, limitée à douze vers, qu'il emprunte au poète de *Gilles et Pasquins* lui offrait des ressources esthétiques particulières qui se verront bientôt mises en évidence par le Comte de Gramont. Ceci étant, Corbière ne cherche pas plus ici que pour le sonnet à s'astreindre à un respect scrupuleux de cette forme à laquelle il apporte quelques variations mineures.

CONCLUSION GÉNÉRALE

[…] grimper au Pinde […]
C'est une chance peu commune.
Et qui montre que la fortune
Jette bien ses dons sans viser.
L. VEUILLOT, *Les Couleuvres*, p. 73.

On ne peut qu'être frappé des différences stylistiques qui opposent l'écriture tourmentée et les ambiguïtés de ses vers à l'aisance et l'intelligibilité de sa prose : elles sont à la fois révélatrices d'une certaine difficulté à se soumettre au carcan du mètre et un changement radical de positionnement auctorial avec l'endossement d'un rôle spécifique qui l'affranchit d'une certaine manière de son être social : le jeune homme Édouard-Joachim s'efface devant le poète dans une émancipation que vient consacrer l'adoption de son nom de plume qui doit moins au fond légendaire de la littérature française qu'à Murger. Comme l'a bien noté M. Lindsay, au moins pour l'essentiel, les libertés qu'il prend avec la versification traditionnelle n'ont rien de révolutionnaire et ne remettent pas fondamentalement en cause l'alexandrin auquel il donne une nouvelle organisation interne, plus expressive[1]. On peut élargir cette analyse à la versification traditionnelle dans son ensemble, dans les aspects prosodiques qui la caractérisaient alors. On ne peut ainsi que lui donner raison pour cette partie de sa conclusion[2] :

> Le désordre était en fait une part de sa personnalité, et cela a déterminé son approche de la poésie. Les libertés particulières qu'il prenait avec les règles

---

1   « The versification », p. 367.
2   Art. cité, p. 368 : « *Yet disorder was part of his personality, and it determined his approach to poetry. The particular liberties he took with traditional rules were characteristic of his inability to adjust rather than of an open and planned rebellion against the tyranny of prosodists.* »

traditionnelles étaient caractéristiques de son inaptitude à s'adapter plutôt que d'une révolte ouverte et planifiée contre la tyrannie des prosodistes.

Mais il faut également prendre en compte sa pratique avant-gardiste de la césure et le caractère parodique de son traitement de la diérèse et du « nombre de la rime » pour prendre la pleine mesure de sa posture de poète antiromantique, et l'on peut rappeler ici ces mots si justes de Burch[3] au terme de sa discussion des conclusions de Lindsay :

> S'il s'est départi des canons établis, c'est pour parvenir à plus de vérité. [...] Le véritable nœud de la révolte du poète a été son refus de se soumettre aux inévitables restrictions qu'exige toute adhésion à une tradition ; le désir de renverser les barrières établies par des écoles déterminées ; le besoin de disposer d'une gamme étendue de sujets, de thèmes, de vocabulaire, de rythmes et d'images.

En publiant *Les Amours jaunes*, Corbière entend bien s'aventurer sur la mer des poètes, mais il le fait *en corsairien*, sans trop y croire, et son poème conclusif, non dépourvu de visée démonstrative par son clin d'œil au lecteur, le dit bien, évoquant « [s]on honteux monstre de livre », idée développée dans l'envoi qu'il ajoute à la main sur son exemplaire personnel où il se traite même d' « [é]*crivain public banal / Qui pouvait si bien le dire... / Et, si bien ne pas l'écrire !* », suggérant d'une part qu'il n'a pas su si bien le dire, d'autre part que sa poésie était davantage faite pour être dite que pour être lue bien qu'il visât clairement la publication comme le disent plus particulièrement les poèmes introductif et conclusif. Toute son attention concentrée vers son cap (imprimer), le poète ne fait pas attention aux détails : orthographe et typographie sont victimes d'une "cécité d'inattention", indisposant le lecteur de bonne volonté, là où un auditeur aurait eu un accès direct à la poésie de Corbière : la satisfaction de Corbière à se voir « IMPRIMÉ » l'a en effet rendu définitivement aveugle sur les innombrables bévues de l'impression au point qu'aucune ne se trouve signalée sur son exemplaire personnel pourtant abondamment annoté et complété en marge dans les mois qui suivirent sa publication[4]. Son *errata*, qui ne comporte que deux *items*, témoigne clairement de ses priorités qui vont à la juste mesure des vers, fût-ce au détriment de la

---

3   *Tristan Corbière*, p. 96.
4   Sur ledit exemplaire, voir Bernardelli, « Il testo contumace », p. 43, et Levi, « New lights ». Sur cette cécité de l'auteur, voir les remarques judicieuses de Bernardelli, *ibid.*, p. 45-46. L'exemple rapporté sans indication est tiré de *La Chute d'un ange* (*Deuxième vision*).

syntaxe. Dans la conception de son recueil, l'ambition de Corbière est simple car elle rejoint celle de tous les poètes. Sa détestation même de Lamartine l'a empêché d'avouer son ambition à la façon d'un Alfred Gabrié, qui, déclare, dans un hommage à l'auteur de *Jocelyn*[5] :

> Oh ! je voudrais chanter, poète, comme toi ;
> Je voudrais, m'éloignant de la commune loi,
> M'élever jusqu'aux cieux sur l'aile de la gloire,
> Et, nouveau favori des Filles de Mémoire,
> Comme toi buriner mon nom dans leur palais !

À côté de ce désir profond de se voir *imprimé*, il y a chez Corbière l'ambition de se confronter à ses anti-modèles, en particulier à Lamartine avec lequel il partage certaines singularités, comme le penchant occasionnel pour les rimes approximatives ou la confrontation aux « rimes du singulier et du pluriel », ou encore la féminisation de *pleurs* lorsqu'il évoque la rosée du matin : « La rosée aura des pleurs matinales », en rime avec *cigales* (*Mirliton*, 5), singularité de la langue poétique que relevait Bescherelle (*DN* II, 911) en commentant :

> Jean-Jacques Rousseau a fait ce mot féminin. […] Lamartine en a fait tout autant, mais ce sont là des licences qu'il faut éviter avec soin.

On peut du reste se souvenir de l'avertissement donné par Lamartine en tête de la première édition de *La Chute d'un ange* qui n'est pas sans échos chez Corbière dont l'excès est la nature même :

> Je sais qu'on me reproche avec une bienveillante colère de ne pas consacrer ma vie entière à écrire, et surtout à polir des vers, dont je n'ai jamais fait ni prétendu faire qu'une consolation rare et accidentelle de ma pensée. Je n'ai rien à répondre, si ce n'est que chacun a reçu sa mission de sa nature.

Mais Corbière s'inscrit d'emblée dans une position antiromantique qui se manifeste avant tout par la dimension satirique de ces *Amours*, jaunes de rire jaune, justifiant d'emblée, par son recours au style bas, le relâchement de sa versification, avec notamment son lot de rimes pauvres et le bousculement occasionnel du rythme, voire, de la structure de l'alexandrin. Les fantaisies du poète visant à respecter la règle du nombre de la rime

---

5   Duportal, *Le Parnasse français contemporain*, p. 31.

ont dû passer pour de pitoyables ruses d'amateur, au détriment de leur intention ironique. Ses synérèses fautives n'auront pas manqué d'être perçues comme les témoins d'un manque d'expérience ou de maturité technique sinon de négligence, tandis que ses diérèses outrancières ajoutaient à ce sentiment les désagréments de la cacophonie : les provocations du poète ne pouvaient qu'atteindre leur but et susciter les conditions d'une nouvelle écoute qui, dépassant la question des conventions poétiques et celle de la correction linguistique et typographique, pourrait accueillir favorablement ce renouvellement radical de l'expression poétique en donnant tout son sens, comme l'a bien vu B. Houzé, à cet « idiome inouï » qu'évoquait Murger, « argot intelligent quoique inintelligible pour tous ceux qui n'en ont pas la clef, et dont l'audace dépasse celle des langues les plus libres[6] ». B. Houzé a eu la bonne fortune d'exhumer le premier compte rendu des *Amours jaunes* dont l'auteur, non identifié, s'inscrit justement dans cette nouvelle génération de lecteurs, affirmant[7] :

> En ouvrant au hasard ce volume de vers, la première impression que l'on éprouve est l'étonnement, pour ne pas dire la stupéfaction. Depuis les beaux jours de l'époque romantique, nos poètes en vogue nous ont plutôt habitués aux mièvreries académiques qu'à cette robu[s]tesse d'idées et à cette vigueur de forme dont toute la pléiade de 1830 a donné l'exemple. Je sais bien que les sentiers battus sont les plus sûrs à suivre, et que trop souvent il ne suffit pas d'être excentrique pour être original. Malgré cela, je considère comme un progrès toute révolte, même avortée, de nos jeunes poètes contre certains potentats du vers qui tendent à convertir le Parnasse en officine à mirlitons.

Quoi qu'il en soit de son assujettissement aux modèles romantiques, et mis de côté les ouvertures du poète sur un imaginaire qui lui est propre, nourri de son expérience de l'univers maritime, de ses voyages et de son séjour parisien, on ne peut plus prétendre que Corbière ignorait la poésie de son temps. Sa connaissance de l'œuvre de Banville, vraisemblablement au moins *Les Exilés* de 1867, transparaît ainsi au travers de l'expérience de rythmes syncopés dans l'album Noir. La connaissance de la seconde édition du *Parnassiculet* apparaît au travers du dispositif ornemental de son recueil, et l'influence de Glatigny apparaît aussi bien au travers d'expressions significatives de *RONDELS POUR APRÈS* que,

---

6   *Scènes de la vie de Bohême*, 4ᵉ éd., p. XIII-XIV. Houzé et Hérisson, *op. cit.*, p. 69.
7   Cité par Houzé, « Un compte rendu inconnu », p. 223 ; paru dans *La Bibliographie contemporaine*, année 1873 (1ᵉʳ octobre), p. 140-141.

peut-être, à travers sa technique de l'alexandrin. On peut également se demander dans quelle mesure le poète n'a pas été influencé par Louis Bouilhet – qui n'est certainement pas le premier poète auquel on songerait pour une influence quelconque sur l'auteur des *Amours jaunes* – dans *Le Crapaud* et les deux derniers poèmes de *RONDELS POUR APRÈS*. Sa fréquentation du comte de Battine et de la bohême parisienne a pu lui donner de nombreuses opportunités pour découvrir des auteurs et des œuvres dont il ignorait sans doute tout jusqu'alors.

L'auteur des *Amours jaunes* aura comblé les attentes du critique de *La Bibliographie contemporaine*, mettant à mal la vieillerie poétique avec des moyens nouveaux qui relèvent plus de la subversion que de la révolution : n'hésitant pas à tourner en dérision les conventions poétiques, il reste dans les limites du syllabisme et de la rime que les poètes symbolistes remettront en cause, même s'il devance Verlaine dans sa manière de s'abandonner ponctuellement à une forme restructurée de l'alexandrin dont l'articulation métrique se déplace alors de deux syllabes vers l'avant. Conscient de ce qui était pour lui un handicap, Corbière ne pensait certainement à « percer le plafond de verre », et, deux ans après la parution de son recueil, il aurait pu opportunément méditer la supplique que son père adressa au secrétaire du Ministre de la marine alors que lui-même n'avait que quelques ans[8] :

> Poëte ou marin, chaque jour,
> D'une main tenant ma supplique,
> De l'autre un poëme comique,
> Je cours implorer tour à tour
> Votre patron qui m'expédie,
> Et le vieux roquet de Thalie,
> Qui garde en jappant l'Odéon.
> Mais, fils réprouvé de Neptune
> Sans être adopté d'Apollon,
> Partout on ferme à mon seul nom
> Et le chemin de la fortune
> Et celui du sacré vallon.
> Daignez au moins, pour que je sorte
> D'un doute pour moi trop fatal,
> Si vous me fermez votre porte,
> M'ouvrir celle de l'hôpital.

---

8   *Brésiliennes*, p. 104-105.

BIBLIOGRAPHIE

OUVRAGES DE RÉFÉRENCE

BESCHERELLE, Louis-Nicolas, *Dictionnaire national ou Dictionnaire universel de la langue française*, 14ᵉ éd., 2 vol., Paris, Garnier frères, 1871.

CARPENTIER, L. J. M., *Gradus français, ou dictionnaire de la langue poétique*, Paris, Alexandre Johanneau, 1822.

CATACH, Nina, *Dictionnaire historique de l'orthographe française*, Paris, Larousse, 1995.

Dictionnaire de l'Académie Française, 7ᵉ éd., 2 vol., Paris, Firmin-Didot, 1878.

DIDEROT, Denis, D'ALEMBERT, Jean Le Rond (dir.), *Encyclopédie ou Dictionnaire raisonné des sciences, des arts et des métiers*, 17 vol., 1751-1765.

GODEFROY, Frédéric, *Dictionnaire de l'ancienne langue française et de tous ses dialectes du IXᵉ au XVᵉ siècle*, Paris, 10 vol., 1881-1902.

GREVISSE, Maurice, *Le Bon Usage*, 11ᵉ éd., Paris–Gembloux, Duculot, 1980.

LAROUSSE, Pierre, *Grand dictionnaire universel du XIXᵉ siècle*, 17 vol., Paris, Administration du Grand dictionnaire universel, 1866-1877.

LITTRÉ, Émile, *Dictionnaire de la langue française*, 4 vol., Paris, Hachette, 1873-1874.

MORIER, Henri, *Dictionnaire de poétique et de rhétorique*, 5ᵉ éd., Paris, PUF, 1998.

SAINT-PRIEST, Ange de, *Encyclopédie du dix-neuvième siècle : répertoire universel des sciences des lettres et des arts, avec la biographie et de nombreuses gravures*, 28 vol., Paris, 1838-1853 ; 3ᵉ éd. 1870-1872.

VAPEREAU, Gustave, *Dictionnaire universel des littératures*, Paris, Hachette, 1876.

VIRMAÎTRE, Charles, *Dictionnaire d'Argot fin-de-siècle*, Paris, A. Charles, 1894.

WARTBURG, Walther von *et al.*, *Französisches Etymologiches Wörterbuch*, 25 v., Bonn–Heidelberg–Leipzig–Berlin–Bâle, 1992-2002.

ŒUVRES CITÉES

AICARD, Jean, *Les Jeunes Croyances*, Paris, Lemerre, 1867.

AICARD, Jean, *Poëmes de Provence*, Paris, Lemerre, 1873.

AICARD, Jean, *Les Rébellions et les Apaisements*, Paris, Lemerre, 1871.

ALLONY, Ed. [E. de Lonlay], *Le Livre défendu*, Paris, E. Dentu, 1873.

BANVILLE, Théodore de, *Les Cariatides*, Paris, Pilout, 1842.

BANVILLE, Théodore de, *Les Exilés*, Paris, Lemerre, 1867.

BANVILLE, Théodore de, *Les Exilés. Les Princesses*, Paris, Lemerre, 1875.

BANVILLE, Théodore de, *Florise*, Paris, Lemerre, 1870.

BANVILLE, Théodore de, *Odes funambulesques*, 2ᵉ éd. Paris, Michel Lévy, 1859.

BANVILLE, Théodore de, *Œuvres complètes*, III : *Les Exilés. Odelettes, Améthystes, Rimes dorées, Rondels, Les Princesses, Trente-six ballades joyeuses*, Paris, Charpentier, 1878.

BANVILLE, Théodore de, *Les Poésies, 1841-1854*. Paris, Poulet-Malassis et de Broise, 1857.

BANVILLE, Théodore de, *Poésies. Occidentales, Rimes dorées, Rondels*, Paris, A. Lemerre, 1875.

BANVILLE, Théodore de, *Les Princesses*, Paris, Lemerre, 1874.

BAUDELAIRE, Charles, *Les Fleurs du Mal*, Paris, Poulet-Malassis et De Broise, 1857.

BAUDELAIRE, Charles, *Les Fleurs du Mal*, Paris, Poulet-Malassis et De Broise, 1861.

BAUDELAIRE, Charles, *Œuvres complètes*, t. I, *Les Fleurs du mal*, Paris, Michel Lévy frères, 1868.

BERGE, Hector, *Les Guirlandes. Poésies diverses*, Paris, C. Vanier, 1863.

BLANCHECOTTE, Mme A[ugustine-] M[alvina], *Les Militantes*, poésies, Paris, Lemerre, 1875.

BLANCHECOTTE, Mme [Augustine-Malvina], *Nouvelles poésies*, Paris, Perrotin, 1861.

BOREL, Pétrus, *Rhapsodies*, Paris, Levavasseur, 1832.

BOUILHET, Louis, *Dernières chansons. Poésies posthumes*, Paris, Michel Lévy, 1872.

BOUILHET, Louis, *Poésies. Festons et Astragales*, Paris, Librairie nouvelle, A. Bourdilliat & Cⁱᵉ, 1859.

BOULAY-PATY, Évariste, *Sonnets*, Paris, H. Féret, 1851.

BRASDOR, Jacques, *Le Far Niente. Rimes et chansons*, Paris, Impr. Émile Voitelain & Cⁱᵉ, 1869.

BRAZIER, Nicolas, CARMOUCHE, Pierre-Frédéric-Adolphe, *Oh ! qu'nenni, ou Le Mirliton fatal*, Paris, R. Riga, 1830.

BRIZEUX, Auguste, *Œuvres complètes*, éd. Saint René Taillandier, Paris, Michel Lévy Frères, 1860.

CARMOUCHE, Pierre-Frédéric-Adolphe, COURCY, Frédéric de, DUPEUTY, Charles, *N,i, Ni ou Le Danger des Castilles*, nouv. éd., Paris, Bezou, 1830.

CAZALIS, Édouard, *Melancholia*, Paris, A. Lemerre, 1868.

CHÂTILLON, Auguste, *A la Grand'Pinte. Poésies*, 2ᵉ éd. très-augmentée, Paris, Librairie du *Petit Journal*, 1860.

CHÂTILLON, Auguste, *Les Poésies*, 3ᵉ éd. très-augmentée, Paris, Librairie du *Petit Journal*, 1866.

COLET, Louise, *Ce qu'on rêve en aimant. Poésies nouvelles*, Paris, Librairie nouvelle, 1854.

COPPÉE, François, *Intimités*, Paris, A. Lemerre, 1868.

COPPÉE, François, *Poëmes modernes*, Paris, A. Lemerre, 1869.

COPPÉE, François, *Le Reliquaire*, Paris, A. Lemerre, 1866.

CORBIÈRE, Édouard, *Brésiliennes*. Seconde édition, augmentée de poésies nouvelles, Paris, Ponthieu, Aimé-André, Charles Béchet, 1825.

CORBIÈRE, Édouard, *Cric-crac*, roman maritime, 2 vol., Paris, Librairie spéciale pour les cabinets de lecture, 1846.

CORBIÈRE, Édouard, *Les Élégies brésiliennes*, suivies de *Poésies diverses* et d'une notice sur la traite des noirs, Paris, Brissot-Thivars, Plancher ; Rouen, Béchet ; Le Havre, Chapelle, 1823.

CORBIÈRE, Édouard, *Les Folles-brises*, roman maritime, 2 vol., Paris, Werdet, 1838.

CORBIÈRE, Édouard, *Les Îlots de Martin Vaz*, roman maritime, 2 vol., Paris, Berquet et Pétion, 1842-1843.

CORBIÈRE, Édouard, *Le Négrier*, 2ᵉ éd., 4 vol., Paris, A.-J. Dénain et Delamare, 1834.

CORBIÈRE, Édouard, *Le Négrier*, 4ᵉ éd. rev. sur un nouveau Manuscrit de l'Auteur, Le Havre, Brindeau & Cⁱᵉ, 1855.

CORBIÈRE, Édouard, *Tribord et bâbord*, roman maritime, 2 vol., Paris, Dumont, 1840.

CORBIÈRE, Édouard, *Les Trois pirates*, 2 vol., Paris, Werdet, 1838.

CORBIÈRE, Tristan, *Les Amours jaunes*, Paris, Glady frères, 1873.

CRÉPET, Eugène (dir.), *Les Poëtes français. Recueil des chefs-d'œuvre de la poésie française depuis les origines jusqu'à nos jours*, 4 vol., Paris, Gide, 1861-1863.

DARASSE, P., *Læta mœsta. Poésies*, Paris, Librairie du XIXᵉ siècle, 1873.

DELVAU, Alfred, *Le Grand et le Petit Trottoir*, Paris, A. Faure, 1866.

DES ESSARTS, Emmanuel, *Les Élévations*, Paris, Librairie du Petit journal, 1864.

DES ESSARTS, Emmanuel, *Le Retour d'un fumiste. Tragi-comédie*, Sens, Impr. Duchemin, 1863.

DIERX, Léon, *Les Lèvres closes*, Paris, Lemerre, 1867.

DIERX, Léon, *Poëmes et poésies*, Paris, E. Sausset, 1864.

DUPORTAL, Georges, *Le Parnasse français contemporain*, Marseille, Impr. typographique Clappier, 1869.

FRANCE, Anatole, *Les Poëmes dorés*, Paris, Lemerre, 1873.

FRANCE, Anatole, *Poésies : Poèmes dorés, Idylles et Légendes, Les Noces Corinthiennes*, Paris, Lemerre, 1896.

FRÉBAULT, Élie, *La Femme à barbe*, Paris, Librairie centrale, 1866.

GAUTIER, Théophile, *Poésies complètes*, 2 vol., Paris, Charpentier, 1875.

GEX, Amélie, *Poésies*, Chambéry, Impr. Ménard, 1879.

GLATIGNY, Albert, *Les Flèches d'or. Poësies*, Paris, Frédéric Henry, 1864.

GLATIGNY, Albert, *Gilles et Pasquins*, Paris, Lemerre, 1872.

GLATIGNY, Albert, *Poésies. Les Vignes folles – Les Flèches d'or – Le Bois*, Paris, Lemerre, 1870.

GLATIGNY, Albert, *Poésies complètes. Les Vignes folles – Les Flèches d'or – Gilles et Pasquins*, Paris, Lemerre, 1879.

GLATIGNY, Albert, *La Presse nouvelle*, Paris, Librairie nouvelle, 1872.

GLATIGNY, Albert, *Les Vignes folles. Poësies*, Paris, Librairie nouvelle, 1860.

HENNEQUIN, Alfred et SILVESTRE, Armand, *Aline*, pièce en un acte, en vers, Paris, Lemerre, 1873.

HERVILLY, Ernest d', *Les Baisers*, Paris, Lemerre, 1872.

HERVILLY, Ernest d', *La Lanterne en vers de couleur*, Paris, L'Éclipse, 1868.

HOUSSAYE, Arsène, *Les Courtisanes du monde*, Paris, Dentu, 1870.

HOUSSAYE, Arsène, *Œuvres poètiques. L'Amour – L'Art – La Nature*, Paris, Hachette, 1857.

HOUSSAYE, Arsène, *Les Poésies*, Paris, Dentu, 1877.

HOUSSAYE, Arsène, *Poésies complètes*, Paris, Charpentier, 1850.

HUGO, Victor, *L'Année terrible*, Paris, M. Lévy, 1872.

HUGO, Victor, *Les Châtiments*, Genève / New York, s.n., 1853.

HUGO, Victor, *Les Contemplations*, 2 vol., Paris, M. Lévy / Pagnerre, 1856.

HUGO, Victor, *Cromwell*, drame, Paris, M. Lévy, 1828.

HUGO, Victor, *Dieu*, Paris, J. Hetzel / A. Quantin, 1891.

HUGO, Victor, *La Légende des siècles*. P.s., 2 vol., Paris, M. Lévy / Hetzel & Cie, 1859.

HUGO, Victor, *La Légende des siècles*. Nouv. s., 2 vol., Paris, Calmann Lévy, 1877.

HUGO, Victor, *Marion de Lorme*, drame, Paris, E. Renduel, 1831.

HUGO, Victor, *Les Quatre Vents de l'Esprit*, 2 vol., Paris, J. Hetzel / A. Quantin, 1881.

HUGO, Victor, *Toute la lyre*, 2 vol., *Œuvres inédites*, Paris, G. Charpentier & Cie, 1889.

HUYSMANS, Joris-Karl, *À rebours*, Paris, Charpentier, 1884.

JACQUEMIN, Winoc, *Sonnets à Ninon. Chair – Lutte – Esprit*, Paris, Lemerre, 1867.

LACAUSSADE, Auguste, *Le Siège de Paris*, Paris, Lemerre, 1871.

LAFENESTRE, Georges, *Idylles et chansons (1864-1870)*, Paris, Lemerre, 1874.

LAFORGUE, Jules, *Œuvres complètes. Mélanges posthumes*, Paris, Mercure de France, 1903.

LAPRADE, Victor de, *Pernette*, 2ᵉ éd., Paris, Didier, 1869.

LAPRADE, Victor de, *Pernette*, éd. ill., Paris, Didier, 1870.

LAPRADE, Victor de, *Œuvres poétiques*, 6 vol., Paris, Lemerre, 1878-1881.

LAPRADE, Victor de, *Poèmes civiques*, 2ᵉ éd., Paris, Didier, 1873.

LAPRADE, Victor de, *Poèmes évangéliques*, 2ᵉ éd., Paris, Charpentier, 1853.

LATOUCHE, Henri de, *Adieux. Poésies*, Paris, Impr. de Lacour et Maistrasse, 1844.

LATOUCHE, Henri de, *Les Agrestes. Poésies*, Paris, Impr. Lange Lévy & Cⁱᵉ, 1845.

LAUZANNE, Auguste de, *Harnali, ou La contrainte par cor*, Paris, J.-N. Barba, 1838 [tiré à part de source non identifiée, p. 765-780].

LECONTE DE LISLE, Charles-Marie, *Poëmes barbares*, Paris, Lemerre, 1872.

LECONTE DE LISLE, Charles-Marie, *Poëmes tragiques*, Paris, Lemerre, 1884.

LECONTE DE LISLE, Charles-Marie, *Poésies antiques*, Paris, Ducloux, 1852.

LECONTE DE LISLE, Charles-Marie, *Poésies barbares*, Paris, Poulet-Malassis, 1862.

LECONTE DE LISLE, Charles-Marie, *Poésies complètes : Poèmes antiques, Poèmes et poésies, Poésies nouvelles*, Paris, Poulet-Malassis et De Broise, 1858.

LEVAVASSEUR, Gustave, PRAROND, Ernest et ARGONNE, A., *Vers*, Paris, Herman frères, 1843.

LONLAY, Eugène de, *Recueil complet de tous les genres de poésies françaises*, Paris, Alcan-Lévy, 1870.

LUZARCHE, Robert, *Les Excommuniés*, Paris, Lemerre, « 1862 » (corr. 1872).

MALLARMÉ, Stéphane, *Album de vers et de prose*, Bruxelles, Librairie nouvelle / Paris, Librairie universelle, 1887.

MALLARMÉ, Stéphane, *L'Après-midi d'un faune : églogue*, Paris, Alphonse Derenne, 1876.

MALLARMÉ, Stéphane, *Pages*, Bruxelles, E. Deman, 1891.

MANCY, [Jean-Baptiste] G[indre] de, *Les Échos du Jura*, Lons-le-Saunier, 1841.

MANUEL, Eugène, *Poëmes populaires*, Paris, M. Lévy, 1872.

MENDÈS, Catulle, *Contes épiques (1870)*, Paris, Librairie des Bibliophiles, 1872.

MENDÈS, Catulle, *Philoméla, livre lyrique*, Paris, J. Hetzel, 1863.

MENDÈS, Catulle, *Poésies*, Paris, Charpentier et Fasquelle, 3 vol., 1892.

MENDÈS, Catulle, *Les Poésies de Catulle Mendès*, Paris, Sandoz et Fischbacher, 1876.

MENDÈS, Catulle, *Théâtre en vers*, Paris, Bibliothèque-Charpentier, E. Fasquelle, 1908.

MÉRAT, Albert, *Les Chimères*, Paris, Achille Faure, 1866.

MÉRAT, Albert, *L'Idole*, Paris, Lemerre, 1869.

MÉRAT, Albert, *Les Souvenirs*, Paris, Lemerre, 1872.

MÉRAT, Albert, *Les Villes de marbre. Poëmes, 1869*, Paris, Lemerre, 1873.

MÉRAT, Albert et VALADE, Léon, *Avril, Mai, Juin. Sonnets*, Paris, Faure, 1863.

MÉRAT, Albert ET VALADE, Léon, *Intermezzo*, Poëme traduit de Henri Heine, Paris, Lemerre, 1863.

MOREAU, Hégésippe, *Le Myosotis*, nouv. éd., précédée d'une notice biographique par M. Sainte-Marie Marcotte, Paris, Paul Masgana, 1851.

MURGER, Henry, *Scènes de la vie de Bohême*, 4ᵉ éd., Paris, Michel Lévy fr., 1852.

MURGER, Henry, *Scènes de la vie de jeunesse*, Paris, Michel Lévy fr., 1851.

Parnasse contemporain (Le). Recueil de vers nouveaux (1866), Paris, Lemerre, 1866.

Parnasse contemporain (Le). Recueil de vers nouveaux (1869), Paris, Lemerre, 1871.

Parnasse contemporain (Le). Recueil de vers nouveaux (1876), Paris, Lemerre, 1876.

Parnassiculet contemporain (Le). Recueil de vers nouveaux, Paris, J. Lemer, 1867.

Parnassiculet contemporain (Le). Recueil de vers nouveaux, 2ᵉ éd., Paris, J. Lemer, 1872.

POPELIN, Claudius, *Cinq octaves de sonnets*, Paris, Lemerre, 1875.

POPELIN, Claudius, *Un livre de sonnets*, Paris, Charpentier, 1888.

RENAUD, Armand, *Caprices de boudoir*, Paris, F. Sartorius, 1864.

RENAUD, Armand, *Les Pensées tristes*, Paris, Hachette, 1865.

RENAUD, Armand, *Les Poèmes de l'amour*, Paris, Librairie nouvelle, 1860.

RICHEPIN, Jean, *La Mer*, Paris, M. Dreyfous et M. Dalsace, 1894.

ROUSSELOT, Gustave, *Le Poëme humain. Chant de Force et de Jeunesse*, Paris, E. Dentu, 1874.

SAINTE-BEUVE, Charles-Augustin, *Vie, poésies et pensées de Joseph Delorme*, Paris, Delangle frères, 1829.

SAINTE-BEUVE, Charles-Augustin, *Vie, poésies et pensées de Joseph Delorme*, nouv. éd. très-augm., Paris, M. Lévy frères, 1863.

SILVESTRE, Armand, *Les Renaissances*, Paris, Lemerre, 1870.

SILVESTRE, Armand, *Rimes neuves et vieilles*, Paris, E. Dentu, 1866.

Sonnets et eaux-fortes, Paris, Lemerre, 1869.

SOULARY, Joséphin, *Œuvres poétiques*, préf. de C.-A. Sainte-Beuve, Paris, Alphonse Lemerre, 3 vol., 1872-1883.

SOULARY, Joséphin, *Sonnets humouristiques*, éd. Andrea Schellino, Paris, Société des textes français modernes, 2018.

THEURIET, André, *Le Chemin des bois*, Paris, Lemerre, 1867.

VACQUERIE, Auguste, *Demi-teintes*, Paris, Garnier frères, 1845.

VACQUERIE, Auguste, *L'Enfer de l'esprit*, Paris, Ébrard, 1840.

VACQUERIE, Auguste, *Mes premières années de Paris*, Paris, Michel Lévy / Librairie nouvelle, 1872.

VACQUERIE, Auguste, *Souvent homme varie, Comédie en deux actes et en vers*, Paris, Librairie nouvelle, 1859.

VACQUERIE, Auguste, *Théâtre complet*, 2 vol., Paris, Calmann-Lévy, 1879.

VALADE, Léon, *À mi-côte*, Paris, Lemerre, 1874.

VALADE, Léon, *Poésies. Avril, Mai, Juin. – À mi-côte*, Paris, Lemerre, 1887.

VAN HASSELT, André, *Nouvelles poésies*, Bruxelles, Bruylant et Comp. / Paris, Borrani et Droz, 1857.

VAN HASSELT, André, *Poëmes, paraboles, odes et études rhythmiques*, Bruxelles, Office de publicité / Paris, A. Goubaud, 1862.

VERLAINE, Paul, *La Bonne Chanson*, Paris, Lemerre, 1870.

VERLAINE, Paul, *Fêtes galantes*, Paris, Lemerre, 1869.

VERLAINE, Paul, *Jadis et Naguère. Poésies*, Paris, Léon Vanier, 1884.

VERLAINE, Paul, *Poëmes saturniens*, Paris, Lemerre, 1866.

VEUILLOT, Louis, *Les Couleuvres*, Paris, Victor Palmé, 1869.

VILLIERS DE L'ISLE-ADAM, Auguste, *Premières poésies, 1856-1858*, Lyon, N. Scheuring, 1859.

ÉDITIONS CRITIQUES CONSULTÉES

BANVILLE, Théodore de, *Œuvres complètes*, dir. Peter J. Edwards, vol. VI : Paris, H. Champion, 1999.

BANVILLE, Théodore de, *Rondels*, éd. Martin Sorrell, University of Exeter, 1973.

BAUDELAIRE, Charle, *Correspondance*, éd. Claude Pichois, avec la collab. de Jean Ziegler, Paris, Gallimard, 1993, 2 vol.

CORBIÈRE, Tristan, *Les Amours jaunes*, suivi de six poèmes retrouvés, de *Casino des trépassé* et *L'Américaine*, éd. Christian Angelet, Paris, Librairie générale française, 2003.

CORBIÈRE, Tristan, *Les Amours jaunes*, éd. Elizabeth Aragon et Claude Bonnin, Toulouse, Presses Universitaires du Mirail, 1992.

CORBIÈRE, Tristan, *Les Amours jaunes*, éd. Jean-Louis Bertrand, Paris, Garnier Flammarion, 2018.

CORBIÈRE, Tristan, *Les Amours jaunes*, suivi de *Poèmes retrouvés* et de *Œuvres en prose*, éd. Jean-Louis Lalanne, préf. Henri Thomas, Paris, Gallimard, 1973.

CORBIÈRE, Tristan, *Les Amours jaunes*, éd. Yves-Gérard Le Dantec, Paris, Gallimard, 1953.

CORBIÈRE, Tristan, *Les Amours jaunes*, éd. René Martineau, Paris, Georges Crès & Cie, 1920.

Corbière, Tristan, *Les Amours jaunes*, [éd. Charles Morice], préf. Charles Le Goffic, Paris, Albert Messein, 1926.

Corbière, Tristan, *Les Amours jaunes* : dans Cros – Corbière, *Œuvres complètes*, éd. Pierre-Olivier Walzer [avec la participation de Francis F. Burch pour Corbière], Paris, Gallimard, 1970.

Corbière, Tristan, *ffocsoR, l'album Louis Noir*, éd. Benoît Houzé, Huelgoat, Françoise Livinec, 2013.

Corbière, Tristan, *Œuvres poétiques complètes*, dans Rimbaud, Cros, Corbière, Lautréamont, *Œuvres poétiques complètes*, éd. Michel Dansel, Paris, R. Laffont, 1980.

Gautier, Théophile, *Poésies complètes*, Nouvelle édition revue et augmentée, éd. René Jasinski, 3 vol., Paris, Nizet, 1970.

Goyet, Francis (éd.). *Traités de poétique et de rhétorique de la Renaissance*, Paris, Le Livre de poche classique, 1990.

Hugo, Victor, *La Légende des Siècles*, éd. Paul Berret, 7 vol., Paris, Hachette, 1920-1927.

Hugo, Victor, *Œuvres complètes*, Paris, Hetzel/Quantin, 1876-1897.

Marot, Clément, *Œuvres*, éd. Charles d'Héricault, Paris, Garnier fr., 1867.

Lamartine, Alphonse de, *Œuvres poétiques complètes*, éd. Marius-François Guyard, Paris, Gallimard, 1965.

L'Escurel, Jehannot de, *Balades, rondeaux et diz entez sus refroiz de rondeaux*, éd. F. Gennrich, Langen bei Frankfurt, 1964.

Mallarmé, Stéphane, *Œuvres complètes*, éd. Marchal, t. I, Paris, Gallimard, 1998.

Orléans, Charles d', *Poësies de Charles d'Orléans, père de Louis XII et oncle de François Ier, rois de France*, éd. Pierre-Vincent Chalvet, Grenoble, J.-L.-A. Giroud 1803.

Orléans, Charles d', *Poésies de Charles d'Orléans*, publiées [...] d'après les manuscrits des bibliothèques du Roi et de l'Arsenal, éd. Joseph-Marie Guichard, Paris, Librairie de Charles Gosselin, 1842.

Orléans, Charles d', *Les Poésies du duc Charles d'Orléans*, publiées sur le manuscrit de la bibliothèque de Grenoble, conféré avec ceux de Paris et de Londres, éd. Aimé Champollion-Figeac, Paris, Librairie J. Belin-Leprieur et Colomb de Batines, 1842.

Orléans, Charles d', *Poésies complètes de Charles d'Orléans*, revues sur les manuscrits, éd. Charles d'Héricault, 2 vol., Paris, A. Lemerre, 1874.

Racine, Jean, *Œuvres complètes*, I : Théâtre – Poésie, Paris, éd. Georges Forestier, Gallimard, 1999.

Rimbaud, Arthur, *Œuvres complètes*, éd. Jules Mouquet et André Rolland de Renéville, Paris, Gallimard, 1967.

Rimbaud, Arthur, *Œuvres complètes*, éd. Steve Murphy, 4 vol., Paris, Honoré Champion, 1999-2002.

VERHAEREN, Émile, *Poèmes. Les Bords de la route – Les Flamandes – Les Moines*, augmentés de plusieurs poèmes, Paris, Société du Mercure de France, 1895.

VERLAINE, Paul, *Correspondance générale*, I : 1857-1885, éd. Michael Pakenham, Paris, Fayard, 2005.

VERLAINE, Paul, *Œuvres complètes*, III, texte définitif collationné sur les originaux et sur les premières éditions, Paris, Messein, 1919.

VERLAINE, Paul, *Œuvres poétiques complètes*, éd. Y.-G. Le Dantec et J. Borel, Paris, Gallimard, 1962.

VERLAINE, Paul, *Poèmes saturniens*, éd. Steve Murphy, Paris, Champion, 2008.

VERLAINE, Paul, *Les Poètes maudits*, éd. Michel Décaudin, Paris, C.D.U. et SEDES, 1982.

VILLON, François, *Œuvres complètes, suivies d'un choix des poésies de ses disciples*, éd. préparée par [Bernard de] La Monnoye, mise au jour, avec notes et glossaire par M. Pierre Jannet, [2ᵉ éd.], Paris, E. Picard, 1867.

BIBLIOGRAPHIE SECONDAIRE

ACKERMANN, Paul, *Traité de l'accent appliqué à la théorie de la versification*, sec. éd., Paris, Aimé-André / Berlin, Asher & Cⁱᵉ, 1843.

ALVIN, Louis, *André Van Hasselt, sa vie et ses travaux*, Bruxelles, Merzbach et Falk, 1877.

ANGELET, Christian, *La Poétique de Tristan Corbière*, Bruxelles, Palais des Académies, 1961.

BALCOU, Jean, « De Baudelaire à Corbière : des "Tableaux parisiens" aux scènes de rue », *Revue d'Histoire Littéraire de la France*, 118 (2018), p. 67-72.

BANVILLE, Théodore de, *Petit traité de poésie française*, Paris, Librairie de l'Écho de la Sorbonne, 1872.

BANVILLE, Théodore de, *Petit traité de poésie française*, Paris, Charpentier, 1881.

BECQ DE FOUQUIÈRES, Louis, *Traité élémentaire de poésie française à l'usage des classes*, Paris, Librairie Ch. Delagrave, 1881.

BELLATI, Giovanna, *Formes fixes et modernité. Structure et esthétique de quelques formes fixes du Moyen Âge à l'époque contemporaine*, Milano, Pubblicazioni dell'I.S.U. Università Cattolica, 2005.

BELLATI, Giovanna, « Le renouveau du rondeau entre Parnasse et symbolisme », dans *Simbolismo e naturalismo fra lingua e testo : atti del Convegno, Università Cattolica di Milano, 25-26-27 settembre 2003*, Milano, Vita e Pensiero, 2010, p. 3-30.

BERNAL, Yann, « Corbière, les coquilles et l'imprimerie. Tératologie de l'édition originale des *Amours jaunes* », *CTC* 3 (2020), p. 19-71.

BERNAL, Yann, « Elzévirien à voir. Du caractère des *Amours jaunes* en 1873 », *CTC* 3 (2020), p. 237-259.

BERNARD, Bernard, *Code poétique*, Paris, Dezobry et E. Mageleine, 1850.

BERNARDELLI, Giuseppe, « Il testo contumace », dans IDEM, *Tre studi su Tristan Corbière*, Udine, Gianfranco Angelico Benvenuto Editore, 1983, p. 30-59.

BERNARDELLI, Giuseppe, « Le esequie del poetino. Intorno ai rondels pour après di Tristan Corbière », *L'Analisi linguistica e letteraria*, 2 (1993), p. 279-357.

BETCHAKU, Akihiko, « À propos de la chanson bretonne Ann hini goz », *CTC* 1 (2018), p. 281-288.

BILLY, Dominique, « *Bien loin d'ici* et ses modèles », dans *La Tradition européenne du sonnet*. Études réunies par Patrick Labarthe et Johannes Bartuschat, Genève, Slatkine, 2019, p. 183-221.

BILLY, Dominique, « Convention and parody in the rhyming of Tristan Corbière », dans *Towards a Typology of Poetic Forms: from language to metrics and beyond*, dir. Jean-Louis Aroui et Andy Arléo, Amsterdam, J. Benjamins, 2009, p. 337-354.

BILLY, Dominique, « Corbière avant Tristan », *CTC* 1 (2018), p. 169-193.

BILLY, Dominique, « Corbière et le vers libéré de *Journal de Bord* », *CTC* 2 (2019), p. 83-111.

BILLY, Dominique, « Des lectures occultées de Baudelaire : le cas d'Élie Mariaker », dans *La Langue de Baudelaire*, dir. Jérôme Hennebert et Vincent Vivès, Valenciennes, Presses Universitaires de Valenciennes, 2002, à par.

BILLY, Dominique, *Les Formes poétiques selon Baudelaire*, Paris, Champion, 2015.

BILLY, Dominique, « *Harmonie du soir* et la postérité formelle de la note XI des *Orientales* », *Studi Francesi* 148 (2006), p. 73-90.

BILLY, Dominique, « Innovation et déconstruction dans l'alexandrin de Rimbaud », dans André Guyaux (dir.), *Rimbaud. Des Poésies à la Saison*, Classiques Garnier, 2009, p. 119-182.

BILLY, Dominique, « L'analyse distributionnelle des vers césurés dans la lyrique française et occitane du moyen âge », dans *Contacts de langues, de civilisations et intertextualité*, actes du IIIᵉ Congrès international d'Études Occitanes (Montpellier, 1990), Montpellier, 1992, t. III, p. 805-828.

BILLY, Dominique, « La Complainte de Geneviève de Brabant ou l'inconstance de la césure », dans *Dai pochi ai molti. Studi in onore di Roberto Antonelli*, dir. Paolo Canettieri et Arianna Punzi, 2 vol. Rome, Viella, 2014, t. I, p. 215-229.

BILLY, Dominique, « Le flottement de la césure dans le décasyllabe des troubadours », *Critica del Testo* III/2 (2000), p. 587-622

BILLY, Dominique, « Le nombre de la rime », *Degrés*, 104 (2000), article *f* (24 p.)

BILLY, Dominique, « Le sabordage de la prosodie française dans les *Amours jaunes* » [version profondément remaniée d'un article de 2005 (*Studi Francesi* 145, p. 73-88)], 2014. https://hal-univ-tlse2.archives-ouvertes. fr/hal-00962229/file/Billy_Sabordage_2014.pdf (consuté le 10/09/2022)

BILLY, Dominique, « Théorie et description de la césure : quelques propositions », dans F. Brugnolo et F. Gambino (dir.), *La lirica romanza del Medioevo. Storia, tradizioni, interpretazioni*, Atti del VI convegno triennale della Società Italiana di Filologia Romanza, Padova, Unipress, 2009, p. 279-299.

BOBILLOT, Jean-Pierre, « "Et la tigresse épou pou pou…" : duplicités métrico-métriques dans les vers de Verlaine », dans *Verlaine. 1896-1996*, dir. Martine Bercot, Paris, Klincksieck, 1998, p. 859-894.

BOSCHOT, Adolphe, « La réforme de la prosodie », *La Revue de Paris*, VIII (1901), IV (juillet-août), p. 859-894.

BOYET, Francis, *Traités de poétique et de rhétorique de la Renaissance*, Paris, Librairie générale française, 1990.

BUISINE, Alain, « Sans rime ni marine », *Revue des sciences humaines*, 177 (1980), p. 131-143.

BURCH, Francis F. *Tristan Corbière*, Paris, Nizet, 1970.

CAMPAUX, Antoine, *François Villon. Sa vie et ses œuvres*, Paris, A. Durand, 1859.

CHAUSSIVERT, Jean-Stéphane, « Esthétique du taratantara verlainien », *Revue des Sciences humaines*, 35 (1970), p. 401-409.

CHEVRIER, Alain, *Le Décasyllabe à césure médiane*, Paris, Classiques Garnier, 2011.

CHEVRIER, Alain, « "Iconicité et symétrie" : inversions et autres variations strophiques du sonnet chez Auguste Brizeux », *Poétique* 143 (2005), p. 323-342.

CHEVRIER, Alain, « Lettre sur le pantoum », *Limon*, 3 (1988), p. 157-163.

CLAYE, Jules, *Manuel de l'apprenti compositeur*, 2ᵉ éd. rev., corr. et augm., Paris, J. Claye, 1874.

CLONTS, Charlène, « Le tiret dans *Les Amours jaunes* de Corbière », *L'Information grammaticale* 164 (2020), p. 14-18.

COCKING, J. M., « The 'invention' of the rondel », *French Studies*, 5 (1951), p. 49-55.

CORNULIER, Benoît de, *Art poëtique. Notions et problèmes de métrique*, Lyon, Presses universitaires de Lyon, 1982.

CORNULIER, Benoît de, « Corbière et la poésie comptable », *CTC* 1 (2018), p. 233-270.

CORNULIER, Benoît de, « Corbière pouëte précieux dans l'album de Roscoff ? », dans S. Murphy (dir.), *Rimbaud, Verlaine et zut. À la mémoire de Jean-Jacques Lefrère*, Paris, Classiques Garnier, 2019, p. 195-214.

CORNULIER, Benoît de, *De la métrique à l'interprétation. Essais sur Rimbaud*, Paris, Classiques Garnier, 2009.

CORNULIER, Benoît de, « Pour une approche de la poésie métrique au XIXe siècle », *Romantisme*, 140 (2008), p. 38-52.

CORNULIER, Benoît de, « Si le mètre m'était compté : sur la notion fallacieuse de mesure du vers », dans L. de Saussure, A. Borillo et M. Vuillaume (dir.), *Grammaire, lexique, référence. Regards sur le sens*, Bern et *al.*, Peter Lang, 2012, p. 355-376.

CORNULIER, Benoît de, « Sur la métrique de Verlaine dans les *Poèmes saturniens* », dans *Lectures de Verlaine. Poèmes saturniens, Fêtes galantes, Romances sans paroles*, dir. S. Murphy, Presses universitaires de Rennes, 2007, p. 195-213.

CORNULIER, Benoît de, « Sur la valeur *taratantara* du mètre 5-5 chez Verlaine, Corbière et Baudelaire », *Revue Verlaine*, 13 (2015), p. 55-72.

CORNULIER, Benoît de, *Théorie du Vers : Rimbaud, Verlaine, Mallarmé*, Paris, Le Seuil, 1982.

DANSEL, Michel, *Langage et modernité chez Tristan Corbière*, Paris, Nizet, 1974.

DE SPOELBERCH DE LOVENJOUL, Charles, *Histoire des œuvres de Théophile Gautier*, 2 vol., Paris, Charpentier, 1887.

DEBAUVE, Jean-Louis, « Autour de la publication des *Amours jaunes* », *La Nouvelle Tour de feu*, 11-13 (1985), p. 55-69.

DEGOTT, Bertrand, « *Les Amours jaunes* à la lumière de l'album Noir », *Op. cit.*, 20 (2019) [En ligne], mis à jour le : 16/12/2019, URL https://revues.univ-pau.fr/op.cit./index.php?id=478 (consulté le 10/09/2022).

DERÊME, Tristan, *La Libellule violette*, Paris, Grasset, 1942.

DESPREZ, Louis, « Les derniers romantiques. I. M. Paul Verlaine », *La Revue indépendante*, I (1884), p. 218-234.

DORCHAIN, Auguste, *L'Art des vers*, nouv. éd. rev. et augm., Paris, Librairie Garnier fr., [1921].

DOMINICY, Marc, « La césure lyrique chez Verhaeren », dans *Le vers français. Histoire, théorie, esthétique*, dir. M. Murat, Paris, Champion, 2000, p. 247-295.

DUCOFFRE, David, « Verlaine et le romantisme », *Revue Verlaine*, 10 (2007), p. 11-13.

DUCONDUT, Abel, *Examen critique de la versification française classique et romantique*, Paris, Dupray de la Mahérie, 1863.

DUCONDUT, Jean-Ambroise, *Essai de rhythmique française*, Paris, Michel Lévy Frères, 1856.

DUFAU, Benoît, « La modernité qui déchante. Railway, chloroforme et télégraphe dans *Les Amours jaunes* de Tristan Corbière », *CTC* 2 (2019), p. 149-174.

DURAND, Pascal, « Avatars de la forme sonnet au XIXe siècle », *Formules*, 12 (2008), p. 257-280.

DUSOLIER, Alcide, « Les Impassibles », *Figaro*, XIII, n° 1169 (29 avril 1866), p. 3.

EDWARDS, Peter J, « Le *Petit Traité de poésie française* de Théodore de Banville : Bible parnassienne ou invitation à l'expérimentation libre ? », *Romantisme*, 163 (2014), p. 91-100.

FERTEL, Martin Dominique, *La Science pratique de l'imprimerie*, Saint-Omer, [chez l'auteur], 1723.

FOGLIA, Aurélie, « Tristan Corbière, enterrement de vie de poète », *CTC* 2 (2019), p. 15-29.

FONGARO, Antoine, « Le poète et le crapaud », *Revue des Lettres Modernes*, 104-107 (1964), p. 113-124.

FONGARO, Antoine, « Sur le texte des *Amours jaunes* », *Littératures*, 14 (1986), p. 77-85.

FOURNIER, Henri, *Traité de la typographie*, 3ᵉ éd. corr. et augm., Tours, 1870.

GAREY, Howard, « The Fifteenth Century Rondeau as aleatory polytext », *Le Moyen Français*, 5 (1980), p. 193-236.

GAUDIN, Paul, *Du rondeau, du triolet, du sonnet*, Paris, Librairie centrale (J. Lemer), 1870.

GAUTIER, Théophile, « Rapport sur les progrès de la poésie », dans S. de Sacy, P. Féval, Th. Gautier et É. Thierry, *Rapport sur le progrès des lettres*, Paris, Imprimerie impériale, 1868, p. 67-141.

GÉNIN, François, *Récréations philologiques, ou Recueil de notes pour servir à l'histoire des mots de la langue française*, 2 vol., Paris, Chamerot, 1858.

GÉRAULT, Iris, « Corbière face à la critique (1873-1885) », *Revue d'Histoire littéraire de la France*, 118, 1 (2018), p. 107-116.

GLACHANT, Paul et Victor, *Essai critique sur le théâtre de Victor Hugo*, Paris, Hachette, 1903.

GLEIZE, Jean-Marie, *Poésie et figuration*, Paris, Le Seuil, 1983.

GOUVARD, Jean-Michel, *Critique du vers*, Paris, Champion, 2000.

GOUVARD, Jean-Michel, « De la sémantique à la métrique : les césures chez Verlaine », *Revue Verlaine*, 1 (1993), p. 125-155.

GOUVARD, Jean-Michel, « Frontières de mot et frontières de morphème dans l'alexandrin », *Langue française*, 99 (1993), p. 45-62.

GOUVARD, Jean-Michel, « L'alexandrin de Victor Hugo. Questions de méthode », dans *Le Sens et la mesure. De la pragmatique à la métrique, Hommages à Benoît de Cornulier*, dir. J.-L. Aroui, Paris, Champion, 2003, p. 365-383.

GOUVARD, Jean-Michel, « Le vers français : de la syllabe à l'accent », *Poétique*, 106 (1996), p. 223-247.

GOUVARD, Jean-Michel, « Les mètres de Jules Laforgue : pour une analyse distributionnelle du vers de 12 syllabes », *Cahiers du Centre d'Études Métriques*, 1 (1992), p. 41-49.

GOUVARD, Jean-Michel, *Recherches sur la métrique interne du vers composé dans la seconde moitié du dix-neuvième siècle*, thèse, Nantes, 1994.

GOUVARD, Jean-Michel, *La Versification*, Paris, PUF, 1999.

GRAMMONT, Maurice, *Le Vers français. Ses moyens d'expression, son harmonie*, 4ᵉ éd. rev. et corr., Paris, Delagrave, 1937.

GRAMONT, Ferdinand, *Les Vers français et leur prosodie*, Paris, Hetzel, 1876.

GRIBENSKI, Michel, « Vers impairs, ennéasyllabe et musique : variations sur un air (mé)connu », dans *Loxias | Loxias 19*, mis en ligne le 6 décembre 2007, URL http://revel.unice.fr/loxias/index.html?id=1988 (consulté le 10/09/2022).

GRIN, Micha, « Un inédit de Tristan Corbière », *Cahiers pour l'art*, 11, p. 10-13.

GRUNDT, Micheline, « Le Poète et la Cigale », *La Nouvelle Tour de feu*, 11-13 (1985), p. 91-95.

GUILBAUD, Jean-Louis, *Métrique du décasyllabe de Voltaire*, mémoire de maîtrise, Université de Nantes, 1995.

GUYAUX, André (éd.), *Un demi-siècle de lectures des Fleurs du mal (1855-1905)*, Paris, Presses universitaires de Paris-Sorbonne, 2007.

HOUZÉ, Benoît, « Corbière créateur d'objets : une dimension méconnue de sa poétique », dans *Revue d'Histoire Littéraire de la France*, 118 (2018), p. 25-36.

HOUZÉ, Benoît, « Corbière lecteur de Verlaine ? Potentialités d'une hypothèse critique », dans S. Murphy (dir.), *Rimbaud, Verlaine et zut. À la mémoire de Jean-Jacques Lefrère*, Paris, Classiques Garnier, 2019, p. 299-315.

HOUZÉ, Benoît, « L'ironie coloriste : jaune et aventure poétique chez Corbière », dans *Fortunes littéraires de Tristan Corbière*, coll. dir. Samuel Lair, L'Harmattan, Paris, 2012, p. 151-172.

HOUZÉ, Benoît, « "La mort de ce pauvre garçon qui s'appelait Tristan Corbière…". Un compte rendu tardif de la première réception des *Amours jaunes* », *CTC*, 4 (2021), p. 381-382.

HOUZÉ, Benoît, « Le dernier Corbière. Nouvelle édition des manuscripts de l'exemplaire de l'auteur des *Amours jaunes* », *CTC* 3 (2020), p. 303-341.

HOUZÉ, Benoît, « Naissances d'une œuvre : deux parodies de chansons par Tristan Corbière », dans S. Murphy (dir.), *Le Chemin des correspondances et le champ poétique. À la mémoire de Michael Pakenham*, Paris, Classiques Garnier, 2016, p. 351-370.

HOUZÉ, Benoît, « Nouvelle édition de trois manuscrits corbiériens », *CTC* 2 (2019), p. 257-273.

HOUZÉ, Benoît, « Traces de Tristan Corbière : documents inédits ou retrouvés », *Histoires littéraires*, 33 (2008), p. 13-34, 8 pl.

HOUZÉ, Benoît, « Tristan Tous Genres », *L'œil bleu*, 11 (2010), p. 3-22.

HOUZÉ, Benoît, « Un compte rendu inconnu des *Amours jaunes* en 1873 », dans *Fortunes littéraires de Tristan Corbière*, dir. S. Lair, Paris, L'Harmattan, 2012, p. 221-225.

HOUZÉ, Benoît, « Un hommage inconnu à Tristan Corbière : quelques *Coups de bâton* de Louis Verbrugghe », *Studi francesi*, 160 (2010), p. 8-12.

HOUZÉ, Benoît, « Un sonnet parodique du Parnasse et du romantisme », *CTC* 3 (2020), p. 379-381.

HOUZÉ, Benoît, HÉRISSON, Armelle, *Tristan Corbière. Les Amours jaunes*, Neuilly, Atlande, 2019.

ISCHI, Stéphane, « Rimbaud et Corbière se sont-ils lus ? », *Romantisme*, 151 (2011), p. 101-112.

JASINSKI, Max, *Histoire du sonnet en France*, Douai, Impr. H. Brugère, A. Dalsheimer & Cie, 1903.

JOB-LAZARE, *Albert Glatigny, sa vie, son œuvre*, Paris, Typographie de A.H. Bécus, 1878.

KILLICK, Rachel, « Banville et le sonnet », *Bulletin d'Études parnassiennes et symbolistes*, 9-10 (1992), p. 87-119.

KUTYLA, Anne-Sophie, *Tristan Corbière. Une curiosité esthétique*, nouv. éd. rev. et corr., Paris, Eurédit, 2010.

LA GRASSERIE, Raoul de, *Des principes scientifiques de la versification française*, Paris, Maisonneuve, 1900.

LA LANDELLE, Gabriel de, *Le Langage des marins*, Paris, E. Dentu, 1859.

LA MADELAINE, Louis Philipon de, *Dictionnaire portatif des rimes*, précédé d'un nouveau *Traité de la versification française* et suivi d'un *Essai sur la langue poétique*, 3e éd., Paris, Saintain, 1822.

LA MOTTE, Antoine de, *Lettres*, suivies d'un recueil de vers du mesme auteur, pour servir de Supplement à ses Œuvres, s.l., s.n., 1754.

LAFORGUE, Jules, « Une étude sur Corbière », *Entretiens politiques et littéraires*, IIe année, III, 16 (juillet 1891), p. 2-13.

LAIR, Samuel, « Le dossier René Martineau dans le fonds Tristan Corbière de la bibliothèque *Les Amours jaunes* », *CTC* 2 (2019), p. 283-295.

LAIR, Samuel, « Tristan Corbière en *fond troué d'Arlequin* », dans *Fortunes littéraires de Tristan Corbière*, dir. S. Lair, Paris, L'Harmattan, 2012, p. 11-18.

[LANCELOT, Claude], « Breve instuction sur les regles de la poësie françoise », dans *Nouvelle méthode pour apprendre facilement la langue latine*, 6e éd., Paris, Le Petit, 1662, p. 861-889.

LAROCHE, Hughes, *Tristan Corbière, ou les voix de la corbière*, Saint-Denis, Presses universitaires de Vincennes, 1997.

LE DUC, Philibert, *Sonnets curieux et sonnets célèbres : étude anthologique et didactique suivie de sonnets inédits*, Paris, L. Willem / Bourg, Francisque Martin, 1879.

LE GOFFIC, Charles et THIEULIN, Édouard, *Nouveau traité de versification française*, Paris, Masson, 1890.

LEBAIGUE, Charles, *La Réforme orthographique et l'Académie française*, 2ᵉ édition, Paris, Delagrave, 1890.

LESCANE, Laurent, « Comment peut-on publier Corbière ? Du manuscrit à l'image textuelle », *CTC* 3 (2020), p. 99-126.

LESCANE, Laurent, « Écrire, peindre, ponctuer. Caractères de Corbière », *CTC* 1 (2018), p. 95-119.

LESCANE, Laurent, « Revoir la ponctuation des *Amours jaunes* », dans J.-M. Hovasse et H. Scepi (dir.), *« Les Amours jaunes » de Tristan Corbière*, <www.crp19.org>.

LESCANE, Laurent, « Trois enregistrements administratifs des *Amours jaunes* en 1873 », *CTC* 3 (2020), p. 285-296.

LESCLIDE, Richard, *Propos de table de Victor Hugo*, 3ᵉ édition, Paris, E. Dentu, 1885.

LEVI, Ida, « New lights on Tristan Corbière », *French Studies*, 5 (1951), p. 233-244.

LINDSAY, Marshall, « Notes pour une édition critique des Amours jaunes », *Revue des langues vivantes*, 6 (1962), p. 490-509.

LINDSAY, Marshall, « The versification of Corbière's *Les Amours jaunes* », *PMLA*, 4 (1963), p. 358-368.

LOTE, G. *En préface à « Hernani ». Cent ans après*, Paris, Librairie universitaire J. Gamber, 1930.

LOTE, G, « Le vers romantique », *Revue des cours et conférences*, 32 (1930-1931), p. 44-58 et 179-192 ; 33 (1931-1932), p. 214-226 et 466-480.

LOUBIER, Pierre, « Deux flâneurs, parallèlement. Paul Verlaine, Tristan Corbière », *Revue Verlaine*, 17 (2019), p. 91-103.

LUBARSCH, E.O., *Über Deklamation und Rhthmus der französischen Verse*, Oppeln et Leipzig, G. Maske, 1888.

MACFARLANE, Keith H. *Tristan Corbière dans 'Les Amours jaunes'*, Minard, Lettres modernes, 1974.

MARTHA, Constant, « La poésie du jour », *Revue des Deux Mondes*, 36 (15 avril 1866), p. 1013-1038.

MARTIN, Gaston, « Trois variantes de Tristan Corbière », *L'Archer*, 4 (1929), p. 55-65.

MARTINEAU, René, *Tristan Corbière*, avec de nombreux documents inédits, Paris, Le Divan, 1925.

MARTINEAU, René, *Tristan Corbière. Essai de biographie et de bibliographie*, Paris, Société du Mercure de France, 1904.

MARTINON, Philippe, « Le trimètre : ses limites, son histoire, ses lois », *Mercure de France*, 77 (1909), p. 620-640 [1], et 78 (1909), p. 40-58 [2].

MARTINON, Philippe, *Les Strophes. Étude historique et critique sur les formes de la poésie lyrique en France depuis la Renaissance*, Paris, Champion, 1912.

MAZALEYRAT, Jean, *Éléments de métrique française*, Paris, Armand-Collin, 1974.

MEITINGER, Serge, « L'ironie antiromantique de Tristan Corbière », *Littérature*, 51 (1983), p. 41-58.

MEJJATI, Naïma, « Les lignes de points. Un aspect peu exploré des *Amours jaunes* », *CTC* 2 (2019), p. 223-234.

MENDÈS, Catulle, *Œuvres*, t. XIV : *Le mouvement poétique français de 1867 à 1900, Dictionnaire des principaux poètes français du XIXᵉ siècle*, éd. Ida Merello, Paris, Classiques Garnier, 2016.

MENDÈS, Catulle, *Rapport à M. le ministre de l'Instruction publique et des beaux-arts sur le mouvement poétique français de 1867 à 1900*, précédé de *Réflexions sur la personnalité de l'esprit poétique de France* ; suivi d'un *Dictionnaire bibliographique et critique* et d'une nomenclature chronologique de la plupart des poètes français du XIXᵉ siècle, Paris, Imprimerie Nationale, 1902.

MITCHELL, Robert L, « Tristan Corbière's "I Sonnet" as Ars (Im)poetica », *The French Review*, 50 (1976), p. 35-45.

MORTELETTE, Yann, « Corbière, Hugo et les poètes du Parnasse », *Revue d'Histoire littéraire de la France*, 1 (2018), p. 73-84.

MORTELETTE, Yann, *Histoire du Parnasse*, Paris, Fayard, 2005.

MORTELETTE, Yann, « Le prédécadentisme des *Amours jaunes* », *CTC* 3 (2020), p. 143-158.

MORTELETTE, Yann (éd.). *Le Parnasse*, textes réunis, préfacés et annotés par Y.M., Paris, Presses de l'Université Paris-Sorbonne, 2006.

MOURGUES, Michel, *Traité de la poesie françoise*, Paris, Chez Guillaume de Luyne, 1685.

MOUQUET, Jules, Charles Baudelaire, *Vers retrouvés (juvenilia – sonnets), Manoël*, Paris, Émile-Paul frères, 1929.

MURPHY, Steve, « Effets et motivations : quelques excentricités de la versification baudelairienne », dans P. Labarthe (dir.), *Baudelaire, une alchimie de la douleur, études sur Les Fleurs du Mal*, Paris, Eurédit, 2003, Eurédit, p. 265-298.

MURPHY, Steve, « Langues jaunes et vertes : dans le bazar de Corbière », dans J.-M. Hovasse et H. Scepi (dir.), *'Les Amours jaunes' de Tristan Corbière*, <www.crp19.org>.

MURPHY, Steve, « Le premier Verlaine : documents, variantes et exégèses », *Revue Verlaine*, 6 (2000), p. 115-214.

MURPHY, Steve, « Versifications "parnassiennes" (?) », *Romantisme*, 140 (2008), p. 67-84.

NATTA, Marie-Christine, *Baudelaire*, Paris, Perrin, 2017.

NUITEN, Henk, *Les Variantes des « Fleurs du mal » et des « Épaves » de Charles Baudelaire (1821-1867)*. *Étude de stylistique génétique*, Amsterdam, Holland University Press, 1979.

OLMSTED, Everett Ward, *The Sonnet in French Literature and the Development of the French Sonnet Form*, Diss. Ithaca, N.Y., 1897.

OZAWA, Makoto « Rondels pour après ». Berceuses pour demain, *CTC* 1 (2018), p. 211-217.

PICHOIS, Claude et DUPONT, Jacques, *L'Atelier de Baudelaire : « Les Fleurs du Mal », édition diplomatique*, 4 vol., Paris, Champion, 2005.

PIRON, A. *Cours complet de littérature à l'usage des séminaires et des collèges. Poétique*, 3ᵉ éd., Paris, J. Lecoffre, 1881.

PLOQUIN, Jean-François, « Étude sur *Les Amours jaunes* de Tristan Corbière. La poésie : la métrique, le chant », *Bulletin d'Études Parnassiennes et Symbolistes*, 5 (1990), p. 69-96.

POIRION, Daniel, *Le Poète et le prince. L'évolution du lyrisme courtois de Guillaume de Machaut à Charles d'Orléans*, Paris, PUF, 1965.

PORCHER, Edmond, « L'alexandrin et le vers libre », *Recueil de la Société libre d'Agriculture, Sciences, Arts et Belles-Lettres de l'Eure*, VIIᵉ s., II (1914), p. 67-98.

QUELLIEN, Narcisse, *Chansons et danses des Bretons*, Paris, J. Maisonneuve et Ch. Leclerc, 1889.

QUICHERAT, Louis, *Petit traité de versification*, Paris, Hachette, 1838.

QUICHERAT, Louis, *Traité de versification*, 2ᵉ éd. revue et considérablement augmentée, Paris, Hachette, 1850.

RANNOU, Pascal, *De Corbière à Tristan. « Les Amours jaunes » : une quête de l'identité*, Paris, Champion, 2006.

RAYNAUD, Gaston (éd.), *Rondeaux et autres poésies du XVᵉ siècle*, Paris, Libr. Firmin Didot & Cⁱᵉ, 1889.

RICHARD, Pierre E, « Deux nouveaux envois de Corbière retrouvés », *CTC* 1 (2018), p. 299-304 + 2 planches n.p.

ROBB, Graham, *La Poésie de Baudelaire et la poésie française 1838-1852*, Paris, Aubier, 1993.

ROCHETTE, Auguste, *L'Alexandrin chez Victor Hugo*, Paris, Hachette, 1911.

ROGER, Thierry, *La Muse au couteau. Lecture des 'Amours jaunes' de Tristan Corbière*, Mont-Saint-Aignan, Presses universitaires de Rouen et du Havre, 2019.

ROSA, Guy, « Hugo et l'alexandrin de théâtre aux années 30 : une question secondaire », *Cahiers de l'Association internationale des études francaises*, 52 (2000), p. 307-328.

ROUBAUD, Jacques, *La Vieillesse d'Alexandre. Essai sur quelques états du vers français récent*, rééd., Paris, Ivrea, 2000.

ROUDAUT, Jean, *Ce qui nous revient. Relais critique*, Paris, Gallimard, 1980.

Roussel, Olivier, « Lettres de Glatigny », *Histoires littéraires*, 67 (2016), p. 13-45.

Rousselot, Jean, *Tristan Corbière*, Paris, Seghers, 1951.

Sainte-Beuve, Charles-Augustin, *Causeries du lundi*, 3ᵉ éd., 15 vol., Paris, Garnier, s.d. 1851-1862

Sainte-Beuve, Charles-Augustin, *Tableau historique et critique de la poésie française et du théâtre français au seizième siècle*, 2ᵉ éd., 2 vol., Paris, 1838.

Scott, David H. T. *Sonnet Theory and Practice in Nineteenth-century France : Sonnets on the Sonnet*, Hull, University of Hull Publications, 1977.

Souriau, Maurice, *L'Évolution du vers français au dix-septième siècle*, Paris, Hachette, 1893.

Souriau, Maurice, « La versification de Lamartine », *Revue des cours et conférences*, 2ᵉ s., VII (1898-1899), p. 841-860.

Stapfer, Paul, « La poésie française contemporaine », *Le Temps*, 13ᵉ année, nº 4366 (28 mars), 4379 (10 avril) et 4382 (13 avril 1873).

Stapfer, Paul, *Racine et Victor Hugo*, Paris, Armand Colin & Cⁱᵉ, 1887.

Steinmetz, Jean-Luc, « Corbière en vue : perspectives de recherches », *Revue d'Histoire littéraire de la France*, 118, 1 (2018), p. 11-16.

Steinmetz, Jean-Luc, *Tristan Corbière : une vie à-peu-près*, Paris, Fayard, 2011.

Stephan, Philip, « Problems of structure in the poetry of Tristan Corbière », *Modern language quatterly*, 22 (1961), p. 333-344.

Sully Prudhomme, *Réflexions sur l'art des vers*, Paris, Lemerre, 1892.

Ténint, Wilhem, *Prosodie de l'école moderne*, Paris, Didier, 1844.

Theuriet, *Les Paysans de l'Argonne*, Paris, Lemerre, 1870.

Thomas, Antoine, « La versification de la *Chirurgie* provençale de Raimon d'Avignon », *Romania*, XI (1882), p. 203-212.

Trigon, Jean de, *Tristan Corbière*, Paris, Le Cercle du livre, 1950.

Valazza, Nicolas, *La Poésie délivrée. Le livre en question du Parnasse à Mallarmé*, Genève, Droz, 2018.

Vareille, Armand, « Tristan Corbière au miroir du *Rapport sur le mouvement poétique français* de 1867 à 1900 (1902) de Catulle Mendès », dans *Fortunes littéraires de Tristan Corbière*, dir. S. Lair, Paris, L'Harmattan, 2012, p. 73-95.

Verluyten, S. Paul, « L'analyse de l'alexandrin. Mètre ou rythme ? », dans *Le Souci des apparences. Neuf études de poétique et de métrique*, dir. M. Dominicy, Bruxelles, Éditions de l'Université de Bruxelles, 1989, p. 31-74.

Veyrières, Louis de, *Sonnettistes anciens et modernes suivis de quatre-vingt sonnets*, 2 vol., Paris, Bachelin-Deflorenne, 1869.

Villemain, Abel-François, *Cours de littérature française*, 2 vol., Paris, Pichon et Didier, 1830.

Weigand, Gustave, *Traité de versification française*, Bromberg, Louis Levit, 1863.

INDEX DES NOTIONS
ET DES FORMES DISCUTÉES

INDEX DES NOMS PROPRES

INDEX DES TITRES DE POÈMES, DE PARTIES DU RECUEIL, DE PROSES DE CORBIÈRE, DES TITRES DE SON PÈRE, DES TITRES DE RECUEILS COLLECTIFS ET DE REVUES CITÉS

Les titres de sections figurent en majuscules. L'index inclut les titres de recueils collectifs mentionnés dans l'ouvrage. Les titres peuvent se présenter sous une forme raccourcie dans l'ouvrage.

TABLE DES FIGURES ET TABLEAUX

TABLE DES MATIÈRES

DEUXIÈME PARTIE

LE VERS VÉREUX DES *AMOURS JAUNES*

TROISIÈME PARTIE

UN TRAITEMENT POSTROMANTIQUE DE LA CÉSURE

QUATRIÈME PARTIE

L'ÉVOLUTION DE L'ALEXANDRIN
DE 1830 À 1873

CINQUIÈME PARTIE

CORBIÈRE ET LE MOUVEMENT PARNASSIEN

SIXIÈME PARTIE

LE SONNET DANS *LES AMOURS JAUNES*

SEPTIÈME PARTIE

RONDELS POUR APRÈS

Achevé d'imprimer par Corlet,
Condé-en-Normandie (Calvados),
en Février 2023
N° d'impression : 179550 - dépôt légal : Février 2023
Imprimé en France

90 0360451 9

CITIZENSHIP, WORK AND WELFARE

By the same author

LOCAL HEALTH AND WELFARE SERVICES

PORTRAIT OF SOCIAL WORK (*with B. N. Rodgers*)

SOCIAL POLICY AND CITIZENSHIP

WOMEN AND WELFARE